KV-419-022

STATUTORY INSTRUMENTS 1971

PART III
(in two Sections)

SECTION 2

Published by Authority

LONDON
HER MAJESTY'S STATIONERY OFFICE
1972

PRINTED AND PUBLISHED BY HER MAJESTY'S STATIONERY OFFICE

To be purchased from

49 High Holborn, LONDON, WC1V 6HB

13a Castle Street, EDINBURGH, EH2 3AR
109 St. Mary Street, CARDIFF, CF1 1JW
Brazennose Street, MANCHESTER, M60 8AS
50 Fairfax Street, BRISTOL, BS1 3DE
258 Broad Street, BIRMINGHAM, B1 2HE
80 Chichester Street, BELFAST, BT1 4JY

or through booksellers

1972

Price for the two Sections: £15·40 net

PRINTED IN ENGLAND

SBN 11 840093 2*

Contents of the Volume

PART I, Section 1

PART I, Section 2

PART II, Section 1

PART II, Section 2

PART III, Section 1

PART III, Section 2

1971 No. 1895

AGRICULTURE

The Price Stability of Imported Products (Rates of Levy) (Eggs) (No. 27) Order 1971

Made - - - *22nd November* 1971

Coming into Operation *23rd November* 1971

The Minister of Agriculture, Fisheries and Food, in exercise of the powers conferred upon him by section 1(2), (4), (5), (6) and (7) of the Agriculture and Horticulture Act 1964 (**a**) and of all other powers enabling him in that behalf, hereby makes the following order:—

1. This order may be cited as the Price Stability of Imported Products (Rates of Levy) (Eggs) (No. 27) Order 1971, and shall come into operation on 23rd November 1971.

2.—(1) In this order—

" the Principal Order " means the Price Stability of Imported Products (Levy Arrangements) (Eggs) Order 1970 (**b**) as amended (**c**) and as amended by any subsequent order, and if any such order is replaced by any subsequent order the expression shall be construed as a reference to such subsequent order;

AND other expressions have the same meaning as in the Principal Order.

(2) The Interpretation Act 1889 (**d**) shall apply to the interpretation of this order as it applies to the interpretation of an Act of Parliament and as if this order and the order hereby revoked were Acts of Parliament.

3. In accordance with and subject to the provisions of the Principal Order (which provides for the charging of levies on imports of those eggs and egg products which are specified commodities for the purposes of the Agriculture and Horticulture Act 1964) the rate of general levy for such imports into the United Kingdom of any specified commodity as are described in column 2 of the Schedule to this order in relation to a tariff heading indicated in column 1 of that Schedule shall be the rate set forth in relation thereto in column 3 of that Schedule.

4. The Price Stability of Imported Products (Rates of Levy) (Eggs) (No. 26) Order 1971 (**e**) is hereby revoked.

In Witness whereof the Official Seal of the Minister of Agriculture, Fisheries and Food is hereunto affixed on 22nd November 1971.

(L.S.)

B. D. Hayes,
Authorised by the Minister.

(**a**) 1964 c. 28. (**b**) S.I. 1970/359 (1970 I, p. 1277).
(**c**) S.I. 1971/947, 1642 (1971 II, p. 2709; III, p. 4505). (**d**) 1889 c. 63.
(**e**) S.I. 1971/1778 (1971 III, p. 4901).

SCHEDULE

1. Tariff Heading	2. Description of Imports	3. Rate of General Levy
	Imports of:—	
04.05	*Birds' eggs (in shell or not in shell), fresh, dried or otherwise preserved, sweetened or not, other than egg yolks:*	(per 120 eggs)
	A. Eggs in shell:	*p*
	1. Not exceeding 11 lb. in weight per 120 ..	5
	2. Over 11 lb. but not exceeding 12½ lb. in weight per 120	5
	3. Over 12½ lb. but not exceeding 14 lb. in weight per 120	5
	B. Eggs not in shell:	(per ton)
	Whole dried	£325
	Whole frozen or liquid	£50

EXPLANATORY NOTE

(*This Note is not part of the Order.*)

This order, which comes into operation on 23rd November 1971, supersedes the Price Stability of Imported Products (Rates of Levy) (Eggs) (No. 26) Order 1971. It—

(*a*) removes the general levy on imports of eggs in shell in the weight grades over 14 lb. per 120 eggs;

(*b*) reduces the rate of general levy to be charged on imports of dried whole egg not in shell; and

(*c*) reimposes unchanged the rates of general levy to be charged on imports of eggs in shell in the weight grades numbered 1 to 3 in the Schedule to the order and on imports of frozen or liquid whole egg not in shell.

STATUTORY INSTRUMENTS

1971 No. 1896

INCOME TAX

The Income Tax (Employments) (No. 8) Regulations 1971

Made - - - - - -	23*rd November* 1971
Laid before the House of Commons	30*th November* 1971
Coming into Operation - -	6*th April* 1972

The Commissioners of Inland Revenue, in exercise of the powers conferred upon them by section 204 of the Income and Corporation Taxes Act 1970**(a)**, hereby make the following Regulations:—

1.—(1) These Regulations shall come into operation on 6th April 1972 and may be cited as the Income Tax (Employments) (No. 8) Regulations 1971.

(2) The Interpretation Act 1889**(b)** shall apply for the interpretation of these Regulations as it applies for the interpretation of an Act of Parliament.

(3) In these Regulations the expression "the Principal Regulations" means the Income Tax (Employments) Regulations 1965**(c)** as amended **(d)**.

2. The Principal Regulations shall be varied by deleting from paragraph (1) of Regulation 2, in the definition of "simplified tax tables", the words "under Regulations 20 and 21" and substituting therefor "under Regulation 20".

3. The following definition shall be added to paragraph (1) of Regulation 2 of the Principal Regulations:—

"pension emoluments" means any payment of emoluments comprising a pension or annuity assessable to income tax under Schedule E.

4. In paragraph (1) of Regulation 16 of the Principal Regulations there shall be inserted after sub-paragraph (*b*) the following sub-paragraph:—

"(*c*) payments of pension emoluments in the year in which retirement takes place unless the Inspector directs that Regulation 13 shall apply; and"

and sub-paragraph (*c*) of paragraph (1) of the said Regulation 16 shall be redesignated (*d*).

5. Regulation 17 of the Principal Regulations shall have effect as if paragraph (7) of that Regulation were deleted and the following paragraphs were inserted:—

"(7) Retirement on pension shall not be treated as a cessation of employment for the purposes of this Regulation if the emoluments are paid by the same person both before and after retirement but any such person shall—

(a) 1970 c. 10. **(b)** 1889 c. 63.
(c) S.I. 1965/516 (1965 I, p. 1321).
(d) The amending Regulations are not relevant to the subject matter of these Regulations.

(*a*) within 14 days after retirement send to the Inspector a certificate on the prescribed form containing the following, viz:—

(i) the name of the employee;

(ii) the date of the employee's retirement;

(iii) the cumulative emoluments at the date of retirement;

(iv) the amount of pension payable weekly or monthly as the case may be; and

(*b*) on making payments of pension emoluments to the employee after retirement deduct tax in accordance with Regulation 16.

(8) If the 2 copies of the certificate given to the employee in accordance with paragraph 2 of this Regulation are delivered to an employer who pays or will pay pension emoluments to that employee the employer shall—

(*a*) complete one copy of the certificate in accordance with paragraph (3)(*a*) of this Regulation and send it to the Inspector indicated therein; and

(*b*) deduct tax by reference to the code shown on the certificate and in accordance with Regulation 16."

6. Regulation 21 and paragraph (2) of Regulation 24 of the Principal Regulations are hereby revoked.

By Order of the Commissioners of Inland Revenue.

G. Wolters,
Secretary.

23rd November 1971.

EXPLANATORY NOTE

(*This Note is not part of the Regulations.*)

These Regulations further amend the Income Tax (Employments) Regulations 1965.

Regulations 3 to 5 make provision for the code number in operation against the emoluments of an employee immediately prior to retirement to be applied to an occupational pension (whether paid direct from the former employer or from a pension fund) on a non-cumulative basis (instead of the normal cumulative basis) pending instructions from the Inspector of Taxes.

Regulations 2 and 6 withdraw the provision for a modified procedure for deducting tax in the case of certain employees paid weekly.

1971 No. 1897

CUSTOMS AND EXCISE

The Anti-Dumping Duty (No. 5) Order 1971

Made - - -	*23rd November* 1971
Laid before the House of Commons	*23rd November* 1971
Coming into Operation	*23rd November* 1971

Whereas by the Anti-Dumping (Provisional Charge to Duty) (No. 4) Order 1971(**a**) which came into operation on the 24th August 1971, goods of the description set out in the Schedule hereto were made subject to a provisional charge in respect of an anti-dumping duty of £50 per ton :

And whereas the said Order remains in force :

Now, therefore, the Secretary of State in exercise of his powers under sections 1, 2, 8(1), 9(3) and 15(4) of the Customs Duties (Dumping and Subsidies) Act 1969(**b**) hereby makes the following Order :—

1.—(1) This Order may be cited as the Anti-Dumping Duty (No. 5) Order 1971 and shall come into operation on the 23rd November 1971.

(2) The Interpretation Act 1889(**c**) shall apply to the interpretation of this Order as it applies to the interpretation of an Act of Parliament and as if this Order and the Order hereby revoked were Acts of Parliament.

2. There shall be charged on the importation into the United Kingdom of any goods of the description set out in the Schedule hereto (being goods classified in the Customs Tariff 1959(**d**) under the heading mentioned in the first column of that Schedule) a duty of customs at the rate set out in the third column ; and the said duty shall be chargeable from 24th August 1971.

3. Section 2 of the Customs Duties (Dumping and Subsidies) Act 1969 shall apply to the duty imposed by this Order.

4. The Anti-Dumping (Provisional Charge to Duty) (No. 4) Order 1971 is hereby revoked.

Anthony Grant,
Parliamentary Under Secretary of State,
Department of Trade and Industry.

23rd November 1971.

(**a**) S.I. 1971/1357 (1971 II, p. 3837). (**b**) 1969 c. 16.
(**c**) 1889 c. 63.
(**d**) See S.I. 1971/1971 (1971 III, p. 5330).

SCHEDULE

Relevant Tariff Heading	Description of Goods	Rate of Duty
Ex 28.21(B)	Chromic anhydride (CrO_3) originating in the Union of Soviet Socialist Republics	£50 per ton

EXPLANATORY NOTE

(*This Note is not part of the Order.*)

This Order imposes an anti-dumping duty of £50 per ton on imports of chromic anhydride (also known as chromium trioxide or chromic acid) originating in the Union of Soviet Socialist Republics. The duty is chargeable retrospectively from 24th August 1971 (when such goods became subject to a provisional charge).

The Order applies to the duty section 2 of the Customs Duties (Dumping and Subsidies) Act 1969, which enables relief to be granted where particular goods have not been dumped or the margin of dumping is less than the amount of the duty.

STATUTORY INSTRUMENTS

1971 No. 1898

LOCAL GOVERNMENT, ENGLAND AND WALES

The Rate Support Grant (Amendment) Regulations 1971

Made - - - -	23*rd November* 1971
Laid before Parliament	30*th November* 1971
Coming into Operation	21*st December* 1971

The Secretary of State for the Environment, in exercise of his powers under section 5(1)(*a*) of the Local Government Act 1966**(a)**, and of all other powers enabling him in that behalf, hereby makes the following regulations:—

Title and commencement

1. These regulations may be cited as the Rate Support Grant (Amendment) Regulations 1971 and shall come into operation on the 21st December 1971.

Interpretation

2.—(1) The Interpretation Act 1889**(b)** shall apply for the interpretation of these regulations as it applies for the interpretation of an Act of Parliament.

(2) In these regulations "the principal regulations" means the Rate Support Grant Regulations 1967**(c)** as amended **(d)** and "the Secretary of State" means the Secretary of State for the Environment.

Amendment of regulation 4 *of the principal regulations*

3. In paragraph (1) of regulation 4 of the principal regulations (which provides for estimating the population of an area) after the words "as at 30th June in the year" there shall be added the words "and certified by him to the Secretary of State for rate support grant purposes."

Amendment of the schedule to the principal regulations

4. In the schedule to the principal regulations (which provides for calculating the number of education units for an area)—

(*a*) for paragraphs 1, 2 and 6 there shall be substituted the following paragraphs:—

"1. For the purpose of calculating the numbers of education units for an area for any year, each of the persons and items referred to in column (1) of the following table shall constitute the number of education units specified in relation thereto in column (2).

(a) 1966 c. 42.
(b) 1889 c. 63.
(c) S.I. 1967/363 (1967 I, p. 1235).
(d) S.I. 1969/105, 1970/1010 (1969 I, p. 339; 1970 II, p. 3154).

(1)	(2)
(*a*) Primary and nursery school pupil	1·00
(*b*) Secondary and special school pupil—	
under 16 years of age	1·79
16 years of age and over	2·87
(*c*) Further education establishment student ...	2·83
(*d*) University or other student award	3·09
(*e*) 1,000 main mid-day meals for day pupils provided in any year in maintained schools ...	0·68

2.—(1) The provisions of this paragraph shall have effect for the purpose of estimating for an area the number of pupils under heads (*a*) and (*b*) of the foregoing table

(2) Regard shall be had to—

(*a*) pupils on the registers of any school which is maintained or assisted by the local education authority for the area;

(*b*) pupils at any other school, the fees for whose tuition are paid by that authority; and

(*c*) children receiving education otherwise than at school, under arrangements made under section 56 of the Education Act 1944**(a)**.

(3) Pupils who fall within sub-paragraph (2)(*a*) above shall be treated as secondary school pupils where—

(*a*) proposals with respect to the school have been approved by the Secretary of State for Education and Science under section 1 of the Education Act 1964**(b)** (which relates to new schools with special age limits) and

(*b*) they were 11 years of age on the 1st September preceding the time as at which, pursuant to paragraph 7 of this schedule, numbers are required to be estimated

and otherwise shall be treated as primary school pupils.

(4) Pupils or children who fall within sub-paragraph (2)(*b*) or (*c*) above shall be treated as primary school pupils if under 12 years of age and as secondary school pupils if 12 years of age or over.

(5) The number of pupils at schools recognised as direct grant grammar schools by the Secretary of State for Education and Science for the purposes of any regulations made by him for the payment of grant to such schools, the fees for whose tuition are paid by the local education authority for the area, shall be taken as 70 per cent. of the full number.

6. For the purposes of paragraphs 2 and 3 of this Schedule children or further education establishment students belonging to the area of one local education authority who are pupils on the register of a school or are enrolled at an establishment of further education maintained or assisted by the local education authority for another area shall be

(a) 1944 c. 31. **(b)** 1964 c. 82.

treated as if the school or further education establishment were maintained or assisted by the authority for the first mentioned area and not by the authority for the other area."

(*b*) paragraph 8 shall be deleted.

Transitional provision

5. Nothing in regulation 4 of these regulations shall affect any calculation required to be made in connection with the payment of rate support grants for any year earlier than 1971-72.

Peter Walker,
Secretary of State for the Environment.

23rd November 1971.

EXPLANATORY NOTE

(*This Note is not part of the Regulations.*)

The Rate Support Grant Regulations 1967 provide for the carrying into effect of sections 1 to 4 of the Local Government Act 1966 (under which rate support grants are paid to local authorities). They provide for estimates to be made of population in any area and also determine inter alia the method of calculating the number of education units for any area, for the purpose of assessing the amounts payable to individual authorities in respect of the needs element of rate support grants.

These Regulations

(*a*) provide for estimates of population to be certified for rate support grant purposes only;

(*b*) amend the method of calculating education units for the years 1971-72 onwards by providing a new table specifying the number of education units to be constituted by each of the persons and items indicated (e.g. school pupils and university awards); and

(*c*) make amendments to the schedule to the Rate Support Grant Regulations 1967 which are consequential upon the coming into force of the provisions of the Education (Handicapped Children) Act 1970 (c. 52).

1971 No. 1899 (C.51)

FRIENDLY SOCIETIES

The Friendly Societies Act 1971 (Commencement) Order 1971

Made - - - *22nd November* 1971

The Treasury, in exercise of the powers conferred on them by section 15(6) of the Friendly Societies Act 1971(**a**), hereby make the following Order:—

1. This Order may be cited as the Friendly Societies Act 1971 (Commencement) Order 1971.

2. Subject to the following article, the Friendly Societies Act 1971 shall come into force on 31st December 1971.

3. Section 9 of the said Act shall come into force on 1st December 1971.

V. H. Goodhew,
P. L. Hawkins,

Two of the Lords Commissioners
of Her Majesty's Treasury.

22nd November 1971.

EXPLANATORY NOTE

(*This Note is not part of the Order.*)

This Order brings into force on the 1st December 1971 section 9 of the Friendly Societies Act 1971 (which confers power on the Treasury to charge fees on registration of societies) and brings into force on the 31st December 1971 all the other provisions of the Act.

(a) 1971 c. 66.

STATUTORY INSTRUMENTS

1971 No. 1900

FRIENDLY SOCIETIES

The Friendly Societies (Fees) Order 1971

Made - - -	22*nd November* 1971
Laid before Parliament	30*th November* 1971
Coming into Operation	1*st December* 1971

The Treasury pursuant to the powers conferred upon them by section 9(1) of the Friendly Societies Act 1971(**a**) and to all other powers enabling them in that behalf hereby make the following Order:—

1.—(1) This Order may be cited as the Friendly Societies (Fees) Order 1971 and shall come into operation on 1st December 1971.

(2) The Interpretation Act 1889(**b**) shall apply for the interpretation of this Order as it applies for the interpretation of an Act of Parliament.

2. Fees may be charged on the registration of a friendly society, benevolent society, cattle insurance society, working-men's club or old people's home society, and on the registration of an amendment of the rules thereof, in accordance with a scale determined by the Treasury under section 96(1) of the Friendly Societies Act 1896(**c**).

V. H. Goodhew,

P. L. Hawkins,

Two of the Lords Commissioners of Her Majesty's Treasury.

22nd November 1971.

EXPLANATORY NOTE

(*This Note is not part of the Order.*)

This Order empowers the Treasury to charge fees on the registration of, and on the registration of an amendment of rules of, any friendly society, benevolent society, cattle insurance society, working-men's club or old people's home society registered under the Friendly Societies Act 1896.

(**a**) 1971 c. 66. (**b**) 1889 c. 63. (**c**) 1896 c. 25.

1971 No. 1901

POLICE

The Police (Amendment) (No. 3) Regulations 1971

Made - - - -	*22nd November* 1971
Laid before Parliament	*1st December* 1971
Coming into Operation	*6th December* 1971

In exercise of the powers conferred on me by section 33 of the Police Act 1964(**a**), and after consulting the Police Council for the United Kingdom in accordance with section 4(4) of the Police Act 1969(**b**), I hereby make the following Regulations:—

PART I

CITATION, OPERATION ETC.

1. These Regulations may be cited as the Police (Amendment) (No. 3) Regulations 1971.

2. These Regulations shall come into operation on 6th December 1971 and, for the purposes of each Regulation contained in Part II or III thereof, shall have effect as from the date specified in the Regulation in question.

3. In these Regulations any reference to the Regulations of 1971 is a reference to the Police Regulations 1971(**c**), as amended(**d**), and any reference to the Regulations of 1968 is a reference to the Police Regulations 1968(**e**), as amended(**f**), so far as they remain in force under Regulation 2(1) of the Regulations of 1971, that is to say, for the purposes of regulating pay and allowances in respect of a period before the Regulations of 1971 came into operation on 15th February 1971.

PART II

AMENDMENTS TO REGULATIONS OF 1971

4.—(1) This Regulation shall have effect as from 6th December 1971.

(2) For Regulation 37 of the Regulations of 1971 (deductions from pay of sickness or injury benefit) there shall be substituted the Regulation set out in Schedule 1 hereto.

(**a**) 1964 c. 48. (**b**) 1969 c. 63.
(**c**) S.I. 1971/156 (1971 I, p. 439).
(**d**) S.I. 1971/659, 1141 (1971 I, p. 1744; II, p. 3373).
(**e**) S.I. 1968/26 (1968 I, p. 38).
(**f**) The relevant amending instruments are S.I. 1969/137, 1970/417, 601, 1971/659 (1969 I, p. 369; 1970 I, pp. 1446, 1923; 1971 I, p. 1744).

5.—(1) This Regulation shall have effect as from 6th December 1971.

(2) In paragraph (1) of Regulation 47 of the Regulations of 1971 (removal allowance) for the words "otherwise than on voluntary transfer from one force to another" there shall be substituted the words "except as a consequence of joining the force otherwise than on being statutorily transferred thereto".

(3) In paragraph (2) of the said Regulation 47 for the words "on voluntary transfer" there shall be substituted the words "in consequence of his voluntarily transferring".

6.—(1) This Regulation shall have effect as from 1st September 1971.

(2) In Regulation 49 of the Regulations of 1971 (boot allowance) for the rate "£0·188 a week" there shall be substituted the rate "£0·24 a week".

7.—(1) This Regulation shall have effect as from 15th February 1971.

(2) In Part II of Schedule 5 to the Regulations of 1971 (scales of pay for women), as set out in Appendix 1 to the Police (Amendment) Regulations 1971, after paragraph 1 (2) there shall be inserted the sub-paragraph set out in Schedule 2 hereto.

PART III

AMENDMENTS TO REGULATIONS OF 1968

8.—(1) This Regulation shall have effect as from 1st April 1970.

(2) Except in the case of a member of the City of London or metropolitan police force, Part II of Schedule 3 to the Regulations of 1968 (scales of pay for women) shall have effect as if it were provided therein that the annual pay of a chief superintendent assigned to duties designated for the purposes hereof by the Secretary of State should be—

(*a*) in respect of any period beginning on or after 1st April 1970 and ending before 1st September 1970, £2,770;

(*b*) in respect of any period beginning on or after 1st September 1970 and ending before 15th February 1971, £3,255.

R. Maudling,
One of Her Majesty's Principal
Secretaries of State.

Home Office,
Whitehall.

22nd November 1971.

SCHEDULE 1

Regulation substituted for Regulation 37 of the Regulations of 1971

Deductions from pay of national insurance benefits

37.—(1) There shall be deducted from the pay of a member of a police force the amount of any such national insurance benefit as is mentioned in paragraph (3) to which he is entitled.

(2) For the purposes of paragraph (1) a policewoman who, as a married woman or a widow, is excepted from liability to pay contributions under section 3 of the National Insurance Act 1965(**a**) shall be deemed to be entitled to any national insurance benefit mentioned in paragraph (3) to which she would have been entitled had she not been so excepted.

(3) The national insurance benefits referred to in this Regulation are—

(*a*) any sickness benefit under the National Insurance Act 1965 together with any supplement thereto payable under section 2 of the National Insurance Act 1966(**b**);

(*b*) any invalidity pension or allowance payable under the said Act of 1965, and

(*c*) any injury benefit under the National Insurance (Industrial Injuries) Act 1965(**c**) together with any supplement thereto payable under section 2 of the said Act of 1966.

SCHEDULE 2

Sub-Paragraph inserted in Paragraph 1 of Part II of Schedule 5 to the Regulations of 1971

(2A) Except in the case of a member of the City of London or metropolitan police force and notwithstanding anything in sub-paragraph (2), the annual pay of a chief superintendent assigned to duties designated for the purposes hereof by the Secretary of State shall be—

(*a*) before completing one year of service in the performance of those duties, £3,255;

(*b*) after one year of such service, £3,363;

(*c*) after 2 years of such service, £3,471;

(*d*) after 3 years of such service, £3,579;

but, for the purposes hereof, a chief superintendent who was first assigned to those duties after 1st July 1971 shall be treated as if she had completed one year of service in the performance of those duties immediately she was in fact assigned thereto—

(i) in the case of a chief superintendent who was first appointed in, or promoted to, that rank before 1st May 1971, if before being first assigned to those duties she had completed 3 years of service in that rank;

(ii) in the case of any other chief superintendent, if before being first assigned to those duties she had completed 2 years of service in that rank.

(**a**) 1965 c. 51. (**b**) 1966 c. 6.
(**c**) 1965 c. 52.

EXPLANATORY NOTE

(This Note is not part of the Regulations.)

These Regulations relate to the emoluments of members of police forces. In so far as they have retrospective effect they are made in exercise of the power conferred by section 33(4) of the Police Act 1964.

Regulation 4 provides that there shall be deducted from a policeman's pay not only (as at present) any national insurance sickness or injury benefit but also any invalidity benefit to which he is entitled.

Regulation 5 restricts the payment of a removal allowance on a policeman joining his force to cases of compulsory transfer.

Regulation 6 increases the rate of boot allowance with effect from 1st September 1971.

Regulations 7 and 8 increase, with effect from 1st April 1970, the pay of a woman chief superintendent assigned to duties designated by the Secretary of State.

1971 No. 1903 (L.40)

INDUSTRIAL RELATIONS

The Industrial Court (Appeals) Order 1971

Laid before Parliament in draft

Made - - -	*24th November* 1971
Coming into Operation	*1st December* 1971

Whereas a draft of the following Order was laid before Parliament and approved by resolution of each House:

Now, therefore, the Lord Chancellor, in exercise of the powers conferred on him by section 114(2) and (4) of the Industrial Relations Act 1971(**a**), hereby makes the following Order:—

Citation and commencement

1. This Order may be cited as the Industrial Court (Appeals) Order 1971 and shall come into operation on 1st December 1971.

Interpretation

2. The Interpretation Act 1889(**b**) shall apply to the interpretation of this Order as it applies to the interpretation of an Act of Parliament.

Appeals from Industrial Tribunals to Industrial Court

3. An appeal on a question of law arising in any proceedings before, or arising from any decision of, an industrial tribunal in England and Wales—

(*a*) under the Contracts of Employment Act 1963(**c**); or

(*b*) under the Redundancy Payments Act 1965(**d**); or

(*c*) under the Equal Pay Act 1970(**e**); or

(*d*) on a complaint under the Industrial Relations Act 1971

shall, subject to paragraph 6 of this Order, lie to the Industrial Court and not to any other court.

Supplementary

4. Subject to paragraph 6 of this Order, section 13(1) of the Tribunals and Inquiries Act 1971(**f**) (which confers on parties to proceedings before certain tribunals a right to appeal to the High Court on a point of law, or to require

(**a**) 1971 c. 72. (**b**) 1889 c. 63. (**c**) 1963 c. 49.
(**d**) 1965 c. 62. (**e**) 1970 c. 41. (**f**) 1971 c. 62.

the tribunal to state a case for the opinion of the High Court) shall not apply to proceedings before an industrial tribunal in England and Wales exercising any of the jurisdictions mentioned in paragraph 3 of this Order.

Transitional provisions

5.—(1) Without prejudice to paragraph 6 of this Order, an appeal (or motion for the determination of a case stated) in respect of any such decision or proceedings as are mentioned in paragraph 3 of this Order which is pending in the High Court on 1st December 1971 shall on that date be transferred to the Industrial Court and be dealt with as an appeal instituted in accordance with Industrial Court Rules on the date on which it was entered in the High Court.

(2) The Industrial Court shall have the same power to award costs in respect of an appeal or motion transferred to it by virtue of sub-paragraph (1) above as the High Court would have had in respect of such an appeal or motion if it had not been so transferred.

Savings

6. Nothing in this Order shall apply to an appeal, or the statement of a case, in respect of any decision made before 1st December 1971 if the High Court has, before that date, entered upon the consideration of the appeal or of the case.

Dated 24th November 1971.

Hailsham of St. Marylebone, C.

EXPLANATORY NOTE

(This Note is not part of the Order.)

This Order confers on parties to proceedings before industrial tribunals in England and Wales a right to appeal on a question of law to the Industrial Court, instead of the High Court, from a decision under the Contracts of Employment Act 1963, the Redundancy Payments Act 1965 or the Equal Pay Act 1970, or on a complaint under the Industrial Relations Act 1971.

1971 No. 1904 (L.41)

LEGAL AID AND ADVICE, ENGLAND

The Legal Aid (Extension of Proceedings) Regulations 1971

Made - - -	21*st October* 1971
Laid before Parliament	3*rd November* 1971
Coming into Operation	1*st December* 1971

The Lord Chancellor, in exercise of the powers conferred on him by sections 1(3) and 12(1) of the Legal Aid and Advice Act 1949(**a**), hereby makes the following Regulations:—

1.—(1) These Regulations may be cited as the Legal Aid (Extension of Proceedings) Regulations 1971 and shall come into operation on 1st December 1971.

(2) The Interpretation Act 1889(**b**) shall apply to these Regulations as it applies to the interpretation of an Act of Parliament.

2. The proceedings in which legal aid may be given shall include proceedings in the National Industrial Relations Court.

Dated 21st October 1971.

Hailsham of St. Marylebone, C.

EXPLANATORY NOTE

(*This Note is not part of the Regulations.*)

These Regulations make legal aid available for proceedings in the National Industrial Relations Court.

(**a**) 1949 c. 51. (**b**) 1889 c. 63.

STATUTORY INSTRUMENTS

1971 No. 1912 (S.204)

LEGAL AID AND ADVICE, SCOTLAND

The Legal Aid (Scotland) (Extension of Proceedings) (No. 2) Regulations 1971

Made - - -	*29th October* 1971
Laid before Parliament	*3rd November* 1971
Coming into Operation	*1st December* 1971

In exercise of the powers conferred on me by sections 1 and 15 of the Legal Aid (Scotland) Act 1967(**a**) and of all other powers enabling me in that behalf, I hereby make the following regulations :—

1.—(1) These regulations may be cited as the Legal Aid (Scotland) (Extension of Proceedings) (No. 2) Regulations 1971 and shall come into operation on 1st December 1971.

(2) The Interpretation Act 1889(**b**) shall apply for the interpretation of these regulations as it applies for the interpretation of an Act of Parliament.

2. The proceedings in which legal aid may be given shall include proceedings before the National Industrial Relations Court.

Gordon Campbell,
One of Her Majesty's Principal
Secretaries of State.

St. Andrew's House,
Edinburgh.
29th October 1971.

EXPLANATORY NOTE

(*This Note is not part of the Regulations.*)

These Regulations make legal aid available for proceedings before the National Industrial Relations Court.

(**a**) 1967 c. 43.

(**b**) 1889 c. 63.

1971 No. 1913 (S.205)

INDUSTRIAL RELATIONS

The Industrial Court (Appeals) (Scotland) Order 1971

Laid before Parliament in draft

Made - - - *24th November* 1971

Coming into Operation *1st December* 1971

In exercise of the powers conferred on me by section 114(3) and (4) of the Industrial Relations Act 1971(**a**), I hereby make the following order, a draft of which has been laid before Parliament and approved by resolution of each House :—

Citation and commencement

1. This order may be cited as the Industrial Court (Appeals) (Scotland) Order 1971 and shall come into operation on 1st December 1971.

2. The Interpretation Act 1889(**b**) applies for the interpretation of this order as it applies for the interpretation of an Act of Parliament.

Appeals from Industrial Tribunals to Industrial Court

3. An appeal on a question of law arising in any proceedings before, or arising from any decision of, an industrial tribunal in Scotland—

(*a*) under the Contracts of Employment Act 1963(**c**) ; or

(*b*) under the Redundancy Payments Act 1965(**d**) ; or

(*c*) under the Equal Pay Act 1970(**e**) ; or

(*d*) on a complaint under the Industrial Relations Act 1971

shall, subject to paragraph 6 of this order, lie to the Industrial Court and shall not lie to any other court.

Supplementary

4. Subject to paragraph 6 of this order, section 13(1) as read with section 13(6) of the Tribunals and Inquiries Act 1971(**f**) (which confers on parties to proceedings before certain tribunals a right to appeal to the Court of Session on a point of law, or to require the tribunal to state a case for the opinion of the Court of Session) shall not apply to proceedings before an industrial tribunal in Scotland exercising any of the jurisdictions mentioned in paragraph 3 of this order.

(**a**) 1971 c. 72.
(**b**) 1889 c. 63.
(**c**) 1963 c. 49.
(**d**) 1965 c. 62.
(**e**) 1970 c. 41.
(**f**) 1971 c. 62.

Transitional Provisions

5.—(1) Without prejudice to paragraph 6 of this order, any appeal to, or case stated for the opinion of, the Court of Session arising out of any such decision or proceedings as are mentioned in paragraph 3 of this order which is pending in the Court of Session on 1st December 1971 shall on that date be transferred to the Industrial Court and be dealt with as if it had been an appeal instituted in accordance with Industrial Court Rules on the date on which it was lodged in the Court of Session.

(2) The Industrial Court shall have the same power to award expenses in respect of an appeal (or case stated) transferred to it by virtue of sub-paragraph (1) above as the Court of Session would have had in respect of such an appeal (or case stated) if it had not been so transferred.

Savings

6. Nothing in this order shall apply to an appeal, or the statement of a case, in respect of any decision made before 1st December 1971 if the Court of Session has, before that date, entered upon the consideration of the appeal or of the case.

Gordon Campbell,
One of Her Majesty's Principal
Secretaries of State.

St. Andrew's House,
Edinburgh.
24th November 1971.

EXPLANATORY NOTE

(*This Note is not part of the Order.*)

The Order confers on parties to proceedings before industrial tribunals in Scotland a right to appeal on a question of law to the Industrial Court, instead of the Court of Session, from a decision under the Contracts of Employment Act 1963 or the Redundancy Payments Act 1965 or the Equal Pay Act 1970, or on a complaint under the Industrial Relations Act 1971.

1971 No. 1914 (S.206)

LEGAL AID AND ADVICE, SCOTLAND

The Legal Aid (Scotland) (General) Amendment (No. 2) Regulations 1971

Made - - - -	*24th November* 1971
Laid before Parliament	*30th November* 1971
Coming into Operation	*1st December* 1971

In exercise of the powers conferred on me by section 15 of the Legal Aid (Scotland) Act 1967(**a**), and of all other powers enabling me in that behalf, and with the concurrence of the Treasury, I hereby make the following regulations:

1.—(1) These regulations may be cited as the Legal Aid (Scotland) (General) Amendment (No. 2) Regulations 1971 and shall come into operation on 1 December 1971.

(2) The Interpretation Act 1889(**b**) shall apply for the interpretation of these regulations as it applies for the interpretation of an Act of Parliament.

(3) In these regulations a regulation referred to by number means a regulation so numbered in the Legal Aid (Scotland) (General) Regulations 1960(**c**) as amended(**d**).

2. In the Arrangement of Regulations at the beginning of the Legal Aid (Scotland) (General) Regulations 1960, after "4. Applications for legal aid" there shall be inserted "4A. Applications for legal aid in connection with proceedings before the National Industrial Relations Court".

3. Regulation 3 shall be amended by the addition of the following paragraph :—

"(2) For the purpose of subsection (4) of section 3 of the Act the expression "property" shall be taken not to include any moneys payable under an order made by the National Industrial Relations Court established under section 99 of the Industrial Relations Act 1971(**e**)."

(**a**) 1967 c. 43.
(**b**) 1889 c. 63.
(**c**) S.I. 1960/2195 (1960 II, p. 1817).
(**d**) S.I. 1971/194 (1971 I, p. 570).
(**e**) 1971 c. 72.

4. The following regulation shall be inserted after regulation 4:—

"*Applications for legal aid in connection with proceedings before the National Industrial Relations Court*

4A—(1) In this regulation the expression "the Industrial Court" means the National Industrial Relations Court established under section 99 of the Industrial Relations Act 1971 and the expresssion "the secretary of the court" means the person appointed to be secretary of the Industrial Court and includes any officer of the Industrial Court authorised to act as his deputy.

(2) Except in so far as otherwise provided by this regulation, these regulations shall apply to applications for legal aid in connection with proceedings in the Industrial Court in like manner as they apply to applications for legal aid in connection with proceedings in any other court.

(3)(*a*) Where it appears to the appropriate committee that an application for legal aid relates to proceedings which are likely to be conducted in England and Wales, they shall transmit the application forthwith to the Law Society in England and Wales and shall notify the applicant and his solicitor that they have done so.

(*b*) Where it appears to the appropriate Committee doubtful whether the proceedings to which an application for a certificate relates will be conducted in England and Wales or in Scotland, they shall request the secretary of the court to determine that question and that determination shall be binding upon the Committee.

(4) Where a certificate has been issued and there is a change of circumstances regarding the conduct of proceedings in that, by direction of the court, they will be wholly or partly conducted in England and Wales, the assisted person's certificate shall remain in force and he may continue to be represented for the proceedings in England and Wales by the solicitor and counsel, if any, who represented him in Scotland; and any counsel subsequently appointed to represent him may be selected from the appropriate list of counsel willing to act for assisted persons which is maintained by the Society.

(5) Where on the coming into force of these regulations a certificate has been granted in respect of an appeal to the Court of Session from a decision of an industrial tribunal and that appeal has been transferred to the Industrial Court in pursuanee of any order made under section 114 of the Industrial Relations Act 1971, the certificate shall be deemed to have been granted in respect of an appeal to the Industrial Court."

5. For regulation 8(2) there shall be substituted the following:—

"(2) Where a legal aid certificate is suspended or discharged by a Committee acting under the powers given to them by these regulations or by paragraphs (5) or (6) of article 16 of the Legal Aid (Scotland) Scheme 1958, or by paragraphs (5) or (6) of article 8 of the Legal Aid (Scotland) (House of Lords) Scheme 1960, or by paragraphs (5) or (6) of article 9 of the Legal Aid (Scottish Land Court) Scheme 1971 or by paragraphs (5) or (6) of article 9 of the Legal Aid (Lands Tribunal for Scotland) Scheme 1971 or paragraphs (5) or (6) of article 9 of the Legal Aid (Scotland) (National Industrial Relations Court) Scheme 1971 or under a direction given by a court under rule 5 of the Act of Sederunt (Legal Aid Rules) 1958**(a)** or otherwise, the assisted person shall remain liable to pay to the Society so much of his contribution as is required to defray the expenses incurred up to the date of suspension or discharge:

(a) S.I. 1958/1872 (1958 I, p. 389).

Provided that where a certificate is discharged under paragraph (6) of article 16 of the Legal Aid (Scotland) Scheme 1958 or paragraph (6) of article 8 of the Legal Aid (Scotland) (House of Lords) Scheme 1960 or paragraph (6) of article 9 of the Legal Aid (Scottish Land Court) Scheme 1971 or paragraph (6) of article 9 of the Legal Aid (Lands Tribunal for Scotland) Scheme 1971 or paragraph (6) of article 9 of the Legal Aid (Scotland) (National Industrial Relations Court) Scheme 1971 or the direction of a court requiring discharge of a certificate is given under sub-paragraph (*c*) of paragraph (1) of the said rule 5 or where, in any other case, a court so directs, the Society shall have the right to recover from the person by whom the certificate was held any sum over and above the amount of his contribution which may be required to meet the sums paid or payable by the Society on his account in respect of the proceedings to which the discharged certificate related."

6. For regulation 10(5) there shall be substituted the following:—

"(5) Where, at any stage in proceedings, a party who is an assisted person ceases to receive legal aid, he shall be deemed to be an assisted person for the purpose of any award of expenses made against him only to the extent that those expenses were incurred before he ceased to receive legal aid:

Provided that where an assisted person's legal aid certificate is discharged under paragraph (6) of article 16 of the Legal Aid (Scotland) Scheme 1958 or paragraph (6) of article 8 of the Legal Aid (Scotland) (House of Lords) Scheme 1960 or paragraph (6) of article 9 of the Legal Aid (Scottish Land Court) Scheme 1971 or paragraph (6) of article 9 of the Legal Aid (Lands Tribunal for Scotland) Scheme 1971 or paragraph (6) of article 9 of the Legal Aid (Scotland) (National Industrial Relations Court) Scheme 1971 or the direction of a court requiring discharge of his certificate is given under sub-paragraph (*c*) of paragraph (1) of rule 5 of the Act of Sederunt (Legal Aid Rules) 1958, the provisions of paragraph (e) of sub-section (6) of section 2 of the Legal Aid (Scotland) Act 1967 shall not apply to him."

Gordon Campbell,
One of Her Majesty's Principal
Secretaries of State.

St. Andrew's House,
Edinburgh.
22nd November 1971.

We concur,

Walter Clegg,
P. L. Hawkins,
Two of the Lords Commissioners of
Her Majesty's Treasury.

24th November 1971.

EXPLANATORY NOTE

(This Note is not part of the Regulations.)

These Regulations apply the Legal Aid (Scotland) (General) Regulations 1960 with certain modifications to proceedings in the National Industrial Relations Court and make provision for legal aid certificates granted in Scotland to remain in force in the event of proceedings being transferred to England.

1971 No. 1917

PATENTS

The Patents (Amendment No. 2) Rules 1971

Made - - -	*24th November* 1971
Laid before Parliament	*2nd December* 1971
Coming into Operation	*1st January* 1972

The Secretary of State in exercise of his powers under section 94(1) of the Patents Act 1949(**a**) and of all other powers enabling him in that behalf hereby makes the following Rules:—

1.—(1) These Rules may be cited as the Patents (Amendment No. 2) Rules 1971 and shall come into operation on 1st January 1972.

(2) The Interpretation Act 1889(**b**) shall apply to the interpretation of these Rules as it applies to the interpretation of an Act of Parliament.

2. The Patents Rules 1968(**c**), as amended (**d**), shall have effect subject to the following further amendments:—

(*a*) for Rule 67 there shall be substituted:—

"**67.** On receipt of the prescribed renewal fee accompanied by Patents Form No. 24 and No. 26, and if the particulars specified in the margin of Form No. 26 have been duly provided, the Comptroller shall issue a certificate of payment on that form.";

(*b*) for Rule 68 there shall be substituted:—

"**68.**—(1) Where the period for payment of a renewal fee pursuant to Rule 64 has expired the Comptroller shall not later than six weeks after the last date for payment under that Rule, and if the fee still remains unpaid, send to the patentee a notice reminding him that payment is overdue and of the consequences of non-payment.

(2) The notice shall be sent to the address in the United Kingdom specified for that purpose by the patentee when last paying a renewal fee in respect of the patent or, if no such address was specified, to the relevant address for service entered in the register of patents.";

(*c*) for Rule 127 there shall be substituted:—

"**127.** Upon the payment of a renewal fee within the time prescribed by these Rules or provided for late payment by section 22 of the Act, the Comptroller shall record the payment and its date in the register.";

(**a**) 1949 c. 87.
(**b**) 1889 c. 63.
(**c**) S.I. 1968/1389 (1968 II, p. 3958).
(**d**) The only relevant amending instrument is S.I. 1971/263 (1971 I, p. 918).

(*d*) the fees specified in paragraph 25 of Schedule 1 as payable on application for a certificate of payment of a renewal fee shall be payable upon the application for renewal of a patent whether or not a certificate of payment is sought and accordingly, in item 25 in Schedule 1, the words "certificate of payment of" and "fee" shall be omitted ; and

(*e*) in Schedule 2 for the forms prescribed as Forms Nos. 24 and 26 there shall be substituted the combined Form No. 24 and No. 26 set out in the Schedule hereto.

Nicholas Ridley,
Parliamentary Under Secretary of State,
Department of Trade and Industry.

24th November 1971.

SCHEDULE

PATENTS FORM NO. 24

This Form does not become effective as a renewal fee payment until left at the Patent Office.

PATENTS ACTS, 1949 to 1961

Payments of Renewal Fee

(a) State name of person tendering the fee.

(b) Insert name of patentee(s).

I/We (a)..

hereby transmit the fee prescribed for the continuation in force of

(b)...

Patent No.......................for a further period of........................and request that the Certificate of Payment may be sent to me (us) at the address specified at (f) in Patents Form No. 26 below.

NOTE—Unless this is completed a Certificate of payment will not be issued.

To be completed when payment is made by or on behalf of the patentee

(c) Delete as appropriate.

(d) Insert address if different from address for service in the register.

I/We specify (c) the United Kingdom address for service entered in the register of Patents

(c) the following address in the United Kingdom

for receipt of a reminder not later than six weeks after the payment of the next renewal fee becomes due (d).......................................

....

NOTE—If the address specified at (c) above or at (f) below is not that entered in the Register of Patents as the Patentee's Address for Service and it is desired to amend the entry in the Register, application therefor must be made on Patents Form No. 57.

To the Comptroller,
The Patent Office, 25 Southampton Buildings
London WC2A 1AY.

The following Patents Form No. 26 is not to be detached from the above Patents Form No. 24. It will be returned to the payer on receipt of the prescribed fee if he fills in the details specified at (e) and (f) in the margin of the Patents Form No. 26.

PATENTS FORM NO. 26

PATENTS ACTS, 1949 to 1961

Certificate of Payment of Renewal Fee

(e) Here complete Patent Number.

(f) Here complete name and full postal address to which the Certificate is to be sent.

Letters Patent No. (e)................................

This is to certify that the prescribed fee has been duly paid and the patent renewed until........................when the next renewal fee will be due

To

(f) ....

....

....

Patent Office
Date Stamp

EXPLANATORY NOTE

(This Note is not part of the Rules.)

These Rules further amend the Patents Rules 1968 with effect from 1st January 1972.

The Comptroller is no longer required to issue a certificate of payment in relation to a patent renewal fee unless one is specifically sought by the person paying the fee.

The requirement that the Comptroller issue a reminder that a renewal fee is due at least one month before the date of payment is replaced by a requirement to issue one not more than six weeks after the due date of payment if the fee remains unpaid.

1971 No. 1918

WAGES COUNCILS

The Wages Regulation (Corset) Order 1971

Made - - - - 24*th November* 1971

Coming into Operation 13*th December* 1971

Whereas the Secretary of State has received from the Corset Wages Council the wages regulation proposals set out in the Schedule hereto;

Now, therefore, the Secretary of State in exercise of his powers under section 11 of the Wages Councils Act 1959**(a)**, and of all other powers enabling him in that behalf, hereby makes the following Order:—

1. This Order may be cited as the Wages Regulation (Corset) Order 1971.

2.—(1) In this Order the expression "the specified date" means the 13th December 1971, provided that where, as respects any worker who is paid wages at intervals not exceeding seven days, that date does not correspond with the beginning of the period for which the wages are paid, the expression "the specified date" means, as respects that worker, the beginning of the next such period following that date.

(2) The Interpretation Act 1889**(b)** shall apply to the interpretation of this Order as it applies to the interpretation of an Act of Parliament and as if this Order and the Order hereby revoked were Acts of Parliament.

3. The wages regulation proposals set out in the Schedules hereto shall have effect as from the specified date and as from that date the Wages Regulation (Corset) (No. 2) Order 1970**(c)** shall cease to have effect.

Signed by order of the Secretary of State.
24th November 1971.

J. R. Lloyd Davies,
Assistant Secretary,
Department of Employment.

(a) 1959 c. 69. **(b)** 1889 c. 63.
(c) S.I. 1970/1529 (1970 III, p. 5280).

Article 3

SCHEDULE 1

The following minimum remuneration shall be substituted for the statutory minimum remuneration fixed by the Wages Regulation (Corset) (No. 2) Order 1970 (Order K. (70)).

STATUTORY MINIMUM REMUNERATION

PART I

GENERAL

1. The minimum remuneration payable to a worker to whom this Schedule applies for all work except work to which a minimum overtime rate applies under Part IV of this Schedule is:—

(1) in the case of a time worker, the general minimum time rate payable to the worker under Part II or Part III of this Schedule;

(2) in the case of a worker employed on piece work, piece rates each of which would yield, in the circumstances of the case, to an ordinary worker at least the same amount of money as the general minimum time rate applicable to the worker under Part II or Part III of this Schedule.

PART II

FEMALE WORKERS

GENERAL MINIMUM TIME RATES

2. Subject to the provisions of this Schedule, the general minimum time rates payable to female time workers are as follows:—

(1) LEARNERS (as defined in paragraph 8) during the following periods of employment in the trade:—

	First six months of employment per hour	Second six months of employment per hour	Second year of employment per hour
(*a*) *Up to and including 2nd January 1972:—*			
Entering the trade	p	p	p
Aged 15 and under 16 years	*16·23*	*18·86*	*23·68*
„ 16 „ „ 17 „	*17·55*	*20·18*	*25·00*
„ 17 „ „ 18 „	*18·86*	*21·49*	*25·00*
„ 18 years or over	*22·81*	*24·12*	*28·50*
(*b*) *On and after 3rd January 1972:—*			
Entering the trade	p	p	p
Aged 15 and under 16 years	*17·08*	*19·85*	*24·93*
„ 16 „ „ 17 „	*18·47*	*21·24*	*26·32*
„ 17 „ „ 18 „	*19·85*	*22·62*	*26·32*
„ 18 years or over	*24·01*	*25·39*	*30·00*

(2) ALL OTHER WORKERS

(*a*) *Up to and including 2nd January 1972* ... ... *28·50p per hour*

(*b*) *On and after 3rd January 1972* ... ... *30·00p per hour*

PART III

MALE WORKERS

GENERAL MINIMUM TIME RATES

3. Subject to the provisions of this Schedule, the general minimum time rates payable to male time workers are as follows:—

	General Minimum Time Rates per hour	
	Up to and including 2nd January 1972	*On and after 3rd January 1972*
	p	p
(1) Workers employed in CUTTING, MARKING-OUT (other than process working), HAND PRESSING, MATCHING-UP or SHADING whose experience in any of the said occupations after the age of 18 years is:—		
(*a*) Not less than 5 years	*37·25*	*38·75*
(*b*) Less than 5 years but not less than 3 years	*36·50*	*38·00*
Provided that in reckoning such experience, there shall be included any experience of a worker after the age of 18 years in folding, hand-fitting, parting, separating or making-up, up to a maximum of 12 months.		
(2) Workers employed in FOLDING, HAND-FITTING, PARTING, SEPARATING or MAKING-UP, with not less than three years' experience in any of the said occupations after the age of 18 years	*36·00*	*37·50*
(3) WAREHOUSEMEN OR PACKERS aged 21 years or over with not less than two years' experience as warehousemen or packers	*36·00*	*37·50*
(4) ALL OTHER WORKERS (including process workers):—		
Aged 21 years or over	*35·25*	*36·75*
" 20 and under 21 years	*31·33*	*32·66*
" 19 " " 20 "	*29·81*	*31·08*
" 18 " " 19 "	*26·98*	*28·13*
" 17 " " 18 "	*22·63*	*23·59*
" 16 " " 17 "	*19·80*	*20·64*
" under 16 years	*16·97*	*17·69*
Provided that the minimum rates applicable during his first year's employment in the trade to a male worker who enters, or has entered, the trade for the first time at or over the age of 19 years shall be:—		
Aged 21 years or over	*29·81*	*31·08*
Aged under 21 years	*26·98*	*28·13*

PART IV

OVERTIME AND WAITING TIME

NORMAL NUMBER OF HOURS

4. Subject to the provisions of this Part of this Schedule, the minimum overtime rates set out in paragraph 5 are payable to a worker in respect of any time worked—

(1) in excess of the hours following, that is to say,

(*a*) in any week ... ... 40 hours

(*b*) on any day other than a Saturday, Sunday or customary holiday—

(i) where the normal working hours exceed 8½ ... ... 9 hours

or

(ii) where the normal working hours are more than 8, but not more than 8½ ... ... 8½ hours

or

(iii) where the normal working hours are not more than 8 ... 8 hours

(2) on a Saturday, Sunday or customary holiday.

MINIMUM OVERTIME RATES

5.—(1) Minimum overtime rates are payable to any worker as follows:—

(*a*) on any day other than a Sunday or customary holiday—

(i) for the first 2 hours of overtime worked ... ... time-and-a-quarter

(ii) for the next 2 hours ... ... time-and-a-half

(iii) thereafter ... ... double time

(*b*) on a Sunday or customary holiday—
for all time worked ... ... double time

(*c*) in any week, exclusive of any time in respect of which any minimum overtime rate is payable under the foregoing provisions of this sub-paragraph—

for all time worked in excess of 40 hours ... ... time-and-a-quarter

(2) The minimum overtime rates set out in sub-paragraph (1)(*a*) or (*b*) of this paragraph are payable in any week whether or not the minimum overtime rate set out in sub-paragraph (1)(*c*) is also payable.

6. In this Schedule—

(1) the expression "customary holiday" means—

A. *in relation to the year ending on 31st December 1971, the following days:—*

(*a*) (i) in England and Wales—

Christmas Day, Boxing Day, Good Friday, Easter Monday, Whit Monday (or where another day is substituted therefor by national proclamation, that day) and August Bank Holiday;

(ii) in Scotland—

New Year's Day;
the local Spring holiday;
the local Autumn holiday; and
three other days (being days of the week on which the worker normally works for the employer), in the course of the year, to be fixed by the employer and notified to the worker not less than three weeks before the holiday; or

(*b*) in the case of each of the said days, a day substituted by the employer therefor, being a day recognised by local custom as a day of holiday in substitution for the said day;

B. *in relation to the year ending on 31st December 1972 and in relation to each subsequent year ending on 31st December, the following days:—*

(*a*) (i) in England and Wales—

Christmas Day (or, if Christmas Day falls on a Sunday, such weekday as may be appointed by national proclamation, or, if none is so appointed, the next following Tuesday), Boxing Day, Good Friday, Easter Monday, Whit Monday (or where another day is substituted therefor by national proclamation, that day), August Bank Holiday *and one other day*

(being a day of the week on which the worker normally works for the employer) in the course of such year, to be fixed by the employer and notified to the worker not less than three weeks before the holiday;

(ii) in Scotland—

New Year's Day (or, if New Year's Day falls on a Sunday, the following Monday);
the local Spring holiday;
the local Autumn holiday; and
four other days (being days of the week on which the worker normally works for the employer) in the course of such year, to be fixed by the employer and notified to the worker not less than three weeks before the holiday; or

(*b*) in the case of each of the said days a day substituted by the employer therefor, being a day recognised by local custom as a day of holiday in substitution for the said day;

(2) the expressions "time-and-a-quarter", "time-and-a-half" and "double time" mean respectively—

(*a*) in the case of a time worker, one and a quarter times, one and a half times and twice the general minimum time rate otherwise payable to the worker;

(*b*) in the case of a worker employed on piece work—

(i) a time rate equal respectively to one quarter, one half and the whole of the general minimum time rate which would be payable to the worker under Part II or Part III of this Schedule if the worker were a time worker and a minimum overtime rate did not apply, and, in addition thereto,

(ii) the piece rates otherwise payable to the worker under paragraph 1(2).

WAITING TIME

7.—(1) A worker is entitled to payment of the minimum remuneration specified in this Schedule for all time during which he is present on the premises of his employer, unless he is present thereon in any of the following circumstances:—

(*a*) without the employer's consent, express or implied;

(*b*) for some purpose unconnected with his work and other than that of waiting for work to be given to him to perform;

(*c*) by reason only of the fact that he is resident thereon;

(*d*) during normal meal times in a room or place in which no work is being done, and he is not waiting for work to be given to him to perform.

(2) The minimum remuneration payable under sub-paragraph (1) of this paragraph to a piece worker when not engaged on piece work is that which would be payable if he were a time worker.

PART V

INTERPRETATION

8. In this Schedule—

(1) the expression "LEARNER" means a female worker who—

(*a*) is employed during the whole or a substantial part of her time in learning any branch of the trade by an employer who provides her with reasonable facilities for such learning, and

(*b*) does not work in a room used for dwelling purposes except where she is in the employment of her parent or guardian.

(2) "THE TRADE" means the corset trade as specified in the next following paragraph.

APPLICABILITY OF STATUTORY MINIMUM REMUNERATION

9. Subject to the provisions of paragraph 10, this Schedule applies to workers in relation to whom the Corset Wages Council operates, that is to say, workers employed in Great Britain in the trade specified in the Schedule to the Trade Boards (Corset Trade, Great Britain) (Amendment) Regulations 1927**(a)**, which is as follows:—

"1. All work in connection with—

(*a*) the manufacture of corsets, corselettes, stays, children's corset bodies, and infants' staybands.

(*b*) the manufacture of bust confiners.

(*c*) the manufacture of support or abdominal belts or similar articles.

(*d*) the manufacture (including assembling) of stocking suspenders, suspender belts and suspender pads, when carried on in conjunction with, or in association with the manufacture of any of the above articles.

2. Work in connection with the manufacture specified in paragraph 1 hereof shall include—

(*a*) the altering, repairing, renovating or remaking of any of the articles specified in paragraph 1 hereof, when carried on in conjunction with or in association with such manufacture.

(*b*) warehousing, packing, marking, letter-press stamping, when incidental to such manufacture.

3. Notwithstanding anything in this Schedule the following operations shall not be operations in the Corset Trade:—

(*a*) the manufacture of bust confiners, when carried on in a department mainly engaged on the making of articles specified in the Appendix to the Trade Boards (Women's Clothing) Order 1919**(b)**;

(*b*) the manufacture of any of the articles specified in paragraph 1 hereof when made in association with or in conjunction with the manufacture of surgical instruments or appliances;

(*c*) the manufacture of corset steels and busks;

(*d*) printing, clerical work, cleaning, caretaking, and general maintenance work."

TRAINING UNDER THE GOVERNMENT VOCATIONAL TRAINING SCHEME

10. Notwithstanding anything hereinbefore contained, this Schedule shall not apply to—

(1) female workers employed on Machining, Pressing, Eyeletting and Boning;

(2) male workers employed on Cutting, Marking-out, Folding and Parting,

during any period in respect of which they are in receipt of allowances as provided under the Government Vocational Training Scheme for resettlement training if they are trainees who have been placed by the Department of Employment with the employer for a period of approved training and if the requirements of the said Scheme are duly complied with.

SCHEDULE 2

HOLIDAYS AND HOLIDAY REMUNERATION

The Wages Regulation (Corset) (Holidays) Order 1967**(c)** (Order K. (64)) shall have effect as if in the Schedule thereto:—

(a) S.R. & O. 1927/534 (1927, p. 1814).
(b) S.R. & O. 1919/1263 (1919 II, p. 531).
(c) S.I. 1967/1362 (1967 III, p. 4011).

1. For sub-paragraph (2) of paragraph 2 (which relates to customary holidays) there were substituted the following sub-paragraph:—

"(2) The said customary holidays are:—

A. *in relation to the year ending on 31st December 1971, the following days:—*

(*a*) (i) in England and Wales—

Christmas Day, Boxing Day, Good Friday, Easter Monday, Whit Monday (or where another day is substituted therefore by national proclamation, that day) and August Bank Holiday;

(ii) in Scotland—

New Year's Day;
the local Spring holiday;
the local Autumn holiday; and
three other days (being days of the week on which the worker normally works for the employer) in the course of the year, to be fixed by the employer and notified to the worker not less than three weeks before the holiday; or

(*b*) in the case of each of the said days, a day substituted by the employer therefor, being a day recognised by local custom as a day of holiday in substitution for the said day;

B. *in relation to the year ending on 31st December 1972, and in relation to each subsequent year ending on 31st December, the following days:—*

(*a*) (i) in England and Wales—

Christmas Day (or, if Christmas Day falls on a Sunday, such weekday as may be appointed by national proclamation, or, if none is so appointed, the next following Tuesday), Boxing Day, Good Friday, Easter Monday, Whit Monday (or where another day is substituted therefor by national proclamation, that day), August Bank Holiday *and one other day (being a day of the week on which the worker normally works for the employer) in the course of such year, to be fixed by the employer and notified to the worker not less than three weeks before the holiday;*

(ii) in Scotland—

New Year's Day (or, if New Year's Day falls on a Sunday, the following Monday);
the local Spring holiday;
the local Autumn holiday; and
four other days (being days of the week on which the worker normally works for the employer) in the course of such year, to be fixed by the employer and notified to the worker not less than three weeks before the holiday; or

(*b*) in the case of each of the said days a day substituted by the employer therefor, being a day recognised by local custom as a day of holiday in substitution for the said day;".

2. For the reference in paragraph 6(1)(*a*) to the provisions of sub-paragraph (2)(*b*) of paragraph 2 (which relates to the substitution by the employer of a day of holiday recognised by local custom), there were substituted a reference to A(*b*) and B(*b*) of sub-paragraph (2) of paragraph 2.

EXPLANATORY NOTE

(This Note is not part of the Order.)

This Order has effect from 13th December 1971. Schedule 1 sets out the statutory minimum remuneration payable in substitution for that fixed by the Wages Regulation (Corset) (No. 2) Order 1970 (Order K. (70)), which Order is revoked. Schedule 2 amends the Wages Regulation (Corset) (Holidays) Order 1967 (Order K. (64)) by providing for an additional day of customary holiday.

New provisions are printed in italics.

1971 No. 1919

WAGES COUNCILS

The Wages Regulation (Shirtmaking) Order 1971

Made - - - -	24*th November* 1971
Coming into Operation	13*th December* 1971

Whereas the Secretary of State has received from the Shirtmaking Wages Council (Great Britain) the wages regulation proposals set out in Schedules 1 and 2 hereto;

Now, therefore, the Secretary of State in exercise of his powers under section 11 of the Wages Councils Act 1959**(a)**, and of all other powers enabling him in that behalf, hereby makes the following Order:—

1. This Order may be cited as the Wages Regulation (Shirtmaking) Order 1971.

2.—(1) In this Order the expression "the specified date" means the 13th December 1971, provided that where, as respects any worker who is paid wages at intervals not exceeding seven days, that date does not correspond with the beginning of the period for which the wages are paid, the expression "the specified date" means, as respects that worker, the beginning of the next such period following that date.

(2) The Interpretation Act 1889**(b)** shall apply to the interpretation of this Order as it applies to the interpretation of an Act of Parliament and as if this Order and the Order hereby revoked were Acts of Parliament.

3. The wages regulation proposals set out in Schedules 1 and 2 hereto shall have effect as from the specified date and as from that date the Wages Regulation (Shirtmaking) (No. 2) Order 1970**(c)** shall cease to have effect.

Signed by order of the Secretary of State.
24th November 1971.

J. R. Lloyd Davies,
Assistant Secretary,
Department of Employment.

Article 3

SCHEDULE 1

The following minimum remuneration shall be substituted for the statutory minimum remuneration fixed by the Wages Regulation (Shirtmaking) (No. 2) Order 1970 (Order S. (75)).

(a) 1959 c. 69. **(b)** 1889 c. 63.
(c) S.I. 1970/1528 (1970 III, p. 5272).

STATUTORY MINIMUM REMUNERATION

PART I

GENERAL

1. The minimum remuneration payable to a worker to whom this Schedule applies for all work except work to which a minimum overtime rate applies under Part IV of this Schedule is:—

(1) in the case of a time worker, the general minimum time rate payable to the worker under Part II or Part III of this Schedule;

(2) in the case of a worker employed on piece work, piece rates each of which would yield in the circumstances of the case, to an ordinary worker at least the same amount of money as the general minimum time rate which would be payable if the worker were a time worker.

PART II

MALE WORKERS

GENERAL MINIMUM TIME RATES

2. Subject to the provisions of this Schedule, the general minimum time rates payable to male time workers are as follows:—

	General minimum time rates Per hour p
(1) SPECIAL OR MEASURE CUTTERS, PATTERN CUTTERS OR PATTERN TAKERS, who are employed as such during the whole or a substantial part of their time and have had after the age of 18 years not less than three years' employment as a cutter of any class specified in this or the next following sub-paragraph including not less than two years as a measure cutter	*38·75*
(2) CUTTERS, aged 21 years or over, who are employed as such during the whole or a substantial part of their time and have had not less than four years' employment as a cutter of any class specified in this or the last preceding sub-paragraph	*38·00*
(3) TIE CUTTERS, aged 22 years or over, who are employed during the whole or a substantial part of their time in tie cutting and have had at least five years' experience therein...	*38·75*
(4) TIE CUTTERS (not being workers to whom sub-paragraph (3) applies) aged 21 years or over, who are employed during the whole or a substantial part of their time in tie cutting and have had at least four years' experience therein	*38·00*
(5) ALL OTHER WORKERS being aged—	
21 years or over	*36·25*
20 and under 21 years	*32·75*
19 „ „ 20 „	*31·00*
18 „ „ 19 „	*28·00*
17 „ „ 18 „	*23·50*
16 „ „ 17 „	*20·50*
under 16 years	*17·75*

PART III

FEMALE WORKERS

GENERAL MINIMUM TIME RATES

3.—(1) Subject to the provisions of this Schedule, the general minimum time rates payable to female time workers are as follows:—

(*a*) LEARNERS during the following periods of employment in the trade:—

	First 6 months Per hour p	Second 6 months Per hour p	Second year Per hour p
Entering the trade			
Aged 15 and under 16 years ...	*17·00*	*19·75*	*25·00*
„ 16 „ „ 17 „ ...	*18·50*	*21·25*	*26·25*
„ 17 „ „ 18 „ ...	*19·75*	*22·50*	*26·25*
„ 18 years or over	*24·00*	*25·50*	*30·00*

(*b*) ALL OTHER WORKERS
(including home-workers) ... ... *30·00p* per hour

(2) For the purpose of determining the period of a learner's employment in the trade and the date on which she ceases to be a learner, there shall be reckoned as employment in the trade any employment in any branch of the trade or in the making, wherever carried on, of overalls for male or female persons.

PART IV

OVERTIME AND WAITING TIME

NORMAL NUMBER OF HOURS

4. Subject to the provisions of this Part of this Schedule, the minimum overtime rates set out in paragraph 5 are payable to a worker in respect of any time worked—

(1) in excess of the hours following, that is to say,

(*a*) in any week ... ... 40 hours

(*b*) on any day other than a Saturday, Sunday or customary holiday—

where the normal working hours exceed 8½ ... ... 9 hours

or

where the normal working hours are more than 8, but not more than 8½ ... ... 8½ hours

or

where the normal working hours are not more than 8 ... 8 hours

(2) on a Saturday, Sunday or customary holiday.

MINIMUM OVERTIME RATES

5.—(1) Minimum overtime rates are payable to any worker as follows:—

(*a*) on any day other than a Sunday or customary holiday—

(i) for the first 2 hours of overtime worked ... ... time-and-a-quarter

(ii) for the next 2 hours... ... ... time-and-a-half

(iii) thereafter ... ... double time

(*b*) on a Sunday or customary holiday—
for all time worked ... ... double time

(*c*) in any week, exclusive of any time in respect of which any minimum overtime rate is payable under the foregoing provisions of this sub-paragraph—

for all time worked in excess of 40 hours... ... time-and-a-quarter

(2) The minimum overtime rates set out in sub-paragraph (1)(*a*) or (*b*) of this paragraph are payable in any week whether or not the minimum overtime rate set out in sub-paragraph (1)(*c*) is also payable.

6. In this Part of this Schedule—

(1) the expression "CUSTOMARY HOLIDAY" means:—

In relation to the year ending on 31st December 1971, the days specified in (a) or (b) of this sub-paragraph:—

(*a*) (i) in England and Wales—

Christmas Day (or, if Christmas Day falls on a Sunday, such weekday as may be appointed by national proclamation, or, if none is so appointed, the next following Tuesday), Boxing Day, Good Friday, Easter Monday, Whit Monday (or where another day is substituted therefor by national proclamation, that day), and August Bank Holiday;

(ii) in Scotland—

New Year's Day (or, if New Year's Day falls on a Sunday, the following Monday);
the local Spring holiday;
the local Autumn holiday; and
three other days (being days of the week on which the worker normally works for the employer), in the course of a calendar year, to be fixed by the employer and notified to the worker not less than three weeks before the holiday;

or (*b*) in the case of each of the said days a day substituted by the employer therefor, being a day recognised by local custom as a day of holiday in substitution for the said day.

In relation to the year ending on 31st December 1972 and in relation to each subsequent year the days specified in (c) or (d) of this sub-paragraph:—

(*c*) (i) in England and Wales—

Christmas Day (or, if Christmas Day falls on a Sunday, such weekday as may be appointed by national proclamation, or, if none is so appointed, the next following Tuesday), Boxing Day, Good Friday, Easter Monday, Whit Monday (or where another day is substituted therefor by national proclamation, that day), August Bank Holiday *and one other day (being a day of the week on which the worker normally works for the employer) in the course of a calendar year, to be fixed by the employer and notified to the worker not less than three weeks before the holiday;*

(ii) in Scotland—

New Year's Day (or, if New Year's Day falls on a Sunday, the following Monday);
the local Spring holiday;
the local Autumn holiday; and
four other days (being days of the week on which the worker normally works for the employer) in the course of a calendar year, to be fixed by the employer and notified to the worker not less than three weeks before the holiday;

or (*d*) in the case of each of the said days a day substituted by the employer therefor, being a day recognised by local custom as a day of holiday in substitution for the said day.

(2) the expressions "TIME-AND-A-QUARTER", "TIME-AND-A-HALF" and "DOUBLE TIME" mean respectively—

(*a*) in the case of a time worker, one and a quarter times, one and a half times and twice the general minimum time rate otherwise payable to the worker;

(*b*) in the case of a worker employed on piece work—

(i) a time rate equal respectively to one quarter, one half and the whole of the general minimum time rate which would be payable to him if he were a time worker and a minimum overtime rate did not apply and, in addition thereto,

(ii) the piece rates otherwise payable to him under paragraph 1(2).

WAITING TIME

7.—(1) A worker is entitled to payment of the minimum remuneration specified in this Schedule for all time during which he is present on the premises of his employer unless he is present thereon in any of the following circumstances:—

(*a*) without the employer's consent, express or implied;

(*b*) for some purpose unconnected with his work and other than that of waiting for work to be given to him to perform;

(*c*) by reason only of the fact that he is resident thereon;

(*d*) during normal meal times in a room or place in which no work is being done, and he is not waiting for work to be given to him to perform.

(2) The minimum remuneration payable under sub-paragraph (1) of this paragraph to a piece worker when not engaged on piece work is that which would be payable if he were a time worker.

PART V

INTERPRETATION

8. In this Schedule, unless the context otherwise requires, the following expressions have the meanings hereby expressly assigned to them:—

(1) A CUTTER is a worker (other than a special or measure cutter, a pattern cutter or a pattern taker) substantially employed in one or more of the following processes:—

(*a*) marking-in or marking-out or marking-up materials;

(*b*) laying-up or hooking-up or folding materials;

(*c*) cutting materials; and

(*d*) dividing, that is to say, the process ordinarily carried on by cutters or their assistants of dividing, parting or separating parts of garments which are being cut and of assembling them into suitable bundles for making-up;

(2) A LEARNER is a female worker who—

(*a*) is employed during the whole or a substantial part of her time in learning any branch or process of the trade by an employer who provides her with reasonable facilities for such learning; and

(*b*) does not work in a room used for dwelling purposes, except where she is in the employment of her parent or guardian;

(3) A SPECIAL OR MEASURE CUTTER is a worker who—

(*a*) is able to take a complete set of measures and cut from model patterns; and

(*b*) has sufficient technical knowledge to alter patterns (excluding stock patterns);

(4) "THE TRADE" means the shirtmaking trade as specified in paragraph 10.

EXPERIENCE UNDER THE GOVERNMENT VOCATIONAL TRAINING SCHEME

9. A worker who has completed his period of training under the Government Vocational Training Scheme as a male cutter or as a female machinist shall, for the purpose of this Schedule be treated—

(1) in the case of a male worker, as a cutter or a tie cutter as the case may be, aged 21 years or over who has had not less than four years' employment as a cutter or tie cutter;

(2) in the case of a female worker, as a worker who has worked for *two* years as a learner in the trade.

APPLICABILITY OF STATUTORY MINIMUM REMUNERATION

10. Subject to the provisions of paragraph 11, this Schedule applies to workers in relation to whom the Shirtmaking Wages Council (Great Britain) operates, that is to say, workers employed in Great Britain in any branch of the trade specified in the Trade Boards (Shirtmaking Trade, Great Britain) (Constitution and Proceedings) Regulations 1929(**a**), namely:—

(1) The making from textile fabrics of shirts, collars, cuffs, pyjamas, aprons, chefs' caps, hospital ward caps, and other washable clothing worn by male persons;

(2) the making of women's collars and cuffs and of nurses' washing belts where carried on in association with or in conjunction with the making of the before mentioned articles;

(3) the making of neckties worn by male persons, and of neckties worn by female persons where made in association with or in conjunction with the making of neckties worn by male persons;

including:—

Laundering, smoothing, folding, ornamenting, boxing, packing, warehousing, and all other operations incidental to or appertaining to the making of any of the above mentioned articles;

but excluding:—

(1) the making of articles which are knitted or are made from knitted fabrics;

(2) the making of handkerchiefs, mufflers, gloves, socks, stockings, spats, gaiters, bonnets, hats or caps (other than chefs' caps and hospital ward caps);

(3) the making of boys' washing suits;

(4) the making of washable clothing to be worn by children without distinction of sex;

(5) the making of any articles, the making of which is included in the Trade Boards (Tailoring) Order 1919(**b**).

(**a**) S.R. & O. 1929/825 (1929, p. 1374). (**b**) S.R. & O. 1919/1201 (1919 II, p. 528).

TRAINING UNDER THE GOVERNMENT VOCATIONAL TRAINING SCHEME

11. Notwithstanding anything hereinbefore contained, this Schedule shall not apply to—

(1) female workers employed as machinists, or

(2) male workers employed as cutters—

during any period in respect of which they are in receipt of allowances as provided under the Government Vocational Training Scheme for resettlement training if they are trainees who have been placed by the Department of Employment with the employer for a period of approved training and if the requirements of the said Scheme are duly complied with.

Article 3

SCHEDULE 2

HOLIDAYS AND HOLIDAY REMUNERATION

The Wages Regulation (Shirtmaking) (Holidays) Order 1967**(a)** (Order S. (69)) shall have effect as if in the Schedule thereto:—

1. For sub-paragraph (2) of paragraph 2 (which relates to customary holidays) there were substituted the following:—

"(2) The said customary holidays are:—

A. In relation to the year ending on 31st December 1971 the days specified in (a) or (b) of this sub-paragraph:—

(*a*) (i) in England and Wales—

Christmas Day (or, if Christmas Day falls on a Sunday, such weekday as may be appointed by national proclamation, or, if none is so appointed, the next following Tuesday), Boxing Day, Good Friday, Easter Monday, Whit Monday (or where another day is substituted therefor by national proclamation, that day) and August Bank Holiday;

(ii) in Scotland—

New Year's Day (or, if New Year's Day falls on a Sunday, the following Monday);
the local Spring holiday;
the local Autumn holiday; and
three other days (being days of the week on which the worker normally works for the employer) in the course of a calendar year, to be fixed by the employer and notified to the worker not less than three weeks before the holiday; or

(*b*) in the case of each of the said days a day substituted by the employer therefor, being a day recognised by local custom as a day of holiday in substitution for the said day.

B. In relation to the year ending on 31st December 1972, and in relation to each subsequent year, the days specified in (a) or (b) of this sub-paragraph:—

(*a*) (i) in England and Wales—

Christmas Day (or, if Christmas Day falls on a Sunday, such weekday as may be appointed by national proclamation, or, if none is so appointed, the next following Tuesday), Boxing Day, Good Friday, Easter Monday, Whit Monday (or where another day is substituted therefor by national proclamation, that day), August Bank Holiday *and one other day (being a day on which the worker normally works for the employer) in the course of a calendar year, to be fixed by the employer and notified to the worker not less than three weeks before the holiday:*

(a) S.I. 1967/1361 (1967 III, p. 4002).

(ii) in Scotland—

New Year's Day (or, if New Year's Day falls on a Sunday, the following Monday);
the local Spring holiday;
the local Autumn holiday; and
four other days (being days on which the worker normally works for the employer) in the course of a calendar year, to be fixed by the employer and notified to the worker not less than three weeks before the holiday;

or (*b*) in the case of each of the said days a day substituted by the employer therefor, being a day recognised by local custom as a day of holiday in substitution for the said day."

2. For the reference in paragraph 6(1)(*a*) to the provisions of sub-paragraph (2)(*b*) of paragraph 2 (which relates to the substitution by the employer of a day of holiday recognised by local custom), there were substituted a reference to sub-paragraph A(*b*) and B(*b*) of sub-paragraph (2) of paragraph 2.

EXPLANATORY NOTE

(*This Note is not part of the Order.*)

This Order has effect from 13th December 1971. Schedule 1 sets out the statutory minimum remuneration payable in substitution for that fixed by the Wages Regulation (Shirtmaking) (No. 2) Order 1970 (Order S.(75)), which Order is revoked. Schedule 2 amends the Wages Regulation (Shirtmaking) (Holidays) Order 1967 (Order S. (69)) by providing for an additional day of customary holiday.

New provisions are printed in italics.

1971 No. 1920

FOOD AND DRUGS

The Welfare Food (Amendment) Order 1971

Made - - -	*25th November* 1971
Laid before Parliament	*3rd December* 1971
Coming into Operation	*2nd January* 1972

The Secretary of State for Social Services, the Secretary of State for Wales and the Secretary of State for Scotland, acting jointly in exercise of their powers under sections 4 and 7 of the Emergency Laws (Re-enactments and Repeals) Act 1964(**a**) and of all other powers enabling them in that behalf, hereby order as follows:—

Title, commencement and extent

1.—(1) This order may be cited as the Welfare Food (Amendment) Order 1971 and shall come into operation on 2nd January 1972.

(2) This order shall not extend to Northern Ireland.

Interpretation

2. In this order the expression "the principal order" means the Welfare Food Order 1971(**b**).

Amendments of the principal order

3.—(1) In article 2(1) of the principal order—

(i) after the words "otherwise requires—" there shall be added—

" 'approved child-minder' means a child-minder who is for the time being approved by the Secretary of State for the purposes of this order;"

" 'approved day nursery' means a day nursery or playgroup which is for the time being approved by the Secretary of State for the purposes of this order;";

(ii) for paragraph (*b*) of the definition of "handicapped child" there shall be substituted "(*b*) by reason of disability of mind or body is not a registered pupil at a school in accordance with the provisions of the Education Acts 1944 to 1971 and the Education (Scotland) Acts 1939 to 1971;";

(iii) the definition of "registered day nursery" shall be deleted;

(iv) for the definition of "vitamin tablets" there shall be substituted " 'vitamin tablets' means vitamin A, D and C tablets;".

(**a**) 1964 c. 60.

(**b**) S.I. 1971/457 (1971 I, p. 1358).

(2) For article 6 of the principal order (arrangements which the Secretary of State may make for children attending day nurseries to receive free milk) there shall be substituted—

"*Milk for young children in day care*

6. The Secretary of State may make arrangements for each young child attending an approved day nursery or who is minded by an approved child-minder at premises approved by the Secretary of State for the purposes of this order to receive free of charge (without prejudice to his entitlement under article 4) one-third of a pint of milk, or dried milk made up to provide one-third of a pint, in respect of each day of attendance."

(3) In Schedule 2 to the principal order (which specifies the entitlement to welfare food other than liquid milk)—

(i) in column (3) for the expression "2½p per packet" wherever it occurs there shall be substituted the expression "6p per container";

(ii) in column (4) for the word "packets" wherever it occurs there shall be substituted the word "containers".

Keith Joseph,
Secretary of State for Social Services.

24th November 1971.

Peter Thomas,
Secretary of State for Wales.

24th November 1971.

Gordon Campbell,
Secretary of State for Scotland.

25th November 1971.

EXPLANATORY NOTE

(*This Note is not part of the Order.*)

This Order amends the Welfare Food Order 1971 by altering the composition of vitamin tablets which are included in welfare food and specifying their price. In addition "approved day nursery" has been substituted for "registered day nursery" as a place of attendance where young children may receive milk free of charge. Young children who attend an approved playgroup or who are minded by an approved child-minder at approved premises may also receive free milk.

1971 No. 1921

CUSTOMS AND EXCISE

The Developing Countries (Origin of Goods) Regulations 1971

Made - - - -	*25th November* 1971
Laid before the House of Commons	*3rd December* 1971
Coming into Operation	*1st January* 1972

The Secretary of State in exercise of his powers under section 12(2) of the Import Duties Act 1958(**a**), and all other powers enabling him in that behalf, hereby makes the following Regulations :—

Citation, commencement and interpretation

1.—(1) These Regulations may be cited as the Developing Countries (Origin of Goods) Regulations 1971 and shall come into operation on 1st January 1972.

—(2) In these Regulations—

"exhibition" means a trade, industrial, agricultural or crafts exhibition, fair or similar show or display other than an exhibition, fair, show or display organised for private purposes in a shop or on business premises with a view to the sale of goods foreign to the country where the exhibition is held ;

"originating" refers, in relation to materials and parts, to materials and parts which would, if these Regulations were applicable to them, fall to be treated as produced or manufactured in the country in which the articles in whose production or manufacture they have been used are claimed to have been produced or manufactured ; and

references to Chapters and tariff headings are references to the Chapters and headings of the Customs Tariff 1959(**b**).

(3) Schedule 1 hereto shall have effect for defining the application of terms used in, and rules mentioned in, Schedules 2 and 3 hereto.

(4) The Interpretation Act 1889(**c**) shall apply to the interpretation of these Regulations as it applies to the interpretation of an Act of Parliament.

2.—(1) For the purpose of any order made under section 1 of the Finance Act 1971(**d**), the question whether goods are to be treated as produced or manufactured in a country shall be determined in accordance with these Regulations.

(**a**) 1958 c. 6.
(**b**) See S.I. 1971/1971(1971 III, p.5330).
(**c**) 1889 c. 63.
(**d**) 1971 c. 68.

(2) Materials and parts shall, for the purpose of these Regulations, be treated as having been imported into a country unless they are shown to the satisfaction of the Commissioners not to have been so imported.

Goods wholly produced or manufactured in a developing country

3.—(1) Goods which have been wholly produced or manufactured in a country without the use of any imported materials or parts shall be treated as produced or manufactured in that country :

Provided that they shall not be so treated by virtue of this paragraph if they have been used in another country for any purpose other than display or demonstration under customs control at an exhibition.

(2) For the purpose of paragraph (1),—

(*a*) used articles fit only for the recovery of materials therefrom shall be treated as wholly produced in a developing country from materials produced there if they are collected in that country ; and

(*b*) scrap or waste shall be treated as so produced if it results from the carrying on of any process of manufacture in that country.

Production or manufacture from imported materials or parts of a different tariff heading

4. Goods produced or manufactured in a country from imported materials or parts not falling within the same tariff heading as those goods shall be treated as produced or manufactured in that country except in the following cases,—

(*a*) if the goods have undergone further processing in another country or have been used in another country otherwise than for display or demonstration under customs control at an exhibition ; or

(*b*) being goods mentioned in column 1 of Schedule 2 hereto,—

(i) if they fall to be classified in a different tariff heading by reason only of the performance of the process mentioned in relation to them in column 2 of that Schedule or a combination of such a process and a process or processes mentioned in head (*c*) of this paragraph ; or

(ii) if they have not undergone in that country the process, or do not satisfy the rule, mentioned in relation to them in column 3 of that Schedule, as the case may be ; or

(*c*) if they fall to be classified in a different tariff heading by reason only of the performance of one or more of the following minor processes, namely,—

(i) operations intended solely to ensure that the goods remain in good condition during transit or storage, including chilling, placing in brine or any other solution, drying, spreading out, ventilating and removing damaged parts ;

(ii) sorting, classifying, matching (including the making up of sets of articles), sifting, screening, removing dust, washing, painting or cutting in pieces ;

(iii) packing, repacking, or splitting up into, or assembling into, consignments;

(iv) marking or labelling;

(v) mixing; or

(vi) simple assembly.

Processing not involving a change of tariff heading

5. Goods mentioned in column 1 of Schedule 3 hereto which have undergone in a country the process mentioned in column 2 of that Schedule shall be treated as produced or manufactured in that country unless they have subsequently undergone a further process in another country or have been used in another country otherwise than for display or demonstration under customs control at an exhibition.

Anthony Grant,
Parliamentary Under Secretary of State,
Department of Trade and Industry.

25th November 1971.

SCHEDULE 1

INTERPRETATION OF SCHEDULES 2 AND 3

1. The descriptions of goods in column 1 of Schedules 2 and 3 hereto shall,—

(*a*) if preceded by a reference to a Chapter, be taken to comprise all goods classified in that Chapter other than goods specifically excluded by the terms of the description; and

(*b*) if preceded by a reference to a tariff heading be taken to comprise all goods classified in that heading or, where the description does not coincide with the description of that heading in the Customs Tariff 1959, be taken to include all goods falling within a sub-heading of that heading in the terms of the description in the column.

2. Where, for the purpose of any entry in column 2 or 3 of Schedule 2 hereto, it is necessary to determine the value of exported goods that value shall be taken—

(*a*) in a case where the goods have been sold for delivery at the place of production or manufacture and the contract of sale is a sale in the open market, to be the price payable under that contract; or

(*b*) in any other case, to be the price which in the opinion of the Commissioners they would have fetched if they had been so sold,

less, in any case, an amount equal to any internal taxes or charges refundable upon the export of the goods from the country of production or manufacture.

3. Where, for any such purpose as aforesaid, it is necessary to determine the value of any imported materials or parts, their value shall—

(*a*) if the material or part is known to have been imported, be taken to be the value attributed to it for customs purposes at the time of importation; or (*b*) if the origin of the material or part is uncertain or it is otherwise impossible to ascertain its value pursuant to head (*a*) and if the price at which it was sold under the first contract for its sale after importation can be proved, be taken to be that price, or

(*c*) in any other case, be such value as the Commissioners may determine.

4. Where, for any such purpose as aforesaid, it is necessary to calculate the value attributable to originating materials or parts, that value shall be taken to be—

(*a*) (i) where the price paid under the first contract for the sale of any originating materials or parts used in the production or manufacture of the exported goods can be proved, that price less an amount equal to the value of any imported materials or parts used in the production or manufacture of those materials or parts; plus

(ii) where the price paid under the first contract for the sale of any originating materials or parts employed in the processing of imported materials and parts used in the production or manufacture of the exported goods can be proved, that price; or

(*b*) where any price cannot be proved in accordance with head (*a*) such amount as the Commissioners may determine.

5. In Schedule 2,—

(i) "the 40% imported materials rule" means that the value of the imported materials and parts employed in the production or manufacture of the goods does not exceed 40% of their value;

(ii) "the 50% imported materials rule" means that the value of the imported materials and parts so employed does not exceed 50% of the value of the goods; and

(iii) "the 40%/50% rule" means—

(*a*) that the value of the imported materials and parts employed in the production or manufacture of the goods does not exceed 40% of their value; and

(*b*) that at least 50% of the value of all the materials and parts so employed is attributable to originating materials and parts.

SCHEDULE 2

Tariff Heading	(1) *Exported products*	(2) *Process of production or manufacture from imported materials or parts that does not qualify the goods for treatment as goods of a developing country*	(3) *Process required to qualify the goods for treatment as goods of a developing country or rule as to the use of imported materials or parts*
02.05	Pig fat free of lean meat and poultry fat (not rendered or solvent-extracted), fresh, chilled, frozen, salted, in brine, dried or smoked	manufacture from products of Chapter 1 or 2	
02.06	Meat and edible offals (except poultry liver), salted, in brine, dried or smoked	manufacture from products of Chapter 1 or 2	
07.02	Vegetables (whether or not cooked), preserved by freezing	freezing	
07.03	Vegetables provisionally preserved in brine, in sulphur water or in other preservative solutions, but not specially prepared for immediate consumption	placing in brine or other solutions	
07.04	Dried vegetables, whole, cut, sliced, broken or in powder, but not further prepared	drying, dehydration, evaporation, cutting, breaking or powdering	
07.05	Dried leguminous vegetables, shelled, whether or not skinned or split	drying, dehydration or evaporation	
08.10	Fruit (whether or not cooked), preserved by freezing, not containing added sugar	freezing	

08.11	Bilberries and nuts provisionally preserved, but unsuitable for immediate consumption		
08.11	Citrus fruits (other than grapefruit, orange, clementine, mandarin or tangerine pulp not containing the peel and lemons comminuted entire), provisionally preserved otherwise than in brine, but unsuitable for immediate consumption	placing in brine or other solutions	
08.11	Fruit (other than blackberries, currants, gooseberries, loganberries, pears, plums, damsons, bullace, greengages and mirabelles, raspberries and mixtures containing any of these fruits or apples or strawberries), provisionally preserved but unsuitable for immediate consumption		
08.12	Fruit, dried, other than that falling within heading No. 08.01, 08.02, 08.03, 08.04 or 08.05	drying	
11.01	Cereal flours	manufacture from products of Chapter 10	
11.02	Cereal grouts and cereal meal; other worked cereal grains (for example, rolled, flaked, polished, pearled or kibbled, but not further prepared), except husked, glazed, polished or broken rice; germ of cereals, whole, rolled, flaked or ground	manufacture from products of Chapter 10	
11.03	Flours of the leguminous vegetables falling within heading No. 07.05	manufacture from dried leguminous vegetables	

SCHEDULE 2—*continued*

	(1)	(2)	(3)
	Exported products	*Process of production or manufacture from imported materials or parts that does not qualify the goods for treatment as goods of a developing country*	*Process required to qualify the goods for treatment as goods of a developing country or rule as to the use of imported materials or parts*
Tariff Heading			
11.04	Flours of the fruits falling within any heading in Chapter 8	manufacture from the fruit	
11.06	Flour and meal of sago and of manioc, arrowroot, salep and other roots and tubers falling within heading No. 07.06	manufacture from products of heading No. 07.06	
11.07	Malt, roasted or not	manufacture from products of Chapter 10	
11.08	Starches; inulin	manufacture from products of Chapter 7, 10 or 11	
12.02	Flours or meals of oil seeds or oleaginous fruit, non-defatted (excluding mustard flour)	manufacture from products of Chapter 12	
15.01	Lard, other pig fat and poultry fat, rendered or solvent-extracted	manufacture from products of Chapter 1 or heading No. 02.05	
15.13	Margarine, imitation lard and other prepared edible fats	manufacture from products of Chapter 15	
16.02	Other prepared or preserved meat or meat offal	manufacture from products of Chapter 1 or 2	
16.04	Prepared or preserved fish, including caviar and caviar substitutes	manufacture from products of Chapter 3	

17.02	Other sugars; sugar syrups; artificial honey (whether or not mixed with natural honey); caramel	manufacture from any product
17.04	Sugar confectionery, not containing cocoa	manufacture from other products of Chapter 17
17.05	Flavoured or coloured sugars, syrups and molasses, but not including fruit juices containing added sugar in any proportion	manufacture from any product
18.06	Chocolate and other food preparations containing cocoa	manufacture from products of Chapter 17 or manufacture from products of heading No. 18.01, 18.02, 18.03, 18.04 or 18.05 where the value of the imported products of those headings used exceeds 40% of the value of the exported product
19.01	Malt extracts	manufacture from products of heading No. 11.07
19.02	Preparations of flour, meal, starch or malt extract, of a kind used as infant food or for dietetic or culinary purposes, containing less than 50 per cent by weight of cocoa	manufacture from cereals and derived products, meat, milk and sugars
19.03	Macaroni, spaghetti and similar products	manufacture from any product
19.05	Prepared foods obtained by the swelling or roasting of cereals or cereal products (puffed rice, cornflakes and similar products)	manufacture from any product

SCHEDULE 2—*continued*

	(1) *Exported products*	(2) *Process of production or manufacture from imported materials or parts that does not qualify the goods for treatment as goods of a developing country*	(3) *Process required to qualify the goods for treatment as goods of a developing country or rule as to the use of imported materials or parts*
Tariff Heading			
19.06	Communion wafers, empty cachets of a kind suitable for pharmaceutical use, sealing wafers, rice paper and similar products	manufacture from products of Chapter 11	
19.07	Bread, ships' biscuits and other ordinary bakers' wares, not containing added sugar, honey, eggs, fats, cheese or fruit	manufacture from products of Chapter 11	
19.08	Pastry, biscuits, cakes and other fine bakers' wares, whether or not containing cocoa in any proportion	manufacture from products of Chapter 11	
20.01	Vegetables and fruit, prepared or preserved by vinegar or acetic acid, with or without sugar, whether or not containing salt, spices or mustard		manufacture from originating products of Chapters 7 and 8
20.02	Vegetables prepared or preserved otherwise than by vinegar or acetic acid		manufacture from originating products of Chapter 7
20.04	Fruit, fruit peel and parts of plants, preserved by sugar (drained, glacé or crystallised)		manufacture from originating products of Chapters 8 and 17

20.06	Fruit otherwise prepared or preserved whether or not containing added sugar or spirit		manufacture from originating products of Chapters 8, 9, 17 and 22
20.07	Fruit juices (including grape must) and vegetable juices, whether or not containing added sugar, but unfermented and not containing spirit		manufacture from originating products of Chapters 7, 8 and 17
21.04	Sauces; mixed condiments and mixed seasonings		manufacture in which the value of any imported tomato concentrate used does not exceed 50% of the value of the exported product
21.05	Soups and broths, in liquid, solid or powder form; homogenised composite food preparations	manufacture from products of heading No. 20.02	
22.02	Lemonade, flavoured spa waters and flavoured aerated waters, and other non-alcoholic beverages, not including fruit and vegetable juices falling within heading No. 20.07	manufacture from fruit juices	
22.04	Grape must, in fermentation or with fermentation arrested otherwise than by the addition of alcohol	manufacture from fruit juices	
22.10	Vinegar and substitutes for vinegar	manufacture from products of Chapter 22 or heading No. 29.14	
23.01	Flours and meals, of meat, offals, fish, crustaceans or molluscs, unfit for human consumption; greaves		the 40% imported materials rule
28.13	Hydrobromic acid	manufacture from products of heading No. 28.01	
28.19	Zinc oxide	manufacture from products of heading No. 79.01	

SCHEDULE 2—*continued*

Tariff Heading	(1) Exported products	(2) *Process of production or manufacture from imported materials or parts that does not qualify the goods for treatment as goods of a developing country*	(3) *Process required to qualify the goods for treatment as goods of a developing country or rule as to the use of imported materials or parts*
28.27	Lead oxides; red lead and orange lead	manufacture from products of heading No. 78.01	
28.28	Lithium hydroxide	manufacture from products of heading No. 28.42	
28.29	Lithium fluoride	manufacture from products of heading No. 28.28 or 28.42	
28.30	Lithium chloride	manufacture from products of heading No. 28.28 or 28.42	
28.33	Bromides	manufacture from products of heading No. 28.01 or 28.13	
28.38	Aluminium sulphate	manufacture from products of heading No. 28.20	
28.42	Lithium carbonate	manufacture from products of heading No. 28.28	
29.02	Organic bromides	manufacture from products of heading No. 28.01 or 28.13	
29.02	Trichlorodi(chloro-phenyl)ethane		transformation of ethanol into chloral and condensation of chloral with monochlorobenzene

29.35	Pyridine; alpha—picoline; beta—picoline; gamma—picoline		transformation of acetylene into acetaldehyde and transformation of acetaldehyde into pyridine or picoline
29.35	Vinylpyridine		transformation of acetaldehyde into picolines and transformation of picolines into vinylpyridine
29.38	Nicotinic acid (Vitamin PP)		transformation of acetaldehyde into beta-picoline and transformation of beta-picoline into nicotinic acid
30.03	Medicaments (including veterinary medicaments)	manufacture from active substances, i.e. any substances which form part of the goods and in respect of which any therapeutic or prophylactic claim is made by the producer or exporter	
30.04	Wadding, gauze, bandages and similar articles (for example, dressings, adhesive plasters, poultices) impregnated or coated with pharmaceutical substances for medical or surgical purposes, other than goods specified in Note 3 to Chapter 30		manufacture from originating pharmaceutical substances
31.05	Other fertilisers; goods of Chapter 31 in tablets, lozenges and similar prepared forms or in packings of a gross weight not exceeding 10 kg		the 50% imported materials rule
32.06	Colour lakes	manufacture from materials of heading No. 32.04 or 32.05	
32.07	Other colouring matter; inorganic products of a kind used as luminophores	mixing of oxides or salts of Chapter 28 with extenders such as natural barium sulphate or carbonate, chalk, and satin white	

SCHEDULE 2—*continued*

	(1)	(2)	(3)
Tariff Heading	*Exported products*	*Process of production or manufacture from imported materials or parts that does not qualify the goods for treatment as goods of a developing country*	*Process required to qualify the goods for treatment as goods of a developing country or rule as to the use of imported materials or parts*
32.10	Artists', students' and signboard painters' colours, modifying tints, amusement colours and the like, in tablets, tubes, jars, bottles, pans or in similar forms of packings, including such colours in sets or outfits, with or without brushes, palettes or other accessories	manufacture from products of heading No. 32.04, 32.05, 32.06, 32.07, 32.08 or 32.09	
32.12	Glaziers' putty; grafting putty; painters' fillings; non-refractory surfacing preparations; stopping, sealing and similar mastics, including resin mastics and cements	manufacture from products of heading No. 32.09	
32.13	Inks other than printing inks	manufacture from products of heading No. 32.09	
33.02	Terpenic by-products of the deterpenation of essential oils	manufacture from products of heading No. 33.01	
33.05	Aqueous distillates and aqueous solutions of essential oils, including such products suitable for medicinal uses	manufacture from products of heading No. 33.01	

34.01	Soap; organic surface-active products and preparations for use as soap, in the form of bars, cakes or moulded pieces or shapes, whether or not combined with soap	manufacture from products of heading No. 34.02 or 34.05	
34.02	Organic surface-active agents; surface-active preparations and washing preparations, whether or not containing soap	manufacture from products of heading No. 34.01 or 34.05	
36.08	Other combustible preparations and products	manufacture from combustible preparations and products	
37.01	Photographic plates and film in the flat, sensitised, unexposed, of any material other than paper, paperboard or cloth	manufacture from products of heading No. 37.02	
37.02	Film in rolls, sensitised, unexposed, perforated or not	manufacture from products of heading No. 37.01	
37.04	Sensitised plates and film, exposed but not developed, negative or positive	manufacture from products of heading No. 37.01 or 37.02	
38.11	Disinfectants, insecticides, fungicides, weed-killers, anti-sprouting products, rat poisons and similar products, put up in forms or packings for sale by retail or as preparations or as articles (for example, sulphur-treated bands, wicks and candles, fly-papers)		the 50% imported materials rule
38.12	Prepared glazings, prepared dressings and prepared mordants, of a kind used in the textile, paper, leather or like industries, excluding prepared glazings and prepared dressings with a basis of amylaceous substances		the 50% imported materials rule

SCHEDULE 2—*continued*

Tariff Heading	(1) *Exported products*	(2) *Process of production or manufacture from imported materials or parts that does not qualify the goods for treatment as goods of a developing country*	(3) *Process required to qualify the goods for treatment as goods of a developing country or rule as to the use of imported materials or parts*
38.13	Pickling preparations for metal surfaces, fluxes and other auxiliary preparations for soldering, brazing or welding; soldering, brazing or welding powders and pastes consisting of metal and other materials; preparations of a kind used as cores or coatings for welding rods and electrodes		the 50% imported materials rule
38.14	Anti-knock preparations, oxidation inhibitors, gum inhibitors, viscosity improvers, anti-corrosive preparations and similar prepared additives for mineral oils, excluding prepared additives for lubricants		the 50% imported materials rule
38.15	Prepared rubber accelerators		the 50% imported materials rule
38.17	Preparations and charges for fire-extinguishers; charged fire-extinguishing grenades		the 50% imported materials rule
38.18	Composite solvents and thinners for varnishes and similar products		the 50% imported materials rule

38.19	Chemical products and preparations of the chemical or allied industries (including those consisting of mixtures of natural products), not elsewhere specified or included; residual products of the chemical or allied industries, not elsewhere specified or included, excluding: Fusel oil and Dippel's oil; Naphthenic acids and their non-water-soluble salts, esters of naphthenic acids; Sulphonaphthenic acids and their non-water-soluble salts, esters of sulphonaphthenic acids; Petroleum sulphonates, excluding petroleum sulphonates of alkali metals, of ammonium or of ethanolamines, thiophenated sulphonic acids of oils obtained from bituminous minerals, and their salts; Mixed alkylenes; Mixed alkylbenzenes and mixed alkylnaphthalenes; Ion exchangers; Catalysts; Getters for vacuum tubes; Refractory cements or mortars and similar preparations; Alkaline iron oxide for the purification of gas; Carbon (excluding that in artificial graphite of heading Nò. 38.01) in metallo-graphite or other compounds, in the form of small plates, bars or other semi-manufactures		the 50% imported materials rule

SCHEDULE 2—*continued*

Tariff Heading	(1) *Exported products*	(2) *Process of production or manufacture from imported materials or parts that does not qualify the goods for treatment as goods of a developing country*	(3) *Process required to qualify the goods for treatment as goods of a developing country or rule as to the use of imported materials or parts*
39.02	Polymers	manufacture from monomers of Chapter 29	
39.07	Articles of materials of the kinds described in headings Nos. 39.01 to 39.06	working of artificial plastic materials, cellulose ethers and esters, and artificial resins	
40.05	Plates, sheets and strip, of unvulcanised natural or synthetic rubber, other than smoked sheets and crepe sheets of heading No. 40.01 or 40.02; granules of unvulcanised natural or synthetic rubber compounded ready for vulcanisation; unvulcanised natural or synthetic rubber, compounded before or after coagulation either with carbon black (with or without the addition of mineral oil) or with silica (with or without the addition of mineral oil), in any form, of a kind known as masterbatch		the 50% imported materials rule

41.02	Bovine cattle leather (including buffalo leather) and equine leather, except leather falling within heading No. 41.06, 41.07 or 41.08	tanning of raw hides and skins of heading No. 41.01	
41.03	Sheep and lamb skin leather, except leather falling within heading No. 41.06, 41.07 or 41.08	tanning of raw hides and skins of heading No. 41.01	
41.04	Goat and kid skin leather, except leather falling within heading No. 41.06, 41.07 or 41.08	tanning of raw hides and skins of heading No. 41.01	
41.05	Other kinds of leather, except leather falling within heading No. 41.06, 41.07 or 41.08	tanning of raw hides and skins of heading No. 41.01	
43.03	Articles of furskin	making up from furskins in plates, crosses and similar forms falling within heading No. 43.02	
44.21	Complete wooden packing cases, boxes, crates, drums and similar packings		manufacture from boards not cut to size
45.03	Articles of natural cork		manufacture from materials of heading No. 45.01
48.06	Paper and paperboard, ruled, lined or squared, but not otherwise printed, in rolls or sheets		manufacture from paper pulp
48.07	Paper and paperboard, printed (not being merely ruled, lined or squared and not constituting printed matter within Chapter 49), in rolls or sheets		manufacture from paper pulp

SCHEDULE 2—*continued*

Tariff Heading	(1) Exported products	(2) *Process of production or manufacture from imported materials or parts that does not qualify the goods for treatment as goods of a developing country*	(3) *Process required to qualify the goods for treatment as goods of a developing country or rule as to the use of imported materials or parts*
48.14	Writing blocks, envelopes, plain letter cards, plain postcards, correspondence cards; boxes, pouches, wallets and writing compendiums, of paper or paperboard, containing only an assortment of paper stationery		the 50% imported materials rule
48.15	Other paper and paperboard (including cellulose wadding), cut to size or shape		manufacture from paper pulp
48.16	Boxes, bags and other packing containers, of paper or paperboard		the 50% imported materials rule
49.09	Picture postcards and pictorial greeting cards, printed, with or without trimmings	manufacture from products of heading No. 49.11	
49.10	Calendars of any kind, of paper or paperboard, including calendar blocks	manufacture from products of heading No. 49.11	
50.04	Silk yarn, other than yarn of noil or other waste silk, not put up for retail sale		manufacture from natural textile fibres or their waste not carded or combed falling within heading No. 50.01, 53.01, 53.02, 53.03, 54.01, 54.02, 55.01, 55.02, 55.03, 57.01, 57.02, 57.03 or 57.04 or from chemical products or textile pulp

50.05	Yarn spun from silk waste other than noil, not put up for retail sale	manufacture from natural textile fibres or their waste not carded or combed falling within heading No. 50.03, 53.01, 53.02, 53.03, 54.01, 54.02, 55.01, 55.02, 55.03, 57.01, 57.02, 57.03 or 57.04 or from chemical products or textile pulp
50.06	Yarn spun from noil silk, not put up for retail sale	
50.07	Silk yarn and yarn spun from noil or other waste silk, put up for retail sale	manufacture from natural textile fibres or their waste not carded or combed falling within heading No. 50.01, 50.03, 53.01, 53.02, 53.03, 54.01, 54.02, 55.01, 55.02, 55.03, 57.01, 57.02, 57.03 or 57.04 or from chemical products or textile pulp
50.08	Silk worm gut; imitation catgut of silk	
57.06	Yarn of jute or of other textile bast fibres of heading No. 57.03	manufacture from natural textile fibres or their waste not carded or combed falling within heading No. 50.01, 53.01, 53.02, 53.03, 54.01, 54.02, 55.01, 55.02, 55.03, 57.01, 57.02, 57.03 or 57.04 or from chemical products or textile pulp
57.07	Yarn of other vegetable textile fibres	
57.08	Paper yarn	manufacture from products of Chapter 47, chemical products, textile pulp, natural textile fibres, discontinuous man-made fibres or their waste, neither carded nor combed
57.10	Woven fabrics of jute or of other textile bast fibres of heading No. 57.03	manufacture from natural textile fibres, discontinuous man-made fibres or their waste falling within heading No. 50.01, 53.01, 53.02, 53.03, 53.04, 53.05, 54.01, 54.02, 55.01, 55.02, 55.03, 55.04, 56.01, 56.02, 56.03, 57.01, 57.02, 57.03 or 57.04 or from chemical products or textile pulp
57.11	Woven fabrics of other vegetable textile fibres	

SCHEDULE 2—*continued*

Tariff Heading	(1) *Exported products*	(2) *Process of production or manufacture from imported materials or parts that does not qualify the goods for treatment as goods of a developing country*	(3) *Process required to qualify the goods for treatment as goods of a developing country or rule as to the use of imported materials or parts*
57.12	Woven fabrics of paper yarn		manufacture from paper, from chemical products, textile pulp, natural textile fibres, discontinuous man-made fibres or their waste
58.01	Carpets, carpeting and rugs, knotted (made up or not)		manufacture from materials falling within heading No. 50.01, 50.02, 50.03, 51.01, 53.01, 53.02, 53.03, 53.04, 53.05, 54.01, 55.01, 55.02, 55.03, 55.04, 56.01, 56.02, 56.03, 57.01, 57.02, 57.03 or 57.04
58.02	Other carpets, carpeting, rugs, mats and matting, and "Kelem", "Schumacks" and "Karamanie" rugs and the like (made up or not)		manufacture from materials falling within heading No. 50.01, 50.02, 50.03, 51.01, 53.01, 53.02, 53.03, 53.04, 53.05, 54.01, 55.01, 55.02, 55.03, 55.04, 56.01, 56.02, 56.03, 57.01, 57.02, 57.03 or 57.04
58.05	Narrow woven fabrics, and narrow fabrics (bolduc) consisting of warp without weft assembled by means of an adhesive, other than goods falling within heading No. 58.06		manufacture from materials falling within heading No. 50.01, 50.02, 50.03, 53.01, 53.02, 53.03, 53.04, 53.05, 54.01, 55.01, 55.02, 55.03, 55.04, 56.01, 56.02, 56.03, 57.01, 57.02, 57.03 or 57.04 or from chemical products or textile pulp

58.08	Tulle and other net fabrics (but not including woven, knitted or crocheted fabrics), plain		manufacture from materials of heading No. 50.01, 50.02, 50.03, 53.01, 53.02, 53.03, 53.04, 53.05, 54.01, 55.01, 55.02, 55.03, 55.04, 56.01, 56.02 or 56.03 or from chemical products or textile pulp
59.01	Wadding and articles of wadding; textile flock and dust and mill neps		manufacture either from natural fibres or from chemical products or textile pulp
59.02	Felt and articles of felt, whether or not impregnated or coated		
59.03	Bonded fibre fabrics, similar bonded yarn fabrics, and articles of such fabrics, whether or not impregnated or coated		
59.04	Twine, cordage, ropes and cables, plaited or not		
59.05	Nets and netting made of twine, cordage or rope and made up fishing nets of yarn, twine, cordage or rope		
59.06	Other articles made from yarn, twine, cordage, rope or cables, other than textile fabrics and articles made from such fabrics		
59.07	Textile fabrics coated with gum or amylaceous substances, of a kind used for the outer-covers of books and the like; tracing cloth; prepared painting canvas; buckram and similar fabrics for hat foundations and similar uses		manufacture from yarn
59.08	Textile fabrics impregnated, coated, covered or laminated with preparations of cellulose derivatives or of other artificial plastic materials		manufacture from yarn

SCHEDULE 2—*continued*

	(1)	(2)	(3)
	Exported products	*Process of production or manufacture from imported materials or parts that does not qualify the goods for treatment as goods of a developing country*	*Process required to qualify the goods for treatment as goods of a developing country or rule as to the use of imported materials or parts*
Tariff Heading			
59.09	Textile fabrics coated or impregnated with oil or preparations with a basis of drying oil		manufacture from yarn
59.10	Linoleum and materials prepared on a textile base in a similar manner to linoleum, whether or not cut to shape or of a kind used as floor coverings; floor coverings consisting of a coating applied on a textile base, cut to shape or not		manufacture either from yarn or from textile fibres
59.11	Rubberised textile fabrics, other than rubberised knitted or crocheted goods		manufacture from yarn
59.12	Textile fabrics otherwise impregnated or coated; painted textile fabrics being theatrical scenery, studio backcloths or the like		manufacture from yarn
59.13	Elastic fabrics and trimmings (other than knitted or crocheted goods) consisting of textile materials combined with rubber threads		manufacture from single yarn

59.14	Wicks, of woven, plaited or knitted textile materials for lamps, stoves, lighters, candles and the like; tubular knitted gas mantle fabric and incandescent gas mantles		manufacture from single yarn
59.15	Textile hosepiping and similar tubing, with or without lining, armour or accessories of other materials		manufacture from materials of heading No. 50.01, 50.02, 50.03, 53.01, 53.02, 53.03, 53.04, 53.05, 54.01, 55.01, 55.02, 55.03, 55.04, 56.01, 56.02, 56.03, 57.01, 57.02, 57.03 or 57.04 or from chemical products or textile pulp
59.16	Transmission, conveyor or elevator belts or belting, of textile material, whether or not strengthened with metal or other material		
59.17	Textile products and textile articles of a kind commonly used in machinery or plant		
62.03	Sacks and bags, of a kind used for the packing of goods		manufacture from chemical products, textile pulp or from natural textile fibres, discontinuous man-made fibres or their waste
64.01	Footwear with outer soles and uppers of rubber or artificial plastic material	manufacture from products of heading No. 64.05	
64.02	Footwear with outer soles of leather or composition leather, footwear (other than footwear falling within heading No. 64.01) with outer soles of rubber or artificial plastic material	manufacture from products of heading No. 64.05	
64.03	Footwear with outer soles of wood or cork	manufacture from products of heading No. 64.05	
64.04	Footwear with outer soles of other material	manufacture from products of heading No. 64.05	

SCHEDULE 2—*continued*

	(1)	(2)	(3)
	Exported products	*Process of production or manufacture from imported materials or parts that does not qualify the goods for treatment as goods of a developing country*	*Process required to qualify the goods for treatment as goods of a developing country or rule as to the use of imported materials or parts*
Tariff Heading			
66.01	Umbrellas and sunshades (including walking-stick umbrellas, umbrella tents and garden and similar umbrellas)		the 50% imported materials rule
68.04, 68.05 and 68.06	Articles of artificial abrasives with a basis of silicon carbide	any manufacture from silicon carbide falling within heading No. 28.56	
70.06	Cast, rolled, drawn or blown glass (including flashed or wired glass) in rectangles, surface ground or polished but not further worked	manufacture from drawn, cast or rolled glass of heading No. 70.04 or 70.05	
70.07	Cast, rolled, drawn or blown glass (including flashed or wired glass) cut to shape other than rectangular shape, or bent or otherwise worked (for example, edge worked or engraved) whether or not surface ground or polished; multiple-walled insulating glass; leaded lights and the like	manufacture from drawn, cast or rolled glass of heading No. 70.04, 70.05 or 70.06	
70.08	Safety glass consisting of toughened or laminated glass, shaped or not	manufacture from drawn, cast or rolled glass of heading No. 70.04, 70.05, 70.06 or 70.07	
70.09	Glass mirrors (including rear-view mirrors), unframed, framed or backed	manufacture from products of heading No. 70.04, 70.05, 70.06, 70.07 or 70.08	

71.15	Articles consisting of, or incorporating, pearls, precious or semi-precious stones (natural, synthetic or reconstructed)		the 50% imported materials rule
73.07	Blooms, billets, slabs and sheet bars (including tinplate bars), of iron or steel; pieces roughly shaped by forging of iron or steel	manufacture from products of heading No. 73.06	
73.08	Iron or steel coils for re-rolling	manufacture from products of heading No. 73.07	
73.09	Universal plates of iron or steel	manufacture from products of heading No. 73.07 or 73.08	
73.10	Bars and rods (including wire rod), of iron or steel, hot-rolled, forged, extruded, cold-formed or cold-finished (including precision-made); hollow mining drill steel	manufacture from products of heading No. 73.07	
73.11	Angles, shapes and sections, of iron or steel, hot-rolled, forged, extruded, cold-formed or cold-finished; sheet piling of iron or steel, whether or not drilled, punched or made from assembled elements	manufacture from products of heading No. 73.07, 73.08, 73.09, 73.10, 73.12 or 73.13	
73.12	Hoop and strip, of iron or steel, hot-rolled or cold-rolled	manufacture from products of heading No. 73.07, 73.08, 73.09 or 73.13	
73.13	Sheets and plates, of iron or steel hot-rolled or cold-rolled	manufactured from products of heading No. 73.07, 73.08 or 73.09	
73.14	Iron or steel wire, whether or not coated, but not insulated	manufacture from products of heading No. 73.10	

SCHEDULE 2—*continued*

Tariff Heading	(1) *Exported products*	(2) *Process of production or manufacture from imported materials or parts that does not qualify the goods for treatment as goods of a developing country*	(3) *Process required to qualify the goods for treatment as goods of a developing country or rule as to the use of imported materials or parts*
73.16	Railway and tramway track construction material of iron or steel, the following: rails, check-rails, switch blades, crossings (or frogs), crossing pieces, point rods, rack rails, sleepers, fishplates, chairs, chair wedges, sole plates (base plates), rail clips, bed-plates, ties and other materials specialised for joining or fixing rails		manufacture from materials of heading No. 73.06
73.18	Tubes and pipes and blanks therefor, of iron (other than of cast iron) or steel, excluding high-pressure hydro-electric conduits		manufacture from materials of heading No. 73.06 or 73.07 or of heading No. 73.15 in a form specified in heading No. 73.06 or 73.07
Chapter 74	Copper and articles thereof *excluding products of headings Nos.* 74.01 *and* 74.02		
Chapter 75	Nickel and articles thereof *excluding products of heading No.* 75.01		
Chapter 76	Aluminium and articles thereof *excluding products of heading No.* 76.01		
Chapter 77	Magnesium and articles thereof *excluding products of heading No.* 77.01		the 50% imported materials rule
Chapter 78	Lead and articles thereof *excluding products of heading No.* 78.01		

Chapter 79	Zinc and articles thereof *excluding pro-eucts of heading No.* 79.01		the 50% imported materials rule
Chapter 80	Tin and articles thereof *excluding products of headings Nos.* 80.01 *and* 80.06		
82.05	Interchangeable tools for hand tools, for machine tools or for power-operated hand tools (for example, for pressing, stamping, drilling, tapping, threading, boring, broaching, milling, cutting, turning, dressing, morticing or screw-driving), including dies for wire drawing, extrusion dies for metal, and rock drilling bits		the 40% imported materials rule
82.06	Knives and cutting blades, for machines or for mechanical appliances		the 40% imported materials rule
Chapter 84	Boilers, machinery and mechanical appliances and parts thereof, *excluding products of heading No. 84.15 and sewing machines and furniture specially designed for sewing machines falling within heading 84.41*		the 40% imported materials rule
84.15	Refrigerators and refrigerating equipment (electrical and other)		the 40%/50% rule
84.41	Sewing machines; furniture specially designed for sewing machines		compliance with the 40% imported materials rule and— (*a*) a head (motor excluded) assembled from materials and parts at least 50% of the value of which is attributable to originating materials and parts (*b*) production with only originating thread tension, crochet or zigzag mechanism

SCHEDULE 2—*continued*

(1)		(2)	(3)
	Exported products	*Process of production or manufacture from imported materials or parts that does not qualify the goods for treatment as goods of a developing country*	*Process required to qualify the goods for treatment as goods of a developing country or rule as to the use of imported materials or parts*
Tariff Heading			
Chapter 85	Electrical machinery and equipment and parts thereof, *excluding products of headings Nos. 85.14 and 85.15*		the 40% imported materials rule
85.14	Microphones and stands therefor; loud-speakers; audio-frequency electric amplifiers		compliance with the 40%/50% rule and production with only originating transistors
85.15	Radiotelegraphic and radiotelephonic transmission and reception apparatus; radiobroadcasting and television transmission and reception apparatus (including receivers incorporating sound recorders or reproducers) and television cameras; radio navigational aid apparatus, radar apparatus and radio remote control apparatus		compliance with the 40%/50% rule and production with only originating transistors
Chapter 86	Railway and tramway locomotives, rolling-stock and parts thereof; rail-way and tramway track fixtures and fittings; traffic signalling equipment of all kinds (not electrically powered)		the 40% imported materials rule

Chapter 87	Vehicles, other than railway or tramway rolling-stock, and parts thereof, *excluding products of heading No. 87.09*		the 40% imported materials rule
87.09	Motor-cycles, auto-cycles and cycles fitted with an auxiliary motor, with or without side-cars; side-cars of all kinds		the 40%/50% rule
Chapter 90	Optical, photographic, cinematographic, measuring, checking, precision, medical and surgical instruments and apparatus and parts thereof, *excluding products of headings Nos. 90.05, 90.07, 90.08, 90.12 and 90.26*		the 40% imported materials rule
90.05	Refracting telescopes (monocular and binocular), prismatic or not		the 40%/50% rule
90.07	Photographic cameras; photographic flashlight apparatus		the 40%/50% rule
90.08	Cinematographic cameras, projectors, sound recorders and sound reproducers but not including rerecorders or film editing apparatus; any combination of these articles		the 40%/50% rule
90.12	Compound optical microscopes, whether or not provided with means for photographing or projecting the image		the 40%/50% rule
90.26	Gas, liquid and electricity supply or production meters; calibrating meters therefor		the 40%/50% rule

SCHEDULE 2—*continued*

Tariff Heading	(1) Exported products	(2) *Process of production or manufacture from imported materials or parts that does not qualify the goods for treatment as goods of a developing country*	(3) *Process required to qualify the goods for treatment as goods of a developing country or rule as to the use of imported materials or parts*
Chapter 91	Clocks and watches and parts thereof, *excluding products of headings Nos. 91.04 and 91.08*		the 40% imported materials rule
91.04	Other clocks		the 40%/50% rule
91.08	Clock movements (including secondary movements), assembled		the 40%/50% rule
Chapter 92	Musical instruments; sound recorders and reproducers; television image and sound recorders and reproducers, magnetic; parts and accessories of such articles, *excluding products of heading No. 92.11*		the 40% imported materials rule
92.11	Gramophones, dictating machines and other sound recorders and reproducers, including record-players and tape decks, with or without sound-heads; television image and sound recorders and reproducers, magnetic		compliance with the 40%/50% rule and production with only originating transistors
Chapter 93	Arms and ammunition; parts thereof		the 50% imported materials rule
96.01	Brooms and brushes, consisting of twigs or other vegetable materials merely bound together and not mounted in a head (for example, besoms and whisks), with or without handles		the 50% imported materials rule

96.02	Other brooms and brushes (including brushes of a kind used as parts of machines); paint rollers; squeegees (other than roller squeegees) and mops		the 50% imported materials rule
97.03	Other toys; working models of a kind used for recreational purposes		the 50% imported materials rule
98.01	Buttons and button moulds, studs, cuff-links, and press-fasteners, including snap-fasteners and press-studs; blanks and parts of such articles		the 50% imported materials rule
98.08	Typewriter and similar ribbons, whether or not on spools, ink pads, with or without boxes		the 50% imported materials rule
98.15	Vacuum flasks and other vacuum vessels, complete with cases		manufacture from products of heading No. 70.12

SCHEDULE 3

Tariff Heading	Exported product	Working or processing operations which, even if not resulting in a change of tariff heading of the materials or parts, qualify the goods for treatment as goods of a developing country if carried out there
21.03	Prepared mustard	manufacture from mustard flour
25.09	Earth colours, calcined or powdered	crushing and calcination or powdering of earth colours
25.15	Marble squared by sawing, of a thickness of 25 cm or less	sawing into slabs or sections, polishing, grinding and cleaning of marble, including marble not further worked than roughly split, roughly squared or squared by sawing, more than 25 cm in thickness
25.16	Granite, porphyry, basalt, sandstone and other monumental and building stone, squared by sawing, of a thickness of 25 cm or less	sawing of granite, porphyry, basalt, sandstone and other building stone, including such stone not further worked than roughly split, roughly squared or squared by sawing, more than 25 cm in thickness
25.18	Calcined dolomite; agglomerated dolomite (including tarred dolomite)	calcination of unworked dolomite
38.05	Refined tall oil	refining of crude tall oil
40.01	Slabs of crêpe rubber for soles	lamination of crêpe sheets of natural rubber
40.07	Rubber thread and cord, textile-covered	manufacture from rubber thread or cord
41.01	Sheep and lamb skins without the wool	removing wool from sheep and lamb skins in the wool
41.03	Retanned skin leather of crossed Indian sheep	retanning of crossed Indian sheep skin leather not further prepared than tanned

41.04	Retanned Indian goat or kid skin leather	retanning of Indian goat or kid skin leather not further prepared than tanned
68.03	Articles of slate, including articles of agglomerated slate	manufacture of articles of slate
68.13	Articles of asbestos; articles of mixtures with a basis of asbestos or of mixtures with a basis of asbestos and magnesium carbonate	manufacture of articles of asbestos or of mixtures with a basis of asbestos, or of mixtures with a basis of asbestos and magnesium carbonate
68.15	Articles of mica, including bonded mica splittings on a support of paper or fabric	manufacture of articles of mica
70.10	Cut-glass bottles	cutting of imported bottles the value of which does not exceed 50% of the value of the exported product
70.13	Cut glassware (other than articles falling in heading No. 70.19) of a kind commonly used for table, kitchen, toilet or office purposes, for indoor decoration, or for similar uses	cutting of imported glassware the value of which does not exceed 50% of the value of the exported product
70.20	Articles made from glass fibre	manufacture from unworked glass fibre
71.02	Precious and semi-precious stones, cut or otherwise worked, but not mounted, set or strung (except ungraded stones temporarily strung for convenience of transport)	manufacture from unworked precious and semi-precious stones
71.03	Synthetic or reconstructed precious or semi-precious stones, cut or otherwise worked, but not mounted, set or strung (except ungraded stones temporarily strung for convenience of transport)	manufacture from unworked synthetic or reconstructed precious or semi-precious stones
71.05	Silver and silver alloys, semi-manufactured	rolling, drawing, beating or grinding of unwrought silver and silver alloys
71.06	Rolled silver, semi-manufactured	rolling, drawing, beating or grinding of unworked rolled silver
71.07	Gold, including platinum-plated gold, semi-manufactured	rolling, drawing, beating or grinding of unwrought gold, including platinum-plated gold
71.08	Rolled gold on base metal or silver, semi-manufactured	rolling, drawing, beating or grinding of unworked rolled gold on base metal or silver

SCHEDULE 3 (*continued*)

Tariff Heading	Exported product	Working or processing operations which, even if not resulting in a change of tariff heading of the materials or parts, qualify the goods for treatment as goods of a developing country if carried out there
71.09	Platinum and other metals of the platinum group, semi-manufactured	rolling, drawing, beating or grinding of unwrought platinum and other metals of the platinum group
71.10	Rolled platinum or other platinum group metals, on base metal or precious metal, semi-manufactured	rolling, drawing, beating or grinding of unworked rolled platinum or other platinum group metals on base metal or precious metal
73.15	Alloy steel and high carbon steel:	
	—in the forms mentioned in headings Nos. 73.07 to 73.13	manufacture from products in a form mentioned in heading No. 73.06
	—in the forms mentioned in heading No. 73.14	manufacture from products in a form mentioned in heading No. 73.06 or 73.07
74.01	Unrefined copper (blister copper and other)	smelting of copper matte
74.01	Refined copper	fire-refining or electrolytic refining of unrefined copper (blister copper and other), copper waste or scrap
74.01	Copper alloy	fusion and thermal treatment of refined copper, copper waste or scrap
75.01	Unwrought nickel	refining by electrolysis, by fusion or chemically, of nickel mattes, nickel speiss and other intermediate products of nickel metallurgy

		the value of which does not exceed 50% of the value of the exported product
81.01	Tungsten, wrought	manufacture from imported unwrought tungsten the value of which does not exceed 50% of the value of the exported product
81.02	Molybdenum, wrought	manufacture from imported unwrought molybdenum the value of which does not exceed 50% of the value of the exported product
81.03	Tantalum, wrought	manufacture from imported unwrought tantalum the value of which does not exceed 50% of the value of the exported product
81.04	Other base metals, wrought	manufacture from other imported base metals, unwrought, the value of which does not exceed 50% of the value of the exported product
Chapter 84	Boilers, machinery and mechanical appliances and parts thereof *excluding products of headings Nos. 84.06, 84.08 and 84.41 specified in the following three items in this Schedule*	incorporation of imported materials and parts *falling within the same tariff heading* as the exported product provided that— (*a*) the value of *such* materials and parts does not exceed 5% of the value of the exported product; and (*b*) the value of the imported materials and parts *which do not fall within the same tariff heading* as the exported product does not exceed 40% of its value; and, (*c*) in the case of goods of heading No. 84.15, at least 50% of the value of all the materials and parts is attributable to originating materials and parts
84.06	Internal combustion piston engines	working, processing or assembly in which *either*— (*a*) (i) the value of imported materials and parts employed *which fall within the same tariff heading* as the exported product does not exceed 5% of its value; and (ii) the value of imported materials and parts employed *which do not fall within the same tariff heading* as the exported product does not exceed 40% of its value *or* (*b*) the value of all imported materials and parts employed (irrespective of their tariff heading) does not exceed 40% of the value of the exported product

SCHEDULE 3 (*continued*)

Tariff Heading	Exported product	Working or processing operations which, even if not resulting in a change of tariff heading of the materials or parts, qualifying the goods for treatment as goods of a developing country if carried out there
84.08	Engines and motors, excluding reaction engines and gas turbines	working, processing or assembly in which *either*— (*a*) (i) the value of imported materials and parts employed *which fall within the same tariff heading* as the exported product does not exceed 5% of its value; and (ii) the value of imported materials and parts employed *which do not fall within the same tariff heading* as the exported product does not exceed 40% of its value *or* (*b*) the value of the imported materials and parts employed (irrespective of their tariff heading) does not exceed 40% of the value of the exported product and at least 50% of the value of the materials and parts employed is attributable to originating materials and parts
84.41	Sewing machines; furniture specially designed for sewing machines	working, processing or assembly in which— (*a*) *either*— (i) the value of imported materials and parts employed *which fall within the same tariff heading* as the exported product does not exceed 5% of its value; and the value of imported materials and parts employed *which do not fall within the same tariff heading* as the exported product does not exceed 40% of its value *or*

		(ii) the value of all the imported materials and parts employed (irrespective of their tariff heading) does not exceed 40% of the value of the exported product, *and* (*b*) at least 50% of the value of the materials and parts employed in the assembly of the head (motor excluded) is attributable to originating materials and parts and the thread tension and any crochet or zig zag mechanism are originating
Chapter 85	Electrical machinery and equipment and parts thereof	incorporation of imported materials and parts *which fall within the same tariff heading* as the exported product provided that— (*a*) the value of *such* materials and parts does not exceed 5% of the value of the exported product; (*b*) the value of the imported materials and parts *which do not fall within the same tariff heading* as the exported product does not exceed 40% of the value of the product; (*c*) in the case of products of headings Nos. 85.14, 85.15, 87.09, 90.05, 90.07, 90.08, 90.12, 90.26, 91.04, 91.08 and 92.11, at least 50% of the value of all the materials or parts employed is attributable to originating materials and parts; and (*d*) in the case of products of headings Nos. 85.14, 85.15 and 92.11, only originating transistors are incorporated
Chapters 86 to 89	Vehicles, aircraft and parts thereof, vessels and certain associated transport equipment	
Chapters 90 to 92	Optical, photographic, cinematographic, measuring, checking, precision, medical and surgical instruments and apparatus; clocks and watches; musical instruments; sound recorders and reproducers; television image and sound recorders and reproducers, magnetic; and parts thereof	
95.01	Articles of tortoise-shell	manufacture from worked tortoise-shell
95.02	Articles of mother of pearl	manufacture from worked mother of pearl
95.03	Articles of ivory	manufacture from worked ivory
95.04	Articles of bone (excluding whalebone)	manufacture from worked bone (excluding whalebone)
95.05	Articles of horn, coral (natural or agglomerated) or of other animal carving material	manufacture from worked horn, coral (natural or agglomerated) or other animal carving material

SCHEDULE 3 (*continued*)

Tariff Heading	Exported product	Working or processing operations which, even if not resulting in a change of tariff heading of the materials or parts, qualifying the goods for treatment as goods of a developing country if carried out there
95.06	Articles of vegetable carving material (for example, corozo)	manufacture from vegetable carving material (for example, corozo)
95.07	Articles of jet (and mineral substitutes for jet), amber, meerschaum, agglomerated amber and agglomerated meerschaum	manufacture from worked jet (and mineral substitutes for jet), amber, meerschaum, agglomerated amber and agglomerated meerschaum
98.11	Smoking pipes, pipe bowls	manufacture from roughly shaped blocks of wood or root

EXPLANATORY NOTE

(This Note is not part of the Regulations.)

These Regulations, which come into force on 1st January 1972, prescribe the conditions under which goods are to be treated as goods produced or manufactured in a developing country for the purpose of any order under section 1 of the Finance Act 1971 relieving goods of such a country either wholly or in part from the duties normally chargeable under the Import Duties Act 1958.

Regulation 3 relates to goods which are to be regarded as wholly produced or manufactured in such a country.

Regulation 4 provides that generally goods which incorporate imported materials or parts shall be treated as produced or manufactured in a developing country if they have undergone in that country a sufficient change to cause them to be classified in a different tariff heading. This rule is qualified in the case of goods mentioned in Schedule 2. The performance of a process mentioned in the second column of that Schedule does not suffice to cause goods to be treated as produced or manufactured in the country in which it is carried out; where a rule or requirement is mentioned in the third column, that rule or requirement must also be satisfied.

Regulation 5 provides that goods mentioned in Schedule 3 shall be treated as produced or manufactured in a developing country if they have undergone there the relevant process mentioned in that Schedule (notwithstanding that the process may not cause them to be classified in a different tariff heading).

1971 No. 1922

WAGES COUNCILS

The Wages Regulation (Wholesale Mantle and Costume) Order 1971

Made - - -	25*th November* 1971
Coming into Operation	20*th December* 1971

Whereas the Secretary of State has received from the Wholesale Mantle and Costume Wages Council (Great Britain) the wages regulation proposals set out in the Schedule hereto ;

Now, therefore, the Secretary of State in exercise of his powers under section 11 of the Wages Councils Act 1959(**a**), and of all other powers enabling him in that behalf, hereby makes the following Order :—

1. This Order may be cited as the Wages Regulation (Wholesale Mantle and Costume) Order 1971.

2.—(1) In this Order the expression "the specified date" means the 20th December 1971, provided that where, as respects any worker who is paid wages at intervals not exceeding seven days, that date does not correspond with the beginning of the period for which the wages are paid, the expression "the specified date" means, as respects that worker, the beginning of the next such period following that date.

(2) The Interpretation Act 1889(**b**) shall apply to the interpretation of this Order as it applies to the interpretation of an Act of Parliament and as if this Order and the Order hereby revoked were Acts of Parliament.

3. The wages regulation proposals set out in the Schedule hereto shall have effect as from the specified date and as from that date the Wages Regulation (Wholesale Mantle and Costume) (No. 2) Order 1970(**c**) shall cease to have effect.

Signed by order of the Secretary of State.
25th November 1971.

J. R. Lloyd Davies,
Assistant Secretary,
Department of Employment.

Article 3

SCHEDULE

The following minimum remuneration shall be substituted for the statutory minimum remuneration fixed by the Wages Regulation (Wholesale Mantle and Costume) (No. 2) Order 1970 (Order W.M. (86)).

(**a**) 1959 c. 69. (**b**) 1889 c. 63.
(**c**) S.I. 1970/1848 (1970 III, p. 6001).

STATUTORY MINIMUM REMUNERATION

PART I

GENERAL

1. The minimum remuneration payable to a worker to whom this Schedule applies for all work except work to which a minimum overtime rate applies under Part IV of this Schedule is:—

(1) in the case of a time worker, the general minimum time rate payable to the worker under Part II or Part III of this Schedule;

(2) in the case of a worker employed on piece work, piece rates each of which would yield, in the circumstances of the case, to an ordinary worker at least the same amount of money as the general minimum time rate otherwise applicable to the worker under Part II or Part III of this Schedule.

PART II

MALE WORKERS

GENERAL MINIMUM TIME RATES

2. Subject to the provisions of this Schedule, the general minimum time rates payable to male workers with the qualifications specified in Column 2 of the next following Table when employed on time work are those set out in Column 3 of the said Table.

Column 1	Column 2	Column 3
Class of Worker	Qualifying Period of Employment or Age of Worker	General Minimum Time Rates
		Per Hour
(1) MEASURE CUTTER, that is to say, a person employed in any process of measure cutting who is capable of taking a complete set of measures and of cutting all garments for a female person from patterns.	Not less than three years' employment after the age of 18 years as a measure cutter, but excluding designing.	p *39·08*

Column 1	Column 2	Column 3
Class of Worker	Qualifying Period of Employment or Age of Worker	General Minimum Time Rates
		Per Hour
		p
(2) CUTTER or TRIMMER, that is to say, a person substantially employed in one or more of the following processes:— (*a*) marking-in or marking-up cloth or linings or other materials; (*b*) laying-up, hooking-up or folding cloth or linings or other materials; (*c*) cutting cloth or linings or other materials or cutting out patterns of any description to be used afterwards for the cutting out of garments; and (*d*) dividing (that is to say, the process ordinarily carried on by cutters or their assistants of dividing, parting or separating the parts of garments after being cut and of assembling them into suitable bundles for making up), other than a measure cutter to whom the minimum rates specified in (1) of this Table apply or a knife cutter or knifeman.	Not less than three years' employment after the age of 18 years as a cutter of any of the classes specified in Column 1 or as a knifeman.	*38·25*
(3) KNIFE CUTTER or KNIFEMAN, that is to say, a person wholly or mainly employed on band, electric or hand-knife processes.	Not less than three years' employment after the age of 18 years as a cutter of any of the classes specified in Column 1 or as a knifeman.	*38·25*

(4) FITTER-UP, that is to say, a person employed in fitting-up (which is a process between that of cutting and that of sewing, baisting or machining, and which consists of preparing or fitting accurately the various parts of the garments before being baisted, sewn or machined, such work of preparing or fitting being always done by shears or knives or other cutting appliances—sewing, baisting or machining forming no part or process of fitting-up).	Not less than three years' employment after the age of 18 years as a fitter-up or tailor.	*38·25*
(5) TAILOR, that is to say, a person employed in sewing by hand in a process of:— (*a*) making a garment or portion of a garment, or (*b*) altering, repairing, renovating or re-making a garment or portion of a garment, when such process is carried out in a factory.	Not less than three years' employment after the age of 18 years as a tailor.	*39·08*
(6) PRESSER, that is to say, a person employed in pressing-off by hand or by machine.	Not less than three years' employment after the age of 18 years in the processes of pressing-off or under-pressing.	*38·25*
(7) MACHINIST, that is to say, a person employed in machining other than as a plain machinist and capable of machining any one garment or portion of a garment.	Not less than three years' employment after the age of 18 years as a machinist.	*38·25*
(8) PASSER, that is to say, a person employed in examining garments, either in the course of being made up or upon completion.	Not less than three years' employment after the age of 18 years as a passer or tailor.	*38·25*
(9) UNDER-PRESSER, that is to say, a person employed in pressing processes other than pressing-off.	Not less than three years' employment after the age of 18 years as an under-presser or presser.	*36·79*
(10) PLAIN MACHINIST, that is to say, a person employed in the process of making up plain sleeves, facings, linings, inside pockets, quilting or padding.	Not less than three years' employment after the age of 18 years as a plain machinist or machinist.	*36·79*
(11) WAREHOUSEMAN, that is to say, a person employed, wholly or mainly, upon one or more of the operations of assembling, keeping, storing and distributing stock, and cutting off lengths of cloth, linings or other materials.	Not less than three years' employment as a warehouseman after the age of 18 years.	*37·42*
(12) PACKER, that is to say, a person employed, wholly or mainly, in packing goods and materials.	Not less than three years' employment as a packer after the age of 18 years.	*37·42*

Column 1	Column 2	Column 3
Class of Worker	Qualifying Period of Employment or Age of Worker	General Minimum Time Rates
		Per Hour
		p
(13) LEARNERS (as defined in paragraph 10)	Aged 21 years or over	*35·54*
	„ 20 and under 21 years	*32·75*
	„ 19 „ „ 20 „	*31·29*
	„ 18 „ „ 19 „	*28·08*
	„ 17 „ „ 18 „	*23·63*
	„ 16 „ „ 17 „	*20·88*
	„ under 16 years	*17·67*
Provided that the general minimum time rate payable during his first year's employment to a learner who enters or has entered the trade for the first time at or over the age of 19 years shall be	(*a*) Aged under 21 years	*28·08*
	(*b*) „ 21 years or over	*31·29*

(13) LEARNERS (as defined in paragraph 10)	Aged 21 years or over	*35·54*
	„ 20 and under 21 years	*32·75*
	„ 19 „ „ 20 „	*31·29*
	„ 18 „ „ 19 „	*28·08*
	„ 17 „ „ 18 „	*23·63*
	„ 16 „ „ 17 „	*20·88*
	„ under 16 years	*17·67*
Provided that the general minimum time rate payable during his first year's employment to a learner who enters or has entered the trade for the first time at or over the age of 19 years shall be	(*a*) Aged under 21 years	*28·08*
	(*b*) „ 21 years or over	*31·29*

PART III

FEMALE WORKERS

GENERAL MINIMUM TIME RATES

3. Subject to the provisions of this Schedule, the general minimum time rates payable to female workers are as follows:—

(1) LEARNERS (as defined in paragraph 10) during the following periods of employment in the trade—

	During 1st six months	During 2nd six months	During 2nd Year
	Per Hour	Per Hour	Per Hour
Entering the trade:	p	p	p
Aged 15 and under 16 years	*17·33*	*20·08*	*25·00*
„ 16 „ „ 17 „	*18·58*	*21·58*	*26·50*
„ 17 „ „ 18 „	*20·08*	*23·08*	*26·50*
„ 18 years and over	*24·33*	*26·08*	*30·33*

(2) ALL OTHER WORKERS ... ... *30·33*p per hour

PART IV

OVERTIME AND WAITING TIME

ALL WORKERS OTHER THAN ALTERATION HANDS WHO ARE NORMALLY REQUIRED TO ATTEND ON 6 DAYS IN THE WEEK

NORMAL NUMBER OF HOURS

4. Subject to the provisions of this Part of this Schedule, the minimum overtime rates set out in paragraph 5 are payable to workers other than alteration hands referred to in paragraphs 6 and 7 in respect of any time worked—

(1) in excess of the hours following, that is to say,

(*a*) in any week ... ... 40 hours

(*b*) on any day other than a Saturday, Sunday or customary holiday—

where the normal working hours exceed 8½ ... ... 9 hours

or

where the normal working hours are more than 8 but not more than 8½ ... ... 8½ hours

or

where the normal working hours are not more than 8 ... 8 hours

(2) on a Saturday, Sunday or customary holiday.

MINIMUM OVERTIME RATES

5.—(1) Minimum overtime rates are payable to a worker other than an alteration hand referred to in paragraphs 6 and 7 as follows:—

(*a*) on any day other than a Sunday or customary holiday—

(i) for the first 2 hours of overtime worked ... ... time-and-a-quarter

(ii) for the next 2 hours ... ... time-and-a-half

(iii) thereafter ... ... double time

(*b*) on a Sunday or customary holiday—

for all time worked ... ... double time

Provided that where it is the practice in a Jewish undertaking for the employer to require attendance on Sunday instead of Saturday the provisions of this paragraph shall apply as if in such provisions the word "Saturday" were substituted for "Sunday", except where such substitution is unlawful.

(*c*) in any week, exclusive of any time in respect of which any minimum overtime rate is payable under the foregoing provisions of this sub-paragraph—

for all time worked in excess of 40 hours ... ... time-and-a-quarter

(2) The minimum overtime rates set out in sub-paragraph (1)(*a*) or (*b*) of this paragraph are payable in any week whether or not the minimum overtime rate set out in sub-paragraph (1)(*c*) is also payable.

ALTERATION HANDS WHO ARE NORMALLY REQUIRED TO ATTEND ON 6 DAYS IN THE WEEK

NORMAL NUMBER OF HOURS

6. Subject to the provisions of this Part of this Schedule, the minimum overtime rates set out in paragraph 7 are payable to workers who are normally required to attend on 6 days in the week and who are employed solely in the alteration (including repairing and renovating) of any of the garments specified in inclusion (1) in paragraph 12 and who are employed in or about a shop engaged in the retail sale of the garments so specified in respect of any time worked—

(1) in excess of the hours following, that is to say,

(*a*) in any week ... ... 40 hours

(*b*) on any day other than a Saturday, Sunday or customary holiday ... ... 8 hours

(*c*) on a Saturday, not being a customary holiday ... ... 4 hours

(2) on a Sunday or customary holiday.

MINIMUM OVERTIME RATES

7.—(1) Minimum overtime rates are payable to a worker who is normally required to attend on 6 days in the week and who is employed solely in the alteration (including repairing and renovating) of any of the garments specified in inclusion (1) in paragraph 12 and who is employed in or about a shop engaged in the retail sale of the garments so specified as follows:—

(*a*) on any day other than a Saturday, Sunday or customary holiday—

(i) for the first 2 hours worked in excess of 8 hours ... time-and-a-quarter

(ii) for the next 2 hours ... ... time-and-a-half

(iii) thereafter ... ... double time

(*b*) on a Saturday, not being a customary holiday—

(i) for the first 4 hours worked in excess of 4 hours ... time-and-a-half

(ii) thereafter ... ... double time

(*c*) on a Sunday or customary holiday—

for all time worked ... ... double time

(*d*) in any week, exclusive of any time in respect of which any minimum overtime rate is payable under the foregoing provisions of this sub-paragraph—

for all time worked in excess of 40 hours ... ... time-and-a-quarter

(2) The minimum overtime rates set out in sub-paragraph (1)(*a*), (*b*) or (*c*) of this paragraph are payable in any week whether or not the minimum overtime rate set out in sub-paragraph (1)(*d*) is also payable.

(3) Where the employer normally requires the worker's attendance on Sunday and not on Saturday, for the purposes of this Part of this Schedule (except where such attendance is unlawful) Saturday shall be treated as a Sunday and, subject to the provisions of sub-paragraph (4) of this paragraph, Sunday shall be treated as a Saturday.

(4) Where an ordinary week-day is substituted for Saturday or, in a case where the provisions of sub-paragraph (3) of this paragraph apply, for Sunday, as the worker's weekly short day, for the purposes of this Part of this Schedule (except where such substitution is unlawful) that ordinary week-day shall be treated as a Saturday, and Saturday or Sunday, as the case may be, shall be treated as an ordinary week-day.

8. In this Part of this Schedule—

(1) The expression "customary holiday" means—

(*a*) (i) In England and Wales—

Christmas Day (or, if Christmas Day falls on a Sunday, such week-day as may be appointed by national proclamation, or, if none is so appointed, the next following Tuesday), Boxing Day, Good Friday, Easter Monday, Whit Monday (or where another day is substituted therefor by national proclamation, that day), August Bank Holiday, and one other day (being a day of the week on which the worker normally works for the employer) in the course of a calendar year, to be fixed by the employer and notified to the worker not less than three weeks before the holiday;

(ii) In Scotland—

New Year's Day (or, if New Year's Day falls on a Sunday, the following Monday);
the local Spring holiday;
the local Autumn holiday;

and four other days (being days of the week on which the worker normally works for the employer) in the course of a calendar year, to be fixed by the employer and notified to the worker not less than three weeks before the holiday; or

(*b*) in the case of each of the said days a day substituted by the employer therefor, being a day recognised by local custom as a day of holiday in substitution for the said day.

(2) The expressions "time-and-a-quarter", "time-and-a-half" and "double time" mean respectively—

(*a*) in the case of a time worker, one and a quarter times, one and a half times and twice the general minimum time rate otherwise payable to the worker;

(*b*) in the case of a worker who is employed on piece work,

(i) a time rate equal respectively to one quarter, one half and the whole of the general minimum time rate which would be payable if the worker were a time worker and a minimum overtime rate did not apply and in addition thereto,

(ii) the piece rates otherwise payable to the worker under paragraph 1(2).

WAITING TIME

9.—(1) A worker is entitled to payment of the minimum remuneration specified in this Schedule for all time during which he is present on the premises of his employer unless he is present thereon in any of the following circumstances:—

(*a*) without the employer's consent, express or implied;

(*b*) for some purpose unconnected with his work and other than that of waiting for work to be given to him to perform;

(*c*) by reason only of the fact that he is resident thereon;

(*d*) during normal meal times in a room or place in which no work is being done and he is not waiting for work to be given to him to perform.

(2) The minimum remuneration payable under sub-paragraph (1) of this paragraph to a piece worker when not engaged on piece work is that which would be payable if he were a time worker.

PART V

INTERPRETATION

10. In this Schedule—

(1) A LEARNER is a worker who:—

(*a*) is employed during the whole or a substantial part of his time in learning any branch or process of the trade by an employer who provides him with reasonable facilities for such learning; and

(*b*) does not work in a room used for dwelling purposes, except where he is in the employment of his parent or guardian.

(2) "THE TRADE" means the trade of wholesale mantle and costume making as specified in paragraph 12.

RECKONING OF EMPLOYMENT

11. For the purpose of determining whether a worker has completed any period of employment specified in paragraph 2 or paragraph 3, there shall be taken into account—

(1) any such employment as a worker in relation to whom there operated one or more of the following Wages Councils (or of the Trade Boards which respectively

preceded them), that is to say, the Wholesale Mantle and Costume Wages Council (Great Britain), the Retail Bespoke Tailoring Wages Councils for England and Wales and for Scotland and the Readymade and Wholesale Bespoke Tailoring Wages Council (Great Britain) and

(2) in the case of a male worker employed as a cutter of any description or as a knifeman any such employment in the rubberised waterproof trade.

APPLICABILITY OF STATUTORY MINIMUM REMUNERATION

12. This Schedule applies to workers in relation to whom the Wholesale Mantle and Costume Wages Council (Great Britain) operates, that is to say, workers employed in Great Britain in wholesale mantle and costume making as specified in the Regulations made by the Minister of Labour and dated 20th November 1919, with respect to the constitution and proceedings of the Trade Board for the Wholesale Mantle and Costume Trade (Great Britain)**(a)**, namely:—

"Women's, girls' and children's ready-made and wholesale bespoke tailoring, and all women's, girls' and children's retail bespoke tailoring carried on in a factory where garments are made up for three or more retail establishments, and any other branch of women's, girls' and children's tailoring which is not included within the scope of the Trade Boards (Tailoring) Order 1919**(b)**,

including:—

(1) All operations and processes of cutting, making or finishing by hand or machine of coats, costumes, tailored skirts, coat-frocks, mantles, service clothing or similar garments made by tailoring processes;

(2)(*a*) The altering, repairing, renovating or remaking of any of the above-mentioned tailored garments, except where included within the scope of the Retail Bespoke Tailoring Trade Board;

(*b*) The cleaning of such garments where carried out in association with or in conjunction with the altering, repairing, renovating or remaking of the garments;

(3) The lining with fur of any of the above-mentioned garments where carried out in association with or in conjunction with the making of such garments;

(4)(*a*) All processes of embroidery or decorative needlework where carried on in association with or in conjunction with the making, altering, repairing, renovating or remaking of any of the above-mentioned tailored garments other than hand-embroidery or hand-drawn thread work on garments made of linen or cotton or of mixed linen and cotton;

(*b*) The following processes if done by machine, namely, thread-drawing, thread clipping, top-sewing, scalloping, nickelling and paring;

(5) Warehousing, packing and all other operations incidental to or appertaining to any of the above-mentioned branches of tailoring,

but excluding:—

(1) Those branches of women's or girls' bespoke tailoring, and all operations or processes covered by the Trade Boards (Tailoring) Order 1919;

(2) The making of head-gear;

(3) The making of rubberised or oilskin garments;

(4) Warehousing, packing and other similar operations carried on in shops mainly engaged in the retail distribution of articles of any description that are not made on the premises."

(a) S.R. & O. 1919/2218 (1919 II, p. 576). **(b)** S.R. & O. 1919/1201 (1919 II, p. 528).

EXPLANATORY NOTE

(*This Note is not part of the Order.*)

This Order, which has effect from 20th December 1971, sets out the statutory minimum remuneration payable in substitution for that fixed by the Wages Regulation (Wholesale Mantle and Costume) (No. 2) Order 1970 (Order W.M. (86)), which Order is revoked.

New provisions are printed in italics.

STATUTORY INSTRUMENTS

1971 No. 1923 (L.42)

MATRIMONIAL CAUSES
SUPREME COURT OF JUDICATURE, ENGLAND
COUNTY COURTS

The Matrimonial Causes (Amendment) Rules 1971

Made - - - - - - -	17*th November* 1971
Laid before Parliament - - -	3*rd December* 1971
Coming into Operation - -	1*st January* 1972

We, the authority having power to make rules of court for the purposes mentioned in section 7(1) of the Matrimonial Causes Act 1967**(a)**, hereby exercise that power as follows:—

1.—(1) These Rules may be cited as the Matrimonial Causes (Amendment) Rules 1971.

(2) In these Rules a rule referred to by number means the rule so numbered in the Matrimonial Causes Rules 1971**(b)**; "Appendix 1" and "Appendix 2" mean respectively Appendices 1 and 2 to those Rules, and a form referred to by number means the form so numbered in Appendix 2.

(3) The Interpretation Act 1889**(c)** shall apply to the interpretation of these Rules as it applies to the interpretation of an Act of Parliament.

2. Rule 2(2) shall be amended as follows:—

(1) For the definition of "divorce registry" there shall be substituted the following definition:—

"“divorce registry" means the principal registry of the Family Division".

(2) For the definition of "divorce town" there shall be substituted the following definition:—

"“divorce town", in relation to any matrimonial proceedings, means a town at which sittings of the High Court are authorised to be held outside the Royal Courts of Justice for the hearing of those proceedings or proceedings of the class to which they belong".

(3) In the definition of "judge" the letter (*a*) and paragraph (*b*) shall be omitted.

(a) 1967 c. 56.
(b) S.I. 1971/953 (1971 II, p. 2713).
(c) 1889 c. 63.

(4) The definition of "long cause" shall be omitted.

(5) In the definition of "the President" for the words "Probate, Divorce and Admiralty Division" there shall be substituted the words "Family Division".

(6) The definition of "short cause" shall be omitted.

3. For paragraph (4) of rule 9 there shall be substituted the following paragraph:—

"(4) A petition for a decree of nullity under section 2(*e*) or (*f*) of the Nullity of Marriage Act 1971**(a)** shall state whether the petitioner was at the time of the marriage ignorant of the facts alleged".

4. In rule 18(4) for the words "section 9(1)(*b*) of the Act of 1965" there shall be substituted the words "section 2(*d*) of the Nullity of Marriage Act 1971".

5. In rule 21(1) for the words "(11) and (14)" there shall be substituted the words "and (11)".

6. In rule 30(1), (2) and (3) the words "impotence or" shall be omitted wherever they appear.

7. In rule 34 the existing paragraph (8) shall be omitted and paragraph (9) shall stand as paragraph (8).

8. Rule 43 shall be amended as follows:—

(1) In paragraph (2) the words from "except that" to the end shall be omitted.

(2) For paragraph (3) there shall be substituted the following paragraph:—

"(3) A judge or the district registrar of the registry for the divorce town at which any cause has been set down for trial may, where it appears to him that the cause cannot conveniently be tried at that town, change the place of trial to some other divorce town.

The power conferred by this paragraph may be exercised by the judge or district registrar of his own motion or on the application of a party, but before acting of his own motion the judge or district registrar shall give the parties an opportunity of being heard on the question of change, and for that purpose the district registrar may give the parties notice of a date, time and place at which the question will be considered".

9. In rule 44 the following paragraph shall be substituted for paragraph (4):—

"(4) In these Rules any reference to the registry for the divorce town at which a cause is to be tried shall, in relation to a divorce town in which there is no district registry, be construed as a reference to such district registry as the Lord Chancellor may designate for the purpose."

10. Rule 46 shall be amended as follows:—

(1) In paragraph (1) for the words from "a short cause list" to "the long causes" there shall be substituted the words "a list of the causes".

(a) 1971 c. 44.

(2) For paragraphs (3), (4), (5) and (6) there shall be substituted the following paragraph:—

"(3) The district registrar of the registry for the divorce town at which a cause has been set down for trial may, if it appears to him to be desirable having regard to the proximity of the date of the trial or otherwise, exercise in the cause any jurisdiction of the registrar of the registry in which the cause is proceeding."

11. In rule 47 paragraph (1) and the figure "(2)" shall be omitted.

12. In rule 62(1) the words from "and, in the case" to the end shall be omitted.

13. The following paragraph shall be added to rule 79:—

"(5) Where, before the registrar has made his report, the parties come to an agreement as to the terms of the order to be made on the application, an order in those terms may be made by the registrar and the foregoing provisions of this rule shall not apply."

14. In rule 102 the following proviso shall be added to paragraph (7):—

"Provided that where, before the registrar has made his report, the parties come to an agreement as to the terms of the order to be made on the application, an order in those terms may be made by the registrar."

15. In rule 107(1) for the words from "the respondent at the time" to "epilepsy" there shall be substituted the words "at the time of the marriage the respondent was suffering from mental disorder within the meaning of the Mental Health Act 1959**(a)** of such a kind or to such an extent as to be unfitted for marriage".

16. Appendix 1 shall be omitted.

17. In Form 2 paragraph (14) shall be omitted.

18. In Form 4 for item (i) of the first paragraph there shall be substituted:—

"(i) residence [*state where the child is living, particulars of the accommodation, what other persons (naming them) live there and who looks after the child*]".

19. Form 9 shall be amended as follows:—

(1) For the words from "be pronounced and declared" to "with the said respondent " there shall be substituted the words "[*in the case of a void marriage* be pronounced and declared to have been by law void and the said petitioner be pronounced to have been and to be free of all bond of marriage with the said respondent] [*in the case of a voidable marriage* be annulled]".

(2) For the words "and that the said marriage" to the end there shall be substituted the words "[*in the case of a void marriage* and that the said marriage was by law void and that the said petitioner was and is free from all bond of marriage with the said respondent] [*in the case of a voidable marriage* and that the said petitioner was from that date and is free from all bond of marriage with the said respondent]".

(a) 1959 c. 72.

20. In the title of Forms 14, 20 and 21 for the words "Probate, Divorce and Admiralty Division" there shall be substituted the words "Family Division".

21.—(1) Subject to paragraph (2), these Rules shall come into operation on 1st January 1972.

(2) Nothing in rules 3, 4 and 15 shall apply in relation to a marriage which took place before 1st August 1971.

Dated 17th November 1971.

Hailsham of St. Marylebone, C.
George Baker, P.
John Latey, J.
Ifor Lloyd.
Irvon Sunderland.
W. D. S. Caird.
J. L. Willams.
Joseph Jackson.
Harold Law.
J. D. Clarke.
D. E. Morris.

EXPLANATORY NOTE

(*This Note is not part of the Rules.*)

These Rules amend the Matrimonial Causes Rules 1971 for the purposes of Part I of the Administration of Justice Act 1970 (c.31), the Courts Act 1971 (c.23) and the Nullity of Marriage Act 1971. Among the amendments consequential on the second of these Acts are the substitution of a new definition of "divorce town" which takes account of the Lord Chancellor's power under section 2 of the Act to fix the places of sitting of the High Court outside London (rule 2(2)), the abolition of the distinction between long and short defended causes (rules 2(4), (6) and 10(1)) and the introduction of new provisions enabling the district registrar of a divorce town to change the place of trial and make interlocutory orders in a cause set down for trial at his town (rules 8(2) and 10(2)). The Rules also enable the registrar, in certain matters referred to him for investigation, to make an order by consent without reporting back to the judge (rules 13 and 14) and provide for more detailed information to be given in the Statement as to Arrangements for Children (rule 19).

1971 No. 1930

LOCAL LOANS

The Local Loans (Increase of Limit) Order 1971

Laid before the House of Commons in draft

Made - - -	26*th November* 1971
Coming into Operation	1*st December* 1971

The Treasury, in exercise of the powers conferred upon them by section 4(2) of the National Loans Act 1968**(a)** and of all other powers enabling them in that behalf, hereby make the following Order, a draft of which has been laid before the Commons House of Parliament and has been approved by resolution of that House:—

1. This Order may be cited as the Local Loans (Increase of Limit) Order 1971, and shall come into operation on 1st December 1971.

2. The Interpretation Act 1889**(b)** shall apply for the interpretation of this Order as it applies for the interpretation of an Act of Parliament.

3. The limit specified in section 4(2) of the National Loans Act 1968 (being a limit on local loans of £1,000 million increased on two occasions by £1,000 million by Orders **(c)** under the said section 4(2)) shall be further increased by the sum of £1,000 million to £4,000 million.

V. H. Goodhew,
Walter Clegg,
Two of the Lords Commissioners
of Her Majesty's Treasury.

26th November 1971.

EXPLANATORY NOTE

(*This Note is not part of the Order.*)

This Order increases the limit on lending by the Public Works Loan Commissioners to local authorities and other eligible borrowers from £3,000 million to £4,000 million as from 1st December 1971.

1971 No. 1933

INSURANCE

The Employers' Liability (Compulsory Insurance) Exemption Regulations 1971

Made - - - - *26th November* 1971

Laid before Parliament *7th December* 1971

Coming into Operation *1st January* 1972

The Secretary of State, in exercise of his powers under section 3(1)(*c*) of the Employers' Liability (Compulsory Insurance) Act 1969**(a)** and of all other powers enabling him in that behalf, hereby makes the following Regulations:—

Commencement and citation

1. These Regulations may be cited as the Employers' Liability (Compulsory Insurance) Exemption Regulations 1971 and shall come into operation on 1st January 1972.

Interpretation

2.—(1) The Interpretation Act 1889**(b)** shall apply to the interpretation of these Regulations as it applies to the interpretation of an Act of Parliament.

(2) In these Regulations—

"the Act" means the Employers' Liability (Compulsory Insurance) Act 1969;

"joint subsidiary" has the same meaning as in section 51(5) of the Transport Act 1968**(c)**; and

"subsidiary" has the same meaning as in section 154 of the Companies Act 1948**(d)** (taking references in that section to a company as being references to any body corporate).

Exemptions

3. The following employers are hereby exempted from the requirement of the Act to insure and maintain insurance:—

(*a*) any body which is for the time being a body holding a certificate issued by a government department (not being a certificate which has been revoked) stating that claims established against that body in respect of any liability of the kind mentioned in section 1(1) of the Act will, to any extent to which they are incapable of being satisfied by that body, be satisfied out of moneys provided by Parliament;

(a) 1969 c. 57.
(b) 1889 c. 63.
(c) 1968 c. 73.
(d) 1948 c. 38.

(*b*) the Government of any foreign state or Commonwealth country;

(*c*) any inter-governmental organisation which by virtue of any statute or Order in Council has the legal capacities of a body corporate;

(*d*) any subsidiary of any such body as is mentioned in section 3(1)(*b*) of the Act (which exempts any body corporate established by or under any enactment for the carrying on of any industry or part of an industry, or of any undertaking, under national ownership or control) and any company of which two or more such bodies are members and which would, if those bodies were a single body corporate, be a subsidiary of that body corporate;

(*e*) any passenger transport executive established under the Transport Act 1968 and any subsidiary thereof;

(*f*) the London Transport Executive, any subsidiary and any joint subsidiary thereof;

(*g*) Cable and Wireless Limited;

(*h*) companies which are statutory water undertakers within the meaning of the Water Acts 1945 and 1948(**a**);

(*i*) the Metropolitan Water Board;

(*j*) the Lee Conservancy Catchment Board;

(*k*) the Conservators of the River Thames;

(*l*) any regional water board and any water development board within the meaning of the Water (Scotland) Act 1967(**b**);

(*m*) any river authority established under the Water Resources Act 1963(**c**);

(*n*) any river purification board within the meaning of the Rivers (Prevention of Pollution) (Scotland) Act 1951(**d**);

(*o*) any development corporation within the meaning of the New Towns Act 1965(**e**) or the New Towns (Scotland) Act 1968(**f**);

(*p*) the Commission for the New Towns;

(*q*) the Letchworth Garden City Corporation;

(*r*) the Schools Council for Curriculum and Examinations;

(*s*) the Scottish Certificate of Education Examination Board;

(*t*) any managing committee of an approved probation home or an approved probation hostel within the meaning of the Criminal Justice Act 1948(**g**);

(*u*) any licensing compensation committee appointed under section 16 of the Licensing Act 1964(**h**);

(*v*) any magistrates' courts committee and the Committee of Magistrates for inner London established under the Justices of the Peace Act 1949(**i**);

(*w*) any probation and after-care committee established under the Criminal Justice Act 1948;

(**a**) 1945 c. 42; 1948 c. 22.
(**b**) 1967 c. 78.
(**c**) 1963 c. 38.
(**d**) 1951 c. 66.
(**e**) 1965 c. 59.
(**f**) 1968 c. 16.
(**g**) 1948 c. 58.
(**h**) 1964 c. 26.
(**i**) 1949 c. 101.

(*x*) any employer who is a member of a mutual insurance association of shipowners or of shipowners and others, in respect of any liability to an employee of the kind mentioned in section 1(1) of the Act against which the employer is insured for the time being with that association for an amount not less than that required by the Act and regulations thereunder, being an employer who holds a certificate issued by that association to the effect that he is so insured in relation to that employee;

(*y*) any licensee within the meaning of the Nuclear Installations Act 1965**(a)**, in respect of any liability to pay compensation under that Act to any of his employees in respect of a breach of duty imposed on him by virtue of section 7 of that Act.

26th November 1971.

Robert Carr,

Secretary of State for Employment.

EXPLANATORY NOTE

(*This Note is not part of the Regulations.*)

These Regulations specify the employers who are exempted from the requirement of the Employers' Liability (Compulsory Insurance) Act 1969 to insure and maintain insurance against liability for bodily injury or disease sustained by their employees and arising out of and in the course of their employment. The exemptions are additional to those contained in section 3 of the Act itself.

(a) 1965 c. 57.

STATUTORY INSTRUMENTS

1971 No. 1937

AGRICULTURE

The Price Stability of Imported Products (Rates of Levy) (Cereals) (No. 12) Order 1971

Made - - - -	*29th November* 1971
Coming into Operation	*1st December* 1971

The Minister of Agriculture, Fisheries and Food, in exercise of the powers conferred upon him by section 1(2), (4), (5), (6) and (7) of the Agriculture and Horticulture Act 1964(**a**) and of all other powers enabling him in that behalf, hereby makes the following order:—

1. This order may be cited as the Price Stability of Imported Products (Rates of Levy) (Cereals) (No. 12) Order 1971, and shall come into operation on 1st December 1971.

2.—(1) In this order—

" the Principal Order " means the Price Stability of Imported Products (Levy Arrangements) (Cereals) Order 1971(**b**), as amended by any subsequent order and if any such order is replaced by any subsequent order the expression shall be construed as a reference to such subsequent order;

AND other expressions have the same meaning as in the Principal Order.

(2) The Interpretation Act 1889(**c**) shall apply to the interpretation of this order as it applies to the interpretation of an Act of Parliament and as if this order and the order hereby revoked were Acts of Parliament.

3. In accordance with and subject to the provisions of Part II of the Principal Order (which provides for the charging of levies on imports of certain specified commodities) the rate of levy for such imports into the United Kingdom of any specified commodity as are described in column 2 of the Schedule to this order in relation to a tariff heading indicated in column 1 of that Schedule shall be the rate set forth in relation thereto in column 3 of that Schedule.

4. The Price Stability of Imported Products (Rates of Levy) (Cereals) (No. 11) Order 1971(**d**) is hereby revoked.

In Witness whereof the Official Seal of the Minister of Agriculture, Fisheries and Food is hereunto affixed on 29th November 1971.

(L.S.)

M. E. Johnston,
Authorised by the Minister.

(**a**) 1964 c. 28. (**b**) S.I. 1971/631 (1971 I, p. 1660). (**c**) 1889 c. 63.
(**d**) S.I. 1971/1774 (1971 III, p. 4811).

SCHEDULE

1. Tariff Heading	2. Description of Imports	3. Rate of Levy
	Imports of:—	per ton £
10.01	Denatured wheat	2·00
	Wheat (other than denatured wheat)..	5·75
10.03	Barley other than barley having a potential diastatic activity of not less than 170 degrees	5·25
10.04	Oats	4·00
10.05	Maize (other than sweet corn on the cob)	3·50
10.07	Grain sorghum	1·75
11.02	Cereal groats, meals (including denatured wheat meal), kibbled or cut cereals, rolled, flaked, crushed or bruised cereals and other processed cereals—	
	of wheat	7·00
	of barley	6·00
	of maize	4·75
	of oats	6·00
	other	6·00

EXPLANATORY NOTE

(*This Note is not part of the Order.*)

This order, which comes into operation on 1st December 1971, supersedes the Price Stability of Imported Products (Rates of Levy) (Cereals) (No. 11) Order 1971. It—

(*a*) increases the rates of levy to be charged on imports of wheat and denatured wheat, oats, grain sorghum and processed maize within tariff heading 11·02; and

(*b*) reimposes unchanged the remaining rates of levy in force immediately before the commencement of the order.

STATUTORY INSTRUMENTS

1971 No. 1938

AGRICULTURE

The Price Stability of Imported Products (Rates of Levy) (Eggs) (No. 28) Order 1971

Made - - - *29th November* 1971

Coming into Operation *30th November* 1971

The Minister of Agriculture, Fisheries and Food, in exercise of the powers conferred upon him by section 1(2), (4), (5), (6) and (7) of the Agriculture and Horticulture Act 1964 (**a**) and of all other powers enabling him in that behalf, hereby makes the following order:—

1. This order may be cited as the Price Stability of Imported Products (Rates of Levy) (Eggs) (No. 28) Order 1971, and shall come into operation on 30th November 1971.

2.—(1) In this order—

" the Principal Order " means the Price Stability of Imported Products (Levy Arrangements) (Eggs) Order 1970 (**b**) as amended (**c**) and as amended by any subsequent order, and if any such order is replaced by any subsequent order the expression shall be construed as a reference to such subsequent order;

AND other expressions have the same meaning as in the Principal Order.

(2) The Interpretation Act 1889 (**d**) shall apply to the interpretation of this order as it applies to the interpretation of an Act of Parliament and as if this order and the order hereby revoked were Acts of Parliament.

3. In accordance with and subject to the provisions of the Principal Order (which provides for the charging of levies on imports of those eggs and egg products which are specified commodities for the purposes of the Agriculture and Horticulture Act 1964) the rate of general levy for such imports into the United Kingdom of any specified commodity as are described in column 2 of the Schedule to this order in relation to a tariff heading indicated in column 1 of that Schedule shall be the rate set forth in relation thereto in column 3 of that Schedule.

4. The Price Stability of Imported Products (Rates of Levy) (Eggs) (No. 27) Order 1971 (**e**) is hereby revoked.

In Witness whereof the Official Seal of the Minister of Agriculture, Fisheries and Food is hereunto affixed on 29th November 1971.

(L.S.)

D. F. Williamson,
Assistant Secretary.

(**a**) 1964 c. 28. (**b**) S.I. 1970/359 (1970 I, p. 1277).
(**c**) S.I. 1971/947, 1642 (1971 II, p. 2709; III, p. 4505). (**d**) 1889 c. 63.
(**e**) S.I. 1971/1895 (1971 III, p. 5145).

SCHEDULE

1. Tariff Heading	2. Description of Imports	3. Rate of General Levy
	Imports of:—	
04.05	*Birds' eggs (in shell or not in shell), fresh, dried or otherwise preserved, sweetened or not, other than egg yolks:*	
	B. Eggs not in shell:	(per ton)
	Whole dried	£325
	Whole frozen or liquid	£50

EXPLANATORY NOTE

(*This Note is not part of the Order.*)

This order, which comes into operation on 30th November 1971, supersedes the Price Stability of Imported Products (Rates of Levy) (Eggs) (No. 27) Order 1971. It—

(*a*) removes the general levy on imports of eggs in shell; and

(*b*) reimposes unchanged the rates of general levy to be charged on imports of dried, frozen or liquid whole egg not in shell.

1971 No. 1939

MERCHANT SHIPPING

The Shipbuilding Industry Board (Dissolution Provisions) Order 1971

Made - - -	*29th November* 1971
Coming into Operation	*15th December* 1971

The Secretary of State, in exercise of his powers under section 9(4) of the Shipbuilding Industry Act 1967(**a**), and all other powers in that behalf enabling him, hereby orders as follows:

Citation and commencement

1. This Order may be cited as The Shipbuilding Industry Board (Dissolution Provisions) Order 1971 and shall come into operation on 15th December 1971.

Interpretation

2.—(1) In this Order—

"the Act" means the Shipbuilding Industry Act 1967;

"the Board" means the Shipbuilding Industry Board;

"the dissolution year" means the period of twelve months ending with 31st March 1972;

"the final period" means the period beginning with 1st April 1971 and ending with 31st December 1971.

(2) The Interpretation Act 1889(**b**) shall apply for the interpretation of this Order as it applies for the interpretation of an Act of Parliament.

Report for the final period

3.—(1) The general report mentioned in section 8(1) of the Act shall not be made in respect of the dissolution year, but the Board shall on 31st December 1971 make a general report to the Secretary of State for Trade and Industry on the exercise by the Board of its functions during the final period.

(2) Section 8(2) and (3) of the Act shall apply to the report for the final period as if it were a report for a financial year, the references to a financial year in the said section 8(2) being for the purposes of such application construed as references to the final period.

Accounts for the final period

4.—(1) The Board shall keep proper accounts and other records for the final period.

(2) A statement of accounts of the Board for the final period shall—

(a) be prepared by the Secretary of State for Trade and Industry in such form as he may with the approval of the Treasury determine,

(**a**) 1967 c. 40. (**b**) 1889 c. 63.

(b) be sent by the Secretary of State for Trade and Industry to the Comptroller and Auditor General not later than the end of November 1972, and

(c) thereafter be dealt with by the Comptroller and Auditor General as if it were a statement of accounts sent to him in pursuance of section 8(5) of the Act.

(3) Except to the extent provided by the foregoing paragraphs of this Article, section 8(4) and (5) of the Act shall not apply in respect of the Board's accounts, records or statement of accounts for the dissolution year.

Other provisions relating to the dissolution of the Board

5. Every contract, agreement, licence and authority, whether written or not, and every deed, bond, instrument and document made before 31st December 1971 and still in effect on that date relating to property, rights or liabilities of the Board vested in the Secretary of State for Trade and Industry by virtue of section 9(3) of the Act shall continue in effect but subject to the following modifications so far as they are applicable—

(a) if the Board is a party thereto, the Secretary of State for Trade and Industry shall be substituted as that party;

(b) for a reference (however worded and whether express or implied) to the Board there shall as respects anything falling to be done or occurring after that date be substituted a reference to the Secretary of State for Trade and Industry;

(c) for a reference (however worded and whether express or implied) to the members or any member, or to any officer or officers of the Board there shall be substituted as respects anything done or falling to be done or occurring after that date a reference to such officer or officers as the Secretary of State shall appoint for the purpose;

(d) for a reference to the office or place of business of the Board there shall be substituted a reference to the principal offices of the Department of Trade and Industry.

Dated 29th November 1971.

John Eden,
Minister for Industry,
Department of Trade and Industry

EXPLANATORY NOTE

(*This Note is not part of the Order.*)

This Order makes provision consequential upon the dissolution of the Shipbuilding Industry Board, which is due to take place on 31st December 1971.

STATUTORY INSTRUMENTS

1971 No. 1942

WAGES COUNCILS

The Wages Regulation (Retail Newsagency, Tobacco and Confectionery) (England and Wales) (Amendment) Order 1971

Made - - -	*29th November* 1971
Coming into Operation	*10th January* 1972

Whereas the Secretary of State has received from the Retail Newsagency, Tobacco and Confectionery Trades Wages Council (England and Wales) the wages regulation proposals set out in the Schedule hereto ;

Now, therefore, the Secretary of State in exercise of his powers under section 11 of the Wages Councils Act 1959(**a**), and of all other powers enabling him in that behalf, hereby makes the following Order :—

1. This Order may be cited as the Wages Regulation (Retail Newsagency, Tobacco and Confectionery) (England and Wales) (Amendment) Order 1971.

2.—(1) In this Order the expression "the specified date" means the 10th January 1972, provided that where, as respects any worker who is paid wages at intervals not exceeding seven days, that date does not correspond with the beginning of the period for which the wages are paid, the expression "the specified date" means, as respects that worker, the beginning of the next such period following that date.

(2) The Interpretation Act 1889(**b**) shall apply to the interpretation of this Order as it applies to the interpretation of an Act of Parliament.

3. The wages regulation proposals set out in the Schedule hereto shall have effect as from the specified date.

Signed by order of the Secretary of State.
29th November 1971.

J. R. Lloyd Davies,
Assistant Secretary,
Department of Employment.

(**a**) 1959 c. 69. (**b**) 1889 c. 63.

Article 3

SCHEDULE

Statutory Minimum Remuneration

The Wages Regulation (Retail Newsagency, Tobacco and Confectionery) (England and Wales) Order 1971(a) (Order R.N.T. (48)) shall have effect as if in the Schedule thereto for paragraph 3 there were substituted the following paragraph:—

"ALL WORKERS OTHER THAN TRANSPORT WORKERS AND STREET NEWSVENDORS REMUNERATED ON A SESSIONAL AND PIECE RATE BASIS

3.—(1) Subject to the provisions of this paragraph and of paragraph 1, the minimum remuneration payable to male or female workers of the classes specified in Column 1 of the next following table employed in the London Area, Provincial A Area or Provincial B Area, as the case may be, shall be the appropriate amount set out in Column 2.

Column 1	Column 2					
	LONDON AREA		PROVINCIAL A AREA		PROVINCIAL B AREA	
	Per week		Per week		Per week	
	Male	Female	Male	Female	Male	Female
(*a*) SHOP MANAGERS and SHOP MANAGERESSES where the number of staff (computed in accordance with the provisions of sub-paragraph (2) of this paragraph) is:—	£	£	£	£	£	£
One or none	14·65	12·40	14·35	12·10	13·80	11·55
Two	15·00	12·80	14·70	12·50	14·15	11·95
Three	15·40	13·20	15·10	12·85	14·55	12·35
(*b*) CLERKS GRADE I, aged 24 years or over	13·80	11·35	13·45	11·05	12·95	10·50
(*c*) CLERKS GRADE I, aged under 24 years, CLERKS GRADE II and all other workers (other than transport workers and street newsvendors remunerated on a sessional and piece rate basis) being workers aged:—						
23 years or over	13·40	11·05	13·10	10·75	12·55	10·20
22 and under 23 years	12·75	10·50	12·45	10·20	11·90	9·70
21 " " 22 "	12·45	10·20	12·10	9·95	11·60	9·45
20 " " 21 "	11·40	9·40	11·15	9·15	10·65	8·65
19 " " 20 "	10·70	8·85	10·50	8·60	10·05	8·15
18 " " 19 "	10·05	8·30	9·85	8·05	9·40	7·65
17 " " 18 "	8·70	7·20	8·50	7·00	8·15	6·65
16 " " 17 "	8·05	6·65	7·85	6·45	7·55	6·10
15 " " 16 "	7·35	6·15	7·20	5·90	6·90	5·60

Provided that where a worker to whom (*c*) of the foregoing table applies enters, or has entered, the retail newsagency, tobacco and confectionery trades for the first time at or over the age of 20 years, the minimum remuneration payable shall be—

(i) during the first three months of the employment, 50p per week less, and

(ii) during the second three months of the employment, 25p per week less than the minimum remuneration otherwise applicable to the worker under (*c*) of the said table.

(a) S.I. 1971/1443 (1971 III, p. 4058).

(2) In Column 1 of the foregoing table 'number of staff' means the number of persons (excluding the shop manager or shop manageress) normally employed by the employer for whose control the shop manager or shop manageress is responsible to the employer and in computing that number—

(*a*) each worker who normally works for the employer for more than 24 hours in a week shall be counted as one unit;

(*b*) each worker who normally works for the employer for 24 hours or less in a week shall be counted as half a unit but where such calculation results in a fraction the next whole number above shall be the number to be counted for the purpose of the table aforesaid;

(*c*) a delivery worker employed for not more than 2 hours per day and for not more than 12 hours per week shall not be counted;

(*d*) a cleaner employed for not more than 2 hours per day and for not more than 12 hours per week shall not be counted."

EXPLANATORY NOTE

(*This Note is not part of the Order.*)

This Order, which has effect from 10th January 1972, amends the Wages Regulation (Retail Newsagency, Tobacco and Confectionery) (England and Wales) Order 1971 (Order R.N.T. (48)) by increasing the statutory minimum remuneration for certain workers aged 23 or below fixed by that Order.

New rates are printed in italics.

1971 No. 1946

FRIENDLY SOCIETIES

The Friendly Societies (Proxy Voting) Regulations 1971

Made - - -	1*st December* 1971
Laid before Parliament	9*th December* 1971
Coming into Operation	31*st December* 1971

The Chief Registrar of Friendly Societies pursuant to the powers conferred upon him by section 4(2) of the Friendly Societies Act 1971(**a**) and to all other powers enabling him in that behalf hereby makes the following Regulations:—

1.—(1) These Regulations may be cited as the Friendly Societies (Proxy Voting) Regulations 1971 and shall come into operation on 31st December 1971.

(2) In these Regulations—

"registered society" means a society registered under the Friendly Societies Act 1896(**b**);

"resolution" means a resolution which, if passed as mentioned in section 4(1)(*b*) of the Friendly Societies Act 1971, would be a special resolution.

(3) The Interpretation Act 1889(**c**) shall apply to the interpretation of these Regulations as it applies to the interpretation of an Act of Parliament.

2. The procedure adopted by a registered society for proxy voting on a resolution shall comply with the following requirements—

(*a*) The instrument appointing a proxy (who need not be a member of the society and shall not, in the case of a collecting society, be a collector or superintendent thereof) shall be in writing under the hand of the appointer or of his agent duly authorised in writing,

(*b*) The instrument appointing a proxy and the power of attorney or other authority, if any, under which it is signed, or a notarially certified copy of that power or authority, shall be deposited at the registered office of the society, or at such other place within the United Kingdom as is specified for that purpose in the notice convening the meeting, not less than 48 hours before the time for holding the meeting, or adjourned meeting, at which the person named in the instrument proposes to vote, and in default the instrument of proxy shall not be valid.

(**a**) 1971 c. 66. (**b**) 1896 c. 25.
(**c**) 1889 c. 63

(c) An instrument appointing a proxy shall be in the following form or a form as near thereto as circumstances admit—

"I/We of

, being a member/members of the Society, hereby appoint

of , or failing him

of , as my/our proxy to vote for me/us on

my/our behalf at the meeting of the society, to be held on

19 , and at any adjournment thereof.

Signed

Date

This form is to be used in favour of / against * the resolution.

Unless otherwise instructed the proxy will vote as he thinks fit.

* Strike out whichever is not desired. "

(d) A vote given in accordance with the terms of an instrument of proxy shall be valid notwithstanding the previous death or insanity of the principal or revocation of the proxy or of the authority under which the proxy was executed, provided that no intimation in writing of such death, insanity or revocation shall have been received by the society at its registered office before the commencement of the meeting or adjourned meeting at which the proxy is used.

S. D. Musson,
Chief Registrar of Friendly Societies.

Date 1st December 1971.

EXPLANATORY NOTE

(*This Note is not part of the Regulations.*)

These Regulations prescribe the procedure to be adopted by societies registered under the Friendly Societies Act 1896 for proxy voting on special resolutions.

1971 No. 1947

INCOME TAX

The Income Tax (Employments) (No. 9) Regulations 1971

Made - - -	1*st December* 1971
Laid before the House of Commons	8*th December* 1971
Coming into Operation	6*th April* 1972

The Commissioners of Inland Revenue, in exercise of the powers conferred upon them by section 204 of the Income and Corporation Taxes Act 1970(**a**), hereby make the following Regulations :—

1. These Regulations shall come into operation on 6th April 1972, and may be cited as the Income Tax (Employments) (No. 9) Regulations 1971. These Regulations are supplemental to the Income Tax (Employments) Regulations 1965(**b**), as amended (**c**) (hereinafter referred to as "the Principal Regulations").

2.—(1) The Interpretation Act 1889(**d**) shall apply for the interpretation of these Regulations as it applies for the interpretation of an Act of Parliament.

(2) In these Regulations, unless the context otherwise requires, words and expressions to which meanings are assigned by the Principal Regulations, or in which other words or expressions are stated in the Principal Regulations to be included, are to be interpreted in accordance with the Principal Regulations.

Application of Part VI of the Principal Regulations

3. Regulation 43 of the Principal Regulations shall apply subject to the deletion of the words " "forces tables" means the tables prepared by the Commissioners of Inland Revenue for the purposes of deduction of tax from forces emoluments".

4. Parts II and III of the Principal Regulations shall apply in relation to forces emoluments with the modifications set out in these Regulations.

5. Regulations 44, 45, 46 and 47 of the Principal Regulations shall cease to have effect from 6th April 1972.

(**a**) 1970 c. 10. (**b**) S.I. 1965/516 (1965 I, p. 1321).
(**c**) The amending Regulations are not relevant to the subject matter of these Regulations
(**d**) 1889 c. 63.

6. An appeal under Regulation 10 of the Principal Regulations may be made to the Special Commissioners.

7.—(1) Regulation 48 of the Principal Regulations shall not apply but the following provisions shall have effect. If the employee ceases, otherwise than by forfeiture during the period of service, to be entitled to any forces emoluments or is granted furlough preparatory to that event, the public department responsible for the payment of those emoluments shall, as soon as possible after they cease to be payable or furlough is granted as aforesaid, deliver to the employee a certificate as prescribed by the Commissioners of Inland Revenue indicating that he has served in the armed forces.

(2) When the final payment is made the public department shall deliver to the employee two copies of a certificate prepared in accordance with paragraph (1) of Regulation 17 of the Principal Regulations for production to his new employer.

(3) If the employee commences new employment before the certificate referred to in paragraph (2) of this Regulation is received he may deliver the certificate referred to in paragraph (1) of this Regulation to the new employer who shall send the certificate to the Inspector.

By Order of the Commissioners of Inland Revenue.

G. Wolters,
Secretary.

1st December 1971.

EXPLANATORY NOTE

(This Note is not part of the Regulations.)

These Regulations re-enact, with amendments, Part VI of the Income Tax (Employments) Regulations 1965, which contains the special PAYE provisions applicable to the armed forces. The amendments to the previous Regulations bring the operation of PAYE for members of the armed forces more closely into line with that for other employees. The Regulations will come into effect at the start of the 1972-73 tax year.

1971 No. 1953

SEA FISHERIES

The White Fish Subsidy (Deep Sea Vessels) (United Kingdom) Scheme 1971

Made - - -	*22nd October* 1971
Laid before Parliament	*3rd November* 1971
Coming into Operation	*1st December* 1971

The Minister of Agriculture, Fisheries and Food and the Secretaries of State for Scotland and Wales (being the Secretaries of State respectively concerned with the sea fishing industry in Scotland and Wales) in exercise of the powers conferred upon them by section 49 of the Sea Fish Industry Act 1970(**a**) and of all other powers enabling them in that behalf, with the approval of the Treasury, hereby make the following scheme :—

Citation, extent and commencement

1. This scheme, which may be cited as the White Fish Subsidy (Deep Sea Vessels) (United Kingdom) Scheme 1971, shall apply to the United Kingdom and shall come into operation on the day following the day on which it is approved by Parliament.

Interpretation

2.—(1) In this scheme, unless the context otherwise requires—

"aggregate operating profits" has the meaning assigned to it by paragraph 8 ;

"the appropriate Minister"—

(*a*) in relation to England and Northern Ireland, means the Minister of Agriculture, Fisheries and Food ;

(*b*) in relation to Scotland, means the Secretary of State concerned with the sea fishing industry in Scotland ;

(*c*) in relation to Wales, means—

(i) for the purpose of the actual making of any payment under this scheme, the Minister of Agriculture, Fisheries and Food, and

(ii) for all the other purposes of this scheme, the said Minister and the Secretary of State concerned with the sea fishing industry in Wales acting jointly ;

"approved" means approved by the appropriate Minister ;

(**a**) 1970 c. 11.

"the exclusive fishery limits" does not include waters within the fishery limits of the British Islands which are adjacent to the Isle of Man or any of the Channel Islands ;

"fish" includes shellfish ;

"length", in relation to a vessel, means the length in relation to which its tonnage was calculated for the purposes of registration under Part IV of the Merchant Shipping Act 1894(**a**) ;

"the Ministers" means the Minister of Agriculture, Fisheries and Food and the Secretaries of State respectively concerned with the sea fishing industry in Scotland and Wales ;

"paragraph" means a paragraph of this scheme ;

"products", in relation to fish, means anything produced by processing the fish and "processing" includes preserving or preparing fish, or producing any substance or article wholly or partly from fish, by any method for human or animal consumption ;

"reference period" has the meaning assigned to it by paragraph 8 ;

"subsidy period" has the meaning assigned to it by paragraph 4 ;

"white fish" means fish of any kind found in the sea, except herring, salmon, migratory trout and shellfish.

(2) In this scheme, in relation to a vessel to which this scheme applies which has completed a voyage, being a voyage for such a purpose as is mentioned in paragraph 3(2), terminating during any reference period :—

"gross proceeds" means the gross proceeds from the first-hand sale of the fish caught by the vessel on that voyage or the products of such fish together with, in any case where during the voyage the vessel was employed for a purpose other than that mentioned in paragraph 3(2) and a payment has been or will be received as a result of such employment, the whole or such part of such payment to the extent to which the appropriate Minister shall consider appropriate having regard to the loss of fishing time resulting from such employment :

Provided that where the first-hand sale of any of the said fish or products landed as aforesaid takes place at a time other than immediately after they were landed the gross proceeds of such fish or products shall for the purposes of this scheme be taken to be such a sum as shall appear to the appropriate Minister to be that which would have been received had such fish or products been sold immediately after they were landed ;

"operating costs" means the total of all approved costs incurred in respect of that voyage including such proportion of the costs of management, of the training of officers and crew and of overhead expenses (or provision for such expenses) as the appropriate Minister may approve as referable to the voyage but excluding the payment of interest on, and the depreciation of, capital ;

"operating loss" means any amount by which the gross proceeds of that voyage are less than the operating costs of the voyage ;

"operating profit" means any amount by which the gross proceeds of that voyage exceed the operating costs of the voyage.

(3) The Interpretation Act 1889(**b**) shall apply for the interpretation of this scheme as it applies for the interpretation of an Act of Parliament.

(**a**) 1894 c. 60. (**b**) 1889 c. 63.

General conditions of Grant

3.—(1) This scheme applies to every fishing vessel of 80 feet or over in length, registered in the United Kingdom, being a vessel engaged on voyages falling within sub-paragraph (2) of this paragraph.

(2) The voyages to which sub-paragraph (1) of this paragraph relates are voyages made for the purpose of catching white fish where it is part of the purpose that the fish or the products of the fish are to be landed in the United Kingdom whether by the vessel which caught them or by another vessel or are to be trans-shipped in a port in the United Kingdom or within the exclusive fishery limits by the vessel which caught them or by another vessel.

4. A grant may be paid by the appropriate Minister in accordance with the following provisions of this scheme to the owner (or his agent) or, where there is a charter-party, to the charterer (or his agent), of a vessel to which this scheme applies in respect of each such period (hereinafter referred to as "the subsidy period") as the Ministers may determine, being a period not exceeding 12 months in duration, which commences—

(*a*) in the case of the first subsidy period, on 1st August 1971 ;

(*b*) in the case of subsequent subsidy periods, on the termination of the immediately preceding subsidy period

and which, in the case of the last subsidy period, terminates on 31st July 1973.

5.—(1) Application for payment of a grant under this scheme shall be made by the owner or charterer or his duly authorised agent in such form and within such period as the appropriate Minister may from time to time require and shall be completed and certified in all respects as so required and shall be delivered to the appropriate Minister at such address as he may specify for the purpose.

(2) Notice that a person is authorised to make application for and receive payment of grants under this scheme on behalf of an owner or charterer shall be given in writing signed by the owner or charterer in such form as the appropriate Minister may from time to time require and shall be sent to the address specified by the appropriate Minister for the purpose of this paragraph.

6. The owner or charterer of a vessel (or his duly authorised agent) who applies for payment of a grant under this scheme or any person acting on behalf of such owner or charterer and appointed by him for the purpose shall, within such time in such form and for such period as may be specified by the appropriate Minister, supply such information and make such returns concerning fishing operations, costs and trading results as may be required by the appropriate Minister, including detailed accounts of the financial results of the operation of all vessels to which this scheme applies owned or chartered by such owner or charterer, and shall when required at any time during the period comprising the remainder of the calendar year current when an application for grant is made in respect of any such vessel and the two years immediately following that year, make any relevant books and records open to examination by any person authorised by the appropriate Minister.

7. Without prejudice to the discretion of the appropriate Minister in the payment of grants under this scheme, if any owner or charterer or any person acting on his behalf makes a statement or produces a document which is false in a material particular or refuses to supply any information, make any return or produce any document in respect of any of the matters required to be disclosed either in connection with an application for payment of grant under this scheme or in accordance with the provisions of paragraph 6 or if any of the conditions relating to the payment of grants under this scheme are not complied with by any owner or charterer or person acting on behalf of an owner or charterer, the payment of grants to that owner, charterer or person at any time may be refused.

Total amount of grant

8. The Ministers may in respect of any subsidy period make available for payment of grant a sum (hereinafter referred to as "the total amount of grant") calculated in accordance with the next following paragraph related to the aggregate operating profits of all vessels to which this scheme applies from all voyages which terminated during the relevant reference period.

In this and the succeeding paragraphs of this scheme the "reference period" in relation to any subsidy period means such period, having the same duration as that subsidy period, as the Ministers may determine, and "aggregate operating profits" for a reference period means the sum, if any, by which the total operating profits of all such vessels from the voyages which terminated during that reference period exceed the total operating losses of such vessels from such voyages.

9.—(1) Subject to the following provisions of this paragraph, the total amount of grant made available in respect of a subsidy period, being a sub sidy period of 12 months, shall be—

(*a*) if the aggregate operating profits for the relevant reference period do not exceed £4,800,000, the sum representing the total of the sum of £2,000,000 and one half of the amount by which the aggregate operating profits are less than £4,800,000 ;

(*b*) if the aggregate operating profits for the relevant reference period exceed £4,800,000, the sum remaining after deducting from the sum of £2,000,000 one half of the amount by which the aggregate operating profits exceed the sum of £4,800,000 :

Provided that the total amount of grant in respect of such a subsidy period shall not exceed the sum of £4,000,000 nor such a sum as taken together with the aggregate operating profits for the relevant reference period will amount to the sum of £7,800,000.

(2) Where the duration of a subsidy period is less than 12 months the provisions of the last foregoing sub-paragraph shall have effect as if for the sums of £2,000,000, £4,000,000, £4,800,000 and £7,800,000 mentioned therein there were substituted respectively such sums as bear the same proportion to £2,000,000, £4,000,000, £4,800,000 and £7,800,000 as the subsidy period bears to a period of 12 months.

Grant payable in respect of each vessel

10. The amount of grant payable in respect of a vessel to which this scheme applies in respect of any subsidy period shall be a sum equal to the relevant fraction of the added value, if any, attributable to the employment of the vessel during the relevant reference period.

In this paragraph—

(*a*) the "relevant fraction" means the fraction which represents the proportion which the total amount of grant made available in respect of the subsidy period bears to the total amount of added value attributable to the employment during the relevant reference period of all vessels to which this scheme applies ;

(*b*) the added value attributable to the employment of a vessel during any reference period shall be the sum, if any, by which the total of the gross proceeds from the employment of the vessel on all the voyages which terminated during that reference period exceeds the total of the operating costs of the vessel in respect of such voyages other than—

(i) wages, holiday pay and other remuneration of, or payments for the provision of benefits to, the officers and crew of the vessel ;

(ii) national insurance payments made by the owner or charterer in respect of the officers and crew of the vessel ;

(iii) victualling expenses, and

(iv) the approved costs of the training of officers and crew.

11. The appropriate Minister may during the course of any subsidy period make a payment on account of grant in respect of a vessel in relation to such period and if, after the expiration of that period, the payment so made exceeds the amount payable under this scheme in respect of the vessel in respect of the subsidy period the amount of the overpayment shall be repaid to the appropriate Minister by the person to whom it was paid.

12. In the event of a dispute as to the purpose of a voyage undertaken by a vessel to which this scheme applies, as to the day on which such a voyage terminated or as to the ascertainment of the amount of any gross proceeds or operating costs the determination of the appropriate Minister shall be conclusive.

13. If, at the time when they propose to make a calculation for any reference period of the aggregate operating profits for the purposes of paragraph 9 or of the total amount of added value for the purposes of paragraph 10, there shall not be available to the Ministers any return, or a return appearing to the appropriate Minister to be adequate for the purpose, of the gross proceeds or any of the costs of any vessel to which this scheme applies for that reference period the appropriate Minister may estimate the gross proceeds or, as the case may be, costs from such information as is available to him and the amounts so estimated may be treated by the Ministers as the gross proceeds or, as the case may be, costs of that vessel for the purposes of either of the calculations aforesaid.

14. Where in any case the added value attributable to the employment of any vessel during any reference period has been estimated in accordance with the provisions of paragraph 13, the value so estimated may, if the appropriate Minister so thinks fit, be treated as the added value attributable to the employment of that vessel during that reference period for the purpose of payment of grant in respect of that vessel in respect of that period.

15. If at any time after 1st August 1968 any structural alteration shall be made or shall have been made to any vessel which increases or has increased its length to 80 feet or over, such vessel shall not be treated as one to which this scheme applies unless the appropriate Minister is satisfied that the alteration was likely to be conducive to the increased fishing efficiency of the vessel.

In witness whereof the Official Seal of the Minister of Agriculture, Fisheries and Food is hereunto affixed on 18th October 1971.

(L.S.)

J. M. L. Prior,
Minister of Agriculture, Fisheries and Food.

Gordon Campbell,
19th October 1971. Secretary of State for Scotland.

Peter Thomas,
21st October 1971. Secretary of State for Wales.

Approved on 22nd October 1971.

Walter Clegg,
P. L. Hawkins,
Two of the Lords Commissioners of
Her Majesty's Treasury.

EXPLANATORY NOTE

(This Note is not part of the Scheme.)

This scheme which is made under the powers contained in section 49 of the Sea Fish Industry Act 1970 provides for the payment of grants to the owners and charterers of fishing vessels of 80 feet or over in length registered in the United Kingdom and engaged in catching white fish. It provides for grants for the two years from 1st August 1971 to 31st July 1973.

The grants payable will be calculated by reference to the results of fishing during specified periods, for which vessel owners will make returns.

The total amount of grant to be paid in respect of a period of one year will be calculated by reference to the aggregate operating profits of all vessels to which the scheme applies. A basic grant of £2m will be increased by one half of the amount by which those profits, in any one year, fall short of £4·8m or reduced by one half of the amount by which the profits exceed £4·8m. The total amount of grant will in no case exceed £4m and the scheme provides that the total amount of grant shall be limited to ensure that the grant plus the aggregate operating profits shall not exceed £7·8m. In respect of a period of less than one year the sums referred to will be reduced proportionately.

The amount payable to individual owners or charterers will be assessed on the basis of the added value contributed by each vessel towards the aggregate added value of all the vessels. The added value will be the total of the operating profits and the costs of officers' and crews' remuneration and training.

Provision is made for the making of returns by the owners and charterers of vessels and the scheme provides which receipts and expenditure are to be taken into account in assessing the gross proceeds and operating costs of a vessel.

This scheme was approved by resolutions of the House of Lords on the 30th November 1971 and of the House of Commons on the 18th November 1971 and came into operation on 1st December 1971.

1971 No. 1954 (L. 43)

MATRIMONIAL CAUSES

COUNTY COURTS

The Divorce County Courts Order 1971

Made - - - *29th November* 1971

Coming into Operation *1st January* 1972

The Lord Chancellor, in exercise of the powers conferred on him by section 1(1) of the Matrimonial Causes Act 1967**(a)** and section 2 of the County Courts Act 1959**(b)**, hereby makes the following Order:—

1.—(1) This Order may be cited as the Divorce County Courts Order 1971 and shall come into operation on 1st January 1972.

(2) The Interpretation Act 1889**(c)** shall apply to the interpretation of this Order as it applies to the interpretation of an Act of Parliament.

2. The county courts mentioned in Schedule 1 are hereby designated as divorce county courts, and those marked "T" shall be courts of trial for the purposes of section 1(1) of the Matrimonial Causes Act 1967.

3. In the case of the county courts mentioned in Column 1 of Schedule 2 (being courts held at more than one place) the jurisdiction conferred by virtue of paragraph 2 of this Order shall be exercised only at the places mentioned in Column 2 of that Schedule opposite the names of those courts.

4. The Orders specified in Schedule 3 are hereby revoked.

Dated 29th November 1971.

Hailsham of St. Marylebone, C.

(a) 1967 c. 56. **(b)** 1959 c. 22. **(c)** 1889 c. 63.

SCHEDULE 1

Divorce County Courts and Courts of Trial

Aberystwyth (T)
Barnet (T)
Barnsley (T)
Barnstaple
Barrow in Furness and Ulverston (T)
Bath (T)
Bedford (T)
Birkenhead
Birmingham (T)
Blackburn (T)
Blackpool (T)
Bodmin (T)
Bolton (T)
Boston
Bournemouth (T)
Bradford (T)
Bridgend (T)
Brighton (T)
Bristol (T)
Bromley (T)
Burnley (T)
Bury
Caernarvon (T)
Cambridge (T)
Canterbury (T)
Cardiff (T)
Carlisle (T)
Carmarthen (T)
Chester (T)
Chesterfield
Chichester (T)
Coventry (T)
Crewe
Croydon (T)
Darlington
Derby (T)
Dewsbury
Doncaster (T)
Dudley
Durham (T)
Eastbourne
Edmonton (T)
Epsom (T)
Exeter (T)
Gloucester (T)
Great Grimsby (T)
Guildford (T)
Halifax
Harlow (T)
Harrogate (T)
Hastings
Hereford (T)
Huddersfield
Ilford (T)
Ipswich (T)
Keighley
Kendal
Kingston upon Hull (T)
Kingston upon Thames (T)
Lancaster (T)
Leeds (T)
Leicester (T)
Lincoln (T)
Liverpool (T)
Luton (T)
Maidstone (T)
Manchester (T)
Merthyr Tydfil
Newcastle upon Tyne (T)
Newport (Mon.) (T)
Newport, Isle of Wight (T)
Northampton (T)
Norwich (T)
Nottingham (T)
Oldham (T)
Oxford (T)
Peterborough (T)
Plymouth (T)
Pontefract
Pontypridd and Ystradyfodwg (T)
Portsmouth (T)
Preston (T)
Reading (T)
Rhyl (T)
Rochdale
Rochester (T)
Saint Helens
Salford (T)
Scarborough
Scunthorpe
Sheffield (T)
Shrewsbury (T)
Slough (T)
Southampton (T)
Southend (T)
Southport
Stafford
Stockport (T)
Stockton on Tees (T)
Stoke on Trent (T)
Sunderland (T)
Swansea (T)
Swindon (T)
Taunton (T)
Torquay (T)
Truro and Falmouth (T)
Tunbridge Wells (T)
Wakefield
Walsall
Warrington (T)
Watford (T)
Wigan (T)
Winchester (T)
Wolverhampton (T)
Worcester (T)
Worthing (T)
Wrexham (T)
Yeovil
York (T)

SCHEDULE 2

Courts held at more than one place

Column 1	*Column* 2
Barrow in Furness and Ulverston	Barrow in Furness
Chichester	Chichester
Darlington	Darlington
Norwich	Norwich
Peterborough	Peterborough
Plymouth	Plymouth
Pontypridd and Ystradyfodwg	Pontypridd
Swindon	Swindon
Truro and Falmouth	Truro

SCHEDULE 3

Orders Revoked

Title	*Reference*
The Divorce County Courts Order 1968	S.I. 1968/314 (1968 I, p. 940)
The Divorce County Courts (Amendment) Order 1968	S.I. 1968/1934 (1968 III, p. 5244)
The Divorce County Courts (Amendment) Order 1969	S.I. 1969/1816 (1969 III, p. 5636)
The Divorce County Courts (Amendment) Order 1970	S.I. 1970/2032 (1970 III, p. 6624)

EXPLANATORY NOTE

(*This Note is not part of the Order.*)

This Order supersedes the Divorce County Courts Order 1968 consolidating a number of amending Orders. The Order designates the divorce county courts in which matrimonial causes may be commenced in pursuance of the Matrimonial Causes Act 1967. The courts marked "T" in Schedule 1 are those at which undefended matrimonial causes may be tried. The courts mentioned in Schedule 2 are held at more than one place and jurisdiction under the Act is exercisable only at the places mentioned in Column 2 of that Schedule. The Harlow County Court is designated as a divorce county court, and the Chichester, Great Grimsby, Harlow, Harrogate and Lancaster County Courts have been added to the list of those at which undefended causes may be tried.

1971 No. 1955 (L.44)

SUPREME COURT OF JUDICATURE, ENGLAND

PROCEDURE

The Rules of the Supreme Court (Amendment No. 5) 1971

Made - - - -	*29th November* 1971
Laid before Parliament	*10th December* 1971
Coming into Operation	
All except rule 42	*1st January* 1972
Rule 42	*1st March* 1972

We, the Rule Committee of the Supreme Court, being the authority having for the time being power under section 99(4) of the Supreme Court of Judicature (Consolidation) Act 1925**(a)** to make, amend or revoke rules regulating the practice and procedure of the Supreme Court of Judicature, hereby exercise these powers and all other powers enabling us in that behalf as follows:—

PART I

CITATION, COMMENCEMENT AND INTERPRETATION

1.—(1) These Rules may be cited as the Rules of the Supreme Court (Amendment No. 5) 1971.

(2) These Rules (except rule 42) shall come into operation on 1st January 1972, and rule 42 shall come into operation on 1st March 1972.

(3) In these Rules an Order referred to by number means the Order so numbered in the Rules of the Supreme Court 1965**(b)**, as amended **(c)** and a form referred to by number means the form so numbered in Appendix A to those Rules.

(4) The Interpretation Act 1889**(d)** shall apply to the interpretation of these Rules as it applies to the interpretation of an Act of Parliament.

PART II

AMENDMENTS CONSEQUENTIAL ON THE COURTS ACT 1971(e)

2. The following definition shall be inserted in Order 1, rule 4(1), after the definition of "folio":—

" "the Lancashire area" means the area comprising the districts of the district registries of Barrow in Furness, Blackburn, Blackpool, Bolton, Burnley, Bury, Lancaster, Liverpool, Manchester, Oldham, Preston, Rochdale, St. Helens, Southport, Warrington and Wigan."

(a) 1925 c. 49. **(b)** S.I. 1965/1776 (1965 III, p. 4995).
(c) The relevant amending instruments are 1966/1514, 1967/1809, 1968/1244, 1970/1861, 1971/1269 (1966 III, p. 4196; 1967 III, p. 4832; 1968 II, p. 3360; 1970 III, p. 6081; 1971 II, p. 3634). **(d)** 1889 c. 63. **(e)** 1971 c. 23.

3. Order 4 shall be amended as follows:—

(1) For paragraph (3) of rule 1 there shall be substituted the following paragraph:—

"(3) A cause or matter begun in the district registry of Leeds, Liverpool, Manchester, Newcastle upon Tyne or Preston shall be assigned to the group of judges known as group B, unless by virtue of any other provision of these rules it is required to be assigned to the group of judges known as group A."

(2) In rule 6(4) after the word "matter" there shall be inserted the words "(whether begun by writ, originating summons or otherwise)".

(3) At the beginning of rule 6(5) there shall be inserted the words "Without prejudice to paragraph (4)".

4. In Order 6, rule 4, after the words "that registry" there shall be inserted the words "(or, in the case of a writ issued out of the Liverpool, Manchester or Preston district registry, in the Lancashire area)".

5. In Order 7, rule 5(2), Order 9, rule 3(1), Order 42, rule 6(3), Order 86, rule 3, Order 92, rule 5(4), Order 102, rule 18, and Order 106, rule 2(3), for the words "Liverpool or the district registry of Manchester" there shall be substituted the words "Leeds, Liverpool, Manchester, Newcastle upon Tyne or Preston".

6. For paragraph (4) of Order 8, rule 3, there shall be substituted the following paragraphs:—

"(4) The notice of an originating motion by which proceedings assigned to the Queen's Bench Division are begun must be issued in the Central Office.

(5) The notice of an originating motion by which proceedings assigned to the Chancery Division are begun may be issued either out of the Central Office or out of the district registry of Leeds, Liverpool, Manchester, Newcastle upon Tyne, or Preston.

(6) Issue of the notice of an originating motion takes place upon its being sealed by an officer of the office out of which it is issued."

7. The following paragraph shall be added to Order 12, rule 2:—

"(6) In relation to a writ in the Chancery Division which is issued out of the district registry of Liverpool, Manchester or Preston, paragraphs (2), (3) and (5) shall have effect as if for the references to the district of that registry there were substituted references to the Lancashire area."

8. In Order 22, rule 1(7), for the words "an assize town" where they appear in sub-paragraphs (*a*) and (*b*) there shall be substituted the words "a town"; and for the words "the assize town" there shall be substituted the words "the town".

9. Order 28, rule 9, shall be amended as follows:—

(1) In paragraph (2) for the words from "the cause clerk" to "that clerk" there shall be substituted the words "the proper officer, who".

(2) In paragraph (3) the words from the beginning to "Family Division" shall be omitted.

10. Order 32 shall be amended as follows:—

(1) The following paragraph shall be added to rule 2(3):—

"For the purposes of this paragraph, a cause or matter in which any jurisdiction is to be exercised by virtue of Order 34, rule 5(4), by a master or by the registrar of a district registry shall be treated, in relation to that jurisdiction, as proceeding in the Central Office or in that district registry respectively."

(2) Rule 25 shall be revoked.

(3) In rule 26 for the words "Liverpool or in the district registry of Manchester", there shall be substituted the words "Leeds, Liverpool, Manchester, Newcastle upon Tyne or Preston" and for the words "Group B" there shall be substituted the words "the group to which the cause or matter is assigned".

11. Order 33 shall be amended as follows:—

(1) In rule 1 for the words "or such" to the end there shall be substituted the words "or one of the other places at which sittings of the High Court are authorised to be held for the trial of those proceedings or proceedings of the class to which they belong".

(2) In rule 4 paragraph (3) shall be omitted and paragraphs (4) and (5) shall be renumbered accordingly.

12. Order 34 shall be amended as follows:—

(1) In rule 1 the figure "(1)" and paragraph (2) shall be omitted.

(2) In rule 3(5) for sub-paragraphs (*b*) and (*c*) there shall be substituted the following sub-paragraph:—

"(*b*) in relation to an action (in whatever Division) which is to be tried outside the Royal Courts of Justice, the district registrar for the district comprising the place of trial;"

and sub-paragraph (*d*) shall stand as sub-paragraph (*c*).

(3) In rule 4(*b*) for the words "that Division" there shall be substituted the words "the Chancery Division".

(4) For rule 5 there shall be substituted the following rule:—

"*Further provisions as to lists*

5.—(1) The district registrar for the district comprising each place at which sittings of the High Court are held outside the Royal Courts of Justice shall keep a list of the actions for the time being set down for trial before a judge at that place.

(2) Where, after an action has been set down for trial—

(*a*) an order is made under Order 33, rule 4(1), varying the order determining the place of trial; or

(*b*) the place of trial is changed under paragraph (5) of this rule,

the action shall be treated, unless the Court otherwise directs, as having been set down at the new place of trial on the date on which it was first set down for trial elsewhere.

(3) At any time after an action has been set down for trial and before it is tried, the Court may require the parties to furnish the Court or an officer thereof, by personal attendance or otherwise, with such information as may be necessary to show whether the action is ready for trial, and if any party fails to comply with any such requirement, the Court may—

(*a*) of its own motion, on 7 days' notice to the parties, direct that the action be removed from the list, or

(*b*) on the application of any party, dismiss the action for want of prosecution or strike out the defence or counterclaim or make such other order as the Court thinks fit.

Where a direction is given under sub-paragraph (*a*), the Court may subsequently direct the action to be restored to the list on such terms, if any, as it thinks fit.

(4) Where an action proceeding in a district registry has been set down for trial at the Royal Courts of Justice or at a place comprised in the district of another district registry, or an action proceeding in the Central Office has been set down for trial outside the Royal Courts of Justice, a master or the district registrar at the place where the action has been set down for trial may, if it appears to him to be desirable having regard to the proximity of the date of trial or otherwise, exercise any jurisdiction which is exercisable in the action by a master or the district registrar at the place where the action is proceeding.

(5) Without prejudice to Order 33, rule 4(1), a judge, or a master or the district registrar at the place where an action has been set down for trial, may, if it appears to him that the action cannot conveniently be tried at the place of trial which has been ordered, change the place of trial to some other place mentioned in Order 33, rule 1.

(6) The power conferred by paragraph (5) may be exercised by the Court of its own motion or on the application of a party, but before acting of its own motion the Court shall give to every party concerned an opportunity of being heard on the question whether the power should be exercised and for that purpose the Court may cause him to be given notice of a date, time and place at which the question will be considered."

(5) Rule 7 shall be omitted.

(6) In rule 8(1) the words from "and must also" to the end shall be omitted.

13. Order 35 shall be amended as follows:—

(1) Rules 4, 5 and 6 shall be omitted.

(2) In rule 10 for the words "at assizes" there shall be substituted the words "outside the Royal Courts of Justice".

14. In Order 38, rule 14(3), for the words "at any assizes" there shall be substituted the words "outside the Royal Courts of Justice".

15. In Order 53, rule 2(1),—

(1) for the words "quarter sessions" there shall be substituted the words "the Crown Court"; and

(2) for the words "first day of the sessions at which" there shall be substituted the words "the day on which".

16. Order 56 shall be amended as follows:—

(1) In rule 1(1), (3) and (5) and rules 4 and 4A for the words "a court of quarter sessions", "quarter sessions" and "the court of quarter sessions", wherever they appear, there shall be substituted the words "the Crown Court".

(2) Paragraph (2) of rule 1, and rule 3, shall be omitted.

(3) In rule 2 for the words "a court of quarter sessions" there shall be substituted the words "the Crown Court"; and for the words "over the court of quarter sessions" there shall be substituted the words "at the hearing in the Crown Court".

17. Order 62 shall be amended as follows:—

(1) In rule 2(1) the words "other than proceedings to which section 15 of the Costs in Criminal Cases Act 1952 applies" shall be omitted.

(2) In rule 12(5), for the words "the registrar of the district registry of Liverpool and the registrar of the district registry of Manchester" there shall be substituted the words "the registrar of each of the following district registries, namely Leeds, Liverpool, Manchester, Newcastle upon Tyne and Preston".

18. In Order 63 rule 12(2), for the words "Liverpool or Manchester" there shall be substituted the words "Leeds, Liverpool, Manchester, Newcastle upon Tyne or Preston".

19. The following rule shall be substituted for Order 64, rule 5:—

"*Exclusion of trial outside Royal Courts of Justice*

5. The foregoing rules of this Order shall not apply in relation to the trial or hearing of causes, matters or applications outside the Royal Courts of Justice."

20. In Order 67, rule 8(1), the words "with the omission of sub-paragraphs (*e*) and (*f*) thereof" shall be omitted.

21. In Order 68, rule 1(1), the words "(including any such proceeding tried or heard by a court of assize)" shall be omitted.

22. Order 72, rule 9, shall be omitted.

23. Order 79 shall be amended as follows:—

(1) Rules 1 to 7 shall be omitted.

(2) In rule 9(8)(*a*) and (10)(*a*), for the words "clerk of the court to which the defendant stands committed" there shall be substituted the words "appropriate officer of the Crown Court".

(3) In rule 9(11) for the words "a court of quarter sessions" there shall be substituted the words "the Crown Court".

24. In Order 102, rules 2(4), 3(3), 4(2) and 5(2), for the words "the district registry of Liverpool or the district registry of Manchester" there shall be substituted the words "or the district registry of Leeds, Liverpool, Manchester, Newcastle upon Tyne or Preston".

25. In relation to a writ in the Chancery Division which is issued out of the district registry of Liverpool, Manchester or Preston, Forms 2, 7 and 15 shall have effect as if for the references to the district of that registry there were substituted references to the Lancashire area.

26. In Form No. 28 (Writ of subpoena) for the words from "[at the Royal Courts of Justice" to "for the county of]" there shall be substituted the words "at the sittings of the Division of Our High Court of Justice [at the Royal Courts of Justice, Strand, London] *or* [at *name of town and address of Court outside the Royal Courts of Justice*]."

27. In Form No. 46 (Judgment after trial before judge with jury) the words "of the county of " shall be omitted.

28. Form 60 (Writ of fieri facias on order of quarter sessions removed into Queen's Bench Division) and Form 61 (Writ of fieri facias on judgment of Mayor's and City of London Court) shall be omitted.

29. In Form No. 97 (Summons to admit to bail) for the words "court of quarter sessions for the county or borough of" there shall be substituted the words "Crown Court at".

30. Form No. 98 (Order of judge in chambers to admit prisoner to bail) shall be amended as follows:—

(1) For the words "to the next quarter sessions for the county of" there shall be substituted the words "to the Crown Court at".

(2) For the words "appeal to quarter sessions" there shall be substituted the words "appeal to the Crown Court".

(3) For the words "at the next quarter sessions for the county of" there shall be substituted the words "before the Crown Court at".

(4) For the words "clerk of the peace" there shall be substituted the word "Court".

(5) For the words "court of quarter sessions for the county of" there shall be substituted the words "Crown Court at".

31. In Form No. 98A (Order varying arrangements for bail) for the words "next quarter sessions for the county of" there shall be substituted the words "Crown Court at", and for the words "appeal to quarter sessions" there shall be substituted the words "appeal to the Crown Court".

32. Form No. 101 (Witness summons) shall be amended as follows:—

(1) In the heading for the words "Central Criminal Court or Assizes (Crown Court)" there shall be substituted the words "Crown Court".

(2) For the words from "Central Criminal Court" to "county of]" there shall be substituted the words "Crown Court at [*name of town and address of court*] [*or* the Central Criminal Court in the Old Bailey, Newgate Street, London E.C.4.]".

33. Form No. 102 (Witness summons—Court of quarter sessions) shall be omitted.

34. Form No. 103 (Witness summons—Court of quarter sessions: appeal) shall be amended as follows:—

(1) In the heading for the words "Court of quarter sessions" there shall be substituted the words "Crown Court".

(2) For the words "before the court of quarter sessions for the [county] [borough] of at [*address of court*]" there shall be substituted the words "before the Crown Court at [*name of town and address of court*]".

35. Any proceedings begun in the Lancaster Palatine Court or the Durham Palatine Court which are continued in the High Court by virtue of paragraph 2 of Schedule 5 to the Courts Act 1971 shall be treated—

(*a*) in the case of a cause or matter which was proceeding in the Liverpool, Manchester or Preston registry of the Lancaster Palatine Court, as proceeding in the corresponding district registry of the High Court;

(*b*) in the case of a cause or matter which was proceeding in the Durham Palatine Court, as proceeding in the district registry of Newcastle upon Tyne;

(*c*) in the case of a cause or matter which, if it had been begun in the High Court on or after 1st October 1971, would have been assigned to the Family Division, as assigned to that Division;

(*d*) in any case not mentioned in paragraph (*c*), as assigned to the Chancery Division and to the group of judges to which the proceedings would have been assigned if they had been begun in the High Court.

Part III

Miscellaneous Amendments

36. In Order 11, rule 1(1), the following sub-paragraph shall be inserted after sub-paragraph (*m*):—

"(*n*) if the action begun by the writ is brought to enforce a claim in respect of a liability incurred under the Merchant Shipping (Oil Pollution) Act 1971(**a**)."

37. In Order 15, the following rule shall be added after rule 17:—

"*Stay of proceedings under Industrial Relations Act* 1971

18. In deciding whether to stay proceedings in tort under section 131 of the Industrial Relations Act 1971(**b**), the Court shall take into account all relevant circumstances, including the question whether, notwithstanding that the proceedings are framed in tort, the complaint is in substance one of an unfair industrial practice within the meaning of that Act, or whether the matters in issue in the proceedings are for any other reason more suitable to be determined by the National Industrial Relations Court or an industrial tribunal than by the appropriate mode of trial in the High Court (including, where applicable, trial with a jury)."

38. Order 29, rule 7A, shall be amended as follows:—

(1) For paragraph (1) there shall be substituted the following paragraph:—

"(1) An application for an order under section 21(1) of the Administration of Justice Act 1969(**c**) in respect of property which may become

(**a**) 1971 c. 59. (**b**) 1971 c. 72. (**c**) 1969 c. 58.

the subject-matter of subsequent proceedings in the High Court or as to which any question may arise in any such proceedings shall be made by originating summons and the person against whom the order is sought shall be made defendant to the summons."

(2) Paragraphs (2) and (8) shall be omitted.

(3) For paragraph (4) there shall be substituted the following paragraph:—

"(3) A summons under paragraph (1) or (2) shall be supported by affidavit which must specify or describe the property in respect of which the order is sought and show, if practicable by reference to any pleading served or intended to be served in the proceedings or subsequent proceedings, that it is property which is or may become the subject-matter of the proceedings or as to which any question arises or may arise in the proceedings."

(4) Paragraphs (3), (5), (6) and (7) shall stand as paragraphs (2), (4), (5) and (6) respectively and in paragraph (6) as so re-numbered for the references to paragraphs (2) and (3) there shall be substituted references to paragraphs (1) and (2) respectively.

39. Order 39, rule 19, shall be amended as follows:—

(1) The following table shall be substituted for the table set out in paragraph (1):—

"TABLE OF EXAMINERS' FEES

	£
1. Upon giving an appointment to take an examination ...	10.00
2. For each hour or part thereof (after the first hour) occupied in an examination within 3 miles from the principal entrance of the Royal Courts of Justice	2.50
3. For each day of 6 hours or part of a day occupied in an examination beyond 3 miles from the principal entrance of the Royal Courts of Justice	17.00"

(2) In paragraph (3) for the words "3 guineas" and "5 guineas" there shall be substituted the words "£7" and "£10" respectively.

40. In Order 90, rule 14(7), for the words "divorce registry" there shall be substituted the words "principal registry".

41. In Order 90, rule 16(1) and (4), for the word "two", wherever it appears, there shall be substituted the word "three".

42. After Order 111 there shall be inserted the following Order:—

"ORDER 112

APPLICATIONS FOR USE OF BLOOD TESTS IN DETERMINING PATERNITY

Interpretation

1. In this Order—

"the Act" means Part III of the Family Law Reform Act 1969(**a**);

"blood samples" and "blood tests" have the meanings assigned to them by section 25 of the Act;

(**a**) 1969 c. 46.

"direction" means a direction for the use of blood tests under section 20(1) of the Act;

"the proper officer" means the officer of the court who draws up a direction.

Application for direction

2.—(1) Except with the leave of the Court, an application in any proceedings for a direction shall be made on notice to every party to the proceedings (other than the applicant) and to any other person from whom the direction involves the taking of blood samples.

(2) If the application is made otherwise than at the hearing of the proceedings it shall be made by summons.

(3) Any notice or summons required by this rule to be served on a person who is not a party to the proceedings shall be served on him personally.

Applications involving persons under disability

3. Where an application is made for a direction in respect of a person (in this rule referred to as a person under disability) who is either—

(*a*) under 16, or

(*b*) suffering from a mental disorder within the meaning of the Mental Health Act 1959**(a)** and incapable of understanding the nature and purpose of blood tests,

the notice of application or summons shall state the name and address of the person having the care and control of the person under disability and shall be served on him instead of on the person under disability.

Joinder of person to be tested

4. Where an application is made for a direction involving the taking of blood samples from a person who is not a party to the proceedings in which the application is made, the Court may at any time direct that person to be made a party to the proceedings.

Service of direction and adjournment of proceedings

5. Where the Court gives a direction in any proceedings, the proper officer shall send a copy to every party to the proceedings and to every other person from whom the direction involves the taking of blood samples and, unless otherwise ordered, further consideration of the proceedings shall stand adjourned until the court receives a report pursuant to the direction.

Service of copy of report

6. On receipt by the court of a report made pursuant to a direction, the proper officer shall send a copy to every party to the proceedings and to every other person from whom the direction involved the taking of blood samples."

(a) 1959 c. 72.

43. In Form 37 in Appendix A for the words "Principal Probate Registry" there shall be substituted the words "Principal Registry of the Family Division".

Dated 29th November 1971.

Hailsham of St. Marylebone, C.
Widgery, C. J.
Denning, M. R.
George Baker, P.
Cyril Salmon, L. J.
John Pennycuick, V-C.
Nigel Bridge, J.
James Fox-Andrews.
Donald K. Rattee.
H. Montgomery-Campbell.

EXPLANATORY NOTE

(*This Note is not part of the Rules.*)

The amendments in Part II of these Rules are consequential on the coming into operation of the Courts Act 1971. A cause or matter may be fixed for trial either at the Royal Courts of Justice or at one of the places at which sittings of the High Court are authorised to be held for the hearing of the particular proceedings or proceedings of the class to which they belong (rule 11(1)). The district registrar of the place of trial is given power to call for information about the readiness of an action for trial and, where desirable, to make interlocutory orders and to change the venue (rule 12(4)). For the purpose of Chancery proceedings the districts of the Liverpool, Manchester and Preston district registries are to comprise the whole of the Lancashire area (rules 2, 4, 7 and 25), and the district registries of Leeds, Newcastle upon Tyne and Preston are given in most respects the same jurisdiction in Chancery proceedings as the district registries of Liverpool and Manchester (rules 3(1), 5, 6, 10(3), 17(2), 18 and 24). Special provision is made for the hearing of Chancery proceedings at those places (rules 9 and 11(2)). Account is taken of the transfer of quarter sessions jurisdiction to the Crown Court (rules 15, 16, 23(2) and (3), 28 to 31, 33 and 34) and the new arrangements for summoning jurors (rules 12(6), 22 and 27).

In Part III the Court is empowered to grant leave to serve the writ out of the jurisdiction in an action under the Merchant Shipping (Oil Pollution) Act 1971 (rule 36). The circumstances to be taken into account by the Court in deciding whether to stay proceedings in tort under the Industrial Relations Act 1971 are defined (rule 37). The rule relating to the inspection etc. of property before the commencement of proceedings is extended to all kinds of actions instead of being confined to actions for personal injuries (rule 38). The fees for examiners of the Court are increased (rule 39). A new Order 112 is introduced to regulate the procedure on an application to the High Court for the use of blood tests to determine paternity under Part III of the Family Law Reform Act 1969 (rule 42).

A number of minor and consequential amendments are also made.

1971 No. 1956

FRIENDLY SOCIETIES

The Friendly Societies (Forms and Fees) Regulations 1971

Made - - - -	2*nd December* 1971
Laid before Parliament	15*th December* 1971
Coming into Operation	31*st December* 1971

The Treasury pursuant to the powers conferred upon them by sections 96(1 and 99(1) of the Friendly Societies Act 1896**(a)** (as amended by paragraphs 2 and 31(1) of Schedule 2 to the Friendly Societies Act 1971**(b)**) and by regulation of the Friendly Societies (Fees) Order 1971**(c)** and to all other powers enablin them in that behalf hereby make the following Regulations:—

Citation, commencement and interpretation.

1.—(1) These Regulations may be cited as the Friendly Societies (Forms and Fees) Regulations 1971 and shall come into operation on 31st December 1971.

(2) The Interpretation Act 1889**(d)** shall apply to the interpretation of these Regulations as it applies to the interpretation of an Act of Parliament.

Applications to register special resolutions.

2. Every application to register a special resolution passed by a society on or after 31st December 1971 shall be in such of the forms contained in Schedule 1 hereto as are appropriate to the special resolution which has been passed.

3. Every application in Form BA to register a special resolution for the amalgamation of societies shall be made by each of the societies in duplicate and shall be sent to the Central Office accompanied by statutory declarations from officers of each society in Form BB. No acknowledgment of registration shall be given to any amalgamating society until special resolutions in like terms have been submitted for registration by the other society or societies.

4. Every application in Form BC to register a special resolution for the transfer of the engagements of a society to another society shall be made in duplicate and shall be sent to the Central Office accompanied by a statutory declaration in Form BB and, where appropriate, by a statutory declaration in Form BD.

5. Every application in Form BE to register a special resolution undertaking to fulfil the engagements of another society shall be made in duplicate and shall be sent to the Central Office accompanied by a statutory declaration in Form BB.

6. Every application in Form BF to register a special resolution for converting a society into a company shall be made in triplicate and shall be sent to the Central Office accompanied by a statutory declaration in Form BB.

(a) 1896 c. 25.
(b) 1971 c. 66.
(c) S.I. 1971/1900 (1971 III, p. 5155)
(d) 1889 c. 63.

7. Every application to register a special resolution for the transfer of the engagements of a society to a company shall be made in duplicate in Form BC, with necessary modifications to suit the facts, and shall be sent to the Central Office accompanied by a statutory declaration in Form BB and by a statutory declaration of an officer of the company in Form AC contained in the Regulations**(a)**, dated 1st January 1897, made by the Treasury under the Friendly Societies Act 1896 and the Collecting Societies and Industrial Assurance Companies Act 1896**(b)** (hereinafter referred to as "the Friendly Societies Regulations 1897"), as amended**(c)**.

Miscellaneous forms.

8. The forms contained in Schedule 2 hereto shall be used for the appropriate matters to which the forms relate.

Fees.

9. The fees set out in Schedule 3 hereto shall be payable in advance to the Central Office or, in Scotland, to the Assistant Registrar for Scotland in respect of the matters specified in that Schedule.

Amendments, revocations and savings.

10. For Forms AO and AOb contained in the Schedule to the Friendly Societies Regulations 1897 there shall be substituted the forms contained in Schedule 4 hereto.

11. The Regulations mentioned in Schedule 5 hereto are hereby revoked to the extent specified in the third column of that Schedule.

12. Nothing in these Regulations shall affect the regulations repealed thereby in their operation in relation to a special resolution passed and confirmed in accordance with section 74 of the Friendly Societies Act 1896 before 31st December 1971.

Tim Fortescue,
Keith Speed,
Two of the Lords Commissioners of
Her Majesty's Treasury.

2nd December, 1971.

(a) S.R. & O. 1897/6 (Rev. VIII, p. 815: 1897, p. 181).
(b) 1896 c. 26.
(c) The relevant amending instruments are S.R. & O. 1897/428, (Rev. VIII, p. 815: 1897, p. 231); S.I. 1971/461 (1971 I, p. 1376).

Regulation 2

SCHEDULE 1

FORM BA

FRIENDLY SOCIETIES ACT 1896

Application for registration of Special Resolution for Amalgamation of Societies pursuant to section 75 of the above mentioned Act.
(To be sent in duplicate by each society, accompanied by Form BB)

Name of Society...

Register No..................

Name of Society...

Register No..................

(and so on, if more than two societies are amalgamating).

To the Central Office

1. Application for registration of a special resolution for the amalgamation of the above-named societies is made by [Name of Society]

2. The following is a copy of a resolution passed

(*a*) at a general meeting of the applicant society, held on.......................19 , of which notice, specifying the intention to propose that resolution, was duly given in accordance with the society's rules, and

(*b*) by not less than three-quarters of those members of the society for the time being entitled under the society's rules to vote who voted either in person or by proxy at the meeting:—

[Where the meeting was of delegates, substitute for paragraph (*b*) "by not less than three-quarters of the delegates who voted at the meeting:—"]

Omit where exemption from this requirement has been obtained.

In accordance with section 1(4)(*a*) of the Friendly Societies Act 1971 a notice in terms approved by the Chief Registrar has been sent to each member of the applicant society.

.... Signature of Chairman of Applicant Society

.... Signature of Secretary of Applicant Society

Date............................

Form BB

Friendly Societies Act 1971

Statutory Declaration to accompany Application for Registration of a Special Resolution pursuant to the Friendly Societies (Forms and Fees) Regulations 1971.

Name of Society..

Register No......................

I...of..

....

an officer of the above-named society, do solemnly and sincerely declare that in passing the special resolution, application for registration of which is appended to this declaration marked..................the provisions of section 4(1) of the Friendly Societies Act 1971 have been duly complied with.

And I make this solemn declaration conscientiously believing the same to be true, and by virtue of the provisions of the Statutory Declarations Act 1835.

Signature of Declarant......................................

Declared at...........................
....
the............day of.................
one thousand nine hundred and
....
before me,

....
A Commissioner for Oaths*
*or Notary Public or Justice of the Peace.

FORM BC

FRIENDLY SOCIETIES ACT 1896

Application for Registration of a Special Resolution for Transfer of Engagements of one society to another society pursuant to section 75 of the above-mentioned Act. (To be sent in duplicate accompanied by Form BB and, where appropriate, Form BD)

Name of transferor society...
Register No..................
Name of transferee society...
Register No..................

To the Central Office

1. Application for registration of a special resolution for transfer of engagements is made by [Name of transferor society].

2. The following is a copy of a resolution passed

(*a*) at a general meeting of the society, held on.......................................19 , of which notice, specifying the intention to propose that resolution, was duly given in accordance with the society's rules, and

(*b*) by not less than three-quarters of those members of the society for the time being entitled under the society's rules to vote who voted either in person or by proxy at the meeting:—

[Where the meeting was of delegates, substitute for paragraph (*b*) "by not less than three-quarters of the delegates who voted at the meeting:—"]

Omit where exemption from this requirement has been obtained.	In accordance with section 1(4)(*a*) of the Friendly Societies Act 1971 a notice in terms approved by the Chief Registrar has been sent to each member of the applicant society.

3. [Name of transferee society] has [state in what manner]................................ undertaken to fulfil the said engagements as testified by the signature of the secretary of the society hereto and by his statutory declaration submitted herewith.

Registered Office of Transferor Society	.... Signature of Chairman of Transferor Society
....	
....	.... Signature of Secretary of Transferor Society
....	
....	
....	.... Signature of Secretary of Transferee Society
Date.............................	

Form BD

Friendly Societies Act 1896

Statutory Declaration by Officer of Society accepting Transfer of Engagements pursuant to regulation 4 of the Friendly Societies (Forms and Fees) Regulations 1971.

Name of Society...
Register No..................

I...of..
....an officer of the above-named society, do solemnly and sincerely declare that the above-named society has, in the manner authorised by its rules, viz. by resolution of...
passed..19 , undertaken to fulfil the engagements of [name of transferor society].

And I make this solemn declaration conscientiously believing the same to be true, and by virtue of the provisions of the Statutory Declarations Act 1835.

Signature of Declarant.............................

Declared at..................................
....
the...
one thousand nine hundred and.........
.... before me,
....
A Commissioner for Oaths*
*or Notary Public or Justice of the Peace

Form BE

Friendly Societies Act 1896

Application for Registration of a Special Resolution undertaking to fulfil the engagements of another society pursuant to section 75 of the above-mentioned Act. (To be sent in duplicate, accompanied by Form BB)

Name of Society...
Register No..................

To the Central Office

1. Application is made by the above-named society for registration of a special resolution undertaking to fulfil the engagements of [name of transferor society].

2. The following is a copy of a resolution passed

(*a*) at a general meeting held on............................19 of which notice, specifying the intention to propose that resolution, was duly given in accordance with the society's rules, and

(*b*) by not less than three-quarters of those members of the society for the time being entitled to vote who voted either in person or by proxy at the meeting:—

[Where the meeting was of delegates, substitute for paragraph (*b*) "by not less than three-quarters of the delegates who voted at the meeting:—"]

....
Signature of Chairman of Society

Date.............................

....
Signature of Secretary of Society

FORM BF

FRIENDLY SOCIETIES ACT 1896

Application for Registration of Special Resolution for Conversion into a Company.
(To be sent in triplicate, accompanied by Form BB)

Name of Society..
Register No..................

To the Central Office

1. Application for registration of a special resolution for conversion of the above-named society into a company is made by the said society.

2. The following is a copy of a resolution passed

(*a*) at a general meeting held on............................19 , of which notice, specifying the intention to propose that resolution, was duly given in accordance with the society's rules, and

(*b*) by not less than three-quarters of those members of the society for the time being entitled to vote who voted either in person or by proxy at the meeting:—

[Where the meeting was of delegates, substitute for paragraph (*b*) "by not less than three-quarters of the delegates who voted at the meeting:—"].

....
Signature of Chairman of Society

....
Signature of Secretary of Society

Date.............................

Regulation 8

SCHEDULE 2

FORM BG

FRIENDLY SOCIETIES ACT 1896

Acknowledgment of registration of copy of Special Resolution

Name of Society..

Register No..................

The copy of the special resolution appended hereto is this day registered under the Friendly Societies Act 1896.

(Seal of Central Office)

Date.............................

FORM BH

FRIENDLY SOCIETIES ACT 1896

Approval of Change of Name pursuant to section 69 of the above-mentioned Act

Register No..................

The change of the name of..
to...effected by the amendment of rules registered this day is hereby approved.

Signature of Chief Registrar
(or Assistant Registrar of Friendly
Societies for Scotland)

Date..............................

FORM BI

FRIENDLY SOCIETIES ACT 1896

Acknowledgment of Registration of Change in Situation of Registered Office of Society or Branch

Register No..................

The change in the situation of the registered office of [Name of Society or Branch]
to ....
is this day registered as an amendment of rules under the Friendly Societies Act 1896.

(Seal of Central Office or signature of
Assistant Registrar for Scotland)

Date..............................

Form BJ

Friendly Societies Act 1896

Notice of proceedings to set aside Dissolution pursuant to section 83(1) of the above mentioned Act.

Name of Society or Branch..

Register No..................

To the Central Office [or, where the society or branch is registered in Scotland, the Assistant Registrar for Scotland]

Whereas on.............................19 ,

Delete as necessary

the instrument of dissolution of the above-named society/branch was registered

the Chief Registrar made an award that the above-named society/branch be dissolved

I hereby give you notice that on.............................19 , I commenced proceedings in the..County Court [or Sheriff Court, as the case may be] to set aside the said dissolution.

Signature..
Address..
....

Date.............................

Form BK

Friendly Societies Act 1896

Notice of Order to set aside Dissolution pursuant to section 83(2) of the above mentioned Act

Name of Society or Branch..

Register No..................

To the Central Office [or, where the society or branch is registered in Scotland, the Assistant Registrar for Scotland]

The above-named society/branch hereby gives you notice that by an order of the ....County Court [or Sheriff Court, as the case may be] dated.............................19 , a copy whereof is hereto annexed, the dissolution of the said society/branch was set aside.

Signed on behalf of the society/branch
..........................Secretary

Date.............................

SCHEDULE 3

Regulation 9

Fees payable for registration and sundry other matters

	£
1. For the acknowledgment of registry of a society	15
2. For the acknowledgment of registry of a branch	5
3. For registration of an annual return (except where the society or branch concerned has by written notice sent to the Central Office or the Assistant Registrar for Scotland irrevocably elected to pay the fees specified in paragraph 4 of this Schedule)—	
where it relates to a society	2.50
where it relates to a branch	1
4. The fees specified in this paragraph shall be payable where the society or branch concerned has by notice elected as aforesaid.	
(*a*) For the acknowledgment of registry of an alteration of rules—	
if the alteration substitutes an entire set of rules for the existing set of rules	
where made by a society	12
where made by a branch	4
if the alteration does not substitute an entire set of rules for the existing set of rules (and including approval of name in the case of an alteration effecting a change of name of a society or branch)	
where made by a society	6
where made by a branch	2
(*b*) For the registry of a notice of change in the situation of the registered office—	
of a society	2
of a branch	1
(*c*) For a receipt issued in respect of a notice of appointment of a trustee or trustees—	
of a society	2
of a branch	1
5. For the registry of a special resolution—	
(1) where the special resolution relates to an amalgamation or a transfer of engagements and the society passing it has—	
(*a*) 100 members or less	4
(*b*) more than 100 members but not more than 500	6
(*c*) more than 500 members but not more than 1,000	8
(*d*) more than 1,000 members	10
(2) where the special resolution relates to a conversion...	10
6. For the appointment of an inspector or calling of a special meeting by a Registrar under section 76 of the Friendly Societies Act 1896 ...	10

Regulation 9

7. For registry of an instrument of dissolution or alteration therein where a society or branch has— £

(*a*) 100 members or less 4

(*b*) more than 100 members but not more than 500 6

(*c*) more than 500 members but not more than 1,000 8

(*d*) more than 1,000 members 10

8. For the determination of a Registrar on a dispute or for the award of a Registrar for dissolution where the matter is settled without a hearing or upon one hearing without an adjournment 3

9. Where on a dispute or on an application for an award of dissolution more than one hearing is required or where the hearing is adjourned—

the same fee as where the matter is settled upon one hearing without adjournment and in addition for every hearing after the first and for every adjournment 3

10. For an award or direction of a Registrar for the appropriation or division of the assets of a society or branch, an additional fee as follows:—

where the value of the assets is less than £300, 5% of that value.
where the value of the assets is £300 or more, £15 with an additional £1 for every £100 or part thereof in excess of £300.

11. Where application is made for an investigation into the affairs of a society or branch with a view to an award of dissolution thereof, the Chief Registrar may, if he thinks fit, at any time before making his award, require the payment of such further fee as he may deem reasonable not exceeding—

where the number of members does not exceed 150 30

where the number of members exceeds 150 but does not exceed 250... 45

where the number of members exceeds 250 but does not exceed 350... 60

where the number of members exceeds 350 but does not exceed 500... 75

where the number of members exceeds 500 but does not exceed 700... 120

where the number of members exceeds 700 but does not exceed 1,000... 165

where the number of members exceeds 1,000 but does not exceed 2,500, £165 for the first 1,000 members, and £25 for every 500 members, or part thereof, exceeding 1,000 members.

where the number of members exceeds 2,500 a special fee may be determined by the Chief Registrar.

12. For every inspection on the same day of documents in the custody of the Registrar relating to one and the same society or branch 0.10

13. For every document (except as otherwise provided) required to be signed by a Registrar, or to bear the seal of the Central Office, not chargeable with any other fee to the Registrar 1
provided that such fee shall not be paid by a society or branch which has not by notice elected as in paragraph 4 of this Schedule.

14. For a copy or extract of any document in the custody of the Registrar, not exceeding 216 words, 50p, and if exceeding that number, 10p per folio of 72 words, in addition to the fee for the signature of a Registrar, or for the seal of the Central Office; provided that where a photocopy is supplied the fee charged therefor may be of an amount less than the fee payable on the basis of word content.

Regulation 9

15. For any document certified as a true copy of a document in the custody of the Registrar, where the copy so certified is not made by the Registrar, 25p for the examination of such copy, and if the copy exceeds 216 words, for every additional folio of 72 words, 5p (in addition to the fee for the signature of a Registrar, or the seal of the Central Office).

The Chief Registrar may, at his discretion, reduce or waive the fee for an award on a dispute.

No fees shall be payable in respect of the examination or authentication of copies of rules or alterations of rules to be used for recording under section 14(1) of the Friendly Societies Act 1896.

SCHEDULE 4

Regulation 10

Form AO

Friendly Societies Act 1896

Instrument of Dissolution

(To be signed in duplicate and accompanied by Form AP)

Name of Society..

Register No..................

Instrument of dissolution of the above-named society made the.................... day of...................................19 , pursuant to section 79 of the Friendly Societies Act 1896.

It is declared and agreed as follows:—

1. This instrument is signed by three fourths of the members.

2. The liabilities and assets of the society are the following:—

3. The number of members is

4. The society has no creditors [or, if there are creditors, state the amount due to them and the provision to be made for their payment].

5. The funds and property of the society shall be appropriated and divided in the following manner [or, in such manner as the Chief Registrar may award].

6. It is desired that this instrument be advertised in the [state some newspaper in general circulation in the neighbourhood of the registered office of the society]. as well as the London [Edinburgh] Gazette, and the cost of such advertisements is herewith transmitted.

[Here insert any other provisions the society desires to make as to the Dissolution].

Signatures of members.

SCHEDULE

List of members who have not signed the foregoing instrument—

Form AOb

Friendly Societies Act 1896

Instrument of Dissolution of Branch

(To be signed in duplicate and accompanied by Form AP)

Name of Society..

Register No..................
Name and number (if any) of branch

Instrument of dissolution of the above-named branch made the...................... day of..................................19 , pursuant to section 79 of the Friendly Societies Act 1896.

It is declared and agreed as follows:—

1. This instrument is signed by three fourths of the members.

2. The liabilities and assets of the branch are the following:—

3. The number of members is

4. The branch has no creditors [or, if there are creditors, state the amount due to them and the provision to be made for their payment].

5. The funds and property of the branch shall be appropriated and divided in the following manner [or, in such manner as the Chief Registrar may award].

6. It is desired that this instrument be advertised in the [state some newspaper in general circulation in the neighbourhood of the registered office of the branch] as well as the London [Edinburgh] Gazette, and the cost of such advertisements is herewith transmitted.

[Here insert any other provisions the branch desires to make as to the Dissolution].

Signatures of members.

SCHEDULE

List of members who have not signed the foregoing instrument—

The consent of the central body of the society has been given to the dissolution.

Signature of the secretary of the society.

Date..........................

SCHEDULE 5

Regulation 11

REVOCATIONS

Regulations revoked	References	Extent of revocation
The Friendly Societies Regulations 1897.	S.R. & O. 1897/6 (Rev. VIII, p. 815; 1897, p. 181).	Regulation 18
		Regulations 21 to 24
		Regulations 33 to 43
		In Regulation 44, the words "amalgamation with".
		Regulation 46
		Regulation 49
		Regulation 54
		Regulation 59
		Regulation 68
		Regulation 70
		In Regulation 75, the words "special resolutions and transfers of engagements from one society to another".
		In the Schedule, Forms J, K, L, T, U, V, W, X, Y, Z, AA, AX, AY, CI, UI and XI.
The Friendly Societies (Amendment) Regulations 1971.	S.I. 1971/461 (1971 I, p. 1376).	In Regulation 3, para (*d*) Schedule 1.

EXPLANATORY NOTE

(*This Note is not part of the Regulations.*)

These Regulations prescribe the forms to be used under the Friendly Societies Act 1971 and the fees to be paid for matters to be transacted, and for the inspection of documents, under the Friendly Societies Acts 1896 to 1971. The fees supersede those prescribed by the Friendly Societies (Amendment) Regulations 1971, Sch. 1.

1971 No. 1961

CONSUMER PROTECTION

The Electric Blankets (Safety) Regulations 1971

Made - - -	1*st December* 1971
Laid before Parliament	10*th December* 1971
Coming into Operation—	
All but Regulation 5	1*st January* 1972
Regulation 5	1*st September* 1972

In pursuance of sections 1 and 2(4) and (6) of the Consumer Protection Act 1961(**a**) and of the Schedule to that Act as amended by the London Government Act 1963(**b**), and after consulting with such persons and bodies of persons as appear to me to be requisite, I hereby make the following Regulations :—

1. These Regulations may be cited as the Electric Blankets (Safety) Regulations 1971 and (with the exception of Regulation 5 which shall come into operation on 1st September 1972) shall come into operation on 1st January 1972.

2.—(1) In these Regulations, except where the context otherwise requires, the expression—

"the Act" means the Consumer Protection Act 1961 as amended by the London Government Act 1963, the Hire-Purchase Act 1965(**c**), the Hire-Purchase (Scotland) Act 1965(**d**) and the Consumer Protection Act 1971(**e**) ;

"electric blanket" means an electrical appliance designed or suitable for household use which has as its principal part an electrically heated blanket (which exceeds 0·15 square metres in area and does not exceed 100 mm in thickness) and is intended to be connected to an electricity supply having a voltage not exceeding 250 volts ;

"the Standard of 1971" means the British Standard Specification for the Testing and Approval of Household Electrical Appliances Section A4 Electrically-Heated Blankets BS 3456 : Section A4 : 1971, as published on 4th February 1971, with the exception of Appendix D to that specification (which contains recommendations relating to radio interference).

(2) Any reference in these Regulations to any requirement or test specified in the Standard of 1971 includes a reference to any requirement or test incorporated in that specification by reference to one or more other British Standard specifications.

(**a**) 1961 c. 40.
(**b**) 1963 c. 33.
(**c**) 1965 c. 66.
(**d**) 1965 c. 67.
(**e**) 1971 c. 15.

(3) For the purposes of these Regulations, any reference to a British Standard specification (other than the Standard of 1971) is to be construed as a reference to that specification as amended before the said 4th February 1971.

(4) The Interpretation Act 1889(a) applies for the interpretation of these Regulations as it applies for the interpretation of an Act of Parliament.

3.—(1) This Regulation applies to any electric blanket (whether it is of a kind mentioned in clause 1 of the Standard of 1971 or not) other than one which bears a certification mark of the British Electrotechnical Approvals Board for Household Equipment (formerly known as the British Electrical Approvals Board for Domestic Appliances), indicating that the blanket conforms to BS 3456.

(2) An electric blanket to which this Regulation applies shall be such as to comply with the requirements of the Standard of 1971 and be capable of satisfying any of the tests specified in that specification:

Provided that clauses 3, 5 and 7 of that specification (which relate to performance generally, voltage rating and marks and explanatory literature) shall not have effect for the purposes of this Regulation.

(3) In the case of an electric blanket to which this Regulation applies and of which the principal part is intended to be used as an under-blanket and to be kept switched on notwithstanding that a person is occupying the bed upon which it is used, the electric blanket shall have an isolating transformer and be so designed that no electricity other than electricity having an alternating voltage not exceeding 30 volts A.C. will be applied to that part.

4. An electric blanket shall on some part thereof be legibly and durably marked so as to indicate the matters specified in the Schedule to these Regulations.

5. Where an electric blanket is individually packed in a box or other container, that box or container shall be conspicuously marked so as to indicate in words whether the blanket is for use as an over-blanket or as an under-blanket and, if as an under-blanket, whether the blanket is or is not suitable to be kept switched on when a person is occupying the bed upon which it is used.

6. As respects the requirements of these Regulations, subsections (1) and (2) of section 2 of the Act (which prohibit sales and possession for sale of goods and component parts not complying with regulations) shall apply in relation to goods and component parts manufactured before the imposition of these requirements notwithstanding anything in subsection (4) of that section (which exempts such goods and parts unless regulations otherwise provide).

7. Section 2(1), (2) and (3) (other than paragraphs (*d*) and (*e*) of subsection (3)) of the Act (which relate to sale and possession for sale of goods and component parts not complying with regulations) shall, except as provided by the proviso to section 2(6), apply in relation to goods to which these Regulations apply as if references to selling or to a sale included references to letting under a hire-purchase agreement or on hire, and the reference to a sale under a credit-sale agreement were a reference to a letting under a hire-purchase agreement.

(a) 1889 c. 63.

8.—(1) The Schedule to the Act shall have effect in relation to goods to which these Regulations apply.

(2) Any test of goods to which these Regulations apply, being a test such as is referred to in paragraph 2 of the Schedule to the Act (which empowers a local authority to purchase goods for the purpose of a test) shall be carried out, at the expense of the local authority, by such person or body as may be authorised by the Secretary of State under this Regulation to carry out such tests.

(3) In relation to goods to which these Regulations apply, "local authority" in the Schedule to the Act means the council of a county borough, the council of a London borough or the Common Council of the City of London ; as respects any non-county borough or urban district which has according to the last published census for the time being a population of 60,000 or upwards, the council of the borough or urban district ; as respects any other area in England and Wales, the council of the county ; and, in Scotland, the council of any county or any town.

R. Maudling,
One of Her Majesty's Principal
Secretaries of State.

Home Office,
Whitehall.
1st December 1971.

Regulation 4

SCHEDULE

MARKINGS REQUIRED ON ELECTRIC BLANKETS

The rated voltage or voltage range in volts.

The rated input in watts.

A warning against using the blanket when folded, rucked or creased.

A warning against laundering, or against dry-cleaning, or against both laundering and dry-cleaning, as the case may require.

In the case of a blanket to be connected only to an A.C. electricity supply or only to a D.C. electricity supply, the type of current (A.C. or D.C.) to be used.

ADDITIONAL REQUIREMENTS

In the case of an over-blanket

A warning against using the blanket otherwise than as an over-blanket.

A warning against switching on the blanket when it is wet.

In the case of an under-blanket for heating a bed even when occupied

A warning against using the blanket otherwise than as an under-blanket.

In the case of an under-blanket for heating a bed only when unoccupied

A warning against using the blanket otherwise than as an under-blanket.

A warning against switching on the blanket when it is wet.

A warning either that the blanket must be disconnected from the electricity supply before the user gets into bed or that the blanket must be switched off before the user gets into bed.

EXPLANATORY NOTE

(*This Note is not part of the Regulations.*)

The Consumer Protection Act 1961 gives the Secretary of State power to make regulations imposing requirements, in respect of any class of goods, to prevent or reduce risk of death or personal injury. These Regulations impose such requirements in relation to electric blankets for household use, and accordingly under the Act, subject to certain exceptions, no person may sell or have in his possession for sale an appliance not complying with the Regulations. By virtue of Regulation 7, letting on hire or hire-purchase is similarly prohibited.

The Regulations apply to electric blankets as defined in Regulation 2. Regulation 3 requires electric blankets which do not bear the appropriate certification mark to comply with certain of the requirements of the relevant British Standard. Regulation 4 and the Schedule specify the information and warnings to be marked, in all cases, on the blanket itself, and Regulation 5 specifies the information to be given on the box in which the blanket is packed.

Copies of the British Standard Specifications referred to in the Regulations can be obtained from the British Standards Institution.

1971 No. 1963

PLANT HEALTH

The Dutch Elm Disease (Local Authorities) (Amendment) (No. 2) Order 1971

Made - - - -	3*rd December* 1971
Laid before Parliament	9*th December* 1971
Coming into Operation	14*th December* 1971

The Forestry Commissioners, by virtue and in exercise of the powers vested in them by sections 3(1), (2) and (4) and 5(1) of the Plant Health Act 1967**(a)**, and of every other power enabling them in that behalf, hereby make the following Order:—

1. This Order, which may be cited as the Dutch Elm Disease (Local Authorities) (Amendment) (No. 2) Order 1971, shall come into operation on 14th December 1971.

2. The Interpretation Act 1889**(b)** shall apply for the interpretation of this Order as it applies for the interpretation of an Act of Parliament.

3. The Schedule to the Dutch Elm Disease (Local Authorities) Order 1971**(c)**, as amended **(d)**, shall be further amended by the addition thereto of the local authorities specified in the Schedule hereto.

IN WITNESS whereof the Official Seal of the Forestry Commissioners is hereunto affixed on 3rd December 1971.

J. J. V. Summers,
Secretary to
the Forestry Commissioners.

(a) 1967 c. 8. **(b)** 1889 c 63.
(c) S.I. 1971/1708 (1971 III, p. 4994).
(d) The relevant amending instrument is S.I. 1971/1823 (1971 III, p. 4994).

THE SCHEDULE

Local Authorities

County Councils

Berkshire
Cambridgeshire and Isle of Ely
Glamorgan
Leicestershire
Norfolk

County Borough Councils

Cardiff
Leicester
Liverpool
Southend-on-Sea

Non-county Borough Councils

Gravesend
Lowestoft

London Borough Councils

Brent
Camden
Ealing
Tower Hamlets

EXPLANATORY NOTE

(This Note is not part of the Order.)

This Order amends the Dutch Elm Disease (Local Authorities) Order 1971 by adding further local authorities to the local authorities who are empowered by that Order as amended by the Dutch Elm Disease (Local Authorities) (Amendment) Order 1971 to take steps in connection with the disease of elm trees known as Dutch elm disease.

1971 No. 1964

SUGAR

The Sugar (Rates of Surcharge and Surcharge Repayments) (No. 9) Order 1971

Made	- - - - -	*3rd December* 1971
Laid before Parliament	-	*6th December* 1971
Coming into Operation	-	*7th December* 1971

The Minister of Agriculture, Fisheries and Food, in exercise of the powers conferred on him by sections 7(4), 8(6) and 33(4) of the Sugar Act 1956(**a**) having effect subject to the provisions of section 3 of, and Part II of Schedule 5 to, the Finance Act 1962(**b**), and section 58 of the Finance Act 1968(**c**) and of all other powers enabling him in that behalf, with the concurrence of the Treasury, on the advice of the Sugar Board, hereby makes the following order:—

1.—(1) This order may be cited as the Sugar (Rates of Surcharge and Surcharge Repayments) (No. 9) Order 1971; and shall come into operation on 7th December 1971.

(2) The Interpretation Act 1889(**d**) shall apply for the interpretation of this order as it applies for the interpretation of an Act of Parliament.

2. Notwithstanding the provisions of Article 2 of the Sugar (Rates of Surcharge and Surcharge Repayments) (No. 8) Order 1971(**e**), the rates of surcharge payable under and in accordance with the provisions of section 7 of the Sugar Act 1956, having effect as aforesaid, in respect of sugar and invert sugar imported or home produced or used in the manufacture of imported composite sugar products shall on and after 7th December 1971 be the appropriate rates specified in Schedule 1 to this order.

3. For the purpose of section 8(3)(*b*) of the Sugar Act 1956, having effect as aforesaid, the rates of surcharge repayments in respect of invert sugar produced in the United Kingdom from materials on which on or after 7th December 1971 sugar duty has been paid or, by virtue of paragraph 1 of Part II of Schedule 5 to the Finance Act 1962, is treated as having been paid shall, notwithstanding the provisions of Article 3 of the Sugar (Rates of Surcharge and Surcharge Repayments) (No. 8) Order 1971 be the appropriate rates specified in Schedule 2 to this order.

(**a**) 1956 c. 48.
(**b**) 1962 c. 44.
(**c**) 1968 c. 44.
(**d**) 1889 c. 63.
(**e**) S.I. 1971/1769 (1971 III, p. 4793).

In Witness whereof the Official Seal of the Minister of Agriculture, Fisheries and Food is hereunto affixed on 2nd December 1971.

(L.S.)

E. J. G. Smith,
Authorised by the Minister.

We concur.
3rd December 1971.

V. H. Goodhew,
P. L. Hawkins,
Two of the Lords Commissioners of Her Majesty's Treasury.

SCHEDULE 1

Part I

Surcharge Rates for Sugar

Polarisation	Rate of Surcharge per ton
	£
Exceeding—	
99°	12·000
98° but not exceeding 99°	11·316
97° " " " 98°	11·040
96° " " " 97°	10·752
95° " " " 96°	10·464
94° " " " 95°	10·176
93° " " " 94°	9·888
92° " " " 93°	9·600
91° " " " 92°	9·312
90° " " " 91°	9·024
89° " " " 90°	8·736
88° " " " 89°	8·448
87° " " " 88°	8·208
86° " " " 87°	7·968
85° " " " 86°	7·752
84° " " " 85°	7·536
83° " " " 84°	7·320
82° " " " 83°	7·104
81° " " " 82°	6·912
80° " " " 81°	6·720
79° " " " 80°	6·528
78° " " " 79°	6·336
77° " " " 78°	6·144
76° " " " 77°	5·952
Not exceeding 76°	5·760

Part II

Surcharge Rates for Invert Sugar

Sweetening matter content by weight	Rate of Surcharge per cwt.
	£
70 per cent. or more	0·38
Less than 70 per cent. and more than 50 per cent.	0·27
Not more than 50 per cent.	0·13

SCHEDULE 2

Surcharge Repayment Rates for Invert Sugar

Sweetening matter content by weight	Rate of Surcharge Repayment per cwt.
	£
More than 80 per cent.	0·45
More than 70 per cent. but not more than 80 per cent.	0·38
More than 60 per cent. but not more than 70 per cent.	0·27
More than 50 per cent. but not more than 60 per cent.	0·21
Not more than 50 per cent. and the invert sugar not being less in weight than 14 lb. per gallon	0·13

EXPLANATORY NOTE

(This Note is not part of the Order.)

This order prescribes—

(*a*) reductions equivalent to 10p per cwt. of refined sugar in the rates of surcharge payable on sugar and invert sugar which become chargeable with surcharge on or after 7th December 1971;

(*b*) correspondingly reduced rates of surcharge repayment in respect of invert sugar produced in the United Kingdom from materials on which surcharge has been paid.

STATUTORY INSTRUMENTS

1971 No. 1965

SUGAR

The Composite Sugar Products (Surcharge and Surcharge Repayments—Average Rates) (No. 9) Order 1971

Made	-	*3rd December* 1971
Laid before Parliament	-	*6th December* 1971
Coming into Operation	-	*7th December* 1971

Whereas the Minister of Agriculture, Fisheries and Food (hereinafter called " the Minister ") has on the recommendation of the Commissioners of Customs and Excise (hereinafter called " the Commissioners ") made an order(**a**) pursuant to the powers conferred upon him by sections 9(1) and 9(4) of the Sugar Act 1956(**b**), having effect subject to the provisions of section 3 of, and Part II of Schedule 5 to, the Finance Act 1962(**c**), to the provisions of section 52(2) of the Finance Act 1966(**d**), and to the provisions of section 58 of the Finance Act 1968(**e**), providing that in the case of certain descriptions of composite sugar products surcharge shall be calculated on the basis of an average quantity of sugar or invert sugar taken to have been used in the manufacture of the products, and that certain other descriptions of composite sugar products shall be treated as not containing any sugar or invert sugar, and that in the case of certain descriptions of goods in the manufacture of which sugar or invert sugar is used, surcharge repayments shall be calculated on the basis of an average quantity of sugar or invert sugar taken to have been so used:

Now, therefore, the Minister, on the recommendation of the Commissioners and in exercise of the powers conferred upon him by sections 9(1), 9(4) and 33(4) of the Sugar Act 1956, having effect as aforesaid, and of all other powers enabling him in that behalf, hereby makes the following order:—

1.—(1) This order may be cited as the Composite Sugar Products (Surcharge and Surcharge Repayments—Average Rates) (No. 9) Order 1971, and shall come into operation on 7th December 1971.

(2) The Interpretation Act 1889(**f**) shall apply for the interpretation of this order as it applies for the interpretation of an Act of Parliament.

2. Surcharge payable on or after 7th December 1971 under and in accordance with the Sugar Act 1956, having effect as aforesaid, in respect of sugar and invert sugar used in the manufacture of the descriptions of imported composite sugar products specified in the second column of Schedule 1 to this order shall, notwithstanding the provisions of the Sugar (Rates of Surcharge and Surcharge Repayments) (No 9) Order 1971(**g**) and the Composite Sugar Products (Surcharge and Surcharge Repayments—Average Rates) (No. 8) Order 1971(**a**), be calculated by reference to the weight of the products at the appropriate rates specified in relation thereto in the third column of the said Schedule.

(**a**) S.I. 1971/1770 (1971 III, p. 4796). (**b**) 1956 c. 48. (**c**) 1962 c. 44.
(**d**) 1966 c. 18. (**e**) 1968 c. 44. (**f**) 1889 c. 63.
(**g**) S.I. 1971/1964 (1971 III, p. 5304).

3. Imported composite sugar products other than those of a description specified in Schedules 1 and 2 to this order shall be treated as not containing any sugar or invert sugar for the purposes of surcharge payable on or after 7th December 1971.

4. Surcharge repayments payable on and after 7th December 1971 under and in accordance with the provisions of section 8 of the Sugar Act 1956, having effect as aforesaid, in respect of sugar and invert sugar used in the manufacture of the descriptions of goods specified in the first column of Schedule 3 to this order shall, notwithstanding the provisions of the Sugar (Rates of Surcharge and Surcharge Repayments) (No. 9) Order 1971(**a**) and the Composite Sugar Products (Surcharge and Surcharge Repayments—Average Rates) (No. 8) Order 1971(**b**), be calculated by reference to the quantity of the goods at the appropriate rates specified in relation thereto in the second column of the said Schedule.

In Witness whereof the Official Seal of the Minister of Agriculture, Fisheries and Food is hereunto affixed on 3rd December 1971.

(L.S.)

E. J. G. Smith,
Authorised by the Minister.

SCHEDULE 1

In this Schedule:—

" Tariff heading " means a heading or, where the context so requires, a subheading of the Customs Tariff 1959 (see paragraph (1) of Article 2 of the Import Duties (General) (No. 7) Order 1970(**c**)).

Tariff heading	Description of Imported Composite Sugar Products	Rate of Surcharge
		Per cwt. £
04.02 ..	Milk and cream, preserved, concentrated or sweetened, containing more than 10 per cent. by weight of added sugar	0·26

(**a**) S.I. 1971/1964 (1971 III, p. 5304). (**b**) S.I. 1971/1770 (1971 III, p. 4796.)
(**c**) S.I. 1970/1522 (1970 III, p. 4935).

Tariff heading	Description of Imported Composite Sugar Products	Rate of Surcharge
		Per cwt. £
17.02 (B) (2) and 17.05 (B)	Syrups containing sucrose sugar, whether or not flavoured or coloured, but not including fruit juices containing added sugar in any proportion:—	
	containing 70 per cent. or more by weight of sweetening matter	0·38
	containing less than 70 per cent., and more than 50 per cent., by weight of sweetening matter	0·27
	containing not more than 50 per cent. by weight of sweetening matter	0·13
17.02 (F) ..	Caramel:—	
	Solid	0·60
	Liquid	0·41
17.04 ..	Sugar confectionery, not containing cocoa ..	0·48
18.06 ..	Chocolate and other food preparations containing cocoa and added sugar:—	
	Chocolate couverture not prepared for retail sale; chocolate milk crumb, liquid ..	0·26
	Chocolate milk crumb, solid	0·32
	Solid chocolate bars or blocks, milk or plain, with or without fruit or nuts; other chocolate confectionery consisting wholly of chocolate or of chocolate and other ingredients not containing added sugar, but not including such goods when packed together in retail packages with goods liable to surcharge at a higher rate	0·26
	Other	0·34
19.08 ..	Pastry, biscuits, cakes and other fine bakers' wares containing added sugar:—	
	Biscuits, wafers and rusks containing more than 12½ per cent. by weight of added sugar, and other biscuits, wafers and rusks included in retail packages with such goods	0·15
	Cakes with covering or filling containing added sugar; meringues	0·19
	Other	0·07
20.01 ..	Vegetables and fruit, prepared or preserved by vinegar or acetic acid, containing added sugar:—	
	Containing 10 per cent. or more by weight of added sugar	0·21
	Other	0·04
20.03 ..	Fruit preserved by freezing, containing added sugar	0·07
20.04 ..	Fruit, fruit-peel and parts of plants, preserved by sugar (drained, glacé or crystallised)	0·39
20.05 ..	Jams, fruit jellies, marmalades, fruit purée and fruit pastes, being cooked preparations, containing added sugar	0·37
20.06 ..	Fruit otherwise prepared or preserved, containing added sugar:—	
	Ginger	0·30
	Other	0·07

SCHEDULE 2

Tariff heading	Description of Imported Composite Sugar Products
17.05 (A) and (B)	Sugar and invert sugar, flavoured or coloured.

SCHEDULE 3

Description of goods	Rate of surcharge repayment per bulk barrel of 36 gallons
Lager	£0·044
All beer other than lager	£0·027

EXPLANATORY NOTE

(This Note is not part of the Order.)

This order provides for reductions on and after 7th December 1971 in the average rates of surcharge payable on imported composite sugar products of the descriptions specified in Schedule 1 and in the average rates of surcharge repayment in respect of exported goods of the descriptions specified in Schedule 3. These correspond to the reductions in surcharge rates effected by the Sugar (Rates of Surcharge and Surcharge Repayments) (No. 9) Order 1971 (S.I. 1971/1964). Provision is also made for certain imported composite sugar products to be treated as not containing any sugar or invert sugar.

STATUTORY INSTRUMENTS

1971 No. 1967

ANIMALS

DISEASES OF ANIMALS

The Brucellosis Payments Scheme 1971

Made - - - -	*3rd December* 1971
Laid before Parliament	*9th December* 1971
Coming into Operation	*10th December* 1971

The Minister of Agriculture, Fisheries and Food and the Secretaries of State for Scotland and Wales respectively, acting jointly, in pursuance of subsections (1), (2), (9) and (10) of section 106 of the Agriculture Act 1970(**a**) and of all their other enabling powers, with the consent of the Treasury, hereby make the following scheme:

Citation, commencement and extent

1. This scheme, which may be cited as the Brucellosis Payments Scheme 1971, shall come into operation on 10th December 1971 and shall apply to Great Britain.

Interpretation

2.—(1) In this scheme, unless the context otherwise requires—

"accredited herd" means a herd of cattle in Great Britain which, to the satisfaction of the appropriate Minister, either—

(*a*) has been found to be free from brucellosis by means of a series of diagnostic tests carried out by him or on his behalf and has been, since the date of commencement of such tests, the subject of adequate precautions against the introduction or re-introduction and consequent spreading of brucellosis, or

(*b*) has been wholly constituted by the transfer of animals from other accredited herds in Great Britain or from such similar herds outside Great Britain as the Minister of Agriculture, Fisheries and Food, in relation to herds in England and Wales, or the Secretary of State, in relation to herds in Scotland, may either generally or in any special case allow, and has been, since being so constituted, the subject of such precautions as aforesaid;

and "accredited" and "unaccredited" shall be construed accordingly;

"area eradication agreement" means a voluntary arrangement between the appropriate Minister and the owner of a herd kept in an eradication area, providing for the eradication of brucellosis from the herd upon terms which include the slaughter by the owner of any reactors found in the herd, the payment to him of a replacement grant, but no other compensation, for each reactor so slaughtered, and the taking by him of precautions against the introduction or re-introduction and consequent spreading of brucellosis;

(**a**) 1970 c. 40.

"the appropriate Minister" means the Minister of Agriculture, Fisheries and Food or, in relation to herds kept in Scotland or sums required for making payments to producers in Scotland, the Secretary of State;

"beef cow scheme" means a scheme made under section 12 of the Agriculture Act 1967(**a**);

"beef incentive payments" means incentive payments made under paragraph 4 of this scheme;

"board" means a board constituted by a scheme relating to the marketing of milk made or having effect as if made under the Agricultural Marketing Act 1958(**b**);

"dairy incentive payments" means incentive payments made under paragraph 5 of this scheme;

"eradication area" means an area which is for the time being an eradication area for purposes connected with the control of brucellosis by virtue of an order made under section 5 of the Diseases of Animals Act 1950(**c**) and to which the Brucellosis (Area Eradication) (England and Wales) Order 1971(**d**) or the Brucellosis (Area Eradication) (Scotland) Order 1971(**e**), or any order revoking and substantially re-enacting either of those orders, for the time being applies;

"first compulsory test" means the first compulsory blood test made by or on behalf of the appropriate Minister for the presence of brucellosis in a herd kept in an eradication area;

"hill cattle scheme" means a scheme made under section 13(1)(*b*) of the Hill Farming Act 1946(**f**);

"incentive payments" has the meaning assigned to it by paragraph 3 of this scheme;

"prescribed date" means a prescribed date for the purposes of a beef cow scheme;

"qualifying day" means a qualifying day for the purposes of a hill cattle scheme;

"reactor" means an animal which, when tested for brucellosis by or on behalf of the appropriate Minister, gives rise to a reaction consistent with its being affected with that disease;

"replacement grant" means a grant made by the appropriate Minister to the owner of a slaughtered reactor at a flat rate unrelated to the value of the animal;

"test" means a test made by or on behalf of the appropriate Minister for the purpose of determining whether brucellosis is present in a herd.

(2) The Interpretation Act 1889(**g**) shall apply to the interpretation of this scheme as it applies to the interpretation of an Act of Parliament.

(**a**) 1967 c. 22.
(**b**) 1958 c. 47.
(**c**) 1950 c. 36.
(**d**) S.I. 1971/1717 (1971 III, p. 4763).
(**e**) S.I. 1971/1752 (1971 III, p. 4769).
(**f**) 1946 c. 73.
(**g**) 1889 c. 63.

Incentive payments for herds in eradication areas

3. Payments, to be known as incentive payments, may be made in accordance with the provisions of this scheme in respect of herds of cattle which are kept in eradication areas and from which brucellosis is being, or has been, eradicated under area eradication agreements.

Beef incentive payments

4.—(1) Incentive payments may be made by the appropriate Minister in respect of a herd which qualifies for subsidy payments under a hill cattle or beef cow scheme by way of supplement to such subsidy payments, and shall be subject to the terms and conditions governing the subsidy payments to which they are supplemental.

(2) Such incentive payments may be made in respect of a herd when a qualifying day for the purposes of a hill cattle scheme or a prescribed date for the purposes of a beef cow scheme, as the case may be, falls within the appropriate qualifying period specified in paragraph 6 below.

(3) The amount of any such incentive payment shall be £5 for each animal which qualifies for the subsidy payment to which the incentive payment is supplemental.

(4) Where in the case of any herd (except such a herd as is referred to in paragraph 6(5) below) the period referred to in sub-paragraph (2) above contains only one qualifying day for the purposes of a hill cattle scheme, or only one prescribed date for the purposes of a beef cow scheme, and incentive payments made in respect of the herd are supplemental to subsidy payments made under that scheme, an additional incentive payment of £5 per animal may be made in respect of the first qualifying day or the first prescribed date, as the case may be, after the termination of that period.

Dairy incentive payments

5.—(1) Incentive payments in respect of a herd from which milk is produced shall be made by a board to the producer of that milk, if he is registered as a milk producer under the scheme constituting the board, at a rate of 0.8p for each gallon of milk which is—

(*a*) produced from cows in the herd, and

(*b*) made the subject of a payment to or by him under that scheme, and

(*c*) either sold under the provisions of that scheme, or deemed for the purposes of any payments under the scheme to have been produced from that herd, during the appropriate qualifying period specified in paragraph 6 below.

(2) Every board shall keep or cause to be kept records of payments made by them under this paragraph and of the administrative cost of making such payments in such form as may be approved by the appropriate Minister and shall make such records available for inspection at all reasonable times by any duly authorised officer, servant or agent of the appropriate Minister or the Comptroller and Auditor General.

(3) Every board shall submit to the appropriate Minister, in such form as he may specify, a statement, certified by the board's auditors, of payments made by the board under this scheme and of the administrative cost of making such payments.

(4) Any such statement as is referred to in the preceding sub-paragraph shall be rendered annually and at such lesser intervals, and covering such periods, as the appropriate Minister may specify in a written notice to that board.

Qualifying periods for incentive payments

6.—(1) Subject to paragraphs 7 and 8(2) below, the qualifying period for incentive payments in respect of a herd shall commence in the case of beef incentive payments with the appropriate date specified in relation to that herd in sub-paragraph (2) below and in the case of dairy incentive payments with the beginning of the first calendar month after that date.

(2) The date referred to in sub-paragraph (1) above shall be—

(*a*) where the owner of the herd has entered into an area eradication agreement within such period after the first compulsory test as appears to the appropriate Minister to be reasonable for the purpose, the date of that test;

(*b*) where the owner has entered into such an agreement after the expiry of that period, the date of the first test after the agreement has been entered into.

(3) Subject to sub-paragraph (5) below, the qualifying period shall end in the case of beef incentive payments one year after the appropriate date specified in relation to that herd in sub-paragraph (4) below, and in the case of dairy incentive payments with the expiry of the twelfth complete calendar month after that date.

(4) The date referred to in sub-paragraph (3) above shall be—

(*a*) in the case of such a herd as is referred to under head (*a*) of the definition of an accredited herd in paragraph 2 above, the date of the last test before it becomes an accredited herd;

(*b*) in the case of such a herd as is referred to under head (*b*) of that definition, the date on which the first animal to be comprised in the herd is moved on to the premises where the herd is to be kept.

(5) Where an area eradication agreement ceases to apply to a herd before the end of the qualifying period as determined in accordance with sub-paragraphs (3) and (4) above, the qualifying period shall end in the case of beef incentive payments with the date on which the agreement ceases to apply to the herd and in the case of dairy incentive payments with the expiry of the calendar month in which that date occurs, without prejudice to the resumption of such payments under a further area eradication agreement.

(6) For the purposes of this paragraph the date of a test is the date when samples are first taken from cattle for use in the test.

Interrupted agreements

7. Where an area eradication agreement has ceased to apply to a herd before the end of the qualifying period and a further such agreement is subsequently entered into in respect of the same herd—

(*a*) any beef incentive payments falling due under the subsequent agreement shall be reduced by the amount of any such payments made under the previous agreement, and

(*b*) the qualifying period for dairy incentive payments under the subsequent agreement shall be reduced by the length of the qualifying period under the previous agreement, the commencement of the subsequent qualifying period being deferred accordingly.

Reductions to take account of previous payments directed against brucellosis

8.—(1) Any beef incentive payments falling due under this scheme shall be reduced by the difference between—

(*a*) the amount of any subsidy payments made in respect of the same herd under a hill cattle scheme or beef cow scheme at a rate determined by reference to the fact that the animals were comprised in a herd which was, or which was subsequently to become, an accredited herd as defined in that scheme, and

(*b*) the amount of the corresponding subsidy payments which would have been made under that scheme if the herd were never such an accredited herd.

(2) A qualifying period for dairy incentive payments under this scheme shall be reduced by the sum of—

(*a*) five-eighths (rounded off to the nearest month) of any period before 1st April 1971 in respect of which payments have been made in respect of the same herd under a scheme, other than this scheme, made under section 106(2) of the Agriculture Act 1970, and

(*b*) the whole of any period commencing on or after 1st April 1971 in respect of which such payments have been made,

the commencement of the qualifying period being deferred accordingly.

Advance payments

9.—(1) Where an unaccredited herd is in the opinion of the appropriate Minister likely to be eligible for incentive payments under this scheme, and the total number of reactors in the herd disclosed by the first compulsory test and subsequent tests made before the herd becomes accredited amounts to 10 per cent or more of the number of animals tested at the first compulsory test, the appropriate Minister may, on application by the owner of the herd made at such time and in such manner as the appropriate Minister may from time to time require, make to him an advance payment of incentive payments—

(*a*) in the case of a herd which is, in the opinion of the appropriate Minister, wholly or predominantly eligible for beef incentive payments, at the rate of £5 for each animal in the herd which has been tested, and found not to be a reactor, at the relevant test;

(*b*) in the case of a herd which is, in the opinion of the appropriate Minister, wholly or predominantly eligible for dairy incentive payments, at the rate of £6.50 for each such animal.

(2) Where an advance payment has been made under sub-paragraph (1) above—

(*a*) the amount of any beef incentive payments falling due during the year after the date of the entry of the herd in the Register of Brucellosis Accredited Herds kept jointly by the Minister of Agriculture, Fisheries and Food and the Secretary of State shall be reduced by such part of the advance payment as, in the opinion of the appropriate Minister, represents an advance payment of beef incentive payments;

(*b*) the amount of any dairy incentive payments falling due during the period of 12 calendar months commencing, at the discretion of the board making the payments, with either the first or second calendar month after they have been notified by the appropriate Minister of the entry of the herd in the said Register, shall be reduced, so far as possible by equal instalments, by such part of the advance payment as, in the opinion of the appropriate Minister, represents an advance payment of dairy incentive payments.

(3) Where, as a result of the insufficiency of dairy incentive payments in any month, a board is not able to reduce such payments in accordance with the preceding sub-paragraph, the part of any advance payment thereby unaccounted for, unless otherwise recovered by or on behalf of the appropriate Minister, shall be accounted for by the reduction of such payments in respect of subsequent months as the opportunity arises.

(4) For the purposes of this paragraph "the relevant test" means the test at which the total number of reactors disclosed by that and previous tests, if any, first exceeds 10 per cent of the number of animals tested at the first compulsory test.

In Witness whereof the Official Seal of the Minister of Agriculture, Fisheries and Food is hereunto affixed on 29th November 1971.

(L.S.)

J. M. L. Prior,
Minister of Agriculture, Fisheries and Food.

Gordon Campbell,
Secretary of State for Scotland.

29th November 1971.

Given under my hand on 30th November 1971.

Peter Thomas,
Secretary of State for Wales.

We approve,

3rd December 1971.

P. L. Hawkins,
Walter Clegg,
Two of the Lords Commissioners of Her Majesty's Treasury.

EXPLANATORY NOTE

(This Note is not part of the scheme.)

This scheme, which is made under section 106 of the Agriculture Act 1970, enables payments to be made in connection with the elimination of brucellosis from herds of cattle in eradication areas.

First, it provides for payments, to be known as incentive payments, to be made by the Minister of Agriculture, Fisheries and Food and the Secretary of State for Scotland as supplements to hill cattle and beef cow subsidy payments at the rate of £5 per animal and, where milk is the subject of payments under a milk marketing scheme, by the appropriate board at the rate of .8p. per gallon. These will be paid in respect of herds whose owners agree with the appropriate Minister on or after 1st November 1971 to undertake voluntary eradication on terms which include a replacement grant, but no other compensation, for each slaughtered reactor. They will start with the commencement of eradication and finish approximately one year after the herd qualifies for accreditation.

Secondly, advance payments may be made where the number of reactors in the herd is not less than 10 per cent of the number of animals tested. These will be paid on animals not found to be reactors and will be at the rate of £5 per animal in predominantly beef herds and £6.50 in predominantly dairy herds. Provision is made for a corresponding reduction of subsequent incentive payments.

1971 No. 1968

CIVIL AVIATION

The Civil Aviation (Aerial Advertising) Regulations 1971

Made - - - -	2*nd December* 1971
Laid before Parliament	10*th December* 1971
Coming into Operation	31*st December* 1971

The Secretary of State, in exercise of his powers under section 7(1) of the Civil Aviation (Licensing) Act 1960**(a)**, and of all other powers enabling him in that behalf, hereby makes the following Regulations:—

1. These Regulations may be cited as the Civil Aviation (Aerial Advertising) Regulations 1971, and shall come into operation on 31st December 1971.

2.—(1) In these Regulations, unless the context otherwise requires, the expression "local authority" means, in relation to England and Wales, the council of a county, county borough, London borough or county district, the Greater London Council or the Common Council of the City of London and, in relation to Scotland, any county or town council; and "operator", in relation to an aircraft, means the person for the time being having the management of the aircraft.

(2) The Interpretation Act 1889**(b)**, shall apply for the interpretation of these Regulations as it applies for the interpretation of an Act of Parliament.

(3) Section 38(2) of the Interpretation Act 1889 (which relates to the effect of repeals) shall apply to these Regulations as if these Regulations were an Act of Parliament and as if the Regulations revoked by Regulation 3 of these Regulations were an Act of Parliament thereby repealed.

3. The Civil Aviation (Aerial Advertising) Regulations 1961**(c)** and the Civil Aviation (Aerial Advertising) (Amendment) Regulations 1970**(d)** are hereby revoked.

4. For the purposes of section 7 of the Civil Aviation (Licensing) Act 1960 (which prohibits aerial advertising and propaganda, save in such circumstances as may be prescribed), the following circumstances are hereby prescribed—

(1) The use of aircraft for the emission or display of any communication solely for one or more of the following purposes:—

(*a*) complying with the law of the United Kingdom or any other country, being law in force in relation to the aircraft;

(a) 1960 c. 38.
(b) 1889 c. 63.
(c) S.I. 1961/2102 (1961 III, p. 3835).
(d) S.I. 1970/1444 (1970 III, p. 4704).

(*b*) securing the safety of the aircraft or any person or property therein;

(*c*) identifying by a mark or inscription on the aircraft any one or more of the following:—

(i) the owner of the aircraft;

(ii) the charterer of the aircraft by demise;

(iii) the charterer of the aircraft otherwise than by demise, if the charterer is an operator of aircraft;

(iv) the manufacturer of the aircraft;

(v) the manufacturer of any of the aircraft's engines;

(vi) the type of the aircraft;

(vii) the type of any of the aircraft's engines:

Provided that nothing in this sub-paragraph shall permit the use of any aircraft for the display of an illuminated sign, or the use of a kite or captive balloon for the emission or display of any communication;

(*d*) the furtherance, by or on behalf of a Government department, a local authority or a person providing ambulance or rescue facilities by air, of measures in connection with circumstances then existing or imminent which are calculated to cause danger to persons or property;

(*e*) civil defence, military or police purposes.

(2) The use of any balloon which at any stage of its flight is not more than one metre in any linear dimension for the display of any mark or inscription on the body of the balloon.

Michael Noble,
Minister for Trade,
2nd December 1971. Department of Trade and Industry.

EXPLANATORY NOTE

(*This Note is not part of the Regulations.*)

These Regulations revoke the Civil Aviation (Aerial Advertising) Regulations 1961, as amended. They reproduce the substance of the 1961 Regulations as amended, except that balloons, other than captive balloons, may now be used for the emission or display of communications of a type prescribed by these Regulations.

1971 No. 1970 (S.209)

PENSIONS

The Superannuation (Teaching and Public Transport Services) Interchange (Scotland) Rules 1971

Made - - - -	26*th November* 1971
Laid before Parliament	10*th December* 1971
Coming into Operation	10*th January* 1972

ARRANGEMENT OF RULES

In exercise of the powers conferred on me by sections 2 and 15 of the Superannuation (Miscellaneous Provisions) Act 1948**(a)** as amended by section 11 of the Superannuation (Miscellaneous Provisions) Act 1967**(b)** and of all other powers enabling me in that behalf and with the consent of the Minister for the Civil Service, I hereby make the following rules:—

Part I

General

Citation and Commencement

1. These rules may be cited as the Superannuation (Teaching and Public Transport Services) Interchange (Scotland) Rules 1971 and shall come into operation on 10th January 1972.

Interpretation

2.—(1) In these rules, unless the context otherwise requires—

"the Act of 1948" means the Superannuation (Miscellaneous Provisions) Act 1948;

"the Act of 1968" means the Teachers Superannuation (Scotland) Act 1968**(c)**;

"contributing service" and "contributory employee" have the same respective meanings as in the Local Government Superannuation (Scotland) Acts 1937 to 1953**(d)**;

"national service", in relation to any person, means—

service which is relevant service within the meaning of the Reserve and Auxiliary Forces (Protection of Civil Interests) Act 1951**(e)**; and any similar service immediately following relevant service entered into with the consent of the body or person by whom he was last employed before undertaking the service;

"operative date" means the date of the coming into operation of these rules;

"pension" has the meaning assigned to it by the Act of 1948;

"prescribed period" has the meaning assigned to that expression by rule 3;

"reckonable service" means such service as is by virtue of the Teachers Regulations of 1969 reckonable service for all the purposes of Part I of the Act of 1968;

"superannuation fund" means a superannuation fund named in column (1) of the Schedule;

(a) 1948 c. 33.
(b) 1967 c. 28.
(c) 1968 c. 12.
(d) 1937 c. 69; 1939 c. 18; 1953 c. 25.
(e) 1951 c. 65.

"the Teachers Regulations of 1957" means the Teachers (Superannuation) (Scotland) Regulations 1957**(a)** as amended **(b)**;

"the Teachers Regulations of 1969" means the Teachers Superannuation (Scotland) Regulations 1969**(c)** as amended **(d)**;

"the Teachers Schemes" means the Superannuation Scheme for Teachers in Scotland dated 5th June 1919**(e)**, the Superannuation Scheme for Teachers (Scotland) 1926**(f)** and the Superannuation Scheme for Teachers (Scotland) 1952**(g)**;

"teaching service" means—

(*a*) reckonable service; and

(*b*) service which for the purposes of the Teachers Regulations of 1969 is service as an organiser;

"the Transfer Value Regulations" means the Local Government Superannuation (Transfer Value) (Scotland) Regulations 1954**(h)**;

"transport authority", in relation to a person employed in transport employment, means the authority or body responsible for the administration of the superannuation fund of which he is, or may become, a member;

"transport employment", in relation to any person, means employment in which he is, or may become, a member of a superannuation fund.

(2) Any reference in these rules to the provisions of any enactment, rules or regulations shall, unless the context otherwise requires, be construed as a reference to those provisions as amended, modified, affected, applied or re-enacted by any subsequent enactment, rules or regulations.

(3) Any reference in these rules to a rule, to a paragraph of a rule, to a Part, or to the Schedule shall, unless the context otherwise requires, be construed as a reference to that rule or to that paragraph of the rule in which the reference occurs, to a Part of, or to the Schedule to, these rules, as the case may be.

(4) The Interpretation Act 1889**(i)** shall apply for the interpretation of these rules as it applies for the interpretation of an Act of Parliament.

Prescribed Period

3.—(1) For the purposes of these rules, subject as provided hereafter in this rule, the expression "prescribed period" shall mean—

(*a*) in the case of a person who immediately after leaving his employment in teaching service or in transport employment became engaged in national service, a period of six months after the date of termination of the national service; and

(*b*) in the case of any other person, a period of twelve months after the date on which he left his employment in teaching service or in transport employment.

(a) S.I. 1957/356 (1957 I, p. 733).
(b) S.I. 1958/1595, 1963/2111, 1965/1166, 1966/1229, 1967/1736 (1958 I, p. 1077; 1963 III, p. 4685; 1965 II, p. 3284; 1966 III, p. 3295; 1967 III, p. 4657).
(c) S.I. 1969/77 (1969 I, p. 133).
(d) S.I. 1969/659 (1969 II, p. 1820).
(e) S.R. & O. 1919/1105 (1919 I, p. 688).
(f) S.R. & O. 1926/363 (1926 p. 449).
(g) S.I. 1952/464 (1952 I, p. 873).
(h) S.I. 1954/1256 (1954 II, p. 1736).
(i) 1889 c. 63.

(2) The Secretary of State and the transport authority may in any particular case extend any period specified in paragraph (1).

(3) Subject as provided in paragraph (4)—

(*a*) in reckoning the periods of six months and twelve months mentioned in paragraph (1) no account shall be taken of any period spent by a person on a course of study or training which he undertook after leaving his former employment; and

(*b*) if a person left his former employment in order to undertake a course of study or training and on completion of that course became engaged in national service, he shall be deemed, for the purposes of paragraph (1), to have left his former employment at the time when he completed the said course of study or training.

(4) The provisions of paragraph (3) shall not apply—

(*a*) to a person whose new employment is transport employment unless the transport authority is satisfied that by reason of his having undertaken the said course of study or training he is better fitted for the duties of his new employment;

(*b*) to a person who in his new employment is in teaching service unless—

(i) before leaving his former employment (or, if between leaving that employment and undertaking the said course of study or training he was engaged in national service, before the end of that service) he gave notice in writing to his former employer of his intention to undertake the said course of study or training; and

(ii) the Secretary of State is satisfied that by reason of his having undertaken the said course of study or training he is better fitted for employment in teaching service.

Part II

Transfer from Teaching Service to Transport Employment

Application

4.—(1) Except as provided in rule 5, this Part shall apply to a person who—

(*a*) becomes, or before the operative date became, employed in transport employment within the prescribed period after ceasing to be employed in teaching service;

(*b*) within three months of becoming a member of a superannuation fund or six months after the operative date, whichever period shall last expire, or within such longer period as the transport authority may with the agreement of the Secretary of State in any particular case allow, notifies that authority in writing that he desires this Part to apply to him and furnishes that authority with particulars in writing of his teaching service; and

(*c*) within the period specified in paragraph (*b*), or within such longer period as the transport authority may in any particular case allow, pays to that authority an amount equal to any repaid contributions paid to him after he last ceased to be employed in teaching service, together with compound interest thereon of an amount determined in accordance with paragraph (2).

(2) For the purposes of paragraph (1)(*c*)—

(*a*) compound interest shall not be payable unless the period between a person's ceasing to be employed in teaching service and becoming a member of a superannuation fund exceeds one year;

(*b*) if the aforesaid period exceeds one year, compound interest shall be calculated on the amount of the repaid contributions at three per cent per annum with yearly rests from the date one year after that on which the person ceased to be employed in teaching service or from the day on which the amount was paid to him, whichever shall be the later, to the date on which he became a member of a superannuation fund; and

(*c*) if the amount of compound interest calculated as aforesaid exceeds a sum equal to one-half of the difference between the amount of the transfer value payable under rule 6 and the amount of the transfer value which would have been so payable if calculated by reference to the person's age on ceasing to be employed in teaching service, it shall be reduced to that sum.

(3) In this rule "repaid contributions" means any sum paid by way of repayment of contributions paid under the Teachers Schemes, the Teachers Regulations of 1957 or the Teachers Regulations of 1969 and includes both any interest added thereto and any sum deducted therefrom in respect of liability to income tax arising by reason of the payment.

Excepted Cases

5. This Part shall not apply to a person who—

(*a*) has become entitled to any benefit (other than repayment of contributions) under the Teachers Schemes or the Teachers Regulations of 1957 or the Teachers Regulations of 1969;

(*b*) became a member of a superannuation fund specified in Part I of the Schedule;

(*c*) became a member of a superannuation fund specified in Part II of the Schedule before the date specified in column (2) thereof against the name of that fund; or

(*d*) became employed in transport employment before the operative date, unless the Secretary of State and the transport authority agree that this Part shall apply to him.

Transfer Value

6.—(1) In respect of a person to whom this Part applies the Secretary of State shall, out of moneys provided by Parliament, pay to the transport authority a transfer value of an amount calculated in accordance with the following provisions of this rule.

(2) Subject as provided hereafter in this rule, the transfer value shall be an amount equal to the transfer value which would have been payable under the Transfer Value Regulations if the person, at the date when he ceased to be employed in teaching service, had ceased to be a contributory employee under one local authority and had become such an employee under another local authority and had been entitled to reckon as contributing service his reckonable service and his service reckonable for the purposes of Part VII of the Teachers Regulations of 1969 at the length at which it is so reckonable.

(3) For the purposes of paragraph (2), teaching service which is reckoned as contributing service shall be deemed to have been affected or modified in accordance with regulations applicable to contributing service made under section 110 of the National Insurance Act 1965**(a)**, or under any provision corresponding thereto contained in an enactment repealed by that Act, in like manner and to the like extent, as nearly as may be, as it was affected or modified by other such regulations.

(4) In calculating the amount of a transfer value there shall be excluded any period of war service within the meaning of the Education (Scotland) (War Service Superannuation) Act 1939**(b)** and of national service within the meaning of the Teachers' Pensions (National Service) (Scotland) Rules 1952**(c)** in respect of which, at the time the amount thereof is determined, the contributions remain unpaid.

(5) The amount of the transfer value shall be calculated by reference to the person's age—

(*a*) on the operative date if he ceased to be employed in teaching service more than twelve months before that date and sub-paragraph (*b*) does not apply; or

(*b*) on the date on which he became a member of a superannuation fund if that date is after the operative date and more than twelve months after the date on which he ceased to be employed in teaching service.

(6) The transfer value shall be reduced by—

(*a*) any sum payable by the Secretary of State by way of income tax in respect thereof; and

(*b*) an amount equal to any compound interest payable in accordance with rule 4(2).

Benefits under Teachers Regulations of 1969

7. Subject to the provisions of Part III and of other rules made under section 2 of the Act of 1948 no payment of any benefit shall be made under the Teachers Regulations of 1969 to any person or his personal representatives in respect of any service which is taken into account in calculating the amount of a transfer value under rule 6.

PART III

TRANSFER FROM TRANSPORT EMPLOYMENT TO TEACHING SERVICE

Application

8. Except as provided in rule 9 this Part shall apply to a person who—

(*a*) becomes, or before the operative date became, employed in teaching service within the prescribed period after ceasing to be employed in transport employment;

(*b*) within three months of becoming employed in teaching service or six months after the operative date, whichever period shall last expire, or

---

(a) 1965 c. 51. **(b)** 1939 c. 96.
(c) S.I. 1952/518 (1952 I, 928).

within such longer period as the Secretary of State may with the agreement of the transport authority in any particular case allow, notifies the Secretary of State in writing that he desires this Part to apply to him and furnishes the Secretary of State with particulars in writing of his transport employment; and

(*c*) is a person in respect of whom the Secretary of State receives from the transport authority a sum by way of transfer value.

Excepted Cases

9. This Part shall not apply to a person who—

(*a*) has become entitled to a pension (other than repayment of contributions) in respect of his transport employment;

(*b*) last ceased to be employed in transport employment before the date specified in column (3) of the Schedule against the name of the superannuation fund of which he was a member in respect of that employment; or

(*c*) became employed in teaching service before the operative date unless the Secretary of State agrees that this Part shall apply to him.

Reckoning of Transport Employment

10.—(1) In relation to a person to whom this Part applies there shall be reckoned as reckonable service such period as is equal to the period of contributing service which would, on the basis of his age and rate of remuneration on the date of becoming employed in teaching service, have resulted in the payment under the Transfer Value Regulations of a transfer value equal to the sum paid in respect of him by the transport authority to the Secretary of State if on that date he had ceased to be a contributory employee under one local authority and had become such an employee under another local authority.

(2) In the case of a person who became employed in teaching service before the operative date, a reference to his age on that date shall be substituted for the reference in paragraph (1) to his age on becoming employed in teaching service.

(3) Any period reckonable by a person to whom this Part applies for any purpose under the rules regulating the superannuation fund of which he was a member in respect of his former employment shall, so far as not included in the period reckoned as reckonable service under paragraph (1), be reckoned as class C external service for the purposes of the Teachers Regulations of 1969.

Average Salary

11. For the purpose of calculating under section 4(3) of the Act of 1968 the average salary of a person to whom this Part applies whose teaching service after ceasing to be employed in transport employment amounts to less than three years—

(*a*) so much of his transport employment immediately prior to ceasing to be employed therein as, together with any teaching service after so ceasing, amounts to three years shall be reckoned as teaching service; and

(*b*) his salary during any period so reckoned shall be such salary as was taken into account for the purposes of the superannuation fund of which he was a member.

Commencement of Employment

12. For the purposes of regulation 40(1)(*a*)(ii) of the Teachers Regulations of 1969 the date on which a person to whom this Part applies became employed in transport employment or, if earlier, the date of commencement of the period reckoned as reckonable service under rule 10(1) shall be deemed to be a date on which he became employed in teaching service.

Repayment of Contributions

13.—(1) Where a person to whom this Part applies ceases to be employed in teaching service or dies, then, in computing any sum payable to him or his personal representatives under the Teachers Regulations of 1969 by way of repayment of the balance of his contributions, there shall be included a sum equal to that which would have been payable by way of repayment of contributions under the rules regulating the superannuation fund of which he was a member in respect of his transport employment if, on ceasing to hold that employment, he had been entitled to such a repayment.

(2) In computing the amount of the sum so included for the purposes of this rule compound interest shall be calculated—

(*a*) as respects the period ending immediately before the date on which the person became employed in teaching service, in the manner in which such interest, if any, would have been calculated if the occasion for making the calculation had occurred immediately before that date; and

(*b*) as respects the period beginning with that date, in accordance with the provisions of Part IV of the Teachers Regulations of 1969.

Payment into Consolidated Fund

14. All sums received by the Secretary of State in respect of a person to whom this Part applies shall be paid into the Consolidated Fund.

Gordon Campbell,
One of Her Majesty's Principal
Secretaries of State.

St Andrew's House,
Edinburgh.
22nd November 1971.

Consent of the Minister for the Civil Service given under his Official Seal on 26th November 1971.

(L.S.)

K. H. McNeill,
Authorised by the Minister for
the Civil Service.

Rules 2, 5 and 9

SCHEDULE

Transport Superannuation Funds

Title of Superannuation Fund (1)	Date for purposes of Rule 5(*c*) (2)	Date for purposes of Rule 9(*b*) (3)
Part I		
British Railways Superannuation Fund —L.M.S.R. Section (formerly the London Midland and Scottish Railway Superannuation Fund)	—	1st June 1957
—G.W.R. Section (formerly the Great Western Railway Superannuation Fund)	—	1st June 1957
—S.R. Section (formerly the Southern Railway Superannuation Fund)	—	1st June 1957
Railway Clearing System Superannuation Fund	—	4th March 1959
Part II		
British Railways Superannuation Fund		
—L.N.E.R. Section (formerly the London and North Eastern Railway Superannuation Fund)	1st June 1957	1st June 1957
—New Section	14th September 1970	14th September 1970
British Transport Police Force Superannuation Fund and Retirement Benefit Fund	1st October 1968	1st October 1968
British Railways (Wages Grades) Pension Fund	14th August 1967	14th August 1967
Scottish Transport Group Staff Pension Fund (formerly the Scottish Bus Group Pension Fund)	1st April 1960	1st April 1960

EXPLANATORY NOTE

(*This Note is not part of the Rules.*)

These Rules provide for preservation of the superannuation rights of persons who transfer from service pensionable under the Teachers Superannuation (Scotland) Regulations 1969 as amended to pensionable employment in certain public transport services or vice versa. Where such a transfer takes place and an appropriate transfer value is paid, the person is credited with previous service for pension purposes under the superannuation scheme to which he becomes subject.

Under the powers conferred by section 2(5) of the Superannuation (Miscellaneous Provisions) Act 1948 provision is made for transfers which took place before the coming into operation of the Rules subject to the agreement of the employee and the former employer, and to certain restrictions indicated by the Rules.

1971 No. 1971

CUSTOMS AND EXCISE

The Import Duties (General) (No. 7) Order 1971

Made - - - -	*4th December* 1971
Laid before the House of Commons	*6th December* 1971
Coming into Operation	*1st January* 1972

The Lords Commissioners of Her Majesty's Treasury, by virtue of the powers conferred on them by sections 1, 2 and 13 of the Import Duties Act 1958(**a**), and of all other powers enabling them in that behalf, on the recommendation of the Secretary of State hereby make the following Order:—

1.—(1) This Order may be cited as the Import Duties (General) (No. 7) Order 1971.

(2) The Interpretation Act 1889(**b**) shall apply for the interpretation of this Order as it applies for the interpretation of an Act of Parliament.

(3) Nothing in this Order shall be construed as affecting the operation of any instrument made under the Import Duties Act 1958 and not revoked by this Order, or as affecting any relief to which any person is or may become entitled under any provisions of that Act.

(4) This Order shall come into operation on 1st January 1972.

2.—(1) The form of customs tariff set out in column 1 of Schedule 1 to this Order (being the form prescribed by the Import Duties (General) (No. 7) Order 1970(**c**) as amended by subsequent Orders under the Import Duties Act 1958(**d**), and with other amendments required to give effect to the Geneva agreements, and to impose duty on certain Commonwealth cotton textiles, or consisting of the omission of unnecessary subheadings or other minor modifications) may continue to be referred to as the Customs Tariff 1959 and to be used in classifying goods for customs purposes in cases where some other method is not required under any enactment.

In this paragraph " the Geneva agreements " means the agreements dated 30th June 1967(**e**) entered into at Geneva between Her Majesty's Government in the United Kingdom and the Governments of certain other countries and amending the General Agreement on Tariffs and Trade concluded in Geneva in 1947(**f**).

(2) The form so set out shall be interpreted and applied in accordance with the interpretative rules preceding it in the said Schedule 1, but the Index of General Definitions etc. appended to those rules shall not be taken as part of that form or affect its interpretation.

(**a**) 1958 c. 6. (**b**) 1889 c. 63. (**c**) S.I. 1970/1522 (1970 III, p. 4935).
(**d**) See the Orders revoked by Art. 4 of this Order. (**e**) Cmnd. 3347.
(**f**) Cmd. 7258.

(3) Where goods are to be classified in accordance with that form and the classification depends on the rate of duty, then, unless the contrary intention appears, account shall be taken of all customs duties for the time being chargeable, other than duty under the Customs Duties (Dumping and Subsidies) Act 1969(**a**), and the classification shall be made by a comparison of the amounts chargeable on goods not qualifying for any preferential rate of duty.

3.—(1) Where in any heading or subheading of Schedule 1 to this Order a rate of duty is shown in column 2, then, on the importation into the United Kingdom of goods classified in that heading or subheading, there shall, subject to the following provisions of this Article, be charged an import duty at the rate so shown:

Provided that—

(*a*) no import duty shall be charged in the case of goods of the Republic of Ireland consigned to the United Kingdom from that country;

(*b*) in the case of goods qualifying for Commonwealth preference (not being goods falling within paragraph (*a*) above), no import duty shall be charged unless a rate is shown in column 3 prefixed by the letter " C " and, if a rate is so shown, import duty shall be charged at that rate;

(*c*) in the case of goods of Convention area origin within the meaning of the European Free Trade Association Act 1960(**b**), but subject to section 2 of that Act, no import duty shall be charged unless a rate is shown in the said column 3 prefixed by the letter " E " and, if a rate is so shown, import duty shall be charged at that rate; and

(*d*) where a heading or subheading limits a rate of duty to a specified period, or shows different rates for different periods, the duty shall be charged accordingly.

(2) Goods falling within both paragraph (*b*) and paragraph (*c*) of the proviso to paragraph (1) above shall, if less import duty would be chargeable if they were treated as falling solely within one of those paragraphs than if they were treated as falling solely within the other, be treated for the purposes of this Order as excluded from that other paragraph.

(3) Where—

(*a*) any import duty is by this Order expressed to be chargeable on goods of any description, and

(*b*) any goods of that description are chargeable with a revenue duty (not being a duty in addition to which the import duty is expressed to be chargeable) but those goods are not exempt from import duties,

then import duty shall be charged on those goods at a rate less by the amount of any such revenue duty chargeable on them than the rate at which the import duty is expressed to be chargeable or, if that amount is equal to or greater than the duty at the last-mentioned rate, shall not be charged on those goods.

(4) Any reference in Schedule 1 to this Order to a rate of duty expressed as a percentage, other than one expressed as a percentage of the full rate, is a reference to the percentage of the value of the goods; and the expression " full rate ", where used in column 3 of that Schedule in relation to goods of any description, means the rate shown for goods of that description in column 2.

(**a**) 1969 c. 16. (**b**) 1960 c. 19.

(5) In this Article and in Schedule 1 to this Order, " revenue duty " means a duty of customs chargeable under any enactment other than the Import Duties Act 1958 and the Customs Duties (Dumping and Subsidies) Act 1969.

4. The Import Duties (General) Orders specified in Schedule 2 to this Order are hereby revoked.

P. L. Hawkins,
V. H. Goodhew,
Two of the Lords Commissioners of Her Majesty's Treasury.

4th December, 1971.

SCHEDULE 1

FORM OF CUSTOMS TARIFF, AND RATES OF IMPORT DUTY

[For list of section and chapter titles, see end of Schedule.]

INTERPRETATIVE RULES

1. The titles of Sections, Chapters and sub-Chapters are provided for ease of reference only; for legal purposes, classification (as between headings) shall be determined according to the terms of the headings and any relative Section or Chapter notes and, provided such headings or notes do not otherwise require, according to Rules 2 to 5 below.

2.(*a*) Any reference in a heading to an article shall be taken to include a reference to that article incomplete or unfinished, provided that, as imported, the incomplete or unfinished article has the essential character of the complete or finished article. It shall also be taken to include a reference to that article complete or finished (or falling to be classified as complete or finished by virtue of this Rule), imported unassembled or disassembled.

(*b*) Any reference in a heading to a material or substance shall be taken to include a reference to mixtures or combinations of that material or substance with other materials or substances. Any reference to goods of a given material or substance shall be taken to include a reference to goods consisting wholly or partly of such material or substance. The classification of goods consisting of more than one material or substance shall be according to the principles of Rule 3.

3. When for any reason, goods are, *prima facie*, classifiable under two or more headings, classification shall be effected as follows:

(*a*) The heading which provides the most specific description shall be preferred to headings providing a more general description (subheadings being disregarded).

(*b*) Mixtures and composite goods which consist of different materials or are made up of different components and which cannot be classified by reference to 3(*a*) shall be classified as if they consisted of the material or component which gives the goods their essential character, in so far as this criterion is applicable.

(*c*) When goods cannot be classified by reference to 3(*a*) or 3(*b*), they shall be classified under the heading which involves the highest rate of duty.

4. Goods not falling within any heading of the Schedule shall be classified under the heading appropriate to the goods to which they are most akin.

5. Except as provided in a note to a Section or Chapter expressed to be a special note applying to subheadings only, the classification of goods within a heading is to be determined by applying as between subheadings the like Rules as are to be applied between headings, and, except in so far as the contrary intention appears, terms used in a subheading are to be interpreted in the same way as in the heading.

Index of General Definitions etc.

Phrase or matter	Defined or explained in
1. Alloys (how classified in Sections XIV and XV)	Chapter 71, Note 5 Section XV, Note 3
2. Artificial fur	Chapter 43, Note 5
3. Base metal	Section XV, Notes 4, 5 and 7
4. Composition leather	Chapter 41, Note 2
5. Embroidery	Chapter 58, Note 5
6. Fine animal hair	Note to Chapter 53
7. Furskins	Chapter 43, Note 1
8. Glass	Chapter 70, Note 4
9. Horsehair	Chapter 5, Note 4
10. Hydrocarbon oil	Chapter 27, Special Note
11. Ivory	Chapter 5, Note 3
12. Light oil	Chapter 27, Special Note
13. Made up (used of textiles in Section XI)	Section XI, Note 6
14. Man-made fibres	Chapter 51, Note 1
15. Mixed textiles (how classified in Chapters 50 to 57)	Section XI, Note 2
16. Parts of general use (of base metal)	Section XV, Note 2
17. Pearls	Chapter 71, Note 4
18. Precious metal	Chapter 71, Notes 4, 6 and 7
19. Put up for retail sale (used of yarn in Chapters 50, 51 and 53 to 56)	Section XI, Note 4
20. Rubber	Chapter 40, Notes 1 and 4
21. Sweetening matter	Special Note to Section IV
22. Twine, cordage, ropes and cables (in Section XI)	Section XI, Note 3
23. Waste and scrap (used of base metal in Section XV)	Section XV, Note 6

SECTION I

Live Animals; Animal Products

Chapter 1

Live Animals

Notes

1. This Chapter covers all live animals except:

(*a*) Fish, crustaceans and molluscs, of headings Nos. 03.01 and 03.03;

(*b*) Microbial cultures and other products of heading No. 30.02; and

(*c*) Animals of heading No. 97.08.

2. Any reference in this Chapter to a particular genus or species, except where the context otherwise requires, includes a reference to the young of that genus or species.

Tariff Heading	*Rate of Import Duty (if any)*	
	Full	*Commonwealth (C)* *E.F.T.A. (E)*
01.01 Live horses, asses, mules and hinnies ...	—	—
01.02 Live animals of the bovine species ...	—	—
01.03 Live swine	—	—
01.04 Live sheep and goats	—	—
01.05 Live poultry, that is to say, fowls, ducks, geese, turkeys and guinea fowls	10%	C — E 10%
01.06 Other live animals:		
(A) Quadrupeds	—	—
(B) Bees	—	—
(C) Other	10%	C — E 10%

Chapter 2

Meat and Edible Meat Offals

Note

This Chapter does not cover:

(*a*) Products of the kinds described in headings Nos. 02.01, 02.02, 02.03, 02.04 and 02.06, unfit or unsuitable for human consumption;

(*b*) Guts, bladders or stomachs of animals (heading No. 05.04) and animal blood (heading No. 05.15); or

(*c*) Animal fat, other than products of heading No. 02.05 (Chapter 15).

Tariff Heading	*Rate of Import Duty (if any)*	
	Full	*Commonwealth (C)* *E.F.T.A. (E)*
02.01 Meat and edible offals of the animals falling within heading No. 01.01, 01.02, 01.03 or 01.04, fresh, chilled or frozen:		
(A) Meat:		
(1) Beef and veal:		
(*a*) Boned or boneless	5%	C — E 5%
(*b*) Other:		
(i) Chilled	£0·3500 per cwt.	C — E £0·3500 per cwt.
(ii) Fresh or frozen	£0·3110 per cwt.	C — E £0·3110 per cwt.
(2) Mutton and lamb:		
(*a*) Mutton, bone-in carcases, whole		
from 1*st January* 1972 *to* 30*th June* 1972	£0·4667 per cwt.	C £0·4667 per cwt E £0·4667 per cwt
from 1*st July* 1972 *onwards*	£0·7000 per cwt.	C £0·7000 per cwt E £0·7000 per cwt
(*b*) Other		
from 1*st January* 1972 *to* 30*th June* 1972	£0·9335 per cwt.	C £0·9335 per cwt E £0·9335 per cwt
from 1*st July* 1972 *onwards*	£1·4000 per cwt.	C £1·4000 per cwt E £1·4000 per cwt
(3) Horsemeat	5%	C — E 5%
(4) Other	10%	C — E 10%
(B) Edible offals:		
(1) Beef and veal:		
(*a*) Sweetbreads and tongues ...	—	—
(*b*) Other	10%	C — E 10%
(2) Other	—	—
02.02 Dead poultry (that is to say, fowls, ducks, geese, turkeys and guinea fowls) and edible offals thereof (except liver), fresh, chilled or frozen:		
(A) Dead poultry:		
(1) Guinea fowl	10%	C — E 10%
(2) Other	£0·0125 per lb.	C — E £0·0125 per lb
(B) Edible poultry offals	10%	C — E 10%

Tariff Heading	*Rate of Import Duty (if any)*	
	Full	*Commonwealth (C)* *E.F.T.A. (E)*
02.03 Poultry liver, fresh, chilled, frozen, salted or in brine	10%	C — E 10%
02.04 Other meat and edible meat offals, fresh, chilled or frozen:		
(A) Rabbit, fresh	5%	C — E 5%
(B) Edible meat offals	—	—
(C) Whale meat	10%	—
(D) Other	10%	C — E 10%
02.05 Pig fat free of lean meat and poultry fat (not rendered or solvent-extracted), fresh, chilled, frozen, salted, in brine, dried or smoked	10%	C — E 10%
02.06 Meat and edible meat offals (except poultry liver), salted, in brine, dried or smoked:		
(A) Meat:		
(1) Beef and veal:		
(*a*) Boned or boneless	20%	C — E 20%
(*b*) Other	£0·3110 per cwt.	C — E £0·3110 per cwt.
(2) Mutton and lamb	—	—
(3) Hams, whole:		
(*a*) In airtight containers	10%	C — E 10%
(*b*) Other	—	—
(4) Other:		
(*a*) Pork (including ham and bacon), not canned or bottled	10%	—
(*b*) Horsemeat	5%	C — E 5%
(*c*) Other	10%	C — E 10%
(B) Edible offals:		
(1) Beef and veal:		
(*a*) Sweetbreads and tongues ...	—	—
(*b*) Other	20%	C — E 20%
(2) Other	—	—

Chapter 3

Fish, Crustaceans and Molluscs

Note

This Chapter does not cover:

(*a*) Marine mammals (heading No. 01.06) or meat thereof (heading No. 02.04 or 02.06);

(*b*) Fish (including livers and roes thereof), crustaceans and molluscs, dead, unfit or unsuitable for human consumption either by reason of their species or their condition (Chapter 5); or

(*c*) Caviar or caviar substitutes (heading No. 16.04).

Tariff Heading	*Rate of Import Duty (if any)*		
	Full	*Commonwealth (C)* *E.F.T.A. (E)*	
03.01 Fish, fresh (live or dead), chilled or frozen:			
(A) Salmon, chilled or frozen	—		—
(B) Fish roes	5%	C	—
		E	5%
(C) Other:			
(1) Fillets, chilled or frozen; portions, weighing not less than 1 ounce each, prepared by cutting blocks of fillets, chilled or frozen	10%		—
(2) Other	10%	C	—
		E	10%
03.02 Fish, dried, salted or in brine; smoked fish, whether or not cooked before or during the smoking process:			
(A) Wet salted split fish	—		—
(B) Fish roes	5%	C	—
		E	5%
(C) Other	10%	C	—
		E	10%
03.03 Crustaceans and molluscs, whether in shell or not, fresh (live or dead), chilled, frozen, salted, in brine or dried; crustaceans, in shell, simply boiled in water:			
(A) Clams, cockles, crabs, crawfish, crayfish, lobsters, mussels, Norway lobsters (Dublin Bay prawns), scallops (including queen scallops), shrimps, whelks, winkles:			
(1) Frozen or dried	10%	C	—
		E	10%
(2) Other	30%	C	—
		E	30%
(B) Oysters:			
(1) In shell:			
(*a*) Of the kind *Ostrea virginica* *from 1st June to last day of February*	15%	C	—
		E	15%
(*b*) Other kinds *from 1st June to last day of February*	30%	C	—
		E	30%
(2) Not in shell	30%	C	—
		E	30%

Tariff Heading	Rate of Import Duty (if any)	
	Full	Commonwealth (C) E.F.T.A. (E)
03.03 Crustaceans and molluscs, etc.—*contd.*		
(C) Prawns:		
(1) Peeled prawns, chilled or frozen...	10%	—
(2) Other	10%	C — E 10%
(D) Other	10%	C — E 10%

Chapter 4

Dairy Produce; Birds' Eggs; Natural Honey; Edible Products of Animal Origin, not elsewhere specified or included

Notes

1. The expression " milk " means whole milk (full cream) or skimmed milk (separated), buttermilk, whey, kephir, yoghourt and similar fermented milk.

2. Milk and cream put up in hermetically sealed cans are regarded as preserved within the meaning of heading No. 04.02. However, milk and cream are not regarded as so preserved merely by reason of being pasteurised, sterilised or peptonised, if they are not put up in hermetically sealed cans.

Tariff Heading	*Rate of Import Duty (if any)*		
	Full	*Commonwealth (C)* *E.F.T.A. (E)*	
04.01 Milk and cream, fresh, not concentrated or sweetened	10%	C E	— 10%
04.02 Milk and cream, preserved, concentrated or sweetened:			
(A) Milk (other than buttermilk, whey, kephir, yoghourt and similar fermented milk):			
(1) Evaporated or condensed:			
(*a*) Whole:			
(i) Not containing added sweetening matter	£0·3000 per cwt.	C E	— £0·3000 per cwt.
(ii) Other	£0·3790 per cwt.	C E	— £0·3790 per cwt.
(*b*) Skimmed	10%	C E	— 10%
(2) Dried milk, block milk and other	£0·3000 per cwt.	C E	— £0·3000 per cwt.
(B) Other:			
(1) Canned cream	10%		—
(2) Other	10%	C E	— 10%
04.03 Butter	—		—
04.04 Cheese and curd:			
(A) Cheese:			
(1) Blue veined	10%		—
(2) Other	15%	C E	— 15%
(B) Curd	10%	C E	— 10%

Tariff Heading	*Rate of Import Duty (if any)*	
	Full	*Commonwealth (C)* *E.F.T.A. (E)*
04.05 Birds' eggs and egg yolks, fresh, dried or otherwise preserved, sweetened or not:		
(A) Eggs in shell:		
(1) Not exceeding 14 lb. in weight per 120	£0·0500 per 120	C — E £0·0500 per 120
(2) Over 14 lb. but not exceeding 17 lb. in weight per 120	£0·0750 per 120	C — E £0·0750 per 120
(3) Over 17 lb. in weight per 120 ...	£0·0875 per 120	C — E £0·0875 per 120
(B) Eggs not in shell and egg yolks ...	10%	C — E 10%
04.06 Natural honey	£0·2500 per cwt.	C — E £0·2500 per cwt.
04.07 Edible products of animal origin, not elsewhere specified or included	10%	C — E 10%

Chapter 5

Products of Animal Origin, not elsewhere specified or included

Notes

1. This Chapter does not cover:

(*a*) Edible products (other than guts, bladders and stomachs of animals, whole and pieces thereof, and animal blood, liquid or dried);

(*b*) Hides or skins (including furskins) other than goods falling within heading No. 05.05, 05.06 or 05.07 (Chapter 41 or 43);

(*c*) Animal textile materials, other than horsehair and horsehair waste (Section XI); or

(*d*) Prepared knots or tufts for broom or brush making (heading No. 96.03).

2. For the purposes of heading No. 05.01, the sorting of hair by length (provided the root ends and tip ends respectively are not arranged together) shall be deemed not to constitute working.

3. Throughout this Schedule elephant, mammoth, mastodon, walrus, narwhal and wild boar tusks, rhinoceros horns and the teeth of all animals are regarded as ivory.

4. Throughout this Schedule, references to " horsehair " are to be taken to include not only references to the hair of the manes and tails of equine animals but also such hair of bovine animals.

Tariff Heading	*Rate of Import Duty (if any)*	
	Full	*Commonwealth (C)* *E.F.T.A. (E)*
05.01 Human hair, unworked, whether or not washed or scoured; waste of human hair	—	—
05.02 Pigs', hogs' and boars' bristles or hair; badger hair and other brush making hair; waste of such bristles and hair:		
(A) Raw, whether or not cleaned or washed	—	—
(B) Bristles in bundles or bunches, consisting exclusively of bristles laid parallel	—	—
(C) Other	7·5%	—
05.03 Horsehair and horsehair waste, whether or not put up in a layer or between two layers of other material:		
(A) Raw, whether or not cleaned or washed	—	—
(B) Other	7·5%	—
05.04 Guts, bladders and stomachs of animals (other than fish), whole and pieces thereof:		
(A) Sausage casings:		
(1) Hog...	—	—
(2) Other	10%	C — E 10%
(B) Other:		
(1) Of bovine animals	10%	—
(2) Other	—	—
05.05 Fish waste:		
(A) Herring offals	—	—
(B) Other	5%	—

Tariff Heading	Rate of Import Duty (if any)	
	Full	Commonwealth (C) E.F.T.A. (E)
05.06 Sinews and tendons; parings and similar waste, of raw hides or skins	—	—
05.07 Skins and other parts of birds, with their feathers or down, feathers and parts of feathers (whether or not with trimmed edges) and down, not further worked than cleaned, disinfected or treated for preservation; powder and waste of feathers or parts of feathers:		
(A) Skins and pieces thereof, with their down	—	—
(B) Feathers in bales, sacks or similar packages, without internal containers; down:		
(1) Cleaned to the standard prescribed in paragraph 8 of Part 12 of British Standard 1425 : 1960 (with its supplement), as amended up to and including November, 1967	5%	—
(2) Other	—	—
(C) Barbs, quills and scapes	5%	—
(D) Other	10%	—
05.08 Bones and horn-cores, unworked, defatted, simply prepared (but not cut to shape), treated with acid or degelatinised; powder and waste of these products:		
(A) Ossein	—	—
(B) Bone meal	5%	—
(C) Other	5%	—
05.09 Horns, antlers, hooves, nails, claws and beaks of animals, unworked or simply prepared but not cut to shape, and waste and powder of these products; whalebone and the like, unworked or simply prepared but not cut to shape, and hair and waste of these products	5%	—
05.10 Ivory, unworked or simply prepared but not cut to shape; powder and waste of ivory	—	—
05.11 Tortoise-shell (shells and scales), unworked or simply prepared but not cut to shape; claws and waste of tortoise-shell	5%	—
05.12 Coral and similar substances, unworked or simply prepared but not otherwise worked; shells, unworked or simply prepared but not cut to shape; powder and waste of shells	—	—
05.13 Natural sponges	—	—

Tariff Heading	Rate of Import Duty (if any)	
	Full	*Commonwealth (C)* *E.F.T.A. (E)*
05.14 Ambergris, castoreum, civet and musk; cantharides; bile, whether or not dried; animal products, fresh, chilled or frozen, or otherwise provisionally preserved, of a kind used in the preparation of pharmaceutical products:		
(A) Pancreas glands	—	—
(B) Other	10%	—
05.15 Animal products not elsewhere specified or included; dead animals of Chapter 1 or Chapter 3, unfit for human consumption:		
(A) Cochineal	—	—
(B) Salted fish roes	10%	—
(C) Blood powder and blood plasma ...	10%	—
(D) Other	10%	C — E 10%

SECTION II

Vegetable Products

Chapter 6

Live Trees and Other Plants; Bulbs, Roots and the Like; Cut Flowers and Ornamental Foliage

Notes

1. This Chapter covers only live trees and goods (including seedling vegetables) of a kind commonly supplied by nursery gardeners or florists for planting or for ornamental use; nevertheless it does not include potatoes, onions, shallots, garlic and other products of Chapter 7.

2. Any reference in heading No. 06.03 or 06.04 to goods of any kind shall be construed as including a reference to bouquets, floral baskets, wreaths and similar articles made wholly or partly of goods of that kind, account not being taken of accessories of other materials.

3. In this Chapter, " gross " means inclusive of the weight of any earth or other growing medium in which the goods are imported.

Tariff Heading	*Rate of Import Duty (if any)*	
	Full	*Commonwealth (C)* *E.F.T.A. (E)*
06.01 Bulbs, tubers, tuberous roots, corms, crowns and rhizomes, dormant, in growth or in flower:		
(A) Dry:		
(1) Lily of the valley crowns and roots	10%	C — E 10%
(2) Bulbs, corms, rhizomes and tubers:		
(*a*) Begonia and gloxinia	5%	C — E 5%
(*b*) Other	10%	C — E 10%
(3) Other, including dahlia and other tuberous roots	£0·0625 per lb.	C — E £0·0625 per lb.
(B) Other:		
(1) Ixia ... ... Narcissus (polyanthus types) ... Roman hyacinth ... ... Snowdrop ... ... Star of Bethlehem	£2·1000 per cwt. (gross)	C — E £2·1000 per cwt. (gross)
(2) Ranunculus	£3·2665 per cwt. (gross)	C — E £3·2665 per cwt. (gross)
(3) Hyacinth (other than roman hyacinth), iris, narcissus (other than polyanthus types but including daffodil), tulip		
from 1st December to last day of February	£15·8665 per cwt. (gross)	C — E £15·8665 per cwt. (gross)
from 1st March to 30th April	£12·6000 per cwt. (gross)	C — E £12·6000 per cwt. (gross)

Tariff Heading	Rate of Import Duty (if any) Full	Commonwealth (C) E.F.T.A. (E)
06.01 Bulbs, tubers, tuberous roots, etc.—*contd.*		
(B) Other:—*contd.*		
(3) Hyacinth, etc.—*contd.*		
from 1st May to 30th November	£9·3330 per cwt. (gross)	C — E £9·3330 per cwt. (gross)
(4) Freesia		
from 1st September to 30th April	25%	C — E 25%
from 1st May to 31st August...	10%	C — E 10%
(5) Other	£9·3330 per cwt. (gross)	C — E £9·3330 per cwt. (gross)
06.02 Other live plants, including trees, shrubs, bushes and roots; buds, eyes and stems for grafting and budding; cuttings and slips; mushroom spawn:		
(A) Buds, eyes and stems for grafting and budding; cuttings and slips; mushroom spawn	10%	C — E 10%
(B) Rose stocks and rose trees, shrubs, bushes and plants:		
(1) Rose stocks neither budded nor grafted, the following: Rooted single stems of rosa canina or rosa rugosa, not less than 4 feet in length; seedlings of rosa canina or rosa laxa	5%	C — E 5%
(2) Other:		
(*a*) Standard trees, including half standards, quarter standards and weeping standards	£12 per 100	C — E £12 per 100
(*b*) Other	£3 per 100	C — E £3 per 100
(C) Fruit stocks and fruit trees, shrubs, bushes and plants	£2·2500 per cwt. (gross)	C — E £2·2500 per cwt. (gross)
(D) Azalea indica:		
(1) Not in flower	—	—
(2) In flower	£9·3330 per cwt. (gross)	C — E £9·3330 per cwt. (gross)
(E) Broussonetia papyrifera (paper mulberry) and grafts on Broussonetia papyrifera stock; sweet bays	10%	C — E 10%

Tariff Heading	Rate of Import Duty (if any)	
	Full	Commonwealth (C) E.F.T.A. (E)
06.02 Other live plants, etc.—*contd.*		
(F) Other:		
(1) Not in flower:		
(*a*) Trees, shrubs and bushes ...	£2·2500 per cwt. (gross)	C — E £2·2500 per cwt. (gross)
(*b*) Other	£0·0625 per lb. (gross)	C — E £0·0625 per lb. (gross)
(2) In flower:		
(*a*) Gypsophila ... ... Heather... ... ... Marguerite ... ... Marigold ... ... Stock	£2·1000 per cwt. (gross)	C — E £2·1000 per cwt. (gross)
(*b*) Other	£9·3330 per cwt. (gross)	C — E £9·3330 per cwt. (gross)
06.03 Cut flowers and flower buds of a kind suitable for bouquets or for ornamental purposes, fresh, dried, dyed, bleached, impregnated or otherwise prepared:		
(A) Mimosa	£0·9330 per cwt.	C — E £0·9330 per cwt.
(B) Gypsophila ... ... Heather ... ... Ixia ... ... Marguerite ... ... Marigold ... ... Roman hyacinth ... ... Snowdrop ... ... Star of Bethlehem ... ... Stock	£2·1000 per cwt.	C — E £2·1000 per cwt.
(C) Lilac	£0·0150 per lb.	C — E £0·0150 per lb.
(D) Narcissus (polyanthus types)... ... Peony ... ... Ranunculus	£3·2665 per cwt.	C — E £3·2665 per cwt.
(E) Hyacinth (other than roman hyacinth), iris, narcissus (other than polyanthus types, but including daffodil), tulip *from 1st December to last day of February*	£15·8665 per cwt.	C — E £15·8665 per cwt.
from 1st March to 30th April ...	£12·6000 per cwt.	C — E £12·6000 per cwt.
from 1st May to 30th November ...	£9·3330 per cwt.	C — E £9·3330 per cwt.

Tariff Heading	Rate of Import Duty (if any)	
	Full	*Commonwealth (C)* *E.F.T.A. (E)*
06.03 Cut flowers and flower buds, etc.—*contd.*		
(F) Freesia		
from 1st September to 30th April		
(*a*) Of a value exceeding £0·9000 per lb.	£0·3500 per lb.	C — E £0·3500 per lb.
(*b*) Other	25%	C — E 25%
from 1st May to 31st August	£0·1250 per lb.	C — E £0·1250 per lb.
(G) Anemone ... ... Carnation ... ... Rose	£0·1250 per lb.	C — E £0·1250 per lb.
(H) Other	£0·1000 per lb.	C — E £0·1000 per lb.
06.04 Foliage, branches and other parts (other than flowers or buds) of trees, shrubs, bushes and other plants, and mosses, lichens and grasses, being goods of a kind suitable for bouquets or ornamental purposes, fresh, dried, dyed, bleached, impregnated or otherwise prepared:		
(A) Foliage:		
(1) Cycas ... ... Magnolia ... ... Holly ... ... Mistletoe ... ... Golden palm	10%	C — E 10%
(2) Asparagus	£9·3330 per cwt.	C — E £9·3330 per cwt.
(3) Other	£2·1000 per cwt.	C — E £2·1000 per cwt.
(B) Branches (other than foliage) and other parts	10%	C — E 10%
(C) Mosses and lichens	£2·1000 per cwt.	C — E £2·1000 per cwt.
(D) Grasses:		
(1) Agrostis ... ... Erianthus ... ... Eulalia ... ... Pampas ... ... Stipa ... ... Tropini (lagurus)	10%	C — E 10%
(2) Other	£2·1000 per cwt.	C — E £2·1000 per cwt

Chapter 7

Edible Vegetables and Certain Roots and Tubers

Note

In headings Nos. 07.01, 07.02 and 07.03, the word " vegetables " is to be taken to include edible mushrooms, truffles, rhubarb, olives, capers, tomatoes, potatoes, salad beetroot, cucumbers, gherkins, marrows, pumpkins, aubergines, sweet peppers, fennel, parsley, chervil, tarragon, cress, sweet marjoram (*Majorana hortensis* or *Origanum majorana*), horse-radish and garlic.

Heading No. 07.04 covers all dried, dehydrated or evaporated vegetables of the kinds falling within headings Nos. 07.01 to 07.03, other than:

(*a*) Dried leguminous vegetables, shelled (heading No. 07.05);

(*b*) Ground sweet peppers (heading No. 09.04);

(*c*) Flours of the dried leguminous vegetables of heading No. 07.05 (heading No. 11.03);

(*d*) Flour, meal and flakes of potato (heading No. 11.05).

Tariff Heading	*Rate of Import Duty (if any)*		
	Full	*Commonwealth (C) E.F.T.A. (E)*	
07.01 Vegetables, fresh or chilled:			
(A) Asparagus			
from 16th April to 30th June ...	£2·8000 per cwt.	C	—
		E	£2·8000 per cwt.
from 1st July to 15th April ...	10%	C	—
		E	10%
(B) Broccoli and cauliflowers			
from 1st March to 30th June ...	£0·4000 per cwt.	C	—
		E	£0·4000 per cwt.
from 1st July to last day of February	£0·3000 per cwt.	C	—
		E	£0·3000 per cwt.
(C) Carrots			
from 1st April to 30th April ...	10%	C	—
		E	10%
from 1st May to 30th June ...	£1 per cwt.	C	—
		E	£1 per cwt.
from 1st July to 31st October ...	10%	C	—
		E	10%
from 1st November to 31st March	5%	C	—
		E	5%
(D) Cucumbers (other than gherkins)			
from 1st March to 30th September	£1 per cwt.	C	—
		E	£1 per cwt.
from 1st October to last day of February	10%	C	—
		E	10%
(E) Green peas, unshelled			
from 1st June to 31st July ...	£0·9330 per cwt.	C	—
		E	£0·9330 per cwt.
from 1st August to 31st May ...	10%	C	—
		E	10%

Tariff Heading	Rate of Import Duty (if any)	
	Full	Commonwealth (C) E.F.T.A. (E)
07.01 Vegetables, fresh or chilled:—*contd.*		
(F) Lettuce and endive		
from 1st March to 30th April ...	£1·5000 per cwt.	C — E £1·5000 per cwt.
from 1st May to 31st May ...	£1 per cwt.	C — E £1 per cwt.
from 1st June to 31st October ...	£0·8000 per cwt.	C — E £0·8000 per cwt.
from 1st November to last day of February	£0·5000 per cwt.	C — E £0·5000 per cwt.
(G) Chicory (salad)		
from 1st November to 31st March	£0·4000 per cwt.	C — E £0·4000 per cwt.
from 1st April to 31st October ...	10%	C — E 10%
(H) Mushrooms		
from 1st October to 30th April ...	20%	C — E 20%
from 1st May to 30th September	10%	C — E 10%
(IJ) Potatoes		
from 16th May to 30th June:		
(*a*) New Potatoes	£0·4665 per cwt.	C — E £0·4665 per cwt.
(*b*) Other	£0·0500 per cwt.	C — E £0·0500 per cwt.
from 1st July to 31st August ...	£0·1000 per cwt.	C — E £0·1000 per cwt.
from 1st September to 15th May	£0·0500 per cwt.	C — E £0·0500 per cwt.
(K) Tomatoes		
from 1st May to 15th May:		
(*a*) Of a value exceeding £7 per cwt.	£1·8665 per cwt.	C — E £1·8665 per cwt.
(*b*) Other	10%	C — E 10%
from 16th May to 31st May:		
(*a*) Of a value exceeding £5·6000 per cwt.	£2·8000 per cwt.	C — E £2·8000 per cwt.
(*b*) Other	10%	C — E 10%
from 1st June to 15th June ...	£2·8000 per cwt.	C — E £2·8000 per cwt.
from 16th June to 31st July ...	£2·3330 per cwt.	C — E £2·3330 per cwt.
from 1st August to 31st August	£1·8665 per cwt.	C — E £1·8665 per cwt.
from 1st September to 31st October	£0·9330 per cwt.	C — E £0·9330 per cwt.
from 1st November to 15th November	10%	C — E 10%

Tariff Heading	Rate of Import Duty (if any)		
	Full	Commonwealth (C) E.F.T.A. (E)	
07.01 Vegetables, fresh or chilled:—*contd.*			
(K) Tomatoes:—*contd.*			
from 16th November to 31st March	8%	C	—
		E	8%
from 1st April to 30th April ...	10%	C	—
		E	10%
(L) Dry-bulb onions and shallots			
from 1st February to 30th June ...	5%	C	—
		E	5%
from 1st July to 31st July ...	10%	C	—
		E	10%
from 1st August to 30th November	£0·2330 per cwt.	C	—
		E	£0·2330 per cwt.
from 1st December to 31st January	10%	C	—
		E	10%
(M) Horse-radish	2·5%	C	—
		E	2·5%
(N) Herbs	£2·1000 per cwt.	C	—
		E	£2·1000 per cwt.
(O) Garlic	10%		—
(P) Celery	5%	C	—
		E	5%
(Q) Other	10%	C	—
		E	10%
07.02 Vegetables (whether or not cooked), preserved by freezing	10%	C	—
		E	10%
07.03 Vegetables provisionally preserved in brine, in sulphur water or in other preservative solutions, but not specially prepared for immediate consumption:			
(A) Cauliflowers:			
(1) In brine, not being in airtight containers	£0·3000 per cwt. of the vegetable content	C	—
		E	£0·3000 per cwt. of the vegetable content
(2) Other	10%	C	—
		E	10%
(B) Gherkins, olives, capers, sweet peppers	—		—
(C) Onions	10%	C	—
		E	10%
(D) Other	10%	C	—
		E	10%
07.04 Dried vegetables, whole, cut, sliced, broken or in powder, but not further prepared:			
(A) Horse-radish	2·5%	C	—
		E	2·5%
(B) Herbs, not in powder	£2·1000 per cwt.	C	—
		E	£2·1000 per cwt.
(C) Tomatoes, leeks	10%		—
(D) Garlic, sweet peppers	—		—

Tariff Heading	Rate of Import Duty (if any)		
	Full	Commonwealth (C) E.F.T.A. (E)	
07.04 Dried vegetables, etc.—*contd.*			
(E) Other:			
(1) Vegetables (other than asparagus) in airtight containers:			
(*a*) Broad, kidney and runner beans; beetroot; broccoli and cauliflowers; Brussels sprouts; carrots; cucumbers (other than gherkins); herbs in powder; lettuce and endive; mushrooms; dry-bulb onions and shallots; peas; potatoes; rhubarb; spinach; turnips; mixtures containing any of these vegetables	15%	C E	— 15%
(*b*) Other	15%	C E	— 15%
(2) Other:			
(*a*) Asparagus; broad, kidney and runner beans; beetroot; broccoli and cauliflowers; Brussels sprouts; carrots; cucumbers (other than gherkins); herbs in powder; lettuce and endive; mushrooms; dry-bulb onions and shallots; peas; potatoes; rhubarb; spinach; turnips; mixtures containing any of these vegetables	10%	C E	— 10%
(*b*) Other	10%	C E	— 10%
07.05 Dried leguminous vegetables, shelled, whether or not skinned or split:			
(A) Peas:			
(1) Split peas	15%	C E	— 15%
(2) Whole peas (other than peas of the varieties commonly known as maple peas, dun peas and yellow or white peas)	£0·3750 per cwt. or 10%, whichever is the greater	C E	— £0·3750 per cwt. or 10%, whichever is the greater
(3) Other	10%	C E	— 10%
(B) Beans, dried, white (including haricot) other than butter	4%	C E	— 4%
(C) Other	5%	C E	— 5%
07.06 Manioc, arrowroot, salep, Jerusalem artichokes, sweet potatoes and other similar roots and tubers with high starch or inulin content, fresh or dried, whole or sliced; sago pith:			
(A) Manioc	—		—
(B) Sago pith	5%	C E	— 5%
(C) Other:			
(1) Dried	5%	C E	— 5%
(2) Other	5%	C E	— 5%

Chapter 8

Edible Fruit and Nuts; Peel of Melons or Citrus Fruit

Notes

1. This Chapter does not cover inedible nuts or fruits.
2. The word " fresh " is to be taken to extend to goods which have been chilled.

Tariff Heading	*Rate of Import Duty (if any)*		
	Full	*Commonwealth (C) E.F.T.A. (E)*	
08.01 Dates, bananas, coconuts, Brazil nuts, cashew nuts, pineapples, avocados, mangoes, guavas and mangosteens, fresh or dried, shelled or not:			
(A) Brazil nuts and coconuts:			
(1) Whole, shelled or not	—		—
(2) Other:			
(*a*) Dried	10%	C	—
		E	10%
(*b*) Other	10%	C	—
		E	10%
(B) Bananas:			
(1) Fresh	£0·3750 per cwt.	C	—
		E	£0·3750 per cwt.
(2) Dried	10%	C	—
		E	10%
(C) Pineapples, dried	5%	C	—
		E	5%
(D) Dates	—		—
(E) Mangoes, guavas, mangosteens, avocados:			
(1) Fresh	5%	C	—
		E	5%
(2) Dried	5%	C	—
		E	5%
(F) Cashew nuts, dried	10%	C	—
		E	10%
(G) Other	10%	C	—
		E	10%
08.02 Citrus fruit, fresh or dried:			
(A) Fresh:			
(1) Grapefruit	£0·2500 per cwt.	C	—
		E	£0·2500 per cwt.
(2) Oranges, clementines, mandarins and tangerines			
from 1st April to 30th November	£0·1750 per cwt.	C	—
		E	£0·1750 per cwt.
from 1st December to 31st March	5%	C	—
		E	5%
(3) Other	5%	C	—
		E	5%
(B) Dried	10%	C	—
		E	10%
08.03 Figs, fresh or dried:			
(A) Fresh	£0·1500 per cwt.		—
(B) Dried	£0·3000 per cwt.	C	—
		E	£0·3000 per cwt.

Tariff Heading	Rate of Import Duty (if any)	
	Full	Commonwealth (C) E.F.T.A. (E)
08.04 Grapes, fresh or dried:		
(A) Currants	£0·1000 per cwt.	C — E £0·1000 per cwt.
(B) Raisins, sultanas and other dried grapes	£0·2000 per cwt.	C — E £0·2000 per cwt.
(C) Other:		
(1) Hothouse		
from 1st February to 30th June ...	£0·7000 per cwt.	C — E £0·7000 per cwt.
from 1st July to 31st January ...	20%	C — E 20%
(2) Other		
from 1st February to 30th June ...	£0·7000 per cwt.	C — E £0·7000 per cwt.
from 1st July to 31st August ...	10%	C — E 10%
from 1st September to 31st January	5%	C — E 5%
08.05 Nuts other than those falling within heading No. 08.01, fresh or dried, shelled or not:		
(A) Hazel nuts, not in shell; almonds, not in shell; pecans	—	—
(B) Other	10%	—
08.06 Apples, pears and quinces, fresh:		
(A) Apples		
from 16th April to 15th August	£0·2250 per cwt.	C — E £0·2250 per cwt.
(B) Pears		
from 1st February to 31st July...	£0·2250 per cwt.	C — E £0·2250 per cwt.
from 1st August to 31st January	£0·1500 per cwt.	C — E £0·1500 per cwt.
(C) Quinces	10%	C — E 10%
08.07 Stone fruit, fresh:		
(A) Cherries		
from 1st June to 15th August ...	£1·8665 per cwt.	C — E £1·8665 per cwt.
from 16th August to 31st May ...	10%	C — E 10%
(B) Peaches and nectarines:		
(1) Hothouse		
from 1st April to 30th November	10%	C — E 10%
from 1st December to 31st March	£0·7000 per cwt.	C — E £0·7000 per cwt.
(2) Other		
from 1st April to 30th November	5%	C — E 5%
from 1st December to 31st March	£0·7000 per cwt.	C — E £0·7000 per cwt.

Tariff Heading	Rate of Import Duty (if any)		
	Full	*Commonwealth (C)* *E.F.T.A. (E)*	
08.07 Stone fruit, fresh:—*contd.*			
(C) Plums (including bullace, damsons, greengages and mirabelles)			
from 16th June to 31st October	£0·8350 per cwt.	C	—
		E	£0·8350 per cwt.
from 1st November to 15th June	6%	C	—
		E	6%
(D) Other	10%	C	—
		E	10%
08.08 Berries, fresh:			
(A) Bilberries	—		—
(B) Currants			
from 16th June to 31st August ...	£1·8665 per cwt.	C	—
		E	£1·8665 per cwt.
from 1st September to 15th June	10%	C	—
		E	10%
(C) Gooseberries			
from 1st May to 31st July ...	£0·9330 per cwt.	C	—
		E	£0·9330 per cwt.
from 1st August to 30th April ...	5%	C	—
		E	5%
(D) Strawberries			
from 1st June to 9th June ...	£1·8665 per cwt.	C	—
		E	£1·8665 per cwt.
from 10th June to 31st July ...	£2·8000 per cwt.	C	—
		E	£2·8000 per cwt.
from 1st August to 31st May ...	10%	C	—
		E	10%
(E) Raspberries and loganberries			
from 1st July to 31st August ...	10%	C	—
		E	10%
from 1st September to 30th June	5%	C	—
		E	5%
(F) Other	5%	C	—
		E	5%
08.09 Other fruit, fresh:			
(A) Melons	5%		—
(B) Other	5%	C	—
		E	5%
08.10 Fruit (whether or not cooked), preserved by freezing, not containing added sugar:			
(A) Apples:			
(1) Pulp...	£0·1750 per cwt. or 15%, whichever is the less	C	—
		E	£0·1750 per cwt. or 15%, whichever is the less
(2) Other	£0·1750 per cwt. or 25%, whichever is the less	C	—
		E	£0·1750 per cwt. or 25%, whichever is the less

Tariff Heading	Rate of Import Duty (if any)	
	Full	*Commonwealth (C)* *E.F.T.A. (E)*
08.10 Fruit (whether or not cooked), etc.—*contd.*		
(B) Bilberries; grapefruit; orange, clementine, mandarin or tangerine pulp not containing the peel	—	—
(C) Strawberries	£0·7500 per cwt.	C — E £0·7500 per cwt.
(D) Other	15%	C — E 15%
08.11 Fruit provisionally preserved (for example, by sulphur dioxide gas, in brine, in sulphur water or in other preservative solutions), but unsuitable in that state for immediate consumption:		
(A) Apples:		
(1) Pulp...	£0·1750 per cwt. or 15%, whichever is the less	C — E £0·1750 per cwt. or 15%, whichever is the less
(2) Other	£0·1750 per cwt. or 25%, whichever is the less	C — E £0·1750 per cwt. or 25%, whichever is the less
(B) Bilberries and nuts	10%	C — E 10%
(C) Cherries	—	—
(D) Citrus fruits:		
(1) Grapefruit; orange, clementine, mandarin or tangerine pulp not containing the peel	—	—
(2) Lemons, oranges, clementines, mandarins and tangerines, comminuted entire	—	—
(3) Other:		
(*a*) In brine...	—	—
(*b*) Otherwise preserved	12·5%	C — E 12·5%
(E) Strawberries	£0·7500 per cwt.	C — E £0·7500 per cwt
(F) Blackberries, currants, gooseberries, loganberries, pears, plums (including bullace, damsons, greengages and mirabelles), raspberries; mixtures containing any of these fruits or apples or strawberries	15%	C — E 15%
(G) Other	15%	C — E 15%

Tariff Heading	Rate of Import Duty (if any)	
	Full	Commonwealth (C) E.F.T.A. (E)
08.12 Fruit, dried, other than that falling within heading No. 08.01, 08.02, 08.03, 08.04 or 08.05:		
(A) Apples, pears, peaches, nectarines, prunes and bilberries	—	—
(B) Apricots:		
(1) Pulp...	10%	C — E 10%
(2) Other	£0·4000 per cwt.	C — E £0·4000 per cwt.
(C) Other	10%	C — E 10%
08.13 Peel of melons and citrus fruit, fresh, frozen, dried, or provisionally preserved in brine, in sulphur water or in other preservative solutions	—	—

Chapter 9

Coffee, Tea, Maté and Spices

Notes

1. Mixtures of the products of headings Nos. 09.04 to 09.10 are to be classified as follows:

(*a*) Mixtures of two or more of the products falling within the same heading are to be classified in that heading;

(*b*) Mixtures of two or more of the products falling within different headings are to be classified under heading No. 09.10.

The addition of other substances to the products of headings Nos. 09.04 to 09.10 (or to the mixtures referred to in paragraph (*a*) or (*b*) above) shall not affect their classification provided that the resulting mixtures retain the essential character of the goods falling in those headings. Otherwise such mixtures are not classified in this Chapter; those constituting mixed condiments or mixed seasonings are classified in heading No. 21.04.

2. This Chapter does not cover:

(*a*) Sweet peppers, unground (Chapter 7);

(*b*) Cubeb pepper (*Piper cubeba*) and other products of heading No. 12.07.

Tariff Heading	*Rate of Import Duty (if any)*	
	Full	*Commonwealth (C)* *E.F.T.A. (E)*
09.01 Coffee, whether or not roasted or freed of caffeine; coffee husks and skins; coffee substitutes containing coffee in any proportion:		
(A) Coffee, unmixed:		
(1) Roasted or ground	£0·3150 per cwt.	C £0·2350 per cwt E £0·2350 per cwt
(2) Other	£0·2350 per cwt.	C — E £0·2350 per cwt
(B) Coffee husks and skins	5%	C — E 5%
(C) Coffee and chicory, roasted and ground, mixed but without other ingredients	£0·7000 per cwt.	C £0·6250 per cwt E £0·7000 per cwt
(D) Other	10%	C — E 10%
09.02 Tea	—	—
09.03 Maté	—	—
09.04 Pepper of the genus *Piper;* pimento of the genus *Capsicum* or the genus *Pimenta:*		
(A) Peppercorns, the fruit of *Piper nigrum*, unground	—	—
(B) Other	10%	C — E 10%
09.05 Vanilla	10%	C — E 10%

Tariff Heading	*Rate of Import Duty (if any)*	
	Full	*Commonwealth (C)* *E.F.T.A. (E)*
09.06 Cinnamon and cinnamon-tree flowers ...	5%	C — E 5%
09.07 Cloves (whole fruit, cloves and stems) ...	10%	C — E 10%
09.08 Nutmeg, mace and cardamoms	10%	C — E 10%
09.09 Seeds of anise, badian, fennel, coriander, cumin, caraway and juniper	—	—
09.10 Thyme, saffron and bay leaves; other spices:		
(A) Saffron (*Crocus sativus*) stigmas and styles, dried but not chopped, ground, manufactured or prepared	—	—
(B) Thyme and bay leaves, not ground ...	£2·1000 per cwt.	C — E £2·1000 per cwt.
(C) Other	10%	C — E 10%

Chapter 10

Cereals

Note

Headings in this Chapter, except heading No. 10.06, are to be taken not to apply to grains which have been ground to remove the husk or pericarp or otherwise worked. Heading No. 10.06 is to be taken to apply to unworked rice and also rice, husked, glazed, polished or broken, but not otherwise worked.

Tariff Heading	*Rate of Import Duty (if any)*	
	Full	*Commonwealth (C)* *E.F.T.A. (E)*
10.01 Wheat and meslin (mixed wheat and rye):		
(A) Wheat	—	—
(B) Meslin	10%	C — E 10%
10.02 Rye	10%	C — E 10%
10.03 Barley	10%	C — E 10%
10.04 Oats	£0·1500 per cwt.	C — E £0·1500 per cwt
10.05 Maize:		
(A) Flat white	10%	C — E 10%
(B) Sweet corn on the cob	5%	C — E 5%
(C) Other	—	—
10.06 Rice:		
(A) Whole, further processed after husking	£0·1500 per cwt.	C — E £0·1500 per cwt
(B) Other	—	—
10.07 Buckwheat, millet, canary seed and grain sorghum; other cereals:		
(A) Grain sorghum	—	—
(B) Other	10%	C — E 10%

Chapter 11

Products of the Milling Industry; Malt and Starches; Gluten; Inulin

Notes

1. This Chapter does not cover:

(*a*) Roasted malt put up as coffee substitutes (heading No 09.01 or 21.01);

(*b*) Flours and meal prepared for use as infant food or for dietetic or culinary purposes of heading No. 19.02;

(*c*) Corn flakes and other products falling within heading No. 19.05;

(*d*) Pharmaceutical products (Chapter 30); or

(*e*) Starches having the character of perfumery, cosmetics or toilet preparations falling within heading No. 33.06.

2.(A) Products from the milling of the cereals listed in the table below fall within this Chapter if they have, by weight on the dry product:

(*a*) a starch content (determined by the modified Ewers polarimetric method) exceeding that indicated in Column 2; and

(*b*) an ash content (after deduction of any added minerals) not exceeding that indicated in Column 3.

Otherwise, they fall to be classified in heading No. 23.02.

(B) Products falling within this Chapter under the above provisions shall be classified in heading No. 11.01 (cereal flours) if the percentage passing through a silk gauze or man-made textile sieve with the aperture indicated in Column 4 or 5 is not less, by weight, than that shown against the cereal concerned.

Otherwise they fall to be classified in heading No. 11.02.

Cereal	*Starch content*	*Ash content*	*Rate of passage through a sieve with an aperture of*	
			315 *micrometres*	500 *micrometres*
(1)	(2)	(3)	(4)	(5)
Wheat and rye	45%	2·5%	80%	—
Barley	45%	3 %	80%	—
Oats	45%	5 %	80%	—
Maize and sorghum ...	45%	2 %	—	90%
Rice	45%	1·6%	80%	—
Buckwheat	45%	4 %	80%	—

Tariff Heading	*Rate of Import Duty (if any)*	
	Full	*Commonwealth (C)* *E.F.T.A. (E)*
11.01 Cereal flours:		
(A) Oat flour	£0·2500 per cwt.	C — E £0·2500 per cwt.
(B) Other	10%	C — E 10%

Tariff Heading	Rate of Import Duty (if any)	
	Full	Commonwealth (C) E.F.T.A. (E)
11.02 Cereal groats and cereal meal; other worked cereal grains (for example, rolled, flaked, polished, pearled or kibbled, but not further prepared), except husked, glazed, polished or broken rice; germ of cereals, whole, rolled, flaked or ground:		
(A) Oat groats; oatmeal; oats, ground, rolled or flaked	£0·2500 per cwt.	C — E £0·2500 per cwt.
(B) Pearled barley (including blocked, pot and pearl barley); flaked barley	20%	C — E 20%
(C) Other	10%	C — E 10%
11.03 Flours of the leguminous vegetables falling within heading No. 07.05	10%	C — E 10%
11.04 Flours of the fruits falling within any heading in Chapter 8	10%	C — E 10%
11.05 Flour, meal and flakes of potato	10%	C — E 10%
11.06 Flour and meal of sago and of manioc, arrowroot, salep and other roots and tubers falling within heading No. 07.06:		
(A) Of manioc or of sago	—	—
(B) Other	10%	C — E 10%
11.07 Malt, roasted or not	10%	—
11.08 Starches; inulin:		
(A) Rice, millet and buckwheat starches...	£0·3750 per cwt.	C — E £0·3750 per cwt.
(B) Maize and milo starches	7·5%	C — E 7·5%
(C) Sago starch	5%	C — E 5%
(D) Manioc starch	—	—
(E) Potato starch (farina)	—	—
(F) Other	10%	—
11.09 Wheat gluten, whether or not dried ...	10%	C — E 10%

Chapter 12

Oil Seeds and Oleaginous Fruit; Miscellaneous Grains, Seeds and Fruit; Industrial and Medical Plants; Straw and Fodder

Notes

1. Heading No. 12.01 is to be taken to apply, *inter alia*, to ground-nuts, soya beans, mustard seeds, oil poppy seeds, poppy seeds and copra. It is to be taken not to apply to coconuts or other products of heading No. 08.01 or to olives (Chapter 7 or Chapter 20).

2. For the purposes of heading No. 12.03, beet seeds, grass and other herbage seeds, seeds of ornamental flowers, vegetable seeds, seeds of forest trees, seeds of fruit trees, seeds of vetches and of lupines are to be regarded as seeds of a kind used for sowing.

Heading No. 12.03 is, however, to be taken not to apply to the following even if for sowing:

(*a*) Leguminous vegetables (Chapter 7);
(*b*) Spices and other products of Chapter 9;
(*c*) Cereals (Chapter 10); or
(*d*) Products falling within heading No. 12.01 or 12.07.

3. Heading No. 12.07 is to be taken to apply, *inter alia*, to the following plants or parts thereof: basil, borage, hyssop, all species of mint, rosemary, rue, sage and wormwood.

Heading No. 12.07 is, however, to be taken not to apply to:

(*a*) Oil seeds and oleaginous fruit (heading No. 12.01);
(*b*) Medicaments falling within Chapter 30;
(*c*) Perfumery or toilet preparations falling within Chapter 33; or
(*d*) Disinfectants, insecticides, fungicides, weed-killers or similar products falling within heading No. 38.11.

Tariff Heading	*Rate of Import Duty (if any)*		
	Full	*Commonwealth (C)* *E.F.T.A. (E)*	
12.01 Oil seeds and oleaginous fruit, whole or broken:			
(A) Cotton seed; rape seed; tung nuts; soya beans	—		—
(B) Sesamum seed	5%	C	—
		E	5%
(C) Castor seed	7·5%	C	—
		E	7·5%
(D) Mustard seed	10%		—
(E) Other	10%	C	—
		E	10%
12.02 Flours or meals of oil seeds or oleaginous fruit, non-defatted (excluding mustard flour)	10%	C	—
		E	10%
12.03 Seeds, fruit and spores, of a kind used for sowing:			
(A) Seeds of coniferous species	5%		—
(B) Other	10%	C	—
		E	10%
12.04 Sugar beet, whole or sliced, fresh, dried or powdered; sugar cane:			
(A) Sugar beet, dried or powdered ...	10%	C	—
		E	10%
(B) Other	10%	C	—
		E	10%

Tariff Heading	*Rate of Import Duty (if any)*	
	Full	*Commonwealth (C)* *E.F.T.A. (E)*
12.05 Chicory roots, fresh or dried, whole or cut, unroasted:		
(A) Dried	£0·9500 per cwt.	C £0·8395 per cwt. E £0·9500 per cwt.
(B) Other	£0·9500 per cwt.	C £0·8395 per cwt. E £0·9500 per cwt.
12.06 Hop cones and lupulin:		
(A) Hops	£4 per cwt.	C £2·6665 per cwt E £4 per cwt.
(B) Lupulin	10%	C — E 10%
12.07 Plants and parts (including seeds and fruit) of trees, bushes, shrubs or other plants, being goods of a kind used primarily in perfumery, in pharmacy, or for insecticidal, fungicidal or similar purposes, fresh or dried, whole, cut, crushed, ground or powdered:		
(A) The following in a dried state, not ground or powdered: Aconite root Agrimony herb Aletris root Angelica root Arnica flowers Balmony herb and leaves Bayberry bark Bearberry (*Uva ursi*) leaves Belladonna root, herb and leaves Beth root Black cohosh root Black haw bark Blood root Blue cohosh root Boldo leaves Boneset herb Burdock root Calamus rhizome Calumba root Cascara sagrada bark Cassia pods Cocillana bark Colchicum corms and seeds Colocynth pulp Comfrey leaves and roots Condurango bark Cubeb berries Damiana leaves Dandelion root	—	—

Tariff Heading	*Rate of Import Duty (if any)*	
	Full	*Commonwealth (C)* *E.F.T.A. (E)*
12.07 Plants and parts, etc.—*contd.*		
(A) The following in a dried state, not ground or powdered:—*contd.*		
Datura metel leaves, tops and seeds		
Deer tongue leaves		
Digitalis leaves and seeds		
Drosera		
Echinacea root		
Elder leaves and flowers		
Ephedra stems and branches		
Ergot of rye		
Euonymus bark		
Frangula bark		
Fringe tree bark		
Galanga root		
Gelsem root		
Gentian root		
Grindelia leaves and flowers		
Henbane (*Hyoscyamus muticus*)		
Henbane (*Hyoscyamus niger*)		
Horehound		
Hydrastis rhizomes		
Ipomoea (Orizaba jalap) root		
Jaborandi leaves		
Jalap root		
Kava kava rhizomes		
Krameria root		
Lavender flowers		
Leptandra root		
Lime tree flowers		
Liquorice root		
Lobelia		
Male fern (*Dryopteris filix-mas*) rhizomes		
Marshmallow leaves and roots		
Nux vomica seeds		
Orris root		
Passion flower		
Pichi tops		
Pleurisy root		
Podophyllum and Indian podophyllum rhizomes		
Prickly ash bark and berries		
Quince seeds		
Rauwolfia vomitoria root and root bark		
Rhubarb (*Rheum palmatum*) rhizomes		
Rhubarb (*Rheum rhaponticum*) rhizomes		
Rhus aromaticus bark		
Sabadilla seeds		
Sarsaparilla root		

Tariff Heading	Rate of Import Duty (if any)	
	Full	Commonwealth (C) E.F.T.A. (E)
12.07 Plants and parts, etc.—*contd.*		
(A) The following in a dried state, not ground or powdered:—*contd.*		
Sassafras bark		
Saw palmetto berries		
Scammony root		
Scullcap		
Senna leaves and pods		
Serpentaria root		
Slippery elm bark		
Squills		
Stillingia root		
Stone root		
Stramonium leaves		
Tonquin beans (or Cumaru seeds)		
Valerian root		
White pine bark		
Wild cherry bark		
Witch hazel (*Hamamelis*) bark and leaves		
Yerba Santa leaves	—	—
(B) Araroba, crude; chamomile flowers, dried; cinchona bark; coca leaves; cubé (*Lonchocarpus nicou*) bark and root; ipecacuanha root; pyrethrum flowers		
(C) Basil, borage, mint (excluding dried peppermint and penny royal), rosemary and sage:		
(1) Not ground or powdered... ...	£2·1000 per cwt.	C — E £2·1000 per cwt
(2) Ground or powdered	10%	C — E 10%
(D) Other	10%	—
12.08 Locust beans, fresh or dried, whether or not kibbled or ground, but not further prepared; fruit kernels and other vegetable products of a kind used primarily for human food, not falling within any other heading:		
(A) Locust bean kernels, whole and apricot kernels, whole	—	—
(B) Other	10%	C — E 10%
12.09 Cereal straw and husks, unprepared, or chopped but not otherwise prepared	—	—
12.10 Mangolds, swedes, fodder roots; hay, lucerne, clover, sainfoin, forage kale, lupines, vetches and similar forage products:		
(A) Hay	—	—
(B) Other	10%	C — E 10%

Chapter 13

Raw Vegetable Materials of a Kind Suitable for Use in Dyeing or in Tanning; Lacs; Gums, Resins and Other Vegetable Saps and Extracts

Note

Heading No. 13.03 is to be taken to apply, *inter alia*, to liquorice extract and extract of pyrethrum, extract of hops, extract of aloes and opium. The heading is to be taken not to apply to:

(*a*) Liquorice extract containing more than ten per cent. by weight of sucrose or when put up as confectionery (heading No. 17.04);

(*b*) Malt extract (heading No. 19.01);

(*c*) Extracts of coffee, tea or maté (heading No. 21.02);

(*d*) Alcoholic saps and extracts constituting beverages, and compound alcoholic preparations (known as " concentrated extracts ") for the manufacture of beverages (Chapter 22);

(*e*) Camphor, glycyrrhizin and other products of headings Nos. 29.13 and 29.41;

(*f*) Medicaments falling within heading No. 30.03 or blood-grouping reagents (heading No. 30.05);

(*g*) Tanning or dyeing extracts (heading No. 32.01 or 32.04);

(*h*) Essential oils, concretes, absolutes and resinoids (heading No. 33.01) or aqueous distillates and aqueous solutions of essential oils (heading No. 33.05); or

(*ij*) Rubber, balata, gutta-percha or similar natural gums (heading No. 40.01).

Tariff Heading	*Rate of Import Duty (if any)*	
	Full	*Commonwealth (C)* *E.F.T.A. (E)*
13.01 Raw vegetable materials of a kind used primarily in dyeing or in tanning:		
(A) Persian berries; gall nuts; sumach leaves; myrobalans	—	—
(B) Henna leaves, dried, not chopped or ground	—	—
(C) Tara (*Caesalpinia spinosa*) pods and powder	—	—
(D) Other	5%	—
13.02 Shellac, seed lac, stick lac and other lacs; natural gums, resins, gum-resins and balsams:		
(A) Shellac, seed lac, stick lac and other lacs; solid natural resins (other than gum resins and damar); balsam of Copaiba, balsam of Peru and balsam of Tolu; storax, crude	—	—
(B) Gum arabic; gum ammoniacum; gum asafetida; gum euphorbium; gum galbanum; gum myrrh; gum olibanum; gum opoponax; gum tragacanth	—	—
(C) Other	5%	—

Tariff Heading	Rate of Import Duty (if any)	
	Full	*Commonwealth (C)* *E.F.T.A. (E)*
13.03 Vegetable saps and extracts; pectic substances, pectinates and pectates; agar-agar and other mucilages and thickeners, derived from vegetable products:		
(A) Aloes; cassia pulp; liquorice extract	—	—
(B) Hop extracts	£4	C £2·6665 E —
	for every cwt. of hops which, in the opinion of the Commissioners of Customs and Excise, has been used in the manufacture of the extract.	
(C) Agar-agar	5%	—
(D) Other	10%	—

Chapter 14

Vegetable Plaiting and Carving Materials; Vegetable Products not elsewhere specified or included

Notes

1. This Chapter does not cover the following products which are to be classified in Section XI: vegetable materials or fibres of vegetable materials of a kind used primarily in the manufacture of textiles, however prepared, or other vegetable materials which have undergone treatment so as to render them suitable for use only as textile materials.

2. Heading No. 14.01 is to be taken to apply, *inter alia,* to split osier, reeds, bamboos and the like, to rattan cores and to drawn or split rattans. The heading is to be taken not to apply to chipwood (heading No. 44.09).

3. Heading No. 14.02 is to be taken not to apply to wood wool (heading No. 44.12).

4. Heading No. 14.03 is to be taken not to apply to prepared knots or tufts for broom or brush making (heading No. 96.03).

Tariff Heading	*Rate of Import Duty (if any)*	
	Full	*Commonwealth (C) E.F.T.A. (E)*
14.01 Vegetable materials of a kind used primarily for plaiting (for example, cereal straw, cleaned, bleached or dyed, osier, reeds, rushes, rattans, bamboos, raffia and lime bark):		
(A) Raffia; common reeds (*Phragmites communis*)	—	—
(B) Rattan cane	7·5%	—
(C) Other	10%	—
14.02 Vegetable materials, whether or not put up in a layer or between two layers of other material, of a kind used primarily as stuffing or as padding (for example, kapok, vegetable hair and eel-grass):		
(A) Eel-grass	—	—
(B) Other	5%	—
14.03 Vegetable materials of a kind used primarily in brushes or in brooms (for example, sorgho, piassava, couch-grass and istle), whether or not in bundles or hanks:		
(A) Vegetable fibres of the following varieties, not further dressed after scutching or decorticating: Bahia piassava (*Attalea funifera*) Para piassava (*Leopoldinia piassaba*) Gumati or Gomuti fibre (*Arenga saccharifera*) Madagascar fibre (*Dictyosperma fibrosum*)	—	—
(B) Mexican fibre or istle (*Agave lecheguilla* or *Agave funkiana*) scutched, decorticated, sorted to approximate length, or put up into tails with the butt end cut and the flag end untrimmed or roughly tip-trimmed, but not further prepared or dressed	—	—

Tariff Heading	*Rate of Import Duty (if any)*	
	Full	*Commonwealth (C) E.F.T.A. (E)*
14.03 Vegetable materials, etc.—*contd.*		
(C) Broomcorn and broomcorn tops (*Sorghum vulgare*)	—	—
(D) Other	5%	—
14.04 Hard seeds, pips, hulls and nuts, of a kind used for carving (for example, corozo and dom)	5%	—
14.05 Vegetable products not elsewhere specified or included:		
(A) Esparto, albardin grass and diss or vine-tie grass (*Ampelodesma tenax*)	—	—
(B) Seaweed, raw, unground, dried or bleached, but not further prepared or treated	—	—
(C) Quillaia bark, in a dried state, not ground or powdered	—	—
(D) Other	5%	—

SECTION III

Animal and Vegetable Fats and Oils and their Cleavage Products; Prepared Edible Fats; Animal and Vegetable Waxes

Chapter 15

Animal and Vegetable Fats and Oils and their Cleavage Products; Prepared Edible Fats; Animal and Vegetable Waxes

Notes

1. This Chapter does not cover:

(*a*) Pig fat or poultry fat of heading No. 02.05;

(*b*) Cocoa butter (fat or oil) (heading No. 18.04);

(*c*) Greaves (heading No. 23.01) and residues of heading No. 23.04;

(*d*) Fatty acids in an isolated state, prepared waxes, medicaments, paints, varnishes, soap, perfumery, cosmetics or toilet preparations, sulphonated oils or other goods falling within any heading in Section VI; or

(*e*) Factice derived from oils (heading No. 40.02).

2. Soapstocks, oil foots and dregs, stearin, wool grease and glycerol residues are to be aken to fall in heading No. 15.17.

Tariff Heading	*Rate of Import Duty (if any)*		
	Full	*Commonwealth (C) E.F.T.A. (E)*	
5.01 Lard, other pig fat and poultry fat, rendered or solvent-extracted:			
(A) Lard	—		—
(B) Other	10%	C	—
		E	10%
5.02 Fats of bovine cattle, sheep or goats, unrendered; rendered or solvent-extracted fats (including "*premier jus*") obtained from those unrendered fats	10%	C	—
		E	10%
.03 Lard stearin, oleostearin and tallow stearin; lard oil, oleo-oil and tallow oil, not emulsified or mixed or prepared in any way	10%	C	—
		E	10%
.04 Fats and oils, of fish and marine mammals, whether or not refined:			
(A) Whale oil (not including sperm oil)...	—		—
(B) Cod liver oil:			
(1) In casks, drums or other receptacles capable of holding at least 84 kilogrammes of cod liver oil and without internal containers	£0·0119 per kilogramme		—
(2) Other	£0·0158 per kilogramme		—
(C) Herring oil	5%		—
(D) Other	10%		—
.05 Wool grease and fatty substances derived therefrom (including lanolin)	5%		—

Tariff Heading	Rate of Import Duty (if any)	
	Full	Commonwealth (C) E.F.T.A. (E)
15.06 Other animal oils and fats (including neat's-foot oil and fats from bones or waste):		
(A) Bone oil; neat's-foot oil	10%	—
(B) Other	10%	C — E 10%
15.07 Fixed vegetable oils, fluid or solid, crude, refined or purified:		
(A) Oiticica oil, raw or liquid; stillingia oil (tallow-seed oil), raw; tung oil (china wood oil), raw	—	—
(B) Castor oil	12·5%	C — E 12·5%
(C) Coconut oil; ground-nut oil; linseed oil; rape oil; sesamum oil; soya bean oil; sunflower seed oil; safflower seed oil	15%	C — E 15%
(D) Olive oil extracted by means of solvents	10%	—
(E) Other	10%	C — E 10%
15.08 Animal and vegetable oils, boiled, oxidised, dehydrated, sulphurised, blown or polymerised by heat in vacuum or in inert gas, or otherwise modified:		
(A) Whale oil (not including sperm oil) ...	—	—
(B) Castor oil	12·5%	—
(C) Coconut oil; ground-nut oil; linseed oil; rape oil; sesamum oil; soya bean oil; sunflower seed oil; safflower seed oil	15%	—
(D) Other	10%	—
15.09 Degras	5%	—
15.10 Fatty acids; acid oils from refining; fatty alcohols:		
(A) Normal aliphatic alcohols containing eight or more carbon atoms in the molecule and having an iodine value not greater than 10:		
(1) Having a radioactivity of less than 3 disintegrations per minute per gramme of total carbon from β particles of energy between 18 kiloelectronvolts and 156 kiloelectronvolts and containing an even number of carbon atoms in each molecule, not less than 70 per cent. by weight of the alcohols having 12 and 14 carbon atoms per molecule and not more than 5 per cent. by weight of the alcohols having 8 carbon atoms per molecule	10%	—
(2) Other	20%	—
(B) Other	10%	—

Tariff Heading	*Rate of Import Duty (if any)*	
	Full	*Commonwealth (C)* *E.F.T.A. (E)*
15.11 Glycerol and glycerol lyes	5%	—
15.12 Animal or vegetable oils and fats, wholly or partly hydrogenated, or solidified or hardened by any other process, whether or not refined, but not further prepared:		
(A) Whale oil (not including sperm oil) ...	—	—
(B) Coconut oil; ground-nut oil; linseed oil; rape oil; sesamum oil; soya bean oil; sunflower seed oil; safflower seed oil	15%	C — E 15%
(C) Other:		
(1) Fats and oils wholly obtained from fish or marine mammals	10%	—
(2) Other	10%	C — E 10%
15.13 Margarine, imitation lard and other prepared edible fats	10%	C — E 10%
15.14 Spermaceti, crude, pressed or refined, whether or not coloured	5%	—
15.15 Beeswax and other insect waxes, whether or not coloured	5%	—
15.16 Vegetable waxes, whether or not coloured:		
(A) Carnauba wax; candelilla wax; esparto wax; ouricury wax	—	—
(B) Other	5%	—
15.17 Residues resulting from the treatment of fatty substances or animal or vegetable waxes	5%	—

SECTION IV

PREPARED FOODSTUFFS; BEVERAGES, SPIRITS AND VINEGAR; TOBACCO

Special note applying to subheadings only

The expression "sweetening matter" includes only glucose, sucrose and invert sugar. For the purposes of this Section the weight of sweetening matter contained in any goods shall be determined as follows: in so far as the sweetening matter is sucrose the weight shall be taken to be the actual weight of the sucrose or, if the sucrose is of a polarisation not exceeding 98°, 95 per cent. of the actual weight of the sucrose; in so far as it is liquid glucose the weight shall be taken to be 48 per cent. of the actual weight of the glucose; and in so far as it is solid glucose or invert sugar the weight shall be taken to be 75 per cent of the actual weight of the glucose or sugar.

Chapter 16

Preparations of Meat, of Fish, of Crustaceans or Molluscs

Note

This Chapter does not cover meat, meat offal, fish, crustaceans or molluscs, prepared or preserved by the processes specified in Chapters 2 and 3.

Tariff Heading	*Rate of Import Duty (if any)*		
	Full	*Commonwealth (C)* *E.F.T.A. (E)*	
16.01 Sausages and the like, of meat, meat offal or animal blood	15%	C E	— 15%
16.02 Other prepared or preserved meat or meat offal:			
(A) Pastes; poultry liver:			
(1) Pastes wholly of pork (including ham and bacon) apart from any curing or seasoning ingredients, in airtight containers	5%	C E	— 5%
(2) Pastes of meat offal, not canned...	15%		—
(3) Other	15%	C E	— 15%
(B) Other:			
(1) In airtight containers:			
(*a*) Pigs' tongues	—		—
(*b*) Ground or chopped pork (including ham and bacon):			
(i) Wholly of pork (including ham and bacon) apart from any curing or seasoning ingredients	5%		—
(ii) Wholly of pork (including ham and bacon) and farinaceous fillers apart from any curing or seasoning ingredients	10%		—
(iii) Other	10%	C E	— 10%

Tariff Heading	*Rate of Import Duty (if any)*	
	Full	*Commonwealth (C)* *E.F.T.A. (E)*
16.02 Other prepared or preserved meat or meat offal:—*contd.*		
(B) Other:—*contd.*		
(1) In airtight containers:—*contd.*		
(*c*) Beef and veal (including edible offals, but excluding tongues and jellied veal)	15%	C — E 15%
(*d*) Poultry (not including guinea fowl)	£0·0125 per lb.	C — E £0·0125 per lb.
(*e*) Other	10%	C — E 10%
(2) Not in airtight containers:		
(*a*) Hams, whole	—	—
(*b*) Other	15%	C — E 15%
16.03 Meat extracts and meat juices; fish extracts:		
(A) Meat extracts and meat juices derived wholly or in part from beef or veal	10%	C — E 10%
(B) Whalemeat extract	10%	—
(C) Other	10%	C — E 10%
16.04 Prepared or preserved fish, including caviar and caviar substitutes:		
(A) Caviar and caviar substitutes ...	30%	—
(B) Other roes	5%	—
(C) Salmon, canned	2·5%	—
(D) Tuna, canned	8%	—
(E) Other	10%	—
16.05 Crustaceans and molluscs, prepared or preserved:		
(A) Oysters	15%	—
(B) Clams, cockles, crabs, crawfish, crayfish, lobsters, mussels, Norway lobsters (Dublin Bay prawns), scallops (including queen scallops), shrimps, whelks and winkles:		
(1) Shrimps, canned	7·5%	—
(2) Other:		
(*a*) Frozen, or preserved in vinegar or airtight containers	10%	—
(*b*) Other	30%	—
(C) Prawns, canned	7·5%	—
(D) Other	10%	—

Chapter 17

Sugars and Sugar Confectionery

Notes

1. This Chapter does not cover:

(*a*) Sugar confectionery containing cocoa (heading No. 18.06);

(*b*) Chemically pure sugars (other than sucrose, glucose and lactose) and other products of heading No. 29.43; or

(*c*) Medicaments and other products of Chapter 30.

2. Chemically pure sucrose, whatever its origin, is to be classified in heading No. 17.01.

Tariff Heading	*Rate of Import Duty (if any)*	
	Full	*Commonwealth (C)* *E.F.T.A. (E)*
17.01 Beet sugar and cane sugar, solid:		
(A) Sugar of which the polarisation has at any time been reduced either as a result of the sugar having been treated (whether by the addition of invert sugar or otherwise) or as the result of the development of invert sugar or other substance in the sugar	£6·9000 per ton	C £1·0665 per ton E £6·9000 per ton
(B) Other:		
Of a polarisation:		
Exceeding—		
99°	£6·9000 per ton	C £1·0665 per ton E £6·9000 per ton
98° but not exceeding 99° ...	£6·9000 per ton	C — E As full rate.
97° but not exceeding 98° ...	£3·9415 per ton	C — E As full rate.
96° but not exceeding 97° ...	£3·8330 per ton	C — E As full rate.
95° but not exceeding 96° ...	£3·7330 per ton	C — E As full rate.
94° but not exceeding 95° ...	£3·6330 per ton	C — E As full rate.
93° but not exceeding 94° ...	£3·5250 per ton	C — E As full rate.
92° but not exceeding 93° ...	£3·4250 per ton	C — E As full rate.
91° but not exceeding 92° ...	£3·3250 per ton	C — E As full rate.
90° but not exceeding 91° ...	£3·2165 per ton	C — E As full rate.
89° but not exceeding 90° ...	£3·1165 per ton	C — E As full rate.
88° but not exceeding 89° ...	£3·0165 per ton	C — E As full rate.

Tariff Heading	*Rate of Import Duty (if any)*	
	Full	*Commonwealth (C)* *E.F.T.A. (E)*
17.01 Beet sugar and cane sugar, solid:—*contd.*		
(B) Other:—*contd.*		
87° but not exceeding 88° ...	£2·9250 per ton	C — E As full rate
86° but not exceeding 87° ...	£2·8415 per ton	
85° but not exceeding 86° ...	£2·7665 per ton	
84° but not exceeding 85° ...	£2·6915 per ton	
83° but not exceeding 84° ...	£2·6080 per ton	
82° but not exceeding 83° ...	£2·5330 per ton	
81° but not exceeding 82° ...	£2·4665 per ton	
80° but not exceeding 81° ...	£2·4000 per ton	
79° but not exceeding 80° ...	£2·3330 per ton	
78° but not exceeding 79° ...	£2·2580 per ton	
77° but not exceeding 78° ...	£2·1915 per ton	
76° but not exceeding 77° ...	£2·1250 per ton	
Not exceeding 76°	£2·0550 per ton	
17.02 Other sugars; sugar syrups; artificial honey (whether or not mixed with natural honey); caramel:		
(A) Sucrose sugar, solid, which can be completely tested by the polariscope:		
(1) Sugar of which the polarisation has at any time been reduced either as a result of the sugar having been treated (whether by the addition of invert sugar or otherwise) or as the result of the development of invert sugar or other substance in the sugar	£6·9000 per ton	C £1·0665 per ton E £6·9000 per ton
(2) Other:		
Of a polarisation:		
Exceeding—		
99°	£6·9000 per ton	C £1·0665 per ton E £6·9000 per ton
98° but not exceeding 99°...	£6·9000 per ton	C — E As full rate
97° but not exceeding 98°...	£3·9415 per ton	

Tariff Heading	Rate of Import Duty (if any)	
	Full	Commonwealth (C) E.F.T.A. (E)
17.02 Other sugars; sugar syrups, etc.—*contd.* (A) Sucrose sugar, solid, which can be completely tested by the polariscope: —*contd.* (2) Other:—*contd.*		
96° but not exceeding 97°...	£3·8330 per ton	C — E As full rate
95° but not exceeding 96°...	£3·7330 per ton	
94° but not exceeding 95°...	£3·6330 per ton	
93° but not exceeding 94°...	£3·5250 per ton	
92° but not exceeding 93°...	£3·4250 per ton	
91° but not exceeding 92°...	£3·3250 per ton	
90° but not exceeding 91°...	£3·2165 per ton	
89° but not exceeding 90°...	£3·1165 per ton	
88° but not exceeding 89°...	£3·0165 per ton	
87° but not exceeding 88°...	£2·9250 per ton	
86° but not exceeding 87°...	£2·8415 per ton	
85° but not exceeding 86°...	£2·7665 per ton	
84° but not exceeding 85°...	£2·6915 per ton	
83° but not exceeding 84°...	£2·6080 per ton	
82° but not exceeding 83°...	£2·5330 per ton	
81° but not exceeding 82°...	£2·4665 per ton	
80° but not exceeding 81°...	£2·4000 per ton	
79° but not exceeding 80°...	£2·3330 per ton	
78° but not exceeding 79°...	£2·2580 per ton	
77° but not exceeding 78°...	£2·1915 per ton	
76° but not exceeding 77°...	£2·1250 per ton	
Not exceeding 76°	£2·0550 per ton	
(B) Invert sugar; syrups containing sucrose: (1) Concentrated cane juice, partly inverted, of the kind known as high test, invert or fancy molasses	—	—

Tariff Heading	Rate of Import Duty (if any)	
	Full	Commonwealth (C) E.F.T.A. (E)
17.02 Other sugars; sugar syrups, etc.—*contd.*		
(B) Invert sugar; syrups containing sucrose:—*contd.*		
(2) Other:		
(*a*) Containing 70 per cent. or more by weight of sweetening matter	£0·1850 per cwt.	C — E £0·1850 per cwt.
(*b*) Containing less than 70 per cent. and more than 50 per cent. by weight of sweetening matter	£0·1330 per cwt.	C — E £0·1330 per cwt.
(*c*) Containing not more than 50 per cent. by weight of sweetening matter	£0·0645 per cwt.	C — E £0·0645 per cwt.
(C) Other sucrose and extracts from sucrose, other than dextrose, which cannot be completely tested by the polariscope	—	—
(D) Glucose:		
(1) Solid	£0·1850 per cwt.	C — E £0·1850 per cwt.
(2) Liquid	£0·1330 per cwt.	C — E £0·1330 per cwt.
(E) Artificial honey (whether or not mixed with natural honey)	£0·2500 per cwt.	C — E £0·2500 per cwt.
(F) Caramel:		
(1) Solid	£0·2915 per cwt.	C — E £0·2915 per cwt.
(2) Liquid	£0·2040 per cwt.	C — E £0·2040 per cwt.
(G) Other:		
(1) Lactose	£1·4000 per cwt.	C — E £1·4000 per cwt.
(2) Other	10%	C — E 10%
17.03 Molasses, whether or not decolourised ...	—	—
17.04 Sugar confectionery, not containing cocoa:		
(A) Fondants, pastes, creams and similar intermediate products, in bulk, containing 80 per cent. or more by weight of added sweetening matter:		
(1) Not flavoured or coloured ...	£0·2375 per cwt.	—

Tariff Heading	Rate of Import Duty (if any)	
	Full	Commonwealth (C) E.F.T.A. (E)
17.04 Sugar confectionery, etc.—*contd.*		
(A) Fondants, etc.—*contd.*		
(2) Other	£0·2375 per cwt. plus 10%, in addition to any revenue duty	—
(B) Other	£0·2375 per cwt. plus 10%, in addition to any revenue duty	—
17.05 Flavoured or coloured sugars, syrups and molasses, but not including fruit juices containing added sugar in any proportion:		
(A) Sucrose sugar, solid, which can be completely tested by the polariscope:		
(1) Sugar of which the polarisation has at any time been reduced either as a result of the sugar having been treated (whether by the addition of invert sugar or otherwise) or as the result of the development of invert sugar or other substance in the sugar	£6·9000 per ton	C £1·0665 per ton E £6·9000 per ton
(2) Other:		
Of a polarisation:		
Exceeding—		
99°	£6·9000 per ton	C £1·0665 per ton E £6·9000 per ton
98° but not exceeding 99°...	£6·9000 per ton	C — E As full rate
97° but not exceeding 98°...	£3·9415 per ton	
96° but not exceeding 97°...	£3·8330 per ton	
95° but not exceeding 96°...	£3·7330 per ton	
94° but not exceeding 95°...	£3·6330 per ton	
93° but not exceeding 94°...	£3·5250 per ton	
92° but not exceeding 93°...	£3·4250 per ton	
91° but not exceeding 92°...	£3·3250 per ton	
90° but not exceeding 91°...	£3·2165 per ton	
89° but not exceeding 90°...	£3·1165 per ton	

Tariff Heading	Rate of Import Duty (if any)	
	Full	Commonwealth (C) E.F.T.A. (E)
17.05 Flavoured or coloured sugars, syrups and molasses, etc.—*contd.*		
(A) Sucrose sugar, solid, which can be completely tested by the polariscope: —*contd.*		
(2) Other:—*contd.*		
88° but not exceeding 89° ...	£3·0165 per ton	C — E As full rate
87° but not exceeding 88° ...	£2·9250 per ton	
86° but not exceeding 87° ...	£2·8415 per ton	
85° but not exceeding 86° ...	£2·7665 per ton	
84° but not exceeding 85° ...	£2·6915 per ton	
83° but not exceeding 84° ...	£2·6080 per ton	
82° but not exceeding 83° ...	£2·5330 per ton	
81° but not exceeding 82° ...	£2·4665 per ton	
80° but not exceeding 81° ...	£2·4000 per ton	
79° but not exceeding 80° ...	£2·3330 per ton	
78° but not exceeding 79° ...	£2·2580 per ton	
77° but not exceeding 78° ...	£2·1915 per ton	
76° but not exceeding 77° ...	£2·1250 per ton	
Not exceeding 76°	£2·0550 per ton	
(B) Invert sugar; syrups containing sucrose:		
(1) Containing 70 per cent. or more by weight of sweetening matter	£0·1850 per cwt.	C — E £0·1850 per cwt.
(2) Containing less than 70 per cent. and more than 50 per cent. by weight of sweetening matter	£0·1330 per cwt.	C — E £0·1330 per cwt.
(3) Containing not more than 50 per cent. by weight of sweetening matter	£0·0645 per cwt.	C — E £0·0645 per cwt.
(C) Molasses; other sucrose and extracts from sucrose, other than dextrose, which cannot be completely tested by the polariscope	—	—

Tariff Heading	Rate of Import Duty (if any)	
	Full	*Commonwealth (C)* *E.F.T.A. (E)*
17.05 Flavoured or coloured sugars, syrups and molasses, etc.—*contd.*		
(D) Glucose:		
(1) Solid	£0·1850 per cwt.	C — E £0·1850 per cwt.
(2) Liquid	£0·1330 per cwt.	C — E £0·1330 per cwt.
(E) Other:		
(1) Lactose	£1·4000 per cwt.	C — E £1·4000 per cwt.
(2) Other	10%	C — E 10%

Chapter 18

Cocoa and Cocoa Preparations

Notes

1. This Chapter does not cover the preparations described in heading No. 19.02, 19.08, 22.02, 22.09 or 30.03 containing cocoa or chocolate.

2. Heading No. 18.06 includes sugar confectionery containing cocoa and, subject to Note 1 of this Chapter, other food preparations containing cocoa.

Tariff Heading	*Rate of Import Duty (if any)*	
	Full	*Commonwealth (C)* *E.F.T.A. (E)*
18.01 Cocoa beans, whole or broken, raw or roasted	—	—
18.02 Cocoa shells, husks, skins and waste ...	—	—
18.03 Cocoa paste (in bulk or in block), whether or not defatted	—	—
18.04 Cocoa butter (fat or oil)	—	—
18.05 Cocoa powder, unsweetened	—	—
18.06 Chocolate and other food preparations containing cocoa:		
(A) Chocolate milk crumb	£0·3000 per cwt.	—
(B) Cocoa powder with added sweetening matter	£0·2500 per cwt.	—
(C) Other:		
(1) Consisting wholly of cocoa and one or more of the following: added sweetening matter, milk, coffee, chicory, saccharin, salt, vanilla, vanillin and lecithin	£0·2000 per cwt.	—
(2) Other	£0·2000 per cwt. plus 10%, in addition to any revenue duty	—

Chapter 19

Preparations of Cereals, Flour or Starch; Pastrycooks' Products

Notes

1. This Chapter does not cover:

(*a*) Preparations of flour, starch or malt extract, of a kind used as infant food or for dietetic or culinary purposes, containing 50 per cent. or more by weight of cocoa (heading No. 18.06);

(*b*) Biscuits or other articles made from flour or from starch, specially prepared for use as animal feeding stuffs (heading No. 23.07); or

(*c*) Medicaments and other products of Chapter 30.

2. In this Chapter the expression " flour " includes the flour of fruits or of vegetables, and products of such flour are to be classified with similar products of cereal flour.

Tariff Heading	*Rate of Import Duty (if any)*		
	Full	*Commonwealth (C) E.F.T.A. (E)*	
19.01 Malt extract	10%		—
19.02 Preparations of flour, meal, starch or malt extract, of a kind used as infant food or for dietetic or culinary purposes, containing less than 50 per cent. by weight of cocoa	10%		—
19.03 Macaroni, spaghetti and similar products...	10%	C E	— 10%
19.04 Tapioca and sago; tapioca and sago substitutes obtained from potato or other starches	—		—
19.05 Prepared foods obtained by the swelling or roasting of cereals or cereal products (puffed rice, corn flakes and similar products)	10%		—
19.06 Communion wafers, empty cachets of a kind suitable for pharmaceutical use, sealing wafers, rice paper and similar products	10%		—
19.07 Bread, ships' biscuits and other ordinary bakers' wares, not containing added sugar, honey, eggs, fats, cheese or fruit:			
(A) Ships' biscuits, crumbs and rusks ...	10%		—
(B) Other	10%	C E	— 10%
19.08 Pastry, biscuits, cakes and other fine bakers' wares, whether or not containing cocoa in any proportion:			
(A) Biscuits, wafers, rusks, cakes without covering or filling, and pastry of the kind known as Danish pastry	10%		—
(B) Other	10%	C E	— 10%

Chapter 20

Preparations of Vegetables, Fruit or Other Parts of Plants

Notes

1. This Chapter does not cover:

(*a*) Vegetables or fruit, prepared or preserved by the processes specified in Chapters 7 and 8; or

(*b*) Fruit jellies, fruit pastes or the like in the form of sugar confectionery (heading No. 17.04) or chocolate confectionery (heading No. 18.06).

2. The vegetables of headings Nos. 20.01 and 20.02 are those which fall in headings Nos. 07.01 to 07.05 when imported in the states provided for in those headings.

3. Edible plants, parts of plants and roots of plants conserved in syrup (for example, ginger and angelica) are to be classified with the preserved fruit falling under heading No. 20.06; roasted ground-nuts are also to be classified in heading No. 20.06.

4. Tomato juice the dry weight content of which is 7 per cent. or more is to be classified under heading No. 20.02.

Tariff Heading	*Rate of Import Duty (if any)*		
	Full	*Commonwealth (C) E.F.T.A. (E)*	
20.01 Vegetables and fruit, prepared or preserved by vinegar or acetic acid, with or without sugar, whether or not containing salt, spices or mustard:			
(A) Beetroot, cauliflowers, onions ...	10%	C	—
		E	10%
(B) Other	10%	C	—
		E	10%
20.02 Vegetables prepared or preserved otherwise than by vinegar or acetic acid:			
(A) Olives	7·5%		—
(B) Tomato juice	5%	C	—
		E	5%
(C) Other:			
(1) In airtight containers:			
(*a*) Asparagus; beans (not being beans in pod); peas:			
(i) Beans, other than broad beans	10%	C	—
		E	10%
(ii) Other	10%	C	—
		E	10%
(*b*) Tomatoes:			
(i) Pulp or paste, wholly of tomato and water apart from salt or any other preserving, seasoning or flavouring ingredients, the dry weight of the tomato in any container being not less than 25 per cent. of the weight of its entire contents	—		—
(ii) Other	5%	C	—
		E	5%
(*c*) Potato crisps	15%		—

Tariff Heading	Rate of Import Duty (if any)		
	Full	Commonwealth (C) E.F.T.A. (E)	
20.02 Vegetables prepared or preserved, etc.— *contd.*			
(C) Other:—*contd.*			
(1) In airtight containers:—*contd.*			
(*d*) Kidney and runner beans; beetroot; broccoli and cauliflowers; Brussels sprouts; carrots; cucumbers (other than gherkins); herbs; lettuce and endive; mushrooms; dry-bulb onions and shallots; potatoes; rhubarb; spinach; turnips; mixtures containing any of these vegetables	15%	C E	— 15%
(*e*) Other	15%	C E	— 15%
(2) Not in airtight containers:			
(*a*) Potato crisps	10%		—
(*b*) Asparagus; broad, kidney and runner beans; beetroot; broccoli and cauliflowers; Brussels sprouts; carrots; cucumbers (other than gherkins); herbs; lettuce and endive; mushrooms; dry-bulb onions and shallots; peas; potatoes; rhubarb; spinach; turnips; mixtures containing any of these vegetables	10%	C E	— 10%
(*c*) Other	10%	C E	— 10%
20.03 Fruit preserved by freezing, containing added sugar:			
(A) Strawberries in containers, the contents of each weighing not less than 12 lb.	£0·8000 per cwt.	C E	— £0·8000 per cw[t.]
(B) Other	15%	C E	— 15%
20.04 Fruit, fruit-peel and parts of plants, preserved by sugar (drained, glacé or crystallised):			
(A) Apricots; figs; plums (including bullace, damsons, greengages and mirabelles, but not prunes)	£0·3750 per cwt.	C E	— £0·3750 per cw[t.]
(B) Cherries; fruit peels	20%	C E	— 20%
(C) Other	10%	C E	— 10%
20.05 Jams, fruit jellies, marmalades, fruit purée and fruit pastes, being cooked preparations, whether or not containing added sugar	10%	C E	— 10%

Tariff Heading	*Rate of Import Duty (if any)*	
	Full	*Commonwealth (C) E.F.T.A. (E)*
20.06 Fruit otherwise prepared or preserved, whether or not containing added sugar or spirit:		
(A) Apples:		
(1) Containing added sweetening matter	£0·1375 per cwt.	C — E £0·1375 per cwt.
(2) Other	£0·1750 per cwt. or 25%, whichever is the less	C — E £0·1750 per cwt. or 25%, whichever is the less
(B) Apricots:		
(1) Containing added sweetening matter	12%	C — E 12%
(2) Other	—	—
(C) Cherries:		
(1) Containing added sweetening matter:		
(*a*) Not stoned:		
(i) In a solution of sulphur dioxide	10%	C — E 10%
(ii) Other	15%	C — E 15%
(*b*) Stoned	10%	C — E 10%
(2) Other:		
(*a*) Canned	—	—
(*b*) Not canned	15%	C — E 15%
(D) Ginger	10%	C — E 10%
(E) Grapefruit	—	—
(F) Lemons:		
(1) Comminuted entire	—	—
(2) Other	15%	C — E 15%
(G) Loganberries:		
(1) Containing added sweetening matter	£0·2375 per cwt.	C — E £0·2375 per cwt.
(2) Other	15%	C — E 15%
(H) Nuts	7·5%	—
(IJ) Oranges, clementines, mandarins and tangerines:		
(1) Comminuted entire	—	—
(2) Pulp not containing the peel ...	—	—
(3) Other	7·5%	C — E 7·5%

Tariff Heading	*Rate of Import Duty (if any)*	
	Full	*Commonwealth (C)* *E.F.T.A. (E)*
20.06 Fruit otherwise prepared, etc.—*contd.*		
(K) Peaches:		
(1) Containing added sweetening matter	6%	C — E 6%
(2) Other	—	—
(L) Pears:		
(1) Containing added sweetening matter	12%	C — E 12%
(2) Other	15%	C — E 15%
(M) Pineapples	£0·2750 per cwt.	C — E £0·2750 per cwt.
(N) Strawberries:		
(1) Containing added sweetening matter	15%	C — E 15%
(2) Other	£0·7500 per cwt.	C — E £0·7500 per cwt.
(O) Mixtures of fruit (including fruit pulp) which contain not less than four separate descriptions of fruit (no one of which exceeds 60 per cent. by weight of the fruit in the mixture) and not less than 25 pieces of fruit per four ounce portion of the drained fruit	£0·1500 per cwt.	C — E £0·1500 per cwt.
(P) Mixtures of fruit (including fruit pulp) other than mixtures falling within subheading (O) above, which contain not less than four separate descriptions of fruit, in which each of at least four descriptions constitutes at least 8 per cent., and no one description represents more than 50 per cent. by weight, of all the fruit in the mixture:		
(1) Where not less than 80 per cent. by weight of all fruit in the mixture consists of all or any of the following fruits, viz. peaches, nectarines, pears, apricots, cherries	—	—
(2) Other	£0·1500 per cwt.	C — E £0·1500 per cwt
(Q) Other:		
(1) Blackberries, currants, gooseberries, plums (including bullace, damsons, greengages and mirabelles), raspberries	15%	C — E 15%
(2) Other	15%	C — E 15%

Tariff Heading	*Rate of Import Duty (if any)*	
	Full	*Commonwealth (C)* *E.F.T.A. (E)*
20.07 Fruit juices (including grape must) and vegetable juices, whether or not containing added sugar, but unfermented and not containing spirit:		
(A) Citrus fruit juices:		
(1) Grapefruit juice; orange, lemon, clementine, mandarin or tangerine juice whether containing the detached cells of the fruit or not:		
(*a*) Not containing more than 20 per cent. by weight of added sweetening matter	—	—
(*b*) Other	3%	C — E 3%
(2) Other:		
(*a*) Not containing more than 20 per cent. by weight of added sweetening matter	15%	C — E 15%
(*b*) Other	18%	C — E 18%
(B) Pineapple juice; tomato juice ...	5%	C — E 5%
(C) Apple juice; blackcurrant juice; pear juice	10%	C — E 10%
(D) Other	10%	C — E 10%

Chapter 21

Miscellaneous Edible Preparations

Notes

1. This Chapter does not cover:

(*a*) Mixed vegetables of heading No. 07.04;

(*b*) Roasted coffee substitutes containing coffee in any proportion (heading No. 09.01);

(*c*) Spices and other products of headings Nos. 09.04 to 09.10; or

(*d*) Yeast put up as a medicament and other products of heading No. 30.03.

2. Extracts of the substitutes referred to in Note 1 (*b*) above are to be classified in heading No. 21.02.

3. For the purposes of heading No. 21.05, the expression "homogenised composite food preparations" means preparations of a kind used as infant food or for dietetic purposes, consisting of a finely homogenised mixture of two or more basic ingredients such as meat (including meat offal), fish, vegetables and fruit. For the application of this definition, no account is to be taken of small quantities of any ingredients which may be added to the mixture for seasoning, preservation or other purposes. Such preparations may contain a small quantity of visible pieces of ingredients other than meat, meat offal or fish.

Tariff Heading	*Rate of Import Duty (if any)*	
	Full	*Commonwealth (C)* *E.F.T.A. (E)*
21.01 Roasted chicory and other roasted coffee substitutes; extracts, essences and concentrates thereof:		
(A) Roasted chicory, unmixed	£0·7000 per cwt.	C £0·6250 per cwt. E —
(B) Preparations consisting wholly or partly of extracts, essences or other concentrates of roasted chicory	£2 per cwt. on the total dry weight of the goods	C £1·7500 per cwt. on the total dry weight of the goods E —
(C) Other	10%	—
21.02 Extracts, essences or concentrates, of coffee, tea or maté; preparations with a basis of those extracts, essences or concentrates:		
(A) Extracts, essences or concentrates of coffee	£2 per cwt. on the total dry weight of the goods	C £1·7500 per cwt. on the total dry weight of the goods E —
(B) Preparations with a basis of extracts, essences or concentrates of coffee	£2 per cwt. on the total dry weight of the goods	C £1·7500 per cwt. on the total dry weight of the goods E —
(C) Other	10%	—
21.03 Mustard flour and prepared mustard ...	10%	—
21.04 Sauces; mixed condiments and mixed seasonings	10%	—

Tariff Heading	Rate of Import Duty (if any)		
	Full	Commonwealth (C) E.F.T.A. (E)	
21.05 Soups and broths, in liquid, solid or powder form; homogenised composite food preparations:			
(A) Soups and broths, in liquid, solid or powder form:			
(1) Canned, but not including tomato soups or dried soups	7·5%		—
(2) Other	10%		—
(B) Homogenised composite food preparations:			
(1) Containing meat or meat offal ...	10%	C	—
		E	10%
(2) Other:			
(*a*) Containing fish	10%		—
(*b*) Other	10%		—
21.06 Natural yeasts (active or inactive); prepared baking powders:			
(A) Natural yeasts	£0·3936 per 100 kilogrammes		—
(B) Prepared baking powders	10%		—
21.07 Food preparations not elsewhere specified or included:			
(A) Sweetfat (mixtures of edible fats and sugar)	10%	C	—
		E	10%
(B) Ice cream (containing fat) but not including ice cream powder	10%	C	—
		E	10%
(C) Mixtures of water and emulsifying agents with fat or oil (not including synthetic cream)	10%	C	—
		E	10%
(D) Coffee pastes (mixtures of ground, roasted coffee with vegetable fats, with or without other ingredients)	10%	C	—
		E	10%
(E) Ravioli, macaroni, spaghetti and the like, cooked (other than rice and other whole cereal grains), whether or not stuffed with other substances or admixed with tomato sauce:			
(1) Ravioli	5%	C	—
		E	5%
(2) Other	10%	C	—
		E	10%
(F) Yoghourt with added flavouring or fruit	10%	C	—
		E	10%
(G) Maize, including maize on cob (sweet corn), frozen or in airtight containers	5%		—
(H) Other:			
(1) Mixtures of chemicals and foodstuffs of a kind used in the preparation of human foodstuffs	8%		—
(2) Other	10%		—

Chapter 22

Beverages, Spirits and Vinegar

Notes

1. This Chapter does not cover:

(*a*) Sea water (heading No. 25.01);

(*b*) Distilled and conductivity water and water of similar purity (heading No. 28.58);

(*c*) Acetic acid of a concentration exceeding 10 per cent. by weight of acetic acid (heading No. 29.14);

(*d*) Medicaments of heading No. 30.03; or

(*e*) Perfumery or toilet preparations (Chapter 33).

2. For the purposes of headings Nos. 22.08 and 22.09, the alcoholic strength is to be taken to be that shown on test by Sikes' hydrometer.

Tariff Heading	*Rate of Import Duty (if any)*	
	Full	*Commonwealth (C) E.F.T.A. (E)*
22.01 Waters, including spa waters and aerated waters; ice and snow:		
(A) Waters, including spa waters and aerated waters	5%	—
(B) Other	—	—
22.02 Lemonade, flavoured spa waters and flavoured aerated waters, and other non-alcoholic beverages, not including fruit and vegetable juices falling within heading No. 20.07	10%	—
22.03 Beer made from malt:		
(A) Of any description (other than mum, spruce, black beer, Berlin white beer or other preparations of a similar character, of an original gravity of 1200° or more) where the worts thereof were before fermentation of a gravity:		
(1) Of 1030° or less	—	—
(2) Exceeding 1030°	—	—
(B) Of the descriptions called or similar to mum, spruce, black beer, Berlin white beer, or other preparations of a similar character, where the worts thereof were before fermentation of a gravity of 1200° or more	—	—
22.04 Grape must, in fermentation or with fermentation arrested otherwise than by the addition of alcohol	10%	C — E 10%

Tariff Heading	Rate of Import Duty (if any)	
	Full	Commonwealth (C) E.F.T.A. (E)
22.05 Wine of fresh grapes (including grape must with fermentation arrested by the addition of alcohol):		
(A) Light wine:		
(1) Still:		
(a) Not in bottle	—	—
(b) In bottle	—	—
(2) Sparkling	—	—
(B) Wine of the Republic of Ireland exceeding 27° but not exceeding 32° of proof spirit:		
(1) Still	—	—
(2) Sparkling	—	—
(C) Other wine not exceeding 42°:		
(1) Still:		
(a) Not in bottle	—	—
(b) In bottle	—	—
(2) Sparkling	—	—
(D) Wine exceeding 42°:		
(1) Still:		
(a) Not in bottle	—	—
(b) In bottle	—	—
(2) Sparkling	—	—
" Light wine " means wine not exceeding 25 degrees or, in the case of wine qualifying for Commonwealth preference or Irish Republic rates, 27 degrees of proof spirit		
22.06 Vermouths, and other wines of fresh grapes flavoured with aromatic extracts:		
(A) Light wine:		
(1) Still:		
(a) Not in bottle	—	—
(b) In bottle	—	—
(2) Sparkling	—	—
(B) Wine of the Republic of Ireland exceeding 27° but not exceeding 32° of proof spirit:		
(1) Still	—	—
(2) Sparkling	—	—
(C) Other wine not exceeding 42°:		
(1) Still:		
(a) Not in bottle	—	—
(b) In bottle	—	—
(2) Sparkling	—	—
(D) Wine exceeding 42°:		
(1) Still:		
(a) Not in bottle	—	—
(b) In bottle	—	—
(2) Sparkling	—	—
" Light wine " means wine not exceeding 25 degrees or, in the case of wine qualifying for Commonwealth preference or Irish Republic rates, 27 degrees of proof spirit		

Tariff Heading	*Rate of Import Duty (if any)*		
	Full	*Commonwealth (C)* *E.F.T.A. (E)*	
22.07 Other fermented beverages (for example, cider, perry and mead):			
(A) Beer:			
(1) Of any description (other than mum, spruce, black beer, Berlin white beer, or other preparations of a similar character, of an original gravity of 1200° or more) where the worts thereof were before fermentation of a gravity:			
(*a*) Of 1030° or less	—		—
(*b*) Exceeding 1030°	—		—
(2) Of the descriptions called or similar to mum, spruce, black beer, Berlin white beer, or other preparations of a similar character where the worts thereof were before fermentation of a gravity of 1200° or more	—		—
(B) Wine:			
(1) Light wine:			
(*a*) Still:			
(i) Not in bottle	—		—
(ii) In bottle	—		—
(*b*) Sparkling	—		—
(2) Wine of the Republic of Ireland exceeding 27° but not exceeding 32° of proof spirit:			
(*a*) Still	—		—
(*b*) Sparkling	—		—
(3) Other wine not exceeding 42°:			
(*a*) Still:			
(i) Not in bottle	—		—
(ii) In bottle	—		—
(*b*) Sparkling	—		—
(4) Wine exceeding 42°:			
(*a*) Still:			
(i) Not in bottle	—		—
(ii) In bottle	—		—
(*b*) Sparkling	—		—
" Light wine " means wine not exceeding 25 degrees or, in the case of wine qualifying for Commonwealth preference or Irish Republic rates, 27 degrees of proof spirit			
(C) Cider and perry containing no added spirit or spirit derived from the addition of sugar	10%	C E	— 10%
(D) Other	10%	C E	— 10%

Tariff Heading	Rate of Import Duty (if any)	
	Full	Commonwealth (C) E.F T.A. (E)
22.08 Ethyl alcohol (ethanol) or neutral spirits, undenatured, of a strength of one hundred and forty degrees proof or higher; denatured spirits (including ethyl alcohol (ethanol) and neutral spirits) of any strength:		
(A) If warehoused 3 years or more ...	—	—
(B) If not warehoused, or warehoused less than 3 years	—	—
22.09 Spirits (other than those of heading No. 22.08); liqueurs and other spirituous beverages; compound alcoholic preparations (known as " concentrated extracts ") for the manufacture of beverages:		
(A) Liqueurs, cordials, mixtures and other preparations in bottle, entered in such a manner as to indicate that the strength is not to be tested:		
(1) If warehoused 3 years or more ...	—	—
(2) If not warehoused, or warehoused less than 3 years	—	—
(B) Other spirits (including spirituous beverages having the character of spirits, and liqueurs):		
(1) If warehoused 3 years or more ...	—	—
(2) If not warehoused, or warehoused less than 3 years	—	—
(C) Other	5%	—
22.10 Vinegar and substitutes for vinegar ...	23%	—

Chapter 23

Residues and Waste from the Food Industries; Prepared Animal Fodder

Tariff Heading	*Rate of Import Duty (if any)*	
	Full	*Commonwealth (C) E.F.T.A. (E)*
23.01 Flours and meals, of meat, offals, fish, crustaceans or molluscs, unfit for human consumption; greaves:		
(A) Herring meal	—	—
(B) Flours and meals of meat or offals ...	10%	—
(C) Other	10%	—
23.02 Bran, sharps and other residues derived from the sifting, milling or working of cereals or of leguminous vegetables	10%	C — E 10%
23.03 Beet-pulp, bagasse and other waste of sugar manufacture; brewing and distilling dregs and waste; residues of starch manufacture and similar residues:		
(A) Bagasse	—	—
(B) Other	10%	C — E 10%
23.04 Oil-cake and other residues (except dregs) resulting from the extraction of vegetable oils	10%	C — E 10%
23.05 Wine lees; argol:		
(A) Wine lees:		
(1) Light wine	—	—
(2) Wine of the Republic of Ireland exceeding 27° but not exceeding 32° of proof spirit	—	—
(3) Other wine not exceeding 42° of proof spirit	—	—
(4) Wine exceeding 42° of proof spirit	—	—
"Light wine" means wine not exceeding 25 degrees or in the case of wine qualifying for Commonwealth preference or Irish Republic rates, 27 degrees of proof spirit		
(B) Other	—	—
23.06 Products of vegetable origin of a kind used for animal food, not elsewhere specified or included:		
(A) Dried apple pomace, unground ...	—	—
(B) Dried citrus fruit waste	—	—
(C) Other	10%	C — E 10%

Tariff Heading	Rate of Import Duty (if any)	
	Full	*Commonwealth (C) E.F.T.A. (E)*
3.07 Sweetened forage; other preparations of a kind used in animal feeding:		
(A) Vitamin supplements:		
(1) Where the vitamin content consists of natural vitamin concentrates	5%	C — E 5%
(2) Other	22% of the value of the vitamin content (other than natural vitamin concentrates) or 5%, whichever is the greater	C — E 22% of the value of the vitamin content (other than natural vitamin concentrates) or 5%, whichever is the greater
(B) Liquefied herring wholly of herring apart from preserving and liquefying ingredients	—	—
(C) Other:		
(1) Fish solubles	10%	—
(2) Other	10%	C — E 10%

Chapter 24

Tobacco

Tariff Heading	*Rate of Import Duty (if any)*	
	Full	*Commonwealth (C) E.F.T.A. (E)*
24.01 Unmanufactured tobacco; tobacco refuse:		
(A) Containing 10 per cent. or more by weight of moisture	—	—
(B) Other	—	—
24.02 Manufactured tobacco; tobacco extracts and essences:		
(A) Manufactured tobacco:		
(1) Cigars	—	—
(2) Cigarettes	—	—
(3) Cavendish or negrohead:		
(*a*) Manufactured in bond ...	—	—
(*b*) Other	—	—
(4) Snuff and snuff work (including tobacco dust or powder and ground tobacco)	—	—
(5) Other	—	—
(B) Extracts and essences	—	—

SECTION V

MINERAL PRODUCTS

Chapter 25

Salt; Sulphur ; Earths and Stone; Plastering Materials, Lime and Cement

Notes

1. Except where the context otherwise requires, the headings of this Chapter are to be aken to apply only to goods which are in the crude state, or which have been washed including washing with chemical substances to remove impurities provided that this does ıot change the character of the product), crushed, ground, powdered, levigated, sifted, creened, concentrated by flotation, magnetic separation or other mechanical or physical processes (not including crystallisation) but not calcined or subjected to any further process ther than a process specially mentioned in any heading in respect of the goods described herein.

2. This Chapter does not cover:

(*a*) Sublimed sulphur, precipitated sulphur or colloidal sulphur (heading No. 28.02);

(*b*) Ferrous earth colours containing 70 per cent. or more by weight of combined iron evaluated as Fe_2O_3 (heading No. 28.23);

(*c*) Medicaments and other products of Chapter 30;

(*d*) Perfumery, cosmetics or toilet preparations of heading No. 33.06;

(*e*) Road and paving setts, curbs and flagstones (heading No. 68.01), mosaic cubes (heading No. 68.02) and roofing, facing and damp course slates (heading No. 68.03);

(*f*) Precious or semi-precious stones (Chapter 71);

(*g*) Cultured sodium chloride crystals (other than optical elements) weighing not less than two and a half grammes each, of heading No. 38.19; optical elements of sodium chloride (heading No. 90.01); or

(*h*) Writing, drawing, tailors' and billiards chalks (heading No. 98.05).

Tariff Heading	*Rate of Import Duty (if any)*	
	Full	*Commonwealth (C)* *E.F.T.A. (E)*
5.01 Common salt (including rock salt, sea salt and table salt); pure sodium chloride; salt liquors; sea water:		
(A) Fishery salt, being salt in coarse crystals of a kind used for curing fish	—	—
(B) Other	5%	—
5.02 Iron pyrites (including cupreous iron pyrites), unroasted	—	—
5.03 Sulphur of all kinds, other than sublimed sulphur, precipitated sulphur and colloidal sulphur	—	—

Tariff Heading	*Rate of Import Duty (if any)*	
	Full	*Commonwealth (C)* *E.F.T.A. (E)*
25.04 Natural graphite:		
(A) Flake graphite containing not less than 83 per cent. by weight of carbon and of which not more than 15 per cent. by weight passes a sieve having a nominal width of aperture of 105 micrometres, and being graphite such that, if a cylindrical container with an internal diameter of 5 centimetres and a capacity of 100 cubic centimetres is filled by funnelling the graphite through a circular orifice of 13 millimetres diameter placed centrally 63 millimetres above the top of the container, the contents of the container will have a density of less than 60 grammes per 100 cubic centimetres	—	—
(B) Other	10%	—
25.05 Natural sands of all kinds, whether or not coloured, other than metal-bearing sands falling within heading No. 26.01	5%	—
25.06 Quartz (other than natural sands); quartzite, including quartzite not further worked than roughly split, roughly squared or squared by sawing:		
(A) Quartz:		
(1) Ground or powdered	5%	—
(2) Other	—	—
(B) Quartzite	5%	—
25.07 Clay (for example, kaolin and bentonite), andalusite, kyanite and sillimanite, whether or not calcined, but not including expanded clays falling within heading No. 68.07; mullite; chamotte and dinas earths:		
(A) Attapulgite clay of which not more than 0·1 per cent. by weight of the dry material is retained, after sieving in the wet state, on a sieve having a nominal width of aperture of 45 micrometres	—	—
(B) Other	4%	—
25.08 Chalk:		
(A) Whiting...	10%	—
(B) Other	5%	—
25.09 Earth colours, whether or not calcined or mixed together; natural micaceous iron oxides	5%	—

Tariff Heading	Rate of Import Duty (if any)	
	Full	Commonwealth (C) E.F.T.A. (E)
25.10 Natural mineral calcium phosphates, natural aluminium calcium phosphates, apatite and phosphatic chalk	—	—
25.11 Natural barium sulphate (barytes); natural barium carbonate (witherite), whether or not calcined	5%	—
25.12 Siliceous fossil meals and similar siliceous earths (for example, kieselguhr, tripolite or diatomite), whether or not calcined, of an apparent specific gravity of 1 or less:		
(A) Not bagged or otherwise packed, containing not less than 35 per cent. by weight of moisture	—	—
(B) Other	4%	—
25.13 Pumice stone; emery; natural corundum, natural garnet and other natural abrasives, whether or not heat-treated:		
(A) Garnet	—	—
(B) Emery, not crushed, ground, powdered or graded	—	—
(C) Other	5%	—
25.14 Slate, including slate not further worked than roughly split, roughly squared or squared by sawing	5%	—
25.15 Marble, travertine, ecaussine and other calcareous monumental and building stone of an apparent specific gravity of 2·5 or more and alabaster, including such stone not further worked than roughly split, roughly squared or squared by sawing	5%	—
25.16 Granite, porphyry, basalt, sandstone and other monumental and building stone, including such stone not further worked than roughly split, roughly squared or squared by sawing:		
(A) Granite:		
(1) Not sawn	5%	—
(2) Sawn on three or more sides:		
(a) Pieces of a volume not exceeding 500 cubic centimetres	—	—
(b) Other	25%	—
(3) Other	10%	—

Tariff Heading	Rate of Import Duty (if any)	
	Full	Commonwealth (C) E.F.T.A. (E)
25.16 Granite, etc.—*contd.*		
(B) Other	5%	—
25.17 Pebbles and crushed or broken stone (whether or not heat-treated), gravel, macadam and tarred macadam, of a kind commonly used for concrete aggregates, for road metalling or for railway or other ballast; flint and shingle, whether or not heat-treated; granules and chippings (whether or not heat-treated) and powder of stones falling within heading No. 25.15 or 25.16:		
(A) Flint, not crushed, ground or powdered	—	—
(B) Chippings of calcareous stones falling within heading No. 25.15 or 25.16 and chippings of serpentine	—	—
(C) Other	5%	—
25.18 Dolomite, whether or not calcined, including dolomite not further worked than roughly split, roughly squared or squared by sawing; agglomerated dolomite (including tarred dolomite):		
(A) Calcined dolomite which, on boiling with 2N hydrochloric acid, yields not more than 0·3 per cent. by weight of insoluble residue	—	—
(B) Other	5%	—
25.19 Natural magnesium carbonate (magnesite), whether or not calcined:		
(A) Dead-burned	5%	—
(B) Other	—	—
25.20 Gypsum; anhydrite; calcined gypsum, and plasters with a basis of calcium sulphate, whether or not coloured, but not including plasters specially prepared for use in dentistry	5%	—
25.21 Limestone flux and calcareous stone, commonly used for the manufacture of lime or cement	5%	—
25.22 Quicklime, slaked lime and hydraulic lime	5%	—
25.23 Portland cement, high alumina cement, slag cement, supersulphate cement and similar hydraulic cements, whether or not coloured or in the form of clinker	5%	—
25.24 Asbestos	10%	—
25.25 Meerschaum (whether or not in polished pieces) and amber; agglomerated meerschaum and agglomerated amber, in plates, rods, sticks or similar forms, not worked after moulding; jet	5%	—

Tariff Heading	Rate of Import Duty (if any)	
	Full	*Commonwealth (C) E.F.T.A. (E)*
25.26 Mica, including splittings; mica waste:		
(A) Blocks, films and splittings	—	—
(B) Other	5%	—
25.27 Natural steatite, including natural steatite not further worked than roughly split, roughly squared or squared by sawing; talc	—	—
25.28 Natural cryolite and natural chiolite ...	—	—
25.29 Natural arsenic sulphides	4%	—
25.30 Crude natural borates and concentrates thereof (calcined or not), but not including borates separated from natural brine; crude natural boric acid containing not more than 85 per cent. of H_3BO_3 calculated on the dry weight	—	—
25.31 Felspar, leucite, nepheline and nepheline syenite; fluorspar:		
(A) Felspar:		
(1) Ground or powdered	2·5%	—
(2) Other	—	—
(B) Other	5%	—
25.32 Strontianite (whether or not calcined), other than strontium oxide; mineral substances not elsewhere specified or included; broken pottery:		
(A) Siliceous fossil meals and similar siliceous earths, not bagged or otherwise packed, containing not less than 35 per cent. by weight of moisture	—	—
(B) Perlite, obsidian and pitchstone, crushed, ground, powdered or graded	—	—
(C) Rare earth minerals and concentrates thereof containing not less than 40 per cent., and not more than 95 per cent., by weight of rare earth compounds calculated as rare earth oxides	—	—
(D) Mineral substances containing not less than 20 per cent. by weight of talc and not less than 25 per cent. by weight and not more than 65 per cent. by weight of tremolite	—	—
(E) Other	5%	—

Chapter 26

Metallic Ores, Slag and Ash

Notes

1. This Chapter does not cover:

(*a*) Slag and similar industrial waste prepared as macadam (heading No. 25.17);

(*b*) Natural magnesium carbonate (magnesite), whether or not calcined (heading No. 25.19);

(*c*) Basic slag of Chapter 31;

(*d*) Slag wool, rock wool or similar mineral wools (heading No. 68.07);

(*e*) Goldsmiths', silversmiths' and jewellers' sweepings, residues, lemels and other waste and scrap, of precious metal (heading No. 71.11); or

(*f*) Copper, nickel or cobalt mattes produced by any process of smelting (Section XV).

2. For the purposes of heading No. 26.01, the term " metallic ores " means minerals of those mineralogical species used for the extraction on an industrial scale of mercury, of the metals of heading No. 28.50 or of the metals of Section XIV or XV; minerals which have undergone a process rendering them more suitable for a purpose other than the extraction of metal on an industrial scale are, however, excluded from the heading.

3. Heading No. 26.03 is to be taken to apply only to ash and residues of a kind used on an industrial scale either for the extraction of metals or as a basis for the manufacture of chemical compounds of metals.

Tariff Heading	*Rate of Import Duty (if any)*	
	Full	*Commonwealth (C)* *E.F.T.A. (E)*
26.01 Metallic ores and concentrates thereof; roasted iron pyrites, including roasted cupreous iron pyrites	—	—
26.02 Slag, dross, scalings and similar waste from the manufacture of iron or steel	—	—
26.03 Ash and residues (other than from the manufacture of iron or steel), containing metals or metallic compounds	—	—
26.04 Other slag and ash, including kelp ...	—	—

Chapter 27

Mineral Fuels, Mineral Oils and Products of their Distillation; Bituminous Substances; Mineral Waxes

Notes

1. This Chapter does not cover:

(*a*) Separate chemically defined organic compounds, other than chemically pure methane and propane which are to be classified in heading No. 27.11;

(*b*) Medicaments falling within heading No. 30.03; or

(*c*) Mixed unsaturated hydrocarbons falling within heading No. 33.01, 33.02, 33.04 or 38.07.

2. In heading No. 27.07 the expression " similar oils and products obtained by other processes " is to be taken to refer to products similar to those obtained by the distillation of high temperature coal tar but which are obtained by the distillation of low temperature coal tar or other mineral tars, by processing petroleum or by any other process, provided that the weight of the aromatic constituents exceeds that of non-aromatic constituents.

3. References in heading No. 27.10 to petroleum oils and oils obtained from bituminous minerals are to be taken to include not only petroleum oils and oils obtained from bituminous minerals but also similar oils, as well as those consisting of mixed unsaturated hydrocarbons, obtained by any process, provided that the weight of the non-aromatic constituents exceeds that of the aromatic constituents.

4. Heading No. 27.13 is to be taken to include not only paraffin wax and the other products specified therein, but also similar products obtained by synthesis or by other processes.

Special note applying to subheadings only

Throughout this Schedule:

(*a*) " Hydrocarbon oil " means petroleum oils, coal tar, and oils produced from coal, shale, peat or any other bituminous substance, and all liquid hydrocarbons, but does not include such hydrocarbons or bituminous or asphaltic substances as are—

(i) solid or semi-solid at a temperature of 60° F.; or

(ii) gaseous at a temperature of 60° F. and under a pressure of one atmosphere.

The expression also includes products which, apart from small proportions of colouring matter or of additives, consist wholly of hydrocarbon oil as defined above. For this purpose, " additive " means any substance commonly added in small proportions to hydrocarbon oil for the purpose of improving or modifying its quality or characteristics as a fuel or a lubricant.

(*b*) " Light oil " has the meaning given by section 1(3) of the Hydrocarbon Oil (Customs and Excise) Act 1971 as for the time being in force.

(*c*) Except as provided in paragraph (*a*) of this Note, references to hydrocarbon oil do not include mixtures or combinations of such oil with other substances.

Tariff Heading	*Rate of Import Duty (if any)*	
	Full	*Commonwealth (C)* *E.F.T.A. (E)*
27.01 Coal; briquettes, ovoids and similar solid fuels manufactured from coal	—	—
27.02 Lignite, whether or not agglomerated ...	—	—
27.03 Peat (including peat litter), whether or not agglomerated	8%	—

Tariff Heading	Rate of Import Duty (if any)	
	Full	Commonwealth (C) E.F.T.A. (E)
27.04 Coke and semi-coke of coal, of lignite or of peat	—	—
27.05 Retort carbon	4%	—
27.05 (*bis*) Coal gas, water gas, producer gas and similar gases	4%	—
27.06 Tar distilled from coal, from lignite or from peat, and other mineral tars, including partially distilled tars and blends of pitch with creosote oils or with other coal tar distillation products:		
(A) Hydrocarbon oil	—	—
(B) Other	4%	—
27.07 Oils and other products of the distillation of high temperature coal tars and similar oils and products obtained by other processes (for example, benzole, creosote, cresylic acid and solvent naphtha):		
(A) Hydrocarbon oil	—	—
(B) Other	5%	—
27.08 Pitch and pitch coke, obtained from coal tar or from other mineral tars	5%	—
27.09 Petroleum oils and oils obtained from bituminous minerals, crude:		
(A) Solid and semi-solid petroleum oils...	—	—
(B) Other	—	—
27.10 Petroleum oils and oils obtained from bituminous minerals, other than crude; preparations not elsewhere specified or included, containing not less than 70 per cent. by weight of petroleum oils or of oils obtained from bituminous minerals, these oils being the basic constituents of the preparations:		
(A) Hydrocarbon oil	—	—
(B) Other:		
(1) Containing light oil	3%, in addition to any hydrocarbon oil duty	—
(2) Other	5%	—
27.11 Petroleum gases and other gaseous hydrocarbons:		
(A) Methane	—	—
(B) Ethylene of a purity not less than 90 per cent.; propane of a purity not less than 95 per cent.	8%	—
(C) Propylene of a purity not less than 90 per cent.	23%	—
(D) Other	5%	—

Tariff Heading	Rate of Import Duty (if any)	
	Full	Commonwealth (C) E.F.T.A. (E)
27.12 Petroleum jelly:		
(A) Hydrocarbon oil	—	—
(B) Other	5%	—
27.13 Paraffin wax, micro-crystalline wax, slack wax, ozokerite, lignite wax, peat wax and other mineral waxes, whether or not coloured:		
(A) Lignite (montan) wax	—	—
(B) Petroleum waxes containing not less than 10 per cent. by weight of oil when determined by the Institute of Petroleum Method No. 158/69	—	—
(C) Paraffin wax and micro-crystalline wax	10%	—
(D) Other	5%	—
27.14 Petroleum bitumen, petroleum coke and other residues of petroleum oils or of oils obtained from bituminous minerals:		
(A) Petroleum coke, calcined, not containing by weight more than 0·8 per cent. of ash, 0·01 per cent. of manganese, 0·02 per cent. of nickel or of vanadium, one part per million of boron or 50 parts per million of titanium	—	—
(B) Hydrocarbon oil	—	—
(C) Other	5%	—
27.15 Bitumen and asphalt, natural; bituminous shale, asphaltic rock and tar sands	5%	—
27.16 Bituminous mixtures based on natural asphalt, on natural bitumen, on petroleum bitumen, on mineral tar or on mineral tar pitch (for example, bituminous mastics, cut-backs):		
(A) Hydrocarbon oil	—	—
(B) Other	5%	—

SECTION VI

Products of the Chemical and Allied Industries

Notes

1. (*a*) Goods (other than radio-active ores) answering to a description in heading No. 28.50 or 28.51 are to be classified in those headings and in no other heading of this Schedule.

(*b*) Subject to paragraph (*a*) above, goods answering to a description in heading No. 28.49 or 28.52 are to be classified in those headings and in no other heading of this Section.

2. Subject to Note 1 above, goods classifiable within heading No. 30.03, 30.04, 30.05, 32.09, 33.06, 35.06, 37.08 or 38.11 by reason of being put up in measured doses or for sale by retail are to be classified in those headings and in no other heading of this Schedule.

Chapter 28

Inorganic Chemicals; Organic and Inorganic Compounds of Precious Metals, of Rare Earth Metals, of Radio-Active Elements and of Isotopes

Notes

1. Except where their context or these Notes otherwise require, the headings of this Chapter are to be taken to apply only to:

(*a*) Separate chemical elements and separate chemically defined compounds, whether or not containing impurities;

(*b*) Products mentioned in (*a*) above dissolved in water;

(*c*) Products mentioned in (*a*) above dissolved in other solvents provided that the solution constitutes a normal and necessary method of putting up these products adopted solely for reasons of safety or for transport and that the solvent does not render the product particularly suitable for some types of use rather than for general use;

(*d*) The products mentioned in (*a*), (*b*) or (*c*) above with an added stabiliser necessary for their preservation or transport;

(*e*) The products mentioned in (*a*), (*b*), (*c*) or (*d*) above with an added anti-dusting agent or a colouring substance added to facilitate their identification or for safety reasons, provided that the additions do not render the product particularly suitable for some types of use rather than for general use.

2. In addition to dithionites stabilised with organic substances and to sulphoxylates (heading No. 28.36), carbonates and percarbonates of inorganic bases (heading No. 28.42), cyanides and complex cyanides of inorganic bases (heading No. 28.43), fulminates, cyanates and thiocyanates, of inorganic bases (heading No. 28.44), organic products included in headings Nos. 28.49 to 28.52 and metal and non-metal carbides (heading No. 28.56), only the following compounds of carbon are also to be classified in the present Chapter:

(*a*) Oxides of carbon; hydrocyanic, fulminic, isocyanic, thiocyanic and other simple or complex cyanogen acids (heading No. 28.13);

(*b*) Oxyhalides of carbon (heading No. 28.14);

(*c*) Carbon disulphide (heading No. 28.15);

(*d*) Thiocarbonates, selenocarbonates, tellurocarbonates, selenocyanates, tellurocyanates, tetrathiocyanatodiamminochromates (reineckates) and other complex cyanates, of inorganic bases (heading No. 28.48);

(*e*) Solid hydrogen peroxide (heading No. 28.54), carbon oxysulphide, thiocarbonyl halides, cyanogen, cyanogen halides and cyanamide and its metallic derivatives (heading No. 28.58) other than calcium cyanamide containing not more than 25 per cent. by weight of nitrogen, calculated on the dry anhydrous product (Chapter 31).

3. This Chapter does not cover:

(*a*) Sodium chloride or other mineral products falling within Section V;

(*b*) Organo-inorganic compounds other than those mentioned in Note 2 above;

(*c*) Products mentioned in Note 1, 2, 3 or 4 of Chapter 31;

(*d*) Inorganic products of a kind used as luminophores, falling within heading No. 32.07;

(e) Artificial graphite (heading No. 38.01); activated carbon (heading No. 38.03); products put up as charges for fire-extinguishers or put up in fire-extinguishing grenades, of heading No. 38.17; ink removers put up in packings for sale by retail, of heading No. 38.19; cultured crystals (other than optical elements) weighing not less than two and a half grammes each, of magnesium oxide or of the halides of the alkali or of the alkaline-earth metals, of heading No. 38.19;

(f) Precious or semi-precious stones (natural, synthetic or reconstructed) or dust or powder of such stones (headings Nos. 71.02 to 71.04), and precious metals falling within Chapter 71;

(g) The metals, whether or not chemically pure, falling within any heading of Section XV; or

(h) Optical elements, for example, of magnesium oxide or of the halides of the alkali or of the alkaline-earth metals (heading No. 90.01).

4. Chemically defined complex acids consisting of a non-metal acid falling within sub-Chapter II and a metallic acid falling within sub-Chapter IV are to be classified in heading No. 28.13.

5. Headings Nos. 28.29 to 28.48 inclusive are to be taken to apply only to metallic or ammonium salts or peroxysalts. Except where the context otherwise requires, double or complex salts are to be classified in heading No. 28.48.

6. Heading No. 28.50 is to be taken to apply only to:

(a) The following fissile chemical elements and isotopes:

natural uranium and uranium isotopes 233 and 235, plutonium and plutonium isotopes;

(b) The following radio-active chemical elements:

technetium, promethium, polonium, astatine, radon, francium, radium, actinium, protactinium, neptunium, americium and other elements of higher atomic number;

(c) All other radio-active isotopes, natural or artificial, including those of the precious metals and of the base metals of Sections XIV and XV;

(d) Compounds, inorganic or organic, of these elements or isotopes, whether or not chemically defined and whether or not mixed together;

(e) Alloys (other than ferro-uranium), dispersions and cermets, containing any of these elements or isotopes or their inorganic or organic compounds;

(f) Nuclear reactor cartridges, spent or irradiated.

The term " isotopes " mentioned above and in headings Nos. 28.50 and 28.51 includes " enriched isotopes ", but does not include chemical elements which occur in nature as pure isotopes nor uranium depleted in uranium-235.

7. Heading No. 28.55 is to be taken to include ferro-phosphorus containing 15 per cent. or more by weight of phosphorus and phosphor copper containing more than 8 per cent. by weight of phosphorus.

8. Chemical elements (for example, silicon and selenium) doped for use in electronics are to be classified in the present Chapter, provided that they are in forms unworked as drawn, or in the form of cylinders or rods. When cut in the form of discs, wafers or similar forms, they fall in heading No. 38.19.

Tariff Heading	*Rate of Import Duty (if any)*	
	Full	*Commonwealth (C)* *E.F.T.A. (E)*
I. Chemical elements		
28.01 Halogens (fluorine, chlorine, bromine and iodine):		
(A) Fluorine; chlorine	8%	—
(B) Bromine; iodine	—	—

Tariff Heading	Rate of Import Duty (if any)	
	Full	Commonwealth (C) E.F.T.A. (E)
28.02 Sulphur, sublimed or precipitated; colloidal sulphur:		
(A) Colloidal sulphur	8%	—
(B) Other	—	—
28.03 Carbon (including carbon black):		
(A) Acetylene black	14%	—
(B) Other	8%	—
28.04 Hydrogen, rare gases and other non-metals:		
(A) Silicon; selenium:		
(1) Silicon, monocrystalline	14%	—
(2) Other	—	—
(B) Other	8%	—
28.05 Alkali and alkaline-earth metals; rare earth metals, yttrium and scandium and inter-mixtures or interalloys thereof; mercury:		
(A) Mercury	—	—
(B) Other	8%	—
II. Inorganic acids and oxygen compounds of non-metals		
28.06 Hydrochloric acid and chlorosulphuric acid	8%	—
28.07 Sulphur dioxide	8%	—
28.08 Sulphuric acid; oleum	8%	—
28.09 Nitric acid; sulphonitric acids:		
(A) Nitric acid	12%	—
(B) Sulphonitric acids	8%	—
28.10 Phosphorus pentoxide and phosphoric acids (meta-, ortho- and pyro-):		
(A) Phosphorus pentoxide	23%	—
(B) Phosphoric acids:		
(1) Metaphosphoric acid	8%	—
(2) Other	17·5%	—
28.11 Arsenic trioxide, arsenic pentoxide and acids of arsenic:		
(A) Arsenic trioxide	—	—
(B) Other	23%	—

Tariff Heading	Rate of Import Duty (if any)	
	Full	Commonwealth (C) E.F.T.A. (E)
28.12 Boric oxide and boric acid:		
(A) Boric oxide	23%	—
(B) Boric acid	14·5%	—
28.13 Other inorganic acids and oxygen compounds of non-metals (excluding water):		
(A) Carbon dioxide; carbon monoxide ...	8%	—
(B) Chlorine dioxide	8%	—
(C) Fluorosulphonic acid	8%	—
(D) Hexafluorophosphoric acid	8%	—
(E) Hydrofluoric acid	8%	—
(F) Hydrogen fluoride; hydrogen sulphide	8%	—
(G) Metaboric acid	8%	—
(H) *di*Nitrogen tetroxide	8%	—
(IJ) Nitrosylsulphuric acid	8%	—
(K) Nitric oxide; nitrous oxide	8%	—
(L) Per*mono*sulphuric acid	8%	—
(M) Selenium dioxide	8%	—
(N) Silicic acid; silicon dioxide; silicon monoxide	8%	—
(O) Sulphur trioxide	8%	—
(P) Sulphurous acid	8%	—
(Q) Other	17·5%	—
III. Halogen and sulphur compounds of non-metals		
28.14 Halides, oxyhalides and other halogen compounds of non-metals:		
(A) Boron trifluoride	8%	—
(B) Bromine pentafluoride; bromine trifluoride	8%	—
(C) Chlorine trifluoride	8%	—
(D) Nitrosyl chloride	8%	—
(E) Phosphoryl bromide	8%	—
(F) Selenium bromide	8%	—
(G) Sulphur chloride; sulphur dichloride; sulphur hexafluoride	8%	—
(H) Sulphuryl chloride	8%	—
(IJ) Thionyl bromide	8%	—
(K) Other	23%	—
28.15 Sulphides of non-metals; phosphorus trisulphide:		
(A) Arsenic disulphide; arsenic pentasulphide; arsenic trisulphide	8%	—
(B) Phosphorus trisulphide	8%	—
(C) Other	17·5%	—

Tariff Heading	Rate of Import Duty (if any)	
	Full	Commonwealth (C) E.F.T.A. (E)
IV. Inorganic bases and metallic oxides, hydroxides and peroxides		
28.16 Ammonia, anhydrous or in aqueous solution	16%	—
28.17 Sodium hydroxide (caustic soda); potassium hydroxide (caustic potash); peroxides of sodium or potassium:		
(A) Sodium hydroxide	10%	—
(B) Sodium peroxide	23%	—
(C) Other	8%	—
28.18 Oxides, hydroxides and peroxides, of strontium, barium or magnesium:		
(A) Barium oxide and peroxide; magnesium oxide; strontium peroxide	8%	—
(B) Magnesium peroxide	17·5%	—
(C) Other	23%	—
28.19 Zinc oxide and zinc peroxide:		
(A) Zinc oxide	12%	—
(B) Zinc peroxide	23%	—
28.20 Aluminium oxide and hydroxide; artificial corundum:		
(A) Aluminium hydroxide	12·5%	—
(B) Other	9%	—
28.21 Chromium oxides and hydroxides:		
(A) Chromic oxide	16%	—
(B) Other	17·5%	—
28.22 Manganese oxides	8%	—
28.23 Iron oxides and hydroxides; earth colours containing 70 per cent. or more by weight of combined iron evaluated as Fe_2O_3:		
(A) Iron oxides and hydroxides	12·5%	—
(B) Earth colours	8%	—
28.24 Cobalt oxides and hydroxides:		
(A) Cobalt oxides	15%	—
(B) Cobalt hydroxides	23%	—
28.25 Titanium oxides	12%	—
28.26 Tin oxides (stannous oxide and stannic oxide)	16%	—

Tariff Heading	*Rate of Import Duty (if any)*	
	Full	*Commonwealth (C)* *E.F.T.A. (E)*
28.27 Lead oxides; red lead and orange lead:		
(A) Lead dioxide	17·5%	—
(B) Red lead and orange lead	12·5%	—
(C) Other	9%	—
28.28 Hydrazine and hydroxylamine and their inorganic salts; other inorganic bases and metallic oxides, hydroxides and peroxides:		
(A) Antimony oxides	£39·3680 per tonne or 25%, whichever is the greater	—
(B) Calcium oxide; calcium hydroxide ...	8%	—
(C) Cupric or cuprous oxide; cupric hydroxide	8%	—
(D) Germanium dioxide	16%	—
(E) Hydrazine, anhydrous	8%	—
(F) Hydroxylammonium nitrate	8%	—
(G) Lead hydroxide	8%	—
(H) Mercuric oxide	8%	—
(IJ) Metastannic acid	8%	—
(K) Nickel oxides	8%	—
(L) Rhenium dioxide	8%	—
(M) Sodium monoxide	8%	—
(N) Thallium hydroxide	8%	—
(O) Zinc hydroxide	8%	—
(P) Other	17·5%	—
V. Metallic salts and peroxysalts, of inorganic acids		
28.29 Fluorides; fluorosilicates, fluoroborates and other complex fluorine salts:		
(A) Aluminium calcium fluoride; aluminium sodium fluoride	8%	—
(B) Ammonium copper fluorides ...	8%	—
(C) Antimony sodium fluoride; antimony trifluoride	8%	—
(D) Beryllium fluoride	8%	—
(E) Bismuth fluoride	8%	—
(F) Cadmium fluoroborate	8%	—
(G) Calcium fluoride	8%	—
(H) Copper fluoroborates	8%	—
(IJ) Lead fluoroborate	8%	—
(K) Magnesium fluorosilicate	8%	—
(L) Potassium hydrogen difluoride ...	8%	—
(M) Sodium fluorotitanate; sodium fluorozirconate	8%	—
(N) Stannous fluoroborate	8%	—
(O) Zinc fluoroborate	8%	—
(P) Other	17·5%	—

Tariff Heading	Rate of Import Duty (if any)	
	Full	Commonwealth (C) E.F.T.A. (E)
28.30 Chlorides and oxide chlorides:		
(A) Aluminium chloride, other than anhydrous	8%	—
(B) Aluminium chlorohydrate	8%	—
(C) Ammonium chloride	16%	—
(D) Barium chloride	8%	—
(E) Calcium chloride	16%	—
(F) Ferric or ferrous chloride; ferric oxide chloride	8%	—
(G) Gallium trichloride	8%	—
(H) Lead chloride; lead oxide chloride ...	8%	—
(IJ) Magnesium chloride	—	—
(K) Magnesium oxide chloride	8%	—
(L) Manganous chloride	8%	—
(M) Stannic or stannous chloride; stannic oxide chloride	8%	—
(N) Zinc chloride	8%	—
(O) Other	23%	—
28.31 Chlorites and hypochlorites	8%	—
28.32 Chlorates and perchlorates:		
(A) Ammonium chlorate	8%	—
(B) Barium chlorate	8%	—
(C) Ferrous perchlorate	8%	—
(D) Lead perchlorate	8%	—
(E) Lithium perchlorate	8%	—
(F) Magnesium perchlorate	8%	—
(G) Potassium chlorate	6·5%	—
(H) Potassium perchlorate	8%	—
(IJ) Sodium chlorate; sodium perchlorate	8%	—
(K) Other	17·5%	—
28.33 Bromides, oxide bromides, bromates and perbromates, and hypobromites:		
(A) Ferric or ferrous bromide	—	—
(B) Chromous bromide	8%	—
(C) Other	23%	—
28.34 Iodides, oxide iodides, iodates and periodates:		
(A) Cupric or cuprous iodide	—	—
(B) Barium periodate	8%	—
(C) Other	23%	—
28.35 Sulphides; polysulphides:		
(A) Sulphides:		
(1) Ammonium sulphide; ammonium hydrogen sulphide	8%	—
(2) Antimony pentasulphide; antimony trisulphide	12·5%	—
(3) Barium sulphide	8%	—

Tariff Heading	Rate of Import Duty (if any)	
	Full	Commonwealth (C) E.F.T.A. (E)
28.35 Sulphides; polysulphides:—*contd.*		
(A) Sulphides—*contd.*		
(4) Cadmium sulphide	12·5%	—
(5) Calcium sulphide; calcium hydrogen sulphide	8%	—
(6) Cupric or cuprous sulphide ...	8%	—
(7) Ferrous sulphide	8%	—
(8) Lead sulphide	8%	—
(9) Mercuric sulphide:		
(*a*) Red	12·5%	—
(*b*) Other	8%	—
(10) Sodium sulphide; sodium hydrogen sulphide	8%	—
(11) Zinc sulphide	16%	—
(12) Other	17·5%	—
(B) Polysulphides	8%	—
28.36 Dithionites, including those stabilised with organic substances; sulphoxylates:		
(A) Zinc dithionite	8%	—
(B) Other	23%	—
28.37 Sulphites and thiosulphates:		
(A) Aluminium thiosulphate	8%	—
(B) Calcium sulphite; calcium hydrogen sulphite	8%	—
(C) Sodium sulphite; sodium hydrogen sulphite (aqueous solution)	8%	—
(D) Sodium thiosulphate, other than photographic quality	8%	—
(E) Other	23%	—
28.38 Sulphates (including alums) and persulphates:		
(A) Sulphates (including alums):		
(1) Aluminium ammonium sulphate; aluminium potassium sulphate; aluminium sodium sulphate; aluminium sulphate	5%	—
(2) Barium sulphate	16%	—
(3) Calcium sulphate	16%	—
(4) Chromic sulphate	10%	—
(5) Chromic potassium sulphate ...	8%	—
(6) Cupric or cuprous sulphate ...	8%	—
(7) Ferric or ferrous sulphate; iron sulphates, basic	8%	—
(8) Gallium sulphate	8%	—
(9) Lead sulphate	8%	—
(10) Lead sulphate, basic	12·5%	—
(11) Magnesium sulphate	8%	—
(12) Manganic or manganous sulphate	8%	—
(13) Potassium sulphate	—	—

Tariff Heading	Rate of Import Duty (if any)	
	Full	Commonwealth (C) E.F.T.A. (E)
28.38 Sulphates (including alums), etc.—*contd.*		
(A) Sulphates (including alums):—*contd.*		
(14) Sodium sulphate; sodium hydrogen sulphate	8%	—
(15) Zinc sulphate	8%	—
(16) Other	23%	—
(B) Persulphates	23%	—
28.39 Nitrites and nitrates:		
(A) Calcium nitrate	—	—
(B) Ferric nitrate	8%	—
(C) Gallium nitrate	8%	—
(D) Lead nitrate	8%	—
(E) Potassium nitrate:		
(1) Synthetic	8%	—
(2) Other than synthetic	—	—
(F) Sodium nitrate:		
(1) Synthetic	16%	—
(2) Other than synthetic	—	—
(G) Sodium nitrite	10%	—
(H) Stannic nitrate	8%	—
(IJ) Other	23%	—
28.40 Phosphites, hypophosphites and phosphates:		
(A) Aluminium metaphosphate	10%	—
(B) *tetra*Ammonium pyrophosphate ...	9%	—
(C) Antimony phosphate	10%	—
(D) Cadmium metaphosphate; *di*cadmium pyrophosphate	10%	—
(E) *tri*Calcium diorthophosphate ...	10%	—
(F) Calcium hydrogen orthophosphate ...	10%	—
(G) Calcium hydroxyphosphate	10%	—
(H) Calcium metaphosphate; *di*calcium pyrophosphate	10%	—
(IJ) Calcium tetrahydrogen diorthophosphate, other than baking powder quality	10%	—
(K) Chromium metaphosphates	10%	—
(L) Magnesium dihydrogen pyrophosphate	10%	—
(M) *tri*Potassium orthophosphate; *penta*-potassium triphosphate	10%	—
(N) *di*Sodium hydrogen orthophosphate	2·5%	—
(O) *tri*Sodium orthophosphate	2·5%	—
(P) Other	23%	—
28.41 Arsenites and arsenates:		
(A) Antimony arsenate	8%	—
(B) Barium arsenite; barium arsenate ...	8%	—

Tariff Heading	Rate of Import Duty (if any)	
	Full	Commonwealth (C) E.F.T.A. (E)
28.41 Arsenites and arsenates:—*contd.*		
(C) Bismuth arsenate	8%	—
(D) Copper arsenites	8%	—
(E) Lead arsenite; lead arsenate ...	8%	—
(F) Sodium arsenite; sodium arsenate	8%	—
(G) Other	23%	—
28.42 Carbonates and percarbonates; commercial ammonium carbonate containing ammonium carbamate:		
(A) Aluminium carbonate	8%	—
(B) Barium carbonate	16%	—
(C) Calcium carbonate	8%	—
(D) Chromous carbonate	8%	—
(E) Copper carbonates, basic	12·5%	—
(F) Ferrous carbonate	8%	—
(G) Lead carbonate	8%	—
(H) Lead carbonate, basic	12·5%	—
(IJ) Potassium carbonate	—	—
(K) Sodium carbonate; sodium hydrogen carbonate; sodium percarbonate; sodium sesquicarbonate	8%	—
(L) Zinc carbonate	8%	—
(M) Other	23%	—
28.43 Cyanides and complex cyanides:		
(A) Calcium cyanide; calcium ferrocyanide; calcium potassium ferrocyanide	8%	—
(B) Copper sodium cyanides	8%	—
(C) Ferric ferrocyanide	16%	—
(D) Ferrous ferricyanide	16%	—
(E) Magnesium ferrocyanide	8%	—
(F) Potassium cyanide; potassium ferrocyanide; potassium zinc ferrocyanide	8%	—
(G) Sodium cyanide; sodium ferrocyanide; sodium zinc cyanide	8%	—
(H) Zinc ferrocyanide	8%	—
(IJ) Other	23%	—
28.44 Fulminates, cyanates and thiocyanates:		
(A) Aluminium thiocyanate	8%	—
(B) Barium thiocyanate	8%	—
(C) Cupric or cuprous thiocyanate ...	8%	—
(D) Strontium thiocyanate	8%	—
(E) Other	23%	—

Tariff Heading	Rate of Import Duty (if any)	
	Full	Commonwealth (C) E.F.T.A. (E)
28.45 Silicates; commercial sodium and potassium silicates:		
(A) Barium silicate	17·5%	—
(B) Cadmium silicate	17·5%	—
(C) Chromic or chromous silicate ...	17·5%	—
(D) Cobalt silicate	17·5%	—
(E) Cupric or cuprous silicate	17·5%	—
(F) Lead silicate	17·5%	—
(G) Magnesium silicate	17·5%	—
(H) Manganic or manganous silicate ...	17·5%	—
(IJ) Nickel silicate	17·5%	—
(K) Strontium silicate	17·5%	—
(L) Zinc silicate	17·5%	—
(M) Other	8%	—
28.46 Borates and perborates:		
(A) Cadmium borate	8%	—
(B) Calcium perborate	8%	—
(C) Cobalt borate	8%	—
(D) Ferric borate	8%	—
(E) Manganic or manganous borate ...	8%	—
(F) Potassium pentaborate	8%	—
(G) Sodium borates:		
(1) Sodium metaborate	17·5%	—
(2) *di*Sodium tetraborate, such that reduced to the dry anhydrous form it would be of a purity not less than 99 per cent.:		
(*a*) Anhydrous	—	—
(*b*) Hydrated	14·5%	—
(3) Other	8%	—
(H) Sodium perborate	8%	—
(IJ) Zinc borate	8%	—
(K) Other	23%	—
28.47 Salts of metallic acids (for example, chromates, permanganates, stannates):		
(A) Aluminium chromate	10%	—
(B) Ammonium perrhenate	8%	—
(C) Barium stannate; barium titanate; barium zirconate	8%	—
(D) Cadmium dichromate...	10%	—
(E) Caesium chromate; caesium dichromate	10%	—
(F) Calcium stannate; calcium titanate; calcium zirconate	8%	—
(G) Chromium chromates...	10%	—
(H) Cobalt aluminate; cobalt zincate ...	12·5%	—
(IJ) Lead chromate; lead chromate, basic	13·5%	—
(K) Lead titanate	12·5%	—
(L) Lead dichromate	10%	—
(M) Lead zirconate	8%	—
(N) Lithium tungstate	8%	—

Tariff Heading	Rate of Import Duty (if any)	
	Full	Commonwealth (C) E.F.T.A. (E)
28.47 Salts of metallic acids (for example, chromates, permanganates, stannates):—*contd.*		
(O) Magnesium stannate; magnesium titanate; magnesium zirconate	8%	—
(P) Potassium dichromate	10%	—
(Q) Potassium manganate; potassium perrhenate	8%	—
(R) Rubidium dichromate	10%	—
(S) Sodium aluminate; sodium manganate; sodium permanganate; sodium stannate; sodium titanate; sodium zincate	8%	—
(T) Sodium chromate; sodium dichromate	10%	—
(U) Strontium stannate; strontium titanate; strontium zirconate	8%	—
(V) Zinc chromate; zinc tetroxychromate	13·5%	—
(W) Other	17·5%	—
28.48 Other salts and peroxysalts of inorganic acids, but not including azides:		
(A) Salts of inorganic acids:		
(1) Aluminium selenate; aluminium potassium selenate; aluminium sodium silicate and other double or complex silicates; aluminium sulphamate; aluminium telluride	8%	—
(2) Ammonium chlorostannite; ammonium cobalt chloride; ammonium cobalt sulphate; ammonium copper carbonates; ammonium reineckate; ammonium sulphamate; ammonium zinc chloride; ammonium zinc phosphate	8%	—
(3) Ammonium cobalt phosphate ...	12·5%	—
(4) Barium selenite	8%	—
(5) Caesium iodobismuthate	8%	—
(6) Calcium magnesium phosphate; calcium selenate; calcium sodium iodide	8%	—
(7) Cupric or cuprous lead arsenate; cupric or cuprous magnesium sulphate; cupric or cuprous sulphamate; cupric or cuprous zinc chromate	8%	—
(8) Ferric magnesium sulphate; ferric sodium phosphate	8%	—
(9) Ferrous selenate	8%	—
(10) Lead sulphamate	8%	—

Tariff Heading	*Rate of Import Duty (if any)*	
	Full	*Commonwealth (C)* *E.F.T.A. (E)*
28.48 Other salts and peroxysalts, etc.—*contd.*		
(A) Salts and inorganic acids:—*contd.*		
(11) Lithium potassium sulphate ...	8%	—
(12) Magnesium potassium chloride; magnesium potassium sulphate; magnesium selenate	8%	—
(13) Manganese sulphamates	8%	—
(14) Potassium chlorostannate; potassium sodium sulphate; potassium thioantimonate; potassium tetrathionate	8%	—
(15) Sodium hydrogen selenite; sodium sulphamate; sodium thiostannate	8%	—
(16) Strontium selenate	8%	—
(17) Zinc selenite	8%	—
(18) Other	17·5%	—
(B) Peroxysalts of inorganic acids ...	8%	—
VI. Miscellaneous		
28.49 Colloidal precious metals; amalgams of precious metals; albuminates, proteinates, tannates and similar compounds of precious metals, whether or not chemically defined; other salts and compounds, inorganic or organic, of precious metals:		
(A) Colloidal precious metals	8%	—
(B) Amalgams of precious metals ...	8%	—
(C) Other:		
(1) Silver chloride and silver sulphide of purity of less than 95 per cent., excluding moisture	8%	—
(2) Other	23%	—
28.50 Fissile chemical elements and isotopes; other radio-active chemical elements and radio-active isotopes; compounds, inorganic or organic, of such elements or isotopes, whether or not chemically defined; alloys, dispersions and cermets, containing any of these elements, isotopes or compounds:		
(A) Radium compounds; compounds of natural uranium, the following: Ammonium diuranate; Magnesium diuranate; Sodium diuranate; *tri*Uranium octaoxide; mixtures consisting wholly or mainly of the foregoing	—	—

Tariff Heading	Rate of Import Duty (if any) Full	Commonwealth (C) E.F.T.A. (E)
28.50 Fissile chemical elements and isotopes, etc.—*contd.*		
(B) Natural uranium:		
(1) Waste and scrap	—	—
(2) Other	8%	—
(C) Nuclear reactor cartridges, spent or irradiated	—	—
(D) Other	23%	—
28.51 Isotopes and their compounds, inorganic or organic, whether or not chemically defined, other than isotopes and compounds falling within heading No. 28.50	23%	—
28.52 Compounds, inorganic or organic, of thorium, of uranium depleted in uranium-235, of rare earth metals, of yttrium or of scandium, whether or not mixed together	23%	—
28.53 Liquid air (whether or not rare gases have been removed); compressed air	8%	—
28.54 Hydrogen peroxide (including solid hydrogen peroxide)	8%	—
28.55 Phosphides:		
(A) Calcium phosphide	8%	—
(B) Iron phosphides	8%	—
(C) Other	17·5%	—
28.56 Carbides (for example, silicon carbide, boron carbide, metal carbides):		
(A) Calcium carbide	—	—
(B) Silicon carbide	—	—
(C) Molybdenum carbide	17·5%	—
(D) Vanadium carbide	23%	—
(E) Other	8%	—
28.57 Hydrides, nitrides and azides, silicides and borides:		
(A) Aluminium lithium hydride; aluminium nitride	8%	—
(B) Barium azide	8%	—
(C) Boron nitride	8%	—
(D) Calcium hydride; calcium boride ...	8%	—
(E) Calcium silicide	—	—
(F) Chromium borides	8%	—
(G) Lithium hydride	8%	—
(H) Niobium hydride	8%	—
(IJ) Potassium borohydride	8%	—
(K) Sodium hydride; sodium borohydride	8%	—
(L) Tantalum hydride	8%	—

Tariff Heading	*Rate of Import Duty (if any)*	
	Full	*Commonwealth (C)* *E.F.T.A. (E)*
28.57 Hydrides, nitrides and azides, silicides and borides:—*contd.*		
(M) Titanium hydride; titanium nitride; titanium boride	8%	—
(N) Zirconium hydride; zirconium boride	8%	—
(O) Manganese nitrides containing not less than 4 per cent. by weight of nitrogen in all	—	—
(P) Other	23%	—
28.58 Other inorganic compoumds (including distilled and conductivity water and water of similar purity); amalgams, except amalgams of precious metals:		
(A) Amalgams	8%	—
(B) Boron phosphate	8%	—
(C) Calcium cyanamide	—	—
(D) Cyanamide	8%	—
(E) Lead cyanamide	16%	—
(F) Thiocarbonyl chloride	8%	—
(G) Water, distilled, conductivity or of similar purity	8%	—
(H) Other	17·5%	—

Chapter 29

Organic Chemicals

Notes

1. Except in so far as the context otherwise requires, the headings of this Chapter are to be taken to apply only to:

(*a*) Separate chemically defined organic compounds, whether or not containing impurities;

(*b*) Mixtures of two or more isomers of the same organic compound (whether or not containing impurities), except mixtures of acyclic hydrocarbon isomers (other than stereoisomers), whether or not saturated (Chapter 27);

(*c*) The products of headings Nos. 29.38 to 29.42 inclusive, or the sugar ethers and sugar esters, and their salts, of heading No. 29.43, or the products of heading No. 29.44, whether or not chemically defined;

(*d*) Products mentioned in (*a*), (*b*) or (*c*) above dissolved in water;

(*e*) Products mentioned in (*a*), (*b*) or (*c*) above dissolved in other solvents provided that the solution constitutes a normal and necessary method of putting up these products adopted solely for reasons of safety or for transport and that the solvent does not render the product particularly suitable for some types of use rather than for general use;

(*f*) The products mentioned in (*a*), (*b*), (*c*), (*d*) or (*e*) above with an added stabiliser necessary for their preservation or transport;

(*g*) The products mentioned in (*a*), (*b*), (*c*), (*d*), (*e*) or (*f*) above with an added anti-dusting agent or a colouring or odoriferous substance added to facilitate their identification or for safety reasons, provided that the additions do not render the product particularly suitable for some types of use rather than for general use;

(*h*) Diazonium salts, arylides used as couplers for these salts, and fast bases for azoic dyes, diluted to standard strengths.

2. This Chapter does not cover:

(*a*) Goods falling within heading No. 15.04, or glycerol (heading No. 15.11);

(*b*) Ethyl alcohol (ethanol) (heading No. 22.08 or 22.09);

(*c*) Methane and propane (heading No. 27.11);

(*d*) The compounds of carbon mentioned in Note 2 of Chapter 28;

(*e*) Urea (heading No. 31.02 or 31.05 as the case may be);

(*f*) Colouring matter of vegetable or animal origin (heading No. 32.04); synthetic organic dyestuffs (including pigment dyestuffs), synthetic organic products of a kind used as luminophores and products of the kind known as optical bleaching agents substantive to the fibre and natural indigo (heading No. 32.05) and dyes or other colouring matter put up in forms or packings of a kind sold by retail (heading No. 32.09);

(*g*) Metaldehyde, hexamine and similar substances put up in forms (for example, tablets, sticks or similar forms) for use as fuels, and liquid fuels of a kind used in mechanical lighters in containers of a capacity not exceeding 300 cubic centimetres (heading No. 36.08);

(*h*) Products put up as charges for fire-extinguishers or put up in fire-extinguishing grenades, of heading No. 38.17; ink removers put up in packings for sale by retail, of heading No. 38.19; or

(*ij*) Optical elements, for example, of 1,2-diaminoethane tartrate (heading No. 90.01).

3. Goods which could be included in two or more of the headings of this Chapter are to be classified in the latest of those headings.

4. In headings Nos. 29.03 to 29.05, 29.07 to 29.10 and 29.12 to 29.21 inclusive, any reference to halogenated, sulphonated, nitrated or nitrosated derivatives is to be taken to include a reference to any combinations of these derivatives (for example, sulphohalogenated, nitrohalogenated, nitrosulphonated and nitrosulphohalogenated derivatives).

Nitro and nitroso groups are not to be taken as nitrogen-functions for the purpose of heading No. 29.30.

5. (*a*) The esters of acid-function organic compounds falling within sub-Chapters I to VII with organic compounds of these sub-Chapters are to be classified with that compound which is classified in the heading placed last in the sub-Chapters.

(*b*) Esters of ethyl alcohol (ethanol) or glycerol with acid-function organic compounds of sub-Chapters I to VII are to be classified with the corresponding acid-function compounds.

(*c*) The salts of the esters referred to in paragraph (*a*) or (*b*) above with inorganic bases are to be classified with the corresponding esters.

(*d*) The salts of other acid- or phenol-function organic compounds falling within sub-Chapters I to VII with inorganic bases are to be classified with the corresponding acid- or phenol-function organic compounds.

(*e*) Halides of carboxylic acids are to be classified with the corresponding acids.

6. The compounds of headings Nos. 29.31 to 29.34 are organic compounds the molecules of which contain, in addition to atoms of hydrogen, oxygen or nitrogen, atoms of other non-metals or of metals (such as sulphur, arsenic, mercury or lead) directly linked to carbon atoms.

Heading No. 29.31 (organo-sulphur compounds) and heading No. 29.34 (other organo-inorganic compounds) are to be taken not to include sulphonated or halogenated derivatives (including compound derivatives) which, apart from hydrogen, oxygen and nitrogen, only have directly linked to carbon the atoms of sulphur and of halogens which give them their nature of sulphonated or halogenated derivatives (or compound derivatives).

7. Heading No. 29.35 (heterocyclic compounds) is to be taken not to include internal ethers, internal hemi-acetals, methylene ethers of orthodihydric phenols, epoxides with three or four member rings, cyclic acetals, cyclic polymers of aldehydes, of thioaldehydes or of aldimines, anhydrides of polybasic acids, cyclic esters of polyhydric alcohols with polybasic acids, cyclic ureides and cyclic thioureides, imides of polybasic acids, hexamine and hexahydro-1,3,5-trinitro-1,3,5-triazine.

Special notes applying to subheadings only

1. Where any esters, salts or halides mentioned in Note 5 above fall within a heading of this Chapter divided into subheadings, they shall be classified in the final subheading unless mentioned in any other subheading.

2. Throughout this Schedule where there is any reference to an organic compound which has a normal isomer, that reference shall be taken to include only the normal isomer, unless the contrary intention appears.

Tariff Heading	*Rate of Import Duty (if any)*	
	Full	*Commonwealth (C)* *E.F.T.A. (E)*
I. Hydrocarbons and their halogenated, sulphonated, nitrated or nitrosated derivatives		
29.01 Hydrocarbons:		
(A) "Hydrocarbon oil" as defined in paragraph (*a*) of the special note to Chapter 27:		
(1) The following: Benzene Dicyclopentadiene Dipentene Heptane Hexane Indene (+)-Limonene; (−)-limonene 2-Methylbutane Octadecane Octane	—	—

Tariff Heading	Rate of Import Duty (if any)	
	Full	Commonwealth (C) E.F.T.A. (E)
29.01 Hydrocarbons:—*contd.*		
(A) " Hydrocarbon oil ", etc.—*contd.*		
(1) The following:—*contd.* Pentane Pinene Terpinolene Toluene Xylene, mixed isomers		
(2) Styrene monomer	8%, in addition to any hydrocarbon oil duty	—
(3) Other	8%	—
(B) Other:		
(1) The following: Anthracene Butane Ethane Ethylene Naphthalene Phenanthrene	8%	—
(2) Buta-1,2-diene; buta-1,3-diene ...	16%	—
(3) Other	23%	—
29.02 Halogenated derivatives of hydrocarbons	23%	—
29.03 Sulphonated, nitrated or nitrosated derivatives of hydrocarbons	23%	—
II. Alcohols and their halogenated, sulphonated, nitrated or nitrosated derivatives		
29.04 Acyclic alcohols and their halogenated, sulphonated, nitrated or nitrosated derivatives:		
(A) Methanol:		
(1) Synthetic	19%	—
(2) Other	8%	—
(B) Other	23%	—

Tariff Heading	*Rate of Import Duty (if any)*	
	Full	*Commonwealth (C) E.F.T.A. (E)*
29.05 Cyclic alcohols and their halogenated, sulphonated, nitrated or nitrosated derivatives:		
(A) Menthol, not containing more than 10 per cent. by weight of isomers of menthol other than (−)-menthol	—	—
(B) Other	23%	—
III. Phenols, phenol-alcohols, and their halogenated, sulphonated, nitrated or nitrosated derivatives		
29.06 Phenols and phenol-alcohols:		
(A) Cresol, mixed isomers	8%	—
(B) Phenol, other than synthetic or pharmaceutical quality	8%	—
(C) 2,2-Di-(4-hydroxyphenyl)propane ...	17·5%	—
(D) Other	23%	—
29.07 Halogenated, sulphonated, nitrated or nitrosated derivatives of phenols or phenol-alcohols	23%	—
IV. Ethers, alcohol peroxides, ether peroxides, epoxides with a three or four member ring, acetals and hemiacetals, and their halogenated, sulphonated, nitrated or nitrosated derivatives		
29.08 Ethers, ether-alcohols, ether-phenols, ether-alcohol-phenols, alcohol peroxides and ether peroxides, and their halogenated, sulphonated, nitrated or nitrosated derivatives:		
(A) Diethyl ether	28%	—
(B) Other	23%	—
29.09 Epoxides, epoxyalcohols, epoxyphenols and epoxyethers, with a three or four member ring, and their halogenated, sulphonated, nitrated or nitrosated derivatives	23%	—

Tariff Heading	Rate of Import Duty (if any)	
	Full	Commonwealth (C) E.F.T.A. (E)
29.10 Acetals and hemiacetals and single or complex oxygen-function acetals and hemiacetals, and their halogenated, sulphonated, nitrated or nitrosated derivatives	23%	—
V. Aldehyde-function compounds		
29.11 Aldehydes, aldehyde-alcohols, adlehyde-ethers, aldehyde-phenols and other single or complex oxygen-function aldehydes; cyclic polymers of aldehydes; paraformaldehyde	23%	—
29.12 Halogenated, sulphonated, nitrated or nitrosated derivatives of products falling within heading No. 29.11	23%	—
VI. Ketone-function compounds and quinone-function compounds		
29.13 Ketones, ketone-alcohols, ketone-phenols, ketone-aldehydes, quinones, quinone-alcohols, quinone-phenols, quinone-aldehydes and other single or complex oxygen-function ketones and quinones, and their halogenated, sulphonated, nitrated or nitrosated derivatives:		
(A) Camphor, natural or synthetic ...	8%	—
(B) Acetone	17·5%	—
(C) Other	23%	—
VII. Carboxylic acids, and their anhydrides, halides, peroxides and peracids, and their halogenated, sulphonated, nitrated or nitrosated derivatives		
29.14 Monocarboxylic acids and their anhydrides, halides, peroxides and peracids, and their halogenated, sulphonated, nitrated or nitrosated derivates:		
(A) Ethyl acetate	25%	—
(B) Ethyl butyrate; ethyl *iso*butyrate ...	28%	—
(C) Lead acetate; lead acetate, basic ...	17·5%	—
(D) Chromic or chromous acetate ...	8%	—
(E) Cupric or cuprous acetate; copper acetates, basic	8%	—

Tariff Heading	*Rate of Import Duty (if any)*	
	Full	*Commonwealth (C) E.F.T.A. (E)*
29.14 Monocarboxylic acids and their anhydrides, etc.—*contd.*		
(F) 2-Ethylbutyric acid	8%	—
(G) Ferric or ferrous acetate	8%	—
(H) Sodium acetate	8%	—
(IJ) Acrylic acid	17·5%	—
(K) Propionic acid	17·5%	—
(L) Sorbic acid	17·5%	—
(M) Other	23%	—
29.15 Polycarboxylic acids and their anhydrides, halides, peroxides and peracids, and their halogenated, sulphonated, nitrated or nitrosated derivatives	23%	—
29.16 Carboxylic acids with alcohol, phenol, aldehyde or ketone function and other single or complex oxygen-function carboxylic acids and their anhydrides, halides, peroxides and peracids, and their halogenated, sulphonated, nitrated or nitrosated derivatives:		
(A) Calcium tartrate	—	—
(B) Calcium gluconate	19%	—
(C) Methyl, ethyl and propyl 4-hydroxybenzoate	17·5%	—
(D) Aluminium ammonium citrate ...	8%	—
(E) Antimony barium tartrate; antimony potassium tartrate; antimony strontium tartrate; antimony tartrate	8%	—
(F) Citric acid	8%	—
(G) Potassium dihydrogen citrate; *di*potassium hydrogen citrate	8%	—
(H) Potassium hydrogen tartrate ...	8%	—
(IJ) (+)-Tartaric acid	8%	—
(K) Other	23%	—
VIII. Inorganic esters and their salts, and their halogenated, sulphonated, nitrated or nitrosated derivatives		
29.17 Sulphuric esters and their salts, and their halogenated, sulphonated, nitrated or nitrosated derivatives	23%	—
29.18 Nitrous and nitric esters, and their halogenated, sulphonated, nitrated or nitrosated derivatives	23%	—
29.19 Phosphoric esters and their salts, including lactophosphates, and their halogenated, sulphonated, nitrated or nitrosated derivatives	23%	—

Tariff Heading	Rate of Import Duty (if any)	
	Full	Commonwealth (C) E.F.T.A. (E)
9.20 Carbonic esters and their salts, and their halogenated, sulphonated, nitrated or nitrosated derivatives	23%	—
9.21 Other esters of mineral acids (excluding halides) and their salts, and their halogenated, sulphonated, nitrated or nitrosated derivatives	23%	—
IX. Nitrogen-function compounds		
9.22 Amine-function compounds	23%	—
9.23 Single or complex oxygen-function amino-compounds:		
(A) Aluminium glutamate	8%	—
(B) Glutamic acid hydrochloride ...	8%	—
(C) Sodium hydrogen glutamate ...	8%	—
(D) Glycine	17·5%	—
(E) Triethanolamine	17·5%	—
(F) Other	23%	—
9.24 Quaternary ammonium salts and hydroxides; lecithins and other phosphoaminolipins:		
(A) Lecithins and other phosphoaminolipins	8%	—
(B) Other	23%	—
9.25 Carboxyamide-function compounds; amide-function compounds of carbonic acid	23%	—
9.26 Carboxyimide-function compounds (including ortho-benzoicsulphimide and its salts) and imine-function compounds (including hexamethylenetetramine and trimethylenetrinitramine)	23%	—
9.27 Nitrile-function compounds:		
(A) Dicyandiamide	—	—
(B) Other	23%	—
9.28 Diazo-, azo- and azoxy-compounds ...	23%	—
9.29 Organic derivatives of hydrazine or of hydroxylamine	23%	—
9.30 Compounds with other nitrogen-functions	23%	—
X. Organo-inorganic compounds and heterocyclic compounds		
9.31 Organo-sulphur compounds	23%	—

Tariff Heading	Rate of Import Duty (if any) Full	Commonwealth (C) E.F.T.A. (E)
29.32 Organo-arsenic compounds	23%	—
29.33 Organo-mercury compounds	23%	—
29.34 Other organo-inorganic compounds ...	23%	—
29.35 Heterocyclic compounds; nucleic acids:		
(A) Amidopyrin	8%	—
(B) Catechin	6·5%	—
(C) Nucleic acids	8%	—
(D) Pyrrole	6·5%	—
(E) Santonin	8%	—
(F) 1,6–Hexanolactam	16%	—
(G) Quassin	8%	—
(H) Other	22%	—
29.36 Sulphonamides	17·5%	—
29.37 Sultones and sultams	23%	—
XI. Provitamins, vitamins, hormones and enzymes, natural or reproduced by synthesis		
29.38 Provitamins and vitamins, natural or reproduced by synthesis (including natural concentrates), derivatives thereof used primarily as vitamins, and intermixtures of the foregoing, whether or not in any solvent:		
(A) Natural vitamin concentrates ...	8%	—
(B) Other	22%	—
29.39 Hormones, natural or reproduced by synthesis; derivatives thereof, used primarily as hormones; other steroids used primarily as hormones:		
(A) Insulin and its salts		
(B) Chorionic gonadotrophin; serum gonadotrophin	8%	—
(C) Corticotrophin; thyrotrophin ...	8%	—
(D) Other	23%	—
29.40 Enzymes	8%	—
XII. Glycosides and vegetable alkaloids, natural or reproduced by synthesis, and their salts, ethers, esters and other derivatives		
29.41 Glycosides, natural or reproduced by synthesis, and their salts, ethers, esters and other derivatives:		
(A) Aesculin	23%	—
(B) Aloin	23%	—
(C) Amygdalin	23%	—
(D) Arbutin; arbutin benzoate	23%	—

Tariff Heading	Rate of Import Duty (if any)	
	Full	Commonwealth (C) E.F.T.A. (E)
29.41 Glycosides, natural or reproduced by synthesis, etc.—*contd.*		
(E) Colocynthin	23%	—
(F) Digitalin	23%	—
(G) Digitonin	23%	—
(H) Digitoxin	23%	—
(IJ) Digoxin	23%	—
(K) Ouabain	23%	—
(L) Phloridzin	23%	—
(M) Rutin	23%	—
(N) Salicin	23%	—
(O) Salicylaldehyde glucoside	23%	—
(P) Sinigrin	23%	—
(Q) Other	8%	—
29.42 Vegetable alkaloids, natural or reproduced by synthesis, and their salts, ethers, esters and other derivatives:		
(A) Caffeine and its salts	16%	—
(B) Theobromine and its salts	16%	—
(C) Emetine and its salts	16%	—
(D) Nicotine; nicotine sulphate	16%	—
(E) Quinine sulphate of vegetable origin	8%	—
(F) Other:		
(1) Chemically defined compounds ...	22%	—
(2) Other	6·5%	—
XIII. Other organic compounds		
29.43 Sugars, chemically pure, other than sucrose, glucose and lactose; sugar ethers and sugar esters, and their salts, other than products of headings Nos. 29.39, 29.41 and 29.42:		
(A) Fructose	—	—
(B) Sugar ethers and sugar esters, and their salts:		
(1) Chemically defined compounds ...	23%	—
(2) Other	8%	—
(C) Other	23%	—
29.44 Antibiotics	17·5%	—
29.45 Other organic compounds:		
(A) Sodium antimonylgluconate	8%	—
(B) Other	23%	—

Chapter 30

Pharmaceutical Products

Notes

1. For the purposes of heading No. 30.03, " medicaments " means goods (other than foods or beverages such as dietetic, diabetic or fortified foods, tonic beverages, spa water) not falling within heading No. 30.02 or 30.04 which are either:

(*a*) Products comprising two or more constituents which have been mixed or compounded together for therapeutic or prophylactic uses; or

(*b*) Unmixed products suitable for such uses put up in measured doses or in forms or in packings of a kind sold by retail for therapeutic or prophylactic purposes.

For the purposes of these provisions and of Note 3 (*d*) to this Chapter, the following are to be treated:

(A) As unmixed products:

(1) Unmixed products dissolved in water;

(2) All goods falling in Chapter 28 or 29; and

(3) Simple vegetable extracts falling in heading No. 13.03, merely standardised or dissolved in any solvent;

(B) As products which have been mixed:

(1) Colloidal solutions and suspensions (other than colloidal sulphur);

(2) Vegetable extracts obtained by the treatment of mixtures of vegetable materials; and

(3) Salts and concentrates obtained by evaporating natural mineral waters.

2. The headings of this Chapter are to be taken not to apply to:

(*a*) Aqueous distillates and aqueous solutions of essential oils, suitable for medicinal uses (heading No. 33.05);

(*b*) Dentifrices of all kinds, including those having therapeutic or prophylactic properties which are to be considered as falling within heading No. 33.06; or

(*c*) Soap or other products of heading No. 34.01 containing added medicaments.

3. Heading No. 30.05 is to be taken to apply and to apply only, to:

(*a*) Sterile surgical catgut and similar sterile suture materials;

(*b*) Sterile laminaria and sterile laminaria tents;

(*c*) Sterile absorbable surgical haemostatics;

(*d*) Opacifying preparations for X-ray examinations and other diagnostic reagents (excluding those of heading No. 30.02) designed to be administered to the patient, being unmixed products put up in measured doses or products consisting of two or more constituents which have been mixed or compounded together for such uses;

(*e*) Blood-grouping reagents;

(*f*) Dental alloys, dental cements and other dental fillings; and

(*g*) First-aid boxes and kits.

Tariff Heading	*Rate of Import Duty (if any)*	
	Full	*Commonwealth (C* *E.F.T.A. (E*
30.01 Organo-therapeutic glands or other organs, dried, whether or not powdered; organo-therapeutic extracts of glands or other organs or of their secretions; other animal substances prepared for therapeutic or prophylactic uses, not elsewhere specified or included	8%	—

Tariff Heading	Rate of Import Duty (if any) Full	Commonwealth (C) E.F.T.A. (E)
30.02 Antisera; microbial vaccines, toxins, microbial cultures (including ferments but excluding yeasts) and similar products	8%	—
30.03 Medicaments (including veterinary medicaments):		
(A) Products comprising two or more constituents which have been mixed or compounded together for therapeutic or prophylactic uses:		
(1) Insulin preparations	—	—
(2) Products not included above containing one or more constituents which have been used in their manufacture or preparation and have not lost their identity and which, if imported separately, would be classified in Chapter 28 or 29 and be chargeable with import duty amounting *at the full rate* to 17·5 per cent. or more of the value of the constituent	6·5% or such greater rate as is equal to the amount or aggregate amount of the duty chargeable on such constituents	—
(3) Other	6·5%	—
(B) Unmixed products put up in measured doses or in forms or in packings of a kind sold by retail for therapeutic or prophylactic purposes	The rate applicable to the products when not put up in measured doses or in forms or in packings of a kind sold by retail	C E { The rate applicable to the products when not put up in measured doses or in forms or in packings of a kind sold by retail
30.04 Wadding, gauze, bandages and similar articles (for example, dressings, adhesive plasters, poultices), impregnated or coated with pharmaceutical substances or put up in retail packings for medical or surgical purposes, other than goods specified in Note 3 to this Chapter:		
(A) Wadding:		
(1) Of cellulose	14%	—
(2) Of other materials	10%	—
(B) Other	16%	—
30.05 Other pharmaceutical goods:		
(A) First-aid boxes and kits	16%	—
(B) Dental alloys, dental cements and other dental fillings:		
(1) Containing base metal	16%	—
(2) Not containing base metal ...	10%	—
(C) Other:		
(1) Blood-grouping reagents	8%	—
(2) Other	10%	—

Chapter 31

Fertilisers

Notes

1. Heading No. 31.02 is to be taken to apply, and to apply only, to the following goods, provided that they are not put up in the forms or packings described in heading No. 31.05:

(*a*) Goods which answer to one or other of the descriptions given below:

(i) Sodium nitrate containing not more than 16·3 per cent. by weight of nitrogen;

(ii) Ammonium nitrate, whether or not pure;

(iii) Ammonium sulphonitrate, whether or not pure;

(iv) Ammonium sulphate, whether or not pure;

(v) Calcium nitrate containing not more than 16 per cent. by weight of nitrogen;

(vi) Calcium nitrate-magnesium nitrate, whether or not pure;

(vii) Calcium cyanamide containing not more than 25 per cent. by weight of nitrogen, whether or not treated with oil;

(viii) Urea, whether or not pure.

(*b*) Fertilisers consisting of any of the goods described in (*a*) above, but without quantitative criteria, mixed together.

(*c*) Fertilisers consisting of ammonium chloride or of any of the goods described in (*a*) or (*b*) above, but without quantitative criteria, mixed with chalk, gypsum or other inorganic non-fertilising substances.

(*d*) Liquid fertilisers consisting of the goods of sub-paragraphs 1 (*a*) (ii) or (viii) above, or of mixtures of those goods, in an aqueous or ammonia solution.

2. Heading No. 31.03 is to be taken to apply, and to apply only, to the following goods, provided that they are not put up in the forms or packings described in heading No. 31.05:

(*a*) Goods which answer to one or other of the descriptions given below:

(i) Basic slag;

(ii) Disintegrated (calcined) calcium phosphates (thermophosphates and fused phosphates) and calcined natural aluminium calcium phosphates;

(iii) Superphosphates (single, double or triple);

(iv) Calcium hydrogen phosphate containing not less than 0·2 per cent. by weight of fluorine.

(*b*) Fertilisers consisting of any of the goods described in (*a*) above, but without quantitative criteria, mixed together.

(*c*) Fertilisers consisting of any of the goods described in (*a*) or (*b*) above, but without quantitative criteria, mixed with chalk, gypsum or other inorganic non-fertilising substances.

3. Heading No. 31.04 is to be taken to apply, and to apply only, to the following goods provided that they are not put up in the forms or packings described in heading No. 31.05:

(*a*) Goods which answer to one or other of the descriptions given below:

(i) Crude natural potassium salts (for example, carnallite, kainite and sylvinite);

(ii) Crude potassium salts obtained by the treatment of residues of beet molasses;

(iii) Potassium chloride, whether or not pure, except as provided in Note 6 (*c*) below

(iv) Potassium sulphate containing not more than 52 per cent. by weight of K_2O;

(v) Magnesium sulphate-potassium sulphate containing not more than 30 per cent by weight of K_2O.

(*b*) Fertilisers consisting of any of the goods described in (*a*) above, but without quantitative criteria, mixed together.

4. Monoammonium and diammonium orthophosphates, whether or not pure, and mixtures thereof, are to be classified in heading No. 31.05.

5. For the purposes of the quantitative criteria specified in Notes 1(*a*), 2(*a*) and 3(*a*) above, the calculation is to be made on the dry anhydrous product.

6. This Chapter does not cover:

(*a*) Animal blood;

(*b*) Separate chemically defined compounds (other than those answering to the descriptions in Note 1 (*a*), 2 (*a*), 3 (*a*) or 4 above); or

(*c*) Cultured potassium chloride crystals (other than optical elements) weighing not less than two and a half grammes each, of heading No. 38.19; optical elements of potassium chloride (heading No. 90.01).

Tariff Heading	*Rate of Import Duty (if any)*	
	Full	*Commonwealth (C)* *E.F.T.A. (E)*
31.01 Guano and other natural animal or vegetable fertilisers, whether or not mixed together, but not chemically treated	8%	—
31.02 Mineral or chemical fertilisers, nitrogenous:		
(A) Calcium cyanamide; calcium nitrate; sodium nitrate, natural	—	—
(B) Ammonium nitrate	12·5%	—
(C) Urea, whether or not mixed with chalk, gypsum or other inorganic non-fertilising substances or in an aqueous or ammonia solution	17·5%	—
(D) Other	19%	—
31.03 Mineral or chemical fertilisers, phosphatic:		
(A) Superphosphates	11%	—
(B) Other	6·5%	—
31.04 Mineral or chemical fertilisers, potassic	—	—
31.05 Other fertilisers; goods of the present Chapter in tablets, lozenges and similar prepared forms or in packings of a gross weight not exceeding 10 kilogrammes:		
(A) Other fertilisers:		
(1) Fertilisers consisting solely of two or more potassic fertilising salts or of natural potassium nitrate and natural sodium nitrate	—	—
(2) Monoammonium orthophosphate (ammonium dihydrogen orthophosphate) containing less than 6 milligrammes of arsenic per kilogramme; monoammonium orthophosphate (ammonium dihydrogen orthophosphate) containing not more than 0·5 per cent. by weight of material insoluble in water and containing not less than 59 per cent. by weight of phosphorus calculated as P_2O_5	23%	—

Tariff Heading	*Rate of Import Duty (if any)*	
	Full	*Commonwealth (C)* *E.F.T.A. (E)*
31.05 Other fertilisers; etc.—*contd.*		
(A) Other fertilisers:—*contd.*		
(3) Diammonium orthophosphate (diammonium hydrogen orthophosphate) containing less than 6 milligrammes of arsenic per kilogramme	9%	—
(4) Other	12·5%	—
(B) Goods of the present Chapter in tablets, lozenges and similar prepared forms or in packings of a gross weight not exceeding 10 kilogrammes	The rate applicable to the products when not in tablets, lozenges and similar prepared forms or when in packings of a gross weight exceeding 10 kilogrammes	—

Chapter 32

Tanning and Dyeing Extracts; Tannins and their Derivatives; Dyes, Colours, Paints and Varnishes; Putty, Fillers and Stoppings; Inks

Notes

1. This Chapter does not cover:

(*a*) Separate chemically defined elements and compounds (except those falling within heading No. 32.04 or 32.05, inorganic products of a kind used as luminophores (heading No. 32.07), and also dyes or other colouring matter in forms or packings of a kind sold by retail falling within heading No. 32.09); or

(*b*) Tannates and other tannin derivatives of products falling within headings Nos. 29.38 to 29.42, 29.44 or 35.01 to 35.04.

2. Heading No. 32.05 is to be taken to include mixtures of stabilised diazonium salts and coupling compounds for the production of insoluble azoic dyestuffs on the fibre.

3. Headings Nos. 32.05, 32.06 and 32.07 are to be taken to apply also to preparations based on, respectively, synthetic organic dyestuffs (including pigment dyestuffs), colour lakes and other colouring matter, of a kind used for colouring in the mass artificial plastics, rubber or similar materials or as ingredients in preparations for printing textiles. The headings are not to be applied, however, to prepared pigments falling within heading No. 32.09.

4. Heading No. 32.09 is to be taken to include solutions (other than collodions) consisting of any of the products specified in headings Nos. 39.01 to 39.06 in volatile organic solvents if, and only if, the weight of the solvent exceeds 50 per cent. of the weight of the solution.

5. The expression " colouring matter " in this Chapter does not include products of a kind used as extenders in oil paints, whether or not they are also suitable for colouring distempers.

6. The expression " stamping foils " in heading No. 32.09 is to be taken to apply only to products of a kind used for printing, for example, book covers or hat bands, and consisting of:

(*a*) Thin sheets composed of metallic powder (including powder of precious metal), or pigment, agglomerated with glue, gelatin or other binder; or

(*b*) Metal (for example, gold or aluminium), or pigment, deposited on paper, artificial plastic material or other support.

Tariff Heading	*Rate of Import Duty (if any)*	
	Full	*Commonwealth (C)* *E.F.T.A. (E)*
32.01 Tanning extracts of vegetable origin:		
(A) Gambier (extract from *Uncaria gambier*)	—	—
(B) Other	8%	—
32.02 Tannins (tannic acids), including water-extracted gall-nut tannin, and their salts, ethers, esters and other derivatives	8%	—

Tariff Heading	Rate of Import Duty (if any)	
	Full	Commonwealth (C) E.F.T.A. (E)
32.03 Synthetic organic tanning substances, and inorganic tanning substances; tanning preparations, whether or not containing natural tanning materials; enzymatic preparations for pre-tanning (for example, of enzymatic, pancreatic or bacterial origin)	8%	—
32.04 Colouring matter of vegetable origin (including dyewood extract and other vegetable dyeing extracts, but excluding indigo) or of animal origin:		
(A) Quercitron bark extract	—	—
(B) Pearl essence containing 5 per cent. or more by weight of guanine	—	—
(C) Other	8%	—
32.05 Synthetic organic dyestuffs (including pigment dyestuffs); synthetic organic products of a kind used as luminophores; products of the kind known as optical bleaching agents, substantive to the fibre; natural indigo:		
(A) Natural indigo	8%	—
(B) Luminophores consisting of synthetic organic dyestuffs (including pigment dyestuffs) dispersed or dissolved in artificial plastic material	16%	—
(C) Synthetic organic dyestuffs (including pigment dyestuffs) dispersed or dissolved in cellulose nitrate (plasticised or not)	16%	—
(D) Other	15%	—
32.06 Colour lakes	16%	—
32.07 Other colouring matter; inorganic products of a kind used as luminophores:		
(A) Other colouring matter:		
(1) Ultramarine blue	11%	—
(2) Mixtures consisting wholly of inorganic substances, containing not less than 94 per cent. by weight of titanium dioxide	12%	—
(3) Mixtures containing not less than 85 per cent. by weight of antimony oxides expressed as antimony trioxide	£39·3680 per tonne or 25%, whichever is the greater	—
(4) Other	16%	—
(B) Inorganic products of a kind used as luminophores:		
(1) Barium tungstate; calcium tungstate; magnesium tungstate	23%	—
(2) Other	8%	—

Tariff Heading	Rate of Import Duty (if any)	
	Full	Commonwealth (C) E.F.T.A. (E)
32.08 Prepared pigments, prepared opacifiers and prepared colours, vitrifiable enamels and glazes, liquid lustres and similar products, of the kind used in the ceramic, enamelling and glass industries; engobes (slips); glass frit and other glass, in the form of powder, granules or flakes:		
(A) Powder consisting of glass and polyethylene glycol wax, which contains not less than 85 per cent. by weight nor more than 95 per cent. by weight of glass and of which, after washing and drying, at least 80 per cent. by weight is capable of passing a sieve having a nominal width of aperture of 150 micrometres	10%	—
(B) Other	16%	—
32.09 Varnishes and lacquers; distempers; prepared water pigments of the kind used for finishing leather; paints and enamels; pigments in linseed oil, white spirit, spirits of turpentine, varnish or other paint or enamel media; stamping foils; dyes or other colouring matter in forms or packings of a kind sold by retail:		
(A) " Hydrocarbon oil " as defined in paragraph (*a*) of the Special Note to Chapter 27	—	—
(B) Pearl essence:		
(1) Containing 5 per cent. or more by weight of guanine	—	—
(2) Other	12·5%	—
(C) Stamping foils:		
(1) Consisting of precious metal, deposited on paper, artificial plastic material or other support	8%	—
(2) Other	12·5%	—
(D) Other:		
(1) Varnishes, lacquers, paints and enamels:		
(*a*) Solutions of alkyd resins (whether modified or not)	7·5%	—
(*b*) Other	10·5%	—
(2) Dyes in forms or packings of a kind sold by retail:		
(*a*) Synthetic organic dyestuffs ...	15%	—
(*b*) Other	8%	—
(3) Goods referred to in Note 4 to this Chapter, other than varnishes and lacquers:		
(*a*) Solutions of alkyd resins (whether modified or not)	5%	—
(*b*) Other	8%	—

Tariff Heading	*Rate of Import Duty (if any)*	
	Full	*Commonwealth (C)* *E.F.T.A. (E)*
32.09 Varnishes and lacquers; etc.—*contd.*		
(D) Other:—*contd.*		
(4) Other:		
(*a*) Containing " light oil " as defined in paragraph (*b*) of the Special Note to Chapter 27	15%	—
(*b*) Other	12·5%	—
32.10 Artists', students' and signboard painters' colours, modifying tints, amusement colours and the like, in tablets, tubes, jars, bottles, pans or in similar forms or packings, including such colours in sets or outfits, with or without brushes, palettes or other accessories	16%	—
32.11 Prepared driers	8%	—
32.12 Glaziers' putty; grafting putty; painters' fillings; non-refractory surfacing preparations; stopping, sealing and similar mastics, including resin mastics and cements	8%	—
32.13 Writing ink, printing ink and other inks:		
(A) Printing ink	10·5%	—
(B) Drawing ink	12%	—
(C) Other	16%	—

Chapter 33

Essential Oils and Resinoids; Perfumery, Cosmetics and Toilet Preparations

Notes

1. This Chapter does not cover:

(*a*) Compound alcoholic preparations (known as "concentrated extracts"), for the manufacture of beverages, of heading No. 22.09;

(*b*) Soap or other products falling within heading No 34.01; or

(*c*) Spirits of turpentine or other products falling within heading No. 38.07.

2. Heading No. 33.06 is to be taken to apply, *inter alia*, to:

(*a*) Prepared room deodorisers, whether or not perfumed;

(*b*) Products, whether or not mixed (other than those of heading No. 33.05), suitable for use as perfumery, cosmetics, or toilet preparations, or as room deodorisers, put up in packings of a kind sold by retail for such use.

Tariff Heading	*Rate of Import Duty (if any)*	
	Full	*Commonwealth (C)* *E.F.T.A. (E)*
33.01 Essential oils (terpeneless or not); concretes and absolutes; resinoids:		
(A) Essential oils:		
(1) Hop oil	£3·5200 per 100 grammes	C £2·3500 per 100 grammes E —
(2) Lime oil	25%	—
(3) Other:		
(*a*) Not terpeneless:		
(i) The following: Bay Cedarwood Citronella Clove Eucalyptus Ginger Gingergrass Lemongrass Litsea cubeba Ninde Onion Orange Palmarosa Patchouli Pimento Sandalwood	8%	—
(ii) Other	—	—
(*b*) Terpeneless	8%	—
(B) Concretes and absolutes; resinoids ...	—	—
33.02 Terpenic by-products of the deterpenation of essential oils	6·5%	—
33.03 Concentrates of essential oils in fats, in fixed oils, or in waxes or the like, obtained by cold absorption or by maceration	8%	—

Tariff Heading	Rate of Import Duty (if any)	
	Full	Commonwealth (C) E.F.T.A. (E)
33.04 Mixtures of two or more odoriferous substances (natural or artificial) and mixtures (including alcoholic solutions) with a basis of one or more of these substances, of a kind used as raw materials in the perfumery, food, drink or other industries:		
(A) Containing synthetic organic chemicals or natural isolates of essential oils	8%, or 23% of the value of the constituents referred to in Column 1, whichever is the greater	—
(B) Other	8%	—
33.05 Aqueous distillates and aqueous solutions of essential oils, including such products suitable for medicinal uses	12%	—
33.06 Perfumery, cosmetics and toilet preparations:		
(A) Perfumed spirits:		
(1) In cask:		
(*a*) If warehoused 3 years or more	—	—
(*b*) If warehoused 2 and less than 3 years	—	—
(*c*) If not warehoused, or warehoused less than 2 years	—	—
(2) In bottle:		
(*a*) If warehoused 3 years or more	—	—
(*b*) If warehoused 2 and less than 3 years	—	—
(*c*) If not warehoused, or warehoused less than 2 years	—	—
(B) Bath salts and essences	17·5%	—
(C) Dental plate fixative preparations ...	9%	—
(D) Other	12%	—

Chapter 34

Soap, Organic Surface-Active Agents, Washing Preparations, Lubricating Preparations, Artificial Waxes, Prepared Waxes, Polishing and Scouring Preparations, Candles and Similar Articles, Modelling Pastes and "Dental Waxes"

Notes

1. This Chapter does not cover:

(*a*) Separate chemically defined compounds; or

(*b*) Dentifrices, shaving creams or shampoos containing soap or organic surface-active agents (heading No. 33.06).

2. For the purposes of heading No. 34.01, the expression " soap " is to be taken to apply only to soap soluble in water. Soap and the other products falling within heading No. 34.01 may contain added substances (for example, disinfectants, abrasive powders, fillers or medicaments). Products containing abrasive powders remain classified in heading No. 34.01 only if in the form of bars, cakes or moulded pieces or shapes. In other forms they are to be classified in heading No. 34.05 as " scouring powders and similar preparations ".

3. The reference in heading No. 34.03 to petroleum oils and oils obtained from bituminous minerals is to be taken to apply to the products defined in Note 3 of Chapter 27.

4. In heading No. 34.04 the expression " prepared waxes, not emulsified or containing solvents " is to be taken to apply only to:

(A) Mixtures of animal waxes, mixtures of vegetable waxes or mixtures of artificial waxes;

(B) Mixtures of different classes of waxes (animal, vegetable, mineral or artificial); and

(C) Mixtures of waxy consistency not emulsified or containing solvents, with a basis of one or more waxes, and containing fats, resins, mineral substances or other materials.

The heading is to be taken not to apply to:

(*a*) Waxes falling within heading No. 27.13; or

(*b*) Separate animal waxes and separate vegetable waxes, merely coloured.

Tariff Heading	*Rate of Import Duty (if any)*	
	Full	*Commonwealth (C)* *E.F.T.A. (E)*
34.01 Soap; organic surface-active products and preparations for use as soap, in the form of bars, cakes or moulded pieces or shapes, whether or not combined with soap:		
(A) For shaving:		
(1) In which the soap content predominates by weight	13%	—
(2) Other	10%	—
(B) For toilet use:		
(1) In which the soap content predominates by weight	17·5%	—
(2) Other	10%	—
(C) Other:		
(1) Soap flakes; soft soap	13%	—
(2) Blocks, bars, tablets or similar forms, not containing abrasive materials	10%	—
(3) Other:		
(*a*) In which the soap content predominates by weight	16%	—
(*b*) Other	10%	—

Tariff Heading	*Rate of Import Duty (if any)*	
	Full	*Commonwealth (C)* *E.F.T.A. (E)*
34.02 Organic surface-active agents; surface-active preparations and washing preparations, whether or not containing soap:		
(A) Products of the condensation of normal aliphatic alcohols containing eight or more carbon atoms in the molecule with epoxyalkanes or alkanediols, and preparations and mixtures containing not less than 90 per cent. by weight of such products	20%	—
(B) Other:		
(1) Consisting solely of polyethylene glycol ethers or of polyethylene glycol ether-esters	—	—
(2) Other	10%	—
34.03 Lubricating preparations, and preparations of a kind used for oil or grease treatment of textiles, leather or other materials, but not including preparations containing 70 per cent. or more by weight of petroleum oils or of oils obtained from bituminous minerals:		
(A) Containing 50 per cent. or more by weight of siloxanes	8%	—
(B) Other:		
(1) Containing "light oil" as defined in paragraph (*b*) of the Special Note to Chapter 27	3%, in addition to any hydrocarbon oil duty	—
(2) Other	8%	—
34.04 Artificial waxes (including water-soluble waxes); prepared waxes, not emulsified or containing solvents:		
(A) Consisting solely of polyethylene glycol ethers or of polyethylene glycol ether-esters	—	—
(B) Other	8%	—
34.05 Polishes and creams, for footwear, furniture or floors, metal polishes, scouring powders and similar preparations, but excluding prepared waxes falling within heading No. 34.04:		
(A) Cleaning and washing pastes based on soap with added abrasives	16%	—
(B) Other	8%	—
34.06 Candles, tapers, night-lights and the like...	16%	—
34.07 Modelling pastes (including those put up for children's amusement and assorted modelling pastes); preparations of a kind known as "dental wax" or as "dental impression compounds", in plates, horseshoe shapes, sticks and similar forms:		
(A) Modelling pastes put up for children's amusement	17·5%	—
(B) Other	8%	—

Chapter 35

Albuminoidal Substances; Glues

Notes

1. This Chapter does not cover:

(*a*) Protein substances put up as medicaments (heading No. 30.03); or

(*b*) Gelatin postcards and other products of the printing industry (Chapter 49).

2. For the purposes of heading No. 35.05, the term " dextrins " is to be taken to apply to starch degradation products with a reducing sugar content, expressed as dextrose on the dry substance, not exceeding 10 per cent.

Such products with a reducing sugar content exceeding 10 per cent. fall in heading No. 17.02.

Tariff Heading	*Rate of Import Duty (if any)*	
	Full	*Commonwealth (C)* *E.F.T.A. (E)*
35.01 Casein, caseinates and other casein derivatives; casein glues:		
(A) Casein glues	8%	—
(B) Other	10%	C —
		E 10%
35.02 Albumins, albuminates and other albumin derivatives	10%	—
35.03 Gelatin (including gelatin in rectangles, whether or not coloured or surface-worked) and gelatin derivatives; glues derived from bones, hides, nerves, tendons or from similar products; fish glues; isinglass:		
(A) Gelatin derivatives; isinglass ...	8%	—
(B) Gelatin and glue	16%	—
35.04 Peptones and other protein substances and their derivatives; hide powder, whether or not chromed	8%	—
35.05 Dextrins and dextrin glues; soluble or roasted starches; starch glues	10%	—
35.06 Prepared glues, not elsewhere specified or included; products suitable for use as glues put up for sale by retail as glues in packages not exceeding a net weight of one kilogramme:		
(A) Put up for sale by retail in packages not exceeding a net weight of one kilogramme:		
(1) Stationery pastes and mucilages...	13%	—
(2) Other	16%	—
(B) Other:		
(1) Containing natural or synthetic rubber or containing synthetic resins (including silicones)	10%	—
(2) Other	16%	—

Chapter 36

Explosives; Pyrotechnic Products; Matches; Pyrophoric Alloys; certain Combustible Preparations

Notes

1. This Chapter does not cover separate chemically defined compounds other than those described in Note 2 (*a*) or (*b*) below.

2. Heading No. 36.08 is to be taken to apply only to:

(*a*) Metaldehyde, hexamine and similar substances, put up in forms (for example, tablets, sticks or similar forms) for use as fuels; fuels with a basis of alcohol, and similar prepared fuels, in solid or semi-solid form;

(*b*) Liquid fuels (for example, petrol, liquid butane) of a kind used in mechanical lighters, in containers of a capacity not exceeding 300 cubic centimetres; and

(*c*) Resin torches, firelighters and the like.

3. " Heavy oil " in subheading 36.08 (C) has the meaning given by Section 1(4) of the Hydrocarbon Oil (Customs and Excise) Act 1971 as for the time being in force.

Tariff Heading	*Rate of Import Duty (if any)*	
	Full	*Commonwealth (C)* *E.F.T.A. (E)*
36.01 Propellent powders	8%	—
36.02 Prepared explosives, other than propellent powders	8%	—
36.03 Mining, blasting and safety fuses	16%	—
36.04 Percussion and detonating caps; igniters; detonators	16%	—
36.05 Pyrotechnic articles (for example, fireworks, railway fog signals, amorces, rain rockets):		
(A) Bengal matches	—	—
(B) Other	16%	—
36.06 Matches (excluding Bengal matches) ...	—	—
36.07 Ferro-cerium and other pyrophoric alloys in all forms:		
(A) In pieces weighing not more than 110 grammes	16%	—
(B) Other	8%	—
36.08 Other combustible preparations and products:		
(A) " Hydrocarbon oil " as defined in paragraph (*a*) of the Special Note to Chapter 27	—	—
(B) Metaldehyde and hexamine	23%	—
(C) Firelighters containing heavy oil ...	8%, in addition to any hydrocarbon oil duty	—
(D) Other	8%	—

Chapter 37

Photographic and Cinematographic Goods

Notes

1. This Chapter does not cover waste or scrap materials.
2. Heading No. 37.08 is to be taken to apply only to:

(*a*) Chemical products mixed or compounded for photographic uses (for example, sensitised emulsions, developers and fixers); and

(*b*) Unmixed substances suitable for such uses and put up in measured portions or put up for sale by retail in a form ready for use.

The heading does not apply to photographic pastes or gums, varnishes or similar products.

Tariff Heading	*Rate of Import Duty (if any)*	
	Full	*Commonwealth (C) E.F.T.A. (E)*
37.01 Photographic plates and film in the flat, sensitised, unexposed, of any material other than paper, paperboard or cloth	16%	—
37.02 Film in rolls, sensitised, unexposed, perforated or not:		
(A) Of a length of 12 feet or more ...	9%	C 6% E —
(B) Of a length less than 12 feet	16%	—
37.03 Sensitised paper, paperboard and cloth, unexposed or exposed but not developed	16%	—
37.04 Sensitised plates and film, exposed but not developed, negative or positive	—	—
37.05 Plates, unperforated film and perforated film (other than cinematograph film), exposed and developed, negative or positive:		
(A) Microfilm, being film for optical projection, consisting wholly of microphotographs of books, publications or other documents, other than trade advertising material	—	—
(B) Aerial survey film depicting only topographical features, of a kind suitable for use in making maps or charts	—	—
(C) Plates and film imported in a packet not exceeding 8 ounces in gross weight which does not form part of a larger consignment	—	—
(D) Other	8%	—
37.06 Cinematograph film, exposed and developed, consisting only of sound track, negative or positive	—	—

Tariff Heading	Rate of Import Duty (if any)	
	Full	*Commonwealth (C)* *E.F.T.A. (E)*
37.07 Other cinematograph film, exposed and developed, whether or not incorporating sound track, negative or positive:		
(A) Negative film	—	—
(B) Positive film:		
(1) Film of a width of less than 35 millimetres, depicting only private and personal records of a kind not suitable for public commercial exhibition or sale	—	—
(2) Film, without sound track of any description, in two or more lengths representing the same objects, imported together and designed for use as a set, each complementary to the other or others, in the production of a coloured film	—	—
(3) Film of a width of 16 millimetres, bearing not more than one frame across the width, with double perforation but without sound track of any description	—	—
(4) Film, not falling within subheading (B) (1), (B) (2) or (B) (3) of this heading, with or without incorporated sound track, bearing not more than one frame across the width	£0·3540 per 100 linear feet	C £0·0790 per 100 linear feet E —
(5) Other	£0·3540 per 100 linear feet	C £0·0790 per 100 linear feet E —
	for film of a width not greater than 35 millimetres, and for other film a rate increased in proportion to the extent to which the width is greater than 35 millimetres	
37.08 Chemical products and flash light materials, of a kind and in a form suitable for use in photography	12%	—

Chapter 38

Miscellaneous Chemical Products

Notes

1. This Chapter does not cover:

(*a*) Separate chemically defined elements or compounds with the exception of the following:

(1) Artificial graphite (heading No. 38.01); activated carbon (decolourising, depolarising or adsorbent) (heading No. 38.03);

(2) Disinfectants, insecticides, fungicides, weed-killers, anti-sprouting products, rat poisons and similar products put up as described in heading No. 38.11;

(3) Products put up as charges for fire-extinguishers or put up in fire-extinguishing grenades (heading No. 38.17);

(4) Products specified in Note 2 (*a*), 2 (*c*), 2 (*d*) or 2 (*f*) below.

(*b*) Mixtures of chemicals and foodstuffs of a kind used in the preparation of human foodstuffs (generally, heading No. 21.07).

(*c*) Medicaments (heading No. 30.03).

2. Heading No. 38.19 is to be taken to include the following goods which are to be taken not to fall within any other heading of this Schedule:

(*a*) Cultured crystals (other than optical elements) weighing not less than two and a half grammes each, of magnesium oxide or of the halides of the alkali or of the alkaline-earth metals;

(*b*) Fusel oil;

(*c*) Ink removers put up in packings for sale by retail;

(*d*) Stencil correctors put up in packings for sale by retail;

(*e*) Ceramic firing testers, fusible (for example, Seger cones);

(*f*) Plasters specially prepared for use in dentistry; and

(*g*) Chemical elements of Chapter 28 (for example, silicon and selenium) doped for use in electronics, in the form of discs, wafers or similar forms, polished or not, whether or not coated with a uniform epitaxial layer.

Tariff Heading	*Rate of Import Duty (if any)*	
	Full	*Commonwealth (C)* *E.F.T.A. (E)*
38.01 Artificial graphite; colloidal graphite, other than suspensions in oil	8%	—
38.02 Animal black (for example, bone black and ivory black), including spent animal black	8%	—
38.03 Activated carbon (decolourising, depolarising or adsorbent); activated diatomite, activated clay, activated bauxite and other activated natural mineral products:		
(A) Activated carbon, not being of animal origin	17·5%	—
(B) Activated aluminium oxide	9%	—
(C) Other	8%	—
38.04 Ammoniacal gas liquors and spent oxide produced in coal gas purification	8%	—
38.05 Tall oil	8%	—
38.06 Concentrated sulphite lye	8%	—

Tariff Heading	*Rate of Import Duty (if any)*	
	Full	*Commonwealth (C)* *E.F.T.A. (E)*
38.07 Spirits of turpentine (gum, wood and sulphate) and other terpenic solvents produced by the distillation or other treatment of coniferous woods; crude dipentene; sulphite turpentine; pine oil (excluding " pine oils " not rich in terpineol):		
(A) " Hydrocarbon oil " as defined in paragraph (*a*) of the Special Note to Chapter 27	—	—
(B) Other	8%	—
38.08 Rosin and resin acids, and derivatives thereof other than ester gums included in heading No. 39.05; rosin spirit and rosin oils:		
(A) " Hydrocarbon oil " as defined in paragraph (*a*) of the Special Note to Chapter 27	—	—
(B) Other:		
(1) Rosin and resin acids	—	—
(2) Disproportionated, hydrogenated, polymerised or oxidised rosin and resin acids	—	—
(3) Other	8%	—
38.09 Wood tar; wood tar oils (other than the composite solvents and thinners falling within heading No. 38.18); wood creosote; wood naphtha; acetone oil	8%	—
38.10 Vegetable pitch of all kinds; brewers' pitch and similar compounds based on rosin or on vegetable pitch; foundry core binders based on natural resinous products	6·5%	—
38.11 Disinfectants, insecticides, fungicides, weed-killers, anti-sprouting products, rat poisons and similar products, put up in forms or packings for sale by retail or as preparations or as articles (for example, sulphur-treated bands, wicks and candles, fly-papers):		
(A) Unmixed products put up in forms or packings for sale by retail	The rate applicable to the products when not put up as mentioned in this heading	C E The rate applicable to the products when not put up as mentioned in this heading.
(B) Other:		
(1) Products containing one or more constituents which have been used in their manufacture or preparation and have not lost their identity and which, if imported separately, would be classified in Chapter 28 or 29 and be chargeable with import duty amounting *at the full rate* to 17·5 per cent. or more of the value of the constituent	8% or such greater rate as is equal to the amount or aggregate amount of the duty chargeable on such constituents	—
(2) Other	8%	—

Tariff Heading	Rate of Import Duty (if any)	
	Full	*Commonwealth (C)* *E.F.T.A. (E)*
38.12 Prepared glazings, prepared dressings and prepared mordants, of a kind used in the textile, paper, leather or like industries	8%	—
38.13 Pickling preparations for metal surfaces; fluxes and other auxiliary preparations for soldering, brazing or welding; soldering, brazing or welding powders and pastes consisting of metal and other materials; preparations of a kind used as cores or coatings for welding rods and electrodes:		
(A) Soldering, brazing or welding powders and pastes consisting of metal and other materials	12·5%	—
(B) Other	8%	—
38.14 Anti-knock preparations, oxidation inhibitors, gum inhibitors, viscosity improvers, anti-corrosive preparations and similar prepared additives for mineral oils:		
(A) " Hydrocarbon oil " as defined in paragraph (*a*) of the Special Note to Chapter 27	—	—
(B) Products containing one or more constituents which have been used in their manufacture or preparation and have not lost their identity and which, if imported separately, would be classified in Chapter 28 or 29 and be chargeable with import duty amounting *at the full rate* to 17·5 per cent. or more of the value of the constituent	8% or such greater rate as is equal to the amount or aggregate amount of the duty chargeable on such constituents	—
(C) Other	8%	—
38.15 Prepared rubber accelerators	23%	—
38.16 Prepared culture media for development of micro-organisms	8%	—
38.17 Preparations and charges for fire-extinguishers; charged fire-extinguishing grenades	8%	—
38.18 Composite solvents and thinners for varnishes and similar products:		
(A) " Hydrocarbon oil " as defined in paragraph (*a*) of the Special Note to Chapter 27	—	—

Tariff Heading	Rate of Import Duty (if any)	
	Full	Commonwealth (C) E.F.T.A. (E)
38.18 Composite solvents and thinners, etc.— *contd.*		
(B) Other:		
(1) Products containing one or more constituents which have been used in their manufacture or preparation and have not lost their identity and which, if imported separately, would be classified in Chapter 28 or 29 and be chargeable with import duty amounting *at the full rate* to 17·5 per cent. or more of the value of the constituent:		
(*a*) Containing " light oil " as defined in paragraph (*b*) of the Special Note to Chapter 27	3% or such greater rate as is equal to the amount or aggregate amount by which the duty chargeable on such constituents exceeds 7%, in addition to any hydrocarbon oil duty	—
(*b*) Other	8% or such greater rate as is equal to the amount or aggregate amount of the duty chargeable on such constituents	—
(2) Other:		
(*a*) Containing " light oil " as defined in paragraph (*b*) of the Special Note to Chapter 27	3%, in addition to any hydrocarbon oil duty	—
(*b*) Other	8%	—
38.19 Chemical products and preparations of the chemical or allied industries (including those consisting of mixtures of natural products), not elsewhere specified or included; residual products of the chemical or allied industries, not elsewhere specified or included:		
(A) " Hydrocarbon oil " as defined in paragraph (*a*) of the Special Note to Chapter 27	—	—
(B) Getters and the like for vacuum tubes	23%	—
(C) Compounded extenders for paints ...	16%	—

Tariff Heading	Rate of Import Duty (if any)	
	Full	Commonwealth (C) E.F.T.A. (E)
38.19 Chemical products and preparations of the chemical or allied industries, etc.—*contd.*		
(D) Silicon alloys containing not less than 90 per cent. by weight of silicon; products containing more than 99·9 per cent. by weight of silicon:		
(1) Products containing more than 99·9 per cent. by weight of silicon	14%	—
(2) Other	—	—
(E) Products consisting solely of polyethylene glycol ethers or of polyethylene glycol ether-esters	—	—
(F) Mixtures containing 50 per cent. or more by weight of siloxanes	8%	—
(G) Catalysts, containing platinum dispersed with alumina, or with alumina and silica, or with aluminium silicate, which contain by weight— not less than 0·10 per cent. nor more than 1·0 per cent. of platinum; and not less than 0·20 per cent. nor more than 8·0 per cent. of chlorine, or of fluorine, or of chlorine and fluorine together; and are in the form of rods, pellets, granules or spheres, having no axial dimension less than 0·075 centimetres nor more than 2·6 centimetres	£0·2380 per kilogramme	—
(H) Pearl essence containing 5 per cent. or more by weight of guanine	—	—
(IJ) Other:		
(1) Products and preparations containing one or more constituents which have been used in their manufacture or preparation and have not lost their identity and which, if imported separately, would be classified in Chapter 28 or 29 and be chargeable with import duty amounting *at the full rate* to 17·5 per cent. or more of the value of the constituent	8% or such greater rate as is equal to the amount or aggregate amount of the duty chargeable on such constituents	—
(2) Other	8%	—

SECTION VII

ARTIFICIAL RESINS AND PLASTIC MATERIALS, CELLULOSE ESTERS AND ETHERS, AND ARTICLES THEREOF; RUBBER, SYNTHETIC RUBBER, FACTICE, AND ARTICLES THEREOF

Chapter 39

Artificial Resins and Plastic Materials, Cellulose Esters and Ethers; Articles thereof

Notes

1. This Chapter does not cover:

(*a*) Stamping foils of heading No. 32.09;

(*b*) Artificial waxes (heading No. 34.04);

(*c*) Synthetic rubber, as defined for the purposes of Chapter 40, or articles thereof;

(*d*) Saddlery or harness (heading No. 42.01) or travel goods, handbags or other receptacles falling within heading No. 42.02;

(*e*) Plaits, wickerwork or other articles falling within Chapter 46;

(*f*) Goods falling within Section XI (textiles and textile articles);

(*g*) Footwear, headgear, umbrellas, sunshades, walking-sticks, whips, riding-crops, fans or parts thereof or other articles falling within Section XII;

(*h*) Imitation jewellery falling within heading No. 71.16;

(*ij*) Articles falling within Section XVI (machines and mechanical or electrical appliances);

(*k*) Parts of aircraft or vehicles falling within Section XVII;

(*l*) Optical elements of artificial plastics, spectacle frames, drawing instruments or other articles falling within Chapter 90;

(*m*) Articles falling within Chapter 91 (for example, clock or watch cases);

(*n*) Musical instruments or parts thereof or other articles falling within Chapter 92;

(*o*) Furniture and other articles of Chapter 94;

(*p*) Brushes or other articles falling within Chapter 96;

(*q*) Articles falling within Chapter 97 (for example, toys, games and sports requisites); or

(*r*) Buttons, slide fasteners, combs, mouthpieces or stems for smoking pipes, cigarette-holders or the like, parts of vacuum flasks or the like, pens, propelling pencils or other articles falling within Chapter 98.

2. Headings Nos. 39.01 and 39.02 are to be taken to apply only to goods of a kind produced by chemical synthesis answering to one of the following descriptions:

(*a*) Artificial plastics including artificial resins;

(*b*) Silicones;

(*c*) Resols, liquid polyisobutylene, and similar artificial polycondensation or polymerisation products.

3. Headings Nos. 39.01 to 39.06 are to be taken to apply to materials in the following forms only:

(*a*) Liquid or pasty, including emulsions, dispersions and solutions (but not including solutions in which the weight of the volatile organic solvent exceeds 50 per cent. of the weight of the solution);

(*b*) Blocks, lumps, powders (including moulding powders), granules, flakes and similar bulk forms;

(*c*) Monofil of which any cross-sectional dimension exceeds 1 millimetre; seamless tubes, rods, sticks and profile shapes, whether or not surface-worked but not otherwise worked;

(*d*) Plates, sheets, film, foil and strip (other than that classified in heading No. 51.02 by the application of Note 4 to Chapter 51), whether or not printed or otherwise surface worked, uncut or cut into rectangles but not further worked (even if, when so cut, they become articles ready for use);

(*e*) Waste and scrap.

Tariff Heading	Rate of Import Duty (if any)	
	Full	Commonwealth (C) E.F.T.A. (E)
39.01 Condensation, polycondensation and polyaddition products, whether or not modified or polymerised, and whether or not linear (for example, phenoplasts, aminoplasts, alkyds, poly(allyl esters) and other unsaturated polyesters, silicones):		
(A) Melamine-formaldehyde	17·5%	—
(B) Phenoplast and aminoplast moulding powders and laminates	15%	—
(C) Consisting solely of polyethylene glycol ethers	—	—
(D) Other:		
(1) Solutions of alkyd resins (whether modified or not)	5%	—
(2) Other	10%	—
39.02 Polymerisation and copolymerisation products (for example, polyethylene, polytetrahaloethylenes, polyisobutylene, polystyrene, poly(vinyl chloride), poly(vinyl acetate), poly(vinyl chloroacetate) and other poly (vinyl derivatives), poly(acrylic derivatives), poly(methacrylic derivatives), coumarone-indene resins):		
(A) " Hydrocarbon oil " as defined in paragraph (*a*) of the Special Note to Chapter 27	—	—
(B) Other:		
(1) Copolymers solely of acrylonitrile with 5-vinyl-2-picoline and containing not less than 40 per cent. and not more than 60 per cent. by weight of acrylonitrile	—	—
(2) Other:		
(*a*) Strip not exceeding 100 millimetres in width coated with adhesive, other than strip suitable for use with embossing devices of subheading 98.07 (B)	14·5%	—
(*b*) Other	10%	—
39.03 Regenerated cellulose; cellulose nitrate, cellulose acetate and other cellulose esters, cellulose ethers and other chemical derivatives of cellulose, plasticised or not (for example, collodions, celluloid); vulcanised fibre:		
(A) Cellulose acetate, but not including transparent wrapping:		
(1) Not plasticised or otherwise compounded	23%	—
(2) Other:		
(*a*) Waste and scrap	23%	—

Tariff Heading	Rate of Import Duty (if any)	
	Full	*Commonwealth* (C) *E.F.T.A.* (E)
39.03 Regenerated cellulose, etc.—*contd.*		
(A) Cellulose acetate, etc.—*contd.*		
(2) Other:—*contd.*		
(*b*) Photographic (including cinematograph) film base	£0·1278 per kilogramme or 10%, whichever is the greater	—
(*c*) Strip not exceeding 100 millimetres in width coated with adhesive	14·5%	—
(*d*) Other	£0·0826 per kilogramme or 10%, whichever is the greater	—
(B) Cellulose ethers, not plasticised or otherwise compounded	23%	—
(C) Cellulose nitrate (collodion cotton) ...	14%	—
(D) Transparent wrapping:		
(1) Of plasticised ethylcellulose, or of plasticised cellulose esters (other than cellulose acetate)	12·5%	—
(2) Of regenerated cellulose, of cellulose acetate or of other materials	16%	—
(E) Vulcanised fibre	10%	—
(F) Other:		
(1) Strip not exceeding 100 millimetres in width coated with adhesive	14·5%	—
(2) Other	10%	—
39.04 Hardened proteins (for example, hardened casein and hardened gelatin)	8%	—
39.05 Natural resins modified by fusion (run gums); artificial resins obtained by esterification of natural resins or of resinic acids (ester gums); chemical derivatives of natural rubber (for example, chlorinated rubber, rubber hydrochloride, oxidised rubber, cyclised rubber)	10%	—
39.06 Other high polymers, artificial resins and artificial plastic materials, including alginic acid, its salts and esters; linoxyn:		
(A) Heparin	17·5%	—
(B) Alpha-cellulose in powder form, having a residue on ignition of more than 0·15 per cent. by weight	—	—
(C) Alginic acid and its salts and esters ...	8%	—
(D) Other	10%	—
39.07 Articles of materials of the kinds described in headings Nos. 39.01 to 39.06:		
(A) Clock and watch glasses	23%	C 8·5% E —

Tariff Heading	Rate of Import Duty (if any)	
	Full	Commonwealth (C) E.F.T.A. (E)
39.07 **Articles of materials, etc.**—*contd.*		
(B) Objects of personal adornment ...	17·5%	—
(C) Articles of apparel and clothing accessories	16%	—
(D) Lighting appliances and fittings ...	16%	—
(E) Bobbins, cones, cops, cores, spools and similar supports, of a kind used on textile machinery	16%	—
(F) Beads and bead trimmings:		
(1) Beads of a size and shape adapted for use in jewellery or imitation jewellery, not mounted, set or strung	—	—
(2) Other:		
(*a*) Of vulcanised fibre, hardened proteins or chemical derivatives of rubber	12%	—
(*b*) Of other materials	15%	—
(G) Other	10%	—

Chapter 40

Rubber, Synthetic Rubber, Factice, and Articles thereof

Notes

1. Except where the context otherwise requires, throughout this Schedule the expression " rubber " means the following products, whether or not vulcanised or hardened: natural rubber, balata, gutta-percha and similar natural gums, synthetic rubber, and factice derived from oils, and such substances reclaimed.

2. This Chapter does not cover the following products of rubber and textiles, which fall generally within Section XI:

(*a*) Knitted or crocheted fabric or articles thereof, elastic or rubberised (other than transmission, conveyor and elevator belts or belting, of rubberised knitted or crocheted fabric of heading No. 40.10); other elastic fabric or articles thereof;

(*b*) Textile hosepiping and similar textile tubing, internally coated or lined with rubber (heading No. 59.15);

(*c*) Woven textile fabrics (other than the goods of heading No. 40.10) impregnated, coated, covered or laminated with rubber:

(i) Weighing not more than one and a half kilogrammes per square metre; or

(ii) Weighing more than one and a half kilogrammes per square metre and containing more than 50 per cent. by weight of textile material;

and articles of those fabrics;

(*d*) Felt impregnated or coated with rubber and containing more than 50 per cent. by weight of textile material, and articles thereof;

(*e*) Bonded fibre fabrics and similar bonded yarn fabrics impregnated or coated with rubber, or in which rubber forms the bonding substance, irrespective of their weight per square metre, and articles thereof;

(*f*) Fabrics composed of parallel textile yarns agglomerated with rubber, irrespective of their weight per square metre, and articles thereof.

However, plates, sheets and strip, of expanded, foam or sponge rubber, combined with textile fabric, and articles thereof, are to be classified in Chapter 40 provided that the textile fabric is present merely for reinforcing purposes.

3. The following are also not covered by this Chapter:

(*a*) Footwear or parts thereof falling within Chapter 64;

(*b*) Headgear or parts thereof (including bathing caps) falling within Chapter 65;

(*c*) Mechanical or electrical appliances or parts thereof (including electrical goods of all kinds), of hardened rubber, falling within Section XVI;

(*d*) Articles falling within Chapter 90, 92, 94 or 96;

(*e*) Articles falling within Chapter 97 (other than sports gloves and goods falling within heading No. 40.11); or

(*f*) Buttons, combs, smoking pipe stems, pens or other articles falling within Chapter 98

4. In Note 1 to this Chapter and in headings Nos. 40.02, 40.05 and 40.06, the expression " synthetic rubber " is to be taken to apply to:

(*a*) Unsaturated synthetic substances which can be irreversibly transformed into non thermoplastic substances by vulcanisation with sulphur and which, when so vulcanise as well as may be (without the addition of any substances such as plasticisers, fillers o reinforcing agents not necessary for the cross-linking), can produce substances which at a temperature between 18° and 29° C, will not break on being extended to three time their original length and will return, after being extended to twice their original length within a period of five minutes, to a length not greater than one and a half times thei original length.

Such substances include *cis*-polyisoprene (IR), polybutadiene (BR), polychloro butadiene (CR), polybutadiene-styrene (SBR), polychlorobutadiene-acrylonitril (NCR), polybutadiene-acrylonitrile (NBR) and butyl rubber (IIR);

(*b*) Thioplasts (TM); and

(*c*) Natural rubber modified by grafting or mixing with artificial plastic material, de polymerised natural rubber, and mixtures of unsaturated synthetic substances wit saturated synthetic high polymers, provided that all the above-mentioned produc comply with the requirements concerning vulcanisation, elongation and recovery in (above.

5. Headings Nos. 40.01 and 40.02 are to be taken not to apply to:

(a) Natural or synthetic rubber latex (including pre-vulcanised rubber latex) compounded with vulcanising agents or accelerators, fillers or reinforcing agents, plasticisers, colouring matter (other than colouring matter added solely for the purpose of identification), or with any other substance; however, latex merely stabilised or concentrated, and thermo-sensitive and electro-positive latex are to be classified in heading No. 40.01 or 40.02 as the case may be;

(b) Rubber which has been compounded with carbon black (with or without the addition of mineral oil) or with silica (with or without the addition of mineral oil) before coagulation or with any substance after coagulation; or

(c) Mixtures of any of the products specified in Note 1 to the present Chapter, whether or not compounded with any other substance.

6. Thread wholly of vulcanised rubber, of any cross-section of which any dimension exceeds five millimetres, is to be classified as strip, rod or profile shape, falling within heading No. 40.08.

7. Heading No. 40.10 is to be taken to include transmission, conveyor or elevator belts or belting of textile fabric impregnated, coated, covered or laminated with rubber or made from textile yarn or cord impregnated or coated with rubber.

8. For the purpose of heading No. 40.06, pre-vulcanised rubber latex is to be deemed to be unvulcanised rubber latex.

For the purposes of headings Nos. 40.07 to 40.14, balata, gutta-percha and similar natural gums, and factice derived from oils, and such substances reclaimed, are to be deemed to be vulcanised rubber whether or not they have been vulcanised.

9. In headings Nos. 40.05, 40.08 and 40.15, the expressions " plates ", " sheets " and " strip " are to be taken to apply, and to apply only, to plates, sheets and strip, whether or not printed or otherwise surface-worked but not cut to shape or otherwise worked, and rectangular articles cut therefrom not further worked.

In heading No. 40.08 the expressions " rods " and " profile shapes " and in heading No. 40.15 the expressions " rods ", " profile shapes " and " tubes " are to be taken to apply, and to apply only, to such products, whether or not cut to length or surface-worked but not otherwise worked.

Tariff Heading	*Rate of Import Duty (if any)*	
	Full	*Commonwealth (C)* *E.F.T.A. (E)*
I. Raw rubber		
40.01 Natural rubber latex, whether or not with added synthetic rubber latex; pre-vulcanised natural rubber latex; natural rubber, balata, gutta-percha and similar natural gums:		
(A) Natural rubber latex:		
(1) Mixtures of natural rubber latex and synthetic rubber latex	4%	—
(2) Other	—	—
(B) Natural rubber, balata, gutta-percha, and similar natural gums:		
(1) Natural rubber, balata in pieces not less than 50 millimetres thick, and gutta-percha	—	—
(2) Other	4%	—

Tariff Heading	Rate of Import Duty (if any) Full	Commonwealth (C) E.F.T.A. (E)
40.02 Synthetic rubber latex; pre-vulcanised synthetic rubber latex; synthetic rubber; factice derived from oils	4%	—
40.03 Reclaimed rubber	8%	—
40.04 Waste and parings of unhardened rubber; scrap of unhardened rubber, fit only for the recovery of rubber; powder obtained from waste or scrap of unhardened rubber	—	—
II. Unvulcanised rubber		
40.05 Plates, sheets and strip, of unvulcanised natural or synthetic rubber, other than smoked sheets and crepe sheets of heading No. 40.01 or 40.02; granules of unvulcanised natural or synthetic rubber compounded ready for vulcanisation; unvulcanised natural or synthetic rubber, compounded before or after coagulation either with carbon black (with or without the addition of mineral oil) or with silica (with or without the addition of mineral oil), in any form, of a kind known as masterbatch	5%	—
40.06 Unvulcanised natural or synthetic rubber, including rubber latex, in other forms or states (for example, rods, tubes and profile shapes, solutions and dispersions); articles of unvulcanised natural or synthetic rubber (for example, coated or impregnated textile thread; rings and discs):		
(A) Blocks and similar bulk forms; rods, tubes and profile shapes	5%	—
(B) Coated or impregnated thread of silk or man-made fibres	£0·0300 per lb. or 13%, whichever is the greater	C 85% of the full rate E —
(C) Other	10%	—
III. Articles of unhardened vulcanised rubber		
40.07 Vulcanised rubber thread and cord, whether or not textile covered, and textile thread covered or impregnated with vulcanised rubber	8%	—
40.08 Plates, sheets, strip, rods and profile shapes, of unhardened vulcanised rubber:		
(A) Plates, sheets and strip with a textile backing	17·5%	—

Tariff Heading	*Rate of Import Duty (if any)*	
	Full	*Commonwealth (C)* *E.F.T.A. (E)*
40.08 Plates, sheets, strip, etc.—*contd.*		
(B) Other	10%	—
40.09 Piping and tubing, of unhardened vulcanised rubber	5%	—
0.10 Transmission, conveyor or elevator belts or belting, of vulcanised rubber:		
(A) Containing more than 5 per cent. by weight of man-made fibres	17·5%	C 85% of the full rate E —
(B) Other	7·5%	—
0.11 Rubber tyres, tyre cases, interchangeable tyre treads, inner tubes and tyre flaps, for wheels of all kinds:		
(A) Suitable for motor vehicles	12%	C 8% E —
(B) Other	12%	—
0.12 Hygienic and pharmaceutical articles (including teats), of unhardened vulcanised rubber, with or without fittings of hardened rubber	10%	—
0.13 Articles of apparel and clothing accessories (including gloves), for all purposes, of unhardened vulcanised rubber:		
(A) Articles and accessories containing more than 25 per cent. by weight of man-made fibres, but not including gloves	12%	C 85% of the full rate E —
(B) Other	12%	—
0.14 Other articles of unhardened vulcanised rubber:		
(A) Articles of stationery of the following types, viz. bands and erasers	7·5%	—
(B) Other	10%	—
V. Hardened rubber (ebonite and vulcanite); articles made thereof		
.15 Hardened rubber (ebonite and vulcanite), in bulk, plates, sheets, strip, rods, profile shapes or tubes; scrap, waste and powder, of hardened rubber	5%	—
.16 Articles of hardened rubber (ebonite and vulcanite)	10%	—

SECTION VIII

RAW HIDES AND SKINS, LEATHER, FURSKINS AND ARTICLES THEREOF; SADDLERY AND HARNESS; TRAVEL GOODS, HANDBAGS AND SIMILAR CONTAINERS; ARTICLES OF GUT (OTHER THAN SILK-WORM GUT)

Chapter 41

Raw Hides and Skins (other than Furskins) and Leather

Notes

1. This Chapter does not cover:

(*a*) Parings or similar waste, of raw hides or skins (heading No. 05.05 or 05.06);

(*b*) Birdskins or parts of birdskins, with their feathers or down, falling within heading No. 05.07 or 67.01; or

(*c*) Hides or skins, with the hair on, raw, tanned or dressed (Chapter 43); the following are, however, to be classified in heading No. 41.01, namely, raw hides or skins, with the hair on, of bovine cattle (including buffalo), of equine animals, of sheep and lambs (except Persian, Astrakhan, Caracul and similar lambs, Indian, Chinese, Mongolian and Tibetan lambs), of goats and kids (except Yemen, Mongolian and Tibetan goats and kids), of swine (including peccary), of reindeer, of chamois, of gazelle, of deer, of elk, of roebucks or of dogs.

2. Throughout this Schedule the expression "composition leather" is to be taken to mean only substances of the kind referred to in heading No. 41.10.

Tariff Heading	*Rate of Import Duty (if any)*	
	Full	*Commonwealth (C)* *E.F.T.A. (E)*
41.01 Raw hides and skins (fresh, salted, dried, pickled or limed), whether or not split, including sheepskins in the wool	—	—
41.02 Bovine cattle leather (including buffalo leather) and equine leather, except leather falling within heading No. 41.06, 41.07 or 41.08:		
(A) Box and willow calf, box and willow sides and other chrome tanned leather, imported in skins or pieces weighing less than 4 lb. each, but not including wet blue chrome tanned leather	16%	—
(B) Other:		
(1) Dressed	12%	—
(2) Other	8%	—

Tariff Heading	Rate of Import Duty (if any)	
	Full	Commonwealth (C) E.F.T.A. (E)
41.03 Sheep and lamb skin leather, except leather falling within heading No. 41.06, 41.07 or 41.08:		
(A) Dressed:		
(1) Chrome tanned and coloured black, of a thickness not exceeding 0·20 millimetre	—	—
(2) Other	12%	—
(B) Other	8%	—
41.04 Goat and kid skin leather, except leather falling within heading No. 41.06, 41.07 or 41.08:		
(A) Dressed:		
(1) Glacé kid, being chrome tanned goat skin of smooth, polished finish	8%	—
(2) Other	12%	—
(B) Other	8%	—
41.05 Other kinds of leather, except leather falling within heading No. 41.06, 41.07 or 41.08	8%	—
41.06 Chamois-dressed leather	12%	—
41.07 Parchment-dressed leather	12%	—
41.08 Patent leather and imitation patent leather; metallised leather	7·5%	—
41.09 Parings and other waste, of leather or of composition or parchment-dressed leather, not suitable for the manufacture of articles of leather; leather dust, powder and flour	—	—
41.10 Composition leather with a basis of leather or leather fibre, in slabs, in sheets or in rolls	5%	—

Chapter 42

Articles of Leather; Saddlery and Harness; Travel Goods, Handbags and Similar Containers; Articles of Animal Gut (other than Silk-Worm Gut)

Notes

1. This Chapter does not cover:

(*a*) Sterile surgical catgut and similar sterile suture materials (heading No. 30.05);

(*b*) Articles of apparel and clothing accessories (except gloves), lined with furskin or artificial fur or to which furskin or artificial fur is attached on the outside except as mere trimming (heading No. 43.03 or 43.04);

(*c*) String or net bags of Section XI;

(*d*) Articles falling within Chapter 64;

(*e*) Headgear or parts thereof falling within Chapter 65;

(*f*) Whips, riding-crops or other articles of heading No. 66.02;

(*g*) Strings, skins for drums and the like, and other parts of musical instruments (heading No. 92.09 or 92.10);

(*h*) Furniture or parts of furniture (Chapter 94);

(*ij*) Articles falling within Chapter 97 (for example, toys, games and sports requisites); or

(*k*) Buttons, studs, cuff-links, press-fasteners, including snap-fasteners and press-studs, and blanks and parts of such articles, falling within heading No. 98.01 or Chapter 71.

2. For the purposes of heading No. 42.03, the expression " articles of apparel and clothing accessories " is to be taken to apply, *inter alia*, to gloves (including sports gloves), aprons and other protective clothing, braces, belts, bandoliers and wrist straps, including watch straps.

Tariff Heading	*Rate of Import Duty (if any)*	
	Full	*Commonwealth (C)* *E.F.T.A. (E)*
42.01 Saddlery and harness, of any material (for example, saddles, harness, collars, traces, knee-pads and boots), for any kind of animal	10%	—
42.02 Travel goods (for example, trunks, suit-cases, hat-boxes, travelling-bags, rucksacks), shopping-bags, handbags, satchels, brief-cases, wallets, purses, toilet-cases, tool-cases, tobacco-pouches, sheaths, cases, boxes (for example, for arms, musical instruments, binoculars, jewellery, bottles, collars, footwear, brushes) and similar containers, of leather or of composition leather, of vulcanised fibre, of artificial plastic sheeting, of paperboard or of textile fabric:		
(A) Women's handbags and pochettes of leather, material resembling leather, composition leather, artificial plastic sheeting or paperboard	£0·0750 each or 10%, whichever is the greater	—
(B) Other	10%	—

Tariff Heading	Rate of Import Duty (if any)	
	Full	Commonwealth (C) E.F.T.A. (E)
42.03 Articles of apparel and clothing accessories, of leather or of composition leather:		
(A) Gloves, including gloves of leather and furskin or of leather and artificial fur	25%	—
(B) Other	20%	—
42.04 Articles of leather or of composition leather of a kind used in machinery or mechanical appliances or for industrial purposes:		
(A) Machinery belting (including conveyor and elevator bands)	7·5%	—
(B) Other	10%	—
42.05 Other articles of leather or of composition leather	10%	—
42.06 Articles made from gut (other than silk-worm gut), from goldbeater's skin, from bladders or from tendons	10%	—

Chapter 43

Furskins and Artificial Fur; Manufactures thereof

Notes

1. Throughout this Schedule references to furskins, other than to raw furskins of heading No. 43.01, are to be taken to apply to hides or skins of all animals which have been tanned or dressed with the hair on.

2. This Chapter does not cover:

(*a*) Birdskins or parts of birdskins, with their feathers or down, falling within heading No. 05.07 or 67.01;

(*b*) Raw hides or skins, with the hair on, of a kind falling within Chapter 41 (see Note 1 (*c*) to that Chapter);

(*c*) Gloves consisting of leather and furskin or of leather and artificial fur (heading No. 42.03);

(*d*) Articles falling within Chapter 64;

(*e*) Headgear or parts thereof falling within Chapter 65; or

(*f*) Articles falling within Chapter 97 (for example, toys, games and sports requisites).

3. For the purposes of heading No. 43.02, the expression " plates, crosses and similar forms " means furskins or parts thereof (excluding " dropped " skins) sewn together in rectangles, crosses or trapeziums, without the addition of other materials. Other assembled skins ready for immediate use (or requiring only cutting to become ready for use), and skins or parts of skins sewn together in the form of garments or parts or accessories of garments or of other articles fall within heading No. 43.03.

4. Articles of apparel and clothing accessories (except those excluded by Note 2) lined with furskin or artificial fur or to which furskin or artificial fur is attached on the outside except as mere trimming are to be classified under heading No. 43.03 or 43.04 as the case may be.

5. Throughout this Schedule the expression " artificial fur " means any imitation of furskin consisting of wool, hair or other fibres gummed or sewn on to leather, woven fabric or other materials, but does not include imitation furskins obtained by weaving (heading No. 58.04, for example).

Tariff Heading	*Rate of Import Duty (if any)*	
	Full	*Commonwealth (C)* *E.F.T.A. (E)*
43.01 Raw furskins	—	—
43.02 Furskins, tanned or dressed, including furskins assembled in plates, crosses and similar forms; pieces or cuttings, of furskin, tanned or dressed, including heads, paws, tails and the like (not being fabricated):		
(A) Furskins assembled in plates, crosses and similar forms	20%	—
(B) Other	6%	—
43.03 Articles of furskin	20%	—
43.04 Artificial fur and articles made thereof ...	20%	—

SECTION IX

Wood and Articles of Wood; Wood Charcoal; Cork and Articles of Cork; Manufactures of Straw, of Esparto and of other Plaiting Materials; Basketware and Wickerwork

Chapter 44

Wood and Articles of Wood; Wood Charcoal

Notes

1. This Chapter does not cover:

(*a*) Wood of a kind used primarily in perfumery, in pharmacy, or for insecticidal, fungicidal or similar purposes (heading No. 12.07);

(*b*) Wood of a kind used primarily in dyeing or in tanning (heading No. 13.01);

(*c*) Activated charcoal (heading No. 38.03);

(*d*) Articles falling within Chapter 46;

(*e*) Footwear or parts thereof falling within Chapter 64;

(*f*) Goods falling within Chapter 66 (for example, umbrellas and walking-sticks and parts thereof);

(*g*) Goods falling within heading No. 68.09;

(*h*) Imitation jewellery falling within heading No. 71.16;

(*ij*) Goods falling within Section XVII (for example, wheelwrights' wares);

(*k*) Goods falling within Chapter 91 (for example, clocks and clock cases);

(*l*) Musical instruments or parts thereof (Chapter 92);

(*m*) Parts of firearms (heading No. 93.06);

(*n*) Furniture or parts thereof falling within Chapter 94;

(*o*) Articles falling within Chapter 97 (for example, toys, games and sports requisites); or

(*p*) Smoking pipes or the like or parts thereof, buttons, pencils or other articles falling within Chapter 98.

2. In this Chapter, the expression " improved wood " means wood which has been subjected to chemical or physical treatment (being, in the case of layers bonded together, treatment in excess of that needed to ensure a good bond), and which has thereby acquired increased density or hardness together with improved mechanical strength or resistance to chemical or electrical agencies.

3. Headings Nos. 44.19 to 44.28 are to be taken to apply to articles of the respective descriptions of plywood, cellular wood, " improved " wood or reconstituted wood as they apply to such articles of wood.

4. Heading No. 44.25 shall be taken not to apply to tools in which metal parts form the blade, working edge, working surface or other working part.

Tariff Heading	*Rate of Import Duty (if any)*	
	Full	*Commonwealth (C)* *E.F.T.A. (E)*
44.01 Fuel wood, in logs, in billets, in twigs or in faggots; wood waste, including sawdust	4%	—

Tariff Heading	Rate of Import Duty (if any)	
	Full	*Commonwealth (C) E.F.T.A. (E)*
44.02 Wood charcoal (including shell and nut charcoal), agglomerated or not	5%	—
44.03 Wood in the rough, whether or not stripped of its bark or merely roughed down:		
(A) Logs not exceeding 2·16 metres in length and 1·22 metres in girth at the narrower end and not being of ash	—	—
(B) Telegraph poles not less than 6·0 metres in length, not less than 127 millimetres in top diameter and not less than 152 millimetres in diameter 1·52 metres down from the butt end	—	—
(C) Other:		
(1) Of the following species, namely, species of *Acer, Betula, Fagus, Fraxinus, Juglans, Populus, Quercus* and *Ulmus; Castanea sativa; Eucalyptus diversicolor; Eucalyptus marginata*	4%	—
(2) Other	—	—
44.04 Wood, roughly squared or half-squared, but not further manufactured:		
(A) Of the following species, namely, species of *Acer, Betula, Fagus, Fraxinus, Juglans, Populus, Quercus* and *Ulmus; Castanea sativa; Eucalyptus diversicolor; Eucalyptus marginata*	4%	—
(B) Other	—	—
44.05 Wood sawn lengthwise, sliced or peeled, but not further prepared, of a thickness exceeding five millimetres:		
(A) Of the following species, namely, coniferous species; species of *Acer, Betula, Fagus, Fraxinus, Juglans, Populus, Quercus* and *Ulmus; Castanea sativa; Eucalyptus diversicolor; Eucalyptus marginata:*		
(1) Feather-edged boards	6%	—
(2) Boxboards	5%	—
(3) Pencil slats:		
(*a*) Of incense cedar, not exceeding 191 millimetres in length and 77 millimetres in width	—	—
(*b*) Other	5%	—
(4) Other:		
(*a*) Of coniferous species	—	—
(*b*) Other	4%	—

Tariff Heading	Rate of Import Duty (if any)	
	Full	Commonwealth (C) E.F.T.A. (E)
44.05 Wood sawn lengthwise, sliced or peeled, but not further prepared, of a thickness exceeding five millimetres:—*contd.*		
(B) Other	—	—
44.06 Wood paving blocks	4%	—
44.07 Railway or tramway sleepers of wood:		
(A) Of coniferous species	—	—
(B) Other	5%	—
44.08 Riven staves of wood, not further prepared than sawn on one principal surface; sawn staves of wood, of which at least one principal surface has been cylindrically sawn, not further prepared than sawn	4%	—
44.09 Hoopwood; split poles; piles, pickets and stakes of wood, pointed but not sawn lengthwise; chipwood; pulpwood in chips or particles; wood shavings of a kind suitable for use in the manufacture of vinegar or for the clarification of liquids:		
(A) Hoopwood	5%	—
(B) Pulpwood, in the form of chips, with an uncompacted bulk density of not less than 160 kilogrammes per cubic metre when measured by a loose weight method using the apparatus described in British Standard 812: 1967, and of which not more than 5 per cent. by weight passes a sieve having a nominal width of aperture of 2·00 millimetres and imported in consignments of not less than 508 tonnes each	—	—
(C) Other	8%	—
44.10 Wooden sticks, roughly trimmed but not turned, bent nor otherwise worked, suitable for the manufacture of walking-sticks, whips, golf club shafts, umbrella handles, tool handles or the like	5%	—
44.11 Drawn wood; match splints; wooden pegs or pins for footwear	10%	—

Tariff Heading	*Rate of Import Duty (if any)*	
	Full	*Commonwealth (C)* *E.F.T.A. (E)*
44.12 Wood wool and wood flour:		
(A) Wood wool	£1·3530 per tonne	—
(B) Wood flour	7·5%	—
44.13 Wood (including blocks, strips and friezes for parquet or wood block flooring, not assembled), planed, tongued, grooved, rebated, chamfered, V-jointed, centre V-jointed, beaded, centre-beaded or the like, but not further manufactured:		
(A) Hardwood flooring blocks, strips and friezes, planed and tongued and grooved, or planed and otherwise manufactured	15%	—
(B) Other	5%	—
44.14 Wood sawn lengthwise, sliced or peeled, but not further prepared, of a thickness not exceeding five millimetres; veneer sheets and sheets for plywood, of a thickness not exceeding five millimetres:		
(A) Boxboards; veneer sheets and sheets for plywood	5%	—
(B) Pencil slats:		
(1) Of incense cedar, not exceeding 191 millimetres in length and 77 millimetres in width	—	—
(2) Other	5%	—
(C) Other:		
(1) Of coniferous species	—	—
(2) Other	5%	—
44.15 Plywood, blockboard, laminboard, battenboard and similar laminated wood products (including veneered panels and sheets); inlaid wood and wood marquetry:		
(A) Plywood, blockboard, laminboard and battenboard, containing no material other than wood and bonding material	5%	—
(B) Other	10%	—
44.16 Cellular wood panels, whether or not faced with base metal	10%	—
44.17 " Improved " wood, in sheets, blocks or the like	5%	—

Tariff Heading	Rate of Import Duty (if any)	
	Full	Commonwealth (C) E.F.T.A. (E)
44.18 Reconstituted wood, being wood shavings, wood chips, sawdust, wood flour or other ligneous waste agglomerated with natural or artificial resins or other organic binding substances, in sheets, blocks or the like:		
(A) Flaxboard	10%	—
(B) Other	18%	—
44.19 Wooden beadings and mouldings, including moulded skirting and other moulded boards	7·5%	—
44.20 Wooden picture frames, photograph frames, mirror frames and the like:		
(A) Carved	7·5%	—
(B) Other	10%	—
44.21 Complete wooden packing cases, boxes, crates, drums and similar packings:		
(A) Imported unassembled, and consisting of softwood boxboards not dovetailed, morticed or tenoned at the ends	5%	—
(B) Other	8%	—
44.22 Casks, barrels, vats, tubs, buckets and other coopers' products and parts thereof, of wood, other than staves falling within heading No. 44.08:		
(A) Sections of cask-heads not dowel-holed or pegged, and cask-heads consisting of a single circular sheet of wood	5%	—
(B) Empty palm oil casks, assembled, with staves not less than 0·99 metre and not more than 1·12 metres in length and heads not less than 0·86 metre and not more than 1·02 metres in diameter, which have been used to contain palm oil	5%	—
(C) Used casks and barrels of oak, whether assembled or not; staves and heads, being parts of such casks and barrels	—	—
(D) Other	8%	—
44.23 Builders' carpentry and joinery (including prefabricated and sectional buildings and assembled parquet flooring panels):		
(A) Hardwood parquet flooring panels, assembled	15%	—
(B) Other	7·5%	—

Tariff Heading	*Rate of Import Duty (if any)*	
	Full	*Commonwealth (C)* *E.F.T.A. (E)*
44.24 Household utensils of wood	15%	—
44.25 Wooden tools, tool bodies, tool handles, broom and brush bodies and handles; boot and shoe lasts and trees, of wood:		
(A) Last blocks roughly shaped by sawing or turning but not further manufactured	—	—
(B) Fork, shovel and spade handles of the box or 'D' Type, whether riveted or not	—	—
(C) Other	10%	—
44.26 Spools, cops, bobbins, sewing thread reels and the like, of turned wood:		
(A) Sewing thread reels and reel blocks, not exceeding 127 millimetres in length and 64 millimetres in diameter, punched longitudinally	2·5%	—
(B) Other	8%	—
44.27 Standard lamps, table lamps and other lighting fittings, of wood; articles of furniture, of wood, not falling within Chapter 94; caskets, cigarette boxes, trays, fruit bowls, ornaments and other fancy articles, of wood; cases for cutlery, for drawing instruments or for violins, and similar receptacles, of wood; articles of wood for personal use or adornment, of a kind normally carried in the pocket, in the handbag or on the person; parts of the foregoing articles, of wood:		
(A) Beads and bead trimming; carved pictures and wall plaques	7·5%	—
(B) Caskets, cigarette boxes, trays, fruit bowls, ornaments (including statuettes and figures but not including candlesticks) and other fancy articles of wood	15%	—
(C) Other	10%	—
44.28 Other articles of wood:		
(A) Pallets of a kind used with fork lift trucks having two-tongue forks	—	—
(B) Softwood boxboards, other than those covered by headings Nos. 44.05, 44.13, 44.14 and 44.21, not dove-tailed, mortised or tenoned at the ends	5%	—
(C) Spring blind or shade rollers, whether with brackets or laths or not, and whether in sets or not, and rollers therefor bored at one or both ends or further manufactured	5%	—

Tariff Heading	Rate of Import Duty (if any)	
	Full	*Commonwealth (C)* *E.F.T.A. (E)*
44.28 Other articles of wood:—*contd.*		
(D) Stems of turned ash, being straight lengths of not less than 0·45 metre and not more than 1·07 metres, of circular cross-section of diameter (uniform throughout the length) not less than 34 millimetres and not more than 43 millimetres, not further prepared or manufactured	5%	—
(E) Other	15%	—

Chapter 45

Cork and Articles of Cork

Notes

1. This Chapter does not cover:

(*a*) Footwear or parts of footwear falling within Chapter 64;

(*b*) Headgear or parts of headgear falling within Chapter 65; or

(*c*) Articles falling within Chapter 97 (for example, toys, games and sports requisites).

2. Natural cork roughly squared or deprived of the outer bark is to be taken to fall within heading No. 45.02 and not within heading No. 45.01.

Tariff Heading	*Rate of Import Duty (if any)*	
	Full	*Commonwealth (C)* *E.F.T.A. (E)*
45.01 Natural cork, unworked, crushed, granulated or ground; waste cork	—	—
45.02 Natural cork in the form of rectangular blocks, plates, sheets or strips (including cubes or square slabs, cut to size for corks or stoppers)	5%	—
45.03 Articles of natural cork:		
(A) Discs not exceeding 31 millimetres in diameter nor 5 millimetres in thickness	—	—
(B) Stoppers containing no material other than natural cork, wax and adhesives	—	—
(C) Other:		
(1) Stoppers not containing metal, rubber or wood	5%	—
(2) Other	10%	—
45.04 Agglomerated cork (being cork agglomerated with or without a binding substance) and articles of agglomerated cork:		
(A) Stoppers not containing metal, rubber or wood	5%	—
(B) Tiles, not exceeding 10 millimetres in thickness, and of which neither the length nor the width exceeds 331 millimetres, tongued and grooved and surface smoothed, but not further prepared or manufactured	5%	—
(C) Rectangular blocks, plates, sheets or strips, made wholly from cork	5%	—
(D) Other	10%	—

Chapter 46

Manufactures of Straw, of Esparto and of Other Plaiting Materials; Basketware and Wickerwork

Notes

1. In this Chapter the expression " plaiting materials " includes straw, osier or willow, bamboos, rattans, rushes, reeds, strips of wood, strips of vegetable fibre or bark, unspun textile fibres, monofil and strip of artificial plastic materials and strips of paper, but not strips of leather, of composition leather or of felt, human hair, horsehair, textile rovings or yarns, or monofil or strip of Chapter 51.

2. This Chapter does not cover:

(*a*) Twine, cordage, ropes or cables, plaited or not (heading No. 59.04);

(*b*) Footwear or headgear or parts thereof falling within Chapter 64 or 65;

(*c*) Vehicles and bodies for vehicles, of basketware (Chapter 87); or

(*d*) Furniture or parts thereof (Chapter 94).

3. For the purposes of heading No. 46.02, " plaiting materials bound together in parallel strands " means " plaiting materials " placed side by side and bound together, in the form of sheets, whether the binding materials are of spun textile fibre or not.

Tariff Heading	*Rate of Import Duty (if any)*	
	Full	*Commonwealth (C)* *E.F.T.A. (E)*
46.01 Plaits and similar products of plaiting materials, for all uses, whether or not assembled into strips	5%	—
46.02 Plaiting materials (other than products falling within heading No. 46.01) bound together in parallel strands or woven, in sheet form, including matting, mats and screens; straw envelopes for bottles:		
(A) Mats and matting, of rush, reed, straw or grass	2·5%	—
(B) Woven material and mats and matting, of raffia; straw envelopes for bottles	5%	—
(C) Other	10%	—
46.03 Basketwork, wickerwork and other articles of plaiting materials, made directly to shape; articles made up from goods falling within heading No. 46.01 or 46.02; articles of loofah:		
(A) Baskets of osier, willow, cane or wicker	30%	—
(B) Mats and matting, of rush, reed, straw or grass	2·5%	—
(C) Other	10%	—

SECTION X

PAPER-MAKING MATERIAL; PAPER AND PAPERBOARD AND ARTICLES THEREOF

Chapter 47

Paper-making Material

Tariff Heading	*Rate of Import Duty (if any)*	
	Full	*Commonwealth (C)* *E.F.T.A. (E)*
47.01 Pulp derived by mechanical or chemical means from any fibrous vegetable material:		
(A) Wood pulp; straw pulp, bleached; bagasse pulp; pulp of esparto, albardin grass or diss (vine-tie) grass; reed or rush pulp, bleached	—	—
(B) Bleached fibrous hydroxyethylated cotton linter pulp, which is insoluble in water and in which the ethylene oxide which is combined with the cotton linters amounts to not less than 1·2 per cent. and not more than 7·5 per cent. by weight of the finished product	—	—
(C) Other	5%	—
47.02 Waste paper and paperboard; scrap articles of paper or of paperboard, fit only for use in paper-making	10%	—

Chapter 48

Paper and Paperboard; Articles of Paper Pulp, of Paper or of Paperboard

Notes

1. This Chapter does not cover:

(*a*) Stamping foils of heading No. 32.09;

(*b*) Perfume and cosmetic papers (heading No. 33.06);

(*c*) Soap papers (heading No. 34.01), papers impregnated or coated with detergent (heading No. 34.02) and cellulose wadding impregnated with polishes, creams or similar preparations (heading No. 34.05);

(*d*) Paper or paperboard, sensitised (heading No. 37.03);

(*e*) Paper-reinforced stratified artificial plastic sheeting (headings Nos. 39.01 to 39.06), or vulcanised fibre (heading No. 39.03), or articles of such materials (heading No. 39.07);

(*f*) Goods falling within heading No. 42.02 (for example, travel goods);

(*g*) Articles falling within any heading in Chapter 46 (manufactures of plaiting material);

(*h*) Paper yarn or textile articles of paper yarn (Section XI);

(*ij*) Abrasive paper (heading No. 68.06) or paper-backed mica splittings (heading No. 68.15) (paper coated with mica powder is, however, to be classified in heading No. 48.07);

(*k*) Metal foil backed with paper or paperboard (Section XV);

(*l*) Perforated paper or paperboard for musical instruments (heading No. 92.10); or

(*m*) Goods falling within any heading in Chapter 97 (for example, toys, games and sports requisites) or Chapter 98 (for example, buttons).

2. Subject to the provisions of Note 3, headings Nos. 48.01 and 48.02 are to be taken to include paper and paperboard which have been subjected to calendering, super-calendering, glazing or similar finishing, including tub-sizing or false water-marking and also to paper and paperboard coloured or marbled throughout the mass by any method. They do not apply to paper or paperboard which has been further processed, for example, by coating or impregnation.

3. Paper or paperboard answering to a description in two or more of the headings Nos. 48.01 to 48.07 is to be classified under that one of such headings which occurs latest in this Chapter.

4. Headings Nos. 48.01 to 48.07 are to be taken not to apply to paper, paperboard or cellulose wadding:

(*a*) In strips or rolls of a width not exceeding fifteen centimetres; or

(*b*) In rectangular sheets (unfolded if necessary) of which no side exceeds thirty-six centimetres; or

(*c*) Cut into shapes other than rectangular shapes.

Except that hand-made paper in any size or shape as made directly and having all its edges deckled remains classified, subject to the provisions of Note 3, within heading No. 48.02.

5. For the purposes of heading No. 48.11 " wallpaper and lincrusta " are to be taken to apply only to:

(*a*) Paper in rolls, suitable for wall or ceiling decoration, being:

(i) Paper with one or with two margins, with or without guide marks; or

(ii) Paper without margins, surface-coloured or design-printed, coated or embossed, of a width not exceeding sixty centimetres;

(*b*) Borders, friezes and corners of paper, of a kind used for wall or ceiling decoration.

6. Heading No. 48.15 is to be taken to apply, *inter alia*, to paper wool, paper strip (whether or not folded or coated) of a kind used for plaiting, and to toilet paper in rolls or packets, but not to the articles mentioned in Note 7.

7. Heading No. 48.21 is to be taken to apply, *inter alia*, to cards for statistical machines, perforated paper and paperboard cards for Jacquard and similar machines, paper lace, shelf edging, paper tablecloths, serviettes and handkerchiefs, paper gaskets, moulded or pressed goods of wood pulp, and dress patterns.

8. Paper, paperboard and cellulose wadding, and articles thereof, printed with characters or pictures which are not merely incidental to the primary use of the goods are regarded as printed matter falling within Chapter 49.

Tariff Heading	*Rate of Import Duty (if any)*	
	Full	*Commonwealth* (*C*) *E.F.T.A.* (*E*)
I. Paper and paperboard, in rolls or in sheets		
48.01 Paper and paperboard (including cellulose wadding), machine-made, in rolls or sheets:		
(A) Weighing more than 220 grammes per square metre:		
(1) Board manufactured wholly of unbleached, undyed sulphate cellulose fibre, in reels	10%	—
(2) Strawboard, being board containing not less than 90 per cent. by weight of unbleached cereal straw pulp	12%	—
(3) Other	18%	—
(B) Weighing not more than 220 grammes per square metre:		
(1) Paper manufactured wholly of bleached or unbleached sulphate cellulose fibre	10%	—
(2) Machine glazed paper (excluding paper comprised in subheading (1) above and fully bleached white poster paper)	12%	—
(3) Other:		
(*a*) Tissue paper	15%	—
(*b*) Printing paper:		
(i) Newsprint, that is to say, paper in rolls, having a water absorbency when tested by the one-minute Cobb method of not less than 45 grammes per square metre, containing not less than 70 per cent of mechanical wood pulp and of a weight not less than 48 nor more than 62 grammes per square metre	—	—
(ii) Other	15%	—
(*c*) Writing or duplicating paper in sheets	15%	—
(*d*) Strawpaper, being paper manufactured entirely from unbleached cereal straw pulp	15%	—
(*e*) Other	18%	—

Tariff Heading	Rate of Import Duty (if any)	
	Full	Commonwealth (C) E.F.T.A. (E)
48.02 Hand-made paper and paperboard:		
(A) Writing or printing paper in sheets measuring more than 36 centimetres in either length or breadth	15%	—
(B) Tissue paper	15%	—
(C) Other	18%	—
48.03 Parchment or greaseproof paper and paperboard, and imitations thereof, and glazed transparent paper, in rolls or sheets:		
(A) Greaseproof paper and imitation greaseproof paper	12%	—
(B) Other	18%	—
48.04 Composite paper or paperboard (made by sticking flat layers together with an adhesive), not surface-coated or impregnated, whether or not internally reinforced, in rolls or sheets:		
(A) Weighing more than 220 grammes per square metre and, apart from adhesive, consisting wholly of strawboards containing not less than 90 per cent. by weight of unbleached cereal straw pulp	12%	—
(B) Other	18%	—
48.05 Paper and paperboard, corrugated (with or without flat surface sheets), creped, crinkled, embossed or perforated, in rolls or sheets:		
(A) Of a weight when fully extended equivalent to not more than 220 grammes per square metre, not being corrugated with flat surface sheets:		
(1) Paper manufactured wholly of bleached or unbleached sulphate cellulose fibre	10%	—
(2) Machine glazed paper (excluding paper comprised in subheading (1) above and fully bleached white poster paper)	12%	—
(3) Other:		
(*a*) Tissue paper	15%	—
(*b*) Printing paper	15%	—
(*c*) Writing paper in sheets ...	15%	—
(*d*) Strawpaper, being paper manufactured entirely from unbleached cereal straw pulp	15%	—
(*e*) Greaseproof and imitation greaseproof paper	12%	—
(*f*) Other	18%	—

Tariff Heading	Rate of Import Duty (if any)	
	Full	Commonwealth (C) E.F.T.A. (E)
48.05 Paper and paperboard, etc.—*contd.*		
(B) Other:		
(1) Board manufactured wholly of unbleached, undyed sulphate cellulose fibre, in reels, not being corrugated with flat surface sheets	10%	—
(2) Other	18%	—
48.06 Paper and paperboard, ruled, lined or squared, but not otherwise printed, in rolls or sheets:		
(A) Writing or duplicating paper in sheets	15%	—
(B) Printing paper	15%	—
(C) Other	18%	—
48.07 Paper and paperboard, impregnated, coated, surface-coloured, surface-decorated or printed (not being merely ruled, lined or squared and not constituting printed matter within Chapter 49), in rolls or sheets:		
(A) Weighing not more than 220 grammes per square metre:		
(1) Paper manufactured wholly of bleached or unbleached sulphate cellulose fibre	10%	—
(2) Machine glazed paper (excluding paper comprised in subheading (1) above and fully bleached white poster paper)	12%	—
(3) Other:		
(*a*) Tissue paper	15%	—
(*b*) Printing paper	15%	—
(*c*) Writing or duplicating paper in sheets	15%	—
(*d*) Strawpaper, being paper manufactured entirely from unbleached cereal straw pulp	15%	—
(*e*) Greaseproof and imitation greaseproof paper	12%	—
(*f*) Other	18%	—
(B) Weighing more than 220 grammes per square metre:		
(1) Board manufactured wholly of unbleached, undyed sulphate cellulose fibre, in reels, not being composite board	10%	—
(2) Strawboard, being board containing not less than 90 per cent. by weight of unbleached cereal straw pulp	12%	—
(3) Other	18%	—
48.08 Filter blocks, slabs and plates, of paper pulp	18%	—

Tariff Heading	Rate of Import Duty (if any)	
	Full	Commonwealth (C) E.F.T.A. (E)
48.09 Building board of wood pulp or of vegetable fibre, whether or not bonded with natural or artificial resins or with similar binders	18%	—
II. Paper and paperboard cut to size or shape and articles of paper or paperboard		
48.10 Cigarette paper, cut to size, whether or not in the form of booklets or tubes	15%	—
48.11 Wallpaper and lincrusta; window transparencies of paper	10%	—
48.12 Floor coverings prepared on a base of paper or of paperboard, whether or not cut to size, with or without a coating of linoleum compound	10%	—
48.13 Carbon and other copying papers (including duplicator stencils) and transfer papers, cut to size, whether or not put up in boxes	18%	—
48.14 Writing blocks, envelopes, plain letter cards, plain postcards, correspondence cards; boxes, pouches, wallets and writing compendiums, of paper or paperboard, containing only an assortment of paper stationery	15%	—
48.15 Other paper and paperboard (including cellulose wadding), cut to size or shape:		
(A) Weighing not more than 220 grammes per square metre:		
(1) Toilet paper	18%	—
(2) Paper manufactured wholly of bleached or unbleached sulphate cellulose fibre, in strips, rolls or in square-cut or angle-cut sheets	10%	—
(3) Machine glazed paper (excluding paper comprised in subheadings (1) or (2) above and fully bleached white poster paper) in strips, rolls or in square-cut or angle-cut sheets	12%	—
(4) Greaseproof and imitation greaseproof paper in strips, rolls or in square-cut or angle-cut sheets	12%	—
(5) Other:		
(*a*) Tissue paper in strips, rolls or rectangular sheets	15%	—
(*b*) Writing or printing paper in parallelograms of which all sides exceed 36 centimetres	15%	—

Tariff Heading	Rate of Import Duty (if any)	
	Full	Commonwealth (C) E.F.T.A. (E)
48.15 Other paper and paperboard, etc.—*contd.*		
(A) (5) Other:—*contd.*		
(*c*) Strawpaper, being paper manufactured entirely from unbleached cereal straw pulp	15%	—
(*d*) Other	18%	—
(B) Weighing more than 220 grammes per square metre	18%	—
48.16 Boxes, bags and other packing containers, of paper or paperboard	12%	—
48.17 Box files, letter trays, storage boxes and similar articles, of paper or paperboard, of a kind commonly used in offices, shops and the like	12%	—
48.18 Registers, exercise books, note books, memorandum blocks, order books, receipt books, diaries, blotting-pads, binders (loose-leaf or other), file covers and other stationery of paper or paperboard; sample and other albums and book covers, of paper or paperboard:		
(A) Printed book covers (other than trade advertising material) for books of a kind falling within heading No. 49.01, 49.03, 49.04 or 49.05	—	—
(B) Printed forms	—	—
(C) Trade advertising material:		
(1) Material the primary purpose of which is to stimulate travel outside the United Kingdom	—	—
(2) Other	12%	—
(D) Other	10%	—
48.19 Paper or paperboard labels, whether or not printed or gummed	18%	—
48.20 Bobbins, spools, cops and similar supports of paper pulp, paper or paperboard (whether or not perforated or hardened)	10%	—
48.21 Other articles of paper pulp, paper, paperboard or cellulose wadding:		
(A) Paper dress patterns, including the paper envelopes in which they are enclosed	10%	—
(B) Face and hand towels, made wholly of paper weighing not less than 24 grammes per square metre	10%	—

Tariff Heading	*Rate of Import Duty (if any)*	
	Full	*Commonwealth (C)* *E.F.T.A. (E)*
48.21 Other articles of paper pulp, paper, paper-board or cellulose wadding:—*contd.*		
(C) Serviettes and handkerchiefs, not printed, of an area not exceeding 2,580 square centimetres, made wholly of paper weighing not less than 17 grammes per square metre	10%	—
(D) Sanitary napkins of cellulose wadding	10%	—
(E) Cards, tapes and other articles on which information has been recorded by means of perforated holes and which are for use in statistical and other machines (but not including articles for use in Jacquard and similar machines)	—	—
(F) Other	18%	—

Chapter 49

Printed Books, Newspapers, Pictures and other Products of the Printing Industry; Manuscripts, Typescripts and Plans

Notes

1. This Chapter does not cover:

(*a*) Paper, paperboard, or cellulose wadding, or articles thereof, in which printing is merely incidental to their primary use (Chapter 48);

(*b*) Playing cards or other goods falling within any heading in Chapter 97; or

(*c*) Original engravings, prints or lithographs (heading No. 99.02), postage, revenue or similar stamps falling within heading No. 99.04, antiques of an age exceeding 100 years or other articles falling within any heading in Chapter 99.

2. Newspapers, journals and periodicals which are bound otherwise than in paper, and sets of newspapers, journals or periodicals comprising more than one number under a single cover are to be treated as falling within heading No. 49.01 and not within heading No. 49.02.

3. Heading No. 49.01 is to be extended to apply to:

(*a*) A collection of printed reproductions of, for example, works of art or drawings, with a relative text, put up with numbered pages in a form suitable for binding into one or more volumes;

(*b*) A pictorial supplement accompanying, and subsidiary to, a bound volume; and

(*c*) Printed parts of books or booklets, in the form of assembled or separate sheets or signatures, constituting the whole or a part of a complete work and designed for binding.

However, printed pictures or illustrations not bearing a text, whether in the form of signatures or separate sheets, fall in heading No. 49.11.

4. Headings Nos. 49.01 and 49.02 are to be taken not to apply to publications issued for advertising purposes by or for an advertiser named therein, or to publications which are primarily devoted to advertising (including tourist propaganda). Such publications are to be taken as falling within heading No. 49.11.

5. For the purposes of heading No. 49.03, the expression " children's picture books " means books for children in which the pictures form the principal interest and the text is subsidiary.

6. For the purposes of heading No. 49.06, the expression " manuscripts and typescripts " is to be taken to extend to carbon copies or copies on sensitised paper of manuscripts and typescripts. References in this Chapter to printed matter of any kind include references to any matter of that kind which is reproduced by means of a duplicating machine.

7. For the purposes of heading No. 49.09, the expression " picture postcards " means cards consisting essentially of an illustration and bearing printed indications of their use.

Tariff Heading	*Rate of Import Duty (if any)*	
	Full	*Commonwealth (C)* *E.F.T.A. (E)*
49.01 Printed books, booklets, brochures, pamphlets and leaflets	—	—
49.02 Newspapers, journals and periodicals, whether or not illustrated	—	—

Tariff Heading	Rate of Import Duty (if any)	
	Full	Commonwealth (C) E.F.T.A. (E)
49.03 Children's picture books and painting books	—	—
49.04 Music, printed or in manuscript, whether or not bound or illustrated	—	—
49.05 Maps and hydrographic and similar charts of all kinds, including atlases, wall maps and topographical plans, printed; printed globes (terrestrial or celestial)	—	—
49.06 Plans and drawings, for industrial, architectural, engineering, commercial or similar purposes, whether original or reproductions on sensitised paper; manuscripts and typescripts	—	—
49.07 Unused postage, revenue and similar stamps of current or new issue in the country to which they are destined; paper impressed with such stamps; banknotes, stock, share and bond certificates and similar documents of title; cheque books and cheque forms	—	—
49.08 Transfers	10%	—
49.09 Picture postcards and pictorial greeting cards, printed, with or without trimmings:		
(A) Trade advertising material the primary purpose of which is to stimulate travel outside the United Kingdom	—	—
(B) Other	10%	—
49.10 Calendars of any kind, of paper or paperboard, including calendar blocks:		
(A) Trade advertising material:		
(1) Material the primary purpose of which is to stimulate travel outside the United Kingdom	—	—
(2) Other	7·5%	—
(B) Other	10%	—
49.11 Other printed matter, including printed pictures and photographs:		
(A) Trade advertising material, the following:		
(1) Catalogues and lists of books and publications offered for sale by publishers or booksellers established outside the United Kingdom	—	—

Tariff Heading	Rate of Import Duty (if any)	
	Full	Commonwealth (C) E.F.T.A. (E)
49.11 Other printed matter, etc.—*contd.*		
(A) Trade advertising material, etc.—*contd.*		
(2) Publications, illustrated or not, the primary purpose of which is to stimulate study or travel outside the United Kingdom, or to advertise exhibitions held outside the United Kingdom	—	—
(3) Other catalogues, lists, books, publications and documents:		
(*a*) Imported either in a packet not exceeding 2¼ lb. in gross weight or in a packet containing not more than one copy of any catalogue, list, book, publication or document, being in either case a postal packet or a packet which does not form part of a larger consignment	—	—
(*b*) Other	12%	—
(4) Printed parts of catalogues, lists, books, publications and documents	12%	—
(B) Less than full-size reproductions of articles falling within headings Nos. 49.01, 49.02, 49.03, 49.04, 49.05, 49.06, 49.07 or subheadings 49.09 (A), 49.10 (A) (1), 49.11 (A) (1), 49.11 (A) (2), 49.11 (C) (2) (*a*), 49.11 (C) (2) (*b*)	—	—
(C) Other:		
(1) Photographic prints:		
(*a*) Imported in a packet not exceeding 8 ounces in gross weight which does not form part of a larger consignment	—	—
(*b*) Other	5%	—
(2) Other printed matter:		
(*a*) Parts of books or booklets in the form of printed pictures or illustrations not bearing a text	—	—
(*b*) Printed documents, printed diagrams, and printed architectural, engineering and similar industrial designs or plans, not being trade advertising material	—	—
(*c*) Other	12%	—

SECTION XI

Textiles and Textile Articles

Notes

1. This Section does not cover:

(*a*) Animal brush making bristles or hair (heading No. 05.02); horsehair or horsehair waste (heading No. 05.03);

(*b*) Human hair or articles of human hair (heading No. 05.01, 67.03 or 67.04), except straining cloth of a kind commonly used in oil presses and the like (heading No. 59.17);

(*c*) Vegetable materials falling within Chapter 14;

(*d*) Asbestos of heading No. 25.24 or articles of asbestos and other products of heading No. 68.13 or 68.14;

(*e*) Articles falling within heading No. 30.04 or 30.05 (for example, wadding, gauze, bandages and similar articles for medical or surgical purposes, sterile surgical suture materials);

(*f*) Sensitised textile fabric (heading No. 37.03);

(*g*) Monofil of which any cross-sectional dimension exceeds 1 millimetre and strip (artificial straw and the like) of a width exceeding 5 millimetres, of artificial plastic material (Chapter 39) or plaits or fabrics of such monofil or strip (Chapter 46);

(*h*) Woven textile fabrics, felt, bonded fibre fabrics or similar bonded yarn fabrics, impregnated, coated, covered or laminated with rubber, and articles thereof, falling within Chapter 40;

(*ij*) Skins with their wool on (Chapter 41 or 43) or articles of furskin, artificial fur or articles thereof, falling within heading No. 43.03 or 43.04;

(*k*) Articles of textile materials falling within heading No. 42.01 or 42.02;

(*l*) Products and articles of Chapter 48 (for example, cellulose wadding);

(*m*) Footwear or parts of footwear, gaiters or leggings or similar articles classified in Chapter 64;

(*n*) Headgear or parts thereof falling within Chapter 65;

(*o*) Hair nets (heading No. 65.05 or 67.04, as the case may be);

(*p*) Goods falling within Chapter 67;

(*q*) Abrasive-coated threads, cords or fabric (heading No. 68.06);

(*r*) Glass fibre or articles of glass fibre, other than embroidery with glass thread on a visible ground of fabric (Chapter 70);

(*s*) Articles falling within Chapter 94 (furniture and bedding); or

(*t*) Articles falling within Chapter 97 (for example, toys, games and sports requisites).

2. (A) Goods classifiable in any heading in Chapters 50 to 57 and of a mixture of two or more different textile materials are to be classified according to the following rules:

(*a*) Goods containing more than 10 per cent. by weight of silk, noil or other waste silk or any combination thereof are to be classified in Chapter 50, and, for the purposes of classification in that Chapter, as if consisting wholly of that one of those materials which predominates in weight;

(*b*) All other goods are to be classified as if consisting wholly of that one textile material which predominates in weight over any other single textile material.

(B) For the purposes of the above rules:

(*a*) Metallised yarn is to be treated as a single textile material and its weight is to be taken as the aggregate of the weight of the textile and metal components, and, for the classification of woven fabrics, metal thread is to be regarded as a textile material;

(*b*) Where a heading refers to a particular form of a textile material (for example, carded sheep's or lambs' wool), that form is to be treated as a single textile material. However, where a heading refers to two or more textile materials (or different forms of the same textile material), all those materials are to be treated as a single textile material;

(*c*) Except as provided in (B) (*a*), the weight of constituents other than textile materials is not to be included in the weight of the goods.

(C) The provisions of paragraphs (A) and (B) above are to be applied also to the yarns referred to in Notes 3 and 4 below.

3. (A) For the purposes of this Section, and subject to the exceptions in paragraph (B) below, yarns (single, multiple or cabled) of the following descriptions are to be treated as " twine, cordage, ropes and cables ":

(*a*) Of silk, noil or other waste silk, of a weight exceeding 2 grammes per metre (18,000 denier);

(*b*) Of man-made fibres (including yarn of two or more monofil of Chapter 51), of a weight exceeding 1 gramme per metre (9,000 denier);

(*c*) Of true hemp or flax:

(i) Polished or glazed, of which the length per kilogramme, multiplied by the number of constituent strands, is less than 7,000 metres;

(ii) Not polished or glazed and of a weight exceeding 2 grammes per metre;

(*d*) Of coir, consisting of three or more plies;

(*e*) Of other vegetable fibres, of a weight exceeding 2 grammes per metre; or

(*f*) Reinforced with metal.

(B) Exceptions:

(*a*) Yarn of sheep's or lambs' wool or other animal hair and paper yarn, other than yarn reinforced with metal;

(*b*) Continuous filament tow for the manufacture of man-made fibres (discontinuous), and multi-filament yarn without twist or with a twist of less than 5 turns per metre;

(*c*) Silk worm gut, imitation catgut of silk or of man-made fibres, and monofil of Chapter 51;

(*d*) Metallised yarn, not being yarn reinforced with metal; and

(*e*) Chenille yarn and gimped yarn.

4. (A) For the purposes of Chapters 50, 51, 53, 54, 55 and 56, the expression " put up for retail sale " in relation to yarn means, subject to the exceptions in paragraph (B) below, yarn put up:

(*a*) In balls or on cards, reels, tubes or similar supports, of a weight (including support) not exceeding:

(i) 200 grammes in the case of flax and ramie;

(ii) 85 grammes in the case of silk, noil or other waste silk, and man-made fibres (continuous); or

(iii) 125 grammes in other cases;

(*b*) In hanks or skeins of a weight not exceeding:

(i) 85 grammes in the case of silk, noil or other waste silk, and man-made fibres (continuous); or

(ii) 125 grammes in other cases;

(*c*) In hanks or skeins comprising several smaller hanks or skeins separated by dividing threads which render them independent one of the other, each of uniform weight not exceeding:

(i) 85 grammes in the case of silk, noil or other waste silk, and man-made fibres (continuous); or

(ii) 125 grammes in other cases.

(B) Exceptions:

(*a*) Single yarn of any textile material, except:

(i) Single yarn of sheep's or lambs' wool or of fine animal hair, unbleached; and

(ii) Single yarn of sheep's or lambs' wool or of fine animal hair, bleached, dyed or printed, of a length less than 2,000 metres per kilogramme;

(*b*) Multiple or cabled yarn, unbleached:

(i) Of silk, noil or other waste silk, however put up; or

(ii) Of other textile material except sheep's or lambs' wool or fine animal hair, in hanks or skeins;

(*c*) Multiple or cabled yarn of silk, noil or other waste silk, bleached, dyed or printed, of a length not less than 75,000 metres per kilogramme, measured multiple; and

(*d*) Single, multiple or cabled yarn of any textile material:

(i) In cross-reeled hanks or skeins; or

(ii) Put up on supports or in some other manner indicating its use in the textile industry (for example, on cops, twisting mill tubes, pirns, conical bobbins or spindles, or reeled in the form of cocoons for embroidery looms).

5. (*a*) For the purposes of heading No. 55.07, " gauze " means a fabric with a warp composed wholly or in part of standing or ground threads and crossing or doup threads which cross the standing or ground threads making a half turn, a complete turn or more to form loops through which weft threads pass.

(*b*) For the purposes of heading No. 58.08, " plain " means consisting solely of a single series of regular meshes of the same shape or size without any pattern or filling-in of the meshes. In applying this definition no account is to be taken of any minor open spaces which are inherent in the formation of the meshes.

6. For the purposes of this Section, the expression " made up " means:

(*a*) Cut otherwise than into rectangles;

(*b*) Made and finished by weaving and ready for use (or merely needing separation by cutting dividing threads) and not requiring sewing or further fabrication (for example, certain dusters, towels, table cloths, scarf squares and blankets);

(*c*) Hemmed or with rolled edges (except fabrics in the piece which have been cut from wider pieces and hemmed or rolled merely to prevent unravelling), or with a knotted fringe at any of the edges;

(*d*) Cut to size and having undergone a process of drawn thread work;

(*e*) Assembled by sewing, gumming or otherwise (other than piece goods consisting of two or more lengths of identical material joined end to end and piece goods composed of two or more fabrics assembled in layers, whether or not padded).

7. The headings of Chapters 50 to 57 and, except where the context otherwise requires, the headings of Chapters 58 to 60, are to be taken not to apply to goods made up within the meaning of Note 6 above. Chapters 50 to 57 are to be taken not to apply to goods falling within Chapter 58 or 59.

8. Any import duty at a rate fixed by reference to the weight of any silk or man-made fibres is to be calculated on the weight inclusive of any loading or dressing, but exclusive of any waterproofing; and in the case of goods containing both silk and man-made fibres, or other fibres in addition to silk or man-made fibres, the total weight of loading or dressing in the goods is to be apportioned between the different types of fibre in the goods according to their respective weights.

Chapter 50

Silk and Waste Silk

Tariff Heading	*Rate of Import Duty (if any)*	
	Full	*Commonwealth (C)* *E.F.T.A. (E)*
50.01 Silk-worm cocoons suitable for reeling ...	—	—
50.02 Raw silk (not thrown)	—	—
50.03 Silk waste (including cocoons unsuitable for reeling, silk noils and pulled or garnetted rags):		
(A) Wholly of silk	—	—
(B) Other:		
(1) Not carded or combed:		
(*a*) In which the textile material which predominates in weight is man-made fibre	10%	C 85% of the full rate E —
(*b*) Other	—	—
(2) Carded or combed:		
(*a*) Containing man-made fibres	10%	C 85% of the full rate E —
(*b*) Not containing man-made fibres	10%	—
50.04 Silk yarn, other than yarn of noil or other waste silk, not put up for retail sale:		
(A) Containing more than 50 per cent. by weight of man-made fibres	£0·0300 per lb. or 13%, whichever is the greater	C 85% of the full rate E —
(B) Other	13%	C 85% of the full rate E —
50.05 Yarn spun from silk waste other than noil, not put up for retail sale:		
(A) Containing more than 50 per cent. by weight of man-made fibres	£0·0300 per lb. or 13%, whichever is the greater	C 85% of the full rate E —
(B) Other	13%	C 85% of the full rate E —
50.06 Yarn spun from noil silk, not put up for retail sale:		
(A) Containing more than 50 per cent. by weight of man-made fibres	£0·0300 per lb. or 13%, whichever is the greater	C 85% of the full rate E —
(B) Other	13%	C 85% of the full rate E —

Tariff Heading	*Rate of Import Duty (if any)*	
	Full	*Commonwealth (C)* *E.F.T.A. (E)*
50.07 Silk yarn and yarn spun from noil or other waste silk, put up for retail sale:		
(A) Containing more than 50 per cent. by weight of man-made fibres	£0·0300 per lb. or 13%, whichever is the greater	C 85% of the full rate E —
(B) Other	13%	C 85% of the full rate E —
50.08 Silk-worm gut; imitation catgut of silk:		
(A) Silk-worm gut	—	—
(B) Imitation catgut	£0·0300 per lb. or 13%, whichever is the greater	C 85% of the full rate E —
50.09 Woven fabrics of silk or of waste silk other than noil:		
(A) Containing more than 50 per cent. by weight of silk or of silk and man-made fibres	£0·0200 per square yard or 17·5%, whichever is the greater	C 85% of the full rate E —
(B) Other	17·5%	C 85% of the full rate E —
50.10 Woven fabrics of noil silk:		
(A) Containing more than 50 per cent. by weight of silk or of silk and man-made fibres	£0·0200 per square yard or 17·5%, whichever is the greater	C 85% of the full rate E —
(B) Other	17·5%	C 85% of the full rate E —

Chapter 51

Man-made Fibres (Continuous)

Notes

1. Throughout this Schedule, the term " man-made fibres " means fibres or filaments of organic polymers produced by manufacturing processes, either:

(*a*) By polymerisation or condensation of organic monomers, for example, polyamides, polyesters, polyurethanes and polyvinyl derivatives; or

(*b*) By chemical transformation of natural organic polymers (such as cellulose, casein, proteins and algae), for example, viscose rayon, cuprammonium rayon (cupra), cellulose acetate and alginates.

2. Heading No. 51.01 is to be taken not to apply to continuous filament tow of man-made fibres falling within Chapter 56.

3. The expression " yarn of man-made fibres (continuous) " is to be taken not to apply to yarn (known as " ruptured filament yarn ") of which the majority of the filaments have been ruptured by passage through rollers or other devices (Chapter 56).

4. Monofil of man-made fibre materials of which no cross-sectional dimension exceeds 1 millimetre is to be classified in heading No. 51.01 when of a weight less than 6·6 milligrammes per metre (60 denier) and in heading No. 51.02 in other cases. Monofil of which any cross-sectional dimension exceeds 1 millimetre is to be classified in Chapter 39.

Strip (artificial straw and the like) of man-made fibre materials is to be classified in heading No. 51.02 when of a width not exceeding 5 millimetres and in Chapter 39 in other cases.

Tariff Heading	Rate of Import Duty (if any)	
	Full	*Commonwealth (C)* *E.F.T.A. (E)*
51.01 Yarn of man-made fibres (continuous), not put up for retail sale	£0·0661 per kilogramme or 13%, whichever is the greater	C 85% of the full rate E —
51.02 Monofil, strip (artificial straw and the like) and imitation catgut, of man-made fibre materials	£0·0661 per kilogramme or 13%, whichever is the greater	C 85% of the full rate E —
51.03 Yarn of man-made fibres (continuous), put up for retail sale	£0·0661 per kilogramme or 13%, whichever is the greater	C 85% of the full rate E —
51.04 Woven fabrics of man-made fibres (continuous), including woven fabrics of monofil or strip of heading No. 51.01 or 51.02	£0·0200 per square yard or 17·5%, whichever is the greater	C 85% of the full rate E —

Chapter 52

Metallised Textiles

Tariff Heading	*Rate of Import Duty (if any)*	
	Full	*Commonwealth (C)* *E.F.T.A. (E)*
52.01 Metallised yarn, being textile yarn spun with metal or covered with metal by any process:		
(A) Containing silk or man-made fibres...	13%	C 85% of the full rate E —
(B) Not containing silk or man-made fibres	7·5%	—
52.02 Woven fabrics of metal thread or of metallised yarn, of a kind used in articles of apparel, as furnishing fabrics or the like:		
(A) Containing silk or man-made fibres...	17·5%	C 85% of the full rate E —
(B) Not containing silk or man-made fibres	17·5%	—

Chapter 53

Wool and other Animal Hair

Note

In this Schedule, the expression " fine animal hair " means hair of alpaca, llama, vicuna, yak, camel, Angora, Tibetan, Kashmir and similar goats (but not common goats), rabbit (including Angora rabbit), hare, beaver, nutria and musk rat.

Tariff Heading	*Rate of Import Duty (if any)*	
	Full	*Commonwealth (C)* *E.F.T.A. (E)*
53.01 Sheep's or lambs' wool, not carded or combed:		
(A) Raw, cleaned, scoured or carbonised, but not otherwise worked	—	—
(B) Other	5%	—
53.02 Other animal hair (fine or coarse), not carded or combed:		
(A) Raw, cleaned, scoured or carbonised, but not otherwise worked	—	—
(B) Other:		
(1) Hatters' fur	—	—
(2) Other	5%	—
53.03 Waste of sheep's or lambs' wool or of other animal hair (fine or coarse), not pulled or garnetted	—	—
53.04 Waste of sheep's or lambs' wool or of other animal hair (fine or coarse), pulled or garnetted (including pulled or garnetted rags)	5%	—
53.05 Sheep's or lambs' wool or other animal hair (fine or coarse), carded or combed:		
(A) Containing man-made fibres ...	10%	C 85% of the full rate E —
(B) Not containing man-made fibres ...	10%	—
53.06 Yarn of carded sheep's or lambs' wool (woollen yarn), not put up for retail sale:		
(A) Containing silk or man-made fibres	13%	C 85% of the full rate E —
(B) Not containing silk or man-made fibres	7·5%	—
53.07 Yarn of combed sheep's or lambs' wool (worsted yarn), not put up for retail sale:		
(A) Containing silk or man-made fibres	13%	C 85% of the full rate E —
(B) Not containing silk or man-made fibres	7·5%	—

Tariff Heading	*Rate of Import Duty (if any)*	
	Full	*Commonwealth (C)* *E.F.T.A. (E)*
53.08 Yarn of fine animal hair (carded or combed), not put up for retail sale:		
(A) Containing silk or man-made fibres	13%	C 85% of the full rate E —
(B) Not containing silk or man-made fibres	7·5%	—
53.09 Yarn of horsehair or of other coarse animal hair, not put up for retail sale:		
(A) Containing silk or man-made fibres	13%	C 85% of the full rate E —
(B) Not containing silk or man-made fibres	7·5%	—
53.10 Yarn of sheep's or lambs' wool, of horsehair or of other animal hair (fine or coarse), put up for retail sale:		
(A) Containing silk or man-made fibres	13%	C 85% of the full rate E —
(B) Not containing silk or man-made fibres	7·5%	—
53.11 Woven fabrics of sheep's or lambs' wool or of fine animal hair:		
(A) Containing silk or man-made fibres	17·5%	C 85% of the full rate E —
(B) Not containing silk or man-made fibres	17·5%	—
53.12 Woven fabrics of coarse animal hair other than horsehair:		
(A) Containing silk or man-made fibres	17·5%	C 85% of the full rate E —
(B) Not containing silk or man-made fibres	17·5%	—
53.13 Woven fabrics of horsehair:		
(A) Containing silk or man-made fibres	17·5%	C 85% of the full rate E —
(B) Not containing silk or man-made fibres	17·5%	—

Chapter 54

Flax and Ramie

Tariff Heading	Rate of Import Duty (if any)	
	Full	Commonwealth (C) E.F.T.A. (E)
54.01 Flax, raw or processed but not spun; flax tow and waste (including pulled or garnetted rags):		
(A) Flax, flax tow and flax waste, not hackled, carded or combed	—	—
(B) Other:		
(1) Containing man-made fibres ...	5%	C 85% of the full rate E —
(2) Not containing man-made fibres...	5%	—
54.02 Ramie, raw or processed but not spun; ramie noils and waste (including pulled or garnetted rags):		
(A) Ramie, ramie noils and ramie waste, not carded or combed	—	—
(B) Other:		
(1) Containing man-made fibres ...	5%	C 85% of the full rate E —
(2) Not containing man-made fibres...	5%	—
54.03 Flax or ramie yarn, not put up for retail sale:		
(A) Containing silk or man-made fibres...	13%	C 85% of the full rate E —
(B) Not containing silk or man-made fibres:		
(1) Of flax, polished or glazed ...	10%	—
(2) Other	7·5%	—
54.04 Flax or ramie yarn, put up for retail sale:		
(A) Containing silk or man-made fibres...	13%	C 85% of the full rate E —
(B) Not containing silk or man-made fibres:		
(1) Of flax, polished or glazed ...	10%	—
(2) Other	7·5%	—
54.05 Woven fabrics of flax or of ramie:		
(A) Containing silk or man-made fibres	17·5%	C 85% of the full rate E —
(B) Not containing silk or man-made fibres	17·5%	—

Chapter 55

Cotton

Tariff Heading	*Rate of Import Duty (if any)*	
	Full	*Commonwealth (C)* *E.F.T.A. (E)*
55.01 Cotton, not carded or combed:		
(A) Not bleached or dyed...	—	—
(B) Bleached or dyed	5%	—
55.02 Cotton linters:		
(A) Unbleached	—	—
(B) Bleached	5%	—
55.03 Cotton waste (including pulled or garnetted rags), not carded or combed	—	—
55.04 Cotton, carded or combed:		
(A) Containing man-made fibres ...	5%	C 85% of the full rate E —
(B) Not containing man-made fibres ...	5%	—
55.05 Cotton yarn, not put up for retail sale:		
(A) Containing more than 5 per cent. by weight of silk, of man-made fibres, or of both together	13%	C 85% of the full rate E —
(B) Other	7·5%	C 85% of the full rate E —
55.06 Cotton yarn, put up for retail sale:		
(A) Containing more than 5 per cent. by weight of silk, of man-made fibres, or of both together	13%	C 85% of the full rate E —
(B) Other	7·5%	C 85% of the full rate E —
55.07 Cotton gauze	25%	C 20% E —
55.08 Terry towelling and similar terry fabrics, of cotton	17·5%	C 85% of the full rate E —
55.09 Other woven fabrics of cotton	17·5%	C 85% of the full rate E —

Chapter 56

Man-made Fibres (Discontinuous)

Note

Heading No. 56.02 is to be taken to apply only to continuous filament tow of man-made fibres, consisting of parallel filaments of a uniform length equal to the length of the tow meeting the following specification:

(*a*) Length of tow exceeding 2 metres;

(*b*) Twist less than 5 turns per metre;

(*c*) Weight per filament less than 6·6 milligrammes per metre (60 denier);

(*d*) In the case of filaments described in Note 1 (*a*) to Chapter 51, the tow must be drawn, that is to say, be incapable of being stretched by more than 100 per cent. of its length;

(*e*) Total weight of tow more than 2 grammes per metre (18,000 denier).

Tow of a length not exceeding 2 metres is to be classified in heading No. 56.01.

Tariff Heading	*Rate of Import Duty (if any)*	
	Full	*Commonwealth (C)* *E.F.T.A. (E)*
56.01 Man-made fibres (discontinuous), not carded, combed or otherwise prepared for spinning:		
(A) Produced by a process mentioned in Note 1(*a*) to Chapter 51:		
(1) Of copolymerised vinyl chloride and vinyl acetate, in lengths not exceeding 2 centimetres	—	—
(2) Other	£0·0551 per kilogramme	C 85% of the full rate E —
(B) Produced by a process mentioned in Note 1(*b*) to Chapter 51:		
(1) Of regenerated protein including casein	—	—
(2) Other	£0·0330 per kilogramme	C 85% of the full rate E —
56.02 Continuous filament tow for the manufacture of man-made fibres (discontinuous):		
(A) Produced by a process mentioned in Note 1(*a*) to Chapter 51	£0·0300 per lb. or 13%, whichever is the greater	C 85% of the full rate E —
(B) Produced by a process mentioned in Note 1(*b*) to Chapter 51	£0·0150 per lb.	C 85% of the full rate E —
56.03 Waste (including yarn waste and pulled or garnetted rags) of man-made fibres (continuous or discontinuous), not carded, combed or otherwise prepared for spinning	10%	C 85% of the full rate E —
56.04 Man-made fibres (discontinuous or waste), carded, combed or otherwise prepared for spinning	10%	C 85% of the full rate E —

Tariff Heading	*Rate of Import Duty (if any)*	
	Full	*Commonwealth (C)* *E.F.T.A. (E)*
56.05 Yarn of man-made fibres (discontinuous or waste), not put up for retail sale	£0·0300 per lb. or 13%, whichever is the greater	C 85% of the full rate E —
56.06 Yarn of man-made fibres (discontinuous or waste), put up for retail sale	£0·0300 per lb. or 13%, whichever is the greater	C 85% of the full rate E —
56.07 Woven fabrics of man-made fibres (discontinuous or waste)	£0·0200 per sq. yd. or 17·5%, whichever is the greater	C 85% of the full rate E —

Chapter 57

Other Vegetable Textile Materials; Paper Yarn and Woven Fabrics of Paper Yarn

Tariff Heading	*Rate of Import Duty (if any)*	
	Full	*Commonwealth (C)* *E.F.T.A. (E)*
57.01 True hemp (*Cannabis sativa*), raw or processed but not spun; tow and waste of true hemp (including pulled or garnetted rags or ropes):		
(A) True hemp, tow and waste of true hemp, not carded or combed	—	—
(B) Other:		
(1) Containing man-made fibres ...	5%	C 85% of the full rate E —
(2) Not containing man-made fibres...	5%	—
57.02 Manila hemp (abaca) (*Musa textilis*), raw or processed but not spun; tow and waste of manila hemp (including pulled or garnetted rags or ropes):		
(A) Manila hemp, tow and waste of manila hemp, not carded or combed	—	—
(B) Other	5%	—
57.03 Jute and other textile bast fibres not elsewhere specified or included, raw or processed but not spun; tow and waste thereof (including pulled or garnetted rags or ropes):		
(A) Not carded or combed	—	—
(B) Other:		
(1) Containing man-made fibres ...	5%	C 85% of the full rate E —
(2) Not containing man-made fibres...	5%	—
57.04 Other vegetable textile fibres, raw or processed but not spun; waste of such fibres (including pulled or garnetted rags or ropes):		
(A) Coir fibre	10%	—
(B) Other:		
(1) Not carded or combed	—	—
(2) Carded or combed:		
(*a*) Containing man-made fibres ...	5%	C 85% of the full rate E —
(*b*) Not containing man-made fibres	5%	—

Tariff Heading	Rate of Import Duty (if any)	
	Full	Commonwealth (C) E.F.T.A. (E)
57.05 Yarn of true hemp:		
(A) Containing man-made fibres ...	15%	C 85% of the full rate E —
(B) Not containing man-made fibres:		
(1) Polished or glazed...	15%	—
(2) Other	7·5%	—
57.06 Yarn of jute or of other textile bast fibres of heading No. 57.03:		
(A) Containing man-made fibres ...	15%	C 85% of the full rate E —
(B) Not containing man-made fibres:		
(1) Singles, not polished or glazed ...	10%	—
(2) Singles, polished or glazed; multiples, whether or not polished or glazed	15%	—
57.07 Yarn of other vegetable textile fibres:		
(A) Containing man-made fibres ...	15%	C 85% of the full rate E —
(B) Not containing man-made fibres:		
(1) Hard fibre singles, polished or glazed singles and all multiples (but not including yarn of coir)	15%	—
(2) Other	10%	—
57.08 Paper yarn	10%	—
57.09 Woven fabrics of true hemp:		
(A) Containing man-made fibres ...	20%	C 15% E —
(B) Not containing man-made fibres ...	20%	—
57.10 Woven fabrics of jute or of other textile bast fibres of heading No. 57.03:		
(A) Containing man-made fibres ...	20%	C 15% E —
(B) Not containing man-made fibres ...	20%	—
57.11 Woven fabrics of other vegetable textile fibres:		
(A) Containing man-made fibres ...	20%	C 15% E —
(B) Not containing man-made fibres ...	20%	—
57.12 Woven fabrics of paper yarn	17·5%	—

Chapter 58

Carpets, Mats, Matting and Tapestries; Pile and Chenille Fabrics; Narrow Fabrics; Trimmings; Tulle and other Net Fabrics; Lace; Embroidery

Notes

1. The headings of this Chapter are to be taken not to apply to coated or impregnated fabrics, elastic fabrics or elastic trimmings, machinery belting or other goods falling within Chapter 59. However, embroidery on any textile base falls within heading No. 58.10.

2. In headings Nos. 58.01 and 58.02, the words " carpets " and " rugs " are to be taken to extend to similar articles having the characteristics of floor coverings but intended for use for other purposes. These headings are to be taken not to apply to felt carpets, which fall within Chapter 59.

3. For the purposes of heading No. 58.05, the expression " narrow woven fabrics " means:

(*a*) Woven fabrics of a width not exceeding 30 centimetres, whether woven as such or cut from wider pieces, provided with selvedges (woven, gummed or made otherwise) on both edges;

(*b*) Tubular woven fabrics of a flattened width not exceeding 30 centimetres; and

(*c*) Bias binding with folded edges, of a width when unfolded not exceeding 30 centimetres.

Narrow woven fabrics in the form of fringes are to be treated as falling within heading No. 58.07.

4. Heading No. 58.08 is to be taken not to apply to nets or netting in the piece made of twine, cordage or rope, which are to be taken as falling within heading No. 59.05.

5. In heading No. 58.10, and elsewhere in this Schedule, the expression " embroidery " means, *inter alia*, embroidery with metal or glass thread on a visible ground of textile fabric, and sewn appliqué work of sequins, beads or ornamental motifs of textile or other materials. The heading is to be taken not to apply to needlework tapestry (heading No. 58.03).

6. The headings of this Chapter are to be taken to include goods of the descriptions specified therein when made of metal thread and of a kind used in apparel, as furnishings or the like.

Tariff Heading	*Rate of Import Duty (if any)*		
	Full	*Commonwealth (C)* *E.F.T.A. (E)*	
58.01 Carpets, carpeting and rugs, knotted (made up or not):			
(A) Hand-made:			
(1) Containing more than 5 per cent. by weight of silk, of man-made fibres, or of both together	£0·2250 per sq. yd. exclusive of fringes or 20%, whichever is the greater	C E	17% —
(2) Other	£0·2250 per sq. yd. exclusive of fringes		—
(B) Other:			
(1) Containing more than 20 per cent. by weight of silk, of man-made fibres, or of both together	£0·0500 per sq. yd. exclusive of fringes or 30%, whichever is the greater	C E	25% —

Tariff Heading	Rate of Import Duty (if any)	
	Full	*Commonwealth (C) E.F.T.A. (E)*
58.01 Carpets, carpeting and rugs, etc.—*contd.*		
(B) Other:—*contd.*		
(2) Containing more than 5 per cent. but not more than 20 per cent. by weight of silk, of man-made fibres, or of both together	£0·0500 per sq. yd. exclusive of fringes or 25%, whichever is the greater	C 21% E —
(3) Other	£0·0500 per sq. yd. exclusive of fringes or 17·5%, whichever is the greater	—
58.02 Other carpets, carpeting, rugs, mats and matting, and " Kelem ", " Schumacks " and " Karamanie " rugs and the like (made up or not):		
(A) Coir mats and matting	20%	—
(B) Other:		
(1) Containing more than 20 per cent. by weight of silk, of man-made fibres, or of both together	£0·0500 per sq. yd. exclusive of fringes or 30%, whichever is the greater	C 25·5% E —
(2) Containing more than 5 per cent. but not more than 20 per cent. by weight of silk, of man-made fibres, or of both together	£0·0500 per sq. yd. exclusive of fringes or 25%, whichever is the greater	C 21% E —
(3) Other	£0·0500 per sq. yd. exclusive of fringes or 17·5%, whichever is the greater	—
58.03 Tapestries, hand-made, of the type Gobelins, Flanders, Aubusson, Beauvais and the like, and needle-worked tapestries (for example, petit point and cross stitch) made in panels and the like by hand:		
(A) Containing more than 5 per cent. by weight of silk, of man-made fibres, or of both together	20%	C 85% of the full rate E —
(B) Other	20%	—
58.04 Woven pile fabrics and chenille fabrics (other than terry towelling or similar terry fabrics of cotton falling within heading No. 55.08 and fabrics falling within heading No. 58.05):		
(A) Containing silk or man-made fibres	17·5%	C 85% of the full rate E —

Tariff Heading	Rate of Import Duty (if any)	
	Full	Commonwealth (C) E.F.T.A. (E)
58.04 Woven pile fabrics, etc.—*contd.*		
(B) Not containing silk or man-made fibres:		
(1) Containing more than 50 per cent. by weight of cotton	17·5%	C 85% of the full rate E —
(2) Other	17·5%	—
58.05 Narrow woven fabrics, and narrow fabrics (bolduc) consisting of warp without weft assembled by means of an adhesive, other than goods falling within heading No. 58.06:		
(A) Containing silk or man-made fibres ...	17·5%	C 85% of the full rate E —
(B) Not containing silk or man-made fibres:		
(1) Containing more than 50 per cent. by weight of fibres falling within heading No. 57.03 or 57.04	17·5%	—
(2) Other	17·5%	—
58.06 Woven labels, badges and the like, not embroidered, in the piece, in strips or cut to shape or size:		
(A) Containing silk or man-made fibres...	17·5%	C 85% of the full rate E —
(B) Not containing silk or man-made fibres	17·5%	—
58.07 Chenille yarn (including flock chenille yarn), gimped yarn (other than metallised yarn of heading No. 52.01 and gimped horsehair yarn); braids and ornamental trimmings in the piece; tassels, pompons and the like:		
(A) Chenille yarn and gimped yarn:		
(1) Containing silk or man-made fibres	13%	C 85% of the full rate E —
(2) Not containing silk or man-made fibres	7·5%	—
(B) Braids and ornamental trimmings in the piece:		
(1) Containing silk or man-made fibres	17·5%	C 85% of the full rate E —
(2) Not containing silk or man-made fibres	17·5%	—
(C) Tassels, pompons and the like:		
(1) Containing more than 5 per cent. by weight of silk, of man-made fibres, or of both together	20%	C 85% of the full rate E —
(2) Other	20%	—

Tariff Heading	Rate of Import Duty (if any)	
	Full	Commonwealth (C) E.F.T.A. (E)
58.08 Tulle and other net fabrics (but not including woven, knitted or crocheted fabrics), plain:		
(A) Knotted:		
(1) Containing silk or man-made fibres:		
(a) Containing more than 10 per cent. by weight of silk, of man-made fibres, or of both together	£0·0250 per sq. yd. or 22·5%, whichever is the greater	C 85% of the full rate E —
(b) Other	20%	C 85% of the full rate E —
(2) Not containing silk or man-made fibres	20%	—
(B) Other:		
(1) Containing silk or man-made fibres	20%	C 85% of the full rate E —
(2) Not containing silk or man-made fibres	20%	—
58.09 Tulle and other net fabrics (but not including woven, knitted or crocheted fabrics), figured; hand or mechanically made lace, in the piece, in strips or in motifs:		
(A) Containing silk or man-made fibres	20%	C 85% of the full rate E —
(B) Not containing silk or man-made fibres	20%	—
58.10 Embroidery, in the piece, in strips or in motifs:		
(A) Containing silk or man-made fibres	20%	C 85% of the full rate E —
(B) Not containing silk or man-made fibres:		
(1) Containing woven fabric of which the cotton content exceeds 50 per cent. by weight of the total textile fabric content	20%	C 85% of the full rate E —
(2) Other	20%	—

Chapter 59

Wadding and Felt; Twine, Cordage, Ropes and Cables; Special Fabrics; Impregnated and Coated Fabrics; Textile Articles of a kind suitable for Industrial Use

Notes

1. For the purposes of this Chapter, the expression "textile fabric" is to be taken to apply only to the textile fabrics of Chapters 50 to 57 and headings Nos. 58.04 and 58.05, the braids and trimmings in the piece of heading No. 58.07, the tulle and other net fabrics of headings Nos. 58.08 and 58.09, lace of heading No. 58.09 and the knitted and crocheted fabrics of heading No. 60.01.

2. (A) Heading No. 59.08 is to be taken to apply to textile fabrics impregnated, coated, covered or laminated with preparations of cellulose derivatives or of other artificial plastic materials whatever the weight per square metre and whatever the nature of the plastic material (compact, foam, sponge or expanded).

It does not, however, cover:

(*a*) Fabrics in which the impregnation, coating or covering cannot be seen with the naked eye (usually Chapters 50 to 58 and 60); for the purpose of this provision, no account should be taken of any resulting change of colour;

(*b*) Products which cannot, without fracturing, be bent manually around a cylinder of a diameter of seven millimetres, at a temperature between 15° and 30°C (usually Chapter 39); or

(*c*) Products in which the textile fabric is either completely embedded in artificial plastic material or coated or covered on both sides with such material (Chapter 39).

(B) Heading No. 59.12 does not apply to:

(*a*) Fabrics in which the impregnation or coating cannot be seen with the naked eye (usually Chapters 50 to 58 and 60); for the purpose of this provision, no account should be taken of any resulting change of colour;

(*b*) Fabrics painted with designs (other than theatrical scenery, studio backcloths and the like);

(*c*) Fabrics covered with flock, dust, powdered cork or the like and bearing designs resulting from these treatments; or

(*d*) Fabrics finished with normal dressings having a basis of amylaceous or similar substances.

3. In heading No. 59.11 "rubberised textile fabrics" means:

(*a*) Textile fabrics impregnated, coated, covered or laminated with rubber:

(i) Weighing not more than 1½ kilogrammes per square metre; or

(ii) Weighing more than 1½ kilogrammes per square metre and containing more than 50 per cent. by weight of textile material;

(*b*) Fabrics composed of parallel textile yarns agglomerated with rubber, irrespective of their weight per square metre; and

(*c*) Plates, sheets and strip, of expanded, foam or sponge rubber, combined with textile fabric, other than those falling in Chapter 40 by virtue of the last paragraph of Note 2 to that Chapter.

4. Heading No. 59.16 is to be taken not to apply to:

(*a*) Transmission, conveyor or elevator belting of a thickness of less than 3 millimetres; or

(*b*) Transmission, conveyor or elevator belts or belting of textile fabric impregnated, coated, covered or laminated with rubber or made from textile yarn or cord impregnated or coated with rubber (heading No. 40.10).

5. Heading No. 59.17 is to be taken to apply to the following goods which are to be taken as not falling within any other heading of Section XI:

(*a*) Textile products (other than those having the character of the products of headings Nos. 59.14 to 59.16), the following only:

(i) Textile fabric, felt and felt-lined woven fabric, coated, covered or laminated with rubber, leather or other material, of a kind commonly used for card clothing, and similar fabric of a kind commonly used in machinery or plant;

(ii) Bolting cloth;

(iii) Straining cloth of a kind commonly used in oil presses and the like, of textile fibres or of human hair;

(iv) Woven textile felts, whether or not impregnated or coated, of a kind commonly used in paper-making or other machinery, tubular or endless with single or multiple warp or weft, or flat woven with multiple warp or weft;

(v) Textile fabrics reinforced with metal, of a kind commonly used in machinery or plant;

(vi) Textile fabrics of the metallised yarn falling within heading No. 52.01, of a kind commonly used in paper-making or other machinery;

(vii) Cords, braids and the like, whether or not coated, impregnated or reinforced with metal, of a kind commonly used in machinery or plant as packing or lubricating materials;

(*b*) Textile articles (other than those of headings Nos. 59.14 to 59.16) of a kind commonly used in machinery or plant (for example, gaskets, washers, polishing discs and other machinery parts).

Tariff Heading	*Rate of Import Duty (if any)*	
	Full	*Commonwealth (C)* *E.F.T.A. (E)*
59.01 Wadding and articles of wadding; textile flock and dust and mill neps:		
(A) Textile flock and dust:		
(1) Containing man-made fibres ...	£0·0150 per lb. of man-made fibres	C 85% of the full rate E —
(2) Not containing man-made fibres...	—	—
(B) Other:		
(1) Containing man-made fibres ...	15%	C 85% of the full rate E —
(2) Not containing man-made fibres...	5%	—
59.02 Felt and articles of felt, whether or not impregnated or coated:		
(A) Felt, not made up:		
(1) Containing man-made fibres ...	17·5%	C 85% of the full rate E —
(2) Not containing man-made fibres...	17·5%	—
(B) Articles of felt:		
(1) Containing more than 5 per cent. by weight of silk, of man-made fibres, or of both together	20%	C 85% of the full rate E —
(2) Other	20%	—

Tariff Heading	Rate of Import Duty (if any) Full	Commonwealth (C) E.F.T.A. (E)
59.03 Bonded fibre fabrics, similar bonded yarn fabrics, and articles of such fabrics, whether or not impregnated or coated:		
(A) Bonded fibre fabrics and similar bonded yarn fabrics, not made up:		
(1) Containing man-made fibres ...	17·5%	C 85% of the full rate E —
(2) Not containing man-made fibres...	17·5%	—
(B) Articles of bonded fibre fabrics or of similar bonded yarn fabrics:		
(1) Containing more than 5 per cent. by weight of silk, of man-made fibres, or of both together	20%	C 85% of the full rate E —
(2) Other	20%	—
59.04 Twine, cordage, ropes and cables, plaited or not:		
(A) Containing silk or man-made fibres:		
(1) Multiple, cabled or plaited ...	20%	C 85% of the full rate E —
(2) Other	15%	C 85% of the full rate E —
(B) Not containing silk or man-made fibres:		
(1) Of paper yarn, cotton, flax, ramie or coir	10%	—
(2) Of true hemp:		
(*a*) If singles, not polished or glazed	7·5%	—
(*b*) Otherwise	15%	—
(3) Other	15%	—
59.05 Nets and netting made of twine, cordage or rope, and made up fishing nets of yarn, twine, cordage or rope:		
(A) Nets, including made up fishing nets:		
(1) Containing more than 20 per cent. by weight of silk, of man-made fibres, or of both together	30%	C 85% of the full rate E —
(2) Containing more than 5 per cent. but not more than 20 per cent. by weight of silk, of man-made fibres, or of both together	25%	C 85% of the full rate E —
(3) Other	20%	—

Tariff Heading	Rate of Import Duty (if any)	
	Full	*Commonwealth (C)* *E.F.T.A. (E)*
59.05 Nets and netting made of twine, etc.—*contd.*		
(B) Netting:		
(1) Containing silk or man-made fibres:		
(*a*) Containing more than 10 per cent. by weight of silk, of man-made fibres, or of both together	£0·0250 per sq. yd. or 22·5%, whichever is the greater	C 85% of the full rate E —
(*b*) Other	20%	C 85% of the full rate E —
(2) Not containing silk or man-made fibres	20%	—
59.06 Other articles made from yarn, twine, cordage, rope or cables, other than textile fabrics and articles made from such fabrics:		
(A) Containing more than 5 per cent. by weight of silk, of man-made fibres, or of both together	25%	C 85% of the full rate E —
(B) Other	20%	—
59.07 Textile fabrics coated with gum or amylaceous substances, of a kind used for the outer covers of books and the like; tracing cloth; prepared painting canvas; buckram and similar fabrics for hat foundations and similar uses:		
(A) Containing silk or man-made fibres	17·5%	C 85% of the full rate E —
(B) Not containing silk or man-made fibres:		
(1) Containing woven fabric of which the cotton content exceeds 50 per cent. by weight of the total textile fabric content	17·5%	C 85% of the full rate E —
(2) Other	17·5%	—
59.08 Textile fabrics impregnated, coated, covered or laminated with preparations of cellulose derivatives or of other artificial plastic materials:		
(A) Containing silk or man-made fibres	17·5%	C 85% of the full rate E —
(B) Not containing silk or man-made fibres:		
(1) Containing woven fabric of which the cotton content exceeds 50 per cent. by weight of the total textile fabric content	17·5%	C 85% of the full rate E —
(2) Other	17·5%	—

Tariff Heading	Rate of Import Duty (if any)	
	Full	Commonwealth (C) E.F.T.A. (E)
59.09 Textile fabrics coated or impregnated with oil or preparations with a basis of drying oil:		
(A) Containing silk or man-made fibres	17·5%	C 85% of the full rate E —
(B) Not containing silk or man-made fibres:		
(1) Containing woven fabric of which the cotton content exceeds 50 per cent. by weight of the total textile fabric content	17·5%	C 85% of the full rate E —
(2) Other	17·5%	—
59.10 Linoleum and materials prepared on a textile base in a similar manner to linoleum, whether or not cut to shape or of a kind used as floor coverings; floor coverings consisting of a coating applied on a textile base, cut to shape or not	10%	—
59.11 Rubberised textile fabrics, other than rubberised knitted or crocheted goods:		
(A) Containing silk or man-made fibres	17·5%	C 85% of the full rate E —
(B) Not containing silk or man-made fibres:		
(1) Containing woven fabric of which the cotton content exceeds 50 per cent. by weight of the total textile fabric content	17·5%	C 85% of the full rate E —
(2) Other	17·5%	—
59.12 Textile fabrics otherwise impregnated or coated; painted textile fabrics being theatrical scenery, studio back-cloths or the like:		
(A) Fabrics:		
(1) Containing silk or man-made fibres	17·5%	C 85% of the full rate E —
(2) Not containing silk or man-made fibres:		
(*a*) Containing woven fabric of which the cotton content exceeds 50 per cent. by weight of the total textile fabric content	17·5%	C 85% of the full rate E —
(*b*) Other	17·5%	—
(B) Theatrical scenery, studio back-cloths or the like	17·5%	—

Tariff Heading	Rate of Import Duty (if any)	
	Full	*Commonwealth (C)* *E.F.T.A. (E)*
.13 Elastic fabrics and trimmings (other than knitted or crocheted goods) consisting of textile materials combined with rubber threads:		
(A) Containing silk or man-made fibres	17·5%	C 85% of the full rate E —
(B) Not containing silk or man-made fibres:		
(1) Woven fabric containing more than 50 per cent. by weight of cotton	17·5%	C 85% of the full rate E —
(2) Other	17·5%	—
.14 Wicks, of woven, plaited or knitted textile materials, for lamps, stoves, lighters, candles and the like; tubular knitted gas-mantle fabric and incandescent gas mantles:		
(A) Containing man-made fibres... ...	17·5%	C 85% of the full rate E —
(B) Not containing man-made fibres:		
(1) Of woven fabric containing more than 50 per cent. by weight of cotton	17·5%	C 85% of the full rate E —
(2) Other	17·5%	—
.15 Textile hosepiping and similar tubing, with or without lining, armour or accessories of other materials:		
(A) Containing more than 5 per cent. by weight of silk, of man-made fibres, or of both together	17·5%	C 85% of the full rate E —
(B) Other:		
(1) Containing woven fabric of which the cotton content exceeds 50 per cent. by weight of the total textile fabric content	17·5%	C 85% of the full rate E —
(2) Other	17·5%	—
.16 Transmission, conveyor or elevator belts or belting, of textile material, whether or not strengthened with metal or other material:		
(A) Containing more than 5 per cent. by weight of silk, of man-made fibres, or of both together	17·5%	C 85% of the full rate E —
(B) Other:		
(1) Containing woven fabric of which the cotton content exceeds 50 per cent. by weight of the total textile fabric content	14%	C 85% of the full rate E —
(2) Other	14%	—

Tariff Heading	Rate of Import Duty (if any)	
	Full	Commonwealth (C E.F.T.A. (E
59.17 Textile products and textile articles, of a kind commonly used in machinery or plant:		
(A) Bolting cloth, not treated or operated upon, containing no other fibre than silk	—	—
(B) Woven textile felts of a kind used in paper-making machinery, in the form of tubes or endless bands, whether woven as such or assembled by splicing, sewing or otherwise, or in the form of flat fabrics fitted with eyelets or other means of fastening, ready for assembly into tubes or endless bands by such fastening	6%	—
(C) Other textile fabrics; cords, braids and the like of a kind used as packing or lubricating materials:		
(1) Containing silk or man-made fibres	17·5%	C 85% of the fu rate E —
(2) Not containing silk or man-made fibres	17·5%	—
(D) Other:		
(1) Containing more than 5 per cent. by weight of silk, of man-made fibres, or of both together	20%	C 85% of the fu rate E —
(2) Other:		
(*a*) Containing woven fabric of which the cotton content exceeds 50 per cent. by weight of the total textile fabric content	20%	C 85% of the fu rate E —
(*b*) Other	20%	—

Chapter 60

Knitted and Crocheted Goods

Notes

1. This Chapter does not cover:

(*a*) Crochet lace of heading No. 58.09;

(*b*) Knitted or crocheted goods falling within Chapter 59;

(*c*) Corsets, corset-belts, suspender-belts, brassières, braces, suspenders, garters or the like (heading No. 61.09);

(*d*) Old clothing or other articles falling within heading No. 63.01; or

(*e*) Orthopaedic appliances, surgical belts, trusses or the like (heading No. 90.19).

2. Headings Nos. 60.02 to 60.06 are to be taken to apply to knitted or crocheted articles and to parts thereof:

(*a*) Knitted or crocheted directly to shape, whether imported as separate items or in the form of a number of items in the length;

(*b*) Made up, by sewing or otherwise.

3. For the purposes of heading No. 60.06, knitted or crocheted articles are not considered to be elastic articles only by reason of their containing rubber thread or elastic forming merely a supporting band.

4. The headings of this Chapter are to be taken to include goods of the descriptions specified therein when made of metal thread and of a kind used in apparel, as furnishings or the like.

5. For the purposes of this Chapter:

(*a*) " Elastic " means consisting of textile materials combined with rubber threads; and

(*b*) " Rubberised " means impregnated, coated, covered or laminated with rubber, or made with textile thread impregnated, coated or covered with rubber.

Tariff Heading	*Rate of Import Duty (if any)*	
	Full	*Commonwealth (C)* *E.F.T.A. (E)*
60.01 Knitted or crocheted fabric, not elastic nor rubberised:		
(A) Net of a kind used in articles of apparel, furnishings or the like, and fabric resembling lace:		
(1) Containing silk or man-made fibres	20%	C 85% of the full rate E —
(2) Not containing silk or man-made fibres	20%	—

Tariff Heading	Rate of Import Duty (if any)	
	Full	*Commonwealth (C)* *E.F.T.A. (E)*
60.01 Knitted or crocheted fabric, etc.—*contd.*		
(B) Other fabric:		
(1) Containing silk or man-made fibres:		
(*a*) Exceeding 30 centimetres in width and containing more than 50 per cent. by weight of silk, of man-made fibres, or of both together	£0·0200 per sq. yd. or 17·5%, whichever is the greater	C 85% of the full rate E —
(*b*) Other	17·5%	C 85% of the full rate E —
(2) Not containing silk or man-made fibres	17·5%	—
60.02 Gloves, mittens and mitts, knitted or crocheted, not elastic nor rubberised:		
(A) Containing more than 20 per cent. by weight of silk, of man-made fibres, or of both together	£0·2500 per lb. or 25%, whichever is the greater	C 90% of the full rate E —
(B) Containing more than 5 per cent. but not more than 20 per cent. by weight of silk, of man-made fibres, or of both together:		
(1) Wholly or partly cut out of fabric containing cotton and sewn up (but excluding gloves known as astrakhan gloves and gloves, mittens and mitts in which the fabric containing cotton is present in the lining only)	£0·1250 per lb. or 25%, whichever is the greater	C £0·1100 per lb. or 20%, whichever is the greater E —
(2) Other	£0·1250 per lb. or 22·5%, whichever is the greater	C £0·1100 per lb. or 20%, whichever is the greater E —
(C) Other:		
(1) Wholly or partly cut out of fabric containing cotton and sewn up (but excluding gloves known as astrakhan gloves and gloves, mittens and mitts in which the fabric containing cotton is present in the lining only)	25%	—
(2) Other	20%	—

Tariff Heading	Rate of Import Duty (if any)	
	Full	*Commonwealth (C)* *E.F.T.A. (E)*
[6]0.03 Stockings, under stockings, socks, ankle-socks, sockettes and the like, knitted or crocheted, not elastic nor rubberised:		
(A) Containing more than 20 per cent. by weight of silk, of man-made fibres, or of both together	£0·3000 per dozen pairs or 25%, whichever is the greater	C 90% of the full rate E —
(B) Containing more than 5 per cent. but not more than 20 per cent. by weight of silk, of man-made fibres, or of both together	20%	C 18% E —
(C) Other	20%	—
[6]0.04 Under garments, knitted or crocheted, not elastic nor rubberised:		
(A) Containing more than 20 per cent. by weight of silk, of man-made fibres, or of both together	£0·2500 per lb. or 20%, whichever is the greater	C 90% of the full rate E —
(B) Containing more than 5 per cent. but not more than 20 per cent. by weight of silk, of man-made fibres, or of both together	20%	C 18% E —
(C) Other	20%	—
[6]0.05 Outer garments and other articles, knitted or crocheted, not elastic nor rubberised:		
(A) Articles of apparel:		
(1) Containing more than 20 per cent. by weight of silk, of man-made fibres, or of both together	£0·2500 per lb. or 20%, whichever is the greater	C 90% of the full rate E —
(2) Containing more than 5 per cent. but not more than 20 per cent. by weight of silk, of man-made fibres, or of both together	20%	C 18% E —
(3) Other	20%	—
(B) Other articles:		
(1) Containing more than 5 per cent. by weight of silk, of man-made fibres, or of both together	20%	C 18% E —
(2) Other	20%	—
[60].06 Knitted or crocheted fabric and articles thereof, elastic or rubberised (including elastic knee-caps and elastic stockings):		
(A) Fabric:		
(1) Containing silk or man-made fibres	17·5%	C 85% of the full rate E —
(2) Not containing silk or man-made fibres	17·5%	—
(B) Made-up articles:		
(1) Containing more than 5 per cent. by weight of silk, of man-made fibres, or of both together	20%	C 85% of the full rate E —
(2) Other	20%	—

Chapter 61

Articles of Apparel and Clothing Accessories of Textile Fabric, Other Than Knitted or Crocheted Goods

Notes

1. The headings of this Chapter are to be taken to apply to articles of the kinds described therein only when made up of any textile fabric (including felt, bonded fibre fabric, braid or trimmings of heading No. 58.07, tulle or other net fabrics and lace) or of fabric of metal thread, but not including articles of knitted or crocheted material other than those falling within heading No. 61.09.

2. The headings of this Chapter do not cover:

(*a*) Old clothing or other articles falling within heading No. 63.01; or

(*b*) Orthopaedic appliances, surgical belts, trusses or the like (heading No. 90.19).

3. For the purposes of headings Nos. 61.01 to 61.04:

(*a*) Articles which cannot be identified as either men's or boys' garments or as women's or girls' garments are to be classified in heading No. 61.02 or 61.04 as the case may be

(*b*) The expression " infants' garments " is to be taken to apply to:

(i) Garments for young children which are not identifiable as for wear exclusively by boys or by girls, and

(ii) Babies' napkins.

4. Scarves and articles of the scarf type, square or approximately square, of which no side exceeds 60 centimetres are to be classified as handkerchiefs (heading No. 61.05).

Handkerchiefs of which any side exceeds 60 centimetres are to be classified in heading No. 61.06.

5. The headings of this Chapter are to be taken to apply to textile fabrics (other than knitted or crocheted fabric) cut to shape for making articles of this Chapter.

Heading No. 61.09, however, also includes fabrics knitted or crocheted to shape for making articles classified in that heading, whether imported as separate items or in the form of a number of items in the length.

Tariff Heading	Rate of Import Duty (if any)	
	Full	*Commonwealth* (C) *E.F.T.A.* (E)
61.01 Men's and boys' outer garments:		
(A) Containing more than 20 per cent. by weight of silk, of man-made fibres, or of both together	£0·2500 per lb. or 20%, whichever is the greater	C 90% of the full rate E —
(B) Containing more than 5 per cent. but not more than 20 per cent. by weight of silk, of man-made fibres, or of both together	20%	C 18% E —
(C) Other:		
(1) Containing woven fabric of which the cotton content exceeds 50 per cent. by weight of the garment	20%	C 85% of the full rate E —
(2) Other	20%	—

Tariff Heading	Rate of Import Duty (if any)	
	Full	Commonwealth (C) E.F.T.A. (E)
61.02 Women's, girls' and infants' outer garments:		
(A) Containing more than 20 per cent. by weight of silk, of man-made fibres, or of both together	£0·2500 per lb. or 20%, whichever is the greater	C 90% of the full rate E —
(B) Containing more than 5 per cent. but not more than 20 per cent. by weight of silk, of man-made fibres, or of both together	20%	C 18% E —
(C) Other:		
(1) Containing woven fabric of which the cotton content exceeds 50 per cent. by weight of the garment	20%	C 85% of the full rate E —
(2) Other	20%	—
61.03 Men's and boys' under garments, including collars, shirt fronts and cuffs:		
(A) Containing more than 20 per cent. by weight of silk, of man-made fibres, or of both together	£0·2500 per lb. or 20%, whichever is the greater	C 90% of the full rate E —
(B) Containing more than 5 per cent. but not more than 20 per cent. by weight of silk, of man-made fibres, or of both together	20%	C 18% E —
(C) Other:		
(1) Containing woven fabric of which the cotton content exceeds 50 per cent. by weight of the garment	20%	C 85% of the full rate E —
(2) Other	20%	—
61.04 Women's, girls' and infants' under garments:		
(A) Containing more than 20 per cent. by weight of silk, of man-made fibres, or of both together	£0·2500 per lb. or 20%, whichever is the greater	C 90% of the full rate E —
(B) Containing more than 5 per cent. but not more than 20 per cent. by weight of silk, of man-made fibres, or of both together	20%	C 18% E —
(C) Other:		
(1) Containing woven fabric of which the cotton content exceeds 50 per cent. by weight of the garment	20%	C 85% of the full rate E —
(2) Other	20%	—

Tariff Heading	Rate of Import Duty (if any)	
	Full	Commonwealth (C) E.F.T.A. (E)
61.05 Handkerchiefs:		
(A) Containing more than 20 per cent. by weight of silk, of man-made fibres, or of both together	£0·2500 per lb. or 20%, whichever is the greater	C 90% of the full rate E —
(B) Containing more than 5 per cent. but not more than 20 per cent. by weight of silk, of man-made fibres, or of both together	£0·1250 per lb. or 20%, whichever is the greater	C £0·1100 per lb. or 18%, whichever is the greater E —
(C) Other:		
(1) Containing woven fabric of which the cotton content exceeds 50 per cent. by weight of the article	£0·0750 per lb. or 20%, whichever is the greater	C 85% of the full rate E —
(2) Other	£0·0750 per lb. or 20%, whichever is the greater	—
61.06 Shawls, scarves, mufflers, mantillas, veils and the like:		
(A) Containing more than 20 per cent. by weight of silk, of man-made fibres, or of both together	£0·2500 per lb. or 20%, whichever is the greater	C 90% of the full rate E —
(B) Containing more than 5 per cent. but not more than 20 per cent. by weight of silk, of man-made fibres, or of both together	20%	C 18% E —
(C) Other:		
(1) Containing woven fabric of which the cotton content exceeds 50 per cent. by weight of the article	20%	C 85% of the full rate E —
(2) Other	20%	—
61.07 Ties, bow ties and cravats:		
(A) Containing more than 20 per cent. by weight of silk, of man-made fibres, or of both together	£0·2500 per lb. or 20%, whichever is the greater	C 90% of the full rate E —
(B) Containing more than 5 per cent. but not more than 20 per cent. by weight of silk, of man-made fibres, or of both together	20%	C 18% E —
(C) Other:		
(1) Containing woven fabric of which the cotton content exceeds 50 per cent. by weight of the article	20%	C 85% of the full rate E —
(2) Other	20%	—
61.08 Collars, tuckers, fallals, bodice-fronts, jabots, cuffs, flounces, yokes and similar accessories and trimmings for women's and girls' garments:		
(A) Containing more than 20 per cent. by weight of silk, of man-made fibres, or of both together	£0·2500 per lb. or 20%, whichever is the greater	C 90% of the full rate E —

Tariff Heading	Rate of Import Duty (if any)	
	Full	Commonwealth (C) E.F.T.A. (E)
61.08 Collars, etc.—*contd.*		
(B) Containing more than 5 per cent. but not more than 20 per cent. by weight of silk, of man-made fibres, or of both together	20%	C 18% E —
(C) Other:		
(1) Containing woven fabric of which the cotton content exceeds 50 per cent. by weight of the article	20%	C 85% of the full rate E —
(2) Other	20%	—
61.09 Corsets, corset-belts, suspender-belts, brassières, braces, suspenders, garters and the like (including such articles of knitted or crocheted fabric), whether or not elastic:		
(A) Containing more than 20 per cent. by weight of silk, of man-made fibres, or of both together	£0·2500 per lb. or 20%, whichever is the greater	C 90% of the full rate E —
(B) Containing more than 5 per cent. but not more than 20 per cent. by weight of silk, of man-made fibres, or of both together	20%	C 18% E —
(C) Other:		
(1) Corsets and similar body-supporting under garments and brassières not containing embroidery, net, lace or material resembling lace:		
(*a*) Containing woven fabric of which the cotton content exceeds 50 per cent. by weight of the garment	15%	C 85% of the full rate E —
(*b*) Other	15%	—
(2) Other:		
(*a*) Containing woven fabric of which the cotton content exceeds 50 per cent. by weight of the article	20%	C 85% of the full rate E —
(*b*) Other	20%	—
1.10 Gloves, mittens, mitts, stockings, socks and sockettes, not being knitted or crocheted goods:		
(A) Containing more than 20 per cent. by weight of silk, of man-made fibres, or of both together	£0·2500 per lb. or 25%, whichever is the greater	C 90% of the full rate E —

Tariff Heading	*Rate of Import Duty (if any)*	
	Full	*Commonwealth (C)* *E.F.T.A. (E)*
61.10 Gloves, etc.—*contd.*		
(B) Containing more than 5 per cent. but not more than 20 per cent. by weight of silk, of man-made fibres, or of both together:		
(1) Gloves, mittens and mitts wholly or partly cut out of fabric containing cotton and sewn up (but excluding gloves known as astrakhan gloves and gloves, mittens and mitts in which the fabric containing cotton is present in the lining only)	£0·1250 per lb. or 25%, whichever is the greater	C £0·1100 per lb or 20%, whichever is the greater E —
(2) Other	£0·1250 per lb. or 22·5%, whichever is the greater	C £0·1100 per lb or 20%, whichever is the greate E —
(C) Other:		
(1) Gloves, mittens and mitts wholly or partly cut out of fabric containing cotton and sewn up (but excluding gloves known as astrakhan gloves and gloves, mittens and mitts in which the fabric containing cotton is present in the lining only):		
(*a*) Containing woven fabric of which the cotton content exceeds 50 per cent. by weight of the article	25%	C 85% of the fu rate E —
(*b*) Other	25%	—
(2) Other	20%	—
61.11 Made up accessories for articles of apparel (for example, dress shields, shoulder and other pads, belts, muffs, sleeve protectors, pockets):		
(A) Containing more than 20 per cent. by weight of silk, of man-made fibres, or of both together	£0·2500 per lb. or 20%, whichever is the greater	C 90% of the fu rate E —
(B) Containing more than 5 per cent. but not more than 20 per cent. by weight of silk, of man-made fibres, or of both together	20%	C 18% E —
(C) Other:		
(1) Containing woven fabric of which the cotton content exceeds 50 per cent. by weight of the article	20%	C 85% of the f rate E —
(2) Other	20%	—

Chapter 62

Other Made Up Textile Articles

Notes

1. The headings of this Chapter are to be taken to apply to the articles of the kinds described therein only when made up of any textile fabric (other than felt and bonded fibre or similar bonded yarn fabrics) or of the braids or trimmings of heading No. 58.07, not being knitted or crocheted goods.

2. The headings of this Chapter do not cover:

(*a*) Goods falling within Chapter 58, 59 or 61; or

(*b*) Old clothing or other articles falling within heading No. 63.01.

Tariff Heading	*Rate of Import Duty (if any)*	
	Full	*Commonwealth (C)* *E.F.T.A. (E)*
62.01 Travelling rugs and blankets:		
(A) Containing more than 5 per cent. by weight of silk, of man-made fibres, or of both together	20%	C 17% E —
(B) Other:		
(1) Containing woven fabric of which the cotton content exceeds 50 per cent. by weight of the article	20%	C 85% of the full rate E —
(2) Other	20%	—
62.02 Bed linen, table linen, toilet linen and kitchen linen; curtains and other furnishing articles:		
(A) Containing more than 5 per cent. by weight of silk, of man-made fibres, or of both together	20%	C 17% E —
(B) Other:		
(1) Bedspreads, quilts, sheets, pillow cases, bolster cases, mattress cases, and face, hand and bath towels, wholly of cotton and not containing embroidery, net, lace or material resembling lace	17·5%	C 85% of the full rate E —
(2) Other:		
(*a*) Containing woven fabric of which the cotton content exceeds 50 per cent. by weight of the article	20%	C 85% of the full rate E —
(*b*) Other	20%	—
62.03 Sacks and bags, of a kind used for the packing of goods:		
(A) Used sacks and bags containing 85 per cent. or more by weight of jute	—	—
(B) Other:		
(1) Containing more than 5 per cent. by weight of silk, of man-made fibres, or of both together	25%	C 85% of the full rate E —

Tariff Heading	Rate of Import Duty (if any)	
	Full	*Commonwealth (C)* *E.F.T.A. (E)*
62.03 Sacks, etc.—*contd.*		
(B) Other:—*contd.*		
(2) Other:		
(*a*) Of a weight not less than 4 oz. and not more than 5 oz., measuring not less than 28 inches by 14 inches and not more than 30 inches by 15½ inches, made wholly of woven cotton fabric and indelibly marked with a trade mark covering an area of not less than 80 square inches	17·5%	—
(*b*) Other	20%	—
62.04 Tarpaulins, sails, awnings, sunblinds, tents and camping goods:		
(A) Containing more than 5 per cent. by weight of silk, of man-made fibres, or of both together	20%	C 85% of the full rate E —
(B) Other:		
(1) Tent roofs, each of a weight of not less than two tons	—	—
(2) Other:		
(*a*) Containing woven fabric of which the cotton content exceeds 50 per cent. by weight of the article	20%	C 85% of the full rate E —
(*b*) Other	20%	—
62.05 Other made up textile articles (including dress patterns):		
(A) Containing more than 5 per cent. by weight of silk, of man-made fibres, or of both together	20%	C 90% of the full rate E —
(B) Other:		
(1) Containing woven fabric of which the cotton content exceeds 50 per cent. by weight of the article	20%	C 85% of the full rate E —
(2) Other	20%	—

Chapter 63

Old Clothing and Other Textile Articles; Rags

Tariff Heading	*Rate of Import Duty (if any)*	
	Full	*Commonwealth (C)* *E.F.T.A. (E)*
63.01 Clothing, clothing accessories, travelling rugs and blankets, household linen and furnishing articles (other than articles falling within heading No. 58.01, 58.02 or 58.03), of textile materials, footwear and headgear of any material, showing signs of appreciable wear and imported in bulk or in bales, sacks or similar bulk packings	The rates applicable to the goods when new	C } The rates applicable to the E } goods when new
63.02 Used or new rags, scrap twine, cordage, rope and cables and worn out articles of twine, cordage, rope or cables:		
(A) Containing more than 55 per cent. by weight of man-made fibres	10%	C 85% of the full rate E —
(B) Other	—	—

SECTION XII

Footwear, Headgear, Umbrellas, Sunshades, Whips, Riding-Crops and Parts thereof; Prepared Feathers and Articles made therewith; Artificial Flowers; Articles of Human Hair; Fans

Chapter 64

Footwear, Gaiters and the like; Parts of such Articles

Notes

1. This Chapter does not cover:

(*a*) Footwear, without applied soles, knitted or crocheted (heading No. 60.03) or of other textile fabric (except felt or bonded fibre or similar bonded yarn fabrics) (heading No. 62.05);

(*b*) Old footwear falling within heading No. 63.01;

(*c*) Articles of asbestos (heading No. 68.13);

(*d*) Orthopaedic footwear or other orthopaedic appliances, or parts thereof (heading No. 90.19); or

(*e*) Toys and skating boots with skates attached (Chapter 97).

2. For the purposes of headings Nos. 64.05 and 64.06, the expression " parts " is to be taken not to include pegs, boot protectors, eyelets, boot hooks, buckles, ornaments, braid, laces, pompons or other trimmings (which are to be classified in their appropriate headings) or buttons or other goods falling within heading No. 98.01.

3. For the purposes of heading No. 64.01, the expression " rubber or artificial plastic material " is to be taken to include any textile fabric coated or covered externally with one or both of those materials.

Tariff Heading	*Rate of Import Duty (if any)*	
	Full	*Commonwealth (C)* *E.F.T.A. (E)*
64.01 Footwear with outer soles and uppers of rubber or artificial plastic material:		
(A) If made to cover the ankle:		
(1) Of a length (front of sole to heel tip) exceeding 11 inches	£0·2000 per pair	—
(2) Other	£0·0750 per pair	—
(B) If not made to cover the ankle:		
(1) Of a length (front of sole to heel tip) exceeding 9¼ inches	£0·0500 per pair	—
(2) Other	£0·0400 per pair	—
64.02 Footwear with outer soles of leather or composition leather; footwear (other than footwear falling within heading No. 64.01) with outer soles of rubber or artificial plastic material:		
(A) With outer soles of rubber or artificial plastic material and uppers of material other than leather:		
(1) Containing more than 5 per cent. by weight of silk, of man-made fibres, or of both together	10%	C 9% E —

Tariff Heading	Rate of Import Duty (if any)	
	Full	Commonwealth (C) E.F.T.A. (E)
64.02 Footwear with outer soles of leather, etc.—*contd.*		
(A) With outer soles of rubber, etc.—*contd.*		
(2) Other:		
(*a*) If made to cover the ankle:		
(i) Of a length (front of sole to heel tip) exceeding 11 inches	£0·2000 per pair	—
(ii) Other	£0·0750 per pair	—
(*b*) If not made to cover the ankle:		
(i) Of a length (front of sole to heel tip) exceeding 9¼ inches	£0·0500 per pair	—
(ii) Other	£0·0400 per pair	—
(B) Other:		
(1) Containing more than 5 per cent. by weight of silk, of man-made fibres, or of both together:		
(*a*) Women's	£0·0750 per pair or 10%, whichever is the greater	C 9% E —
(*b*) Other	10%	C 9% E —
(2) Other:		
(*a*) Women's	£0·0750 per pair or 5%, whichever is the greater	—
(*b*) Men's	7·5%	—
(*c*) Other	10%	—
64.03 Footwear with outer soles of wood or cork:		
(A) Containing more than 5 per cent. by weight of silk, of man-made fibres, or of both together:		
(1) Women's	£0·0750 per pair or 10%, whichever is the greater	C 9% E —
(2) Other	10%	C 9% E —
(B) Other:		
(1) Women's	£0·0750 per pair or 5%, whichever is the greater	—
(2) Men's	7·5%	—
(3) Other	10%	—

Tariff Heading	*Rate of Import Duty (if any)*	
	Full	*Commonwealth (C)* *E.F.T.A. (E)*
64.04 Footwear with outer soles of other materials:		
(A) Containing more than 5 per cent. by weight of silk, of man-made fibres, or of both together:		
(1) Women's	£0·0750 per pair or 10%, whichever is the greater	C 9% E —
(2) Other	10%	C 9% E —
(B) Other:		
(1) Women's	£0·0750 per pair or 5%, whichever is the greater	—
(2) Men's	7·5%	—
(3) Other	10%	—
64.05 Parts of footwear, removable in-soles, hose protectors and heel cushions of any material except metal:		
(A) Boot and shoe uppers, mounted on dummy lasts of wood or unmounted, and, in either case, perforated in at least two prominent places by the letters "S.P." so as to render them unsuitable for use as boot or shoe parts	—	—
(B) Other:		
(1) Containing more than 5 per cent. by weight of silk, of man-made fibres, or of both together	10%	C 9% E —
(2) Other	10%	—
64.06 Gaiters, spats, leggings, puttees, cricket pads, shin-guards and similar articles, and parts thereof	20%	—

Chapter 65

Headgear and Parts thereof

otes

1. This Chapter does not cover:

(*a*) Old headgear falling within heading No. 63.01;

(*b*) Hair nets of human hair (heading No. 67.04);

(*c*) Asbestos headgear (heading No. 68.13); or

(*d*) Dolls' hats or other toy hats, or carnival articles of Chapter 97.

2. Heading No. 65.02 is to be taken not to apply to hat-shapes made by sewing (other than ıt-shapes made by the sewing in spirals of plaited or other strips).

3. For the purposes of headings Nos. 65.03 to 65.06, the expression " headgear " is to be .ken to include hoods and hat-shapes not falling within headings Nos. 65.01 and 65.02.

Tariff Heading	*Rate of Import Duty (if any)*	
	Full	*Commonwealth (C) E.F.T.A. (E)*
5.01 Hat-forms, hat bodies and hoods of felt, neither blocked to shape nor with made brims; plateaux and manchons (including slit manchons), of felt:		
(A) Hat-forms and cone-shaped hat bodies:		
(1) Containing silk or man-made fibres	17·5%	C 15% E —
(2) Not containing silk or man-made fibres	15%	—
(B) Other:		
(1) Containing silk or man-made fibres	17·5%	C 10·5% E —
(2) Not containing silk or man-made fibres	17·5%	—
5.02 Hat-shapes, plaited or made from plaited or other strips of any material, neither blocked to shape nor with made brims:		
(A) Containing silk or man-made fibres (including monofil or strip of heading No. 51.01 or 51.02)	17·5%	C 85% of the full rate E —
(B) Not containing silk or man-made fibres:		
(1) Wholly of unspun buntal fibre ...	5%	—
(2) Other	7·5%	—
5.03 Felt hats and other felt headgear, being headgear made from the felt hoods and plateaux falling within heading No. 65.01, whether or not lined or trimmed:		
(A) Containing more than 5 per cent. by weight of silk, of man-made fibres, or of both together:		
(1) Lined or trimmed or decorated in any manner or with edges which have been cut to shape, hemmed or bound	20%	C 18% E —
(2) Other	17·5%	C 10·5% E —

Tariff Heading	Rate of Import Duty (if any)	
	Full	Commonwealth (C E.F.T.A. (E
65.03 Felt hats and other felt headgear, etc. *—contd.*		
(B) Other:		
(1) Lined or trimmed or decorated in any manner or with edges which have been cut to shape, hemmed or bound	20%	—
(2) Other	17·5%	—
65.04 Hats and other headgear, plaited or made from plaited or other strips of any material, whether or not lined or trimmed:		
(A) Containing more than 5 per cent. by weight of silk, of man-made fibres (including monofil or strip of heading No. 51.01 or 51.02), or of both together:		
(1) Lined or trimmed or decorated in any manner or with edges which have been cut to shape, hemmed or bound	20%	C 18% E —
(2) Other	17·5%	C 85% of the fu[ll] rate E —
(B) Other:		
(1) Wholly of unspun buntal fibre, not lined, trimmed or decorated in any manner	5%	—
(2) Other:		
(*a*) Lined or trimmed or decorated in any manner or with edges which have been cut to shape, hemmed or bound	20%	—
(*b*) Other	7·5%	—
65.05 Hats and other headgear (including hair nets), knitted or crocheted, or made up from lace, felt or other textile fabric in the piece (but not from strips), whether or not lined or trimmed:		
(A) Containing more than 5 per cent. by weight of silk, of man-made fibres, or of both together	20%	C 18% E —
(B) Other	20%	—
65.06 Other headgear, whether or not lined or trimmed:		
(A) Bathing caps of rubber	10%	—
(B) Other headgear	20%	—
65.07 Head-bands, linings, covers, hat foundations, hat frames (including spring frames for opera hats), peaks and chinstraps, for headgear	17·5%	—

Chapter 66

Umbrellas, Sunshades, Walking-sticks, Whips, Riding-crops and parts thereof

Notes

1. This Chapter does not cover:

(*a*) Measure walking-sticks or the like (heading No. 90.16);

(*b*) Firearm-sticks, sword-sticks, loaded walking-sticks or the like (Chapter 93); or

(*c*) Goods falling within Chapter 97 (for example, toy umbrellas and toy sunshades).

2. Heading No. 66.03 is to be taken not to apply to parts, trimmings or accessories of textile material, nor to covers, tassels, thongs, umbrella cases or the like, of any material. Such goods imported with, but not fitted to, articles falling within heading No. 66.01 or 66.02 are to be classified separately and are not to be treated as forming part of those articles.

Tariff Heading	*Rate of Import Duty (if any)*	
	Full	*Commonwealth (C)* *E.F.T.A. (E)*
66.01 Umbrellas and sunshades (including walking-stick umbrellas, umbrella tents, and garden and similar umbrellas):		
(A) With covers or cases containing silk or man-made fibres	20%	C 17% E —
(B) Other	20%	—
66.02 Walking-sticks (including climbing-sticks and seat-sticks), canes, whips, riding-crops and the like	10%	—
66.03 Parts, fittings, trimmings and accessories of articles falling within heading No. 66.01 or 66.02	10%	—

Chapter 67

Prepared Feathers and Down and Articles made of Feathers or of Down; Artificial Flowers; Articles of Human Hair; Fans

Notes

1. This Chapter does not cover:

(*a*) Straining cloth of human hair (heading No. 59.17);

(*b*) Floral motifs of lace, of embroidery or other textile fabric (Section XI);

(*c*) Footwear (Chapter 64);

(*d*) Headgear (Chapter 65);

(*e*) Feather dusters (heading No. 96.04), powder-puffs (heading No. 96.05) or hair sieves (heading No. 96.06); or

(*f*) Toys, sports requisites or carnival articles (Chapter 97).

2. Heading No. 67.01 is to be taken not to apply to:

(*a*) Goods (for example, bedding) in which feathers or down constitute only filling or padding;

(*b*) Articles of apparel and accessories thereto in which feathers or down constitute no more than mere trimming or padding;

(*c*) Artificial flowers or foliage or parts thereof or made up articles of heading No. 67.02; or

(*d*) Fans (heading No. 67.05).

3. Heading No. 67.02 is to be taken not to apply to:

(*a*) Articles of glass (Chapter 70);

(*b*) Artificial flowers, foliage or fruit of pottery, stone, metal, wood or other materials obtained in one piece by moulding, forging, carving, stamping or other process, or consisting of parts assembled otherwise than by binding, glueing or similar methods or to articles made of such artificial flowers, foliage or fruit.

Tariff Heading	*Rate of Import Duty (if any)*	
	Full	*Commonwealth (C)* *E.F.T.A. (E)*
67.01 Skins and other parts of birds with their feathers or down, feathers, parts of feathers, down, and articles thereof (other than goods falling within heading No. 05.07 and worked quills and scapes)	10%	—
67.02 Artificial flowers, foliage or fruit and parts thereof; articles made of artificial flowers, foliage or fruit:		
(A) Containing more than 25 per cent. by weight of silk, of man-made fibres, or of both together	21%	C 17·5% E —
(B) Other	12·5%	—

Tariff Heading	*Rate of Import Duty (if any)*	
	Full	*Commonwealth (C) E.F.T.A. (E)*
67.03 Human hair, dressed, thinned, bleached or otherwise worked; wool or other animal hair prepared for use in making wigs and the like	5%	—
67.04 Wigs, false beards, hair pads, curls, switches and the like, of human or animal hair or of textiles; other articles of human hair (including hair nets)	10%	—
67.05 Fans and hand screens, non-mechanical, of any material; frames and handles therefor and parts of such frames and handles, of any material	10%	—

SECTION XIII

ARTICLES OF STONE, OF PLASTER, OF CEMENT, OF ASBESTOS, OF MICA AND OF SIMILAR MATERIALS; CERAMIC PRODUCTS; GLASS AND GLASSWARE

Chapter 68

Articles of Stone, of Plaster, of Cement, of Asbestos, of Mica and of Similar Materials

Notes

1. This Chapter does not cover:

(*a*) Goods falling within Chapter 25;

(*b*) Coated or impregnated paper falling within heading No. 48.07 (for example, paper coated with mica powder or graphite, bituminised or asphalted paper);

(*c*) Coated or impregnated textile fabric falling within Chapter 59 (for example, mica-coated fabric, bituminised or asphalted fabric);

(*d*) Articles falling within Chapter 71;

(*e*) Tools or parts of tools, falling within Chapter 82;

(*f*) Lithographic stones of heading No. 84.34;

(*g*) Electrical insulators (heading No. 85.25) or fittings of insulating material falling within heading No. 85.26;

(*h*) Dental burrs (heading No. 90.17);

(*ij*) Goods falling within Chapter 91 (for example, clocks and clock cases);

(*k*) Articles falling within heading No. 95.07;

(*l*) Articles falling within Chapter 97 (for example, toys, games and sports requisites);

(*m*) Goods falling within heading No. 98.01 (for example, buttons), No. 98.05 (for example, slate pencils) or No. 98.06 (for example, drawing slates); or

(*n*) Works of art, collectors' pieces or antiques (Chapter 99).

2. In heading No. 68.02 the expression " worked monumental or building stone " is to be taken to apply not only to the varieties of stone referred to in headings Nos. 25.15 and 25.16 but also to all other natural stone (for example, quartzite, flint, dolomite and steatite) similarly worked; it is, however, to be taken not to apply to slate.

Tariff Heading	*Rate of Import Duty (if any)*	
	Full	*Commonwealth (C)* *E.F.T.A. (E)*
68.01 Road and paving setts, curbs and flagstones, of natural stone (except slate):		
(A) Granite flagstones	25%	—
(B) Other	10%	—
68.02 Worked monumental or building stone, and articles thereof (including mosaic cubes), other than goods falling within heading No. 68.01 or within Chapter 69:		
(A) Granite, and articles thereof:		
(1) Blocks in the form of rough cylinders, not less than 18 feet in length and not less than 28 inches in diameter, not further worked than scabbled	—	—

Tariff Heading	Rate of Import Duty (if any)	
	Full	Commonwealth (C) E.F.T.A. (E)
68.02 Worked monumental or building stone, etc.—*contd.*		
(A) Granite, and articles thereof:—*contd.*		
(2) Planed, or sawn and planed, on one or two sides only, but not further worked	15%	—
(3) Vases, inkstands (with or without trays or penholders), pen or pencil racks, stands and trays, blotters and letter openers, and bureau sets consisting of two or more of the foregoing articles	10%	—
(4) Other	25%	—
(B) Marble, ecaussine and similar calcareous stone of an apparent specific gravity of 2·5 or more, and articles thereof:		
(1) Tiles of which no side exceeds 2 feet in length; mosaic cubes	10%	—
(2) Other:		
(*a*) Sawn but not otherwise worked (apart from being roughly split or roughly squared)	5%	—
(*b*) Other	15%	—
(C) Other	7·5%	—
68.03 Worked slate and articles of slate, including articles of agglomerated slate	5%	—
68.04 Millstones, grindstones, grinding wheels and the like (including grinding, sharpening, polishing, trueing and cutting wheels, heads, discs and points), of natural stone (agglomerated or not), of agglomerated natural or artificial abrasives, or of pottery, with or without cores, shanks, sockets, axles and the like of other materials, but without frameworks; segments and other finished parts of such stones and wheels, of natural stone (agglomerated or not), of agglomerated natural or artificial abrasives, or of pottery	7%	—
68.05 Hand polishing stones, whetstones, oil stones, hones and the like, of natural stone, of agglomerated natural or artificial abrasives, or of pottery	7%	—
68.06 Natural or artificial abrasive powder or grain, on a base of woven fabric, of paper, of paperboard or of other materials, whether or not cut to shape or sewn or otherwise made up	8%	—

Tariff Heading	Rate of Import Duty (if any)	
	Full	Commonwealth (C) E.F.T.A. (E)
68.07 Slag wool, rock wool and similar mineral wools; exfoliated vermiculite, expanded clays, foamed slag and similar expanded mineral materials; mixtures and articles of heat-insulating, sound-insulating, or sound-absorbing mineral materials, other than those falling in heading No. 68.12 or 68.13, or in Chapter 69	5%	—
68.08 Articles of asphalt or of similar material (for example, of petroleum bitumen or coal tar pitch):		
(A) Pipes, couplings and pipe-fittings containing not less than 20 per cent. by weight of vegetable fibre and not less than 50 per cent. by weight of the asphalt or similar material	10%	—
(B) Other	5%	—
68.09 Panels, boards, tiles, blocks and similar articles of vegetable fibre, of wood fibre, of straw, of wood shavings or of wood waste (including sawdust), agglomerated with cement, plaster or with other mineral binding substances	10%	—
68.10 Articles of plastering material	5%	—
68.11 Articles of cement (including slag cement), of concrete or of artificial stone (including granulated marble agglomerated with cement), reinforced or not	5%	—
68.12 Articles of asbestos-cement, of cellulose fibre-cement or the like	7·5%	—
68.13 Fabricated asbestos and articles thereof (for example, asbestos board, thread and fabric; asbestos clothing, asbestos jointing), reinforced or not, other than goods falling within heading No. 68.14; mixtures with a basis of asbestos and mixtures of, or with a basis of, asbestos and magnesium carbonate, and articles of such mixtures:		
(A) Clothing and parts thereof	10%	—
(B) Other	7·5%	—

Tariff Heading	Rate of Import Duty (if any)	
	Full	*Commonwealth (C)* *E.F.T.A. (E)*
68.14 Friction material (segments, discs, washers, strips, sheets, plates, rolls and the like) of a kind suitable for brakes, for clutches or the like, with a basis of asbestos, other mineral substances or of cellulose, whether or not combined with textile or other materials:		
(A) Unmounted linings suitable for brakes, clutches and other parts of motor vehicles	12%	C 8% E —
(B) Other	7·5%	—
68.15 Worked mica and articles of mica, including bonded mica splittings on a support of paper or fabric (for example, micanite and micafolium)	10%	—
68.16 Articles of stone or of other mineral substances (including articles of peat), not elsewhere specified or included	5%	—

Chapter 69

Ceramic Products

Notes

1. The headings of this Chapter are to be taken to apply only to ceramic products which have been fired after shaping. Headings Nos. 69.04 to 69.14 are to be taken to apply only to such products other than heat-insulating goods and refractory goods.

2. This Chapter does not cover:

(*a*) Goods falling within Chapter 71 (for example, imitation jewellery);

(*b*) Cermets falling within heading No. 81.04;

(*c*) Electrical insulators (heading No. 85.25) or fittings of insulating material falling within heading No. 85.26;

(*d*) Artificial teeth (heading No. 90.19);

(*e*) Goods falling within Chapter 91 (for example, clocks and clock cases);

(*f*) Articles falling within Chapter 97 (for example, toys, games and sports requisites);

(*g*) Smoking pipes, buttons or other articles falling within Chapter 98; or

(*h*) Original statuary, collectors' pieces or antiques (Chapter 99).

Tariff Heading	*Rate of Import Duty (if any)*	
	Full	*Commonwealth (C)* *E.F.T.A. (E)*
I. Heat-insulating and refractory goods		
69.01 Heat-insulating bricks, blocks, tiles and other heat-insulating goods of siliceous fossil meals or of similar siliceous earths (for example, kieselguhr, tripolite or diatomite):		
(A) Bricks and blocks	4%	—
(B) Other	10%	—
69.02 Refractory bricks, blocks, tiles and similar refractory constructional goods, other than goods falling within heading No. 69.01	5%	—
69.03 Other refractory goods (for example, retorts, crucibles, muffles, nozzles, plugs, supports, cupels, tubes, pipes, sheaths and rods), other than goods falling within heading No. 69.01:		
(A) Laboratory wares	17%	—
(B) Other	5%	—
II. Other ceramic products		
69.04 Building bricks (including flooring blocks, support or filler tiles and the like)	5%	—
69.05 Roofing tiles, chimney-pots, cowls, chimney-liners, cornices and other constructional goods, including architectural ornaments:		
(A) Roofing tiles	6%	—
(B) Other	10%	—

Tariff Heading	Rate of Import Duty (if any)	
	Full	Commonwealth (C) E.F.T.A. (E)
69.06 Piping, conduits and guttering (including angles, bends and similar fittings)	10%	—
69.07 Unglazed setts, flags and paving, hearth and wall tiles	7·5%	—
69.08 Glazed setts, flags and paving, hearth and wall tiles:		
(A) All white, flat, rectangular, not figured or embossed	£0·1345 per square metre	—
(B) Other	£0·1345 per square metre or 15%, whichever is the greater	—
69.09 Laboratory, chemical or industrial wares; troughs, tubs and similar receptacles of a kind used in agriculture; pots, jars and similar articles of a kind commonly used for the conveyance or packing of goods:		
(A) Laboratory wares	17%	—
(B) Other	10%	—
69.10 Sinks, wash basins, bidets, water closet pans, urinals, baths and like sanitary fixtures	12·5%	—
69.11 Tableware and other articles of a kind commonly used for domestic or toilet purposes, of porcelain or china (including biscuit porcelain and parian):		
(A) Articles designed for fixing to or setting in the wall	12·5%	—
(B) Articles designed for use primarily in the storage, preparation, serving or consumption of food or drink, the following: Cups (including mugs and beakers) Saucers and plates Teapots and coffee pots Sets of articles of the kinds commonly known as morning sets, dinner sets, hors d'oeuvre sets, tea sets and coffee sets, and articles designed as parts of such sets Cooking utensils and kitchen ware	£1·2302 per 100 kilogrammes	—
(C) Washstand utensils and chamber pots	£1·2302 per 100 kilogrammes	—
(D) Other	£8·8578 per 100 kilogrammes	—

Tariff Heading	Rate of Import Duty (if any)	
	Full	Commonwealth (C) E.F.T.A. (E)
69.12 Tableware and other articles of a kind commonly used for domestic or toilet purposes, of other kinds of pottery:		
(A) Fireproof non-vitrified earthenware cooking utensils	14%	—
(B) Articles designed for fixing to or setting in the wall	12·5%	—
(C) Articles designed for use primarily in the storage, preparation, serving or consumption of food or drink, the following: Cups (including mugs and beakers) Saucers and plates Teapots and coffee pots Sets of articles of the kinds commonly known as morning sets, dinner sets, hors d'oeuvre sets, tea sets and coffee sets, and articles designed as parts of such sets Cooking utensils, not comprised in subheading (A) above, and kitchen ware	£1·2302 per 100 kilogrammes	—
(D) Washstand utensils and chamber pots	£1·2302 per 100 kilogrammes	—
(E) Other	£8·8578 per 100 kilogrammes	—
69.13 Statuettes and other ornaments, and articles of personal adornment; articles of furniture:		
(A) Statuettes and other ornaments ...	£8·8578 per 100 kilogrammes	—
(B) Other	10%	—
69.14 Other articles	10%	—

Chapter 70

Glass and Glassware

Notes

1. This Chapter does not cover:
(*a*) Ceramic enamels (heading No. 32.08);
(*b*) Goods falling within Chapter 71 (for example, imitation jewellery);
(*c*) Electrical insulators (heading No. 85.25) or fittings of insulating material falling within heading No. 85.26;
(*d*) Hypodermic syringes, artificial eyes, thermometers, barometers, hydrometers, optically worked optical elements or other articles falling within Chapter 90;
(*e*) Toys, games, sports requisites, Christmas tree ornaments or other articles falling within Chapter 97 (excluding glass eyes without mechanisms for dolls or for other articles of Chapter 97); or
(*f*) Buttons, fitted vacuum flasks, scent or similar sprays or other articles falling within Chapter 98.

2. The reference in heading No. 70.07 to " cast, rolled, drawn or blown glass (including flashed or wired glass) cut to shape other than rectangular shape, or bent or otherwise worked (for example, edge worked or engraved), whether or not surface ground or polished " is to be taken to apply to articles made from such glass, provided they are not framed or fitted with other materials.

3. For the purposes of heading No. 70.20, the expression " wool " means:
(*a*) Mineral wools with a silica (SiO_2) content not less than 60 per cent. by weight;
(*b*) Mineral wools with a silica (SiO_2) content less than 60 per cent. but with an alkaline oxide (K_2O and/or Na_2O) content of more than 5 per cent. by weight or a boric oxide (B_2O_3) content of more than 2 per cent. by weight.
Mineral wools which do not comply with the above specifications fall in heading No. 68.07.

4. For the purposes of this Schedule, the expression " glass " is to be taken to extend to fused quartz and fused silica.

Tariff Heading	*Rate of Import Duty (if any)*	
	Full	*Commonwealth (C)* *E.F.T.A. (E)*
70.01 Waste glass (cullet); glass in the mass (excluding optical glass)	5%	—
70.02 Glass of the variety known as " enamel " glass, in the mass, rods and tubes	10%	—
70.03 Glass in balls, rods and tubes, unworked (not being optical glass):		
(A) Balls	5%	—
(B) Other	15%	—
70.04 Unworked cast or rolled glass (including flashed or wired glass), whether figured or not, in rectangles	7·5%	—
70.05 Unworked drawn or blown glass (including flashed glass), in rectangles	7·5%	—
70.06 Cast, rolled, drawn or blown glass (including flashed or wired glass) in rectangles, surface ground or polished, but not further worked	7·5%	—

Tariff Heading	Rate of Import Duty (if any)	
	Full	Commonwealth (C) E.F.T.A. (E)
70.07 Cast, rolled, drawn or blown glass (including flashed or wired glass) cut to shape other than rectangular shape, or bent or otherwise worked (for example, edge worked or engraved), whether or not surface ground or polished; multiple-walled insulating glass; leaded lights and the like	7·5%	—
70.08 Safety glass consisting of toughened or laminated glass, shaped or not:		
(A) In sizes and shapes ready for incorporation in motor vehicles	10%	C 7% E —
(B) Other	10%	—
70.09 Glass mirrors (including rear-view mirrors), unframed, framed or backed:		
(A) Suitable for motor vehicles	15%	C 10% E —
(B) Other	10%	—
70.10 Carboys, bottles, jars, pots, tubular containers and similar containers, of glass, of a kind commonly used for the conveyance or packing of goods; stoppers and other closures, of glass	12·5%	—
70.11 Glass envelopes (including bulbs and tubes) for electric lamps, electronic valves or the like:		
(A) For filament lamps	5%	—
(B) For mercury arc rectifiers of the mercury pool cathode type	5%	—
(C) Other	12·5%	—
70.12 Glass inners for vacuum flasks or for other vacuum vessels	15%	—
70.13 Glassware (other than articles falling in heading No. 70.19) of a kind commonly used for table, kitchen, toilet or office purposes, for indoor decoration, or for similar uses:		
(A) Cooking utensils, kitchen and tableware, of glass-ceramic, being a crystalline ceramic material made from glass	£1·2302 per 100 kilogrammes	—
(B) Other	15·5%	—
70.14 Illuminating glassware, signalling glassware and optical elements of glass, not optically worked nor of optical glass:		
(A) Optical elements	20%	—
(B) Other	10%	—

Tariff Heading	Rate of Import Duty (if any)	
	Full	*Commonwealth (C) E.F.T.A. (E)*
70.15 Clock and watch glasses and similar glasses (including glass of a kind used for sunglasses but excluding glass suitable for corrective lenses), curved, bent, hollowed and the like; glass spheres and segments of spheres, of a kind used for the manufacture of clock and watch glasses and the like:		
(A) Clock and watch glasses	17%	C 11% E —
(B) Other	5%	—
70.16 Bricks, tiles, slabs, paving blocks, squares and other articles of pressed or moulded glass, of a kind commonly used in building; multi-cellular glass in blocks, slabs, plates, panels and similar forms	5%	—
70.17 Laboratory, hygienic and pharmaceutical glassware, whether or not graduated or calibrated; glass ampoules	17%	—
70.18 Optical glass and elements of optical glass, other than optically worked elements; blanks for corrective spectacle lenses	20%	—
70.19 Glass beads, imitation pearls, imitation precious and semi-precious stones, fragments and chippings, and similar fancy or decorative glass smallwares, and articles of glassware made therefrom; glass cubes and small glass plates, whether or not on a backing, for mosaics and similar decorative purposes; artificial eyes, of glass, including those for toys but excluding those for wear by humans; ornaments and other fancy articles of lamp-worked glass; glass grains (ballotini):		
(A) Glass beads, imitation pearls, imitation precious and semi-precious stones, fragments and chippings, and similar fancy or decorative glass smallwares:		
(1) Not mounted, set or strung, but including ungraded goods temporarily strung for convenience of transport	—	—
(2) Other	12·5%	—
(B) Articles of glassware made from the goods within subheading (A) above:		
(1) Bead trimmings	7·5%	—
(2) Other	12·5%	—

Tariff Heading	*Rate of Import Duty (if any)*	
	Full	*Commonwealth (C)* *E.F.T.A. (E)*
70.19 Glass beads, etc.—*contd.*		
(C) Ornaments and other fancy articles of lamp-worked glass	12·5%	—
(D) Other	5%	—
70.20 Glass fibre (including wool), yarns, fabrics, and articles made therefrom	10%	—
70.21 Other articles of glass:		
(A) Face plates, cones or necks, being parts of glass envelopes for cathode ray tubes	12·5%	—
(B) Other	10%	—

SECTION XIV

Pearls, Precious and Semi-Precious Stones, Precious Metals, Rolled Precious Metals, and Articles thereof; Imitation Jewellery; Coin

Chapter 71

Pearls, Precious and Semi-Precious Stones, Precious Metals, Rolled Precious Metals, and Articles thereof; Imitation Jewellery

Notes

1. Subject to Note 1 (*a*) to Section VI and except as provided below, all articles consisting wholly or partly:

(*a*) Of pearls or of precious or semi-precious stones (natural, synthetic or reconstructed), or

(*b*) Of precious metal or of rolled precious metal,

are to be classified within this Chapter and not within any other Chapter.

2. (*a*) Headings Nos. 71.12, 71.13 and 71.14 do not cover articles in which precious metal or rolled precious metal is present as minor constituents only, such as minor fittings or minor ornamentation (for example, monograms, ferrules and rims), and paragraph (*b*) of the foregoing Note does not apply to such articles.

(*b*) Heading No. 71.15 does not cover articles containing precious metal or rolled precious metal (other than as minor constituents).

3. This Chapter does not cover:

(*a*) Amalgams of precious metal, and colloidal precious metal (heading No. 28.49);

(*b*) Sterile surgical suture materials, dental fillings and other goods falling in Chapter 30;

(*c*) Goods falling in Chapter 32 (for example, lustres);

(*d*) Handbags and other articles falling within heading No. 42.02 or 42.03;

(*e*) Goods of heading No. 43.03 or 43.04;

(*f*) Goods falling within Section XI (textiles and textile articles);

(*g*) Footwear (Chapter 64) and headgear (Chapter 65);

(*h*) Umbrellas, walking-sticks and other articles falling within Chapter 66;

(*ij*) Fans and hand screens of heading No. 67.05;

(*k*) Coin (Chapter 72 or 99);

(*l*) Abrasive goods falling within headings Nos. 68.04, 68.05, 68.06 or Chapter 82, containing dust or powder of precious or semi-precious stones (natural or synthetic); goods of Chapter 82 with a working part of precious or semi-precious stones (natural, synthetic or reconstructed) on a support of base metal; machinery, mechanical appliances and electrical goods, and parts thereof, falling within Section XVI, not being such articles wholly of precious or semi-precious stones (natural, synthetic or reconstructed);

(*m*) Goods falling within Chapter 90, 91 or 92 (scientific instruments, clocks and watches, or musical instruments);

(*n*) Arms or parts thereof (Chapter 93);

(*o*) Articles covered by Note 2 to Chapter 97;

(*p*) Articles falling within headings of Chapter 98 other than headings Nos. 98.01 and 98.12; or

(*q*) Original sculptures and statuary (heading No. 99.03), collectors' pieces (heading No. 99.05) and antiques of an age exceeding 100 years (heading No. 99.06), other than pearls or precious or semi-precious stones.

4. (*a*) The expression " pearls " is to be taken to include cultured pearls.

(*b*) The expression " precious metal " means silver, gold, platinum and other metals of the platinum group.

(*c*) The expression " other metals of the platinum group " means iridium, osmium, palladium, rhodium and ruthenium.

5. For the purposes of this Chapter, any alloy (including a sintered mixture) containing precious metal is to be treated as an alloy of precious metal if, and only if, any one precious metal constitutes as much as 2 per cent., by weight, of the alloy.

Alloys of precious metal are to be classified according to the following rules:

(*a*) An alloy containing 2 per cent. or more, by weight, of platinum is to be treated only as an alloy of platinum.

(*b*) An alloy containing 2 per cent. or more, by weight, of gold but no platinum, or less than 2 per cent., by weight, of platinum, is to be treated only as an alloy of gold.

(*c*) Other alloys containing 2 per cent. or more, by weight, of silver are to be treated as alloys of silver.

For the purposes of this Note, metals of the platinum group are to be regarded as one metal and are to be treated as though they were platinum.

6. Except where the context otherwise requires, any reference in these Notes or elsewhere in this Schedule to precious metal or to any particular precious metal is to be taken to include a reference to alloys treated as alloys of precious metal or of the particular metal in accordance with the rules in Note 5 above, but not to rolled precious metal or to base metal or non-metals coated or plated with precious metal.

7. The expression " rolled precious metal " means material made with a base of metal upon one or more surfaces of which there is affixed by soldering, brazing, welding, hot-rolling or similar mechanical means a covering of precious metal. The expression is also to be taken to cover base metal inlaid with precious metal.

8. In this Chapter the expression " articles of jewellery " means:

(*a*) Any small objects of personal adornment (gem-set or not) (for example, rings, bracelets, necklaces, brooches, ear-rings, watch-chains, fobs, pendants, tie-pins, cuff-links, dress-studs, religious or other medals and insignia); and

(*b*) Articles of personal use of a kind normally carried in the pocket, in the handbag or on the person (such as cigarette cases, powder boxes, chain purses, cachou boxes).

9. For the purposes of heading No. 71.13, the expression " articles of goldsmiths' or silversmiths' wares " includes such articles as ornaments, tableware, toilet-ware, smokers' requisites and other articles of household, office or religious use.

10. For the purposes of heading No. 71.16, the expression " imitation jewellery " means articles of jewellery within the meaning of paragraph (*a*) of Note 8 above, not incorporating pearls, precious or semi-precious stones (natural, synthetic or reconstructed) nor (except as plating or as minor constituents) precious metal or rolled precious metal, and composed:

(*a*) Wholly or partly of base metal, whether or not plated with precious metal; or

(*b*) Of at least two materials (for example, wood and glass, bone and amber, mother of pearl and artificial plastic material), no account being taken of materials (for example, necklace strings) used only for assembly, or of paint, varnish, pearl essence or similar coating materials.

However, heading No. 71.16 does not cover buttons, studs or cuff-links (heading No. 98.01), dress combs or hair slides (heading No. 98.12) or buckles, buckle clasps or clasps.

11. Cases, boxes and similar containers imported with articles of this Chapter are to be classified with such articles if they are of a kind normally sold therewith. Cases, boxes and similar containers imported separately are to be classified under their appropriate headings.

Tariff Heading	Rate of Import Duty (if any)	
	Full	Commonwealth (C) E.F.T.A. (E)
I. Pearls and precious and semi-precious stones		
71.01 Pearls, unworked or worked, but not mounted, set or strung (except ungraded pearls temporarily strung for convenience of transport)	—	—
71.02 Precious and semi-precious stones, unworked, cut or otherwise worked, but not mounted, set or strung (except ungraded stones temporarily strung for convenience of transport):		
(A) Diamonds drilled so as to be adapted for use in wire-drawing dies	10%	—
(B) Piezo-electric quartz in the form of plates, bars or rods	5%	—
(C) Other	—	—
71.03 Synthetic or reconstructed precious or semi-precious stones, unworked, cut or otherwise worked, but not mounted, set or strung (except ungraded stones temporarily strung for convenience of transport):		
(A) Piezo-electric quartz in the form of plates, bars or rods	5%	—
(B) Other	—	—
71.04 Dust and powder of natural or synthetic precious or semi-precious stones	—	—
II. Precious metals and rolled precious metals, unwrought, unworked or semi-manufactured		
71.05 Silver, including silver gilt and platinum-plated silver, unwrought or semi-manufactured:		
(A) Silver bullion	—	—
(B) Other	5%	—
71.06 Rolled silver, unworked or semi-manufactured	5%	—
71.07 Gold, including platinum-plated gold, unwrought or semi-manufactured:		
(A) Gold bullion	—	—
(B) Other	5%	—
71.08 Rolled gold on base metal or silver, unworked or semi-manufactured	5%	—

Tariff Heading	Rate of Import Duty (if any)	
	Full	Commonwealth (C) E.F.T.A. (E)
71.09 Platinum and other metals of the platinum group, unwrought or semi-manufactured:		
(A) Platinum in grain, ingot, bar or powder; platinum sponge	—	—
(B) Other	5%	—
71.10 Rolled platinum or other platinum group metals, on base metal or precious metal, unworked or semi-manufactured	5%	—
71.11 Waste and scrap (including goldsmiths', silversmiths' and jewellers' sweepings, residues and lemels) of precious metal, fit only for the recovery of metal or for use in the manufacture of chemicals	—	—
III. Jewellery, goldsmiths' and silversmiths' wares and other articles		
71.12 Articles of jewellery and parts thereof, of precious metal or rolled precious metal	12·5%	—
71.13 Articles of goldsmiths' or silversmiths' wares and parts thereof, of precious metal or rolled precious metal, other than goods falling within heading No. 71.12:		
(A) Articles of rolled precious metal on a base of non-precious metal	10%	—
(B) Other	15%	—
71.14 Other articles of precious metal or rolled precious metal	10%	—
71.15 Articles consisting of, or incorporating, pearls, precious or semi-precious stones (natural, synthetic or reconstructed):		
(A) Diamond-set used or defective drill bits, reaming shells and other articles, being parts of tools, fit only for recovery of the diamonds set therein	—	—
(B) Machinery and instrument parts made wholly of precious or semi-precious stones:		
(1) Bearings and parts of bearings prepared for mounting and setting, wholly of natural stones	—	—
(2) Other	7·5%	—

Tariff Heading	*Rate of Import Duty (if any)*	
	Full	*Commonwealth (C)* *E.F.T.A. (E)*
71.15 Articles consisting of, or incorporating, pearls, etc.—*contd.*		
(C) Other:		
(1) Made wholly or partly of jade, onyx, lapis lazuli, agate, rose quartz, cornelian or other similar stones; made partly of ivory, tortoise-shell, mother of pearl, amber or coral	15%	—
(2) Other	12·5%	—
71.16 Imitation jewellery	12·5%	—

Chapter 72

Coin

Note This Chapter does not cover collectors' pieces (heading No. 99.05)

Tariff Heading	*Rate of Import Duty (if any)*	
	Full	*Commonwealth* (*C*) *E.F.T.A.* (*E*)
72.01 Coin	—	—

SECTION XV

Base Metals and Articles of Base Metal

Notes

1. This Section does not cover:

(*a*) Prepared paints, inks or other products with a basis of metallic flakes or powder falling within heading No. 32.08, 32.09, 32.10 or 32.13;

(*b*) Ferro-cerium or other pyrophoric alloys (heading No. 36.07);

(*c*) Headgear or parts thereof falling within heading No. 65.06 or 65.07;

(*d*) Umbrella frames and other goods of heading No. 66.03;

(*e*) Goods falling within Chapter 71 (for example, precious metal alloys, rolled precious metal and imitation jewellery);

(*f*) Subject to the operation of Note 1 (*f*) to Chapter 84, articles falling within Section XVI (machinery, mechanical appliances and electrical goods);

(*g*) Assembled railway or tramway track (heading No. 86.10) or other articles falling within Section XVII (vehicles, ships and boats, aircraft);

(*h*) Instruments or apparatus of base metal of a kind falling within Section XVIII, including clock and watch springs;

(*ij*) Lead shot prepared for ammunition (heading No. 93.07) or other articles falling within Section XIX (arms and ammunition);

(*k*) Articles falling within Chapter 94 (furniture and mattress supports);

(*l*) Hand sieves (heading No. 96.06);

(*m*) Articles falling within Chapter 97 (for example, toys, games and sports requisites); or

(*n*) Buttons, pens, pencil-holders, pen nibs or other articles falling within Chapter 98.

2. Throughout this Schedule, the expression " parts of general use " means:

(*a*) Goods described in headings Nos. 73.20, 73.25, 73.29, 73.31 and 73.32 and similar goods of other base metals;

(*b*) Springs and leaves for springs, of base metal, other than watch and clock springs (heading No. 91.11); and

(*c*) Goods described in headings Nos. 83.01, 83.02, 83.07, 83.09, 83.12 and 83.14.

In Chapters 73 to 82 (but not in heading No. 73.29 or 74.13) references to parts of goods do not include references to parts of general use as defined above.

Subject to the preceding paragraph and to the Note to Chapter 83, the headings in Chapters 73 to 81 are to be taken not to apply to any goods falling within Chapter 82 or 83.

3. Classification of alloys (other than ferro-alloys and master alloys as defined in Chapters 73 and 74):

(*a*) An alloy of base metals containing more than 10 per cent., by weight, of nickel is to be classified as an alloy of nickel, except in the case of an alloy in which iron predominates by weight over each of the other metals.

(*b*) Any other alloy of base metals is to be classified as an alloy of the metal which predominates by weight over each of the other metals.

(*c*) An alloy composed of base metals of this Section and of elements not falling within this Section is to be treated as an alloy of base metals of this Section if the total weight of such metals equals or exceeds the total weight of the other elements present.

(*d*) In this Section the term " alloy " is to be taken to include sintered mixtures of metal powders and heterogeneous intimate mixtures obtained by melting (other than cermets).

4. Unless the context otherwise requires, any reference in this Schedule to a base metal is to be taken to include a reference to alloys which, by virture of Note 3 above, are to be classified as alloys of that metal.

5. Classification of Composite Articles:

Except where the headings otherwise require, articles of base metal (including articles of mixed materials treated as articles of base metal under the Interpretative Rules) containing two or more base metals are to be treated as articles of the base metal predominating by weight.

For this purpose:

(*a*) Iron and steel, or different kinds of iron or steel, are regarded as one and the same metal;

(*b*) An alloy is regarded as being entirely composed of that metal as an alloy of which, by virtue of Note 3, it is classified, and

(*c*) A cermet of heading No. 81.04 is regarded as a single base metal.

6. For the purposes of this Section, the expression " waste and scrap " means waste and scrap metal fit only for the recovery of metal or for use in the manufacture of chemicals.

7. In this Section, any reference to base metal, or to a particular base metal, is to be taken as including base metal plated with precious metal.

Chapter 73

Iron and Steel and Articles thereof

Notes

1. In this Chapter the following expressions have the meanings hereby assigned to them:

(*a*) **Pig iron and cast iron** (heading No. 73.01):

A ferrous product containing, by weight, 1·9 per cent. or more of carbon, and which may contain one or more of the following elements within the weight limits specified:

less than 15 per cent. phosphorus,
not more than 8 per cent. silicon,
not more than 6 per cent. manganese,
not more than 30 per cent. chromium,
not more than 40 per cent. tungsten, and
an aggregate of not more than 10 per cent. of other alloy elements (for example, nickel, copper, aluminium, titanium, vanadium, molybdenum).

However, the ferrous alloys known as " non-distorting tool steels ", containing, by weight, 1·9 per cent. or more of carbon and having the characteristics of steel, are to be classified as steels, under their appropriate headings.

(*b*) **Spiegeleisen** (heading No. 73.01):

A ferrous product containing, by weight, more than 6 per cent. but not more than 30 per cent. of manganese and otherwise conforming to the specification at (*a*) above.

(*c*) **Ferro-alloys** (heading No. 73.02):

Alloys of iron (other than master alloys as defined in Note 1 to Chapter 74) which are not usefully malleable and are commonly used as raw material in the manufacture of ferrous metals and which contain, by weight, separately or together:

more than 8 per cent. of silicon, or
more than 30 per cent. of manganese, or
more than 30 per cent. of chromium, or
more than 40 per cent. of tungsten, or
a total of more than 10 per cent. of other alloy elements (aluminium, titanium, vanadium, copper, molybdenum, niobium or other elements, subject to a maximum content of 10 per cent. in the case of copper),

and which contain, by weight, not less than 4 per cent. in the case of ferro-alloys containing silicon, not less than 8 per cent. in the case of ferro-alloys containing manganese but no silicon or not less than 10 per cent. in other cases, of the element iron.

(*d*) **Alloy steel** (heading No. 73.15):

Steel containing, by weight, one or more elements in the following proportions:
more than 2 per cent. of manganese and silicon, taken together, or
2·00 per cent. or more of manganese, or
2·00 per cent. or more of silicon, or
0·50 per cent. or more of nickel, or
0·50 per cent. or more of chromium, or
0·10 per cent. or more of molybdenum, or
0·10 per cent. or more of vanadium, or
0·30 per cent. or more of tungsten, or
0·30 per cent. or more of cobalt, or
0·30 per cent. or more of aluminium, or
0·40 per cent. or more of copper, or
0·10 per cent. or more of lead, or
0·12 per cent. or more of phosphorus, or
0·10 per cent. or more of sulphur, or
0·20 per cent. or more of phosphorus and sulphur, taken together, or
0·10 per cent. or more of other elements, taken separately.

(*e*) **High carbon steel** (heading No. 73.15):

Steel containing, by weight, not less than 0·60 per cent. of carbon and having a content, by weight, less than 0·04 per cent. of phosphorus and sulphur taken separately and less than 0·07 per cent. of these elements taken together.

(*f*) **Puddled bars and pilings** (heading No. 73.06):

Products for rolling, forging or re-melting obtained either:

(i) By shingling balls of puddled iron to remove the slag arising during puddling, or

(ii) By roughly welding together by means of hot-rolling, packets of scrap iron or steel or puddled iron.

(*g*) **Ingots** (heading No. 73.06):

Products for rolling or forging obtained by casting into moulds.

(*h*) **Blooms and billets** (heading No. 73.07):

Semi-finished products of rectangular section, of a cross-sectional area exceeding 1,225 square millimetres and of such dimensions that the thickness exceeds one quarter of the width.

(*ij*) **Slabs and sheet bars (including tinplate bars)** (heading No. 73.07):

Semi-finished products of rectangular section, of a thickness not less than 6 millimetres, of a width not less than 150 millimetres and of such dimensions that the thickness does not exceed one quarter of the width.

(*k*) **Coils for re-rolling** (heading No. 73.08):

Coiled semi-finished hot-rolled products, of rectangular section, not less than 1·5 millimetres thick, of a width exceeding 500 millimetres and of a weight of not less than 500 kilogrammes per piece.

(*l*) **Universal plates** (heading No. 73.09):

Products of rectangular section, hot-rolled lengthwise in a closed box or universal mill, of a thickness exceeding 5 millimetres but not exceeding 100 millimetres, and of a width exceeding 150 millimetres but not exceeding 1,200 millimetres.

(*m*) **Hoop and strip** (heading No. 73.12):

Rolled products with sheared or unsheared edges, of rectangular section, of a thickness not exceeding 6 millimetres, of a width not exceeding 500 millimetres and of such dimensions that the thickness does not exceed one tenth of the width, in straight strips, coils or flattened coils.

(*n*) **Sheets and plates** (heading No. 73.13):

Rolled products (other than coils for re-rolling as defined in paragraph (*k*) above) of any thickness and, if in rectangles, of a width exceeding 500 millimetres.

Heading No. 73.13 is to be taken to apply, *inter alia*, to sheets or plates which have been cut to non-rectangular shape, perforated, corrugated, channelled, ribbed, polished or coated, provided that they do not thereby assume the character of articles or of products falling within other headings.

(*o*) **Wire** (heading No. 73.14):

Cold-drawn products of solid section of any cross-sectional shape, of which no cross-sectional dimension exceeds 13 millimetres. In the case of headings Nos. 73.26 and 73.27, however, the term " wire " is deemed to include rolled products of the same dimensions.

(*p*) **Bars and rods (including wire rod)** (heading No. 73.10):

Products of solid section which do not conform to the entirety of any of the definitions (*h*), (*ij*), (*k*), (*l*), (*m*), (*n*) and (*o*) above, and which have cross-sections in the shape of circles, segments of circles, ovals, isosceles triangles, rectangles, hexagons, octagons or quadrilaterals with only two sides parallel and the other sides equal.

The expression also includes concrete reinforcing bars which apart from minor indentations, flanges, grooves or other deformations produced during the rolling process correspond to the above definition.

(*q*) **Hollow mining drill steel** (heading No. 73.10):

Steel hollow bars of any cross-section, suitable for mining drills, of which the greatest external dimension exceeds 15 millimetres but does not exceed 50 millimetres, and of which the greatest internal dimension does not exceed one third of the greatest external dimension. Other steel hollow bars are to be treated as falling within heading No. 73.18.

(*r*) **Angles, shapes and sections** (heading No. 73.11):

Products, other than those falling within heading No. 73.16, which do not conforn to the entirety of any of the definitions (*h*), (*ij*), (*k*), (*l*), (*m*), (*n*) and (*o*) above, and whicl do not have cross-sections in the form of circles, segments of circles, ovals, isoscele triangles, rectangles, hexagons, octagons or quadrilaterals with only two sides paralle and the other two sides equal, and which are not hollow.

2. Headings Nos. 73.06 to 73.14 are to be taken not to apply to goods of alloy or hig carbon steel (heading No. 73.15).

3. Iron and steel products of the kind described in any of the headings Nos. 73.06 to 73.1 inclusive, clad with another ferrous metal, are to be classified as products of the ferrou metal predominating by weight.

4. Iron obtained by electrolytic deposition is classified according to its form an dimensions with the corresponding products obtained by other processes.

5. The expression " high-pressure hydro-electric conduits of steel " (heading No. 73.19 means riveted, welded or seamless circular steel tubes or pipes and bends therefor, of a internal diameter exceeding 400 millimetres and of a wall thickness exceeding 10·5 mill metres.

Tariff Heading	*Rate of Import Duty (if any)*	
	Full	*Commonwealth (C E.F.T.A. (E*
73.01 Pig iron, cast iron and spiegeleisen, in pigs, blocks, lumps and similar forms:		
(A) Pig iron, smelted wholly with charcoal	—	—
(B) Vanadium-titanium pig iron produced in an electric furnace	—	—
(C) Pig iron produced in an electric furnace and containing more than 0·1 per cent. by weight of cobalt but not more than 0·025 per cent. by weight of phosphorus and not more than 0·02 per cent. by weight of sulphur	—	—

Tariff Heading	Rate of Import Duty (if any)	
	Full	Commonwealth (C) E.F.T.A. (E)
73.01 Pig iron, etc.—*contd.*		
(D) Pig iron produced in an electric furnace and containing not more than 0·025 per cent. by weight of phosphorus, not more than 0·02 per cent. by weight of sulphur and not more than 2·5 per cent. by weight of total carbon	—	—
(E) Other pig iron; cast iron:		
(1) Forge and foundry; haematite ...	£1·9680 per tonne or 8%, whichever is the greater	—
(2) Other	£1·9680 per tonne or 8%, whichever is the greater	—
(F) Spiegeleisen	£3·1490 per tonne or 8%, whichever is the greater	—
73.02 Ferro-alloys:		
(A) Ferro-chromium	—	—
(B) Ferro-silicon containing not less than 20 per cent. by weight of silicon	—	—
(C) Silico-manganese	—	—
(D) Ferro-silico-chromium containing not less than 20 per cent. by weight of silicon and not less than 10 per cent. by weight of chromium	—	—
(E) Calcium-silicon containing not less than 20 per cent. by weight of calcium, not less than 55 per cent. by weight of silicon and not more than 5 per cent. by weight of aluminium, and otherwise consisting mainly of iron	—	—
(F) Calcium-manganese-silicon containing not less than 15 per cent. by weight of calcium, not less than 8 per cent. by weight of manganese and not less than 50 per cent. by weight of silicon, and otherwise consisting mainly of iron	—	—
(G) Silicon-manganese-zirconium containing not less than 55 per cent. by weight of silicon, not less than 4 per cent. by weight of manganese and not less than 4 per cent. by weight of zirconium, and otherwise consisting mainly of iron	—	—
(H) Ferro-nickel	—	—
(IJ) Ferro-manganese:		
(1) Containing less than 3 per cent. by weight of carbon	—	—

Tariff Heading	*Rate of Import Duty (if any)*	
	Full	*Commonwealth (C)* *E.F.T.A. (E)*
73.02 Ferro-alloys:—*contd.*		
(IJ) Ferro-manganese:—*contd.*		
(2) Other:		
(*a*) Containing less than 65 per cent. by weight of manganese	£3·1490 per tonne or 8%, whichever is the greater	—
(*b*) Other	£6·8890 per tonne or 8%, whichever is the greater	—
(K) Ferro-molybdenum; ferro-titanium containing not more than 2 per cent. by weight of carbon; ferro-tungsten; ferro-vanadium	15%	—
(L) Other	5%	—
73.03 Waste and scrap metal of iron or steel ...	—	—
73.04 Shot and angular grit, of iron or steel, whether or not graded; wire pellets of iron or steel:		
(A) Shot and angular grit	8%	—
(B) Wire pellets	25%	—
73.05 Iron or steel powders; sponge iron or steel:		
(A) Sponge iron in the form of cakes, briquettes or powder, containing not less than 94 per cent. by weight of total iron and not more than 0·2 per cent. by weight of total carbon	—	—
(B) Other	8%	—
73.06 Puddled bars and pilings; ingots, blocks, lumps and similar forms, of iron or steel:		
(A) Puddled bars and pilings:		
(1) Of wrought iron produced by puddling with charcoal from pig iron smelted wholly with charcoal	—	—
(2) Other	£3·1490 per tonne or 8%, whichever is the greater	—
(B) Ingots, blocks, lumps and similar forms:		
(1) Manufactured entirely from pig iron smelted wholly with charcoal	—	—
(2) Other	£2·5585 per tonne or 8%, whichever is the greater	—

Tariff Heading	Rate of Import Duty (if any)	
	Full	Commonwealth (C) E.F.T.A. (E)
73.07 Blooms, billets, slabs and sheet bars (including tinplate bars), of iron or steel; pieces roughly shaped by forging, of iron or steel:		
(A) Blooms, billets, slabs and sheet bars	£3·1490 per tonne or 8%, whichever is the greater	—
(B) Pieces roughly shaped by forging ...	12%	—
73.08 Iron or steel coils for re-rolling	£4·9210 per tonne or 8%, whichever is the greater	—
73.09 Universal plates of iron or steel	£3·7395 per tonne or 8%, whichever is the greater	—
73.10 Bars and rods (including wire rod), of iron or steel, hot-rolled, forged, extruded, cold-formed or cold-finished (including precision-made); hollow mining drill steel:		
(A) Bars and rods of wrought iron produced by puddling with charcoal from pig iron smelted wholly with charcoal	—	—
(B) Cut bars of iron or steel, not exceeding 152 millimetres in length, 152 millimetres in width and 32 millimetres in thickness, and containing not more than 0·03 per cent. by weight of sulphur and not more than 0·025 per cent. by weight of phosphorus	—	—
(C) Bright steel bars	£5·5115 per tonne or 8%, whichever is the greater	—
(D) Other bars and rods; hollow mining drill steel	£3·5430 per tonne or 8%, whichever is the greater	—
3.11 Angles, shapes and sections, of iron or steel, hot-rolled, forged, extruded, cold-formed or cold-finished; sheet piling of iron or steel, whether or not drilled, punched or made from assembled elements:		
(A) Fluted or U-section form sections of a kind suitable for use in the manufacture of umbrella ribs, whether or not hardened, tempered or annealed, cut into lengths not exceeding 915 millimetres but not further manufactured	8%	—

Tariff Heading	Rate of Import Duty (if any)	
	Full	Commonwealth (C) E.F.T.A. (E)
73.11 Angles, shapes and sections, etc.—*contd.*		
(B) Other angles, shapes and sections:		
(1) Not drilled, punched or otherwise fabricated	£3·5430 per tonne or 8%, whichever is the greater	—
(2) Other	£5·9050 per tonne or 8%, whichever is the greater	—
(C) Sheet piling	£3·5430 per tonne or 8%, whichever is the greater	—
73.12 Hoop and strip, of iron or steel, hot-rolled or cold-rolled:		
(A) Bandsaw strip 267 millimetres wide and over and from 1·6 millimetres to 2·5 millimetres in thickness	—	—
(B) Other hoop and strip:		
(1) 3 millimetres or more in thickness	£3·7395 per tonne or 8%, whichever is the greater	—
(2) Less than 3 millimetres in thickness:		
(*a*) Not plated, coated or clad, nor cold-rolled	£3·5430 per tonne or 8%, whichever is the greater	—
(*b*) Other	£5·5115 per tonne or 8%, whichever is the greater	—
73.13 Sheets and plates, of iron or steel, hot-rolled or cold-rolled:		
(A) 3 millimetres or more in thickness ...	£3·7395 per tonne or 8%, whichever is the greater	—
(B) Less than 3 millimetres in thickness:		
(1) Not plated, coated or clad ...	£4·9210 per tonne or 8%, whichever is the greater	—
(2) Other	£5·7080 per tonne or 8%, whichever is the greater	—
73.14 Iron or steel wire, whether or not coated, but not insulated	25%	—

Tariff Heading	Rate of Import Duty (if any)	
	Full	Commonwealth (C) E.F.T.A. (E)
73.15 Alloy steel and high carbon steel in the forms mentioned in headings Nos. 73.06 to 73.14:		
(A) Bandsaw strip 267 millimetres wide and over and from 1·6 millimetres to 2·5 millimetres in thickness	—	—
(B) Machinery belting (including conveyor and elevator bands) of cold-rolled strip, exceeding 254 millimetres in width, imported in coils, of stainless steel, or hardened and tempered, of charcoal steel	8%	—
(C) Heat resisting wire, not plated, coated or covered, of metal alloy containing by weight the following: not less than per cent. / not more than per cent. Chromium ... 19·5 / 26·0 Aluminium ... 3·5 / 6·5 Cobalt ... ... 1·5 / 4·0 and not more than a total of 3 per cent. by weight of substances other than chromium, aluminium, cobalt and iron	12%	—
(D) Other:		
(1) Ingots, blocks, lumps and similar forms	£2·5585 per tonne or 8%, whichever is the greater	—
(2) Blooms, billets, slabs and sheet bars	£3·1490 per tonne or 8%, whichever is the greater	—
(3) Pieces roughly shaped by forging	12%	—
(4) Coils for re-rolling	£4·9210 per tonne or 8%, whichever is the greater	—
(5) Universal plates	£3·7395 per tonne or 8%, whichever is the greater	—
(6) Bars and rods (including wire rod):		
(a) Bright steel bars	£5·5115 per tonne or 8%, whichever is the greater	—
(b) Other	£3·5430 per tonne or 8%, whichever is the greater	—

Tariff Heading	*Rate of Import Duty (if any)*	
	Full	*Commonwealth (C)* *E.F.T.A. (E)*
73.15 Alloy steel, etc.—*contd.*		
(D) Other:—*contd.*		
(7) Hollow mining drill steel ...	£3·5430 per tonne or 8%, whichever is the greater	—
(8) Angles, shapes and sections:		
(*a*) Not drilled, punched or otherwise fabricated	£3·5430 per tonne or 8%, whichever is the greater	—
(*b*) Other	£5·9050 per tonne or 8%, whichever is the greater	—
(9) Sheet piling	£3·5430 per tonne or 8%, whichever is the greater	—
(10) Hoop and strip:		
(*a*) 3 millimetres or more in thickness	£3·7395 per tonne or 8%, whichever is the greater	—
(*b*) Less than 3 millimetres in thickness:		
(i) Not plated, coated or clad, nor cold-rolled	£3·5430 per tonne or 8%, whichever is the greater	—
(ii) Other	£5·5115 per tonne or 8%, whichever is the greater	—
(11) Sheets and plates:		
(*a*) 3 millimetres or more in thickness	£3·7395 per tonne or 8%, whichever is the greater	—
(*b*) Less than 3 millimetres in thickness:		
(i) Not plated, coated or clad	£4·9210 per tonne or 8%, whichever is the greater	—
(ii) Other	£5·7080 per tonne or 8%, whichever is the greater	—
(12) Wire	25%	—

Tariff Heading	Rate of Import Duty (if any)	
	Full	Commonwealth (C) E.F.T.A. (E)
73.16 Railway and tramway track construction material of iron or steel, the following: rails, check-rails, switch blades, crossings (or frogs), crossing pieces, point rods, rack rails, sleepers, fishplates, chairs, chair wedges, sole plates (base plates), rail clips, bedplates, ties and other material specialised for joining or fixing rails:		
(A) Rails, check-rails, switch blades, crossings (or frogs) and crossing pieces:		
(1) Used	—	—
(2) Unused	£3·3460 per tonne or 8%, whichever is the greater	—
(B) Sleepers, fishplates and sole plates (base plates)	£4·3300 per tonne or 8%, whichever is the greater	—
(C) Other	12%	—
73.17 Tubes and pipes, of cast iron	17%	—
73.18 Tubes and pipes and blanks therefor, of iron (other than of cast iron) or steel, excluding high-pressure hydro-electric conduits	17%	—
73.19 High-pressure hydro-electric conduits of steel, whether or not reinforced	17%	—
73.20 Tube and pipe fittings (for example, joints, elbows, unions and flanges), of iron or steel	17%	—
73.21 Structures and parts of structures, (for example, hangars and other buildings, bridges and bridge-sections, lock-gates, towers, lattice masts, roofs, roofing frameworks, door and window frames, shutters, balustrades, pillars and columns), of iron or steel; plates, strip, rods, angles, shapes, sections, tubes and the like, prepared for use in structures, of iron or steel:		
(A) Tubes	17%	—
(B) Other	8%	—
73.22 Reservoirs, tanks, vats and similar containers, for any material (other than compressed or liquefied gas), of iron or steel, of a capacity exceeding 300 litres, whether or not lined or heat-insulated, but not fitted with mechanical or thermal equipment	10%	—

Tariff Heading	*Rate of Import Duty (if any)*	
	Full	*Commonwealth (C)* *E.F.T.A. (E)*
73.23 Casks, drums, cans, boxes and similar containers, of sheet or plate iron or steel, of a description commonly used for the conveyance or packing of goods	10%	—
73.24 Containers, of iron or steel, for compressed or liquefied gas	10%	—
73.25 Stranded wire, cables, cordage, ropes, plaited bands, slings and the like, of iron or steel wire, but excluding insulated electric cables	17%	—
73.26 Barbed iron or steel wire; twisted hoop or single flat wire, barbed or not, and loosely twisted double wire, of kinds used for fencing, of iron or steel	25%	—
73.27 Gauze, cloth, grill, netting, fencing, reinforcing fabric and similar materials, of iron or steel wire	17%	—
73.28 Expanded metal, of iron or steel	8%	—
73.29 Chain and parts thereof, of iron or steel:		
(A) Motor vehicle transmission chain, and parts thereof	12%	C 8% E —
(B) Chain and parts thereof, manufactured of wire (other than welded or forged chain)	17%	—
(C) Other	10%	—
73.30 Anchors and grapnels and parts thereof, of iron or steel	10%	—
73.31 Nails, tacks, staples, hook-nails, corrugated nails, spiked cramps, studs, spikes and drawing pins, of iron or steel, whether or not with heads of other materials, but not including such articles with heads of copper	10%	—
73.32 Bolts and nuts (including bolt ends and screw studs), whether or not threaded or tapped, and screws (including screw hooks and screw rings), of iron or steel; rivets, cotters, cotter-pins, washers and spring washers, of iron or steel	12%	—

Tariff Heading	*Rate of Import Duty (if any)*	
	Full	*Commonwealth (C) E.F.T.A. (E)*
73.33 Needles for hand sewing (including embroidery), hand carpet needles and hand knitting needles, bodkins, crochet hooks, and the like, and embroidery stilettos, of iron or steel	10%	—
73.34 Pins (excluding hatpins and other ornamental pins and drawing pins), hairpins and curling grips, of iron or steel	17%	—
73.35 Springs and leaves for springs, of iron or steel:		
(A) Upholstery and mattress wire springs	17%	—
(B) Other	10%	—
73.36 Stoves (including stoves with subsidiary boilers for central heating or for hot water supply), ranges, cookers, grates, fires and other space heaters, gas-rings, plate warmers with burners, wash boilers with grates or other heating elements, and similar equipment, of a kind used for domestic purposes, not electrically operated, and parts thereof, of iron or steel	10%	—
73.37 Boilers (excluding boilers of heading No. 84.01) and radiators, for central heating, not electrically heated, and parts thereof, of iron or steel; air heaters and hot air distributors (including those which can also distribute cool or conditioned air), not electrically heated, incorporating a motor-driven fan or blower, and parts thereof, of iron or steel	10%	—
73.38 Articles of a kind commonly used for domestic purposes, sanitary ware for indoor use, and parts of such articles and ware, of iron or steel:		
(A) Of wire, but not including boot and shoe trees	17%	—
(B) Other:		
(1) Builders' sanitary ware for indoor use	10%	—
(2) Other	15%	—
73.39 Iron or steel wool; pot scourers and scouring and polishing pads, gloves and the like, of iron or steel	17%	—

Tariff Heading	Rate of Import Duty (if any)	
	Full	Commonwealth (C) E.F.T.A. (E)
73.40 Other articles of iron or steel:		
(A) Empty ribbon spools adapted for use in typewriters (including electric typewriters), accounting, adding, listing, book-keeping and billing machines, cash registers, weighing machines or time recorders, and parts of such spools	5%	—
(B) Other:		
(1) Of wire	25%	—
(2) Other	10%	—

Chapter 74

Copper and Articles thereof

Notes

1. For the purposes of heading No. 74.02, the expression " master alloys " means alloys (except copper phosphide (phosphor copper) containing more than 8 per cent. by weight of phosphorus) containing with other alloy elements more than 10 per cent. by weight of copper, not usefully malleable and commonly used as raw material in the manufacture of other alloys or as de-oxidants, de-sulphurising agents or for similar uses in the metallurgy of non-ferrous metals.

(Copper phosphide (phosphor copper) containing more than 8 per cent. by weight of phosphorus falls within heading No. 28.55 and not within this Chapter).

2. In this Chapter the following expressions have the meanings hereby assigned to them:

(*a*) **Wire** (headings Nos. 74.03, 74.10 and 74.11):

Rolled, extruded or drawn products of solid section of any cross-sectional shape, of which no cross-sectional dimension exceeds six millimetres.

(*b*) **Wrought bars, rods, angles, shapes and sections** (heading No. 74.03):

Rolled, extruded, drawn or forged products of solid section, of which the maximum cross-sectional dimension exceeds six millimetres and which, if they are flat, have a thickness exceeding one tenth of the width. Also cast or sintered products, of the same forms and dimensions, which have been subsequently worked after production (otherwise than by simple trimming or de-scaling), provided that they have not thereby assumed the character of articles or of products falling within other headings.

Wire-bars and billets with their ends tapered or otherwise worked simply to facilitate their entry into machines for converting them into, for example, wire-rod or tubes, are however to be taken to be unwrought copper of heading No. 74.01.

(*c*) **Wrought plates, sheets and strip** (heading No. 74.04):

Flat-surfaced, wrought products (coiled or not), of which the maximum cross-sectional dimension exceeds six millimetres, and of which the thickness exceeds 0·15 millimetre but does not exceed one tenth of the width.

Heading No. 74.04 is to be taken to apply, *inter alia*, to such products, whether or not cut to shape, perforated, corrugated, ribbed, channelled, polished or coated, provided that they do not thereby assume the character of articles or of products falling within other headings.

(*d*) **Foil** (heading No. 74.05):

Products of a thickness (excluding any backing) not exceeding 0·15 millimetre.

Heading No. 74.05 is to be taken to apply, *inter alia*, to such products whether or not embossed, cut to shape, perforated, coated, printed, or backed with paper or other reinforcing material.

3. Heading No. 74.07 is to be taken to apply, *inter alia*, to tubes, pipes and hollow bars which have been polished or coated, or which have been shaped or worked, such as bent, coiled, threaded, drilled, waisted, cone-shaped or finned. Heading No. 74.08 is to be taken to apply, *inter alia*, to tube and pipe fittings which have been similarly treated.

Tariff Heading	*Rate of Import Duty (if any)*	
	Full	*Commonwealth (C)* *E.F.T.A. (E)*
74.01 Copper matte; cement copper; unwrought copper (refined or not); copper waste and scrap:		
(A) Alloys of copper, not being waste and scrap:		
(1) Beryllium alloys	10%	—
(2) Other	5%	—
(B) Other	—	—

Tariff Heading	Rate of Import Duty (if any) Full	Commonwealth (C) E.F.T.A. (E)
74.02 Master alloys:		
(A) Beryllium alloys	10%	—
(B) Other	5%	—
74.03 Wrought bars, rods, angles, shapes and sections, of copper; copper wire:		
(A) Of beryllium alloys	10%	—
(B) Other	8%	—
74.04 Wrought plates, sheets and strip, of copper:		
(A) Of beryllium alloys	15%	—
(B) Other	8%	—
74.05 Copper foil:		
(A) Of beryllium alloys	15%	—
(B) Other	8%	—
74.06 Copper powders and flakes	10%	—
74.07 Tubes and pipes and blanks therefor, of copper; hollow bars of copper:		
(A) Of beryllium alloys	15%	—
(B) Other	10%	—
74.08 Tube and pipe fittings (for example, joints, elbows, sockets and flanges), of copper:		
(A) Of beryllium alloys	15%	—
(B) Other	10%	—
74.09 Reservoirs, tanks, vats and similar containers, for any material (other than compressed or liquefied gas), of copper, of a capacity exceeding 300 litres, whether or not lined or heat-insulated, but not fitted with mechanical or thermal equipment	10%	—
74.10 Stranded wire, cables, cordage, ropes, plaited bands and the like, of copper wire, but excluding insulated electric wires and cables	10%	—
74.11 Gauze, cloth, grill, netting, fencing, reinforcing fabric and similar materials (including endless bands), of copper wire	10%	—
74.12 Expanded metal, of copper	10%	—
74.13 Chain and parts thereof, of copper ...	10%	—
74.14 Nails, tacks, staples, hook-nails, spiked cramps, studs, spikes and drawing pins, of copper, or of iron or steel with heads of copper	10%	—
74.15 Bolts and nuts (including bolt ends and screw studs), whether or not threaded or tapped, and screws (including screw hooks and screw rings), of copper; rivets, cotters, cotter-pins, washers and spring washers, of copper:		
(A) Screws for wood (other than screw hooks and screw rings)	6%	—
(B) Other	10%	—

Tariff Heading	*Rate of Import Duty (if any)*	
	Full	*Commonwealth (C)* *E.F.T.A. (E)*
74.16 Springs, of copper	10%	—
74.17 Cooking and heating apparatus of a kind used for domestic purposes, not electrically operated, and parts thereof, of copper	10%	—
74.18 Other articles of a kind commonly used for domestic purposes, sanitary ware for indoor use, and parts of such articles and ware, of copper	10%	—
74.19 Other articles of copper	10%	—

Chapter 75

Nickel and Articles thereof

Notes

1. In this Chapter the following expressions have the meanings hereby assigned to them:

(*a*) **Wire** (heading No. 75.02):

Rolled, extruded or drawn products of solid section of any cross-sectional shape, of which no cross-sectional dimension exceeds six millimetres.

(*b*) **Wrought bars, rods, angles, shapes and sections** (heading No. 75.02):

Rolled, extruded, drawn or forged products of solid section, of which the maximum cross-sectional dimension exceeds six millimetres and which, if they are flat, have a thickness exceeding one tenth of the width. Also cast or sintered products, of the same forms and dimensions, which have been subsequently machined (otherwise than by simple trimming or de-scaling).

(*c*) **Wrought plates, sheets and strip** (heading No. 75.03):

Flat-surfaced, wrought products (coiled or not), of which the maximum cross-sectional dimension exceeds six millimetres, and of which the thickness exceeds 0·15 millimetre but does not exceed one tenth of the width.

Heading No. 75.03 is to be taken to apply, *inter alia*, to such products, whether or not cut to shape, perforated, corrugated, ribbed, channelled, polished or coated, provided that they do not thereby assume the character of articles or of products falling within other headings.

(*d*) **Foil** (heading No. 75.03):

Products of a thickness (excluding any backing) not exceeding 0·15 millimetre.

Heading No. 75.03 is to be taken to apply, *inter alia*, to such products whether or not embossed, cut to shape, perforated, coated, printed, or backed with paper or other reinforcing material.

2. Heading No. 75.04 is to be taken to apply, *inter alia*, to tubes, pipes, hollow bars and tube and pipe fittings which have been polished or coated, or which have been shaped or worked, such as bent, coiled, threaded, drilled, waisted, cone-shaped or finned.

Tariff Heading	*Rate of Import Duty (if any)*	
	Full	*Commonwealth* (*C*) *E.F.T.A.* (*E*)
75.01 Nickel mattes, nickel speiss and other intermediate products of nickel metallurgy; unwrought nickel (excluding electro-plating anodes); nickel waste and scrap:		
(A) Alloys of nickel, not being waste and scrap:		
(1) Nickel-copper alloys containing more than 60 per cent. by weight of nickel	—	—
(2) Other	5%	—
(B) Other	—	—
75.02 Wrought bars, rods, angles, shapes and sections, of nickel; nickel wire:		
(A) Bars and rods, of nickel-copper alloy containing more than 60 per cent. by weight of nickel	—	—
(B) Other	8%	—

Tariff Heading	*Rate of Import Duty (if any)*	
	Full	*Commonwealth (C)* *E.F.T.A. (E)*
75.03 Wrought plates, sheets and strip, of nickel; nickel foil; nickel powders and flakes:		
(A) Plates, sheets, strip and foil of nickel-copper alloy containing more than 60 per cent. by weight of nickel	—	—
(B) Powders	—	—
(C) Other	8%	—
75.04 Tubes and pipes and blanks therefor, of nickel; hollow bars, and tube and pipe fittings (for example, joints, elbows, sockets and flanges), of nickel:		
(A) Hollow bars and blanks for tubes and pipes, of nickel-copper alloy containing more than 60 per cent. by weight of nickel	—	—
(B) Other	10%	—
75.05 Electro-plating anodes, of nickel, wrought or unwrought, including those produced by electrolysis:		
(A) Unwrought	—	—
(B) Wrought	8%	—
75.06 Other articles of nickel	10%	—

Chapter 76

Aluminium and Articles thereof

Notes

1. In this Chapter the following expressions have the meanings hereby assigned to them:

(*a*) **Wire** (headings Nos. 76.02, 76.12 and 76.13):

Rolled, extruded or drawn products of solid section of any cross-sectional shape, of which no cross-sectional dimension exceeds six millimetres.

(*b*) **Wrought bars, rods, angles, shapes and sections** (heading No. 76.02):

Rolled, extruded, drawn or forged products of solid section, of which the maximum cross-sectional dimension exceeds six millimetres and which, if they are flat, have a thickness exceeding one tenth of the width. Also cast or sintered products, of the same forms and dimensions, which have been subsequently machined (otherwise than by simple trimming or de-scaling).

(*c*) **Wrought plates, sheets and strip** (heading No. 76.03):

Flat-surfaced, wrought products (coiled or not), of which the maximum cross-sectional dimension exceeds six millimetres, and of which the thickness exceeds 0·20 millimetre but does not exceed one tenth of the width.

Heading No. 76.03 is to be taken to apply, *inter alia*, to such products, whether or not cut to shape, perforated, corrugated, ribbed, channelled, polished or coated, provided that they do not thereby assume the character of articles or of products falling within other headings.

(*d*) **Foil** (heading No. 76.04):

Products of a thickness (excluding any backing) not exceeding 0·20 millimetre.

Heading No. 76.04 is to be taken to apply, *inter alia*, to such products whether or not embossed, cut to shape, perforated, coated, printed, or backed with paper or other reinforcing material.

2. Heading No. 76.06 is to be taken to apply, *inter alia*, to tubes, pipes and hollow bars which have been polished or coated, or which have been shaped or worked, such as bent, coiled, threaded, drilled, waisted, cone-shaped or finned. Heading No. 76.07 is to be taken to apply, *inter alia*, to tube and pipe fittings which have been similarly treated.

Tariff Heading	*Rate of Import Duty (if any)*	
	Full	*Commonwealth (C)* *E.F.T.A. (E)*
76.01 Unwrought aluminium; aluminium waste and scrap:		
(A) Alloys of aluminium, not being waste and scrap	5%	—
(B) Other	—	—
76.02 Wrought bars, rods, angles, shapes and sections, of aluminium; aluminium wire	8%	—
76.03 Wrought plates, sheets and strip (including discs and circles), of aluminium	8%	—
76.04 Aluminium foil	10%	—
76.05 Aluminium powders and flakes	10%	—

Tariff Heading	Rate of Import Duty (if any)	
	Full	Commonwealth (C) E.F.T.A. (E)
76.06 Tubes and pipes and blanks therefor, of aluminium; hollow bars of aluminium	8%	—
76.07 Tube and pipe fittings (for example, joints, elbows, sockets and flanges), of aluminium	8%	—
76.08 Structures and parts of structures, (for example, hangars and other buildings, bridges and bridge-sections, towers, lattice masts, roofs, roofing frameworks, door and window frames, balustrades, pillars and columns), of aluminium; plates, rods, angles, shapes, sections, tubes and the like, prepared for use in structures, of aluminium	10%	—
76.09 Reservoirs, tanks, vats and similar containers, for any material (other than compressed or liquefied gas), of aluminium, of a capacity exceeding 300 litres, whether or not lined or heat-insulated, but not fitted with mechanical or thermal equipment	10%	—
76.10 Casks, drums, cans, boxes and similar containers (including rigid and collapsible tubular containers), of aluminium, of a description commonly used for the conveyance or packing of goods	10%	—
76.11 Containers, of aluminium, for compressed or liquefied gas	10%	—
76.12 Stranded wire, cables, cordage, ropes, plaited bands and the like, of aluminium wire, but excluding insulated electric wires and cables	10%	—
76.13 Gauze, cloth, grill, netting, reinforcing fabric and similar materials, of aluminium wire	10%	—
76.14 Expanded metal, of aluminium	10%	—
76.15 Articles of a kind commonly used for domestic purposes, sanitary ware for indoor use, and parts of such articles and ware, of aluminium	10%	—
76.16 Other articles of aluminium	10%	—

Chapter 77

Magnesium and Beryllium and Articles thereof

Tariff Heading	Rate of Import Duty (if any)	
	Full	Commonwealth (C) E.F.T.A. (E)
77.01 Unwrought magnesium; magnesium waste (excluding shavings of uniform size) and scrap:		
(A) Alloys of magnesium, not being waste and scrap	5%	—
(B) Other	—	—
77.02 Wrought bars, rods, angles, shapes and sections, of magnesium; magnesium wire; wrought plates, sheets and strip, of magnesium; magnesium foil; raspings and shavings of uniform size, powders and flakes, of magnesium; tubes and pipes and blanks therefor, of magnesium; hollow bars of magnesium:		
(A) Raspings and shavings of uniform size of alloys of magnesium; powder and flakes of alloys of magnesium	10%	—
(B) Other	8%	—
77.03 Other articles of magnesium	10%	—
77.04 Beryllium, unwrought or wrought, and articles of beryllium:		
(A) Waste and scrap	—	—
(B) Other	10%	—

Chapter 78

Lead and Articles thereof

Notes

1. In this Chapter the following expressions have the meanings hereby assigned to them:

(*a*) **Wire** (heading No. 78.02):

Rolled, extruded or drawn products of solid section of any cross-sectional shape, of which no cross-sectional dimension exceeds six millimetres.

(*b*) **Wrought bars, rods, angles, shapes and sections** (heading No. 78.02):

Rolled, extruded, drawn or forged products of solid section, of which the maximum cross-sectional dimension exceeds six millimetres and which, if they are flat, have a thickness exceeding one tenth of the width. Also cast or sintered products, of the same forms and dimensions, which have been subsequently machined (otherwise than by simple trimming or de-scaling).

(*c*) **Wrought plates, sheets and strip** (heading No. 78.03):

Flat-surfaced, wrought products (coiled or not), of which the maximum cross-sectional dimension exceeds six millimetres, of which the thickness does not exceed one tenth of the width, and which are of a weight exceeding 1,700 grammes per square metre.

Heading No. 78.03 is to be taken to apply, *inter alia*, to such products, whether or not cut to shape, perforated, corrugated, ribbed, channelled, polished or coated, provided that they do not thereby assume the character of articles or of products falling within other headings.

(*d*) **Foil** (heading No. 78.04):

Products of a weight per square metre (excluding any backing) not exceeding 1,700 grammes.

Heading No. 78.04 is to be taken to apply, *inter alia*, to such products whether or not embossed, cut to shape, perforated, coated, printed, or backed with paper or other reinforcing material.

2. Heading No. 78.05 is to be taken to apply, *inter alia*, to tubes, pipes, hollow bars and tube and pipe fittings which have been polished or coated, or which have been shaped or worked, such as bent, coiled, threaded, drilled, waisted, cone-shaped or finned.

Tariff Heading	*Rate of Import Duty (if any)*	
	Full	*Commonwealth (C)* *E.F.T.A. (E)*
78.01 Unwrought lead (including argentiferous lead); lead waste and scrap:		
(A) Alloys of lead containing not more than 12 per cent. by weight of tin, not being waste and scrap	5%	—
(B) Other	—	—
78.02 Wrought bars, rods, angles, shapes and sections, of lead; lead wire	8%	—
78.03 Wrought plates, sheets and strip, of lead ...	8%	—
78.04 Lead foil; lead powders and flakes ...	10%	—

Tariff Heading	Rate of Import Duty (if any)	
	Full	*Commonwealth (C) E.F.T.A. (E)*
78.05 Tubes and pipes and blanks therefor, of lead; hollow bars, and tube and pipe fittings (for example, joints, elbows, sockets, flanges and S-bends), of lead	10%	—
78.06 Other articles of lead	10%	—

Chapter 79

Zinc and Articles thereof

Notes

1. In this Chapter the following expressions have the meanings hereby assigned to them:

(*a*) **Wire** (heading No. 79.02):

Rolled, extruded or drawn products of solid section of any cross-sectional shape, of which no cross-sectional dimension exceeds six millimetres.

(*b*) **Wrought bars, rods, angles, shapes and sections** (heading No. 79.02):

Rolled, extruded, drawn or forged products of solid section, of which the maximum cross-sectional dimension exceeds six millimetres and which, if they are flat, have a thickness exceeding one tenth of the width. Also cast or sintered products, of the same forms and dimensions, which have been subsequently machined (otherwise than by simple trimming or de-scaling).

(*c*) **Wrought plates, sheets and strip** (heading No. 79.03):

Flat-surfaced, wrought products (coiled or not), of which the maximum cross-sectional dimension exceeds six millimetres, and of which the thickness exceeds 0·15 millimetre but does not exceed one tenth of the width.

Heading No. 79.03 is to be taken to apply, *inter alia*, to such products, whether or not cut to shape, perforated, corrugated, ribbed, channelled, polished or coated, provided that they do not thereby assume the character of articles or of products falling within other headings.

(*d*) **Foil** (heading No. 79.03):

Products of a thickness (excluding any backing) not exceeding 0·15 millimetre.

Heading No. 79.03 is to be taken to apply, *inter alia*, to such products whether or not embossed, cut to shape, perforated, coated, printed, or backed with paper or other reinforcing material.

2. Heading No. 79.04 is to be taken to apply, *inter alia*, to tubes, pipes, hollow bars and tube and pipe fittings which have been polished or coated, or which have been shaped or worked, such as bent, coiled, threaded, drilled, waisted, cone-shaped or finned.

Tariff Heading	*Rate of Import Duty (if any)*	
	Full	*Commonwealth (C) E.F.T.A. (E)*
79.01 Unwrought zinc; zinc waste and scrap:		
(A) Zinc, other than alloys of zinc ...	£1·4760 per tonne	—
(B) Alloys of zinc	5%	—
(C) Waste and scrap	—	—
79.02 Wrought bars, rods, angles, shapes and sections, of zinc; zinc wire	8%	—
79.03 Wrought plates, sheets and strip, of zinc; zinc foil; zinc powders and flakes:		
(A) Foil and flakes	10%	—
(B) Other	8%	
79.04 Tubes and pipes and blanks therefor, of zinc; hollow bars, and tube and pipe fittings (for example, joints, elbows, sockets and flanges), of zinc	10%	—

Tariff Heading	Rate of Import Duty (if any)	
	Full	Commonwealth (C) E.F.T.A. (E)
79.05 Gutters, roof capping, skylight frames, and other fabricated building components, of zinc	10%	—
79.06 Other articles of zinc	10%	—

Chapter 80

Tin and Articles thereof

Notes

1. In this Chapter the following expressions have the meanings hereby assigned to them:

(*a*) **Wire** (heading No. 80.02):

Rolled, extruded or drawn products of solid section of any cross-sectional shape, of which no cross-sectional dimension exceeds six millimetres.

(*b*) **Wrought bars, rods, angles, shapes and sections** (heading No. 80.02):

Rolled, extruded, drawn or forged products of solid section, of which the maximum cross-sectional dimension exceeds six millimetres and which, if they are flat, have a thickness exceeding one tenth of the width. Also cast or sintered products, of the same forms and dimensions, which have been subsequently machined (otherwise than by simple trimming or de-scaling).

(*c*) **Wrought plates, sheets and strip** (heading No. 80.03):

Flat-surfaced, wrought products (coiled or not), of which the maximum cross-sectional dimension exceeds six millimetres, of which the thickness does not exceed one tenth of the width, and which are of a weight exceeding one kilogramme per square metre.

Heading No. 80.03 is to be taken to apply, *inter alia*, to such products, whether or not cut to shape, perforated, corrugated, ribbed, channelled, polished or coated, provided that they do not thereby assume the character of articles or of products falling within other headings.

(*d*) **Foil** (heading No. 80.04):

Products of a weight per square metre (excluding any backing) not exceeding one kilogramme.

Heading No. 80.04 is to be taken to apply, *inter alia*, to such products, whether or not embossed, cut to shape, perforated, coated, printed, or backed with paper or other reinforcing material.

2. Heading No. 80.05 is to be taken to apply, *inter alia*, to tubes, pipes, hollow bars and tube and pipe fittings which have been polished or coated, or which have been shaped or worked, such as bent, coiled, threaded, drilled, waisted, cone-shaped or finned.

Tariff Heading	*Rate of Import Duty (if any)*	
	Full	*Commonwealth (C)* *E.F.T.A. (E)*
80.01 Unwrought tin; tin waste and scrap ...	—	—
80.02 Wrought bars, rods, angles, shapes and sections, of tin; tin wire	8%	—
80.03 Wrought plates, sheets and strip, of tin ...	8%	—
80.04 Tin foil; tin powders and flakes	10%	—
80.05 Tubes and pipes and blanks therefor, of tin; hollow bars, and tube and pipe fittings (for example, joints, elbows, sockets and flanges), of tin	10%	—
80.06 Other articles of tin	10%	—

Chapter 81

Other Base Metals employed in Metallurgy and Articles thereof

Note

Heading No. 81.04 is to be taken to apply only to the following base metals: antimony, bismuth, cadmium, chromium, cobalt, gallium, germanium, hafnium, indium, manganese, niobium (columbium), rhenium, thallium, thorium, titanium, uranium depleted in uranium-235, vanadium, zirconium. The heading also covers cobalt mattes, cobalt speiss and other intermediate products of cobalt metallurgy, and cermets.

Tariff Heading	*Rate of Import Duty (if any)*	
	Full	*Commonwealth (C) E.F.T.A. (E)*
81.01 Tungsten (wolfram), unwrought or wrought, and articles thereof	12·5%	—
81.02 Molybdenum, unwrought or wrought, and articles thereof	17%	—
81.03 Tantalum, unwrought or wrought, and articles thereof:		
(A) Tantalum (other than alloys of tantalum) unwrought or in powder, sheets, plates, bars, wire, tubes and other semi-manufactured forms; waste and scrap	—	—
(B) Other	10%	—
81.04 Other base metals, unwrought or wrought, and articles thereof; cermets, unwrought or wrought, and articles thereof:		
(A) Antimony and articles thereof:		
(1) Antimony metal containing not less than 85 per cent. by weight of antimony	£39·3680 per tonne or 25%, whichever is the greater	—
(2) Other:		
(*a*) Waste and scrap	—	—
(*b*) Other	10%	—
(B) Bismuth and articles thereof:		
(1) Unwrought metal; waste and scrap	—	—
(2) Other	10%	—
(C) Chromium and vanadium and articles thereof	12·5%	—
(D) Cobalt and articles thereof:		
(1) Mattes, speiss and other intermediate products of cobalt metallurgy; waste and scrap	—	—
(2) Unwrought metal; powder:		
(*a*) Cobalt, other than alloys of cobalt	—	—
(*b*) Alloys of cobalt	5%	—
(3) Other	10%	—
(E) Germanium and articles thereof:		
(1) Waste and scrap	—	—
(2) Other	8%	—

Tariff Heading	Rate of Import Duty (if any)	
	Full	Commonwealth (C) E.F.T.A. (E)
81.04 Other base metals, etc.—*contd.*		
(F) Manganese and articles thereof:		
(1) Waste and scrap	—	—
(2) Ferro-manganese containing less than 3 per cent. by weight of carbon, and silico-manganese	—	—
(3) Manganese metal, other than alloys, of a purity exceeding 99·5 per cent.	—	—
(4) Other	10%	—
(G) Other metals and articles thereof:		
(1) Waste and scrap	—	—
(2) Uranium depleted in uranium-235	—	—
(3) Other	10%	—
(H) Cermets and articles thereof	10%	—

Chapter 82

Tools, Implements, Cutlery, Spoons and Forks, of Base Metal; Parts thereof

Notes

1. Apart from blow lamps, portable forges, grinding wheels with frameworks, manicure and chiropody sets, and goods classified in headings Nos. 82.07 and 82.15, the present Chapter covers only articles with a blade, working edge, working surface or other working part of:

(*a*) Base metal;
(*b*) Metal carbides;
(*c*) Precious or semi-precious stones (natural, synthetic or reconstructed) on a support of base metal; or
(*d*) Abrasive materials on a support of base metal, provided that the articles have cutting teeth, flutes, grooves, or the like, of base metal, which retain their identity and function after the application of the abrasive.

2. Parts of base metal of the articles falling in the headings of this Chapter are to be classified with the articles of which they are parts, except parts separately specified as such and tool-holders for hand tools (heading No. 84.48). However, parts of general use as defined in Note 2 to Section XV are in all cases excluded from this Chapter.

Cutting plates for electric hair clippers are to be classified in heading No. 82.13 and blades and heads for electric shavers are to be classified in heading No. 82.11.

3. Sets (other than manicure or chiropody sets (heading No. 82.13)) comprising an assortment of tools, cutlery, spoons, forks or other articles of a kind falling within the different headings of this Chapter, fitted in cabinets, boxes, cases or the like, are to be classified as that one of the constituent articles which is chargeable with the highest rate of duty. For this purpose a specific rate of duty shall be converted into its *ad valorem* equivalent rate and where an *ad valorem* equivalent rate is the highest rate of duty, the set shall be charged as a whole at that rate.

4. Cases, boxes and similar containers imported with articles of this Chapter are to be classified with such articles if they are of a kind normally sold therewith. Cases, boxes and similar containers imported separately are to be classified under their appropriate headings.

Tariff Heading	*Rate of Import Duty (if any)*	
	Full	*Commonwealth (C)* *E.F.T.A. (E)*
82.01 Hand tools, the following: spades, shovels, picks, hoes, forks and rakes; axes, bill hooks and similar hewing tools; scythes, sickles, hay knives, grass shears, timber wedges and other tools of a kind used in agriculture, horticulture or forestry	7·5%	—
82.02 Saws (non-mechanical) and blades for hand or machine saws (including toothless saw blades)	10%	—
82.03 Hand tools, the following: pliers (including cutting pliers), pincers, tweezers, tinmen's snips, bolt croppers and the like; perforating punches; pipe cutters; spanners and wrenches (but not including tap wrenches); files and rasps	10%	—

Tariff Heading	Rate of Import Duty (if any)	
	Full	Commonwealth (C) E.F.T.A. (E)
82.04 Hand tools (including glaziers' diamonds but not including needles, bodkins, crochet hooks, embroidery stilettos and the like) not falling within any other heading of this Chapter; blow lamps, anvils; vices and clamps, other than accessories for, and parts of, machine tools; portable forges; grinding wheels with frameworks (hand or pedal operated):		
(A) Knife sharpeners	10%	—
(B) Tyre levers and other appliances for fitting tyres	7·5%	—
(C) Other tools and appliances:		
(1) Of wire, but not including engineers', carpenters' and joiners' tools	17%	—
(2) Other	7·5%	—
(D) Parts of the tools and appliances of subheadings (A), (B) and (C) above:		
(1) Parts of wire of the tools and appliances of subheading (C)(1) above	17%	—
(2) Other	10%	—
82.05 Interchangeable tools for hand tools, for machine tools or for power-operated hand tools (for example, for pressing, stamping, drilling, tapping, threading, boring, broaching, milling, cutting, turning, dressing, morticing or screw driving), including dies for wire drawing, extrusion dies for metal, and rock drilling bits:		
(A) Diamond dies for wire drawing ...	10%	—
(B) Other tools	7·5%	—
(C) Parts of the tools of subheadings (A) and (B) above	10%	—
82.06 Knives and cutting blades, for machines or for mechanical appliances	7·5%	—
82.07 Tool-tips and plates, sticks and the like for tool-tips, unmounted, of sintered metal carbides (for example, carbides of tungsten, molybdenum or vanadium)	10%	—
82.08 Coffee-mills, mincers, juice-extractors and other mechanical appliances, of a weight not exceeding ten kilogrammes and of a kind used for domestic purposes in the preparation, serving or conditioning of food or drink	10%	—

Tariff Heading	Rate of Import Duty (if any)	
	Full	Commonwealth (C) E.F.T.A. (E)
82.09 Knives with cutting blades, serrated or not (including pruning knives), other than knives falling within heading No. 82.06:		
(A) Knives	£0·1000 per dozen or 18%, whichever is the greater	—
(B) Parts of knives	18%	—
82.10 Knife blades	£0·0500 per dozen or 18%, whichever is the greater	—
82.11 Razors and razor blades (including razor blade blanks, whether or not in strips):		
(A) Safety razor blades (including blanks)	15%	—
(B) Other	6%	—
82.12 Scissors (including tailors' shears), and blades therefor	20%	—
82.13 Other articles of cutlery (for example, secateurs, hair clippers, butchers' cleavers, paper knives); manicure and chiropody sets and appliances (including nail files):		
(A) Manicure and chiropody sets and appliances	20%	—
(B) Other	10%	—
82.14 Spoons, forks, fish-eaters, butter-knives, ladles, and similar kitchen or tableware	18%	—
82.15 Handles of base metal for articles falling within heading No. 82.09, 82.13 or 82.14	18%	—

Chapter 83

Miscellaneous Articles of Base Metal

Note

In this Chapter a reference to parts of articles is in no case to be taken as applying to cables, chains, nails, bolts, nuts, screws, springs or other articles of iron or steel of a kind described in heading No. 73.25, 73.29, 73.31, 73.32 or 73.35, nor to similar articles of other base metals (Chapters 74 to 81 inclusive).

Tariff Heading	*Rate of Import Duty (if any)*	
	Full	*Commonwealth (C) E.F.T.A. (E)*
83.01 Locks and padlocks (key, combination or electrically operated), and parts thereof, of base metal; frames incorporating locks, for handbags, trunks or the like, and parts of such frames, of base metal; keys for any of the foregoing articles of base metal	9%	—
83.02 Base metal fittings and mountings of a kind suitable for furniture, doors, staircases, windows, blinds, coachwork, saddlery, trunks, caskets and the like (including automatic door closers); base metal hat-racks, hat-pegs, brackets and the like	9%	—
83.03 Safes, strong-boxes, armoured or reinforced strong-rooms, strong-room linings and strong-room doors, and cash and deed boxes and the like, of base metal	7·5%	—
83.04 Filing cabinets, racks, sorting boxes, paper trays, paper rests and similar office equipment, of base metal, other than office furniture falling within heading No. 94.03	7·5%	—
83.05 Fittings for loose-leaf binders, for files or for stationery books, of base metal; letter clips, paper clips, staples, indexing tags, and similar stationery goods, of base metal	10%	—
83.06 Statuettes and other ornaments of a kind used indoors, of base metal	10%	—
83.07 Lamps and lighting fittings, of base metal, and parts thereof, of base metal (excluding switches, electric lamp holders, electric lamps for vehicles, electric battery or magneto lamps, and other articles falling within Chapter 85 except heading No. 85.22)	8%	—
83.08 Flexible tubing and piping, of base metal ...	10%	—

Tariff Heading	Rate of Import Duty (if any)	
	Full	Commonwealth (C) E.F.T.A. (E)
83.09 Clasps, frames with clasps for handbags and the like, buckles, buckle-clasps, hooks, eyes, eyelets, and the like, of base metal, of a kind commonly used for clothing, travel goods, handbags, or other textile or leather goods; tubular rivets and bifurcated rivets, of base metal:		
(A) Bifurcated rivets of iron or steel ...	12·5%	—
(B) Other	8%	—
83.10 Beads and spangles, of base metal ...	7·5%	—
83.11 Bells and gongs, non-electric, of base metal, and parts thereof of base metal	15%	—
83.12 Photograph, picture and similar frames, of base metal; mirrors of base metal	10%	—
83.13 Stoppers, crown corks, bottle caps, capsules, bung covers, seals and plombs, case corner protectors and other packing accessories, of base metal	8%	—
83.14 Sign-plates, name-plates, numbers, letters and other signs, of base metal	10%	—
83.15 Wire, rods, tubes, plates, electrodes and similar products of base metal or of metal carbides, coated or cored with flux material, of a kind used for soldering, brazing, welding or deposition of metal or of metal carbides; wire and rods, of agglomerated base metal powder, used for metal spraying	8%	—

SECTION XVI

Machinery and Mechanical Appliances ; Electrical Equipment ; Parts Thereof

Notes

1. This Section does not cover:

(*a*) Transmission, conveyor or elevator belts or belting, of artificial plastic material of Chapter 39, or of vulcanised rubber (heading No. 40.10); or other articles of a kind used on machinery, mechanical or electrical appliances, of unhardened vulcanised rubber (for example, washers) (heading No. 40.14);

(*b*) Articles of leather or of composition leather (heading No. 42.04) or of furskin (heading No. 43.03), of a kind used in machinery or mechanical appliances or for industrial purposes;

(*c*) Bobbins, spools, cops, cones, cores, reels and similar supports, of any material (for example, Chapter 39, 40, 44 or 48 or Section XV);

(*d*) Perforated cards of paper or paperboard for Jacquard or similar machines, falling within heading No. 48.21;

(*e*) Transmission, conveyor or elevator belts of textile material (heading No. 59.16) or other articles of textile material of a kind commonly used in machinery or plant (heading No. 59.17);

(*f*) Precious or semi-precious stones (natural, synthetic or reconstituted) of heading No. 71.02 or 71.03, or articles wholly of such stones of heading No. 71.15;

(*g*) Parts of general use, as defined in Note 2 to Section XV, of base metal (Section XV), or similar goods of artificial plastic materials (which are generally classified in heading No. 39.07);

(*h*) Endless belts of metal wire or strip (Section XV);

(*ij*) Articles falling within Chapter 83;

(*k*) Vehicles, aircraft, ships or boats, and parts thereof, of Section XVII;

(*l*) Articles falling within Chapter 90;

(*m*) Clocks, watches and other articles falling within Chapter 91;

(*n*) Brushes of a kind used as parts of machines, falling within heading No. 96.02; interchangeable tools falling within heading No. 82.05; similar interchangeable tools, which are to be classified according to the constituent material of their working part (for example, in Chapter 40, 42, 43, 45 or 59, or heading No. 68.04 or 69.09); or

(*o*) Articles falling within Chapter 97.

2. Subject to Note 1 to this Section, Note 1 to Chapter 84 and to Note 1 to Chapter 5, parts of machines (not being parts of the articles described in headings Nos. 84.64, 85.23, 5.24, 85.25 and 85.27) are to be classified according to the following rules:

(*a*) Goods of a kind described in any of the headings of Chapters 84 and 85 (other than headings Nos. 84.65 and 85.28) are in all cases to be classified in their respective headings.

(*b*) Other parts, if suitable for use solely or principally with a particular kind of machine, or with a number of machines falling within the same heading (including a machine falling within heading No. 84.59 or 85.22) are to be classified with the machines of that kind. However, goods which are equally suitable for use principally with the goods of headings Nos. 85.13 and 85.15 are to be classified in heading No. 85.13.

(*c*) All other parts are to be classified in heading No. 84.65 or 85.28.

3. Unless the headings otherwise require, composite machines consisting of two or more ıachines fitted together to form a whole and other machines adapted for the purpose of erforming two or more complementary or alternative functions are to be classified as if onsisting only of that component or as being that machine which performs the principal ınction.

4. Motors and transmission, conveyor or elevator belts, for machinery or appliances to hich they are fitted, or, if packed separately for convenience of transport, which are clearly ıtended to be fitted to or mounted on a common base with the machine or appliance with hich they are imported, are to be classified under the same heading as such machinery r appliances.

5. For the purposes of these Notes, the expression "machine" means any machine, pparatus or appliance of a kind falling within Section XVI.

Chapter 84

Boilers, Machinery and Mechanical Appliances; Parts thereof

Notes

1. This Chapter does not cover:

(*a*) Millstones, grindstones and other articles falling within Chapter 68;

(*b*) Appliances and machinery (for example, pumps) and parts thereof, of ceramic material (Chapter 69);

(*c*) Laboratory glassware of heading No. 70.17; machinery and appliances and parts thereof, of glass (heading No. 70.20 or 70.21);

(*d*) Articles falling within heading No. 73.36 or 73.37 and similar articles of other base metals (Chapters 74 to 81);

(*e*) Tools for working in the hand of heading No. 85.05 or electro-mechanical domestic appliances of heading No. 85.06; or

(*f*) Articles falling within Chapter 82, not being articles falling within heading No. 84.21, 84.22, 84.49 or 84.50.

2. Subject to the operation of Notes 3 and 4 to Section XVI, a machine or appliance which answers to a description in one or more of the headings Nos. 84.01 to 84.21 and at the same time to a description in one or other of the headings Nos. 84.22 to 84.60, is to be classified under the appropriate heading of the former group and not the latter.

Heading No. 84.17 is, however, to be taken not to apply to:

(*a*) Germination plant, incubators and brooders (heading No. 84.28);

(*b*) Grain dampening machines (heading No. 84.29);

(*c*) Diffusing apparatus for sugar juice extraction (heading No. 84.30);

(*d*) Machinery for the heat-treatment of textile yarns, fabrics or made up textile articles (heading No. 84.40); or

(*e*) Machinery or plant, designed for a mechanical operation, in which a change of temperature, even if necessary, is subsidiary.

Heading No. 84.19 is to be taken not to apply to:

(*a*) Sewing machines for closing bags or similar containers (heading No. 84.41); or

(*b*) Office machinery of heading No. 84.54.

3.(A) For the purposes of heading No. 84.53, the expression " automatic data processing machines " means:

(*a*) Digital machines having storages capable of storing not only the processing program or programs and the data to be processed but also a program for translating the formal programming language in which the programs are written into machine language. These machines must have a main storage which is directly accessible for the execution of a program and which has a capacity at least sufficient to store those parts of the processing and translating programs and the data immediately necessary for the current processing run. They must also be able themselves, on the basis of the instructions contained in the initial program, to modify, by logical decision, its execution during the processing run;

(*b*) Analogue machines capable of simulating mathematical models and comprising at least: analogue elements, control elements and programming elements;

(*c*) Hybrid machines consisting of either a digital machine with analogue elements or an analogue machine with digital elements.

(B) Automatic data processing machines may be in the form of systems consisting of a variable number of separately-housed units. A unit is to be regarded as being a part of the complete system if it meets all the following conditions:

(*a*) it is connectable to the central processing unit either directly or through one or more other units;

(*b*) it is specifically designed as part of such a system (it must, in particular, unless it is a power supply unit, be able to accept or deliver data in a form (code or signals) which can be used by the system).

Such units imported separately are also to be classified in heading No. 84.53.

4. Heading No. 84.62 is to be taken to apply, *inter alia*, to polished steel balls, the maximum nd minimum diameters of which do not differ from the nominal diameter by more than per cent. or by more than 0·05 millimetre, whichever is less. Other steel balls are to be lassified under heading No. 73.40.

5. A machine which is used for more than one purpose is, for the purposes of classification, o be treated as if its principal purpose were its sole purpose.

Subject to Note 2 to this Chapter and Note 3 to Section XVI, a machine whose principal urpose is not described in any heading or for which no one purpose is the principal purpose , unless the context otherwise requires, to be classified in heading No. 84.59. Heading No. 84.59 is also to be taken to cover machines for making rope or cable (for example, tranding, twisting or cabling machines) from metal wire, textile yarn or any other material r from a combination of such materials.

6. Heading No. 84.16 is to be taken to apply, *inter alia*, to machines for rolling into sheet orm material fed to the rollers in a plastic condition.

Tariff Heading	*Rate of Import Duty (if any)*	
	Full	*Commonwealth (C) E.F.T.A. (E)*
4.01 Steam and other vapour generating boilers (excluding central heating hot water boilers capable also of producing low pressure steam); super-heated water boilers	7·5%	—
4.02 Auxiliary plant for use with boilers of heading No. 84.01 (for example, economisers, superheaters, soot removers, gas recoverers and the like); condensers for vapour engines and power units	9%	—
4.03 Producer gas and water gas generators, with or without purifiers; acetylene gas generators (water process) and similar gas generators, with or without purifiers	10%	—
4.04 Steam engines (including mobile engines, but not steam tractors falling within heading No. 87.01 or mechanically propelled road rollers) with self-contained boilers	9%	—
4.05 Steam and other vapour power units, not incorporating boilers	9%	—
4.06 Internal combustion piston engines:		
(A) Motor vehicle engines, other than track-laying tractor engines, and parts suitable for use therein (but not including piston rings of a diameter of 127 millimetres or over when compressed)	14%	C 9% E —
(B) Other engines and parts	7·5%	—
4.07 Hydraulic engines and motors (including water wheels and water turbines)	7·5%	—

Tariff Heading	Rate of Import Duty (if any)	
	Full	Commonwealth (C) E.F.T.A. (E)
84.08 Other engines and motors:		
(A) Motor vehicle engines	12%	C 8% E —
(B) Musical instrument (including gramophone) motors	10%	—
(C) Camera and cinematograph motors...	20%	—
(D) Other	7·5%	—
84.09 Mechanically propelled road rollers ...	7·5%	—
84.10 Pumps (including motor pumps and turbo pumps) for liquids, whether or not fitted with measuring devices; liquid elevators of bucket, chain, screw, band and similar kinds	7·5%	—
84.11 Air pumps, vacuum pumps and air or gas compressors (including motor and turbo pumps and compressors, and free-piston generators for gas turbines); fans, blowers and the like:		
(A) Parts and accessories of motor vehicles, other than vacuum pumps and air or gas compressors	12%	C 8% E —
(B) Other	7·5%	—
84.12 Air conditioning machines, self-contained, comprising a motor-driven fan and elements for changing the temperature and humidity of air	7·5%	—
84.13 Furnace burners for liquid fuel (atomisers), for pulverised solid fuel or for gas; mechanical stokers, mechanical grates, mechanical ash dischargers and similar appliances	9%	—
84.14 Industrial and laboratory furnaces and ovens, non-electric	7·5%	—
84.15 Refrigerators and refrigerating equipment (electrical and other)	7·5%	—
84.16 Calendering and similar rolling machines (other than metal-working and metal-rolling machines and glass-working machines) and cylinders therefor	7·5%	—
84.17 Machinery, plant and similar laboratory equipment, whether or not electrically heated, for the treatment of materials by a process involving a change of temperature such as heating, cooking, roasting, distilling, rectifying, sterilising, pasteurising, steaming, drying, evaporating, vapourising, condensing or cooling, not being machinery or plant of a kind used for domestic purposes; instantaneous or storage water heaters, non-electrical	7·5%	—

Tariff Heading	Rate of Import Duty (if any)	
	Full	*Commonwealth (C) E.F.T.A. (E)*
84.18 Centrifuges; filtering and purifying machinery and apparatus (other than filter funnels, milk strainers and the like), for liquids or gases:		
(A) Centrifuges:		
(1) Dryers of the types used in dry cleaning and laundering	7·5%	—
(2) Cream separators	7·5%	—
(3) Other	9%	—
(B) Filtering and purifying machinery and apparatus:		
(1) Parts of motor vehicles	12%	C 8% E —
(2) Other	9%	—
84.19 Machinery for cleaning or drying bottles or other containers; machinery for filling, closing, sealing, capsuling or labelling bottles, cans, boxes, bags or other containers; other packing or wrapping machinery; machinery for aerating beverages; dish washing machines	7·5%	—
84.20 Weighing machinery (excluding balances of a sensitivity of 5 centigrammes or better), including weight-operated counting and checking machines; weighing machine weights of all kinds:		
(A) Weights of a kind used with the balances of heading No. 90.15	17%	—
(B) Other	9%	—
84.21 Mechanical appliances (whether or not hand operated) for projecting, dispersing or spraying liquids or powders; fire extinguishers (charged or not); spray guns and similar appliances; steam or sand blasting machines and similar jet projecting machines	7·5%	—
84.22 Lifting, handling, loading or unloading machinery, telphers and conveyors (for example, lifts, hoists, winches, cranes, transporter cranes, jacks, pulley tackle, belt conveyors and teleferics), not being machinery falling within heading No. 84.23:		
(A) Rolling mill (metal-working) machinery, the following: Working and transporter roller racks and tables; ingot, slab, bar and plate tilters and manipulators	12·5%	—
(B) Other	7·5%	—

Tariff Heading	Rate of Import Duty (if any)	
	Full	Commonwealth (C) E.F.T.A. (E)
84.23 Excavating, levelling, tamping, boring and extracting machinery, stationary or mobile, for earth, minerals or ores (for example, mechanical shovels, coal-cutters, excavators, scrapers, levellers and bulldozers); pile-drivers; snow-ploughs, not self-propelled (including snow-plough attachments)	7·5%	—
84.24 Agricultural and horticultural machinery for soil preparation or cultivation (for example, ploughs, harrows, cultivators, seed and fertiliser distributors); lawn and sports ground rollers	6%	—
84.25 Harvesting and threshing machinery; straw and fodder presses; hay or grass mowers; winnowing and similar cleaning machines for seed, grain or leguminous vegetables and egg-grading and other grading machines for agricultural produce (other than those of a kind used in the bread grain milling industry falling within heading No. 84.29):		
(A) Root topping machines, root lifters and root harvesters	6%	—
(B) Other:		
(1) Agricultural and commercial horticultural machines, other than hay or grass mowers	12%	—
(2) Other	7·5%	—
84.26 Dairy machinery (including milking machines)	7·5%	—
84.27 Presses, crushers and other machinery, of a kind used in wine-making, cider-making, fruit juice preparation or the like	9%	—
84.28 Other agricultural, horticultural, poultry-keeping and bee-keeping machinery; germination plant fitted with mechanical or thermal equipment; poultry incubators and brooders	7·5%	—
84.29 Machinery of a kind used in the bread grain milling industry, and other machinery (other than farm type machinery) for the working of cereals or dried leguminous vegetables	9%	—
84.30 Machinery, not falling within any other heading of this Chapter, of a kind used in the following food or drink industries: bakery, confectionery, chocolate manufacture, macaroni, ravioli or similar cereal food manufacture, the preparation of meat, fish, fruit or vegetables (including mincing or slicing machines), sugar manufacture or brewing	7·5%	—

Tariff Heading	Rate of Import Duty (if any)	
	Full	Commonwealth (C) E.F.T.A. (E)
84.31 Machinery for making or finishing cellulosic pulp, paper or paperboard	7·5%	—
84.32 Book-binding machinery, including book-sewing machines	7·5%	—
84.33 Paper or paperboard cutting machines of all kinds; other machinery for making up paper pulp, paper or paperboard	7·5%	—
84.34 Machinery, apparatus and accessories for type-founding or type-setting; machinery, other than the machine-tools of heading No. 84.45, 84.46 or 84.47, for preparing or working printing blocks, plates or cylinders; printing type, impressed flongs and matrices, printing blocks, plates and cylinders; blocks, plates, cylinders and lithographic stones, prepared for printing purposes (for example, planed, grained or polished):		
(A) Impressed flongs and matrices for the production of complete printed pages, each page, without margins, being not less than 500 millimetres long and not less than 380 millimetres wide	—	—
(B) Other	7·5%	—
84.35 Other printing machinery; machines for uses ancillary to printing	7·5%	—
84.36 Machines for extruding man-made textiles; machines of a kind used for processing natural or man-made textile fibres; textile spinning and twisting machines; textile doubling, throwing and reeling (including weft-winding) machines	7·5%	—
84.37 Weaving machines, knitting machines and machines for making gimped yarn, tulle, lace, embroidery, trimmings, braid or net; machines for preparing yarns for use on such machines, including warping and warp sizing machines	7·5%	—
84.38 Auxiliary machinery for use with machines of heading No. 84.37 (for example, dobbies, Jacquards, automatic stop motions and shuttle changing mechanisms); parts and accessories suitable for use solely or principally with the machines of the present heading or with machines falling within heading No. 84.36 or 84.37 (for example, spindles and spindle flyers, card clothing, combs, extruding nipples, shuttles, healds and heald-lifters and hosiery needles):		

Tariff Heading	*Rate of Import Duty (if any)*	
	Full	*Commonwealth (C)* *E.F.T.A. (E)*
84.38 Auxiliary machinery for use with, etc. —*contd.*		
(A) Inset mails of a kind used in the manufacture of wire healds for textile looms	—	—
(B) Bearded needles, and narrowing points, running-on points and welthooks, adapted for use in conjunction therewith	20%	—
(C) Hosiery latch needles	17%	—
(D) Other	7·5%	—
84.39 Machinery for the manufacture or finishing of felt in the piece or in shapes, including felt-hat making machines and hat-making blocks	9%	—
84.40 Machinery for washing, cleaning, drying, bleaching, dyeing, dressing, finishing or coating textile yarns, fabrics or made-up textile articles (including laundry and dry-cleaning machinery); fabric folding, reeling or cutting machines; machines of a kind used in the manufacture of linoleum or other floor coverings for applying the paste to the base fabric or other support; machines of a type used for printing a repetitive design, repetitive words or overall colour on textiles, leather, wallpaper, wrapping paper, linoleum or other materials, and engraved or etched plates, blocks or rollers therefor	7·5%	—
84.41 Sewing machines; furniture specially designed for sewing machines; sewing machine needles	12·5%	—
84.42 Machinery (other than sewing machines) for preparing, tanning or working hides, skins or leather (including boot and shoe machinery)	7·5%	—
84.43 Converters, ladles, ingot moulds and casting machines, of a kind used in metallurgy and in metal foundries	7·5%	—
84.44 Rolling mills and rolls therefor	10%	—
84.45 Machine-tools for working metal or metal carbides, not being machines falling within heading No. 84.49 or 84.50:		
(A) Flying shears of a kind used in rolling mills	12·5%	—
(B) Other	9%	—

Tariff Heading	Rate of Import Duty (if any)	
	Full	Commonwealth (C) E.F.T.A. (E)
84.46 Machine-tools for working stone, ceramics, concrete, asbestos-cement and like mineral materials or for working glass in the cold, other than machines falling within heading No. 84.49	9%	—
84.47 Machine-tools for working wood, cork, bone, ebonite (vulcanite), hard artificial plastic materials or other hard carving materials, other than machines falling within heading No. 84.49	12%	—
84.48 Accessories and parts suitable for use solely or principally with the machines falling within headings Nos. 84.45 to 84.47, including work and tool holders, self-opening dieheads, dividing heads and other appliances for machine-tools; tool holders for any type of tool or machine-tool for working in the hand:		
(A) Parts of flying shears of a kind used in rolling mills	12·5%	—
(B) Other	9%	—
84.49 Tools for working in the hand, pneumatic or with self-contained non-electric motor	7·5%	—
84.50 Gas-operated welding, brazing, cutting and surface tempering appliances	7·5%	—
84.51 Typewriters, other than typewriters incorporating calculating mechanisms; cheque-writing machines	7·5%	—
84.52 Calculating machines; accounting machines, cash registers, postage-franking machines, ticket-issuing machines and similar machines, incorporating a calculating device:		
(A) Cash registers	5%	—
(B) Other	7·5%	—
84.53 Automatic data processing machines and units thereof; articles of the following descriptions, unless specified or included in the first part of this heading or elsewhere, namely, magnetic and optical readers, machines for transcribing data onto data media in coded form and machines for processing such data:		
(A) Automatic data processing machines and units thereof:		
(1) Automatic data processing machines (including systems)	14%	—
(2) Units of automatic data processing machines:		
(*a*) Card punches and card readers	7·5%	—
(*b*) Power supply units	10%	—
(*c*) Other units	14%	—
(B) Other	7·5%	—

Tariff Heading	Rate of Import Duty (if any)	
	Full	Commonwealth (C) E.F.T.A. (E)
84.54 Other office machines (for example, hectograph or stencil duplicating machines, addressing machines, coin-sorting machines, coin-counting and wrapping machines, pencil-sharpening machines, perforating and stapling machines):		
(A) Cash registers	5%	—
(B) Other	7·5%	—
84.55 Parts and accessories (other than covers, carrying cases and the like) suitable for use solely or principally with machines of a kind falling within heading No. 84.51, 84.52, 84.53 or 84.54:		
(A) Parts of the following machines (not being electronic machines or machines operated in conjunction with punched cards): Typewriters (including electric typewriters) Machines of the types used for the automatic production of typewritten correspondence Accounting machines Calculating machines Adding machines Listing machines Book-keeping machines Billing machines Posting machines Cheque-writing machines	£0·0850 per lb. or 7·5%, whichever is the less	—
(B) Parts of cash registers	5%	—
(C) Parts of automatic data processing machines and units thereof:		
(1) Of goods of subheading 84.53(A)(2)(*a*)	7·5%	—
(2) Of goods of subheading 84.53(A)(2)(*b*)	10%	—
(3) Other	14%	—
(D) Other	7·5%	—
84.56 Machinery for sorting, screening, separating, washing, crushing, grinding or mixing earth, stone, ores or other mineral substances, in solid (including powder and paste) form; machinery for agglomerating, moulding or shaping solid mineral fuels, ceramic paste, unhardened cements, plastering materials or other mineral products in powder or paste form; machines for forming foundry moulds of sand	7·5%	—

Tariff Heading	Rate of Import Duty (if any)	
	Full	Commonwealth (C) E.F.T.A. (E)
84.57 Glass-working machines (other than machines for working glass in the cold); machines for assembling electric filament and discharge lamps and electronic and similar tubes and valves	7·5%	—
84.58 Automatic vending machines (for example, stamp, cigarette, chocolate and food machines), not being games of skill or chance	7·5%	—
84.59 Machines and mechanical appliances, having individual functions, not falling within any other heading of this Chapter:		
(A) Strip coilers of a kind used in rolling mills	12·5%	—
(B) Other	7·5%	—
84.60 Moulding boxes for metal foundry; moulds of a type used for metal (other than ingot moulds), for metal carbides, for glass, for mineral materials (for example, ceramic pastes, concrete or cement) or for rubber or artificial plastic materials	7·5%	—
84.61 Taps, cocks, valves and similar appliances, for pipes, boiler shells, tanks, vats and the like, including pressure reducing valves and thermostatically controlled valves	8%	—
84.62 Ball, roller or needle roller bearings ...	9%	—
84.63 Transmission shafts, cranks, bearing housings, plain shaft bearings, gears and gearing (including friction gears and gear-boxes and other variable speed gears), flywheels, pulleys and pulley blocks, clutches and shaft couplings	7·5%	—
84.64 Gaskets and similar joints of metal sheeting combined with other material (for example, asbestos, felt and paperboard) or of laminated metal foil; sets or assortments of gaskets and similar joints, dissimilar in composition, for engines, pipes, tubes and the like, put up in pouches, envelopes or similar packings	7·5%	—
84.65 Machinery parts, not containing electrical connectors, insulators, coils, contacts or other electrical features and not falling within any other heading in this Chapter	7·5%	—

Chapter 85

Electrical Machinery and Equipment; Parts thereof

Notes

1. This Chapter does not cover:

(*a*) Electrically warmed blankets, bed pads, foot-muffs and the like; electrically warmed clothing, footwear and ear pads and other electrically warmed articles worn on or about the person;

(*b*) Articles of glass of heading No. 70.11;

(*c*) Electrically heated furniture of Chapter 94.

2. Heading No. 85.01 is to be taken not to apply to goods described in heading No. 85.08, 85.09 or 85.21, other than metal tank mercury arc rectifiers which remain classified in heading No. 85.01.

3. Heading No. 85.06 is to be taken to apply only to the following electro-mechanical machines of types commonly used for domestic purposes:

(*a*) Vacuum cleaners, floor polishers, food grinders and mixers, fruit juice extractors and fans, of any weight;

(*b*) Other machines provided the weight of such other machines does not exceed 20 kilogrammes.

The heading does not, however, apply to dish washing machines (heading No. 84.19), centrifugal and other clothes washing machines (heading No. 84.18 or 84.40), roller and other ironing machines (heading No. 84.16 or 84.40), sewing machines (heading No. 84.41) or to electro-thermic appliances (heading No. 85.12).

4. For the purposes of heading No. 85.19, " printed circuits " are to be taken to be circuits obtained by forming on an insulating base, by any printing process (for example embossing, plating-up, etching) or by the " film circuit " technique, conductor elements, contacts or other printed components (for example, inductances, resistors, capacitors) alone or interconnected according to a pre-established pattern, other than elements which can produce, rectify, modulate or amplify an electrical signal (for example, semi-conductor elements).

The term " printed circuits " does not cover circuits combined with elements other than those obtained during the printing process. Printed circuits may, however, be fitted with non-printed connecting elements.

Thin- or thick-film circuits comprising passive and active elements obtained during the same technological process are to be classified in heading No. 85.21.

5. For the purposes of heading No. 85.21:

(A) " Diodes, transistors and similar semi-conductor devices " are to be taken to be those devices the operation of which depends on variations in resistivity on the application of an electric field;

(B) " Electronic micro-circuits " are to be taken to be:

(*a*) Microassemblies of the " fagot " module, moulded module, micromodule and similar types, consisting of discrete, active or both active and passive miniaturised components which are combined and interconnected;

(*b*) Monolithic integrated circuits in which the circuit elements (diodes, transistors, resistors, capacitors, interconnections, etc.) are created in the mass (essentially) and on the surface of a semi-conductor material (doped silicon, for example) and are inseparably associated;

(*c*) Hybrid integrated circuits in which passive and active elements, some obtained by thin- or thick-film technology (resistors, capacitors, interconnections, etc.), others by semi-conductor technology (diodes, transistors, monolithic integrated circuits, etc.), are combined, to all intents and purposes indivisibly, on a single insulating substrate (glass, ceramic, etc.). These circuits may also include miniaturised discrete components.

For the classification of the articles defined in this Note, heading No. 85.21 shall take precedence over any other heading in the Nomenclature which might cover them by reference to, in particular, their function.

Tariff Heading	Rate of Import Duty (if any)	
	Full	Commonwealth (C) E.F.T.A. (E)
5.01 Electrical goods of the following descriptions: generators, motors, converters (rotary or static), transformers, rectifiers and rectifying apparatus, inductors:		
(A) Motor and generator casings and unwound rotors and stators	5%	—
(B) Transformers rated at not less than 1 KVA on continuous load	7·5%	—
(C) Metal tank mercury arc rectifiers ...	7·5%	—
(D) Inductors, calibrated	12·5%	—
(E) Other	10%	—
5.02 Electro-magnets; permanent magnets and articles of special materials for permanent magnets, being blanks of such magnets; electro-magnetic and permanent magnet chucks, clamps, vices and similar work holders; electro-magnetic clutches and couplings; electro-magnetic brakes; electro-magnetic lifting heads:		
(A) Chucks and vices	7·5%	—
(B) Other	10%	—
.03 Primary cells and primary batteries ...	12·5%	—
.04 Electric accumulators	7·5%	—
.05 Tools for working in the hand, with self-contained electric motor	7·5%	—
.06 Electro-mechanical domestic appliances, with self-contained electric motor	7·5%	—
.07 Shavers and hair clippers, with self-contained electric motor:		
(A) Shavers and hair clippers	7·5%	—
(B) Parts of shavers and hair clippers ...	10%	—
.08 Electrical starting and ignition equipment for internal combustion engines (including ignition magnetos, magneto-dynamos, ignition coils, starter motors, sparking plugs and glow plugs); generators (dynamos and alternators) and cut-outs for use in conjunction with such engines:		
(A) Parts of motor vehicles other than ignition magnetos	12%	C 8% E —
(B) Other	10%	—

Tariff Heading	Rate of Import Duty (if any)	
	Full	Commonwealth (C) E.F.T.A. (E)
85.09 Electrical lighting and signalling equipment and electrical windscreen wipers, defrosters and demisters, for cycles or motor vehicles:		
(A) Equipment for cycles (other than motor cycles)	14%	—
(B) Other	12%	C 8% E —
85.10 Portable electric battery and magneto lamps, other than lamps falling within heading No. 85.09	10%	—
85.11 Industrial and laboratory electric furnaces, ovens and induction and dielectric heating equipment; electric welding, brazing and soldering machines and apparatus and similar electric machines and apparatus for cutting:		
(A) Welding machines or apparatus (other than tube-making machines or apparatus)	7·5%	—
(B) Heating and cooking apparatus ...	7·5%	—
(C) Other machines and apparatus ...	10%	—
(D) Parts of the goods of subheadings (A), (B) and (C) above	10%	—
85.12 Electric instantaneous or storage water heaters and immersion heaters; electric soil heating apparatus and electric space heating apparatus; electric hair dressing appliances (for example, hairdryers, hair curlers, curling tong heaters) and electric smoothing irons; electro-thermic domestic appliances; electric heating resistors, other than those of carbon:		
(A) Heating and cooking apparatus ...	7·5%	—
(B) Other apparatus and appliances ...	10%	—
(C) Parts of the goods of subheadings (A) and (B) above	10%	—
85.13 Electrical line telephonic and telegraphic apparatus (including such apparatus for carrier-current line systems)	7·5%	—
85.14 Microphones and stands therefor; loudspeakers; audio-frequency electric amplifiers:		
(A) Microphones and stands therefor; loudspeakers and amplifiers, not being sound amplification apparatus of a kind used for the reproduction of music	10%	—
(B) Other loudspeakers and amplifiers ...	10%	C 7% E —
(C) Parts of the goods of subheadings (A) and (B) above	10%	—

Tariff Heading	Rate of Import Duty (if any)	
	Full	Commonwealth (C) E.F.T.A. (E)
85.15 Radiotelegraphic and radiotelephonic transmission and reception apparatus; radio-broadcasting and television transmission and reception apparatus (including receivers incorporating sound recorders or reproducers) and television cameras; radio navigational aid apparatus, radar apparatus and radio remote control apparatus:		
(A) Transmitting sets, receiving sets and combined transmitting and receiving sets, designed or adapted for fitting to motor vehicles	15%	C 10% E —
(B) Parts of the sets of subheading (A) above	15%	—
(C) Radiogramophones; combined recorders and reproducers for magnetic sound recording on tape or wire, incorporated with radio receivers of the domestic type or with radio-gramophones	15%	C 10% E —
(D) Other	15%	—
85.16 Electric traffic control equipment for railways, roads or inland waterways and equipment used for similar purposes in port installations or upon airfields	10%	—
85.17 Electric sound or visual signalling apparatus (such as bells, sirens, indicator panels, burglar and fire alarms), other than those of heading No. 85.09 or 85.16	10%	—
85.18 Electrical capacitors, fixed or variable ...	12·5%	—
85.19 Electrical apparatus for making and breaking electrical circuits, for the protection of electrical circuits, or for making connections to or in electrical circuits (for example, switches, relays, fuses, lightning arresters, surge suppressors, plugs, lamp-holders and junction boxes); resistors, fixed or variable (including potentiometers), other than heating resistors; printed circuits; switchboards (other than telephone switchboards) and control panels:		
(A) Parts of motor vehicles	12%	C 8% E —
(B) Resistors, standard and laboratory ...	17%	—
(C) Printed circuits	12·5%	—
(D) Other	8%	—

Tariff Heading	Rate of Import Duty (if any)	
	Full	Commonwealth (C) E.F.T.A. (E)
85.20 Electric filament lamps and electric discharge lamps (including infra-red and ultra-violet lamps); arc-lamps; electrically ignited photographic flashbulbs:		
(A) Discharge lamps	12·5%	—
(B) Arc-lamps for cinematograph projectors	12·5%	—
(C) Other	8%	—
85.21 Thermionic, cold cathode and photo-cathode valves and tubes (including vapour or gas filled valves and tubes, cathode-ray tubes, television camera tubes and mercury arc rectifying valves and tubes); photocells; mounted piezo-electric crystals; diodes, transistors and similar semi-conductor devices; electronic microcircuits:		
(A) Mercury arc rectifiers, being rectifiers with mercury pool cathodes	8%	—
(B) Thermionic, cold cathode and photo-cathode valves and tubes other than those described in subheading (A) above	12·5%	—
(C) Mounted piezo-electric crystals of quartz	5%	—
(D) Microcircuit audio amplifiers:		
(1) Amplifiers not being sound amplification apparatus of a kind used for the reproduction of music	10%	—
(2) Other	10%	C 7% E —
(E) Other	20%	—
85.22 Electrical appliances and apparatus, having individual functions, not falling within any other heading of this Chapter:		
(A) Standard signal generators, radio type; oscillators, laboratory and standard	17%	—
(B) Other	12·5%	—
85.23 Insulated (including enamelled or anodised) electric wire, cable, bars, strip and the like (including co-axial cable), whether or not fitted with connectors:		
(A) Cable core, whether bound with brass tape or not, produced by stripping used submarine cables	—	—
(B) Other	8%	—

Tariff Heading	*Rate of Import Duty (if any)* Full	Commonwealth (C) E.F.T.A. (E)
85.24 Carbon brushes, arc-lamp carbons, battery carbons, carbon electrodes and other carbon articles of a kind used for electrical purposes:		
(A) Arc-lamp carbons and parts thereof:		
(1) Arc-lamp carbons which are externally covered with copper and do not exceed 14 millimetres in diameter and parts thereof	£0·4078 per kilogramme	—
(2) Other	£0·1322 per kilogramme	—
(B) Amorphous carbon electrodes, but not including primary battery carbons or arc-lamp carbons	12·5%	—
(C) Carbon brushes fitted with metal terminals or metal connectors	6%	—
(D) Other	8%	—
85.25 Insulators of any material	10%	—
85.26 Insulating fittings for electrical machines, appliances or equipment, being fittings wholly of insulating material apart from any minor components of metal incorporated during moulding solely for purposes of assembly, but not including insulators falling within heading No. 85.25:		
(A) Parts of motor vehicles	12%	C 8% E —
(B) Other	10%	—
85.27 Electrical conduit tubing and joints therefor, of base metal lined with insulating material	8%	—
85.28 Electrical parts of machinery and apparatus, not being goods falling within any of the preceding headings of this Chapter	10%	—

SECTION XVII

VEHICLES, AIRCRAFT, AND PARTS THEREOF; VESSELS AND CERTAIN ASSOCIATED TRANSPORT EQUIPMENT

Notes

1. This Section does not cover articles falling within heading No. 97.01, 97.03 or 97.08, or bobsleighs, toboggans and the like falling within heading No. 97.06.

2. Throughout this Section the expressions " parts " and " parts and accessories " are to be taken not to apply to the following articles, whether or not they are identifiable as for the goods of this Section:

(*a*) Joints, washers and the like (classified according to their constituent material or in heading No. 84.64);

(*b*) Parts of general use, as defined in Note 2 to Section XV, of base metal (Section XV), or similar goods of artificial plastic materials (which are generally classified in heading No. 39.07);

(*c*) Articles falling within Chapter 82 (tools);

(*d*) Articles falling within heading No. 83.11;

(*e*) Machines and mechanical appliances and other articles falling within headings Nos. 84.01 to 84.59, 84.61 or 84.62 and parts of engines and motors falling within heading No. 84.63;

(*f*) Electrical machinery and equipment (Chapter 85);

(*g*) Articles falling within Chapter 90;

(*h*) Clocks (Chapter 91);

(*ij*) Arms (Chapter 93);

(*k*) Brushes of a kind used as parts of vehicles (heading No. 96.02).

3. References in Chapters 86 to 88 to parts or accessories are to be taken not to apply to parts or accessories which are not suitable for use solely or principally with the articles of those Chapters. A part or accessory which answers to a description in two or more of the headings of those Chapters is to be classified under that heading which corresponds to the principal use of that part or accessory.

4. Flying machines specially constructed so that they can also be used as road vehicles are classified as flying machines. Amphibious motor vehicles are classified as motor vehicles.

5. Air-cushion vehicles are to be classified within this Section with the vehicles to which they are most akin as follows:

(*a*) In Chapter 86 if designed to travel on a guide-track (hovertrains);

(*b*) In Chapter 87 if designed to travel over land or over both land and water;

(*c*) In Chapter 89 if designed to travel over water, whether or not able to land on beaches or landing-stages or also able to travel over ice.

Parts and accessories of air-cushion vehicles are to be classified in the same way as those of vehicles falling within the heading in which the air-cushion vehicles are classified under the above provisions.

Hovertrain track fixtures and fittings are to be classified as railway track fixtures and fittings, and traffic control equipment for hovertrain transport systems as traffic control equipment for railways.

Chapter 86

Railway and Tramway Locomotives, Rolling-stock and Parts Thereof; Railway and Tramway Track Fixtures and Fittings; Traffic Signalling Equipment of All Kinds (Not Electrically Powered)

Notes

1. This Chapter does not cover:

(*a*) Railway or tramway sleepers of wood or of concrete, or concrete guide-track sections for hovertrains (heading No. 44.07 or 68.11);

(*b*) Railway or tramway track construction material of iron or steel falling within heading No. 73.16; or

(*c*) Electrically powered signalling apparatus falling within heading No. 85.16.

2. Heading No. 86.09 is to be taken to apply, *inter alia*, to:

(*a*) Axles, wheels, metal tyres, hoops and hubs and other parts of wheels;

(*b*) Frames, underframes and bogies;

(*c*) Axle boxes; brake gear;

(*d*) Buffers for rolling-stock; coupling gear and corridor connections;

(*e*) Coachwork.

3. Subject to the provisions of Note 1 above, heading No. 86.10 is to be taken to apply, *inter alia*, to:

(*a*) Assembled track, turntables, platform buffers, loading gauges;

(*b*) Semaphores, mechanical signal discs, level crossing control gear, signal and point controls, whether or not they are fitted for electric lighting.

Tariff Heading	*Rate of Import Duty (if any)*	
	Full	*Commonwealth (C)* *E.F.T.A. (E)*
86.01 Steam rail locomotives and tenders ...	8%	—
86.02 Electric rail locomotives, battery operated or powered from an external source of electricity	8%	—
86.03 Other rail locomotives	8%	—
86.04 Mechanically propelled railway and tramway coaches, vans and trucks; mechanically propelled track inspection trolleys	8%	—
86.05 Railway and tramway passenger coaches and luggage vans; hospital coaches, prison coaches, testing coaches, travelling post office coaches and other special purpose railway coaches	8%	—
86.06 Railway and tramway rolling-stock, the following: workshops, cranes and other service vehicles	8%	—

Tariff Heading	*Rate of Import Duty (if any)*	
	Full	*Commonwealth (C)* *E.F.T.A. (E)*
86.07 Railway and tramway goods vans, goods wagons and trucks:		
(A) For use on railways not exceeding 900 millimetres in gauge	17%	—
(B) Other	10%	—
86.08 Containers specially designed and equipped for carriage by one or more modes of transport	10%	—
86.09 Parts of railway and tramway locomotives and rolling-stock:		
(A) Of vans, wagons and trucks for use on railways not exceeding 900 millimetres in gauge	17%	—
(B) Other	10%	—
86.10 Railway and tramway track fixtures and fittings; mechanical equipment, not electrically powered, for signalling to or controlling road, rail or other vehicles, ships or aircraft; parts of the foregoing fixtures, fittings or equipment	10%	—

Chapter 87

Vehicles, other than Railway or Tramway Rolling-stock, and parts thereof

Notes

1. For the purposes of this Chapter, tractors are deemed to be vehicles constructed essentially for hauling or pushing another vehicle, appliance or load, whether or not they contain subsidiary provision for the transport, in connection with the main use of the tractor, of tools, seeds, fertilisers or other goods.

2. Motor chassis fitted with cabs are to be treated as falling within heading No. 87.02 and not within heading No. 87.04.

3. Headings Nos. 87.10 and 87.14 are to be taken not to apply to children's cycles which are not fitted with ball bearings nor to children's cycles which, though fitted with ball bearings, are not constructed in the normal form of adults' cycles. Such children's cycles are to be treated as falling within heading No. 97.01.

4. The headings of this Chapter are to be taken not to apply to railway or tramway rolling-stock designed solely for running on rails.

Tariff Heading	*Rate of Import Duty (if any)*		
	Full	*Commonwealth (C)* *E.F.T.A. (E)*	
87.01 Tractors (other than those falling within heading No. 87.07), whether or not fitted with power take-offs, winches or pulleys:			
(A) Track-laying tractors; one or two wheeled tractors	7·5%		—
(B) Other tractors:			
(1) Agricultural tractors	7·5%	C E	7·5% —
(2) Other	22%	C E	15% —
87.02 Motor vehicles for the transport of persons, goods or materials (including sports motor vehicles, other than those of heading No. 87.09):			
(A) Air-cushion vehicles	7%		—
(B) Other:			
(1) Dumpers designed solely for use in excavating and levelling operations	7·5%		—
(2) Agricultural vehicles of a kind mainly used for hauling or pushing another vehicle, appliance or load	7·5%	C E	7·5% —
(3) Other:			
(*a*) Motor vehicles for the transport of persons including vehicles designed for the transport of both passengers and goods:			

Tariff Heading	Rate of Import Duty (if any)		
	Full	*Commonwealth (C) E.F.T.A. (E)*	
87.02 Motor vehicles for the transport of persons, etc.—*contd.*			
(B) Other:—*contd.*			
(3) Other:—*contd.*			
(*a*) Motor vehicles, etc.—*contd.*			
(i) With a seating capacity of 15 or more and either a spark ignition engine of a cylinder capacity of 2,800 cubic centimetres or more or a compression ignition engine of a cylinder capacity of 2,500 cubic centimetres or more	22%	C E	15% —
(ii) Other	11%	C E	7·5% —
(*b*) Motor vehicles for the transport of goods or materials:			
(i) With either a spark ignition engine of a cylinder capacity of 2,800 cubic centimetres or more or a compression ignition engine of a cylinder capacity of 2,500 cubic centimetres or more	22%	C E	15% —
(ii) Other	11%	C E	7·5% —
87.03 Special purpose motor lorries and vans (such as breakdown lorries, fire-engines, fire-escapes, road sweeper lorries, snow-ploughs, spraying lorries, crane lorries, searchlight lorries, mobile workshops and mobile radiological units), but not including the motor vehicles of heading No. 87.02:			
(A) Air-cushion vehicles	7%		—
(B) Other	11%	C E	7·5% —
87.04 Chassis fitted with engines, for the motor vehicles falling within heading No. 87.01, 87.02 or 87.03:			
(A) For track-laying tractors or the dumpers of subheading No. 87.02 (B) (1)	7·5%		—
(B) Other:			
(1) For motor vehicles for the transport of persons including vehicles designed for the transport of both passengers and goods:			
(*a*) With a seating capacity of 15 or more and either a spark ignition engine of a cylinder capacity of 2,800 cubic centimetres or more or a compression ignition engine of a cylinder capacity of 2,500 cubic centimetres or more	22%	C E	15% —

Tariff Heading	Rate of Import Duty (if any)	
	Full	Commonwealth (C) E.F.T.A. (E)
87.04 Chassis fitted with engines, etc.—*contd.*		
(B) Other:—*contd.*		
(1) For motor vehicles, etc.—*contd.*		
(*b*) Other	11%	C 7·5% E —
(2) For other motor vehicles:		
(*a*) With either a spark ignition engine of a cylinder capacity of 2,800 cubic centimetres or more or a compression ignition engine of a cylinder capacity of 2,500 cubic centimetres or more	22%	C 15% E —
(*b*) Other	11%	C 7·5% E —
87.05 Bodies (including cabs), for the motor vehicles falling within heading No. 87.01, 87.02 or 87.03	11%	C 7·5% E —
87.06 Parts and accessories of the motor vehicles falling within heading No. 87.01, 87.02 or 87.03:		
(A) Of track-laying tractors, of one or two wheeled tractors, or of the dumpers of subheading No. 87.02 (B) (1)	7·5%	—
(B) Other	11%	C 7·5% E —
87.07 Works trucks, mechanically propelled, of the types used in factories, warehouses, dock areas or airports for short distance transport or handling of goods (for example, platform trucks, fork-lift trucks and straddle carriers); tractors of the type used on railway station platforms; parts of the foregoing vehicles:		
(A) Scissor lift vehicles of the type used in airports; freight container straddle carriers designed to handle containers not less than 19 feet 9 inches in length, and parts thereof	7·5%	—
(B) Side loaders for top lifting freight containers; straddle carriers other than those of subheading (A) above	22%	C 15% E —
(C) Parts of the goods of subheading (B) above	11%	C 7·5% E —
(D) Other	9%	—
87.08 Tanks and other armoured fighting vehicles, motorised, whether or not fitted with weapons, and parts of such vehicles	10%	—

Tariff Heading	*Rate of Import Duty (if any)*		
	Full	*Commonwealth (C) E.F.T.A. (E)*	
87.09 Motor-cycles, auto-cycles and cycles fitted with an auxiliary motor, with or without side-cars; side-cars of all kinds	18%	C E	18% —
87.10 Cycles, not motorised	20%		—
87.11 Invalid carriages, fitted with means of mechanical propulsion (motorised or not)	9%		—
87.12 Parts and accessories of articles falling within heading No. 87.09, 87.10 or 87.11:			
(A) Of motor-cycles, side-cars, auto-cycles, cycles fitted with an auxiliary motor, or motorised invalid carriages	18%	C E	12% —
(B) Of cycles (not motorised), or invalid carriages (not motorised)	20%		—
87.13 Baby carriages and invalid carriages (other than motorised or otherwise mechanically propelled) and parts thereof	10%		—
87.14 Other vehicles (including trailers), not mechanically propelled, and parts thereof:			
(A) Air-cushion vehicles	7%		—
(B) Other:			
(1) Trailer units of flexible or articulated motor vehicles and parts thereof	22%	C E	15% —
(2) Other	11%		—

Chapter 88

Aircraft and parts thereof; Parachutes; Catapults and similar Aircraft Launching Gear; Ground Flying Trainers

Tariff Heading	*Rate of Import Duty (if any)*	
	Full	*Commonwealth (C) E.F.T.A. (E)*
88.01 Balloons and airships	9%	—
88.02 Flying machines, gliders and kites; roto-chutes:		
(A) Helicopters of an empty weight of 2,000 kilogrammes or less	14%	—
(B) Other	7%	—
88.03 Parts of goods falling in heading No. 88.01 or 88.02	7%	—
88.04 Parachutes and parts thereof and accessories thereto:		
(A) Of silk or man-made fibres	17%	C 14% E —
(B) Other	8%	—
88.05 Catapults and similar aircraft launching gear; ground flying trainers; parts of any of the foregoing articles	8%	—

Chapter 89

Ships, Boats and Floating Structures

Note

A hull, unfinished or incomplete vessel, assembled, unassembled or disassembled, or a complete vessel unassembled or disassembled, is to be classified within heading No. 89.01 if it does not have the essential character of a vessel of a particular kind.

Special Note applying to subheadings only

References in this Chapter to gross tonnage are references thereto as ascertained in accordance with the Merchant Shipping Acts as for the time being in force or, where not capable of being ascertained under those Acts, as ascertained by such methods as the Commissioners of Customs and Excise may determine.

Tariff Heading	*Rate of Import Duty (if any)*	
	Full	*Commonwealth* (*C*) *E.F.T.A.* (*E*)
89.01 Ships, boats and other vessels not falling within any of the following headings of this Chapter:		
(A) Air-cushion vehicles	5%	—
(B) Other:		
(1) Of a gross tonnage of 80 tons or more	—	—
(2) Fishing vessels of a kind commonly known as Danish-type seiners with a fuel carrying capacity of not less than 500 gallons	—	—
(3) Other	5%	—
89.02 Vessels specially designed for towing (tugs) or pushing other vessels:		
(A) Of a gross tonnage of 80 tons or more	—	—
(B) Other	5%	—
89.03 Light-vessels, fire-floats, dredgers of all kinds, floating cranes and other vessels the navigability of which is subsidiary to their main function; floating docks:		
(A) Air-cushion vehicles	5%	—
(B) Other:		
(1) Of a gross tonnage of 80 tons or more	—	—
(2) Other	5%	—
89.04 Ships, boats and other vessels for breaking up	The same rate as if not for breaking up	—
89.05 Floating structures other than vessels (for example, coffer-dams, landing stages, buoys and beacons)	8%	—

SECTION XVIII

Optical, Photographic, Cinematographic, Measuring, Checking, Precision, Medical and Surgical Instruments and Apparatus; Clocks and Watches; Musical Instruments; Sound Recorders and Reproducers; Television Image and Sound Recorders and Reproducers, Magnetic; Parts Thereof

Chapter 90

Optical, Photographic, Cinematographic, Measuring, Checking, Precision, Medical and Surgical Instruments and Apparatus; Parts Thereof

Notes

1. This Chapter does not cover:

(*a*) Articles of a kind used in machines, appliances, instruments or apparatus, of unhardened vulcanised rubber, falling within heading No. 40.14, of leather or of composition leather, falling within heading No. 42.04, or of textile material (heading No. 59.17);

(*b*) Refractory goods of heading No. 69.03; laboratory, chemical or industrial wares of heading No. 69.09;

(*c*) Glass mirrors, not optically worked, falling within heading No. 70.09, and mirrors of base metal or of precious metal, not being optical elements, falling within heading No. 83.12 or Chapter 71;

(*d*) Goods falling within heading No. 70.07, 70.11, 70.14, 70.15, 70.17 or 70.18;

(*e*) Parts of general use, as defined in Note 2 to Section XV, of base metal (Section XV) or similar goods of artificial plastic materials (which are generally classified in heading No. 39.07);

(*f*) Pumps incorporating measuring devices, of heading No. 84.10; weighing machinery, including weight-operated counting and checking machinery, and separately imported weights for balances (heading No. 84.20); lifting and handling machinery of heading No. 84.22; fittings for adjusting work or tools on machine-tools, of heading No. 84.48, including fittings with optical devices for reading the scale (for example, " optical " dividing heads) but not those which are in themselves essentially optical instruments (for example, alignment telescopes); valves and other appliances of heading No. 84.61;

(*g*) Searchlights and spotlights, of a kind used on motor vehicles, of heading No. 85.09, and radio navigational aid or radar apparatus of heading No. 85.15;

(*h*) Cinematographic sound recorders, reproducers and re-recorders, operating solely by a magnetic process (heading No. 92.11); magnetic sound-heads (heading No. 92.13);

(*ij*) Articles of Chapter 97;

(*k*) Capacity measures, which are to be classified according to the material of which they are made; or

(*l*) Spools, reels or similar supports (which are to be classified according to their constituent material, for example, in heading No. 39.07 or Section XV).

2. Subject to Note 1 above, parts or accessories which are suitable for use solely or principally with machines, appliances, instruments, or apparatus falling within any heading of this Chapter are to be classified as follows:

(*a*) Parts or accessories constituting in themselves machines, appliances, instruments or apparatus (including optical elements of heading No. 90.01 or 90.02) of any particular heading of the present Chapter or of Chapter 84, 85 or 91 (other than headings Nos. 84.65 and 85.28) are to be classified in that heading;

(*b*) Other parts or accessories are to be classified in heading No. 90.29 if they answer to the terms of that heading; otherwise they are to be classified in the heading appropriate to the machine, appliance, instrument or apparatus itself.

3. Heading No. 90 05 is to be taken not to apply to astronomical telescopes of a kind unsuitable for terrestrial observation (heading No. 90.06), or to telescopic sights for fitting to firearms, periscopic telescopes for fitting to submarines or tanks, or to telescopes for machines, appliances, instruments or apparatus of this Chapter; such telescopic sights and telescopes are to be classified in heading No. 90.13.

4. Measuring or checking optical instruments, appliances or machines which, but for this Note, could be classified both in heading No. 90.13 and in heading No. 90.16, are to be classified in heading No. 90.16.

5. Heading No. 90.28 is to be taken to apply, and apply only, to the following goods (other than electronic microcircuits defined in Note 5 to Chapter 85) which are to be taken not to fall within any other heading of this Schedule:

(*a*) Instruments or apparatus for measuring or checking electrical quantities;

(*b*) Machines, appliances, instruments or apparatus of a kind described in heading No. 90.14, 90.15, 90.16, 90.22, 90.23, 90.24, 90.25 or 90.27 (other than stroboscopes), the operation of which depends on an electrical phenomenon which varies according to the factor to be ascertained or automatically controlled;

(*c*) Instruments or apparatus for measuring or detecting alpha, beta, gamma, X-ray, cosmic or similar radiations; and

(*d*) Automatic regulators of electrical quantities, and instruments or apparatus for automatically controlling non-electrical quantities the operation of which depends on an electrical phenomenon varying according to the factor to be controlled.

6. Cases, boxes and similar containers imported with articles of this Chapter are to be classified with such articles if they are of a kind normally sold therewith. Cases, boxes and similar containers when imported separately are not to be treated as parts of or accessories to their articles but are to be classified within heading No. 42.02 or according to their constituent material as appropriate.

Tariff Heading	*Rate of Import Duty (if any)*	
	Full	*Commonwealth (C)* *E.F.T.A. (E)*
90.01 Lenses, prisms, mirrors and other optical elements, of any material, unmounted, other than such elements of glass not optically worked; sheets or plates, of polarising material	25%	—
90.02 Lenses, prisms, mirrors and other optical elements, of any material, mounted, being parts of or fittings for instruments or apparatus, other than such elements of glass not optically worked	25%	—
90.03 Frames and mountings, and parts thereof, for spectacles, pince-nez, lorgnettes, goggles and the like	10%	—
90.04 Spectacles, pince-nez, lorgnettes, goggles and the like, corrective, protective or other	10%	—

Tariff Heading	Rate of Import Duty (if any)	
	Full	Commonwealth (C) E.F.T.A. (E)
90.05 Refracting telescopes (monocular and binocular), prismatic or not	20%	—
90.06 Astronomical instruments (for example, reflecting telescopes, transit instruments and equatorial telescopes), and mountings therefor, but not including instruments for radio-astronomy	20%	—
90.07 Photographic cameras; photographic flashlight apparatus:		
(A) Photographic cameras	20%	—
(B) Photographic flashlight apparatus; tripods and other stands for articles of this heading; pistol grips for cameras of this heading	10%	—
90.08 Cinematographic cameras, projectors, sound recorders and sound reproducers but not including re-recorders or film editing apparatus; any combination of these articles:		
(A) Tripods and other stands for articles of this heading; pistol grips for cameras of this heading	10%	—
(B) Cinematographic projectors	12·5%	—
(C) Cinematographic sound reproducers (photo-electric)	12·5%	C 8% E —
(D) Cinematographic projectors combined with sound reproducers (photo-electric or magnetic)	12·5%	—
(E) Other	20%	—
90.09 Image projectors (other than cinematographic projectors); photographic (except cinematographic) enlargers and reducers:		
(A) Tripods and other stands for image projectors	10%	—
(B) Other	20%	—
90.10 Apparatus and equipment of a kind used in photographic or cinematographic laboratories, not falling within any other heading in this Chapter; photo-copying apparatus (whether incorporating an optical system or of the contact-type) and thermo-copying apparatus; screens for projectors:		
(A) Cinematographic editing machines incorporating means of projection	20%	—

Tariff Heading	Rate of Import Duty (if any)	
	Full	Commonwealth (C) E.F.T.A. (E)
90.10 Apparatus and equipment, etc.—*contd.*		
(B) Other:		
(1) Cinematographic enlargers and reducers (optical printers); re-recorders; other optical projection apparatus	20%	—
(2) Film viewing magnifiers	20%	—
(3) Other	7·5%	—
90.11 Microscopes and diffraction apparatus, electron and proton	17%	—
90.12 Compound optical microscopes, whether or not provided with means for photographing or projecting the image:		
(A) Micro-manipulators	17%	—
(B) Other	25%	—
90.13 Optical appliances and instruments (but not including lighting appliances other than searchlights or spotlights), not falling within any other heading of this Chapter	20%	—
90.14 Surveying (including photogrammetrical surveying), hydrographic, navigational, meteorological, hydrological and geophysical instruments; compasses; range-finders:		
(A) Instruments incorporating optical elements but not including instruments in which the optical element is for viewing a scale or for some other subsidiary function	25%	—
(B) Other:		
(1) Compasses	17%	—
(2) Other	12·5%	—
90.15 Balances of a sensitivity of five centigrammes or better, with or without their weights	17%	—
90.16 Drawing, marking-out and mathematical calculating instruments (for example, drafting machines, pantographs, slide rules, disc calculators, centre punches, scribers and carpenters' marking gauges); measuring or checking instruments, appliances and machines, not falling within any other heading of this Chapter (for example, micrometers, callipers, gauges, measuring rods, balancing machines); profile projectors:		

Tariff Heading	*Rate of Import Duty (if any)*	
	Full	*Commonwealth (C)* *E.F.T.A. (E)*
90.16 Drawing, marking-out and mathematical, etc.—*contd.*		
(A) Instruments, appliances and machines incorporating optical elements but not including instruments, appliances or machines in which the optical element is for viewing a scale or for some other subsidiary function:		
(1) Profile projectors	20%	—
(2) Other	25%	—
(B) Other instruments, appliances and machines:		
(1) Calculating cylinders, dials and rules; isographs; half sets; compasses (including beam compasses); dividers (including proportional dividers); bows; spring bows; ruling pens; pantographs and eidographs; slide rules	17%	—
(2) Other	12·5%	—
90.17 Medical, dental, surgical and veterinary instruments and appliances (including electro-medical apparatus and ophthalmic instruments):		
(A) Instruments and appliances incorporating optical elements but not including instruments or appliances in which the optical element is for viewing a scale or for some other subsidiary function:		
(1) Mirrors, mouth, not optically worked	8%	—
(2) Other	20%	—
(B) Other	10%	—
90.18 Mechano-therapy appliances; massage apparatus; psychological aptitude-testing apparatus; artificial respiration, ozone therapy, oxygen therapy, aerosol therapy or similar apparatus; breathing appliances (including gas masks and similar respirators)	7·5%	—
90.19 Orthopaedic appliances, surgical belts, trusses and the like; splints and other fracture appliances; artificial limbs, eyes, teeth and other artificial parts of the body; deaf-aids and other appliances which are worn or carried, or implanted in the body, to compensate for a defect or disability	8%	—

Tariff Heading	Rate of Import Duty (if any)	
	Full	Commonwealth (C) E.F.T.A. (E)
90.20 Apparatus based on the use of X-rays or of the radiations from radio-active substances (including radiography and radiotherapy apparatus); X-ray generators; X-ray tubes; X-ray screens; X-ray high tension generators; X-ray control panels and desks; X-ray examination or treatment tables, chairs and the like	12·5%	—
90.21 Instruments, apparatus or models, designed solely for demonstrational purposes (for example, in education or exhibition), unsuitable for other uses	8%	—
90.22 Machines and appliances for testing mechanically the hardness, strength, compressibility, elasticity and the like properties of industrial materials (for example, metals, wood, textiles, paper or plastics)	10%	—
90.23 Hydrometers and similar instruments; thermometers, pyrometers, barometers, hygrometers, psychrometers, recording or not; any combination of these instruments:		
(A) Pyrometers, optical	25%	—
(B) Other	12·5%	—
90.24 Instruments and apparatus for measuring, checking or automatically controlling the flow, depth, pressure or other variables of liquids or gases, or for automatically controlling temperature (for example, pressure gauges, thermostats, level gauges, flow meters, automatic oven-draught regulators), not being articles falling within heading No. 90.14; heat meters of a type used with central heating systems and the like	8%	—
90.25 Instruments and apparatus for physical or chemical analysis (such as polarimeters, refractometers, spectrometers, gas analysis apparatus); instruments and apparatus for measuring or checking viscosity, porosity, expansion, surface tension or the like (such as viscometers, porosimeters, expansion meters); instruments and apparatus for measuring or checking quantities of heat, light or sound (such as photometers (including exposure meters), calorimeters); microtomes:		
(A) Instruments and apparatus incorporating optical elements but not including instruments or apparatus in which the optical element is for viewing a scale or for some other subsidiary function	20%	—
(B) Environmental test chambers ...	7·5%	—
(C) Other instruments and apparatus ...	17%	—

Tariff Heading	Rate of Import Duty (if any)	
	Full	Commonwealth (C) E.F.T.A. (E)
90.26 Gas, liquid and electricity supply or production meters; calibrating meters therefor	8%	—
90.27 Revolution counters, production counters, taximeters, mileometers, pedometers and the like, speed indicators (including magnetic speed indicators) and tachometers (other than articles falling within heading No. 90.14); stroboscopes:		
(A) Stroboscopes	25%	—
(B) Mileometers, revolution indicators and speed indicators, suitable for use on motor vehicles	12%	C 8% E —
(C) Other	10%	—
90.28 Electrical measuring, checking, analysing or automatically controlling instruments and apparatus:		
(A) Instruments and apparatus incorporating optical elements but not including instruments or apparatus in which the optical element is for viewing a scale or for some other subsidiary function	20%	—
(B) Other	12·5%	—
90.29 Parts or accessories suitable for use solely or principally with one or more of the articles falling within heading No. 90.23, 90.24, 90.26, 90.27 or 90.28	The rate of duty applicable to the article of which the goods are parts or accessories	—

Chapter 91

Clocks and Watches and Parts Thereof

Notes

1. For the purposes of headings Nos. 91.02 and 91.07, the expression " watch movements " means movements regulated by a balance-wheel and hairspring or by any other system capable of determining intervals of time, not exceeding twelve millimetres in thickness when measured with the plate, the bridges and any additional outer plates.

2. Headings Nos. 91.07 and 91.08 are to be taken not to apply to spring-operated or weight-operated motors not fitted, nor adapted to be fitted, with escapements (heading No. 84.08).

3. Headings Nos. 91.09, 91.10 and 91.11 are to be taken not to include:

(*a*) Weights, clock or watch glasses, watch chains or straps, ball bearings or bearing balls;

(*b*) Electric motors, electro-magnets and other electrical parts of the kinds used both in clocks or watches and in other articles, whether or not suitable for use only in clocks or watches;

(*c*) Parts of general use, as defined in Note 2 to Section XV, of base metal (Section XV), or similar goods of artificial plastic materials (which are generally classified in heading No. 39.07).

Clock or watch springs are to be classified as clock or watch parts (heading No. 91.11).

4. Except as provided in Notes 2 and 3, movements and other parts suitable for use both in clocks or watches and in other articles (for example, precision instruments) are to be taken as falling within this Chapter and not within any other Chapter.

5. Cases, boxes and similar containers imported with articles of this Chapter are to be classified with such articles if they are of a kind normally sold therewith. Cases, boxes and similar containers imported separately are to be classified under their appropriate headings.

Tariff Heading	*Rate of Import Duty (if any)*		
	Full	*Commonwealth (C)* *E.F.T.A. (E)*	
91.01 Pocket-watches, wrist-watches and other watches, including stop-watches:			
(A) Watches capable of indicating the time of day	17%	C E	11% —
(B) Other	10%		—
91.02 Clocks with watch movements (excluding clocks of heading No. 91.03):			
(A) Alarm clocks:			
(1) Of a value not less than £0·6000 each	£0·1250 each or 12·5%, whichever is the greater	C E	£0·0850 each or 8%, whichever is the greater —
(2) Other	£0·1250 each	C E	£0·0850 each —
(B) Other	16%	C E	11% —
91.03 Instrument panel clocks and clocks of a similar type, for vehicles, aircraft or vessels	17%	C E	11% —

Tariff Heading	Rate of Import Duty (if any)		
	Full	Commonwealth (C) E.F.T.A. (E)	
91.04 Other clocks:			
(A) Alarm clocks:			
(1) Of a value not less than £0·6000 each	£0·1250 each or 12·5%, whichever is the greater	C	£0·0850 each or 8%, whichever is the greater
		E	—
(2) Other	£0·1250 each	C	£0·0850 each
		E	—
(B) Other	16%	C	11%
		E	—
91.05 Time of day recording apparatus; apparatus with clock or watch movement (including secondary movement) or with synchronous motor, for measuring, recording or otherwise indicating intervals of time:			
(A) Apparatus capable of indicating the time of day	17%	C	11%
		E	—
(B) Other	10%		—
91.06 Time switches with clock or watch movement (including secondary movement) or with synchronous motor	10%		—
91.07 Watch movements (including stop-watch movements), assembled:			
(A) Movements suitable for articles capable of indicating the time of day	17%	C	11%
		E	—
(B) Other	10%		—
91.08 Clock movements (including secondary movements), assembled:			
(A) Movements suitable for articles capable of indicating the time of day	17%	C	11%
		E	—
(B) Other	10%		—
91.09 Watch cases and parts of watch cases ...	17%	C	11%
		E	—
91.10 Clock cases and cases of a similar type for other goods of this Chapter, and parts thereof	17%	C	11%
		E	—
91.11 Other clock and watch parts	17%	C	11%
		E	—

Chapter 92

Musical Instruments; Sound Recorders and Reproducers; Television Image and Sound Recorders and Reproducers, Magnetic; Parts and Accessories of such Articles

Notes

1. This Chapter does not cover:

(*a*) Film wholly or partly sensitised for photographic or photo-electric recording or such film exposed, whether or not developed (Chapter 37);

(*b*) Parts of general use, as defined in Note 2 to Section XV, of base metal (Section XV), or similar goods of artificial plastic materials (which are generally classified in heading No. 39.07);

(*c*) Microphones, amplifiers, loudspeakers, head-phones, switches, stroboscopes and other accessory instruments, apparatus or equipment falling within Chapter 85 or 90, for use with but not incorporated in or housed in the same cabinet as instruments of the present Chapter; sound recorders or reproducers combined with a radio or television receiver (heading No. 85.15);

(*d*) Brushes (for cleaning musical instruments) falling within heading No. 96.02;

(*e*) Toy instruments (heading No. 97.03);

(*f*) Collectors' pieces or antiques (heading No. 99.05 or 99.06); or

(*g*) Spools, reels or similar supports (which are to be classified according to their constituent material, for example, in heading No. 39.07 or Section XV).

2. Bows and sticks and similar devices used in playing the musical instruments of headings Nos. 92.02 and 92.06 imported with such instruments in numbers normal thereto and clearly intended for use therewith, are to be classified in the same heading as the relative instruments.

Perforated music rolls (heading No. 92.10) and gramophone records and the like (heading No. 92.12) imported with an instrument are to be treated as separate articles and not as forming a part of such instrument.

3. Cases, boxes and similar containers imported with articles of this Chapter are to be classified with such articles if they are of a kind normally sold therewith. Cases, boxes and similar containers imported separately are classified elsewhere in this Schedule, in general according to their constituent material, and not under heading No. 92.10 or 92.13.

Tariff Heading	*Rate of Import Duty (if any)*	
	Full	*Commonwealth (C)* *E.F.T.A. (E)*
92.01 Pianos (including automatic pianos, whether or not with keyboards); harpsichords and other keyboard stringed instruments; harps but not including aeolian harps:		
(A) Harps	—	—
(B) Other	17%	C 11% E —
92.02 Other string musical instruments	12·5%	C 8% E —

Tariff Heading	Rate of Import Duty (if any)		
	Full	*Commonwealth (E)* *E.F.T.A. (C)*	
92.03 Pipe and reed organs, including harmoniums and the like:			
(A) Reed organs, including harmoniums	12·5%		—
(B) Other	12·5%	C	8%
		E	—
92.04 Accordions, concertinas and similar musical instruments; mouth organs:			
(A) Piano accordions	8%	C	5%
		E	—
(B) Other	10%	C	7%
		E	—
92.05 Other wind musical instruments	12·5%	C	8%
		E	—
92.06 Percussion musical instruments (for example, drums, xylophones, cymbals, castanets)	17%	C	11%
		E	—
92.07 Electro-magnetic, electrostatic, electronic and similar musical instruments (for example, pianos, organs, accordions)	12·5%	C	8%
		E	—
92.08 Musical instruments not falling within any other heading of this Chapter (for example, fairground organs, mechanical street organs, musical boxes, musical saws); mechanical singing birds; decoy calls and effects of all kinds; mouth-blown sound signalling instruments (for example, whistles and boatswains' pipes):			
(A) Musical instruments:			
(1) Musical boxes	15%	C	10%
		E	—
(2) Other	17%	C	11%
		E	—
(B) Mechanical singing birds; decoy calls and effects of all kinds; mouth-blown sound signalling instruments	10%		—
92.09 Musical instrument strings:			
(A) For keyboard instruments	17%	C	11%
		E	—
(B) Other	12·5%	C	8%
		E	—

Tariff Heading	Rate of Import Duty (if any)	
	Full	Commonwealth (C) E.F.T.A. (E)
92.10 Parts and accessories of musical instruments (other than strings), including perforated music rolls and mechanisms for musical boxes; metronomes, tuning forks and pitch pipes of all kinds:		
(A) Parts and accessories of musical instruments (including pitch pipes and tuning forks of a kind designed for musical purposes):		
(1) Parts of organs (other than reeds) but not including parts of mouth organs	5%	C 3% E —
(2) Reeds, and reed plates incorporating reeds, not comprised in subheading (1) above	10%	C 7% E —
(3) Drum head skins	7·5%	—
(4) Mechanical movements for musical boxes	12·5%	C 8% E —
(5) Other parts and accessories:		
(*a*) Specialised for use with concertinas, accordions, wind or string instruments	12·5%	C 8% E —
(*b*) Other	17%	C 11% E —
(B) Metronomes; tuning forks and pitch pipes not comprised in subheading (A) above	10%	—
92.11 Gramophones, dictating machines and other sound recorders and reproducers, including record-players and tape decks, with or without sound-heads; television image and sound recorders and reproducers, magnetic:		
(A) Dictating machines, and reproducing machines adapted for use therewith (but not including machines suitable for the recording or reproduction of music)	10%	—
(B) Television image and sound recorders and reproducers, magnetic	8%	—
(C) Other	10%	C 7% E —

Tariff Heading	Rate of Import Duty (if any)		
	Full	Commonwealth (C) E.F.T.A. (E)	
92.12 Gramophone records; other articles having recordings (whether of sound or not) or data embodied therein by means similar to those used for the recording of sound; matrices for the production of records, prepared record blanks, film for mechanical sound recording, prepared tapes, wires, strips and like articles of a kind commonly used for embodying recordings or data by means similar to those used for the recording of sound:			
(A) Matrices, impressed	—		—
(B) Gramophone records for the reproduction of speech, specially adapted for the use of the blind	—		—
(C) Other:			
(1) Sound recordings for reproducing music:			
(*a*) Gramophone records	7·5%	C E	5% —
(*b*) Other	12·5%	C E	8% —
(2) Other	5%		—
92.13 Other parts and accessories of apparatus falling within heading No. 92.11:			
(A) Record shaving machines adapted for use in connection with dictating machines	10%		—
(B) Parts and accessories of the apparatus of subheading No. 92.11(B)	8%		—
(C) Other	10%	C E	7% —

SECTION XIX

ARMS AND AMMUNITION; PARTS THEREOF

Chapter 93

Arms and Ammunition; Parts thereof

Notes

1. This Chapter does not cover:

(*a*) Goods falling within Chapter 36 (for example, percussion caps, detonators, signalling flares);

(*b*) Parts of general use, as defined in Note 2 to Section XV, of base metal (Section XV), or similar goods of artificial plastic materials (which are generally classified in heading No. 39.07);

(*c*) Armoured fighting vehicles (heading No. 87.08);

(*d*) Telescopic sights and other optical devices suitable for use with arms, unless mounted on a firearm or imported with the firearm on which they are designed to be mounted (Chapter 90);

(*e*) Bows, arrows, fencing foils or toys falling within Chapter 97; or

(*f*) Collectors' pieces or antiques (heading No. 99.05 or 99.06).

2. In heading No. 93.07, the reference to " parts thereof " is to be taken not to include radio or radar apparatus of heading No. 85.15.

3. Cases, boxes and similar containers imported with articles of this Chapter are to be classified with such articles if they are of a kind normally sold therewith. Cases, boxes and similar containers imported separately are to be classified under their appropriate headings.

Tariff Heading	*Rate of Import Duty (if any)*	
	Full	*Commonwealth (C)* *E.F.T.A. (E)*
93.01 Side-arms (for example, swords, cutlasses and bayonets) and parts thereof and scabbards and sheaths therefor	12·5%	—
93.02 Revolvers and pistols, being firearms ...	10%	—
93.03 Artillery weapons, machine-guns, sub-machine-guns and other military firearms and projectors (other than revolvers and pistols)	10%	—
93.04 Other firearms, including Very light pistols, pistols and revolvers for firing blank ammunition only, line-throwing guns and the like	10%	—
93.05 Arms of other descriptions, including air, spring and similar pistols, rifles and guns:		
(A) Air, spring and similar pistols, rifles and guns	20%	—
(B) Other	10%	—

Tariff Heading	*Rate of Import Duty (if any)*	
	Full	*Commonwealth (C)* *E.F.T.A. (E)*
93.06 Parts of arms, including gun barrel blanks, but not including parts of side-arms:		
(A) Wooden stock blocks, roughly sawn or planed or polished but not further manufactured	5%	—
(B) Other parts	10%	—
93.07 Bombs, grenades, torpedoes, mines, guided weapons and missiles and similar munitions of war, and parts thereof; ammunition and parts thereof, including cartridge wads; lead shot prepared for ammunition	10%	—

SECTION XX

Miscellaneous Manufactured Articles

Chapter 94

Furniture and parts thereof; Bedding, Mattresses, Mattress Supports, Cushions and similar Stuffed Furnishings

Notes

1. This Chapter does not cover:

(*a*) Pneumatic or water mattresses, pillows or cushions, falling within Chapter 39, 40 or 62;

(*b*) Standard lamps, table lamps, wall lamp brackets and other lighting fittings;

(*c*) Articles of stone, ceramic or any other material referred to in Chapter 68 or 69, used as seats, tables or columns, of the kind used in parks, gardens or vestibules (Chapter 68 or 69);

(*d*) Mirrors designed for placing on the floor or ground (for example, cheval-glasses (swing-mirrors)) falling within heading No. 70.09;

(*e*) Parts of general use, as defined in Note 2 to Section XV, of base metal (Section XV), or similar goods of artificial plastic materials (which are generally classified in heading No. 39.07); and safes falling within heading No. 83.03;

(*f*) Furniture specially designed as parts of refrigerators of heading No. 84.15; furniture specially designed for sewing machines (heading No. 84.41);

(*g*) Furniture specially designed as parts of radio-gramophones, wireless sets or television sets (heading No. 85.15);

(*h*) Dentists' spittoons falling within heading No. 90.17;

(*ij*) Goods falling within Chapter 91 (for example, clocks and clock cases);

(*k*) Furniture specially designed as parts of gramophones, of dictating machines or of other sound reproducers or recorders, falling within heading No. 92.13; or

(*l*) Toy furniture (heading No. 97.03), billiard tables and other furniture specially constructed for games (heading No. 97.04) or for conjuring tricks (heading No. 97.05).

2. The articles (other than parts) referred to in headings Nos. 94.01, 94.02 and 94.03 are to be classified in those headings only if they are designed for placing on the floor or ground.

This provision is, however, to be taken not to apply to the following which are still to be classified in the above-mentioned headings even if they are designed to be hung, to be fixed to the wall or to stand one on the other:

(*a*) Kitchen cabinets and similar cupboards;

(*b*) Seats and beds;

(*c*) Unit bookcases and similar unit furniture.

3. (*a*) In this Chapter references to parts of goods do not include references to sheets (whether or not cut to shape but not combined with other parts) of glass (including mirrors) or of marble or other stone.

(*b*) Goods described in heading No. 94.04, imported separately, are not to be classified in heading No. 94.01, 94.02 or 94.03 as parts of goods.

Tariff Heading	*Rate of Import Duty (if any)*	
	Full	*Commonwealth (C)* *E.F.T.A. (E)*
94.01 Chairs and other seats (other than those falling within heading No. 94.02), whether or not convertible into beds, and parts thereof	10%	—
94.02 Medical, dental, surgical or veterinary furniture (for example, operating tables, hospital beds with mechanical fittings); dentists' and similar chairs with mechanical elevating, rotating or reclining movements; parts of the foregoing articles	10%	—
94.03 Other furniture and parts thereof	10%	—
94.04 Mattress supports; articles of bedding or similar furnishing fitted with springs or stuffed or internally fitted with any material, or of expanded, foam or sponge rubber or of expanded, foam or sponge artificial plastic material, whether or not covered (for example, mattresses, quilts, eiderdowns, cushions, pouffes and pillows):		
(A) Containing more than 5 per cent. by weight of silk, of man-made fibres, or of both together	20%	C 17% E —
(B) Other	20%	—

Chapter 95

Articles and Manufactures of Carving or Moulding Material

Note

This Chapter does not cover:

(*a*) Articles falling within Chapter 66 (for example, parts of umbrellas, walking-sticks);

(*b*) Fans or hand screens, non-mechanical (heading No. 67.05);

(*c*) Articles falling within Chapter 71 (for example, imitation jewellery);

(*d*) Cutlery or other articles falling within Chapter 82, with handles or other parts of carving or moulding materials; the headings of the present Chapter apply, however, to separately imported handles or other parts of such articles;

(*e*) Articles falling within Chapter 90 (for example, spectacle frames);

(*f*) Articles falling within Chapter 91 (for example, clock or watch cases);

(*g*) Articles falling within Chapter 92 (for example, musical instruments and parts thereof);

(*h*) Articles falling within Chapter 93 (arms and parts thereof);

(*ij*) Articles falling within Chapter 94 (furniture and parts thereof);

(*k*) Brushes, powder-puffs or other articles falling within Chapter 96;

(*l*) Articles falling within Chapter 97 (toys, games and sports requisites);

(*m*) Articles falling within Chapter 98 (for example, buttons, cuff-links, smoking pipes, combs); or

(*n*) Collectors' pieces or antiques (Chapter 99).

Tariff Heading	*Rate of Import Duty (if any)*	
	Full	*Commonwealth (C) E.F.T.A. (E)*
95.01 Worked tortoise-shell and articles of tortoise-shell	15%	—
95.02 Worked mother of pearl and articles of mother of pearl:		
(A) Mother of pearl discs, cut from simply prepared shell, not polished or otherwise worked	5%	—
(B) Other	15%	—
95.03 Worked ivory and articles of ivory ...	15%	—
95.04 Worked bone (excluding whalebone) and articles of bone (excluding whalebone):		
(A) Unstrung beads	—	—
(B) Other	8%	—

Tariff Heading	Rate of Import Duty (if any)	
	Full	Commonwealth (C) E.F.T.A. (E)
95.05 Worked horn, coral (natural or agglomerated) and other animal carving material, and articles of horn, coral (natural or agglomerated) or of other animal carving material:		
(A) Unstrung beads made of shells ...	—	—
(B) Unmounted cameos made of natural coral or of shell and of a size and shape suitable for use in articles of jewellery or imitation jewellery	—	—
(C) Other:		
(1) Coral (natural or agglomerated) and articles thereof	15%	—
(2) Other	8%	—
95.06 Worked vegetable carving material (for example, corozo) and articles of vegetable carving material:		
(A) Unstrung beads made of seeds ...	—	—
(B) Other	8%	—
95.07 Worked jet (and mineral substitutes for jet), amber, meerschaum, agglomerated amber and agglomerated meerschaum, and articles of those substances:		
(A) Unmounted cameos made of amber and of a size and shape suitable for use in articles of jewellery or imitation jewellery	—	—
(B) Other	15%	—
95.08 Moulded or carved articles of stearin, of natural gums or natural resins (for example, copal or rosin) or of other non-mineral substances, not elsewhere specified or included; moulded or carved articles of wax or of modelling pastes; worked, unhardened gelatin (except gelatin falling within heading No. 35.03) and articles of unhardened gelatin	10%	—

Chapter 96

Brooms, Brushes, Feather Dusters, Powder-puffs and Sieves

Notes

1. This Chapter does not cover:
(*a*) Articles falling within Chapter 71;
(*b*) Brushes of a kind specialised for use in dentistry or for medical, surgical or veterinary purposes, falling within heading No. 90.17; or
(*c*) Toys (Chapter 97).

2. In heading No. 96.03, the expression "prepared knots and tufts for broom or brush making" is to be taken to apply only to unmounted knots and tufts of animal hair, vegetable fibre or other material, which are ready for incorporation without division in brooms or brushes, or which require only such further minor processes as glueing or coating the butts, or trimming to shape at the top, to render them ready for such incorporation.

Tariff Heading	*Rate of Import Duty (if any)*		
	Full	*Commonwealth (C)* *E.F.T.A. (E)*	
96.01 Brooms and brushes, consisting of twigs or other vegetable materials merely bound together and not mounted in a head (for example, besoms and whisks), with or without handles	10%		—
96.02 Other brooms and brushes (including brushes of a kind used as parts of machines); paint rollers; squeegees (other than roller squeegees) and mops:			
(A) Paint rollers, squeegees and mops ...	10%		—
(B) Brooms, household and toilet brushes:			
(1) With filling of man-made fibres (including monofil of heading No. 51.01 or 51.02)	20%	C E	18% —
(2) With filling of iron or steel wire ...	20%		—
(3) Other	£0·3000 per gross or 20%, whichever is the greater		—
(C) Other:			
(1) Brushes with filling of man-made fibres (including monofil of heading No. 51.01 or 51.02)	17%	C E	15% —
(2) Other	17%		—
96.03 Prepared knots and tufts for broom or brush making	10%		—
96.04 Feather dusters	10%		—
96.05 Powder-puffs and pads for applying cosmetics or toilet preparations	10%		—
96.06 Hand sieves and hand riddles	12·5%		—

Chapter 97

Toys, Games and Sports Requisites; Parts thereof

Notes

1. This Chapter does not cover:

(*a*) Christmas tree candles (heading No. 34.06);

(*b*) Fireworks or other pyrotechnic articles falling within heading No. 36.05;

(*c*) Yarns, monofil, cords or gut and the like for fishing, cut to length but not made up into fishing lines, falling within Chapter 39, heading No. 42.06 or Section XI;

(*d*) Rubber tyres (heading No. 40.11); sports bags or other containers of heading No. 42.02 or 43.03;

(*e*) Sports clothing or fancy dress, of textiles, falling within Chapter 60 or 61;

(*f*) Textile flags or bunting, or sails for boats or land craft, falling within Chapter 62;

(*g*) Sports footwear (other than skating boots with skates attached), cricket pads, shin-guards or the like, falling within Chapter 64, or sports headgear falling within Chapter 65;

(*h*) Climbing sticks, whips, riding crops or the like (heading No. 66.02), or parts thereof (heading No. 66.03);

(*ij*) Unmounted glass eyes for dolls or other toys, falling within heading No. 70.19;

(*k*) Parts of general use, as defined in Note 2 to Section XV, of base metal (Section XV), or similar goods of artificial plastic materials (which are generally classified in heading No. 39.07);

(*l*) Articles falling within heading No. 83.11;

(*m*) Sports vehicles (other than bobsleighs, toboggans and the like) falling within Section XVII;

(*n*) Children's cycles fitted with ball bearings and in the normal form of adults' cycles (heading No. 87.10);

(*o*) Sports craft such as canoes and skiffs (Chapter 89), or their means of propulsion (Chapter 44 for such articles made of wood);

(*p*) Spectacles, goggles and the like, for sports and outdoor games (heading No. 90.04);

(*q*) Decoy calls and whistles (heading No. 92.08);

(*r*) Arms or other articles of Chapter 93; or

(*s*) Racket strings, tents or other camping goods, or gloves (classified, in general, according to the material of which they are made).

2. The headings of this Chapter are to be taken to include articles in which pearls, precious or semi-precious stones (natural, synthetic or reconstructed), precious metals or rolled precious metals constitute only minor constituents.

3. In heading No. 97.02 the term " dolls " is to be taken to apply only to such articles as are representations of human beings.

4. Subject to Note 1 above, parts and accessories which are suitable for use solely or principally with articles falling within any heading of this Chapter are to be classified with those articles.

Tariff Heading	Rate of Import Duty (if any)	
	Full	*Commonwealth (C)* *E.F.T.A. (E)*
97.01 Wheeled toys designed to be ridden by children (for example, toy bicycles and tricycles and pedal motor cars); dolls' prams and dolls' push chairs:		
(A) Containing more than 20 per cent. by weight of silk, of man-made fibres, or of both together	12·5%	C 10% E —
(B) Other	12·5%	—
97.02 Dolls:		
(A) Containing more than 20 per cent. by weight of silk, of man-made fibres, or of both together	12·5%	C 10% E —
(B) Other	12·5%	—
97.03 Other toys; working models of a kind used for recreational purposes:		
(A) Containing more than 20 per cent. by weight of silk, of man-made fibres, or of both together	12·5%	C 10% E —
(B) Other	12·5%	—
97.04 Equipment for parlour, table and funfair games for adults or children (including billiard tables and pintables and table-tennis requisites):		
(A) Playing cards, exceeding 45 millimetres in length and 32 millimetres in width, being any of the 13 cards of a conventional suit	£0·1250 per 100 packs (each of 52 cards), and so in proportion for any other number of cards	C £0·1250 per 100 packs (each of 52 cards), and so in proportion for any other number of cards E —
(B) Coin or disc operated machines ...	10%	—
(C) Other	12·5%	—
97.05 Carnival articles; entertainment articles (for example, conjuring tricks and novelty jokes); Christmas tree decorations and similar articles for Christmas festivities, (for example, artificial Christmas trees, Christmas stockings, imitation yule logs, Nativity scenes and figures therefor):		
(A) Christmas tree decorations and similar articles for Christmas festivities, electrical	10%	—
(B) Other:		
(1) Containing more than 20 per cent. by weight of silk, of man-made fibres, or of both together	12·5%	C 10% E —
(2) Other	12·5%	—

Tariff Heading	*Rate of Import Duty (if any)*	
	Full	*Commonwealth (C)* *E.F.T.A. (E)*
97.06 Appliances, apparatus, accessories and requisites for gymnastics or athletics, or for sports and outdoor games (other than articles falling within heading No. 97.04):		
(A) Wooden golf club head blocks roughly shaped by sawing but not further manufactured	5%	—
(B) Rackets, exceeding 255 grammes in weight	£0·2500 per racket or 20%, whichever is the greater	—
(C) Unstrung racket frames	£0·1500 per frame or 20%, whichever is the greater	—
(D) Other	20%	—
97.07 Fish-hooks, line fishing rods and tackle; fish landing nets and butterfly nets; decoy " birds " and similar lures:		
(A) Fishing rods of iron or steel	7·5%	—
(B) Other	15%	—
97.08 Roundabouts, swings, shooting galleries and other fairground amusements; travelling circuses, travelling menageries and travelling theatres	12·5%	—

Chapter 98

Miscellaneous Manufactured Articles

Notes

1. This Chapter does not cover:

(*a*) Eyebrow and other cosmetic pencils (heading No. 33.06);

(*b*) Buttons, studs, cuff-links or other articles of a kind described in heading No. 98.01 or 98.12, if made wholly or partly of precious metal or rolled precious metal (subject to the provisions of Note 2 (*a*) to Chapter 71) or if containing pearls or precious or semi-precious stones (natural, synthetic or reconstructed) (Chapter 71);

(*c*) Parts of general use, as defined in Note 2 to Section XV, of base metal (Section XV), or similar goods of artificial plastic materials (which are generally classified in heading No. 39.07);

(*d*) Mathematical drawing pens (heading No. 90.16); or

(*e*) Toys falling within Chapter 97.

2. Subject to Note 1 above, the headings in this Chapter are to be taken to apply to goods of the kind described whether or not composed wholly or partly of precious metal or rolled precious metal or of pearls or precious or semi-precious stones (natural, synthetic or reconstructed).

3. Cases, boxes and similar containers imported with articles of this Chapter are to be classified with such articles if they are of a kind normally sold therewith. Cases, boxes and similar containers imported separately are to be classified under their appropriate headings.

Tariff Heading	*Rate of Import Duty (if any)*	
	Full	*Commonwealth (C)* *E.F.T.A. (E)*
98.01 Buttons and button moulds, studs, cuff-links, and press-fasteners, including snap-fasteners and press-studs; blanks and parts of such articles:		
(A) Buttons and button moulds, and parts and blanks thereof	25%	—
(B) Cuff-links and parts and blanks thereof:		
(1) Decorative glass smallwares, unmounted	—	—
(2) Decorative plastic smallwares, unmounted	10%	—
(3) Other	12·5%	—
(C) Other	7·5%	—
98.02 Slide fasteners and parts thereof:		
(A) Slide fasteners	£0·0250 per dozen plus, for any length in excess of 2½ inches, £0·0050 per dozen for each inch or part of an inch of such excess	—

Tariff Heading	Rate of Import Duty (if any)	
	Full	Commonwealth (C) E.F.T.A. (E)
98.02 Slide fasteners, etc.—*contd.*		
(B) Parts of slide fasteners:		
(1) Metal chain scoops mounted on tape or other material	£0·0025 per foot length of single tape or 10%, whichever is the greater	—
(2) Unmounted metal chain scoops and all other metal components	£0·0750 per lb. or 10%, whichever is the greater	—
(3) Other	5%	—
98.03 Fountain pens, stylograph pens and pencils (including ball point pens and pencils) and other pens, pen-holders, pencil-holders and similar holders, propelling pencils and sliding pencils; parts and fittings thereof, other than those falling within heading No. 98.04 or 98.05	10%	—
98.04 Pen nibs and nib points	7·5%	—
98.05 Pencils (other than pencils of heading No. 98.03), pencil leads, slate pencils, crayons and pastels, drawing charcoals and writing and drawing chalks; tailors' and billiards chalks:		
(A) Pencil leads and tailors' chalks ...	5%	—
(B) Other	10%	—
98.06 Slates and boards, with writing or drawing surfaces, whether framed or not	10%	—
98.07 Date, sealing or numbering stamps, and the like (including devices for printing or embossing labels), designed for operating in the hand; hand-operated composing sticks and hand printing sets incorporating such composing sticks:		
(A) Hand-operated daters and numberers with metal figures over 6 millimetres in height, and self-inking hand-operated daters and numberers with rubber letters or figures	6%	—
(B) Devices for making labels by printing or embossing, otherwise than by stamping the whole legend simultaneously	7%	—
(C) Other	10%	—

Tariff Heading	Rate of Import Duty (if any)	
	Full	Commonwealth (C) E.F.T.A. (E)
98.08 Typewriter and similar ribbons, whether or not on spools; ink-pads, with or without boxes	10%	—
98.09 Sealing wax (including bottle-sealing wax) in sticks, cakes or similar forms; copying pastes with a basis of gelatin, whether or not on a paper or textile backing	10%	—
98.10 Mechanical lighters and similar lighters, including chemical and electrical lighters, and parts thereof, excluding flints and wicks:		
(A) Portable lighters, being portable mechanical, chemical, electrical or similar contrivances intended to provide a means of ignition, whether by spark, flame or otherwise, and parts thereof:		
(1) Portable lighters constructed solely for the purpose of igniting gas for domestic use, whether complete or incomplete (including stems of electrical lighters and rigid or spring frames of flint lighters)	—	—
(2) Other portable lighters, complete or incomplete (including bodies)	—	—
(3) Parts not specified above ...	10%	—
(B) Other lighters and parts thereof ...	10%	—
98.11 Smoking pipes; pipe bowls, stems and other parts of smoking pipes (including roughly shaped blocks of wood or root); cigar and cigarette holders and parts thereof:		
(A) Briar root blocks, roughly shaped by sawing but not further manufactured; briar pipe bowls, with stem either undrilled or drilled to a bore of 4 millimetres or less	—	—
(B) Other	8%	—
98.12 Combs, hair-slides and the like	10%	—
98.13 Corset busks and similar supports for articles of apparel or clothing accessories	10%	—
98.14 Scent and similar sprays of a kind used for toilet purposes, and mounts and heads therefor:		
(A) Of glass, or containing precious metal (not including base metal rolled, coated or plated with precious metal)	15%	—
(B) Other	10%	—

Tariff Heading	Rate of Import Duty (if any)	
	Full	Commonwealth (C) E.F.T.A. (E)
98.15 Vacuum flasks and other vacuum vessels, complete with cases; parts thereof, other than glass inners	15%	—
98.16 Tailors' dummies and other lay figures; automata and other animated displays of a kind used for shop window dressing	8%	—

SECTION XXI

Works of Art, Collectors' Pieces, and Antiques

Chapter 99

Works of Art, Collectors' Pieces, and Antiques

Notes

1. This Chapter does not cover:

(*a*) Unused postage, revenue or similar stamps of current or new issue in the country to which they are destined (heading No. 49.07);

(*b*) Theatrical scenery, studio back-cloths or the like, of painted canvas (heading No. 59.12); or

(*c*) Pearls or precious or semi-precious stones (heading No. 71.01 or 71.02).

2. For the purposes of heading No. 99.02, the expression " original engravings, prints and lithographs " means impressions produced directly, in black and white or in colour, of one or of several plates wholly executed by hand by the artist, irrespective of the process or of the material employed by him, but not including any mechanical or photo-mechanical process.

3. Heading No. 99.03 is to be taken not to apply to mass-produced reproductions or works of conventional craftsmanship of a commercial character.

4. (*a*) Subject to Notes 1 to 3 above, articles falling within headings of this Chapter are to be classified in whichever of those headings is appropriate and not in any other heading o this Schedule.

(*b*) Heading No. 99.06 is to be taken not to apply to articles falling within any of the preceding headings of this Chapter.

5. Frames around paintings, drawings, pastels, engravings, prints or lithographs are to be treated as forming part of those articles, provided they are of a kind and of a value normal to those articles.

Tariff Heading	*Rate of Import Duty (if any)*	
	Full	*Commonwealth (C)* *E.F.T.A. (E)*
99.01 Paintings, drawings and pastels, executed entirely by hand (other than industrial drawings falling within heading No. 49.06 and other than hand-painted or hand-decorated manufactured articles)	—	—
99.02 Original engravings, prints and lithographs:		
(A) Of an age exceeding 100 years ...	—	—
(B) Other	10%	—

Tariff Heading	*Rate of Import Duty (if any)*	
	Full	*Commonwealth (C)* *E.F.T.A. (E)*
99.03 Original sculptures and statuary, in any material:		
(A) Of an age exceeding 100 years ...	—	—
(B) Other	10%	—
99.04 Postage, revenue and similar stamps (including stamp-postmarks and franked envelopes, letter-cards and the like), used, or if unused not of current or new issue in the country to which they are destined	—	—
99.05 Collections and collectors' pieces of zoological, botanical, mineralogical, anatomical, historical, archaeological, paleontological, ethnographic or numismatic interest	—	—
99.06 Antiques of an age exceeding one hundred years	—	—

LIST OF SECTION AND CHAPTER TITLES

Section I

Live Animals; Animal Products

Chapter

1 Live animals.
2 Meat and edible meat offals.
3 Fish, crustaceans and molluscs.
4 Dairy produce; birds' eggs; natural honey; edible products of animal origin, not elsewhere specified or included.
5 Products of animal origin, not elsewhere specified or included.

Section II

Vegetable Products

6 Live trees and other plants; bulbs, roots and the like; cut flowers and ornamental foliage.
7 Edible vegetables and certain roots and tubers.
8 Edible fruit and nuts; peel of melons or citrus fruit.
9 Coffee, tea, maté and spices.
10 Cereals.
11 Products of the milling industry; malt and starches; gluten; inulin.
12 Oil seeds and oleaginous fruit; miscellaneous grains, seeds and fruit; industrial and medical plants; straw and fodder.
13 Raw vegetable materials of a kind suitable for use in dyeing or in tanning; lacs; gums, resins and other vegetable saps and extracts.
14 Vegetable plaiting and carving materials; vegetable products not elsewhere specified or included.

Section III

Animal and Vegetable Fats and Oils and their Cleavage Products; Prepared Edible Fats; Animal and Vegetable Waxes

15 Animal and vegetable fats and oils and their cleavage products; prepared edible fats; animal and vegetable waxes.

Section IV

Prepared Foodstuffs; Beverages, Spirits and Vinegar; Tobacco

16 Preparations of meat, of fish, of crustaceans or molluscs.
17 Sugars and sugar confectionery.
18 Cocoa and cocoa preparations.
19 Preparations of cereals, flour or starch; pastrycooks' products.
20 Preparations of vegetables, fruit or other parts of plants.
21 Miscellaneous edible preparations.
22 Beverages, spirits and vinegar.
23 Residues and waste from the food industries; prepared animal fodder.
24 Tobacco.

Section V

Mineral Products

25 Salt; sulphur; earths and stone; plastering materials, lime and cement.
26 Metallic ores, slag and ash.
27 Mineral fuels, mineral oils and products of their distillation; bituminous substances mineral waxes.

Section VI

Products of the Chemical and Allied Industries

Chapter

28 Inorganic chemicals; organic and inorganic compounds of precious metals, of rare earth metals, of radio-active elements and of isotopes.
29 Organic chemicals.
30 Pharmaceutical products.
31 Fertilisers.
32 Tanning and dyeing extracts; tannins and their derivatives; dyes, colours, paints and varnishes; putty, fillers and stoppings; inks.
33 Essential oils and resinoids; perfumery, cosmetics and toilet preparations.
34 Soap, organic surface-active agents, washing preparations, lubricating preparations, artificial waxes, prepared waxes, polishing and scouring preparations, candles and similar articles, modelling pastes and " dental waxes ".
35 Albuminoidal substances; glues.
36 Explosives; pyrotechnic products; matches; pyrophoric alloys; certain combustible preparations.
37 Photographic and cinematographic goods.
38 Miscellaneous chemical products.

Section VII

Artificial Resins and Plastic Materials, Cellulose Esters and Ethers, and Articles thereof; Rubber, Synthetic Rubber, Factice, and Articles thereof

39 Artificial resins and plastic materials, cellulose esters and ethers; articles thereof.
40 Rubber, synthetic rubber, factice, and articles thereof.

Section VIII

Raw Hides and Skins, Leather, Furskins and Articles thereof; Saddlery and Harness; Travel Goods, Handbags and Similar Containers; Articles of Gut (other than Silk-Worm Gut)

41 Raw hides and skins (other than furskins) and leather.
42 Articles of leather; saddlery and harness; travel goods, handbags and similar containers; articles of animal gut (other than silk-worm gut).
43 Furskins and artificial fur; manufactures thereof.

Section IX

Wood and Articles of Wood; Wood Charcoal; Cork and Articles of Cork; Manufactures of Straw, of Esparto and of other Plaiting Materials; Basketware and Wickerwork

44 Wood and articles of wood; wood charcoal.
45 Cork and articles of cork.
46 Manufactures of straw, of esparto and of other plaiting materials; basketware and wickerwork.

Section X

Paper-Making Material; Paper and Paperboard and Articles thereof

47 Paper-making material.
48 Paper and paperboard; articles of paper pulp, of paper or of paperboard.
49 Printed books, newspapers, pictures and other products of the printing industry; manuscripts, typescripts and plans.

Section XI

Textiles and Textile Articles

Chapter

50 Silk and waste silk.
51 Man-made fibres (continuous).
52 Metallised textiles.
53 Wool and other animal hair.
54 Flax and ramie.
55 Cotton.
56 Man-made fibres (discontinuous).
57 Other vegetable textile materials; paper yarn and woven fabrics of paper yarn.
58 Carpets, mats, matting and tapestries; pile and chenille fabrics; narrow fabrics; trimmings; tulle and other net fabrics; lace; embroidery.
59 Wadding and felt; twine, cordage, ropes and cables; special fabrics; impregnated and coated fabrics; textile articles of a kind suitable for industrial use.
60 Knitted and crocheted goods.
61 Articles of apparel and clothing accessories of textile fabric, other than knitted or crocheted goods.
62 Other made up textile articles.
63 Old clothing and other textile articles; rags.

Section XII

Footwear, Headgear, Umbrellas, Sunshades, Whips, Riding-crops and Parts thereof; Prepared Feathers and Articles made therewith; Artificial Flowers; Articles of Human Hair; Fans

64 Footwear, gaiters and the like; parts of such articles.
65 Headgear and parts thereof.
66 Umbrellas, sunshades, walking-sticks, whips, riding-crops and parts thereof.
67 Prepared feathers and down and articles made of feathers or of down; artificial flowers; articles of human hair; fans.

Section XIII

Articles of Stone, of Plaster, of Cement, of Asbestos, of Mica and of Similar Materials; Ceramic Products; Glass and Glassware

68 Articles of stone, of plaster, of cement, of asbestos, of mica and of similar materials.
69 Ceramic products.
70 Glass and glassware.

Section XIV

Pearls, Precious and Semi-Precious Stones, Precious Metals, Rolled Precious Metals, and Articles thereof; Imitation Jewellery; Coin

71 Pearls, precious and semi-precious stones, precious metals, rolled precious metals, and articles thereof; imitation jewellery.
72 Coin.

Section XV

Base Metals and Articles of Base Metal

73 Iron and steel and articles thereof.
74 Copper and articles thereof.
75 Nickel and articles thereof.
76 Aluminium and articles thereof.
77 Magnesium and beryllium and articles thereof.
78 Lead and articles thereof.
79 Zinc and articles thereof.
80 Tin and articles thereof.
81 Other base metals employed in metallurgy and articles thereof.
82 Tools, implements, cutlery, spoons and forks, of base metal; parts thereof.
83 Miscellaneous articles of base metal.

Section XVI

Machinery and Mechanical Appliances; Electrical Equipment; Parts thereof

Chapter

84 Boilers, machinery and mechanical appliances; parts thereof.
85 Electrical machinery and equipment; parts thereof.

Section XVII

Vehicles, Aircraft, and Parts thereof; Vessels and certain associated Transport Equipment

86 Railway and tramway locomotives, rolling-stock and parts thereof; railway and tramway track fixtures and fittings; traffic signalling equipment of all kinds (not electrically powered).
87 Vehicles, other than railway or tramway rolling-stock, and parts thereof.
88 Aircraft and parts thereof; parachutes; catapults and similar aircraft launching gear; ground flying trainers.
89 Ships, boats and floating structures.

Section XVIII

Optical, Photographic, Cinematographic, Measuring, Checking, Precision, Medical and Surgical Instruments and Apparatus; Clocks and Watches; Musical Instruments; Sound Recorders and Reproducers; Television Image and Sound Recorders and Reproducers, Magnetic; Parts thereof

90 Optical, photographic, cinematographic, measuring, checking, precision, medical and surgical instruments and apparatus; parts thereof.
91 Clocks and watches and parts thereof.
92 Musical instruments; sound recorders and reproducers; television image and sound recorders and reproducers, magnetic; parts and accessories of such articles.

Section XIX

Arms and Ammunition; Parts thereof

93 Arms and ammunition; parts thereof.

Section XX

Miscellaneous Manufactured Articles

94 Furniture and parts thereof; bedding, mattresses, mattress supports, cushions and similar stuffed furnishings.
95 Articles and manufactures of carving or moulding material.
96 Brooms, brushes, feather dusters, powder-puffs and sieves.
97 Toys, games and sports requisites; parts thereof.
98 Miscellaneous manufactured articles.

Section XXI

Works of Art, Collectors' Pieces, and Antiques

99 Works of art, collectors' pieces, and antiques.

SCHEDULE 2

Import Duties (General) Orders Revoked

Number and Year of Order	*Reference*
No. 7 of 1970	S.I. 1970/1522 (1970 III, p. 4935).
No. 1 of 1971	S.I. 1971/115 (1971 I, p. 209).
No. 2 of 1971	S.I. 1971/272 (1971 I, p. 934).
No. 3 of 1971	S.I. 1971/851 (1971 II, p. 2458)
No. 4 of 1971	S.I. 1971/858 (1971 II, p. 2478).
No. 5 of 1971	S.I. 1971/1056 (1971 II, p. 3145).
No. 6 of 1971	S.I. 1971/1387 (1971 II, p. 3901).

EXPLANATORY NOTE

(This Note is not part of the Order.)

This Order, which comes into operation on 1st January 1972—

(1) consolidates the Import Duties (General) (No. 7) Order 1970 and the Orders amending it,

(2) completes the process begun by the Import Duties (General) (No. 4) Order 1968 and continued in subsequent Orders, in that it again reduces, as the fourth and last of a series of reductions, the full rate of import duty (and, where applicable the Commonwealth preference rate) on a wide range of goods in accordance with the undertakings given by the United Kingdom at Geneva and set out in the June 1967 Protocol to the General Agreement on Tariffs and Trade (the Kennedy Round; Cmnd. 3347),

(3) effects some further simplifications of the tariff by again reducing the number of sub-divisions in certain headings and entirely eliminating those in others where previously differing rates of duty have been brought to the same level as a result of the reductions referred to in (2) above,

(4) imposes new duties, generally at the rate of 85 per cent. of the full rates, on imports of certain cotton textiles (as defined in the Order) from countries in the Commonwealth Preference Area other than the Republic of Ireland,

(5) provides in some descriptions and rates of duty for a change to metric units where consultation has shown their use to be desired by the industries concerned,

(6) adapts the text of certain chapter notes and headings to take account of the consolidation of the law relating to the hydrocarbon oil duty in the Hydrocarbon Oil (Customs and Excise) Act 1971 (c. 12),

(7) effects minor alterations to the tariff, including modifications in certain headings to facilitate implementation of the provisions of section 1 of the Finance Act 1971 (c. 68) introducing the Generalised System of Preferences and

(8) incorporates amendments to tariff headings, section and chapter notes and the interpretative rules to give effect to a Recommendation of the Customs Co-operation Council designed to bring the Brussels Nomenclature (on which the United Kingdom Tariff is based) abreast of various technological developments and in other respects to improve its texts.

These amendments are too numerous to explain in detail in this Note but they include, for example, new and specific provisions for the classification of computers (Chapter 84), printed circuits and microcircuits (Chapter 85), air-cushion vehicles (Chapters 86, 87, 89) and new-type watch movements (Chapter 91). They also introduce, to mention two further examples, criteria for distinguishing between various products of the cereal milling industry (Chapter 11) and for classifying goods in which textiles and artificial plastic materials are combined (Chapter 59).

Some of the amendments transfer goods to headings bearing a different rate of duty. Where such transfers involve goods of known trade importance new subheadings have been raised to preserve the rate which, but for the amendment, would apply. The amendment of Note 4 to Chapter 31, by deletion of the reference to arsenic content, will, for example, result in certain ammonium phosphates, at present classified in heading 28.40 with rates of duty of 23 per cent. and 9 per cent., being transferred to heading 31.05. New subheadings have therefore been raised in heading 31.05 to preserve these rates.

1971 No. 1972

CIVIL AVIATION

The Rules of the Air and Air Traffic Control (Third Amendment) Regulations 1971

Made - - - - *3rd December* 1971

Coming into Operation *6th January* 1972

The Secretary of State in exercise of his powers under Article 60(1) of the Air Navigation Order 1970(**a**), as amended(**b**), and of all other powers enabling him in that behalf, hereby makes the following Regulations.

1. These Regulations may be cited as the Rules of the Air and Air Traffic Control (Third Amendment) Regulations 1971 and shall come into operation on 6th January 1972.

2. The Interpretation Act 1889(**c**) applies for the purpose of the interpretation of these Regulations as it applies for the purpose of the interpretation of an Act of Parliament.

3. The Schedule to the Rules of the Air and Air Traffic Control Regulations 1970(**d**), as amended(**e**), shall be further amended as follows:—

For Rule 16 (excluding the proviso) there shall be substituted:

"16. Every aircraft (not being a glider or a helicopter) when flying within such airspace as may be notified for the purposes of this Rule shall be provided with radio apparatus of a design approved by the Secretary of State capable of replying to an interrogation from secondary surveillance radar units on the surface and set in accordance with such instructions as may be given to the aircraft by the appropriate air traffic control unit:".

D. F. Hubback,
A Deputy Secretary,
Department of Trade and Industry.

3rd December 1971.

(**a**) S.I. 1970/954 (1970 II, p. 2964).
(**b**) There is no relevant amending instrument.
(**c**) 1889 c. 63.
(**d**) S.I. 1970/1082 (1970 II, p. 3366).
(**e**) The relevant amending instrument is S.I. 1970/1448 (1970 III, p. 4748).

EXPLANATORY NOTE

(*This Note is not part of the Regulations.*)

These Regulations further amend the Schedule to the Rules of the Air and Air Traffic Control Regulations 1970, as amended, by extending to the airspace below flight level 250 the requirement that aircraft should carry secondary surveillance radar transponders. The exception which previously applied only to gliders is now extended to helicopters.

1971 No. 1974

CUSTOMS AND EXCISE

The Customs Duty (Personal Reliefs) (No. 4) Order 1968 (Amendment) Order 1971

Made - - -	*3rd December* 1971
Laid before the House of Commons	*10th December* 1971
Coming into Operation	*1st January* 1972

The Commissioners of Customs and Excise in exercise of the powers conferred on them by section 7 of the Finance Act 1968(**a**) and of all other powers enabling them in that behalf, hereby make the following Order—

1. This Order may be cited as the Customs Duty (Personal Reliefs) (No. 4) Order 1968 (Amendment) Order 1971 and shall come into operation on the 1st day of January 1972.

2. The Interpretation Act 1889(**b**) applies for the interpretation of this Order as it applies for the interpretation of an Act of Parliament.

3. The Customs Duty (Personal Reliefs) (No. 4) Order 1968(**c**) shall be amended—

(*a*) to add after paragraph 1(1)(*a*)(ii)—

"(iii) goods which are relieved wholly or partly from duty by Orders made under section 1 of the Finance Act 1971(**d**) or which would be so relieved if consigned to the United Kingdom from a place specified in such Orders ; and"

(*b*) to add after paragraph 2(*c*)— " ; or
(*d*) relief under section 1 of the Finance Act 1971" and

(*c*) to add at the end of paragraph 2 after the words "Republic of Ireland" and before the words "as the case may be" the words—"or a designated place under section 1 of the Finance Act 1971".

Dated this 3rd day of December 1971.

C. H. Blake,
Commissioner of Customs and Excise.

King's Beam House,
Mark Lane,
London, EC3R 7HE.

(**a**) 1968 c. 44.
(**b**) 1889 c. 63.
(**c**) S.I. 1968/1561 (1968 III, p. 4349).
(**d**) 1971 c. 68.

EXPLANATORY NOTE

(This Note is not part of the Order.)

By Orders made under section 1 of the Finance Act 1971 goods which originate in certain designated countries may be relieved wholly or partly from Customs duty. This Order waives, in respect of personal effects originating in the designated countries and imported in baggage, the normal rule whereby the preferential rate of duty can be claimed only if the goods concerned are consigned direct from the designated country. It also accords to such effects the simplified assessment of customs charges accorded to other effects eligible for preferential rates of Customs duty.

1971 No. 1975

JUSTICES OF THE PEACE

The Justices' Allowances (Amendment) Regulations 1971

Made - - -	*3rd December* 1971
Laid before Parliament	*13th December* 1971
Coming into Operation	*1st January* 1972

In exercise of the powers conferred upon me by section 8(6) and (7) of the Justices of the Peace Act 1949(**a**) as extended by section 4 of the Justices of the Peace Act 1968(**b**), I hereby make the following Regulations :—

1. These Regulations may be cited as the Justices' Allowances (Amendment) Regulations 1971 and shall come into operation on 1st January 1972.

2. Regulation 5 of the Justices' Allowances Regulations 1971(**c**) shall be amended by the substitution of the words "£2·375" and "£4·75" for the words "£2·00" and "£4·00" respectively.

R. Maudling,
One of Her Majesty's Principal
Secretaries of State.

Home Office,
Whitehall.
3rd December 1971.

EXPLANATORY NOTE

(*This Note is not part of the Regulations.*)

These Regulations increase the minimum rates of financial loss allowances payable to justices of the peace. The new minimum rates are £4·75, if the time involved exceeds 4 hours in a 24 hour period, and £2·375 in other cases.

(**a**) 1949 c. 101. (**b**) 1968 c. 69.
(**c**) S.I. 1971/413 (1971 I, p. 1217).

STATUTORY INSTRUMENTS

1971 No. 1976

PROBATION AND AFTER-CARE

The Probation (Allowances) (Amendment) Rules 1971

Made - - -	*3rd December* 1971
Coming into Operation	*1st January* 1972

In exercise of the powers conferred upon me by Schedule 5 to the Criminal Justice Act 1948(**a**), as extended by section 36 of the Justices of the Peace Act 1949(**b**) (as amended by section 4 of the Justices of the Peace Act 1968(**c**)), I hereby make the following Rules:—

1. These Rules may be cited as the Probation (Allowances) (Amendment) Rules 1971 and shall come into operation on 1st January 1972.

2. Rule 5 of the Probation (Allowances) Rules 1971(**d**) shall be amended by the substitution of the words "£2·375" and "£4·75" for the words "£2·00" and "£4·00" respectively.

R. Maudling,
One of Her Majesty's Principal
Secretaries of State.

Home Office,
Whitehall.

3rd December 1971.

EXPLANATORY NOTE

(This Note is not part of the Rules.)

These Rules increase the minimum rates of financial loss allowances payable to members of probation and after-care committees and case committees. The new minimum rates are £4·75, if the time involved exceeds 4 hours in a 24 hour period, and £2·375 in other cases.

(**a**) 1948 c. 58.
(**b**) 1949 c. 101.
(**c**) 1968 c. 69.
(**d**) S.I. 1971/414 (1971 I, p. 1225).

1971 No. 1977 (L.45)

SUPREME COURT OF JUDICATURE, ENGLAND

PROCEDURE

The Non-Contentious Probate (Amendment) Rules 1971

Made - - -	6*th December* 1971
Laid before Parliament	13*th December* 1971
Coming into Operation	1*st January* 1972

The President of the Family Division, in exercise of the powers conferred on him by section 2(5) of the Colonial Probates Act 1892(**a**) and section 100 of the Supreme Court of Judicature (Consolidation) Act 1925(**b**), as amended by paragraph 6 of Schedule 2 to the Administration of Justice Act 1970(**c**), and with the concurrence of the Lord Chancellor and the Lord Chief Justice, hereby makes the following Rules :—

1.—(1) These Rules may be cited as the Non-Contentious Probate (Amendment) Rules 1971 and shall come into operation on 1st January 1972.

(2) The Interpretation Act 1889(**d**) shall apply to the interpretation of these Rules as it applies to the interpretation of an Act of Parliament.

(3) The amendments set out in these Rules shall be made to the Non-Contentious Probate Rules 1954(**e**), as amended (**f**).

2. Paragraph (2) of rule 2 (which relates to interpretation) shall be amended as follows :—

(*a*) In the definition of "The President", for the word "Probate" there shall be substituted the word "Family".

(*b*) The definition of "The principal probate registrar" shall be deleted.

(*c*) For the definition of "The principal registry" there shall be substituted the following definition :—

" "The principal registry" means the principal registry of the Family Division".

(*d*) After the definition of "Registry" there shall be inserted the following definition :—

" "The Senior Registrar" means the principal registrar of the Family Division or, in his absence, the senior of the registrars in attendance."

(**a**) 1892 c. 6. (**b**) 1925 c. 49. (**c**) 1970 c. 31.
(**d**) 1889 c. 63. (**e**) S.I. 1954/796 (1954 II, p. 2202).
(**f**) The only relevant amending instruments are S.I. 1961/72, 1967/748, 1969/1689 (1961 I, p. 143; 1967 II, p. 2225; 1969 III, p. 5319).

(*e*) In the definition of "Statutory guardian", for the words "section 4 of the Guardianship of Infants Act 1925" there shall be substituted the words "section 3 of the Guardianship of Minors Act 1971"(**a**).

(*f*) In the definition of "Testamentary guardian", for the words "section 5 of the Guardianship of Infants Act 1925" there shall be substituted the words "section 4 of the Guardianship of Minors Act 1971".

3. In paragraph (7) of rule 4 (which relates to personal applications), for the word "bond" there shall be substituted the word "guarantee" and for the word "obligors" there shall be substituted the word "sureties".

4. In rule 5 (which relates to the duty of the registrar on receiving an application for a grant) there shall be added the following paragraph :—

"(4) The registrar shall not require a guarantee under section 167 of the Act as a condition of granting administration to any person without giving that person or, where the application for the grant is made through a solicitor, the solicitor an opportunity of being heard with respect to the requirement."

5. In rule 6 (which relates to the oath in support of a grant), paragraphs (4) and (5) shall be omitted and there shall be substituted the following paragraph :—

"(4) Unless otherwise directed by a registrar, the oath shall state where the deceased died domiciled."

6. Rule 21 (which relates to the order of priority for a grant on intestacy) shall be amended as follows :—

(*a*) After paragraph (5) there shall be inserted the following new paragraph :—

"(5A) The provisions of the Adoption Act 1958(**b**) shall apply in determining the entitlement to a grant as they apply to the devolution of property on intestacy."

(*b*) In paragraph (6), for the words "legitimated and adopted" there shall be substituted the words "and legitimated".

7. In paragraph (1) of rule 34 (which relates to grants to trust corporations and other corporate bodies), for the words "principal probate registrar" there shall be substituted the words "Senior Registrar."

8. For rule 38 (which relates to administration bonds) there shall be substituted the following rule :—

"*Guarantee*

38.—(1) The registrar shall not require a guarantee under section 167 of the Act as a condition of granting administration except where it is proposed to grant it—

(*a*) by virtue of rule 19(v) or rule 21(4) to a creditor or the personal representative of a creditor or to a person who has no immediate beneficial interest in the estate of the deceased but may have such an interest in the event of an accretion to the estate ;

(*b*) under rule 27 to a person or some of the persons who would, if the person beneficially entitled to the whole of the estate died intestate, be entitled to his estate ;

(**a**) 1971 c. 3. (**b**) 1958 c. 5.

(*c*) under rule 30 to the attorney of a person entitled to a grant;

(*d*) under rule 31 for the use and benefit of a minor;

(*e*) under rule 33 for the use and benefit of a person who is by reason of mental or physical incapacity incapable of managing his affairs;

(*f*) to an applicant who appears to the registrar to be resident elsewhere than in the United Kingdom;

or except where the registrar considers that there are special circumstances making it desirable to require a guarantee.

(2) Notwithstanding that it is proposed to grant administration as aforesaid, a guarantee shall not be required, except in special circumstances, on an application for administration where the applicant or one of the applicants is—

(*a*) a trust corporation;

(*b*) a solicitor holding a current practising certificate under the Solicitors Acts 1957 to 1965(**a**);

(*c*) a servant of the Crown acting in his official capacity;

(*d*) a nominee of a public department or of a local authority within the meaning of the Local Government Act 1933(**b**).

(3) Every guarantee entered into by a surety for the purposes of section 167 of the Act shall be in Form 1.

(4) Except where the surety is a corporation, the signature of the surety on every such guarantee shall be attested by an authorised officer, commissioner for oaths or other person authorised by law to administer an oath.

(5) Unless the registrar otherwise directs—

(*a*) if it is decided to require a guarantee, it shall be given by two sureties, except where the gross value of the estate does not exceed £500 or a corporation is a proposed surety, and in those cases one will suffice;

(*b*) no person shall be accepted as a surety unless he is resident in the United Kingdom;

(*c*) no officer of a registry or sub-registry shall become a surety;

(*d*) the limit of the liability of the surety or sureties under a guarantee given for the purposes of section 167 of the Act shall be the gross amount of the estate as sworn on the application for the grant;

(*e*) every surety, other than a corporation, shall justify.

(6) Where the proposed surety is a corporation there shall be filed an affidavit by the proper officer of the corporation to the effect that it has power to act as surety and has executed the guarantee in the manner prescribed by its constitution, and containing sufficient information as to the financial position of the corporation to satisfy the registrar that its assets are sufficient to satisfy all claims which may be made against it under any guarantee which it has given or is likely to give for the purposes of section 167 of the Act:

Provided that the Senior Registrar may, instead of requiring an affidavit in every case, accept an affidavit made not less often than once in every

(**a**) 1957 c. 27; 1959 c. 42; 1965 c. 31. (**b**) 1933 c. 51.

year together with an undertaking by the corporation to notify the Senior Registrar forthwith in the event of any alteration in its constitution affecting its power to become surety under that section."

9. Rule 39 (particulars of estate to be filed and sureties to justify in certain cases) is hereby revoked.

10. Rule 40 (which relates to the resealing of Scottish confirmations and Northern Irish grants, etc.) is hereby revoked.

11. In paragraph (2) of rule 41 (which relates to resealing under the Colonial Probates Acts 1892 and 1927(**a**)), sub-paragraph (*c*) and the proviso are hereby revoked, and after paragraph (2) there shall be inserted the following paragraph :—

"(2A) On an application for the resealing of a grant of administration—

(*a*) the registrar shall not require sureties under section 11 of the Administration of Estates Act 1971(**b**) as a condition of resealing the grant except where it appears to him that the grant is made to a person or for a purpose mentioned in paragraphs (*a*) to (*f*) of rule 38(1) or except where he considers that there are special circumstances making it desirable to require sureties ;

(*b*) rules 5(4) and 38(2), (4), (5) and (6) shall apply with any necessary modifications ; and

(*c*) a guarantee entered into by a surety for the purposes of the said section 11 shall be in Form 2."

12. After rule 41 there shall be inserted the following rule :—

"*Application for leave to sue on guarantee*

41A. An application for leave under section 167(3) of the Act or under section 11(5) of the Administration of Estates Act 1971 to sue a surety on a guarantee given for the purposes of either of those sections shall, unless the registrar otherwise directs under rule 60, be made by summons to a registrar of the principal registry, and notice of the application shall in any event be served on the administrator, the surety and any co-surety."

13. Rule 44 (which relates to the entry of caveats) shall be amended as follows :—

(*a*) In paragraph (5), for the words "principal probate registrar" there shall be substituted the words "Senior Registrar."

(*b*) In paragraph (14), the words "a Scottish confirmation and" shall be deleted.

14. In paragraph (2) of rule 47 (which relates to citation to propound a will), for the words "on motion" there shall be substituted the words "by summons to a registrar of the principal registry".

15. In paragraph (1) of rule 49 (which relates to an application for an order to bring in a will or to attend for examination), for the words "may be made" to the end of the paragraph there shall be substituted the words "may, unless a probate action has been commenced, be made to a registrar of the principal registry by summons, which shall be served on every such person as aforesaid."

(**a**) 1892 c. 6; 1927 c. 43. (**b**) 1971 c. 25.

16. In paragraph (1) of rule 56 (which relates to notice of election by a surviving spouse to redeem a life interest), for the words "principal probate registrar" there shall be substituted the words "Senior Registrar".

17. In the First Schedule (which relates to Forms), for Forms 1 and 2 there shall be substituted the Forms so numbered in the Schedule to these Rules.

18. The following amendments shall be made to Forms 3, 4, 5, 6 and 7 in the First Schedule :—

(*a*) In Form 3, for the words "Great Britain" there shall be substituted the words "the United Kingdom".

(*b*) In marginal note (3) to Form 4, for the words "Name(s) of party or parties" there shall be substituted the words "Name of party".

(*c*) In Forms 4, 5, 6 and 7, for the words "Probate, Divorce and Admiralty Division" there shall be substituted the words "Family Division" ; and from the words "Principal Probate Registry" and "Probate Registry" wherever they appear, the word "Probate" shall be deleted.

(*d*) At the foot of Form 7, for the words "Principal Probate Registrar" there shall be substituted the words "Principal Registrar of the Family Division".

Dated 6th December 1971.

George Baker, P.

We concur,

Dated 6th December 1971.

Hailsham of St. Marylebone, C.

Dated 6th December 1971.

Widgery, C. J.

SCHEDULE

FORM 1

SURETY'S GUARANTEE

In the High Court of Justice
Family Division

The (1)Registry

In the Estate of (2)deceased

Whereas (2) of (3)

died on the day of 19

and [and](4)

(hereinafter called "the administrator(s)") is/are(5) the intended administrator(s) of his estate.

Now Therefore:

1. I/We(5) of

[and of](6)

hereby [jointly and severally](7) guarantee that I/we(5) will, when lawfully required to do so(8) make good any loss which any person interested in the administration of the estate of the deceased may suffer in consequence of the breach by the administrator(s) of his/her/their(5) duty—

(a) to collect and get in the estate of the deceased and administer it according to law;

(b) when required to do so by the court, to exhibit on oath in the court a full inventory of the estate and, when so required, to render an account of the estate; or

(c) when so required by the court, to deliver up the grant to the court.

2. The giving of time to the administrator(s) or any other forbearance or indulgence shall not in any way affect my/our(5) liability under this guarantee.

3. The liability under this guarantee shall be continuing and shall be for the whole amount of the loss mentioned in paragraph 1 above, but [my] [our aggregate] total liability shall not in any event exceed the sum of £ .(9)

Dated this day of 19 .

Signed, sealed and delivered by the above named

in the presence of

Commissioner for Oaths.
[or *other person authorised by law to administer an oath*](10)

[The Common Seal of
was hereunto affixed in the presence of].

(1) Insert "Principal" or ". . . . District Probate" (stating name).

(2) Full name of deceased.

(3) Address of deceased.

(4) Full name(s) and address(es) and description(s) of proposed administrator(s).

(5) Delete whichever is inapplicable.

(6) Full name(s), address(es) and description(s) of suret(y)(ies).

(7) Delete if only one surety.

(8) An action on the guarantee may only be brought with the leave of the court.

(9) Insert gross value of estate (unless a Registrar has directed otherwise).

(10) Attestation is not required in the case of a corporation.

FORM 2

SURETY'S GUARANTEE
ON APPLICATION FOR RESEALING UNDER
COLONIAL PROBATES ACTS 1892 AND 1927

In the High Court of Justice
Family Division
The Principal Registry

(1) Full name of deceased.

In the Estate of (1) deceased

(2) Address of deceased.

Whereas (1) of (2)

died on the day of 19

and letters of administration of his estate were on the

(3) Description of court by which grant was issued.

day of 19 granted by the (3)

to

[and

(4) Full name(s) and address(es) and description(s) of administrator(s).

](4) and are about to be sealed in England and Wales under the Colonial Probates Acts 1892 and 1927.

Now Therefore:

(5) Delete whichever is inapplicable.

1. I/We(5) of

[and

(6) Full name(s), address(es) and description(s) of suret(y)(ies).

of](6)

(7) Delete if only one surety.

(8) An action on the guarantee may only be brought with the leave of the court.

hereby [jointly and severally](7) guarantee that I/we(5) will, when lawfully required to do so(8), make good any loss which any person interested in the administration of the estate of the deceased in England and Wales may suffer in consequence of the breach by the administrator(s) of his/her/their(5) duty—

(*a*) to collect and get in the estate of the deceased which is situated in England and Wales and administer it according to law;

(*b*) when required to do so by the court, to exhibit on oath in the court a full inventory of the estate which is situated in England and Wales and, when so required, to render an account of that estate.

2. The giving of time to the administrator(s) or any other forbearance or indulgence shall not in any way affect my/our(5) liability under this guarantee.

3. The liability under this guarantee shall be continuing and shall be for the whole amount of the loss mentioned in paragraph 1 above, but [my] [our aggregate] total liability shall not in any event exceed the sum of £ .(9)

(9) Insert gross value of estate in England and Wales (unless a Registrar has directed otherwise).

Dated this day of 19

Signed, sealed and delivered by the above named

in the presence of

a Commissioner for Oaths.
[*or other person authorised by law to administer an oath*](10)

(10) Attestation is not required in the case of a coporation.

[The Common Seal of
was hereunto affixed in the presence of]

EXPLANATORY NOTE

(*This Note is not part of the Rules.*)

These Rules make amendments to the Non-Contentious Probate Rules 1954 most of which are required on the coming into force on 1st January 1972 of the Administration of Estates Act 1971. That Act abolishes the resealing of grants of probate and letters of administration as between the courts of the United Kingdom, and does away with the need for administration bonds under the law of England and Wales, although in certain cases specified in the Rules a guarantee may be required.

In addition, amendments are made to rules 47 and 49 which provide that certain applications at present made to a judge may in future be made to a registrar of the principal registry. A number of minor drafting amendments are consequential on the redistribution of business in the High Court and the creation of the Family Division under section 1 of the Administration of Justice Act 1970 which came into operation on the 1st October 1971.

These Rules come into force on 1st January 1972.

1971 No. 1979

ROAD TRAFFIC

The Motor Vehicles (Minimum Age for Driving) (Motor Cycles) Regulations 1971

Made - - -	6*th December* 1971
Laid before Parliament	15*th December* 1971
Coming into Operation	16*th December* 1971

The Secretary of State for the Environment, in exercise of his powers under section 97(2) of the Road Traffic Act 1960**(a)** as amended by section 1 of the Road Traffic (Driving of Motor Cycles) Act 1960**(b)** and of all other enabling powers, and after consultation with representative organisations in accordance with section 260(2) of the Road Traffic Act of 1960, hereby makes the following Regulations:—

1.—(1) These Regulations shall come into operation on 16th December 1971, and may be cited as the Motor Vehicles (Minimum Age for Driving) (Motor Cycles) Regulations 1971.

(2) The Interpretation Act 1889**(c)** shall apply for the interpretation of these Regulations as it applies for the interpretation of an Act of Parliament.

2.—(1) The table in section 97(1) of the Road Traffic Act 1960 (which specifies the minimum age for driving certain classes or descriptions of motor vehicles) shall have effect as if it specified the age of 17 (instead of the age of 16) in relation to all motor cycles other than—

(a) motor cycles whereof the cylinder capacity of the engine does not exceed 50 cubic centimetres, being cycles equipped with pedals by means whereof they are capable of being propelled,

(b) motor cycles being mowing machines, or

(c) motor cycles being vehicles controlled by a pedestrian.

(2) In this Regulation "controlled by a pedestrian" means that the vehicle either—

(a) is constructed or adapted for use only under such control, or

(b) is constructed or adapted for use either under such control or under the control of a person carried on it but is not for the time being in use under, or proceeding under, the control of a person carried on it.

Signed by authority of the Secretary of State.

John Peyton,
Minister for Transport Industries,
Department of the Environment.

6th December 1971.

(a) 1960 c. 16. **(b)** 1960 c. 69. **(c)** 1889 c. 63.

EXPLANATORY NOTE

(*This Note is not part of the Regulations.*)

These Regulations amend section 97 of the Road Traffic Act 1960 (which specifies the minimum age for driving certain vehicles) so as to raise from 16 to 17 the minimum age for driving motor cycles (other than those having an engine capacity not exceeding 50 cc and equipped with pedals (commonly known as "mopeds"), those which are mowing machines or are vehicles controlled by a pedestrian).

1971 No. 1980

CIVIL AVIATION

The Air Navigation (Fees) (Third Amendment) Regulations 1971

Made - - - *6th December* 1971

Coming into Operation *1st February* 1972

The Secretary of State with the consent of the Treasury and in exercise of his powers under Article 78 of the Air Navigation Order 1970(**a**), as amended (**b**), and of all other powers enabling him in that behalf, hereby makes the following Regulations:

1. These Regulations may be cited as the Air Navigation (Fees) (Third Amendment) Regulations 1971 and shall come into operation on 1st February 1972.

2. The Interpretation Act 1889(**c**) shall apply for the purpose of the interpretation of these Regulations as it applies for the purpose of the interpretation of an Act of Parliament.

3. The Schedule to the Air Navigation (Fees) Regulations 1970(**d**), as amended (**e**), shall be further amended as follows:

(1) In paragraph 1 for "6,000 lb." wherever it appears there shall be substituted "2,730 kg."; for "12,500 lb." wherever it appears there shall be substituted "5,700 kg."; for "30,000 lb." wherever it appears there shall be substituted "13,600 kg." and for "100,000 lb." wherever it appears there shall be substituted "45,500 kg.";

(2) In paragraph 3 for "£1 per lb." there shall be substituted "£2·20 per kg.";

(3) In paragraph 4:

(*a*) for "£1 per lb." there shall be substituted "£2·20 per kg.";

(*b*) for "1,000 lb." there shall be substituted "455 kg."; and for "2,000 lb." wherever it appears there shall be substituted "910 kg.";

(4) In paragraph 6 for "1,000 lb." there shall be substituted "455 kg." and for "2,000 lb." wherever it appears there shall be substituted "910 kg.";

(**a**) S.I. 1970/954 (1970 II, p. 2964).
(**b**) There is no relevant amending instrument.
(**c**) 1889 c. 63.
(**d**) S.I. 1970/1085 (1970 II, p. 3426).
(**e**) The relevant amending instruments are S.I. 1971/468, 1971/1105 (1971 I, p. 1387; 1971 II, p. 3287).

(5) In paragraph 12 for "12,500 lb." wherever it appears there shall be substituted "5,700 kg." ; for "75,000 lb." wherever it appears there shall be substituted "34,000 kg." and for "200,000 lb." wherever it appears there shall be substituted "91,000 kg." ;

(6) In paragraph 15 :

(*a*) for "three days" wherever it appears there shall be substituted "8 days" ;

(*b*) for "6,500 lb." wherever it appears there shall be substituted "2,950 kg." and for "15,000 lb." wherever it appears there shall be substituted "6,800 kg.".

D. F. Hubback,
A Deputy Secretary,
Department of Trade and Industry.

6th December 1971.

We consent to the making of these Regulations.

Walter Clegg,
P. L. Hawkins,
Lords Commissioners of
Her Majesty's Treasury.

6th December 1971.

EXPLANATORY NOTE

(*This Note is not part of the Regulations.*)

These Regulations further amend the Schedule to the Air Navigation (Fees) Regulations 1970, as amended. The imperial units of measurement of the weight of aircraft are replaced by the approximate metric equivalents and fees to be charged with reference to such weights have been decimalised. Temporary aerodrome licences at a reduced fee will now be valid for up to 8 days instead of 3 days.

1971 No. 1981

CIVIL AVIATION

The Civil Aviation (Licensing) (Fifth Amendment) Regulations 1971

Made - - -	*6th December* 1971
Laid before Parliament	*14th December* 1971
Coming into Operation	*1st January* 1972

The Secretary of State, in exercise of his powers under section 5 of the Civil Aviation (Licensing) Act 1960(**a**), and of that Act as extended to the Isle of Man by the Civil Aviation (Licensing) Act 1960 (Isle of Man) Order 1961(**b**) and to the Channel Islands by the Civil Aviation (Licensing) Act 1960 (Channel Islands) Order 1961(**c**), and of all other powers enabling him in that behalf, hereby makes the following Regulations, with the approval of the Treasury :—

1. These Regulations shall come into operation on 1st January 1972 and may be cited as the Civil Aviation (Licensing) (Fifth Amendment) Regulations 1971.

2. The Interpretation Act 1889(**d**) shall apply for the interpretation of these Regulations as it applies for the interpretation of an Act of Parliament.

3. The Civil Aviation (Licensing) Regulations 1964(**e**), as amended (**f**), shall be further amended as follows :—

(1) For paragraph 1 of Schedule 2 there shall be substituted the following :—

"1. The Table referred to in this Schedule is as follows :—

1 Description of Licence	2 Application Fee	3 Fee for grant, variation suspension or revocation	4 Annual Fee
	£	£	£
Class A Licence for—			
Area I Service	35	35	60
Area II Service	80	80	120
Area III Service	150	300	240
Area IV Service	300	600	600
Area V Service	150	300	240
Class C Licence	6	Nil	Nil
Any other Licence—			
(*a*) for a restricted number of journeys	35	Nil	20
(*b*) for an unrestricted number of journeys	35	80	90"

(**a**) 1960 c. 38.
(**b**) S.I. 1961/575 (1961 I, p. 1262).
(**c**) S.I. 1961/574 (1961 II, p. 1260).
(**d**) 1889 c. 63.
(**e**) S.I. 1964/1116 (1964 II, p. 2484).
(**f**) The relevant amendment is S.I. 1970/1365 (1970 III, p. 4561).

(2) In paragraph 3(4) of Schedule 2 for "£5" there shall be substituted "£6".

Michael Noble,
Minister for Trade,
Department of Trade and Industry.

6th December 1971.

We approve the making of these Regulations.

Walter Clegg,
P. L. Hawkins,
Lords Commissioners of
Her Majesty's Treasury.

6th December 1971.

EXPLANATORY NOTE

(This Note is not part of the Regulations.)

These Regulations amend the Civil Aviation (Licensing) Regulations 1964, as amended, by increasing the fees payable to the Air Transport Licensing Board in connection with air services licences and applications relating to such licences.

1971 No. 1983 (L.46)

COUNTY COURTS

The County Courts (Bankruptcy and Companies Winding-up Jurisdiction) (Amendment) Order 1971

Made - - - *3rd December* 1971

Coming into Operation 1*st January* 1972

The Lord Chancellor, in exercise of the powers conferred on him by section 96 of the Bankruptcy Act 1914**(a)** and section 218(5) of the Companies Act 1948**(b)**, hereby makes the following Order:—

1.—(1) This Order may be cited as the County Courts (Bankruptcy and Companies Winding-up Jurisdiction) (Amendment) Order 1971 and shall come into operation on 1st January 1972.

(2) In this Order "the principal Order" means the County Courts (Bankruptcy and Companies Winding-up Jurisdiction) Order 1971**(c)**.

(3) The Interpretation Act 1889**(d)** shall apply to the interpretation of this Order as it applies to the interpretation of an Act of Parliament.

2. After the entry relating to Matlock in Schedule 1 to the principal Order, there shall be inserted the following entry:—

Column 1	*Column* 2
"Mayor's and City of London Court	High Court"

Dated 3rd December 1971.

Hailsham of St. Marylebone, C.

EXPLANATORY NOTE

(*This Note is not part of the Order.*)

This Order amends the County Courts (Bankruptcy and Companies Winding-up Jurisdiction) Order 1971 by adding the Mayor's and City of London Court to the list of courts which are excluded from exercising jurisdiction in bankruptcy and the winding-up of companies and attaches its district to the High Court for these purposes.

(a) 1914 c. 59.
(b) 1948 c. 38.
(c) 1971/656 (1971 I, p. 1737).
(d) 1889 c. 63.

1971 No. 1984 (L.47)

COUNTY COURTS

The County Courts (Admiralty Jurisdiction) (Amendment) Order 1971

Made - - -	*3rd December* 1971
Coming into Operation	*1st January* 1972

The Lord Chancellor, in exercise of the powers conferred on him by section 55 of the County Courts Act 1959(**a**), hereby makes the following Order:—

1.—(1) This Order may be cited as the County Courts (Admiralty Jurisdiction) (Amendment) Order 1971 and shall come into operation on 1st January 1972.

(2) In this Order "the principal Order" means the County Courts (Admiralty Jurisdiction) Order 1971(**b**).

(3) The Interpretation Act 1889(**c**) shall apply to the interpretation of this Order as it applies to the interpretation of an Act of Parliament.

2. In column 1 of the Schedule to the principal Order, the reference to the Mayor's and City of London Court shall stand as a reference to the county court for the district of the City of London as constituted by section 42(2) of the Courts Act 1971(**d**).

Dated 3rd December 1971.

Hailsham of St. Marylebone, C.

(**a**) 1959 c. 22.
(**b**) S.I. 1971/1152 (1971 II, p. 3389).
(**c**) 1889 c. 63.
(**d**) 1971 c. 23.

EXPLANATORY NOTE

(This Note is not part of the Order.)

This Order provides for the county court for the district of the City of London, which will be known as the Mayor's and City of London Court by virtue of section 42(3) of the Courts Act 1971, to exercise Admiralty jurisdiction in the place of the court of the same name which is abolished by section 42(1) of that Act.

1971 No. 1985 (L.48)

COUNTY COURTS

The County Courts (Race Relations Jurisdiction) (Amendment No. 2) Order 1971

Made - - - *3rd December* 1971

Coming into Operation *1st January* 1972

The Lord Chancellor, in exercise of the powers conferred on him by section 19(2) and (3) of the Race Relations Act 1968(**a**), hereby makes the following Order:—

1.—(1) This Order may be cited as the County Courts (Race Relations Jurisdiction) (Amendment No. 2) Order 1971 and shall come into operation on 1st January 1972.

(2) In this Order "the principal Order" means the County Courts (Race Relations Jurisdiction) Order 1968(**b**), as amended by the County Courts (Race Relations Jurisdiction) (Amendment) Order 1971(**c**).

(3) The Interpretation Act 1889(**d**) shall apply to the interpretation of this Order as it applies to the interpretation of an Act of Parliament.

2. In column 2 of the Schedule to the principal Order, in the entry opposite the entry relating to Westminster in column 1, the words "City of London" shall be inserted after the reference to Chelmsford and the words "Mayor's & City of London" shall be deleted.

Dated 3rd December 1971.

Hailsham of St. Marylebone, C.

EXPLANATORY NOTE

(This Note is not part of the Order.)

This Order amends the County Courts (Race Relations Jurisdiction) Order 1968 by including the county court district of the City of London in the enlarged district of the Westminster County Court for the purpose of the exercise of jurisdiction under the Race Relations Act 1968 and deletes a reference to the district of the former Mayor's and City of London Court which is abolished by section 42(1) of the Courts Act 1971 (c.23).

(**a**) 1968 c. 71.
(**b**) S.I. 1968/1978 (1968 III, p. 5388).
(**c**) S.I. 1971/454 (1971 I, p. 1355).
(**d**) 1889 c. 63.

1971 No. 1986

AGRICULTURE

The Price Stability of Imported Products (Rates of Levy) (Cereals) (No. 13) Order 1971

Made - - - -	*7th December* 1971
Coming into Operation	*8th December* 1971

The Minister of Agriculture, Fisheries and Food, in exercise of the powers conferred upon him by section 1(2), (4), (5), (6) and (7) of the Agriculture and Horticulture Act 1964(**a**) and of all other powers enabling him in that behalf, hereby makes the following order:—

1. This order may be cited as the Price Stability of Imported Products (Rates of Levy) (Cereals) (No. 13) Order 1971, and shall come into operation on 8th December 1971.

2.—(1) In this order—

"the Principal Order" means the Price Stability of Imported Products (Levy Arrangements) (Cereals) Order 1971(**b**), as amended by any subsequent order and if any such order is replaced by any subsequent order the expression shall be construed as a reference to such subsequent order;

AND other expressions have the same meaning as in the Principal Order.

(2) The Interpretation Act 1889(**c**) shall apply to the interpretation of this order as it applies to the interpretation of an Act of Parliament and as if this order and the order hereby revoked were Acts of Parliament.

3. In accordance with and subject to the provisions of Part II of the Principal Order (which provides for the charging of levies on imports of certain specified commodities) the rate of levy for such imports into the United Kingdom of any specified commodity as are described in column 2 of the Schedule to this order in relation to a tariff heading indicated in column 1 of that Schedule shall be the rate set forth in relation thereto in column 3 of that Schedule.

4. The Price Stability of Imported Products (Rates of Levy) (Cereals) (No. 12) Order 1971(**d**) is hereby revoked.

In Witness whereof the Official Seal of the Minister of Agriculture, Fisheries and Food is hereunto affixed on 7th December 1971.

(L.S.)

A. Jeffrey Smith,
Assistant Secretary.

(**a**) 1964 c. 28. (**b**) S.I. 1971/631 (1971 I, p. 1660). (**c**) 1889 c. 63.
(**d**) S.I. 1971/1937 (1971 III, p. 5251).

SCHEDULE

1. Tariff Heading	2. Description of Imports	3. Rate of Levy
		per ton £
	Imports of:—	
10.01	Denatured wheat	2·00
	Wheat (other than denatured wheat)	5·75
10.03	Barley other than barley having a potential diastatic activity of not less than 170 degrees	5·25
10.04	Oats	4·00
10.05	Maize (other than sweet corn on the cob)	3·75
10.07	Grain sorghum	1·75
11.02	Cereal groats, meals (including denatured wheat meal), kibbled or cut cereals, rolled, flaked, crushed or bruised cereals and other processed cereals—	
	of wheat	7·00
	of barley	6·00
	of maize	4·75
	of oats	6·00
	other	6·00

EXPLANATORY NOTE

(*This Note is not part of the Order.*)

This order, which comes into operation on 8th December 1971, supersedes the Price Stability of Imported Products (Rates of Levy) (Cereals) (No. 12) Order 1971. It—

(*a*) increases to £3·75 per ton the rate of levy to be charged on imports of maize (other than sweet corn on the cob); and

(*b*) reimposes unchanged the remaining rates of levy in force immediately before the commencement of the order.

1971 No. 1987

INJURIES IN WAR COMPENSATION

The Injuries in War (Shore Employments) Compensation (Amendment) Scheme 1971

Made - - - *3rd December* 1971

The Defence Council, in exercise of the powers conferred on them by section 1 of the Injuries in War Compensation Act, 1914 (Session 2)(**a**) (as amended by the Defence (Transfer of Functions) (No. 1) Order 1964(**b**)) and section 1(1) and (3) of the Defence (Transfer of Functions) Act 1964(**c**) and of all other powers enabling them in that behalf, hereby make the following Scheme :—

1. The Injuries in War (Shore Employments) Compensation Scheme 1914 as amended (**d**) shall be further amended as follows :—

In paragraph (3) thereof for the figures "168s. 0d." wherever they occur, there shall be substituted the figures "£10.00.".

2. This Scheme shall have effect as from 20th September 1971 so, however, that no payment shall be made thereunder in respect of any period before that date.

3. This Scheme may be cited as the Injuries in War (Shore Employments) Compensation (Amendment) Scheme 1971 and the Injuries in War (Shore Employments) Compensation Schemes 1914 to 1969 and this Scheme may be cited together as the Injuries in War (Shore Employments) Compensation Schemes 1914 to 1971.

Dated 29th November 1971.

Consent of the Minister for the Civil Service given under his Official Seal.

Balniel
Michael Carver

Dated 3rd December 1971.

K. H. McNeill,
Authorised by the Minister for the Civil Service.

(**a**) 5 & 6 Geo. 5. c. 18.
(**b**) S.I. 1964/488 (1964 I, p. 769).
(**c**) 1964 c. 15.
(**d**) The relevant amending instrument is S.I. 1969/1861 (1969 III, p. 5807).

EXPLANATORY NOTE

(This Note is not part of the Scheme.)

The Injuries in War (Shore Employments) Compensation Schemes 1914 to 1969 provide for the payment of weekly allowances to small numbers of ex-members of the Women's Auxiliary Forces who suffered disablement from their service overseas during the 1914-18 war. The amending scheme provides that the maximum weekly allowance payable shall be increased from 168s. 0d. to £10.00 and that other allowances shall be increased proportionately. The increases will take effect as from 20th September 1971 in accordance with section 1(5) of the Injuries in War Compensation Act, 1914 (Session 2).

1971 No. 1990 (S.210)

JUSTICES OF THE PEACE

The Justices Allowances (Scotland) Amendment Regulations 1971

Made - - - -	*3rd December* 1971
Laid before Parliament	*14th December* 1971
Coming into Operation	*1st January* 1972

In exercise of the powers conferred upon me by section 8(6) and (7) of the Justices of the Peace Act 1949**(a)**, as amended by section 31 of the Administration of Justice Act 1964**(b)**, and of all other powers enabling me in that behalf, I hereby make the following regulations:—

1.—(1) These regulations may be cited as the Justices Allowances (Scotland) Amendment Regulations 1971, and shall come into operation on 1st January 1972.

(2) The Interpretation Act 1889**(c)** shall apply for the interpretation of these regulations as it applies for the interpretation of an Act of Parliament.

2. In Schedule 3 to the Justices Allowances (Scotland) Regulations 1971**(d)** (which sets out the rate of financial loss allowance payable to justices of the peace) for the expressions "£2·00" and "£4·00", there shall be substituted the expressions "£2·37½" and "£4·75" respectively.

Gordon Campbell,
One of Her Majesty's Principal
Secretaries of State.

St Andrew's House,
Edinburgh.
3rd December 1971.

EXPLANATORY NOTE

(This Note is not part of the Regulations.)

These Regulations increase the rate of financial loss allowance payable to justices of the peace.

(a) 1949 c. 101.
(b) 1964 c. 42.
(c) 1889 c. 63.
(d) S.I. 1971/490 (1971 I, p. 1440).

1971 No. 1991 (L. 49)

MAGISTRATES' COURTS

PROCEDURE

The Magistrates' Courts (Blood Tests) Rules 1971

Made - - -	*6th December* 1971
Laid before Parliament	*16th December* 1971
Coming into Operation	*1st March* 1972

The Lord Chancellor, in exercise of the power conferred on him by section 15 of the Justices of the Peace Act 1949**(a)** as extended by section 122 of the Magistrates' Courts Act 1952**(b)**, after consultation with the Rule Committee appointed under the said section 15, hereby makes the following Rules:—

1. These Rules may be cited as the Magistrates' Courts (Blood Tests) Rules 1971 and shall come into operation on 1st March 1972.

2.—(1) In these Rules save where the context otherwise requires—

"the Act" means the Family Law Reform Act 1969**(c)**;

"the applicant" means an applicant for a direction;

"blood samples" and "blood tests" have the same meaning as in Part III of the Act;

"complaint" means a complaint in the hearing of which the paternity of any person falls to be determined;

"court" means a magistrates' court;

"direction" means a direction given in accordance with the provisions of section 20(1) of the Act;

"direction form" means Form 1 in Schedule 1 to the Blood Tests (Evidence of Paternity) Regulations 1971**(d)**;

"photograph" means a recent photograph, taken full face without a hat, of the size required for insertion in a passport;

"proceedings" means any proceedings in a magistrates' court for the hearing of a complaint;

"sampler" means a registered medical practitioner or tester, nominated in a direction form to take blood samples for the purpose of the direction;

"subject" means a person from whom a court directs that blood samples shall be taken;

"tester" means a person appointed by the Secretary of State to carry out blood tests.

(2) Any reference in these Rules to a form other than a direction form is a reference to a form contained in the Schedule to these Rules.

(a) 1949 c. 101.
(b) 1952 c. 55.
(c) 1969 c. 46.
(d) S.I. 1971/1861 (1971 III, p. 5093)

(3) Any reference in these Rules to a person who is under a disability is a reference to a person who has not attained the age of 16 years or who is suffering from a mental disorder within the meaning of the Mental Health Act 1959**(a)** and is incapable of understanding the nature and purpose of blood tests.

(4) The Interpretation Act 1889**(b)** shall apply to the interpretation of these Rules as it applies to the interpretation of an Act of Parliament.

3. Form 1 shall be served on any person who makes a complaint under the Affiliation Proceedings Act 1957**(c)** or any other complaint in the hearing of which it appears to the justices' clerk that the paternity of any person falls to be determined and on any person who is served with a summons to answer such a complaint.

4. A party to any proceedings may apply in writing to the court for a direction at any time after the making of the complaint, and, on receipt of the application, the justices' clerk shall inform the other party to the proceedings that the application has been made and that he may consent to the court giving a direction before the commencement of the hearing of the complaint.

5. A court may give a direction in the absence of the applicant and the other party to the proceedings if it appears to the court that that other party, or, where he is under a disability, the person having the care and control of him has consented to the giving of the direction.

6. The court, when giving a direction, shall name the person appearing to the court to have the care and control of any subject who is under a disability.

7. A direction shall be in Form 2 and a copy of it shall be served on every subject or, where the subject is under a disability, on the person named in the direction as having the care and control of him.

8. Within 14 days, or such longer period as the court may order, of the giving of the direction, the applicant, unless he has been granted legal aid under the Legal Aid and Advice Act 1949**(d)**, shall pay to the justices' clerk such sum as appears to the justices' clerk to be sufficient to pay the fees of the sampler and tester in respect of taking and testing samples for the purpose of giving effect to the direction.

9. Within 14 days, or such longer period as the court may order, of service of a copy of the direction, each subject who is not under a disability and the person having the care and control of a subject who is under a disability but has attained the age of 12 months by the date of the direction shall furnish to the justices' clerk a photograph of the subject:

Provided that this requirement shall not apply in the case of a subject who is suffering from a mental disorder if the medical practitioner in whose care he is certifies that a photograph cannot or should not be taken of the subject.

10.—(1) If any person fails to comply with the provisions of Rule 8 or 9 of these Rules, the justices' clerk shall not take any further steps required of him by these Rules without first informing the court and receiving its instructions to do so.

(a) 1959 c. 72. **(b)** 1889 c. 63. **(c)** 1957 c. 55. **(d)** 1949 c. 51.

(2) If the court is informed by the justices' clerk in accordance with paragraph (1) of this Rule, it may vary or revoke the direction or may make such order as to the hearing or the continuation of the hearing of the complaint as appears to the court to be appropriate in all the circumstances and shall cause the parties to be notified.

11. Where a court has given a direction and the justices' clerk is satisfied that the requirements of Rule 8 of these Rules (where applicable) have been met and he is in possession of a photograph (or a certificate under the proviso to Rule 9 of these Rules) in respect of each subject who has attained the age of 12 months by the date of the direction, the justices' clerk shall arrange for blood samples to be taken and for blood tests to be made on those samples, or shall arrange for the parties' solicitors to make the arrangement on his behalf.

12. When arrangements have been made for the taking of samples, the justices' clerk shall—

(*a*) give notice in Form 3 to each subject or, where a subject is under a disability, the person having the care and control of the subject, of the arrangements made for the taking of samples from the subject and shall require him, or where he is under a disability, the person having the care and control of him, to comply with the arrangements;

(*b*) complete Parts I and II of a direction form in respect of each subject and send the direction form to the sampler who is to take the blood sample from that subject.

13. When a direction form is returned to the court by a sampler, or by a tester, unless it is accompanied by a report under section 20(2) of the Act, the court shall cause a copy of the form to be served on each party to the proceedings and shall consider any entries made on the direction form by the sampler, tester or any other person and may vary or revoke the direction or make such order as to the hearing or the continuation of the hearing of the complaint as appears to the court to be appropriate in all the circumstances.

14. On receipt of the report by the tester under section 20(2) of the Act, the justices' clerk shall serve a copy of the report on each of the parties to the proceedings.

15. The justices' clerk shall use any sum paid to him under Rule 8 of these Rules in paying the fees due to the sampler and tester and shall repay the balance, if any, to the applicant.

16. Service of any document required to be served by these Rules may be effected by delivering it to the person upon whom it is required to be served or to his solicitor or by sending it by first class post to him at his last known or usual place of abode or to his solicitor at his office.

Dated 6th December 1971.

Hailsham of St. Marylebone, C.

Rule 2 (2)

SCHEDULE

FORM 1

FAMILY LAW REFORM ACT 1969

An explanation of the use of blood tests in paternity disputes
(M.C.(B.T.) Rules 1971, *r.*3.)

Introduction

In a case where there is a dispute about the paternity of a child blood tests may provide important evidence and courts now have power to order their use if a party in a case asks for them. This leaflet explains about blood tests and how to get them.

Evidence from blood tests

A small amount of blood is taken from the mother, her child and the man said to be the child's father. Tests upon this blood can show that the man is not the father of the child. They cannot definitely prove that a man is the father, but they can in some cases show that he is likely to be the father. Giving blood for this purpose is simple and not harmful to the health.

Applying for blood tests

Any party in a case where the paternity of a child is disputed can apply for blood tests. If both parties agree, the court may order tests before the case is heard. If one party does not agree, the case must come before the court which will then decide whether or not to order tests.

Refusal to comply with an order

No-one can be forced to give a blood sample. But if a person does not comply with the court's order, the court will consider his reason, and if it does not think he has good reason for not complying, it can draw its own conclusions. One of these may be that the person knew that the result of tests might not support his case.

Arrangements for giving blood

When blood tests are ordered, the parties (and the person looking after the child, if not one of the parties) will be told to attend a named doctor at a stated time and place. Anyone who cannot keep the appointment must tell the doctor immediately so that another appointment can be made. Failure to do this may be taken as a refusal to undergo tests. It is important that the three samples of blood are taken by the same doctor at the same time. Distance may make this impossible, but if the mother, child and man said to be the father are living in the same area they will have to attend the same doctor on the same day.

Identification of parties

It is essential that the right people are tested. For this purpose a passport size photograph must be provided of all parties over 12 months old. A child under 12 months is identified by the person who is looking after it. Giving a blood sample instead of someone else or allowing the wrong child to be tested is a serious offence. The penalty is a fine of up to £400 or imprisonment for up to two years. The blood test itself can show that the wrong person has been tested.

Cost of blood tests

The cost of blood tests may be as much as £36. This must be paid by the person asking for the tests before they will be carried out. However, a party to a case where the paternity of a child is disputed may be entitled to legal aid, and if he or she is, the cost of the test may be paid by the legal aid fund. Anyone involved in this type of case should consult a solicitor about this possibility.

Effect of blood transfusion

Blood transfusion within 3 months of the tests can effect their value. If a person has had a recent transfusion, his solicitor or the clerk of the court should be informed before the court orders tests.

Report

When tests have been carried out, the tester will send a written report to the court and a copy of this will be sent to the parties to the case.

Further information

Further information about the procedure may be obtained from a solicitor or from the clerk of the court which is dealing with the case.

FORM 2

FAMILY LAW REFORM ACT 1969

Blood test direction (*M.C.*(*B.T.*) *Rules* 1971, *r.*7.)

In the .... Magistrates' Court

.... *Complainant*

and

.... *Defendant*

By virtue of the power conferred upon the court by section 20(1) of the Family Law Reform Act 1969 and on the application of ....
the court hereby directs that blood tests be used to ascertain whether such tests show that .... is or is not excluded from being the father of .... and that for that purpose blood samples shall be taken from:—

And it is further ordered that such samples shall be taken before the day of 19 .

By order of the court,

....

Justices' Clerk.

Dated 19 . Address ....

The person appearing to the court to have the care and control of ....
.... being a person who [has not attained the age of sixteen years] [is suffering from a mental disorder within the meaning of the Mental Health Act 1959 and is incapable of understanding the nature and purpose of blood tests] is ....

FORM 3

FAMILY LAW REFORM ACT 1969

Requirement to give blood sample (M.C.(B.T.) Rules 1971, *r*.12.)

To .... (*Name of subject/person having care and control of subject*).

Further to the direction for the carrying out of blood tests given on .... 19 by the .... Magistrates' Court, a copy of which has been served on you, you are hereby required, for the purpose of giving effect to the direction, to attend on .... (*insert title and name of sampler*) at ....(*insert address at which sample is to be taken*) at ....a.m./p.m. on .... 19 for a blood sample to be taken from you.

....

Justices' Clerk.

Address ....

Note.—Any travelling or other expenses reasonably incurred in complying with this requirement are payable in the first instance by the person who applied to the court for the direction, namely whose solicitors are of . The court has power to deal with these expenses when it makes an order for costs at the end of the proceedings.

EXPLANATORY NOTE

(*This Note is not part of the Rules.*)

Part III of the Family Law Reform Act 1969 (which comes into force on 1st March 1972) makes provisions for the use of blood tests in determining paternity in civil proceedings. These Rules prescribe the practice and procedure to be adopted in magistrates' courts in civil proceedings in which the paternity of any person falls to be determined.

STATUTORY INSTRUMENTS

1971 No. 1992 (C.52)

CIVIL AVIATION

The Civil Aviation Act 1971 (Commencement No. 3) Order 1971

Made - - - *8th December* 1971

The Secretary of State, in exercise of the powers conferred on him by section 70(2) of the Civil Aviation Act 1971(**a**) hereby orders as follows :—

1. This Order may be cited as the Civil Aviation Act 1971 (Commencement No. 3) Order 1971.

2. The provisions of the Civil Aviation Act 1971 specified in the Schedule to this Order shall, for the purposes therein respectively specified, come into force on 20th December 1971.

P. G. Hudson,
An Under Secretary,
Department of Trade and Industry.

8th December 1971.

SCHEDULE

The whole of Part I.
Section 21(2)—for the purpose of making instruments.
Section 21(3).
Section 22(1) and (6)—for the purpose of publishing notices and making regulations.
Section 22(7).
Section 23(1) and (4)—for the purpose of making regulations.
Section 24(1), (3) and (6)—for the purpose of making regulations.
Section 26.
Section 27(2)—for the purpose of making regulations.
Section 27(3), (4) and (5).
Section 28(2)—for the purpose of giving a direction.
Sections 31 to 36.
Section 61.
Section 62(2) to (5).
Sections 63 to 68.
Section 69(1)—for the purposes for which it is not already in force.
Schedules 1, 2, 3, 5, 6, 7 and 9.
Schedule 10—paragraphs 1, 4 and 13 to 15;
—paragraphs 6 and 7 in so far as they are not already in force.

(**a**) 1971 c. 75.

EXPLANATORY NOTE

(This Note is not part of the Order.)

This Order brings into force those provisions of the Civil Aviation Act 1971 which relate to the constitution and finances of the Civil Aviation Authority and the power of the Secretary of State to make regulations, together with a number of minor or ancillary provisions. The provisions now brought into force do not include those which would require the Authority to start its regulatory functions, the operation of aerodromes or the provision of air navigation services.

STATUTORY INSTRUMENTS

1971 No. 1993

ACQUISITION OF LAND

COMPENSATION

The Acquisition of Land (Rate of Interest after Entry) (No. 4) Regulations 1971

Made - - -	7*th December* 1971
Laid before Parliament	16*th December* 1971
Coming into Operation	17*th December* 1971

The Treasury, in exercise of the powers conferred upon them by section 32(1) of the Land Compensation Act 1961**(a)**, and of all other powers enabling them in that behalf, hereby make the following Regulations:—

1. These Regulations may be cited as the Acquisition of Land (Rate of Interest after Entry) (No. 4) Regulations 1971, and shall come into operation on 17th December 1971.

2. The Interpretation Act 1889**(b)** shall apply for the interpretation of these Regulations as it applies for the interpretation of an Act of Parliament.

3. The rate of interest on any compensation in respect of the compulsory acquisition of an interest in any land on which entry has been made before the payment of the compensation shall be 7 per cent. per annum.

4. The Acquisition of Land (Rate of Interest after Entry) (No. 3) Regulations 1971**(c)** are hereby revoked.

V. H. Goodhew,

Walter Clegg,

Two of the Lords Commissioners of Her Majesty's Treasury.

7th December 1971.

EXPLANATORY NOTE

(*This Note is not part of the Regulations.*)

These Regulations reduce from 7½ per cent. to 7 per cent. per annum, in respect of any period after the coming into operation of these Regulations, the rate of interest payable where entry is made, before payment of compensation, on land in England and Wales which is being purchased compulsorily, and revoke the Acquisition of Land (Rate of Interest after Entry) (No. 3) Regulations 1971.

(a) 1961 c. 33. **(b)** 1889 c. 63. **(c)** S.I. 1971/1544 (1971 III, p. 4359).

1971 No. 1994

ACQUISITION OF LAND

COMPENSATION

The Acquisition of Land (Rate of Interest after Entry) (Scotland) (No. 4) Regulations 1971

Made - - -	7*th December* 1971
Laid before Parliament	16*th December* 1971
Coming into Operation	17*th December* 1971

The Treasury, in exercise of the powers conferred upon them by section 40(1) of the Land Compensation (Scotland) Act 1963**(a)**, and of all other powers enabling them in that behalf, hereby make the following Regulations:—

1.—(1) These Regulations may be cited as the Acquisition of Land (Rate of Interest after Entry) (Scotland) (No. 4) Regulations 1971, and shall come into operation on 17th December 1971.

(2) These Regulations shall extend to Scotland only.

2. The Interpretation Act 1889**(b)** shall apply for the interpretation of these Regulations as it applies for the interpretation of an Act of Parliament.

3. The rate of interest on any compensation in respect of the compulsory acquisition of an interest in any land on which entry has been made before the payment of the compensation shall be 7 per cent. per annum.

4. The Acquisition of Land (Rate of Interest after Entry) (Scotland) (No. 3) Regulations 1971**(c)** are hereby revoked.

V. H. Goodhew,
Walter Clegg,
Two of the Lords Commissioners
of Her Majesty's Treasury.

7th December 1971.

EXPLANATORY NOTE

(*This Note is not part of the Regulations.*)

These Regulations reduce from 7½ per cent. to 7 per cent. per annum, in respect of any period after the coming into operation of these Regulations, the rate of interest payable where entry is made, before payment of compensation, on land in Scotland which is being purchased compulsorily, and revoke the Acquisition of Land (Rate of Interest after Entry) (Scotland) (No. 3) Regulations 1971.

(a) 1963 c. 51 **(b)** 1889 c. 63. **(c)** S.I. 1971/1545 (1971 III, p. 4360).

STATUTORY INSTRUMENTS

1971 No. 1995 (S.211)

EDUCATION, SCOTLAND

The Teachers Superannuation (Scotland) Amendment Regulations 1971

Made - - - -	1*st December* 1971
Laid before Parliament	15*th December* 1971
Coming into Operation	10*th January* 1972

(1) In exercise of the powers conferred upon me by sections 1, 4, 11 and 18 of the Teachers Superannuation (Scotland) Act 1968**(a)** and of all other powers enabling me in that behalf, and after consultation with representatives of education authorities, teachers and other bodies appearing to me to be likely to be affected, as required by section 18(5) of the said Act, and with the consent of the Minister for the Civil Service, I hereby make the following regulations, except regulation 12; and

(2) having made the consultations required by section 62(3) of the National Insurance Act 1965**(b)** and having been determined by the Minister for the Civil Service to be the appropriate Minister of the Crown under section 110(1) of that Act, in exercise of the powers conferred upon me by those sections and of all other powers enabling me in that behalf, I hereby make regulation 12 of the following regulations—

Citation and commencement

1.—(1) These regulations may be cited as the Teachers Superannuation (Scotland) Amendment Regulations 1971 and shall come into operation on 10th January 1972.

(2) The Teachers Superannuation (Scotland) Regulations 1969**(c)** as amended **(d)** (hereinafter referred to as "the principal Regulations") and these regulations may be cited together as the Teachers Superannuation (Scotland) Regulations 1969 to 1971.

Interpretation

2. The Interpretation Act 1889**(e)** shall apply for the interpretation of these regulations as it applies for the interpretation of an Act of Parliament.

(a) 1968 c. 12.
(b) 1965 c. 51.
(c) S.I. 1969/77 (1969 I, p. 133).
(d) S.I. 1969/659 (1969 II, p. 1820).
(e) 1889 c. 63.

Saving

3. Except as in these regulations expressly provided, the amendment of the Teachers Superannuation (Scotland) Regulations 1969 by these regulations shall not—

(*a*) affect the previous operation of those regulations or anything duly done or suffered under those regulations; or

(*b*) affect any right, obligation or liability acquired, accrued or incurred under those regulations before the coming into operation of these regulations.

Amendments to the principal Regulations

4. Regulation 5 of the principal Regulations (which provides definitions) shall be amended as follows:—

(*a*) the paragraph defining "Salaries Memorandum" shall be deleted and the following paragraph substituted:—

" 'Salaries Memorandum' means a memorandum setting out the scales and other provisions required for determining the relevant remuneration of teachers being a memorandum referred to in an order made by the Secretary of State under section 2 of the Remuneration of Teachers (Scotland) Act 1967**(a)** as applied by section 4 of that Act.";

(*b*) the paragraph defining "approved school" shall be deleted; and

(*c*) after the definition of "registered teacher" there shall be inserted the following paragraph:—

" 'residential establishment' has the meaning assigned to it in the Social Work (Scotland) Act 1968**(b)**."

5. In regulation 7 of the principal Regulations (which relates to reckonable service) paragraphs 2 and 3 shall be deleted and the following paragraphs substituted:—

"(2) Notice in writing by a teacher for the purpose of paragraph (1)(*a*)(ii) of this regulation may be given at any time. The election, if accepted by the Secretary of State, shall be irrevocable, shall have effect from the first day of part-time service or such later date as the teacher may elect, being in any case a date not earlier than 30 days before the receipt by the Secretary of State of the notice, and shall thereafter apply to all part-time service as a teacher before allowances under these regulations first accrue or become payable to him and to all part-time service of a re-employed teacher who, on re-employment, has elected to have his annual allowance in respect of periods of re-employment dealt with under Method A set out in regulation 50(4) to (7) of the principal Regulations.

(3) Except as provided above, nothing in this regulation shall affect an election made by a teacher after 1st April 1965 but before the appointed day under the corresponding provisions of the regulations of 1957."

(a) 1967 c. 36. **(b)** 1968 c. 49.

6. In regulation 8(3) of the principal Regulations (which relates to external service) the following words shall be added:—

"or the teacher has received payment of superannuation allowances by virtue of regulation 40(1)(*a*)."

7. In regulation 14 of the principal Regulations (which relates to intervals of service) the following paragraph shall be added after paragraph (2):—

"(3) A period which is reckonable service by virtue of this regulation shall not be a period of employment for the purposes of paragraphs 4 to 7 of regulation 50."

8. In regulation 28 of the principal Regulations (which relates to the payment of contributions on reduction of salary) for sub-paragraph (*b*) of paragraph (1) there shall be substituted the following sub-paragraph:—

"(*b*) within six months after the commencement of such reduction elects, with the approval of the Secretary of State, that it shall apply to him and has not withdrawn that election by notice in writing to the Secretary of State."

9. In Part I of Schedule 1 to the principal Regulations (which specifies the types of teaching service which shall be recorded as reckonable service) for paragraph 3 there shall be substituted the following paragraph:—

"3. Teacher in a residential establishment where education is provided or in a special school being an occupational centre."

10. In Schedule 3 to the principal Regulations (which specifies the employments which shall be recorded as qualifying service) for paragraph 1 there shall be substituted the following paragraph:—

"1. Service in a school or other educational establishment in Scotland, being either full-time service, or part-time service undertaken after 31st March 1965."

11. For Schedule 4 to the principal Regulations there shall be substituted the following Schedule:—

Regulation 31

SCHEDULE 4

Additional Contributions in Respect of Previous Employment

Age	Method I Periodical Payments			Method II Single Payment		
	Percentage of salary	Annual Reduction in respect of each £1 of reduction of annual allowance by reason of national insurance		Percentage of salary	Reduction in respect of each £1 of reduction of annual allowance by reason of national insurance	
(1)	(2)	(3)		(4)	(5)	
	Men and Women	Men	Women	Men and Women	Men	Women
		£	£		£	£
21 and under 25	·30	0·12	0·18	8·80	2·30	2·65
25 " " 26	·31	0·13	0·20	8·63	2·40	2·80
26 " " 27	·32	0·14	0·21	8·62	2·50	3·05
27 " " 28	·33	0·14	0·23	8·61	2·65	3·30
28 " " 29	·35	0·15	0·24	8·62	2·75	3·55
29 " " 30	·36	0·16	0·26	8·64	2·85	3·85
30 " " 31	·38	0·17	0·27	8·66	3·00	4·15
31 " " 32	·39	0·18	0·30	8·71	3·10	4·45
32 " " 33	·41	0·19	0·32	8·76	3·20	4·80
33 " " 34	·43	0·20	0·34	8·83	3·35	5·10
34 " " 35	·45	0·21	0·36	8·91	3·50	5·40
35 " " 36	·47	0·23	0·38	9·01	3·60	5·75
36 " " 37	·50	0·24	0·41	9·11	3·75	6·05
37 " " 38	·53	0·26	0·44	9·23	3·90	6·35
38 " " 39	·56	0·27	0·47	9·36	4·05	6·70
39 " " 40	·59	0·30	0·51	9·50	4·20	7·00
40 " " 41	·63	0·32	0·55	9·66	4·35	7·30
41 " " 42	·67	0·35	0·59	9·83	4·55	7·65
42 " " 43	·72	0·37	0·64	10·03	4·70	7·95
43 " " 44	·78	0·40	0·69	10·24	4·90	8·25
44 " " 45	·84	0·44	0·75	10·47	5·05	8·60
45 " " 46	·91	0·48	0·82	10·70	5·25	8·90
46 " " 47	·99	0·53	0·90	10·96	5·45	9·25
47 " " 48	1·09	0·58	0·99	11·22	5·65	9·60
48 " " 49	1·20	0·64	1·10	11·50	5·90	9·95
49 " " 50	1·33	0·72	1·23	11·79	6·10	10·35
50 " " 51	1·49	0·81	1·39	12·10	6·35	10·70
51 " " 52	1·69	0·93	1·59	12·41	6·60	11·10
52 " " 53	1·95	1·07	1·83	12·73	6·85	11·55
53 " " 54	2·28	1·27	2·16	13·06	7·10	12·00
54 " " 55	2·73	1·53	2·60	13·40	7·40	12·45

12. Schedule 5 to the principal Regulations (which contains provisions in connection with national insurance) shall be amended as follows:—

(*a*) for the sums of £2:19:— and £2:8:— specified in sub-paragraph (2) of paragraph 3 there shall be substituted the sums of £2·95 and £2·40 respectively;

(*b*) for the Table contained in paragraph 4 there shall be substituted the following Table:—

TABLE

Annual Rate of Salary	Annual Rate of Reduction of Contributions
	£
Not exceeding £468	Nil
Over £468 but not exceeding £520	0·40
Over £520 but not exceeding £572	1·25
Over £572 but not exceeding £624	2·10
Over £624 but not exceeding £676	2·95
Over £676 but not exceeding £728	3·80
Over £728 but not exceeding £780	4·65
Over £780 but not exceeding £832	5·50
Over £832 but not exceeding £884	6·35
Over £884 but not exceeding £936	7·20
Over £936	7·65

(*c*) for the sums of £1:14:— and £67:15:— specified in sub-paragraph (2) of paragraph 5 there shall be substituted the sums of £1·70 and £67·75 respectively;

(*d*) for the Table contained in sub-paragraph (2) of paragraph 6 there shall be substituted the following Table:—

TABLE

Age at date of Modification (1)	Yearly reduction of annual allowance for each completed year of reckonable service after date of modification	
	Men (2)	Women (3)
	£	£
20 or under	1·70	1·70
21	1·65	1·60
22	1·60	1·53
23	1·55	1·45
24	1·50	1·37
25	1·47	1·30
26	1·45	1·23
27	1·43	1·17
28	1·40	1·13
29	1·35	1·07
30	1·33	1·03
31	1·30	0·97
32	1·27	0·95
33	1·25	0·93
34	1·23	0·90
35	1·20	0·87
36	1·17	0·85
37	1·15	0·83
38	1·13	0·80
39	1·10	0·77
40	1·07	0·75
41	1·07	0·73
42	1·05	0·73
43	1·03	0·70
44	1·00	0·70
45	0·97	0·67
46	0·95	0·65
47	0·95	0·65
48	0·93	0·63
49	0·93	0·63
50 and over	0·93	0·60

(*e*) in the Table contained in paragraph 8 for the sum of £2·9 specified in the last column there shall be substituted the sum of £2·90; and

(*f*) for the sum of £2·9 specified in sub-paragraph (*b*) of paragraph 9 there shall be substituted the sum of £2·90.

Gordon Campbell,
One of Her Majesty's Principal
Secretaries of State.

St Andrew's House,
Edinburgh.

23rd November 1971.

Consent of the Minister for the Civil Service given under his Official Seal on 1st December 1971.

(L.S.)

K. H. McNeill,
Authorised by the Minister for
the Civil Service.

EXPLANATORY NOTE

(This Note is not part of the Regulations.)

These Regulations—

(1) alter amounts of money expressed in pounds, shillings and pence to amounts expressed in pounds and new pence (Regulations 11 and 12);

(2) define the circumstances in which an election for the recording of part-time service as reckonable service shall be binding on a teacher who resumes teaching service after retirement (Regulation 5);

(3) impose a time limit within which application must be made to pay contributions on a previous higher salary (Regulation 8);

(4) make minor alterations in respect of external service (Regulation 6), intervals of service (Regulation 7), definitions (Regulations 4 and 9) and qualifying part-time service (Regulation 10).

1971 No. 2000

CUSTOMS AND EXCISE

The Import Duty Reliefs (No. 1) Order 1971

Made - - - -	*9th December* 1971
Laid before the House of Commons -	*15th December* 1971
Coming into Operation	*1st January* 1972

The Lords Commissioners of Her Majesty's Treasury, by virtue of the powers conferred on them by section 5 of the Import Duties Act 1958(**a**), as extended by section 2 of the Finance Act 1971(**b**), and of all other powers enabling them in that behalf, on the recommendation of the Secretary of State, hereby make the following Order:—

1.—(1) This Order may be cited as the Import Duty Reliefs (No. 1) Order 1971.

(2) The Interpretation Act 1889(**c**) shall apply for the interpretation of this Order as it applies for the interpretation of an Act of Parliament.

(3) This Order shall come into operation on 1st January 1972.

2. Import duty shall not be chargeable on the following goods, that is to say, cotton yarn and manufactures of woven cotton, if—

(*a*) they are goods of the Commonwealth preference area, and

(*b*) they are imported on or after 1st January 1972 under the authority of an import licence which restricts the quantity of goods which may be imported thereunder, and

(*c*) the Secretary of State certifies that he is satisfied that they were exported from their country of origin before 1st January 1972, and

(*d*) import duty would not have been chargeable on them if they had been imported on 31st December 1971.

V. H. Goodhew,
Walter Clegg,
Two of the Lords Commissioners of Her Majesty's Treasury.

9th December 1971.

EXPLANATORY NOTE

(*This Note is not part of the Order.*)

This Order provides for relief from import duty on certain cotton yarn and manufactures of woven cotton from the Commonwealth preference area.

(**a**) 1958 c. 6. (**b**) 1971 c. 68. (**c**) 1889 c. 63.

STATUTORY INSTRUMENTS

1971 No. 2001

CUSTOMS AND EXCISE

The Anti-Dumping and Countervailing Duties (Metric Rates) Order 1971

Made - - -	9*th December* 1971
Laid before the House of Commons	14*th December* 1971
Coming into Operation	1*st January* 1972

The Secretary of State, in exercise of his powers under sections 1, 2, 7, 15 and 18(2) of the Customs Duties (Dumping and Subsidies) Act 1969(**a**) and all other powers enabling him in that behalf, hereby makes the following Order :—

1.—(1) This Order may be cited as the Anti-Dumping and Countervailing Duties (Metric Rates) Order 1971 and shall come into operation on 1st January 1972.

(2) The Interpretation Act 1889(**b**) shall apply to the interpretation of this Order as it applies to the interpretation of an Act of Parliament and as if this Order and the Orders hereby revoked were Acts of Parliament.

(3) The Orders specified in Schedule 2 hereto are hereby revoked.

2. The anti-dumping and countervailing duties chargeable immediately before the commencement of this Order by virtue of Orders mentioned in Schedule 2 hereto on the importation into the United Kingdom of goods of the descriptions mentioned in Column 2 of Schedule 1 shall be chargeable on and after 1st January 1972 by virtue of this Order at the relevant rate set out in column 3.

3. No duty shall be chargeable by virtue of this Order on goods of any description unless the goods are classified in the relevant heading of the Customs Tariff 1959(**c**) mentioned in column 1 of Schedule 1.

4. Section 2 of the Customs Duties (Dumping and Subsidies) Act 1969 shall apply to the duties chargeable by virtue of this Order.

Anthony Grant,
Parliamentary Under Secretary of State,
Department of Trade and Industry.

9th December 1971.

(**a**) 1969 c. 16. (**b**) 1889 c. 63.
(**c**) See S.I. 1971/1971 (1971 III, p.5330).

SCHEDULE 1

Anti-dumping Duties

Relevant Tariff Heading	*Description*	*Rate chargeable from 1st January 1972*
28.21 (B)	Chromic anhydride (CrO_3) originating in the Union of Soviet Socialist Republics	£49·2100 per tonne
28.28 (P)	Zirconium dioxide originating in the Union of Soviet Socialist Republics	£270·6565 per tonne
29.26	Saccharin and its salts	
	(*a*) originating in Japan	£0·0917 per kilogramme
	(*b*) originating in the Republic of Korea	£0·5511 per kilogramme
31.02 (D)	Ammonium sulphonitrate originating in the Federal Republic of Germany	£4·9210 per tonne
31.02 (D)	Calcium ammonium nitrate originating in the Republic of South Africa	£14·7630 per tonne
	Countervailing Duties	
84.15	Domestic electrically operated refrigerators with a storage capacity not exceeding 12 cubic feet originating in Italy.	£0·0238 per kilogramme

SCHEDULE 2

Revocations

The Anti-Dumping Duty Order 1965 S.I. 1965/1599 (1965 II, p. 4605).
The Anti-Dumping Duty Order 1970 S.I. 1970/1013 (1970 II, p. 3159).
The Anti-Dumping Duty (No. 2) Order 1970 S.I. 1970/1148 (1970 II, p. 3905).
The Anti-Dumping Duty (No. 3) Order 1970 S.I. 1970/1558 (1970 III, p. 5314).
The Anti-Dumping Duty (No. 4) Order 1970 S.I. 1970/1641 (1970 III, p. 5398).
The Anti-Dumping Duty (No. 5) Order 1970 S.I. 1970/1846 (1970 III, p. 5997).
The Anti-Dumping Duty Order 1971 S.I. 1971/154 (1971 I, p. 436).
The Anti-Dumping Duty (No. 3) Order 1971 S.I. 1971/1048 (1971 II, p. 3133).
The Anti-Dumping Duty (No. 4) Order 1971 S.I. 1971/1635 (1971 III, p. 4501).
The Anti-Dumping Duty (No. 5) Order 1971 S.I. 1971/1897. (1971 III, p. 5149).
The Countervailing Duty Order 1968 S.I. 1968/1240 (1968 II, p. 3350).

EXPLANATORY NOTE

(This Note is not part of the Order.)

This Order replaces certain current anti-dumping and countervailing duty Orders imposing duties at rates expressed by reference to imperial units of measurement. Such duties are to be chargeable on or after 1st January 1972 by reference to metric units. The goods concerned fall within Chapters of the Customs tariff where metric units are to be employed from 1st January 1972. The new rates have been calculated so that they do not involve any increase in duties.

Some spent Orders are included among the Orders revoked.

1971 No. 2002

EXCHANGE CONTROL

The Exchange Control (Scheduled Territories) (Amendment) (No. 3) Order 1971

Made - - - -	*9th December* 1971
Laid before Parliament	*14th December* 1971
Coming into Operation	*15th December* 1971

The Treasury, in exercise of the powers conferred upon them by sections 1(3)(*b*) and 36(5) of the Exchange Control Act 1947(**a**), hereby make the following Order:—

1.—(1) This Order may be cited as the Exchange Control (Scheduled Territories) (Amendment) (No. 3) Order 1971, and shall come into operation on 15th December 1971.

(2) The Interpretation Act 1889(**b**) shall apply for the interpretation of this Order as it applies for the interpretation of an Act of Parliament.

2. Schedule 1 to the Exchange Control Act 1947, as amended by the Exchange Control (Scheduled Territories) Order 1967(**c**) and as further amended (**d**), shall be further amended by deleting paragraph 18 thereof.

3. This Order shall extend to the Channel Islands, and any reference in this Order to the Exchange Control Act 1947 includes a reference to that Act as extended by the Exchange Control (Channel Islands) Order 1947(**e**).

Tim Fortescue,
P. L. Hawkins,
Two of the Lords Commissioners
of Her Majesty's Treasury.

9th December 1971.

(**a**) 1947 c. 14. (**b**) 1889 c. 63.
(**c**) S.I. 1967/1767 (1967 III, p. 4736).
(**d**) S.I. 1968/333, 1399, 1970/748, 1455, 1971/1406, 1556 (1968 I, p. 971; II, p. 4047; 1970 II, p. 2343; III, p. 4785; 1971 II, p. 3943; III, p. 4373).
(**e**) S.R. & O. 1947/2034 (Rev. VI, p. 1001: 1947 I, p. 660).

EXPLANATORY NOTE

(*This Note is not part of the Order.*)

This Order amends the list of scheduled territories contained in Schedule 1 to the Exchange Control Act 1947 by deleting the United Kingdom of Libya.

STATUTORY INSTRUMENTS

1971 No. 2003 (C.53)

HIGHWAYS, ENGLAND AND WALES

The Highways Act 1971 (Commencement No. 2) Order 1971

Made - - - - *3rd December* 1971

The Secretary of State for the Environment (as respects England, except Monmouthshire) and the Secretary of State for Wales (as respects Wales and Monmouthshire) make this Order in exercise of their powers under section 87 of the Highways Act 1971(**a**):—

1. This Order may be cited as the Highways Act 1971 (Commencement No. 2) Order 1971.

2. The provisions of the Highways Act 1971 (hereinafter referred to as "the Act") which are specified in the first column of the Schedule to this Order and which relate to the matters respectively specified in relation to those provisions in the second column of that Schedule shall come into operation in the whole of England and Wales on the 17th January 1972.

SCHEDULE

PROVISIONS OF THE ACT COMING INTO OPERATION ON THE 17TH JANUARY 1972

Provisions of the Act	*Subject matter of provisions*
In Part II,	
section 31	Control of builders' skips.
section 32	Removal of builders' skips.
section 40	Vehicle crossings over footways and verges.
section 41	Provisions relating to placing, etc. of certain apparatus in or under a highway.
section 42	Appeal against certain decisions of a local highway authority under s.41.
section 43	Licence to plant trees, shrubs, etc. in a highway.
In Part IV	
section 86(1) and (2), so far as those sub-sections apply to the provisions of Schedules 11 and 12 which are specified below.	Transitional provisions, repeals etc.

(**a**) 1971 c. 41.

Provisions of the Act	*Subject matter of provisions*
Schedule 3	Provisions with respect to notices under section 40.
In Schedule 11 paragraph 5	Transitional provisions and savings with respect to vehicle crossings.
In Schedule 12 the entries relating to the following provisions of the Highways Act 1959(**a**):— section 155, Schedule 6, and Schedule 18; and the entry relating to paragraph 44 of Schedule 6 to the London Government Act 1963(**b**).	Repeals.

Signed by authority of the Secretary of State for the Environment.

30th November 1971.

W. J. Sharp,
An Under Secretary in the Department of the Environment.

Signed by authority of the Secretary of State for Wales.

3rd December 1971.

D. A. R. Hall,
Director of Highways in the Welsh Office.

(**a**) 1959 c. 25.

(**b**) 1963 c. 33.

EXPLANATORY NOTE

(*This Note is not part of the Order.*)

This Order brings into operation for the whole of England and Wales on the 17th January 1972 the provisions of the Highways Act 1971 which relate to the control of builders' skips on highways (sections 31 and 32), vehicle crossings over footways and verges (section 40, section 86(1) and (2), Schedule 3, paragraph 5 of Schedule 11 and certain entries in Schedule 12), the placing of apparatus in or under highways (sections 41 and 42), and the planting of trees, shrubs etc. in highways (section 43).

1971 No. 2007

RATING AND VALUATION

The Rating (Charitable Institutions) Order 1971

Made - - - -	*9th December* 1971
Laid before Parliament	*17th December* 1971
Coming into Operation	*7th January* 1972

Whereas section 40(2) of the General Rate Act 1967(**a**) provides that no mandatory relief from rating under section 40(1) shall be given in the case of a hereditament falling within section 40(1)(*a*) for any period during which the hereditament is occupied by an institution specified in Schedule 8;

And whereas section 40(3) empowers the Secretary of State for the Environment by order to amend that Schedule by adding any institution which in his opinion ought to be classified with the institutions mentioned therein or omitting any institution;

And whereas paragraph 2 of the said Schedule relates to the colleges, institutions and schools of the universities of Durham, London and Wales except those colleges and institutes excepted therefrom by sub-paragraphs (*a*) and (*b*) thereof;

And whereas the Secretary of State is of the opinion that Heythrop College of the University of London should be excepted:

Now therefore the Secretary of State for the Environment, in exercise of his powers under the said section 40(3) and of all other powers enabling him in that behalf, hereby orders as follows:—

Title and commencement

1.—(1) This order may be cited as the Rating (Charitable Institutions) Order 1971 and shall come into operation on 7th January 1972.

(2) This order shall have effect from 14th May 1971.

Interpretation

2. The Interpretation Act 1889(**b**) shall apply for the interpretation of this order as it applies for the interpretation of an Act of Parliament.

(**a**) 1967 c. 9. (**b**) 1889 c. 63.

Amendment of Schedule 8 *to General Rate Act* 1967

3. The provisions of Schedule 8 to the General Rate Act 1967 as amended **(a)** shall be further amended by adding Heythrop College to the list of excepted colleges and institutes in sub-paragraph (*b*) of paragraph 2.

Peter Walker,
Secretary of State for
the Environment.

9th December 1971.

EXPLANATORY NOTE

(*This Note is not part of the Order.*)

This Order amends Schedule 8 to the General Rate Act 1967 (which excludes certain charities from mandatory relief from rating) by adding Heythrop College to the list of colleges, institutions and schools in paragraph 2 which are exempted from the exclusion. The Order is given retrospective effect to 14th May 1971 under the express powers of section 40(4) of the Act.

(a) There is no amendment which relates expressly to the institution affected by this order.

1971 No. 2008

COMPENSATION

The Courts (Compensation to Officers) Regulations 1971

Made - - - -	10*th December* 1971
Laid before Parliament	17*th December* 1971
Coming into Operation	1*st January* 1972

ARRANGEMENT OF REGULATIONS

PART V

RETIREMENT COMPENSATION AND PAYMENTS ON DEATH

PART VI

ADJUSTMENT, REVIEW AND COMPOUNDING OF COMPENSATION

PART VII

PROCEDURE AND MISCELLANEOUS

SCHEDULE

The Lord Chancellor, in exercise of the powers conferred on him by section 44 of the Courts Act 1971**(a)**, and with the concurrence of the Minister for the Civil Service, hereby makes the following Regulations:—

PART I

PRELIMINARY

Citation and commencement

1. These Regulations may be cited as the Courts (Compensation to Officers) Regulations 1971 and shall come into operation on 1st January 1972.

Interpretation

2.—(1) In these Regulations, unless the context otherwise requires, the following expressions have the meanings hereby respectively assigned to them, that is to say:—

"accrued pension", in relation to a pensionable officer who has suffered loss of employment, means—

(*a*) if his last relevant pension scheme provided benefits in which he had a right to participate, the pension to which he would have become entitled in respect of his pensionable service according to the method of calculation (modified where necessary for the purpose of giving effect to these Regulations) prescribed by that scheme if, at the date on which he ceased to be subject to that scheme, he had attained normal retiring age and complied with any requirement of that scheme as to a minimum period of qualifying service or contribution and completed any additional contributory payments or payments in respect of added years which he was in the course of making; and

(*b*) in any other case, such portion of the pension (if any) of which he had reasonable expectations as the compensating authority consider equitable, having regard to his age, the length of his employment at the date of loss and all the other circumstances of the case;

"accrued retiring allowance", in relation to a pensionable officer who has suffered loss of employment, means—

(*a*) if his last relevant pension scheme provided benefits in which he had a right to participate, any lump sum payment to which he would have become entitled in respect of his pensionable service according to the method of calculation (modified where necessary for the purpose of giving effect to these Regulations) prescribed by that scheme if, at the date on which he ceased to be subject to that scheme, he had attained normal retiring age and complied with any requirement of that scheme as to a minimum period of qualifying service or contribution and completed any additional contributory payments or payments in respect of added years which he was in the course of making; and

(*b*) in any other case, such portion of the lump sum payment (if any) of which he had reasonable expectations as the compensating authority consider equitable, having regard to his age, the length of his employment at the date of loss and all the other circumstances of the case;

(a) 1971 c. 23.

"accrued incapacity pension" and "accrued incapacity retiring allowance" have the same respective meanings as "accrued pension" and "accrued retiring allowance" except that the reference to a person's attaining normal retiring age shall be construed as a reference to his becoming incapable of discharging efficiently the duties of his employment by reason of permanent ill-health or infirmity of mind or body;

"added years", in relation to a person who suffers loss of employment, means—

(*a*) in the case of a contributory employee or local Act contributor, any additional years of service reckonable by him in his employment immediately prior to the loss in question under Regulation 12 of the Local Government Superannuation (Benefits) Regulations 1954**(a)** as amended**(b)**, or any corresponding provision of a local Act scheme, or those Regulations or any such provision as aforesaid as applied by or under any enactment, and includes any additional years of service which, having been granted under any such provision or under any similar provision contained in any other enactment or scheme, have subsequently become and are reckonable under or by virtue of rules made under section 2 of the Superannuation (Miscellaneous Provisions) Act 1948**(c)**, or any other enactment; and

(*b*) in the case of any other person, any additional years of service, similar to those mentioned in paragraph (*a*) of this definition, reckonable by him under the pension scheme associated with the employment he has lost;

"additional contributory payments" means—

(*a*) additional contributory payments of the kind referred to in section 2(3) and (4) of the Local Government Superannuation Act 1953**(d)**; or

(*b*) any similar payments made under a local Act scheme or other pension scheme as a condition of reckoning any period of employment as service or as a period of contribution for the purposes of the scheme, or, where the scheme provides for the reckoning of non-contributing service, as contributing service for the purposes of the scheme; or

(*c*) any payments made for the purpose of increasing the length of which any period of service or of contribution would be reckonable for the purpose of calculating a benefit under a local Act scheme; or

(*d*) any payments similar to any of those mentioned in the foregoing subparagraphs made in pursuance of rules made under section 2 of the Superannuation (Miscellaneous Provisions) Act 1948;

"compensating authority" means the Lord Chancellor;

"compensation question" means a question arising under these Regulations—

(*a*) as to a person's entitlement to compensation for loss of employment, or for loss or diminution of emoluments; or

(*b*) as to the manner of a person's employment or the comparability of his duties;

"contributory employee", "contributing service", "non-contributing service", "local Act contributor" and "local Act scheme" have the same meanings as in the Local Government Superannuation Act 1937**(e)**;

(a) S.I. 1954/1048 (1954 II, p. 1595). **(b)** S.I. 1955/1041 (1955 II, p. 1825).
(c) 1948 c. 33. **(d)** 1953 c. 25. **(e)** 1937 c. 68.

"emoluments" means all salary, wages, fees and other payments paid or made to an officer as such for his own use, and also the money value of any apartments, rations or other allowances in kind appertaining to his employment, but does not include payments for overtime which are not a usual incident of his employment, or any allowances payable to him to cover the cost of providing office accommodation or clerical or other assistance, or any travelling or subsistence allowance or other moneys to be spent, or to cover expenses incurred, by him for the purposes of his employment; and

"net emoluments", in relation to any employment, means the annual rate of the emoluments of that employment less such part of those emoluments as the officer was liable to contribute under a pension scheme, and in relation to any employment which has been lost or the emoluments of which have been diminished, the expression means the annual rate of emoluments as aforesaid immediately before the loss or diminution, as the case may be:

Provided that where fees or other variable payments were paid to an officer as part of his emoluments during any period immediately preceding the loss or diminution, the amount in respect of fees or other variable payments to be included in the annual rate of emoluments shall be the annual average of the fees or other payments paid to him during the period of five years immediately preceding the loss or diminution, or such other period as the compensating authority may think reasonable in the circumstances;

"enactment" means any Act or any instrument made under an Act;

"last relevant pension scheme", in relation to a pensionable officer, means a pension scheme to which he was subject immediately before suffering loss of employment or loss or diminution of emoluments;

"local authority" means the council of a county, county borough, metropolitan borough, London borough, county district, rural parish or borough included in a rural district, the Greater London Council, the Common Council of the City of London and the council of the Isles of Scilly, any two or more of those authorities acting jointly and any joint committee, combined authority or joint board and a police authority for a county, a borough or a combined police area;

"long-term compensation" means compensation payable in accordance with the provisions of Part IV of these regulations for loss of employment or loss or diminution of emoluments;

"material date", in relation to any person who has suffered loss of employment or loss or diminution of emoluments, means, for the purposes of regulations 3 and 5, 30th June 1971, and, for all other purposes, 1st January 1972, or the date on which the loss or diminution occurred, whichever is the earlier;

"minimum pensionable age" means, in relation to a pensionable officer, the earliest age at which, under his last relevant pension scheme, he could have become entitled to receive payment of a pension, other than a pension payable in consequence of his redundancy or the termination of his employment in the interests of efficiency or his incapacity to discharge efficiently the duties of his employment by reason of permanent ill-health or infirmity of mind or body;

"national service" means service which is relevant service within the meaning of the Reserve and Auxiliary Forces (Protection of Civil Interests) Act 1951**(a)** and includes service immediately following such service as aforesaid being

(a) 1951 c. 65.

service in any of Her Majesty's naval, military or air forces pursuant to a voluntary engagement entered into with the consent of the authority or person under whom an officer held his last relevant employment or, where appropriate, the authority by whom such an officer was appointed.

"normal retiring age" means, in the case of a pensionable officer to whom an age of compulsory retirement applied by virtue of any enactment to which he was subject in the employment which he has lost or the emoluments of which have been diminished or by virtue of the conditions of that employment, that age, and, in any other case—

(*a*) in relation to a person claiming compensation in respect of the office of clerk of the peace, deputy clerk of the peace or under-sheriff, seventy years, and,

(*b*) in relation to any other person, the age of sixty-five years if the officer is a male, or sixty years if the officer is a female.

"officer" includes the holder of any place, situation or employment and the expression "office" shall be construed accordingly;

"pensionable officer", in relation to a person who has suffered loss of employment or loss or diminution of emoluments, means a person who immediately before such loss or diminution was subject to a pension scheme;

"pension scheme", in relation to a pensionable officer, means any form of arrangement associated with his employment for the payment of superannuation benefits, whether subsisting by virtue of Act of Parliament, trust, contract or otherwise;

"reckonable service", in relation to a person, means any period of whole-time or part-time employment in any relevant employment and includes any period of war service or national service undertaken on his ceasing to hold any such employment but does not include employment of which account has been taken, or is required to be taken, in calculating the amount of any superannuation benefit to which he has become entitled;

"relevant employment" means employment—

(*a*) under the Crown or in the service of a local authority or of any court abolished or merged under the Courts Act 1971 or in connection with the exercise of any function transferred to the Lord Chancellor or any other Minister by that Act;

(*b*) by any authority or body for the purposes of the Crown or of local government in the United Kingdom;

(*c*) under any officer employed as mentioned in paragraph (*a*) or (*b*) of this definition for the purposes of the functions of the employing authority or body;

(*d*) preceding any of the foregoing employments which was reckonable for the purposes of the last relevant pension scheme; or

(*e*) such other employment as the compensating authority may, in the case of any named officer, approve,

but except as provided in regulations 7(1) and 13(1) does not include service in the armed forces of the Crown;

"resettlement compensation" means compensation payable in accordance with Part III of these Regulations for loss of employment;

"retirement compensation" means compensation payable in accordance with the provisions of regulation 20, 21, 22 or 23;

"tribunal" means a tribunal established under section 12 of the Industrial Training Act 1964(**a**);

"war service" means war service within the meaning of the Local Government Staffs (War Service) Act 1939(**b**), the Teachers Superannuation (War Service) Act 1939(**c**), the Police and Firemen (War Service) Act 1939(**d**), or employment for was purposes within the meaning of the Superannuation Schemes (War Service) Act 1940(**e**), and includes any period of service in the first world was in the armed forces of the Crown or in the forces of the Allied or Associated Powers if such service immediately followed a period of relevant employment and was undertaken either compulsorily or with the permission of the employer in that employment.

(2) The holder of an office or appointment shall, for the purposes of these Regulations, be regarded as employed in that office or appointment and the expression "employment" shall be construed accordingly.

(3)(*a*) Where under any provision of these regulations an annual value is to be assigned to a capital sum or a capital value to an annual amount, the annual or capital value shall be ascertained in accordance with the tables set out in the schedule to these regulations insofar as they provide for the particular case.

(*b*) For the purpose of determining the application of the said tables the headings and the note to each table shall be treated as part of the table.

(*c*) Where the said tables do not provide for a case in which an annual value is to be assigned to a capital sum or a capital value to an annual amount, the annual or capital value shall be such as may be agreed between the compensating authority and the person to whom the capital sum or annual amount is payable.

(4) Unless the context otherwise requires, references in these Regulations to the provisions of any enactment shall be construed as references to those provisions as amended, re-enacted or modified by any subsequent enactment.

(5) References in these Regulations to a numbered regulation shall, unless the reference is to a regulation of specified regulations, be contrued as references to the regulation bearing that number in these Regulations.

(6) References in any of these Regulations to a numbered paragraph shall, unless the reference is to a paragraph of a specified regulation, be construed as references to the paragraph bearing that number in the first mentioned regulation.

(7) The Interpretation Act 1889(**f**) shall apply to the interpretation of these Regulations as it applies to the interpretation of an Act of Parliament.

PART II

ENTITLEMENT TO COMPENSATION

Persons to whom the regulations apply

3. These Regulations shall apply to any person who, for the whole or part only of his time, immediately before the material date—

(*a*) was employed in any office referred to in section 44(1) of the Courts Act 1971; or

(**a**) 1964 c. 16. (**b**) 1939 c. 94. (**c**) 1939 c. 95.
(**d**) 1939 c. 103. (**e**) 1940 c. 26 (**f**) 1889 c. 63.

(*b*) was employed, whether by or under the holder of any such office or otherwise, in connection with the exercise of the functions of any court abolished or merged, or in connection with any function transferred to the Lord Chancellor or to any other Minister, by that Act; or

(*c*) would have been so employed but for any national service on which he was then engaged.

Grounds of entitlement to compensation

4. Subject to the provisions of these Regulations, any person to whom these Regulations apply and who suffers loss of employment or loss or diminution of emoluments which is attributable to—

(*a*) the provisions of section 44(1) of the Courts Act 1971,

(*b*) the abolition or merger of any court by that Act, or

(*c*) the transfer by that Act of any function to the Lord Chancellor or to any other Minister

shall be entitled to have his case considered for the payment of compensation under these regulations, and such compensation shall be determined in accordance with these regulations.

National Service

5.—(1) Where any person to whom these Regulations apply would have been employed immediately before the material date in any capacity referred to in paragraphs (*a*) or (*b*) of regulation 3 but for any national service on which he was then engaged, then if before the expiry of two months after ceasing to be so engaged, or if prevented by sickness or other reasonable cause, as soon as practicable thereafter, he gives notice to the compensating authority that he is available for employment, that person shall be entitled to have his case considered for the payment of compensation on the ground—

(*a*) if he is not given or offered re-employment in his former office or in any reasonably comparable office (whether in the same or in a different service), of loss of employment; or

(*b*) if he is so re-employed with diminished emoluments as compared with the emoluments which he would have enjoyed had he continued in his former employment, of diminution of emoluments.

(2) The loss of employment which is the cause of a claim for compensation under paragraph (1)(*a*) shall be treated as having occurred on the earlier of the two following dates, that is to say, the date of the refusal of re-employment or a date one month after the date on which the person gave notice that he was available for employment; and the person shall be deemed to have been entitled to the emoluments which he would have enjoyed at such earlier date had he continued in his former employment.

PART III

RESETTLEMENT COMPENSATION

Resettlement compensation for loss of employment

6. The compensating authority shall, subject to the provisions of these Regulations, pay resettlement compensation to any person to whom these Regulations apply and who satisfies the conditions set out in regulation 7.

Conditions for payment of resettlement compensation

7.—(1) Without prejudice to any other requirement of these Regulations, the conditions for the payment of resettlement compensation to any person are that—

(*a*) he has suffered loss of employment attributable to any of the matters referred to in regulation 4 on or after 30th June 1971 but not later than ten years after the material date;

(*b*) he had not at the date of the loss attained normal retiring age;

(*c*) he had been for a period beginning on the date three years immediately before the material date and ending on the date when the loss of employment occurred continuously engaged (disregarding breaks not exceeding in the aggregate six months) for the whole or part of his time in relevant employment; and for this purpose the expression "relevant employment" includes any period of national service immediately following such employment;

(*d*) he has made a claim for such compensation in accordance with the provisions of Part VII of these Regulations not later than thirteen weeks after the loss of employment which is the cause of his claim, or thirteen weeks after the coming into operation of these Regulations, whichever is the later, or within such longer period as the compensating authority may allow in any particular case where they are satisfied that the delay in making the claim was due to ill-health or other circumstances beyond the claimant's control;

(*e*) the loss of employment which is the cause of his claim has occurred for some reason other than misconduct or incapacity to perform such duties as, immediately before the loss, he was performing or might reasonably have been required to perform; and

(*f*) he has not, subject to paragraph (3), been offered any reasonably comparable employment under the Crown or in the service of a local authority.

(2) In ascertaining for the purposes of this regulation whether a person has been offered employment which is reasonably comparable with the employment which he has lost, no account shall be taken of the fact that the duties of the employment offered are in relation to a different service from that in connection with which his employment was held or are duties which involve a transfer of his employment from one place to another within England and Wales.

(3) No account shall be taken for the purposes of this regulation of an offer of employment where the compensating authority is satisfied—

(*a*) that acceptance would have involved undue hardship to the person, or

(*b*) that he was prevented from accepting the offer by reason of ill-health or other circumstances beyond his control.

Amount of resettlement compensation

8.—(1) The amount of resettlement compensation which may be paid to a person shall, for each week for which such compensation is payable, be a sum ascertained by taking two-thirds of the weekly rate of the net emoluments which that person has lost and deducting therefrom, in addition to the items mentioned in regulation 33(3) and (4), such of the following items as may be applicable—

(*a*) unemployment, sickness or injury benefit under any Act relating to National Insurance claimable by him in respect of such week (excluding any amount claimable by him in respect of a dependant); and (*b*) two-thirds of the net emoluments received by him in respect of such week from work or employment undertaken as a result of the loss of employment.

(2) For the purposes of this regulation the weekly rate of a person's net emoluments shall be deemed to be seven three hundred and sixty-fifths of those emoluments.

Period for payment of resettlement compensation

9. Subject to the provisions of these Regulations, resettlement compensation shall be payable to a person only in respect of the period of thirteen weeks next succeeding the week in which he lost the employment in respect of which his claim has been made or, in the case of a person who has attained the age of forty-five years, the said thirteen weeks and one additional week for every year of his age after attaining the age of forty-five years and before the date of the loss of employment, subject to a maximum addition of thirteen such weeks.

Additional provisions relating to resettlement compensation

10.—(1) Resettlement compensation shall be payable to a person at intervals equivalent to those at which the emoluments of his employment were previously paid or at such other intervals as may be agreed between the person and the compensating authority.

(2) Resettlement compensation shall be terminated by the compensating authority—

(*a*) if without reasonable cause the recipient fails to comply with any of the provisions of regulation 11, or

(*b*) if on being requested to do so, he fails to satisfy the compensating authority that, so far as he is able, he is seeking suitable employment.

Claimant for resettlement compensation to furnish particulars of employment.

11. Every person claiming or in receipt of resettlement compensation shall (after as well as before the compensation begins to be paid)—

(*a*) forthwith supply the compensating authority in writing with particulars of any employment which he obtains or of any change in his earnings from any such employment, and

(*b*) if the compensating authority so require, so long as he is out of employment and is not receiving sickness or injury benefit, register with the Department of Employment.

PART IV

LONG-TERM COMPENSATION

Long-term compensation for loss of employment or loss or diminution of emoluments

12. The compensating authority shall, subject to the provisions of these Regulations, pay long-term compensation to any person to whom these Regulations apply and who satisfies the conditions set out in regulation 13.

Conditions for payments of long-term compensation

13.—(1) Without prejudice to any other requirement of these Regulations, the conditions for the payment of long-term compensation to any person are that—

(*a*) he has suffered loss of employment or loss or diminution of emoluments attributable to any of the matters referred to in regulation 4 on or after 30th June 1971, but not later than ten years after the material date;

(*b*) he had not, save as is provided in regulation 29, at the date of the loss or diminution attained normal retiring age;

(*c*) he had been for a period beginning on a date not less than eight years immediately before the material date and ending on the date when the loss or diminution occurred continuously engaged (without a break of more than twelve months at any one time) for the whole or part of his time in relevant employment; and for this purpose the expression "relevant employment" includes any period of national service immediately following such employment;

(*d*) he has made a claim for such compensation in accordance with the provisions of Part VII of these Regulations not later than two years after the loss or diminution which is the cause of the claim or two years after the coming into operation of these Regulations whichever is the later; and

(*e*) if the cause of the claim for compensation is loss of employment—

(i) the loss has occurred for some reason other than misconduct or incapacity to perform such duties as, immediately before the loss, he was performing or might reasonably have been required to perform; and

(ii) he has not been offered any reasonably comparable employment under the Crown or in the service of a local authority.

(2) Regulation 7(2) and (3) (which relate to offers of employment) shall apply for the purposes of this regulation in ascertaining whether a person has been offered reasonably comparable employment.

(3) Claims for long-term compensation for loss of employment shall in all respects be treated as claims for such compensation for the loss of emoluments occasioned thereby and the provisions of these Regulations shall apply to all such claims accordingly.

Factors to be considered in determining payment of long-term compensation

14.—(1) For the purpose of determining the amount (subject to the limits set out in these Regulations) of long-term compensation, if any, payable under these Regulations to any person for loss or diminution of emoluments, the compensating authority shall have regard to such of the following factors as may be relevant, that is to say—

(*a*) the conditions upon which the person held the employment which he has lost, including in particular its security of tenure, whether by law or practice;

(*b*) the emoluments and other conditions, including security of tenure, whether by law or practice, of any work or employment undertaken by the person as a result of the loss of employment;

(*c*) the extent to which he has sought suitable employment and the emoluments which he might have acquired by accepting other suitable employment offered to him;

(*d*) all the other circumstances of his case.

(2) In ascertaining for the purposes of paragraph (1)(*c*) whether a person has been offered suitable employment, regulation 7(2) and (3) shall apply as they apply for the purpose of ascertaining whether employment is reasonably comparable with employment which has been lost.

Amount of long-term compensation payable for loss of emoluments

15.—(1) Long-term compensation for loss of emoluments shall, subject to the provisions of these Regulations, be payable until the normal retiring age or death of a person to whom it is payable, whichever first occurs, and shall not exceed a maximum annual sum calculated in accordance with the provisions of paragraphs (2) to (4).

(2) The said maximum annual sum shall, subject as hereinafter provided, be the aggregate of the following sums, namely—

(*a*) for every year of the person's reckonable service, one sixtieth of the net emoluments which he has lost; and

(*b*) in the case of a person who has attained the age of forty years at the date of the loss, a sum calculated in accordance with the provisions of paragraph (3) appropriate to his age at that date,

but the said maximum annual sum shall in no case exceed two-thirds of the net emoluments which the person has lost.

(3) The sum referred to in paragraph (2)(*b*) shall be—

(*a*) in the case of a person who has attained the age of forty years but has not attained the age of fifty years at the date of the loss, the following fraction of the net emoluments which he has lost—

(i) where his reckonable service is less than ten years, one sixtieth for each year of such service, after attaining the age of forty years; or

(ii) where his reckonable service amounts to ten years but is less than fifteen years, one sixtieth for each year of such service after attaining the age of forty years and one additional sixtieth; or

(iii) where his reckonable service amounts to fifteen years but is less than twenty years, one sixtieth for each year of such service after attaining the age of forty years and two additional sixtieths; or

(iv) where his reckonable service amounts to twenty years or more, one sixtieth for each year of such service after attaining the age of forty years and three additional sixtieths;

but the sum so calculated shall not in any case exceed one sixth of the said net emoluments;

(*b*) in the case of a person who has attained the age of fifty years but has not attained the age of sixty years at the date of the loss, one sixtieth of the said net emoluments for each year of his reckonable service after attaining the age of forty years, up to a maximum of fifteen such years; and

(*c*) in the case of a person who has attained the age of sixty years at the date of the loss, one sixtieth of the said net emoluments for each year of his reckonable service after attaining the age of forty-five years.

(4) Where a person has become entitled (whether immediately or prospectively on attaining some greater age) to a superannuation benefit by way of annual amounts under a pension scheme associated with the employment which he has

lost, the maximum annual sum referred to in paragraph (1) shall be the maximum sum calculated under paragraphs (2) and (3) as if he had not become so entitled.

(5) Where long-term compensation is payable in respect of any period and resettlement compensation is also payable in respect of that period, the long-term compensation shall be limited to the amount (if any) by which it exceeds the resettlement compensation payable as aforesaid.

(6) Long-term compensation shall be payable to a person at intervals equivalent to those at which the emoluments of his employment were previously paid or at such other intervals as may be agreed between the person and the compensating authority.

Long-term compensation for diminution of emoluments

16. Long-term compensation for diminution of emoluments in respect of any employment shall, subject to the provisions of these Regulations, be awarded and paid in accordance with the following provisions:—

(*a*) the compensation shall consist of an annual sum which shall be payable to a person at intervals equivalent to those at which the emoluments of his employment are or were previously paid or at such other intervals as may be agreed between the person and the compensating authority, and shall, subject to the provisions of these Regulations, be payable until normal retiring age or death, whichever first occurs; and

(*b*) the said annual sum shall not exceed the maximum annual sum which could have been awarded under regulation 15 if the person had suffered loss of employment and the loss of emoluments occasioned thereby had been equivalent to the amount of the diminution:

Provided that no compensation shall be payable if the emoluments have been diminished by less than 2½ per cent.

Date from which long-term compensation is to be payable

17.—(1) Long-term compensation shall be payable with effect from the date of the claim or from any earlier date permitted by the succeeding provisions of this regulation.

(2) Where a claim for long-term compensation is duly made within thirteen weeks of the occurrence of the loss or diminution which is the cause of the claim, the award shall be made retrospective to the date on which the loss or diminution occurred.

(3) Where a claim for long-term compensation is made after the expiry of the period mentioned in paragraph (2), the award may, at the discretion of the compensating authority, be made retrospective to a date not earlier than thirteen weeks prior to the date on which the claim was made:

Provided that if the compensating authority are satisfied that the failure to make the claim within the period mentioned in paragraph (2) was due to ill-health or other circumstances beyond the claimant's control, the award may be made retrospective to a date not earlier than that on which the loss or diminution occurred.

PART V

RETIREMENT COMPENSATION AND PAYMENTS ON DEATH

Entitlement to retirement compensation and other payments

18.—(1) The compensating authority shall, subject to the provisions of these Regulations, pay retirement compensation to any person to whom this part of these Regulations applies, and shall make the other payments for which provision is made in regulations 26 to 30.

(2) Save as is provided in regulation 29, this Part of these Regulations applies to a pensionable officer who satisfies the conditions set out in regulation 13.

(3) Regulation 14 shall apply in relation to retirement compensation and payments under Part V as it applies in relation to compensation under Part IV.

Additional factors governing payment of retirement compensation

19.—(1) Where retirement compensation is payable under any one of regulations 20, 21, 22 and 23, such compensation shall not be payable under any other of those regulations.

(2) If a person has attained the age of forty years at the date on which he lost his employment or suffered a diminution of his emoluments, the compensating authority, in calculating the amount of the retirement compensation payable to him, shall credit him with additional years of service or an additional period of contribution on the following basis, namely—

(*a*) two years, whether or not he has completed any years of service after attaining the age of forty years, and

(*b*) two years for each of the first four completed years of his reckonable service between the date when he attained the age of forty years and the date of the loss or diminution, and

(*c*) one year for each such year of service after the fourth,

but the additional years of service or period of contribution so credited shall not exceed the shortest of the following periods, namely—

(i) such number of years as, when added to his pensionable service, would amount to the maximum period of such service which would have been reckonable by him had he continued in his employment until attaining normal retiring age, or

(ii) the number of years of his reckonable service, or

(iii) fifteen years;

and in calculating the amount of any retirement compensation payable to him any period so added shall be aggregated with any years of service or period of contribution entailing reduction of the relevant pension or retiring allowance because of a retirement pension payable under section 30 of the National Insurance Act 1965(**a**).

(3) When retirement compensation is awarded, or when an award is reviewed under regulation 35, the additional compensation payable in consequence of any years of service or period of contribution credited to a person under paragraph (2) may be reduced or withheld to such extent as the compensating authority may think reasonable having regard to the pension scheme (if any) associated with any further employment obtained by him.

(4) If under his last relevant pension scheme the amount of any benefit to which a person might have become entitled could have been increased at the discretion of the authority administering the pension scheme or of any other body,

(**a**) 1965 c. 51.

the compensating authority may increase, to an extent not exceeding that to which his accrued pension, accrued retiring allowance, accrued incapacity pension or accrued incapacity retiring allowance might have been increased or supplemented, the corresponding component of any retirement compensation payable to him; and in this connection the compensating authority shall have regard to the terms of any relevant resolutions of the authority or body with regard to the increase of benefits and to the provisions of any enactment protecting the interests of that person.

(5) If under his last relevant pension scheme a person would have been entitled to surrender a proportion of any pension which might have become payable to him in favour of his spouse or any dependant, then, if he so desires and informs the compensating authority by notice in writing accordingly within one month after becoming entitled to retirement compensation under these Regulations, he may surrender a proportion of so much of the said compensation as is payable by way of an annual sum on the like terms and conditions and in consideration of the like payments by the compensating authority as if the said annual sum were a pension to which he had become entitled under the said pension scheme.

(6) In calculating for the purposes of regulation 20, 21 or 22 the amount of the annual sum which is equal to a person's accrued pension, no account shall be taken of any reduction falling to be made in that pension by reason of the provisions of any Act relating to National Insurance until the person reaches the age at which under his last relevant pension scheme the pension would have been so reduced.

(7) In paragraph (2) the expression "reckonable service" includes any period of employment of which account has been taken or is required to be taken in calculating the amount of any superannuation benefit to which a person has become entitled under a pension scheme associated with the employment which he has lost or, as the case may be, the employment in which his emoluments were diminished.

Retirement compensation for loss of emoluments payable to pensionable officer on attainment of normal retiring age

20.—(1) Subject to the provisions of these Regulations, when a person to whom this part of these Regulations applies reaches normal retiring age, the retirement compensation payable to him for loss of emoluments shall be—

(*a*) an annual sum equal to the amount of his accrued pension, and

(*b*) a lump sum equal to the amount of his accrued retiring allowance (if any).

(2) Where an annual sum is payable under this regulation in respect of any period and resettlement compensation is also payable in respect of that period, the said annual sum shall be limited to the amount (if any) by which it exceeds the resettlement compensation so payable as aforesaid.

(3) No compensation shall be payable under this regulation if the person had continued to pay superannuation contributions as if he had suffered no loss of emoluments.

Retirement compensation payable to pensionable officer on his becoming incapacitated or reaching minimum pensionable age

21.—(1) Where a person to whom this part of these Regulations applies and who has suffered loss of employment before attaining what would have been his normal retiring age—

(*a*) becomes incapacitated in circumstances in which, if he had continued in the employment which he has lost, he would have become entitled to a pension under his last relevant pension scheme; or (*b*) attains the age which, had he continued to serve in the employment which he has lost, would have been his minimum pensionable age,

he shall be entitled on the happening of either event to claim, in lieu of any compensation to which he would otherwise be entitled under these Regulations—

(i) in the case mentioned in head (*a*) of this paragraph, an annual sum equal to the amount of his accrued incapacity pension and a lump sum equal to the amount of his accrued incapacity retiring allowance (if any), and

(ii) in the case mentioned in head (*b*) of this paragraph, an annual sum equal to the amount of his accrued pension and a lump sum equal to the amount of his accrued retiring allowance (if any),

subject, however, to the conditions specified in paragraph (5).

(2) On receipt of a claim under paragraph (1) the compensating authority shall consider whether the claimant is a person to whom that paragraph applies, and within thirteen weeks after the date of the receipt of the claim—

(*a*) if they are satisfied that he is not such a person, they shall notify him in writing accordingly; or

(*b*) if they are satisfied that he is such a person, they shall assess the amount of compensation payable to him and notify him in writing accordingly,

and any such notification shall, for the purposes of these Regulations, be deemed to be notification by the authority of a decision on a claim for compensation.

(3) A compensating authority may require any person who makes a claim under paragraph (1)(*a*) to submit himself to a medical examination by a registered medical practitioner selected by that authority, and if they do so, they shall also offer the person an opportunity of submitting a report from his own medical adviser as a result of an examination by him, and the authority shall take that report into consideration together with the report of the medical practitioner selected by them.

(4) If a person wishes to receive compensation under this regulation, he shall so inform the compensating authority in writing within one month from the receipt of a notification under paragraph (2) or, where the claim has been the subject of an appeal, from the decision of the tribunal thereon; and the compensation shall be payable as from the date on which the compensating authority received the claim.

(5) The calculation of compensation under this regulation shall be subject to the following conditions—

(*a*) where the compensating authority, by virtue of regulation 19, have credited the person with additional years of service or an additional period of contribution, no account shall be taken of any additional years or period beyond the number of years which he could have served, had he not lost his employment, before the date on which the claim was received by the compensating authority; and

(*b*) if, by reason of any provision of the relevant pension scheme for a minimum benefit, the amount of any such pension or retiring allowance is in excess of that attributable to the person's actual service, no account shall be taken of any such additional years or period except to the extent (if any) by which they exceed the number of years represented by the difference between his actual service and the period by reference to which the minimum benefit has been calculated; and (*c*) if the number of years by reference to which an accrued incapacity pension or accrued incapacity retiring allowance is to be calculated is less than any minimum number of years of qualifying service prescribed by the relevant pension scheme, the amount of such pension or retiring allowance shall, notwithstanding any minimum benefit prescribed by the pension scheme, not exceed such proportion of such minimum benefit as the number of years of pensionable service bears to the minimum number of years of qualifying service.

Option to take retirement compensation prematurely

22.—(1) If a person to whom this Part of these Regulations applies has suffered loss of employment after attaining the age of fifty years and so requests the compensating authority by notice in writing, he shall be entitled, as from the date on which the compensating authority received such notice, to an annual sum equal to the amount of his accrued pension and a lump sum equal to the amount of his accrued retiring allowance (if any), and in that event he shall not be entitled to receive any further payment of long-term compensation after that date:

Provided that—

(i) in calculating the amount of the compensation payable to a person who has given such notice as aforesaid no account shall be taken of any additional years of service or period of contribution credited to him under regulation 19; and

(ii) where the person has claimed long-term compensation the said notice shall be given not later than two years after the decision on the claim or, where the decision has been reviewed under regulation 35(3), not later than two years after the review, or if there has been more than one such review, after the latest.

(2) Regulation 21(2) shall apply in relation to a notice given under the last foregoing paragraph as it applies to a claim under paragraph (1) of that regulation.

(3) Where an annual sum is payable under this regulation in respect of any period and resettlement compensation is also payable in respect of that period, the said annual sum shall be limited to the amount (if any) by which it exceeds the resettlement compensation payable as aforesaid.

Retirement compensation for diminution of emoluments

23.—(1) A person to whom this Part of these Regulations applies and who has suffered a diminution of his emoluments shall be entitled to receive retirement compensation in accordance with the provisions of this regulation.

(2) The provisions of regulations 20 and 21 shall apply to any such person as if he had suffered loss of employment immediately before the diminution occurred; but the amount of the retirement compensation payable shall be the amount which would have been payable in respect of loss of employment multiplied by a fraction of which—

(*a*) the numerator is the amount by which his emoluments have been diminished, and

(*b*) the denominator is the amount of his emoluments immediately before they were diminished.

For the purposes of this calculation no account shall be taken of any reduction which might otherwise fall to be made in the accrued pension or accrued incapacity pension because of a retirement pension payable under section 30 of the National Insurance Act 1965.

(3) No compensation shall be payable under this regulation—

(*a*) if the person's emoluments have been diminished by less than 2½ per cent; or

(*b*) if the person had continued to pay superannuation contributions as if his emoluments had not been diminished.

Superannuation contributions

24.—(1) A person entitled to retirement compensation under regulation 20, 21 or 22 shall pay to the compensating authority an amount equal to any sum which was paid to him by way of return of superannuation contributions, including any interest, after ceasing to be employed, and the compensating authority may at his request repay that amount to him at any time before he becomes entitled as aforesaid, but if that amount is not paid to the compensating authority, or is repaid by it to the person, the compensation shall be reduced by an annual amount the capital value of which is equal to the amount of the said superannuation contributions.

(2) For the purposes of this regulation the expression "superannuation contributions" shall include payments made by the person in respect of added years and any additional contributory payments made by him.

Retirement compensation of a person who obtains further pensionable employment

25.—(1) Where a person to whom this Part of these Regulations applies, after suffering loss of employment or diminution of emoluments, enters employment in which he is subject to a pension scheme and thereafter becomes entitled to reckon for the purposes of that scheme any service or period of contribution which falls to be taken into account for the purpose of assessing the amount of any retirement compensation payable to him, his entitlement to retirement compensation shall be reviewed and no retirement compensation shall be payable in respect of such service or period unless the annual rate of the emoluments to which he was entitled immediately before such loss or diminution exceeds the annual rate on entry of the emoluments of the new employment by more than 2½ per cent of such first mentioned emoluments, and any retirement compensation so payable to him shall, in so far as it is calculated by reference to remuneration, be calculated by reference to the difference between the said annual rates:

Provided that—

(i) if on entering the new employment a person—

(*a*) becomes a contributory employee or local Act contributor, and

(*b*) becomes entitled to reckon as non-contributing service, or as service at half-length for purposes of a local Act scheme, any service or period of contribution which immediately before the loss of employment or the diminution of emoluments was reckonable as contributing service or a period of contribution,

one-half of that service or period shall not be subject to the provisions of this paragraph;

(ii) this paragraph shall not operate to increase the amount of any retirement compensation payable in respect of diminution of emoluments beyond the amount which would have been payable if the person had attained normal retiring age immediately before he ceased to hold the employment in which he suffered the diminution of emoluments.

(2) No retirement compensation shall be payable in the circumstances mentioned in paragraph (1) if the person has continued to pay superannuation contributions as if his emoluments had not been diminished.

Compensation payable to widow or dependants of a claimant

26.—(1) Payments in accordance with this regulation and regulations 27 and 28 shall be made to or for the benefit of the widow, child or other dependant or to the personal representatives of a person to whom this Part of these Regulations applies or, as the case may be, to trustees empowered by such a person to stand possessed of any benefit under his last relevant pension scheme.

(2) If the widow, child or other dependant of that person might have become entitled but for the loss of his employment to a pension under his last relevant pension scheme, the widow, child or other dependant, as the case may be, shall be entitled to receive—

(*a*) where the pension scheme provides for a prescribed proportion, an annual sum equal to the prescribed proportion of any retirement compensation by way of annual amounts payable to the person under regulation 20, 21 or 22 immediately before his death or, if he dies before becoming entitled to receive compensation under any of those regulations, the prescribed proportion of the compensation by way of annual amounts which he would have received under regulation 21 had he become entitled thereto immediately before his death, and

(*b*) where the pension scheme does not provide for a prescribed proportion, such an annual sum as is provided by paragraph (3):

Provided that—

(i) where any retirement compensation has been surrendered under regulation 19(5) or compounded under regulation 36, any sum payable under sub-paragraph (*a*) shall be calculated as if such surrender or compounding had not taken place, and

(ii) in calculating the sum payable under sub-paragraph (*a*) it shall be assumed that the retirement compensation payable, or which would have been payable, to a person under regulation 20, 21 or 22 had been such sum as would have been payable if the accrued pension or accrued incapacity pension had not been reduced by reason of the provisions of any Act relating to National Insurance.

(3) The sum mentioned in paragraph (2)(*b*) shall be an annual sum equal to the annual amount of the pension (calculated in the manner specified in paragraph (4)) to which the widow, child or other dependant of the person in question would have become entitled if he had died immediately before the date on which he suffered the loss of employment, having then complied with any requirements of the last relevant pension scheme as to a minimum period of qualifying service or contribution and completed any additional contributory payments or payments in respect of added years which he was then in the course of making.

(4) The calculation referred to in paragraph (3) shall be made on the basis of the method prescribed by the last relevant pension scheme of the person in question for the calculation of benefits for a widow, child or other dependant and in so far as the age at which he died is relevant for the purposes of the said calculation, the date on which he died shall be taken to be the actual date of his death, the provisions of paragraph (3) to the contrary notwithstanding.

(5) Any annual sum payable to or for the benefit of a widow, child or other dependant under this regulation shall cease to be payable in any circumstances in which a corresponding pension under the last relevant pension scheme would have ceased to be payable; and where that scheme provides for payment of the pension to any person on behalf of a child or other dependant, any annual sum payable under this regulation to a child or other dependant shall be paid to that person on behalf of the child or dependant in the like manner and for the like period as is provided in the pension scheme.

(6) Except where the compensation has been reduced under regulation 24, compensation payable under this regulation and regulation 27 shall in the aggregate be reduced by an amount the capital value whereof is equal to the amount of any superannuation contributions as defined in regulation 24(2) returned to the person in respect of whom the compensation is payable and either not paid to the compensating authority or repaid to that person by the compensating authority, the compensation under each such regulation being reduced in proportion to the capital value of each amount.

(7) If the person in question suffered a diminution of emoluments, then—

(*a*) where his last relevant pension scheme provides for a prescribed proportion, the provisions of paragraph (2)(*a*) shall apply with the substitution of references to diminution of emoluments for references to loss of employment, and the annual sum payable to a widow, child or other dependant of such a person shall be calculated as if he had suffered loss of employment and as if the loss of emoluments occasioned thereby had been equivalent to the amount of the diminution:

Provided that no sum shall be payable under this sub-paragraph—

(i) if the emoluments have been diminished by less than 2½ per cent; or

(ii) if the person had continued to pay superannuation contributions as if his emoluments had not been diminished;

and

(*b*) where the said scheme does not provide for a prescribed proportion. the provisions of paragraph (2)(*b*) and of regulation 33(4)(*a*) shall apply with the substitution of references to diminution of emoluments for the references to loss of employment and of a reference to employment in which he has suffered such a diminution for the reference to employment which he has lost:

Provided that no sum shall be payable under this sub-paragraph if the sum calculated thereunder amounts to less than 2½ per cent of such sum as would have been payable had the person in question suffered a loss of employment instead of a diminution of emoluments.

(8) In this regulation "prescribed proportion" means the proportion which, by the provisions contained in the last relevant pension scheme of a person to whom this Part of these Regulations applies, the pension payable to his widow, child or other dependant is to bear to that person's pension.

Compensation where death grant would have been payable

27.—(1) If the widow, the personal representatives of a person to whom this part of these Regulations applies or trustees empowered by such a person to stand possessed of any benefit under his last relevant pension scheme, might have become entitled to a death grant under that scheme, she or they, as the case may be, shall be entitled to receive a sum calculated in accordance with the provision of regulation 26(6) and paragraph (2) of this regulation.

(2) The amount of the sum referred to in paragraph (1) shall be ascertained in accordance with the method of calculation prescribed by the last relevant pension scheme for the ascertainment of death grant as if the person had died immediately before losing his employment, subject to the following modifications—

(*a*) except where the person had been in receipt of retirement compensation under regulation 22, account shall be taken of any additional years of service or period of contribution credited to him under regulation 19(2)—

(i) in the case of a person who had been in receipt of retirement compensation under regulation 21, to the extent of the period between the loss of employment and the date of the claim made under that regulation; and

(ii) in any other case, to the extent of the period between the loss of employment and the person's death;

(*b*) if the number of years of the person's service or period of contribution is less than the minimum number of years of qualifying service or period prescribed by the pension scheme for the receipt of a death grant, the said sum shall not exceed such proportion of the death grant calculated as aforesaid as the number of years of the person's pensionable service or period of contribution bears to the minimum number of years of qualifying service or period prescribed by the pension scheme; and

(*c*) there shall be deducted from such sum the amount of any retirement compensation paid to the person under regulation 20, 21 or 22, or where any part of the compensation has been surrendered under regulation 19(5), the amount which would have been so paid but for any such surrender.

(3) For the purpose of calculating such death grant, an annual sum payable under either paragraph (2)(*a*) or paragraph (7)(*a*) of regulation 26 to or for the benefit of the widow, child or other dependant shall be deemed to be a pension payable to or for the benefit of the widow, child or dependant, as the case may be.

(4) This regulation shall apply in the case of a person who has suffered a diminution of emoluments with the substitution of references to diminution of emoluments for references to loss of employment, and the sum payable to the widow, personal representatives or trustees of such a person shall be calculated as if he had lost emoluments equivalent to the amount of the diminution:

Provided that no sum shall be payable under this paragraph—

(i) if the emoluments have been diminished by less than 2½ per cent; or

(ii) if the person has continued to pay superannuation contributions as if his emoluments had not been diminished.

Balance payable to claimant's widow or personal representatives

28.—(1) If no annual sum is payable to the widow, child or other dependant of any person under regulation 26(2)(*a*) or (7)(*a*) and no sum is payable under regulation 27 and the person dies before he has received in the aggregate by way of retirement compensation a sum equivalent to the amount of any contributions repaid by him under regulation 24, together with compound interest thereon calculated at the rate of 3 per cent per annum with half-yearly rests up to the date of his death as from the 1st April or 1st October following the half-year in which the amount was paid, there shall be paid to his personal representatives the difference between the aggregate amount received by way of retirement compensation as aforesaid and the said equivalent sum.

(2) If an annual sum becomes payable to a widow under either paragraph (2)(*a*) or paragraph (7)(*a*) of regulation 26 and on her re-marriage or death the sum ceases to be payable, and any sum payable to a child or other dependant under either of those paragraphs has ceased to be payable, and if the aggregate amount of the payments which were made as aforesaid to her husband by way of retirement compensation and to the widow, personal representatives or trustees under regulation 27 is less than a sum equivalent to the amount which would have been payable to the personal representatives under that regulation if no annual sum had been payable under either of the said paragraph (2)(*a*) or (7)(*a*), there shall be paid to her or her personal representatives the difference between such aggregate amount and the said equivalent sum.

(3) For the purposes of this regulation a person who has surrendered any part of his retirement compensation under regulation 19(5) shall be deemed to have received during any period the amount of compensation for that period which he would have received but for any such surrender.

Compensation payable to non-pensionable officer on reaching retiring age

29.—(1) Where a person who is not a pensionable officer is receiving long-term compensation for loss of employment and attains normal retiring age, the compensating authority may, if satisfied that the person would, but for the loss, have continued in the employment he has lost for a substantial period beyond that age, continue to pay compensation to him for the remainder of his life at half its former rate.

(2) Where a person who is not a pensionable officer suffers loss of employment on or after attaining normal retiring age, the compensating authority may, if satisfied that the person would in the normal course have continued in the employment he has lost for a further substantial period, pay compensation to him for the remainder of his life at half the rate to which he would have been entitled under regulation 15 had he not attained normal retiring age at the date on which he lost his employment.

Persons subject to policy schemes

30.—(1) Regulations 20, 21, 22, 23 and 27 shall not apply to a person (in this regulation referred to as a "policy scheme participant") who had been participating in a scheme associated with his employment for providing superannuation benefits by means of contracts or policies of insurance, and who, after the loss of his employment or the diminution of his emoluments, continued to participate in that scheme, or became entitled to a benefit or prospective benefit thereunder other than a return of contributions.

(2) If a policy scheme participant has lost his employment, the compensating authority may, if the relevant scheme so permits, make such payments to or in respect of him, whether by way of the payment of premiums or otherwise, as are actuarially equivalent to the amounts by which his retirement compensation might have been increased under regulation 19(2) or (4) had he been a person to whom regulation 20, 21 or 22 applied.

(3) If a policy scheme participant has suffered a diminution of his emoluments, the compensating authority may, if the relevant scheme so permits, make such payments to or in respect of him, whether by way of the payment of premiums or otherwise, as will secure to him the like benefits as if his emoluments had not been diminished.

(4) If a policy scheme participant becomes entitled to a benefit under such a scheme as is mentioned in paragraph (1) before reaching normal retiring age, the compensating authority may reduce any long-term compensation payable to him by the amount of such benefit.

Intervals for payment of compensation under Part V

31. Any compensation awarded as an annual sum under this Part of these Regulations to or in respect of any person shall be payable at intervals equivalent to those at which the corresponding benefit would have been payable under the person's last relevant pension scheme or at such other intervals as may be agreed between the person entitled to receive the compensation and the compensating authority.

PART VI

ADJUSTMENT, REVIEW AND COMPOUNDING OF COMPENSATION

Adjustment of compensation where superannuation benefit is also payable

32.—(1) Where any period of service of which account was taken in calculating the amount of any compensation payable under Part IV or V of these Regulations is subsequently taken into account for the purpose of calculating the amount of any superannuation benefit payable to or in respect of any person in accordance with a pension scheme associated with any employment undertaken subsequent to the loss of employment or diminution of emoluments which was the subject of the claim for compensation, the compensating authority may in accordance with this regulation withhold or reduce the compensation payable.

(2) If the part of any superannuation benefit which is attributable to a period of service mentioned in paragraph (1) equals or exceeds the part of any compensation which is attributable to the same period, that part of the compensation may be withheld, or if such part of the superannuation benefit is less than such part of the compensation, the compensation may be reduced by an amount not exceeding such part of the superannuation benefit.

(3) In the case of a death benefit payable in respect of any person, the sum payable under regulation 27 may be reduced by an amount not greater than the proportion of the death benefit which the period of service mentioned in paragraph (1) bears to the total period of service of which account was taken in the calculation of the death benefit.

(4) In addition to any reduction authorised by paragraph (2) or (3), if, in the circumstances mentioned in paragraph (1), compensation is attributable in part to any provision of the relevant pension scheme for a minimum benefit, the compensation may be reduced by an amount not exceeding that part.

(5) Where any additional years of service or period of contribution have been credited to a person under regulation 19(2), if the number of such years or such period is equal to or less than the period spent in the subsequent employment mentioned in paragraph (1), the compensation may be reduced (in addition to any other reduction authorised by this regulation) by an amount not exceeding that attributable to the additional years or period so credited or, if the number of such years or such period is greater than the period spent in the subsequent employment, by such proportion of that amount as the period spent in the subsequent employment, bears to the number of additional years or the period so credited.

(6) Where compensation has been calculated in accordance with regulation 25, the provisions of this regulation shall only apply—

(*a*) in relation to such part (if any) of the superannuation benefit as is attributable to annual emoluments in excess of those to which the person was entitled on entering the new employment referred to in regulation 25, and

(*b*) in relation to any non-contributing service which becomes reckonable as contributing service pursuant to section 2 of the Local Government Superannuation Act 1953.

(7) Where compensation is payable in respect of diminution of emoluments, the provisions of this regulation shall apply only in relation to such part (if any) of the superannuation benefit as is attributable to annual emoluments in excess of those to which the person was entitled immediately prior to the diminution.

Reduction of compensation in certain cases

33.—(1) If under a person's last relevant pension scheme any benefit for which the scheme provided would have been subject to reduction or suspension on his taking up other specified employment, any retirement compensation to which he is entitled for loss of employment or diminution of emoluments shall, where such employment is taken up, be reduced or suspended in the like manner and to the like extent:

Provided that in calculating the amount of the reduction there shall be aggregated with the emoluments of the employment taken up the amount of any superannuation benefit by way of annual amounts payable to the person under a pension scheme associated with the employment which he has lost or, as the case may be. the employment in which the emoluments were diminished.

(2) There shall be deducted from the retirement compensation payable to any person any additional contributory payments remaining unpaid at the date when he suffered loss of employment; and any such payments not recovered at the date of his death shall be deducted from any compensation payable in respect of that person under regulation 26, 27 or 28(2).

(3) Where a person is entitled to compensation under these Regulations and the circumstances are such that he is also entitled to—

(*a*) a redundancy payment under the Redundancy Payments Act 1965(**a**), or

(*b*) any similar payment in consequence of the loss of his employment under any contract or arrangement with the authority by whom he was employed (other than payments by way of a return of contributions under a pension scheme), or

(*c*) any payment under or by virtue of the provisions of any enactment relating to the reinstatement in civil employment of persons who have been in the service of the Crown,

the compensation which would, apart from this paragraph, become due to the person, whether by instalments or lump sum or both, shall in the aggregate be reduced by the amount of the payments referred to in this paragraph.

(4) Where compensation under these Regulations is payable to or in respect of any person, and that person or his widow, child or other dependant or his personal representatives or trustees such as are mentioned in regulation 27(1) is or are also entitled (whether immediately or on the person's attaining some greater age) to a superannuation benefit under a pension scheme associated with the employment which he has lost—

(*a*) any instalment of such compensation which is payable in respect of any period shall be reduced by the amount of the instalment of such superannuation benefit which is payable in respect of the same period; and

(*b*) any such compensation which is payable as a lump sum shall be reduced by the amount of any lump sum superannuation benefit.

(5) For the purposes of paragraph (4) no account shall be taken of any sum payable in consequence of the surrender by any person of part of his superannuation benefit under any provision in that behalf in the relevant pension scheme with a view to obtaining or increasing allowances for his widow, child or other dependant; and the person shall be deemed to have received during any period the amount of superannuation benefit which he would have received but for any such surrender.

(6) Where in any week a person is entitled to long-term compensation for loss or diminution of emoluments and is also entitled to unemployment, sickness or injury benefit under any Act relating to National Insurance, other than a benefit claimable by him in respect of a dependant, there shall be deducted from the long-term compensation payable for that week a sum equal to the amount by which the aggregate of such National Insurance benefits claimable in respect of that week and the weekly rate at which the long-term compensation would be payable but for this regulation exceeds two-thirds of the weekly rate of the net emoluments of the employment which he has lost or in which the emoluments have been diminished:

Provided that this paragraph shall not apply in relation to any such sickness or injury benefit in so far as—

(*a*) an equivalent sum is deducted from the emoluments of his current employment, and

(*b*) such deduction from those emoluments has not occasioned an increase in his long-term compensation.

(7) In paragraph (6) the expression "weekly rate" means seven three hundred and sixty-fifths of the relevant annual rate.

(**a**) 1965 c. 62.

Notification of change of circumstances

34. Where—

(*a*) a pensionable officer after suffering loss of employment or diminution of emoluments enters any employment referred to in regulation 25 or becomes entitled to any superannuation benefit on ceasing to hold such employment, or

(*b*) a person entitled to long-term compensation enters employment the remuneration whereof is payable out of public funds, or ceases to hold such employment, or receives any increase in his remuneration in such employment, or

(*c*) a person entitled to retirement compensation enters employment in which the compensation is subject to reduction or suspension under regulation 33, or ceases to hold such employment, or receives any increase in his remuneration in such employment, or

(*d*) a person entitled to long-term compensation starts to receive any benefit, any increase in benefit or any further benefit, under any Act relating to National Insurance,

he shall forthwith inform the compensating authority in writing of that fact.

Review of awards of long-term or retirement compensation

35.—(1) The compensating authority shall, within a period of two years after the date on which any decision on a claim for long-term or retirement compensation for loss of employment (other than compensation payable under regulation 22) is notified to a claimant under regulation 37, or within such longer period as is specified in the subsequent provisions of this regulation, and at intervals of not more than six months, review its decision or, where the claim has been the subject of an appeal, the decision of the tribunal, and these Regulations shall apply in relation to any such review as they apply in relation to the initial determination of the claim; and on such review, in the light of any material change in the circumstances of the case, compensation may be awarded, or compensation previously awarded may be increased, reduced or discontinued, subject to the limits set out in these Regulations.

(2) The person to whom the decision relates may require the compensating authority to carry out the review mentioned in paragraph (1) at any time within the period of two years mentioned in that paragraph if he considers that there has been a change in the circumstances of his case which is material for the purposes of these Regulations.

(3) The compensating authority shall carry out a review in accordance with paragraph (1), notwithstanding the expiration of the period mentioned in that paragraph, if—

(*a*) the emoluments of employment or work undertaken as a result of the loss of employment had been taken into account in determining the amount of any compensation awarded, and

(*b*) such employment or work has been lost or the emoluments thereof reduced, otherwise than by reason of misconduct or incapacity to perform such duties as the person might reasonably have been required to perform, and

(*c*) the compensating authority is satisfied that such loss or reduction is causing him hardship, and where any decision is so reviewed, the decision shall be subject to further review in accordance with paragraph (1) as if the review carried out under this paragraph had been the initial determination of the claim.

(4) Paragraphs (1) and (2) shall apply in relation to any decision on a claim for long-term or retirement compensation in respect of diminution of emoluments as they apply in relation to any decision mentioned in the said paragraph (1):

Provided that—

(i) where the person to whom the decision relates ceases to hold the employment in which his emoluments were diminished, a review shall be held within three months after that date, but no further review shall be held after the expiry of that period, and

(ii) while that person continues to hold that employment, there shall be no limit to the period within which a review may take place.

(5) Notwithstanding anything contained in the foregoing provisions of this regulation, the compensating authority shall review a decision, whether of the authority or the tribunal, on a claim for long-term compensation for loss of employment or diminution of emoluments after the expiration of any period within which a review is required to be made if at any time—

(*a*) the person to whom the decision relates becomes engaged in employment (hereinafter referred to as "his current employment") the remuneration whereof is payable out of public funds and which he has undertaken subsequent to the loss or diminution, and

(*b*) the aggregate of the net emoluments of his current employment, any superannuation benefit by way of annual amounts payable to him in respect of the employment which he has lost or the employment in which his emoluments have been diminished and the long-term compensation payable to him exceeds the net emoluments of the employment which he has lost or, as the case may be, in which the emoluments have been diminished.

(6) The compensating authority shall further review any decision reviewed under paragraph (5) whenever the net emoluments of the person's current employment are increased.

(7) If on any review under paragraph (5) or (6) the compensation is reduced it shall not be reduced below the amount by which the net emoluments of the person's current employment, together with any superannuation benefit by way of annual amounts payable to him in respect of the employment which he has lost or the employment in which his emoluments have been diminished, falls short of the net emoluments of the employment which he has lost, or, as the case may be, in which the emoluments have been diminished.

(8) The compensating authority shall give to a person to whom a decision relates not less than fourteen days' notice of any review of that decision to be carried out under this regulation unless the review is carried out at his request.

(9) Nothing in this regulation shall preclude the making of any adjustment of compensation required by regulation 32 or 33.

Compounding of awards

36.—(1) In a case where an annual sum which has been or might be awarded under these Regulations does not exceed £35, the compensating authority may, at its discretion, compound its liability in respect thereof by paying a lump sum equivalent to the capital value of the annual sum and, if any lump sum payment has been awarded or might be awarded in addition to such sum under regulation 20, 21 22 or 23, the compensating authority may likewise discharge its liability in respect thereof by an immediate payment.

(2) In any other case, if the person who has been awarded long-term or retirement compensation requests it to do so, the compensating authority may, after having regard to the state of health of that person and the other circumstances of the case, compound up to one quarter of its liability to make payments under the award (other than payments to a widow, child or other dependant under regulation 26) by the payment of an equivalent amount as a lump sum or, where any compensation has been awarded as a lump sum by increasing that compensation to such equivalent amount; and in calculating for this purpose the liability of the authority to make such payments, account shall be taken of the annual value of lump sum payments of compensation.

(3) The making of a composition under paragraph (2) in relation to an award of long-term or retirement compensation shall not prevent the subsequent making of a composition under paragraph (1) in relation to that award but, subject as aforesaid, not more than one composition may be made in relation to any award.

PART VII

PROCEDURE AND MISCELLANEOUS

Procedure on making claims

37.—(1) Every claim for compensation under these Regulations and every request for a review of an award of long-term or retirement compensation shall be made in accordance with this regulation.

(2) Every such claim or request shall be made to the compensating authority in a form approved by that authority and shall state whether any other claim for compensation has been made by the claimant under these Regulations.

(3) Resettlement compensation shall be claimed separately from any other form of compensation claimable under these Regulations.

(4) The compensating authority shall consider any such claim or request in accordance with the relevant provisions of these Regulations and shall notify the person making the claim or request in writing of its decision—

(*a*) in the case of a claim for resettlement compensation, not later than one month after the receipt of the claim, and

(*b*) in the case of a claim for, or request for the review of an award of, compensation under part IV or V of these Regulations, not later than thirteen weeks after the receipt of the claim or request, and

(*c*) in any other case, as soon as possible after the decision;

but the decision of the compensating authority shall not be invalidated by reason of the fact that notice of the decision is given after the expiry of the period mentioned in this paragraph.

(5) Every notification of a decision by the compensating authority (whether granting or refusing compensation or reviewing an award, or otherwise affecting any compensation under these Regulations) shall contain a statement—

(*a*) giving reasons for the decision;

(*b*) showing how any compensation has been calculated and, in particular, if the amount is less than the maximum which could have been awarded under these Regulations, showing the factors taken into account in awarding that amount; and

(*c*) directing the attention of the claimant to his right under regulation 43, if he is aggrieved by the decision, to institute proceedings before a tribunal and giving him the address to which the application instituting such proceedings should be sent.

Claimants to furnish information

38.—(1) Any person claiming or receiving compensation or whose award of compensation is being reviewed shall furnish all such information as the compensating authority may at any time reasonably require; and he shall verify the same in such manner, including the production of books or of original documents in his possession or control, as may be reasonably so required.

(2) Any such person shall, on receipt of reasonable notice, present himself for interview at such place as the compensating authority may reasonably require; any any person who attends for interview may, if he so desires, be represented by his adviser.

Procedure on death of claimant

39.—(1) In the event of the death of a claimant or of a person who, if he had survived, could have been a claimant, a claim for compensation under these Regulations may be continued or made, as the case may be, by his personal representatives.

(2) Where any such claim is continued or made as afoiesaid by personal representatives, the personal representatives shall, as respects any steps to be taken or thing to be done by them in order to continue to make the claim, be deemed for the purposes of these Regulations to be the person entitled to claim, but, save as aforesaid, the person in whose right they continue or make the claim shall be deemed for the purposes of these Regulations to be such person, and the relevant provisions of these Regulations shall be construed accordingly:

Provided that the compensating authority may in any such case extend the period within which a claim is required to be made by regulation 7 or 13.

Calculation of service

40.—(1) For the purpose of determining the amount of any compensation payable in respect of the loss of an office to which, or of any two or more offices to which in the aggregate, a person devoted substantially the whole of his time, any previous period of part-time employment shall be treated as though it were whole-time employment for a proportionately reduced period.

(2) For the purpose of making any calculation under these Regulations in respect of a person's reckonable service, all periods of such service shall be

aggregated and, except where reference is made to completed years of service, if the aggregated service includes a fraction of a year, that fraction shall, if it equals or exceeds six months, be treated as a year, and shall, in any other case be disregarded.

Emoluments of part-time employments

41. In ascertaining for the purposes of these Regulations whether, and how far, the remuneration of alternative employment falls short of emoluments which have been lost where those emoluments were payable in respect of two or more part-time employments, the remuneration of the alternative employment or of the aggregate of two or more such employments shall be apportioned in the proportion which the emoluments of the part-time employments bore to each other.

Compensation not assignable

42. Subject to any statutory provision in that behalf, any compensation to which a person becomes entitled under these Regulations shall be paid by the compensating authority and shall be payable to, or in trust for, the person who is entitled to receive it, and shall not be assignable:

Provided that, without prejudice to any other right of recovery, any compensation paid in error may be recovered by the compensating authority by deduction from any compensation payable under these Regulations.

Right of appeal from decision of compensating authority

43.—(1) Every person who is aggrieved by any decision of the compensating authority with respect to a compensation question or by any failure on the part of the compensating authority to notify him of any such decision within the appropriate time prescribed by these Regulations, may within thirteen weeks of the notification to him of the decision or the expiry of the prescribed time, as the case may be, institute proceedings for the determination of the question by a tribunal in accordance with the Industrial Tribunals (Employment and Compensation) Regulations 1967(**a**) and these Regulations; and the tribunal shall determine the question accordingly.

(2) For the purpose of any such proceedings a person or persons may be appointed to sit with the tribunal as assessor or assessors.

(3) The compensating authority shall give effect to the decision of a tribunal subject to any modifications that may be required in consequence of any appeal from that decision on a point of law.

Dated 9th December 1971.

Hailsham of St. Marylebone, C.

Concurrence of the Minister for the Civil Service given under his Official Seal on 10th December 1971.

(L.S.)

K. H. McNeill,
Authorised by the
Minister for the Civil Service.

(**a**) S.I. 1967/361 (1967 I, p. 1205).

SCHEDULE

Regulation 2(3)

Table I

Factors to be applied to an annual amount payable for life to obtain the capital value

Age	Factor	
	Female	Male
Under 35	15·55	15·15
35 and under 40	15·10	14·60
40 and under 45	14·55	13·95
45 and under 50	13·90	13·10
50	13·45	12·55
51	13·25	12·35
52	13·10	12·15
53	12·90	11·90
54	12·70	11·70
55	12·50	11·45
56	12·30	11·25
57	12·10	11·00
58	11·90	10·75
59	11·65	10·50
60	11·40	10·25
61	11·20	10·00
62	10·95	9·70
63	10·70	9·45
64	10·40	9·15
65	10·15	8·90
66	9·90	8·60
67	9·60	8·35
68	9·35	8·05
69	9·05	7·80
70	8·75	7·50

NOTE:—This table is for use in connection with regulation 36(1) and (2) for the compounding of annual retirement compensation which a person is currently entitled to receive under regulation 20, 21, 22 or 23. Where the compensation is payable before age 60 (females), 65 (males) but will be reduced on the attainment of that age (in connection with National Insurance pension) the tables should be used in conjunction with Table II, i.e. Table II should be used for valuing that part of the compensation which ceases to be payable at 60 (65) and this table should be used for valuing the remainder.

TABLE II

Factors to be applied to annual amounts ceasing
at 65 (males) or 60 (females) to obtain the capital value

Age	Factor	
	Female	Male
Under 35	13·40	14·10
35 and under 40	12·25	13·15
40 and under 45	10·70	11·95
45 and under 50	8·65	10·40
50	7·15	9·30
51	6·60	8·90
52	6·00	8·45
53	5·35	7·95
54	4·65	7·50
55	3·90	6·95
56	3·15	6·40
57	2·30	5·85
58	1·45	5·20
59	·50	4·55
60	—	3·85
61	—	3·10
62	—	2·30
63	—	1·40
64	—	·50

NOTE:—This table is for use in connection with regulation 36(1) and (2) for the compounding of any part of annual retirement compensation which will cease to be payable on the attainment of age 60 (females), 65 (males). Table I should be used in relation to the remainder of such compensation, i.e. the part which is payable for life—see note on that table.

TABLE III

Factors to be applied to annual amounts payable to a widow until death or re-marriage to obtain the capital value

Age of widow at date of widowhood	Factor	Age of widow at date of widowhood	Factor
20	6·00	45	11·90
21	6·00	46	12·05
22	6·00	47	12·15
23	6·00	48	12·25
24	6·00	49	12·30
25	6·25	50	12·30
26	6·60	51	12·30
27	6·95	52	12·25
28	7·30	53	12·20
29	7·65	54	12·15
30	8·00	55	12·05
31	8·40	56	11·95
32	8·75	57	11·80
33	9·10	58	11·65
34	9·40	59	11·50
35	9·75	60	11·30
36	10·05	61	11·15
37	10·30	62	10·95
38	10·55	63	10·70
39	10·80	64	10·40
40	11·05	65	10·15
41	11·25	66	9·90
42	11·45	67	9·60
43	11·60	68	9·35
44	11·75	69	9·05
		70	8·75

NOTE:—This table is for use in connection with regulation 36(1) for compounding annual compensation to a widow under regulation 26. It should also be used, where a reduction of compensation under regulation 26(6) falls to be apportioned between the compensation payable under that regulation and under regulation 27, for ascertaining the capital value of annual compensation to a widow.

TABLE IV

Factors to be applied to lump sums to find
the equivalent annual amount payable for life

Age	Factor	
	Female	Male
Under 35	·0642917	·0660000
35 and under 40	·0662083	·0685000
40 and under 45	·0687083	·0716667
45 and under 50	·0719583	·0763333
50	·0743333	·0796667
51	·0754583	·0809583
52	·0763333	·0822917
53	·0775000	·0840417
54	·0787500	·0854583
55	·0800000	·0873333
56	·0812917	·0888750
57	·0826250	·0909167
58	·0840417	·0930000
59	·0858333	·0952500
60	·0877083	·0975417
61	·0892917	·1000000
62	·0913333	·1030833
63	·0934583	·1058333
64	·0961667	·1092917
65	·0985000	·1123750
66	·1010000	·1162917
67	·1041667	·1197500
68	·1069583	·1242083
69	·1105000	·1282083
70	·1142917	·1333333

NOTE:—This table is for use in connection with regulation 24(1) for ascertaining the annual amount by which retirement compensation under regulation 20, 21 or 22 is to be reduced where a claimant has not paid to the compensating authority an amount equal to any sum paid to him by way of superannuation contributions or that amount has been repaid to him by the compensating authority at his request. It should also be used in connection with regulation 36(2) for calculating for the purposes of that paragraph the annual value of retirement compensation awarded as a lump sum.

Table V

Factors to be applied to lump sums to find the equivalent annual amount payable to a widow until death or re-marriage

Age of widow at date of widowhood	Factor	Age of widow at date of widowhood	Factor
20	·1666667	45	·0840417
21	·1666667	46	·0830000
22	·1666667	47	·0822917
23	·1666667	48	·0816250
24	·1666667	49	·0812917
25	·1600000	50	·0812917
26	·1515000	51	·0812917
27	·1438750	52	·0816250
28	·1370000	53	·0819583
29	·1307083	54	·0822917
30	·1250000	55	·0830000
31	·1190417	56	·0836667
32	·1142917	57	·0847500
33	·1098750	58	·0858333
34	·1063750	59	·0869583
35	·1025833	60	·0885000
36	·0995000	61	·0897083
37	·0970833	62	·0913333
38	·0947917	63	·0934583
39	·0925833	64	·0961667
40	·0905000	65	·0985000
41	·0888750	66	·1010000
42	·0873333	67	·1041667
43	·0862083	68	·1069583
44	·0851250	69	·1105000
		70	·1142917

NOTE:—This table is for use in connection with regulation 26(6) for ascertaining the annual amount by which compensation to a widow is to be reduced in the circumstances described in that paragraph. If a reduction is required to be apportioned between compensation payable under regulations 26 and 27, the capital value of annual compensation to a widow should be ascertained by reference to Table III.

TABLE VI

Factors according to the outstanding period of long-term compensation to be applied to the total amount of long-term compensation compounded to obtain the capital value

Outstanding number of complete years of long term compensation	Factor	
	Female	Male
0	·984	·982
1	·952	·948
2	·921	·915
3	·892	·883
4	·864	·854
5	·838	·827
6	·813	·801
7	·789	·777
8	·767	·754
9	·746	·732
10	·726	·712
11	·706	·693
12	·688	·675
13	·670	·657
14	·653	·641
15	·637	·625
16	·621	·610
17	·606	·596
18	·592	·582
19	·578	·569
20	·565	·556
21	·552	·544
22	·540	·532
23	·528	·520
24	·516	·509
25	·505	·499
26	·494	·489
27	·484	·479
28	·474	·469
29	·464	·459
30	·455	·450

NOTE:—This table is for use in connection with regulation 36(1) and (2) for compounding awards of long-term compensation under Part IV of these Regulations. The total amount of the annual long-term compensation which is to be compounded must first be calculated, i.e. the amount which the person would receive on account of that compensation or the part of it which is to be compounded, if it were paid until "normal retiring age" (as defined in these Regulations). The capital value of that annual long-term compensation will be the total calculated multiplied by the appropriate factor.

EXPLANATORY NOTE

(This Note is not part of the Regulations.)

1. These Regulations, made under section 44 of the Courts Act 1971, provide for the payment of compensation to or in respect of persons who suffer loss of employment or loss or diminution of emoluments in consequence of the provisions of section 44(1) of the Act, the abolition or merger of any court by the Act, or the transfer by the Act of any function to the Lord Chancellor or any other Minister.

2. Part I of the Regulations contains definitions. Part II specifies the persons to whom the Regulations apply and the grounds of entitlement to compensation.

3. The compensation payable is—

(*a*) resettlement compensation for loss of employment (Part III);

(*b*) long-term compensation for loss of employment or loss or diminution of emoluments (Part IV);

(*c*) retirement compensation for loss of employment or loss or diminution of emoluments (Part V);

(*d*) compensation to the widow, child or other dependant or to the personal representatives of a claimant who was a pensionable officer (Part V).

4. Resettlement compensation is payable for a period not exceeding 26 weeks to officers with at least three years' service in relevant employment. The qualifying conditions and factors to be considered are set out in regulation 7. The method of calculating the amount of compensation is contained in regulation 8.

5. Long-term and retirement compensation is payable to officers with at least eight years' service in relevant employment. The qualifying and other conditions are set out in regulation 13.

6. The method of calculating the maximum amount of long-term compensation is laid down in regulations 15 (loss of emoluments) and 16 (diminution of emoluments). This amount is a proportion, not exceeding two-thirds, of the net emoluments lost or of the amount by which emoluments have been diminished, as the case may be. This compensation is payable from a date determined under regulation 17 and can be payable up to normal retiring age. In the case of a non-pensionable officer, compensation not exceeding one-half of the rate of long-term compensation may be paid beyond normal retiring age (regulation 29).

7. Retirement compensation payable to a pensionable officer is based upon his accrued pension rights (regulations 20 and 23) supplemented in the case of persons aged 40 or over at the date of loss by the addition of notional years of service (regulation 19). Special provision is made for any persons whose pension arrangements are by way of policies of insurance (regulation 30). Retirement compensation is ordinarily payable from normal retiring age but in certain circumstances is payable earlier (regulations 21 and 22).

8. Compensation is payable to the widow, child or other dependant or to the personal representatives or trustees of a claimant who dies where such persons would have benefited under the relevant pension scheme (regulations 26 to 28).

9. Part VI provides for long-term and retirement compensation to be reviewed and for awards to be varied in the light of changing circumstances (regulation 35). It also contains provisions for the adjustment, suspension and compounding of compensation in certain circumstances.

10. Part VII contains provisions relating to the procedure for making claims and notifying decisions, and confers upon a claimant who is aggrieved by a decision on a compensation question or the failure of the compensating authority to notify its decision a right to refer the question for determination by a tribunal established under section 12 of the Industrial Training Act 1964.

1971 No. 2009

CUSTOMS AND EXCISE

The Import Duty Drawbacks (No. 3) Order 1971

Made - - - -	13*th December* 1971
Laid before the House of Commons	17*th December* 1971
Coming into Operation	1*st January* 1972

The Lords Commissioners of Her Majesty's Treasury, by virtue of the powers conferred on them by sections 9 and 13 of, and Schedule 5 to, the Import Duties Act 1958(**a**), and of all other powers enabling them in that behalf, on the recommendation of the Secretary of State hereby make the following Order:—

1.—(1) This Order may be cited as the Import Duty Drawbacks (No. 3) Order 1971.

(2) The Interpretation Act 1889(**b**) shall apply for the interpretation of this Order as it applies for the interpretation of an Act of Parliament.

(3) This Order shall come into operation on 1st January 1972.

2. In Schedule 1 to the Import Duty Drawbacks (No. 1) Order 1971(**c**) (which relates to the drawbacks to be allowed on the exportation of imported articles or goods incorporating them), in each of the following entries, in column 2, for the words " on or after 1st January 1972 " there shall be substituted the words " on or after 1st January 1973 "—

(*a*) the entry relating to headings 69.11, 69.12 and 69.13 of the Customs Tariff 1959 (tableware and other articles of a kind commonly used for domestic or toilet purposes, of porcelain, china or other pottery; certain ornaments and furniture of ceramic);

(*b*) the entry relating to heading 70.13 (glassware of a kind commonly used for table, kitchen, toilet or office purposes, for indoor decoration or similar uses); and

(*c*) the entry relating to heading 70.14 (illuminating glassware, signalling glassware and optical elements of glass).

Tim Fortescue,
P. L. Hawkins,
Two of the Lords Commissioners
of Her Majesty's Treasury.

13th December 1971.

(**a**) 1958 c. 6. (**b**) 1889 c. 63 (**c**) S.I. 1971/274 (1971 I, p. 939).

EXPLANATORY NOTE

(*This Note is not part of the Order.*)

This Order extends for one year the period for which drawback of import duty is allowed on the exportation of certain imported ceramic products and glassware.

1971 No. 2010

CUSTOMS AND EXCISE

The Import Duties (Temporary Exemptions) (No. 9) Order 1971

Made - - - -	13*th December* 1971
Laid before the House of Commons	17*th December* 1971
Coming into Operation	1*st January* 1972

The Lords Commissioners of Her Majesty's Treasury, by virtue of the powers conferred on them by sections 3(6) and 13 of the Import Duties Act 1958(**a**), and of all other powers enabling them in that behalf, on the recommendation of the Secretary of State, hereby make the following Order:—

1.—(1) This Order may be cited as the Import Duties (Temporary Exemptions) (No. 9) Order 1971.

(2) The Interpretation Act 1889(**b**) shall apply for the interpretation of this Order as it applies for the interpretation of an Act of Parliament.

(3) This Order shall come into operation on 1st January 1972.

2.—(1) Until the beginning of 1st January 1973 or, in the case of goods in relation to which an earlier day is specified in Schedule 1 to this Order, until the beginning of that day, any import duty which is for the time being chargeable on goods of a heading of the Customs Tariff 1959 specified in that Schedule shall not be chargeable in respect of goods of any description there specified in relation to that heading.

(2) In Schedule 1 to this Order—

(*a*) a reference to the British Pharmacopoeia or the British Pharmaceutical Codex is to the edition thereof current at the date of this Order, with amendments up to (but exclusive of) that date;

(*b*) an item marked with a dagger is an item appearing under a revised classification, as compared with the classification under which exemption from import duty was allowed at the date of this Order.

(3) Any entry in column 2 in Schedule 1 to this Order is to be taken to comprise all goods which would be classified under an entry in the same terms constituting a subheading (other than the final subheading) in the relevant heading in the Customs Tariff 1959.

(4) For the purposes of classification under the Customs Tariff 1959, in so far as that depends on the rate of duty, any goods to which paragraph (1) of this Article applies shall be treated as chargeable with the same duty as if this Order had not been made.

(**a**) 1958 c. 6. (**b**) 1889 c. 63.

3. Until the beginning of 1st January 1973, goods of subheading 39.03(A)(2)(*b*) of the Customs Tariff 1959 (which comprises photographic, including cinematographic, film base of cellulose acetate) shall not be chargeable with import duty of an amount greater than 10 per cent. of their value.

4. The Import Duties (Temporary Exemptions) Orders specified in Schedule 2 to this Order are hereby revoked.

Tim Fortescue,
P. L. Hawkins,
Two of the Lords Commissioners
of Her Majesty's Treasury.

13*th December* 1971.

SCHEDULE 1

Goods Temporarily Exempt from Import Duty

Tariff heading	*Description*
05.15	Blue whiting (Gadus Poutassou)
	Norway Pout (Trisopterus (Gadus) Esmarkii)
	Sand eels (ammodytes)
07.01	Tarragon, fresh or chilled
12.01	Castor seed
15.04	Sperm oil, unrefined
27.07	Anthracene
	Pyridine bases, having a basicity equivalent to not less than 7·0 millilitres and not more than 12·5 millilitres of 1·0 N sulphuric acid solution when estimated by method No. RB. 1–67 of "Standard Methods for Testing Tar and its Products" published by the Standardisation of Tar Products Test Committee
	Pyridine bases, of which, after drying, not less than 70 per cent. by volume distils between 140° and 250° centigrade at normal pressure
28.14	Boron tribromide
	Boron trichloride
	Phosphorus pentabromide
	Phosphorus pentafluoride
	Silicon tetrachloride
	Sulphur tetrafluoride
	Thionyl chloride
28.15	Carbonyl sulphide
28.17	Potassium hydroxide, pharmaceutical quality
	Sodium peroxide
28.20	Aluminium oxide, not being artificial corundum, being in the form of spheres and containing by weight not more than 0·06 per cent. of acid soluble sulphates expressed as SO_3 and not more than 0·005 per cent. of sodium expressed as Na, and all of which passes a sieve having a nominal width of aperture of 4·76 millimetres and not less than 99 per cent. by weight of which is retained by a sieve having a nominal width of aperture of 1·00 millimetre
28.23	γ-Ferric oxide
28.27	Lead monoxide which, when examined by X-ray diffraction is free of the tetragonal form, and which has a specific surface, when determined by air permeability, of not less than 600 square metres per kilogramme
28.28	Beryllium oxide
	Hydroxylammonium sulphate
28.29	Aluminium sodium fluoride
	Potassium fluorosilicate
	Sodium fluoride, which does not contain impurities equivalent to more than 5×10^{-9} grammes of U_3O_8 per gramme, and of which 1 gramme must not contain impurities capable of depressing the estimation of U_3O_8 by more than 1×10^{-8} grammes, when determined fluorimetrically
	Sodium fluorosilicate
	Tungsten hexafluoride
28.32	Ammonium perchlorate
	Sodium perchlorate
28.35	Zinc sulphide
28.38	Magnesium sulphate, anhydrous, containing not less than 0·05 per cent. by weight and not more than 1·0 per cent. by weight of potassium compounds calculated as K
	Mercuric sulphate
	Potassium hydrogen per*mono*sulphate
	Thallous sulphate

Tariff heading	*Description*
28.39	Barium nitrate containing not more than 0·006 per cent. by weight of heavy metals calculated as Pb
	Beryllium nitrate
	Potassium nitrite
28.40	Potassium dihydrogen orthophosphate in the form of single crystals
	*tetra*Potassium pyrophosphate
28.42	Magnesium carbonate, light, in rectangular blocks of a weight not less than 25 grammes and not more than 125 grammes and of a cubic capacity not less than 115 cubic centimetres
	Manganous carbonate
	Nickel carbonate, basic
	Potassium hydrogen carbonate
28.43	Mercuric cyanide
	Potassium ferricyanide
	Sodium nitroprusside
28.44	Ammonium thiocyanate
	Potassium cyanate
	Sodium thiocyanate
28.46	Sodium metaborate tetrahydrate, $Na_2B_2O_4$, $4H_2O$
28.47	Bismuth aluminate containing not less than 52 per cent. by weight and not more than 55 per cent. by weight of bismuth calculated as Bi on the dry anhydrous salt
	Sodium tungstate containing not more than 0·0003 per cent. by weight of arsenic compounds calculated as As and not more than 0·005 per cent. by weight of molybdenum compounds calculated as Mo
28.48	Dihydroxyaluminium sodium carbonate
	Ferric sodium pyrophosphate
28.49	Silver protein, mild, which satisfies the requirements of the British Pharmaceutical Codex
	Silver protein, which satisfies the requirements of the British Pharmaceutical Codex
28.50	All goods of this heading other than radium compounds, natural uranium and compounds thereof and nuclear reactor cartridges, spent or irradiated
28.51	Deuterium oxide
28.52	Compounds of uranium depleted in uranium-235, the following:—
	Uranium hexafluoride
	Mixed rare earth compounds containing not less than 3·5 per cent. by weight and not more than 9·0 per cent. by weight of combined fluorine estimated as F, and not less than 0·5 per cent. by weight and not more than 4·0 per cent. by weight of barium compounds estimated as $BaSO_4$; and of which not less than 10 per cent. by weight is retained by a sieve having a nominal width of aperture of 45 micrometres
28.57	Aluminium sodium hydride
	Lithium borohydride
	Silane
28.58	Trichlorosilane containing not more than 0·002 parts per million by weight of boron compounds calculated as B
29.01	Acenaphthylene
	Allene
	Anthracene
	Azulene
	1,2-Benzanthracene
	Bicyclo[2,2,1]hepta-2,5-diene
	*iso*Butane
	n-But-1-ene
	*cis*But-2-ene

Tariff heading	*Description*
29.01	*trans*But-2-ene
	But-2-ene, mixed isomers
	But-1-yne
	Chrysene
	trans-trans-trans-Cyclododeca-1,5,9-triene
	9,10-Dihydroanthracene
	2,2-Dimethylpropane
	n-Eicosane
	5-Ethylidenebicyclo[2,2,1]hept-2-ene
	Fluoranthene
	Fluorene
	2-Methylpentane
	n-Nonane
	Perylene
	Propyne
	Pyrene
	*trans*Stilbene
	p-Terphenyl
	1,2,3,4-Tetrahydro-1,1,2,4,4,7-hexamethylnaphthalene
	1,2,4,5-Tetramethylbenzene
	n-Undecane
29.02	Aldrin
	Allyl chloride
	1-Bromo-3-chloro-2-methylpropane
	Bromotrifluoromethane
	Carbon tetrafluoride
	Chlordane
	3-Chlorobenzotrifluoride
	4-Chlorobenzotrifluoride
	2-Chlorobuta-1,3-diene
	1-Chloro-*n*-butane
	1-Chloro-*n*-but-1-ene
	3-Chloro-*n*-but-1-ene
	1-Chloro-*n*-but-2-ene
	1-Chloronaphthalene
	1-Chloroprop-1-ene
	3-Chloropropyne
	2-Chlorotoluene
	Decachlorobicyclopenta-2,4-dienyl
	1,4-Dibromobut-2-ene
	2,3-Dibromobut-2-ene
	Dibromodifluoromethane
	Dibromomethane
	1,3-Dichlorobenzene
	2,3-Dichlorobuta-1,3-diene
	1,3-Dichloro-*n*-but-2-ene
	1,4-Dichlorobut-2-ene
	1,1-Dichloro-2,2-di-(4-chlorophenyl)ethane
	1,2-Dichloroethylene
	2,3-Dichloroprop-l-ene
	2,6-Dichlorotoluene
	1,1-Difluoroethane
	Diphenylchloromethane
	Dodecachloropentacyclo[5,2,1,$0^{2,6}$,$0^{3,9}$,$0^{5,8}$]decane
	1,6,7,8,9,14,15,16,17,17,18,18-Dodecachloropentacyclo-[12,2,1,$1^{6,9}$,$0^{2,13}$,$0^{5,10}$]octadeca-7,15-diene
	Fluorobenzene
	Heptachlor
	1,2,5,6,9,10-Hexabromocyclododecane

Tariff heading	*Description*
29.02	1,2,3,4,5,6-Hexachlorocyclohexane, mixed isomers, of which either (*a*) the α-isomer content is not more than 50 per cent. by weight, or (*b*) the γ-isomer content is not less than 35 per cent. by weight provided that, in a case where the γ-isomer content is not less than 35 per cent. and not more than 40 per cent. by weight, not less than 90 per cent. by weight of the material passes a sieve having a nominal width of aperture of 53 micrometres
	α-1,2,3,4,5,6-Hexachlorocyclohexane
	γ-1,2,3,4,5,6-Hexachlorocyclohexane
	Hexachlorocyclopentadiene
	Hexafluoropropene
	Methallyl chloride
	Octafluorocyclobutane.
	Pentachloroethane
	1,2,3,4-Tetrachlorobenzene
	1,2,4,5-Tetrachlorobenzene
	1,1,1,2-Tetrachloroethane
	1,1,2,2-Tetrachloroethane
	Tribromofluoromethane
	1,2,3-Trichlorobenzene
	1,2,4-Trichlorobenzene
	Trichlorobenzene, mixed isomers
	1,1,2-Trichloroethane of which not less than 92 per cent. by volume distils between 110° and 115° centigrade at normal pressure
	Trifluoroiodomethane
	Vinyl bromide
	Vinyl fluoride
29.03	1-*tert*Butyl-3,4,5-trimethyl-2,6-dinitrobenzene
	Chloropicrin
	Methanesulphonic acid
	Methanesulphonyl chloride
	Nitroethane
	Nitromethane
	1-Nitronaphthalene
	1-Nitropropane
	2-Nitropropane
	1,1,3,3,5-Pentamethyl-4,6-dinitroindane
	*di*Sodium benzene-1,3-disulphonate
	Sodium 4-chlorobenzenesulphonate
	Sodium 3-chloro-*n*-but-2-ene-1-sulphonate
	Sodium ethylenesulphonate
	Sodium styrenesulphonate, mixed isomers
29.04	Adonitol
	Allyl alcohol
	Amyl alcohol, containing not less than 58 per cent. by weight of *n*-pentan-1-ol and not more than 1 per cent. by weight of aldehydes or ketones calculated as $C_5H_{10}O$
	D-Arabitol
	n-Butane-1,3-diol
	Butane-1,4-diol
	n-Butane-2,3-diol
	Butane-1,2,4-triol
	n-Butan-2-ol
	But-2-ene-1,4-diol
	n-But-2-en-1-ol
	But-2-yne-1,4-diol
	But-3-yn-2-ol
	2-Chloroethanol

Tariff heading	*Description*
29.04	3-Chloropropan-1-ol
	Decane-1,10-diol
	2,2-Di(bromomethyl)propanediol
	2,6-Dimethylheptan-4-ol
	2,5-Dimethylhexane-2,5-diol
	(±)-3,7-Dimethylnona-1,6-dien-3-ol
	Dimethyloctadienol, mixed 2,6,3,5,2- and 3,7,4,6,3- isomers
	3,6-Dimethyloctan-3-ol
	3,7-Dimethyloctan-3-ol
	Dimethyloctanol, mixed 2,6,2- and 3,7,3- isomers
	(−)-3,7-Dimethyloct-6-en-1-ol
	3,7-Dimethyloct-6-en-1-yn-3-ol
	3,6-Dimethyloct-4-yne-3,6-diol
	2,2-Dimethylpropanediol
	2,2-Dimethylpropanol
	Ethchlorvynol
	2-Ethylhexane-1,3-diol
	2-Ethyl-2-hydroxymethylpropanediol
	Farnesol
	n-Heptan-1-ol
	Hexadecyl alcohol, mixed isomers, which freezes at a temperature not higher than −40° centigrade
	2*H*-Hexafluoropropan-2-ol
	Hexane-1,6-diol
	Hexane-1,2,6-triol
	Hexanetriol, mixed isomers
	n-Hexan-1-ol
	n-Hex-3-en-1-ol
	2-Hydroxymethyl-2-methylpropanediol
	2-Hydroxymethyl-2-nitropropanediol
	3-Methylbutan-1-ol, of a purity not less than 90 per cent.
	2-Methylbutan-2-ol
	3-Methylpentyn-3-ol
	2-Methylpropan-2-ol containing not more than 0·007 per cent. by weight of unsaturated compounds calculated as butene
	2-Methylpropan-2-ol containing not less than 10 per cent. by weight and not more than 13 per cent. by weight of water
	Nerolidol
	1*H*,1*H*,5*H*-Octafluoropentan-1-ol
	2-*n*-Octyl-*n*-dodecan-1-ol
	n-Pentan-1-ol
	Phytol
	*iso*Phytol
	Pinacol
	Propane-1,3-diol
	Prop-2-yn-1-ol
	Succinaldehyde di(sodium bisulphite)
	1*H*,1*H*,3*H*-Tetrafluoropropan-1-ol
	3,7,11,15-Tetramethylhexadecane-1,2,3-triol
	3,7,9-Trimethyldeca-1,6-dien-3-ol
	2,2,4-Trimethylhexane-1,6-diol
	n-Undecan-1-ol
	Undec-10-en-1-ol
	Xylitol
29.05	Borneol
	*iso*Borneol
	Dihydrotachysterol
	2,2-Di-(4-hydroxycyclohexyl)propane
	1,4-Di(hydroxymethyl)cyclohexane
	Fenchyl alcohol

Tariff heading	*Description*
29.05	*meso*Inositol
	p-Menth-1-en-4-ol
	2-Methyl-4-phenylbutan-2-ol
	3-Methyl-1-phenylpentan-3-ol
	Nopol
	Phenylethane-1,2-diol
	1-Phenylethanol
	1-Phenylprop-2-yn-1-ol
	α-Terpineol, having a freezing point not less than 20° centigrade
	2,2,2-Trichlorodi-(4-chlorophenyl)ethanol
29.06	2-*tert*Butyl-4-ethylphenol
	4-*sec*Butylphenol
	2-*tert*Butylphenol
	3,5-Di*tert*butyl-4-hydroxybiphenyl
	1,1-Di-(3-*tert*butyl-4-hydroxy-6-methylphenyl)-*n*-butane
	2,6-Di*tert*butylphenol
	Di-(3,5-di*tert*butyl-4-hydroxyphenyl)methane
	3,4-Dihydroxybiphenyl
	1,3-Dihydroxynaphthalene
	1,5-Dihydroxynaphthalene
	2,3-Dihydroxynaphthalene
	3,4-Di-(4-hydroxyphenyl)-*n*-hexane-3,4-diol
	2,4-Di*tert*pentylphenol
	2,5-Di*tert*pentylquinol
	4-Hydroxybiphenyl
	2-Methylquinol
	1-Naphthol
	3-*n*-Pentadecylphenol
	4-*tert*Pentylphenol
	Salicyl alcohol
	Sodium biphenyl-2-yloxide
	Stilboestrol
	2,4,2′,4′-Tetrahydroxybiphenyl
	Thymol
	1,1,3-Tri-(5-*tert*butyl-4-hydroxy-2-methylphenyl)-*n*-butane-toluene complex
	2,4,6-Tri-(3,5-di*tert*butyl-4-hydroxybenzyl)mesitylene
	2,3,5-Trimethylquinol
29.07	3-Chloro-4-hydroxybiphenyl
	3-Chlorophenol
	2,3-Dichlorophenol
	2,2-Di-(3,5-dichloro-4-hydroxyphenyl)propane
	6,7-Dihydroxynaphthalene-2-sulphonic acid
	4,6-Dinitro-*o*-cresol (-OH at 1), ammonium salt
	4-Hydroxynaphthalene-1-sulphonic acid
	5-Hydroxynaphthalene-1-sulphonic acid
	*di*Sodium 1,8-dihydroxynaphthalene-3,6-disulphonate
	Sodium 6,7-dihydroxynaphthalene-2-sulphonate
	Sodium 4-hydroxynaphthalene-1-sulphonate
29.08	4-Allylanisole
	Anethole
	Batyl alcohol
	Benzyl cyclohex-3-enylidenemethyl ether
	*iso*Butyl vinyl ether
	Chloromethyl methyl ether
	Di-*n*-butyldigol
	2,5-Di*tert*butylperoxy-2,5-dimethylhexane
	1,4-Di-(1-*tert*butylperoxy-1-methylethyl)benzene
	Di-(2-chloroethyl) ether
	2,4-Dichlorophenyl 4-nitrophenyl ether

Tariff heading	*Description*
29.08	Di-(αα-dimethylbenzyl) peroxide
	Diethyldigol
	2,2-Di-[4-(2-hydroxyethoxy)phenyl]propane
	1,2-Dimethoxyethane
	Dimethyl ether
	Dimethyltetragol
	Dimethyltrigol
	1,4-Dioxan
	Di(phenoxyphenoxy)benzene, mixed isomers
	Di*iso*propylbenzene hydroperoxide
	2-Ethoxynaphthalene
	Ethyl vinyl ether
	Guaiacol having a melting point of not less than 27° centigrade
	n-Hexyldigol
	p-Menthanyl hydroperoxide
	3-Methoxy-*n*-butan-1-ol
	Methoxyflurane
	2-Methoxynaphthalene
	4-Methoxy-1-naphthol
	Methyl vinyl ether
	Musk ambrette
	Potassium guaiacolsulphonate
	5-Propenylguaethol (-OH at 1)
	1,2,3-Tri-(2-hydroxy-*n*-propoxy)propane
	Tri-α-propylene glycol *mono*methyl ether
29.09	Allyl glycidyl ether
	l-Chloro-2,3-epoxypropane
	Dieldrin
	1,4-Di-(2,3-epoxypropoxy)butane
	Endrin
	1,2-Epoxy-*n*-butane
	Epoxybutane, mixed 1,2- and 2,3- isomers
	1,11-Epoxy-5,5,7,8-tetramethyltricyclo[5,4,0,$0^{4,6}$]undecane
	3,4-Epoxytricyclo[5,2,1,$0^{2,6}$]decanol
	Glycidol
	Styrene oxide
29.10	α-Anhydroglucochloral
	1-Chloro-2,2-diethoxyethane
	1,1-Diethoxy-3,7-dimethylocta-2,6-diene
	1,1-Dimethoxy-3,7-dimethylocta-2,6-diene
	Dimethoxymethane
	1,1-Dimethoxy-*n*-octane
	1,3-Dioxan
	2-Ethyl-2-methyl-1,3-dioxolan
	17α-Ethynyl-3,3-dimethoxyoestr-5(10)-en-17*β*-ol
	Hexahydro-2,3,6,7-tetrahydroxy-1,4,5,8-tetraoxanaphthalene
	1,1,3,3-Tetraethoxypropane
	4,4a,5,9b-Tetrahydroindeno[1,2-*d*]-1,3-dioxin
	4,4a,9,9a-Tetrahydroindeno[2,1-*d*]-1,3-dioxin
	1,1,3,3-Tetramethoxypropane
29.11	Acrylaldehyde
	3-(4-*tert*Butylphenyl)-2-methylpropionaldehyde
	n-Butyraldehyde
	*iso*Butyraldehyde
	Crotonaldehyde containing not more than 4 per cent. by weight of water
	*iso*Cyclocitral
	2,4-Dihydroxybenzaldehyde
	3,4-Dihydroxybenzaldehyde

Tariff heading	*Description*
29.11	2,3-Dimethoxybenzaldehyde
	2,6-Dimethylhept-5-enal
	2-Ethylhexanal
	DL-Glyceraldehyde
	Glyoxal
	n-Hex-2-enal
	4-Hydroxybenzaldehyde
	4-(4-Hydroxy-4-methylpentyl)cyclohex-3-enaldehyde
	n-Octanal
	Terephthalaldehyde
	4-(Tricyclo[5,2,1,$0^{2,6}$]dec-8-ylidene)butyraldehyde
	3,5,5-Trimethylhexanal
	2,6,10-Trimethylundec-10-enal
	1,3,5-Trioxan
	n-Valeraldehyde
	*iso*Valeraldehyde
29.12	Chloroacetaldehyde
	2-Chlorobenzaldehyde
	4-Chlorobenzaldehyde
	2,6-Dichlorobenzaldehyde
	2-Nitrobenzaldehyde
	4-Nitrobenzaldehyde
	5-Nitrosalicylaldehyde
	Sodium 2-formylbenzenesulphonate
29.13	Acetoin
	Acetoin dimer
	Acetonylacetone
	4-Acetyl-6-*tert*butyl-1,1-dimethylindane
	7-Acetyl-6-ethyl-1,2,3,4-tetrahydro-1,1,4,4-tetramethylnaphthalene
	7-Acetyl-2-methyl-5-*iso*propylbicyclo[2,2,2]oct-2-ene
	Benzoin
	Butanedione
	α-*n*-Butoxybenzyl phenyl ketone
	(+)-Camphor
	Canthaxanthin
	L-Carvone
	Chloranil
	2-Chlorocyclohexanone
	2-[α-(4-Chlorophenyl)phenylacetyl]indane-1,3-dione
	Cycloheptadec-9-enone
	Cyclopentadecanone
	1,3-Dihydroxyacetone
	2,4-Dihydroxyacetophenone
	2,2′-Dihydroxy-4,4′-dimethoxybenzophenone
	2,2′-Dihydroxy-4-methoxybenzophenone
	11β,21-Dihydroxypregna-4,17(20)-dien-3-one
	3β,17α-Dihydroxy-5β-pregnane-11,20-dione
	11β,17α-Dihydroxypregn-4-ene-3,20-dione
	3,3-Dimethoxyoestr-5(10)-en-17-one
	2,6-Dimethylheptan-4-one
	3,17-Dioxoandrost-4-en-19-al
	Dithranol
	4-(1-Ethoxyvinyl)-3,3,5,5-tetramethylcyclohexanone
	2-Ethylanthraquinone
	17,17-Ethylenedioxyandrosta-1,4-dien-3-one
	Fenchone
	n-Heptan-2-one
	n-Heptan-3-one
	3H,3H-Hexafluoroacetylacetone

Tariff heading	*Description*
29.13	2-*n*-Hexylcyclopent-2-enone
	2-Hydroxyacetophenone
	4-Hydroxyacetophenone
	4-Hydroxybenzophenone
	2-Hydroxy-3-methylcyclopent-2-enone
	2-Hydroxy-4-*n*-octyloxybenzophenone
	17α-Hydroxypregn-4-ene-3,11,20-trione
	17β-Hydroxy-4,5-seco-19-norandrostane-3,5-dione
	Menaphthone
	(±)-*iso*Menthone
	Mesityl oxide
	4-Methoxy-4-methylpentan-2-one
	5-Methylheptan-3-one
	5-Methylhexan-2-one
	6-Methyl-α-ionone
	3-Methyl-2-(*n*-pent-2-enyl)cyclopent-2-enone
	3-Methyl-2-*n*-pentylcyclopent-2-enone
	4-Methyl-4-phenylpentan-2-one
	Musk ketone
	1,4-Naphthaquinone
	n-Octan-3-one
	Oestr-5(10)-ene-3,17-dione
	Oestr-4-en-17-one
	n-Pentan-2-one
	Pentan-3-one
	Phenacyl bromide
	Pinacolone
	Sodium 2,2′-dihydroxy-4,4′-dimethoxybenzophenone-5-sulphonate
	2,4,2′,4′-Tetrahydroxybenzophenone
	1,1,1-Trifluoroacetylacetone, of a purity not less than 99 per cent.
	n-Undecan-2-one
29.14	Allyl 3-cyclohexylpropionate
	(±)-3-Allyl-2-methyl-4-oxocyclopent-2-enyl *trans*-(+)-chrysanthemum*mono*carboxylate
	Aluminium acetate, basic
	Ammonium pentadecafluoro-*n*-octanoate
	Arachidonic acid
	(−)-Bornyl acetate
	4-*tert*Butylbenzoic acid
	n-Butyl chloroformate
	*sec*Butyl chloroformate
	2-*sec*Butyl-4,6-dinitrophenyl 3-methylcrotonate
	*tert*Butyl 2-ethylperbutyrate
	n-Butyric acid
	*iso*Butyric acid
	Chloroacetyl chloride
	2-Chlorobenzoic acid
	3-Chlorobenzoic acid
	4-Chloro-3-nitrobenzoic acid
	Chrysanthemic acid
	Chrysanthemoyl chloride
	Crotonic acid
	Cyclohexyl chloroformate
	Decahydro-2-naphthyl acetate
	n-Dec-2-enoic acid
	Dichloroacetic acid
	2,4-Dichlorobenzoyl chloride
	Digol dichloroformate
	Dihydrocarveyl acetate
	Dihydrocarveyl propionate

Tariff heading	*Description*
29.14	17α,21-Dihydroxy-16α-methylpregna-1,4,9(11)-triene-3,20-dione 21-acetate
	17α,21-Dihydroxy-5α-pregnane-3,11,20-trione 21-propionate
	3α,20-Dihydroxy-5β-pregn-17(20)-en-11-one diacetate
	1,1-Dimethyl-5-methylenehept-6-enyl acetate
	1,1-Dimethyl-2-phenylethyl *n*-butyrate
	1,1-Dimethyl-3-phenylpropyl acetate
	(±)-1,5-Dimethyl-1-vinylhept-4-enyl acetate
	2-Ethylhexyl chloroformate
	α-Ethyl-3-nitrocinnamic acid
	Ethyl trichloroacetate
	Farnesyl acetate
	Fenchyl acetate
	Glycerol tripropionate
	Heptafluoro-*n*-butyric acid
	n-Heptanoic acid
	Lead tetra-acetate
	Linalyl cinnamate
	3-Methoxy-*n*-butyl acetate
	2-Methoxyethyl chloroformate
	Methyl acetate of a purity not less than 98 per cent.
	Methyl chloroformate
	Methyl formate
	Methyl *p*-toluate
	2-Nitrobenzoic acid
	4-Nitrobenzoic acid
	n-Nonanoic acid
	Nonyl acetate, mixed isomers, having a specific rotation at 20° centigrade to the D line of sodium of between −9° and −13°
	n-Octanoic acid
	n-Oct-2-ynoic acid
	Phenyl chloroformate
	Pivalic acid
	Potassium sorbate
	2-(4-*iso*Propenylcyclohex-l-enyl)ethyl formate
	Propiolic acid
	Propionic anhydride
	n-Propyl acetate
	*iso*Propyl chloroformate
	Sodium fluoroacetate
	Sodium formate
	Sodium trichloroacetate
	Tetragol di-(2-ethylhexanoate)
	Tetragol dimethacrylate
	o-Toluic acid (-COOH at l)
	p-Toluic acid (-COOH at 1)
	Tricyclo[5,2,1,$0^{2,6}$]dec-4-en-8-yl acetate
	Triethyl orthoacetate
	Triethyl orthopropionate
	Trifluoroacetic acid
	Trigol di-(2-ethylbutyrate)
	Trigol dimethacrylate
	Trimethyl orthoformate
	2,2,4-Trimethylpentane-1,3-diol 1-*iso*butyrate
	2,2,4-Trimethylpentane-1,3-diol di*iso*butyrate
	*iso*Valeric acid
	Vinyl *n*-butyrate
	Vinyl chloroacetate
	Vinyl decanoate, mixed isomers

Tariff heading	*Description*
29.14	Vinyl *n*-dodecanoate Vinyl 2-ethylhexanoate Vinyl propionate
29.15	*cis*Aconitic acid Ammonium ferric oxalate Azelaic acid Benzenedicarboxylic acid, mixed isomers Benzene-1,2,4-tricarboxylic anhydride *n*-Butyl hydrogen itaconate Di-*n*-butyl itaconate Dichloromaleic anhydride Dimethyl adipate Dimethyl isophthalate Dimethyl itaconate Dioctyl 2*H*,3*H*-hexachlorobicyclo[2,2,1]hept-5-ene-2,3-dicarboxylate, mixed isomers Dodecane-1,12-dioic acid Dodecenylsuccinic acid, mixed isomers Ethanediol cyclic brassylate Glutaric anhydride Isophthalic acid Itaconic anhydride Malonic acid Methylbicyclo[2,2,1]hept-5-ene-2,3-dicarboxylic anhydride Pimelic acid Pyromellitic dianhydride Sodium oxalate which, in the form in which it is imported, contains not less than 5·0 per cent. by weight of moisture and which contains in the dried material not more than 98·0 per cent. by weight of oxalates expressed as sodium oxalate, $Na_2C_2O_4$ Suberic acid Succinic acid 4-Sulphophthalic acid 4-Sulphophthalic acid, diammonium salt Tetrachlorophthalic anhydride
29.16	4-Allyloxy-3-chlorophenylacetic acid Aluminium hydroxide di-(*O*-acetylsalicylate) Antimony potassium tartrate, which satisfies the requirements of the British Pharmacopoeia 4-Bromo-3,5-dihydroxybenzoic acid *n*-Butoxycarbonylmethyl *n*-butyl phthalate Calcium gluconate lactobionate Calcium D-saccharate Carbenoxolone Carbenoxolone, disodium salt 2,5-Dichloro-6-methoxybenzoic acid Diethyl ethoxymethylenemalonate 2,5-Dihydroxybenzoic acid 3,5-Dihydroxybenzoic acid 2,2-Di(hydroxymethyl)propionic acid 3,5-Di-iodosalicylic acid (-COOH at 1) Dimethyl methoxymethylenemalonate Enoxolone Ethacrynic acid Ethyl sodioacetoacetate Galacturonic acid Glucuronic acid Glycollic acid Glyoxylic acid

Tariff heading	*Description*
29.16	3-Hydroxy-2,2-dimethylpropyl 3-hydroxydimethylpropionate
	1-Hydroxy-2-naphthoic acid
	2-Hydroxy-*m*-toluic acid
	Laevulic acid
	Magnesium gluconate
	L-Malic acid
	L-Mandelic acid
	Methallenoestril
	2-(6-Methoxy-2-naphthyl)propionic acid
	Methyl 3,5-dihydroxybenzoate
	Mucic acid
	Mucochloric acid
	2-Oxoglutaric acid
	Pentaerythritol tetra-3-(3,5-di*tert*butyl-4-hydroxyphenyl)propionate
	Potassium gluconate
	Potassium sodium tartrate
	Prostaglandin E_2
	Pyruvic acid which, in the dry state, contains not more than 97 per cent. by weight of free acid calculated as pyruvic acid
	Quinic acid
	Sodium *cis*-3-bromo-3-(4-methoxybenzoyl)acrylate
	Sodium deoxycholate
	Sodium dihydrogen citrate
	(—)-Tartaric acid
	*meso*Tartaric acid
	2,4,5-Trichlorophenoxyacetic acid
	Triethyl *O*-acetylcitrate
	3,7,12-Trioxo-5β-cholanic acid
29.17	1-*iso*Butyl-4-ethyloctyl sodium sulphate
	n-Dodecyl sodium sulphate
29.19	Barium hydrogen 3-phospho-D-glycerate
	Chloro-1-(2,4-dichlorophenyl)vinyl diethyl phosphate
	trans-2-Chloro-1-(2,4,5-trichlorophenyl)vinyl dimethyl phosphate
	1,2-Dibromo-2,2-dichloroethyl dimethyl phosphate
	Di-*n*-butyl 2,2-dichlorovinyl phosphate
	2,2-Dichlorovinyl dimethyl phosphate
	Di-(2-ethylhexyl) sodium phosphate
	2-Ethylhexyl diphenyl phosphate
	Sodium phytate
	Triethyl phosphate
29.20	Diallyl digol dicarbonate
	Di-(4-*tert*butylcyclohexyl) peroxydicarbonate
	Diethyl pyrocarbonate
	Diphenyl carbonate
	Ethylene carbonate
	Propylene carbonate
29.21	*O*-4-Bromo-2,5-dichlorophenyl *OO*-diethyl phosphorothioate
	O-4-Bromo-2,5-dichlorophenyl *OO*-dimethyl phosphorothioate
	O-2,4-Dichlorophenyl *OO*-diethyl phosphorothioate
	OO-Diethyl *O*-4-nitrophenyl phosphorothioate
	OO-Diethyl phosphorochloridothioate
	OO-Dimethyl *O*-3-methyl-4-nitrophenyl phosphorothioate
	OO-Dimethyl *O*-4-nitrophenyl phosphorothioate
	OO-Dimethyl *O*-2,4,5-trichlorophenyl phosphorothioate
	1,9,10,11,12,12-Hexachloro-4,6-dioxa-5-thiatricyclo[7,2,1,$0^{2,8}$]dodec-10-ene 5-oxide

Tariff heading	*Description*
29.21	Tri-(2-ethylhexyl) phosphite
	Triethyl phosphite
	Trimethyl phosphite
29.22	Allylamine
	2-Aminobiphenyl
	N-2-Amino-3,5-dibromobenzyl-*N*-cyclohexylmethylammonium chloride
	4-Amino-1-diethylamino-*n*-pentane
	4-Aminodiphenylamine
	3-Aminomethyl-3,5,5-trimethylcyclohexylamine
	2-Aminonaphthalene-1-sulphonic acid
	8-Aminonaphthalene-1-sulphonic acid
	8-Aminonaphthalene-2-sulphonic acid
	Amitriptyline embonate
	Amitriptyline hydrochloride
	Benzidine
	Benzidine hydrochloride
	*iso*Butylamine
	*sec*Butylamine
	*tert*Butylamine
	4-Chloro-2-nitroaniline
	4-Chloro-*m*-toluidine-6-sulphonic acid (-NH_2 at 1)
	4-Chloro-2-trifluoromethylaniline
	4-Cyclohexylaminodiphenylamine
	3-Cyclohexylaminopropylamine
	N-Cyclohexyldimethylamine
	N-Cyclohexylmethylamine
	Cyclopentamine hydrochloride
	N-*n*-Decyldimethylamine
	Diallylamine
	1,3-Diaminocyclohexane
	1,12-Diaminododecane
	Di-(4-amino-3-methylcyclohexyl)methane
	1,8-Diaminonaphthalene
	1,2-Diaminopropane
	1,3-Diaminopropane
	Di-(3-aminopropyl)amine
	2,4-Diaminotoluene
	1,6-Diaminotrimethylhexane, mixed 2,2,4- and 2,4,4- isomers
	αα′-Diaminoxylene, mixed isomers
	Diamylamine, mixed isomers
	6,8-Dianilinonaphthalene-1-sulphonic acid
	2,4-Dichloroaniline
	4,5-Dichloro-*o*-phenylenediamine
	Dicyclohexylamine
	NN′-Dicyclohexyl-*p*-phenylenediamine
	1,3-Di(dimethylamino)-*n*-butane
	NN′-Di-(1,4-dimethylpentyl)-*p*-phenylenediamine
	2-Diethylaminoethylamine
	3-Diethylaminopropylamine
	NN′-Di-(l-ethyl-3-methylpentyl)-*p*-phenylenediamine
	NN-Diethyl-*p*-phenylenediamine
	2-Dimethylaminoethylamine
	3-Dimethylaminopropylamine
	NN′-Di-(l-methylheptyl)-*p*-phenylenediamine
	NN-Dimethyl-*n*-octylamine
	NN-Dimethyl-*p*-phenylenediamine
	NN-Dimethyl-*n*-tetradecylamine
	2,6-Dinitro-*NN*-di-*n*-propyl-4-trifluoromethylaniline
	Di-*n*-octylamine

Tariff heading	*Description*
29.22	Di-*n*-propylamine
	N-*n*-Dodecyldimethylamine
	Ethamsylate
	2-Ethylaniline
	N-Ethyldi-(3-phenylpropyl)ammonium dihydrogen citrate
	N-Ethyl-1-naphthylamine
	Fast Red RL Base
	Fast Red TR Base
	Fenfluramine hydrochloride
	4-Fluoroaniline
	n-Hexylamine
	Mephentermine
	3-Methylaminopropylamine
	N-Methylaniline
	3-Methylbenzylamine
	N-1-Methylheptyl-*N'*-phenyl-*p*-phenylenediamine
	N-(2-Methyl-2-nitropropyl)-4-nitrosoaniline
	N-Methyltaurine, sodium salt
	1-Naphthylamine
	2-Naphthylamine
	2-Nitroaniline-4-sulphonic acid
	4-Nitrodiphenylamine
	4-Nitro-*m*-phenylenediamine
	n-Octylamine
	Pargyline hydrochloride
	NNN'N''N''-Pentamethyldiethylenetriamine
	n-Pentylamine
	*iso*Pentylamine
	Phentermine
	m-Phenylenediamine
	p-Phenylenediamine
	p-Phenylenediamine dihydrochloride
	(±)-1-Phenylethylamine
	Prenylamine lactate
	n-Propylamine
	Protriptyline hydrochloride
	Sodium 4-aminonaphthalene-1-sulphonate
	Sodium *N*-benzylsulphanilate
	Taurine
	3,4,3',4'-Tetra-aminobiphenyl tetrahydrochloride
	o-Tolidine
	o-Tolidine dihydrochloride
	m-Tolidine dihydrochloride
	8-*p*-Toluidinonaphthalene-1-sulphonic acid
	Triallylamine
	2,4,5-Trichloroaniline
	Tri-*n*-decylamine
	4-Trifluoromethylaniline
	Tri-*n*-hexylamine
	Tri-*n*-octylamine
	Tri-*n*-pentylamine
	Tri*iso*pentylamine
	Tri-*n*-propylamine
	2,3-Xylidine
	2,5-Xylidine
	3,4-Xylidine
29.23	D-Alanine
	L-Alanine
	DL-Alanine
	4-Aminoacetophenone
	7-(4-Aminoanilino)-4-hydroxynaphthalene-2-sulphonic acid

Tariff heading	*Description*
29.23	4-Aminobenzoic acid
	2-Amino-*n*-butan-1-ol
	4-Aminobutyric acid
	5-Amino-2-chlorobenzoic acid
	2-Amino-5-chlorobenzophenone
	L-2-Amino-3-(3,4-dihydroxyphenyl)-2-methylpropionic acid
	2-(2-Aminoethoxy)ethanol
	2-Aminoethyl dihydrogen phosphate
	2-Amino-2-ethylpropane-1,3-diol
	6-Aminohexanoic acid
	4-Amino-5-hydroxynaphthalene-1,7-disulphonic acid
	6-Amino-4-hydroxynaphthalene-2-sulphonic acid
	2-Amino-2-methylpropane-1,3-diol
	2-Amino-2-methylpropan-l-ol
	2-Amino-5-nitrophenol
	(−)-2-Amino-1-(4-nitrophenyl)propane-1,3-diol
	3-Aminophenol
	4-Aminophenol
	(+)-2-Aminopropan-l-ol
	3-Aminopropan-1-ol
	3-Aminopropionic acid
	4-Aminosalicylic acid (-COOH at 1)
	11-Aminoundecanoic acid
	o-Anisidine
	m-Anisidine
	L-Aspartic acid
	DL-Aspartic acid
	Bamethan sulphate
	Benzocaine
	7-(4-Carboxymethoxyanilino)-4-hydroxynaphthalene-2-sulphonic acid
	5-Chloro-*o*-anisidine (-NH_2 at 1)
	5-Chloroanthranilic acid (-COOH at 1)
	3-Chloro-4-(4-chlorophenoxy)aniline
	4-(4-Chlorophenoxy)aniline
	3-Chloro-6-phenoxyaniline
	Chlorphenoxamine hydrochloride
	Clorprenaline hydrochloride
	2,4-Diaminoanisole
	2,4-Diaminoanisole *mono*sulphate
	1,2-Diaminocyclohexane-*NNN′N′*-tetra-acetic acid
	1,3-Diaminopropan-2-ol-*NNN′N′*-tetra-acetic acid
	3,9-Di-(3-aminopropyl)-2,4,8,10-tetraoxaspiro[5,5]undecane
	o-Dianisidine
	o-Dianisidine dihydrochloride of a purity not greater than 98·5 per cent.
	1,15-Diaza-5,8,11-trioxapentadecane
	2,6-Di*tert*butyl-4-dimethylaminomethylphenol
	3,3′-Di(carboxymethoxy)benzidine, dipotassium salt
	1,2-Di[di-(2-hydroxy-*n*-propyl)amino]ethane
	Di-(2-dimethylaminoethyl) ether
	3-Diethylaminophenol
	5,5′-Dihydroxy-2,2′-dinaphthylamine-7,7′-disulphonic acid
	3-(3,4-Dihydroxyphenyl)-L-alanine
	3-(3,4-Dihydroxyphenyl)-DL-alanine
	2-(3,4-Dimethoxyphenyl)ethylamine
	(+)-4-Dimethylamino-3-methyl-1,2-diphenylbutan-2-ol
	6-Dimethylaminomethyl-2,5-xylenol hydrochloride (−OH at 1)
	1-Dimethylaminopropan-2-ol
	3-(3-Dimethylaminopropyl)-1,2:4,5-dibenzocycloheptadien-3-ol
	1,4-Di-(2,4,6-trimethylanilino)anthraquinone
	Ethomoxane hydrochloride

Tariff heading	*Description*
29.23	Ethyl aminoacetate hydrochloride
	2-Ethylaminoethanol, of which not less than 90 per cent. by volume distils between 165° and 170° centigrade at normal pressure and which contains not more than 0·5 per cent. by weight of water
	Ethylenediamine-*NN'*-diacetic acid, cobalt complex
	Ethylenediamine-*NN'*-di-[α-(2-hydroxyphenyl)acetic acid], iron complex
	Ethylenediamine-*NNN'N'*-tetra-acetic acid, dicobalt complex
	Fast Scarlet RC Base
	D-Glucosamine hydrochloride
	Glutamic acid
	1-(4-Hydroxyphenyl)-2-methylaminoethanol tartrate
	Iopanoic acid
	Isatoic anhydride
	Isoxsuprine hydrochloride
	Ketamine hydrochloride
	L-Leucine
	DL-Leucine
	L-*iso*Leucine
	DL-*iso*Leucine
	L-*nor*Leucine
	DL-*nor*Leucine
	L-Lysine
	L-Lysine L-glutamate
	L-Lysine *mono*hydrochloride
	DL-Lysine *mono*hydrochloride
	Mebeverine hydrochloride
	Methoxyphenamine hydrochloride
	3-Methoxypropylamine
	6-Methoxy-*m*-toluidine (-NH_2 at 1)
	2-Methylaminoethanol
	N-Methyldiethanolamine
	2,3,5,6,2',3',5',6'-Octachlorodi-(2-hydroxyethylamino)biphenyl
	Orciprenaline sulphate
	DL-Ornithine *mono*hydrochloride
	Orphenadrine
	Orphenadrine dihydrogen citrate
	Orphenadrine hydrochloride
	Pentyl 4-dimethylaminobenzoate, mixed isomers
	5-*tert*Pentyl-2-phenoxyaniline
	o-Phenetidine
	m-Phenetidine
	L-3-Phenylalanine
	DL-3-Phenylalanine
	Potassium 4-aminosalicylate (-COOH at 1)
	Potassium 2-methylaminopropionate
	Procaine
	Procaine hydrochloride
	Prostaglandin $F_{2\alpha}$, trometamol salt
	Protokylol hydrochloride
	Sarcosine
	L-Serine
	DL-Serine
	Sodium 4-aminosalicylate (-COOH at 1)
	Sodium hydrogen glutamate
	L-Threonine
	DL-Threonine
	Thymoxamine hydrochloride
	N-[2-(α-*o*-Tolylbenzyloxy)ethyl]methylammonium chloride
	Tri-(2-hydroxy-*n*-propyl)amine
	Trometamol

Tariff heading	*Description*
29.23	Tyramine hydrochloride
	L-Tyrosine
	DL-Tyrosine
	L-Valine
	DL-Valine
	DL-*nor*Valine
29.24	Benzethonium chloride
	Betaine
	Betaine hydrochloride
	Edrophonium chloride
	N-2,3-Epoxypropyltrimethylammonium chloride
	Methylbenzethonium chloride
	Tetraethylammonium chloride
	Tridihexethyl chloride
29.25	*O*-Acetyl-4′-chloro-3,5-di-iodosalicylanilide
	Acrylamide
	Ambenonium chloride
	Ambucetamide
	7-(4-Aminobenzamido)-4-hydroxynaphthalene-2-sulphonic acid
	4-Aminohippuric acid
	L-α-Asparagine
	DL-α-Asparagine
	L-*β*-Asparagine
	Barbitone
	Barbitone sodium
	N-Benzoyl-*N′N′*-di-*n*-propylisoglutamine
	β-Benzyl hydrogen *N*-benzyloxycarbonyl-L-aspartate
	N-Bromoacetamide
	4-Bromo-3,5-dihydroxy-*N*-methylbenzamide
	Bucetin
	*sec*Butylurea
	Carbachol
	Chloroacetamide
	5′-Chloroacetoacet-*o*-anisidide
	α-Chloro-2′,6′-diethyl-*N*-(methoxymethyl)acetanilide
	N-(3-Chloro-4-methoxyphenyl)-*N′N′*-dimethylurea
	2,6-Dichlorobenzamide
	5,2′-Dichloro-2-α-chloroacetamidobenzophenone
	3,3′-Dichloro-5-trifluoromethyl-*NN′*-diphenylurea
	4,4′-Dichloro-3-trifluoromethyl-*NN′*-diphenylurea
	1,2-Di(diacetylamino)ethane
	2,4-Dihydroxybenzamide
	3,5-Dihydroxy-*N*-(2-hydroxyethyl)benzamide
	Dimethylcarbamoyl chloride
	N-(1,1-Dimethyl-3-oxobutyl)acrylamide
	3-(*N′N′*-Dimethylureido)phenyl *tert*butylcarbamate
	Ethosalamide
	Ethotoin
	(−)-1-Ethylcarbamoylethyl phenylcarbamate
	Ethyl *N*-3-(1,2:5,6-dibenzocycloheptatrien-7-yl)propylmethylcarbamate
	1-Ethyl-1-methylprop-2-ynyl carbamate
	Fast Violet B Base
	Fluoroacetamide
	Formamide
	L-Glutamine
	DL-Glutamine
	Glycylglycine
	3-Hydroxy-*NN*-di-(2-hydroxyethyl)-2-naphthamide
	Iocetamic acid

Tariff heading	*Description*
29.25	Iodoacetamide
	Iothalamic acid
	Isopropamide iodide
	Methacrylamide
	Methohexitone
	Methyl 4-acetamido-2-ethoxybenzoate
	Methyl 4-acetamido-5-chloro-2-methoxybenzoate
	Methyl carbamate
	Methyl 3-(*m*-tolylcarbamoyloxy)phenylcarbamate
	Naphthol AS
	Naphthol AS-BG
	Naphthol AS-BS
	Naphthol AS-D
	Naphthol AS-E
	Naphthol AS-G
	Naphthol AS-IRG
	Naphthol AS-ITR
	Naphthol AS-KB
	Naphthol AS-OL
	Naphthol AS-RT
	Naphthol AS-TR
	1-Naphthyl methylcarbamate
	Nealbarbitone
	Niclosamide
	Phenytoin sodium
	2-*iso*Propoxyphenyl methylcarbamate
	Tetramethylurea
	N-[2,2,2-Trichloro-1-(3,4-dichloroanilino)ethyl]formamide
	Tybamate
	N-Vanillyl-*n*-nonanamide
29.26	Acetamidinium chloride
	α-(4-Aminophenyl)-α-ethylglutarimide
	L-Arginine
	L-Arginine L-glutamate
	L-Arginine *mono*hydrochloride
	3,5-Dichloro-*p*-benzoquinonechlorimine
	Di-(2,6-di*iso*propylphenyl)carbodi-imine
	3-Dimethylaminomethyleneaminophenyl methylcarbamate hydrochloride
	n-Dodecylguanidinium acetate
	N-Ethylmaleimide
	Glutethimide
	Guanidinium carbonate
	Guanidinium chloride
	Guanidinium nitrate containing not more than 0·9 per cent. by weight of water
	Hexahydro-1,3,5-tri-(2-hydroxyethyl)-1,3,5-triazine
	Hexamine 3-chloroallylochloride
	N-Phosphonocreatine, sodium salt
	3,4,5,6-Tetrahydrophthalimidomethyl 2,2-dimethyl-3-(2-methylprop-1-enyl)cyclopropanecarboxylate
29.27	(−)-2-Acetamido-2-vanillylpropionitrile
	Acetonitrile
	Benzonitrile
	Chloroacetonitrile
	4-Chlorophenylacetonitrile
	3-Cyano-5-dimethylamino-2-methyl-3-phenylhexane
	2-Cyanoethyl acrylate

Tariff heading	*Description*
29.27	2,3-Dichloro-5,6-dicyanobenzoquinone *NN*-Di-2-cyanoethylformamide 3-Dimethylaminopropionitrile 4,8-Dimethylnon-7-enonitrile 2,2-Dimethylpropionitrile Diphenylacetonitrile Ethyl 2-cyano-3,3-diphenylacrylate 2-Ethylhexyl 2-cyano-3,3-diphenylacrylate Mandelonitrile Methacrylonitrile Phthalonitrile Propionitrile Tetracyanoethylene Verapamil hydrochloride
29.28	Azobenzene 4-*N*-Benzylethylaminophenyldiazonium zinc chloride Sodium 6-diazo-5-hydroxynaphthalene-1-sulphonate *tri*Sodium hydrogen 4,5-dihydroxy-3,6-di-(2-sulphophenylazo)-naphthalene-2,7-disulphonate
29.29	*p*-Benzoquinone dioxime *p*-Benzoquinone dioxime dibenzoate Benzylideneaminoguanidinium tartrate Bufexamac 1-(2-Carboxyphenyl)-5-(2-hydroxy-5-sulphophenyl)-3-phenylformazan *N*-(4-Chlorobenzoyl)-*N*-(4-methoxyphenyl)hydrazine *N*-4-Chlorophenyl-*N′*-methoxy-*N′*-methylurea *O*-α-Cyanobenzylideneamino *OO*-diethyl phosphorothioate Desferrioxamine mesylate 1,3-Di-(4-chlorobenzylideneamino)guanidinium chloride *N*-3,4-Dichlorophenyl-*N′*-methoxy-*N′*-methylurea *NN*-Diethylhydroxylamine Diethyl naphthalimido phosphate *NN*-Dimethylhydrazine Hydroxyurea Phenelzine hydrogen sulphate Phenylhydrazine 1-Phenylsemicarbazide Procarbazine hydrochloride
29.30	4-*tert*Butyl-2-chlorophenyl methyl methylphosphoramidate 1-Chloro-2-*iso*cyanatobenzene *iso*Cyanatobenzene 5-*iso*Cyanato-3-*iso*cyanatomethyl-1,1,3-trimethylcyclohexane *iso*Cyanatocyclohexane *iso*Cyanatomethane 1-*iso*Cyanatonaphthalene 1-*iso*Cyanato-*n*-octadecane Di-(4-*iso*cyanatocyclohexyl)methane 4,4′-Di*iso*cyanatodiphenylmethane of a purity not less than 85 per cent. 1,6-Di*iso*cyanatohexane 1,5-Di*iso*cyanatonaphthalene Dimethylamine-borine Hexamethylphosphoramide 4,4′,4″-Tri*iso*cyanatotriphenylmethane

Tariff heading	*Description*
29.31	Acetyl cyclohexanesulphonyl peroxide
	N-Acetyl-DL-methionine
	Ambazone
	2-Aminobenzenethiol
	Benzenethiol
	Bithionol
	*iso*Bornyl thiocyanatoacetate
	Butane-1,4-dithiol
	n-Butane-1-thiol
	2-*n*-Butoxyethyl 2-thiocyanatoethyl ether
	S-Carboxymethylcysteine
	Chlordantoin
	2-Chloroallyl diethyldithiocarbamate
	4-Chlorophenylthiomethyl *OO*-diethyl phosphorodithioate
	N-Cyclohexanesulphenylphthalimide
	DL-Cystathionine
	L-Cysteine
	L-Cysteme hydrochloride
	L-Cystine
	Dapsone
	n-Decane-1-thiol
	Di-(3-*tert*butyl-4-hydroxy-6-methylphenyl) sulphide
	Di-(2-carboxyphenyl) disulphide
	S-2,3-Dichloroallyl di*iso*propylthiocarbamate
	Di-(4-chlorophenyl) sulphone
	2,6-Dichlorothiobenzamide
	1,2-Di-(3-ethoxycarbonyl-2-thioureido)benzene
	OO-Diethyl 2-ethylthioethyl phosphorodithioate
	OO-Diethyl *O*-2-ethylthioethyl phosphorothioate
	OO-Diethyl ethylthiomethyl phosphorodithioate
	Di-(2-hydroxyethyl) sulphide
	Di-(6-hydroxy-2-naphthyl) disulphide
	Dimercaprol
	1,2-Di-(*N′*-methoxycarbonylthioureido)benzene
	Dimethyl disulphide
	Dimethyl *S*-2-(1-methylcarbamoylethylthio)ethyl phosphorothioate
	OO-Dimethyl methylcarbamoylmethyl phosphorodithioate
	Dimethyl sulphoxide
	Dimethylxanthogen disulphide
	1,4-Dioxan-2,3-dithiol di-(*OO*-diethyl phosphorodithioate)
	Diphenyl disulphide
	Diphenyl sulphide
	NN′-Diphenylthiourea
	3,6-Dithiaoctane-1,8-diol
	Dithio-oxamide
	Dithizone of a purity not less than 99·0 per cent. which yields not more than 0·20 per cent. by weight of sulphated ash
	Di(trichloromethyl) sulphone
	Dodecanethiol, mixed isomers
	Ecothiopate iodide
	Ethane-1,2-dithiol
	Ethanethiol
	L-Ethionine
	DL-Ethionine
	Ethylcarbamoylmethyl *OO*-dimethyl phosphorodithioate
	Ethyl methyl sulphide
	O-2-Ethylthioethyl *OO*-dimethyl phosphorothioate
	S-2-Ethylthioethyl dimethyl phosphorothioate
	Glutathione
	Glutathione disulphide

Tariff heading	*Description*
29.31	*n*-Hexane-1-thiol
	DL-Homocysteine
	3-Mercaptopropane-1,2-diol
	2-Mercaptopropionic acid
	3-Mercaptopropionic acid
	Mercaptosuccinic acid
	Methanethiol
	Methionine
	5-(1-Methylbutyl)-5-(2-methylthioethyl)-2-thiobarbituric acid, sodium derivative
	2-Methyl-2-(methylthio)propionaldehyde *O*-(methylcarbamoyl)oxime
	Methyl phenyl sulphide
	4-(Methylthio)-3,5-xylyl methylcarbamate
	1-Naphthylthiourea
	n-Octane-1-thiol
	n-Pentane-1-thiol
	Potassium ethylxanthate
	Potassium *n*-pentylxanthate
	Propane-1,3-dithiol
	Propane-1-thiol
	Propane-2-thiol
	S-*n*-Propyl *n*-butylethylthiocarbamate
	Sodium toluene-4-sulphinate
	2,4,5,4′-Tetrachlorodiphenyl sulphide
	2,4,5,4′-Tetrachlorodiphenyl sulphone
	N-(1,1,2,2-Tetrachloroethanesulphenyl)cyclohex-4-ene-1,2-dicarboxyimide
	OOO′O′-Tetraethyl methylene di(phosphorodithioate)
	Thioacetamide
	Thiobarbituric acid
	*iso*Thiocyanatobenzene
	*iso*Thiocyanatomethane
	Thiodiacetic acid
	2,2′-Thiodi-(4-*tt*-octylphenolato)-*n*-butylaminenickel(II)
	Thiourea
	Tolnaftate
	Toluene-2-thiol
	Toluenethiol, mixed isomers
	S-2,3,3-Trichloroallyl di*iso*propylthiocarbamate
	Trichloromethanesulphenyl chloride
	N-(Trichloromethanesulphenyl)cyclohex-4-ene-1,2-dicarboxyimide
	N-(Trichloromethanesulphenyl)phthalimide
	Zinc di-(2-benzamidophenyl sulphide)
	Zinc di(pentachlorophenyl sulphide)
	Zinc propylenebisdithiocarbamate
29.32	Bismuth *N*-glycollylarsanilate
	Cacodylic acid
	Phenylarsonic acid
	Sodium cacodylate
29.33	4-Chloromercuribenzoic acid of a purity of not less than 98 per cent. and a melting point of not less than 278° centigrade
	3,2-Mercurioxy-4-nitrotoluene
29.34	Allyltrichlorosilane
	3-Aminopropyltriethoxysilane
	3-Aminopropyltrimethoxysilane
	n-Butyl-lithium
	*sec*Butyl-lithium
	3-Chloropropyltrimethoxysilane

Tariff heading	*Description*
29.34	Di*iso*butylaluminium hydride
	Dicyclopentadienyliron
	Diethyl di-(2-hydroxyethyl)aminomethylphosphonate
	Dimethyl 2,2,2-trichloro-l-hydroxyethylphosphonate
	Diphenyldichlorosilane
	Diphenylsilanediol
	2-(3,4-Epoxycyclohexyl)ethyltrimethoxysilane
	3-Glycidyloxypropyltrimethoxysilane
	3-Mercaptopropyltrimethoxysilane
	3-Methacryloyloxypropyltrimethoxysilane
	Methylcyclopentadienylmanganese tricarbonyl
	Methylphosphonothioic dichloride
	Methylphosphonous dichloride
	Methylvinyldichlorosilane
	Molybdenum hexacarbonyl
	Nitrilotri(methylphosphonic acid)
	Octaphenylcyclotetrasiloxane
	Phenyltrichlorosilane
	*penta*Sodium hydrogen nitrilotri(methylphosphonate)
	Sodium tetraphenylborate
	Tetramethylsilane
	Tri-*n*-butylaluminium
	Tri-*n*-butyl-2,4-dichlorobenzylphosphonium chloride
	Tricyclohexyltin hydroxide
	Triphenylphosphine
	Triphenyltin acetate
	Triphenyltin hydroxide
	Tungsten hexacarbonyl
	Vinyltrichlorosilane
	Vinyltriethoxysilane
	Vinyltri-(2-methoxyethoxy)silane
29.35	Acepromazine hydrogen maleate
	2-Acetyl-1,4-butyrolactone
	Acridine
	Adenine
	Adenine sulphate
	Adenosine
	Adenosine 3′-(dihydrogen phosphate)
	Adenosine 5′-(dihydrogen phosphate)
	Adenosine 5′-(dilithium hydrogen pyrophosphate)
	Adenosine 5′-(dipotassium dihydrogen triphosphate)
	Adenosine 5′-(disodium dihydrogen triphosphate)
	Adenosine 5′-(sodium dihydrogen pyrophosphate)
	Adenosine 5′-tosylate
	Adenosine 5′-(trisodium pyrophosphate)
	Ambrettolide
	2-Aminobenzothiazole
	4-Amino-5-cyano-2-methylpyrimidine
	5-Amino-3,4-dimethyl*iso*oxazole
	4-Amino-2,6-dimethylpyrimidine
	2-Amino-6-methylbenzothiazole
	5-Amino-3-methyl-1-phenylpyrazole
	3-(4-Amino-2-methyl-5-pyrimidyl)methyl-5-(2-hydroxyethyl)-4-methylthiazoline-2-thione
	3-Amino-5-morpholinomethyl-2-oxazolidone
	3-Amino-2-oxazolidone sulphate
	6-Aminopenicillanic acid
	4-Aminophenazone

Tariff heading	*Description*
29.35	5-Amino-l-phenylpyrazole
	1-(4-Amino-2-*n*-propyl-5-pyrimidylmethyl)-2-picolinium chloride *mono*hydrochloride
	4-Aminopyridine
	2-Aminopyrimidine
	2-Aminothiazole
	Angiotensin amide
	D-*iso*Ascorbic acid
	6-Azauridine
	Aziridine
	Benzimidazole
	Benzoguanamine
	5,6-Benzoquinoline
	N-Benzothiazol-2-yl-*NN′*-dimethylurea
	5-Benzyl-3-furylmethanol
	5-Benzyl-3-furylmethyl (±)-chrysanthemate
	5-Benzyl-3-furylmethyl (+)-*trans*chrysanthemate
	Biperiden hydrochloride
	2,2′-Biquinolyl
	Bisacodyl
	5-Bromo-2′-deoxycytidine
	5-Bromo-2′-deoxyuridine
	Brompheniramine hydrogen maleate
	Buclizine dihydrochloride
	Bupivacaine hydrochloride
	2-*n*-Butoxyethyl nicotinate
	*N-tert*Butylbenzothiazole-2-sulphenamide
	*tert*Butyl 1-(4-chlorobenzoyl)-5-methoxy-2-methylindol-3-ylacetate
	2-*n*-Butyldihydro-4,6-dimethylpyran, mixed isomers
	2-(3-*tert*Butyl-2-hydroxy-5-methylphenyl)-5-chlorobenzotriazole
	2-*iso*Butylquinoline
	6-*iso*Butylquinoline
	6-*tert*Butylquinoline
	Butylquinoline, mixed isomers
	2-Carbamoyloxymethyl-1-methyl-5-nitroimidazole
	Carbinoxamine hydrogen maleate
	Chlordiazepoxide
	Chlordiazepoxide *mono*hydrochloride
	2-(4-Chlorobenzyl)pyridine
	2-Chloro-4-(1-cyano-1-methylethylamino)-6-ethylamino-1,3,5-triazine
	5-Chloro-2-(3,5-di*tert*butyl-2-hydroxyphenyl)benzotriazole
	7-Chloro-1-(2-diethylaminoethyl)-5-(2-fluorophenyl)-1,3-dihydrobenzo-1,4-diazepin-2-one dihydrochloride
	7-Chloro-1-(2-diethylaminoethyl)-5-(2-fluorophenyl)-1,3-dihydrobenzo-1,4-diazepin-2-one *mono*hydrochloride
	7-Chloro-10-(2-dimethylaminoethyl)dibenzo[*b*,*e*]-1,4-diazepin-11-one *mono*hydrochloride
	(6-Chloro-2-oxobenzoxazolin-3-yl)methyl *OO*-diethyl phosphorodithioate
	6-Chloropurine
	2-Chloroquinoline
	Chlorprothixene
	Chlorzoxazone
	Cinnarizine
	Clonidine hydrochloride
	Clorazepic acid, dipotassium salt
	Cocarboxylase
	Coenzyme A
	Coenzyme A, trilithium salt

Tariff heading	Description
29.35	2,4,6-Collidine
	Creatinine
	Creatinine hydrochloride
	o-Cresolphthalein-6,6′-di(methylaminodiacetic acid)
	4-Cyano-1-methyl-4-phenylazacycloheptane
	2-Cyanophenothiazine
	Cyanuric chloride
	4-Cyclododecyl-2,6-dimethylmorpholinium acetate
	2-Cyclopentyl-2-(2-thienyl)glycollic acid
	Cyproheptadine hydrochloride
	Cytidine
	Cytosine
	Cytosine-1 β-D-arabinoside hydrochloride
	Debrisoquine sulphate
	Decahydro-4a-hydroxy-2,8,8-trimethyl-2-naphthoic acid lactone
	3,4,5,6,7,8,9,10,11,12-Decahydro-7,14,16-trihydroxy-3-methyl-2-benzoxacyclotetradecin-1-one
	1,5-Decanolactone
	Dehydracetic acid of a purity not less than 96 per cent.
	2′-Deoxyadenosine
	2′-Deoxyadenosine 5′-(disodium dihydrogen triphosphate)
	2′-Deoxycytidine 5′-(sodium trihydrogen triphosphate)
	2′-Deoxyguanosine
	2′-Deoxyguanosine 5′-(tetrasodium triphosphate)
	2′-Deoxyuridine
	Dextromethorphan hydrobromide
	Dextromoramide hydrogen (+)-tartrate
	2,5-Diamino-7-ethoxyacridinium lactate
	Diamthazole
	1,4-Diazabicyclo[2,2,2]octane
	Diazepam
	Diazoxide
	NN′-Di(benzothiazol-2-ylthiomethyl)urea
	3,5-Dibenzyltetrahydro-1,3,5-thiadiazine-2-thione
	2-(3,5-Di*tert*butyl-2-hydroxyphenyl)benzotriazole
	1-(2,3-Dichloroallyl)pyridinium chloride
	1-[2-(2,4-Dichlorobenzyloxy)-2-(2,4-dichlorophenyl)ethyl]imidazolium nitrate
	2,6-Dichloro-3,5-dicyano-4-phenylpyridine
	3,5-Dichloro-4-hydroxylutidine
	2-(3,4-Dichlorophenyl)-4-methyl-1,2,4-oxadiazolidinedione
	1,3-Di-(3-*iso*cyanato-4-methylphenyl)-1,3-diazacyclobutane-2,4-dione
	2,3-Dicyano-1,4-dithia-anthraquinone
	NN-Dicyclohexylbenzothiazole-2-sulphenamide
	OO-Diethyl *O*-4-methyl-2-*iso*propyl-6-pyrimidyl phosphorothioate
	2,4-Diethyl-6-*iso*propoxy-1,3,5-triazine
	OO-Diethyl *O*-pyrazin-2-yl phosphorothioate
	OO-Diethyl *O*-3,5,6-trichloro-2-pyridyl phosphorothioate
	8-[4,4-Di-(4-fluorophenyl)butyl]-1-phenyl-1,3,8-triazaspiro[4,5]decan-4-one
	α-(4-[4,4-Di-(4-fluorophenyl)butyl]piperazin-1-yl)acet-2′,6′-xylidide
	1-(1-[4,4-Di-(4-fluorophenyl)butyl]-4-piperidyl)benzimidazolin-2-one
	Dihydrallazine *mono*sulphate
	4,5-Dihydro-2,3:6,7-dibenzazepine
	3,4-Dihydro-2-methoxypyran
	Dihydronicotinamide-adenine dinucleotide, disodium salt
	Dihydronicotinamide-adenine dinucleotide phosphate, tetrasodium salt
	2,3-Dihydropyran
	3-(3β,17β-Dihydroxyandrost-5-en-17α-yl)propionic acid lactone
	2,4-Dihydroxyquinoline

Tariff heading	*Description*
29.35	2,4-Dihydroxyquinoline, *mono*sodium derivative
	Dimethisoquin *mono*hydrochloride
	11-(3-Dimethylaminopropylidene)-6,11-dihydrodibenz[*b*,*e*]oxepin hydrochloride
	11-(3-Dimethylaminopropylidene)-6,11-dihydrobenzo[*b*,*e*]thiepin hydrochloride
	5,6-Dimethylbenzimidazole
	OO-Dimethyl 4-oxobenzotriazin-3-ylmethyl phosphorodithioate
	2,3-Dimethyl-1-phenyl-4-*iso*propyl-5-pyrazolone
	NN-Dimethyl-2-(tribromopyrazol-1-yl)propionamide
	2,6-Dimethyl-4-*n*-tridecylmorpholine
	1,5-Di-(5-nitro-2-furyl)pentadien-3-one amidinohydrazone hydrochloride
	Diosgenin
	Diperodon
	Diphenoxylate hydrochloride
	Dipyridamole
	Dipyrone
	Dithiazanine iodide
	1,12-Dodecanolactam
	1,5-Dodecanolactone
	Doxapram hydrochloride
	Dropropizine
	Drostanolone tetrahydropyran-2-yl ether
	Ethionamide
	2-Ethoxy-3,4-dihydropyran
	2-Ethylamino-4-methylthio-6-*iso*propylamino-1,3,5-triazine
	2-Ethyl-3-hydroxy-4-pyrone
	5-Ethyl-2-picoline
	Fentanyl dihydrogen citrate
	Flavin-adenine dinucleotide
	Flupromazine *mono*hydrochloride
	Fluorescein-2′,7′-di(methylaminodiacetic acid)
	1-[3-(4-Fluorobenzoyl)propyl]-4-hydroxy-4-(3-trifluoromethylphenyl)-piperidine
	1-[3-(4-Fluorobenzoyl)propyl]-4-hydroxy-4-(3-trifluoromethylphenyl)-piperidinium chloride
	1-(1-[3-(4-Fluorobenzoyl)propyl]-1,2,3,6-tetrahydro-4-pyridyl)-benzimidazolin-2-one
	4′-Fluoro-4-[4-(2-pyridyl)piperazin-1-yl]butyrophenone
	5-Fluorouracil
	Fluphenazine *O*-*n*-decanoate
	Fluphenazine dihydrochloride
	Furan
	Furfuraldehyde
	D-Glucuronolactone
	Glycopyrronium bromide
	Guanethidine *mono*sulphate
	Guanine
	Guanine hydrochloride
	Guanosine 5′-(disodium phosphate)
	Haloperidol
	Hecogenin
	Hecogenin acetate
	10-(3-[4-(2-*n*-Heptanoyloxyethyl)piperazin-1-yl]propyl)-2-trifluoromethylphenothiazine
	1,3,4,6,7,8-Hexahydro-4,6,6,7,8,8-hexamethylindeno[5,6-*c*]pyran
	Hexa(methoxymethyl)melamine
	Hexetidine
	2-*n*-Hexyl-1,4-butyrolactone

Tariff heading	*Description*
29.35	Histamine acid phosphate
	Histamine dihydrochloride
	L-Histidine
	L-Histidine *mono*hydrochloride
	DL-Histidine *mono*hydrochloride
	Hydrallazine hydrochloride
	4-Hydroxy-1-methylpiperidine
	7-Hydroxy-7-(1-methyl-4-piperidyl)-1,2:5,6-dibenzocycloheptatriene hydrochloride
	3-Hydroxy-*N*-(3-morpholinopropyl)-2-naphthamide
	2-(2-Hydroxyphenyl)benzotriazole
	4-Hydroxypiperidine
	L-Hydroxyproline
	3-Hydroxypyridine
	4-Hydroxy-3-(1,2,3,4-tetrahydro-1-naphthyl)coumarin
	5-Hydroxy-DL-tryptophan
	Hydroxyzine dihydrochloride
	Hydroxyzine embonate
	Idoxuridine
	Imidazole
	Indole
	Indomethacin
	Inosine
	Inosine 5′-(disodium phosphate)
	Inosine 5′-(trisodium pyrophosphate)
	Iproniazid *mono*phosphate
	Isatin
	Isocarboxazid
	Isoniazid
	Isothipendyl *mono*hydrochloride
	Levallorphan hydrogen tartrate
	Levorphanol hydrogen tartrate
	Maltol
	Mebhydrolin napadisylate
	Menaphthone hydrogen bisulphite-2-hydroxy-4,6-dimethylpyrimidine complex
	Mepenzolate bzimide
	2-Mercaptobenzimidazole
	6-Mercaptopurine
	Methixene hydrochloride
	Methotrexate
	2-Methoxyphenothiazine
	Methyl 3-amino-5,6-dichloropyrazine-2-carboxylate
	Methyl 5-benzoylbenzimidazol-2-ylcarbamate
	Methyl 1-(*n*-butylcarbamoyl)benzimidazol-2-ylcarbamate
	6-Methyl-1,3-dithiolo[4,5-*b*]quinoxalin-2-one
	Methylenedi-(1,6-hexanolactam), mixed isomers
	2-Methylindole
	Methyl phenidate *mono*hydrochloride
	Methyl 1-(1-phenylethyl)imidazole-5-carboxylate hydrochloride
	1-Methylpiperazine
	1-Methylpyrrole
	1-Methyl-2-pyrrolidone
	2-(4-Methylsulphonylphenyl)imidazo[1,2-*a*]pyridine
	6-Methyl-2-thiouracil
	4-Methylumbelliferone
	Methyprylone
	Metyrapone
	2-(Morpholinodithio)benzothiazole
	1-(2-Morpholinoethyl)-5-nitroimidazole

Tariff heading	*Description*
29.35	Nialamide
	*iso*Nicotinamide
	Nicotinamide-adenine dinucleotide
	Nicotinamide-adenine dinucleotide phosphate, *mono*sodium salt
	Nicotinyl alcohol
	Nifuratel
	Nitrazepam
	Nitrofurantoin of which not more than 5·0 per cent. by weight passes a sieve having a nominal width of aperture of 75 micrometres
	Nitron
	1,8-Octanolactam
	7-Oxabicyclo[2,2,1]heptane-2,3-dicarboxylic acid
	11-Oxa-1,16-hexadecanolactone
	12-Oxa-1,16-hexadecanolactone
	Oxandrolone
	Oxymetazoline hydrochloride
	Oxyphencyclimine hydrochloride
	Pancuronium bromide
	(−)-Pantolactone
	(±)-Pantolactone, which yields on hydrolysis not more than 5 parts per million by weight of cyanides calculated as CN
	Pemoline
	Pentachloropyridine
	1,15-Pentadecanolactone
	Phenazone
	Phenazopyridine *mono*hydrochloride
	Phenbutrazate hydrochloride
	Pheniramine hydrogen maleate
	Phenmetrazine hydrochloride
	Phenolphthalein, which satisfies the requirements of the British Pharmacopoeia
	Phenoperidine hydrochloride
	Phenprocoumon
	Phentolamine *mono*mesylate
	Phenylbutazone
	2-Phenylcinchoninic acid
	2-Phenylindole
	4-(3-Phenylpropyl)pyridine
	α-Phenylpyrrolidinoacetamide
	2-Picoline
	Picoline, mixed isomers
	Picolinic acid
	Pipenzolate bromide
	2-Piperidinoethyl 3-methyl-4-oxo-2-phenylchromene-8-carboxylate hydrochloride
	Piperidolate hydrochloride
	Piritramide
	Potassium 4-amino-3,5,6-trichloropicolinate
	Pramoxine hydrochloride
	Prazepam
	L-Proline
	DL-Proline
	Prolintane hydrochloride
	Propantheline bromide
	1,3-Propiolactone
	*iso*Propyl 2-(thiazol-4-yl)benzimidazol-5-ylcarbamate hydrochloride
	6-*n*-Propylthiouracil
	Prothionamide
	Pyrazinamide
	2-Pyridone

Tariff heading	*Description*
29.35	3-Pyridyl dimethylcarbamate
	Pyrrobutamine pentahydrogen diphosphate
	Pyrrolidine
	2-Pyrrolidone
	Quinuronium sulphate
	Skatole
	Sodium D-*iso*ascorbate
	Sodium dehydracetate
	Sodium deoxyribonucleate
	Sodium ribonucleate
	Spironolactone
	Tetrabenazine
	Tetracosactide hexa-acetate
	Tetra(dichloro-1,3,5-triazinetrione)-trichloro-1,3,5-triazinetrione complex, tetrapotassium derivative
	Tetrahydro-2,5-dimethoxyfuran
	Tetrahydro-3,5-dimethyl-1,3,5-thiadiazine-2-thione
	Tetrahydrofurfuryl alcohol
	(+)-Tetrahydro-4-methyl-2-(2-methylprop-1-enyl)pyran
	(−)-Tetrahydro-4-methyl-2-(2-methylprop-1-enyl)pyran
	(±)-Tetrahydro-4-methyl-2-(2-methylprop-1-enyl)pyran
	1,4,5,6-Tetrahydro-1-methyl-2-[2-(3-methyl-2-thienyl)vinyl]pyrimidine tartrate
	2-(Tetrahydro-5-methyl-5-vinyl-2-furyl)propan-2-ol
	(±)-2,3,5,6-Tetrahydro-6-phenylimidazo[2,1-*b*]thiazole
	2,3,5,6-Tetrahydro-6-phenylimidazo[2,1-*b*]thiazole hydrochloride
	Tetrahydrozoline *mono*hydrochloride
	Thiabendazole
	Thiethylperazine di(hydrogen maleate)
	Thioguanine
	Thioridazine
	Thioridazine *mono*hydrochloride
	Thiotepa
	Thymidine
	Thymidine 5′-(trisodium hydrogen triphosphate)
	Thymine
	Thymolphthalein-2,2′-di(methylaminodiacetic acid)
	Triallyl cyanurate
	2-(3-Trifluoromethylanilino)nicotinic acid
	4,4,4-Trifluoro-1-(2-thienyl)butane-1,3-dione
	Tri-(2-hydroxyethyl)-1,3,5-triazinetrione
	Trimetaphan *mono*-(+)-camphorsulphonate
	Trimetazidine dihydrochloride
	Tri-(2-methylaziridin-1-yl)phosphine oxide
	Tripelennamine *mono*hydrochloride
	4-(Triphenylmethyl)morpholine
	Tryptamine hydrochloride
	L-Tryptophan
	DL-Tryptophan
	Uracil
	Uric acid
	Uridine
	Uridine 3′-(dihydrogen phosphate)
	N-Vinyl-2-pyrrolidone
	Viprynium embonate
	Xanthen-9-carboxylic acid
	Xanthine
	Xylometazoline hydrochloride
	Zinc di-(2-thiobenzimidazole)

Tariff heading	*Description*
29.36	N^1-Acetylsulphamethoxypyridazine
	3-*iso*Butyl-6-chloro-3,4-dihydrobenzo-1,2,4-thiadiazine-7-sulphonamide 1,1-dioxide
	Chloramine T
	5-Chloroaniline-2,4-disulphonamide
	2-Dimethylsulphamoylphenothiazine
	Epithiazide
	Frusemide
	Glibenclamide
	Sulphadimidine esylate, sodium derivative
	Sulphamethoxypyridazine
	Sulphathiazole
	Thiothixene
	Tolazamide
29.37	*o*-Cresolsulphonephthalein-6,6′-di(methylaminodiacetic acid)
	o-Cresolsulphonephthalein-6,6′-di(methylaminodiacetic acid), tetrasodium salt
	1,3-Propanesultone
	Thymolsulphonephthalein-2,2′-di-(methylaminodiacetic acid)
29.38	L-Ascorbic acid
	Ascorbyl palmitate
	D-Biotin
	Calciferol
	Calcium folinate
	Carotene
	Dexpanthenol
	Ergosterol
	(+)-*N*-(3-Ethoxypropyl)-2,4-dihydroxy-3,3-dimethylbutyramide
	Phytomenadione
	Pteroylmonoglutamic acid
	Pyridoxal 5-(dihydrogen phosphate)
	Riboflavine
	Sodium D-pantothenate
	(+)-α-Tocopherol
	(+)-α-Tocopheryl acetate
	(+)-α-Tocopheryl hydrogen succinate
	Vitamin D_2 resin
29.39	17*β*-Acetyl-6-chloro-17α-hydroxyoestra-4,6-dien-3-one acetate
	(+)-Aldosterone
	†17α-Allyloestr-4-en-17*β*-ol
	Betamethasone 17-benzoate
	Chlormadinone acetate
	†4-Chloro-17*β*-hydroxyandrost-4-en-3-one acetate
	3-Cyclopentyloxy-17α-ethynyloestra-1,3,5(10)-trien-17*β*-ol
	3-Cyclopentyloxy-17α-hydroxypregna-3,5-dien-20-one acetate
	3-Cyclopentyloxypregna-3,5-dien-20-one
	Delmadinone acetate
	Deoxycorticosterone acetate
	Deoxycorticosterone 21-D-glucoside
	Deoxycorticosterone pivalate
	Dexamethasone
	Dexamethasone 21-(disodium phosphate)
	Dexamethasone 21-*iso*nicotinate
	Dexamethasone 21-(3-phenylpropionate)
	6α,7α-Difluoromethylene-6*β*-fluoro-17α-hydroxypregna-1,4-diene-3,20-dione acetate
	†11*β*,17α-Dihydroxypregna-1,4-diene-3,20-dione
	†Drostanolone propionate

Tariff heading	*Description*
29.39	†Dydrogesterone
	Edogestrone
	17α-Ethyloestr-4-en-17β-ol
	†Ethynodiol diacetate
	Fluclorolone acetonide
	Fludrocortisone 21-acetate
	†Flumethasone
	†Flumethasone 21-pivalate
	Fluocinolone acetonide
	Fluocinolone acetonide 21-acetate
	†9α-Fluoro-11β,17α-dihydroxypregn-4-ene-3,20-dione 17-acetate
	9α-Fluoro-11β,17α,21-trihydroxypregna-1,4-diene-3,20-dione 21-acetate
	Fluoxymesterone
	†Flurandrenolone
	†3β-Hydroxypregn-5-en-20-one
	Lynoestrenol
	Medroxyprogesterone acetate
	†Methandienone
	Methylprednisolone
	Methylprednisolone 21-acetate
	Nandrolone laurate
	(−)-Noradrenaline
	(−)-Noradrenaline hydrogen tartrate
	Norethandrolone
	Norethisterone
	Norethisterone acetate
	†(±)-Norgestrel
	Oxymesterone
	Oxymetholone
	Oxytocin
	Oxytocin dihydrogen citrate
	Paramethasone 21-acetate
	Quinestradol
	Triamcinolone
	Triamcinolone acetonide
	Triamcinolone acetonide 21-(3,3-dimethylbutyrate)
	Triamcinolone 16,21-diacetate
	Vasopressin
	Vasopressin tannate
29.41	Aesculin
	Digitalin
	Digitonin
	Digitoxin
	Ouabain
	Salicin
29.42	18β-Acetoxy-10β,17α-dimethoxy-16β-methoxycarbonyl-3-oxo-2,3-seco-20α-yohimbane
	Alcuronium chloride
	Arecoline-acetarsol
	Arecoline hydrobromide
	Cinchonidine
	Cinchonidine sulphate
	Cinchonine
	Cocaine, of a purity not greater than 97·5 per cent. by weight
	Colchicine
	Deptropine dihydrogen citrate
	(+)-9-*N'N'*-Diethylureido-4,6,6a,7,8,9-hexahydro-7-methylindolo-[4,3-*f,g*]quinoline hydrogen maleate
	Dihydroergotamine *mono*mesylate

Tariff heading	*Description*
29.42	Dimenhydrinate
	*pseudo*Ephedrine
	*pseudo*Ephedrine hydrochloride
	Ergotamine tartrate
	Ethyl quinine carbonate
	1-*n*-Hexyltheobromine
	Hyoscine *n*-butylobromide
	Lobeline hydrochloride
	Lobeline sulphate
	(+)-Lysergic acid
	Lysergide tartrate-methanol complex
	Papaverine
	Papaverine hydrochloride
	Papaverine hydrogen sulphate
	Phenmetrazine theoclate
	N^4-*n*-Propylajmalinium hydrogen tartrate
	Reserpine
	Vinblastine sulphate
	Vincristine sulphate
	Xanthinol nicotinate
	Yohimbine *mono*hydrochloride
29.43	D-Arabinose
	L-Arabinose
	D-Erythrose
	Fructose 1-(barium phosphate)
	Fructose tetranicotinate, mixed isomers
	L-Fucose
	D-Galactose
	Galactose 6-(barium phosphate)
	Gentiobiose
	*di*Magnesium hydrogen D-ribose 5-phosphate 1-pyrophosphate
	Maltose
	D-Mannose
	Mannose 6-(barium phosphate)
	D-Melezitose dihydrate
	Raffinose
	L-Rhamnose
	D-Ribose
	Ribose 5-(barium phosphate)
	Sorbose
	Sucrose diacetate hexa*iso*butyrate
	Turanose
	D-Xylose
29.44	Amphotericin B
	Bacitracin zinc
	Clindamycin hydrochloride
	Clindamycin 2′-palmitate hydrochloride
	Clomocycline, sodium salt
	Colistin sulphate
	Colistin sulphomethate sodium
	Cycloserine
	Erythromycin ethyl succinate
	Erythromycin lactobionate
	Gentamicin sulphate
	N-(4-Guanidinoformimidoylpiperazin-1-ylmethyl)tetracycline dihydrochloride
	Lincomycin hydrochloride
	Lucensomycin

Tariff heading	*Description*
29.44	Lymecycline 3-(4-Methylpiperazin-1-yliminomethyl)rifamycin SV Natamycin Novobiocin Novobiocin calcium Novobiocin sodium Nystatin Paromomycin sulphates Pristinamycin Rifamycin B diethylamide, *mono*sodium derivative Rolitetracycline nitrate Rubidomycin hydrochloride Sodium fusidate Spectinomycin dihydrochloride Spectinomycin sulphate Spiramycin Vancomycin hydrochloride Viomycin sulphate Virginiamycin
29.45	Boron trifluoride-ethylamine complex Ferrous sulphate-glycine complex Potassium *tert*butoxide Potassium methoxide Sodium dihydridodi-(2-methoxyethoxy)aluminate Sodium ethoxide
32.07	Lithopones, being pigments consisting of barium sulphate and zinc sulphide and containing not less than 28 per cent. by weight of zinc sulphide Pigments, dry, which contain (*a*) hydrated iron oxides as the sole colouring agent and (*b*) not more than 1 per cent. by weight of total silica, and which, when spread evenly over a transparent substrate at a density of 13 grammes of pigment per square metre in a clear binder of refractive index 1·52, have an opacity of not more than 30 per cent. when measured by Ministry of Defence Specification DEF-1053 Method 12 modified by using the red filter of the reflectometer recommended therein
38.03	Acid-activated montmorillonite which, when examined by X-ray powder diffraction, shows four principal lines corresponding to crystal interplanar spacings (*d* values) of 0·44, 0·40, 0·33 and 0·25 nanometres, the line corresponding to 0·40 nanometre being the most intense
38.15	Mixtures consisting of *N-tert*butylbenzothiazole-2-sulphenamide and *N*-cyclohexanesulphenylphthalimide and containing not less than 45 per cent. by weight of each constituent Prepared rubber accelerators, being sulphides of alkylphenols, and containing not less than 20 per cent. by weight and not more than 30 per cent. by weight of sulphur in all Prepared rubber accelerators containing not less than 80 per cent. by weight of *NNN'*-trimethylthiourea
38.19	Amines, mixed primary aromatic, containing not less than 4·5 per cent. by weight and not more than 5·5 per cent. by weight of nitrogen calculated as N Calcined bauxite Chlordane

Tariff heading	*Description*
39.01	Nylon 6 in the forms covered by Note 3(*b*) of Chapter 39, containing not more than 2 per cent. by weight of titanium dioxide and not more than 2·5 per cent. by weight of carbon black, but not otherwise compounded
	Poly-[2,2-di-(4-hydroxyphenyl)propane carbonate] moulding compounds, containing glass fibres which amount to not less than 25 per cent. by weight of the product and not more than 45 per cent. by weight of the product
	Poly-[2,2-di-(4-hydroxyphenyl)propane carbonate], uncompounded, or compounded with other materials which do not exceed 3 per cent. by weight of the product
	Scrap photographic (including cinematographic) and X-ray film
39.02	Acrylic sheet, transparent, colourless, of a thickness not less than 1.5 millimetres and not greater than 25·0 millimetres, which, when kept for 24 hours at a temperature of 110° centigrade, undergoes a linear shrinkage of not more than 10 per cent. and which, when kept for 24 hours at a temperature of 145° centigrade, undergoes a linear shrinkage of not less than 37·5 per cent.
	Copolymers solely of allyl alcohol with styrene, which have an acetyl value of not less than 190
	Poly(vinyl butyral) sheet, of a thickness not greater than 1·2 millimetres and of a width not less than 35 centimetres
	Poly(vinyl chloride) having an apparent density of not more than 0·3 gramme per millilitre and a viscosity number of not less than 170 when tested by the methods described in British Standard 2782:1970 and of which not more than 5 per cent. by weight is retained by a sieve having a nominal width of aperture of 150 micrometres
39.03	Carboxymethylcellulose, aluminium salt
	Cellulose acetate, where the weight of the acetyl content, calculated as acetic acid, is not less than 60 per cent. of the weight of the cellulose acetate, not being cellulose acetate plasticised or otherwise compounded
	Cellulose acetate butyrate compounded with other materials which do not exceed 25 per cent. by weight of the product, in the forms covered by Note 3(*b*) of Chapter 39
	Cellulose acetate butyrate, not plasticised or otherwise compounded
	Cellulose acetate propionate, not plasticised or otherwise compounded
	Cellulose propionate, not plasticised or otherwise compounded
	Ethylcellulose
	Ethylhydroxyethylcellulose
	Hydroxybutylmethylcellulose
	Hydroxyethylcellulose
	Hydroxypropylcellulose
	Scrap photographic (including cinematographic) and X-ray film
44.05	Stavewood of white oak (Quercus alba) not exceeding 1·38 metres long 42 millimetres thick and 204 millimetres wide
44.08	Staves of white oak (Quercus alba) not exceeding 1·38 metres long 42 millimetres thick and 204 millimetres wide
51.01	Yarn wholly of poly(glycollic acid)
58.02	" Synthetic Grass " being a knitted pile fabric with a pile of green polyamide strip of not less than 350 decitex of heading No. 51.02 and a ground of polyester and polyamide man-made fibres

Tariff heading	*Description*
59.03	Bonded fibre fabrics containing not less than 95 per cent. by weight, calculated on the dry material, of synthetic polyamide (fibres and fibrid bonding) materials which do not melt below 300° centigrade
69.09	Catalyst carriers in the form of spheres, consisting of aluminium oxide and silica whether or not combined together, and containing not more than 12·5 per cent. by weight of total silica, and of which (*a*) not less than 99 per cent. by weight passes a sieve having a nominal width of aperture of 2·40 millimetres and (*b*) not less than 99 per cent. by weight is retained by a sieve having a nominal width of aperture of 1·00 millimetre
70.03	Amber-coloured tubing of soda glass, not being glass containing 0·25 per cent. or more of cadmium, free or combined, calculated as Cd
	Tubing of glass which contains not less than 58 per cent. by weight of lead compounds estimated as PbO and not more than 6·5 per cent. by weight of alkali metal compounds estimated as K_2O
	Tubing of neutral glass, in straight lengths and capable of passing a test corresponding with the test for limit of alkalinity of glass prescribed by British Pharmacopoeia, not including (*a*) glass with a content of more than 85 per cent. of silica and boric oxide together, or (*b*) glass of fused silica or fused quartz
70.18	Optical glass in the form of sheets, slabs or moulded lens blanks, having, with reference to the D line of sodium, a refractive index (n_D) not less than 1·5625 and not greater than 1·5650 and a dispersive power (ν_D) not less than 60·0 and not greater than 61·5
	Optical glass in the form of sheets, slabs or moulded lens blanks, having, with reference to the D line of sodium, a refractive index (n_D) not less than 1·612 and not greater than 1·615 and a dispersive power (ν_D) not less than 43·5 and not greater than 45·0; having also at a wavelength of 400 nanometres a light transmission for a 25 millimetres path of not less than 83 per cent.; and which acquires no visible stain when kept for 15 minutes at a temperature of 25° centigrade in contact with a buffered sodium acetate solution having a pH value of 4·6
70.20	Glass fibres, loose, unfelted, having a diameter not greater than 3 micrometres
73.12	Iron or steel strip in coils, completely clad on both sides with alloy steel containing not less than 17 per cent. by weight of chromium and not less than 7 per cent. by weight of nickel the cladding layers each being less than 25 per cent. of the total thickness, of a width of not less than 200 millimetres nor more than 460 millimetres, and of a total thickness of not less than 2·5 millimetres nor more than 6 millimetres
73.23	Tinplate containers, not being circular or rectangular, consisting of a can lipped for sealing, plain or printed externally and lacquered internally, with internal dimensions of not less than 120 millimetres nor more than 168 millimetres in length, not less than 85 millimetres nor more than 120 millimetres at the widest point and not less than 45 millimetres nor more than 70 millimetres in depth, of a minimum capacity of 445 cubic centimetres and a maximum capacity of 940 cubic centimetres scored for opening with opening key attached to base, and related sealing lids
73.40	Sintered alloy steel fibre in the form of flat rectangular porous sheets, re-inforced on one or both sides with alloy steel wire mesh, of an overall thickness of not less than 0·35 millimetre nor more than 1·15 millimetres, and of such length and width that the area of one side of a sheet is not less than 450 square centimetres nor more than 11,620 square centimetres

Tariff heading	*Description*
74.01	Copper alloy containing not less than 99·8 per cent. by weight of copper and not less than 0·08 per cent. nor more than 0·11 per cent. by weight of silver as the major alloying element, in the form of billets of a diameter of not less than 149 millimetres nor more than 156 millimetres and of a length of not less than 1,358 millimetres nor more than 1,385 millimetres
76.03	Aluminium discs of a minimum value of £0·5000 per lb., not less than 6 inches nor more than 18 inches in diameter and not less than 0·033 inch nor more than 0·036 inch in thickness and which, when either face is placed on a flat surface, do not deviate from the flat by more than 0·010 inch at any point
81.02	Cylindrical molybdenum alloy bars containing not less than 98 per cent. by weight of molybdenum and not more than 1 per cent. by weight of titanium as the major alloying element, of a diameter of not less than 5 millimetres nor more than 357 millimetres, and of a length of not more than 508 millimetres
	Cylindrical molybdenum alloy tubes containing not less than 98 per cent. by weight of molybdenum and not more than 1 per cent. by weight of titanium as the major alloying element, of an external diameter of not less than 12 millimetres nor more than 64 millimetres, of a wall thickness of not more than 13 millimetres, and of a length of not more than 381 millimetres
	Molybdenum alloy sheet containing not less than 98 per cent. by weight of molybdenum and not more than 1 per cent. by weight of titanium as the major alloying element, of a thickness not less than 1 millimetre nor more than 5 millimetres, and of such dimensions that the top surface area of the sheet does not exceed 3,600 square millimetres
	Molybdenum alloy slabs containing not less than 98 per cent. by weight of molybdenum and not more than 1 per cent. by weight of titanium as the major alloying element, of a thickness of not less than 12 millimetres nor more than 51 millimetres, and of such dimensions that the top surface area of the slab does not exceed 915 square millimetres
	Molybdenum flat strip in coils, containing not more than 0·05 per cent. by weight of iron and not more than 0·01 per cent. by weight of nickel as major impurities, of a thickness of not less than 0·02 millimetre and not more than 1·3 millimetres, and of a width of not less than 0·5 millimetre and not more than 3·6 millimetres
	Molybdenum, of a purity not less than 99·8 per cent., in the form of rods (whether or not threaded at the ends) not less than 55 inches nor more than 100 inches in length and not less than $1\frac{7}{32}$ inches nor more than $2\frac{1}{16}$ inches in diameter
	Molybdenum, of a purity not less than 99·8 per cent. in the form of rods of not less than 18 inches and not more than 100 inches in length and of not less than $2\frac{1}{4}$ inches and not more than $4\frac{1}{4}$ inches in diameter and whether or not threaded at the ends
81.04	Hafnium crystal bars consisting of hafnium wire on which hafnium crystals have been deposited
	Manganese metal of a purity not less than 96 per cent. and not more than 99·5 per cent. and containing not more than 1·0 per cent. by weight of carbon and not more than 3·0 per cent. by weight of iron
	Zirconium sponge
85.14	Microphones, of a kind for incorporation in deaf aids, approximately rectangular in shape, with a maximum thickness not exceeding 0·165 inch and a total of the length and width not exceeding 0·675 inch, exclusive of sound tube

Tariff heading	*Description*
85.15	The following apparatus for use in aircraft: (*a*) very high frequency omni-directional radio range apparatus (VOR), instrument landing system localiser apparatus (ILS/LOC), instrument landing system glide path apparatus (ILS/G.PATH); (*b*) very high frequency communication apparatus (VHF/COM) (transmitters, receivers, or combined transmitter/receivers) covering a frequency band of at least 118 to 135·95 MHz, with not less than 180 channels and capable of operating in areas where 50 kHz channel spacing is in force; (*c*) apparatus combining the functions and capabilities of any of the apparatus specified in (*a*) and (*b*) above but excluding apparatus combining any of those functions and capabilities with any other function or capability; being in each case apparatus of a type approved by the Secretary of State, at the date of this Order, under Article 13(5) of the Air Navigation Order 1970, as amended, for use in aircraft of not more than 12,500 lb. maximum total weight authorised, flying in controlled airspace in accordance with the Instrument Flight Rules as defined in the said Air Navigation Order, but not for use in other aircraft (until 2nd March 1972)
85.19	Carbon track volume controls of a kind for incorporation in deaf aids, being of drum type with a cylindrical drum not exceeding 12 millimetres in diameter and 4 millimetres in thickness
85.20	Glass neon discharge lamps, having a metal cap fitted to each end and not exceeding 1 inch in overall length and ½ inch in diameter over the caps
85.28	Moving coil receivers having an overall diameter of 52 millimetres, of a kind for use with electro medical apparatus (for example, clinical audiometers)
90.01	Lenses, prisms, mirrors and other optical elements, not optically worked, of barium fluoride Material consisting of a polarising film supported on one or both sides by transparent material Optical windows of zinc sulphide, unmounted
90.19	Aortic heart valves Earphones, of a kind for incorporation in deaf aids, approximately rectangular in shape, with a maximum thickness not exceeding 0·165 inch and a total of the length and width not exceeding 0·675 inch exclusive of sound tube Mitral heart valves
95.05	Coral simply shaped in the form of cabochons, marquises, boutons or the like, polished but not faceted or otherwise worked

SCHEDULE 2

IMPORT DUTIES (TEMPORARY EXEMPTIONS) ORDERS REVOKED

Number and year of Order	*Reference*
No. 11 of 1970	S.I. 1970/1819 (1970 III, p. 5894)
No. 1 of 1970	S.I. 1971/43 (1971 I, p. 36)
No. 2 of 1971	S.I. 1971/273 (1971 I, p. 935)
No. 3 of 1971	S.I. 1971/445 (1971 I, p. 1293)
No. 4 of 1971	S.I. 1971/667 (1971 I, p. 1763)
No. 5 of 1971	S.I. 1971/1012 (1971 II, p. 2951)
No. 6 of 1971	S.I. 1971/1388 (1971 II, p. 3903)
No. 7 of 1971	S.I. 1971/1543 (1971 III, p. 4358)
No. 8 of 1971	S.I. 1971/1712 (1971 III, p. 4658)
The Import Duties (Temporary Exemptions) (Amendment) Order 1971 ...	S.I. 1971/499 (1971 I, p. 1490)

EXPLANATORY NOTE

(*This Note is not part of the Order.*)

This Order provides that the goods listed in Schedule 1 shall continue to be exempt from import duty until 1st January 1973, except for items for which an earlier day is specified.

Items marked † in Schedule 1, formerly classified under headings 29.05, 29.13 and 29.14, have been re-classified under heading 29.39 in the Customs Tariff following a Classification Opinion of the Customs Co-operation Council.

The Order also continues the partial exemption for photographic film base of cellulose acetate.

The more specialist publications referred to in the Order are as follows:—

Standard Methods for Testing Tar and its Products

6th edition published in 1967, by the Standardisation of Tar Products Testing Committee, c/o Coal Tar Research Association, Oxford Road, Gomersal, Cleckheaton, Yorkshire.

Ministry of Defence Specification DEF-1053

Standard Methods of Testing Paint, Varnish, Lacquer and Related Products, Method No. 12, Opacity (Contrast Ratio), current at the date of this Order, published by H.M. Stationery Office.

Radio Equipment for Light Aircraft

Apparatus of a type approved by the Secretary of State for Trade and Industry is listed in Civil Aviation Publication CAP 208, Airborne Radio Apparatus Vol. 2, published by H. M. Stationery Office. This publication is subject to amendment and confirmation that apparatus is of the type approved at the date of this Order should be obtained from the Department of Trade and Industry, Controllerate of National Air Traffic Services, Tels. N3(b), 19–29 Woburn Place, London, WC1H 0LX.

STATUTORY INSTRUMENTS

1971 No. 2011

CUSTOMS AND EXCISE

The Import Duties (Temporary Reductions) (No. 2) Order 1971

Made - - - -	13*th December* 1971
Laid before the House of Commons	17*th December* 1971
Coming into Operation	1*st January* 1972

The Lords Commissioners of Her Majesty's Treasury, by virtue of the powers conferred on them by sections 3(6) and 13 of the Import Duties Act 1958(**a**) and of all other powers enabling them in that behalf, on the recommendation of the Secretary of State hereby make the following Order:—

1.—(1) This Order may be cited as the Import Duties (Temporary Reductions) (No. 2) Order 1971.

(2) The Interpretation Act 1889(**b**) shall apply for the interpretation of this Order as it applies for the interpretation of an Act of Parliament.

(3) This Order shall come into operation on 1st January 1972.

2.—(1) Until the beginning of 1st January 1973 any import duty which is for the time being chargeable on goods of heading 32.05(D) of the Customs Tariff 1959 shall be chargeable (in the case of goods liable for duty at the full rate) at 10% instead of 15%.

(2) For the purposes of classification under the Customs Tariff 1959, in so far as that depends on the rate of duty, any goods to which paragraph (1) above applies shall be treated as chargeable with the same duty as if this Order had not been made.

Tim Fortescue,
P. L. Hawkins,
Two of the Lords Commissioners of Her Majesty's Treasury.

13th December 1971.

EXPLANATORY NOTE

(*This Note is not part of the Order.*)

This Order reduces the import duty on certain synthetic organic dyestuffs and kindred products to 10% ad valorem for the whole of 1972.

(**a**) 1958 c. 6. (**b**) 1889 c. 63.

1971 No. 2012

CUSTOMS AND EXCISE

The Import Duties (Temporary Reductions) (No. 3) Order 1971

Made - - - -	13*th December* 1971
Laid before the House of Commons	17*th December* 1971
Coming into Operation	3*rd January* 1972

The Lords Commissioners of Her Majesty's Treasury, by virtue of the powers conferred on them by sections 3(6) and 13 of the Import Duties Act 1958(**a**) and of all other powers enabling them in that behalf, on the recommendation of the Secretary of State hereby make the following Order:—

1.—(1) This Order may be cited as the Import Duties (Temporary Reductions) (No. 3) Order 1971.

(2) The Interpretation Act 1889(**b**) shall apply for the interpretation of this Order as it applies for the interpretation of an Act of Parliament.

(3) This Order shall come into operation on 3rd January 1972.

2.—(1) Until the beginning of 1st January 1973 any import duty which is for the time being chargeable on goods of heading 20.06(L)(2) of the Customs Tariff 1959 shall be chargeable in the case of canned pears, not containing added sweetening matter, at the rate of 5%, instead of 15% (whether the goods are liable for duty at the full rate or at the rate appropriate to goods of Convention area origin, within the meaning of the European Free Trade Association Act 1960(**c**)).

(2) For the purposes of classification under the Customs Tariff 1959, in so far as that depends on the rate of duty, any goods to which paragraph (1) above applies shall be treated as chargeable with the same duty as if this Order had not been made.

Tim Fortescue,
P. L. Hawkins,
Two of the Lords Commissioners of Her Majesty's Treasury.

13th December 1971.

(**a**) 1958 c. 6. (**b**) 1889 c. 63. (**c**) 1960 c. 19.

EXPLANATORY NOTE

(This Note is not part of the Order.)

This Order reduces the full and E.F.T.A. rates of import duty on unsweetened canned pears from 15% to 5% ad valorem from 3rd January 1972 until 1st January 1973.

1971 No. 2013

PENSIONS

The Superannuation (Civil Service and Northern Ireland Teaching Service) Transfer Rules 1971

Made - - - 10*th December* 1971

Laid before Parliament 16*th December* 1971

Coming into Operation 17*th December* 1971

The Minister for the Civil Service, in exercise of the powers conferred on him by sections 2 and 15 of the Superannuation (Miscellaneous Provisions) Act 1948(**a**) and article 2(1)(*c*) of the Minister for the Civil Service Order 1968(**b**), and of all other powers enabling him in that behalf, hereby makes the following Rules :—

PART I

GENERAL PROVISIONS

Citation and commencement

1. These Rules may be cited as the Superannuation (Civil Service and Northern Ireland Teaching Service) Transfer Rules 1971, and shall come into operation on 17th December 1971.

Interpretation

2.—(1) In these Rules, unless the context otherwise requires—

"civil servant" has the meaning assigned to it by section 98 of the Superannuation Act 1965(**c**) ;

"Northern Ireland teaching employment" in relation to any person, means employment by virtue of which that person is entitled to participate in the benefits provided by the Teachers (Superannuation) Acts (Northern Ireland) 1950 to 1967 ;

"pension" has the meaning assigned to it by section 17(1) of the Superannuation (Miscellaneous Provisions) Act 1948.

(2) The Interpretation Act 1889(**d**) shall apply for the interpretation of these Rules as it applies for the interpretation of an Act of Parliament.

(**a**) 1948 c. 33.
(**b**) S.I. 1968/1656 (1968 III, p. 4485).
(**c**) 1965 c. 74.
(**d**) 1889 c. 63.

Part II

Transfers from Northern Ireland Teaching Service to the Civil Service

Application of Part II

3.—(1) This Part of these Rules shall apply to any person who—

(*a*) becomes employed as a civil servant within twelve months after ceasing to be employed in Northern Ireland teaching employment or within such longer period as the Minister for the Civil Service may allow in any particular case ; and

(*b*) has not become entitled to a pension other than a return of contributions in respect of his service in Northern Ireland teaching employment, or, if he has become so entitled, has not been granted such a pension ; and

(*c*) within three months after the date on which he becomes employed as a civil servant or within six months after the coming into operation of these Rules, whichever period last expires, or within such longer period as the Minister for the Civil Service may allow in any particular case, notifies the Department in which he is employed that he desires these Rules to apply to him ; and

(*d*) if after ceasing to be employed in Northern Ireland teaching employment he has received any payment by way of a return of contributions (other than family benefit contributions) in respect of his service in Northern Ireland teaching employment, pays to the Minister for the Civil Service, within three months after the date on which he becomes employed as a civil servant or within six months after the coming into operation of these Rules, whichever period last expires, or within such longer period as the Minister for the Civil Service may allow in any particular case, a sum equal to such payment, together with compound interest thereon calculated at the rate of $3\frac{1}{2}$ per cent., per annum with yearly rests from the date when he received the payment by way of return of contributions to the date when he makes the payment to the Minister for the Civil Service.

(2) This Part of these Rules shall apply to such person as aforesaid notwithstanding that he ceased to be employed in Northern Ireland teaching employment or became employed as a civil servant before the coming into operation of these Rules :

Provided that—

(*a*) he ceased to be employed in Northern Ireland teaching employment not earlier than 1st April 1950 ; and

(*b*) he has not ceased to be employed as a civil servant before the coming into operation of these Rules.

(3) Where a person who makes a payment to the Minister for the Civil Service in accordance with paragraph (1)(*d*) above became employed as a civil servant more than twelve months before the date of the coming into operation of these Rules or more than twelve months after ceasing to be employed in Northern Ireland teaching employment, the interest payable under paragraph

(1)(*d*) above shall not exceed a sum equal to one-half of the difference between the transfer value payable under these Rules and the transfer value which would be payable if calculated by reference to his age on ceasing to be employed in Northern Ireland teaching employment.

Reckoning of service

4.—(1) If the Minister for the Civil Service receives from the Ministry of Education for Northern Ireland a transfer value, calculated in accordance with the following provisions of this Rule, in respect of service which a person to whom this Part of these Rules applies was entitled to reckon as recognised or contributory service for the purposes of the Teachers (Superannuation) Acts (Northern Ireland) 1950 to 1967 immediately before he ceased to be employed in Northern Ireland teaching employment, the service in respect of which the transfer value is calculated shall, subject to paragraph (5) below, be reckoned for the purposes of the Superannuation Acts 1965 and 1967(**a**) as service in the capacity of a civil servant.

(2) The transfer value referred to in paragraph (1) above shall be calculated by reference to the Tables set out in Schedule 1 to the Local Government Superannuation (Transfer Value) Regulations 1954(**b**), account being taken of any amount by which any pension for which the person may become eligible under the Superannuation Acts 1965 and 1967 will be reduced in consequence of the National Insurance Act 1965(**c**).

(3) Where a person became employed as a civil servant more than twelve months before the date of the coming into operation of these Rules, the transfer value shall be calculated by reference to his age on that date.

(4) Where a person, not being a person to whom paragraph (3) above applies, became employed as a civil servant more than twelve months after ceasing to be employed in Northern Ireland teaching employment, the transfer value shall be calculated by reference to his age on the date on which he became employed as a civil servant.

(5) Where a person to whom this Part of these Rules applies was, at the date on which he ceased to be employed in Northern Ireland teaching employment, in the course of paying, but had not completed paying, additional contributions to the Ministry of Education for Northern Ireland as a condition of reckoning any period of service, and any such contributions which were not paid on or before that date are not paid to the Minister for the Civil Service within such time as he may require, the period of service in respect of which the contributions remain unpaid shall not be reckonable for the purposes of the Superannuation Acts 1965 and 1967 as service in the capacity of a civil servant.

Benefits payable in case of premature retirement or death

5. Where a person to whom this Part of these Rules applies dies, or ceases to be employed as a civil servant in circumstances which do not render him eligible for a superannuation allowance under the Superannuation Acts 1965 and 1967, the Minister for the Civil Service may, provided that he has not

(**a**) 1965 c. 74; 1967 c. 28.
(**b**) S.I. 1954/1212 (1954 II, p. 1723).
(**c**) 1965 c. 51.

been dismissed in consequence of an offence of a fraudulent character or of grave misconduct, pay to or in respect of him whichever is the greater of the following sums :—

(*a*) a sum equal to the sum which might, at the time when he ceased to be employed in Northern Ireland teaching employment, have been paid to or in respect of him by way of a return of contributions and interest thereon ; or

(*b*) such a sum as he may be eligible to receive or as may be paid in respect of him under the Superannuation Act 1965 by way of a death gratuity or a short service gratuity, as the case may be.

PART III

TRANSFERS FROM THE CIVIL SERVICE TO NORTHERN IRELAND TEACHING SERVICE

Application of Part III

6.—(1) This Part of these Rules shall apply to any person who—

(*a*) becomes employed in Northern Ireland teaching employment within twelve months after ceasing to be employed as a civil servant or within such longer period as the Minister for the Civil Service may allow in any particular case ; and

(*b*) has obtained the consent of the head of the Department in which he was last employed to his changing his employment as aforesaid ; and

(*c*) has not become eligible for a pension under the Superannuation Acts 1965 and 1967, or, if he has become so eligible, has not been granted a pension under those Acts ; and

(*d*) within three months after the date on which he becomes employed in Northern Ireland teaching employment or within six months after the coming into operation of these Rules, whichever period last expires, or within such longer period as the Minister for the Civil Service may allow in any particular case, notifies the Ministry of Education for Northern Ireland that he desires these Rules to apply to him.

(2) This Part of these Rules shall apply to such person as aforesaid notwithstanding that he ceased to be employed as a civil servant or became employed in Northern Ireland teaching employment before the coming into operation of these Rules :

Provided that—

(*a*) he ceased to be employed as a civil servant not earlier than 1st April 1950 ; and

(*b*) he has not ceased to be employed in Northern Ireland teaching employment before the coming into operation of these Rules.

Payment of transfer value

7.—(1) If the Minister for the Civil Service is satisfied that a person to whom this Part of these Rules applies will be entitled to reckon as recognised or contributory service for the purposes of the Teachers (Superannuation)

Acts (Northern Ireland) 1950 to 1967 such of his service as is reckonable for the purposes of the Superannuation Acts 1965 and 1967 as service in the capacity of a civil servant, the Minister for the Civil Service may, upon these Rules becoming applicable to him, pay to the Ministry of Education for Northern Ireland a transfer value, calculated in accordance with the following provisions of this Rule, in respect of such of the person's service as is reckonable as aforesaid.

(2) The transfer value referred to in paragraph (1) above shall be calculated by reference to the Tables in Schedule 1 to the Local Government (Transfer Value) Regulations 1954, account being taken of any amount by which any pension for which the person may become eligible under the Teachers (Superannuation) Acts (Northern Ireland) 1950 to 1967 will be reduced in consequence of the National Insurance Act (Northern Ireland) 1966.

(3) Where a person became employed in Northern Ireland teaching employment more than twelve months before the date of the coming into operation of these Rules, the transfer value shall be calculated by reference to his age on that date.

(4) Where a person, not being a person to whom paragraph (3) above applies, became employed in Northern Ireland teaching employment more than twelve months after ceasing to be employed as a civil servant, the transfer value shall be calculated by reference to his age on the date on which he became employed in Northern Ireland teaching employment.

Eligibility for pensions under the Superannuation Acts to cease

8. Where a person to whom this Part of these Rules applies was, on ceasing to be employed as a civil servant, eligible for a pension under the Superannuation Acts 1965 and 1967, he shall, upon the payment by the Minister for the Civil Service of a transfer value in respect of him under Rule 7 above, cease to be so eligible.

Given under the official seal of the Minister for the Civil Service on

10th December 1971.

(L.S.)

K. H. McNeill,
Authorised by the Minister
for the Civil Service.

EXPLANATORY NOTE

(*This Note is not part of the Rules.*)

These Rules provide for the aggregation of service and a single superannuation award in cases where persons transfer from established service in the Civil Service to reckonable service under the Teachers (Superannuation) Acts (Northern Ireland) 1950 to 1967, or vice versa. Where such a transfer is made, the person is enabled to reckon previous service for pension under the superannuation scheme to which he transfers.

Under the powers conferred by section 2(5) of the Superannuation (Miscellaneous Provisions) Act 1948, the Rules apply, subject to conditions specified in the Rules, to persons who have transferred before the coming into operation of the Rules.

1971 No. 2019

PRISONS

The Prison (Amendment) Rules 1971

Made - - -	*9th December* 1971
Laid before Parliament	*20th December* 1971
Coming into Operation	*1st January* 1972

In pursuance of section 47 of the Prison Act 1952(**a**), as amended by the Criminal Justice Act 1961(**b**), the Criminal Justice Act 1967(**c**) and the Courts Act 1971(**d**), I hereby make the following Rules :—

1.—(1) These Rules may be cited as the Prison (Amendment) Rules 1971 and shall come into operation on 1st January 1972.

(2) In these Rules, "the principal Rules" means the Prison Rules 1964(**e**), as amended (**f**).

2. The proviso to Rule 26(2) of the principal Rules (which relates to shaving and haircutting in the case of unconvicted prisoners) shall be amended by inserting after the word "prisoner" the words "or a convicted prisoner who has not yet been sentenced".

3. Rule 6(4) of the principal Rules shall be amended by substituting for the words "at or by assizes or quarter sessions" the words "before or by the Crown Court".

4. The principal Rules shall (in consequence of section 53(3) of the Courts Act 1971, which replaces visiting committees with boards of visitors) be amended as follows :—

(*a*) in Rules 74(4) and 75(2) for the words "visiting committee" there shall be substituted the words "board of visitors" ;

(*b*) Rules 89, 90 and 91 shall be omitted ;

(*c*) in Rule 56(2) the word "committee" shall be omitted ;

(*d*) the words "visiting committee or" and "committee or" shall be omitted wherever they occur in Rules 8(1), 10(2), 19(2), 25, 34(6), 41(1), 43(2), 46(2) and (4), 51, 52, 88, 93, 94, 95, 96 and 97 ;

(*e*) in Rule 96, the words "in the case of a visiting committee, each week, and, in the case of a board of visitors," shall be omitted ; and

(*f*) in Rule 99(1), the definition of "local prison" shall be omitted.

(**a**) 1952 c. 52.
(**b**) 1961 c. 39.
(**c**) 1967 c. 80.
(**d**) 1971 c. 23.
(**e**) S.I. 1964/388 (1964 I, p. 591).
(**f**) S.I. 1968/440 (1968 I, p. 1149).

5. Any charge referred to a visiting committee under Rule 51 or 52 of the principal Rules which is still pending on 1st January 1972 shall be treated as having been referred to the corresponding board of visitors.

R. Maudling,
One of Her Majesty's Principal
Secretaries of State.

Home Office,
Whitehall.
9th December 1971.

EXPLANATORY NOTE

(*This Note is not part of the Rules.*)

Rule 26 of the Prison Rules 1964 provides that an unconvicted prisoner shall not be required to have his hair cut or any beard or moustache usually worn by him shaved off except where the medical officer directs this to be done for the sake of health or cleanliness. These Rules extend this provision to convicted prisoners who have not yet been sentenced.

These Rules also amend the Rules of 1964 to take account of the establishment of the Crown Court and the substitution, by the Courts Act 1971, of boards of visitors for prison visiting committees.

1971 No. 2020

ROAD TRAFFIC

The Goods Vehicles (Prohibitions) (Exemptions and Appeals) Regulations 1971

Made - - -	10*th December* 1971
Laid before Parliament	21*st December* 1971
Coming into Operation	1*st January* 1972

The Secretary of State for the Environment (hereinafter referred to as "the Secretary of State"), in exercise of his powers under sections 185(3) and 190(1) of the Road Traffic Act 1960(**a**), section 16(10) of the Road Safety Act 1967(**b**), and of all other enabling powers, and after consultation with representative organisations in accordance with section 260(2) of the said Act of 1960, hereby makes the following Regulations :—

Commencement and citation

1. These Regulations shall come into operation on the 1st January 1972, and may be cited as the Goods Vehicles (Prohibitions) (Exemptions and Appeals) Regulations 1971.

Revocation

2. The Regulations specified in the Schedule to these Regulations are hereby revoked.

Interpretation

3.—(1) In these Regulations, except where the context otherwise requires, the following expressions have the meanings hereby respectively assigned to them :—

"the 1960 Act" means the Road Traffic Act 1960 ;

"the 1967 Act" means the Road Safety Act 1967 ;

"inspection" means any inspection of a vehicle required for the purposes of section 185(1), (2) or (3) of the 1960 Act ;

"traffic area" means any such area as is a traffic area for the purposes of Part III of the 1960 Act, and "office", in relation to such an area, means an office provided for the use of the Licensing Authority for that area ;

"vehicle testing station" means a station provided by the Secretary of State under section 24 of the 1967 Act.

(**a**) 1960 c. 16. (**b**) 1967 c. 30.

(2) The Interpretation Act 1889(**a**) shall apply for the interpretation of these Regulations as it applies for the interpretation of an Act of Parliament, and as if for the purposes of section 38 of that Act these Regulations were an Act of Parliament and the Regulations revoked by Regulation 2 of these Regulations were Acts of Parliament thereby repealed.

*Exemptions from s.*16(9) *of the* 1967 *Act*

4. The use of a goods vehicle on a road—

(*a*) solely for the purpose of submitting it by previous arrangement for a specified time on a specified date for an inspection at a vehicle testing station or such other place as shall have been agreed between the person proposing to carry out, and the person submitting the vehicle for, the inspection ; or

(*b*) in the course of an inspection for the purpose of taking it to, or bringing it away from, any place where a part of the inspection is to be, or as the case may be, has been carried out, or of carrying out any part of the inspection, the person so using it being a person carrying out the inspection; or

(*c*) for the purpose of its test or trial within three miles of the place where it is being, or has been, repaired with a view to the removal under section 185 of the 1960 Act of a prohibition,

is exempted from section 16(9) of the 1967 Act (which makes it an offence to drive a vehicle on a road in contravention of a prohibition under s.16 of that Act).

*Provisions as to prohibitions under s.*16 *of the* 1967 *Act*

5.—(1) Where a certifying officer has under the provisions of section 185(2) of the 1960 Act inspected a vehicle he shall within seven days of such inspection give his decision, whether or not to remove the prohibition, in writing to the person on whose application he examined the vehicle.

(2) Every appeal to the Secretary of State against the refusal of a certifying officer to remove a prohibition shall be made in writing within fourteen days of the date on which he notified the person in accordance with the provisions of paragraph (1) of this Regulation.

(3) Every such appeal shall be lodged at the office of any traffic area.

Signed by authority of the Secretary of State.
10th December 1971.

John Peyton,
Minister for Transport Industries,
Department of the Environment.

(**a**) 1889 c. 63.

SCHEDULE

Regulations Revoked by Regulation 2

Title	Year and Number
The Goods Vehicles (Licences and Prohibitions) Regulations 1960	S.I. 1960/1505 (1960 III, p. 3020)
The Goods Vehicles (Licences and Prohibitions) (Amendment) Regulations 1962	S.I. 1962/927 (1962 II, p. 1074)
The Goods Vehicles (Licences and Prohibitions) (Amendment) Regulations 1969	S.I. 1969/420 (1969 I, p. 1212)
The Goods Vehicles (Licences and Prohibitions) (Amendment) (No. 2) Regulations 1969	S.I. 1969/1638 (1969 III, p. 5159)

EXPLANATORY NOTE

(*This Note is not part of the Regulations.*)

These Regulations are consequent upon the coming into operation on the 1st January 1972 of s.16 of the Road Safety Act 1967 which gives new powers for goods vehicle examiners to prohibit the driving on roads of unfit goods vehicles.

Regulation 4 exempts from s.16(9) of the 1967 Act (which makes it an offence to drive a goods vehicle on a road in contravention of a prohibition under s.16) the use of a goods vehicle for certain specified purposes.

Regulation 5 deals with certain procedural matters in connection with the removal under s.185 of the Road Traffic Act 1960 of a prohibition under s.16.

The Regulations specified in the Schedule, which dealt with, inter alia, carriers' licences under Part IV of the Road Traffic Act 1960 for goods vehicles and now superseded by operators' licences under Part V of the Transport Act 1968 (c.73), are revoked.

STATUTORY INSTRUMENTS

1971 No. 2021

CUSTOMS AND EXCISE

The Import Duties (General) (No. 9) Order 1971

Made - - - -	13*th December* 1971
Laid before the House of Commons	17*th December* 1971
Coming into Operation	1*st January* 1972

The Lords Commissioners of Her Majesty's Treasury, by virtue of the powers conferred on them by sections 1, 2 and 13 of the Import Duties Act 1958(**a**) and of section 1 of the Finance Act 1971(**b**) and of all other powers enabling them in that behalf, on the recommendation of the Secretary of State, hereby make the following Order:—

1.—(1) This Order may be cited as the Import Duties (General) (No. 9) Order 1971.

(2) The Interpretation Act 1889(**c**) shall apply for the interpretation of this Order as it applies for the interpretation of an Act of Parliament.

(3) This Order shall come into operation on 1st January 1972.

2. Schedule 1 to the Import Duties (General) (No. 7) Order 1971(**d**) (which by reference to the Customs Tariff 1959 sets out the import duties chargeable under the Import Duties Act 1958) shall be amended in accordance with the provisions of the Schedule to this Order.

3. In consequence of the amendment effected by paragraph 2 of the Schedule to this Order, Schedule 2 to the Import Duties (Developing Countries) Order 1971(**e**) shall be amended by substituting for the entry in the second column relating to heading 08.11 the following:—

"All goods falling within subheadings (B), (D)(3), (D)(4)(*b*), (G) and (H)".

V. H. Goodhew,
Walter Clegg,
Two of the Lords Commissioners of Her Majesty's Treasury.

13th December 1971.

(**a**) 1958 c. 6. (**b**) 1971 c. 68. (**c**) 1889 c. 63.
(**d**) S.I. 1971/1971 (1971 III, p. 5330). (**e**) S.I. 1971/1882(1971 III, p. 5125).

SCHEDULE

AMENDMENTS OF SCHEDULE 1 TO NO. 7 ORDER OF 1971

1. In heading 07.04 (dried vegetables, whole, cut, sliced, broken or in powder, but not further prepared) for subheadings (C) and (D) there shall be substituted the following:—

" (C) Leeks	10%	—
(D) Tomatoes, garlic, sweet peppers	—	— "

2.—(1) In heading 08.11 (fruit provisionally preserved, but unsuitable in that state for immediate consumption) in subheading (D), after paragraph (2), there shall be inserted the following:—

" (3) Orange pulp, containing the peel, not in brine	10%	C — E 10% "

and the existing paragraph (3) shall accordingly become (4).

(2) After subheading (F) of that heading there shall be inserted the following:—

" (G) Apricot pulp	10%	C — E 10% "

and the existing subheading (G) shall accordingly become (H).

3. In heading 33.01 (essential oils, terpeneless or not; concretes and absolutes; resinoids), in subheading (A)(3)(*a*)(i) the words " Cedarwood ", " Clove ", " Orange " and " Patchouli " shall be omitted.

4. In heading 47.02 (waste paper and paperboard; scrap articles of paper or of paperboard, fit only for use in paper-making) the rate of duty specified in column 2 shall be omitted.

EXPLANATORY NOTE

(*This Note is not part of the Order.*)

This Order, which comes into operation on 1st January 1972—

(1) removes the import duty on (*a*) dried tomatoes, (*b*) essential oils, not terpeneless, of cedarwood, clove, orange and patchouli, and (*c*) waste paper and paperboard, and scrap articles of paper or of paperboard fit only for use in paper-making:

(2) reduces to 10% the full and E.F.T.A. rates of import duty on (*a*) provisionally preserved apricot pulp and (*b*) provisionally preserved orange pulp, containing the peel, not in brine; and provides for consequential amendment to the Import Duties (Developing Countries) Order 1971.

STATUTORY INSTRUMENTS

1971 No. 2022 (S.212)

JURIES

The Jurors' Allowances (Scotland) Amendment Regulations 1971

Made - - -	*9th December* 1971
Coming into Operation	1*st January* 1972

In exercise of the powers conferred upon me by sections 24(1) and 32(1) of the Juries Act 1949(**a**), as amended by the Juries Act 1954(**b**), I hereby, with the consent of the Treasury, make the following regulations:—

1. These regulations may be cited as the Jurors' Allowances (Scotland) Amendment Regulations 1971 and shall come into operation on 1st January 1972.

2. In regulation 5 of the Jurors' Allowances (Scotland) Regulations 1971(**c**) (which relates to compensation for loss of earnings or additional expense) for the expressions of "£2·00", "£4·00" and "£8·00", there shall be substituted the expressions "£2·37½", "£4·75" and "£9·50" respectively.

Gordon Campbell,
One of Her Majesty's Principal
Secretaries of State.

St. Andrew's House,
Edinburgh.
6th December 1971.

We consent,

V. H. Goodhew,
Walter Clegg,
Two of the Lords Commissioners
of Her Majesty's Treasury.

9th December 1971.

(**a**) 1949 c. 27. (**b**) 1954 c. 41. (**c**) S.I. 1971/220 (1971 I, p. 651).

EXPLANATORY NOTE

(This Note is not part of the Regulations.)

These Regulations amend the Jurors' Allowances (Scotland) Regulations 1971. They provide for an increase in the maximum amount payable to a juror as compensation for loss of earnings or additional expenses.

STATUTORY INSTRUMENTS

1971 No. 2023 (S. 213)

LOCAL GOVERNMENT, SCOTLAND

The Local Government Audit (Scotland) Amendment Regulations 1971

Made - - -	8*th December* 1971
Coming into Operation	1*st January* 1972

In the exercise of the powers conferred upon me by section 207 of the Local Government (Scotland) Act 1947**(a)**, and of all other powers enabling me in that behalf, I hereby make the following regulations:—

1.—(1) These regulations may be cited as the Local Government Audit (Scotland) Amendment Regulations 1971 and shall come into operation on 1st January 1972.

(2) The Interpretation Act 1889**(b)** shall apply for the interpretation of these regulations as it applies for the interpretation of an Act of Parliament, and as if these regulations and the regulation hereby revoked were Acts of Parliament.

2. Regulation 4 of the Local Government Audit (Scotland) Regulations 1948**(c)** is hereby revoked.

Gordon Campbell,
One of Her Majesty's Principal
Secretaries of State.

St. Andrew's House,
Edinburgh.
8th December 1971.

EXPLANATORY NOTE

(*This Note is not part of the Regulations.*)

These Regulations amend the Local Government Audit (Scotland) Regulations 1948, to remove the obligation on the auditor to initial or stamp all vouchers submitted to him and to mark thereon the date of his examination.

(a) 1947 c. 43. **(b)** 1889 c. 63. **(c)** S.I. 1948/712 (Rev. XII, p. 621: 1948 I, p. 1748).

1971 No. 2024 (S.214)

PENSIONS

The Superannuation (Teaching and Public Boards) Interchange (Scotland) Amendment Rules 1971

Made - - -	7*th December* 1971
Laid before Parliament	20*th December* 1971
Coming into Operation	18*th January* 1972

In exercise of the powers conferred upon me by sections 2 and 15 of the Superannuation (Miscellaneous Provisions) Act 1948(**a**), as amended by section 11 of the Superannuation (Miscellaneous Provisions) Act 1967(**b**), and of all other powers enabling me in that behalf, and with the consent of the Minister for the Civil Service, I hereby make the following rules:—

1. These rules may be cited as the Superannuation (Teaching and Public Boards) Interchange (Scotland) Amendment Rules 1971 and shall come into operation on 18th January 1972.

2. Schedule 3 to the Superannuation (Teaching and Public Boards) Interchange (Scotland) Rules 1969(**c**) is hereby amended by the addition thereto of the following bodies and dates:—

The Arts Council of Great Britain	1st January 1967
The British Steel Corporation	1st July 1969
Forth Ports Authority	1st January 1968

3. In relation to a person becoming, or ceasing to be, employed by a body added to Schedule 3 to the Superannuation (Teaching and Public Boards)

(**a**) 1948 c.33 (**b**) 1967 c.28.
(**c**) S.I. 1969/1046 (1969 II, p.3080).

Interchange (Scotland) Rules 1969 by rule 2 the operative date for the purposes of those rules shall be the date of the coming into operation of these rules.

Gordon Campbell,
One of Her Majesty's Principal
Secretaries of State.

St. Andrew's House,
Edinburgh.
1st December 1971.

Consent of the Minister for the Civil Service given under his Official Seal on 7th December 1971.

(L.S.)

K. H. McNeill,
Authorised by the Minister for the
Civil Service.

EXPLANATORY NOTE

(This Note is not part of the Rules.)

These Rules extend to the Arts Council of Great Britain, the British Steel Corporation and the Forth Ports Authority the existing arrangements under the Superannuation (Teaching and Public Boards) Interchange (Scotland) Rules 1969 for the preservation of superannuation rights upon changes of employment between teaching and public boards.

The Rules may have retrospective effect in certain cases under the express powers of, and subject to the safeguards required by, section 2(5) of the Superannuation (Miscellaneous Provisions) Act 1948.

1971 No. 2025 (S.215)

PENSIONS

The Superannuation (Teaching and Local Government) Interchange (Scotland) Rules 1971

Made - - - -	7*th December* 1971
Laid before Parliament	22*nd December* 1971
Coming into Operation	20*th January* 1972

ARRANGEMENT OF RULES

In exercise of the powers conferred on me by sections 2 and 15 of the Superannuation (Miscellaneous Provisions) Act 1948**(a)**, as amended by section 11 of the Superannuation (Miscellaneous Provisions) Act 1967**(b)**, and with the consent of the Minister for the Civil Service, I hereby make the following rules:—

PART I

GENERAL

Citation and Commencement

1. These rules may be cited as the Superannuation (Teaching and Local Government) Interchange (Scotland) Rules 1971 and shall come into operation on 20th January 1972.

Revocation

2. The Superannuation (Teaching and Local Government) Interchange (Scotland) Rules 1962**(c)** are hereby revoked.

Interpretation

3.—(1) In these rules, unless the context otherwise requires—

"the Act of 1909" means the Asylums Officers' Superannuation Act 1909**(d)**;

"the Act of 1937" means the Local Government Superannuation (Scotland) Act 1937**(e)**;

"the Act of 1948" means the Superannuation (Miscellaneous Provisions) Act 1948;

"the Act of 1953" means the Local Government Superannuation Act 1953**(f)**;

"the Acts of 1937 to 1953" means the Local Government Superannuation (Scotland) Acts 1937 to 1953**(g)**;

"the Teachers Regulations of 1957" means the Teachers (Superannuation) (Scotland) Regulations 1957**(h)** as amended **(i)**;

(a) 1948 c. 33.
(b) 1967 c. 28.
(c) S.I. 1962/1000 (1962 II, p. 1125).
(d) 1909 c. 48.
(e) 1937 c. 69.
(f) 1953 c. 25.
(g) 1937 c. 69; 1939 c. 18; 1953 c. 25.
(h) S.I. 1957/356 (1957 I, p. 733).
(i) S.I. 1958/1595, 1963/2111, 1965/1166, 1966/1229, 1967/1736 (1958 I, p. 1077; 1963 III, p. 4685; 1965 II, p. 3284; 1966 III, p. 3295; 1967 III, p. 4657).

"the Teachers Regulations of 1969" means the Teachers Superannuation (Scotland) Regulations 1969**(a)** as amended **(b)**;

"the Teachers Schemes" means the Superannuation Scheme for Teachers in Scotland dated 5th June 1919**(c)**, the Superannuation Scheme for Teachers (Scotland) 1926**(d)** and the Superannuation Scheme for Teachers (Scotland) 1952**(e)**;

"added years" means, in relation to local government employment, any additional years of service reckonable under regulation 12 of the Benefits Regulations or any corresponding provision of a local Act scheme; and includes any additional years of service which, having been granted under any such provision or under any similar provision contained in any other enactment or scheme, have subsequently become and are reckonable under or by virtue of interchange rules;

"benefit" means any superannuation benefit payable to or in respect of any person;

"the Benefits Regulations" means the Local Government Superannuation (Benefits) (Scotland) Regulations 1954**(f)**;

"fund authority" means the local authority maintaining the superannuation fund to which a person first becomes a contributor after ceasing to be employed in teaching service or, as the case may be, was last a contributor before he became employed in teaching service;

"interchange rules" means rules made under section 2 of the Act of 1948 (which provides for the pensions of persons transferring to different employment) and includes provisions similar to those of such rules contained in any instrument made under any other Act;

"local government employment" means employment by virtue of which the person employed is or is deemed to be a contributory employee or local Act contributor within the meaning of the Act of 1937;

"the Modification Regulations" means the National Insurance (Modification of Local Government Superannuation Schemes) (Scotland) Regulations 1970**(g)**;

"national service" means, in relation to any person, service which is relevant service within the meaning of the Reserve and Auxiliary Forces (Protection of Civil Interests) Act 1951**(h)** and any similar service immediately following relevant service entered into with the consent of the authority or person by whom he was last employed before undertaking that service or, in the case of a person who holds an appointment to an office and is not employed under a contract of employment, with the consent of the authority by whom he was appointed;

"operative date" means the date of the coming into operation of these rules;

"prescribed period" has the meaning assigned to that expression by rule 4;

"reckonable service" means such service as is by virtue of the Teachers Regulations of 1969 reckonable service for all purposes of Part I of the Teachers Superannuation (Scotland) Act 1968**(i)**;

(a) S.I. 1969/77 (1969 I, p. 133).
(b) S.I. 1969/659 (1969 II, p. 1820).
(c) S.R. & O. 1919/1105 (1919 I, p. 688).
(d) S.R. & O. 1926/363 (1926, p. 449).
(e) S.I. 1952/464 (1952 I, p. 873).
(f) S.I. 1954/1059 (1954 II, p. 1632).
(g) S.I. 1970/1307 (1970 III, p. 4337).
(h) 1951 c. 65.
(i) 1968 c. 12.

"repaid contributions" means any sum paid to a person under the Teachers Schemes, the Teachers Regulations of 1957 or the Teachers Regulations of 1969, the Acts of 1937 to 1953 or a local Act scheme by way of repayment or return of contributions (other than voluntary contributions and contributions made or deemed to be made for the purpose of securing benefits for a widow, children or other dependants); and includes both any interest included in such sum and any amount deducted therefrom in respect of liability to income tax arising by reason of its payment;

"teaching service" means—

(*a*) reckonable service; and

(*b*) service which for the purposes of the Teachers Regulations of 1969 is service as an organiser;

"the Transfer Value Regulations" means the Local Government Superannuation (Transfer Value) (Scotland) Regulations 1954**(a)**;

"voluntary contributions" means—

(*a*) in relation to employment in teaching service, additional contributions paid or being paid under regulation 31 of the Teachers Regulations of 1969 in respect of a period of previous employment and any contributions being paid as a condition of any other period (not being a period of war service within the meaning of the Education (Scotland) (War Service Superannuation) Act 1939**(b)** or of national service) being reckoned as reckonable service; and

(*b*) in relation to local government employment, payments (other than completed payments, that is to say, payments made in respect of a liability which has been wholly discharged) of any of the following categories—

(i) additional contributory payments of the kind referred to in section 2(3) and (4) of the Act of 1953;

(ii) any similar payments made under a local Act scheme as a condition of reckoning any period of employment as service or as a period of contribution for the purposes of the scheme or, where the local Act scheme provides for the reckoning of non-contributing service, as contributing service for the purposes of the scheme;

(iii) any payments made for the purpose of increasing the length at which any period of service or of contribution would be reckonable for the purpose of calculating a benefit under a local Act scheme; and

(iv) any payments made in respect of added years.

(2) Other expressions which having meanings assigned to them by the Acts of 1937 to 1953 or the Teachers Regulations of 1969 or the Modification Regulations have, unless the context otherwise requires, the same respective meanings for the purposes of these rules.

(3) Any reference in these rules to the provisions of any enactment, rules, regulations or other instrument shall, unless the context otherwise requires, be construed as a reference to those provisions as amended, modified, extended, applied or re-enacted by any subsequent enactment, rules, regulations or instrument.

(a) S.I. 1954/1256 (1954 II, p. 1736). **(b)** 1939 c. 96.

(4) Unless the context otherwise requires, any reference in these rules to a rule, Part or paragraph shall be construed as a reference to that rule or Part of these rules or to that paragraph of the rule in which the reference occurs. as the case may be.

(5) The Interpretation Act 1889(**a**) shall apply for the interpretation of these rules as it applies for the interpretation of an Act of Parliament, and as if these rules and the rules revoked by rule 2 were Acts of Parliament.

Prescribed Period

4.—(1) For the purposes of these rules, subject as provided hereafter in this rule, the expression "prescribed period" shall mean—

(*a*) in the case of a person who, immediately after ceasing to be employed in teaching service or local government employment, became engaged in national service, a period of six months after the date of termination of the national service;

(*b*) in the case of a person to whom section 6 of the Act of 1948 has become applicable, a period of five years after the date on which he ceased to be employed in local government employment or such longer period as the Secretary of State may in any particular case allow; and

(*c*) in the case of any other person, a period of twelve months after the date on which he ceased to be employed in teaching service or local government employment.

(2) The Secretary of State in the case of a person entering teaching service and the fund authority in the case of a person entering local government employment may, with the agreement of the other, extend the periods of six months or twelve months, whichever is appropriate, specified in paragraph (1).

(3) Subject as provided in paragraph (4)—

(*a*) in reckoning the periods of six months and twelve months specified in paragraph (1) of this rule no account shall be taken of any period spent by a person on a course of study or training which he undertook after leaving his former employment; and

(*b*) if a person left his former employment in order to undertake a course of study or training and on completion of that course became engaged in national service, he shall be deemed for the purposes of paragraph (1) to have left his former employment at the time when he completed the said course of study or training.

(4) The provisions of paragraph (3) shall not apply to a person who in his new employment is in local government employment unless the authority employing him are satisfied, or to a person who in his new employment is in teaching service unless the Secretary of State is satisfied, that by reason of his having undertaken the said course of study or training he is better fitted for the duties of his new employment.

(**a**) 1889 c. 63.

PART II

TRANSFER FROM TEACHING SERVICE TO LOCAL GOVERNMENT EMPLOYMENT

Application

5.—(1) Except as provided in rule 6, this Part shall apply to a person who—

(*a*) enters, or on or after 1st February 1969 has entered, local government employment within the prescribed period after ceasing to be employed in teaching service;

(*b*) before or within three months after entering local government employment or six months after the operative date, whichever period shall last expire, or within such longer period as the fund authority may with the agreement of the Secretary of State in any particular case allow, notifies that authority in writing that he desires this Part to apply to him and furnishes that authority with particulars in writing of any national service in which he has been engaged since ceasing to be employed in teaching service; and

(*c*) within three months after entering local government employment or six months after the operative date, whichever period shall last expire, or within such longer period as the fund authority may in any particular case allow, pays to that authority an amount equal to any repaid contributions paid to him after he last ceased to be employed in teaching service, together with any compound interest thereon payable in accordance with paragraph (2) of this rule.

(2) For the purposes of paragraph (1)(*c*)—

(*a*) compound interest shall be paid where the prescribed period exceeds twelve months and shall be calculated on the amount of the repaid contributions at the rate of three per cent per annum with half-yearly rests from the day twelve months after that on which the person ceased to be employed in teaching service or from the day on which repaid contributions were paid to him, whichever shall be the later, to the day on which he notified the fund authority as required by paragraph (1)(*b*); and

(*b*) if the amount of compound interest calculated as aforesaid exceeds a sum equal to one half of the difference between the amount of the transfer value payable under rule 7 and the amount of the transfer value which would have been so payable if calculated by reference to the person's age on ceasing to be employed in teaching service, it shall be reduced to that sum.

Excepted Cases

6. This Part shall not apply to a person who—

(*a*) has received payment of any benefit (other than repaid contributions) under the Teachers Schemes, the Teachers Regulations of 1957 or the Teachers Regulations of 1969; or

(*b*) is a person in respect of whom a transfer value has been paid otherwise than under these rules by the Secretary of State since he last ceased to be employed in teaching service.

Transfer Value

7.—(1) In respect of a person to whom this Part applies the Secretary of State shall, out of moneys provided by Parliament, pay to the fund authority a transfer value of an amount calculated in accordance with the following provisions of this rule.

(2) Subject as provided hereafter in this rule, the transfer value shall be an amount equal to the transfer value which would have been payable under the Transfer Value Regulations if the person, at the date when he ceased to be employed in teaching service, had ceased to be a contributory employee under one local authority and had become such an employee under another local authority in the circumstances described in section 24 of the Act of 1937 and had been entitled to reckon as contributing service his reckonable service and his service reckonable for the purposes of Part VII of the Teachers Regulations of 1969 at the length at which it is so reckonable.

(3) For the purpose of calculating the amount of a transfer value any period of service which, having originally been non-contributing service or non-contributing service for the purposes of regulations made under section 66 of the National Health Service (Scotland) Act 1947**(a)** or section 67 of the National Health Service Act 1946**(b)**, became reckonable as reckonable service by virtue of such regulations or of interchange rules shall be treated as non-contributing service.

(4) In calculating the amount of a transfer value there shall be excluded—

(*a*) any period of war service within the meaning of the Education (Scotland) (War Service Superannuation) Act 1939 and of national service within the meaning of the Teachers Pensions (National Service) (Scotland) Rules 1952**(c)** in respect of which, at the time the transfer value is paid, the contributions remain unpaid; and

(*b*) any period of previous employment and any period additional to actual service in respect of which the person was immediately before ceasing to be employed in teaching service paying voluntary contributions and in respect of which, at the time the transfer value is paid, he has not elected to continue to pay such contributions.

(5) The amount of the transfer value payable in respect of a person shall be calculated by reference to his age—

(*a*) on the operative date if, having ceased to be employed in teaching service more than twelve months before that date, he entered local government employment before that date; or

(*b*) on the date on which he entered local government employment if that date is on or after the operative date and more than twelve months after that on which he ceased to be employed in teaching service.

(6) The amount of the transfer value payable in respect of any person shall be reduced by an amount equal to any compound interest payable by him in accordance with rule 5(2).

Reckoning of Service

8.—(1) Subject as provided hereafter in this rule, so much service as is taken into account as contributing service under rule 7 for the purpose of calculating the amount of the transfer value payable in respect of a person shall be reckoned as contributing service or as service under a local Act scheme or a period of contribution for the purposes of such a scheme.

(2) So much service as is taken into account as non-contributing service under rule 7 for the purpose of calculating the amount of the transfer value payable in respect of a person shall be reckoned as non-contributing service or, for the purpose of a local Act scheme, in the manner and to the extent to which it would have been reckonable if in his employment in teaching service he had been a contributory employee.

(a) 1947 c. 27. **(b)** 1946 c. 81.
(c) S.I. 1952/518 (1952 I, p. 928).

(3) Any service of a person to whom this Part applies which under the Teachers Regulations of 1969 is reckonable only for the purpose of calculating the amount of any benefit payable to or in respect of him or only for the purpose of determining whether he is entitled to any benefit shall be reckoned only for the corresponding like purpose under the Acts of 1937 to 1953 or a local Act scheme.

(4) Except as before provided in this rule, a person to whom this Part applies shall not be entitled under section 12(2) of the Act of 1937 or any corresponding provision of a local Act scheme to reckon as non-contributing service any service as referred to therein prior to the date on which he became employed in teaching service if a transfer value has been paid in respect of that service under rule 17 or under any corresponding provision contained in interchange rules or if a transfer of assets in respect of benefits payable by virtue of his local government employment has been made out of a local authority's superannuation fund under any enactment.

Voluntary Contributions

9.—(1) A person to whom this Part applies may elect to continue to pay voluntary contributions being paid by him immediately before ceasing to be employed in teaching service.

(2) If a person elects as aforesaid and—

(*a*) within three months of becoming employed in local government employment, or within such longer period as the fund authority may in any particular case allow, pays to that authority a sum equal to the aggregate of any sum paid to him by way of return of voluntary contributions on or after ceasing to be employed in teaching service, any interest added thereto and any amount deducted therefrom in respect of liability to income tax by reason of the payment; and

(*b*) thereafter pays to that authority any amounts outstanding in respect of those voluntary contributions as they would have been payable if he had remained in teaching service

his local government employment shall be affected in the manner prescribed by the following provisions of this rule.

(3) In respect of voluntary contributions made in respect of any period of previous employment and any period additional to actual service, the person shall enjoy rights and be subject to liabilities as if any such period were added years in respect of which payments are being made in his local government employment under regulation 12 of the Benefits Regulations or, if in his local government employment he is subject to a local Act scheme, under such provisions corresponding to the said regulation 12 or to regulation 5 of the Local Government Superannuation (Reckoning of Service on Transfer) (Scotland) Regulations 1954**(a)** as are contained in that scheme.

(4) In respect of voluntary contributions other than those to which paragraph (3) applies, the person shall be treated as if those contributions had been completed immediately before he ceased to be employed in teaching service.

(a) S.I. 1954/1241 (1954 II, p. 1680).

Computation of Contributions

10.—(1) Where a person to whom this Part applies ceases to be employed in local government employment or dies, then, in calculating any amount payable to or in respect of him by way of return of contributions, the amount of his contributions in respect of service reckonable in accordance with rule 8(1) shall be taken to include such amount as would have been payable by way of return of contributions under the Teachers Regulations of 1969 if, on his ceasing to be employed in teaching service, he had been entitled to be repaid his contributions without interest.

(2) Where an amount payable by way of return of contributions or by way of benefit is a sum equal to, or which falls to be calculated by reference to, the amount of a person's contributions with compound interest thereon, compound interest shall also be payable in respect of the amount by which those contributions are increased under paragraph (1) calculated—

(*a*) as respects the period ending immediately before the day on which he entered local government employment, at the rate at which it would have been calculated under the Teachers Regulations of 1969, if on ceasing to be employed in teaching service he had been entitled to a return of contributions together with compound interest thereon; and

(*b*) as respects the period beginning with the day on which he entered local government employment, in accordance with the provisions of section 10 of the Act of 1937 or, as the case may be, the corresponding provisions of the relevant local Act scheme.

(3) Notwithstanding anything previously contained in this rule, the sum by which contributions are increased by virtue of paragraph (1) or (2) shall not include—

(*a*) any sum in respect of contributions which, on or after the person's ceasing to be employed in teaching service, were returned to and retained by him; or

(*b*) any amount in respect of voluntary contributions which are not continued in pursuance of rule 9.

Benefits under Teachers Regulations of 1969

11. Subject to the provisions of Part III and of interchange rules, no payment of any benefit shall be made under the Teachers Regulations of 1969 to or in respect of any person by reason of any service which is taken into account in calculating the amount of a transfer value under rule 7 other than a payment by way of return of voluntary contributions.

Provisions relating to National Insurance

12.—(1) A person to whom this Part applies shall for the purposes of the Modification Regulations be—

(*a*) a person subject to flat-rate reduction but not a person entitled to the optant's rate if, on the day on which he ceased to be employed in teaching service, paragraph 3 of Schedule 5 to the Teachers Regulations of 1969 (which paragraph provides for the reduction of contributions at a flat-rate) applied to him and if, for the purpose of determining the amount of any benefit payable to him under the Teachers Regulations of 1969, paragraph 5 of that Schedule (which provides for the reduction of benefits by fixed annual amounts) would have been applicable to him;

(*b*) a person subject to flat-rate reduction and a person entitled to the optant's rate if, on the day on which he ceased to be employed in teaching service, paragraph 3 of Schedule 5 to the Teachers Regulations of 1969 applied to him and if, for the purpose aforesaid, paragraph 6 of that Schedule (which paragraph provides for the reduction of benefits by annual amounts ascertained by reference to a table) would have been applicable to him; or

(*c*) a person who retains unmodified status if, on the day on which he ceased to be employed in teaching service, paragraph 3 of Schedule 5 to the Teachers Regulations of 1969 did not apply to him and if, for the purpose aforesaid, neither paragraph 5 nor paragraph 6 of that Schedule would have been applicable to him.

(2) Where, by virtue of paragraph (1)(*b*), a person to whom this Part applies is a person entitled to the optant's rate the material date for the purposes of Part II of the Modification Regulations shall be the date which was in relation to him the date of modification for the purposes of paragraph 6 of Schedule 5 to the Teachers Regulations of 1969.

Questions and Appeals

13. The provisions of section 30 of the Act of 1937 (which section relates to the decision of questions and appeals) shall have effect in relation to a person (not being a local Act contributor) to whom this Part applies as if the reference therein to regulations made under that Act included a reference to these rules.

PART III

TRANSFER FROM LOCAL GOVERNMENT EMPLOYMENT TO TEACHING SERVICE

Application

14.—(1) Except as provided in rule 15, this Part shall apply to a person who—

(*a*) becomes, or on or after 1st February 1969 has become, employed in teaching service within the prescribed period after ceasing to be employed in local government employment;

(*b*) before or within three months after becoming employed in teaching service or six months after the operative date, whichever period shall last expire, or within such longer period as the Secretary of State may with the agreement of the fund authority in any particular case allow, notifies the Secretary of State in writing that he desires this Part to apply to him and furnishes the Secretary of State with particulars in writing of any national service in which he has been engaged since ceasing to be employed in local government employment; and

(*c*) within three months after becoming employed in teaching service or six months after the operative date, whichever period shall last expire, or within such longer period as the Secretary of State may in any particular case allow, pays to the Secretary of State an amount equal to any repaid contributions paid to him after he last ceased to be employed in local government employment, together with any compound interest thereon payable in accordance with paragraph (2).

(2) For the purposes of paragraph (1)(*c*)—

(*a*) compound interest shall not be payable unless—

(i) the prescribed period exceeds twelve months; and

(ii) the fund authority requires that it be paid;

(*b*) compound interest shall be calculated on the amount of the repaid contributions at the rate of three per cent per annum with half-yearly rests from the day twelve months after that on which the person ceased to be employed in local government employment or from the day on which repaid contributions were paid to him, whichever shall be the later, to the day on which he notified the Secretary of State as required by paragraph (1)(*b*); and

(*c*) if the amount of compound interest calculated as aforesaid exceeds a sum equal to one half of the difference between the amount of the transfer value payable under rule 17 and the amount of the transfer value which would have been so payable if calculated by reference to the person's age on ceasing to be employed in local government employment, it shall be reduced to that sum.

Excepted Cases

15. This Part shall not apply to a person who—

(*a*) ceased to be employed in local government employment before the operative date unless the fund authority consents to its application; or

(*b*) has received payment of any benefit (other than repaid contributions) under the Acts of 1937 to 1953 or a local Act scheme; or

(*c*) is a person in respect of whom a transfer value has been paid otherwise than under these rules by a fund authority since he last ceased to be employed in local government employment.

Discretionary Increase of Benefits

16.—(1) The local authority by whom a person to whom this Part applies was last employed may, within six months after the date on which they are notified by the Secretary of State of such application, exercise in relation to that person any discretion which, with a view to increasing the benefit payable to him, it would have been open to them to exercise at the time when he left their employment if he had then retired and had been entitled to a retirement benefit under regulation 5 of the Benefits Regulations or, if that regulation was not applicable to him, to any corresponding benefit provided under the superannuation provisions which were applicable to him in his former employment.

(2) A decision made in the exercise of any discretion under paragraph (1) shall be subject to the limitations and restrictions (if any) and to the right of appeal (if any) to which it would have been subject if the discretion had been exercised on the person's retirement in the circumstances aforesaid.

(3) Where a discretion has been exercised under paragraph (1) the service reckonable, immediately before he ceased to be employed in local government employment, by a person in whose favour the discretion has been exercised shall be deemed to have been correspondingly increased.

(4) Any increase in service, if attributable to a decision under this rule to increase the benefit payable to the person otherwise than by any notional increase or extension of the service reckonable for the purpose of calculating that benefit or by treating any specified period of non-contributing service as contributing service, or, under a local Act scheme, by similarly converting service of one category to service of another category, shall be ascertained by converting the service in respect of which the higher rate of benefit is payable into contributing service or service for the purposes of the relevant local Act scheme in the manner in which non-contributing service is converted into contributing service under section 2(4) of the Act of 1953.

Transfer Value

17.—(1) In respect of a person to whom this Part applies the fund authority shall, out of the superannuation fund maintained by them, pay to the Secretary of State a transfer value of an amount calculated in accordance with the following provisions of this rule.

(2) Subject as provided hereafter in this rule, the transfer value shall be an amount equal to the transfer value which would have been payable under the Transfer Value Regulations if the person, at the date when he ceased to be a contributory employee or local Act contributor, had become such an employee or contributor under another local authority in the circumstances described in section 24 of the Act of 1937.

(3) In calculating the amount of a transfer value—

(*a*) there shall be included any increase of service of the person by reason of the exercise under rule 16 of a discretion in his favour; and

(*b*) the Transfer Value Regulations shall be deemed to be modified—

(i) by the omission from sub-paragraph (*a*) of the definition of "service" in paragraph 1 of the First Schedule thereto of the words "not being such service as is mentioned in proviso (*a*) to that sub-section"; and

(ii) by the omission, in respect of a person who was an established officer or servant within the meaning of the Act of 1909, of sub-paragraph (*c*) of the said definition.

(4) The amount of the transfer value payable in respect of a person shall be calculated by reference to his age—

(*a*) on the operative date if, having ceased to be employed in local government employment more than twelve months before that date, he became employed in teaching service before that date; or

(*b*) on the date on which he became employed in teaching service if that date is on or after the operative date and more than twelve months after that on which he ceased to be employed in local government employment.

(5) The amount of the transfer value payable in respect of any person shall be reduced by—

(*a*) an amount equal to any compound interest payable by him in accordance with rule 14(2); and

(*b*) an amount equal to any sum payable by the fund authority by way of income tax by reason of the payment of the transfer value.

Supplementary Provisions as to Transfer Value

18.—(1) Where the amount of a transfer value payable under rule 17 is increased by reason of the exercise under rule 16 of a discretion by a local authority, that authority shall pay the amount of the increase to the superannuation fund out of which the transfer value is payable.

(2) When paying a transfer value under rule 17 a fund authority shall furnish to the Secretary of State and to the person in respect of whom it is paid the like particulars relating to that person's pensionable service as would have been given to him if instead of becoming employed in teaching service he had re-entered local government employment.

(3) Where—

(*a*) a transfer value is payable under rule 17 by a fund authority in respect of a person who before entering local government employment had been subject to the Act of 1909; and

(*b*) the body by whom he was last employed while subject to that Act (in this rule called "the hospital body") would, if he had become entitled to a superannuation allowance on leaving local government employment, have been liable to contribute to that allowance

the hospital body shall pay to the fund authority a sum equal to the transfer value which the body would have been liable to pay to the Secretary of State under regulation 52(4) of the National Health Service (Scotland) (Superannuation) Regulations 1950(**a**) if that regulation had become applicable to the person on the date when he became employed in teaching service.

(4) Where the hospital body would have had in respect of any such contribution as aforesaid a right of contribution from any other body, that other body shall pay to the fund authority a sum equal to the transfer value which the other body would have been liable to pay to the Secretary of State under paragraph (5) of the said regulation 52 if that regulation had become applicable to the person on the date when he became employed in teaching service.

(5) Where any body referred to in paragraph (3) or (4) has been dissolved or has ceased to exercise functions as such, references to that body shall be construed as references to the appropriate authority as defined in paragraph (15) of the said regulation 52.

Reckoning of Service

19.—(1) Subject as provided hereafter in this rule, in respect of a person to whom this Part applies—

(*a*) there shall be reckoned as reckonable service—

(i) any period of service which, at the time of his ceasing to be employed in local government employment, is reckonable as contributing service or as service or a period of contribution for the purposes of a local Act scheme;

(ii) any period of national service after ceasing to be employed in local government employment which would have been reckonable as aforesaid if he had again become employed in local government employment after the termination thereof; and

(iii) one half of any period of service which, at the time of his ceasing to be employed in local government employment, is reckonable as non-contributing service; and

(*b*) there shall be reckoned as class C external service for the purposes of the Teachers Regulations of 1969 any period of service which, at the time of his ceasing to be employed in local government employment, is reckonable as non-contributing service, except in so far as that service is reckoned under this rule or those Regulations as reckonable service.

(2) Where a person to whom this Part applies has, during his local government employment, been employed as a part-time employee, the period of his part-time service shall be treated—

(**a**) S.I. 1950/498 (1950 I, p. 1458).

(*a*) for the purpose of determining whether he has served for any minimum period prescribed by the Teachers Regulations of 1969 as necessary for any benefit to be paid to or in respect of him, as if it were whole-time service; and

(*b*) for the purpose of calculating the amount of any benefit payable under the Teachers Regulations of 1969, as if it were whole-time service for a proportionately reduced period.

(3) Where by virtue of a scheme modifying the Act of 1937 any period of service of a person to whom this Part applies is reckoned at a fraction of its actual length for the purpose of calculating the amount of the transfer value payable under rule 17, then, for the purpose of calculating the amount of any benefit payable to or in respect of him under the Teachers Regulations of 1969, only that fraction of that period of service shall be reckoned as reckonable service.

(4) In respect of a person to whom this Part applies there shall not by virtue of this Part be reckoned as reckonable service—

(*a*) any service which he is or was entitled to reckon as contributing or non-contributing service by virtue of section 15 of the Act of 1937 or the corresponding provisions of a local Act scheme if that service is reckonable as reckonable service otherwise than by virtue of these rules;

(*b*) any service which in his case is deemed to be service to which the said section 15 applies by virtue of the Local Government Superannuation (England and Scotland) Regulations 1948**(a)**, if that service is reckonable as reckonable service within the meaning of regulations made under the Teachers Superannuation Act 1967**(b)**; or

(*c*) any service which is the subject of a direction under section 17(3) of the Act of 1953 that all rights enjoyed by or in respect of the person with respect to that service shall be forfeited.

(5) The whole of any period of service to which paragraph (1) applies shall, for the purpose of calculating under section 4(3) of the Teachers Superannuation (Scotland) Act 1968 the average salary of a person to whom this Part applies, be reckoned as a period of employment in reckonable service and his salary during any period so reckoned shall be such amount as would under the Benefits Regulations be taken into account for the purpose of determining the annual average of his remuneration during that period.

(6) Notwithstanding anything before contained in this rule, any service of a person to whom this Part applies which under the Acts of 1937 to 1953 or a local Act scheme was at the time he ceased to be employed in local government employment reckonable only for the purpose of calculating the amount of any benefit payable to or in respect of him or only for the purpose of determining whether he was entitled to any benefit shall be reckoned only for the corresponding like purpose under the Teachers Regulations of 1969.

Voluntary Contributions

20.—(1) A person to whom this Part applies may elect to continue to pay voluntary contributions of any category being paid by him immediately before ceasing to be employed in local government employment.

(2) If a person elects as aforesaid and—

(*a*) within three months of becoming employed in teaching service, or within such longer period as the Secretary of State may in any particular

(a) S.I. 1948/1131(Rev.XVII, p.813:1948, p.3304) (b) 1967 c. 12.

case allow, pays to the Secretary of State a sum equal to the aggregate of any sum paid to him on or after ceasing to be employed in local government employment by way of return of voluntary contributions of any category he has elected to continue to pay, any interest added thereto and any amount deducted therefrom in respect of liability to income tax arising by reason of the payment; and

(*b*) thereafter pays to the Secretary of State any amounts outstanding in respect of voluntary contributions of any category he has elected to continue to pay at the times at which they would have been payable if he had remained in local government employment

his teaching service shall be affected in the manner prescribed by the following provisions of this rule.

(3) In respect of voluntary contributions paid in respect of added years, those years shall be reckoned as reckonable service.

(4) In respect of voluntary contributions paid otherwise than in respect of added years, the service in respect of which they are paid shall be reckoned for the purposes of the Teachers Regulations of 1969 in the manner in which it would under rule 19 have been so reckoned if the payment of the contributions had been completed immediately before the person ceased to be employed in local government.

(5) The provisions of paragraphs (5)(*b*), (6), (7) and (10) of regulation 31 and the provisions of regulation 37 of the Teachers Regulations of 1969 shall apply to voluntary contributions payable under this rule as if they were additional contributions payable in respect of previous employment within the meaning of those Regulations.

(6) If a person does not elect as aforesaid or if voluntary contributions are repaid to him under regulation 37 of the Teachers Regulations of 1969, as applied by this rule, the period in respect of which such contributions were paid shall be reckoned for the purposes of the Teachers Regulations of 1969 only to the extent, if any, to which it would have been so reckoned if no such payments or contributions had been made in respect thereof.

Commencement of Employment

21. For the purposes of regulation 40(1)(*a*)(ii) of the Teachers Regulations of 1969, the date on which a person to whom this Part applies entered any service taken into account for the purpose of calculating the amount of the transfer value payable in respect of him shall be deemed to be a date on which he became employed in teaching service.

Computation of Contributions

22.—(1) Where a person to whom this Part applies ceases to be employed in teaching service or dies, then, in computing the sum to which he or his personal representatives shall be entitled under the Teachers Regulations of 1969, there shall be included a sum in respect of contributions paid by him in respect of service which by virtue of these rules is reckoned as reckonable service and, in the case of a person who has elected in pursuance of rule 20 to continue paying voluntary contributions, in respect also of voluntary contributions paid by him before becoming employed in teaching service which have either not been returned to him or, if returned, have been paid to the Secretary of State under rule 20 and have not subsequently been again returned.

(2) In computing the amount of the sum so included for the purposes of this rule compound interest shall be calculated—

(*a*) as respects the period ending immediately before the date on which the person became employed in teaching service, in the manner in which such interest, if any, would have been calculated if the occasion for making the calculation had occurred immediately before that date; and

(*b*) as respects the period beginning with that date, in accordance with the provisions of Part IV of the Teachers Regulations of 1969.

Benefits under Acts or Scheme

23. Notwithstanding anything in the Acts of 1937 to 1953 or any local Act scheme, a person to whom this Part has become applicable shall cease to be entitled to any payment out of the superannuation fund to which he contributed while in local government employment in respect of any service of which account was taken in calculating the transfer value payable under this Part out of that fund, other than a payment by way of return of voluntary contributions.

Provisions relating to National Insurance

24.—(1) In relation to a person to whom this Part applies—

(*a*) the following paragraphs of Schedule 5 to the Teachers Regulations of 1969, that is to say—

paragraph 3 (which provides for the reduction of contributions),

paragraph 5 (which provides for the reduction of benefits by fixed annual amounts specified therein), and

paragraph 6 (which provides for the reduction of benefits by annual amounts ascertained by reference to a table)

shall not apply if, on the day on which he ceased to be employed in local government employment, he was a person who retained unmodified status;

(*b*) paragraphs 3 and 5 of the said Schedule 5 shall apply if, on the day on which he ceased to be employed in local government employment, he was a person subject to flat rate reduction and, for the purpose of determining the amount of any benefit payable to him under the Acts of 1937 to 1953 or a local Act scheme, would not have been a person entitled to the optant's rate; and

(*c*) paragraphs 3 and 6 of the said Schedule 5 shall apply if, for the purpose aforesaid, he would have been a person entitled to the optant's rate.

(2) Where, by virtue of paragraph (1)(*c*), paragraph 6 of Schedule 5 to the Teachers Regulations of 1969 applies to a person the date of modification for the purposes of the latter paragraph shall be the date which was in relation to him the material date for the purposes of Part II of the Modification Regulations.

PART IV

MISCELLANEOUS

Exclusion of Section 15 *of Act of* 1937

25. In relation to a person who, having been employed in reckonable service, enters local government employment—

(*a*) section 15 of the Act of 1937 (which section as extended by the Teachers Regulations of 1969, provides for the reckoning of reckonable service as contributing service) shall not apply; and (*b*) his service in respect of which contributions were payable under the Teachers Superannuation (Scotland) Act 1968 shall not be reckonable for any purpose of the Acts of 1937 to 1953 or a local Act scheme otherwise than in accordance with these rules.

Application of Section 11(3) *of Act of* 1953

26.—(1) Section 11(3) of the Act of 1953 (which sub-section enables certain persons who would otherwise be debarred on grounds of age from becoming contributory employees or local Act contributors to become such employees or such contributors and to reckon previous pensionable employment) shall apply to a person who before the operative date entered the employment of a local authority after ceasing to be employed in teaching service on or after 1st February 1969.

(2) For the purposes of paragraph (1) section 11(3) of the Act of 1953 shall have effect as if for the references therein to the passing of that Act there were substituted references to the coming into operation of these rules.

Gordon Campbell,
One of Her Majesty's Principal Secretaries of State.

St Andrew's House,
Edinburgh.
1st December 1971.

Consent of the Minister for the Civil Service given under his Official Seal on 7th December 1971.

(L.S.)

K. H. McNeill,
Authorised by the Minister for the Civil Service.

EXPLANATORY NOTE

(*This Note is not part of the Rules.*)

These Rules provide for the preservation of the superannuation rights of persons in Scotland who change their employment in either direction between pensionable teaching service and pensionable local government employment: with modifications and drafting amendments, they continue the arrangements formerly applicable by virtue of the Superannuation (Teaching and Local Government) Interchange (Scotland) Rules 1962, which are revoked.

The principal changes from the previous Rules are:—

(*a*) provision is made enabling the period between employments to be extended (Rule 4(2)); and

(*b*) in certain cases on transfer from teaching service to local government employment interest is required to be paid, and on transfer from local government employment to teaching service may require to be paid, on contributions made by a person in his previous employment, returned to him on his leaving that employment, and required by the Rules to be again paid by him (Rules 5(2) and 14(2)).

The Rules may have retrospective effect in certain cases under the express power of, and subject to the safeguards required by, section 2(5) of the Superannuation (Miscellaneous Provisions) Act 1948.

1971 No. 2026

IRON AND STEEL

The Iron and Steel (Compensation to Employees) (Amendment) Regulations 1971

Laid before Parliament in draft

Made - - - - 13*th December* 1971

Coming into Operation 1*st February* 1972

The Secretary of State, in exercise of his powers under section 41 of the Iron and Steel Act 1949**(a)** as revived and amended by section 31 of the Iron and Steel Act 1967**(b)** and section 8 of the Iron and Steel Act 1969**(c)** and all other powers in that behalf enabling him, and after consultation with the British Steel Corporation and such organisations as appear to him to be representative of persons concerned, hereby makes the following regulations, a draft of which has been laid before Parliament and has been approved by resolution of each House of Parliament in accordance with the said section 41:—

1.—(1) These regulations may be cited as the Iron and Steel (Compensation to Employees) (Amendment) Regulations 1971 and shall come into operation on 1st February 1972.

(2) Regulation 3(*a*) of these regulations shall have effect from 1st February 1972 and regulation 3(*b*) shall have effect from 29th March 1970.

2.—(1) In these regulations "the principal regulations" means the Iron and Steel (Compensation to Employees) Regulations 1968**(d)**.

(2) The Interpretation Act 1889**(e)** shall apply for the interpretation of these regulations as it applies for the interpretation of an Act of Parliament.

3. Regulation 2(1) of the principal regulations is amended:—

(*a*) by adding after paragraphs (*a*) to (i) thereof in the definition of "relevant employment"—

"but except as provided in regulations 5(1)(*c*), 10(1)(*c*), and 16(1)(*c*), does not include service in the armed forces of the Crown:"

(a) 1949 c. 72.
(b) 1967 c. 17.
(c) 1969 c. 45.
(d) S.I. 1968/1170 (1968 II, p. 3156).
(e) 1889 c. 63.

(*b*) by substituting a semi-colon and the word "or" for the comma after the words "that Act" in the definition of "relevant event" and adding thereafter:—

"(*d*) the making of an order under section 8 of the Iron and Steel Act 1969,".

Dated 13th December 1971.

John Eden,
Minister for Industry,
Department of Trade and Industry.

EXPLANATORY NOTE

(*This Note is not part of the Regulations.*)

These regulations amend the Iron and Steel (Compensation to Employees) Regulations 1968.

Service in the armed forces of the Crown, other than in certain specified circumstances, is excluded from employment qualifying for possible entitlement to compensation (regulation 3(*a*)). Persons who suffer loss of employment or loss or diminution of emoluments or pension rights in consequence of the making of a vesting or dissolution order under section 8 of the Iron and Steel Act 1969 are now included among those eligible for the determination and payment of compensation by the British Steel Corporation (regulation 3(*b*)).

In exercise of the power conferred by section 41(2) of the Iron and Steel Act 1949, as revived and amended by section 31 of the Iron and Steel Act 1967, regulation 3(*b*) is to have effect from 29th March 1970. Regulation 3(*a*) will however have effect from the date on which the regulations come into operation (regulation 1).

1971 No. 2029

BETTING AND GAMING

The Gaming Clubs (Permitted Areas) (Amendment) Regulations 1971

Made - - - -	13*th December* 1971
Laid before Parliament	22*nd December* 1971
Coming into Operation	1*st January* 1972

In pursuance of sections 22(3) and 51 of the Gaming Act 1968**(a)**, and after consultation with the Gaming Board for Great Britain, I hereby make the following Regulations:—

1. These Regulations may be cited as the Gaming Clubs (Permitted Areas) (Amendment) Regulations 1971 and shall come into operation on 1st January 1972.

2. Paragraph (*a*) of Regulation 3 of the Gaming Clubs (Permitted Areas) Regulations 1971**(b)** shall be amended by substituting for the words "1st January 1971" the words "1st December 1970".

R. Maudling,
One of Her Majesty's Principal
Secretaries of State.

Home Office,
Whitehall.
13th December 1971.

EXPLANATORY NOTE

(*This Note is not part of the Regulations.*)

The Gaming Clubs (Permitted Areas) Regulations 1971 permit licences for general gaming in any county borough outside Greater London having an estimated population, at any time from 1971 onwards, of 125,000 or more. These Regulations amend the earlier Regulations so as to take account for this purpose of the estimates published in December 1970.

(a) 1968 c. 65.
(b) S.I. 1971/1538 (1971 III, p. 4345).

1971 No. 2031

LOCAL GOVERNMENT, ENGLAND AND WALES

The Rate Support Grant (Increase) (No. 1) Order 1971

Made - - -	18*th November* 1971
Laid before the House of Commons	25*th November* 1971
Coming into Operation	15*th December* 1971

The Secretary of State for the Environment, with the consent of the Treasury and after consultation with the associations of local authorities appearing to him to be concerned and with the local authority with whom consultation appeared to him to be desirable, in exercise of his powers under section 3 of the Local Government Act 1966(**a**), and of all other powers enabling him in that behalf, hereby makes the following order :—

Title, commencement and interpretation

1.—(1) This order may be cited as the Rate Support Grant (Increase) (No. 1) Order 1971 and shall come into operation on the day following the day on which it is approved by a resolution of the Commons House of Parliament.

(2) In this order any reference to a numbered section shall be construed as a reference to the section bearing that number in the Local Government Act 1966 and any reference to a numbered paragraph shall be construed as a reference to the paragraph bearing that number in Part I of Schedule 1 to that Act.

Further amendment of Rate Support Grant Order 1968

2. For the items set out in column (2) of the following table, prescribed by the Rate Support Grant Order 1968(**b**) as amended by the Rate Support Grant (Increase) Order 1969(**c**) and the Rate Support Grant (Increase) Order 1970(**d**) for the purposes of rate support grants for the year 1970-71 in respect of the matters indicated in column (1), there shall be substituted the items specified in column (3).

(**a**) 1966 c. 42.
(**b**) S.I. 1968/1956 (1968 III, p. 5356).
(**c**) S.I. 1969/1806 (1969 III, p. 5618).
(**d**) S.I. 1970/1875 (1970 III, p. 6159).

Relevant matter (1)	Existing item (2)	Substituted item (3)
	£	£
For the year 1970-71		
As the aggregate amount of the rate support grants—	1,873,000,000	1,880,000,000
As the amount of the needs element—	1,506,000,000	1,513,000,000
In relation to the basic payment under paragraph 2		
As the sum to be multiplied by the population—	17·53	17·70
As the sum to be multiplied by the estimated number of persons under 15 years of age in the population—	1·36	1·37
In relation to the supplementary payment under paragraph 3		
As the sum to be multiplied by the estimated number of persons under 5 years of age in the population—	1·22	1·23
In relation to the supplementary payment under paragraph 4		
As the sum to be multiplied by the estimated number of persons over 65 years of age in the population—	1·22	1·23
In relation to the supplementary payment under paragraph 5		
As the sum to be multiplied by the excess and by the population to determine the amount of the payment—	0·094	0·095
In relation to the supplementary payment under paragraph 8		
As the sum by which the road-mileage of the area of the authority (excluding trunk roads) is to be multiplied—	312	315

Relevant matter (1)	Existing item (2)	Substituted item (3)
	£	£
As the sum by which the road-mileage of the roads in the area of the authority classified as principal roads under section 27 (hereinafter called "the prescribed sum") is to be multiplied—	1,526	1,545
As the sum by which the prescribed sum is to be reduced for each 100 persons in the short-fall—	29·50	30·00
As the sum by which the prescribed sum is to be increased for each 100 persons in the excess—	38·46	38·83
As the sum below which the prescribed sum shall not be reduced—	936	945

Peter Walker,
Secretary of State for the Environment.

18th November 1971.

We consent to this order,

V. H. Goodhew,
Walter Clegg,
Two of the Lords Commissioners of Her Majesty's Treasury.

18th November 1971.

EXPLANATORY NOTE

(This Note is not part of the Order.)

This Order came into operation on 15th December 1971 and (under the powers of section 3(1) of the Local Government Act 1966) relates to the financial year 1970-71. It—

(*a*) increases the aggregate amounts of the rate support grants payable under Part I of the Local Government Act 1966 to councils of counties, county boroughs and county districts in England and Wales, the Greater London Council, the councils of London Boroughs, the Common Council of the City of London and the Council of the Isles of Scilly ;

(*b*) increases one of the constituent elements of the rate support grants, namely the needs element (which is not payable to councils of county districts or, subject to the provision to the contrary by regulations under the Act, to the Greater London Council) ; and

(*c*) varies certain of the matters prescribed by the Rate Support Grant Order 1968 as amended by the Rate Support Grant (Increase) Order 1969 and the Rate Support Grant (Increase) Order 1970 in relation to the distribution of the needs element.

STATUTORY INSTRUMENTS

1971 No. 2032

LOCAL GOVERNMENT, ENGLAND AND WALES

The Rate Support Grant (Increase) (No. 2) Order 1971

Made - - -	18*th November* 1971
Laid before the House of Commons	25*th November* 1971
Coming into Operation	15*th December* 1971

The Secretary of State for the Environment, with the consent of the Treasury and after consultation with the associations of local authorities appearing to him to be concerned and with the local authority with whom consultation appeared to him to be desirable, in exercise of his powers under section 3 of the Local Government Act 1966(**a**), section 3(1) of the Education (Milk) Act 1971(**b**) and section 55(4) of the Courts Act 1971(**c**), and of all other powers enabling him in that behalf, hereby makes the following order :—

Title, commencement and interpretation

1.—(1) This order may be cited as the Rate Support Grant (Increase) (No. 2) Order 1971 and shall come into operation on the day following the day on which it is approved by a resolution of the Commons House of Parliament.

(2) In this order any reference to a numbered section shall be construed as a reference to the section bearing that number in the Local Government Act 1966 and any reference to a numbered paragraph shall be construed as a reference to the paragraph bearing that number in Part I of Schedule 1 to that Act.

Amendment of Rate Support Grant Order 1970

2. For the items set out in column (2) of the following table, prescribed by the Rate Support Grant Order 1970(**d**) for the purposes of rate support grants for the years 1971-72 and 1972-73 in respect of the matters indicated in column (1), there shall be substituted the items specified in column (3).

Relevant matter (1)	Existing item (2)	Substituted item (3)
	£	£
For the year 1971-72—		
As the aggregate amount of the rate support grants—	2,004,000,000	2,156,000,000
As the amount of the needs element—	1,607,000,000	1,741,000,000
As the amount of the resources element	280,000,000	298,000,000

(**a**) 1966 c. 42.
(**b**) 1971 c. 74.
(**c**) 1971 c. 23.
(**d**) S.I. 1970/1876 (1970 III, p. 6163).

Relevant matter (1)	Existing item (2)	Substituted item (3)
	£	£
For the year 1972-73—		
As the aggregate amount of the rate support grants—	2,116,000,000	2,303,000,000
As the amount of the needs element—	1,694,000,000	1,861,000,000
As the amount of the resources element—	290,000,000	310,000,000
In relation to the basic payment under paragraph 2		
As the sum to be multiplied by the population—		
For the year 1971-72:	18·19	20·12
For the year 1972-73:	18·63	20·82
As the sum to be multiplied by the estimated number of persons under 15 years of age in the population—		
For the year 1971-72:	1·41	1·56
For the year 1972-73:	1·44	1·61
In relation to the supplementary payment under paragraph 3		
As the sum to be multiplied by the estimated number of persons under 5 years of age in the population—		
For the year 1971-72:	1·26	1·39
For the year 1972-73:	1·29	1·44
In relation to the supplementary payment under paragraph 4		
As the sum to be multiplied by the estimated number of persons over 65 years of age in the population—		
For the year 1971-72:	1·26	1·39
For the year 1972-73:	1·29	1·44
In relation to the supplementary payment under paragraph 5		
As the sum to be multiplied by the excess and by the population to determine the amount of the payment—		
For the year 1971-72:	0·113	0·125
For the year 1972-73:	0·115	0·129

Relevant matter (1)	Existing item (2)	Substituted item (3)
	£	£
In relation to the supplementary payment under paragraph 8		
As the sum by which the road-mileage of the area of the authority (excluding trunk roads) is to be multiplied—		
For the year 1971-72:	323	357
For the year 1972-73:	330	369
As the sum by which the road-mileage of the roads in the area of the authority classified as principal roads under section 27 (hereinafter called "the prescribed sum") is to be multiplied—		
For the year 1971-72:	1,578	1,745
For the year 1972-73:	1,613	1,804
As the sum by which the prescribed sum is to be reduced for each 100 persons in the short-fall—		
For the year 1971-72:	30·45	33·70
For the year 1972-73:	31·15	34·85
As the sum by which the prescribed sum is to be increased for each 100 persons in the excess—		
For the year 1971-72:	39·79	44·00
For the year 1972-73:	40·67	45·50
As the sum below which the prescribed sum shall not be reduced—		
For the year 1971-72:	969	1,071
For the year 1972-73:	990	1,107

Peter Walker,
Secretary of State for the Environment.

18th November 1971.

We consent to this order,

Walter Clegg,
V. H. Goodhew,
Two of the Lords Commissioners of Her Majesty's Treasury.

18th November 1971.

EXPLANATORY NOTE

(This Note is not part of the Order.)

This Order came into operation on 15th December 1971 and (under the powers of section 3(1) of the Local Government Act 1966) relates to the financial years 1971-72 and 1972-73. It—

(*a*) increases the aggregate amounts of the rate support grants payable under Part I of the Local Government Act 1966 to councils of counties, county boroughs and county districts in England and Wales, the Greater London Council, the councils of London Boroughs, the Common Council of the City of London and the Council of the Isles of Scilly ;

(*b*) increases two of the constituent elements of the rate support grants, namely the needs element (which is not payable to councils of county districts or, subject to the provision to the contrary by regulations under the Act, to the Greater London Council) and the resources element ; and

(*c*) varies certain of the matters prescribed by the Rate Support Grant Order 1970 in relation to the distribution of the needs element.

STATUTORY INSTRUMENTS

1971 No. 2034

EXCHANGE CONTROL

The Exchange Control (Authorised Dealers and Depositaries) (Amendment) (No. 4) Order 1971

Made - - - *14th December* 1971

Coming into Operation *31st December* 1971

The Treasury, in exercise of the powers conferred upon them by sections 36(5) and 42(1) of the Exchange Control Act 1947(**a**), hereby make the following Order :—

1.—(1) This Order may be cited as the Exchange Control (Authorised Dealers and Depositaries) (Amendment) (No. 4) Order 1971, and shall come into operation on 31st December 1971.

(2) The Interpretation Act 1889(**b**) shall apply for the interpretation of this Order as it applies for the interpretation of an Act of Parliament.

2. Schedule 2 to the Exchange Control (Authorised Dealers and Depositaries) Order 1971(**c**), as amended (**d**), shall be further amended as follows :—

(*a*) by inserting the words "Bank Hapoalim B.M." after the words "Bangkok Bank Ltd." ;

(*b*) by deleting the words "Barclays Bank D.C.O." and substituting the words "Barclays Bank International Ltd." ;

(*c*) by deleting the words "Eastern Bank, Ltd., The." ; and

(*d*) by inserting the words "Industrial Bank of Japan Ltd., The." after the words "Hongkong & Shanghai Banking Corporation, The."

3. This Order shall extend to the Channel Islands, and any reference in this Order to the Exchange Control Act 1947 includes a reference to that Act as extended by the Exchange Control (Channel Islands) Order 1947(**e**).

Walter Clegg,
V. H. Goodhew,
Two of the Lords Commissioners
of Her Majesty's Treasury.

14th December 1971.

(**a**) 1947 c. 14. (**b**) 1889 c. 63. (**c**) S.I. 1971/477 (1971 I, p. 1425).
(**d**) S.I. 1971/1028, 1370, 1566 (1971 II, pp. 3009, 3855; III, p. 4377).
(**e**) S.R. & O. 1947/2034 (Rev. VI, p. 1001: 1947 I, p. 660).

EXPLANATORY NOTE

(This Note is not part of the Order.)

This Order amends the list of persons authorised by the Treasury under the Exchange Control Act 1947 to act as dealers in gold and foreign currencies and as depositaries for the purpose of the deposit of securities.

1971 No. 2035

PENSIONS

The Increase of Pensions (Governors) Regulations 1971

Made - - - -	14*th December* 1971
Laid before Parliament	21*st December* 1971
Coming into Operation	12*th January* 1972

In exercise of the powers conferred upon me by section 5(3) and (4) of the Pensions (Increase) Act 1971(**a**) and with the approval of the Minister for the Civil Service, I hereby make the following Regulations:—

1. These Regulations may be cited as the Increase of Pensions (Governors) Regulations 1971 and shall come into operation on 12th January 1972.

2. In these Regulations, unless the context otherwise requires, the following expressions have the meanings respectively assigned to them, that is to say—

" The Act " means the Pensions (Increase) Act 1971 ;

" Governor " has the meaning assigned to it by section 1 of the Governors' Pensions Act 1957(**b**) ;

The Interpretation Act 1889(**c**) shall apply for the interpretation of and otherwise in relation to these Regulations as it applies for the interpretation of and otherwise in relation to an Act of Parliament.

3. The provisions of the Act shall apply to any pension payable to or in respect of a Governor under the Governors' Pensions Acts 1957 and 1967 (other than a pension granted under sections 8 or 10 of the Governors' Pensions Act 1957 or a pension to which section 4(6) of the Superannuation (Miscellaneous Provisions) Act 1967(**d**) applies) subject to the modifications specified in regulation 4 of these Regulations.

4. In relation to any pension to which the preceding regulation applies the Act, but not any order made under section 6 of the Act, shall apply as if section 8(2) and (3) and any references in the Act to either of those provisions were omitted and as if—

(*a*) a pension to which section 1(1) of the Pensions (Governors of Dominions, etc.) Act 1929(**e**) applied began on 27th March 1929 ;

(*b*) a pension to which section 2(1) of the Pensions (Governors of Dominions, etc.) Act 1947(**f**) applied either directly or by virtue of section 14 of the Governors' Pensions Act 1956(**g**) began on 18th December 1947 ;

(*c*) a pension granted under the Governors' Pensions Acts 1957 and 1967 began on whichever is the later of—

(i) the date of first appointment of the recipient to the last office of Governor in which he served in respect of which a pension has been granted to him under the Governors' Pensions Acts 1957 and 1967, or

(**a**) 1971 c. 56. (**b**) 1957 c. 62. (**c**) 1889 c. 63. (**d**) 1967 c. 28.
(**e**) 1929 c. 16 (19 & 20 Geo 5). (**f**) 1947 c. 12 (11 & 12 Geo 6). (**g**) 1956 c. 64.

(ii) the date on which the salary enjoyed by him during service in that last office was last revised ; and

(*d*) a substituted pension began on the same date as the original pension is deemed to have begun under this regulation or, if earlier, on the date from which the surrender of the original pension took effect.

5. These Regulations shall be deemed to have taken effect from 1st September 1971.

Alec Douglas-Home,
Secretary of State for Foreign and Commonwealth Affairs.

1st December 1971.

Consent of the Minister for the Civil Service given under his Official Seal on 14th December 1971.

A. W. Wyatt,
Authorised by the Minister for the Civil Service.

EXPLANATORY NOTE

(*This Note is not part of the Regulations.*)

These Regulations apply the provisions of the Pensions (Increase) Act 1971 to pensions payable to or in respect of Governors under the Governors' Pensions Acts 1957 and 1967 subject to modifications in relation to the dates on which pensions are deemed to begin.

The Regulations have retrospective effect from 1st September 1971, in pursuance of the powers conferred by section 5(4) of the Act.

STATUTORY INSTRUMENTS

1971 No. 2036 (S.216)

PENSIONS

The Increase of Pensions (Teachers Family Benefits) (Scotland) Regulations 1971

Made - - - -	10*th December* 1971
Laid before Parliament	20*th December* 1971
Coming into Operation	31*st December* 1971

In exercise of the powers conferred upon me by section 5(3) of the Pensions (Increase) Act 1971**(a)**, and of all other powers enabling me in that behalf and with the consent of the Minister for the Civil Service, I hereby make the following regulations:—

Citation and Commencement

1. These regulations may be cited as the Increase of Pensions (Teachers Family Benefits) (Scotland) Regulations 1971 and shall come into operation on 31st December 1971.

Interpretation

2.—(1) In these regulations, unless the context otherwise requires—

"the Act" means the Pensions (Increase) Act 1971;

"the regulations" means the Teachers Superannuation (Family Benefits) (Scotland) Regulations 1971**(b)**.

(2) A pension shall be deemed for the purposes of these regulations to begin on the day following the last day of the service in respect of which the pension is payable.

(3) A reference in these regulations to a regulation or to a Part shall, unless the context otherwise requires, be construed as a reference to a regulation or to a Part of the regulations, as the case may be.

(4) The Interpretation Act 1889**(c)** shall apply for the interpretation of these regulations as it applies for the interpretation of an Act of Parliament.

Modification of Act

3. In relation to pensions payable under the regulations the provisions of the Act are hereby modified so that the annual rate thereof may, instead of being increased in accordance with those provisions, be increased as in these regulations provided.

(a) 1971 c. 56.
(b) S.I. 1971/1775 (1971 III, p. 4813).
(c) 1889 c. 63.

Widow's Pension

4.—(1) Except as provided in paragraph (2) of this regulation and in regulation 7 of these regulations, the increase in the minimum annual amount of a widow's pension specified in either sub-paragraph (*a*) or sub-paragraph (*b*) of regulation 44(2) shall, if the pension began on or before 1st April 1971, be such as will make that amount £132 in respect of any period beginning on or after 1st September 1971.

(2) Paragraph (1) above shall not apply in relation to any widow's pension if the annual amount thereof, as determined under paragraph (4) or paragraph (5) of regulation 44 and increased in accordance with the provisions of the Act, would exceed £132.

Short Service Widow's Pension

5. Except as provided in regulation 7 of these regulations, the increase in the annual amount of a short service widow's pension which began on or before 1st April 1971 and is payable in a case specified in either paragraph (*a*) or paragraph (*b*) of regulation 47 shall, in respect of any period beginning on or after 1st September 1971, be the amount which, opposite to the number of years of service counting for benefit of her husband specified in column (1) of the following Table, is specified—

(*a*) in column (2) thereof in a case specified in the said paragraph (*a*); and

(*b*) in column (3) thereof in a case specified in the said paragraph (*b*):—

TABLE

(1) Years of Service	(2) Increase (Regulation 47(a))	(3) Increase (Regulation 47(b))
3	£8	£3
4	£9	£4
5	£10	£4
6	£12	£5
7	£13	£5
8	£15	£6
9	£16	£6

Children's Pension

6. Except as provided in regulation 7 of these regulations, the increase in the annual amount of a children's pension which began on or before 1st April 1971 and is payable in a case to which either sub-paragraph (*a*) or sub-paragraph (*b*) of regulation 50(1) applies shall, in respect of any period beginning on or after 1st September 1971, be the amount which, opposite to the number of eligible children to or in respect of whom it is for the time being payable specified in column (1) of the following Table, is specified in column (2) or column (3) thereof, whichever column shall for the time be appropriate—

(*a*) under letter A, in a case to which the said sub-paragraph (*a*) applies; and

(*b*) under letter B, in a case to which the said sub-paragraph (*b*) applies:—

TABLE

(1) Number of Eligible Children	(2) Increase where there is a Surviving Widow of the Contributor		(3) Increase where there is not a Surviving Widow of the Contributor	
	A	B	A	B
1	£8	£3	£15	£5
2	£17	£7	£25	£10
3	£25	£10	£35	£15
4 or more	£33	£13	£51	£21

Increases in respect of Contributors under External Schemes

7.—(1) Except as provided in paragraph (2) of this regulation, in a case to which regulation 52 applies the increase in—

(*a*) the minimum annual amount of a widow's pension specified in either sub-paragraph (*a*) or sub-paragraph (*b*) of regulation 44(2);

(*b*) the annual amount of a short service widow's pension payable in a case specified in either paragraph (*a*) or paragraph (*b*) of regulation 47; and

(*c*) the annual amount of a children's pension payable in a case to which either sub-paragraph (*a*) or sub-paragraph (*b*) of regulation 50(1) applies

being a pension which began on or before 1st April 1971, shall, in respect of any period beginning on or after 1st September 1971, be the amount which bears to the amount of the increase of such a pension under regulation 4, 5 or 6, as the case may be, of these regulations the same proportion as that specified in regulation 52 for the purpose of calculating the annual amount thereof.

(2) Paragraph (1) above shall not apply in relation to any widow's pension if the annual amount thereof, as determined under paragraph (4) or paragraph (5) of regulation 44 and regulation 52 and increased in accordance with the provisions of the Act, would exceed the annual amount thereof as increased under paragraph (1).

Gordon Campbell,
One of Her Majesty's Principal
Secretaries of State.

St Andrew's House,
Edinburgh.

7th December 1971.

Consent of the Minister for the Civil Service given under his Official Seal on 10th December 1971.

A. Wyatt,
Authorised by the Minister for the Civil Service.

EXPLANATORY NOTE

(This Note is not part of the Regulations.)

These Regulations apply to a widow's pension, a short service widow's pension and a children's pension payable under the Teachers Superannuation (Family Benefits) (Scotland) Regulations 1971 where the service of the deceased teacher in respect of which such a pension is payable ended on or before 1st April 1971. Instead of being increased in accordance with the Pensions (Increase) Act 1971, from 1st September 1971 the minimum annual amount of the widow's pension is raised to £132 and the annual amounts of the other pensions by the amounts specified.

Where the deceased teacher also had service in England, Wales, Northern Ireland, the Isle of Man or the Channel Islands the increase is limited to the amount which bears the same proportion to the total increase otherwise authorised as his contributions in respect of his service in Scotland bears to his total contributions.

The Regulations have retrospective effect by virtue of section 5(4) of the Pensions (Increase) Act 1971.

STATUTORY INSTRUMENTS

1971 No. 2040

CUSTOMS AND EXCISE

The European Free Trade Association (Origin of Goods) (Amendment) Regulations 1971

Made - - -	15*th December* 1971
Laid before the House of Commons	22*nd December* 1971
Coming into Operation	1*st January* 1972

The Secretary of State, in exercise of his powers under section 1(1) of the European Free Trade Association Act 1960(**a**), hereby makes the following Regulations :—

1.—(1) These Regulations may be cited as the European Free Trade Association (Origin of Goods) (Amendment) Regulations 1971 and shall come into operation on 1st January 1972.

(2) The Interpretation Act 1889(**b**) shall apply to the interpretation of these Regulations as it applies to the interpretation of an Act of Parliament.

2. The European Free Trade Association (Origin of Goods) Regulations 1964(**c**), as amended (**d**), shall have effect as if the Schedules thereto were further amended in the manner mentioned in the Schedule hereto.

Anthony Grant,
Parliamentary Under Secretary of State,
Department of Trade and Industry.

15th December 1971.

SCHEDULE

PART I

Amendments to descriptions only in Schedule 1 *to the* 1964 *Regulations*

1. In column 1 of Schedule 1, the descriptions of goods shall be amended as follows:—

(**a**) 1960 c. 19. (**b**) 1889 c. 63.
(**c**) S.I. 1964/1966 (1964 III, p. 4296).
(**d**) The previous amending Regulations are not relevant to the subject matter of these Regulations.

Chapter 28

In the description related to heading 28.03 (carbon), the words "anthracene black, acetylene black and lamp black" shall be omitted.

For the description related to heading 28.05, there shall be substituted—

"Alkali and alkaline-earth metals; rare earth metals, yttrium and scandium and intermixtures or interalloys thereof; mercury.".

In the description related to heading 28.06 (acids), for "chlorosulphonic acid" there shall be substituted "chlorosulphuric acid".

In the description related to heading 28.56 (carbides), for "metallic carbides" there shall be substituted "metal carbides".

Chapter 29

At the end of the first description related to heading 29.11 (aldehydes) there shall be added "cyclic polymers of aldehydes; paraformaldehyde".

In the first description related to heading 29.14, for "Monoacids" there shall be substituted "Monocarboxylic acids" and the word "acid" shall be omitted before "halides" and "peroxides".

In the first description related to heading 29.15, for "Polyacids" there shall be substituted "Polycarboxylic acids" and the word "acid" shall be omitted before "halides" and "peroxides".

In the first description related to heading 29.16, for "Alcohol-acids, aldehyde-acids, ketone-acids, phenol-acids" there shall be substituted "Carboxylic acids with alcohol, phenol, aldehyde or ketone function", the word "carboxylic" shall be inserted after "oxygen-function" and the word "acid" omitted before "halides" and "peroxides".

For the description related to heading 29.25 there shall be substituted—

"Carboxyamide—function compounds; amide function compounds of carbonic acid.".

For the description related to heading 29.26 there shall be substituted—

"Carboxyimide-function compounds (including ortho-benzoicsulphimide and its salts) and imine-function compounds (including hexamethylene-tetramine and trimethylenetrinitramine).".

For the first description related to heading 29.39 there shall be substituted—

"Hormones, natural or reproduced by synthesis; derivatives thereof, used primarily as hormones; other steroids used primarily as hormones.".

Chapter 31

For the second description related to heading 31.05 there shall be substituted—

"Monoammonium and diammonium orthophosphates.".

Chapter 32

For the description related to heading 32.03 there shall be substituted—

"Synthetic organic tanning substances, and inorganic tanning substances; tanning preparations, whether or not containing natural tanning materials; enzymatic preparations for pre-tanning (for example, of enzymatic, pancreatic or bacterial origin).".

In the description related to heading 32.12 (putty etc), after "painters' fillings" there shall be inserted "non-refractory surfacing preparations".

Chapter 44

In the description related to heading 44.09 (hoopwood, poles etc), for the words after "chipwood" there shall be substituted "pulpwood in chips or particles; wood shavings of a kind suitable for use in the manufacture of vinegar or for the clarification of liquids".

For the description related to heading 44.21 there shall be substituted—

"Complete wooden packing cases, boxes, crates, drums and similar packings.".

Chapter 68

In the description related to heading 68.04 (millstones etc), for "not mounted on frameworks" there shall be substituted "without frameworks".

Chapter 69

In the description related to heading 69.01 (heat insulating bricks etc), for the words after "other heat insulating goods" there shall be substituted "of siliceous fossil meals or of similar siliceous earths (for example, kieselguhr, tripolite or diatomite)".

In the description related to heading 69.10, for "sanitary fittings" there shall be substituted "sanitary fixtures".

Chapter 70

In the description related to heading 70.12 (inners for vacuum flasks) the words "and blanks therefor" shall be omitted.

Chapters 73 *to* 76

In the descriptions related to headings 73.21 (structures of iron or steel) and 76.08 (aluminium structures), the words "complete or incomplete, whether or not assembled" shall be omitted.

In the descriptions related to headings 73.22 (iron or steel reservoirs and tanks), 74.09 (copper reservoirs and tanks) and 76.09 (aluminium reservoirs and tanks), after 'for any material" there shall be inserted "(other than compressed or liquified gas)".

For the descriptions related to headings 73.24 and 76.11 there shall be substituted respectively:—

"Containers, of iron or steel, for compressed or liquified gas."; and

"Containers, of aluminium, for compressed or liquified gas.".

In the description related to heading 73.33 (needles), "including blanks" shall be omitted.

In the description related to heading 73.37 (boilers), "steam-generating" shall be omitted.

In the descriptions related to headings 74.18 (copper ware) and 76.15 (aluminium ware), "builders" shall be omitted.

Chapter 82

In the description related to heading 82.04 (hand tools), the first "mounted" shall be omitted and for "grinding wheels mounted on frameworks" there shall be substituted "grinding wheels with frameworks".

Chapter 83

In the description related to heading 83.01 (locks and keys), "finished or not" shall be omitted.

Chapter 84

At the end of the description related to heading 84.01 (boilers) there shall be added "superheated water boilers".

In the description related to tariff heading 84.02, for "Auxiliary plant for use with steam and other vapour generating boilers" there shall be substituted "Auxiliary plant for use with boilers of heading No. 84.01".

In the descriptions related to heading 84.45 (machine tools) and 84.60 (moulding boxes), for "metallic carbides" there shall be substituted "metal carbides".

For the description related to heading 84.53 there shall be substituted—

"Automatic data processing machines and units thereof; articles of the following descriptions, unless specified or included in the first part of this heading or elsewhere, namely, magnetic and optical readers, machines for transcribing data on to data media in coded form and machines for processing such data.".

Chapter 85

In the description related to heading 85.08 (starting and ignition equipment), for "dynamos and cut-outs for use in conjunction therewith" there shall be substituted "generators (dynamos and alternators) and cut-outs for use in conjunction with such engines".

In the description related to heading 85.15 (radio equipment), for the words in parenthesis there shall be substituted "(including receivers incorporating sound recorders or reproducers)".

In the description related to heading 85.19 (electrical apparatus), "terminals, terminal strips" shall be omitted and after "heating resistors" there shall be inserted "printed circuits".

In the description related to heading 85.21 (valves), for the words after "photocells" there shall be substituted "mounted piezo-electric crystals; diodes, transistors and similar semi-conductor devices; electronic microcircuits".

Chapter 87

In the description related to heading 87.07 (work trucks), for "of the types used in factories or warehouses" there shall be substituted "of the types used in factories, warehouses, dock areas or airports"; for the words in parenthesis there shall be substituted "(for example, platform trucks, fork-lift trucks and straddle carriers)" and for "trucks and tractors" there shall be substituted "vehicles".

Chapter 89

For the description "Tugs" related to heading 89.02 there shall be substituted "Vessels specially designed for towing (tugs) or pushing other vessels".

Chapter 90

In the description related to heading 90.10 (certain photo apparatus), for the words after "photo-copying apparatus" there shall be substituted "(whether incorporating an optical system or of the contact-type) and thermo-copying apparatus; screens for projectors".

In the description related to heading 90.19 (orthopaedic appliances), after "trusses and the like" there shall be inserted "splints and other fracture appliances" and for the words after "deaf aids" there shall be substituted "and other appliances which are worn or carried, or implanted in the body, to compensate for a defect or disability".

In the description related to heading 91.09 (watch cases and parts of watch cases), "including blanks thereof" shall be omitted.

In the description related to heading 93.06 (parts of arms), "roughly sawn gun stock blocks and" shall be omitted.

PART II

Amendment relating to both descriptions of goods and qualifying processes in Schedule 1 to the 1964 Regulations

In Schedule 1—

(*a*) for the entry related to heading 34.01 there shall be substituted:—

		Qualifying process
"34.01	Soap; organic surface-active products and preparations for use as soap, in the form of bars, cakes or moulded pieces or shapes, whether or not combined with soap	Manufacture from materials not falling in 34.01 or 34.02, provided that any organic surface-active agent present in the finished product has been made in the Area by chemical transformation* or is of Area origin.";

(*b*) for the two entries related to heading 35.06 there shall be substituted the following single entry—

		Qualifying process
"35.06	Prepared glues, not elsewhere specified or included; products suitable for use as glues put up for sale by retail as glues in packages not exceeding a net weight of 1 kg.	Manufacture from casein (35.01) or albumins (35.02) or from materials not falling in 28.45, 32.09, 38.19 or 40.06 or Chapter 35 or 39.";

(*c*) there shall be included before the existing entry related to heading 74.19 the following further entry—

		Qualifying process
"74.19	Reservoirs, tanks, vats and similar containers, of copper, of a capacity exceeding three hundred litres for compressed or liquefied gas	Manufacture from materials not falling in 74.09 other than reservoirs, tanks, vats and similar containers, of copper, of a capacity exceeding three hundred litres for compressed or liquefied gas of 74.19.".

PART III

Amendments to Schedule 2 to the 1964 Regulations

In Schedule 2, the descriptions of goods in column 1 shall be amended as follows:—

1. For the description related to heading 57.03 there shall be substituted—

"Jute and other textile bast fibres not elsewhere specified or included, carded or combed or otherwise prepared for spinning.".

2. At the end of the descriptions related to headings 57.06 and 57.10 there shall be added "or of other textile bast fibres of heading No. 57.03.".

3. In the description related to heading 59.08, for "impregnated or coated" there shall be substituted "impregnated, coated, covered or laminated".

PART IV

Amendments to Schedule 3 *to the* 1964 *Regulations*

The description of materials in Schedule 3 shall be amended as follows:—

1. In the description related to heading 25.12, "Infusorial earths" shall be omitted.

2. In the description related to heading 28.03, all the words after "carbon black" shall be omitted.

3. The whole entry related to heading 38.19 (mixed alkylenes) shall be omitted.

4. For the description related to heading 57.03 there shall be substituted "Jute and other textile bast fibres not elsewhere specified or included, raw or processed but not spun; tow and waste thereof (including pulled or garnetted rags or ropes).".

EXPLANATORY NOTE

(This Note is not part of the Regulations.)

These Regulations further amend the European Free Trade Association (Origin of Goods) Regulations 1964 (S.I. 1964/1966).

They make a number of changes in the descriptions of goods and materials and processes specified in the Schedules to the 1964 Regulations which the E.F.T.A. Council have agreed shall come into operation on 1st January 1972.

All of the amendments reflect nomenclature changes in the Customs tariff.

STATUTORY INSTRUMENTS

1971 No. 2041

CUSTOMS AND EXCISE

The Import Duties (General) (No. 10) Order 1971

Made - - - -	16*th December* 1971
Laid before the House of Commons	17*th December* 1971
Coming into Operation	1*st January* 1972

The Lords Commissioners of Her Majesty's Treasury, by virtue of the powers conferred on them by sections 1, 2 and 13 of the Import Duties Act 1958(**a**) and of all other powers enabling them in that behalf, on the recommendation of the Secretary of State hereby make the following Order:—

1.—(1) This Order may be cited as the Import Duties (General) (No. 10) Order 1971.

(2) The Interpretation Act 1889(**b**) shall apply for the interpretation of this Order as it applies for the interpretation of an Act of Parliament.

(3) This Order shall come into operation on 1st January 1972.

2. In Schedule 1 to the Import Duties (General) (No. 7) Order 1971(**c**) (which by reference to the Customs Tariff 1959 sets out the import duties chargeable under the Import Duties Act 1958) for subheading (B) of heading 20.04 there shall be substituted the following subheading:—

" (B) Cherries; fruit peels:

(1) Drained or glacé cherries ...	10%	C	—
		E	10%
(2) Other	20%	C	—
		E	20%."

3. In article 2 of the Import Duties (General) (No. 8) Order 1971(**d**) the words from " and the like amendment " onwards shall be omitted.

Tim Fortescue,
Walter Clegg,
Two of the Lords Commissioners of Her Majesty's Treasury.

16th December 1971.

EXPLANATORY NOTE

(*This Note is not part of the Order.*)

This Order provides for the continuation after 31st December 1971 of the reduced rate of import duty on drained or glacé cherries.

(**a**) 1958 c. 6. (**b**) 1889 c. 63. (**c**) S.I. 1971/1971(1971 III, p.5330). (**d**) S.I. 1971/1891 (1971 III, p. 5140).

1971 No. 2042

CUSTOMS AND EXCISE

The Import Duties (Temporary Exemptions) (No. 10) Order 1971

Made - - - -	16*th December* 1971
Laid before the House of Commons	23*rd December* 1971
Coming into Operation	1*st January* 1972

The Lords Commissioners of Her Majesty's Treasury, by virtue of the powers conferred on them by sections 3(6) and 13 of the Import Duties Act 1958(**a**), and of all other powers enabling them in that behalf, on the recommendation of the Secretary of State, hereby make the following Order:—

1.—(1) This Order may be cited as the Import Duties (Temporary Exemptions) (No. 10) Order 1971.

(2) The Interpretation Act 1889(**b**) shall apply for the interpretation of this Order as it applies for the interpretation of an Act of Parliament.

(3) This Order shall come into operation on 1st January 1972.

2.—(1) Until the beginning of 1st January 1973, any import duty which is for the time being chargeable on goods of a heading of the Customs Tariff 1959 specified in Schedule 1 to this Order shall not be chargeable in respect of goods of any description there specified in relation to that heading.

(2) The period for which goods of the headings of the Customs Tariff 1959 and descriptions specified in Schedule 2 to this Order are exempt from import duty shall be extended until the beginning of 1st January 1973.

(3) Any entry in column 2 in Schedule 1 or Schedule 2 to this Order is to be taken to comprise all goods which would be classified under an entry in the same terms constituting a subheading (other than the final subheading) in the relevant heading in the Customs Tariff 1959.

(4) For the purposes of classification under the Customs Tariff 1959, in so far as that depends on the rate of duty, any goods to which paragraph (1) or paragraph (2) above applies shall be treated as chargeable with the same duty as if this Order had not been made.

Tim Fortescue,
Walter Clegg,
Two of the Lords Commissioners of Her Majesty's Treasury.

16th December 1971.

(**a**) 1958 c. 6. (**b**) 1889 c. 63.

SCHEDULE 1

Goods Temporarily Exempt from Import Duty

Tariff Heading	*Description*
15.10	Fatty alcohols, normal, containing fourteen or more carbon atoms in the molecule and having an iodine value not less than 40
28.30	Aluminium chloride, anhydrous, containing by weight (*a*) not more than 0·0005 per cent. of lead compounds calculated as Pb, (*b*) not more than 0·0010 per cent. of magnesium compounds calculated as Mg, and (*c*) not more than 0·0020 per cent. of zinc compounds calculated as Zn
28.42	Lithium carbonate
29.02	1-Chloro-*n*-octane of a purity not less than 99·5 per cent., containing not more than 0·2 per cent. by weight of other chloro-octanes and not more than 0·05 per cent. by weight of other alkyl chlorides
	α,4-Dichlorodiphenylmethane
29.03	4-Nitro-*m*-xylene
	*di*Sodium naphthalene-2,7-disulphonate
	*tri*Sodium naphthalenetrisulphonate, mixed isomers, which contains not more than 0·005 per cent. by weight of iron compounds calculated as Fe, and of which an aqueous solution containing 50 grammes per litre has a pH not greater than 7
29.07	3-Hydroxynaphthalene-2,7-disulphonic acid
	2-Nitro-*p*-cresol (-OH at 1)
29.10	2,2-Dimethoxypropane
	1,2-*O*-*iso*Propylidene-D-glucofuranose
29.12	*di*Sodium 4-formylbenzene-1,3-disulphonate
29.13	Dicyclohexyl ketone
	1,5-Dihydroxyanthraquinone
	1,8-Dihydroxyanthraquinone
	9α-Fluoro-11β,17α-dihydroxy-16α-methylpregna-1,4-diene-3,20-dione
29.14	Aluminium formate, solid
	n-Valeric acid
29.15	*n*-Hexadecylsuccinic anhydride
29.16	Dimethyl 4,4′-(ethylenedioxy)dibenzoate
	4,4′-(Ethylenedioxy)dibenzoic acid
	3-Hydroxy-2-naphthoic acid
	n-Octadecyl 3-(3,5-di*tert*butyl-4-hydroxyphenyl)propionate
	Phenyl 1-hydroxy-2-naphthoate
	2-*p*-Toluoylbenzoic acid
29.19	Pyruvic acid enol phosphate, *mono*potassium salt
	Pyruvic acid enol phosphate, *mono*sodium salt
29.22	5-Aminonaphthalene-2-sulphonic acid
	6-Aminonaphthalene-2-sulphonic acid
	Aminonaphthalenesulphonic acid, mixed 5,2- and 8,2- isomers
	4-Aminostilbene-2-sulphonic acid
	Aniline-2,5-disulphonic acid
	8-Anilinonaphthalene-1-sulphonic acid
	N-Benzyl-*N*-ethyl-*m*-toluidine
	2-Chloro-5-nitroaniline
	NN′-Di*sec*butyl-*p*-phenylenediamine

Tariff Heading	*Description*
29.22	Fast Scarlet G Base *N*-Methyl-*n*-octadecylamine *m*-Phenylenediamine-4-sulphonic acid Pyruvic acid enol phosphate, triscyclohexylammonium salt Sodium 8-aminonaphthalene-2-sulphonate Sodium hydrogen 8-aminonaphthalene-1,6-disulphonate Sodium hydrogen aniline-2,5-disulphonate Sulphanilic acid of a purity not less than 98 per cent., and of which an ammoniacal aqueous solution containing 100 grammes per litre shows optical densities which, being measured in a cell of 20 millimetres length at wavelengths of 470 nanometres, 570 nanometres and 680 nanometres and added together, give a sum not greater than 1·26
29.23	3-Amino-5-chloro-2-hydroxybenzenesulphonic acid 2-Amino-*p*-cresol (—OH at 1) 2-Amino-3-hydroxyanthraquinone 3-Amino-4-hydroxybenzenesulphonic acid 4-Amino-5-hydroxynaphthalene-2,7-disulphonic acid 4-Amino-5-hydroxynaphthalene-1-sulphonic acid 7-Amino-4-hydroxynaphthalene-2-sulphonic acid 3-Amino-4-methoxybenzoic acid 2-Amino-6-nitro-*p*-cresol hydrochloride (—OH at 1) *p*-Anisidine-3-sulphonic acid (—NH_2 at 1) Anthranilic acid containing not more than 1 per cent. by weight of water 2,4-Dimethoxyaniline 6-Dimethylamino-4-hydroxynaphthalene-2-sulphonic acid 2,4-Di-*o*-tolyloxyaniline Fast Bordeaux GP Base Fast Red B Base 2-(4-*tert*Pentylphenoxy)aniline Sodium 7-(4-aminoanilino)-4-hydroxynaphthalene-2-sulphonate Sodium hydrogen 4-amino-5-hydroxynaphthalene-1,3-disulphonate
29.25	4-Acetamidoaniline 4-Acetamidoaniline-3-sulphonic acid 3,5-Dinitro-*o*-toluamide (—$CONH_2$ at 1) Ethyl 2-[*N*-(3,4-dichlorophenyl)benzamido]propionate Methyl 7-hydroxy-1-naphthylcarbamate
29.26	Sodium 2-(cyclohexa-1,4-dienyl)-2-(2-methoxycarbonyl-1-methylethylideneamino)acetate
29.27	2-Amino-5-nitrobenzonitrile 2-Chlorobenzonitrile Phenylacetonitrile
29.28	4-Aminoazobenzene 4-Aminoazobenzene-3,4′-disulphonic acid
29.31	2-Amino-4-methylsulphonylphenol Di-(4-aminophenyl) sulphide Tridecane-1-thiol, mixed isomers
29.32	4-Hydroxyphenylarsonic acid
29.34	1,2-Diaminoethane-*NNN′N′*-tetra(methylphosphonic acid)
29.35	Adenosine 3′,5′-(hydrogen cyclic phosphate) 2-Amino-6-chlorobenzothiazole hydrochloride 6-Amino-1,2-dihydroindazol-3-one dihydrochloride 1-(4-Aminophenyl)-3-methyl-5-pyrazolone 3-Amino-1-(2,4,6-trichlorophenyl)-5-pyrazolone

Tariff Heading	*Description*
29.35	Benzothiazole-2-sulphenamide Betahistine dihydrochloride Carbazole 2-(4-Chloroanilino)-5-(4-chlorophenyl)-3,5-dihydro-3-*iso*propyliminophenazine 3-(4-Chlorophenyl)-1-[4-(2-hydroxyethylsulphonyl)phenyl]-2-pyrazoline 4-Chloropyridinium chloride $N^6O^{2'}$-Di-*n*-butyryladenosine 3′,5′-(sodium cyclic phosphate) 2,4-Dichloro-α-5-pyrimidylbenzhydrol 3-Ethoxycarbonyl-1-phenyl-5-pyrazolone 1-(2-Ethylphenyl)-3-methyl-5-pyrazolone Guanosine 5′-(trisodium hydrogen triphosphate) 2-(2-Hydroxy-3,5-di*tert*pentylphenyl)benzotriazole 2-(6-Hydroxy-*m*-tolyl)benzotriazole 3-Methyl-1-phenyl-5-pyrazolone 3-Methyl-1-(3-sulphophenyl)-5-pyrazolone 6-Nitrobenzimidazole 1,3,3-Trimethylindolin-2-ylideneacetaldehyde 1,3,3-Trimethyl-2-methyleneindoline
29.36	Fast Red ITR Base
29.38	Nicotinamide
29.44	Thiostrepton
34.04	Artificial waxes, being partial esters of the acids derived from montan wax, and having an acid value of not less than 10 and not more than 20 and a saponification value of not less than 110
39.02	Poly(vinyl chloride), emulsion-polymerised, in powder form and of natural colour, unplasticised but compounded with not less than 1·3 per cent. by weight and not more than 2·5 per cent. by weight of artificial wax, and having a viscosity number of not less than 150 and not more than 170 when determined by Method 404A of British Standard 2782:1970
50.05	Yarn spun from silk waste other than noil, not dyed and not put up for retail sale
73.14	Nickel plated iron or steel wire, the wire having a diameter of not less than 0·005 inch nor more than 0·250 inch and the nickel plating being not less than 0·0001 inch and not more than 0·0005 inch
73.15	Cold-rolled steel strip, with dressed edges, in coils, the strip being less than 0·004 inch in thickness and not less than ¼ inch nor more than 4 inches in width, containing not less than 16 per cent. by weight nor more than 18 per cent. by weight of chromium and not less than 6 per cent. by weight nor more than 8 per cent. by weight of nickel and being of a tensile strength of more than 115 tons per square inch Cold-rolled steel strip, with dressed edges, in coils, the strip being less than 0·004 inch in thickness and not less than $\frac{1}{16}$ inch nor more than 4 inches in width, containing not less than 16 per cent. by weight nor more than 18 per cent. by weight of chromium, and not less than 6 per cent. by weight nor more than 8 per cent. by weight of nickel, and being of a tensile strength of not less than 120 tons per square inch Cold-rolled steel strip, with dressed edges, in coils, the strip being not less than 0·004 inch nor more than 0·040 inch in thickness and not less than 0·0625 inch nor more than 0·24 inch in width, containing not less than 16 per cent. by weight nor more than 18 per cent. by weight of chromium, and not less than 6 per cent. by weight nor more than 8 per cent. by weight of nickel, and being of a tensile strength of not less than 120 tons per square inch

Tariff Heading	*Description*
76.03	Aluminium alloy strip in coils, containing not less than 18 per cent. by weight and not more than 22 per cent. by weight of tin and not less than 0·7 per cent. by weight and not more than 1·5 per cent. by weight of copper as the major alloying elements, and having a width of not less than 75 millimetres and not more than 230 millimetres and a thickness of not less than 4·5 millimetres and not more than 6·5 millimetres
81.04	Hafnium metal in the form of crushed pieces or sponge, containing not more than 7 per cent. by weight of zirconium and not more than 1 per cent. by weight of other alloying elements
88.02	Helicopters of an empty weight of 5,000 kilogrammes or more

SCHEDULE 2

Goods for which Exemption from Import Duty is Extended

Tariff Heading	*Description*
15.04	Herring oil, falling within subheading (C), and oils falling within subheading (D), except fish liver oils and refined sperm oil
25.11	Natural barium sulphate, not ground or powdered
28.18	Barium oxide
28.38	Aqueous barium sulphate paste containing not less than 70 per cent. and not more than 80 per cent. by weight of barium sulphate and containing in the dried material not more than four parts per million by weight of iron compounds calculated as Fe and not more than forty parts per hundred million by weight of ethanol soluble sulphur
29.02	1,2-Dibromoethane
29.06	3,5-Di*tert*butyl-4-hydroxybenzyl alcohol
29.08	Dipentaerythritol
29.13	Cyclo-octanone Indanetrione hydrate
29.14	Dichloroacetyl chloride Glycidyl methacrylate Methyl chloroacetate
29.16	*n*-Butyl glycollate
29.19	Di-*n*-butyl phenyl phosphate
29.21	4,4′-*iso*Propylidenedicyclohexyl di-(4-[1-(4-hydroxycyclohexyl)-1-methylethyl]cyclohexyl phenyl phosphite)
29.22	2-Nitroaniline Tri-*n*-butylamine
29.23	2-Amino-5,2′-dichlorobenzophenone *p*-Phenetidine *tri*Sodium nitrilotriacetate
29.25	Procainamide hydrochloride
29.31	Di-(4-hydroxyphenyl) sulphone having a melting point not less than 236° centigrade Diphenyl sulphone Hexane-1,6-dithiol

Tariff Heading	*Description*
29.32	*p*-Arsanilic acid
29.34	*O*-Ethyl phenyl ethylphosphonodithioate
29.35	Chloroquine sulphate Hypoxanthine Pyridine 5-Vinyl-2-picoline
29.36	Sulphanilamide
29.42	Theobromine
29.44	Sodium cephalothin
29.45	Sodium methoxide
30.02	Foot-and-mouth disease vaccine
38.05	Tall oil, crude
38.19	Mixed alkyl-substituted benzenesulphonic acids having an acid value not greater than 125
48.03	Genuine vegetable parchment paper of a substance not exceeding 75 grammes per square metre
73.14	Iron-nickel alloy wire, copper-clad and nickel-plated, having an overall diameter of not less than 400 micrometres and not more than 450 micrometres, the nickel plating being not less than 2 micrometres and not more than 15 micrometres in thickness; the whole containing not less than 20 per cent. by weight of copper, not less than 25 per cent. by weight of nickel and not less than 40 per cent. by weight of iron, and having, when measured on an 0·20 metre length, a percentage elongation not less than 18 and not more than 25, and a tensile strength not less than 430 newtons per square millimetre and not more than 530 newtons per square millimetre, the rate of straining being 50 millimetres per minute
81.04	Chromium, electrolytic, in the form of cathode chips, which contains not more than 0·10 per cent. by weight of total oxygen, not more than 0·015 per cent. by weight of total aluminium, and not more than 0·001 per cent. by weight of aluminium compounds insoluble in boiling 5N hydrochloric acid and in boiling fuming perchloric acid, and estimated as Al
85.18	Tantalum capacitors greater than 10 microfarads in capacitance, of a kind for incorporation in deaf aids, with a maximum length not exceeding 7 millimetres exclusive of leads and with a transverse cross section having a circumference not exceeding 14 millimetres Tantalum capacitors greater than 12 microfarads in capacitance of a working voltage of not less than 4 volts, of a kind for incorporation in deaf aids, with a maximum length not exceeding 8 millimetres exclusive of leads with a transverse cross section having a circumference not exceeding 13 millimetres Tantalum capacitors, of a kind for incorporation in deaf aids, with a maximum length not exceeding 7 millimetres exclusive of leads and with a transverse cross section having a circumference not exceeding 10 millimetres

EXPLANATORY NOTE

(This Note is not part of the Order.)

This Order provides that the goods listed in Schedule 1 shall be temporarily exempt from import duty, and those listed in Schedule 2 shall continue to be exempt from import duty, both until 1st January 1973.

STATUTORY INSTRUMENTS

1971 No. 2043

CUSTOMS AND EXCISE

The Import Duties (General) (No. 11) Order 1971

Made - - - -	16*th December* 1971
Laid before the House of Commons	17*th December* 1971
Coming into Operation	1*st January* 1972

The Lords Commissioners of Her Majesty's Treasury, by virtue of the powers conferred on them by sections 1, 2 and 13 of the Import Duties Act 1958(**a**), and of all other powers enabling them in that behalf, on the recommendation of the Secretary of State hereby make the following Order:—

1.—(1) This Order may be cited as the Import Duties (General) (No. 11) Order 1971.

(2) The Interpretation Act 1889(**b**) shall apply for the interpretation of this Order as it applies for the interpretation of an Act of Parliament.

(3) This Order shall come into operation on 1st January 1972.

2. In Schedule 1 to the Import Duties (General) (No. 7) Order 1971(**c**) (which by reference to the Customs Tariff 1959 sets out the import duties chargeable under the Import Duties Act 1958) for sub-paragraph (*b*) of sub-heading (B)(2) of heading 39.02 there shall be substituted the following:—

" (*b*) Other:

(i) Polymerisation and copolymerisation products of ethylene and of a density less than 0·940 grammes per cubic centimetre	16%	—
(ii) Polymerisation and copolymerisation products of styrene other than acrylonitrile-butadiene-styrene	16%	—
(iii) Other	10%	—".

Walter Clegg,
V. H. Goodhew,
Two of the Lords Commissioners of Her Majesty's Treasury.

16th December 1971.

EXPLANATORY NOTE

(*This Note is not part of the Order.*)

This Order increases from 10% to 16% the full rate of import duty on certain polymerisation and copolymerisation products, (1) of ethylene and of a density less than 0·940 grammes per cubic centimetre, and (2) of styrene other than acrylonitrile-butadiene-styrene, as from 1st January 1972.

(**a**) 1958 c. 6. (**b**) 1889 c. 63. (c) S.I. 1971/1971(1971 III, p. 5330).

1971 No. 2044

COMPANIES

The Companies (Accounts) Regulations 1971

Made - - -	15*th December* 1971
Laid before Parliament	23*rd December* 1971
Coming into Operation	7*th February* 1972

The Secretary of State, in exercise of his powers under section 454 of the Companies Act 1948(**a**), hereby makes the following Regulations :—

1. These Regulations may be cited as the Companies (Accounts) Regulations 1971, and shall come into operation on 7th February 1972.

2. In section 6(6) of the Companies Act 1967(**b**) the figure "£15,000" shall be substituted for the figure "£7,500".

3. In paragraph 13(A)(5) of Schedule 8 to the Companies Act 1948, the figure "£250,000" shall be substituted for the figure "£50,000".

Nicholas Ridley,
Parliamentary Under Secretary of State,
Department of Trade and Industry.

15th December 1971.

EXPLANATORY NOTE

(*This Note is not part of the Regulations.*)

These Regulations alter the requirements of the Companies Acts as to the matters to be stated in the accounts of a company which is neither a holding company nor a subsidiary. The changes are :—

(1) A company whose turnover for a period to which the accounts relate does not exceed £250,000 is not required to give particulars of its turnover. This limit was formerly £50,000.

(2) If the aggregate of directors' emoluments shown in the accounts does not exceed £15,000 particulars of the emoluments of individual directors need not be shown. This limit was formerly £7,500.

(**a**) 1948 c. 38. (**b**) 1967 c. 81.

STATUTORY INSTRUMENTS

1971 No. 2045

ANIMALS

DISEASES OF ANIMALS

The Rabies (Importation of Mammals) Order 1971

Made - - - -	15*th December* 1971
Laid before Parliament	20*th December* 1971
Coming into Operation	10*th January* 1972

The Minister of Agriculture, Fisheries and Food and the Secretary of State, acting jointly, in pursuance of the powers conferred on them by sections 1(1), 24(1), 27(1), 33(1), 77(3), 84(1)(*a*) and 85(1) of the Diseases of Animals Act 1950(**a**), as read with the Transfer of Functions (Animal Health) Order 1955(**b**), and as adapted to air transport by section 11 of the Agriculture (Miscellaneous Provisions) Act 1954(**c**), and by Schedule 2 thereto, and, as respects section 24(1) of the Diseases of Animals Act 1950, as amended by section 105(1) of the Agriculture Act 1970(**d**), and of all their other enabling powers, hereby make the following order:—

Citation, extent and commencement

1. This order (which applies to Great Britain) may be cited as the Rabies (Importation of Mammals) Order 1971, and shall come into operation on 10th January 1972.

Interpretation

2.—(1) In this order, unless the context otherwise requires, the following expressions have the meanings hereby respectively assigned to them:—

"the Act" means the Diseases of Animals Act 1950;

"animal" means an animal belonging to any family or species of the orders of mammals specified in Parts I and II of Schedule 1 to this order, other than man or an animal belonging to either the species canis familiaris or to the species felis catus of the order carnivora;

"authorised carrying agent" means a person authorised by the Minister to carry animals in accordance with the provisions of Article 9 of this order;

"authorised quarantine premises" means any premises authorised by the Minister under Article 8 of this order for the purpose of the detention and isolation of imported animals in quarantine;

"inspector" has the meaning assigned to it by section 84(4) of the Act;

"licence" means any licence granted under this order, and includes any permit, approval or other form of authorisation;

(**a**) 1950 c. 36. For change of title of the Minister see S.I. 1955/554 (1955 I, p. 1200).
(**b**) S.I. 1955/958 (1955 I, p. 1184). (**c**) 1954 c. 39. (**d**) 1970 c. 40.

"the Minister" and "the Ministry" mean respectively, in relation to England and Wales, the Minister and the Ministry of Agriculture, Fisheries and Food, and, in relation to Scotland, the Secretary of State and the Department of Agriculture and Fisheries for Scotland;

"registered medical practitioner" means a person included in the Medical Register maintained by the General Medical Council;

"veterinary surgeon" means a veterinary surgeon entered in a register maintained under section 2 of the Veterinary Surgeons Act 1966(**a**).

(2) Other expressions used in this order have, in so far as the context admits, the same meanings as in the Act.

(3) The Animals Importation Order of 1930(**b**) shall not apply to animals imported under this order.

(4) The Interpretation Act 1889(**c**) applies to the interpretation of this order as it applies to the interpretation of an Act of Parliament.

Extension of definition of "animals" for the purposes of the Act and of the Rabies Order of 1938(**d**)

3. For the purposes of the Act and of this order, and for the purposes of the Rabies Order of 1938, the definition of "animals" contained in section 84(1) of the Act is hereby extended so as to comprise any animal (other than man) belonging to any family or species of the orders of mammals specified in Parts I, II and III of Schedule 1 to this order, and shall also include any animal belonging to the species canis familiaris or to the species felis catus of the order carnivora, and Article 12 of the said order of 1938 shall be construed accordingly.

General prohibition on landing of animals

4.—(1) Subject to the provisions of this order, no animal, being an animal brought from any country outside Great Britain other than Northern Ireland, the Republic of Ireland, the Channel Islands or the Isle of Man, shall be landed in Great Britain; and accordingly, Part I of Schedule 1 to the Act (which requires animals to be slaughtered on landing) shall, except in so far as the Minister otherwise directs, apply to any such animal.

(2) For the purposes of the preceding paragraph, an animal which is taken from a place in Great Britain, Northern Ireland, the Republic of Ireland, the Channel Islands or the Isle of Man, to a place which is not situated in any of those countries (whether or not such animal is landed at such place, or comes into contact with any other animal while there, or during the journey thereto or therefrom), shall be deemed to be an animal imported from a country outside Great Britain when landed in Great Britain.

Modification of prohibition on landing of imported animals

5.—(1) Notwithstanding the provisions of Article 4 of this order, an animal to which that Article applies may, in accordance with the terms and conditions of a licence previously granted by the Minister, be landed in Great Britain without being subject to the provisions of the said Part I of Schedule 1 to the Act in the circumstances referred to in the following provisions of this order.

(**a**) 1966 c. 36. (**b**) S.R. & O. 1930/922 (Rev. II, p. 331: 1930, p. 52).
(**c**) 1889 c. 63. (**d**) S.R. & O. 1938/202 (Rev. II, p. 578: 1938 I, p. 206).

(2) Where an animal is landed in accordance with the provisions of the preceding paragraph, then, subject to the provisions of this order, Part II of Schedule 1 to the Act (which requires animals to be kept in quarantine) and paragraph 1 of Part III of the said Schedule (which, in the circumstances mentioned therein, negatives any right to compensation) shall apply to any such animal.

(3) The ports and airports which alone may be used for the landing of animals imported under this Article are the ports and airports respectively specified in Part I and Part II of Schedule 2 to this order, and for the purposes of paragraph 1 of Part II of Schedule 1 to the Act (as applied to this order), so much of any such port or airport as is from time to time set apart by the port or airport authority for the reception of animals landed from outside Great Britain shall constitute an "imported animals quarantine station":

Provided that nothing in this paragraph shall be construed as precluding the Minister, on his being satisfied that exceptional circumstances exist in connection with the importation of a particular animal, from granting a licence for the landing of such animal at a port or airport other than a port or airport specified in the said Schedule 2.

(4) Nothing in the preceding paragraph shall render it unlawful (subject to the authority of an inspector first having been obtained) for an animal to which that paragraph applies to be unloaded at a port or airport in Great Britain (other than the port or airport at which the animal is licensed to be landed) to which the vessel or aircraft, as the case may be, which is bringing the said animal to Great Britain has been ordered to be diverted in the interests of safety, or in the light of other exceptional circumstances.

(5) Article 3 of the Importation of Dogs and Cats (Amendment) (No. 2) Order 1970**(a)** (which prohibits the landing of canine and feline animals in Great Britain) and paragraph (2) of Article 4 of the Importation of Dogs and Cats (Amendment) (No. 3) Order 1970**(b)** (which continues the prohibition on landing of canine and feline animals other than domestic dogs and cats) are hereby revoked; and the Importation of Dogs and Cats (Amendment) Order 1969**(c)** and the Importation of Dogs and Cats (Amendment) (No. 1) Order 1970**(d)** shall cease to have effect in relation to animals to which this order applies.

Detention and isolation in quarantine

6.—(1) Where an animal specified in Part I of Schedule 1 to this order is landed in Great Britain under the provisions of the preceding Article, and in accordance with the terms and conditions of a licence granted thereunder, it shall, after being so landed, be immediately detained and isolated in quarantine at its owner's expense for the rest of its life, at such premises, and subject to such conditions, as may be prescribed in the licence; and in the event of any progeny of any such animal being born in Great Britain, such progeny shall be subject to the same conditions with regard to detention and isolation in quarantine for life, as if they were imported animals.

(2) Where an animal specified in Part II of Schedule 1 to this order is landed in Great Britain under the provisions of the preceding Article, and in accordance with the terms and conditions of a licence granted thereunder, it shall, after being so landed, be immediately detained and isolated in quarantine at its

(a) S.I. 1970/441 (1970 I, p. 1514).
(b) S.I. 1970/1271 (1970 II, p. 4147).
(c) S.I. 1969/1743 (1969 III, p. 5473).
(d) S.I. 1970/358 (1970 I, p. 1275).

owner's expense for six calendar months, at such premises, and subject to such conditions, as may be prescribed in the licence; and in the event of any offspring being born to any such animal during the period of its detention and isolation in quarantine, such offspring shall itself be similarly detained and isolated at its owner's expense for a period coterminous with the period applying in respect of the parent animal, or for such shorter period, and at such premises and subject to such conditions, as the Minister may in any particular case direct.

(3) The Minister may by licence permit other animals to be kept with imported animals which are being detained and isolated in quarantine in accordance with the provisions of the preceding paragraph.

(4) Where any such other animal has been in contact with an imported animal in quarantine, it shall be detained and isolated there at its owner's expense, subject to the terms and conditions of the licence, until the imported animal is released from quarantine, or for such shorter period as the Minister may in any particular case direct, and shall be treated as an imported animal for the purposes of this order.

Control of movement of animals after landing

7.—(1) Where an animal is landed at a port or airport in Great Britain under the provisions of Article 5 of this order, and in accordance with the terms and conditions of a licence granted thereunder, it shall, as soon as practicable, be moved by an authorised carrying agent to the premises specified in the licence at which it is to be detained and isolated in quarantine, and during the period of its detention and isolation in quarantine, it shall not be moved from those premises, except to other premises authorised for the purpose by the Minister, or to a vessel or aircraft for exportation, and in either case, only in accordance with the terms and conditions of a further licence granted by the Minister.

(2) The provisions of Article 6 of this order, and of the preceding paragraph, shall not apply to an animal landed at a port or airport in Great Britain which is intended to be re-exported from that port or airport within a period of 48 hours after its landing, provided that, during its stay at the port or airport, it is detained and isolated at an imported animals quarantine station.

(3) Notwithstanding the provisions of the preceding paragraph, where an animal to which it applies is, during its stay at a port or airport in Great Britain, concerned in any incident involving a human being or another animal whereby the rabies virus could, if present in the said animal, be transmitted, such animal shall not leave Great Britain (unless the Minister otherwise directs) until after it has undergone detention and isolation in quarantine at its owner's expense, at such premises, and for such period and subject to such conditions, as the Minister may direct.

Authorised quarantine premises

8.—(1) No premises shall be used for the detention and isolation in quarantine of any animal to which this order applies unless such premises have been authorised for use for the purpose by a licence granted by the Minister.

(2) A licence shall not be granted under the provisions of the preceding paragraph unless the Minister is satisfied that the premises to which the licence relates are under the supervision of a veterinary surgeon or registered medical practitioner who has been authorised in writing by him to act in that behalf, and any such authorisation may be issued for such period as may be specified therein, and given subject to such conditions as the Minister may think fit.

(3) A licence granted under the provisions of paragraph (1) of this Article shall remain in force for such period as may be specified therein, and shall be granted subject to such terms and conditions as may be so specified:

Provided that nothing in this paragraph shall preclude the Minister from revoking such a licence at any time, or from varying the terms and conditions subject to which it was granted, but without prejudice to anything lawfully done pursuant to the licence before such revocation or variation took effect.

Authorised carrying agents

9.—(1) The Minister may authorise in writing any person to act as an authorised carrying agent in connection with the movement of animals landed in Great Britain in accordance with the provisions of this order from a port or airport to authorised quarantine premises, or in connection with the subsequent movement of such animals in accordance with the said provisions during the period of their detention and isolation in quarantine, and any such authorisation may be issued for such period as may be specified therein, and given subject to such terms and conditions as may be so specified.

(2) An authorisation issued by the Minister under the provisions of the preceding paragraph, may relate generally to the movement of animals to which this order applies, or of any order or species of such animals, or to the movement of a specified animal or specified animals on an occasion or on occasions so specified.

(3) Where the Minister has, in accordance with the foregoing provisions of this Article, authorised a person to act as an authorised carrying agent, he may at any time withdraw such authorisation, or vary the terms and conditions subject to which it was given, but without prejudice to anything lawfully done pursuant to the authorisation before such withdrawal or variation took effect.

Licences

10.—(1) A licence granted by the Minister under any provision of this order shall be granted subject to such terms and conditions specified therein as, in the opinion of the Minister, are necessary or expedient for the purpose of in any manner preventing the introduction and spreading of rabies.

(2) Without prejudice to the generality of the preceding paragraph, the Minister may insert in licences granted under the provisions of this order, conditions—

(*a*) prescribing the port or airport at which the animal to which the licence relates is to be landed;

(*b*) prescribing the type of container to be used for confining the animal to which the licence relates at the time of landing, and in the course of any subsequent movement of the animal during the period of its detention and isolation in quarantine;

(*c*) prescribing the mode of transport to be used for moving the animal to which the licence relates during the period of its detention and isolation in quarantine, and the authorised carrying agent by whom it is to be transported;

(*d*) prescribing and regulating the detention and isolation in quarantine of the animal to which the licence relates, or of animals of any kind or species, in so far as the same is not prescribed and regulated by this order;

(*e*) prescribing and regulating the frequency, and the nature and scope, of the veterinary or medical inspections to which any animal detained and isolated in quarantine shall be subjected;

(*f*) prescribing the mode of isolation of the animal to which the licence relates, or of animals of a specified class or group;

(*g*) prescribing the notice to be given of the death or loss of an animal during the period of its detention and isolation in quarantine, or of any matter arising in connection with the movement, detention or isolation of the said animal, and the person by whom and to whom the notice is to be given; and

(*h*) prescribing the production of a licence granted or notice served in accordance with the provisions of this order for inspection by an officer of the Ministry or of a local authority, or by a police constable or an officer of Customs and Excise, and the taking of a copy of, or an extract from, any such licence or notice.

Records

11.—(1) The person in charge of premises authorised for the detention and isolation in quarantine of animals to which this order applies, shall adopt such system for the identification of every animal received at such premises, and shall keep such records in relation to its receipt, treatment and subsequent despatch (or death) and other matters, as may be required by the Minister, either generally, or in relation to a particular case.

(2) Every entry in such a record shall be made in ink or indelible pencil, within 36 hours of the event which is required by this Article to be recorded.

(3) Every entry in such a record shall be retained by the person whose duty it is to keep such records for a period of at least 12 months from such event, and shall be produced by him for inspection at all reasonable times on demand to an inspector, who shall be entitled to make a copy of such entry.

(4) A local authority may supply forms of record for the purposes of this Article to any person in the district of the local authority.

Detention of animals on vessels in port

12.—(1) Every animal to which this Article applies shall at all times, while on board a vessel in any port in Great Britain, be confined in an enclosed part of the vessel from which it cannot escape, and in no circumstances shall such animal be taken or be permitted to go ashore, or to come into contact with any other animal.

(2) If an animal to which this Article applies is, while on board a vessel in any port in Great Britain, concerned in any incident involving a human being or another animal whereby the rabies virus could, if present in the said animal, be transmitted, the person in charge of the animal shall forthwith give notice of such incident to an officer of the Ministry or of a local authority, or to a police constable, and the animal shall not (unless the Minister otherwise directs) leave Great Britain until after it has undergone detention and isolation in quarantine at its owner's expense, at such premises, and for such period and subject to such conditions, as the Minister may direct.

(3) If an animal to which this Article applies shall die, or be lost from a vessel in any port in Great Britain, the person in charge of the animal shall forthwith give notice of such death or loss to an officer of the Ministry or of a local authority, or to a police constable.

(4) Failure to comply with the foregoing provisions of this Article shall be an offence against the Act.

(5) The provisions of this Article shall apply to any animal which has been brought (whether directly or indirectly) from a place outside Great Britain, Northern Ireland, the Republic of Ireland, the Channel Islands or the Isle of Man, and which is not accompanied by a licence granted by the Minister authorising the landing of such animal in Great Britain.

Animals illegally landed

13.—(1) If an animal is imported into Great Britain in contravention of this order, then, subject to the powers of the Commissioners of Customs and Excise to seize, detain and forfeit the said animal under the Customs and Excise Acts, without prejudice to the provisions of Schedule 1 to the Act relating to slaughter (as applied to this order), an inspector or other officer of the Ministry may serve on any person appearing to him to have the control and custody of the said animal a notice in writing requiring him, at the expense of the owner of the animal or the person on whom the notice is served, immediately to detain and isolate the said animal, and, within the time specified in the notice, to arrange for the animal to be moved in such manner, and subject to such conditions, as may be so specified—

(*a*) to a vessel or aircraft for re-exportation; or

(*b*) to premises authorised by the Minister for the purpose of detention and isolation in quarantine for such period as may be specified in the notice.

(2) A notice served under the provisions of the preceding paragraph may require that the animal to which it relates shall be subjected to such examinations and such tests as may be specified therein.

(3) If any person on whom such a notice is served fails to comply with the requirements thereof, it shall be lawful for an inspector (without prejudice to any proceedings for an offence arising out of such default, or in relation to the illegal landing) to seize the animal to which the notice relates, and to arrange for the requirements of the notice to be complied with.

(4) A person who has failed to comply with the requirements of any such notice shall give all necessary facilities to an inspector to enable him to exercise the power conferred on him by the preceding paragraph, and the reasonable expenses incurred in the exercise of the said power shall be recoverable by the Minister as a civil debt from the owner of the animal, or from the person on whom the notice was served.

(5) Where an animal has been seized in accordance with the provisions of paragraph (3) of this Article, and has been removed to premises authorised by the Minister for the purpose of detention and isolation in quarantine, the expenses arising in connection with such detention and isolation shall be recoverable as a civil debt from the owner of the animal, or from the person on whom the notice was served, and in the event of such expenses not being met, the Minister may, without prejudice to his power of recovery, dispose of such animal in such manner as he may determine, and in determining the manner of disposal of any such animal, the Minister shall have power to require that it be slaughtered or re-exported to the country from which it was landed in Great Britain.

(6) A notice under this Article may be served in any of the ways provided for in section 77(4) and (5) of the Act.

Seizure, detention and disposal of animals found straying in ports or airports

14.—(1) Where an inspector or officer of the Ministry or of a local authority, or a police constable or officer of Customs and Excise, has reason to believe that any animal found straying in a port or airport in Great Britain has come from a place outside Great Britain, Northern Ireland, the Republic of Ireland, the Channel Islands or the Isle of Man, he shall forthwith seize the animal, and arrange for its detention and isolation in quarantine at premises authorised for the purpose, and such animal shall be detained and isolated in quarantine for such period, and subject to such conditions, as the Minister may direct.

(2) Where an animal is seized under the provisions of the preceding paragraph by an officer of a local authority, or by a police constable or officer of Customs and Excise, he shall forthwith report the action he has taken to the Ministry.

(3) Any animal seized in accordance with the provisions of paragraph (1) of this Article, shall be disposed of in such manner as the Minister may determine, and in determining the manner of disposal of any such animal, the Minister shall have power to require that it be slaughtered or re-exported to the country from which he has reason to believe it was landed in Great Britain.

(4) Where the owner or other person in charge of an animal seized in accordance with the provisions of paragraph (1) of this Article is known to the Minister, any expenses incurred by the Minister in relation to the seizure, detention and isolation of the said animal, or in relation to its disposal, shall be recoverable as a civil debt from that person, without prejudice to any proceedings arising in connection with the landing of the animal in Great Britain.

Contact animals

15.—(1) For the purposes of this Article, the expression "animal" shall be extended to mean, in relation to animals which come into contact with other animals in the circumstances described in the following paragraph, any animal (other than man) belonging to any family or species of the orders of mammals specified in Parts I, II and III of Schedule 1 to this order, and shall also include an animal belonging to the species canis familiaris or to the species felis catus of the order carnivora.

(2) Where an animal comes into contact with—

(*a*) an animal which is being detained and isolated in quarantine under the provisions of this order, or which has escaped from such detention and isolation; or

(*b*) an animal awaiting re-exportation at an imported animals quarantine station, in accordance with the provisions of paragraph (2) of Article 7 of this order; or

(*c*) an animal on board a vessel in any port in Great Britain to which Article 12 of this order applies; or

(*d*) an animal which an inspector or other officer of the Ministry or of a local authority, or a police constable or officer of Customs and Excise, has reason to believe may have been landed in Great Britain in contravention of the provisions of this order, or which has been found straying in a port or airport in Great Britain in the circumstances referred to in the preceding Article;

the Minister may inform in writing the person appearing to him to have the control and custody of the said animal of the possibility that rabies infection may have been transmitted as a result of the contact, and may serve on any such person a notice in writing requiring him to notify to the Minister the address of the place at which the animal is at present being kept, and any subsequent change of that address.

(3) A notice served in accordance with the provisions of the preceding paragraph shall remain in force for such period as may be specified therein, or until withdrawn by a further notice served as aforesaid.

Offences

16. The contravention of any provision of this order, or of any notice served or licence granted thereunder, or the failure to comply with any condition of any such notice or licence, or the causing or permitting of any such contravention or non-compliance, shall be an offence against the Act.

Local authority to enforce order

17. This order shall, except where otherwise expressly provided, be executed and enforced by the local authority.

Amendment of the Importation of Dogs and Cats Order of 1928**(a)** *and the Rabies Order of* 1938

18.—(1) Article 12 of the Importation of Dogs and Cats Order of 1928 (Interpretation) shall be amended as follows:—

(*a*) there shall be substituted for the definition of "canine animal" the following definition:—

"'canine animal' means an animal belonging to the species canis familiaris of the order of mammals carnivora;".

(*b*) there shall be substituted for the definition of "feline animal" the following definition:—

"'feline animal' means an animal belonging to the species felis catus of the order of mammals carnivora;".

(2) In Article 2 (service of isolation notices) and Article 4 (compulsory slaughter of diseased dogs and cats) of the Rabies Order of 1938, for references to "dog or cat" there shall be substituted references to "animal".

(3) Article 5 of the said order of 1938 (local authority to secure isolation of animals suspected of rabies, or having been exposed to the infection thereof) shall be amended as follows:—

(*a*) in paragraph (1) thereof, the words from "on the owner" (where they first occur) to"to the like effect)" shall be omitted, together with the word "other" in the eighth line of that paragraph;

(*b*) in paragraph (3) of the said Article, the words "dog, cat, or other" shall be omitted, and for the words "dog or cat" where they subsequently occur, there shall be substituted the word "animal".

(4) In Article 14 of the said order of 1938 (Interpretation), the definition of the expression "animal" shall be amended so as to include any animal (other than man) belonging to any family or species of the orders of mammals specified in Parts I, II and III of Schedule 1 to this order.

(a) S.R. & O. 1928/922 (Rev. II, p. 399: 1928 p. 177).

Revocation of the Exotic Animals (Importation) Order 1969**(a)**

19. The Exotic Animals (Importation) Order 1969 is hereby revoked; but notwithstanding such revocation, any licence granted under that order, and in force immediately before the coming into operation of this order, shall have effect as if granted under this order.

In Witness whereof the Official Seal of the Minister of Agriculture, Fisheries and Food is hereunto affixed on 13th December 1971.

(L.S.)

J. M. L. Prior,
Minister of Agriculture, Fisheries and Food.

Gordon Campbell,
Secretary of State for Scotland.

15th December 1971.

SCHEDULE 1

ANIMALS TO WHICH THE ORDER APPLIES

PART I

ANIMALS SUBJECT TO QUARANTINE FOR LIFE

Order		*Common names of some species* (see note below)
Chiroptera	Desmodontidae only	Vampire bats

PART II

ANIMALS SUBJECT TO 6 MONTHS' QUARANTINE

Order		*Common names of some species* (see note below)
Carnivora	All families and species except canis familiaris (domestic dog) and felis catus (domestic cat)	Jackals, foxes, wolves, bears, raccoons, coatis, pandas, otters, weasels, martens, polecats, badgers, skunks, mink, ratels, genets, civets, linsangs, mongooses, hyaenas, ocelots, pumas, cheetahs, lions, tigers, leopards

(a) S.I. 1969/1737 (1969 III, p. 5450).

Chiroptera	All families except Desmodontidae	Bats, flying foxes
Dermoptera		Flying lemurs
Edentata		Anteaters, sloths, armadillos
Hyracoidea		Hyraxes
Insectivora		Solenodons, tenrecs, otter shrews, golden moles, hedgehogs, elephant shrews, shrews, moles, desmans
Lagomorpha		Pikas, rabbits, hares
Marsupialia		Opossums, marsupial mice, dasyures, marsupial moles, marsupial anteaters, bandicoots, rat opossums, cuscuses, phalangers, koalas, wombats, wallabies, kangaroos
Primates	All families except Hominidae (Man)	Tree-shrews, lemurs, indrises, sifakas, aye-ayes, lorises, bushbabies, tarsiers, titis, uakaris, sakis, howlers, capuchins, squirrel monkeys, marmosets, tamarins, macaques, mangabeys, baboons, langurs, gibbons, great apes
Rodentia		Gophers, squirrels, chipmunks, marmots, scaly-tailed squirrels, pocket mice, kangaroo rats, beavers, mountain beavers, springhaas, mice, rats, hamsters, lemmings, voles, gerbils, water rats, dormice, jumping mice, jerboas, porcupines, cavies, capybaras, chinchillas, spiny rats, gundis

PART III

ADDITIONAL ANIMALS FOR CONTACT PURPOSES (ARTICLE 15)

Order	*Common names of some species* (see note below)
Artiodactyla	Pigs, peccaries, hippopotamuses, camels, llamas, chevrotains, deer, giraffes, pronghorns, cattle, antelopes, duikers, gazelles, goats, sheep
Monotremata	Echidnas, duck-billed platypuses
Perissodactyla	Horses, asses, zebras, tapirs, rhinoceroses
Pholidota	Pangolins
Proboscidea	Elephants
Tubulidentata	Aardvarks

NOTE: Some of the common names of animals included in this Schedule are set out opposite the appropriate reference. The list is for guidance only and does not form part of the order.

SCHEDULE 2

Ports and Airports at which Authorised Landings of Animals may take Place

Part I

Ports

Bristol (Avonmouth)
Dover
Leith
Harwich
Hull
Liverpool
London (including Tilbury)
Southampton

Part II

Airports

Birmingham
Heathrow } London
Gatwick } London
Manchester
Prestwick
Southend

EXPLANATORY NOTE

(This Note is not part of the Order.)

For purposes connected with the prevention of the introduction of rabies into Great Britain this order extends the application of the Diseases of Animals Act 1950 to the ten orders of mammals (excluding man and domestic dogs and cats) prescribed in Part I and Part II of Schedule 1. In respect of such animals, the order imposes a general prohibition on their importation (otherwise than from Northern Ireland, the Republic of Ireland, the Channel Islands and the Isle of Man), and thereby in general requires any such animals which are brought to Great Britain from overseas in contravention of such prohibition to be slaughtered on landing.

However, the Minister of Agriculture, Fisheries and Food, in relation to England and Wales, and the Secretary of State, in relation to Scotland, are given power to allow such animals into the country in accordance with the terms and conditions of a licence previously granted, but, except in exceptional circumstances, they may only be landed at prescribed ports and airports from which they must be moved without delay in accordance with the terms of the licence to authorised quarantine premises.

The order provides for the majority of the animals to which it applies to be detained and isolated in quarantine for a period of at least six months after landing, but in the case of vampire bats, their entry into the country is only permitted on the basis of their being quarantined for life.

The order also contains detailed provisions relating to the movement of animals during quarantine, the licensing of carrying agents and of quarantine premises, the control of animals (including the additional orders of mammals specified in Part III of Schedule 1) which have come into contact with imported animals, the action to be taken in relation to illegally landed animals or animals found straying in ports and airports, and other ancillary matters.

The order replaces the Exotic Animals (Importation) Order 1969, which is accordingly revoked, together with certain provisions of the Importation of Dogs and Cats (Amendment) (No. 2) and (No. 3) Orders 1970 relating to the importation of canine and feline animals other than domestic dogs and cats. In addition, the order provides that the Importation of Dogs and Cats (Amendment) Order 1969 and the Importation of Dogs and Cats (Amendment) (No. 1) Order 1970 shall cease to have effect in relation to animals to which it applies.

Finally, the Rabies Order of 1938 is amended so that its provisions will now apply to all of the animals covered by the present order, whilst an amendment to the Importation of Dogs and Cats Order of 1928 restricts its application to domestic dogs and cats.

The order applies to Great Britain.

1971 No. 2046

JURIES

The Jurors' Allowances (No. 2) Regulations 1971

Made - - - *15th December* 1971
Coming into Operation *1st January* 1972

The Lord Chancellor, in exercise of the powers conferred on him by section 1 of the Juries Act 1949(**a**), as amended by section 1 of the Juries Act 1954(**b**) and section 36 of the Courts Act 1971(**c**), and with the consent of the Treasury, hereby makes the following Regulations :—

1. These Regulations may be cited as the Jurors' Allowances (No. 2) Regulations 1971 and shall come into operation on 1st January 1972.

2.—(1) In these Regulations any reference to a juror shall include a reference to a person who, in obedience to a summons to serve on a jury, attends for service as a juror notwithstanding that he is not subsequently sworn and any reference to service as a juror shall be construed accordingly.

(2) In these Regulations the expression "the Act" means the Juries Act 1949, as amended by the Juries Act 1954 and the Courts Act 1971.

(3) The Interpretation Act 1889(**d**) shall apply to the interpretation of these Regulations as it applies to the interpretation of an Act of Parliament.

3. The travelling allowance to which a juror is entitled under section 1 of the Act shall be in accordance with the rates set out in the Schedule hereto.

4.—(1) The subsistence allowance to which a juror is entitled under section 1 of the Act shall be calculated in accordance with paragraphs (2) and (3) of this regulation.

(2) In respect of any period other than a period in respect of which a subsistence allowance is payable under paragraph (3) of this regulation, the subsistence allowance shall be—

(*a*) if the period on any one day during which a juror is necessarily absent from his place of residence, business or employment for the purpose of serving as a juror does not exceed four hours, 45p in respect of that day ;

(*b*) if the said period on any one day exceeds four hours but does not exceed eight hours, 95p in respect of that day ;

(*c*) if the said period on any one day exceeds eight hours, but does not exceed twelve hours, £1·75 in respect of that day ;

(**a**) 1949 c. 27.
(**b**) 1954 c. 41.
(**c**) 1971 c. 23.
(**d**) 1889 c. 63.

(*d*) if the said period on any one day exceeds twelve hours but does not exceed sixteen hours, £2·50 in respect of that day ;

(*e*) if the said period on any one day exceeds sixteen hours, £2·95 in respect of that day.

(3) If a juror is necessarily absent from his place of residence overnight for the purpose of serving as a juror, the subsistence allowance shall be £5·50 in respect of each period of twenty-four hours or fraction thereof during which he is so absent overnight.

5. The compensation for loss of earnings which a juror would otherwise have made, or additional expense (other than expense on account of travelling or subsistence) to which he would not otherwise have been subject, to which he is entitled under section 1 of the Act, shall be the amount of the said loss or additional expense :

Provided that the amount payable under this Regulation to a person in respect of his services as a juror on any one day shall not exceed—

(*a*) where the period of time over which the earnings are lost or additional expense is incurred does not exceed four hours, the sum of £2·37½ ; or

(*b*) where the said period of time exceeds four hours, the sum of £4·75 ;

except that, where in obedience to a summons to serve on a jury he has served as a juror on more than ten days and the court so directs, the amount so payable in respect of his services as a juror in obedience to the same summons on any one day after the tenth such day may exceed the sum specified above but shall not exceed £9·50.

6. The Jurors' Allowances Regulations 1971(**a**) are hereby revoked except in so far as they apply to service as a juror at a coroner's court.

Dated 14th December 1971.

Hailsham of St. Marylebone, C.

We consent,

Dated 15th December 1971.

Tim Fortescue,
V. H. Goodhew,
Two of the Lords Commissioners
of Her Majesty's Treasury.

(**a**) S.I. 1971/136 (1971 I, p. 315).

SCHEDULE

Regulation 3

TRAVELLING ALLOWANCE

1. Where a person travels by railway or other public conveyance, the allowance shall be the amount of the fare actually paid:

Provided that, unless for a special reason the court otherwise directs, only the amount of the second class fare shall be allowed for travel by railway.

2. Where a person travels by a hired vehicle, the allowance shall be—

(*a*) in a case of urgency or where no public service is reasonably available, the amount of the fare and any reasonable gratuity paid ; and

(*b*) in any other case, the amount of the fare for travel by the appropriate public services.

3. Where a person travels by private conveyance, the allowance shall—

(*a*) in any case where the use of a private conveyance results in a substantial saving of time or is otherwise reasonable, be at a rate not exceeding—

(i) in the case of a vehicle of engine capacity not exceeding 1000 c.c., 3½p a mile each way ;

(ii) in the case of a vehicle of engine capacity exceeding 1000 c.c. but not exceeding 1750 c.c., 4½p a mile each way ;

(iii) in the case of a vehicle of engine capacity exceeding 1750 c.c., 5p a mile each way ; and

(*b*) in any other case, be at a rate not exceeding 2p a mile each way.

EXPLANATORY NOTE

(*This Note is not part of the Regulations.*)

These Regulations revoke and replace the existing Jurors' Allowances Regulations except in so far as they apply to service as a juror at a coroner's court which is covered by regulations made by the Home Secretary. The only changes of substance are the increases in compensation for loss of earnings under Regulation 5. The Lord Chancellor is made responsible for making the Regulations by section 36(2) of the Courts Act 1971.

STATUTORY INSTRUMENTS

1971 No. 2047

PENSIONS

The Circuit Judges' Superannuation (Transitional) Rules 1971

Made - - - -	14*th December* 1971
Laid Before Parliament	22*nd December* 1971
Coming into Operation	1*st January* 1972

The Lord Chancellor, in exercise of the powers conferred on him by section 16 of, and paragraph 9(2) of schedule 2 to, the Courts Act 1971**(a)**, and with the consent of the Minister for the Civil Service, hereby makes the following Rules:—

1.—(1) These Rules may be cited as the Circuit Judges' Superannuation (Transitional) Rules 1971 and shall come into operation on 1st January 1972.

(2) In these Rules, unless the context otherwise requires—

"the Act" means the Courts Act 1971;

"benefits" means superannuation benefits payable to a person who has held judicial office;

"specified office" means any of the judicial offices specified in paragraph 1(2) of schedule 2 to the Courts Act 1971.

(3) The Interpretation Act 1889**(b)** shall apply to the interpretation of these Rules as it applies to the interpretation of an Act of Parliament.

2. These Rules shall apply where—

(*a*) any person becomes a Circuit judge by virtue of having held a specified office; and

(*b*) a pension or derivative benefit becomes payable to, or in respect of, that person under section 19 of the Act; and

(*c*) the period of that person's service which falls to be taken into account in determining the amount of that pension or derivative benefit, includes, by virtue of paragraph 9(1) of schedule 2 to the Act, service in the specified office; and

(*d*) the period of that person's service as a Circuit judge, disregarding any period of service taken into account by virtue of paragraph 9(1) of schedule 2 to the Act, is less than fifteen completed years.

(a) 1971 c. 23. **(b)** 1889 c. 63.

3. In any case where these Rules apply, the Crown shall be entitled to recover from the authority which, before 1st January 1972, was responsible, directly or indirectly, for meeting the whole or any part of the cost of the superannuation benefits payable to or in respect of former holders of the specified office, a contribution which bears to the total amount of benefits payable the same proportion as the period of the person's service in the specified office bears to the total period of service in respect of which benefits are payable:

Provided that the amount of any contribution so recoverable shall not exceed the amount of any contribution which would have been payable by the authority under Rule 7(2) of the Superannuation (Judicial Offices) Rules 1970(**a**) had the person made an election under those Rules.

Dated 14th December 1971.

Hailsham of St. Marylebone, C.

Consent of the Minister for the Civil Service given under his Official Seal on 14th December 1971.

(L.S.)

K. H. McNeill,
Authorised by the
Minister for the Civil Service.

EXPLANATORY NOTE

(*This Note is not part of the Rules.*)

These Rules provide for the recovery by the Crown of contributions towards the cost of superannuation benefits payable to certain Circuit judges. Such contributions are recoverable, in the circumstances defined in rule 2, from the authorities responsible for meeting the cost of benefits payable to former holders of offices listed in paragraph 1(2) of schedule 2 to the Courts Act 1971.

(**a**) S.I. 1970/1021 (1970 II, p. 3171).

1971 No. 2048

POLICE

The Police Authorities (Appointment of Magistrates) Rules 1971

Made - - -	15*th December* 1971
Coming into Operation	1*st January* 1972

In exercise of the powers conferred on me by section 2(4) of the Police Act 1964(**a**), I hereby make the following Rules :—

Citation and commencement

1. These Rules may be cited as the Police Authorities (Appointment of Magistrates) Rules 1971 and shall come into operation on 1st January 1972.

Revocations

2. The Police Authorities (Appointment of Magistrates) Rules 1964(**b**) are hereby revoked.

Interpretation

3.—(1) In these Rules any reference to an enactment is a reference to that enactment as amended by any subsequent enactment.

(2) In these Rules any reference to an appointment in accordance therewith, or with any provision thereof, shall be construed as including a reference to an appointment made before 1st January 1972 in accordance with the Rules revoked by these Rules or, as the case may be, with the corresponding provision thereof.

(3) The Interpretation Act 1889(**c**) shall apply for the interpretation of these Rules as it applies for the interpretation of an Act of Parliament.

Appointments to police committee for a county

4.—(1) The members of a police committee for a county to be appointed by the magistrates for the county, in pursuance of section 2(2) of the Police Act 1964 and in accordance with a scheme made thereunder by the magistrates' courts committee (hereinafter referred to as "the county scheme"), shall be appointed at least seven days before the appropriate date in the year in which the appointments are to take effect.

(2) A member of a police committee appointed in accordance with this Rule shall serve thereon from the appropriate date in the year in which his appointment takes effect until the appropriate date in such one of the three following years as the county scheme may provide ; and in determining the

(**a**) 1964 c. 48.
(**b**) S.I. 1964/1556 (1964 III, p. 3502).
(**c**) 1889 c. 63.

term of an appointment, the magistrates' courts committee shall have regard to the term for which members of the police committee appointed by the council of the county serve thereon.

(3) In this Rule the expression "the appropriate date" means, in relation to a particular year, the date in that year of the annual meeting of the council of the county.

Appointments to watch committee for a borough

5.—(1) The members of a watch committee for a borough to be appointed by the magistrates for the borough, in pursuance of section 2(3) of the Police Act 1964, shall be appointed at the meeting of the magistrates held for the purpose of electing a chairman of the bench, in accordance with rules made under section 13 of the Justices of the Peace Act 1949(**a**), in the year preceding that in which the appointments are to take effect.

(2) A member of a watch committee appointed in accordance with this Rule shall serve thereon from the appropriate date in the year in which his appointment takes effect until the appropriate date in the next following year.

(3) In this Rule the expression "the appropriate date" means, in relation to a particular year, the date in that year of the annual meeting of the council of the borough.

Casual vacancies

6.—(1) If a casual vacancy occurs on a police committee for a county or on a watch committee for a borough among the members appointed in accordance with these Rules, whether through death, resignation or otherwise, then, unless it is determined in accordance with the county scheme or by the magistrates for the borough that it is not necessary so to do, an appointment shall be made as soon as is practicable to fill the vacancy.

(2) A member of a police committee or of a watch committee appointed in accordance with this Rule shall serve thereon for the period for which the member he replaces would have served had the vacancy not occurred and nothing in Rule 4 or 5 shall apply in relation to such an appointment.

Supplementary provisions

7.—(1) If, by reason that the council of the county or borough have not determined the number of persons comprising the police committee or, as the case may be, the watch committee or of other circumstances, appointments to a police committee or watch committee, in accordance with these Rules, are not made when they would otherwise be made, those appointments shall be made as soon as is practicable thereafter.

(2) If the council of the county or borough determine that the number of persons comprising the police committee or, as the case may be, the watch committee shall be varied as from a specified date—

(*a*) additional appointments to the committee may be made, or

(*b*) any appointment to the committee made in accordance with these Rules may be terminated,

(**a**) 1949 c. 101.

as the circumstances may require, in either case with effect from the specified date in accordance with the county scheme or by the magistrates for the borough at any meeting; and, subject as aforesaid, in the case of such an additional appointment these Rules shall apply as if the appointment were made in accordance with Rule 4 or, as the case may be, Rule 5 of these Rules.

(3) Where an appointment to a watch committee falls to be made or terminated in accordance with these Rules by the magistrates for the borough nominations shall be permitted, but where voting is necessary it shall be by ballot and there shall be no disclosure how any magistrate voted:

Provided that where any magistrates receive an equal number of votes and the addition of a vote would result in the appointment of one of them being made or terminated, the clerk to the magistrates shall forthwith decide between those magistrates by lot and the magistrate on whom the lot falls shall be deemed to have received an additional vote.

R. Maudling,
One of Her Majesty's Principal Secretaries of State.

Home Office,
Whitehall.
15th December 1971.

EXPLANATORY NOTE

(This Note is not part of the Rules.)

These Rules make provision as respects the time, manner and term of appointment of magistrates to county and county borough police authorities. They supersede the Police Authorities (Appointment of Magistrates) Rules 1964 with effect from 1st January 1972.

As from that date, appointments of magistrates to a county police authority will, by virtue of section 53(5) of the Courts Act 1971 (c. 23), fall to be made in accordance with a scheme made by the magistrates' courts committee for the county instead of by the court of Quarter sessions. The Rules take account of this change.

1971 No. 2050

SOCIAL SECURITY

The National Insurance (Collection of Graduated Contributions) Amendment Regulations 1971

Made - - - -	16*th December* 1971
Laid before Parliament	6*th January* 1972
Coming into Operation	6*th April* 1972

The Secretary of State for Social Services, in conjunction with the Treasury and with the concurrence of the Commissioners of Inland Revenue, in exercise of powers under sections 11(3), 14(1), 15, 74(2) and 95(12) of the National Insurance Act 1965**(a)**, and of all other powers enabling him in that behalf, after considering the report of the National Insurance Advisory Committee on the preliminary draft submitted to them in accordance with section 108 of that Act, hereby makes the following regulations:—

Citation, interpretation and commencement

1. These regulations, which may be cited as the National Insurance (Collection of Graduated Contributions) Amendment Regulations 1971, shall, unless the context otherwise requires, be read as one with the National Insurance (Collection of Graduated Contributions) Regulations 1970**(b)** (hereinafter referred to as "the principal regulations") and shall come into operation on 6th April 1972.

Amendment of regulations 1(2) *and* 5(2) *of the principal regulations*

2. In regulations 1(2) and 5(2) of the principal regulations for the word "Schedule" there shall be substituted the word "Schedules".

Amendment of regulation 2 *of the principal regulations*

3. In regulation 2 of the principal regulations (collection and recovery of graduated contributions)—

(1) for the word "Schedule" there shall be substituted the word "Schedules";

(2) after the reference to the Income Tax (Employments) Regulations 1965, as amended there shall be added the words "and of the Income Tax (Employments) (No. 6) (Seamen) Regulations 1970**(c)**".

(a) 1965 c. 51.
(b) S.I. 1970/1770 (1970 III, p. 5763).
(c) S.I. 1970/1142 (1970 II, p. 3878).

Amendment of Schedule to the principal regulations and revocation of Part V of that Schedule

4. In the Schedule to the principal regulations (provisions of the Income Tax (Employments) Regulations 1965 as they apply to graduated contributions)—

(1) for the heading "SCHEDULE" there shall be substituted the heading "SCHEDULE 1";

(2) in regulations 19(1), 26(1), 27(1) and (5), 28(1), 29(2)(*c*) and 32(4) after the words "Regulation 13", "Regulation 26", or, as the case may be "Regulation 28" there shall be inserted the words "of this Schedule";

(3) in regulation 29(6)—

(*a*) after the words "Regulation 28" where they first appear there shall be inserted the words "of this Schedule";

(*b*) for the words "Regulation 28" where they next appear there shall be substituted the words "that Regulation".

(4) Part V (special provisions applicable to seamen) is hereby revoked.

Addition of Schedule 2 to the principal regulations

5. After Schedule 1 to the principal regulations there shall be added the provisions set out in the Schedule to these regulations.

Signed by authority of the Secretary of State for Social Services.

Paul Dean,
Parliamentary Under Secretary of State,
Department of Health and Social Security.

10th December 1971.

Tim Fortescue,
V. H. Goodhew,
Two of the Lords Commissioners of
Her Majesty's Treasury.

14th December 1971.

The Commissioners of Inland Revenue hereby concur.
By Order of the Commissioners of Inland Revenue.

A. H. Dalton,
Secretary.

16th December 1971.

Regulation 5

SCHEDULE

SCHEDULE SUBSTITUTED FOR PART V OF SCHEDULE TO THE NATIONAL INSURANCE (COLLECTION OF GRADUATED CONTRIBUTIONS) REGULATIONS 1970

Regulation 2

SCHEDULE 2

CONTAINING THE PROVISIONS OF THE INCOME TAX (EMPLOYMENTS) (NO. 6) (SEAMEN) REGULATIONS 1970 AS THEY APPLY TO GRADUATED CONTRIBUTIONS

Interpretation

2.—(3) In this Schedule unless the context otherwise requires—

"employer" includes the master of a ship;

"Schedule 1" means Schedule 1 to these Regulations;

"seaman" means any person—

(*a*) who has signed the agreement with the crew of a ship to which any determination of the National Maritime Board relating to remuneration applies, not being a member of Her Majesty's naval, military or air forces or a person in the employment of the British Railways Board; or

(*b*) who being the holder of a British Seaman's Identity Card or of a British Seaman's Card to which he is lawfully entitled is employed to work on a ship;

and for the purpose of this definition—

(i) where the crew of a ship are engaged at a place outside the United Kingdom on terms which adopt any determination of the National Maritime Board relating to remuneration, that ship shall be deemed to be a ship to which that determination applies if the determination would have applied to the ship if the crew had been engaged in the United Kingdom;

(ii) where an arrangement has been made for the purposes of deduction of tax from the emoluments of persons resident in the United Kingdom who are employed or engaged in sea-going service in any foreign ship, those persons shall be deemed to be seamen; and

(iii) an apprentice or cadet whose name is entered on the agreement with the crew shall be deemed to be a person who has signed the agreement.

2A. Subject to the provisions of the preceding paragraph the provisions contained in Part I of Schedule 1 shall apply also to the provisions of this Schedule.

Deduction of graduated contributions from seamen's emoluments

4.—(1A) Subject to the provisions of regulation 11 of this Schedule, Parts II and III of Schedule 1 shall not apply in the case of a seaman and every employer, on making any payment of a seaman's emoluments, may deduct graduated contributions therefrom in accordance with the provisions of this Schedule.

(2A) An employer shall not be entitled to recover any graduated contributions paid or to be paid by him on behalf of any seaman otherwise than by deduction in accordance with the provisions of this Schedule.

(3A) On the occasion of the payment of any seaman's emoluments there may be deducted therefrom the amount, if any, of the graduated contributions based thereon which the seaman is liable to pay under those provisions of Part I of the Act which relate to graduated contributions or under those provisions as modified by Part II of the National Insurance (Mariners) Regulations 1967 (**a**) as amended (**b**) (which modifies the statutory provisions in relation to graduated contributions for a seaman).

(**a**) S.I. 1967/386 (1967 I, p. 1294).
(**b**) S.I. 1969/1277; 1970/46, 507 (1969 III, p. 3811; 1970 I, p. 243, 1713).

(4A) If by reason of an error made in good faith the employer, on making any payment of emoluments to a seaman, fails to deduct therefrom the full amount of graduated contributions which by virtue of the provisions of this Schedule he is entitled to deduct, he may recover the amount so underdeducted by deduction from any subsequent payment of emoluments to that employee during the same year:

Provided that—

(*a*) the amount which may be deducted by virtue of the provisions of this paragraph from any payment shall be in addition to but shall not exceed the amount deductible therefrom under the other provisions of this Schedule; and

(*b*) for the purposes of Part IV of Schedule 1 and of Regulations 6 and 8 of this Schedule an additional amount which may be deducted by virtue of the provisions of this paragraph shall be treated as an amount deductible under the provisions of this Schedule only in so far as the amount of the corresponding underdeduction has not been so treated.

Payment of graduated contributions to Collector

6. All amounts of graduated contributions which are deductible from any payment of emoluments under the provisions of this Schedule, together with an equal amount by way of employer's graduated contributions, shall be paid to the Collector within the time limited for the payment of income tax, if any, deductible from that payment of emoluments or, if income tax is not so deductible, the time which would be so limited if income tax were so deductible.

Return to be rendered by employer

7. Every employer who makes any payment of emoluments to a seaman shall, within the time laid down in Regulation 6 of this Schedule for the payment of the graduated contributions, if any, which are deductible therefrom, render a return to the Collector in such form as may be authorised by the Commissioners of Inland Revenue showing as regards every payment of emoluments which he makes to the seaman—

(*a*) the seaman's name;

(*b*) the seaman's rank or rating and discharge book number;

(*c*) the seaman's National Insurance number;

(*d*) the total emoluments paid to the seaman by the employer for the period in respect of which the payment of emoluments is made;

(*e*) the number of employer's contributions which the employer is liable to pay under section 3 of the Act (which provides for the payment of weekly employer's contributions) in respect of the seaman for the period in respect of which the payment of emoluments is made;

(*f*) the total amount of graduated contributions which may be deducted from the emoluments otherwise than under paragraph (4A) of Regulation 4 of this Schedule.

Application of Part IV of Schedule 1

8.—(1) The provisions of Part IV of Schedule 1 shall apply in relation to seamen subject to any necessary modifications and in particular to the modifications set out in the following paragraphs of this Regulation.

(2) Paragraph (1) of Regulation 26 of Schedule 1 shall apply as if—

(*a*) for the reference to payment of graduated contributions within 14 days of the end of every income tax month there were substituted a reference to payment of graduated contributions within the time limited in Regulation 6 of this Schedule; and

(*b*) the words "other than amounts deductible by virtue of the proviso to paragraph (1) of Regulation 13 of this Schedule which he did not deduct" were omitted; and

(*c*) the proviso were omitted.

(3) Regulation 27 of Schedule 1 shall not apply, but the following provisions shall have effect where the employer fails to pay to the Collector within the time limited in Regulation 6 of this Schedule any amount of graduated contributions which he is liable under this Schedule to pay to the Collector, that is to say—

(*a*) the production of the return made by the employer under Regulation 7 of this Schedule shall be sufficient evidence that the amount of graduated contributions shown in that return as deductible by the employer is one half of the amount which the employer is liable to pay to the Collector; and

(*b*) if the amount of graduated contributions shown as deductible in the said return differs from the amount which the employer was entitled to deduct from the payments specified therein under the provision of this Schedule, a certificate of the Collector as to the amount properly deductible shall be sufficient evidence that that amount, and not the amount shown in the said return, is one half of the amount which the employer is liable to pay to the Collector; and any document purporting to be such a certificate as aforesaid shall be deemed to be such a certificate until the contrary is proved.

(4) Regulation 29 of Schedule 1 shall not apply in the case of seamen.

Seamen to whom this Schedule shall not apply

11. Notwithstanding the preceding regulations in this Schedule where, under Regulation 11 of the Income Tax (Employments) (No. 6) (Seamen) Regulations 1970 the Commissioners of Inland Revenue have approved arrangements agreed with an employer in respect of all or some of his employees for the purpose of applying with or without modification the provisions of Parts II, III and IV of the Income Tax (Employments) Regulations 1965(**a**) and in consequence the provisions of the Income Tax (Employments) (No. 6) (Seamen) Regulations 1970 do not apply in respect of those employees, the foregoing provisions of this Schedule shall not apply in respect of them either and the provisions of Parts II, III and of Part IV of Schedule 1 shall, subject to any modifications which may be specified in the said arrangements, apply instead.

EXPLANATORY NOTE

(*This Note is not part of the Regulations.*)

These Regulations revoke Part V of the Schedule to the National Insurance (Collection of Graduated Contributions) Regulations 1970 and replace it in a slightly amended form by a Schedule 2.

That Schedule sets out the provisions of the regulations dealing with the collection and recovery of Income Tax under Pay As You Earn in respect of seamen as modified to apply for the purposes of graduated contributions. In it have been made the consequential amendments necessitated by the making of the Income Tax (Employments) (No. 6) (Seamen) Regulations 1970 which revoked and re-enacted in slightly amended form Part V of the Income Tax (Employments) Regulations 1965.

As in the regulations revoked, the regulations in Schedule 2 are numbered non-consecutively, so that those provisions of the Income Tax (Employments) (No. 6) (Seamen) Regulations 1970, applied or adapted, retain for graduated contributions purposes the numbers which they bear in the regulations last mentioned above.

An amendment of substance is made in regulation 11 of the new Schedule 2, corresponding to a similar provision of the Income Tax (Employments) (No. 6)

(**a**) S.I. 1965/516 (1965 I, p. 1321).

(Seamen) Regulations 1970. Under regulation 11 Parts II, III and IV of Schedule 1 can be applied in certain circumstances instead of the provisions of Schedule 2.

The report of the National Insurance Advisory Committee on the preliminary draft of these Regulations dated 21st October 1971 is contained in Command Paper (Cmnd. 4844) published by Her Majesty's Stationery Office.

1971 No. 2051 (S.217)

BUILDING AND BUILDINGS

The Building Standards (Relaxation by Buildings Authorities) (Scotland) No. 2 Regulations 1971

Made - - - -	13*th* *December* 1971
Laid before Parliament	31*st* *December* 1971
Coming into Operation	14*th* *February* 1972

In exercise of the powers conferred on me by section 4(2) of the Building (Scotland) Act 1959**(a)** as substituted by section 2(1) of the Building (Scotland) Act 1970**(b)**, and of all other powers enabling me in that behalf, I hereby make the following regulations:—

PART I—GENERAL

Citation and commencement

1. These regulations may be cited as the Building Standards (Relaxation by Buildings Authorities) (Scotland) No 2 Regulations 1971 and shall come into operation on 14th February 1972.

Revocation and general savings

2.—(1) The Building Standards (Relaxation by Buildings Authorities) (Scotland) Regulations 1971**(c)** are hereby revoked.

(2) Anything whatsoever done under or by virtue of any regulation revoked by these regulations shall be deemed to have been done under or by virtue of the corresponding provision of these regulations and anything whatsoever begun under any such regulation may be continued under these regulations as if begun under these regulations.

(3) So much of any document, drawing or plan as refers expressly to any regulation revoked by these regulations shall, if and so far as the context permits, be construed as referring to the corresponding provision of these regulations.

(4) Nothing in paragraphs (2) and (3) of this regulation shall be taken as affecting the general application by regulation 3(3) of these regulations of the rules for the construction of Acts of Parliament contained in section 38 of the Interpretation Act 1889**(d)** (effect of repeal) with regard to the effect of revocations.

(a) 1959 c. 24.
(b) 1970 c. 38.
(c) S.I. 1971/745 (1971 II, p. 2067).
(d) 1889 c. 63.

Interpretation

3.—(1) In these regulations unless the context otherwise requires:—

"the Act" means the Building (Scotland) Act 1959 as read with the Building (Scotland) Act 1970;

"buildings authority" has the meaning assigned to it by section 1 of the Act;

"buildings standards regulations" means the regulations referred to in section 3(1) of the Act and for the time being in force;

"change of use" has the meaning assigned to it by section 29 of the Act;

"local authority" has the meaning assigned to it by section 29 of the Act.

(2) Any reference in these regulations to any enactment shall, unless the context otherwise requires, be construed as a reference to that enactment as amended applied or extended by or under any subsequent enactment.

(3) References in these regulations to any occupancy sub-group shall be construed as a reference to the occupancy sub-group within the meaning of regulation A6 of the building standards regulations.

(4) The Interpretation Act 1889 shall apply for the interpretation of these regulations as it applies for the interpretation of an Act of Parliament.

PART II—DELEGATION OF POWER TO RELAX THE BUILDING STANDARDS REGULATIONS

Alteration, extension or change of use of buildings built or approved before 1964

4.—(1) This regulation shall apply to an application made under section 4(1)(*a*) of the Act for a direction dispensing with or relaxing a provision of the building standards regulations in the case of a particular building which was erected or an approval for the erection of which was granted prior to 15th June 1964.

(2) The power to dispense with or relax any provision of the building standards regulations shall be exercisable by a buildings authority instead of by the Secretary of State as regards any provision of Parts D, E, F, G, H, J, K, L, M, P, Q, R or S of the building standards regulations in relation to the alteration or extension or change of use of that particular building:

Provided that this regulation shall not apply where the alteration or extension results—

(*a*) in the case of a particular building within occupancy sub-group A1 or A2, in an increase of more than 50 cubic metres or 10 per cent of the cubic capacity of the building whichever is the greater, or

(*b*) in the case of a particular building within any occupancy sub-group other than sub-group A1 or A2, in an increase of more than 2,800 cubic metres or 20 per cent of the cubic capacity of the building whichever is the less.

(3) The reference in this regulation to cubic capacity shall be taken to be a reference to cubic capacity calculated or measured in accordance with the provisions of Schedule 1 to the building standards regulations.

Erection of buildings ancillary to houses built or approved before 1964

5.—(1) This regulation shall apply to an application made under section 4(1)(*a*) of the Act for a direction dispensing with or relaxing a provision of the building standards regulations in the case of a particular building the use of which is ancillary to the occupancy use of a building in occupancy sub-group A1 or A2 which was erected or an approval for the erection of which was granted prior to 15th June 1964.

(2) The power to dispense with or relax any provision of the building standards regulations shall be exercisable by a buildings authority instead of by the Secretary of State as regards any provision of Parts D, E, F, G, H, J, K, L, M, P, Q, R or S of the building standards regulations in relation to the erection of that particular building.

Disapplication of regulations

6. Nothing in these regulations shall apply—

(*a*) to any application made by a local authority, or

(*b*) where any application for a warrant under section 6 of the Act is referred to the Secretary of State under section 6A of the Act.

Gordon Campbell,
One of Her Majesty's Principal
Secretaries of State.

St Andrew's House,
Edinburgh.
13th December 1971.

EXPLANATORY NOTE

(*This Note is not part of the Regulations.*)

These Regulations, made under the Building (Scotland) Acts 1959 and 1970, revoke and re-enact with certain amendments the Building Standards (Relaxation by Buildings Authorities) (Scotland) Regulations 1971. The principal amendment extends the power of buildings authorities to dispense with or relax provisions of the building standards regulations in relation to the alteration or extension or change of use of a particular building to include not only existing dwelling houses covered by the revoked regulations but also all other existing buildings built or approved before 15th June 1964. The regulations also empower buildings authorities to dispense with or relax provisions of the building standards regulations in relation to the erection of buildings which are ancillary to houses built or approved before 15th June 1964. The delegation extends to any provision covered by Parts D, E, F, G, H, J, K, L, M, P, Q, R or S of the building standards regulations.

STATUTORY INSTRUMENTS

1971 No. 2052 (S.218)

BUILDING AND BUILDINGS

The Building Standards (Scotland) (Consolidation) Regulations 1971

Made - - - 13*th December* 1971

Laid before Parliament 19*th January* 1972

Coming into Operation 9*th February* 1972

ARRANGEMENT OF REGULATIONS

**Note:* Throughout these regulations, the presence of an asterisk against the heading to a regulation denotes that one of the specifications in Schedule 10 is deemed to satisfy a provision of that regulation.

Part C

Structural Strength and Stability

Regulation

C 1. Interpretation of Part C.
C 2.* Foundation and structure above foundation.
C 3.* Further requirements for the structure of certain buildings.
C 4. Loading notices.

Part D

Structural Fire Precautions

D 1. Application of Part D.
D 2. Interpretation of Part D.
D 3. Provision of fire division walls and compartment floors.
D 4. Provision of separating walls and floors.
D 5. Requirements as to fire resistance.
D 6. Requirements as to non-combustibility.
D 7. Additional requirements for fire division walls.
D 8. Additional requirements for separating walls.
D 9. Additional requirements for separating floors and compartment floors.
D10. Protection of service and ventilation ducts and pipes.
D11. Protection of lifts.
D12. Protection of stairways not forming part of an exit and escalators.
D13. Fire-stops in elements of structure of hollow construction.
D14. Connection of elements.
D15. Timber on outer face of external walls.
D16. Special provision as to pends.
D17. Distance of side of building from boundary.
D18. Roofs.
D19. Application for warrant for more than one building.
D20.* Special provisions as to certain groups of garages.
D21. Special provisions as to certain small garages and carports.
D22. Special provisions as to garden huts, greenhouses and other buildings ancillary to houses.
D23.* Fuel oil storage tanks.

Part E

Means of Escape from Fire and Assistance to Fire Service

E 1. Application of Part E.
E 2. Interpretation of Part E.
E 3. Provision of exits.
E 4. Number of exits.
E 5. Travel distance in relation to exits.
E 6. Requirements as to exits.
E 7. Width of exits.
E 8. Width of stairways in exits.
E 9. Enclosure of stairways.
E10. Lobby approach stairways.
E11. Construction of ramps.

Regulation

PART F

CHIMNEYS, FLUES, HEARTHS AND THE INSTALLATION OF HEAT PRODUCING APPLIANCES

Solid Fuel and Oil Burning Appliances

Gas Burning Appliances

Appliances of a High Rating

General

Regulation

PART L

DAYLIGHTING AND SPACE ABOUT HOUSES

PART M

DRAINAGE AND SANITARY APPLIANCES

PART N

ELECTRICAL INSTALLATIONS

Regulation

PART P

PREVENTION OF DANGER AND OBSTRUCTION

PART Q

HOUSING STANDARDS

PART R

ASHPITS AND DUNGSTEADS

Part S

Construction of Stairways, Landings and Balconies

11. Levels of sound insulation in houses.
12. Mechanical ventilation of buildings—rate of fresh air supply.
13. Assumed reflection factors of surfaces in rooms.
14. Minimum distance (in metres) between window openings.
15. Daylighting—minimum width of window openings.
16. Daylighting—percentage additions to window opening widths according to type of window installed.
17. Standards of housing accommodation.
18. Space standards for houses.

SCHEDULE 10

Deemed-to-satisfy specifications.

SCHEDULE 11

General specifications for preparation of sites and resistance to the passage of moisture.

In exercise of the powers conferred on me by sections 3 and 24 of, and the Fourth Schedule to, the Building (Scotland) Act 1959(**a**) as amended by the Building (Scotland) Act 1970(**b**) and of all other powers enabling me in that behalf, I hereby make the following regulations—

PART A

GENERAL

CITATION AND COMMENCEMENT

Citation and Commencement

A1. These regulations which may be cited as the Building Standards (Scotland) (Consolidation) Regulations 1971 shall come into operation on 9th February 1972.

REVOCATION AND GENERAL SAVINGS

Revocation and General Savings

A2.—(1) The Building Standards (Scotland) (Consolidation) Regulations 1970(**c**), the Building Standards (Scotland) Amendment Regulations 1971(**d**), the Building Standards (Scotland) Amendment No. 2 (Metrication) Regulations 1971(**e**) and the Building Standards (Scotland) Amendment No. 3 Regulations 1971(**f**) are hereby revoked.

(2) Anything whatsoever done under or by virtue of any regulation revoked by these regulations shall be deemed to have been done under or by virtue of the corresponding provision of these regulations and anything whatsoever begun under any such regulation may be continued under these regulations as if begun under these regulations.

(3) So much of any document, drawing or plan as refers expressly or by implication to any regulation revoked by these regulations shall, if and so far as the context permits, be construed as referring to the corresponding provision of these regulations.

(4) Nothing in paragraphs (2) and (3) of this regulation shall be taken as affecting the general application by regulation A3(11) of these regulations of the rules for the construction of Acts of Parliament contained in section 38 of the Interpretation Act 1889(**g**) (effect of repeal) with regard to the effect of revocations.

(**a**) 1959 c. 24.
(**b**) 1970 c. 38.
(**c**) S.I. 1970/1137 (1970 II, p. 3635).
(**d**) S.I. 1971/748 (1971 II, p. 2153).
(**e**) S.I. 1971/1032 (1971 II, p. 3013).
(**f**) S.I. 1971/1811 (1971 III, p. 4936).
(**g**) 1889 c. 63.

General Interpretation

Interpretation

A3.—(1) In these regulations—

"the Act" means the Building (Scotland) Acts 1959 and 1970;

"agriculture", "agricultural land" and "agricultural unit" shall have the same meanings as in the Agriculture (Scotland) Act 1948(**a**);

"apartment" has the meaning assigned to that expression by regulation A5;

"appliance" has the meaning assigned to that expression by regulation F2;

"balustrade" has the meaning assigned to that expression by paragraph (1) of regulation S2;

"basement storey" has the meaning assigned to that expression by paragraph (9) of this regulation;

"block of flats" means a building which contains two or more flats and which consists of two or more storeys exclusive of any storey which is constructed for use for purposes other than those of a dwelling; so, however, that where part of such a building is so separated from another part by a vertical wall that no access (other than an access provided only for fire escape purposes) can be obtained from one part to the other, each part shall for the purposes of these regulations be taken to be a block of flats;

"boundary" has the meaning assigned to that expression by regulation A4(2);

"building" means any structure or erection of what kind or nature soever, whether temporary or permanent, and every part thereof, including any fixture affixed thereto, not being a structure or erection or part thereof consisting of, or ancillary to—

(*a*) any road, whether public or private, including in the case of a public road (but not in the case of a private road) any bridge on which the road is carried;

(*b*) any sewer or water main which is, or is to be, vested in a public authority;

(*c*) any aerodrome runway;

(*d*) any railway line;

(*e*) any large reservoir within the meaning of the Reservoirs (Safety Provisions) Act 1930(**b**); or

(*f*) any telegraphic line as defined in section 2 of the Telegraph Act 1878(**c**),

and includes any prospective building; and in relation to the extension, alteration or change of use of a building any reference to the building shall be construed as a reference only to so much of the building as is comprised in the extension or is the subject of alteration or change of use as the case may be;

"caravan" has the same meaning as in the Caravan Sites and Control of Development Act 1960(**d**);

"carport" means a building used for the storage of a motor vehicle or vehicles and having a roof and having or being bounded by not more than two walls over 1·2 metres in height;

"cavity wall" means a wall constructed of two or more leaves with a continuous cavity;

(**a**) 1948 c. 45.
(**b**) 1930 c. 51.
(**c**) 1878 c. 76.
(**d**) 1960 c. 62.

"chalet" means a house which is used and occupied—

(*a*) only for holiday or recreational purposes, and

(*b*) not as a permanent dwelling;

"change of use", in relation to a building, means such change in the use or occupation of the building as will bring it within a class of building to which these regulations apply, or, if it is already within such a class, within a class to which additional or more onerous provisions of these regulations apply, and "change the use" shall be construed accordingly;

"chimney" means a structure, not being a flue-pipe, enclosing one or more flues and includes any opening therein for the accommodation of an appliance, but does not include any chimney can thereon;

"chimney stack" means that part of a chimney which rises above a roof of the building of which it forms part and includes any cope thereon, but does not include any chimney can thereon;

"column" means an isolated loadbearing member whose greatest overall dimension, measured in the horizontal plane, is not more than four times the least overall dimension so measured;

"compartment", in relation to a building or division of a building, means a part of the building, or of the division, separated from the remainder of the building or division by a compartment floor or floors;

"compartment floor" means a floor complying with the provisions of Part D relating to compartment floors and separating a compartment of a building or of a division from the remainder of the building or division;

"construct" includes alter, erect, extend and fit, and "construction" shall be construed accordingly;

"cross-sectional area" in relation to—

(*a*) an opening, ventilator or duct means the unobstructed area of the smallest louvre or grill located within the opening, ventilator or duct;

(*b*) a flue means the smallest cross-sectional area within that flue;

"damp-proof course" means a layer or layers of material impervious to moisture so constructed as to prevent the passage of moisture;

"division", in relation to a building, means any part of the building separated from the remainder of the building by a fire division wall or walls;

"element of structure" means an element which falls within one of the following descriptions—

(*a*) a member forming part of a structural frame or other beam or column, not being a member forming part of a roof structure only;

(*b*) a floor, not being the lowest floor of a building;

(*c*) a fire division wall or separating wall;

(*d*) an internal wall supporting any other structural element in respect of which a standard of fire resistance is prescribed under these regulations;

(*e*) an external wall;

(*f*) any door, shutter, duct enclosure or access cover in respect of which a standard of fire resistance is prescribed under these regulations;

"fire division wall" means a wall complying with the provisions of Part D relating to fire division walls and separating a division of a building from the remainder of the building;

"flat" means a separate and self-contained set of premises, whether or not on the same floor, constructed for use for the purposes of a dwelling and forming part of a building from some other part of which it is divided horizontally;

"flat roof" means a roof whose slope does not exceed 10 degrees from the horizontal;

"foundation" means that part of the structure in direct contact with and transmitting loads to the ground;

"ground storey" has the meaning assigned to that expression by paragraph (9) of this regulation;

"house" includes any part of a building, being a part which is occupied or intended to be occupied as a separate dwelling, and in particular includes a flat;

"instantaneous water heater" means an appliance designed to burn only gaseous fuel and to heat water, having no storage capacity for water therein;

"kitchen" has the meaning assigned to that expression by regulation A5;

"land in different occupation" has the meaning assigned to that expression by regulation A4;

"land in the same occupation" has the meaning assigned to that expression by regulation A4;

"living room" has the meaning assigned to that expression by regulation A5;

"non-combustible" in relation to a material means that the material is either—

(*a*) graded as non-combustible according to the combustibility test of materials specified in clauses 3 and 4 of British Standard 476: Part 1: 1953, "Fire tests on building materials and structures", or

(*b*) classified as non-combustible according to the non-combustibility test for materials specified in British Standard 476: Part 4: 1970, "Non-combustibility test for materials",

and "combustible" shall be construed accordingly;

"occupant capacity" has the meaning assigned to that expression by regulation A7;

"office premises" has the same meaning as in section 1 of the Offices, Shops and Railway Premises Act 1963(**a**);

"open access balcony", in relation to a house, means a balcony giving access to any house or common service area having therein an opening or openings to the external air, which, excluding any structural columns, extend throughout the length and to an aggregate of more than one-third of the height of the balcony;

"passage", in relation to a part of a building, means a part of the building used solely as a means of passage and in particular includes a corridor, lobby or vestibule;

"permanent ventilator" means a permanent ventilation opening which permits an uninterrupted passage of air between a part of a building and the external air either directly or by means of a duct of a length not exceeding 2 metres;

"pier" means a loadbearing member which forms an integral part of a wall and whose width is not more than four times its thickness, including the thickness of the wall;

"pitch line" has the meaning assigned to that expression by paragraph (1) of regulation S2;

(**a**) 1963 c. 41.

"public road" means a road maintainable by the Secretary of State, a county council or a town council, and "private road" means a road not so maintainable whether it comprises a public right of way or not;

"reasonably practicable", in relation to the carrying out of any operation, means reasonably practicable having regard to all the circumstances including the expense involved in carrying out the operation;

"road" includes street and any pavement, footpath, drain, ditch or verge at the side of a road or street;

"roof space" means any space in a building between a part of the roof of the building and the ceiling next below that part;

"room" means any enclosed part of a storey of a building intended for human occupation, not being a part of a storey used solely as a bathroom, washroom, watercloset, stairway or passage, or, where the storey is not divided into separate rooms, means a whole storey excluding any part thereof used solely as aforesaid;

"separating wall" and "separating floor" mean respectively a wall or floor complying with the provisions of Part D relating to separating walls or floors and separating—

(*a*) any two adjoining buildings, or parts of one building, occupied or intended to be occupied by different persons, or

(*b*) any two adjoining buildings, or parts of one building, in different occupancy groups, or

(*c*) any two adjoining parts of one building, where one part is in single occupation and the other is communally occupied;

"shop premises" has the same meaning as in section 1 of the Offices, Shops and Railway Premises Act 1963;

"site", in relation to a building, means the area of ground covered or to be covered by the building, including its foundations;

"socket outlet" means a fixed device containing metal contacts for the purpose of connecting to a supply of electricity the corresponding metal contacts of a plug attached to any current using appliance; and

"multiple socket outlet" means a fixed device containing metal contacts for the purpose of connecting to a supply of electricity the corresponding metal contacts of two or more plugs each of which is attached to a current using appliance;

"storage water heater" means an appliance designed to burn only gaseous fuel and to heat water, having storage capacity for water therein;

"storey" has the meaning assigned to that expression by paragraph (9) of this regulation;

"sun porch" means any glazed structure, not being an apartment or part of an apartment or kitchen, attached to the external walls of a house, and having a roof (excluding the glazing bars) constructed entirely of glass or other translucent material;

"temporary building" means a building intended to have a life not exceeding that specified in regulation A11, that is to say, five years;

"tread" has the meaning assigned to that expression by paragraph (1) of regulation S2;

"upper storey" has the meaning assigned to that expression by paragraph (9) of this regulation;

"utility room" has the meaning assigned to that expression by regulation A5;

"washroom" means any enclosed part of a storey used solely for ablutionary purposes, not being a bathroom ;

"watercloset" means an enclosed part of a storey which has a fixed receptacle for excremental matter connected to a drainage system with provision for flushing the receptacle from a piped supply of water either by the operation of mechanism or by automatic action and includes a urinal or a room combining a watercloset and a bathroom ;

"water service pipe" means so much of any pipe for supplying water from a main to any premises as is subject to water pressure from that main or would be so subject but for the closing of some stop valve, stopcock or tap.

(2) Where in these regulations any meaning is assigned to an expression such meaning shall have effect for the purposes of these regulations only where the context does not otherwise require.

(3) In these regulations, unless the contrary intention appears, words in the singular shall include the plural and words in the plural shall include the singular.

(4) Any reference in these regulations to a British Standard or a British Standard Code of Practice shall be construed as a reference to a British Standard Specification or a British Standard Code of Practice published under authority of the General Council of the British Standards Institution.

(5) Where a British Standard or a British Standard Code of Practice or any other publication referred to in these regulations or in the Schedules to these regulations itself refers to a British Standard or to a British Standard Code of Practice or to any other publication, the reference to such British Standard or to such British Standard Code of Practice or to any other such publication shall be taken to be a reference to the latest edition thereof as at 31st December 1970 including any amendments thereto published at that date.

(6) Any reference in these regulations to a height, area, cubic capacity or other dimension shall, unless the context otherwise requires, be taken to be a reference to a height, area, cubic capacity or other dimension as the case may be, calculated or measured in accordance with the provisions of Schedule 1.

(7) Any reference in these regulations to a value specified in a Table is a reference to the appropriate value shown in that Table having regard to the conditions and other matters by reference to which the Table sets forth different values.

(8) Any reference in these regulations to a Part, regulation or Schedule shall be construed as a reference to a Part or regulation of, or Schedule to these regulations and any reference to a numbered Table shall be construed as a reference to a Table in Schedule 9 to these regulations.

(9) Any reference in these regulations to a storey of a building shall be construed as meaning that part of the building which is situated between the top of any floor and the top of the floor next above it or, if there be no floor above it, that portion between the top of such floor and the ceiling above it (any mezzanine floor being taken to be a separate storey and any open work floor, gallery or catwalk being taken to be part of the storey in which it is situated); and in relation to the storeys of a building—

(*a*) the ground storey shall be taken as the storey in which there is situated an entrance to the building from the level of the adjoining ground or, if there be more than one such storey, the lower or lowest of these ;

(*b*) a basement storey shall be taken to be any storey of the building which is below the level of the ground storey ;

(*c*) an upper storey shall be taken to be any storey of the building which is above the level of the ground storey.

(10) The provisions of these regulations shall be without prejudice to the provisions of any local enactment continued in force by any Order made by the Secretary of State under section 30(2) of the Act.

(11) The Interpretation Act 1889 shall apply for the interpretation of these regulations as it applies for the interpretation of an Act of Parliament.

Land in different occupation

A4.—(1) Any reference in these regulations to land in different occupation in relation to a building shall, subject to regulation L2(2), be taken as a reference to land occupied or to be occupied by a person other than the occupier of the land on which the building has been erected or is to be erected, and any reference to land in the same occupation shall be construed accordingly :

Provided that in relation to the land on which the building has been or is to be erected, none of the following descriptions of land shall be treated as land in different occupation, that is to say—

(i) that portion of any road, access way, river or stream adjacent to the land, but only to the centre line thereof ;

(ii) that portion of any common, public open space, loch, lake or pond adjacent to the land ;

(iii) any portion of the foreshore or area of the sea adjacent to the land.

(2) Any reference in these regulations to a boundary in relation to a building shall, subject to regulations D2(1) and L2(1), be construed as a reference to the boundary between land in the same occupation as the building and land in different occupation.

(3) In this regulation—

"common" includes any town or village green ;

"occupier", in relation to any house on land to which this regulation applies, means the person inhabiting the house, and "occupation" shall be construed accordingly ;

"public open space" includes any land laid out as a public garden or used for the purpose of public recreation or as a burial ground or land being a disused burial ground.

Rooms in houses

A5.—(1) In these regulations the following expressions used to describe rooms forming part of a house shall have the meanings hereby assigned to them respectively—

"apartment" means any habitable room, not being a kitchen ;

"kitchen" means any room used or intended to be used for the preparation or cooking of food ;

"living room", in relation to a house containing two or more apartments, means—

(*a*) where there is in the house one apartment which is neither used nor intended to be used for sleeping, that apartment ;

(*b*) where there is in the house more than one such apartment, the larger or the largest of these apartments ;

(c) where there is in the house no such apartment, the larger or largest apartment ;

"utility room" means any room other than an apartment, kitchen or laundry.

(2) In a room, as defined in regulation A3, where areas thereof are used or intended to be used as any combination of the following, namely, kitchen, utility room or living room, each such area shall be deemed to be a separate room for the purposes of Parts K, L and Q.

Classification of buildings by occupancy

A6.—(1) For the purposes of these regulations buildings shall be classified according to the grouping and sub-grouping of occupancy use set forth in Schedule 2.

(2) Any reference in these regulations to a building or part of a building of a particular occupancy group or sub-group shall, unless the context otherwise requires, be taken to include a reference to any building or part of a building which is put to a use ancillary to any occupancy use falling within the description specified in relation to that occupancy group or sub-group by column (3) of Schedule 2.

(3) Any occupancy use which falls within any of the numbered heads of classification of industry set forth in column (4) of Schedule 2 shall be deemed to form part of the relevant occupancy sub-group—

(a) the reference to numbered heads of classification of industry being a reference to the heads set forth in the Standard Industrial Classification issued by the Central Statistical Office in September 1968, and

(b) any such reference shall include that part of the numbered head appropriate to that occupancy sub-group.

(4) Where any building or any part of a building falls within more than one occupancy sub-group and as a result is required to conform to more than one standard prescribed in any provision of these regulations, that provision shall have effect in relation to the building, or part, as the case may be, as if the building or part were required to conform to the more or most onerous standard :

Provided that no account shall be taken for the purposes of this paragraph of the occupancy use of any part of a building which is separated from the remainder of the building by a separating wall, fire division wall, compartment floor or separating floor or any combination of these.

(5) Where a building or part of a building does not fall into any occupancy group or sub-group the provisions of these regulations shall have effect as if the most onerous requirement applicable to any occupancy group or sub-group applied.

Occupant capacity

A7.—(1) Any reference in these regulations to the occupant capacity of a room or storey shall, subject to regulation E4, be construed as a reference to the number of persons which the room or storey is, for the purposes of these regulations, to be taken as capable of holding, that is to say—

(a) in the case of any part of a storey comprising a flat, the occupant capacity specified in Table 1 ;

(b) in the case of a room or storey of a description mentioned in Table 2, the number obtained by dividing the area in square metres of the room or storey by the occupant load factor specified in column (2) of that Table ;

(*c*) in the case of any other room or storey, the number of persons the room or storey is designed to hold.

(2) Any reference in these regulations to the occupant capacity of a building shall be construed as a reference to the aggregate of the occupant capacities of the rooms or storeys comprised within the building calculated in accordance with paragraph (1) of this regulation.

(3) In calculating the area of any room, storey or flat for the purposes of this regulation there shall be excluded the area of any bathroom, washroom, watercloset or stairway.

Classification of roofs

A8. Any reference in these regulations to a roof or part of a roof of a specified designation, being one of the following designations—

AA	BA	CA	DA
AB	BB	CB	DB
AC	BC	CC	DC
AD	BD	CD	DD

shall, subject to regulation D18(5), be construed as a reference to a roof or part of a roof of a construction which complies with the tests set out in respect of that designation of roof in British Standard 476: Part 3: 1958, "External fire exposure roof tests" as read with Amendment PD 3276, February 1959.

Application

Exempted classes and fixtures for the fitting of which no warrant required

A9.—(1) Subject to the following provisions of these regulations, these regulations shall apply to every building other than a building every part of which falls into one of the exempted classes specified in Schedule 3.

(2) For the purposes of the proviso to section 6(1) of the Act (which provides that nothing in that subsection—which requires warrant to be obtained for the alteration of a building—shall apply to any operations for the alteration of a building which consist solely of the fitting of a fixture of any such kind as may be prescribed) there are prescribed the kinds of fixtures set forth in Schedule 4.

Exclusion from specification in section 11 notices

A10. The provisions of these regulations, so far as they relate to premises in respect of which a licence has been granted under section 2 of the Cinematograph Act 1909(**a**), shall not be subject to specification in a notice served under section 11 of the Act (which enables local authorities to require existing buildings to conform to these regulations).

General

Buildings having a short life

A11. For the purposes of section 3(3)(*b*) of the Act (which enables special provisions to be made in these regulations for buildings intended to have a life not exceeding such period as may be specified) a period of five years is specified.

(**a**) 1909 c. 30.

Deemed-to-satisfy specifications

A12.—(1) Where any element of structure or other part of a building or any fitting affixed thereto specified in the second column of Schedule 10 consists of materials of such type or is constructed by such method as to conform with one of the specifications set forth in relation thereto in the fourth column of that Schedule (but only in the case, or subject to the conditions if any, set out in the third column of that Schedule) the element of structure, part or fitting shall be deemed to satisfy the provisions of the regulation set out in relation thereto in the first column of that Schedule.

(2) Nothing in any specification in Schedule 10 which is deemed to satisfy any provision of these regulations shall be taken to prohibit the use of any other material, component, design, method of construction or operation or any combination of these which satisfies that provision.

(3) Any reference in this regulation to a specification set forth in the fourth column of Schedule 10 shall include a reference to such of the general specifications set forth in Schedule 11 as are referred to in that specification.

PART B

MATERIALS AND DURABILITY

**Selection and use of materials*

B1. All materials used in the construction of any building to which these regulations apply shall be—

(*a*) of a suitable quality and of suitable properties for the purposes for which they are used, and

(*b*) sufficiently resistant to deterioration and wear having regard to the conditions to which they will be subjected and, in the case of a temporary building, to the intended life of the building, and

(*c*) properly prepared, and

(*d*) so applied, fixed or otherwise used that those parts of the building in which they are used attain the standards prescribed in these regulations:

Provided that nothing in this regulation shall prevent the use of a material which does not comply with paragraph (*b*) of this regulation—

(i) where the material can achieve a sufficient standard of durability by added protection, if the material is given such protection as its nature and the conditions to which it will be subjected require, and, where periodic maintenance or renewal of the protective work is necessary, is used only in a position where the protected work will be readily accessible for inspection and maintenance or renewal, or

(ii) where the material itself is readily accessible for inspection and maintenance or renewal,

and in either case such maintenance or renewal is reasonably practicable.

PART C

STRUCTURAL STRENGTH AND STABILITY

Interpretation of Part C

C1. In this Part—

"dead load", in relation to a building, means the weight of all walls, partitions, floors and roofs comprised in the building, including the weight of all other fixed construction therein and any service equipment affixed to the building as a fixture;

"imposed load", in relation to a building, means all static and dynamic loads imposed on the building, and includes floor loads, roof loads other than from wind, wind loads, crane and traffic loads and any load, other than dead load, which will be imposed on the building as a result of the intended use thereof.

**Foundation and structure above foundation*

C2.—(1) The foundation of every building shall be taken down to such a depth and shall be so designed and constructed as to sustain and transmit to the ground the combined dead load and imposed load, in such a manner that the total or differential settlement of the building will not impair the stability of, or cause damage to, the whole or any part of the building.

(2) The structure of a building above the foundation thereof shall be so designed and constructed as to sustain and transmit to the foundation the combined dead load and imposed load, without such deflection or deformation as would impair the stability of, or cause damage to, the whole or any part of the building.

(3) For the purposes of this regulation the dead load and imposed load other than wind loads shall be taken to be the loads calculated on the basis of the recommendations of British Standard Code of Practice CP 3: Chapter V: Part 1: 1967 "Dead and imposed loads" as read with Amendments AMD 141, November 1968 and AMD 587, September 1970:

Provided that in calculating such loads, where under Table 1 of the Code a use to which a building or structure is to be put requires an intensity of distributed load of 1·5 kilonewtons per square metre, the concentrated load referred to in the Table may not be included in the calculation in the case of—

(i) timber floors having joists arranged at 450 millimetres centres supporting 21 millimetres thick flooring or a floor arrangement which will support the same concentrated load as such floors;

(ii) ceiling joists arranged at 450 millimetres centres over which is placed a timber walkway for access purposes comprising a 200 millimetres width of 21 millimetres thick tongued and grooved flooring or a ceiling joist arrangement which will support the same concentrated load as such ceiling joists.

(4) For the purposes of this regulation the wind load shall be taken to be the loads calculated on the basis of the recommendations of British Standard Code of Practice CP 3: Chapter V: Part 2: 1970 "Wind loads" as read with Amendment AMD 645, November 1970.

(5) For the purposes of this regulation where it is known in any case that the actual dead load, imposed load or wind load to which a building will be subject will differ or is likely to differ from the dead load, imposed load or wind load calculated in accordance with this Part, such actual dead load, imposed load or wind load as the buildings authority may in the circumstances determine shall be substituted for the load so calculated.

**Further requirements for the structure of certain buildings*

C3.—(1) In addition to the requirements of regulation C2, the provisions of this regulation shall apply to a building having five or more storeys (including basement storeys, if any).

(2) In this regulation—

"portion", in relation to a structural member, means that part of a member which is situated or spans between adjacent supports or between a support and the extremity of a member:

Provided that, in the case of a wall, a portion shall be taken to have a length which is the lesser of the following, namely, the length determined in accordance with the preceding provisions of this definition or 2·25 times the height of the portion (or, if its height varies, its greatest height);

"structural failure" means the failure of a structural member fully to perform its function in contributing to the structural stability of the building of which it forms part;

"structural member" means a member essential to the structural stability of a building.

(3) In the application of this regulation—

(*a*) dead load and imposed load other than wind load shall be determined in accordance with the provisions of regulations C2(3) and C2(5) except that—

(i) a reduction of not more than 66⅔ per cent in the imposed load other than wind load shall be permitted on all structural members provided that no reduction shall be made for any plant, machinery or equipment which is specifically allowed for nor shall a reduction be made for warehouses, garages or buildings used wholly or predominantly for filing or storage. In the case of factories or workshops the load shall not be reduced below 5 kilonewtons per square metre; and

(ii) for the purposes of paragraph (5) of this regulation the maximum reductions permitted by sub-paragraph (i) above shall be made;

(*b*) wind load may be taken as not less than one-third of the load determined in accordance with the provisions of regulations C2(4) and C2(5); and

(*c*) the load which would cause structural collapse shall exceed the combined dead load and imposed load on the structure together with, for the purposes of paragraph (5) of this regulation, the loads specified in sub-paragraphs (*b*) and (*c*) of that paragraph by at least 5 per cent.

(4) A building to which the provisions of this regulation apply shall be so constructed that if any portion of any one structural member (other than a portion which satisfies the conditions specified in paragraph (5) of this regulation) were to be removed—

(*a*) structural failure consequent on that removal would not occur within any storey other than the storey of which that portion forms part, the storey next above (if any) and the storey next below (if any); and

(*b*) any structural failure would be localised within each such storey.

(5) The conditions referred to in paragraph (4) of this regulation are that the portion should be capable of sustaining without structural failure the following loads applied simultaneously—

(*a*) the combined dead load and imposed load;

(*b*) a load of 34 kilonewtons per square metre applied to that portion from any direction; and

(*c*) the load, if any, which would be directly transmitted to that portion by any immediately adjacent part of the building if that part were subjected to a load of 34 kilonewtons per square metre applied in the same direction as the load specified in sub-paragraph (*b*).

Loading notices

C4.—(1) In any building with a floor supporting an imposed floor load of

2·5 kilonewtons per square metre or greater there shall be exhibited conspicuously at each stairway or doorway giving access to such a floor a notice incised or embossed in letters and figures not less than 13 millimetres high, stating in the following terms, or in terms substantially to the like effect, the imposed floor load for which the floor has been designed—

"NOTICE

The imposed load on [this floor]* [the floor to which this stairway gives access]* must not exceed kilogrammes per square metre.

**Delete as appropriate*":

Provided that where different parts of such a floor have been designed for different imposed loads, a notice complying with this paragraph shall be displayed on each such part stating the load for which that part has been designed.

(2) (*a*) Where any part of the roof of a building is not capable of supporting a concentrated load of 0·9 kilonewtons per 130 millimetres square, there shall be exhibited at some appropriate and conspicuous place visible from any access to that part of the roof a notice in permanent form in letters not less than 50 millimetres high in the following terms—

"DANGER

This roof covering will not support your weight".

(*b*) No such notice shall be required for flat roofs having joists arranged at 450 millimetres centres and supporting 21 millimetres thick timber boarding.

PART D

STRUCTURAL FIRE PRECAUTIONS

Application of Part D

D1.—(1) The provisions of this Part, other than the provisions of regulations D3 to D17 so far as they relate to buildings under head (*b*) of occupancy sub-group E1 or of occupancy sub-group E2, shall not be subject to specification in a notice served under section 11 of the Act (which enables local authorities to require existing buildings to conform to these regulations).

(2) The provisions of regulations D3 to D18, unless specifically provided for by regulation D20, D21, D22 or D23 shall not apply to—

(*a*) any garage to which regulation D20 or D21 applies, any carport to which regulation D21 applies, or any building to which regulation D22 applies;

(*b*) a building comprising only a tank for the storage of fuel oil, or erected solely for housing such a tank, being a tank or building to which regulation D23 applies.

Interpretation of Part D

D2.—(1) In this Part—

"boundary", in relation to any external wall or side of a building, means any part of the boundary within the meaning of regulation A4(2) on the same side of the building as the wall or side, being a part which is either parallel to the wall or side or at an angle with the wall or side of not more than 80 degrees;

"fire-stop" means—

(*a*) a barrier in a cavity, or

(*b*) a seal at the junction of two faces, or

(*c*) a packing between a cable, pipe or duct or a shaft enclosing a duct and any floor or wall through which it passes,

so formed and positioned as to prevent or retard the passage of smoke or flame, and "fire-stopped" shall be construed accordingly;

"opening", in relation to an external wall or side of a building, means a window, door or other aperture in the wall or side, so, however, that—

(*a*) any part of an external wall or side which has a fire resistance less than that required for the wall by this Part, or

(*b*) any part of an external wall which has attached or applied to its external face combustible material of a thickness of more than 1 millimetre, whether for cladding or for any other purpose,

shall for the purposes of this Part be treated as an opening.

(2) Any provision of this Part requiring that an element of structure shall have a fire resistance for a specified period shall be construed as a requirement that the element of structure shall either—

(*a*) in the conditions of test set out in column (3) of Table 5 in relation to the element, be capable of satisfying such of the three requirements of clause 11 of British Standard 476: Part 1: 1953, "Fire tests on building materials and structures" as are so set out in the said column (3), or

(*b*) be of such materials and construction as are stated in Table 3 in relation to that element to have a notional fire resistance for a period not less than the period so specified,

so, however, that nothing in Table 3 shall be taken to prohibit the use of any other material or any other form of construction which has a fire resistance for a period not less than the period so specified.

(3) (*a*) Any beam which is built into and forms part of a floor for which these regulations prescribe a fire resistance shall for the purposes of this Part be taken to be part of the floor.

(*b*) Any column which is built into a wall for which these regulations prescribe a fire resistance and does not project beyond either face of the wall shall for the purposes of this Part be taken to be part of the wall.

Provision of fire division walls and compartment floors

D3.—(1) Subject to the following provisions of this regulation, where—

(*a*) the cubic capacity of a building exceeds that specified in column (4) of Table 4, or

(*b*) the area of any storey of a building exceeds that set forth in column (5) of that Table,

the building shall be so divided by fire division walls or compartment floors that—

(i) the cubic capacity of each division of the building or of each compartment does not exceed that specified in column (4) of Table 4, and

(ii) the area of any storey within a division does not exceed that set forth in column (5) of that Table.

(2) Where the height of a building exceeds 15 metres the building shall be so split up into compartments that—

(*a*) the height of the lowest compartment (irrespective of the number of storeys contained therein) does not exceed 15 metres, and

(*b*) the height of the compartment next above the lowest (irrespective of the number of storeys contained therein) does not exceed 9 metres, and (*c*) the height of any other compartment in the building does not exceed 6 metres:

Provided that nothing in this paragraph shall apply to—

(i) a building comprising only one storey;

(ii) a building consisting of a theatre, cinema, music hall, concert hall, exhibition hall, non-residential school or place of public worship;

(iii) a building for the storage or parking of motor vehicles;

(iv) that part of a building comprising a stairway enclosure provided so as to comply with regulation E9 or a lift enclosure.

(3) There shall in every building be provided such fire division walls and compartment floors as are necessary to comply with regulation D11 and Part E.

Provision of separating walls and floors

D4. Between—

(*a*) any two adjoining buildings, or parts of one building, occupied or intended to be occupied by different persons, or

(*b*) any two adjoining buildings, or parts of one building, in different occupancy groups, or

(*c*) any two adjoining parts of one building, where one part is in a single occupation and the other is communally occupied,

there shall be provided a wall (in these regulations referred to as a "separating wall") which complies with regulations D5, D6 and D8 or, as the case may be, a floor (in these regulations referred to as a "separating floor") which complies with regulations D5, D6 and D9:

Provided that where a building comprises two or more garages each of an area not more than 40 square metres, nothing in this regulation shall require the provision of a separating wall between any two adjacent garages in that building.

Requirements as to fire resistance

D5.—(1) Every element of structure of a building and every part of an exit by way of a flat roof permitted in terms of the proviso to regulation E6(1) shall comply with the following provisions of this regulation as to fire resistance:

Provided that paragraphs (2) and (3) of this regulation shall not apply to—

(i) any structural frame or other beam or column in a single storey building;

(ii) any internal loadbearing wall, being neither a fire division wall nor a separating wall, in a single storey building;

(iii) any part of an external wall which is under regulation D2 treated as an opening for the purposes of this Part.

(2) The element of structure shall throughout its whole extent have a fire resistance not less than the appropriate period specified in Table 6 by reference to column (4) of Table 5.

(3) Where the element of structure forms part of more than one building, division or compartment so that more than one requirement is specified for that element in Table 6, the foregoing paragraph shall have effect as if the higher or highest of these requirements was the requirement so specified.

(4) The element of structure shall, in any event, have a fire resistance for a period not less than that required under this regulation for any part of the structure of the building to which it gives support.

(5) In this regulation and in Table 6, any reference to the building, division or compartment in relation to an element of structure of a building means—

(*a*) where the building is neither divided into divisions nor split up into compartments, the building;

(*b*) where the building is divided into divisions, each division of which the element forms part (not being a division which is split up into compartments);

(*c*) where the building or the division of the building is split up into compartments, each compartment of which the element forms part:

Provided that nothing in sub-paragraph (*c*) of this paragraph shall apply to any requirement in Table 6 based on the height of a division or of a building.

Requirements as to non-combustibility

D6. In every building the following shall be constructed of non-combustible materials—

(*a*) any floor which is a compartment floor or separating floor;

(*b*) any separating wall;

(*c*) any fire division wall which forms a stairway enclosure provided so as to comply with regulation E9 or which separates a lift shaft from the remainder of the building so as to comply with regulation D11;

(*d*) any part of an external wall which is not more than 1 metre from the boundary;

(*e*) any stair forming part of an exit for the purposes of Part E, not being a stairway wholly within a flat;

(*f*) the floor of any landing or passage within a stairway enclosure provided so as to comply with regulation E9;

(*g*) any stair or balcony or the floor of any landing where such stair, balcony or landing forms part of the access to a house provided so as to comply with regulation Q2:

Provided that nothing in this regulation shall—

(i) apply to a floor separating flats in a building of occupancy sub-group A2 not more than four storeys in height;

(ii) apply to any stair in a house in occupancy sub-group A2, not being a flat, not more than three storeys in height or to the floor of any landing or passage within a stairway enclosure of such a stair;

(iii) prevent the addition to the items referred to in (*a*) to (*g*) of this regulation of any combustible floor covering or, subject to regulation E15, of any ceiling or wall lining if with the addition of the covering or lining the items referred to in (*a*) to (*g*) comply with the provisions of regulation D5 as relate to them without such addition;

(iv) apply to the separating floor between a flat and a shop situated below the flat and in the same occupation where—

(A) there is no other flat above the shop, and

(B) the building containing the flat and the shop does not exceed three storeys in height, and

(C) the area of the shop is not greater than the area of the flat, or where the flat comprises two storeys, the lower storey of the flat.

Additional requirements for fire division walls

D7.—(1) Every fire division wall in a building shall, subject to regulation

D10, form a complete vertical separation between the divisions of the building including, where the wall extends to the top storey of the building, the roof space:

Provided that nothing in this paragraph shall—

(i) prevent the formation in a wall of an access opening, including access to a roof space, which complies with paragraph (6) of this regulation;

(ii) require any fire division wall to be extended across any balcony outwith the external walls of the building;

(iii) prevent vertical separation between the divisions of the building by means of a combination of fire division walls and compartment floors.

(2) Where an external wall is carried across the end of a fire division wall—

(*a*) the two walls shall be bonded together, or

(*b*) the junction of the two walls shall be fire-stopped.

(3) Where a fire division wall forms a junction with a roof the wall shall be carried above the upper surface of the roof covering for a distance of not less than 375 millimetres measured normal to the surface of the roof:

Provided that this paragraph shall not apply—

(i) where the wall separates buildings of occupancy sub-group A1 or A2 not exceeding 14 metres in height, and any part of the roof within a distance of 1·5 metres from the wall is designated AA, AB or AC; or

(ii) where each building, or division of a building, on either side of the wall is within occupancy group A or occupancy sub-group C2 or any combination of these and is a division of a height of not more than 12·5 metres and the roof covering is non-combustible; or

(iii) where any part of the roof within a distance of 1·5 metres from the wall is of solid or hollow slab construction of non-combustible material or is an asbestos cement cavity deck with a non-combustible infill and is designated AA, AB or AC; or

(iv) where each building, or division of a building, on either side of the wall is of a height of not more than 12·5 metres and any part of the roof within a distance of 1·5 metres from the wall is of non-combustible, self-supporting, single-skin sheet materials with no supporting deck; or

(v) where each building, or division of a building, on either side of the wall is of a height of not more than 12·5 metres and any part of the roof within a distance of 1·5 metres from the wall has a covering designated AA or AB and is supported by a self-supporting, single-skin deck of non-combustible materials;

if, in any case, either—

(A) the complete surface of the top of the wall is tightly jointed with non-combustible fire resisting materials to the underside of the roof covering; or

(B) the junction between the wall and the roof is fire-stopped, such fire-stopping having the same period of fire resistance as the wall.

(4) No combustible material shall be built into or carried through or across the ends of or over the top of any fire division wall in such a way as to render ineffective the resistance of the wall to the effects of fire and the spread of fire:

Provided that where under the proviso to the last foregoing paragraph a fire division wall is not carried above the surface of the roof covering, nothing in this paragraph shall prevent the continuation over the top of the wall of—

(i) any timber sarking and underslating felt, if the sarking is used as a base for slates or tiles fixed to the sarking without fillets and the sarking is solidly bedded in mortar or other not less suitable material where it rests on the wall;

(ii) any wood wool slabbing and underslating felt, or wood wool slabbing and tiling or slating fillets, if the slabbing is solidly bedded in mortar or other not less suitable material where it rests on the wall;

(iii) any other tiling or slating fillets which are solidly bedded in mortar where they rest on the wall and the space between which is filled with mortar or other not less suitable material up to the underside of the roof covering.

(5) Where in any storey of a building there is a fire division wall or part of a fire division wall separating two divisions of the building, the width of any opening, or the aggregate width of any openings, in the wall, or part, shall not exceed one-quarter of the length of the wall or of the part, as the case may be.

(6) Every opening in a fire division wall shall be protected by a door or shutter, which with its frames and surrounds has a fire resistance for a period of not less than that required by regulation D5:

Provided that—

(i) where the period so required for the door or shutter is not more than one hour there shall be accepted as sufficient compliance with this paragraph the provision of a "fire-check door", that is a door which swings in one direction only, and which is capable of satisfying the requirements of clause 11 of British Standard 476: Part 1: 1953, "Fire tests on building materials and structures", as follows—

a. collapse—for the period so required,

b. passage of flame—for 20 minutes where the period so required is 30 minutes, or for 45 minutes where the period so required is one hour,

when either face is exposed to fire;

(ii) where the period of fire resistance so required is 30 minutes and the openings open into a lobby or corridor from a stairway enclosure provided so as to comply with regulation E9, it shall be accepted as sufficient compliance with this paragraph if there is provided a single or double leaf door without rebates, so, however, that if the door contains any glazed opening the opening shall be protected by wired glass and no pane shall exceed 0·4 square metre in area.

Additional requirements for separating walls

D8.—(1) Every separating wall shall, subject to the following provisions of this regulation and of regulations D10 and D21—

(*a*) in the case of a wall separating parts of a building which does not extend throughout the whole height of the building, form a complete vertical separation between those parts;

(*b*) in the case of any other separating wall, form a complete vertical separation between the buildings, or parts of a building, which it separates, including the roof space:

Provided that—

(i) nothing in this paragraph shall require a wall which separates two buildings or parts of a building to extend across any balcony outwith the external walls of the buildings or building;

(ii) where a building contains a common stair, lift well, landing, passage or other common service area which is separated from the remainder of the building by more than one separating wall, nothing in this paragraph shall require more than one separating wall to be carried into the roof space when there is between the common stair, lift well, landing, passage or other common service area and the roof space a floor which complies with the provisions of this Part relating to separating floors.

(2) The provisions of paragraphs (2) to (4) and (6) of the last foregoing regulation shall apply to a separating wall as they apply to a fire division wall and as if references to divisions of a building were references to separate buildings or parts of a building in different occupancy groups or occupied by different persons.

(3) Nothing in this regulation shall prohibit the formation in a separating wall of any opening required for access where the wall separates—

(*a*) two adjoining buildings, or any two parts of one building which are in different occupancy groups but are occupied or intended to be occupied by the same person, or

(*b*) any two parts of one building where one part is in a single occupation and the other is communally occupied,

unless either—

(i) the wall is a wall separating a building or part of a building in occupancy group A from a building or part of a building in occupancy group D or E, or

(ii) the opening would be an opening giving access between two parts of a roof space.

Additional requirements for separating floors and compartment floors

D9.—(1) Every separating floor or compartment floor shall be of such construction that the requirements of regulation D5 are met without taking into account any suspended ceiling unless the ceiling—

(*a*) is of jointless construction with no openings therein, or

(*b*) is designed and constructed in accordance with the provisions of Schedule 5.

(2) Where an external wall, separating wall or fire division wall is carried across the edge of a separating floor or a compartment floor the junction of the wall and the floor shall be fire-stopped.

(3) Subject to the next succeeding regulation every separating floor or compartment floor shall form a complete horizontal separation between parts separated or the compartments of the building:

Provided that nothing in this paragraph—

(i) shall require any separating floor or compartment floor to be extended outwith the external walls of the building;

(ii) shall be taken to prohibit in a building of occupancy sub-group A2 an opening in a separating floor for a stairway, if—

(A) the stair is constructed of non-combustible material, and

(B) the walls enclosing the stairway are constructed as separating walls.

(4) Subject to the next succeeding regulation no combustible material shall be built into or carried through a separating floor or compartment floor.

Protection of service and ventilation ducts and pipes

D10.—(1) Nothing in regulations D7 to D9 shall prohibit—

(*a*) a duct to which paragraph (2) of this regulation applies, or (*b*) a pipe to which paragraph (3) of this regulation applies

being carried through a separating wall, fire division wall, separating floor or compartment floor.

(2) This regulation shall apply to any duct used for ventilation and to any duct carrying service or other pipes or forming part of a refuse chute if the duct—

(*a*) is enclosed throughout so much of its length as is within each part of the building separated by the wall or floor, as the case may be, by an enclosure—

(i) which with its junction with the wall or floor has a fire resistance for a period of not less than that required by regulation D5, and

(ii) which is imperforate save for any opening for access fitted with a cover having a period of fire resistance of not less than that required by regulation D5, and

(*b*) in the case of a duct used for ventilation which serves a part of the building on each side of the wall or floor, is fitted internally at the wall or floor with shutters or baffles which close automatically in the event of fire.

(3) This regulation shall apply to any pipe which—

(*a*) has a diameter not greater than—

(i) in the case of a pipe of combustible material, 25 millimetres,

(ii) in the case of a pipe of non-combustible material, 150 millimetres, and

(*b*) is fire-stopped and where necessary sleeved where it passes through the wall or floor.

Protection of lifts

D11. Every lift well in a building shall be separated from the remainder of the building by a fire division wall:

Provided that nothing in this regulation shall require the provision of a fire division wall separating a lift well from a stairway enclosure which is so enclosed as to comply with regulation E9.

Protection of stairways not forming part of an exit and escalators

D12. Every stairway to which the requirements for "other stairways" in Part S apply and every escalator shaft in a building shall be separated from the remainder of the building by a fire division wall:

Provided that nothing in this regulation shall require the provision of a fire division wall—

(1) separating an escalator shaft from a stairway which is so enclosed as to comply with regulation E9, or

(2) separating a stairway to which the requirements for "other stairways" in Part S apply or an escalator shaft from the remainder of a building if—

(*a*) the building is of occupancy group B, D or E or of occupancy sub-group C1 or C3, and

(*b*) such stairway or escalator shaft provides access only between storeys within one compartment, or in an uncompartmented building, and

(*c*) there are available from the storeys above the lowest storey of the building, exits being—

(i) not less in number than is required to comply with Part E, and

(ii) in no case less in number than two and giving escape in at least two directions, and

(iii) such that the travel distance from any point on any storey served by such stairway or escalator shaft above the lowest storey is—

(A) where there is only one such storey above the lowest, 30 metres,

(B) where there are two or more such storeys above the lowest, 12·5 metres, and

(iv) in such a position on the perimeter of the storey that an exit can be reached from any part of the storey in a direction away from such stairway or escalator.

Fire-stops in elements of structure of hollow construction

D13. Where in any building an element of structure contains a cavity which is continuous throughout the whole or part of the extent of the element and any surface within the cavity is of combustible material, the cavity shall be fire-stopped at every junction with any other cavity, and

(*a*) where the length of the cavity between such junctions exceeds 8 metres, at intervals of not more than 8 metres, and

(*b*) where the area of the cavity in any one plane between such junctions exceeds 46 square metres, at intervals of not less than 46 square metres:

Provided that nothing in this regulation shall—

(i) prevent the introduction of a combustible filling within such a cavity,

(ii) apply to a cavity between floor joists in a timber floor, provided that the ends of such cavities shall be closed in a manner which constitutes a fire-stop, or

(iii) apply to a cavity where the surface within the cavity is Grade A as specified in paragraph (2) of regulation E15 as read with paragraphs (3) and (4) of that regulation.

Connection of elements

D14. Any connection between two elements of structure each of which is, by this Part, required to have a fire resistance of not less than a specified period shall be so made that the structure comprising the junction of the two elements so connected has a fire resistance of a period not less than that so specified, or if different periods are specified for the two elements, the lower of the two periods.

Timber on outer face of external walls

D15. Any timber used on the outer face of an external wall of a building shall be not less than 9 millimetres thick:

Provided that this regulation shall not apply—

(i) to any timber facing which is of an area of less than 0·1 square metre and is not nearer to any other such timber facing on the same side of the building, division or compartment than 1·5 metres;

(ii) in the case of any building of occupancy group A or occupancy sub-group C2 of a height of not more than 12·5 metres.

Special provisions as to pends

D16. Where a floor or part thereof separates any part of a building from a pend, the provisions of this Part shall apply to the floor as they apply to a separating floor.

Distance of side of building from boundary

D17.—(1) Subject to regulation D19 every building shall be so sited that each external wall or exterior side of the building complies with the following provisions of this regulation in relation to the boundary.

(2) No part of the side of a building, division or compartment shall be nearer to the boundary than one-half of the distance at which the total thermal radiation intensity in still air due to all openings in that side of the building, division or compartment would be 12·6 kilowatts per square metre when the radiation intensity at each such opening is—

(*a*) if the building is of occupancy sub-group B2, C3, D2 or D3 or occupancy group E, 168 kilowatts per square metre;

(*b*) if the building is of occupancy group A or occupancy sub-group B1, C1, C2 or D1, 84 kilowatts per square metre.

(3) Where any part of an external wall is by virtue of the provisions of regulation D2 treated as an opening by reason only of having attached to its external face combustible material of a thickness more than 1 millimetre, whether for cladding or for any other purpose, that part of the wall shall, for the purposes of the last foregoing paragraph, be treated as an opening at which the radiation intensity is one-half of that prescribed in the said paragraph.

(4) For the purpose of paragraph (2) of this regulation, no account shall be taken of any of the following openings, namely—

(*a*) an opening which is of an area less than 0·1 square metre and is not nearer to another such opening in the same side of the building, division or compartment than 1·5 metres;

(*b*) an opening in any part of the side of the building which forms the side of a stairway, being a stairway completely separated from the rest of the building by an enclosure consisting of fire division or separating walls and, where a floor comprises part of the enclosure, a compartment or separating floor;

(*c*) an opening or group of openings if—

(i) the area of the opening or the aggregate area of the group of openings is not more than 0·9 square metre, and

(ii) no part of any opening is nearer to any other opening in the same side of the building, division or compartment than 3·6 metres, unless such other opening is an opening to which sub-paragraph (*a*) of this paragraph applies;

(*d*) any opening or part of an opening in an uncompartmented building, the height of the opening or part being not less than 15 metres above ground level.

(5) No part of the side of a building shall be less than 1 metre from the boundary:

Provided that nothing in this paragraph shall prohibit the side of a building, or part of such a side, being contiguous with the boundary if in the side or part, as the case may be, there is no opening other than such an opening as is mentioned in sub-paragraph (*a*) of the last foregoing paragraph.

(6) Nothing in this regulation shall apply to—

(*a*) the side of a building, or of a division or compartment of a building, if no part of the enclosing rectangle of any opening or of any group of openings in that side is nearer to any point on the boundary than the distance calculated in accordance with the provisions of Schedule 6;

(*b*) the side of a building of occupancy sub-group A1 or A2 which does not exceed three storeys in height or 24 metres in length if no part of the side is nearer to the boundary than—

(i) where the aggregate area of openings in the side does not exceed 5·6 square metres, 1 metre;

(ii) where such aggregate area does not exceed 15 square metres, 2·4 metres;

(iii) where such aggregate area exceeds 15 square metres, 6 metres, or, if the side of the building does not exceed 12·5 metres in length, 4·9 metres.

(7) In this regulation—

(*a*) "enclosing rectangle", in relation to an opening or a group of openings in the exterior side of a building or of a division or compartment of a building, means the smallest rectangle, two sides of which are vertical and of a height set forth in column (1) of Table 8, and two sides of a width set forth in column (2) of Table 8, that will enclose the opening or group of openings;

"overall enclosing rectangle", in relation to the exterior side of a building, division or compartment, means the smallest enclosing rectangle that will enclose all the openings in that side;

"plane of reference", in relation to the side of a building, division or compartment, means the outermost vertical plane on that side which contains the outer surface of an enclosing wall or, where there is no enclosing wall, the outer edge of any floor, including any floor laid directly upon the solum;

"thermal radiation intensity" means the amount of radiant energy per unit area in unit time;

(*b*) any reference to a building, division or compartment in relation to an opening means—

(i) where the building is neither divided into divisions nor split into compartments, the building in the side of which the opening is situated;

(ii) where the building is divided into divisions, the side of the division in which the opening is situated (not being a division which is further split into compartments);

(iii) where a building or a division of a building is split into compartments, the compartment in the side of which the opening is situated;

(*c*) any reference to an opening in the side of a building shall include a reference to any part of a roof which—

(i) slopes at an angle to the horizontal of 70 degrees or more, and

(ii) forms part of the side of a building within the height thereof as measured in accordance with Rule (4) of Schedule 1, and

(iii) does not have a fire resistance for the period required by this Part for the external wall on that side or has attached to its external face combustible material of a thickness of more than 1 millimetre, whether for covering or for any other purpose.

Roofs

D18.—(1) Subject to the provisions of regulation D19, every part of the roof of a building shall comply with the following provisions of this regulation.

(2) No part of the roof—

(*a*) which is designated BA, BB or BC shall be nearer to any boundary than 6 metres;

(*b*) which is designated AD, BD, CA, CB, CC or CD or is covered with thatch or wood shingles shall be nearer to any boundary than a distance of—

(i) where the area of such roof does not exceed 3 square metres and is separated from any other part of the same roof so designated or covered by an area of non-combustible material at no part less than 1·5 metres in width, 6 metres,

(ii) in any other case, 12 metres;

(*c*) which is designated DA, DB, DC or DD shall—

(i) be nearer to any boundary than 22 metres, or

(ii) be nearer to any other part of the same roof so designated than 1·5 metres, or

(iii) be of greater area than 3 square metres,

so, however, that any roof covering separating one part of a roof designated DA, DB, DC or DD from another part so designated shall be non-combustible.

(3) Where the building—

(*a*) is of occupancy group D or E and is of capacity of more than 1130 cubic metres, or

(*b*) is of occupancy sub-group A1 and comprises more than two houses, or

(*c*) is occupied or intended to be occupied by more than one separate occupier,

no part of the roof shall be a roof designated BD, CA, CB, CC, CD, DA, DB, DC or DD or shall be covered with thatch or wood shingles.

(4) Where any part of a roof of a building cannot be designated under regulation A8, that part shall not be nearer to any point on the boundary than—

(*a*) 12 metres, or

(*b*) a distance equal to twice the height of the building,

whichever is the greater:

Provided that, if that part of the roof is—

(i) of an area not greater than 3 square metres, and

(ii) separated from any part of the same roof that is of the same or any similarly unclassifiable material by an area of non-combustible material of not less than 1·5 metres in width,

nothing in this paragraph shall require that part to be distant from the boundary by more than 6 metres.

(5) If a roof conforms to one of the specifications listed in Table 7 it shall, for the purposes of this regulation and notwithstanding the provisions of regulation A8, be deemed to be of the appropriate designation shown in that Table.

(6) Nothing in this regulation shall apply to a wall-head fascia, soffit or barge board.

(7) Nothing in this regulation shall prevent any part of a roof being constructed of either—

(*a*) glass; or

(*b*) rigid polyvinylchloride sheeting which cannot be designated in accordance with regulation A8 but which is classified as self-extinguishing when tested in accordance with method 508A of Part 5 of British Standard 2782: 1970,

if, in either case—

(i) that part of the roof is not less than 6 metres from any boundary; or

(ii) the roof is that of a garage, porch, conservatory, sun porch or shed, having a floor area not exceeding 40 square metres; or

(iii) the roof forms a canopy over, or is the roof of, a balcony, verandah, carport or detached swimming pool or forms a covered way.

Application for warrant for more than one building

D19. Where an application for warrant under section 6 of the Act relates to more than one building to which this Part applies—

(*a*) nothing in regulation D17 shall be taken to regulate the distance between any building to which the application relates and its boundary with any other such building if the two buildings are separated by a distance equal to the sum of the distances calculated in relation to the said boundary under regulation D17(2) in respect of each such building, and

(*b*) nothing in regulation D18 shall be taken to regulate the distance between the roof of any building to which the application relates and the boundary with any other such building if the roofs of the two buildings are separated by a distance equal to the sum of the distances provided in relation to the said boundary under regulation D18 in respect of each such roof.

**Special provisions as to certain groups of garages*

D20.—(1) Every garage used solely for the storage or parking of motor vehicles and having an area not exceeding 19 square metres, or a group of two or more such garages to be built on a site reserved for the erection of such garages, shall comply with the following provisions of this regulation.

(2) For the purpose of regulation D17, a group of not more than 24 garages shall be deemed to form a single building on land in the same occupation having sides with openings therein equal to the aggregate area of the sides of the individual garages facing the boundary:

Provided that nothing in this paragraph shall prohibit a garage being sited on the boundary or within a distance of the boundary less than that required by regulation D17 (or limit the number in a group of such garages), if the sides facing the boundary have no openings, are constructed of non-combustible materials which have a period of fire resistance of not less than one-half hour and if the garage has a roof designated AA, AB or AC.

(3) Notwithstanding anything in this regulation a garage or group of garages may be erected in accordance with regulations D3 to D18.

Special provisions as to certain small garages and carports

D21.—(1) Every garage or carport the area of which does not exceed 40 square metres and which either—

(*a*) forms part of or is attached to a building in occupancy sub-group A1 or A2, not being a block of flats, or

(*b*) is a detached building on land in the same occupation as another building which is in occupancy sub-group A1 or A2, not being a block of flats,

shall comply with the following provisions of this regulation.

(2) Every garage to which paragraph (1)(*a*) of this regulation applies shall be so constructed that—

(*a*) the wall separating the garage from the other part of the building or from the building to which it is attached is a fire division wall with a period of fire resistance of not less than one hour;

(*b*) any opening in the fire division wall required by paragraph (2)(*a*) of this regulation at any point where it separates the garage and the building is—

(i) for access only,

(ii) protected by a fire-check door within the meaning of proviso (i) to regulation D7(6) which with its frames and surrounds has a fire resistance of not less than one-half hour, and

(iii) provided with an upstand between the foot of the door and the floor of the garage of not less than 100 millimetres in height;

(*c*) if any part of the garage is contiguous with the boundary or less than 2 metres from the boundary the external wall of the garage adjacent to or on the boundary is constructed of non-combustible materials and the roof is designated AA, AB or AC;

(*d*) if there is no external wall of the garage contiguous with the boundary there shall be a distance of not less than 500 millimetres between the wall and the boundary;

(*e*) if there is living accommodation above the garage—

(i) the floor of the living accommodation has a period of fire resistance of not less than one hour,

(ii) the external walls of the garage are non-combustible, and

(iii) the ceiling of the garage is constructed of jointless non-combustible materials; and

(*f*) if there is living accommodation below the garage the floor of the garage is constructed of solid non-combustible materials and has a fire resistance of not less than one hour.

(3) Every garage to which paragraph (1)(*b*) of this regulation applies and the walls and roof of which are constructed of the materials described in columns (1) and (2) of the following table shall not be nearer to the boundary or to that house than the distances set forth respectively in columns (3) and (4) thereof opposite those columns provided that the conditions set forth in column (5) thereof in relation thereto are complied with.

Materials of construction		Minimum distance from boundary	Minimum distance from house on land in same occupation	Conditions
Walls	Roof			
(1)	(2)	(3)	(4)	(5)
Non-combustible	Designated AA, AB or AC	500 millimetres except when contiguous with the boundary	500 millimetres	—
	Other than AA, AB or AC	2 metres	2 metres	—
			500 millimetres	The wall of the house adjacent to the garage to be imperforate and constructed of non-combustible materials having a period of fire resistance of not less than one hour.
Combustible	Any designation or materials of construction	2 metres	500 millimetres	The wall of the house adjacent to the garage to be imperforate and constructed of non-combustible materials having a period of fire resistance of not less than one hour.
	Any designation or materials of construction	2 metres	2 metres	—
Any materials of construction	Any designation or materials of construction	500 millimetres	3 metres	No part of garage to be within 3 metres from any opening in any other house.

(4) Every carport to which this regulation applies shall—

(*a*) if contiguous with the boundary or within 2 metres of the boundary have a roof designated AA, AB or AC, and

(*b*) if attached to a house having openings in the wall adjoining the carport have a roof designated AA, AB or AC.

(5) Any reference in this regulation to a roof designated AA, AB or AC shall be construed as including a reference to a roof made of glass or of rigid polyvinylchloride sheeting mentioned in regulation D18(7)(*b*).

(6) Any reference in this regulation to walls constructed of non-combustible materials shall be construed as including a reference in the case of a garage to walls constructed of bricks, concrete or similar materials and of timber framing with non-combustible external cladding.

Special provisions as to garden huts, greenhouses and other buildings ancillary to houses

D22.—(1) This regulation shall apply to any greenhouse, garden hut or other building ancillary to a house, not being a garage or carport to which regulation D21 applies, which—

(*a*) is erected on an area of land in the same occupation as a building in occupancy sub-group A1 or A2 not being a block of flats,

(*b*) is not a building every part of which falls within Class 11 specified in Schedule 3 (Exempted classes of building), and

(*c*) has a floor area not greater than that specified in column (2) of the table following paragraph (2) of this regulation.

(2) Every building described in column (1) of the following table, having a floor area not greater than specified in column (2) thereof and constructed of the materials specified in column (3) thereof shall not be nearer to the boundary or to the house on land in the same occupation than the distances set forth respectively in columns (4) and (5) thereof opposite those columns and in relation thereto.

Building (1)	Floor area not more than (2)	Materials of construction (3)	Minimum distance from boundary (4)	Minimum distance from house on land in same occupation (5)
1. Greenhouses	19 square metres	Not less than three-quarters of the total external area including the roof being of glass (including glazing bars)	500 millimetres except when on boundary	500 millimetres except when attached to house
2. Garden huts and other ancillary buildings	9 square metres	Non-combustible walls (including walls where framing being of timber) and roof designated AA, AB or AC	500 millimetres except when on boundary	2 metres
3. Garden huts, greenhouses and other ancillary buildings	9 square metres	Any materials of construction	1 metre	2 metres
4. Garden huts, greenhouses and other ancillary buildings	19 square metres	Any materials of construction	2 metres	2 metres
5. Covered ways	19 square metres	Roof designated AA, AB or AC	—	—

(3) Any reference in this regulation to a roof designated AA, AB or AC shall

be construed as including a reference to a roof made of glass or of rigid polyvinylchloride sheeting mentioned in regulation D18(7)(*b*).

**Fuel oil storage tanks*

D23.—(1) This regulation shall apply in relation to every tank having a capacity of not less than 90 litres used for storing fuel oil and connected to one or more appliances, the principal use of which is to afford space heating, water heating or cooking facilities within one or more buildings (hereinafter in this regulation referred to as "the building"), not being a building to which the Factories Act 1961 **(a)** applies:

Provided that nothing in this regulation shall apply to any tank serving an appliance the principal use of which forms part of an industrial or manufacturing process.

(2) The tank shall, if—

(*a*) within or forming part of a building, or

(*b*) of a capacity exceeding 1250 litres and neither within nor forming part of a building,

be provided with an oil-tight catchpit of sufficient size to receive and contain the total capacity of the tank, plus one-tenth:

Provided that nothing in this paragraph shall require the provision of a catchpit in the case of a tank which is neither within nor forms part of a building and is—

(i) underground, or

(ii) of a capacity exceeding 1250 litres, but not exceeding 3400 litres,

if there is no danger of the contents of the tank contaminating—

(A) any drains, sewers or water supply, or

(B) any land in different occupation or buildings erected thereon.

(3) If the tank is within or forms part of a building—

(*a*) the tank shall be contained within a tank room or tank chamber which—

(i) is adequately ventilated to the external air, either directly or by means of a duct, and

(ii) does not contain any appliance; and

(*b*) any chamber shall be fully enclosed by a combination of walls, floors and a cover which comply with the requirements of this paragraph, any cover to such chamber conforming to the requirements of this paragraph for floors; and

(*c*) any walls or floors separating the room or chamber from the remainder of the building shall satisfy the requirements of this Part for fire division walls or, as the case may be, compartment floors and shall have a period of fire resistance of not less than—

(i) where the capacity of the tank does not exceed 1250 litres, 1 hour;

(ii) where the capacity of the tank exceeds 1250 litres but does not exceed 3400 litres, 2 hours;

(iii) where the capacity of the tank exceeds 3400 litres, 4 hours:

Provided that nothing in this paragraph shall prohibit any room or chamber being constructed so as to form a catchpit as required by the last foregoing paragraph.

(a) 1961 c. 34.

(4) Subject to the next succeeding paragraph, if the tank is neither within nor forms part of the building—

(*a*) the side of the tank facing the building shall be no nearer to the building than the minimum distance set forth in column (2) of the following table unless the conditions set forth in column (3) of the said table are satisfied in relation to the building;

(*b*) the side of the tank facing the boundary shall be no nearer to the boundary than the minimum distance set forth in column (4) of the said table unless the conditions set forth in column (5) of the said table are satisfied.

Capacity of tank (litres) (1)	Minimum distance of tank from building containing appliance (2)	Conditions (3)	Minimum distance of tank from boundary (4)	Conditions (5)
Exceeding 90 but not exceeding 1250	1·8 metres	(*a*) The tank is underground, or (*b*) there is a screen wall, or (*c*) the external wall of the building is protected.	760 millimetres	(*a*) The tank is underground, or (*b*) there is a screen wall.
Exceeding 1250 but not exceeding 3400	1·8 metres	(*a*) The tank is underground, or (*b*) there is a screen wall, or (*c*) the external wall of the building is protected.	760 millimetres	(*a*) The tank is underground, or (*b*) there is a screen wall.
Exceeding 3400	6 metres	(*a*) The tank is underground, or (*b*) there is a screen wall, or (*c*) the external wall of the building is protected.	6 metres	(*a*) The tank is underground, or (*b*) there is a screen wall.

(5) In this regulation—

(*a*) any reference to a tank being underground shall be construed as a reference to a tank no part of which is above ground level, and which tank, if within or forming part of a building, is provided with a cover having a period of fire resistance of not less than—

(i) in the case of a tank having a capacity exceeding 3400 litres, 2 hours,

(ii) in the case of any other tank, 1 hour;

(*b*) any condition that there is a screen wall shall be construed as a condition that there is provided between the tank and the external wall of the building or the boundary, as the case may be, at a distance of not more than 225 millimetres from the nearest part of the tank, a solid non-combustible wall—

(i) of such length that it extends, on each side of the projected width of the tank in relation to the external wall of the building or the boundary, for a distance of not less than—

(A) in the case of a tank having a capacity exceeding 3400 litres, 900 millimetres,

(B) in the case of any other tank, 300 millimetres, and

(ii) of a height above the height of the tank and throughout its whole length of not less than—

(A) in the case of a tank having a capacity exceeding 3400 litres, 900 millimetres,

(B) in the case of any other tank, 300 millimetres, and

(iii) having a period of fire resistance of not less than—

(A) in the case of a tank having a capacity exceeding 3400 litres, 2 hours,

(B) in the case of any other tank, 1 hour;

(*c*) any condition that the external wall of a building is protected shall be construed as a condition—

(i) in the case of a tank having a capacity exceeding 3400 litres, that every part of such wall within 6 metres of any part of the tank is non-combustible, has no openings and has a period of fire resistance of not less than 2 hours,

(ii) in the case of any other tank, that every part of such wall within 1·8 metres of any part of the tank is non-combustible, has no openings and has a period of fire resistance of not less than 1 hour:

Provided that for the purposes of this regulation no account shall be taken of any opening, within the meaning of regulation D2(1), which is intended solely for the ventilation of an air space below a timber floor.

(6) Every tank to which this regulation applies shall be designed, constructed and fitted with such safety devices as are necessary to enable it to operate efficiently and safely.

(7) All drainage outlet valves and drainage outlet cocks of any tank to which this regulation applies, being a tank neither within nor forming part of a building, shall be capable of being locked.

(8) In this regulation any reference to an "appliance" shall be construed as a reference to an appliance within the meaning of regulation F2(1).

PART E

Means of Escape from Fire and Assistance to Fire Service

Application of Part E

E1.—(1) This Part shall not apply to any building of occupancy sub-group A1:

Provided that nothing in this paragraph shall exclude the application to any building of regulation E15.

(2) Nothing in this Part shall prohibit the provision within a room or storey of a building of an openwork floor or gallery, or a catwalk, or a stairway leading therefrom where regulations E3 to E5 are complied with in relation to that room or storey.

(3) The provisions of this Part, so far as they relate to—

(*a*) any house of more than two storeys not being a flat, or

(*b*) any building to which the Factories Act 1961 applies,

shall not be subject to specification in a notice served under section 11 of the Act (which enables local authorities to require existing buildings to conform to these regulations).

Interpretation of Part E

E2.—(1) In this Part—

"exit" means a route by way of a room or doorway into a passage and thereafter only by way of a passage, including any stairway forming part thereof and at no stage by means of a lift, escalator or doorway containing a revolving door, by which a person may reach a place of safety, and in relation to—

(*a*) any point on a storey of a building, means a route from that point;

(*b*) any room, means a route from a doorway of the room;

(*c*) any storey of a building, means a route from a point of egress from the storey;

(*d*) any flat, means a route from an entrance to the flat;

"independent circuit" means an electrical circuit supplying current to a fire lift or to lights for an exit, being either from an independent source or a separate circuit commencing at the main switch control point, so that a supply of current would be available even in the event of the supply of electricity to the remainder of the building being isolated;

"place of safety" means either—

(*a*) an unenclosed space in the open air at ground level, or

(*b*) an enclosed space in the open air at ground level which has a means of access to such an unenclosed space by means of an exit or exits having a width, or aggregate width, not less than the width, or aggregate width, of the exits leading from the building to the enclosed space;

"protected doorway" means—

(*a*) any doorway containing a self-closing, fire-resisting door—

(i) from a flat on to an open access balcony which gives access to a stairway forming part of an exit, or

(ii) giving access to a protected zone, or

(*b*) any doorway leading directly to a place of safety in the open air at ground level;

"protected zone" in relation to an exit in a building means any part of the exit, not being a part within a room, which extends to a place of safety at ground level and which is completely enclosed—

(*a*) at the top of the zone, by a roof or a compartment floor or a separating floor or the soffit of a stairway or the soffit of a landing or any combination of these, and

(*b*) at the sides of the zone, by fire division walls or separating walls or external walls (openings in external walls, other than ventilation openings provided in accordance with Part K, being fitted with windows or doors) or any combination of these, and

(*c*) at the bottom of the zone, by a compartment floor or a separating floor or the floor of the lowest storey of the building or any combination of these;

"rate of discharge", in relation to any point in an exit, means the number of persons to be taken for the purposes of this Part as passing that point in one minute;

"travel distance" has the meaning assigned to that term by regulation E5;

"unprotected zone", in relation to an exit, means any part of the exit being neither a protected zone nor a part within a room.

(2) In calculating for the purposes of this Part the occupant capacity of a storey containing an exit door from a flat, every part of the flat shall be taken to form part of the storey notwithstanding that—

(*a*) part of the flat is on another storey, or

(*b*) there is another exit from the flat on another storey.

(3) Any reference in this Part to a self-closing fire-resisting door shall be construed as a reference to a door which—

(*a*) with its frames and surrounds has a fire resistance for a period of not less than that required by regulation D5, and

(*b*) is so constructed and fitted as to close automatically from all angles of swing including the fully open position, and

(*c*) is fitted with a suitable quick release device to hold the door open when required, and

(*d*) in the case of any building in occupancy group A or B, not being the door of a flat, has attached to the door on both sides a notice in permanent form in letters not less than 13 millimetres high in the following terms or any terms substantially to the like effect—

"FIRE DOOR—This door must be kept closed at night.".

So, however, that in any case where the provision of such a door as is mentioned in paragraph (i) or (ii) of the proviso to regulation D7(6) is accepted as sufficient compliance with regulation D7(6) this paragraph shall have effect as if for the requirement in sub-paragraph (*a*) of this paragraph there were substituted a requirement that the door should be such a door as is mentioned in either paragraph of that proviso.

Provision of exits

E3. In every building to which this Part applies there shall be available from each room and from each storey not less than such number of exits as are required to comply with the provisions of regulations E4 and E5, each of which exits shall comply with so much of the provisions of regulations E5 to E15 as apply thereto.

Number of exits

E4.—(1) Subject to regulation E3, the number of exits available from any flat or from any ground or upper storey of a house of more than two storeys (not being a flat) shall be not less than the number specified in column (5) of Part I, II or III, as the case may be, of Table 10.

(2) Subject to regulation E3, the number of exits available from—

(*a*) any storey of a building other than the ground or upper storey of a house of more than two storeys, or

(*b*) any room, not being a room in a flat,

shall be not less than whichever is the greater of the following numbers—

(i) in the case of a storey of a description mentioned in Part IV or V of Table 10, the number specified in column (5) of the said Part IV or V, as the case may be, and

(ii) in any case, the number of exits shown in the following table having regard to the occupant capacity of the room or storey—

(1) Occupant capacity of room or storey	(2) Number of exits
1 - 60	1
61 - 600	2
601 - 1000	3
1001 - 1400	4
1401 - 1700	5
1701 - 2000	6
2001 - 2250	7
2251 - 2500	8
2501 - 2700	9
Over 2700	One additional exit over 9 for every 300 persons or part thereof over 2700:

Provided that in a school or part of a school of not more than two storeys, either storey of which has an occupant capacity of not more than 120, nothing in this paragraph shall require more than one exit from that storey.

Travel distance in relation to exits

E5.—(1) Subject to regulation E3 and the following provisions of this regulation, the exits from any storey shall be of such number and so situated that the travel distance from any point on that storey does not exceed—

(*a*) where two or more exits are provided from the point, the distance which can be covered in 2·5 minutes by a person moving at the speed of—

(i) if the storey is a ground storey and is not sub-divided into separate rooms, no part thereof is equipped with fixed or moveable seating, no part of such exit therefrom forms a stairway and no part of such exit comprising a corridor or passage from the point of egress from the storey exceeds 3 metres in length, 18 metres per minute;

(ii) in any other case, 12·5 metres per minute;

(*b*) where only one exit is provided from the point, two-fifths of the distance calculated in accordance with sub-paragraph (*a*) of this paragraph;

(*c*) where in a building of occupancy sub-group A3 or A4 or occupancy group B, C, D or E—

(i) only one exit is provided from the point, and

(ii) within a distance of 12·5 metres from that point the exit enters a passage, and

(iii) escape is possible along that passage in two directions at an angle of not less than 90 degrees to each other,

the distance which can be covered in 2·5 minutes by a person moving at the speed of 12·5 metres per minute:

Provided that nothing in this paragraph shall apply to any storey in a block of flats falling within any one of the descriptions in head 2 of Part I of Table 10 and heads 1, 2, 3, 5 and 6 of Part IV of Table 10.

(2) Where, in the relevant circumstances set forth in the next succeeding paragraph—

(*a*) a room has more than one exit, and

(*b*) any part of an exit from a point in the room is by way of an adjoining room from which it is separated by a fire division wall, the travel distance from that point shall be measured as if any doorway in the fire division wall were a protected doorway.

(3) In relation to any such room and adjoining room the relevant circumstances are that—

(*a*) not less than one-half of the number of exits from the room are by way of a protected doorway, and

(*b*) the floor of the adjoining room is of an area, in square metres, not less than the sum of the occupant capacities of both rooms multiplied by—

(i) in the case of a building of occupancy sub-group A4, 2·23,

(ii) in any other case, 0·3, and

(*c*) in any case, there is in the adjoining room a protected doorway.

(4) In this regulation "travel distance", in relation to any point in a storey of a building, means the distance required to be covered between that point and the nearest protected doorway, whether in that storey or in the storey next to that storey, measured—

(*a*) when the floor area is divided up with fixed seating or other fixed obstruction, by way of the shortest route along open gangways;

(*b*) where not so divided, by way of the shortest route:

Provided that if the travel distance is to be measured from any point on a storey to a protected doorway on the storey next to that storey, any distance required to be covered by way of a stairway shall, for the purposes of this regulation, be taken to be the distance measured along the pitch line from the centre of the nosing of the topmost tread to the lower landing, including the length of any intermediate landing, measured throughout along the centre line of travel.

Requirements as to exits

E6.—(1) Every exit from a room or storey shall lead directly to a place of safety:

Provided that where more than one exit is available from the top storey of a building and that storey is either in a building—

(i) of occupancy sub-group A2, A3 or B1, or of occupancy group D or E, or

(ii) of occupancy sub-group B2 and the public have no access thereto,

nothing in this paragraph shall prevent one of the exits from that storey being by way of a flat roof.

(2) Every exit from a room or storey shall be independent from any other exit to which access may be obtained directly from that room or storey:

Provided that where the occupant capacity of a room, not being a whole storey, does not exceed 100, nothing in this paragraph shall prevent the exits from that room giving access to one common hall or passage from which escape to a protected doorway is possible in more than one direction.

(3) Where part of any exit from the top storey of a building is by way of a roof, that part shall—

(*a*) lead to another exit, not being another exit from the same storey, and

(*b*) comply with regulation D5, and

(*c*) be situated not less than 3 metres from any roof-light, window or other opening which does not have a fire resistance against collapse and the passage of flame of not less than one-half hour, and (*d*) be protected on each side by a suitable wall or balustrade not less than 1·1 metres in height, and

(*e*) if access to the roof exit is obtained from the top of a stairway serving the top storey, be separated from the stairway at the floor of the top storey by a wall having the same fire resistance as the stairway enclosure and containing a self-closing fire-resisting door.

(4) No part of an exit shall be less in height than 2 metres.

(5) Where more than one exit is available from a room in accordance with regulation E4 or E5, these exits shall be so situated that from the furthermost point in the room the angle of direction of travel between at least two of these exits shall be not less than 45 degrees.

Width of exits

E7.—(1) Every exit from a room or storey shall have an unobstructed width not less than whichever of the following is the greater—

(*a*) such width throughout as will, when taken with the width of any other exit or exits from that room or storey, allow the total occupant capacity of the room or storey to discharge in 2·5 minutes when the rate of discharge is taken as 40 persons per minute per 530 millimetres of width of exit, or

(*b*) the width specified by the following table in relation to the occupant capacity of the room or storey within a building of the appropriate occupancy sub-group—

Occupant capacity	Width	
	Sub-group A2	Any other sub-group
Not exceeding 25 or, if forming part of a school, 50	800 millimetres	800 millimetres
Exceeding 25 or, if forming part of a school, 50 but not exceeding 100	800 millimetres	1100 millimetres
Exceeding 100	1100 millimetres	1100 millimetres

(2) For the purposes of paragraph (1)(*b*) of this regulation where a door comprising a single leaf forms part of the exit the width of the door leaf shall be not less than—

(*a*) the width specified by the following table in relation to the occupant capacity of the room or storey within a building of occupancy sub-group A2—

Occupant capacity	Width
Not exceeding 25	700 millimetres
Exceeding 25 but not exceeding 100	700 millimetres
Exceeding 100	900 millimetres

(*b*) 726 millimetres in the case of a building of any occupancy sub-group other than A2 where the occupant capacity of the room or storey does not exceed 25 or, if forming part of a school, 50.

(3) Every exit from a room or storey shall be of an unobstructed width at no part less than the width required by these regulations for any other part of the exit further from the place of safety in the open air to which the exit leads.

(4) Where any part of an exit from the ground storey also forms part of an exit from a stairway the width of the exit shall be not less than the sum of the widths required to allow—

(*a*) the total occupant capacity of the ground storey to discharge according to the manner prescribed in paragraph (1)(*a*) of this regulation, and

(*b*) the total appropriate capacities of any other storey or storeys (including any basement storey) to discharge calculated in accordance with regulation E8(2).

(5) Nothing in this regulation shall apply to that part of an exit in so far as it comprises a stairway the width of which shall be determined in accordance with regulation E8.

Width of stairways in exits

E8.—(1) Subject to the following provisions of this regulation, every stairway from a storey shall be of such width as will allow the appropriate capacity of that storey to discharge in a time not exceeding 2·5 minutes when the rate of discharge is taken as 40 persons per minute per 530 millimetres of width of exit.

(2) The appropriate capacity of a storey in relation to a stairway shall, for the purpose of the last foregoing paragraph, be taken to be—

(*a*) where the stairway does not serve a storey next above that storey, the occupant capacity of that storey;

(*b*) where the stairway also serves the storey next above that storey, the aggregate of—

(i) the occupant capacity of that storey, and

(ii) the occupant capacity of such storey next above, under deduction of the standing capacity of that part of the stairway between that storey and such storey next above:

Provided that where there is available from any storey more than two stairways, there shall, for the appropriate capacity of that storey as determined under this paragraph, be substituted a capacity equal to the appropriate capacity so determined divided by a number equal to one less than the number of stairways so available.

(3) The standing capacity in relation to any part of a stairway between two storeys, for the purposes of the last foregoing paragraph, means the number of persons that part of the stairway, including landings as aftermentioned, can hold and shall be taken to be the sum of—

(*a*) the aggregate in metres of the lengths of all the treads comprised in that part of the stairway (the length of a tread being taken to be the horizontal distance between the two sides of the tread), and

(*b*) the number obtained by dividing by 0·3 the area in square metres of any landing at the level of the higher of the two storeys and of any intermediate landing (the width of a landing being taken as in no case greater than the width of the stairway).

(4) No part of a stairway forming part of an exit from an upper storey shall be of less width than—

(*a*) the width of any higher part of the stairway, other than a landing;

(*b*) at any level below any exit doorway which gives access to the stairway, the width of that exit doorway.

(5) No part of a stairway forming part of an exit from a basement storey shall be of less width than—

(*a*) the width of any lower part of the stairway, other than a landing;

(*b*) at any point above the floor of a storey from which an exit doorway gives access to the stairway, the width of that exit doorway.

(6) For the purposes of this regulation "stairway", in relation to any storey, means—

(*a*) where the stairway serves only that storey, the whole stairway;

(*b*) where the stairway serves other storeys, that part of the stairway which serves the storey.

Enclosure of stairways

E9.—(1) Subject to the following provisions of this regulation, this regulation shall apply to every stairway forming part of an exit being neither a stairway wholly within a flat nor a stairway to which regulation E1(2) applies.

(2) The exit stairway shall be enclosed within a protected zone and, except as after-mentioned, no other part of the building containing that stairway shall be enclosed within that protected zone:

Provided that there may also be enclosed within the protected zone—

(*a*) in the case where two or more exit stairways serve a building, a ticket office or porter's lodge ancillary to the use of the building and intended solely for the control or supervision of persons entering or leaving the building; and

(*b*) in the case of any building—

(i) a washroom or watercloset;

(ii) floor space giving access to the stairway if such floor space is intended for use solely as a means of passage.

In this regulation a protected zone provided in accordance with this paragraph is referred to as a "stairway enclosure".

(3) Where a stairway enclosure projects beyond the external wall of a building and is connected thereto by an access passage, landing, balcony or other common service area and any part of the stairway is not more than 3 metres from the building, then either—

(*a*) the external wall or walls of the building shall conform to the requirements of Part D for fire division walls for a distance equal to the projected width of that part of the stairway enclosure which is less than 3 metres from the external wall of the building, or

(*b*) the external wall or walls of any part of the stairway enclosure, access passage, landing, balcony or other common service area, which is less than 3 metres from the building, shall conform to the requirements of Part D for fire division walls.

(4) Where in a building a passage or other common service area separated from the remainder of the building by a separating wall or walls gives access to an exit stairway, the stairway shall be separated from that passage or other common service area by a wall and self-closing fire-resisting door, both of which shall have a period of fire resistance of not less than one-half hour:

Provided that nothing in this paragraph shall prohibit the inclusion of openings in the wall and door separating the stairway from such passage or other common service area if the said openings are protected with panes of wired glass, each of which does not exceed 0·4 square metre in area, and which are installed in fixed frames.

(5) Every stairway enclosure shall give access at ground level to an exit to the open air, which exit shall be separate from any other exit to which access is given from any other stairway:

Provided that nothing in this paragraph shall prevent a stairway enclosure giving access to another exit by way of a roof exit which complies with regulation E6(3).

(6) Where between a stairway forming part of an exit and the access to the open air at ground level there is a vestibule forming part of the same exit, the stairway enclosure shall be so continued as to separate the vestibule from the remainder of the building.

(7) Where any storey is by this Part required to have more than one exit, the stairway enclosures provided from that storey shall be so constructed and situated that access may be obtained from any point on that storey to at least two stairway enclosures without passing through any stairway enclosure.

(8) Where from any storey of a building there is access to only one stairway, any room on that storey, or on a lower storey of that building which gives access to that stairway, shall be separated from the stairway by not less than two doors, that nearest the stairway being a door in the stairway enclosure.

(9) Where a stairway forming part of the only exit from an upper storey of a building is continued so as to form part of the exit from any basement storey of the building, that part of the stairway enclosure above the level of the floor of the ground storey shall be separated from that part below the level of the ground storey by a wall having the same fire resistance as the stairway enclosure and containing a self-closing fire-resisting door.

(10) Nothing in this regulation shall apply to—

(*a*) a stairway or part thereof between a doorway from the building and the adjoining ground if that stairway or part thereof comprises not more than eight rises; and

(*b*) a stairway within a house of occupancy sub-group A2 where any wall, or as the case may be any floor, separating the kitchen and living room from the stairway has a period of fire resistance of not less than one-half hour, any opening in such a wall being protected by a self-closing fire-resisting door having a period of fire resistance of not less than one-half hour.

Lobby approach stairways

E10.—(1) Where in a building, not being a building of occupancy sub-group A2, a doorway gives access from a storey which is at a height above ground level of more than 24 metres to a stairway to which the last foregoing regulation applies, there shall be provided from every storey in that building access to not less than the relevant number of lobby approach stairways.

For the purposes of this paragraph—

(*a*) "the relevant number" is one for every 900 square metres of floor area of that storey which is at a height above ground level of more than 24 metres or if there is more than one such storey the storey having the greater or greatest floor area, and (*b*) a "lobby approach stairway" is a stairway to which access is obtained only by way of a lobby or lobbies which complies or comply with the following provisions of this regulation.

(2) At least one wall of the lobby shall be an external wall adjacent to an area of cleared ground provided so as to comply with regulation E16(4)(*b*) or with regulation E17(*c*).

(3) The lobby shall have a floor area of not less than 2·8 square metres and shall be separated from the remainder of the building by a fire division wall or walls, any door therein being a self-closing, fire-resisting door and having a period of fire resistance not less than one-half of that required for the wall, and, where applicable, by a compartment floor.

(4) If the lobby is on a ground storey or on a storey above the ground storey it shall be provided with—

(*a*) an opening to the external air of an area of not less than—

(i) where the floor area of the lobby exceeds 11 square metres, one-quarter of the floor area, or

(ii) in any other case, 2·8 square metres, or

(*b*) an openable window providing such an opening of such area and a permanent ventilator or ventilators having an area or aggregate cross-sectional area of not less than 0·7 per cent of the floor area of the lobby.

(5) If the lobby is on a storey below the ground storey it shall be provided with a smoke extract—

(*a*) independent of any other such extract, and

(*b*) having a minimum cross-sectional area of 0·9 square metre, and

(*c*) which discharges direct to the open air at a point not less than 3 metres measured horizontally from any part of any exit from the building.

Construction of ramps

E11.—(1) Any ramp forming part of an exit shall be constructed in unbroken flights, each having a uniform slope not greater than 1 in 10.

(2) The ramp shall be guarded on each side by a wall or a secure balustrade or railing extending in either case to a height of not less than 900 millimetres measured vertically from the upper surface of the ramp.

(3) Between any two successive flights of the ramp there shall be a landing not less in length in the direction of travel and measured on the centre line of the ramp than—

(*a*) in the case of a building of occupancy sub-group A4, 2·1 metres;

(*b*) in the case of any other building, 1·2 metres.

Doors in exits

E12.—(1) Where the occupant capacity of a room or storey exceeds—

(*a*) in the case of a building of occupancy group A, B or C, 50;

(*b*) in the case of any other building, 10,

every door across an exit from that room or storey, not being the entrance door of a flat, shall—

(i) except in the case of a classroom in a school, open in the direction of travel towards the open air;

(ii) if constructed to open both ways, have a transparent upper panel;

(iii) if it is necessary to secure the door against entry from outside the building, be capable of being readily opened from the inside, although so secured, so, however, that in the case of a building or part of a building in occupancy group C the means of securing shall be by bolts that will open to pressure from the inside:

Provided that nothing in sub-paragraph (i) of this paragraph shall prohibit the provision of a sliding door across an exit in a building to which the public have no access, other than a building in occupancy group C, where the door is clearly marked on both sides "SLIDE TO OPEN".

(2) Every door opening on to an exit—

(*a*) if it opens outwards into a passage, shall be so arranged as not to obstruct the passage when fully opened;

(*b*) if it opens on to a landing between flights of stairs, shall not when fully open diminish the effective width of the landing to less than the width of the stair nor at any angle of swing reduce the effective width of the landing either below 900 millimetres or the width of the stair, whichever is the greater.

(3) Every entrance door of a flat shall be a self-closing fire-resisting door.

Lighting of exits

E13.—(1) This regulation shall not apply to—

(*a*) a house in occupancy sub-group A2 other than a flat, or

(*b*) any building which comprises premises to which Part I of the Cinematograph (Safety) (Scotland) Regulations 1955(**a**) applies.

(2) Every part of an exit from a room or storey shall be provided with adequate means of lighting.

(3) Where in any exit any means of lighting is by electricity the current for such lighting shall be supplied by an independent circuit.

(4) Where any stairway forms part of an exit and the lighting in the stairway enclosure is by electricity the current for such lighting shall be supplied by an independent circuit separate from any electrical circuit supplying lighting to any other part of the same exit.

Control of smoke spread

E14.—(1) This regulation shall apply to a house, in a building of occupancy sub-group A2, with a room or storey at a height of 11 metres or more above ground level, where there is provided within the house a system of warm air central heating which serves that room.

(2) Every opening which serves to extract air for re-circulation from the room to any other part of the house shall be so positioned that the top of the opening is not more than one-half the height of the room or 1·4 metres above the floor of the room, whichever is the greater.

(3) The room shall be fitted with a thermostat which will serve to halt the circulation of warm air through the opening when the temperature within the room reaches 27° Celsius.

(**a**) S.I. 1955/1125 (1955 I, p. 326).

Internal linings

E15.—(1) In every building to which this Part applies and in every building in occupancy sub-group A1 any internal lining of a wall or ceiling (excluding doors or finishings) shall be of a grade not lower than—

(*a*) in any protected zone of an exit or in any unprotected zone of an exit (not being an unprotected zone within a part of a house falling within the next succeeding sub-paragraph)—Grade A;

(*b*) in the case of a house in occupancy sub-group A1 which contains a stairway, that part of the house containing the stairway and any landing or passage leading to or from the stairway—Grade B;

(*c*) in the case of walls and ceilings within any room in a building of any of the following occupancy group or sub-groups, that grade specified in the following table—

Occupancy group or sub-group	Grade	
	Walls	Ceilings
A2	B	B
A3	B	C
A4	A	B
B1	C	C
B2	B	C
C1	C	C
C2	C†	C
C3	A	B
D	B	B
E1	C	C
E2	A	A

†In the case of a school—Grade B

Provided that—

(i) in any part of a house to which sub-paragraph (*b*) of this paragraph applies, nothing in this paragraph shall prohibit a percentage of the total area of the wall and ceiling linings, not exceeding 10 per cent, being of Grade D;

(ii) in any room to which sub-paragraph (*c*) applies, nothing in this paragraph shall prohibit—

(A) a percentage of the aggregate area of the wall linings, not exceeding 15 per cent, being of Grade D, and

(B) in the case of a room whose occupant capacity is less than 10, the wall or ceiling lining being of Grade C;

(iii) where a percentage of the aggregate area of the wall linings in—

(A) any room, or

(B) any part of a house to which sub-paragraph (*b*) of this paragraph applies

is of a Grade higher than that required by this paragraph, nothing in this paragraph shall prohibit an equal percentage of the area of the ceiling lining being of the Grade next below that which is required under this paragraph for the ceiling as a whole, but in no case of Grade D;

(iv) nothing in this paragraph shall prohibit the wall and ceiling lining being of Grade C in any building or part of a building used solely for the housing of livestock.

(2) Any provision in this regulation requiring that a wall or ceiling lining shall be of a specified Grade shall be construed as a requirement that the lining shall satisfy the requirements set forth below in relation to that Grade (the Grades being set forth in descending order of degree of resistance to the spread of flame)—

Grade		*Requirement*
A	—	The lining is non-combustible or complies with the conditions set out in paragraph (3) of this regulation.
B	—	The lining is Class 1.
C	—	The lining is Class 2 or Class 3.
D	—	The lining does not fall into any of the foregoing Grades.

(3) The conditions referred to in paragraph (2) of this regulation are—

(*a*) where the base material or background is non-combustible, any surface film of material is not more than 1 millimetre in thickness and the combined product is not lower than Grade B;

(*b*) if the material of the lining has a structural base or background of combustible material, it is finished with a skin of not less than 3 millimetres in thickness of material of Grade A so that the combined product is not lower than Grade B and the other surface is not exposed to the air.

(4) Any reference in paragraphs (2) and (3) of this regulation to a lining of any of the Classes 1, 2 or 3 shall be construed as a reference to a lining which complies with the tests as to the surface spread of flame set forth in relation to that Class in clause 7 of British Standard 476: Part 1: 1953, "Fire tests on building materials and structures".

(5) Any part of a ceiling or soffit that slopes at an angle to the horizontal of 70 degrees or more shall for the purposes of this regulation be treated as if it were a wall.

Construction of and access to windows

E16.—(1) Where in a building of occupancy sub-group A2 or A3 any upper storey is at a height of less than 24 metres above ground level and there is available from that storey only one exit, there shall be provided in an external wall of that storey such windows so positioned and so constructed as to comply with paragraphs (2) and (3) of this regulation and in front of each such window there shall be available an area of cleared ground so as to comply with paragraph (4) of this regulation.

(2) In each such storey there shall be—

(*a*) if the storey contains more than one flat, one such window in each flat;

(*b*) if the storey is in a building of occupancy sub-group A3 and contains more than one bedroom, one such window in each bedroom;

(*c*) in any other case, one such window.

(3) Each window shall be so constructed as to be capable of providing an opening—

(*a*) the bottom of which is not more than 1·1 metres from the floor of the storey, and

(*b*) which measures when the window is open not less than 850 millimetres in height by 550 millimetres in width.

(4) Each area of cleared ground provided so as to comply with paragraph (1)

of this regulation shall be so positioned that between it and the wall of the building containing the window there is no obstruction exceeding 1·8 metres in height, and shall—

(*a*) when the height of the highest storey of the building does not exceed 11 metres—

(i) be not less than 4·5 metres in width and in no part at a distance from the wall on the side of the building on which the window is situated greater than 9 metres or less than 1·5 metres;

(ii) if not itself a public road, be accessible from a public road by a roadway or reinforced surface not less than 2·6 metres in width and having at every part a headroom of not less than 3·5 metres;

(*b*) when the height of the highest storey of the building exceeds 11 metres—

(i) be a roadway or reinforced surface capable of bearing an axle loading of 8 tonnes;

(ii) be not less than 3 metres in width and in no part at a distance from the wall on the side of the building on which the window is situated greater than 13 metres or less than 4·9 metres;

(iii) if not comprising a public road be accessible from such a road by an accessway not less than 3 metres in clear width and having at every part a headroom of not less than 3·5 metres and in which the radius of any bend will provide a turning circle of not less than 8·3 metres radius.

Access to buildings for fire fighting purposes

E17. Where a building falls within occupancy sub-group A4 or occupancy group B, C, D or E there shall be available in respect of that building, or, if the building contains two or more divisions, in respect of each division comprised in the building, an area of cleared ground which—

(*a*) is adjacent to an external wall of the building or, as the case may be, an external wall or part of an external wall comprised in the division, and

(*b*) is not less in length measured parallel to the wall of the building than—

(i) where the cubic capacity of the building exceeds 2800 cubic metres, 2·4 metres for every 90 square metres of ground floor area;

(ii) in any case, 3 metres,

whichever is the greater, and

(*c*) (i) is a roadway or reinforced surface capable of bearing an axle loading of 8 tonnes;

(ii) is not less than 3 metres in width and in no part at a distance from the wall of the building greater than 13 metres or less than 4·9 metres;

(iii) if not comprising a public road is accessible from such a road by an accessway, capable of bearing an axle loading of 8 tonnes, not less than 3 metres in clear width and having at every part a headroom of not less than 3·5 metres and in which the radius of any bend provides a turning circle of not less than 8·3 metres radius:

Provided that nothing in this regulation shall apply to a building, in occupancy group D or occupancy sub-group E1, of not more than one storey and having a floor area of not more than 37 square metres.

Provision of fire mains

E18.—(1) Where—

(*a*) in a building the floor of any storey is at a height exceeding 11 metres, or (*b*) in an undivided building or a division of a building, being an undivided building or a division of more than one storey, the floor area of any storey exceeds—

(i) in the case of an undivided building or a division of occupancy sub-group E2, 230 square metres, or

(ii) in the case of any other undivided building or division, 900 square metres,

there shall be affixed to the building as fixtures such fire mains, provided with such outlets for appliances of the Fire Service, as comply with paragraphs (4) to (9) of this regulation.

(2) Where the total floor area of an undivided building or division of a building, being an undivided building or division of not more than one storey, exceeds—

(*a*) in the case of an undivided building, or a division, of occupancy sub-group E2, 230 square metres, or

(*b*) in the case of any other undivided building or division, 900 square metres,

there shall be provided outside the undivided building or the building containing the division as the case may be but within land in the same occupation as that undivided building or division, ground hydrants so situated that no part of the perimeter of the undivided building or division is at a greater distance from one of those hydrants than 61 metres measured along a route which is both external to the building and suitable for a hose:

Provided that nothing in this paragraph shall prohibit—

(i) any such hydrant being situated within the building if—

(A) the part of the building in which the hydrant is situated is separated from the remainder by fire division or separating walls;

(B) the hydrant is at a distance of not more than 4·5 metres from the entrance to the building and is visible from the entrance; and

(C) there is attached to the building at that entrance a notice indicating the presence of the hydrant;

(ii) the acceptance for the purposes of this paragraph of any hydrant attached to a water main vested in a regional water board if the hydrant is within the distance specified in this paragraph in relation to the perimeter of the building in question.

(3) The hydrants provided in accordance with paragraph (2) of this regulation shall be attached to a water service pipe of not less than 100 millimetres in diameter.

(4) Any part of a fire main which is not within a protected zone of an exit shall be enclosed within a duct or enclosure—

(*a*) which, with its junction with any wall or floor, has a fire resistance for a period not less than that required by Part D, and

(*b*) which is imperforate save for any opening for access fitted with a cover of fire resistance for a period of not less than that so required.

(5) The outlets shall be so situated and of such number that no point on any storey of the building or division is distant from an outlet by more than—

(*a*) 61 metres, measured along a route suitable for a hose, including any distance in that route up or down a stairway, and

(*b*) one storey in height.

(6) If there is fitted in the building a fire lift which complies with regulation E19 no outlet on any storey shall be more than 4·5 metres distant from the entrance to the fire lift on that storey.

(7) Each outlet shall be located in one of the following places—

(*a*) on an open balcony;

(*b*) within the protected zone of an exit;

(*c*) in a lobby giving access to such a stairway, being a lobby which complies with the provisions of regulation E10.

(8) Each inlet to a fire main shall be so sited that—

(*a*) access for a pumping appliance can be obtained to a cleared space which complies with regulation E16(4) or E17(*c*) and is within 18 metres of, and within sight of, an inlet, and

(*b*) it is not more than 12·5 metres measured horizontally from any vertical part of the main.

(9) In this regulation "fire main" means a system of pipes, each being of an internal diameter of not less than 100 millimetres, available for carrying a supply of water for fire fighting purposes and for those purposes only, and "undivided building" means a building which is not sub-divided by fire division walls.

Fire lifts

E19.—(1) In every building any storey of which is at a height of more than 24 metres above ground level there shall be provided, in respect of every storey, at least one lift serving that storey and complying with the following provisions of this regulation:

Provided that nothing in this regulation shall apply in respect of—

(i) a storey in a block of flats on which there is no entrance to any flat,

(ii) the top-most storey of a building—

(A) on which there is a fire mains outlet provided so as to comply with the last foregoing regulation, and

(B) to which there is access by a stair serving also the storey below that storey, and

(C) the lift serving the floor next below that storey is distant from a door in the stairway enclosure of that stair by a horizontal distance of not more than 4·5 metres.

(2) The electrical supply to the lift shall be provided by an independent circuit.

(3) The lift car of the lift shall have an internal area of not less than 1100 millimetres by 1400 millimetres and the lift shall be capable of carrying a load of not less than 600 kilogrammes.

(4) The lift shall be fitted with a fire switch control system incorporating—

(*a*) a device which will enable firemen to take control of the lift without interference from landing call points, and

(*b*) a fire switch positioned at the landing call station at ground floor level and housed in a glass-fronted lock-fast recessed box clearly marked "FIRE SWITCH".

(5) The entrance to the lift on each storey served by the lift shall be—

(*a*) in an open access balcony or other permanently ventilated area, or (*b*) within any stairway enclosure provided so as to comply with regulation E9, or

(*c*) within any lobby provided so as to comply with regulation E10, or

(*d*) not more than—

(i) where there is only one exit from the storey, 4·5 metres, or

(ii) where there is more than one exit from the storey, 15 metres

from a protected doorway giving access to such a stairway enclosure.

PART F

Chimneys, Flues, Hearths and the Installation of Heat Producing Appliances

Application of Part F

F1.—(1) Regulations F3 to F20 shall apply to—

(*a*) any appliance—

(i) designed to burn solid fuel or oil and having an output rating not exceeding 45 kilowatts, or

(ii) comprising an incinerator having a combustion chamber capacity exceeding 0·03 cubic metre but not exceeding 0·08 cubic metre, and

(*b*) any chimney, flue-pipe or hearth used in conjunction with such an appliance.

(2) Regulations F21 to F29 shall apply to—

(*a*) any appliance—

(i) designed to burn only gaseous fuel and having an input rating not exceeding 45 kilowatts, or

(ii) comprising an incinerator having a combustion chamber capacity not exceeding 0·03 cubic metre, and

(*b*) any chimney, flue-pipe or hearth used in conjunction with such an appliance.

(3) Regulation F30 shall apply to—

(*a*) any appliance—

(i) designed to burn solid fuel or oil and having an output rating exceeding 45 kilowatts, or

(ii) designed to burn only gaseous fuel and having an input rating exceeding 45 kilowatts, or

(iii) comprising an incinerator having a combustion chamber capacity exceeding 0·08 cubic metre, and

(*b*) any chimney, flue-pipe or hearth used in conjunction with such an appliance.

(4) The provisions of regulations F5, F10 and F20 shall not be subject to specification in a notice served under section 11 of the Act (which enables local authorities to require existing buildings to conform to these regulations).

Interpretation of Part F

F2.—(1) In this Part—

"air heater" means an appliance designed to burn only gaseous fuel and to distribute warm air by means of a fan forming part of the appliance;

"appliance" means a heat producing appliance, either forming part of a building or affixed to a building as a fixture, not being an appliance designed to burn without being connected to a flue and includes an incinerator;

"appliance ventilation duct" means a flue which in one part serves to convey combustion air to one or more appliances, in another part serves to convey the products of combustion from one or more appliances to the external air, and intermediately serves both purposes;

"aspect ratio", in relation to any part of a flue, means—

(*a*) in the case of a flue of rectangular shape, the ratio of the length of the longer side to the length of the shorter side, or in the case of a square a ratio of 1 to 1,

(*b*) in the case of a flue of any other shape, the ratio of the major axis to the minor axis, or in the case of a circle, a ratio of 1 to 1,

the dimensions in either case being those of the internal cross-section of that part of the flue;

"controlled combustion appliance" means an appliance so designed that the total supply of air thereto can be controlled manually or automatically but does not include an open fire or openable stove;

"convector gas fire" means an appliance designed to burn only gaseous fuel, incorporating an incandescent source of heat and designed to give not less than 10 per cent of its heat output in the form of convected warm air, not being an air heater;

"flue" means a passage which conveys the products of combustion from an appliance to the open air;

"flue-pipe" means a pipe forming a flue, but does not include a pipe fitted as a lining in a chimney;

"openable stove" means a stove fitted with fire doors and which is designed to operate efficiently with the fire doors either open or closed;

"radiant gas fire" means an appliance designed to burn only gaseous fuel and incorporating an incandescent source of heat not being a convector gas fire.

(2) Any reference in this Part to bricks or blocks of a fire-resistant composition shall be construed as a reference to—

(*a*) bricks or blocks of kiln-burnt material or of concrete having a density of not less than 1600 kilogrammes per cubic metre and made with natural aggregate or aggregate composed of crushed kiln-burnt material, or

(*b*) blocks of aerated concrete.

(3) In determining, for the purposes of this Part, whether a material used in particular circumstances is suitable or is of adequate thickness regard shall be had—

(*a*) in the case of appliances, chimneys, flues or hearths to which regulations F3 to F20 apply, to the strength of the material as so used and to—

(i) its ability to withstand a temperature of 1000° Celsius without significant change in its properties, and

(ii) the effect on its properties of rapid heating;

(*b*) in the case of appliances, chimneys, flues or hearths to which regulations F21 to F29 apply, to the permeability and strength of the material so used and to its ability to withstand a temperature of 120° Celsius and the effects of corrosion without significant change in its properties.

Solid Fuel and Oil Burning Appliances

Construction of chimneys

F3. Every part of a chimney to which this regulation applies shall be constructed of suitable non-combustible materials and shall be properly jointed:

Provided that nothing in this regulation shall prevent the use in a chimney of a damp-proof course composed of combustible material if it is solidly bedded in mortar.

**Construction of flue-pipes*

F4.—(1) Every flue-pipe to which this regulation applies shall be—

(*a*) constructed of—

(i) malleable or wrought iron or mild or stainless steel not less than 4·75 millimetres in thickness, or

(ii) cast iron of adequate thickness and strength, and

(*b*) properly jointed and supported, and

(*c*) properly connected to the appliance and to any chimney into which it discharges, and

(*d*) so fitted as to discharge into a flue in a chimney complying with the requirements of this Part or into the open air:

Provided that nothing in this regulation shall prevent—

(i) so much of any flue-pipe, not being a flue-pipe connected with an open fire, as is more than 1·8 metres from the junction of the flue-pipe with the appliance being constructed of asbestos cement conforming to British Standard 835: 1967, "Asbestos cement flue pipes and fittings, heavy quality";

(ii) any part of the flue-pipe which is not more than 460 millimetres in length and connects the outlet of a free-standing open fire to a chimney being constructed of sheet steel having a thickness of not less than 1·6 millimetres.

(2) No part of the flue-pipe, whether encased or not, shall pass through—

(*a*) any floor, or

(*b*) any roof space, other than a space between a roof covering and a ceiling attached as a lining to—

(i) the rafters or purlins of a pitched roof, or

(ii) the joists of a flat roof, or

(*c*) any ceiling, other than such a ceiling as is referred to in the last foregoing sub-paragraph, or

(*d*) any wall, other than—

(i) an external wall of a building, or

(ii) where the flue-pipe discharges into a flue in a chimney, a wall forming part of the chimney:

Provided that nothing in this paragraph shall prevent a flue-pipe from passing through any ceiling and floor where—

(i) the ceiling and floor are constructed of non-combustible materials, and

(ii) the flue-pipe discharges into a flue within a chimney carried by the floor.

(3) Where the flue-pipe passes through a roof or, subject to the provisions of the last foregoing paragraph, passes through a ceiling or wall, it shall—

(*a*) be distant by an amount equal to not less than three times its external diameter from any combustible material forming part of the roof, ceiling or wall, or

(*b*) be separated from any combustible material forming part of the roof, ceiling or wall by solid non-combustible material not less than 200 millimetres thick, so, however, that if the flue-pipe passes through a wall and the combustible material is above the pipe the non-combustible material shall not be less than 300 millimetres thick, or

(*c*) be enclosed in a sleeve of metal or asbestos cement which complies with the provisions of the next succeeding paragraph.

(4) Any sleeve of metal or asbestos cement provided so as to comply with sub-paragraph (*c*) of the last foregoing paragraph shall—

(*a*) be carried through the roof, ceiling or wall to project not less than 150 millimetres beyond any combustible material forming part of the roof, ceiling or wall, and

(*b*) have between it and the flue-pipe a space of not less than 25 millimetres packed with non-combustible thermal insulating material, and

(*c*) where the roof, ceiling or wall contains any combustible material, and—

(i) is of hollow construction—

(A) be so placed that there is an air space between the outer surface of the sleeve and the combustible material, and

(B) be so fitted that the combustible material is at a distance of not less than 25 millimetres from the outer surface of the sleeve and not less than one and a half times the external diameter of the flue-pipe from the outer surface of the pipe,

(ii) is of solid construction—

(A) be so fitted that the combustible material is at a distance of not less than 190 millimetres from the outer surface of the flue-pipe, and

(B) be separated from the outer surface of the sleeve by solid non-combustible material not less than 100 millimetres thick.

(5) Where the flue-pipe is adjacent to any wall which contains any combustible material, the flue-pipe shall be distant from the combustible material by an amount equal to not less than three times the external diameter of the flue-pipe:

Provided that where—

(i) the combustible material is protected by a shield of non-combustible material fixed between the wall and the flue-pipe, and

(ii) the shield projects on either side of the flue-pipe for a distance not less than an amount equal to one and one-half times the external diameter of the flue-pipe, and

(iii) there is an air space of not less than 12·5 millimetres between the shield and the combustible material or between the shield and any non-combustible material which covers the combustible material,

this paragraph shall have effect as if for the amount equal to not less than three times the external diameter of the flue-pipe there were substituted an amount equal to not less than one and one-half times such diameter.

(6) Where the flue-pipe passes under any floor, roof or ceiling which contains any combustible material it shall be distant from the combustible material by an

amount equal to not less than four times the external diameter of the pipe:

Provided that where—

(i) the combustible material is protected by a shield of non-combustible material fixed between the floor, roof or ceiling and the flue-pipe, and

(ii) the shield projects on either side of the flue-pipe for a distance of not less than an amount equal to two and one-half times the external diameter of the flue-pipe, and

(iii) there is an air space of not less than 12·5 millimetres between the shield and the combustible material or between the shield and any non-combustible material which covers the combustible material,

this paragraph shall have effect as if for the amount equal to not less than four times the external diameter of the flue-pipe there were substituted an amount equal to not less than three times such diameter.

(7) Where the flue-pipe discharges in a vertical direction into a flue in a chimney, the flue-pipe shall be separated from any combustible material fixed into the chimney by solid non-combustible material not less than 200 millimetres thick all round the flue-pipe.

(8) Where the flue-pipe discharges into the side of a flue in a chimney it shall be distant from any combustible material fixed into the chimney by an amount of not less than—

(*a*) if the combustible material is below or beside the flue-pipe, 200 millimetres;

(*b*) if the combustible material is above the flue-pipe, 300 millimetres.

(9) There shall be provided in the flue-pipe such number of openings so located and of such size as shall enable the flue to be inspected and cleaned and each such opening shall be fitted with a non-combustible close fitting cover.

Height of chimney stacks and flue-pipes

F5.—(1) Every chimney stack and flue-pipe to which this regulation applies shall extend to such a height and be so positioned that the outlet of—

(*a*) any flue contained in the chimney stack, no account being taken of any attachment to the stack, or

(*b*) any flue-pipe

complies with the following provisions of this regulation.

(2) No part of the outlet shall be within a horizontal distance of 2·3 metres of any part of any building, other than a chimney or parapet wall.

(3) No part of the outlet shall be within a distance of 12 metres measured in any direction from any part of a roof which is covered with materials designated DA, DB, DC or DD.

(4) No part of the outlet shall be less than—

(*a*) 600 millimetres above the highest point of intersection of the chimney stack or flue-pipe with any roof, saddle or gutter, or in the case of a flat roof, 1·5 metres;

(*b*) 1 metre above the level of the top of any dormer window, openable skylight or other roof opening any part of which is within a horizontal distance of 2·3 metres of the flue;

(*c*) 1 metre above the level of any part of a building (other than a roof, chimney or parapet wall) that is within a horizontal distance of 2·3 metres of the flue.

Combustible materials in relation to chimneys

F6.—(1) No timber, or other combustible material, shall be built into the structure of a building within a distance of 200 millimetres from any part of—

(*a*) a fireplace opening in a chimney to which this regulation applies, or

(*b*) a flue in a chimney or flue-pipe to which this regulation applies, or

(*c*) an opening into such a fireplace opening or flue:

Provided that—

(i) in relation to wooden dooks built into the structure of a building, this paragraph shall have effect as if for the distance of 200 millimetres there were substituted a distance of 150 millimetres;

(ii) nothing in this regulation shall prevent the use of a damp-proof course composed of combustible materials if it is solidly bedded in mortar.

(2) No structural timber or other combustible structural material, other than flooring, strapping or sarking, shall be nearer than 38 millimetres to the face of any rendering provided so as to comply with regulation F8.

Metal fastenings

F7. No metal fastening which is in contact with any combustible material forming part of the building shall be placed within a distance of 50 millimetres from any part of—

(*a*) any fireplace opening in a chimney to which this regulation applies, or

(*b*) any flue in a chimney or flue-pipe to which this regulation applies, or

(*c*) any opening into such a fireplace opening or flue.

Sealing the outside of chimneys

F8. Where any part of a chimney to which this regulation applies, not being a chimney which is constructed of concrete cast in situ, is within a building and the thickness in that part from the outer surface of the chimney to the flue is less than 200 millimetres, the outer surface of that part of the chimney shall be rendered with mortar or plaster not less than 7 millimetres in thickness:

Provided that nothing in this regulation shall apply to a chimney the flue of which complies with the provisions of regulation F10(1)(*a*).

Thickness of materials surrounding flues in chimneys

F9.—(1) The following provisions of this regulation shall apply to every flue in a chimney to which this regulation applies.

(2) The flue shall be surrounded by, and separated from every other flue by, solid material—

(*a*) extending from the top of the fireplace opening to the top of the chimney stack, and

(*b*) of a thickness not less than—

(i) in the case of bricks or blocks of a fire-resistant composition, 100 millimetres,

(ii) in any other case, 150 millimetres.

(3) Where the flue is in a chimney forming part of a separating wall, the material surrounding the flue shall, on the side opposite to that of the building

or part of a building served by the flue, be of a thickness of not less than—

(*a*) in the case of bricks or blocks of a fire-resistant composition, 200 millimetres,

(*b*) in any other case, 300 millimetres,

which thickness shall extend from the top of the fireplace opening up to the underside of the roof covering:

Provided that nothing in this paragraph shall prevent the thickness so required being made up of leaves of a wall separated by a cavity or flue if the two leaves together are of the thickness so required, and neither leaf is of a thickness less than—

(i) in the case of bricks or blocks of a fire-resistant composition, 100 millimetres;

(ii) in any other case, 150 millimetres.

(4) No part of the flue shall make an angle with a horizontal plane of less than 45 degrees.

(5) Any reference in this regulation to a thickness shall be construed as a reference to a thickness excluding any lining.

Lining of flues

F10.—(1) Every flue in a chimney to which this regulation applies shall either—

(*a*) be lined continuously throughout its length with any one of the following, namely—

(i) rebated or socketed clay flue linings complying with British Standard 1181: 1961,

(ii) rebated or socket flue linings made from kiln-burnt aggregate and high alumina cement,

(iii) glazed vitrified clay pipes and fittings complying with British Standard 65 & 540: 1966 as read with Amendment PD 6410, May 1968,

(iv) glazed (vitreous) enamelled salt-glazed fireclay pipes and fittings complying with British Standard 65 & 540: 1966 as read with Amendment PD 6410, May 1968,

and be jointed and flush-pointed with cement mortar and so built that the socket of any component having a socket is uppermost, or

(*b*) be constructed of concrete flue blocks made of, or having inside walls made of, kiln-burnt aggregate and high alumina cement and so made that no joints between blocks other than bedding joints adjoin any flue, the blocks being jointed and flush-pointed with cement mortar.

(2) Every flue to which the last foregoing paragraph applies shall—

(*a*) have no openings in it other than—

(i) an inlet in the base which, in the case of a flue not serving an open fire, shall be within a chamber which complies with paragraph (3) of this regulation, and

(ii) an outlet at the top to allow discharge of flue gases to the open air, and

(*b*) if the flue is lined in accordance with sub-paragraph (*a*) of the last foregoing paragraph, and does not serve an open fire, terminate at its lower end in such chamber, into which the lining shall project so as to form a drip for condensate.

(3) The chamber referred to in the last foregoing paragraph shall be—

(*a*) provided with means of access for inspection and cleaning and fitted with a non-combustible close-fitting cover, and

(*b*) connected to the appliance by a flue-pipe which discharges into the chamber through one of its sides, and

(*c*) so constructed as to be capable of containing a condensate collecting vessel.

(4) Where required for the safe burning of a controlled combustion appliance there shall be provided a draught-stabiliser or explosion door which shall open either into such a chamber as complies with the last foregoing paragraph or into the flue-pipe connecting the appliance to such a chamber.

(5) Nothing in this regulation shall require a flue to—

(*a*) be lined in accordance with this regulation if it previously served an appliance to which regulation F1(1) applies, or

(*b*) terminate at its lower end in a chamber if it previously served an open fire.

Access to flues

F11. Where any flue in a chimney or flue-pipe to which this regulation applies serves a fireplace opening capable of containing an open fire, there shall be no opening in the flue which is not an opening of any of the following descriptions—

(*a*) the opening made for the purpose of receiving the products of combustion;

(*b*) any opening made for the purpose of inspection or cleaning and fitted with a non-combustible close-fitting cover;

(*c*) an air inlet made in a part of the chimney either—

(i) in the same room as the fireplace opening, or

(ii) from the external air;

(*d*) the opening made for the purpose of discharging the products of combustion into the external air.

Flues for appliances

F12.—(1) Every appliance to which this regulation applies, not being an incinerator, shall be connected to a separate flue:

Provided that nothing in this regulation shall prevent the connection of two appliances to one flue if—

(i) one of the appliances is auxiliary to the other, and

(ii) both are situated in the same room, and

(iii) both are designed to burn the same type of fuel, that is, either solid fuel or oil, and

(iv) the flue of each appliance is provided with a suitable and adequate baffle or damper to prevent the passage of smoke or gases from one appliance to the other, and

(v) the two appliances are connected to the flue at different levels, the connection from the auxiliary appliance being the lower.

(2) The cross-sectional area of the flue shall be adequate to dispose efficiently of the products of combustion of any appliance which it serves and shall, in any case, be not less than the area of any flue connection on the appliance or, if the flue is used for two appliances, not less than the area of the larger of the flue connections.

**Thickness of materials surrounding fireplace openings*

F13.—(1) Every fireplace opening in a chimney to which this regulation applies shall be constructed in accordance with the following provisions of this regulation.

(2) The jambs at each side of the fireplace opening shall be constructed of solid non-combustible material of a thickness, excluding any part of the appliance, of not less than—

(*a*) in the case of bricks or blocks of a fire-resistant composition, 200 millimetres;

(*b*) in any other case, 300 millimetres.

(3) Subject to Part J, the wall at the back of the fireplace opening shall be constructed of solid non-combustible material of a thickness, excluding any part of the appliance, of not less than—

(*a*) where the wall is exposed on one face to the open air or is common to more than one fireplace opening but does not form part of a separating wall—

(i) in the case of bricks or blocks of a fire-resistant composition, 100 millimetres,

(ii) in any other case, 150 millimetres;

(*b*) where the wall is not so exposed or, if common to more than one fireplace opening, forms part of a separating wall—

(i) in the case of bricks or blocks of a fire-resistant composition, 200 millimetres,

(ii) in any other case, 300 millimetres:

Provided that where under this paragraph a wall is required to be of a thickness of 200 millimetres or more, nothing in this paragraph shall prevent the thickness so required being made up of two leaves separated by a cavity if the two leaves together are of the thickness so required, and neither leaf is of a thickness less than—

(i) in the case of bricks or blocks of fire-resistant composition, 100 millimetres;

(ii) in any other case, 150 millimetres.

(4) The solid non-combustible material provided so as to comply with paragraphs (2) and (3) of this regulation shall extend for the full height of the fireplace opening and up to the underside of the lintel or springing of the arch over the opening.

(5) The walls and jambs forming the fireplace opening shall be lined on the back and sides with fireclay not less than 38 millimetres in thickness:

Provided that this paragraph shall not apply to any fireplace opening in which there is set an appliance which is itself lined with fireclay of a thickness of not less than 38 millimetres.

(6) In this regulation "fireclay" shall include fireclay bricks built and pointed in fireclay cement.

Thickness of materials in proximity to free-standing appliances

F14. Any part of a building which is within 300 millimetres of any part of a free-standing appliance to which this regulation applies shall—

(*a*) in the case of a wall, be constructed of solid non-combustible material and be of a thickness of not less than 100 millimetres, which construction shall extend to a height of not less than 300 millimetres measured vertically above the upper surface of the appliance;

(*b*) in the case of any other part, not being a floor, be constructed of non-combustible materials, unless it is so protected as to ensure that it cannot be ignited by heat from the appliance.

Constructional hearths in fireplace openings

F15.—(1) Subject to paragraph (5) of this regulation, every fireplace opening in a chimney to which this regulation applies shall be provided with a constructional hearth which complies with the following provisions of this regulation.

(2) The hearth shall—

(*a*) be of solid non-combustible construction throughout, and

(*b*) extend throughout the whole base of the fireplace opening, and

(*c*) project not less than 150 millimetres beyond each side of the opening and have a total width of not less than 840 millimetres, and

(*d*) project not less than 500 millimetres in front of the face of the jamb.

(3) The hearth throughout its whole area shall be not less than 125 millimetres thick, exclusive of any part of the appliance, but inclusive of any tiles or other non-combustible surface finish:

Provided that where the floor is constructed as a solid concrete floor laid directly on the ground nothing in this paragraph shall require any hearth in or on that floor to be of a thickness greater than 100 millimetres.

(4) The upper surface of that portion of the hearth projecting beyond the front of that part of the appliance which is designed to contain the fire shall be not lower than the surface of the floor adjoining the hearth.

(5) Nothing in this regulation shall prohibit—

(*a*) the construction of a pit to hold the sunken ash container of an appliance if—

(i) such pit is surrounded with brickwork or concrete not less than 50 millimetres in thickness, and

(ii) there is beneath the pit a solid base of non-combustible material not less than 100 millimetres in thickness, and

(iii) there is no opening in the surround or base of the pit other than—

(A) the outlet of a smoke-tight duct drawing the air supply for the appliance direct from the external air or sub-floor area, or

(B) a smoke-tight opening in the external wall of the building to enable the removal of the container, and

(iv) there is no combustible material nearer to the inner surface of any part of the surround and base of the pit than 225 millimetres, and

(v) between the outer surface of any part of the surround or base of the pit and any combustible material, there is an air space of not less than 50 millimetres;

(*b*) the formation in the hearth of a smoke-tight duct solely for the admission of air to the appliance and constructed of non-combustible materials.

Constructional hearths other than in fireplace openings

F16.—(1) Every free-standing appliance to which this regulation applies shall be provided with a constructional hearth which shall comply with the following provisions of this regulation.

(2) The hearth shall be throughout of solid non-combustible material and, including any tiles or other surface finish, shall be not less than 125 millimetres in thickness.

(3) No part of the upper surface of the hearth shall be below the surface of the floor adjoining the hearth.

(4) The hearth shall have such a width and depth in relation to the appliance as will enable compliance with regulation F19, but in no case shall such width and depth be less than 840 millimetres.

Combustible material under constructional hearths

F17. Any timber or other combustible materials under a constructional hearth provided so as to comply with regulation F15 or the last foregoing regulation shall be so placed that it is separated from the underside of the hearth by an air space of not less than 50 millimetres:

Provided that—

(i) this regulation shall not apply if the timber or other combustible material is separated from the upper surface of the constructional hearth, or superimposed hearth, as the case may be, by solid non-combustible material not less than 250 millimetres in thickness;

(ii) nothing in this regulation shall prevent the placing under a hearth of timber fillets supporting the edges of the hearth at the front and on the sides.

Construction of appliances

F18. Every appliance to which this regulation applies shall be so designed and constructed as to contain the fire and shall be provided with an opening of adequate size for the removal of smoke and noxious fumes and such opening shall be so formed as to permit its connection with the flue or flue-pipe.

Installation of appliances

F19.—(1) Every appliance to which this regulation applies shall be so installed as to comply with the following provisions of this regulation.

(2) The appliance shall be placed either—

(*a*) directly upon the constructional hearth provided so as to comply with regulation F15 or F16, or

(*b*) directly upon a superimposed hearth which is of non-combustible material not less than 48 millimetres in thickness and is placed wholly or partly on the constructional hearth so provided.

(3) The distance between an appliance and the edges of the hearth upon which it is directly placed shall in no case be less than—

(*a*) from the front of the appliance—

(i) if the appliance is or has an open fire, 300 millimetres,

(ii) in any other case, 200 millimetres;

(*b*) from the sides of the appliance, 150 millimetres;

(*c*) from the back of the appliance, 150 millimetres.

(4) Where an appliance is installed directly upon a superimposed hearth no part of the appliance shall project over any edge of the constructional hearth and no combustible material beneath the superimposed hearth shall be nearer any part of the appliance than 150 millimetres measured horizontally.

**Fireguard fittings*

F20. Where in any building of occupancy group A there is a fireplace opening capable of containing an open fire there shall be provided on each side of the fireplace opening screwed bushes or plugs fitted with screwed eyelets so as to enable a fireguard to be securely fitted in front of the opening.

Gas Burning Appliances

**Design and construction of chimneys and flue-pipes*

F21.—(1) Every part of a chimney or flue-pipe to which this regulation applies shall be constructed of suitable non-combustible materials and shall be properly jointed:

Provided that nothing in this paragraph shall prevent the use in a chimney—

(i) of a damp-proof course composed of combustible material if it is solidly bedded in mortar, or

(ii) of combustible jointing collars if the chimney is constructed of blocks and has only horizontal joints.

(2) Every flue-pipe to which this regulation applies shall—

(*a*) be properly supported, and

(*b*) be so fitted as to discharge into a flue of a chimney or flue-pipe which complies with this Part or into the open air, and

(*c*) be properly connected to the appliance and to any flue into which it discharges.

(3) No part of such a flue-pipe shall be nearer to any combustible material than 25 millimetres.

(4) Where such a flue-pipe passes through a roof, floor, ceiling or wall of combustible material it shall be enclosed in a sleeve of non-combustible material which—

(*a*) is carried through the roof, floor, ceiling or wall, and

(*b*) is separated from the pipe by a distance of 25 millimetres.

(5) Where any part of a flue-pipe from an appliance to which this regulation applies passes through any room (other than that in which the appliance is installed) or other enclosed space, that part of the flue-pipe shall be so placed or protected as to prevent damage to the pipe or danger to the occupants of the building.

Flue outlets

F22. Every outlet of a flue of a chimney or flue-pipe to which this regulation applies shall—

(*a*) be so positioned that a free current of air may pass across it at all times, and

(*b*) be fitted with a terminal, that is to say, a device designed to allow free egress to the products of combustion, to minimise downdraught and to prevent the entrance of foreign matter which might cause restriction of the flue:

Provided that nothing in paragraph (*b*) of this regulation shall apply to the outlet of a flue which terminates in the outer face of a wall and is suitably covered to protect it from damage.

Fastenings in relation to chimneys

F23. No fastenings shall be built into or placed in any chimney to which this regulation applies nearer than 25 millimetres to the internal face of any flue.

Thickness of materials surrounding flues in chimneys

F24. Every flue in a chimney to which this regulation applies shall be surrounded by and separated from every other flue by solid material not less than 25 millimetres in thickness:

Provided that nothing in this regulation shall require a flue in a chimney to be separated from another flue in the chimney by solid material if each flue is contained within a flue-pipe fitted in the chimney, being a flue-pipe which complies with this Part.

Access to flues

F25. Where any flue in a chimney or flue-pipe to which this regulation applies serves one or more appliances there shall be no opening in the flue which is not an opening of any of the following descriptions—

(*a*) the opening made for the purpose of receiving the products of combustion from an appliance so served;

(*b*) any opening associated with a draught diverter, that is to say, a device designed to prevent downdraught or static conditions in a flue from interfering with combustion gas in any appliance or to prevent excessive flue pull;

(*c*) any opening made for the purpose of inspecting or cleaning and fitted with a non-combustible gas-tight cover;

(*d*) any air inlet made in that part of the flue which is in a room where an appliance to which it is connected is situated;

(*e*) the opening made for the purpose of discharging the products of combustion into the open air.

Flues for appliances

F26.—(1) Every appliance to which this regulation applies, not being an incinerator, shall be connected to a separate flue:

Provided that nothing in this paragraph shall prevent the connection of two or more appliances—

(i) to a common flue if the appliances are situated in the same room;

(ii) to a common flue by way of separate subsidiary flues in the relevant circumstances;

(iii) to an appliance ventilation duct if—

(A) all of the appliances so connected draw their combustion air from, and discharge their combustion products to, the duct, and

(B) the combustion chambers of the appliances are sealed from the room in which they are fitted except for a gas-tight lighting or access door which is either self-closing or, when open, operates to close automatically the flue from the appliance to the duct, and

(C) the duct is so designed and constructed that under any condition of normal operation of the appliances so connected the discharge from the outlet of the duct does not contain more than 2 per cent in volume of carbon dioxide.

(2) For the purposes of proviso (ii) to paragraph (1) of this regulation the relevant circumstances are all of the following—

(*a*) all the appliances connected to the common flue are of the same type, being one of the types set forth in column (1) of the table in sub-paragraph (*j*) of this paragraph, and each is fitted with a flame failure device;

(*b*) the common flue has a cross-sectional area of not less than 40 000 square millimetres;

(*c*) the outlet of the common flue is in a position which is freely exposed to the external air and which is at no part lower than whichever is the greatest of the following heights—

(i) if the roof is a pitched roof, the height of the ridge thereof, or if the roof is a flat roof, 600 millimetres above the roof;

(ii) if there is any part of a structure within a horizontal distance from the outlet not exceeding 3·4 metres—

(A) if the distance does not exceed 1·5 metres, a height of 600 millimetres above that part;

(B) if the distance exceeds 1·5 metres, a height above that part equal to one-third of the difference between the distance and 3·4 metres;

(*d*) the common flue is not fitted to an external wall;

(*e*) the windows of the rooms in which the appliances are fitted all face in the same direction;

(*f*) between the outlet of each appliance and the point of connection of the subsidiary flue to the common flue there shall be a vertical portion of the subsidiary flue extending to a height of not less than 1·8 metres;

(*g*) the cross-sectional area of each subsidiary flue is not less than the cross-sectional area of the outlet of the appliance;

(*h*) no part of a subsidiary flue, other than a connecting bend no part of which is more than 600 millimetres in length, makes an angle with the horizontal plane of less than 45 degrees;

(*i*) the outlet of the common flue is not less than 6 metres above the outlet of the highest appliance connected thereto;

(*j*) the number of appliances and their aggregate rating does not exceed—

(i) where the cross-sectional area of the common flue is less than 62 000 square millimetres, the number and rating set forth respectively in columns (2) and (3) of the following table, and

(ii) in any other case, the number and rating set forth respectively in columns (4) and (5) of the said table.

Appliance (1)	No. of appliances (2)	Maximum total input rating (kilo-watts) (3)	No. of appliances (4)	Maximum total input rating (kilo-watts) (5)
Convector gas fire with controlled flue flow (42–70 cubic metres) ...	5	30	7	45
Instantaneous water heater ...	10	300	10	450
Storage water heater, circulator or air heater	10	120	10	180

(3) Every flue in a chimney or flue-pipe to which this regulation applies shall be so constructed that at no point in the flue shall—

(*a*) the dimension of any axis of the cross-sectional area thereof be less than 63 millimetres;

(*b*) the aspect ratio exceed—

(i) in the case of a flue serving a convector gas fire or radiant gas fire, 5 to 1;

(ii) in the case of any other flue, 1½ to 1;

(*c*) the cross-sectional area be less than the area of any flue connection on the appliance served by the flue, or, if the flue is used for two appliances, be less than the area of the larger of the flue connections to the common flue.

(4) In this regulation any reference to a roof in relation to the outlet of a common flue shall be construed as a reference to any roof or part of a roof with which the flue-pipe or chimney containing the common flue makes an intersection.

Combustible material in relation to appliances

F27. The back, top and sides of any appliance to which this regulation applies (including any draught divertor associated therewith) shall be separated from any combustible material in the building, other than flooring, by a shield of non-combustible material not less than 25 millimetres in thickness or by a space of not less than 75 millimetres:

Provided that this regulation shall not apply to any appliance designed so that, under any conditions of normal operation, the external surface temperature at no point on the back, top or sides exceeds 100° Celsius.

Hearths for appliances

F28. Between the underside of any appliance to which this regulation applies and any combustible surface finish, or other combustible material, there shall be provided a hearth of non-combustible material not less than 12·5 millimetres thick, which hearth shall—

(*a*) extend beyond each side and the back of the appliance—

(i) not less than 150 millimetres, or

(ii) up to any adjacent wall,

whichever is the less distance, and

(*b*) extend forward from the appliance to a distance of not less than 225 millimetres measured horizontally from the lowest part of any flame or incandescent material within the appliance:

Provided that this regulation shall not apply in the case of an appliance—

(i) of which the lowest portion of any flame or incandescent material is at a distance of 225 millimetres or more above the floor, or

(ii) so designed that under any condition of normal operation the temperature at the base of the appliance does not exceed 100° Celsius.

**Gas burning appliances*

F29. Every appliance to which this regulation applies shall be so designed, constructed and installed as to operate efficiently and safely.

Appliances of a High Rating

Chimneys, flue-pipes and hearths and appliances of a high rating

F30.—(1) Every chimney, flue-pipe and hearth to which this regulation applies shall be constructed of suitable non-combustible materials so put together and arranged as to prevent the ignition of any part of the building of which they form part, and every such chimney or flue-pipe shall be carried upwards to such a height and so positioned as to prevent so far as is reasonably practicable the escape of smoke, grit, dust or gases into any such part or any other adjoining building.

(2) Every appliance to which this regulation applies shall be so designed, constructed and installed as to operate efficiently and safely.

General

Access to roof

F31. Where in the case of any building—

(*a*) the roof is a mansard roof and the flatter portion thereof is, or

(*b*) the roof is a flat roof and is, or

(*c*) the roof is neither a flat roof nor a mansard roof and the eaves are

at a height of more than 4·5 metres above ground level at every part, the building shall be provided with suitable means for obtaining access to the roof and to any chimney stacks forming part of the building:

Provided that nothing in this regulation shall apply to buildings in occupancy sub-group A1 or A2 not exceeding two storeys in height.

Appliances for heating and cooking

F32. No appliance for heating or cooking shall be installed in a building other than an appliance designed to burn coke, anthracite, semi-anthracite, gas or electricity:

Provided that nothing in this regulation shall prohibit—

(i) the installation of a furnace to which section 3 of the Clean Air Act 1956(**a**) applies;

(ii) the installation of an appliance which is itself exempt from the provisions of section 11 of the said Act of 1956, or which belongs to a class or description of appliance which is so exempt;

(iii) the installation of an appliance in a building which is itself so exempt, or which belongs to a class or description of building which is so exempt.

PART G

Preparation of Sites and Resistance to the Passage of Moisture

Application of Part G

G1.—(1) Regulations G3, G5 and G6 shall not apply to any temporary building of occupancy sub-group A3 or A4 or of occupancy group B, C, D or E.

(2) Regulation G7 shall not apply to any temporary building of occupancy group B, C, D or E.

(**a**) 1956 c. 52.

**Protection against ground water and flood water*

G2. The site of every building and the ground in the vicinity of the building shall, so far as is reasonably practicable, be drained or otherwise treated to the extent necessary to prevent any harmful effects on any part of the building from ground water or flood water.

Existing drains

G3. Every drain and agricultural pipe passing under the site of a building shall, if reasonably practicable, be diverted therefrom or, if not so practicable, shall be so reconstructed as to conform to regulation M5.

Removal of matter harmful to health

G4. There shall be removed from the site of any building intended for human use and habitation, and from the ground in the vicinity of the building, any matter which might have harmful effects on the health of the users or occupants of the building.

Removal of surface soil and other matter

G5. There shall be dug out and removed from the site of every building surface soil, vegetable and other similarly harmful matter to the extent necessary to prevent any harmful effects therefrom on any part of the building.

**Treatment of solum*

G6.—(1) The solum shall be treated in such a way as to prevent the growth of vegetable matter and to reduce the evaporation of moisture from the ground to the extent necessary to prevent any harmful effects on any part of the building and on the health of its occupants.

(2) In this regulation "solum" means the area within the containing walls of a building after removal of the soil and other matter so as to comply with the last foregoing regulation.

**Resistance to moisture from the ground*

G7. In every building, that part of the structure in contact with the ground shall—

(*a*) have incorporated therein a layer of material impermeable to moisture and so positioned as to prevent the passage of ground moisture, or

(*b*) be of such material and so constructed that ground moisture cannot penetrate

to the inner surface of the building or to any part of the building that would be harmfully affected thereby.

**Resistance to moisture from rain or snow*

G8. In every building those parts of the structure that are exposed to the effects of rain or snow shall be so designed and comprised of such materials as—

(*a*) to prevent any harmful effect of moisture from rain or snow on the health of the persons using or occupying the building, and

(*b*) (i) in the case of roofs, to prevent, and

(ii) in the case of other parts of the structure, to restrict so far as is reasonably practicable the passage of such moisture to the inner surface of the building or any part thereof that would be harmfully affected thereby:

Provided that this regulation shall not apply to a building or part of a building which is intended to be used in such a manner that the passage of moisture to the inner surface thereof will have no more harmful effect upon the structure of the building or part thereof than that likely to result from the intended use of the building.

PART H

Resistance to the Transmission of Sound

Application of Part H

H1. The provisions of this Part shall not be subject to specification in a notice served under section 11 of the Act (which enables local authorities to require existing buildings to conform to these regulations).

**Separating walls and floors*

H2.—(1) Where a wall separates a house from any other building or where a wall or floor separates a house forming part of a building from any other part of that building, the wall or floor, as the case may be, shall be so constructed that, in conjunction with other components of the structure of the building in association therewith, it reduces the airborne sound by not less than the values given in Part I of Table 11 at all the frequencies stated therein:

Provided that the wall or floor shall be accepted as meeting the requirements of this paragraph if, on a reading being taken at each of the frequencies set out in the said Part I, the aggregate of any amounts by which the reduction of airborne sound falls short of the value given in the said Part I does not exceed 23 decibels.

(2) Where the floor of any part of a building separates that part of the building from a house in the same building, the floor shall be so constructed that in conjunction with other components of the structure in association therewith, it limits the impact sound transmission so that when a sound field is generated in that part of the building by the standard impact method, the sound pressure levels produced in any part of any house do not exceed the values given in Part II of Table 11 at all the frequencies stated therein:

Provided that a floor shall be accepted as meeting the requirements of this paragraph if, on a reading being taken at each of the frequencies set out in the said Part II, the aggregate of any amounts by which the sound pressure level exceeds the value set forth in the said Part II is not greater than 23 decibels.

(3) In this regulation "standard impact method" means the method of generating a sound field described in clause 5*a* of British Standard 2750:1956, "Recommendations for field and laboratory measurement of airborne and impact sound transmission in buildings" as read with Amendment PD 5065, October 1963, used in relation to a floor.

(4) Nothing in this regulation shall apply to any wall separating a house from an open access balcony.

Measurement of sound transmission

H3.—(1) For the purposes of regulation H2 the measurements of sound transmission and the values of sound transmission in relation to any wall or floor shall be determined in accordance with the following provisions of this regulation:

Provided that—

(i) where the construction of any part of a wall or floor differs from that of the remaining part of that wall or floor each part shall be treated for the purposes of this regulation as a separate wall or floor;

(ii) every wall or floor or part of a wall or floor in a building with nominally identical construction shall be treated as forming part of a single wall or floor, as the case may be.

(2) Measurements shall be in accordance with sections two and three of British Standard 2750: 1956 as read with Amendment PD 5065, October 1963, and the method of normalising the results for both airborne and impact sound shall be that given in clause 3*e*(ii) of the said British Standard.

(3) Where a wall or floor in any building separates one or more pairs of apartments the value of the sound transmission of that wall or floor shall be taken to be the average of the measurements between apartments separated by that wall or floor as follows—

(*a*) where the wall or floor separates four pairs of living rooms, the measurements between those four pairs;

(*b*) where the wall or floor separates more than four pairs of living rooms, the measurements between such of those pairs of rooms, being not less than four, as may be selected by the buildings authority;

(*c*) where the wall or floor separates less than four pairs of living rooms but separates other pairs of apartments, the measurements between the pairs of living rooms and such other pairs as may be selected by the buildings authority, being in any case such number as will bring up the number tested to not less than four;

(*d*) where the wall or floor separates less than four pairs of apartments, the measurements between those pairs of apartments.

(4) Where a wall or floor of any construction, in any building, separates any apartments forming part of a house from any other part of that building, not being a part within another house, the value of the sound transmission of that wall or floor shall be that achieved by a wall or floor of such construction, separating apartments in one house from apartments in another, tested in accordance with paragraph (3) of this regulation.

(5) In this regulation "apartment" shall include a reference to "room, bathroom, washroom, watercloset, stairway or passage within a house".

PART J

Resistance to the Transmission of Heat

Application of Part J

J1.—(1) Nothing in this Part shall apply to—

(*a*) any temporary building of occupancy sub-group A3 or A4;

(*b*) any hospital or sanatorium;

(*c*) the roof, external wall or floor of any ancillary accommodation (including a garage, store, wash-house or watercloset) which forms part of a building of occupancy sub-group A1, A2 or A3 but is not entered from within the building;

(*d*) the roof, external wall or floor of a sun porch.

(2) The provisions of regulations J4 and J5 shall not be subject to specification in a notice served under section 11 of the Act (which enables local authorities to require existing buildings to conform to these regulations).

Interpretation of Part J

J2. In this Part—

"surface heat transfer coefficient", in relation to a surface, means the rate of heat transfers in watts between each square metre of the surface and the ambient air when there is a difference in temperature of one degree Celsius between the surface and the ambient air;

"surface resistance" means the reciprocal of the surface heat transfer coefficient;

"thermal transmittance coefficient", in relation to any structure, being a roof, wall or floor, means the rate of heat transfers in watts through one square metre of the structure when there is a difference in temperature of one degree Celsius between the air on the internal and external surfaces of the structure.

**Roofs*

J3.—(1) The roof of every building of occupancy group A shall be so constructed that when the sum of the surface resistances of—

(*a*) the external surface of the roof, and

(*b*) the internal surface of the roof, or the lower surface of the ceiling of the storey immediately below the roof

is taken as 0·15 the thermal transmittance coefficient of the roof, or of the roof in conjunction with any such ceiling, is not more than 1·1.

(2) For the purpose of this regulation "roof" shall not include any roof-light or other opening therein.

(3) Where the floor of a balcony or other structure, or any part of such a floor, forms the roof of any part of a building of occupancy group A and the upper side thereof is exposed to the open air, this regulation shall apply to the floor or that part thereof, as the case may be, as it applies to the roof of the building.

**Walls*

J4.—(1) Every part of external wall of a building of occupancy sub-group A1, A2, A3 or A4, which does not comprise a window or other glazed opening, shall be so constructed that the thermal transmittance coefficient thereof is not more than 1·7.

(2) The external walls of a building of occupancy sub-group A1 or A2, being a wholly detached house, or of occupancy sub-group A3 or A4 shall be so constructed that the average thermal transmittance coefficient over the area of all such walls is not more than 2·4.

(3) The average thermal transmittance coefficient over the area of all the external walls of a building of occupancy sub-group A1 or A2, other than a wholly detached house, shall be not more than—

(*a*) 2·4 where the area of the external walls exceeds 125 per cent of the total area of any internal separating walls;

(*b*) 2·7 where the area of the external walls is between 75 per cent and 125 per cent of the total area of any internal separating walls;

(*c*) 3·3 where the area of the external walls is less than 75 per cent of the total area of any internal separating walls.

(4) For the purposes of paragraphs (2) and (3) of this regulation the area of any external wall shall include the area of any windows or other glazed openings therein.

(5) In calculating the average thermal transmittance coefficient for the purposes of this regulation—

(*a*) the thermal transmittance coefficient of any single glazing shall be taken as 5·7 and of any double glazing as 2·8, and

(*b*) where the average thermal transmittance coefficient over all the windows and other glazed openings in the external walls of the house or building of occupancy sub-group A3 or A4 is 4·3 or more, the average thermal transmittance coefficient over the remaining parts of the walls shall be taken to be not less than 1·1, and

(*c*) where the average thermal transmittance coefficient over all the windows and other glazed openings in the external walls of the house or building of occupancy sub-group A3 or A4 is less than 4·3, the average thermal transmittance coefficient over the remaining parts of the walls shall be taken to be not less than 0·6.

(6) For the purposes of this regulation "wall" shall include any internal or external surface finishes thereon and in any calculation for the purposes of this regulation the sum of the surface resistance of the internal and external surfaces shall be taken as 0·18.

**Floors*

J5.—(1) In any building of occupancy group A every floor or part of a floor next to the ground shall be constructed—

(*a*) as a suspended floor with tongued and grooved boarding or other draught-resisting decking, carried on joists or as a suspended concrete floor, having in either case a space beneath the level of the floor enclosed by walls on all sides (apart from any necessary ventilation openings), or

(*b*) as a floor laid upon the ground or upon hardcore filling.

(2) Where the underside of the floor of any part of a building of occupancy group A is exposed to the open air the floor shall be so constructed that when the sum of the surface resistances of the upper and lower surfaces of the floor is taken as 0·18 the thermal transmittance coefficient of the floor is not more than 1·1.

PART K

VENTILATION

Application of Part K

K1.—(1) This Part shall not apply to any building or part of a building—

(*a*) which comprises premises which are subject to the Factories Act 1961**(a)**, or any regulations made under that Act, or

(*b*) which is a school building as defined in the School Premises (General Requirements and Standards) (Scotland) Regulations 1967**(b)**, or

(a) 1961 c. 34. **(b)** S.I. 1967/1199 (1967 II, p. 3514).

(*c*) which comprises any premises used as a cinema or theatre.

(2) The provisions of regulation K16 shall not be subject to specification in a notice served under section 11 of the Act (which enables local authorities to require existing buildings to conform to these regulations).

Interpretation of Part K

K2.—(1) In this Part—

"air change", in relation to a room or space being ventilated, means a movement of air whereby a quantity of fresh air equal to the cubic capacity of the room or space is admitted thereto;

"mechanical ventilation" means a system of ventilation operated by a power driven mechanism which causes a change of air between any part of the interior of a building and the external air;

"roof-light" means a roof-light so constructed that the whole or part thereof is capable of being opened;

"ventilator" (except in the expression "permanent ventilator") means a louvre, grille or other similar device, each of which is capable of being opened to a varying degree to permit an uninterrupted passage of air between a part of a building and the external air.

(2) Any provision of this Part requiring that a window, roof-light or ventilator shall have an opening area of a given amount shall be construed as a requirement that the window, roof-light or ventilator shall be so constructed as to be capable of being opened to the extent of an area not less than the given amount.

(3) Any provision of this Part requiring a system of mechanical ventilation to provide a fresh air supply at a rate given in Table 12 shall be construed as a requirement that the fresh air supply shall be not less than the rate given in Table 12.

(4) Any provision of this Part requiring—

(*a*) the provision of a window, roof-light or ventilator having a given opening area shall be construed as requiring the provision of one or more windows, roof-lights or ventilators or any combination thereof having an area or aggregate opening area equal to the given area;

(*b*) the provision of a ventilator or a permanent ventilator of a given cross-sectional area shall be construed as requiring the provision of one or more ventilators or permanent ventilators respectively having an area or aggregate cross-sectional area equal to the given area.

(5) Any reference in this Part to—

(*a*) the cubic space per occupant of a room shall be construed as a reference to the cubic space obtained by dividing the cubic capacity of the room by the occupant capacity thereof, and

(*b*) the cross-sectional area per occupant in relation to a permanent ventilator in a room shall be construed as a reference to the cross-sectional area of the ventilator divided by the occupant capacity of the room.

VENTILATION OF HOUSES

**Cross ventilation of houses*

K3.—(1) Every house, whether or not it forms only part of a building, shall be so constructed as to have at least two external walls, being either—

(*a*) on opposite sides of the house, or

(*b*) adjacent to each other, so, however, that the relevant area in the house, or if the house contains more than one storey, in each storey, shall not be less than one-third of the floor area of the house, or as the case may be of that storey.

For the purposes of this paragraph "the relevant area" is the area enclosed on a horizontal plane by the largest assumed triangle created by the adjacent walls and any vertical plane joining the centre lines of the windows or ventilators provided so as to comply with paragraph (2) of this regulation.

(2) In each of these external walls there shall, on each storey of the house bounded by the wall, be a window or ventilator from an apartment, kitchen, passage, stairway or landing to the external air, such window or ventilator having an opening area of 0·1 square metre.

(3) Nothing in this regulation shall apply to a house in which there is installed a system of mechanical ventilation which—

(*a*) will provide a supply of fresh air in each apartment in the house and in the kitchen at the rate set out in Table 12, and

(*b*) is so designed that no air is fed directly into any part of the house from any kitchen, bathroom or watercloset, and

(*c*) is designed so as to be capable of continuous operation.

**Kitchens*

K4. Every kitchen forming part of a house shall be ventilated—

(*a*) direct to the external air by a window, roof-light or ventilator having an opening area of one-twentieth of the floor area of the kitchen, or

(*b*) by mechanical means so as to provide a fresh air supply at the rate set out in Table 12.

**Apartments and other rooms in houses*

K5.—(1) Subject to paragraph (2) of this regulation every apartment or other room (not being a utility room of an area of not more than 3·7 square metres or a kitchen or a sun porch) forming part of a house shall be ventilated—

(*a*) (i) direct to the external air by a window, roof-light or ventilator having an opening area of one-twentieth of the floor area of the apartment or room, and

(ii) by—

(A) a ventilator having a cross-sectional area of not less than 6500 square millimetres opening direct to the external air, or

(B) a permanent ventilation opening having a cross-sectional area of not less than 6500 square millimetres and opening within the house into a passage which is ventilated by a window, roof-light or ventilator or into which there opens an entrance doorway to the house, or

(*b*) by mechanical means so as to provide a fresh air supply at the rate set out in Table 12:

Provided that nothing in paragraph (*a*)(ii) of this regulation shall apply to an apartment or room where there is leading from the apartment or room the flue from an uncloseable appliance if—

(i) the appliance is designed to burn solid fuel, or

(ii) the flue has a cross-sectional area of not less than 19 000 square millimetres.

(2) Every sun porch shall be ventilated direct to the external air by a window or ventilator having an opening area of one-twentieth of the floor area of the sun porch:

Provided that where a sun porch is constructed over an existing window or ventilator of an apartment or other room (not being a sun porch), the sun porch shall be ventilated direct to the external air by a window or ventilator having an opening area equal to the opening area of the existing window or ventilator over which the sun porch is constructed, in addition to the opening area required in terms of this paragraph.

(3) For the purposes of paragraph (2) of this regulation a door opening from the sun porch direct to the external air shall be regarded as if it were an opening window if—

(*a*) such door contains a ventilator having an area of not less than 9500 square millimetres which is capable of being opened without the door being opened, or

(*b*) the sun porch contains one or more windows, roof-lights or ventilators having a total opening area of not less than 9500 square millimetres in addition to the door opening from the sun porch direct to the external air.

**Bathrooms, washrooms and waterclosets*

K6. Every bathroom, washroom or watercloset forming part of a house shall be ventilated—

(*a*) direct to the external air by a window, roof-light or ventilator having an opening area of—

(i) one-twentieth of the floor area of the bathroom, washroom or watercloset, or

(ii) 0·1 square metre,

whichever is the greater, or

(*b*) by mechanical means—

(i) so as to provide a fresh air supply at the rate set out in Table 12, and

(ii) so designed that the outlet is to the external air, and

(iii) in the case of mechanical means serving waterclosets or bathrooms containing a watercloset in more than one house, provided with a duplicate motor, and

(iv) separate from any other ventilating plant installed for any other purpose in the building:

Provided that, subject to regulation Q7, nothing in paragraph (*b*)(ii) of this regulation shall prohibit a bathroom or watercloset opening directly off an apartment other than a living room.

**Ancillary accommodation*

K7.—(1) Every room in which there are provided laundry facilities or clothes drying facilities for communal use in respect of a number of houses shall be ventilated—

(*a*) direct to the external air by—

(i) a window, roof-light or ventilator having an opening area of one-twentieth of the floor area of the room, and

(ii) a permanent ventilator having a cross-sectional area of 2250

square millimetres for each cubic metre of the room so, however, that in no case shall an opening area be less than 48 000 square millimetres, or

(*b*) by mechanical means so as to provide a fresh air supply at the rate set out in Table 12.

(2) Every room which is not—

(*a*) such a room as is referred to in the last foregoing paragraph, or

(*b*) a room forming part of a house, or

(*c*) a garage, or

(*d*) part of a building used only for vehicle parking, or

(*e*) a storage room of an area of not more than 3·7 square metres

shall be ventilated—

(i) direct to the external air by—

(A) a window, roof-light or ventilator having an opening area of one-twentieth of the floor area of the room, and

(B) a permanent ventilator having a cross-sectional area of not less than 300 square millimetres for each cubic metre of the room so, however, that in no case shall an opening area be less than 6500 square millimetres, or

(ii) by mechanical means so as to provide a fresh air supply at the rate set out in Table 12.

VENTILATION OF GARAGES

Small garages

K8. In every garage, used solely for the storage of motor vehicles or to which regulation D20 or D21 applies and the area of which does not exceed 370 square metres, there shall be provided two permanent ventilators or permanent ventilation openings—

(*a*) each having a cross-sectional area of not less than—

(i) in the case of a garage the area of which does not exceed 40 square metres, 6500 square millimetres,

(ii) in any other case, 300 square millimetres for each cubic metre of the garage so, however, that in no case shall an opening area be less than 6500 square millimetres, and

(*b*) so situated as to permit the maximum flow of air within the whole of the garage:

Provided that in the case of a garage the area of which does not exceed 40 square metres nothing in this regulation shall prohibit both permanent ventilators or permanent ventilation openings being situated in any one wall of the garage.

**Garages other than small garages*

K9.—(1) This regulation shall apply to any storey of a building used for vehicle parking or garaging, being neither a garage to which regulation K8 applies nor a storey of a building in which vehicles are moved by mechanical means forming part of the building.

(2) If the storey is the ground storey or an upper storey it shall be ventilated—

(*a*) direct to the external air by two permanent ventilators situated on opposite walls of the storey, and each having a cross-sectional area equal to not less than, in the case of a storey used for—

(i) car parking or for the loading and unloading of vehicles, one-fortieth of the floor area of the storey,

(ii) repairing vehicles, one-sixtieth of the floor area of the storey,

(iii) garaging of commercial or public service vehicles, one-eightieth of the floor area of the storey, or

(*b*) by mechanical means so as to provide a fresh air supply at the rate set out in Table 12.

(3) If the storey is a basement storey ventilated only by mechanical means—

(*a*) it shall be ventilated by two mechanical ventilation systems—

(i) which in aggregate provide a fresh air supply at the rate set out in Table 12, and

(ii) each of which is capable of providing a fresh air supply at one-half of the rate set out in Table 12, and

(*b*) there shall be provided in the storey an audible or visible warning signal which operates automatically in the event of a failure of both such mechanical ventilation systems and which is available even in the event of a failure of the mains power supply to the building, and

(*c*) there shall be exhibited conspicuously at each entrance to the storey a notice incised or embossed with letters of not less than 200 millimetres high, in the following terms or in terms substantially to the like effect—

"DANGER

SWITCH YOUR ENGINE OFF WHEN WARNING SIGNAL [SHOWS] [SOUNDS]†

†*Delete as appropriate*".

(4) If the storey is a basement storey not ventilated solely by mechanical means it shall be ventilated—

(*a*) direct to the external air by two permanent ventilators each having a cross-sectional area equal to not less than one-eightieth of the floor area of the storey or part thereof and situated in opposite walls, and

(*b*) by a mechanical ventilation system so as to provide a fresh air supply at one-half of the rate set out in Table 12.

(5) Any mechanical ventilation system provided so as to comply with this regulation shall—

(*a*) be independent of any ventilating plant for any other part of the building, and

(*b*) have at least one exhaust air outlet for every 190 square metres of area of the floor of the storey served by the system, and

(*c*) be so constructed that at least two-thirds of the exhaust air is extracted from outlets not more than 600 millimetres above the level of the floor.

(6) The provisions of this regulation shall apply to—

(*a*) any passage giving access to a storey to which this regulation applies, or

(*b*) any ramp giving access to such a storey from an adjacent storey

as if that passage or ramp were itself such a storey.

(7) In this regulation any reference to a storey shall include a reference to any part of a storey.

Ventilation of Buildings other than Houses and Garages

**Ventilation of buildings other than houses and garages*

K10.—(1) This regulation shall apply to every room—

(*a*) in a building, being neither a building comprising or containing a house nor a garage;

(*b*) in the case of a building containing a house or garage, in any part which neither forms part of a house or garage nor pertains to a house;

(*c*) in a building or part of a building used for vehicle parking, in which vehicles are moved by mechanical means forming part of the building.

(2) If the room—

(*a*) forms part of a building of occupancy group E, or

(*b*) is used only for the purposes of storage not being for storage which requires a controlled temperature, or

(*c*) is neither a room forming part of a building of a description mentioned in Table 2 nor a room for which there is available a number, being the number of persons the room is designed to hold,

it shall be ventilated—

(i) direct to the external air by a window, roof-light or ventilator having an opening area of 300 square millimetres for each cubic metre of the room so, however, that in no case shall an opening area be less than 6500 square millimetres, or

(ii) by mechanical ventilation to give a fresh air supply at the rate set out in Table 12.

(3) The provisions of regulation K6 shall apply to any room to which this regulation applies and which is used as a bathroom, washroom or watercloset as they apply respectively to any bathroom, washroom or watercloset forming part of a house.

(4) Any other room to which this regulation applies shall, subject to the provisions of regulations K11 and K12, be ventilated—

(*a*) where the cubic space per occupant does not exceed 2·8 cubic metres, by mechanical means to provide a fresh air supply at the rate set out in Table 12;

(*b*) where the cubic space per occupant exceeds 2·8 cubic metres but does not exceed 21 cubic metres—

(i) direct to the external air, by a window, roof-light or ventilator having an opening area of one-twentieth of the floor area of the room and by a ventilator having a cross-sectional area of not less than 6500 square millimetres per occupant, or

(ii) by mechanical means to provide a fresh air supply at the rate set out in Table 12;

(*c*) where the cubic space per occupant exceeds 21 cubic metres—

(i) (A) direct to the external air by a window, roof-light or ventilator having an opening area of one-twentieth of the floor area of the room, and

(B) by a ventilator having a minimum cross-sectional area per occupant as set forth in column (2) of the table annexed to this regulation, or

(ii) by mechanical means to provide a fresh air supply at the rate set out in Table 12.

Table referred to in paragraph (4)(c)(i)(B) of this regulation

Cubic space per occupant (cubic metres) (1)	Minimum cross-sectional area per occupant (square millimetres) (2)
Exceeding 21 but not exceeding 28	6500
Exceeding 28 but not exceeding 35	5850
Exceeding 35 but not exceeding 42	5200
Exceeding 42 but not exceeding 49	4550
Exceeding 49 but not exceeding 56	3900
Exceeding 56 but not exceeding 63	3250
Exceeding 63 but not exceeding 70	2600
Exceeding 70 but not exceeding 77	1950
Exceeding 77 but not exceeding 84	1300
Exceeding 84	650

GENERAL

**Additional requirements for sleeping rooms*

K11.—(1) The provisions of this regulation shall apply to any room used or intended to be used for sleeping but not forming part of a house and shall so apply notwithstanding the provisions of the last foregoing regulation.

(2) The room shall be ventilated by—

(*a*) a roof-light or window opening direct to the external air, and

(*b*) a ventilator

which shall comply with the provisions of paragraph (4)(*b*)(i) or (4)(*c*)(i), as the case may be, of the last foregoing regulation:

Provided that nothing in this paragraph shall require the provision of a ventilator in the case of—

(i) a room whose cubic capacity does not exceed 42 cubic metres and where there is leading from the room the flue of an uncloseable appliance if—

(A) the appliance is designed to burn solid fuel, or

(B) the flue has a cross-sectional area of not less than 19 000 square millimetres;

(ii) a room which is ventilated by mechanical means to provide a fresh air supply at the rate set out in Table 12.

(3) The room shall have a cubic capacity of not less than 14·9 cubic metres.

(4) The provisions of regulation Q6 shall apply to the room as they apply to an apartment forming part of a house.

Additional requirements for rooms with flue-less gas water heaters

K12.—(1) This regulation shall apply only to a room in which there is affixed as a fixture a gas water heater which has no flue from the combustion chamber to the external air, and shall so apply notwithstanding any of the foregoing provisions of this Part.

(2) Any room to which this regulation applies, having a cubic capacity of not more than 11·3 cubic metres, shall be ventilated to the external air by a permanent ventilator having a cross-sectional area of not less than—

(*a*) if the heater is an instantaneous water heater, 3250 square millimetres;

(*b*) if the heater is a storage water heater, 9500 square millimetres.

(3) Any room to which this regulation applies and which has a cubic capacity of more than 11·3 cubic metres but not more than 21 cubic metres shall, if the heater is a storage water heater, be ventilated to the external air by a permanent ventilator having a cross-sectional area of not less than 3250 square millimetres.

**Enclosed access to houses and other buildings*

K13. Every part of an enclosed passage, stairway, landing or balcony providing common access to—

(*a*) any part of a building, or

(*b*) any part of the curtilage of a building containing two or more houses, being a part which is provided for the use of the occupants of two or more houses in that building

shall be ventilated—

(i) direct to the external air by a permanent ventilator having a cross-sectional area of not less than 300 square millimetres for each cubic metre of that part of the access so, however, that in no case shall an opening area be less than 6500 square millimetres, or

(ii) by mechanical means to provide a fresh air supply at the rate set out in Table 12:

Provided that nothing in this regulation shall apply to any part of an enclosed passage, stairway, landing or balcony where opposite ends of the enclosure are formed only by a doorway which opens directly to the external air.

Lift machine rooms and lift wells

K14.—(1) Any room in which there is housed machinery operating a lift shall be ventilated by—

(*a*) two permanent ventilation openings, each having a cross-sectional area of not less than 65 000 square millimetres, to the external air either directly or by means of a vertical duct, or

(*b*) mechanical means to provide a fresh air supply at the rate set out in Table 12.

(2) The lift well of any lift shall be ventilated by a permanent ventilation opening having a cross-sectional area of not less than 6500 square millimetres which permits an uninterrupted passage of air between the lift well and the open air either directly or by means of a duct.

General requirement for windows and ventilators

K15. Every window, ventilator, permanent ventilator and permanent ventilation opening provided so as to comply with this Part shall be so positioned that the top of the opening part or of the permanent ventilation opening is not less than 2 metres above the floor:

Provided that, where two permanent ventilators or permanent ventilation openings are provided in accordance with regulation K8 or K9, nothing in this regulation shall prohibit—

(i) one such permanent ventilator or permanent ventilation opening being positioned so that the top of the opening is not less than 1·7 metres above the floor, and

(ii) the other such permanent ventilator or permanent ventilation opening being positioned so that the top of the opening is not more than 600 millimetres above the floor.

Windows and ventilators opening to courts or passages

K16.—(1) Where a window provided so as to comply with this Part opens into a closed court, open court or passage, it shall be so sited that there is in front of every part of the window and at the level of the sill of the window a horizontal area of open space comprising a square, one side of which is in the plane of the window opening and which has sides of a length not less than—

(*a*) the relevant length set forth in paragraphs (2) to (5) of this regulation, and

(*b*) in any case, 3 metres:

Provided that no area shall for the purposes of this regulation be taken to be an area of open space if it is overhung by a balcony or other projection.

(2) Where the window opens into a closed court the relevant length for the purposes of the last foregoing paragraph shall be equal to one-third of the height of the lowest of the opposite or adjacent walls above the level of the head of the window.

(3) Where the window opens into an open court, the opening of which is on the side opposite the window, the relevant length for the purposes of paragraph (1) of this regulation shall be equal to one-sixth of—

(*a*) the height of the lower of the adjacent walls above the level of the head of the window, or

(*b*) the distance from the plane of the window opening to the plane of the opening of the court,

whichever is the less.

(4) Where the window opens into an open court, the opening of which is on a side adjacent to the window, the relevant length for the purposes of paragraph (1) of this regulation shall be equal to one-quarter of—

(*a*) the height of the lowest wall of the court above the level of the head of the window, or

(*b*) the distance from the plane containing the opening of the court to the nearest part of the window,

whichever is the less.

(5) Where the window opens into a passage the relevant length for the purposes of paragraph (1) of this regulation shall be equal to one-sixth of—

(*a*) the height of the passage wall above the level of the head of the window, or

(*b*) the distance from the nearest point where the passage terminates to the nearest part of the window,

whichever is the less.

(6) In this regulation—

"closed court", in relation to a window, means any space at the level of the sill of the window which is either wholly enclosed by walls or enclosed by walls but has an opening on one side which—

(*a*) is less than 1 metre in width, or

(*b*) opens on to a passage of a width of less than 3 metres;

"open court", in relation to a window, means any space at the level of the sill of the window enclosed by walls, not being a closed court, and includes a recess if, and only if—

(*a*) the window is in the back wall of the recess and the ratio of the length of the back wall to the depth of the recess is less than 1 to 1, or

(*b*) the window is in the side of a recess and the ratio of the length of the back wall of the recess to the depth of the recess is less than 2 to 1;

"passage", in relation to a window, means any space at the level of the sill of the window bounded by walls on two opposite sides where the distance between the opposite walls is not greater than one-quarter of the height of the higher of the two walls above the said level.

(7) This regulation shall apply in relation to a ventilator provided so as to comply with this Part as it applies in relation to a window so provided, and references to the sill of the window shall be taken to include references to the foot of the ventilator, and references to the head of the window shall be taken to include references to the top of the ventilator.

External openings to mechanical ventilation system

K17. Every external opening forming part of a mechanical ventilation system of a building to which this Part applies—

(*a*) shall be so sited in relation to any outlet for smoke, steam or noxious vapours as to reduce as far as practicable the ingress into the system of smoke, steam or noxious vapours therefrom, and

(*b*) shall be so sited in relation to any other opening into the building as to avoid the escape of air from the system into any part of the building, and

(*c*) shall be protected against the passage of snow, rain and vermin.

Construction of ventilation ducts

K18. Every wall of a duct forming part of a mechanical ventilation system of a building to which this Part applies shall be so constructed that it is airtight and the internal surface thereof is smooth.

PART L

Daylighting and Space about Houses

Application of Part L

L1.—(1) This Part shall apply to a building any part of which is of occupancy sub-group A1 or A2.

(2) The provisions of this Part shall not be subject to specification in a notice served under section 11 of the Act (which enables local authorities to require existing buildings to conform to these regulations).

Interpretation of Part L

L2.—(1) In this Part—

"boundary", in relation to a window, means that part of the boundary over which daylight reaches the window;

"daylight area", in relation to a daylight factor, means the area enclosed by a line drawn through all points on the working plane on which the daylight factor is of the given value;

"daylight factor", in relation to any reference point, means the ratio of the daylight illumination (including light reflected from interior and exterior surfaces) on the working plane at that point to that prevailing simultaneously on a horizontal plane due to the whole of an unobstructed sky having a standard luminance distribution as defined by the International Commission on Illumination;

"daylight penetration", in relation to a window in a wall or a roof, means the horizontal distance from the window to any reference point in the room, measured from the outer face of the window frame at the height of the window sill;

"daylighting window" means a window provided so as to comply with regulation L4;

"external obstruction", in relation to a window, means any building or land (including any trees thereon) which obstructs any part of the view of the sky as seen through the window at an angle above the working plane;

"reference point" means any point on the working plane at which a daylight factor is calculated or, as the case may be, any point by reference to which a proportion of obscured sky is calculated;

"reflection factor", in relation to a surface, means the ratio of light reflected from that surface to light incident upon it;

"working plane", in relation to the window of a room, means the horizontal plane 850 millimetres above the floor level of the room, on which a daylight factor is calculated.

(2) The provisions of regulation A4 (which relate to the meaning of the expression "land in different occupation") shall, in relation to this Part, have effect as if there was added at the end of the proviso to paragraph (1) of that regulation the following sub-paragraph—

"(iv) any land, including a private street, over which there exists a servitude of light in favour of the building or of the land on which the building is to be erected".

Rooms in which daylighting to be provided

L3. Regulations L4 to L7 shall apply to every kitchen, living room or other apartment forming part of a house.

Standard of daylighting

L4.—(1) In every room to which this regulation applies there shall be provided a daylighting window so positioned and of such dimensions that—

(*a*) in any kitchen a daylight factor of not less than 2 per cent shall extend over an area of not less than one-half of the floor area of the room or 4·5 square metres whichever is the less;

(*b*) in any living room a daylight factor of not less than 1 per cent shall extend—

(i) over an area of not less than one-half of the floor area of the room, and

(ii) to not less than one-half of the depth of the room;

(*c*) in any other apartment a daylight factor of not less than ½ per cent shall extend—

(i) over an area of not less than one-half of the floor area of the room, and

(ii) to not less than one-half of the depth of the room:

Provided that nothing in sub-paragraph (*b*) of this paragraph shall require a daylight factor to extend over an area greater than one-half of that required for living and cooking by regulation Q5 as read with column (3) of Table 17 when there is deducted therefrom the floor area of the kitchen as specified in column (4) of the said Table.

(2) Nothing in this regulation shall apply to a room in which there is provided a daylighting window or windows which complies or comply with Part I or II of Schedule 7.

Calculation of daylight factor

L5.—(1) Subject to regulation L7, in calculating the daylight factor in any room for the purposes of these regulations—

(*a*) there shall be taken into account in relation to any daylighting window—

(i) any existing external obstruction, or

(ii) the external obstruction assumed to exist in accordance with paragraph (2) of this regulation,

whichever is the greater, and

(*b*) the brightness of any external obstruction shall be assumed to be one-tenth of the sky brightness, and

(*c*) there shall be taken into account any part of the frame of the window and any glazing bar, transom or mullion which obstructs the passage of daylight through the opening of a daylighting window, and

(*d*) the reflection factors of the internal surfaces of the room shall be taken to be those specified in column (2) of Table 13.

(2) In relation to any daylighting window there shall for the purposes of sub-paragraph (*a*) of the last foregoing paragraph be assumed to be an obstruction—

(*a*) on the other side of the boundary, parallel to the line of the boundary and of infinite length, and

(*b*) of such height that at ground level at any point on the line of the boundary it subtends an angle of 43 degrees, and

(*c*) at a distance beyond the boundary equal to the difference between—

(i) the minimum distance of the boundary from the wall of the building as calculated for the purposes of regulation L8, and

(ii) the minimum distance which would have been so calculated if for the external obstruction used for the purpose of calculating the distance in regulation L8 there were substituted an assumed external obstruction which obscured 5 per cent of the unobstructed sky and for the angle of elevation and the horizontal angle so used there were substituted angles of 30 degrees and 45 degrees respectively:

Provided that nothing in this paragraph shall apply in relation to a boundary with land which consists or forms part of an area shown in an operative development plan under the Town and Country Planning (Scotland) Act 1947**(a)** as allocated for a use other than residential.

Windows

L6.—(1) Nothing in regulation L4(1) shall prevent the compliance with the provisions thereof by the provision of two or more windows in the same or in different walls, or, as provided in paragraph (2) of this regulation, in the ceiling of any room.

(2) Every daylighting window shall be situated in an external wall except as provided in regulation L7(3):

Provided that nothing in this paragraph shall prohibit a daylighting window—

(i) in an apartment other than the living room being situated in any part of the roof structure so that the window is inclined at not less than 30 degrees from the horizontal, or

(ii) in a kitchen, from being situated in any part of the roof structure.

(3) If, in any room to which this regulation applies, there is provided in an external wall a glazed door, the glazed part of the door shall, for the purposes of this Part, be taken to be a daylighting window.

Balconies, projections and sun porches

L7.—(1) In calculating the daylight factor in relation to a daylighting window for the purposes of this Part, account shall also be taken of—

(*a*) any horizontal projection beyond the plane of the window opening and over the head of the opening, and

(*b*) any wall or screen flanking the window opening and forward of the plane of the opening, and

(*c*) any balustrade, screen or other external part of the building so constructed as to constitute an obstruction to daylight entering the window.

(2) If, in relation to the opening of a daylighting window of any apartment, there is such a horizontal projection as is mentioned in sub-paragraph (*a*) of the last foregoing paragraph, and—

(*a*) there is a private balcony with access from the apartment of not less projection and width than the horizontal projection, or

(*b*) there is direct access on the same level to an open space intended for the exclusive use of the occupants of the house or joint use with the occupants of other houses in the building only,

an area and depth of the private balcony or open space equal to three-quarters of the area and depth of the projection shall, for the purposes of this Part, be deemed to form part of the daylight area and daylight penetration respectively in relation to the apartment.

(3) Nothing in this regulation shall prohibit the existing daylighting window of any apartment or kitchen from opening into a sun porch on the same storey which has the wall opposite the daylighting window glazed above a height of 840 millimetres above floor level.

Relationship of building to boundary

L8.—(1) Subject to the provisions of regulation D17 and to the following provisions of this regulation, every building to which this Part applies shall be

(a) 1947 c. 53.

so sited in relation to any boundary and so designed that, when the building, together with any existing external obstruction, is taken as the external obstruction in relation to a reference point assumed to be at ground level at any point on the line of the boundary, the part of the sky obscured in relation to the reference point does not exceed 14·5 per cent of the unobstructed sky.

(2) In calculating the percentage of obstructed sky for the purposes of this regulation—

(*a*) there shall be assumed to be between the reference point and the building a vertical unglazed opening so placed in relation to the reference point that—

(i) the foot of the opening is on the same horizontal plane as the reference point, and

(ii) the height of the opening subtends at the reference point an angle of elevation to the horizontal of 45 degrees, and

(iii) each side of the opening makes with the vertical plane perpendicular to the line of the boundary or to the line tangential with the boundary a horizontal angle at the reference point of 57½ degrees, and

(*b*) the plane of the opening shall be assumed to be parallel to the line of the boundary or to a line tangential to the boundary at the reference point, and

(*c*) no account shall be taken of light reaching the reference point—

(i) over land in different occupation, below an angle of 43 degrees above the horizontal, and

(ii) over any land, below an angle of 10 degrees above the horizontal.

(3) Nothing in this regulation shall prevent the erection of any part of the building nearer to any point on the boundary than is required by paragraph (1) of this regulation if—

(*a*) the height of the part of the building does not exceed—

(i) if contiguous with the boundary, 2·9 metres,

(ii) if not so contiguous, the sum of 2·9 metres and an amount equal to one-third of the distance of that part from the boundary,

such height being measured above the ground level at that point on the boundary, or

(*b*) the building forms part of a continuous frontage to the street and the part of the building is—

(i) of a height not greater than the highest part of the remainder of the building, and

(ii) of a depth measured backwards from the front of the building at ground floor level not exceeding 12·5 metres, or

(*c*) the building—

(i) does not exceed three storeys in height, and

(ii) has a frontage aligned with, or set back or forward from, the line of the frontage of an adjacent building on land in different occupation, and

(iii) the side thereof nearest the boundary with that adjacent building—

(A) has no daylighting windows therein, and

(B) is of a depth, measured at right angles to the front of the building—

(I) not exceeding 12·5 metres, or

(II) one-half of the greatest depth of the land in different occupation on which there is such an adjacent building,

whichever is the lesser, or

(*d*) in the last foregoing sub-paragraph for the purpose of measuring the depth of any land in different occupation there shall be excluded from such land—

(i) any portion of any road, access way, river or stream adjacent to the land,

(ii) any portion of any common, public open space, loch, lake or pond adjacent to the land,

(iii) any portion of the foreshore or area of the sea adjacent to the land, or

(*e*) the boundary is a boundary with land which consists or forms part of an area shown in an operative development plan under the Town and Country Planning (Scotland) Act 1947 as allocated for a use other than residential.

(4) Nothing in this regulation shall apply to a building if the distance of the building from any point on the boundary is not less than that determined in accordance with Part III or IV of Schedule 7.

Application for warrant for more than one building

L9. Where an application for warrant under section 6 of the Act relates to more than one building to which this Part applies—

(*a*) the land on which these buildings are to be erected shall, for the purposes of this Part, be deemed to form land in the same occupation, notwithstanding that the buildings are intended for different occupation, and

(*b*) each of the buildings shall, in relation to the other buildings comprised in the application, be deemed to be an existing building for the purposes of regulation L5.

Minimum distance between windows

L10.—(1) Subject to paragraph (2) of this regulation, no part of any window of an apartment or of a kitchen in a house shall be sited nearer to any part of any window of an apartment or of a kitchen in another house than the horizontal distance specified in Table 14 according to each of the horizontal angles included between the shortest line joining any part of one window opening to any part of the other and the vertical plane of the opening of each window:

Provided that, where a window of the kitchen in the house is on a side of the house which contains no window of an apartment, the horizontal distance between any part of the window of the kitchen and any part of the window of an apartment in another house shall not be required to be greater than 12 metres if—

(i) the floor of the kitchen is not less than 2·2 metres below the level of the floor of the apartment in the other house, and

(ii) the top of the sill of the window of the apartment is not less than 800 millimetres above the floor of the apartment.

(2) Nothing in this regulation shall prevent any window of an apartment or a kitchen in a house from being sited nearer to any such window in another house than the distance required by paragraph (1) if—

(*a*) no part of either window below a level of 1·8 metres above floor level can be seen from any part of the other window below a level of 1·8 metres above floor level, or

(*b*) both the windows are windows of kitchens.

PART M

Drainage and Sanitary Appliances

Application of Part M

M1. In this Part the provisions of—

(*a*) regulation M3(2) so far as relating to a building of any class to which section 120 of the Public Health (Scotland) Act 1897(**a**) applies, and

(*b*) regulation M23 and regulation M24 in so far as they apply to any building not being shop premises

shall not be subject to specification in a notice served under section 11 of the Act (which enables local authorities to require existing buildings to conform to these regulations).

Interpretation of Part M

M2. In this Part—

"drain", in relation to a building, means any pipe, forming part of the drainage system of that building, which is either—

(*a*) wholly below ground, or

(*b*) a continuation, in the direction of flow, of part of a drainage system that has been below ground;

"drainage system", in relation to a building, means the system of pipes and drains used for the drainage of the building, including all other fittings, appliances and equipment so used, but excluding sub-soil water drains;

"foul water" means any water contaminated by soil water, waste water or trade effluent;

"gutter" includes a rhone;

"manhole" means any chamber constructed on a drain so as to provide access thereto for inspection and cleaning;

"public sewer" means any sewer provided, constructed or maintained under any provision of the Public Health (Scotland) Act 1897, or of the Burgh Police (Scotland) Acts 1892 to 1903(**b**), or under any corresponding provision of a local enactment, or vested in a local authority under any of those provisions;

"rainwater pipe" means a pipe for conveying only rainwater from any part of a building to a drain;

"soak-away" means a pit or chamber suitably prepared to receive surface water for seepage into the surrounding ground;

"soil appliance" means a sanitary appliance for the collection and discharge of excreted matter;

"soil pipe" means a pipe for conveying soil water to a drain;

"soil-waste pipe" means a pipe for conveying both soil and waste water to a drain;

"soil water" means water containing excreted matter, whether human or animal;

"sub-soil water" means the ground water naturally contained in the subsoil;

"surface water" means the run-off of rainwater from roofs and the ground surface whether paved or unpaved;

(**a**) 1897 c. 38. (**b**) 1892 c. 55; 1901 c. 24; 1903 c. 33.

"surface water drain" means a pipe below the ground for conveying only water from rainwater pipes and the ground, whether paved or unpaved, or from a sub-soil drainage system;

"trade effluent" means any liquid, either with or without particles of matter in suspension therein, which is wholly or in part produced in the course of any trade, industry or research carried on at premises used or intended to be used for carrying on such trade, industry or research, but does not include soil water or waste water;

"ventilating pipe" means a pipe open to the atmosphere at its highest point which ventilates the drainage system or any part thereof;

"waste appliance" means a sanitary appliance for the collection and discharge of water used for ablutionary, culinary and other domestic purposes;

"waste pipe" means a pipe for conveying waste water to a drain;

"waste water" means used water, not being soil water or trade effluent.

**Drainage system of a building*

M3.—(1) Every building shall be provided with such a drainage system as may be necessary for the hygienic and adequate disposal of foul water and surface water from that building and so as to comply with this regulation.

(2) The drainage system shall communicate with a public sewer:

Provided that this paragraph shall not apply in the case of any building where there is within 90 metres of the building no public sewer to which it is reasonably practicable to obtain access and—

(i) any surface water drain from the building communicates with a soak-away, ditch or other means of disposal approved by the local authority, and

(ii) any part of the drainage system conveying foul water discharges to sewage treatment works which are—

(A) at such distance from any building of occupancy group A as to prevent any danger to health therefrom and in any event not nearer such a building than 15 metres, and

(B) so sited as not to endanger any water supply used for domestic purposes, and

(C) provided with suitable access, and

(D) of adequate size and suitable design having regard to the volume and strength of foul water discharging thereto, and

(E) constructed of suitable materials.

(3) No part of the drainage system conveying foul water shall be connected to a public sewer reserved for surface water, and no part of the drainage system conveying surface water shall be connected to a public sewer reserved for foul water.

**Construction of drains*

M4.—(1) Every drain which forms part of a drainage system provided so as to comply with regulation M3 shall be constructed in accordance with this regulation and with regulations M5 to M13:

Provided that nothing in the said regulations shall apply to any open-jointed, porous or perforated drain which is a surface water drain communicating with a soak-away, ditch or other means of disposal approved by the local authority.

(2) The drain shall be constructed of pipes, joints and fittings of suitable materials of sufficient durability and of adequate strength having regard to the nature of the ground through which the drain passes, the matter passing through the drain and the maximum imposed loads to which the drain may be subjected.

(3) The drain shall be—

(*a*) securely jointed, properly supported and protected against damage and laid at such a gradient that all foul, surface and sub-soil water is effectively carried away, and

(*b*) so constructed as to be watertight, and

(*c*) of adequate size with an internal diameter of not less than 75 millimetres, or of the maximum diameter of any connection to it, whichever is the greater, and

(*d*) laid in a straight line between points where changes of direction or gradient are necessary.

(4) The junction between any two portions of the drain having different internal diameters shall be effected by the use of a level invert taper fitting.

(5) There shall be provided on the drain such number of manholes so positioned as to ensure that the drain will be readily accessible for inspection and cleaning, but in any event—

(*a*) a manhole shall be provided at each point where there is such a change of direction or gradient as would prevent any part of the drain being readily inspected or cleaned without a manhole;

(*b*) where no manhole is provided at the point of connection of the drain to a public sewer, a manhole shall be provided not more than 12·5 metres from that point;

(*c*) no part of a drain shall at any point be more than 45 metres distant (measured along the drain) from a manhole on the same drain.

(6) The drain shall—

(*a*) after any jointing material with a setting action has set but before any concrete haunching or encasing is commenced or before the drain track has been infilled, and

(*b*) after the drain track has been infilled,

be capable of satisfying—

(i) in the case of a drain which is to carry no foul water, either of the tests specified in Part I of Schedule 8;

(ii) in the case of a drain which is to carry foul water, either of the tests specified in Part II of Schedule 8:

Provided that in the case of a drain of an internal diameter of more than 600 millimetres, the provisions of this paragraph shall not apply if the drain has been approved by the buildings authority after an internal and external inspection.

(7) Where any contraction joint is provided in the concrete infill of a drain track so as to comply with regulation M6(2), a flexible joint shall be provided in the drain at that point.

**Additional requirements for drains in or under buildings*

M5.—(1) A drain which is not constructed outside and clear of the foundations and supports of any building shall comply with the following provisions of this regulation.

(2) Where the drain passes through or under a building it shall, so far as it is within a distance of 1·2 metres from the building (including the part within or under the building)—

(*a*) be laid in a straight line, or

(*b*) change direction only at a manhole.

(3) Where a drain passes through or under a wall of a building, that part of the drain within or under the wall shall be suitably supported and strengthened and provision made for settlement of either the structure or the drain.

**Drain tracks passing near or under walls*

M6.—(1) Where—

(*a*) the track of a drain or part of a drain, not being a track in solid rock, is adjacent to the foundation of a wall, and

(*b*) the bottom of the track is lower than a depth beneath the foundation equal to the horizontal distance between the nearside of the track and the foundation less 150 millimetres,

the track shall, after the drain is laid, be infilled with concrete of a suitable strength up to that depth:

Provided that where any part of the track lies within 1 metre of the foundation of a wall, the concrete infill in that part shall be carried up to the level of the bottom of that foundation.

(2) The concrete infill provided under the foregoing paragraph shall have such contraction joints as are necessary to ensure that no continuous length of infill exceeds 9 metres.

Junctions and manholes

M7.—(1) Where a drain joins another drain, the drain so joining shall be constructed to meet the other drain obliquely in the direction of flow of that other drain.

(2) Where the buildings authority so require, a manhole or other suitable means of access to the drain shall be provided—

(*a*) at any junction between a drain and any other drain, or

(*b*) at a point as near as may be reasonably practicable to such junction.

(3) No junction with a drain shall be made so as to be opposite to another junction with that drain unless both such junctions are within a manhole.

(4) The foregoing provisions of this regulation shall not apply to a drain carrying sub-soil water only and constructed of open-jointed or porous or perforated pipes, so, however, that where such a drain discharges into the drainage system of any building there shall be provided before the point of entry a suitable catchpit, that is to say a pit or chamber constructed of brick, concrete or fireclay for the purpose of intercepting silt or grit.

**Construction of manholes*

M8.—(1) Every manhole provided in accordance with any provision of these regulations shall—

(*a*) be of such a size and form as to permit ready access to the drain for inspection and cleaning purposes, and

(*b*) be so constructed of brickwork, concrete or other suitable material as to have adequate strength and durability, and be watertight, and (*c*) where the depth of the manhole so requires, be fitted with such step irons, ladder or other fitting as will provide safe access to the level of the drain, and

(*d*) be fitted with a non-ventilating cover of adequate strength, constructed of cast iron or other suitable material, and

(*e*) where the manhole is within a building, be so constructed as to remain airtight under the maximum pressure to which that part of the drain may be subjected.

(2) That part of a drain which is within a manhole provided in accordance with these regulations shall be—

(*a*) (i) constructed with access fittings provided with covers, or

(ii) formed with open channels having a smooth impervious finish, the main channel being of equal diameter to the outlet drain and any branch channel being not less in diameter than the inlet pipe of the branch drain, and

(*b*) completed with sloped benching suitable to the type of manhole.

Ventilation of drains

M9. Every drain or section of a drain exceeding 6 metres in length and used for the conveyance of foul water from a building shall be ventilated by a pipe situated as near as may be practicable to the highest part of the drain or section ventilated thereby:

Provided that nothing in this regulation shall prevent the ventilation of a drain by a soil, soil-waste or waste pipe.

Installation of traps

M10. Every surface water drain shall, before the junction with any drain carrying foul water, be fitted with a trap with a minimum water seal of 50 millimetres so situated as to be easily accessible.

**Oil, grease and silt interceptors*

M11. Every drain which may receive any discharge containing substantial quantities of oil, fat, grease, volatile substances or silt, including the discharge from operations of cleaning, washing and servicing motor vehicles, shall be provided with a suitable trap or tank for the interception and retention of such substances.

Drains conveying steam or hot water

M12.—(1) Every drain which connects with a public sewer and which may convey steam or hot water shall be fitted with a blow-down sump or such other means as may be necessary to reduce the temperature of the effluent from the drain to not more than 45° Celsius.

(2) Any blow-down sump provided in accordance with this regulation shall—

(*a*) be carried upwards to the level of the ground and covered with an open grating, or

(*b*) be ventilated by a shaft.

**Ventilation of traps*

M13. Every trap in a drain, not being a trap within a building, shall be provided with adequate means of ventilation.

**Soil pipes, soil-waste pipes, waste pipes and ventilating pipes*

M14.—(1) Every soil pipe, soil-waste pipe, waste pipe and ventilating pipe shall—

(*a*) be formed of suitable materials of adequate strength and sufficient durability for its function, and

(*b*) have all joints formed in a manner appropriate to the materials of which the pipe is composed and so that the interior of the pipe is free from any obstruction, and

(*c*) be so constructed as to be capable of satisfying the test specified in Part III of Schedule 8.

(2) Every ventilating pipe to a drain, soil, soil-waste or waste pipe shall—

(*a*) be carried upwards to such a height and be so positioned as effectively to prevent the escape of foul air from the drain, soil pipe, soil-waste pipe or waste pipe into any building, and

(*b*) be fitted at its open end with a wire cage or other suitable cover of durable material, which does not restrict the flow of air:

Provided that the provisions of this paragraph shall not apply to a waste pipe from a waste appliance in the ground floor of a building if that waste pipe discharges into a trap with a suitable cover, so that the discharge is effected above the level of the water in the trap but below the level of the cover, and in such a way as not to cause dampness in a wall or foundation of any building.

**Additional requirements for soil, soil-waste and ventilating pipes*

M15.—(1) Subject to paragraph (4) of this regulation, every soil pipe, soil-waste pipe and ventilating pipe shall be of adequate size for its function but in no case shall a soil or soil-waste pipe have an internal diameter less than 75 millimetres, or the maximum diameter of any connection to it, whichever is the greater.

(2) Where any bend occurs in any soil, soil-waste or ventilating pipe—

(*a*) that bend shall be of an obtuse angle and have the largest practicable radius of curvature, and

(*b*) the cross-section of the pipe shall not change throughout the bend.

(3) Every soil, soil-waste and ventilating pipe shall be—

(*a*) adequately supported throughout its length without restraining thermal movement, the supports being securely attached to the building, and

(*b*) so placed as to be reasonably accessible for maintenance throughout its length, and

(*c*) provided with such means of access as are necessary to enable internal cleaning and inspection to take place.

(4) Any soil pipe serving only urinals shall—

(*a*) be constructed of lead, cast iron, or other suitable material not less resistant to corrosion, and

(*b*) have an internal diameter adequate for the number of fittings served and in no case less than that set out in Table 1 of British Standard Code of Practice CP 304: 1968 as read with Amendment AMD 187, January 1969.

**Additional requirements for waste pipes*

M16.—(1) Every waste pipe shall be of adequate size for its function and shall be adequately supported without restraining thermal movement, the supports being securely attached to the building.

(2) Every waste pipe from a waste appliance shall have close to such appliance a readily accessible trap with an adequate water seal and have means of access for internal cleaning:

Provided that this paragraph shall not apply to the waste pipes from—

(i) two adjacent waste appliances, being sinks, tubs, or a sink and tub, or

(ii) not more than six waste appliances fixed in a range, being wash-hand basins or shower trays,

if the waste appliances are served by a common waste pipe not exceeding 5 metres in length on which there is fitted close to the junction or last junction, as the case may be, a trap which has an adequate water seal and there are provided both at the trap and at the higher end of the common waste pipe means of access for internal cleaning.

**Sanitary appliances*

M17.—(1) Every soil appliance and waste appliance shall—

(*a*) be constructed of suitable, durable, impervious and corrosion resistant materials, and

(*b*) have smooth surfaces resistant to abrasion, and

(*c*) be so constructed as to be readily cleansed, and

(*d*) be so designed as to function efficiently, and

(*e*) be securely fixed and supported in position having due regard to thermal movement, and

(*f*) have a suitable outlet and connection to the drainage system, so graded as to ensure the efficient discharge of the soil or waste water, and

(*g*) be watertight when assembled and fixed.

(2) Every soil appliance shall be so constructed and fitted as to pass the discharge through an effective trap having a water seal of not less than 50 millimetres in depth and thence directly to a soil pipe or drain.

**Maintenance of water seal in traps*

M18. Such provision shall be made in every drainage system as may be necessary to prevent, under working conditions, the destruction of the water seal of any drain trap or trap of a soil or waste appliance.

Machines for the wet disposal of solid refuse and food processing machines

M19.—(1) Every machine installed for the purpose of macerating solid refuse shall be so designed and constructed as to produce an effluent which can be readily disposed of through the drainage system.

(2) Where the waste water from a food processing machine contains matter which cannot readily be disposed of through the drainage system, a suitable interceptor for the removal of such matter shall be interposed between the machine and the drainage system.

Disposal of rainwater from buildings

M20. Adequate means shall be provided for the collection and disposal of the rainwater which may fall upon a building so as to prevent dampness or damage thereto.

**Gutters and channels for roofs, canopies and balconies*

M21.—(1) Every channel and gutter provided for collecting rainwater from roofs, canopies and balconies shall be—

(*a*) of suitable material of adequate strength and durability, and

(*b*) of adequate size for its function, and

(*c*) securely attached to the building, and

(*d*) jointed in a manner appropriate to the material of which it is constructed so as to be watertight, and

(*e*) provided with a suitable outlet of adequate size.

(2) Every valley gutter having a slope of not more than 10 degrees from the horizontal and every enclosed parapet gutter shall be provided with a suitable and adequate overflow.

**Rainwater pipes*

M22.—(1) Every rainwater pipe shall—

(*a*) be of suitable material of adequate strength and durability, and

(*b*) be of adequate size for its function, and

(*c*) be securely attached to the building, and

(*d*) be jointed in a manner appropriate to the material of which the pipe is constructed, and

(*e*) to the extent to which it is situated within a building, be constructed and jointed so as to comply with regulation M14(1), and

(*f*) discharge into a drain or into a rainwater storage receptacle which has an overflow pipe discharging into a drain:

Provided that nothing in this paragraph shall prevent the use of a rainwater pipe for the conveyance of rainwater from a higher to a lower roof where adequate provision is made for its disposal from the lower roof.

(2) A rainwater pipe shall not be used for soil or waste water or be connected to or used as a ventilating pipe:

Provided that nothing in this paragraph shall prevent the use of a soil pipe, soil-waste pipe, waste pipe or ventilating pipe for the conveyance of rainwater, where—

(i) the rainwater inlet complies with regulation M14(2)(*a*), or in the case of a waste pipe being used to convey rainwater, the pipe is provided or fitted with a trap before its junction with the drain, and

(ii) the rainwater inlet is above the level of the highest soil or waste appliance, and

(iii) the drainage system does not make separate provision for surface water and foul water, and

(iv) in the case of a block of flats containing five or more storeys the pipes connecting the soil and waste appliances in the ground storey are connected directly to the drain.

Ducts for services

M23.—(1) Where any soil pipe, soil-waste pipe, waste pipe or ventilating pipe serves an appliance provided so as to comply with Part Q of these regulations within a building of occupancy sub-group A1 or A2 and comprising two storeys or more, the pipe shall be within the area bounded by the external walls of the building.

(2) Where any such pipe passes through—

(*a*) an apartment or kitchen, not being a pipe serving only a fitting in that room, or

(*b*) any part of an access to a house, being a part within a building,

the pipe shall be enclosed in a duct.

(3) Any duct provided so as to comply with the foregoing paragraph shall be fitted with such access panel or panels as are necessary for the inspection and maintenance of the pipes contained therein.

**Provision of sanitary conveniences in buildings*

M24.—(1) This regulation shall apply to every building used as a filling station or every building of occupancy sub-group A3 or A4 or of occupancy group B or C.

(2) There shall be provided in the building suitable and sufficient sanitary conveniences with separate accommodation for persons of each sex, so situated, of such a type and of such number as may be necessary having regard to the number of persons likely to be employed in the building and to the number of persons likely to frequent the building:

Provided that nothing in this regulation shall—

(i) prejudice the operation of any other enactment relating to the provision of sanitary conveniences in buildings to which this regulation applies, or

(ii) require the provision of—

(A) separate accommodation for persons of each sex in the case of any building in which less than six persons are employed, or

(B) washrooms in buildings of occupancy sub-group C1 used as grandstands or stadia, or

(C) sanitary conveniences for customers in shop premises which are within occupancy sub-group B2.

(3) For the purposes of this regulation "sanitary conveniences" include waterclosets, urinals and washrooms.

PART N

ELECTRICAL INSTALLATIONS

Application of Part N

N1.—(1) This Part shall not apply to any building or part of a building—

(*a*) which comprises premises which are subject to the Factories Act 1961 or any regulations made under that Act;

(*b*) which comprises premises to which Part I of the Cinematograph (Safety) (Scotland) Regulations 1955**(a)** applies;

(*c*) which forms part of or is deemed to form part of a mine or quarry under the Mines and Quarries Act 1954**(b)**.

(2) Nothing in this Part shall apply to—

(*a*) a conductor or apparatus forming part of the works of an undertaker to whom the Electricity Supply Regulations 1937 apply;

(*b*) a conductor, apparatus or appliance which does not form part of a building or is not a fixture affixed thereto;

(a) S.I. 1955/1125 (1955 I, p. 326). **(b)** 1954 c. 70.

(*c*) a conductor, apparatus or appliance forming part of a radio, telephone, bell and call, or sound distribution circuit or apparatus, not being a conductor, apparatus or appliance connected to a public or private power distribution supply.

Interpretation of Part N

N2. In this Part—

"apparatus" means electrical apparatus, and includes all machines, apparatus and fittings in which conductors are used or of which they form a part;

"appliance" means any device which utilises electricity for a particular purpose, excluding a lighting fitting or a motor;

"circuit" means an arrangement of conductors for the purpose of carrying electrical current;

"circuit-breaker" means a mechanical device for making and breaking a circuit which under abnormal conditions breaks the circuit automatically;

"conductor", in relation to a core or cable, means the conducting portion whether consisting of a single wire or a group of wires in contact with each other;

"earthed", in relation to a connection, means effectually connected with the general mass of the earth;

"fuse" means a device for opening a circuit by means of a conductor designed to melt when an excessive current flows;

"insulation" means suitable non-conducting material enclosing, surrounding or supporting a conductor;

"linked switch" means a switch, the blades of which are so linked mechanically as to make or break all poles simultaneously or in a definite sequence;

"live", in relation to a conductor, means that, under working conditions—

(*a*) a difference of voltage exists between the conductor and earth, or

(*b*) it is connected to the middle wire, common return wire or neutral wire of a supply system in which that wire is not permanently and solidly earthed;

"switch" means a device, other than a fuse or circuit-breaker, for closing or opening a circuit;

"switch-fuse" means a unit comprising a switch and one or more fuses, the fuses not being carried on the moving part of the switch.

**Electrical conductors and apparatus*

N3.—(1) All electrical conductors shall be of sufficient size and current rating for the purposes for which they are to be used.

(2) All electrical apparatus shall be of sufficient power rating for the purposes for which the apparatus is to be used.

(3) All live conductors, including conductors forming part of apparatus, shall be either—

(*a*) so insulated, and where necessary, further effectively protected, or

(*b*) so placed and safeguarded

as to prevent danger so far as is reasonably practicable.

(4) Every electrical joint and connection shall be of proper construction as regards conductance, insulation, mechanical strength and protection.

**Fuses, switches and circuit-breakers*

N4.—(1) Every electrical circuit and sub-circuit shall be protected against excess current by fuses, circuit-breakers, or other similar devices which—

(*a*) will operate automatically at current values which are suitably related to the safe current ratings of the circuit, and

(*b*) are of adequate breaking capacity, and

(*c*) are suitably located and of such construction as to prevent danger from overheating, arcing or the scattering of hot metal when they come into operation, and as to permit ready renewal of the fusible metal without danger.

(2) Where the possible earth fault leakage current from a circuit is insufficient to operate the fuses, circuit-breakers or other similar devices provided so as to comply with paragraph (1) of this regulation, the circuit shall be protected against the persistence of earth leakage currents liable to cause danger by an earth leakage circuit-breaker or equivalent device.

(3) No fuse or circuit-breaker other than a linked circuit-breaker shall be inserted in a conductor connected with earth and any linked circuit-breaker inserted in a conductor connected with earth shall be arranged to break every live conductor.

(4) Any single pole switch shall be inserted only in a live conductor and any switch inserted in the conductor connected with earth shall be a linked switch and shall be arranged to break every live conductor.

**Precautions against metal becoming live*

N5. Where metal work, other than current-carrying conductors, is liable to become charged with electricity in such a manner as to create a danger if the insulation of a conductor should become defective or if a defect should occur in any apparatus—

(*a*) the metal work shall be earthed in such manner as will ensure immediate electrical discharge without danger, or

(*b*) other adequate precautions shall be taken to prevent danger.

**Isolation of systems and apparatus*

N6. Effective means, suitably placed for ready operation, shall be provided so that all voltage may be cut off from every circuit and sub-circuit and from all apparatus, as may be necessary to prevent danger.

**Installation of apparatus*

N7.—(1) Every piece of apparatus which requires operation or attention in normal use shall be so installed that adequate means of access and working space are afforded for such operation or attention.

(2) All parts of a building in which such apparatus is placed shall be adequately lighted to prevent danger.

(3) Every electric motor shall be controlled by an efficient switch for starting and stopping, such switch to be readily accessible and easily operated and so placed as to prevent danger.

**Connection of appliances to supply*

N8.—(1) Every appliance, other than a heating appliance, shall be—

(*a*) controlled by means of a switch, which shall be additional to any automatic control device, and shall be arranged to disconnect the appliance from all live conductors, or

(*b*) where the supply of electricity is alternating current, connected by means of a plug and socket outlet:

Provided that nothing in this paragraph shall apply to—

(i) an electric clock, or

(ii) a bell transformer fed from a separate circuit.

(2) Every heating appliance shall be controlled by a linked switch arranged to break the supply conductors:

Provided that this paragraph shall not apply to an appliance the heating elements of which are so screened that they cannot be touched.

**Precautions against special conditions*

N9.—(1) All apparatus and conductors exposed to weather, corrosive atmosphere or other adverse conditions shall be so constructed or protected as may be necessary to prevent danger arising from such exposure.

(2) Where a conductor or apparatus is, or is likely to be, exposed to flammable surroundings or an explosive atmosphere, it shall be protected by a flameproof enclosure or be otherwise so designed and constructed as to prevent danger.

(3) For the purposes of the last foregoing paragraph a "flameproof enclosure", in relation to any conductor or apparatus, means an enclosure or casing which will withstand without injury any explosion of a flammable gas that may occur within it (in the case of apparatus under conditions of operation within the rating of the apparatus and recognised overloads, if any, associated therewith) and will prevent the transmission of flame such as would ignite any flammable gas that may be present in the surrounding atmosphere.

**Voltages exceeding 250 volts*

N10. Conductors and apparatus operating at voltages between conductors or to earth exceeding 250 volts shall either—

(*a*) be completely enclosed in earthed metal which is electrically continuous and adequately protected against mechanical damage, or

(*b*) be so constructed, installed and protected as to prevent danger so far as is reasonably practicable.

**Electrical appliances*

N11. Every fixed appliance to which this Part applies shall be so designed, constructed and installed as to operate efficiently and safely.

Light fittings or appliances in rooms containing baths or showers

N12.—(1) Any light fitting or appliance in a room containing a fixed bath or shower shall comply with the following provisions of this regulation.

(2) Any part of a lamp-holder likely to be touched by a person replacing a lamp shall be constructed of or shrouded in insulating material and fitted with a protective shield.

(3) Any switch or other means of control or adjustment associated with a light or electrical appliance in the room shall be either—

(*a*) of the type operated by an insulating cord, or

(*b*) be placed in an accessible position outside and immediately adjacent to the normal access door of the room, but shall in any event be so situated as to be out of the reach of a person in the bath or under the shower:

Provided that nothing in this paragraph shall prohibit the provision in the room of a shaver supply unit—

(i) complying with British Standard 3052: 1958, "Electric shaver supply units" as read with Amendments PD 4386, November 1961 and AMD 455, March 1970, and

(ii) so situated as to be out of the reach of a person in the bath or under the shower, and

(iii) having its earth terminal so earthed as to comply with regulation N5, and

(iv) having its secondary circuit isolated both from the supply mains and earth.

(4) Save as provided for in the last foregoing paragraph, no provision shall be made in the room for the use of any portable appliance.

(5) Any heating appliance or other apparatus in the room shall be so situated as to be out of the reach of a person in the bath or under the shower.

Wiring diagrams

N13. In every building or part of a building to which this Part applies, not being a building or part of a building comprising a house, there shall be displayed on the wall beside the main supply switch for that building, or part thereof, or at some other suitable place, a schematic diagram, in permanent form and of a suitable size, showing the main distribution circuits and controls of the wiring of the building.

PART P

Prevention of Danger and Obstruction

Projections and fixtures

P1. Where any part of a building or any fixture affixed to a building—

(*a*) projects, or is capable of being projected, over or on to any place to which the persons inhabiting or frequenting the building or adjacent buildings or places, or the public generally, have access, or

(*b*) opens or is capable of being opened over or on to such a place, or

(*c*) is affixed to a wall or roof which faces on to such a place,

such part or fixture shall be so situated, fixed and secured as to cause no obstruction or danger—

(i) in the case of a footway or other place to which pedestrian access only is available, to any person;

(ii) in the case of any other place, to any person or vehicle.

Pipes for the discharge of smoke, etc.

P2. No pipe for the discharge of gas, steam, hot water or smoke or other gaseous product of combustion shall be—

(*a*) fixed to a building against the outside of, or taken through, any wall in such a manner as to cause obstruction or danger to any member of the public, or

(*b*) so fixed as to discharge through a window or door.

Steam pipes

P3. All waste steam from high pressure engines in or connected with any building shall be conveyed and carried away by a high chimney.

Windows

P4. In every building—

(*a*) every window above the ground storey of the building, not being a roof-light, and

(*b*) every roof-light to which Part L applies

shall be so constructed as to enable the outside of the window or roof-light to be cleaned safely from inside the building:

Provided that nothing in this regulation shall apply—

(i) in the case of a house, to a window or roof-light where access to the outside thereof for cleaning can be safely obtained from a balcony, platform or flat roof, or

(ii) in the case of any other building, to a window where—

(A) access to the outside thereof for cleaning can be safely obtained from a balcony, platform or flat roof, or

(B) such other facilities, forming part of the building, are provided as will enable the safe cleaning of the window from outwith the building.

PART Q

HOUSING STANDARDS

Application of Part Q

Q1.—(1) This Part shall apply only in relation to a building or part of a building of occupancy sub-group A1 or A2.

(2) In this Part, the provisions of regulations Q3, Q4 to Q6, Q8 to Q13, Q18 and Q19 shall not be subject to specification in a notice served under section 11 of the Act (which enables local authorities to require existing buildings to conform to these regulations).

(3) Regulations Q5, Q8(3) and Q11 shall not apply to any house to which regulation Q19 applies.

**Access to houses—general*

Q2.—(1) There shall be provided in respect of each house access from a public road to—

(*a*) at least one entrance door into that house, and

(*b*) any refuse collection point serving that house,

by means of a roadway, footpath, passage, stairway, landing or balcony, being an access which complies with the following provisions of this regulation and with the relevant provisions of Part S.

(2) Any part of the access to a house which is at a distance, measured along the access, of more than—

(*a*) if the house is served by a common ground floor entrance doorway or a common stairway, 46 metres from that entrance doorway or from the bottom step of the stairway, or if the house is not so served, 46 metres from the door of the house, and

(*b*) if the house is served by a communal refuse storage container, 9 metres from the refuse collection point, or if the house is not so served, 46 metres from the refuse collection point

shall be a roadway at least 3 metres wide and capable of carrying a vehicle of an axle load of 5 tonnes.

(3) The access shall, subject to the last foregoing paragraph, be of an unrestricted width of not less than—

(*a*) in the case of a footpath—

(i) providing access only to one house, 900 millimetres,

(ii) providing access to two houses, 1·2 metres,

(iii) providing access to more than two houses, 1·8 metres;

(*b*) in the case of a passage, landing or balcony—

(i) providing access only to one house, 900 millimetres,

(ii) providing access to two or more houses, 1 metre;

(*c*) in the case of any part providing access only—

(i) to a refuse collection point which serves only one house, 900 millimetres,

(ii) to any other refuse collection point, 1·2 metres.

(4) The access shall be so constructed as to prevent an accumulation of water thereon and provide a safe and adequate surface for pedestrian traffic.

(5) Where any part of the access is a footpath providing access to a communal refuse storage container the footpath shall—

(*a*) either be level or have a fall-away from the refuse collection point not exceeding 1 in 14 at any part, and

(*b*) be constructed with an even continuous finish.

(6) Where in the wall of any part of an access comprising a passage there is a window, any part of the glazed portion of which is less than 1·1 metres above the floor, the window shall be guarded by a secure railing or balustrade extending to a height of 1·2 metres above the floor.

(7) No opening in any balustrade or between any railings provided in accordance with paragraph (6) of this regulation shall be of such a size as will permit the passage through it of a sphere 100 millimetres in diameter.

(8) In this regulation "refuse collection point" means the point, if any, from which the refuse of a house will be collected by the appropriate public authority.

Access within houses—general

Q3. Within every house of more than one storey there shall be provided between such storeys access by means of a stairway complying with the relevant provisions of Part S:

Provided that nothing in this regulation shall require the provision of a stairway to any storey within a house if that storey is used only as general storage accommodation other than that provided so as to comply with regulation Q11.

Lifts

Q4.—(1) This regulation shall apply to every block of flats in which the entrance door of any house is vertically distant from any entrance to the block by not less than either—

(*a*) the height of four storeys of the building, or

(*b*) 9 metres,

so, however, that where an entrance to a block of flats is higher than the ground level adjacent to that entrance, the vertical distance of the entrance door of any house in the block in relation to that entrance shall be measured from that ground level.

(2) Subject to regulation E19, in any block of flats to which this regulation applies—

(*a*) there shall be provided access by passenger lift to within one storey of the entrance door of every house in that block;

(*b*) the number of lifts so provided shall be not less than—

(i) where in the block of flats there are more than 70 houses or the occupant capacity of the block exceeds 160, the number required to provide a scale of either one lift to 70 houses or one lift to 160 occupants;

(ii) where the entrance door of any house in the block of flats is vertically distant from any entrance to the block by a distance not less than either—

(A) the height of eight storeys of the building, or

(B) 19 metres,

two lifts;

(iii) in any other case, one lift;

(*c*) each lift so provided shall comply with the following provisions of this regulation.

(3) The lift shall be capable of carrying not less than eight adults at any one time by means of a guided lift-car which shall be mechanically operated in an enclosed well.

(4) The lift shall be fitted with—

(*a*) if its travel range does not exceed 8 storeys, automatic push button control;

(*b*) if its travel range exceeds 8 storeys, automatic directional-collective control.

(5) The lift shall be capable of a speed of—

(*a*) if its travel range does not exceed 10 storeys, 0·5 metre per second;

(*b*) if its travel range exceeds 10 storeys but does not exceed 18 storeys, 0·75 metre per second;

(*c*) if its travel range exceeds 18 storeys but does not exceed 24 storeys, 1 metre per second;

(*d*) if its travel range exceeds 24 storeys, 1·5 metres per second.

(6) The lift shall have arrangements for the automatic parking of the lift-car when not in use at a floor containing an entrance to the building.

(7) The lift shall be fitted with such control devices as may be necessary to prevent—

(*a*) the movement of the lift-car in the well unless all the landing doors by which access to that lift-car is obtained and the doors of the lift-car itself are closed, and

(*b*) the opening of a landing door unless the lift-car is at rest opposite it:

Provided that nothing in this paragraph shall be so construed as to prevent the incorporation in the mechanism of safety devices such as to permit in an emergency the opening, subject to suitable safeguards, of the doors of a lift-car or landing doors.

(8) The lift-car of the lift shall—

(*a*) have an internal area of not less than 1100 millimetres by 1400 millimetres and an internal height of not less than 2200 millimetres, and

(*b*) be fitted with an imperforate and self-closing door, and

(*c*) be equipped with means of ventilation but otherwise be a fully enclosed structure, and

(*d*) be equipped with means of artificial lighting, available both in normal operation and on the failure of the main power supply to the lift, and

(*e*) be fitted with a suitable device for making an alarm signal capable of being heard outside the lift well, and

(*f*) have displayed conspicuously therein a notice stating the maximum working load and the maximum number of passengers which can be safely permitted to be carried in the car.

(9) Each landing door shall be self-closing and so constructed as to open by sliding or by sliding-and-folding.

(10) The lift well of the lift shall not contain any pipes, wires or other equipment unless these form part of the lift or are necessary for its operation and maintenance.

(11) The machinery operating the lift shall be—

(*a*) housed in a separate room which is capable of being secured against access by unauthorised persons and in which provision is made for artificial lighting, and

(*b*) effectively insulated from the floor of the machine room in relation to sound and vibration.

(12) In this regulation "travel range", in relation to a lift fitted in a building, means the number of storeys between the level of the storey containing the main entrance to the building and the highest storey at which access is provided by the lift.

Space requirements for houses

Q5.—(1) In any house—

(*a*) the total area of the accommodation provided for living and cooking shall not be less than that set out in column (3) of Table 17, and

(*b*) the aggregate area of the apartments, other than the living room, shall be not less than that set out in column (5) of Table 17.

(2) No apartment or kitchen shall have an area of less than—

(*a*) in the case of an apartment, 7 square metres;

(*b*) in the case of a kitchen, that specified in column (4) of Table 17.

(3) Where—

(*a*) in an apartment other than the living room, or

(*b*) in the case of a house of one apartment, in the apartment

there is fitted any built-in wardrobe accommodation the floor area thereof shall, for the purposes of this regulation, be included as part of the floor area of that apartment but not to any extent greater than—

(i) in the case of an apartment having an area of 11 square metres or more, 0·9 square metre;

(ii) in the case of any other apartment, 0·5 square metre.

Height of rooms

Q6.—(1) Subject to the following provisions of this regulation—

(*a*) (i) every apartment, kitchen and bathroom forming part of a house, and

(ii) every room in which there are provided communal laundry facilities or heated drying cabinets or tumbler dryers so as to comply with regulation Q12 or Q13,

shall at no part be less than 2·3 metres in height;

(*b*) every watercloset forming part of a house shall be at no part less than 2·06 metres in height.

(2) There shall be accepted as complying with this regulation—

(*a*) a living room, if it is not less than 2·3 metres in height over nine-tenths of the floor area thereof and is at no part less than 2·1 metres in height;

(*b*) any other apartment if—

(i) it has a cubic capacity of not less than 14·9 cubic metres, and

(ii) it is not less than 2·3 metres in height over at least one-half of its floor area and not less than 1·9 metres over at least three-quarters of such area;

(*c*) a kitchen if—

(i) over the area specified in column (4) of Table 17, or

(ii) over one-half of the area of the kitchen,

whichever is the greater, it is not less than 2·3 metres in height and is at no part less than 1·5 metres in height;

(*d*) a bathroom, if it is not less than 2·3 metres in height over at least three-quarters of its floor area and is at no part less than 1·5 metres in height;

(*e*) a watercloset, if it is not less than 2·06 metres in height over at least three-quarters of its floor area and is at no part less than 1·5 metres in height.

(3) Nothing in this regulation shall be taken to prohibit the provision of a stairway rising from the floor of an apartment or kitchen to the storey above.

**Bathrooms and waterclosets*

Q7.—(1) There shall, within every house, be provided the following equipment—

(*a*) a bath of one of the following types—

(i) a bath of rectangular or tub pattern measuring not less than 1·5 metres in length overall;

(ii) a shower bath which complies with paragraph (2) of this regulation;

(iii) a sitz-bath measuring at least 1 metre in length overall, 685 millimetres in width overall and 600 millimetres in depth at its deepest part and installed so that the top of the roll of the bath is not more than 530 millimetres above the floor of the bathroom or a raised step or platform adjacent to the bath, and (*b*) a wash-hand basin of adequate size, and

(*c*) a watercloset pan connected to a suitable flushing system.

(2) Any shower bath provided so as to comply with the last foregoing paragraph shall be equipped with a spray operated by an anti-scald valve and contained in a compartment—

(*a*)(i) which is enclosed or capable of being enclosed by materials impervious to the passage of moisture, and

(ii) which has a cross-sectional area of not less than 0·49 square metre above a height of 600 millimetres above floor level and is at no part less than 660 millimetres in width, and

(*b*) the floor of which is—

(i) composed of a material impervious to the passage of moisture, and

(ii) not less than 90 millimetres below the level of the top of a kerb surrounding it or the level of the floor of the bathroom, and

(iii) graded to an outlet.

(3) Subject to the next succeeding paragraph, the bath and the wash-hand basin provided so as to comply with paragraph (1) of this regulation shall be fitted in a separate bathroom which shall not open directly into any apartment or kitchen:

Provided that in the case of a house containing only one apartment, nothing in this paragraph shall be taken to prohibit a bathroom which does not contain a watercloset pan opening directly into that apartment.

(4) If a house contains a bathroom in addition to that provided so as to comply with paragraph (3) of this regulation it shall not open into a living room or kitchen, but nothing in the said paragraph (3) shall prohibit it opening directly into any apartment other than the living room.

(5) The watercloset pan provided so as to comply with paragraph (1) of this regulation shall be fitted either—

(*a*) in the bathroom provided so as to comply with paragraph (3) of this regulation, or

(*b*) in a separate watercloset which complies with the two next succeeding paragraphs.

(6) Every watercloset forming part of a house shall be fitted with a wash-hand basin:

Provided that nothing in this paragraph shall require the fitting of a wash-hand basin in a watercloset where there is a wash-hand basin fitted in any room giving access directly to the watercloset.

(7) No watercloset forming part of a house shall open directly into—

(*a*) in the case of the watercloset referred to in paragraph (5) of this regulation, any apartment or kitchen;

(*b*) in any other case, a living room or kitchen.

**Kitchens*

Q8.—(1) There shall be provided in every house a kitchen which shall comply with the following provisions of this regulation.

(2) The kitchen shall be fitted with—

(*a*) a sink of adequate size, and

(*b*) a draining board fixed on one side of the sink and having a total area of not less than 0·28 square metre, and

(c) cooking facilities in the form of either—

(i) such piping, cables or other apparatus as may be necessary to enable a gas, electric or oil cooker to be used, or

(ii) a solid fuel cooker designed for continuous burning.

(3) The kitchen shall be provided with—

(a) a larder complying with the next succeeding regulation, and

(b) a dry goods cupboard or cupboards

having an aggregate cubic capacity of not less than that specified in column (6) of Table 17.

Larders

Q9.—(1) Any larder required to be provided under the last foregoing regulation shall comply with the provisions of this regulation.

(2) The cubic capacity of the larder shall be not less than 0·34 cubic metre:

Provided that where there are fitted in the house such piping, cables or other apparatus as may be necessary to enable a refrigerator to be used, the cubic capacity of the larder and the cubic capacity specified in column (6) of Table 17 may both be reduced by 0·17 cubic metre.

(3) The larder shall be ventilated to the external air by a permanent ventilator which—

(a) has a cross-sectional area of not less than 3250 square millimetres,

(b) is fitted with a fly-proof cover so constructed as to allow a free flow of air, and

(c) has a smooth internal surface which is accessible for cleaning.

(4) No part of any hot water pipe, flue or other source of heat shall be within the larder or within 460 millimetres of any part thereof unless there is provided such insulation as will prevent the emission of heat therefrom into the larder.

(5) No window shall be placed in any wall of the larder which forms part of the external wall of the house unless the wall faces in a northerly direction within the limits between east and north-west and all openable parts of any window in the larder shall be fitted with a fly-proof cover.

(6) The larder shall be provided with shelves so constructed and fitted as to allow a free flow of air within the larder.

Fuel stores

Q10. Every house containing an appliance designed to burn solid fuel, fitted for the purpose of complying with regulation Q15, shall be provided with a fuel store which—

(a) is adjacent to or within the house but does not enter directly from any habitable room or any room used for the preparation of food, and

(b) is capable of containing not less than 1·13 cubic metres of fuel, and

(c) has a suspended floor of reinforced concrete not less than 100 millimetres in thickness or a solid floor of concrete or paving stone not less than 75 millimetres in thickness, and

(d) has pointed or cement plastered walls constructed of bricks, stone or building blocks or concrete cast in situ, and

(e) if within the house, is accessible for fuel delivery purposes by a hatch or doorway from outside the house or from a utility room, passage or vestibule, having direct entry from outside the house:

Provided that—

(i) in the case of a house having a ground floor where access thereto is otherwise than by way of a common stair or passage, this regulation shall not apply if there is provided for that house a fuel store which is capable of containing not less than 1·13 cubic metres of fuel situated either—

(A) outside the house, or

(B) in a utility room within the house having direct entry from outside the house;

(ii) nothing in paragraph (*a*) of this regulation shall prohibit the provision of a hopper or other suitable device so as to withdraw fuel from a fuel store directly into an apartment or a kitchen in which there is an appliance designed to burn solid fuel.

Linen and general storage

Q11. In respect of every house there shall, in addition to the dry goods cupboard required under regulation Q8(3), be provided—

(*a*) a linen cupboard or cupboards within the house, and

(*b*) general storage accommodation, enclosed and floored, within the house or in the curtilage of the house or of the building containing the house,

having an aggregate cubic capacity of not less than that specified in column (7) of Table 17.

**Laundry facilities*

Q12.—(1) In every house there shall be provided in the kitchen, or in a separate laundry room, facilities for the washing of clothes comprising—

(*a*) a sink of adequate size, and

(*b*) adjacent to a sink either—

(i) a tub of adequate size, or

(ii) such piping, cables or other apparatus as may be necessary to enable the use of a washing machine:

Provided that—

(i) where these facilities are provided in the kitchen nothing in this regulation shall require the provision of a sink in addition to that required under regulation Q8;

(ii) this paragraph shall not apply to—

(A) any house in respect of which there is provided within the same building communal laundry facilities which comply with paragraph (2) of this regulation;

(B) any house having an area not exceeding 42 square metres.

(2) The communal laundry facilities referred to in the proviso to the last foregoing paragraph—

(*a*) shall comprise the facilities specified under either head (A) or head (B) of the following table—

Appliance	Capable of dealing in one operation with dry weight of washing	Scale—number of houses to each appliance not more than—
(A)		
(i) Combined washing and rinsing machines powered by electricity and heated by gas, electricity or steam	(*a*) 4 kilogrammes or (*b*) 9 kilogrammes	(*a*) 15 or (*b*) 30
and		
(ii) Tubs	—	15
and		
(iii) Hydro-extractors powered by electricity, or wringers	(*a*) 4 kilogrammes or (*b*) 6 kilogrammes	(*a*) 30 or (*b*) 60
(B)		
(i) Combined washing, boiling, rinsing and spin-drying machines powered by electricity and heated by gas, electricity or steam	4 kilogrammes	15
and		
(ii) Tubs	—	15

(*b*) shall be provided in a room which—

(i) is naturally lighted, and

(ii) has provision for artificial lighting, and

(iii) has a ceiling, floor and walls of impervious finish, and

(iv) has a solid floor laid with falls to trapped gullies.

Drying facilities

Q13.—(1) There shall be provided in respect of every house such drying facilities or combination of drying facilities as are set forth under one of the heads in column (3) of the following table, sited as shown in column (4) thereof—

Description of house (1)	Head (2) Drying facilities (3)	Sited (4)
Not in blocks of flats	(1) Drying area of not less than 4·2† square metres.	On ground adjacent to house or building.
In a block of flats of less than 5 storeys	(2) Individual drying area not less than 4·2† square metres or communal drying area on scale of not less than 4·2† square metres per house.	On ground adjacent to building.
In a block of flats	(3) Individual drying area not less than 4·2† square metres or communal drying area on scale of not less than 4·2† square metres per house.	On a balcony or On a flat roof or In a room or other part of the block set aside for the purpose.
	(4)(*a*) Individual drying cabinet or tumbler dryer and	(*a*) Within house.
	(*b*) Individual drying area not less than 2·8 square metres or communal drying area on scale of not less than 2·8 square metres per house.	(*b*) On a balcony or On a flat roof or In a room or other part of the block set aside for the purpose.
	(5) Individual drying cabinet or tumbler dryer and Hydro-extractor capable of dealing with 2·7 kilogrammes dry weight of washing in one operation and powered by electricity.	Within house.
	(6)(*a*) Communal heated drying cabinets or tumbler dryers and	(*a*) In the block.
	(*b*) Individual drying area not less than 2·8 square metres or communal drying area on scale of not less than 2·8 square metres per house.	(*b*) On a balcony or On a flat roof or In a room or other part of the block set aside for the purpose.
In a block of flats in respect of which there is provided communal laundry facilities such as are mentioned in regulation Q12(2)(*a*)	(7) Communal heated drying cabinets or tumbler dryers.	In the block.

†*Note:* This area to be 2·8 square metres in relation to a house in a block of flats comprising—

(i) one or two apartments, or

(ii) three apartments, two of which have a floor area of less than 10 square metres.

(2) In the foregoing table—

(*a*) any reference to a drying area shall be construed as a reference to an area—

(i) suitable for use for drying clothes and equipped with posts or other suitable fittings for the fixing and suspension of a clothes line;

(ii) if on a balcony or flat roof, exposed to the open air and provided with suitable means of disposing of surface water;

(iii) in no case less than 2·7 metres in length, and

(*b*) any reference to a drying cabinet or a tumbler dryer shall be construed as a reference to a heated drying cabinet ventilated to the external air or, as the case may be, a heated tumbler dryer, and

(*c*) any reference to communal drying cabinets or tumbler dryers shall be construed as a reference to heated drying cabinets or, as the case may be, heated tumbler dryers—

(i) provided on a scale of one cabinet or tumbler dryer for every 15 houses they are intended to serve, and

(ii) in the case of drying cabinets, each capable of dealing with 5·4 kilogrammes dry weight of washing in one operation, and

(iii) fitted in a room which is naturally lighted, has provision for artificial lighting, has a ceiling, floor and walls of impervious finish, and has a solid floor laid with falls to trapped gullies.

Water supply to baths, sinks, tubs and wash-hand basins

Q14.—(1) Every bath, sink, tub and wash-hand basin provided so as to comply with these regulations shall have a piped supply of both hot and cold water with tap outlets, the piped supply of cold water to the sink being connected directly to the water service pipe for the house:

Provided that nothing in this paragraph shall require the provision of a piped supply of—

(i) hot water to a wash-hand basin fitted in a watercloset to which access can be obtained only from outside the house;

(ii) cold water to the sink from the water service pipe for the house when the pressure in the main supply pipe is insufficient to provide a constant supply of water.

(2) In every sink provided so as to comply with regulation Q8 there shall be a clearance of not less than 300 millimetres between the outlet of the fittings supplying water to the sink and the bottom of the sink on the inside.

Heating

Q15.—(1) There shall be provided—

(*a*) in the living room of every house, and

(*b*) in the case of a house of three or more apartments where no public electricity supply is available and no central heating system is installed, in one other apartment,

a space heating appliance which complies with this regulation.

(2) The appliance shall be—

(*a*) a solid fuel stove or open fire, or

(*b*) an electric or gas heating appliance affixed to the house as a fixture, or

(*c*) an appliance forming part of a central heating system, or

(*d*) a flued oil burning convector heating appliance, not being an integral tank convector appliance.

(3) Where there is provided in the house any power point of the descrip-
available for heating the room not less than 2 kilowatts.

(4) Any electric appliance provided so as to comply with this regulation shall be permanently connected to the electrical supply system and any gas appliance so provided shall be connected to the gas supply with fixed non-flexible metal tubing and fittings.

(5) In this regulation "central heating system" shall include any system of heating by means of warm air or under-floor heating.

Artificial lighting

Q16.—(1) Every house to which a public supply of electricity is available shall be provided with an efficient electric lighting system which complies with the following provisions of this regulation.

(2) The system shall include at least one terminal point for lighting in every room having an area of 1·9 square metres or more and in every bath-room, watercloset, entrance vestibule, hall, passage and stairway terminal landing.

(3) Where any light forming part of the system is at a stairway terminal landing, switches controlling the light shall be provided—

(*a*) at the landing itself, and

(*b*) at any other terminal landing on the stairway.

**Power points*

Q17.—(1) Every house shall be provided with power points, so installed that they shall be safe and efficient under normal conditions of use, for the attachment and use of portable domestic appliances:

Provided that nothing in this paragraph shall apply to a house to which it is not reasonably practicable to provide a supply of electricity or gas from a public supply.

(2) Subject to paragraph (3) of this regulation, the number of power points provided shall not be less than that specified in the appropriate column of the following table—

Position	Minimum number of points	
	Houses with electricity or both electricity and gas	Houses with gas only
Living room	4 power points, 2 of which to be electricity points or 2 power points and 1 multiple socket outlet.	1 gas point.
Every other apartment	2 power points.	1 gas point.
Kitchen	3 power points†.	3 gas points.
In any part of the house	2 power points in addition to those referred to above.	—

†2 power points in the case of any house of—

(a) not more than two apartments, or

(b) not more than three apartments, of which each of the apartments other than the living room has a floor area less than 10 square metres.

(3) Where there is provided in the house any power point of the description mentioned in—

(*a*) regulation Q8(2)(*c*)(i) (for cooking facilities);

(*b*) regulation Q9(2) (for a refrigerator);

(*c*) regulation Q12(1)(*b*)(ii) (for a washing machine),

the requirements of paragraph (2) shall be in addition to the provision of that point.

(4) In this regulation—

"electricity point" means a suitable electricity socket outlet which shall provide safely a current of 13 amperes by means of a ring or radial circuit;

"gas point" means a gas outlet fitted with a safety tap;

"power point" means an electricity point or a gas point.

**Refuse disposal arrangements*

Q18.—(1) Where in a block of flats the entrance door of any house is vertically distant from any entrance to the block by not less than either—

(*a*) the height of four storeys of the building, or

(*b*) 9 metres

there shall be provided in respect of every house in that block, refuse disposal arrangements by means of a system which complies with the following provisions of this regulation.

(2) The system shall be so designed as to—

(*a*) afford access for the purposes of refuse disposal by means of a hopper or other suitable device either within the house or at a point within a distance of not more than one storey from every house served by the system, and

(*b*) carry or dispose of the refuse efficiently, without damage to the building or danger or offence to the persons in the building, and

(*c*) allow access for cleansing and for clearing obstructions.

(3) Any chute or refuse container chamber forming part of the system shall be so ventilated as to prevent the escape of foul air into the building.

(4) Where the system includes a refuse container, the container shall be housed in a chamber—

(*a*) formed of solid non-combustible materials, and

(*b*) the inner surface of which comprises a material impervious to the passage of moisture, and

(*c*) so designed as to permit convenient removal and replacement of containers and to prevent spillage of refuse on to the floor of the chamber.

**Alternative space standards for houses*

Q19.—(1) This regulation shall apply to every house which is—

(*a*) provided with such adequate and suitably located and planned accommodation as is necessary to enable it to fulfil its function satisfactorily for the number of persons which the house is designed to accommodate; and

(*b*) constructed in accordance with the following provisions of this regulation.

(2) In this regulation—

"general storage space" excludes any dust bin store, fuel store, kitchen storage (including any ventilated larder and broom cupboard), cupboard for linen storage and pram space located in a store;

"maisonette" means a flat on more than one storey;

"net space" means the area of one or more floors enclosed by the external walls and any separating walls of the house, and includes the area of any floor taken up by any staircase, partition, chimney breast, flue and heating appliance, and any watercloset provided in addition to the watercloset required by regulation Q7, but excludes the area of any floor occupied by—

(i) the general storage space;

(ii) any dust bin store, fuel store, garage or balcony;

(iii) in a room with a sloping ceiling, such part of the floor as is covered by any part of the ceiling which does not exceed 1·5 metres in height;

(iv) any porch, lobby or covered way, any of which is open to the external air; and

(v) any sun porch; and

"single access house" means a house with public access from one side only.

(3) The net space of a house of a type described in column (1) in Part A of Table 18 shall be not less than the area prescribed for net space in column (3) thereof for the number of persons that house is designed to accommodate.

(4) A house of a type described in column (1) in Part A of Table 18 shall be provided with—

(*a*) general storage space not less than the area prescribed for general storage space in column (3) thereof for the number of persons that house is designed to accommodate;

(*b*) kitchen storage space (including a ventilated larder and a broom cupboard) which shall be enclosed and have a cubic capacity not less than that prescribed in column (2) in Part B of Table 18 in respect of the ventilated larder and a total cubic capacity not less than that prescribed in column (3) thereof for the number of persons that house is designed to accommodate; and

(*c*) one or more cupboards for linen storage having in aggregate a cubic capacity not less than that prescribed in column (2) in Part C of Table 18 for the number of persons that house is designed to accommodate.

(5) Net space shall be measured to the finished internal faces of the external walls and any separating walls of the house, and general storage space shall be measured to the internal faces of the enclosing walls and door.

(6) Where in the case of a single access house any space within the general storage space forms part of a means of passage from one side of the house to any other side of the house, the space shall be deemed to be 700 millimetres wide and shall not be taken to contribute to the area of net space or general storage space prescribed in Part A of Table 18.

(7) The general storage space shall—

(*a*) be enclosed and floored, and

(*b*) have a minimum height, measured from the floor to the ceiling, of 1·5 metres.

(8) In any house other than a flat or maisonette—

(*a*) not less than 2·5 square metres of general storage space shall be provided at ground storey level ;

(*b*) any general storage space provided on an upper storey shall be enclosed separately from the space provided for linen storage ; and

(*c*) where there is a garage adjoining the house, any area in the garage in excess of 12 square metres may be taken to be general storage space.

(9) In the case of a flat or maisonette—

(*a*) not more than 1·5 square metres of the general storage space may be provided outside the house ; and

(*b*) where there is a garage adjoining the flat or maisonette, any area in the garage in excess of 12 square metres may be treated as general storage space permitted under sub-paragraph (*a*) of this paragraph to be outside the house.

PART R

Ashpits and Dungsteads

Ashpits

R1. Any ashpit provided in relation to a building of occupancy sub-group A1, A2 or A3 shall—

(*a*) be so sited that neither it nor any drainage system therefrom endangers any water supply used for domestic purposes, and

(*b*) be no nearer to any part of a house than 6 metres, and

(*c*) be so sited as to afford ready means of access for cleansing and for the removal of its contents without passing through the interior of any building, and

(*d*) have walls constructed of suitable impervious materials finished smooth on the inner surfaces, and

(*e*) have a floor not less than 75 millimetres above the surface of the adjoining ground at the entrance thereto constructed of suitable impervious material, finished smooth, and graded to an outlet which is so constructed as to allow the passage of liquid only and is connected to a channel leading to a drainage system, and

(*f*) be roofed in such a manner and be provided with a door or doors so fitted as to prevent the escape of the contents, and

(*g*) be ventilated to the external air.

Dungsteads

R2. Every dungstead shall—

(*a*) be so sited that neither it nor any drainage system therefrom endangers any water supply used for domestic purposes, and

(*b*) be no nearer to any part of a house than 18 metres, and

(*c*) have walls and a floor constructed of suitable impervious material, and

(*d*) be properly drained.

PART S

Construction of Stairways, Landings and Balconies

Application of Part S

S1.—(1) The provisions of this Part shall apply to all stairways, landings and balconies in buildings to which these regulations apply.

(2) The provisions of this Part, in so far as they relate to—

(*a*) exit stairways in houses of more than two storeys and in buildings to which the Factories Act 1961(**a**) applies,

(*b*) access and private stairways (other than the provisions of paragraphs (6) and (8) of regulation S3), and

(*c*) other stairways (other than the provisions of paragraphs (6) and (8) of regulation S3 and heads B and L of the table in regulation S4)

shall not be subject to specification in a notice served under section 11 of the Act (which enables local authorities to require existing buildings to conform to these regulations).

Interpretation of Part S

S2.—(1) In this Part—

"exit stairway" means a stairway forming part of an exit for the purposes of Part E ;

"access stairway" means a stairway which—

(*a*) forms part of an access provided so as to comply with regulation Q2, or

(*b*) provides access to any part of—

(i) a building containing two or more houses, or

(ii) the curtilage of such a building,

being a part which is provided for the use of the occupants of two or more houses in the building ;

"private stairway" means—

(*a*) a stairway wholly within a house, or

(*b*) a stairway providing access to any part of a building or of the curtilage of a building being a part which is available for the use only of the occupants of one house within the building and not being a stairway forming part of an access provided for the purposes of regulation Q2 ;

"other stairway" means a stairway not being an exit, access or private stairway ;

"balcony" includes a gallery ;

"balustrade" means a protective barrier so designed as to give a satisfactory degree of safety and rigidity and includes a wall or railing ;

"flight" means a stair or part of a stair uninterrupted by any landing ;

"going" means the horizontal distance between the nosings of two consecutive treads or between the nosing of a tread and the nosing of a landing next above it ;

"handrail" means a rail attached to a wall or balustrade and so designed as to afford a means of support to persons using the stair ;

(**a**) 1961 c. 34.

"pitch" means the angle between the pitch line and the horizontal;

"pitch line" means a notional line connecting the nosings of the treads;

"rise" means the vertical distance between the tops of two consecutive treads or between the top of a tread and the top of a landing next above it;

"stair" means the structure formed by the walls, balustrades or railings, handrails, risers, treads, and stringers if any;

"stairway" means the route of travel and includes the stair and any landings and balconies forming part of that route;

"tread" means the upper surface of a step within the width of the stairway.

(2) The minimum width of—

(*a*) an exit stairway or an access stairway shall be taken to be the unobstructed width thereof, provided that no account shall be taken of any obstruction caused by handrails where such obstruction does not exceed 100 millimetres;

(*b*) a private stairway or other stairway shall be taken to be the overall width thereof, provided that no account shall be taken of any obstruction caused by handrails, balustrades, stringers or newel post where such obstruction does not exceed 90 millimetres.

(3) The length of a landing shall be measured horizontally along the centre line of the direction of travel.

(4) The length of a tread shall be taken to be the horizontal distance between the two sides of the tread.

(5) Where a stairway or part of a stairway falls within more than one of the definitions in paragraph (1) of this regulation and is required to conform to more than one standard prescribed by this Part, that standard shall have effect in relation to the stairway or part, as the case may be, as if the stairway or part were required to conform to the more or most onerous standard.

General requirements for stairs

S3.—(1) Every stair shall have a clear headroom of 2050 millimetres measured vertically from the pitch line.

(2) Every stair shall be constructed in straight flights having a uniform rise and going:

Provided that nothing in this paragraph shall prohibit tapered treads with uniform going which comply with the requirements of head G of the table in regulation S4.

(3) A landing complying with regulation S5 shall be provided at each end of a flight:

Provided that nothing in this paragraph shall—

(i) apply to any flight between the external door of a building and the ground or an access balcony where the aggregate rise in each case does not exceed 600 millimetres and the door opens inwards; or

(ii) prohibit a landing being common to two flights.

(4) Where a stair is formed having open rises the nosing of the tread of any step or landing shall overlap the back edge of the tread below by not less than 16 millimetres.

(5) The width of a tread (which shall be measured from the front of the tread to the face of the riser, or to the back of the tread if there is no riser) shall be not less than the going.

(6) Every stair which rises more than 600 millimetres above an adjacent floor or landing or above ground external to a building shall be guarded on each side by a wall or by a secure balustrade or railing complying with the requirements in head J of the table in regulation S4.

(7) Where a stair open to the external air descends for more than 600 millimetres below an opening at ground level in which it is constructed, that opening shall be guarded at ground level by a wall or secure balustrade or railing extending above the ground level to a height of not less than 1·1 metres.

(8) (*a*) Every stair which rises more than 600 millimetres shall be provided with a handrail on one side where the width of the stair is not more than 1·1 metres and on each side where the width is greater than 1·1 metres; and

(*b*) the handrail shall be fixed securely at a height of not less than 840 millimetres nor more than 1 metre measured vertically above the pitch line and shall be continuous throughout each flight.

(9) A glazed area in the wall of a stair shall be guarded by a secure balustrade or railing of a height not less than that required by head J of the table in regulation S4 for balustrades or railings for that stair:

Provided that this paragraph shall not apply to a glazed area constructed of glass blocks or wired or toughened glass.

Specific requirements for stairs

S4. Every stair forming part of an exit, access, private or other stairway shall comply with the requirements set forth in the second, third, fourth or fifth columns respectively of the following table in relation to the corresponding head in the first column thereof—

Head (1)	Exit stairways (2)	Access stairways (3)	Private stairways (4)	Other stairways (5)
A. Width	Not less than the width determined in accordance with the provisions of regulations E7 and E8.	(*a*) Not less than 900 millimetres if the stairway serves only one house. (*b*) Not less than 1·1 metres in any other case.	(*a*) Not less than 890 millimetres. (*b*) Not less than 600 millimetres if the stairway provides access only— (i) to one room, not being a living room or kitchen, or (ii) to a bathroom, washroom or water-closet.	Not less than 600 millimetres.
B. Additional requirements for stairways over 1·8 metres in width.	(*a*) The stair to be so constructed as to permit of separate sections not less than 1·1 metres nor more than 1·8 metres in width. (*b*) The stair to be divided into such sections by a handrail or handrails. (*c*) The upper end of any such handrail to be supported by an upright rigidly secure post carried to the ceiling or to a height of not less than 2·1 metres.	—	—	(*a*) The stair to be so constructed as to permit of separate sections not less than 900 millimetres nor more than 1·8 metres in width. (*b*) The stair to be divided into such sections by a handrail or handrails. (*c*) The upper end of any such handrail— (i) to be supported by an upright rigidly secure post carried to the ceiling or to a height of not less than 2·1 metres, or (ii) to be ramped to the floor, or (iii) to be a scroll end. (*d*) These requirements not to apply to buildings in occupancy sub-groups A3, B1, B2 or C2.

Head (1)	Exit stairways (2)	Access stairways (3)	Private stairways (4)	Other stairways (5)
C. Pitch	(*a*) Not exceeding 33 degrees in buildings in occupancy sub-groups A4, C1, C2 and C3. (*b*) Not exceeding 38 degrees in any other building.	Not exceeding 38 degrees.	Not exceeding 42 degrees.	(*a*) Not exceeding 33 degrees in a building in occupancy sub-group A4 or in a part of a building in occupancy group C to which the public have access. (*b*) Not exceeding 38 degrees in any other building or part of a building.
D. Number of rises per flight. The requirement for a minimum of 3 rises not to apply to a flight of one or two rises between the external door of a building and the ground or an access balcony.	Not fewer than 3 and not more than 16.	As for exit stairways.	(*a*) Not fewer than 3 and not more than 22. (*b*) Not fewer than 3 and not more than 16 if the stairway is open to the external air.	(*a*) Not fewer than 3 and not more than 16 in flats (occupancy sub-group A2) and in buildings in occupancy sub-groups A4 and C1. (*b*) Not fewer than 3 and not more than 22 in other buildings.
E. Going (subject to the provisions of head G).	At every part of the stair not less than— (*a*) 280 millimetres in a building in occupancy sub-group C3; or (*b*) 250 millimetres in any other building.	At every part of the stair not less than— (*a*) 250 millimetres where the stairway forms part of an access provided so as to comply with regulation Q2; or (*b*) 230 millimetres in any other case.	At every part of the stair not less than 220 millimetres.	At every part of the stair not less than 250 millimetres at the points 270 millimetres from each end of the tread.
F. Aggregate of going and twice the rise (subject to the provisions of head G).	Not less than 550 millimetres nor more than 700 millimetres.	As for exit stairways.	As for exit stairways, except that the rise to be not more than 220 millimetres.	As for exit stairways.

G. Going and rise of tapered treads. Consecutive tapered treads of different lengths to be deemed to have a length equal to the length of the shortest part of the treads. The deemed length to be measured from the tapered ends of the treads.	Aggregate of going and twice the rise not less than 550 millimetres nor more than 720 millimetres at the points 270 millimetres from each end of the tread (or where applicable the deemed length).	As for exit stairways.	(*a*) Aggregate of going and twice the rise as for exit stairways but measured along the centre line of the stair. (*b*) Where the stair is not more than 1 metre in width, the minimum going to be not less than 75 millimetres.	As for exit stairways, but where a stair is not more than 1·1 metres in width the going and rise may be measured along the centre line of the stair.
H. Openings between adjacent treads in open rise stairs.	In buildings in occupancy sub-group A2; residential schools (occupancy sub-group A3); children's homes and special schools for handicapped children (occupancy sub-group A4); shop premises (occupancy sub-group B2); and non-residential schools (occupancy sub-group C2), no opening to be of such a size as will permit the passage through it of a sphere 100 millimetres in diameter.	No opening to be of such a size as will permit the passage through it of a sphere 100 millimetres in diameter.	As for access stairways.	As for exit stairways.

Head (1)	Exit stairways (2)	Access stairways (3)	Private stairways (4)	Other stairways (5)
J. Heights of walls, balustrades or railings. (Measurements to be taken vertically above the pitch line. Where a handrail is fixed to the top of the balustrade or railing the measurements may be taken to the top of the handrail).	Not less than 900 millimetres.	Not less than 900 millimetres.	Not less than 840 millimetres.	Not less than 900 millimetres.
K. Openings in balustrades or between railings. These requirements not to apply to the space bounded by the riser and the lowest edge of the balustrade or railing if the lowest edge is not more than 50 millimetres above and parallel to the pitch line.	In buildings in occupancy sub-group A2; residential schools (occupancy sub-group A3); children's homes and special schools for handicapped children (occupancy sub-group A4); shop premises (occupancy sub-group B2); and non-residential schools (occupancy sub-group C2), no opening to be of such a size as will permit the passage through it of a sphere 100 millimetres in diameter.	No opening to be of such a size as will permit the passage of a sphere 100 millimetres in diameter.	As for access stairways.	In buildings in occupancy sub-group B2—as for access stairways.
L. Additional requirements for handrails.	Unless forming part of a balustrade the handrail at both ends to be wreathed back to the wall.	—	—	Unless forming part of a balustrade the handrail at both ends to be wreathed back to the wall or ramped to the floor.

Requirements for landings

S5.—(1) A landing forming part of a stairway shall be of a width not less than the width required for the stair by this Part.

(2) A landing forming part of an access provided for the purposes of regulation Q2 shall be of an unrestricted width not less than the width required by paragraph (3)(*b*) of that regulation.

(3) A landing required to comply with regulation S3(3) shall be of a length not less than that set forth in the second column of the following table in relation to the stairway described in the first column thereof—

A landing forming part of:— (1)	Minimum length (2)
An exit stairway	1·1 metres or the width of the stairway, whichever is the greater.
An access stairway	The width of the stairway.
A private stairway	800 millimetres.
An other stairway	1·8 metres or the width of the stairway, whichever is the lesser.

(4) A landing shall be guarded on every side by a wall or secure balustrade or railing, falling either within head A or head B of the first column of the following table, not less in height than that set forth in the third column thereof in relation to the landing described in the second column thereof—

Head (1)	Description or position of landing (2)	Minimum height (3)
A. Walls, balustrades or railings where the landing is open to the external air.	A landing forming part of a stairway in a house (occupancy sub-groups A1 and A2), a residential school (occupancy sub-group A3), a children's home or special school for handicapped children (occupancy sub-group A4), or a non-residential school (occupancy sub-group C2).	(*a*) 1·2 metres, or (*b*) 1·1 metres where any part of the landing is guarded by a wall, balustrade or railing the coping or top rail of which is of an overall width of not less than 230 millimetres.
B. Walls, balustrades or railings irrespective of whether the landing, other than one referred to in head A, is open to the external air.	A landing forming part of an exit.	1·1 metres.
	A landing forming part of an access stairway or of an access provided for the purposes of regulation Q2.	1·1 metres.
	A landing which— (i) is within a house, or (ii) provides access to any part of a building or the curtilage of a building being a part which is available for the use only of the occupants of one house within the building and is not part of an access provided for the purposes of regulation Q2.	900 millimetres.
	Any other landing.	1·1 metres.

(5) A glazed area in the wall of a landing shall be guarded by a secure balustrade or railing of a height not less than that required by paragraph (4) of this regulation for balustrades or railings for that landing:

Provided that this paragraph shall not apply to a glazed area constructed of glass blocks or wired or toughened glass or to a glazed portion of a door.

(6) No opening in any balustrade or between any railings provided in accordance with paragraphs (4) or (5) of this regulation shall be of such a size as will permit the passage through it of a sphere 100 millimetres in diameter.

Requirements for balconies

S6.—(1) A balcony forming part of an access provided for the purposes of regulation Q2 shall be of an unrestricted width not less than the width required by paragraph (3)(*b*) of that regulation.

(2) Where a balcony in a house, residential school (occupancy sub-group A3), children's home or special school for handicapped children (occupancy sub-group A4) or non-residential school (occupancy sub-group C2) is open to the external air and is at first storey level or above, the wall, balustrade or railing shall not be less than 1·2 metres in height:

Provided that where any part of the balcony is guarded by a wall, balustrade or railing, the coping or top rail of which is of an overall width of not less than 230 millimetres, this paragraph shall have effect in relation to that part as if for the words "1·2 metres" there were substituted the words "1·1 metres".

(3) Except as provided in paragraph (2) of this regulation every balcony shall be guarded on every side by a wall or secure balustrade or railing not less than 1·1 metres in height.

(4) A glazed area in the wall of a balcony shall be guarded by a secure balustrade or railing of a height not less than that required by paragraphs (2) and (3) of this regulation for balustrades or railings for that balcony:

Provided that this paragraph shall not apply to a glazed area constructed of glass blocks or wired or toughened glass or to a glazed portion of a door.

(5) No opening in any balustrade or between any railings provided in accordance with paragraph (2), (3) or (4) of this regulation where the balcony forms—

(*a*) part of an access provided for the purposes of regulation Q2, or

(*b*) part of a house, residential school (occupancy sub-group A3), children's home or special school for handicapped children (occupancy sub-group A4), or non-residential school (occupancy sub-group C2)

shall be of such a size as will permit the passage through it of a sphere 100 millimetres in diameter.

Gordon Campbell,
One of Her Majesty's Principal
Secretaries of State.

St. Andrew's House,
Edinburgh.
13th December 1971.

Regulation A3(6)

SCHEDULE 1

GENERAL RULES OF MEASUREMENT

Thickness

(1) The thickness of timber shall be taken to be the actual thickness.

(2) The thickness of any plaster shall be taken to be the least thickness of the plaster.

(3) The thickness of a wall or leaf of a cavity wall shall be taken to be the actual thickness exclusive of any applied surface finish.

Height

(4) The height of—

(*a*) a building, or division of a building, shall be taken to be the vertical measurement from the upper surface of the floor of the lowest storey to the underside of the ceiling of the topmost storey or, where there is no such ceiling, to the highest part of the roof less one-half of the vertical measurement between the lowest and the highest parts of the roof;

(*b*) a compartment of a building shall be taken to be the vertical measurement from the upper surface of the floor of the lowest storey in the compartment to the underside of the ceiling of the topmost storey in the compartment or, where the compartment is the topmost compartment of a building and there is no such ceiling, to the highest part of the roof less one-half of the vertical measurement between the lowest and highest parts of the roof;

(*c*) the roof of a building above ground level shall be taken to be the vertical measurement from the mean ground level to the highest part of the roof less, in the case of a building with a pitched roof, one-half of the vertical measurement between the lowest and the highest parts of the roof:

Provided that where any building has more than one roof any reference in this rule to the roof shall, in relation to that building, be construed as a reference to the higher or highest roof as the case may be.

(5) The height of a wall shall be measured—

(*a*) where there is a parapet, to the top of the parapet,

(*b*) in any other case, to the wallhead,

and where a wall is not of uniform height the height of the wall shall be taken to be the average height over its length.

(6) The height of a storey above ground level shall be taken to be the vertical measurement from the upper surface of the floor of the storey to the finished surface of the ground adjacent to the building containing the storey or, if such ground is not level, the least such measurement.

(7) The height of any part of a room shall be measured vertically from the upper surface of the floor to the underside of the ceiling or to the underside of any beam, bulkhead or other projection.

(8) The height of any part of a chimney or flue-pipe above an appliance shall be measured vertically from the highest part of the junction of the appliance with a chimney or flue-pipe.

(9) The height of any part of an exit except for the height appertaining to stairs required by regulation S3(1) shall be the clear unobstructed height measured vertically from the upper surface of the floor to the soffit of any obstruction.

Area

(10) The area of any storey of a building, division or compartment shall be taken to be the total area in that storey bounded by the finished inner surfaces of the enclosing walls or, on any side where there is no enclosing wall, by the outermost edge of the floor on that side.

(11) The area of any room or lobby shall be taken to be the total area of the floor thereof bounded by the inner finished surfaces of the walls forming the room or lobby:

SCHEDULE 1—*continued*

Provided that in calculating the area of—

(i) any room of a house, there shall be excluded—

(A) the area of any passage, watercloset, washroom, bathroom or store room, and

(B) the area of any part of a room where the height is less than 1·5 metres, and

(C) where there is within any apartment or kitchen a stair or part of a stair, the area of any space occupied by any part of the stair in any horizontal plane within that room, and

(D) the area of any larder, bulkhead, chimney, cupboard, press or fixture that extends to a height of more than 900 millimetres above the floor;

(ii) any room, not being a room of a house, there shall be excluded the area of any built-in storage space which extends from the floor to the ceiling.

(12) The area of any window or glazed opening shall be taken to be the area of the glass therein clear of any frame, sash or glazing bars.

Cubic capacity

(13) The cubic capacity of a building shall be taken to be the space contained by—

(*a*) the finished inner surfaces of its enclosing walls or, on any side where there is no enclosing wall, a plane extending vertically from the outermost edge of the floor on that side, and

(*b*) the upper surface of the floor of the lowest storey of the building, and

(*c*) if the roof over the building is non-combustible, the internal surface of the roof, or if combustible, the external surface.

(14) The cubic capacity of any room, larder, cupboard or general storage accommodation shall be taken to be the internal cubic capacity thereof:

Provided that, for the purposes of Parts K and Q of these regulations, in calculating the cubic capacity of—

(i) any room, no account shall be taken of any part of the room at a height of less than 1·5 metres, or

(ii) any general storage accommodation, no account shall be taken of any space at a height of more than 2·3 metres above the floor, or

(iii) any garage or part of a building used for vehicle parking, no account shall be taken of any space at a height of more than 3 metres above the floor, or

(iv) any room of a building, not being a garage or part of a building used for vehicle parking, no account shall be taken of any space at a height of more than 6 metres above the floor.

General

(15) Any distance from any point on the boundary of land in different occupation shall be measured horizontally.

(16) A rise, slope or fall away shall be taken to be one unit of measurement vertically in a given number of such units horizontally.

(17) Any reference to a width of cavity in a cavity wall shall be taken to be a reference to the distance between the inner face of the outer leaf and the outer face of the inner leaf.

(18) The width of a window shall be measured over the window opening.

(19) Any regulation which requires the provision of equipment or appliances to a scale of one item of equipment or one appliance to a given number of houses shall be construed in any particular case as requiring the provision of one such item of equipment or appliance for every whole such number in that case, and one for any remainder left over.

Regulation A6

SCHEDULE 2

Classification of Buildings by Occupancy

Occupancy group (1)	Occupancy sub-group (2)	Description of occupancy use (3)	Standard Industrial Classification (4)
A (Residential)	1	Houses of not more than 2 storeys—other than flats—including any surgeries, consulting rooms, offices and other accommodation not exceeding an aggregate of 46 square metres, forming part of the house of any person providing professional or scientific services and used in his professional or scientific capacity	871†, 872†, 873†, 874†, 875†, 876†, 879†
	2	Houses of more than 2 storeys and flats—including any surgeries, consulting rooms, offices and other accommodation not exceeding an aggregate of 46 square metres, forming part of the house of any person providing professional or scientific services and used in his professional or scientific capacity	871†, 872†, 873†, 874†, 875†, 876†, 879†
	3	Residential clubs	887†
		Residential colleges and schools ...	872†
		Residential ecclesiastical buildings ...	875†
		Hotels ... ... Motels ... ... Hostels ... ... Lodging houses ... ... Boarding houses	884, 899(3)†
		Bothies and chaumers	—
		Chalets	—
		Fire stations with sleeping or residential accommodation attached ...	906(2)†
		Police stations with sleeping or residential accommodation attached ...	906(1)†
	4	Children's homes ... ... Old people's homes ... ... Special schools for handicapped children	899(3)†
		Hospitals ... ... Private nursing homes ... ... Sanatoria	874†
B (Commercial)	1	Office premises (including Post Office sorting offices and telephone exchanges)	708†, 709†, 860–866, 871†, 873†, 874†, 875†, 876†, 879†, 881†, 899†, 906(3)†

†*Note:* Throughout this Schedule the presence of a dagger against a numbered head in column (4) denotes that the numbered head is common to more than one occupancy group or sub-group.

SCHEDULE 2—*continued*

Occupancy group (1)	Occupancy sub-group (2)	Description of occupancy use (3)	Standard Industrial Classification (4)
B (Commercial)—*cont.*	2	Shop premises (including sub-post offices attached thereto but excluding shop premises to which other occupancy sub-groups apply)	810–812†, 820, 821, 831†, 895†
		Licensed betting offices	883†
		Beauty parlours...	889
		Hairdressers	889
		Television, radio, recording and film studios...	881†
		Laboratories	874†, 876†, 879†
		Launderettes (self-service)	892†
		Dry cleaning (self-service)	893†
C (Assembly)	1	Bus passenger roadside shelters ...	702(1)†
		Passenger stations	701, 702(1)†
		Public conveniences	906(3)†
		Grandstands	882†
		Stadia	882†
		Sports pavilions...	882†
		Gymnasia	882†
		Indoor bowling alleys	882†
		Indoor games courts	882†
		Riding schools	882†
		Skating rinks	882†
		Swimming baths (including any swimming pool, changing rooms, slipper baths, turkish baths or similar facilities pertaining thereto)	882†
		Funfairs	882†
		Menageries and zoos	882†
		Amusement arcades	883†
	2	Non-residential clubs	887†
		Non-residential colleges and schools ...	872†
		Clinics, surgeries, consulting rooms and related accommodation (other than those covered in occupancy sub-groups A1 and A2)	874†, 876†, 879†
		Ecclesiastical buildings, meeting houses	875†
		Court rooms	906(3)†
		Museums, art galleries	899(4)†
		Libraries to which persons other than employees have access	899(4)†, 906(3)†
		Public houses	886
		Fire stations (other than those covered in occupancy sub-group A3) ...	906(2)†
		Police stations (other than those covered in occupancy sub-group A3) ...	906(1)†
	3	Theatres, cinemas, radio and television studios to which the public are admitted	881†
		Casinos and bingo halls	883†
		Concert halls	881†
		Restaurants, cafes, canteens	885, 887†, 888
		Exhibition halls	899(4)†
		Dance halls, dancing schools	882†

SCHEDULE 2—*continued*

Occupancy group (1)	Occupancy sub-group (2)	Description of occupancy use (3)	Standard Industrial Classification (4)
D (Industrial)	1	Mining and quarrying other than coal and shale mining	102, 103, 109
		Manufacture, process or repair of any of the following—	
		tobacco;	240
		steel tubes;	312
		aluminium and aluminium alloys;...	321
		mechanical handling equipment; ...	337
		mechanical equipment or parts not elsewhere specified;	349
		photographic and document copying equipment;...	351
		watches and clocks;	352
		surgical instruments and appliances;	353
		scientific and industrial instruments and systems;	354
		electrical machinery;...	361
		insulated wires and cables;	362
		telegraph and telephone apparatus and equipment;	363, 708†
		radio and electronic components; ...	364
		broadcast receiving and sound reproducing equipment;	365
		electronic computers;	366
		radio, radar and electronic capital goods;	367
		electric appliances primarily for domestic use;	368
		other electrical goods;	369
		aerospace equipment;	383
		locomotives and railway track equipment;	384
		railway carriages, wagons and trams;	385
		cutlery;	392
		bolts, nuts, screws, rivets etc; ...	393
		wire and wire products;	394
		cans and metal boxes;	395
		metal goods not elsewhere specified;	399
		hosiery and other knitted goods; ...	417
		glass;	463
		cement;...	464
		abrasives and building materials not elsewhere specified;	469
		plaster cast, image and models ...	499(2)

SCHEDULE 2—*continued*

Occupancy group (1)	Occupancy sub-group (2)	Description of occupancy use (3)	Standard Industrial Classification (4)
D (Industrial)—*cont.*	2	Agriculture and horticulture	001
		Coal mining	101
		Exploration (including boring) for and extracting petroleum; mining oil shale	104
		Shipbuilding and marine engineering...	370†
		Paper, printing and publishing ...	481–486, 489
		Laundries and dry cleaners	892†, 893†
		Slaughterhouses and abattoirs ...	810(2)†
		Motor repairers, distributors, garages and filling stations	894
		Manufacture, process or repair of any of the following—	
		food and drink;	211–218, 229, 231, 232, 239
		chemicals and allied industries; ...	261–263, 271–274, 276–279
		metal;	311, 313, 322, 323
		engineering and electrical goods; ...	331–336, 338, 339, 341, 342
		vehicles;	380–382, 494(2), 708†
		tools and implements;	390, 391
		jewellery and precious metals; ...	396
		textiles;	411–415, 418, 419, 423, 429
		fur;	433
		clothing and footwear;	441–445, 449, 450, 895†
		bricks, fire clay and refractory goods;	461
		pottery;	462
		rubber;	491†
		brushes and brooms;	493†
		stationers' goods;	495
		gas, electricity and water	601–603
		Any other industry not separately classified in occupancy sub-groups D1 or D3	

SCHEDULE 2—*continued*

Occupancy group (1)	Occupancy sub-group (2)	Description of occupancy use (3)	Standard Industrial Classification (4)
D (Industrial)—*cont.*	3	Manufacture, process or repair of any of the following—	
		animal and poultry foods;	219
		vegetable and animal oils and fats;	221
		soap and detergents;...	275
		rope, twine and net;...	416
		narrow fabrics;	421
		made-up textiles;	422
		leather (tanning and dressing); ... sheepskin wool (fellmongery); ...	431
		leather goods;	432
		hats, caps and millinery;	446
		timber;	471
		furniture and upholstery;	472
		bedding and similar goods;... ...	473
		shop and office fittings;	474
		wooden containers and baskets; ...	475
		miscellaneous wood and cork goods;	479
		linoleum, plastic floor covering; ... leather cloth and similar material;...	492
		toys, games and sports equipment;	494(1) and (3)
		plastic products not elsewhere specified;...	370†, 491†, 493†, 496
		musical instruments	499(1)
E (Storage)	1	(*a*) Storage of goods and materials not specified as hazardous in occupancy sub-group E2	708†, 810†, 812†, 831†, 832†
		(*b*) Garages used solely for the storage or parking of motor vehicles, multi-storey car parks, transit sheds and transport services other than any used for the storage of vehicles loaded with hazardous materials or for the storage of hazardous materials in transit	702†, 703–707, 708†, 709(1) and (3)
		(*c*) Libraries (other than those covered in occupancy sub-group C2) ...	872†, 899(4)†, 906(3)†
	2	(*a*) Storage of hazardous materials including— (i) any compressed, liquified or dissolved gas; (ii) any substance which becomes dangerous by interaction with either water or air; (iii) any liquid substance with a flash point below 65° Celsius including whisky or other spirituous liquor; (iv) any corrosive substance; (v) any substance that emits poisonous fumes when heated; (vi) any oxidising agent;	709(2), 811†, 831†, 832†

SCHEDULE 2—*continued*

Occupancy group (1)	Occupancy sub-group (2)	Description of occupancy use (3)	Standard Industrial Classification (4)
E (Storage)—*cont.*	2 *cont.*	(vii) any substance liable to spontaneous combustion; (viii) any substance that changes or decomposes readily giving out heat when doing so; (ix) any combustible solid substance with a flash point less than 121° Celsius; (x) any substance likely to spread fire by flowing from one part of a building to another (*b*) Transit sheds and transport services used for the storage of hazardous materials or vehicles loaded with hazardous materials	709(2), 811†, 831†, 832†

SCHEDULE 3

Regulation A9(1)

EXEMPTED CLASSES OF BUILDINGS

Description	Limitations
Class 1. A building erected on agricultural land having an area of more than 0·4 hectare and comprised in an agricultural unit, being a building required for the use of that land for the purposes of agriculture and of which every part falls within one or more of the following descriptions— (*a*) building for housing cattle (other than milking dairy cattle), horses, sheep or dogs; (*b*) barn, shed or other building for storage purposes in which no feeding stuffs for livestock are prepared; (*c*) gate, fence, wall or other means of enclosure not exceeding 2·1 metres in height.	(i) In the case of a building falling under head (*a*) or (*b*)— (A) the cubic capacity does not exceed 1130 cubic metres; (B) no part thereof is nearer to the boundary of the agricultural unit than 13 metres. (ii) In the case of a wall falling under head (*c*), no part of the wall which is over 1·2 metres in height adjoins any road or other place to which the public have access as of right.

SCHEDULE 3—*continued*

Description	Limitations
Class 2. A building erected on land used for the purposes of forestry (including afforestation), being a building required for the use of the land for such purposes and of which every part falls within one or more of the following descriptions— (*a*) building for housing animals; (*b*) shed or other building for storage purposes; (*c*) gate, fence, wall or other means of enclosure not exceeding 2·1 metres in height.	(i) In the case of a building falling under head (*a*) or (*b*)— (A) the cubic capacity does not exceed 1130 cubic metres; (B) no part thereof is nearer to the boundary than 13 metres. (ii) In the case of a wall falling under head (*c*), no part of the wall which is over 1·2 metres in height adjoins any road or other place to which the public have access as of right.
Class 3. A building consisting only of plant or machinery or of a structure or erection of the nature of plant or machinery.	No part of the building is nearer to any point on the boundary than— (A) 13 metres, or (B) the height of the building, whichever is the less, unless at that point the boundary is a boundary with agricultural land on which there is no building nearer to the point than 13 metres.
Class 4. An electricity transformer not exceeding 1000 kVA capacity and switchgear and control pillars associated therewith.	No part of the apparatus is nearer to the boundary of the site than 1 metre.
Class 5. A building used only to house fixed plant or machinery in which there is no human occupation or no human occupation other than intermittent occupation for the purposes of maintenance.	As for Class 3.
Class 6. A building essential for the operation of a railway and comprising or erected within— (*a*) a locomotive depot; (*b*) a carriage depot; (*c*) a goods yard; (*d*) a marshalling yard; (*e*) a signal box: Provided that a building shall not be excluded from this class by reason only that a part thereof of a cubic capacity not exceeding one-tenth of the total cubic capacity of the building does not conform to this description.	There shall not be included in this Class any building of occupancy sub-group D1.

SCHEDULE 3—*continued*

Description	Limitations
Class 7. A bus passenger roadside shelter providing no facilities other than a waiting room.	(i) The building does not exceed 9 square metres in area. (ii) The building is constructed of non-combustible materials, or if constructed of combustible materials, is sited not less than 6 metres from any other building.
Class 8. A building essential for the operation of a dock, harbour or pier and erected within the area of the dock, harbour or pier undertaking.	There shall not be included in this Class any building in respect of the construction of which the approval or consent of the local authority would have been required under a local act in force immediately before the coming into operation of these regulations.
Class 9. A work of civil engineering construction including dock, wharf, harbour, pier, quay, sea defence work, lighthouse, embankment, river work, dam, bridge, tunnel, filter station (including filter bed), inland navigation, water works, viaduct, aqueduct, reservoir, pipe line, sewerage work, sewage treatment works, gas holder, gas main, electric supply line and supports.	
Class 10. A building in respect of which there is constructional control by virtue of the powers under the Explosives Acts 1875 and 1923(**a**).	
Class 11. A garden hut, greenhouse or other building ancillary to a house including one used or intended to be used for the keeping of poultry, bees, birds or other animals for the domestic needs or personal enjoyment of the occupants of the house.	(i) There shall not be included in this Class any garage, carport, sun porch or sun lounge. (ii) The building is erected on land in the same occupation as a building in occupancy sub-group A1 or A2. (iii) The height of the building does not exceed 2·3 metres. (iv) The floor area of the building does not exceed 4·5 square metres or 9 square metres in the case of a greenhouse of which not less than three-quarters of the total external area is of glass (including glazing bars). (v) The building is at a distance of not less than 500 millimetres from the boundary:

(**a**) 1875 c. 17; 1923 c. 17.

SCHEDULE 3—*continued*

Description	Limitations
Class 11.—*cont.*	Provided that in the case of a building an external wall of which is situated on the boundary— (*a*) such external wall shall have no opening in terms of regulation D2(1); and (*b*) the building shall be of non-combustible material (other than the internal framing which may be of timber).
Class 12. A building constructed to be used only in connection with and during the construction, alteration, demolition or repair of any building or other work.	The building is neither used nor intended to be used for human habitation.
Class 13. A moveable dwelling including a tent, caravan, shed or similar structure used for human habitation.	
Class 14. A building erected on a site during a period of not more than 28 days in any period of 12 months.	
Class 15. (*a*) A gate or fence not exceeding 2·1 metres in height; (*b*) a wall or other means of enclosure not exceeding 1·2 metres in height.	In the case of a building falling under head (*a*)—the gate or fence does not adjoin any road or other place to which the public have access as of right.
Class 16. A pipe, cable or other apparatus laid underground.	There shall not be included in this Class— (*a*) a drain provided so as to comply with Part M; (*b*) a conductor or apparatus provided so as to comply with Part N.

Regulation A9(2)

SCHEDULE 4

FIXTURES FOR THE FITTING OF WHICH NO WARRANT REQUIRED

(1) No warrant shall be required for the fitting of any of the following—

(*a*) any fixture or notice of a kind for which no standard is prescribed in these regulations;

(*b*) any outdoor sign whether illuminated or not which is subject to the requirements of the Town and Country Planning (Control of Advertisements) (Scotland) Regulations 1961(a);

(*c*) any fixture of the same pattern or type as an existing fixture which it is replacing:

(a) S.I. 1961/195 (1961 I, p. 308).

Provided that there shall not be included in this head any replacement of—

(i) any internal linings to which the provisions of regulation E15 apply,
(ii) any fire mains to which the provisions of regulation E18 apply,
(iii) any lift to which the provisions of regulation E19 or Q4 apply,
(iv) any solid fuel appliance of the type mentioned in regulation F1(3),
(v) any refuse chute to which the provisions of regulation Q18 apply;

(*d*) any heating appliance of a type mentioned in regulation F1(1) or (2);

(*e*) the fitting to any flue outlet of a terminal so as to comply with regulation F22;

(*f*) any sanitary appliance or any part of a drainage system complying with Part M provided as a replacement and not involving any alteration to the drainage system which would adversely affect the efficiency in operation of the system or any part thereof;

(*g*) any notice provided so as to comply with regulation C4, E2 or K9;

(*h*) any fixture provided so as to comply with Part K:

Provided that there shall not be included in this head any installation of ducting, piping or trunking, forming part of a mechanical ventilation system, permanently fixed to the building;

(*i*) any fixture provided so as to comply with Part N or to which any provision of that Part applies;

(*j*) any fixture provided so as to comply with Part Q:

Provided that there shall not be included in this head any lift or refuse chute.

(2) Notwithstanding anything in this Schedule—

(*a*) a warrant shall be required for the fitting of any fixture, sign or notice mentioned in heads (*a*) to (*i*) of the foregoing paragraph which constitutes a change of use, and

(*b*) any fixture for which no warrant is required shall be fitted in accordance with any relevant requirements of these regulations.

SCHEDULE 5

Regulation D9(1)(*b*)

Structural Fire Precautions

The design and construction of suspended ceilings contributing to the fire resistance of separating floors and compartment floors

For the purpose of regulation D9(1) any suspended ceiling accepted as contributing to the fire resistance of a separating floor or compartment floor shall be designed and constructed as follows—

1. The separating or compartment floor and the ceiling thereto throughout their whole extent shall have a fire resistance not less than that required for the floor by regulation D5.

2. Any grid suspension system intended to support a suspended ceiling shall be designed so as to—

(*a*) provide in the event of fire for the linear expansion of the whole panel grid system in any direction so that the integrity of the ceiling is maintained, and shall take account of the degree of expansion in any specimen of the material which has been tested in accordance with British Standard 476: Part 1: 1953, and

(*b*) ensure that all panels are supported on two or more edges.

3. All supporting members, grid suspension systems or other fixings shall be of non-combustible material.

4. All surfaces exposed within the cavity formed by the floor and suspended ceiling, including any insulating material applied thereto, shall be of a grade not lower than Grade B as specified in regulation E15(2) as read with paragraphs (3) and (4) of that regulation.

5. Any cavity formed by a suspended ceiling shall be fire-stopped, and the areas enclosed by such fire-stopping shall extend to not more than 46 square metres:

Provided that nothing in this paragraph shall require the provision of fire-stopping within any such cavity—

(i) if the cavity is not more than 50 millimetres in depth measured from the underside of the floor to the upper surface of the panels forming the ceiling; or

(ii) if all surfaces exposed within the cavity are Grade A as specified in regulation E15(2).

6. The external surface of panels forming a suspended ceiling shall be imperforate throughout.

7. Nothing in the provisions of the last foregoing paragraph shall prevent the forming of openings in the external surface of panels forming a suspended ceiling—

(*a*) extending to more than 65 000 square millimetres in area, for—

(i) ducts used for ventilation, constructed of sheet steel and forming a fire-tight joint at the ceiling level,

(ii) purposes of maintenance of any services within the cavity formed by the suspended ceiling, the integrity of the fire resistance being maintained within the cavity formed by the ceiling, and

(iii) recessed light fittings, the integrity of the fire resistance being maintained within the cavity formed by the ceiling;

(*b*) extending to not more than 65 000 square millimetres in area in every 9 square metres of the ceiling, for pipes, ducts or electrical outlets.

Regulation D17(6)(*a*)

SCHEDULE 6

STRUCTURAL FIRE PRECAUTIONS

DISTANCE OF SIDE OF BUILDING FROM BOUNDARY CALCULATED BY REFERENCE TO ENCLOSING RECTANGLE OF OPENINGS

1. For the purposes of regulation D17(6) the minimum distance between any part of the enclosing rectangle of any opening or any group of openings in the side of a building, or of a division or compartment of a building, and any point on the boundary shall, where all of the side is in the plane of reference of that side, be the distance specified in Table 8:

Provided that, if in any side of a building, compartment or division two adjacent enclosing rectangles are separated by a space which contains no opening and extends horizontally to more than four times the distance specified in Table 8 in relation to the overall enclosing rectangle of that side, no account shall be taken of the overall enclosing rectangle of that side for the purposes of this paragraph.

2. Where any part of the side of a building, division or compartment is recessed or set back but—

(*a*) is less than 1·5 metres behind the plane of reference, or

(*b*) if more than 1·5 metres behind the plane of reference, has no openings therein,

the foregoing paragraph shall apply as if that part were in the plane of reference.

3. Where any part of the side of a building, division or compartment consists of a recess which—

(*a*) extends to more than 1·5 metres behind the plane of reference of the side, and

(*b*) has openings in either of the side walls of the recess (whether or not there is any opening in the back wall), paragraph 1 of this Schedule shall apply as if that part were in the plane of reference but contained an opening—

(i) of an area equal to the aggregate of the areas of all the openings in the recess, but in any case not greater than the area of that part of the aperture of the recess that is included in the overall enclosing rectangle of that side;

(ii) the enclosing rectangle of which is co-incident with the said part of the aperture of the recess.

4. Where any part of the side of a building, division or compartment consists of a recess which extends to more than 1·5 metres behind the plane of reference of that side and has an opening or openings only in the back wall, paragraph 1 of this Schedule shall have effect as if such opening or openings were in the plane of reference:

Provided that where the distance specified in Table 8 in respect of the enclosing rectangle of such opening or openings is less than the distance set forth in—

(i) Part I of Table 9, there may for the purposes of the said paragraph 1 be substituted the distance specified in Table 8 as if the percentage of openings in the enclosing rectangle were reduced by 10;

(ii) Part II of Table 9, there may for the purposes of the said paragraph 1 be substituted the distance specified in Table 8 as if the percentage of openings in the enclosing rectangle were reduced by 20.

5. Where any part of the side of a building or division is set back from the plane of reference of that side by more than 1·5 metres and the set back is uniform throughout the height of the building or division, the provisions of paragraph 1 of this Schedule shall apply—

(*a*) in relation to that part of the side within the plane of reference of the side as if the side terminated at the commencement of the set back, and

(*b*) in relation to the set back as if the building had a side with a plane of reference extending along the diagonal of the sides of the set back and containing an opening—

(i) the enclosing rectangle of which is that rectangle in the plane of reference enclosing the projections of the extreme edges of the outermost openings in the set back, the upper edge of the topmost opening and the lower edge of the lowest opening, all the projections being normal to the plane of reference, and

(ii) equal in area to the aggregate of the areas of actual openings in the set back, but in any case not greater than the area of the enclosing rectangle referred to in the last foregoing sub-paragraph.

6. For the purposes of this Schedule—

(*a*) no account shall be taken of any of the openings mentioned in regulation D17(4) whether in a plane of reference, recess or set back;

(*b*) the provisions of regulation D17(7) shall have effect for the purposes of this Schedule as they have effect for the purposes of that regulation;

(*c*) where any part of an external wall is by virtue of the provisions of regulation D2 treated as an opening by reason only of having attached to its external face combustible material of a thickness more than 1 millimetre, whether for cladding or for any other purpose, that part of the wall shall be treated as an opening but only to the extent of one-half of its area:

Provided that nothing in this sub-paragraph shall affect the dimensions of the enclosing rectangle or the overall enclosing rectangle of that external wall.

Regulations L4(2) and L8(4) SCHEDULE 7

Daylighting Standards and Permissible Height Indicators

Part I

Standard of daylighting using permissible height indicators—
all buildings containing houses

1. A room shall comply with this Part of this Schedule if there is provided a window or windows—

(*a*) of not less width, or in the aggregate of not less width, than that specified in Table 15, increased by the percentage specified in Table 16, and

(*b*) at a distance from—

(i) any existing obstruction, and

(ii) the obstruction assumed to exist in accordance with paragraph 3 of this Schedule

not less than the minimum distance determined in the manner described in the next following paragraph by test with four permissible height indicators which have been constructed in accordance with the measurements given in head (*a*) of paragraph 11 of this Schedule.

2. The minimum distance referred to in sub-paragraph (*b*) of the last foregoing paragraph is the least distance given by any one of the four permissible height indicators when—

(*a*) the indicator is laid on the plan with the point P over the centre of the window opening which is being tested, and

(*b*) the indicator is rotated in either direction about the point P, so, however, that neither of the lines PA or PD crosses the line of the external face of the wall containing the window opening, and

(*c*) with the indicator rotated to any position between the limits defined in the last foregoing sub-paragraph no part of the obstruction which lies on the plan between the lines PB and PC is of greater height above the floor level of the room lighted by the window than the height given by any arc (or interpolated arc) which lies over that part of the obstruction.

3. There shall for the purposes of this Part of this Schedule be assumed to be an obstruction—

(*a*) on the other side of the boundary parallel to the line of the boundary and of infinite length, and

(*b*) of such height that at ground level at any point on the line of the boundary it subtends an angle of 43 degrees to the horizontal, and

(*c*) at a distance beyond the boundary equal to the difference between—

(i) the least distance of the boundary from the wall of the building as determined under Part III of this Schedule by test with permissible height indicators constructed in accordance with the measurements given in head (*b*) of paragraph 11 of this Schedule, and

(ii) the least distance of the boundary from the wall of the building which would have been determined under Part III of this Schedule had the permissible height indicators been constructed in accordance with the measurements given in head (*a*) of paragraph 11 of this Schedule.

4. For the purposes of this Part of this Schedule no account shall be taken of any window if—

(*a*) the angle above the horizontal subtended at the reference point appropriate to the use and floor area of the room by the lower edge of any balcony or projection above the window is less than—

(i) in the case of a kitchen, 30 degrees,

(ii) in the case of a living room, 25 degrees,

(iii) in the case of any other apartment, 25 degrees;

(*b*) the horizontal angle subtended at such reference point by the forward edges of any walls or screens flanking the window opening and forward of the plane of opening is less than—

(i) in the case of a kitchen, 50 degrees,

(ii) in the case of a living room, 45 degrees,

(iii) in the case of any other apartment, 30 degrees, or

(*c*) the height above the level of the floor of the room of any balustrade or screens in front of the window exceeds the sum of—

(i) 850 millimetres, and

(ii) one-third of the distance of such balustrade or screen from the wall containing the window.

PART II

Standard of daylighting without using permissible height indicators—buildings under 12·5 metres containing houses

5. Where a room forms part of a building not exceeding 12·5 metres in height, that room shall comply with this Part of this Schedule if there is provided therein a window or windows—

(*a*) of not less width, or in the aggregate of not less width, than that specified in Table 15, increased by the percentage specified in Table 16, and

(*b*) at a distance from—

(i) any existing obstruction, and

(ii) the obstruction assumed to exist in accordance with paragraph 6 of this Schedule

not less than a distance equal to twice that part of the height of the building above the floor of the room, plus 300 millimetres.

6. There shall for the purposes of this Part of this Schedule be assumed to be an obstruction—

(*a*) on the other side of the boundary parallel to the boundary and of infinite length, and

(*b*) of a height above the ground level at the boundary equal to the height of the building, and

(*c*) at a distance beyond the boundary equal to the height of the building.

7. Paragraph 4 of this Schedule shall have effect for the purposes of this Part of this Schedule as it has effect for the purposes of Part I of this Schedule.

PART III

Relationship of building to boundary using permissible height indicators—all buildings containing houses

8. A building shall comply with this Part of this Schedule if the distance of the building from any point on the boundary is not less than the minimum distance determined as set forth in the next following paragraph by test with four permissible height indicators which have been constructed in accordance with the measurements given in head (*b*) of paragraph 11 of this Schedule.

9. The minimum distance of the building from the boundary is the least distance given by any one of the four permissible height indicators when—

(*a*) the indicator is laid on the plan with the point P over any point on the line of the boundary, and

(*b*) the indicator is rotated in either direction about the point P provided that neither of the lines PA or PD crosses the line of the boundary, and (*c*) with the indicator rotated to any position between the limits defined in the last foregoing sub-paragraph, no part of the building which lies on the plan between the lines PB and PC is of greater height above the point of the boundary at P than the height given by any arc (or interpolated arc) which lies over that part of the building.

PART IV

Relationship of building to boundary without using permissible height indicators—buildings under 12·5 metres containing houses

10. Where the height of a building does not exceed 12·5 metres that building shall comply with this Part of this Schedule if the distance of the building from any point on the boundary is not less than a distance equal to the height of the building above the level of the ground at that point on the boundary.

PART V

Permissible height indicators

11. In this Schedule "permissible height indicator", in relation to a window or a building, means one of a series of four figures drawn to the scale of a plan of the building and its boundary as shown in the following diagram—

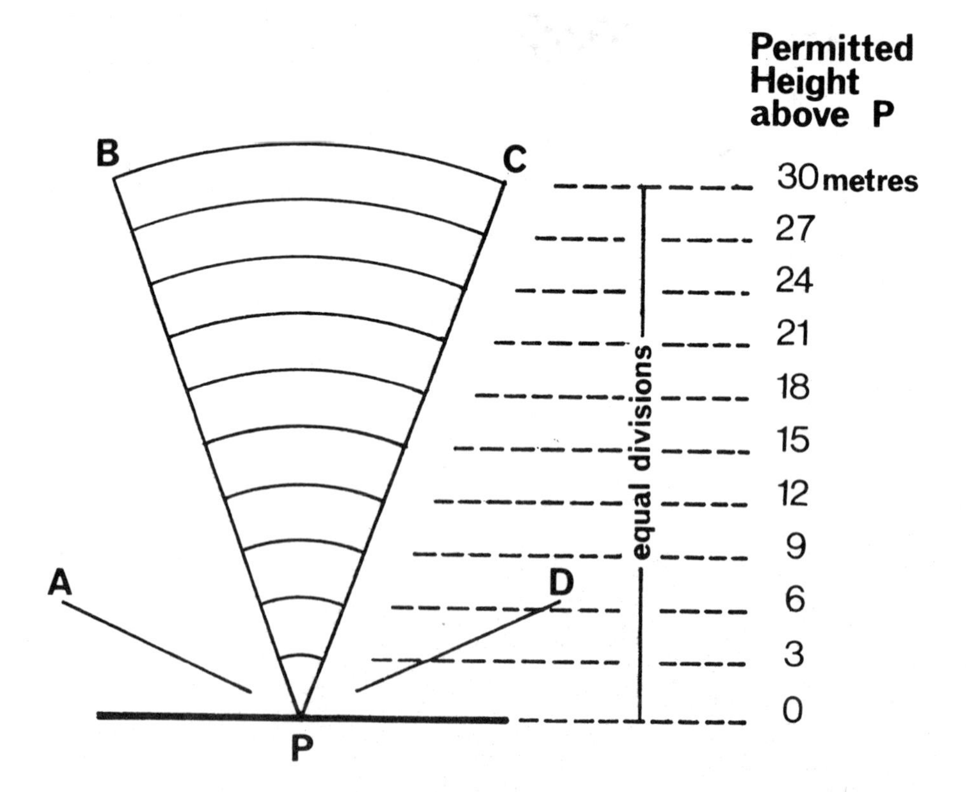

Diagram of a permissible height indicator

in which the angles APB, BPC and CPD and the dimensions of PB and PC are as follows—

(a)—if testing windows in relation to obstructions

	Indicator number—			
	1	2	3	4
Angles: APB, CPD	45°	45°	45°	45°
BPC	45°	35°	25°	20°
Distance PB & PC	64 metres	82 metres	112 metres	170 metres

(b)—if testing siting of buildings in relation to boundaries

	Indicator number—			
	1	2	3	4
Angles: APB, CPD	25°	25°	25°	25°
BPC	65°	45°	30°	20°
Distance PB & PC	32 metres	41 metres	56 metres	86 metres

SCHEDULE 8 Regulations M4(6) and M14(1)

Drainage Tests

Part I

Tests for drains of an internal diameter of 600 millimetres or less which are to carry no foul water

Test 1

The drain or section thereof to be tested shall be suitably plugged and filled with water at a pressure equivalent to a head of 600 millimetres of water at the highest part of the drain or section under test. The test shall be so arranged that a pressure of 234 millibars (equivalent to a head of 2·4 metres of water) is not exceeded at any point in the drain or section under test. After sufficient time has elapsed to permit the absorption of water by the pipes, joints and fittings the pressure shall be restored to that equivalent to a head of 600 millimetres of water.

This test shall be satisfied if the drain thereafter maintains that pressure for a period of at least 10 minutes.

Test 2

The drain or section thereof to be tested shall be suitably plugged and filled with air (with or without smoke) at a pressure equivalent to a head of 50 millimetres of water.

This test shall be satisfied if the drain for 5 minutes thereafter maintains a pressure equivalent to a head of at least 38 millimetres of water.

Part II

Tests for drains to carry foul water

Test 3

The drain or section thereof to be tested shall be suitably plugged and filled with water at a pressure equivalent to a head of 1·5 metres of water at the highest part of the drain or section under test. The test shall be so arranged that a pressure of 234 millibars (equivalent to a head of 2·4 metres of water) is not exceeded at any point in the drain or section under test. After sufficient time has elapsed to permit the absorption of water by the pipes and joints, the pressure shall be restored to that equivalent to a head of 1·5 metres of water.

This test shall be satisfied if the drain thereafter maintains that pressure for a period of at least 10 minutes.

Test 4

The drain or section thereof to be tested shall be suitably plugged and filled with air (with or without smoke) at a pressure equivalent to a head of 50 millimetres of water.

This test shall be satisfied if the drain for 5 minutes thereafter maintains a pressure equivalent to a head of at least 38 millimetres of water.

Part III

Test for soil pipes, soil-waste pipes, waste pipes and ventilating pipes

Test 5

The soil pipes, soil-waste pipes, waste pipes and ventilating pipes or any section thereof to be tested shall be suitably plugged and filled with air (with or without smoke) at a pressure equivalent to a head of 50 millimetres of water.

This test shall be satisfied if this pressure remains constant for a period of 5 minutes thereafter.

SCHEDULE 9

Tables

Regulation A7 — Table 1—Occupant capacity of flats

Size of flat (1)	Number of apartments (other than living room) less than 10 square metres (2)	Occupant capacity (3)
One apartment	—	1
Two apartments	Nil	2
	One	1
Three apartments	Nil	4
	One	3
	Two	2
Four apartments	Nil	6
	One	5
	Two	4
	Three	3
Five apartments	Nil	8
	One	7
	Two	6
	Three	5
	Four	4
Six or more apartments ...	—	For each apartment (other than the living room)— (i) if less than 10 square metres, one; (ii) if not less than 10 square metres, two.

SCHEDULE 9—*continued*

TABLE 2—OCCUPANT LOAD FACTORS

Regulation A7

Description of room or storey (1)	Occupant load factor‡ (2)
Assembly halls (moveable or no seating)	0·5
Bars (including public and lounge bars)	0·5
Bedrooms (in buildings other than those classified A1 or A2)	4·6
Bowling alleys and billiard rooms	9·3
Canteens	1·1
Clubs	0·5
Common rooms	1·1
Concourses	0·7
Conference rooms and committee rooms	1·1
Crush halls and queuing lobbies	0·7
Dance halls	0·7
Dining rooms	1·1
Dormitories	4·6
Enquiry rooms	3·7
Factory shop floors—workrooms and storage	4·6
Grandstands (without fixed seating)	0·5
Kitchens	9·3
Libraries, museums, art galleries	4·6
Lounges	1·9
Messrooms	1·1
Offices (*a*) for storeys not divided into rooms...	5·1
(*b*) for individual rooms...	3·7
Reading rooms	1·9
Restaurants, cafes	1·1
Shops trading in the common type of consumer goods (including Standard Industrial Classifications 820/1, 820/2, 821/1, 821/2, 821/3 and 821/5 and including shops trading in chemists' wares, fancy goods, toys, games and sports goods)†	
(*a*) basement storeys...	1·4*
(*b*) ground and upper storeys	1·9*
Shops specialising in more expensive or exclusive trades (including Standard Industrial Classification 821/4 and including shops trading in furniture and carpets)†	7·0*
Shops for personal services including hairdressing	1·9
Stadia (without fixed seating)	0·5
Staff rooms	1·1
Studios (radio, film, television, recording)	1·4
Warehouses	27·9
Writing rooms	1·9

*The factors are to be applied to the gross sales floor area.

†These references to numbered heads of classification of industry are references to the heads set forth in the third edition of the Standard Industrial Classification issued by the Central Statistical Office in September 1968.

‡Where any room or storey is used or is likely to be used for a variety of purposes the more or, as the case may be, the most onerous occupant load factor shall be applied.

SCHEDULE 9—*continued*

TABLE 3—NOTIONAL PERIODS OF FIRE RESISTANCE

Regulation D2

In this Table—

(*a*) "Class 1 aggregate" means foamed slag, pumice, blast furnace slag, pelleted fly ash, crushed brick and burnt clay products including expanded clay, well-burnt clinker and crushed limestone;
"Class 2 aggregate" means flint-gravel, granite and all crushed natural stones other than limestones;

(*b*) any reference to plaster means—
(i) in the case of an external wall 1 metre or more from the boundary, plaster applied on the internal face only;
(ii) in the case of any other wall, plaster applied to both faces;
(iii) if to plaster of a given thickness on the external face of a wall, except in the case of a reference to vermiculite-gypsum or perlite-gypsum plaster, a reference to rendering on the external face of the same thickness;
(iv) if to vermiculite-gypsum plaster, shall be construed as a reference to vermiculite-gypsum plaster of a mix within the range of 1½ to 2:1 by volume;

(*c*) any reference to sprayed asbestos means sprayed asbestos conforming to BS 3590: 1970;

(*d*) the imposed load is assumed to be shared by both leaves for periods of fire resistance in excess of 2 hours.

Part I: Walls

A. *Masonry construction*

Materials and construction	Minimum thickness in millimetres (excluding plaster) for a period of fire resistance of											
	Loadbearing						Non-loadbearing					
	4 hours	3 hours	2 hours	1½ hours	1 hour	½ hour	4 hours	3 hours	2 hours	1½ hours	1 hour	½ hour
1. Reinforced concrete, minimum concrete cover to main reinforcement of 25 millimetres—												
(*a*) unplastered	180	150	100	100	75	75						
(*b*) 12·5 millimetres cement-sand plaster	180	150	100	100	75	75						
(*c*) 12·5 millimetres gypsum-sand plaster	180	150	100	100	75	75						
(*d*) 12·5 millimetres vermiculite-gypsum plaster	125	100	75	75	63	63						

2. No-fines concrete of Class 2 aggregate—												
(*a*) 12·5 millimetres concrete-sand plaster ..							150					
(*b*) 12·5 millimetres gypsum-sand plaster.. ..							150					
(*c*) 12·5 millimetres vermiculite-gypsum plaster ..							150					
3. Brickwork of clay, concrete or sand-lime bricks unreinforced—												
(*a*) unplastered	200	200	100	100	100	100	170	170	100	100	75	75
(*b*) 12·5 millimetres cement-sand plaster	200	200	100	100	100	100	170	170	100	100	75	75
(*c*) 12·5 millimetres gypsum-sand plaster.. ..	200	200	100	100	100	100	170	170	100	100	75	75
(*d*) 12·5 millimetres vermiculite-gypsum or perlite-gypsum plaster	100	100	100	100	100	100	100	100	100	100	75	75
4. Blockwork of solid concrete blocks of Class 1 aggregate—												
(*a*) unplastered	150	150	100	100	100	100	150	130	75	75	75	50
(*b*) 12·5 millimetres cement-sand plaster	150	150	100	100	100	100	100	100	75	75	75	50
(*c*) 12·5 millimetres gypsum-sand plaster.. ..	150	150	100	100	100	100	100	100	75	75	75	50
(*d*) 12·5 millimetres vermiculite-gypsum plaster ..	100	100	100	100	100	100	75	75	75	62	50	50
5. Blockwork of solid concrete blocks of Class 2 aggregate—												
(*a*) unplastered			100	100	100	100	150	150	100	100	75	50
(*b*) 12·5 millimetres cement-sand plaster			100	100	100	100	150	100	100	100	75	50
(*c*) 12·5 millimetres gypsum-sand plaster.. ..			100	100	100	100	150	100	100	100	75	50
(*d*) 12·5 millimetres vermiculite-gypsum plaster ..	100	100	100	100	100	100	100	100	75	75	75	50
6. Blockwork of solid autoclaved aerated concrete blocks unplastered, density 475-1200 kilogrammes per cubic metre	180	150	100	100	100	100	100	75	62	62	50	50
7. Blockwork of hollow concrete blocks of Class 1 aggregate—												
(*a*) unplastered			100	100	100	100	150	150	100	100	100	75
(*b*) 12·5 millimetres cement-sand plaster			100	100	100	100	150	150	100	75	75	75
(*c*) 12·5 millimetres gypsum-sand plaster.. ..			100	100	100	100	150	150	100	75	75	75
(*d*) 12·5 millimetres vermiculite-gypsum plaster ..			100	100	100	100	100	100	75	75	62	62

SCHEDULE 9—*continued*

TABLE 3—*continued*

Part I: Walls—continued

Materials and construction	Minimum thickness in millimetres (excluding plaster) for period of fire resistance of											
	Loadbearing						Non-loadbearing					
	4 hours	3 hours	2 hours	1½ hours	1 hour	½ hour	4 hours	3 hours	2 hours	1½ hours	1 hour	½ hour
8. Blockwork of hollow concrete blocks of Class 2 aggregate—												
(*a*) unplastered							150	150	150	125	125	125
(*b*) 12·5 millimetres cement-sand plaster							150	150	150	125	125	100
(*c*) 12·5 millimetres gypsum-sand plaster							150	150	150	125	125	100
(*d*) 12·5 millimetres vermiculite-gypsum plaster ..							125	125	100	100	100	75
9. Blockwork of cellular clay blocks—												
(*a*) one cell not less than 50 per cent solid 12·5 millimetres cement-sand or gypsum-sand plaster											100	75
(*b*) one cell not less than 30 per cent solid 12·5 millimetres cement-sand or gypsum-sand plaster											150	150
(*c*) two cells not less than 70 per cent solid 12·5 millimetres cement-sand or gypsum-sand plaster			100	100	100	100			100	100	100	75
(*d*) two cells not less than 45 per cent solid 12·5 millimetres cement-sand or gypsum-sand plaster									230	230	150	150
(*e*) three cells not less than 70 per cent solid 12·5 millimetres cement-sand or gypsum-sand plaster	150	150	150	150	150	150	150	150	150	150	150	150

10. Cavity wall with outer leaf of brickwork or blockwork of clay, composition, concrete, or sand-lime bricks or blocks minimum 100 millimetres thick and—												
(*a*) inner leaf of solid brickwork or blockwork of clay, composition, concrete or sand-lime bricks or blocks other than those specified below	100	100	100	100	100	100	75	75	75	75	75	75
(*b*) inner leaf of solid concrete blockwork of blocks of Class 1 aggregate	100	100	100	100	100	100	75	75	75	75	75	50
(*c*) inner leaf of hollow concrete blockwork of blocks of Class 1 aggregate	100	100	100	100	100	100	100	75	75	75	75	62
(*d*) inner leaf of solid concrete blockwork of blocks of Class 2 aggregate			100	100	100	100	75	75	75	75	75	50
(*e*) inner leaf of blockwork of aerated concrete blocks, including autoclaved aerated concrete blocks density 475-1200 kilogrammes per cubic metre	150	150	100	100	100	100	75	75	62	62	50	50

SCHEDULE 9—*continued*

TABLE 3—*continued*

Part I: Walls—continued

B. *Framed and composite construction*

Materials of construction	Period of fire resistance in hours
1. Steel frame with external cladding of 16 millimetres rendering on metal lathing and internal lining of autoclaved aerated concrete blocks, density 480–1120 kilogrammes per cubic metre of thickness of—	
50 millimetres	2
62 millimetres	3
75 millimetres	4
2. Steel frame with external cladding of 100 millimetres concrete blocks and internal lining of 16 millimetres gypsum plaster on metal lathing ...	4
3. Steel frame with external cladding of bricks of clay, concrete or sand-lime 100 millimetres thick and internal lining of asbestos insulation board of thickness of—	
9 millimetres	3
4. Steel frame with external cladding of 16 millimetres rendering on metal lathing and internal lining of—	
9 millimetres asbestos insulation board	½
16 millimetres gypsum plaster on metal lathing...	1
5. Steel or timber frame with facings on each side of—	
(*a*) metal lathing with cement-sand or gypsum plaster of thickness of:	
19 millimetres	1
12·5 millimetres	½
(*b*) metal lathing with vermiculite-gypsum or perlite-gypsum plaster of thickness of:	
25 millimetres	2
19 millimetres	1½
12·5 millimetres	1
(*c*) 9·5 millimetres plasterboard with gypsum plaster of thickness of:	
5 millimetres	½
(*d*) 9·5 millimetres plasterboard with vermiculite-gypsum plaster of thickness of:	
25 millimetres	2
16 millimetres	1½
10 millimetres	1
5 millimetres	½
(*e*) 12·5 millimetres plasterboard with gypsum plaster of thickness of:	
12·5 millimetres	1
nil	½
(*f*) 12·5 millimetres plasterboard with vermiculite-gypsum plaster of thickness of:	
25 millimetres	2
16 millimetres	1½
10 millimetres	1
(*g*) 19 millimetres plasterboard (or two layers of 9·5 millimetres) fixed to break joint without finish	1

SCHEDULE 9—*continued*

TABLE 3—*continued*

Part I: Walls—continued

	Materials of construction	Period of fire resistance in hours
	(*h*) 19 millimetres plasterboard (or two layers of 9·5 millimetres) with vermiculite-gypsum plaster of thickness of:	
	16 millimetres	2
	10 millimetres	1½
	(*i*) 12·5 millimetres fibre insulation board with gypsum plaster of thickness of:	
	12·5 millimetres	½
	(*j*) (i) 9 millimetres asbestos insulation board fixed to 9 millimetres asbestos insulation board fillets planted on face of studs ...	½
	(ii) 12 millimetres asbestos insulation board...	½
	(*k*) 25 millimetres wood wool slabs with gypsum plaster of thickness of: 12·5 millimetres	1
6.	Compressed straw slabs in timber frames finished on both faces with gypsum plaster of thickness of—	
	5 millimetres	1
7.	Plasterboard 9·5 millimetres thick on each side of cellular core—	
	(*a*) unplastered	½
	(*b*) 12·5 millimetres gypsum plaster	½
	(*c*) 22 millimetres vermiculite-gypsum plaster	2
8.	Plasterboard 12·5 millimetres thick on each side of cellular core—	
	(*a*) unplastered	½
	(*b*) 12·5 millimetres gypsum plaster	1
	(*c*) 16 millimetres vermiculite-gypsum plaster	2
9.	Plasterboard 19 millimetres finished on both faces with 16 millimetres gypsum plaster...	1
10.	Plasterboard 12·5 millimetres bonded with neat gypsum plaster to each side of 19 millimetres plasterboard	1½
11.	Three layers of 19 millimetres plasterboard bonded with gypsum plaster	2
12.	Wood wool slab with 12·5 millimetres render or plaster of thickness of—	
	75 millimetres	2
	50 millimetres	1
13.	Compressed straw slabs with 75 millimetres by 12·5 millimetres wood cover strips to joints, of thickness of—	
	50 millimetres	½
C.	*External walls not on the boundary*	
1.	Steel frame with external cladding of non-combustible sheets with internal lining of—	
	(*a*) asbestos insulation board of thickness of 9 millimetres	4
	(*b*) metal lathing with cement-sand or gypsum plaster of thickness of 12·5 millimetres	4
	(*c*) sprayed asbestos of thickness of 12·5 millimetres	4
	(*d*) two layers of 9·5 millimetres plasterboard	½
	(*e*) 9·5 millimetres plasterboard finished with gypsum plaster of thickness of 12·5 millimetres	½

SCHEDULE 9—*continued*

TABLE 3—*continued*

Part 1: Walls—continued

	Materials of construction	Period of fire resistance in hours
	(*f*) 12·5 millimetres plasterboard finished with 5 millimetres gypsum plaster	½
	(*g*) 50 millimetres compressed straw slabs	½
	(*h*) 50 millimetres compressed straw slabs finished with 5 millimetres gypsum plaster	1
†2.	Timber frame with external cladding of 10 millimetres cement-sand or cement-lime rendering and internal cladding of—	
	(*a*) 9 millimetres asbestos insulation board	1
	(*b*) 16 millimetres gypsum plaster on metal lathing	1
	(*c*) 9·5 millimetres plasterboard finished with 12·5 millimetres gypsum plaster	1
	(*d*) 12·5 millimetres plasterboard finished with 5 millimetres gypsum plaster	1
	(*e*) 50 millimetres compressed straw slabs	1
	(*f*) aerated concrete blocks:	
	50 millimetres	3
	62 millimetres	4
	75 millimetres	4
	100 millimetres	4
3.	Timber frame with external cladding of 100 millimetres clay, concrete or sand-lime bricks or blocks, finished internally with—	
	(*a*) asbestos insulation board	4
	(*b*) 16 millimetres gypsum plaster on metal lathing	4
†4.	Timber frame with external cladding of weather boarding or 9·5 millimetres exterior grade plywood and internal lining of—	
	(*a*) 9 millimetres asbestos insulation board	½
	(*b*) 16 millimetres gypsum plaster on metal lathing	½
	(*c*) 9·5 millimetres plasterboard finished with 12·5 millimetres gypsum plaster	½
	(*d*) 12·5 millimetres plasterboard finished with 5 millimetres gypsum plaster	½
	(*e*) 50 millimetres compressed straw slabs	½
	(*f*) 75 millimetres wood wool slabs faced each side with asbestos cement	2
	(*g*) aerated concrete blocks:	
	50 millimetres	3
	62 millimetres	4
	75 millimetres	4
	100 millimetres	4

†The presence of a combustible vapour barrier within the thickness of these constructions will not affect these periods of fire resistance.

SCHEDULE 9—*continued*

TABLE 3—*continued*

Part II: Reinforced concrete columns

Construction and materials	Minimum dimension§ of concrete column without finish (in millimetres) for a fire resistance in accordance with Table 5 for a period of—					
	4 hours	3 hours	2 hours	1½ hours	1 hour	½ hour
1.—(*a*) without plaster	450	400	300	250	200	150
(*b*) finished with 12·5 millimetres encasement of vermiculite-gypsum plaster	275	225	200	150	120	120
(*c*) with 12·5 millimetres cement-sand or gypsum-sand plaster on mesh reinforcement fixed round column	300	275	225	150	150	150
(*d*) with hard drawn steel wire fabric 2·5 millimetres of maximum 150 millimetres pitch in each direction placed in concrete cover to main reinforcement	300	275	225	200	150	150
(*e*) with limestone or lightweight aggregate as coarse aggregate	300	275	225	200	200	150
2. Built into† a separating wall, fire division wall, external wall on the boundary or other external walls‡—						
(*a*) without plaster	180	150	100	100	75	75
(*b*) finished with 12·5 millimetres vermiculite-gypsum plaster	125	100	75	75	63	63

†No part of column projecting beyond either face of wall.
‡Extending to its full height and not less than 600 millimetres on each side of column.
§The minimum dimension of a circular column is the diameter.

Part III: Reinforced concrete beams

Construction and materials	Minimum concrete cover (in millimetres) (without finish) to main reinforcement for a fire resistance in accordance with Table 5 for a period of—					
	4 hours	3 hours	2 hours	1½ hours	1 hour	½ hour
(*a*) without plaster	63	55	45	35	25	12·5
(*b*) finished with 12·5 millimetres vermiculite-gypsum plaster	25	12·5	12·5	12·5	12·5	12·5
(*c*) with 12·5 millimetres cement-sand or gypsum-sand plaster, on mesh reinforcement fixed round beam	50	40	30	20	12·5	12·5

SCHEDULE 9—*continued*

TABLE 3—*continued*

Part IV: Prestressed concrete beams

Additional protection	Minimum average thickness† of concrete cover (in millimetres) for a fire resistance in accordance with Table 5 for a period of –					
	4 hours	3 hours	2 hours	1½ hours	1 hour	½ hour
1. No additional protection	100‡	83‡	63‡	50‡	38	25
2. Vermiculite concrete slabs, as permanent shuttering, 12·5 millimetres thick	75‡	63	45	32	25	12·5
3. Vermiculite concrete slabs, as permanent shuttering, 25 millimetres thick	63	50	38	25	12·5	12·5
4. Gypsum plaster on mesh reinforcement fixed around beams, 12·5 millimetres thick ...	90‡	70	50	38	25	12·5
5. Vermiculite-gypsum plaster 12·5 millimetres thick or sprayed asbestos 12·5 millimetres thick	75‡	63	45	32	25	12·5
6. Vermiculite-gypsum plaster 25 millimetres thick or sprayed asbestos 25 millimetres thick ...	50	45	32	20	12·5	12·5

†This part of the Table gives minimum average thicknesses which shall be assessed as the arithmetic mean distance of each element of prestressing steel in the member from the nearest outside concrete face which may be exposed to fire.

‡Mesh reinforcement or continuous arrangement of stirrups must be incorporated in the beams to retain the concrete in position around the prestressing steel. This reinforcement should have a concrete cover of minimum average thickness of 25 millimetres.

Part V: Prestressed concrete slabs

Additional protection	Minimum average thickness† of concrete cover (in millimetres) for a fire resistance in accordance with Table 5 for a period of—					
	4 hours	3 hours	2 hours	1½ hours	1 hour	½ hour
1. No additional protection	63‡	50‡	38	32	25	12·5
2. Gypsum plaster on metal lath as a jointless suspended ceiling with non-combustible fixing, 12·5 millimetres thick	38	25	12·5	12·5	12·5	12·5
3. Vermiculite-gypsum plaster or sprayed asbestos applied direct to soffit, 12·5 millimetres thick...	38	25	12·5	12·5	12·5	12·5

†This part of the Table gives minimum average thicknesses which shall be assessed as the arithmetic mean distance of each element of prestressing steel in the member from the nearest outside concrete face which may be exposed to fire.

‡Mesh reinforcement must be incorporated in the slab in the soffit to retain the concrete in position around the prestressing steel. This reinforcement should have a concrete cover of minimum average thickness of 25 millimetres.

SCHEDULE 9—*continued*

TABLE 3—*continued*

Part VI: Structural steel

(1) *Encased steel stanchions* (*Weight of steel not less than 45 kilogrammes per metre*)

Construction and materials	Minimum thickness (in millimetres) of protection for a fire resistance in accordance with Table 5 for a period of—					
	4 hours	3 hours	2 hours	1½ hours	1 hour	½ hour
A. *Solid protection*† (*unplastered*)						
1. Reinforced concrete not leaner than 1:2:4 mix with natural aggregates—						
(*a*) concrete not assumed to be loadbearing...	50	38	25	25	25	25
(*b*) concrete assumed to be loadbearing in accordance with BS 449: Part 2: 1969 as read with Amendments AMD 416, January 1970, AMD 523, May 1970 and AMD 661, December 1970	75	50	50	50	50	50
2. Solid bricks of clay composition or sand-lime	75	50	50	50	50	50
3. Solid blocks of foamed slag or pumice concrete reinforced‡ in every horizontal joint... ...	62	62	50	50	50	50
4. Sprayed asbestos—140 to 240 kilogrammes per cubic metre	44	32	19	15	10	10
5. Sprayed vermiculite-cement			38	32	19	12·5
B. *Hollow protection*§						
1. Solid bricks of clay composition or sand-lime reinforced in every horizontal joint, unplastered	100	75	50	50	50	50
2. Solid blocks of foamed slag or pumice concrete reinforced‡ in every horizontal joint, unplastered	75	62	50	50	50	50
3. Metal lath with gypsum or cement-lime plaster of thickness of			38‖	25	19	12·5
4. (*a*) Metal lath with vermiculite-gypsum or perlite-gypsum plaster of thickness of ...	50‖	35‖	19	16	12·5	12·5
(*b*) metal lath spaced 25 millimetres from flanges with vermiculite-gypsum or perlite-gypsum plaster of thickness of	44	32	19	12·5	12·5	12·5
5. Gypsum plasterboard with 1·6 millimetres wire binding at 100 millimetres pitch—						
(*a*) 9·5 millimetres plasterboard with gypsum plaster of thickness of					12·5	12·5
(*b*) 19 millimetres plasterboard with gypsum plaster of thickness of			12·5	10	7	7
6. Gypsum plasterboard with 1·6 millimetres wire binding at 100 millimetres pitch—						
(*a*) 9·5 millimetres plasterboard with vermiculite-gypsum plaster of thickness of ...			16	12·5	10	7
(*b*) 19 millimetres plasterboard with vermiculite-gypsum plaster of thickness of ...	32‖	19	10	10	7	7
7. Metal lath with sprayed asbestos of thickness of...	44	32	19	15	10	10
8. Vermiculite-cement slabs of 4:1 mix reinforced with wire mesh and finished with plaster skim. Slabs of thickness of	63	44	25	25	25	25
9. Asbestos insulation boards of density 510 to 880 kilogrammes per cubic metre (screwed to 25 millimetres thick asbestos battens for ½-hour and 1 hour periods)			25	19	12	9

†Solid protection means a casing which is bedded close up to the steel without intervening cavities and with all joints in that casing made full and solid.

‡Reinforcement. Where reinforcement is required in this Table, that reinforcement shall consist of steel binding wire not less than 2·3 millimetres in thickness, or a steel mesh weighing not less than 0·48 kilogrammes per square metre. In concrete protection the spacing of that reinforcement shall not exceed 150 millimetres in any direction.

§Hollow protection means that there is a void between the protective material and the steel. All hollow protection to columns shall be effectively sealed at each floor level.

‖Light mesh reinforcement required 12·5 to 19 millimetres below surface unless special corner beads are used.

SCHEDULE 9—*continued*
TABLE 3—*continued*
Part VI: Structural steel—continued

(2) *Encased steel beams* (*Weight of steel not less than 30 kilogrammes per metre*)

Construction and materials	Minimum thickness (in millimetres) of protection for a fire resistance in accordance with Table 5 for a period of—					
	4 hours	3 hours	2 hours	1½ hours	1 hour	½ hour
A. *Solid protection*† (*unplastered*)						
1. Reinforced concrete not leaner than 1:2:4 mix with natural aggregates—						
(*a*) concrete not assumed to be loadbearing...	63	50	25	25	25	25
(*b*) concrete assumed to be loadbearing in accordance with BS 449: Part 2: 1969 as read with Amendments AMD 416, January 1970, AMD 523, May 1970 and AMD 661, December 1970	75	50	50	50	50	50
2. Sprayed asbestos—140 to 240 kilogrammes per cubic metre	44	32	19	15	10	10
3. Sprayed vermiculite-cement			38	32	19	12·5
B. *Hollow protection*‡						
1. Metal lathing—						
(*a*) with cement-lime plaster of thickness of...			38	25	19	12·5
(*b*) with gypsum plaster of thickness of ...			22	19	16	12·5
(*c*) with vermiculite-gypsum or perlite-gypsum plaster of thickness of	32	19	12·5	12·5	12·5	12·5
2. Gypsum plasterboard with 1·6 millimetres wire binding at 100 millimetres pitch—						
(*a*) 9·5 millimetres plasterboard with gypsum plaster of thickness of					12·5	12·5
(*b*) 19 millimetres plasterboard with gypsum plaster of thickness of			12·5	10	7	7
3. Plasterboard with 1·6 millimetres wire binding at 100 millimetres pitch—						
(*a*) 9·5 millimetres plasterboard nailed to wooden brackets finished with gypsum plaster of thickness of						12·5
(*b*) 9·5 millimetres plasterboard with vermiculite-gypsum plaster of thickness of ...			16	12·5	10	7
(*c*) 19 millimetres plasterboard with vermiculite-gypsum plaster of thickness of ...	32§	19	10	10	7	7
(*d*) 19 millimetres plasterboard with gypsum plaster of thickness of			12·5			
4. Metal lathing with sprayed asbestos—140 to 240 kilogrammes per cubic metre of thickness of...	44	32	19	15	10	10
5. Asbestos insulation boards of density 510 to 880 kilogrammes per cubic metre (screwed to 25 millimetres thick asbestos battens for ½-hour and 1 hour periods)			25	19	12	9
6. Vermiculite-cement slabs of 4:1 mix reinforced with wire mesh and finished with plaster skim. Slabs of thickness of	63	44	25	25	25	25
7. Gypsum-sand plaster 12·5 millimetres thick applied to heavy duty (Type B as designated in BS 1105: 1963) wood wool slabs of thickness of			50	38	38	38

†Solid protection means a casing which is bedded close up to the steel without intervening cavities and with all joints in that casing made full and solid.

‡Hollow protection means that there is a void between the protective material and the steel. All hollow protection to columns shall be effectively sealed at each floor level.

§Light mesh reinforcement required 12·5 to 19 millimetres below surface unless special corner beads are used.

SCHEDULE 9—*continued*

TABLE 3—*continued*

Part VII: Structural aluminium

Encased aluminium alloy stanchions and beams

Construction and materials	Minimum thickness (in millimetres) of protection for a fire resistance in accordance with Table 5 for a period of—					
	4 hours	3 hours	2 hours	1½ hours	1 hour	½ hour
A. *Solid protection*†						
1. Sprayed asbestos—140 to 240 kilogrammes per cubic metre...			48	32	19	10
2. Sprayed vermiculite-cement					44	19
B. *Hollow protection*‡						
1. Metal lath with vermiculite-gypsum or perlite-gypsum plaster of thickness of		50	32	22	16	12·5
2. Metal lath finished with neat gypsum plaster of thickness of					19	12·5
3. Gypsum plasterboard 19 millimetres thick with 1·6 millimetres wire binding at 100 millimetres pitch finished with gypsum-vermiculite plaster of thickness of		38	22	16	10	10
4. Asbestos insulation board of density 510 to 880 kilogrammes per cubic metre (screwed to 25 millimetres thick asbestos battens for the ½-hour period)				34	21	9

†Solid protection means a casing which is bedded close up to the alloy without intervening cavities and with all joints in that casing made full and solid.

‡Hollow protection means that there is a void between the protective material and the alloy. All hollow protection to columns shall be effectively sealed at each floor level.

SCHEDULE 9—*continued*

TABLE 3—*continued*

Part VIII: Timber floors

A. *All floors other than compartment and separating floors except floors in flats up to four storeys (Sub-group A2)*

Minimum width of joist (millimetres) (1)	Minimum thickness of tongued and grooved boarding (millimetres)† (2)	Ceiling base (3)	Ceiling finish for a fire resistance in accordance with the requirements set out in Table 5 for a period of— (4)			
			2 hours	1½ hours	1 hour	½ hour
37‡	16	two layers plasterboard of total thickness of 19 millimetres				nil
		9 millimetres asbestos insulation board				nil
		12 millimetres asbestos insulation board			25 millimetres glass fibre or mineral wool on top	nil
		9·5 millimetres plaster-board			12·5 millimetres vermiculite-gypsum plaster	12·5 millimetres gypsum plaster
		12·5 millimetres plaster-board				5 millimetres gypsum plaster
		19 millimetres plaster-board				nil
		metal lathing fixed direct to joists			22 millimetres gypsum plaster or 12·5 millimetres vermiculite-gypsum plaster	15 millimetres gypsum plaster or 12·5 millimetres vermiculite-gypsum plaster
		25 millimetres wood wool slabs			10 millimetres vermiculite-gypsum plaster	5 millimetres gypsum plaster
	16 as floating floor on 25 millimetres glass fibre or mineral wool quilt	12·5 millimetres plaster-board with metal lath or brandering			19 millimetres gypsum plaster	12·5 millimetres gypsum plaster

49‡	21	6 millimetres asbestos insulation board				nil
		12·5 millimetres fibre insulation board†				5 millimetres gypsum plaster
		metal lathing fixed direct to joists	38 millimetres sprayed asbestos§	30 millimetres sprayed asbestos§	19 millimetres sprayed asbestos§	12·5 millimetres sprayed asbestos§
		metal lath			19 millimetres sprayed asbestos§	15 millimetres gypsum plaster or 12·5 millimetres sprayed asbestos§
49	21	19 millimetres plasterboard			12·5 millimetres vermiculite-gypsum plaster	12·5 millimetres gypsum plaster
		12·5 millimetres plasterboard				5 millimetres gypsum plaster
		19 millimetres plasterboard in two layers laid to break bond				nil
		12·5 millimetres fibre insulation board				12·5 millimetres gypsum plaster
		6 millimetres asbestos insulation board				nil
		25 millimetres wood wool slabs			10 millimetres vermiculite-gypsum plaster	5 millimetres gypsum plaster

SCHEDULE 9—*continued*

TABLE 3—*continued*

Part VIII: Timber floors—continued

B. *For a floor above the lowest in a small house (Sub-group A1)*

Minimum width of joist (millimetres) (1)	Minimum thickness of tongued and grooved boarding (millimetres)† (2)	Ceiling base (3)	Ceiling finish for a fire resistance in accordance with the requirements set out in Table 5 (4)
37‡	16	9·5 millimetres plasterboard	nil
		12·5 millimetres plasterboard	nil
		12·5 millimetres fibre insulation board†	12·5 millimetres gypsum plaster
49	21	12·5 millimetres fibre insulation board†	nil

†Or an equal thickness of wood chipboard.

‡All forms of ceiling protection for 38 millimetres joists are suitable for 50 millimetres joists.

§Sprayed asbestos in accordance with **BS 3590: 1970.**

SCHEDULE 9—*continued*

TABLE 3—*continued*

Part IX: Concrete floors

Construction (1)	Minimum thickness of solid substance including screed (millimetres) (2)	Ceiling finish (in millimetres) for a fire resistance in accordance with the requirements set out in Table 5 for a period of— (3)					
		4 hours	3 hours	2 hours	1½ hours	1 hour	½ hour
Solid flat slab or filler joist floor.	90	25V or 25A	19V or 19A	10V or 12·5A	10V or 12·5A	7V or 10A	nil
Units of channel or T section	100	19V or 19A	12·5V	7V	7V	nil	nil
	125	10V or 12·5A	7V	nil	nil	nil	nil
	150	nil	nil	nil	nil	nil	nil
Solid flat slab or filler joist floor with 25 millimetres wood wool slab ceiling base	90				12·5G	nil	nil
	100		12·5G	nil	nil	nil	nil
	125	12·5G	nil	nil	nil	nil	nil
	150	nil	nil	nil	nil	nil	nil
Units of inverted U section with minimum thickness at crown	63						nil
	75					nil	nil
	100			nil	nil	nil	nil
	150	nil	nil	nil	nil	nil	nil
Hollow block construction or units of box or I section	63						nil
	75					nil	nil
	90			nil	nil	nil	nil
	125	nil					
Cellular steel with concrete topping	63	12·5V suspended on metal lathing or 12·5A (direct)	12·5V suspended on metal lathing or 12·5A	12·5G suspended on metal lathing	12·5G suspended on metal lathing	12·5G suspended on metal lathing	nil

"V"—vermiculite-gypsum plaster "A"—sprayed asbestos in accordance with BS 3590: 1970 "G"—gypsum plaster

SCHEDULE 9—*continued*

Regulation D3

TABLE 4—LIMITS OF CUBIC CAPACITY OF BUILDING AND AREA OF STOREY IN RELATION TO STRUCTURAL FIRE PRECAUTIONS

Occupancy		Number of storeys	Maximum cubic capacity of building, division or compartment (cubic metres)	Maximum area of storey in the building or within division (square metres)
Group	Sub-group			
(1)	(2)	(3)	(4)	(5)
A (Residential)	1	Not more than two storeys ...	N.L.	230
	2	One or more storeys	N.L.	460
	3	One or more storeys	14 000	1 900
	4	One or more storeys	8 500	1 400
B (Commercial)	1	One or more storeys	28 000	4 600
	2	One or more storeys	7 100†	2 800†
C (Assembly)	1	One or more storeys	N.L.	N.L.
	2	One or more storeys	21 000	1 900
	3	One or more storeys	N.L.	1 900
D (Industrial)	1	One storey	N.L.	93 000
		More than one storey	84 000	7 400
	2	One storey	N.L.	33 000
		More than one storey	28 000	2 800
	3	One storey	N.L.	9 000
		More than one storey	8 500	900
E (Storage)	1	One storey	N.L.	14 000
		More than one storey	21 000	2 800
	2	One storey	N.L.	900
		More than one storey	4 200	460

N.L. No upper limit is imposed.

†In the case of a shop in occupancy sub-group B2 the maximum cubic capacity stated in column (4) shall be doubled, and the maximum area stated in column (5) shall be increased to 3700 square metres if the building, division or compartment, or storey in the building or within the division, as the case may be, is fitted throughout, save in protected zones as defined in regulation E2, with an automatic sprinkler system complying with the recommendations of CP 402.201: 1952 as read with Amendments PD 2998, March 1958, PD 4054, January 1961 and PD 5724, January 1966.

SCHEDULE 9—*continued*

TABLE 5—FIRE RESISTANCE REQUIREMENTS

Regulations D2(2) and D5(2)

Element of structure (1)	(2)	Period of fire resistance, conditions of test and requirements of British Standard 476: Part 1: 1953, "Fire tests on building materials and structures", clause 11, to be satisfied *a.* collapse, *b.* passage of flame and *c.* insulation (3)	Column in Table 6 which specifies basic period of fire resistance (4)
Frame members—structural frames, beams and columns	In an uncompartmented building	The element is capable of satisfying requirement— *a.* collapse—for the period specified when subjected to fire from all radial directions at once.	(5)
	In a building which is split up into compartments		(6)
Floors	Separating and compartment floors in all buildings Floors of garages to which regulation D21(2)(*f*) applies	The element‡ is capable of satisfying each of the three requirements *a.*, *b.* and *c.* for the period specified when the underside is exposed to fire.	(6)
	Floor above the lowest in a house in a building of occupancy sub-group A1	The element‡ is capable of satisfying each of the three requirements when the underside is exposed to fire, thus— *a.* collapse—for the period specified; *b.* passage of flame—for 15 minutes†; *c.* insulation—for 15 minutes†.	(5)
	All other floors being floors above the lowest	The element‡ is capable of satisfying each of the three requirements *a.*, *b.* and *c.* for the period specified when the underside is exposed to fire.	(5)
Walls	Separating and fire division walls External walls on the boundary Internal loadbearing walls in a building which is split up into compartments Walls of garages to which regulation D21(2)(*a*) applies	The element is capable of satisfying each of the three requirements *a.*, *b.* and *c.* for the period specified when either side is exposed to fire.	(6)

SCHEDULE 9—*continued*

TABLE 5—*continued*

Element of structure (1)	Element of structure (2)	Period of fire resistance, conditions of test and requirements of British Standard 476: Part 1: 1953, "Fire tests on building materials and structures", clause 11, to be satisfied *a.* collapse, *b.* passage of flame and *c.* insulation (3)	Column in Table 6 which specifies basic period of fire resistance (4)
Walls—*cont.*	Internal loadbearing walls in an uncompartmented building	The element is capable of satisfying each of the three requirements *a.*, *b.* and *c.* for the period specified when either side is exposed to fire.	(5)
	External walls 1 metre or more from the boundary	The element is capable of satisfying each of the three requirements when only the internal side is exposed to fire, thus— *a.* collapse—for the period specified or 30 minutes, whichever is the greater; *b.* passage of flame—for the period specified or 30 minutes, whichever is the greater; *c.* insulation—for 15 minutes†.	(5)
Doors, shutters, ducts and access covers	Where protecting openings in a fire division wall enclosing a stairway or lift shaft; or protecting openings in a separating wall between a flat and a common accessway; or comprising the enclosure of, or the access cover to, a duct carried through a separating wall, fire division wall, separating floor or compartment floor	Subject in the case of doors and shutters to regulation D7(6) the element is capable of satisfying requirements— *a.* collapse, *b.* passage of flame, both for one-half of the period specified for the wall or floor, as the case may be or 30 minutes, whichever is the greater, when either side is exposed to fire: Provided that where the period required by this Table for a door or shutter would otherwise be 45 minutes the door or shutter shall not be required to have a fire resistance greater than 30 minutes.	(6)
	Where protecting openings in any other fire division or separating wall	Subject in the case of doors and shutters to regulation D7(6) the element is capable of satisfying requirements— *a.* collapse, *b.* passage of flame, both for the period specified when either side is exposed to fire.	(6)

†Notwithstanding the period specified.

‡Taken together with any suspended ceiling which is of jointless construction with no openings therein or which is designed and constructed in accordance with the provisions of Schedule 5.

SCHEDULE 9—*continued*

TABLE 6—PERIODS OF FIRE RESISTANCE Regulation D5

Part I: Periods of fire resistance according to height and cubic capacity of all buildings of occupancy groups A, B and C

Occupancy		The following are not exceeded:—		Specified period of fire resistance†	
Group (1)	Sub-group (2)	Height of building or division (metres) (3)	Capacity of undivided building or of division or of compartment (cubic metres) (4)	hours (5)	hours (6)
A (Residential)	1	Not more than two storeys	N.L.	½	1
	2	15 24 N.L.	N.L. N.L. N.L.	½ 1 1½	1 1 1½
	3	9 24 N.L.	4 200 8 500 14 000	½ 1 1½	1 1 1½
	4	9 24 N.L.	2 800 5 700 8 500	½ 1 1½	1 1 1½
B (Commercial)	1	6 12 24 N.L.	1 130 4 200 14 000 28 000	Nil‡ ½ 1 1½	1 1 1 1½
	2	6 12 24 N.L.	708 2 120 4 200 7 100	½ 1 2 3	1 1½ 2 3
C (Assembly)	1	N.L.	N.L.	½	½
	2	7·5 18 30 N.L.	4 200 8 500 14 000 21 000	Nil‡ ½ 1 1½	1 1 1 1½
	3	6 12 24 N.L.	566 2 800 14 000 N.L.	Nil‡ ½ 1 2	1 1 1 2

†If more than one period specified for any element, higher or highest to apply (see regulation D5(3)).

‡A minimum of ½-hour for external walls (see Table 5).

N.L. No upper limit is imposed.

SCHEDULE 9—*continued*

TABLE 6—*continued*

Part II: Periods of fire resistance according to floor area of single storey buildings of occupancy groups D and E

Occupancy		Floor area of undivided building or of division not exceeding:—	Specified period of fire resistance†	
Group	Sub-group	(square metres)	hours	hours
(1)	(2)	(3)	(5)	(6)
D (Industrial)	1	9 000 93 000	½ 1	½ 1
	2	1 400 7 000 33 000	½ 1 1½	1 1 1½
	3	460 900 2 300 9 000	½ 1 1½ 2	1 1½ 1½ 2
E (Storage)	1	900 2 300 14 000	½ 1 2	1 1 2
	2	90 190 280 460 900	½ 1 1½ 3 4	1½ 1½ 2 3 4

†If more than one period specified for any element, higher or highest to apply (see regulation D5(3)).

SCHEDULE 9—*continued*

TABLE 6—*continued*

Part III: Periods of fire resistance according to height and cubic capacity of buildings of more than one storey of occupancy groups D and E

Occupancy		The following are not exceeded:—		Specified period of fire resistance†	
Group (1)	Sub-group (2)	Height of undivided building or division (metres) (3)	Capacity of undivided building or of division or of compartment (cubic metres) (4)	hours (5)	hours (6)
D (Industrial)	1	9 15 N.L.	8 500 28 000 84 000	Nil‡ ½ 1	½ ½ 1
	2	9 12 15 24 N.L.	1 700 4 200 8 500 17 000 28 000	Nil‡ ½ 1 1½ 2	1 1 1 1½ 2
	3	9 12 15 24 N.L.	708 1 410 2 800 4 200 8 500	½ 1 1½ 2 3	1 1½ 1½ 2 3
E (Storage)	1	9 12 15 24 N.L.	850 1 410 2 800 8 500 21 000	Nil‡ ½ 1 2 3	1 1 1 2 3
	2	9 12 15 24 N.L.	425 850 1 410 2 120 4 200	½ 1 1½ 3 4	1½ 1½ 2 3 4

†If more than one period specified for any element, higher or highest to apply (see regulation D5(3)).

‡A minimum of ½-hour for external walls (see Table 5).

N.L. No upper limit is imposed.

SCHEDULE 9—*continued*

TABLE 7—NOTIONAL DESIGNATIONS OF ROOF COVERINGS

Regulation D18

Part 1: Pitched roofs covered with slates or tiles

Covering material (1)	Supporting structure (2)	Designation (3)
1. Natural slates 2. Asbestos-cement slates 3. Clay tiles 4. Concrete tiles	1. Timber rafters with or without underfelt, sarking, boarding, wood wool slabs, compressed straw slabs, plywood, wood or flax chipboard, or fibre insulating board	AA
5. Bitumen felt strip slates (asbestos or fibre based)	2. Timber rafters and boarding, plywood, wood wool slabs, compressed straw slabs, wood or flax chipboard, or fibre insulating board	CC
6. Bitumen felt strip slates Type 2E, with underlayer of bitumen felt Type 2B or 2C	3. Timber rafters and boarding, plywood, wood wool slabs, compressed straw slabs, wood or flax chipboard, or fibre insulating board	BB

Note: Any reference in this Part of the Table to bitumen felt strip slates or to underfelt is a reference to materials of this description complying with BS 747: Part 2: 1970.

SCHEDULE 9—*continued*

TABLE 7—*continued*

Part II: Pitched roofs covered with preformed self-supporting sheets

Details of covering		Supporting structure (3)	Designation (4)
Material (1)	Construction (2)		
Corrugated sheets of— (i) galvanised steel; (ii) aluminium; (iii) composite steel and asbestos; (iv) asbestos-cement; or (v) PVC coated metal	1. Single-skin without underlay or with underlay of— (i) asbestos insulating board; (ii) plasterboard; (iii) fibre insulating board; (iv) compressed straw slab; or (v) wood wool slab	Structure of timber, steel or concrete	AA
	2. Double-skin without interlayer or with interlayer of— (i) resin-bonded glass fibre; (ii) bitumen-bonded glass fibre; (iii) mineral wool slab or blanket; (iv) polystyrene; or (v) polyurethane	Structure of timber, steel or concrete	AA

Part III: Pitched or flat roofs covered with fully supported material

Covering material (1)	Supporting structure (2)	Designation (3)
1. Aluminium sheet 2. Copper sheet 3. Zinc sheet 4. Lead sheet 5. Mastic asphalt 6. Vitreous enamelled steel sheet	1. Timber joists and— (i) tongued and grooved boarding; or (ii) plain edged boarding	AA*
	2. Steel or timber joists with deck of— (i) wood wool slab; (ii) compressed straw slab; (iii) wood or flax chipboard; (iv) fibre insulating board; or (v) 9·5 millimetres plywood	AA
	3. Concrete or clay pot slab (cast in situ or precast); or non-combustible deck of steel, aluminium or asbestos-cement (with or without insulation)	AA

**Note:* Lead sheet supported by timber joists and plain edged boarding shall be deemed to be of designation BA.

SCHEDULE 9—*continued*

TABLE 7—*continued*

Part IV: A. Flat roofs covered with bitumen felt

Any bitumen felt roofing specification applied to the roof deck materials prescribed in the Table in Part IV B and having a surface finish of (*a*) bitumen bedded stone chippings covering the whole surface to a depth of not less than 12·5 millimetres, (*b*) bitumen bedded tiles of a non-combustible material, (*c*) sand and cement screed or (*d*) macadam, shall be deemed to be of designation AA.

Part IV: B. Pitched roofs covered with bitumen felt

DETAILS OF FELT			COMBUSTIBLE DECK			NON-COMBUSTIBLE DECK		
Number of layers	Type of upper layer	Type of under-layer or layers	Deck of any of the following (having minimum thickness stated)—plywood (6 millimetres); wood or flax chipboard (12·5 millimetres); T & G boarding (16 millimetres finished); or PE boarding (19 millimetres finished)	Deck of compressed straw slab	Deck of screeded wood wool slab	Asbestos-cement or steel single-skin or cavity deck (without overlay or with overlay of fibre insulating board)	Aluminium single-skin or cavity deck (without overlay or with overlay of fibre insulating board)	Concrete or clay pot slab (cast in situ or precast)
(1)	(2)	(3)	(4)	(5)	(6)	(7)	(8)	(9)
1. Two or three layers built-up in accordance with CP 144: Part 3: 1970	1. Type 1E	Type 1B, C or D (Minimum weight 13 kg/10m²)	CC	AC	AC	AC	AC	AB
	2. Type 2E	Type 1B, C or D (Minimum weight 13 kg/10m²)	BB	AB	AB	AB	AB	AB
	3. Type 2E	Type 2B or C	AB	AB	AB	AB	AB	AB
	4. Type 3E	Type 3B or G	BC	AC	AB	AB	AB	AB
2. Single layer	Type 1E		CC	AC	AC	AC	AC	AC

Note: Any reference to bitumen felt of a specified type is a reference to bitumen felt as so designated in BS 747: Part 2: 1970.

SCHEDULE 9—*continued*

Regulation D17 and Schedule 6

TABLE 8—STRUCTURAL FIRE PRECAUTIONS—MINIMUM DISTANCE BETWEEN ENCLOSING RECTANGLE OF OPENINGS IN THE SIDE OF A BUILDING AND THE BOUNDARY

Part I: Buildings of occupancy sub-group B2, C3, D2 or D3 or occupancy group E

Height (in metres) of enclosing rectangle not exceeding	Width (in metres) of enclosing rectangle not exceeding	Percentage of openings not exceeding—								
		20	30	40	50	60	70	80	90	100
		Distance (in metres) from boundary								
3	3	1·1	1·5	1·8	2·0	2·3	2·5	2·7	2·9	3·0
3	6	1·5	2·0	2·4	2·8	3·2	3·4	3·7	4·0	4·2
3	9	1·7	2·3	2·8	3·3	3·8	4·1	4·5	4·8	5·0
3	12	1·8	2·5	3·1	3·7	4·2	4·7	5·0	5·4	5·6
3	15	1·8	2·6	3·3	3·9	4·5	5·0	5·4	5·9	6·2
3	18	1·8	2·7	3·5	4·2	4·8	5·2	5·8	6·3	6·7
3	21	1·8	2·8	3·6	4·3	5·0	5·5	6·0	6·6	7·1
3	24	1·8	2·8	3·7	4·5	5·1	5·7	6·2	6·9	7·4
3	27	1·8	2·9	3·8	4·6	5·3	5·9	6·5	7·1	7·7
3	30	1·8	2·9	3·8	4·7	5·4	6·0	6·7	7·4	7·9
3	40	1·8	2·9	3·9	4·8	5·7	6·4	7·2	7·8	8·6
3	50	1·8	2·9	3·9	4·9	5·8	6·7	7·5	8·2	9·0
3	60	1·8	2·9	3·9	5·0	5·9	6·8	7·7	8·5	9·3
3	80	1·8	2·9	3·9	5·0	6·0	7·0	7·9	8·9	9·7
3	100	1·8	2·9	3·9	5·0	6·0	7·0	7·9	9·0	10·0
3	N.L.	1·8	2·9	3·9	5·0	6·0	7·0	7·9	9·0	10·0
6	3	1·5	2·0	2·4	2·8	3·2	3·4	3·7	4·0	4·2
6	6	2·2	2·9	3·5	4·0	4·5	4·9	5·3	5·7	6·0
6	9	2·6	3·5	4·3	4·9	5·5	6·0	6·5	6·9	7·2
6	12	3·0	4·0	4·8	5·5	6·3	6·8	7·4	7·9	8·3
6	15	3·2	4·3	5·3	6·2	7·0	7·5	8·2	8·8	9·1
6	18	3·3	4·5	5·7	6·6	7·5	8·2	8·9	9·5	10·0
6	21	3·4	4·8	6·0	7·0	8·0	8·8	9·5	10·2	10·6
6	24	3·5	5·0	6·2	7·2	8·4	9·3	10·0	10·7	11·2
6	27	3·5	5·1	6·4	7·6	8·7	9·7	10·4	11·2	11·8
6	30	3·6	5·2	6·7	7·8	9·0	10·0	11·0	11·8	12·5
6	40	3·6	5·5	7·1	8·5	10·0	11·0	12·0	13·0	14·0
6	50	3·7	5·7	7·4	9·0	10·5	11·5	12·8	14·0	15·0
6	60	3·7	5·7	7·5	9·3	11·0	12·0	13·5	15·0	16·0
6	80	3·7	5·9	7·7	9·7	11·3	13·0	14·3	15·8	17·3
6	100	3·7	5·9	7·8	10·0	11·8	13·3	15·0	16·5	18·0
6	120	3·7	5·9	7·8	10·0	11·8	13·8	15·3	17·0	18·8
6	140	3·7	5·9	7·8	10·0	12·0	14·0	16·0	18·0	19·0
6	160	3·7	5·9	7·8	10·0	12·0	14·0	16·0	18·0	20·0
6	N.L.	3·7	5·9	7·8	10·0	12·0	14·0	16·0	18·0	20·0

N.L. No upper limit is imposed.

SCHEDULE 9—*continued*

TABLE 8—*continued*

Part I—continued

Height (in metres) of enclosing rectangle not exceeding	Width (in metres) of enclosing rectangle not exceeding	Percentage of openings not exceeding—								
		20	30	40	50	60	70	80	90	100
		Distance (in metres) from boundary								
9	3	1·7	2·3	2·8	3·3	3·8	4·1	4·5	4·8	5·0
9	6	2·6	3·5	4·3	4·9	5·5	6·0	6·5	6·9	7·2
9	9	3·3	4·4	5·3	6·0	6·7	7·3	8·0	8·5	9·0
9	12	3·7	5·0	6·0	6·9	7·7	8·4	9·2	9·7	10·5
9	15	4·1	5·5	6·7	7·7	8·5	9·3	10·2	11·0	11·5
9	18	4·4	6·0	7·2	8·4	9·4	10·2	11·0	12·0	12·5
9	21	4·7	6·3	7·7	9·0	10·2	11·0	12·0	12·8	13·5
9	24	4·8	6·6	8·0	9·5	10·8	11·8	12·8	13·5	14·3
9	27	5·0	6·8	8·5	10·0	11·3	12·3	13·3	14·3	15·0
9	30	5·1	7·0	8·8	10·3	11·8	13·0	14·0	15·0	15·8
9	40	5·3	7·5	9·5	11·3	13·0	14·3	15·5	16·8	17·5
9	50	5·5	7·9	10·2	12·3	14·0	15·5	16·8	18·3	19·5
9	60	5·5	8·2	10·8	12·8	14·8	16·5	18·0	19·5	20·8
9	80	5·5	8·5	11·3	13·5	15·8	17·5	19·5	21·3	22·8
9	100	5·6	8·6	11·5	14·3	16·5	18·5	20·8	22·5	24·5
9	120	5·6	8·6	11·5	14·5	17·0	19·3	21·5	23·5	25·8
9	140	5·6	8·6	11·5	14·8	17·3	19·8	22·3	24·3	26·8
9	160	5·6	8·6	11·8	15·0	18·0	20·0	23·0	25·0	28·0
9	180	5·6	8·6	11·8	15·0	18·0	21·0	23·0	26·0	28·0
9	200	5·6	8·6	11·8	15·0	18·0	21·0	24·0	26·0	29·0
9	240	5·6	8·6	11·8	15·0	18·0	21·0	24·0	26·0	29·0
9	280	5·6	8·6	11·8	15·0	18·0	21·0	24·0	26·0	30·0
9	320	5·6	8·6	11·8	15·0	18·0	21·0	24·0	26·0	30·0
9	N.L.	5·6	8·6	11·8	15·0	18·0	21·0	24·0	26·0	30·0
12	3	1·8	2·5	3·1	3·7	4·2	4·7	5·0	5·4	5·6
12	6	3·0	4·0	4·8	5·5	6·3	6·8	7·4	7·9	8·3
12	9	3·7	5·0	6·0	6·9	7·7	8·4	9·2	9·7	10·5
12	12	4·3	5·8	7·0	8·0	9·0	9·7	10·8	11·5	12·0
12	15	4·8	6·4	7·8	9·0	10·0	11·0	12·0	12·8	13·3
12	18	5·2	7·0	8·5	9·8	11·0	12·0	13·0	13·8	14·5
12	21	5·6	7·5	9·2	10·5	12·0	12·8	14·0	15·0	15·8
12	24	5·8	7·9	9·7	11·3	12·5	13·8	14·8	15·8	16·5
12	27	6·2	8·2	10·3	11·8	13·3	14·5	15·8	16·8	17·5
12	30	6·3	8·5	10·5	12·3	14·0	15·0	16·5	17·5	18·3
12	40	6·7	9·4	11·8	13·8	15·5	17·3	18·5	20·0	21·0
12	50	7·0	9·9	12·8	14·8	17·0	18·8	20·3	22·8	23·0
12	60	7·1	10·5	13·3	15·8	18·0	20·0	21·5	23·5	24·8
12	80	7·2	11·0	14·3	17·0	19·5	21·5	23·5	25·8	27·5
12	100	7·4	11·3	14·8	18·0	20·8	23·0	25·5	27·8	29·8
12	120	7·5	11·5	15·0	18·5	21·8	24·0	26·8	29·5	31·5
12	140	7·5	11·8	15·3	19·0	22·3	25·0	27·8	30·5	34·0
12	160	7·5	11·8	15·5	20·0	23·0	26·0	29·0	32·0	35·0
12	180	7·5	11·8	15·5	20·0	23·0	26·0	30·0	33·0	36·0
12	200	7·5	11·8	15·5	20·0	23·0	27·0	31·0	33·0	37·0
12	240	7·5	11·8	15·5	20·0	24·0	27·0	32·0	34·0	38·0
12	280	7·5	11·8	15·5	20·0	24·0	28·0	32·0	35·0	38·0
12	320	7·5	11·8	15·5	20·0	24·0	28·0	32·0	36·0	39·0
12	360	7·5	11·8	15·5	20·0	24·0	28·0	32·0	36·0	39·0
12	400	7·5	11·8	15·5	20·0	24·0	28·0	32·0	36·0	40·0
12	N.L.	7·5	11·8	15·5	20·0	24·0	28·0	32·0	36·0	40·0

N.L. No upper limit is imposed.

SCHEDULE 9—*continued*

TABLE 8—*continued*

Part I—continued

Height (in metres) of enclosing rectangle not exceeding	Width (in metres) of enclosing rectangle not exceeding	Percentage of openings not exceeding—								
		20	30	40	50	60	70	80	90	100
		Distance (in metres) from boundary								
15	3	1·8	2·6	3·3	3·9	4·5	5·0	5·4	5·9	6·2
15	6	3·2	4·3	5·3	6·2	7·0	7·5	8·2	8·8	9·1
15	9	4·1	5·5	6·7	7·7	8·5	9·3	10·2	11·0	11·5
15	12	4·8	6·4	7·8	9·0	10·0	11·0	12·0	12·8	13·3
15	15	5·5	7·2	8·8	10·0	11·3	12·3	13·3	14·3	15·0
15	18	5·9	7·9	9·6	11·0	12·3	13·3	14·5	15·5	16·3
15	21	6·3	8·5	10·5	12·0	13·3	14·3	15·8	16·5	17·5
15	24	6·7	9·0	11·0	12·8	14·3	15·3	16·8	17·8	18·8
15	27	7·0	9·4	11·5	13·3	15·0	16·3	17·8	18·8	19·8
15	30	7·3	10·0	12·0	14·0	15·8	17·0	18·5	19·8	20·8
15	40	8·0	11·0	13·5	15·8	18·0	19·5	21·0	22·5	23·5
15	50	8·4	11·8	14·8	17·3	19·5	21·5	23·0	24·8	26·0
15	60	8·7	12·5	15·5	18·0	20·8	23·3	25·0	26·8	28·0
15	80	8·9	13·3	16·8	20·0	23·0	25·5	27·8	30·0	31·5
15	100	9·0	13·8	17·8	21·3	24·5	27·3	29·8	32·5	34·5
15	120	9·1	14·0	18·5	22·3	25·5	28·5	31·3	34·3	36·8
15	140	9·1	14·5	19·0	23·0	27·0	30·0	34·0	36·0	39·0
15	160	9·1	14·5	19·0	24·0	28·0	31·0	35·0	38·0	41·0
15	180	9·1	14·5	19·0	24·0	28·0	32·0	35·0	39·0	42·0
15	200	9·1	14·5	19·5	24·8	29·0	32·0	36·0	40·0	43·0
15	240	9·1	14·5	19·5	24·8	29·0	33·0	37·0	41·0	45·0
15	280	9·1	14·5	19·5	24·8	30·0	34·0	38·0	42·0	46·0
15	320	9·1	14·5	19·5	24·8	30·0	34·0	39·0	43·0	47·0
15	360	9·1	14·5	19·5	24·8	30·0	35·0	39·0	44·0	48·0
15	400	9·1	14·5	19·5	24·8	30·0	35·0	40·0	45·0	48·0
15	460	9·1	14·5	19·5	24·8	30·0	35·0	40·0	45·0	49·0
15	520	9·1	14·5	19·5	24·8	30·0	35·0	40·0	45·0	50·0
15	N.L.	9·1	14·5	19·5	24·8	30·0	35·0	40·0	45·0	50·0

N.L. No upper limit is imposed.

SCHEDULE 9—*continued*

TABLE 8—*continued*

Part II: Buildings of occupancy group A or occupancy sub-group B1, C1, C2 or D1

Height (in metres) of enclosing rectangle not exceeding	Width (in metres) of enclosing rectangle not exceeding	Percentage of openings not exceeding—								
		20	30	40	50	60	70	80	90	100
		Distance (in metres) from boundary								
3	3	1·0	1·0	1·1	1·3	1·5	1·6	1·8	1·9	2·0
3	6	1·0	1·2	1·5	1·8	2·0	2·2	2·4	2·7	2·8
3	9	1·0	1·2	1·7	2·0	2·3	2·6	2·8	3·1	3·3
3	12	1·0	1·3	1·8	2·2	2·5	2·8	3·1	3·4	3·7
3	15	1·0	1·3	1·8	2·3	2·6	3·0	3·3	3·7	3·9
3	18	1·0	1·3	1·8	2·3	2·7	3·1	3·5	3·8	4·2
3	21	1·0	1·3	1·8	2·4	2·8	3·2	3·6	3·9	4·3
3	24	1·0	1·3	1·8	2·4	2·8	3·3	3·7	4·1	4·5
3	27	1·0	1·3	1·8	2·4	2·9	3·3	3·8	4·1	4·6
3	30	1·0	1·3	1·8	2·4	2·9	3·4	3·8	4·2	4·7
3	40	1·0	1·3	1·8	2·4	2·9	3·4	3·9	4·2	4·8
3	60	1·0	1·3	1·8	2·4	2·9	3·5	3·9	4·2	5·0
3	N.L.	1·0	1·3	1·8	2·4	2·9	3·5	3·9	4·2	5·0
6	3	1·0	1·2	1·5	1·8	2·0	2·2	2·4	2·7	2·8
6	6	1·0	1·7	2·2	2·6	2·9	3·2	3·5	4·0	4·0
6	9	1·1	2·0	2·6	3·1	3·5	4·0	4·3	4·7	4·9
6	12	1·3	2·3	3·0	3·5	4·0	4·5	4·8	5·2	5·5
6	15	1·3	2·4	3·2	3·8	4·3	5·0	5·3	5·7	6·2
6	18	1·3	2·4	3·3	4·0	4·5	5·2	5·7	6·2	6·6
6	21	1·3	2·5	3·4	4·2	4·8	5·4	6·0	6·6	7·0
6	24	1·3	2·5	3·5	4·3	5·0	5·6	6·2	6·8	7·2
6	27	1·4	2·5	3·5	4·4	5·1	5·8	6·4	7·1	7·6
6	30	1·4	2·6	3·6	4·4	5·2	5·9	6·7	7·2	7·8
6	40	1·4	2·6	3·6	4·6	5·5	6·3	7·1	7·8	8·5
6	50	1·4	2·6	3·7	4·7	5·7	6·6	7·4	8·1	9·0
6	60	1·4	2·6	3·7	4·8	5·7	6·7	7·5	8·4	9·3
6	80	1·4	2·6	3·7	4·8	5·9	6·8	7·7	8·6	9·7
6	100	1·4	2·6	3·7	4·8	5·9	6·9	7·8	8·6	10·0
6	N.L.	1·4	2·6	3·7	4·8	5·9	6·9	7·8	8·6	10·0
9	3	1·0	1·2	1·7	2·0	2·3	2·6	2·8	3·1	3·3
9	6	1·1	2·0	2·6	3·1	3·5	4·0	4·3	4·7	4·9
9	9	1·3	2·5	3·3	3·9	4·4	4·8	5·3	5·7	6·0
9	12	1·5	2·9	3·7	4·4	5·0	5·5	6·0	6·5	6·9
9	15	1·8	3·2	4·1	4·9	5·5	6·1	6·7	7·2	7·7
9	18	1·9	3·4	4·4	5·2	6·0	6·6	7·2	7·9	8·4
9	21	1·9	3·5	4·7	5·5	6·3	7·0	7·7	8·4	9·0
9	24	1·9	3·6	4·8	5·7	6·6	7·4	8·0	8·8	9·5
9	27	2·0	3·6	5·0	5·9	6·8	7·7	8·5	9·3	10·0
9	30	2·0	3·7	5·1	6·2	7·0	8·0	8·8	9·7	10·3
9	40	2·0	3·7	5·3	6·5	7·5	8·6	9·5	10·6	11·3
9	50	2·0	3·8	5·5	6·7	7·9	9·1	10·2	11·3	12·3
9	60	2·0	3·8	5·5	6·8	8·2	9·5	10·8	11·7	12·8
9	80	2·0	3·9	5·5	7·1	8·5	9·9	11·3	12·3	13·5
9	100	2·0	3·9	5·6	7·1	8·6	10·2	11·5	12·6	14·3
9	120	2·0	3·9	5·6	7·2	8·6	10·3	11·8	12·6	15·0
9	N.L.	2·0	3·9	5·6	7·2	8·6	10·3	11·8	12·6	15·0

N.L. No upper limit is imposed.

SCHEDULE 9—*continued*

TABLE 8—*continued*

Part II—continued

Height (in metres) of enclosing rectangle not exceeding	Width (in metres) of enclosing rectangle not exceeding	Percentage of openings not exceeding—								
		20	30	40	50	60	70	80	90	100
		Distance (in metres) from boundary								
12	3	1·0	1·3	1·8	2·2	2·5	2·8	3·1	3·4	3·7
12	6	1·3	2·3	3·0	3·5	4·0	4·5	4·8	5·2	5·5
12	9	1·5	2·9	3·7	4·4	5·0	5·5	6·0	6·5	6·9
12	12	1·7	3·3	4·3	5·1	5·8	6·3	7·0	7·6	8·0
12	15	2·0	3·7	4·8	5·7	6·4	7·1	7·8	8·5	9·0
12	18	2·3	4·0	5·2	6·2	7·0	7·7	8·5	9·1	9·8
12	21	2·4	4·2	5·6	6·5	7·5	8·3	9·2	9·8	10·5
12	24	2·5	4·5	5·8	7·0	7·9	8·7	9·7	10·5	11·3
12	27	2·5	4·6	6·2	7·2	8·2	9·2	10·3	11·0	11·8
12	30	2·6	4·7	6·3	7·5	8·5	9·6	10·5	11·5	12·3
12	40	2·6	4·9	6·7	8·2	9·4	10·6	11·8	13·0	13·8
12	50	2·7	5·0	7·0	8·6	9·9	11·1	12·8	13·8	14·8
12	60	2·7	5·1	7·1	8·9	10·5	11·8	13·3	14·5	15·8
12	80	2·7	5·1	7·2	9·2	11·0	12·8	14·3	15·8	17·0
12	100	2·7	5·2	7·4	9·4	11·3	13·3	14·8	16·3	18·0
12	120	2·7	5·2	7·5	9·5	11·5	13·5	15·0	16·8	18·5
12	140	2·7	5·2	7·5	9·6	11·8	13·8	15·3	17·0	19·0
12	160	2·7	5·2	7·5	9·6	11·8	13·8	15·5	17·0	20·0
12	N.L.	2·7	5·2	7·5	9·6	11·8	13·8	15·5	17·0	20·0
15	3	1·0	1·3	1·8	2·3	2·6	3·0	3·3	3·7	3·9
15	6	1·3	2·4	3·2	3·8	4·3	5·0	5·3	5·7	6·2
15	9	1·8	3·2	4·1	4·9	5·5	6·1	6·7	7·2	7·7
15	12	2·0	3·7	4·8	5·7	6·4	7·1	7·8	8·5	9·0
15	15	2·1	4·1	5·5	6·4	7·2	7·9	8·8	9·5	10·0
15	18	2·4	4·5	5·9	7·0	7·9	8·7	9·6	10·3	11·0
15	21	2·7	4·9	6·3	7·5	8·5	9·3	10·5	11·1	12·0
15	24	2·9	5·2	6·7	7·9	9·0	10·0	11·0	11·8	12·8
15	27	3·0	5·3	7·0	8·3	9·4	10·5	11·5	12·5	13·3
15	30	3·1	5·6	7·3	8·7	10·0	10·9	12·0	13·3	14·0
15	40	3·2	6·0	8·0	9·5	11·0	12·3	13·5	14·8	15·8
15	50	3·3	6·1	8·4	10·2	11·8	13·3	14·8	16·3	17·3
15	60	3·3	6·3	8·7	10·7	12·5	14·0	15·5	17·0	18·0
15	80	3·3	6·4	8·9	11·2	13·3	15·0	16·8	18·5	20·0
15	100	3·4	6·4	9·0	11·5	13·8	16·0	17·8	19·5	21·3
15	120	3·4	6·5	9·1	11·7	14·0	16·5	18·5	20·3	22·3
15	140	3·4	6·5	9·1	11·8	14·5	17·0	19·0	20·8	23·0
15	160	3·4	6·5	9·1	11·9	14·5	17·3	19·0	21·0	24·0
15	180	3·4	6·5	9·1	12·0	14·5	17·3	19·0	21·0	24·0
15	200	3·4	6·5	9·1	12·0	14·5	17·3	19·5	21·0	24·8
15	N.L.	3·4	6·5	9·1	12·0	14·5	17·3	19·5	21·0	24·8

N.L. No upper limit is imposed.

SCHEDULE 9—*continued*

Regulation D17 and Schedule 6

TABLE 9—STRUCTURAL FIRE PRECAUTIONS—LIMITING DISTANCE (IN METRES) IN RESPECT OF A RECESS HAVING OPENINGS ONLY IN THE BACK WALL

Part I: For a reduction in percentage effective opening of 10 per cent

Depth of recess (in metres) exceeding	Percentage of openings not exceeding—								
	15	20	25	30	40	50	60	80	100
1	1·0	1·2	1·7	2·2	3·2	4·2	5·2	7·2	9·2
3	2·0	3·6	5·1	6·6	9·6	12·6	15·7	21·6	27·6
5	3·4	6·0	8·5	11·0	16·0	21·1	26·2	36·1	46·1
7	4·7	8·4	12·0	15·5	22·5	29·5	36·5	50·5	—
9	6·1	10·8	15·4	20·0	29·0	38·0	47·0	—	—
15	10·2	18·0	25·7	33·2	48·0	—	—	—	—
30	20·4	36·0	51·5	—	—	—	—	—	—

Part II: For a reduction in percentage effective opening of 20 per cent

Depth of recess (in metres) exceeding	Percentage of openings not exceeding—					
	30	40	50	60	80	100
1	1·0	1·2	1·7	2·2	3·2	4·2
3	2·0	3·6	5·1	6·6	9·6	12·6
5	3·4	6·0	8·5	11·0	16·0	21·1
7	4·7	8·4	12·0	15·5	22·5	29·5
9	6·1	10·8	15·4	20·0	29·0	38·0
15	10·2	18·0	25·7	33·2	48·0	—
30	20·4	36·0	51·5	—	—	—

SCHEDULE 9—*continued*

TABLE 10—MINIMUM NUMBER OF EXITS Regulation E4

Occupancy group (1)	Occupancy sub-group (2)	Head no. (3)	Description of flat or storey to which requirement applies (4)	Minimum number of exits (5)
			Part I: Exits from a flat with all rooms on one floor	
A	2	1	The floor is at a height not greater than 11 metres.	1
		2	(*a*) The exit from every apartment other than the living room is directly to a private entrance hall, and (*b*) the entrance door of the flat can be reached from every apartment other than the living room without passing across or within 900 millimetres of the doorway of the living room or kitchen, and (*c*) the doors of any living room or kitchen opening into the entrance hall are self-closing fire-resisting doors.	1
		3	Any other flat on one floor.	2
			Part II: Exits from a flat with rooms on two or more floors	
		1	(*a*) No apartment other than the living room is at a height greater than 11 metres, and (*b*) the stairway descends directly into a private entrance hall.	1
		2	(*a*) Every apartment other than the living room and the normal entrance to the flat are on the lowest floor, and (*b*) the lowest floor is at a height not greater than 24 metres, and (*c*) the living room and kitchen are not on the lowest floor.	1
		3	(*a*) Every apartment other than the living room and the normal entrance to the flat are on the same floor, and (*b*) the living room or kitchen are on a floor below the floor containing any other apartment, and (*c*) the landing of the stairway at the level of the floor above the living room floor is protected by a partition of 30 minutes fire resistance and a self-closing fire-resisting door at the upper or lower level, and (*d*) the level of the floor above the living room floor is at a height not greater than 24 metres.	1
		4	(*a*) Any apartment other than the living room is on a floor other than that on which the normal entrance to the flat is situated, and (*b*) the stairway and private entrance hall are separated from the living room and kitchen by a partition of 30 minutes fire resistance and a self-closing fire-resisting door, and (*c*) no apartment other than the living room is at a height greater than 24 metres.	1
		5	Any other flat on two or more floors.	2

SCHEDULE 9—*continued*

TABLE 10—*continued*

Occupancy group (1)	Occupancy sub-group (2)	Head no. (3)	Description of flat or storey to which requirement applies (4)	Minimum number of exits (5)
A	2		*Part III: Exits from a ground or upper storey of a house of more than two storeys (not being a flat)*	
		1	Any exit from any upper storey is through the living room.	2
		2	Any other case.	1
			Part IV: Exits from the ground and upper storeys of a building other than a storey to which Part III applies	
		1	A storey— (*a*) containing flats of which the rooms are on one floor; and (*b*) at any height; and (*c*) in which the entrance door of every flat— (i) opens into a ventilated common lobby, and (ii) is not more than 4·5 metres from a self-closing fire-resisting door which opens into a common hall or passage from which access to the stairway is by way of a protected doorway, and (iii) is not more than 15 metres from the protected doorway, measured along the route of travel.	1
		2	A storey— (*a*) containing flats of which the rooms are on one floor; and (*b*) at any height; and (*c*) in which the entrance door of every flat— (i) opens into a common hall or passage, and (ii) is not more than 4·5 metres from a self-closing fire-resisting door which gives access to the stairway by way of a ventilated lobby and a protected doorway, and (iii) is not more than 15 metres from the protected doorway, measured along the route of travel.	1
		3	A storey— (*a*) containing flats of which the rooms are on one floor; and (*b*) at any height; and (*c*) in which the entrance door of every flat— (i) opens into a ventilated private lobby, and (ii) is not more than 4·5 metres from a self-closing fire-resisting door which opens into a common hall or passage from which access to the stairway is by way of a protected doorway, and (iii) is not more than 15 metres from the protected doorway, measured along the route of travel.	1

SCHEDULE 9—*continued*

TABLE 10—*continued*

Occupancy group (1)	Occupancy sub-group (2)	Head no. (3)	Description of flat or storey to which requirement applies (4)	Minimum number of exits (5)
A	2	4	A storey— (*a*) containing flats of which the rooms are on one or more floors; and (*b*) at a height not greater than 11 metres; and (*c*) in which the entrance doors of not more than eight flats open into a common hall or passage.	1
		5	A storey— (*a*) containing flats of which the rooms are on one or more floors; and (*b*) at a height not greater than 24 metres; and (*c*) in which two or more flats have access to the stairway by an open access balcony on one side of the block.	1
		6	A storey— (*a*) containing flats of which the rooms are on one or more floors; and (*b*) at any height; and (*c*) in which every flat has access to the stairway by open access balconies on different sides of the block.	1
		7	Any other storey containing flats.	2
	3	8	A storey— (*a*) the floor of which is at a height not greater than 11 metres, and (*b*) whose occupant capacity does not exceed 25.	1
		9	Any other storey.	2
	4	10	Any storey.	2
B	1	11	A storey— (*a*) the floor of which is at a height not greater than 11 metres, and (*b*) whose occupant capacity does not exceed 60, and (*c*) whose area does not exceed 370 square metres.	1
	2	12	A storey— (*a*) the floor of which is at a height not greater than 4·5 metres, and (*b*) in which the travel distance does not exceed 12·5 metres.	1
	1 and 2	13	Any other storey.	2
C	1	14	Any storey.	2

SCHEDULE 9—*continued*

TABLE 10—*continued*

Occupancy group (1)	Occupancy sub-group (2)	Head no. (3)	Description of flat or storey to which requirement applies (4)	Minimum number of exits (5)
C	2	15	A storey— (*a*) the floor of which is at a height not greater than 4·5 metres, and (*b*) whose occupant capacity does not exceed 60 (or, in the case of a storey in a school or part of a school of not more than two storeys, the occupant capacity of that storey does not exceed 120), and (*c*) whose area does not exceed 370 square metres.	1
		16	Any other storey.	2
	3	17	Any storey.	2
D and E	—	18	A storey— (*a*) the floor of which is at a height not greater than 4·5 metres, and (*b*) whose occupant capacity does not exceed 60, and (*c*) whose area does not exceed 370 square metres.	1
		19	Any other storey.	2
			Part V: Basement storeys	
All occupancy groups		1	A basement storey— (*a*) which is used solely for storage purposes or as a heating chamber, and (*b*) the floor of which is not more than 3 metres below the level of the ground to which the exit serving that basement storey gives access.	1
		2	Any other basement storey.	2

In this Table—

"self-closing fire-resisting door" has the meaning assigned to that expression by regulation E2(3);

"ventilated lobby", "ventilated common lobby" and "ventilated private lobby" means, as the case may be, a lobby, common lobby or private lobby which adjoins an external wall and has a permanent ventilation opening in that wall of an area of not less than 1·4 square metres.

SCHEDULE 9—*continued*

TABLE 11—LEVELS OF SOUND INSULATION IN HOUSES Regulation H2

Part I: Airborne sound

Frequency in hertz	Minimum sound reduction in decibels	
	Separating walls—houses other than flats	Separating walls and floors—flats
100	40	36
125	41	38
160	43	39
200	44	41
250	45	43
315	47	44
400	48	46
500	49	48
630	51	49
800	52	51
1000	53	53
1250	55	54
1600	56	56
2000	56	56
2500	56	56
3150	56	56

Part II: Impact sound

Frequency in hertz	Maximum octave-band sound pressure level in decibels for separating floors—flats
100	63
125	64
160	65
200	66
250	66
315	66
400	66
500	66
630	65
800	64
1000	63
1250	61
1600	59
2000	57
2500	55
3150	53

SCHEDULE 9—*continued*

Regulations K3–K7, K9–K11, and K13

TABLE 12—MECHANICAL VENTILATION OF BUILDINGS—RATE OF FRESH AIR SUPPLY

	Minimum rate of supply in cubic metres of fresh air per hour per person		Minimum rate of supply in no. of air changes per hour
A. *Room or apartment (excluding kitchen) with cubic space per occupant*—		Laboratory	4
		Changing room	3
		Gymnasium	3
exceeding 0·25 cubic metre but		Swimming bath	4
not exceeding 8	28	Shower bath	10
exceeding 8 cubic metres but not exceeding 11	20	Anaesthetic room .. .. / Sterilising room .. .. / Operating theatre	10
exceeding 11 cubic metres but not exceeding 14	17	X-ray room .. .. .. / First-aid room .. .. .. / Recovery room	3
exceeding 14 cubic metres ..	12		
	Minimum rate of supply in no. of air changes per hour	Drying room	10
		Cloakroom	2
		Stairway or access way —in building of occupancy sub-group A1 or A2	1
B. *Room with no occupant capacity (including kitchen)*—		—in any other building.. ..	2
Watercloset .. .. .. / Bathroom with W.C. pan ..	3	Storage room	1
		Building for car parking ..	8
Bathroom without W.C. pan .. / Washroom	2	Garage —for repair of vehicles	6
Kitchen—in building of occupancy sub-group A1 or A2	6	—for commercial or public service vehicles	4
—in any other building	20		
Pantry / Larder (exceeding 1·5 cubic metres)	2	Lift machine room	3
		Any other room	1
Servery / Scullery	2		
Laundry	10		
Boiler room	10		

SCHEDULE 9—*continued*

TABLE 13—ASSUMED REFLECTION FACTORS OF SURFACES IN ROOMS

Regulation L5

Room (1)	Assumed reflection factors of surfaces (2)
Kitchen Living room Any other apartment	Walls .. .. 40 per cent Floor .. .. 15 per cent Ceiling .. .. 70 per cent

TABLE 14—MINIMUM DISTANCE (IN METRES) BETWEEN WINDOW OPENINGS

Regulation L10

Angle† at window of house to be erected not more than—

Angle† at window of any other house not more than—		90°	80°	70°	60°	50°	40°	30°	20°	10°	0°
	90°	18	18	18	18	13	9	6	4	3	2
	80°	18	18	18	13	9	6	4	3	2	
	70°	18	18	13	9	6	4	3	2		
	60°	18	13	9	6	4	3	2			
	50°	13	9	6	4	3	2				
	40°	9	6	4	3	2					
	30°	6	4	3	2						
	20°	4	3	2							
	10°	3	2								
	0°	2									

Distances shall be interpolated for intermediate angles

†That is, the horizontal angle included between—

(i) the shortest line joining any part of one window opening to any part of the other, and

(ii) the vertical plane of the opening of the window (see regulation L10).

Schedule 7

SCHEDULE 9—*continued*

TABLE 15—DAYLIGHTING—MINIMUM WIDTH OF WINDOW OPENINGS (ROOMS WITH ONE WINDOW SITUATED IN THE MIDDLE OF THE EXTERNAL WALL)

Part I: Living rooms

Height of head of window opening above floor†		Floor area of room		Width of room measured parallel to window, exceeding (metres)												
Exceeding (metres)	Not exceeding (metres)	Exceeding (square metres)	Not exceeding (square metres)	2·7	3·0	3·3	3·6	3·9	4·2	4·5	4·8	5·1	5·4	5·7	6·0	6·3
(1)	(2)	(3)	(4)	Minimum width of window opening (metres) (5)												
2·4	2·5	23	24	—	—	—	3·25	2·65	2·30	2·07	1·92	1·83	1·80	1·80	1·80	1·80
		22	23	—	—	—	2·80	2·40	2·10	1·85	1·75	1·72	1·71	1·71	1·71	1·71
		21	22	—	—	—	2·57	2·12	1·90	1·67	1·64	1·62	1·62	1·62	1·62	1·62
		20	21	—	—	2·67	2·22	2·00	1·67	1·59	1·55	1·53	1·53	1·53	1·53	1·53
		19	20	—	2·55	2·45	2·00	1·65	1·55	1·48	1·44	1·44	1·44	1·44	1·44	1·44
		18	19	—	2·27	2·05	1·70	1·52	1·42	1·38	1·35	1·35	1·35	1·35	1·35	1·35
		17	18	2·45	1·96	1·75	1·52	1·35	1·29	1·26	1·26	1·26	1·26	1·26	1·26	1·26
		16	17	2·07	1·72	1·57	1·40	1·22	1·20	1·19	1·18	1·18	1·18	1·18	1·18	1·18
		15	16	1·85	1·47	1·42	1·20	1·15	1·12	1·10	1·10	1·10	1·10	1·10	1·10	1·10
		14	15	1·52	1·22	1·17	1·10	1·05	1·02	1·02	1·02	1·02	1·02	1·02	1·02	1·02
		13	14	1·30	1·10	1·05	0·97	0·94	0·93	0·93	0·93	0·93	0·93	0·93	0·93	0·93
		—	13	1·10	0·94	0·88	0·85	0·85	0·85	0·85	0·85	0·85	0·85	0·85	0·85	0·85

2·3	2·4	23	24	—	—	—	—	3·37	2·77	2·45	2·20	2·10	2·07	2·05	2·05	2·05
		22	23	—	—	—	—	2·87	2·55	2·17	2·02	1·98	1·95	1·95	1·95	1·95
		21	22	—	—	—	3·22	2·60	2·20	2·00	1·95	1·88	1·85	1·85	1·85	1·85
		20	21	—	—	—	2·75	2·35	1·97	1·82	1·78	1·75	1·75	1·75	1·75	1·75
		19	20	—	—	3·10	2·45	2·00	1·85	1·72	1·65	1·65	1·65	1·65	1·65	1·65
		18	19	—	2·75	2·52	2·02	1·87	1·62	1·57	1·54	1·54	1·54	1·54	1·54	1·54
		17	18	—	2·40	2·27	1·85	1·60	1·52	1·46	1·44	1·44	1·44	1·44	1·44	1·44
		16	17	—	2·07	1·87	1·62	1·42	1·37	1·34	1·34	1·34	1·34	1·34	1·34	1·34
		15	16	2·30	1·80	1·65	1·42	1·32	1·26	1·24	1·24	1·24	1·24	1·24	1·24	1·24
		14	15	1·85	1·45	1·33	1·23	1·14	1·14	1·14	1·14	1·14	1·14	1·14	1·14	1·14
		13	14	1·55	1·27	1·18	1·08	1·05	1·05	1·05	1·05	1·05	1·05	1·05	1·05	1·05
		—	13	1·30	1·10	1·05	1·00	0·97	0·97	0·97	0·97	0·97	0·97	0·97	0·97	0·97
2·2	2·3	23	24	—	—	—	—	—	3·60	2·92	2·67	2·52	2·44	2·40	2·37	2·37
		22	23	—	—	—	—	3·70	3·15	2·75	2·52	2·34	2·27	2·25	2·25	2·25
		21	22	—	—	—	—	3·37	2·72	2·40	2·22	2·16	2·13	2·13	2·13	2·13
		20	21	—	—	—	—	2·82	2·50	2·15	2·07	2·03	2·02	2·02	2·02	2·02
		19	20	—	—	—	3·15	2·55	2·22	1·97	1·92	1·90	1·90	1·90	1·90	1·90
		18	19	—	—	—	2·57	2·30	1·92	1·85	1·82	1·78	1·78	1·78	1·78	1·78
		17	18	—	—	2·80	2·35	1·87	1·75	1·69	1·65	1·65	1·65	1·65	1·65	1·65
		16	17	—	2·60	2·37	1·92	1·72	1·62	1·55	1·52	1·52	1·52	1·52	1·52	1·52
		15	16	—	2·25	1·95	1·72	1·53	1·47	1·42	1·40	1·40	1·40	1·40	1·40	1·40
		14	15	2·32	1·80	1·70	1·50	1·40	1·35	1·32	1·30	1·30	1·30	1·30	1·30	1·30
		13	14	1·90	1·52	1·42	1·27	1·25	1·23	1·21	1·21	1·21	1·21	1·21	1·21	1·21
		—	13	1·62	1·30	1·25	1·19	1·14	1·12	1·12	1·12	1·12	1·12	1·12	1·12	1·12
2·1	2·2	23	24	—	—	—	—	—	—	3·95	3·47	3·05	2·86	2·80	2·80	2·80
		22	23	—	—	—	—	—	—	3·62	3·07	2·80	2·68	2·65	2·65	2·65
		21	22	—	—	—	—	—	3·65	3·05	2·72	2·60	2·55	2·50	2·50	2·50
		20	21	—	—	—	—	—	3·35	2·72	2·55	2·45	2·40	2·35	2·35	2·35
		19	20	—	—	—	—	3·40	2·72	2·42	2·30	2·24	2·20	2·20	2·20	2·20
		18	19	—	—	—	—	2·77	2·45	2·27	2·15	2·07	2·05	2·05	2·05	2·05
		17	18	—	—	—	2·97	2·47	2·17	2·02	1·91	1·91	1·91	1·91	1·91	1·91
		16	17	—	—	—	2·50	2·07	1·90	1·83	1·78	1·78	1·78	1·78	1·78	1·78
		15	16	—	—	2·52	2·25	1·87	1·75	1·70	1·67	1·67	1·67	1·67	1·67	1·67
		14	15	—	2·35	2·20	1·80	1·66	1·59	1·55	1·55	1·55	1·55	1·55	1·55	1·55
		13	14	2·42	1·92	1·72	1·57	1·50	1·45	1·42	1·42	1·42	1·42	1·42	1·42	1·42
		—	13	2·12	1·57	1·52	1·35	1·30	1·27	1·27	1·27	1·27	1·27	1·27	1·27	1·27

†(a) Height of foot of glazed portion of opening not exceeding 1·15 metres.

(b) The table gives minimum widths for ground floor windows on a level site; the height of window head may be reduced by up to 0·30 metre on floors above the ground floor.

SCHEDULE 9—*continued*

TABLE 15—*continued*

Part I: Living rooms—continued

Height of head of window opening above floor†		Floor area of room		Width of room measured parallel to window, exceeding (metres)												
Exceeding (metres)	Not exceeding (metres)	Exceeding (square metres)	Not exceeding (square metres)	2·7	3·0	3·3	3·6	3·9	4·2	4·5	4·8	5·1	5·4	5·7	6·0	6·3
(1)	(2)	(3)	(4)	Minimum width of window opening (metres) (5)												
2·0	2·1	23	24	—	—	—	—	—	—	—	—	4·05	3·68	3·45	3·37	3·37
		22	23	—	—	—	—	—	—	—	4·17	3·70	3·42	3·21	3·15	3·15
		21	22	—	—	—	—	—	—	4·22	3·60	3·27	3·12	3·02	2·96	2·96
		20	21	—	—	—	—	—	—	3·77	3·17	2·87	2·80	2·80	2·80	2·80
		19	20	—	—	—	—	—	3·75	3·27	2·87	2·70	2·65	2·65	2·65	2·65
		18	19	—	—	—	—	—	3·37	2·77	2·61	2·49	2·49	2·49	2·49	2·49
		17	18	—	—	—	—	3·45	2·67	2·52	2·38	2·32	2·32	2·32	2·32	2·32
		16	17	—	—	—	—	2·75	2·37	2·27	2·18	2·14	2·14	2·14	2·14	2·14
		15	16	—	—	—	2·97	2·37	2·15	2·05	1·97	1·97	1·97	1·97	1·97	1·97
		14	15	—	—	—	2·30	2·00	1·88	1·82	1·82	1·82	1·82	1·82	1·82	1·82
		13	14	—	2·52	2·32	2·05	1·75	1·70	1·67	1·67	1·67	1·67	1·67	1·67	1·67
		—	13	—	2·12	2·07	1·67	1·57	1·52	1·52	1·52	1·52	1·52	1·52	1·52	1·52
—	2·0	23	24	—	—	—	—	—	—	—	—	—	5·02	4·55	4·45	4·40
		22	23	—	—	—	—	—	—	—	—	—	4·52	4·35	3·98	3·95
		21	22	—	—	—	—	—	—	—	—	4·57	4·22	3·77	3·67	3·65
		20	21	—	—	—	—	—	—	—	4·60	4·12	3·65	3·44	3·41	3·41
		19	20	—	—	—	—	—	—	—	4·07	3·65	3·36	3·18	3·18	3·18
		18	19	—	—	—	—	—	—	4·05	3·50	3·20	2·95	2·95	2·95	2·95

	17	18	—	—	—	—	—	—	3·60	3·02	2·82	2·75	2·75	2·75	2·75
	16	17	—	—	—	—	—	3·70	2·87	2·65	2·55	2·55	2·55	2·55	2·55
	15	16	—	—	—	—	3·57	2·82	2·47	2·42	2·37	2·37	2·37	2·37	2·37
	14	15	—	—	—	—	2·70	2·37	2·27	2·22	2·22	2·22	2·22	2·22	2·22
	13	14	—	—	—	2·75	2·30	2·15	2·09	2·07	2·07	2·07	2·07	2·07	2·07
	—	13	—	—	2·77	2·20	2·07	1·97	1·92	1·92	1·92	1·92	1·92	1·92	1·92

†(*a*) Height of foot of glazed portion of opening not exceeding 1·15 metres.
(*b*) The table gives minimum widths for ground floor windows on a level site; the height of window head may be reduced by up to 0·30 metre on floors above the ground floor.

SCHEDULE 9—*continued*

TABLE 15—*continued*

Part II: Kitchens

Height of head of window opening above floor†		Floor area of room		Width of room measured parallel to window, exceeding (metres)									
Exceeding (metres)	Not exceeding (metres)	Exceeding (square metres)	Not exceeding (square metres)	1·2	1·5	1·8	2·1	2·4	2·7	3·0	3·3	3·6	3·9
(1)	(2)	(3)	(4)	Minimum width of window opening (metres) (5)									
2·4	2·5	16	17	—	—	—	1·84	1·33	1·14	1·10	1·10	1·10	1·10
		15	16	—	—	—	1·82	1·33	1·14	1·10	1·10	1·10	1·10
		14	15	—	—	—	1·81	1·33	1·14	1·09	1·09	1·09	1·09
		13	14	—	—	—	1·79	1·32	1·13	1·09	1·09	1·09	1·09
		12	13	—	—	—	1·78	1·32	1·13	1·08	1·08	1·08	1·08
		11	12	—	—	—	1·76	1·32	1·13	1·08	1·08	1·08	1·08
		10	11	—	—	—	1·74	1·31	1·12	1·07	1·07	1·07	1·07
		9	10	—	—	—	1·70	1·30	1·10	1·06	1·06	1·06	1·06
		8	9	—	—	—	1·59	1·23	1·07	1·03	1·03	1·03	1·03
		7	8	—	—	1·65	1·20	1·00	0·93	0·91	0·91	0·91	0·91
		6	7	—	—	1·20	0·92	0·81	0·79	0·79	0·79	0·79	0·79
		5	6	—	1·10	0·88	0·74	0·69	0·68	0·68	0·68	0·68	0·68
		4	5	1·15	0·72	0·63	0·59	0·57	0·57	0·57	0·57	0·57	0·57
		3	4	0·72	0·49	0·47	0·46	0·46	0·46	0·46	0·46	0·46	0·46
		—	3	0·44	0·35	0·35	0·35	0·35	0·35	0·35	0·35	0·35	0·35
2·3	2·4	16	17	—	—	—	—	1·55	1·32	1·24	1·24	1·24	1·24
		15	16	—	—	—	—	1·55	1·31	1·24	1·24	1·24	1·24
		14	15	—	—	—	—	1·54	1·30	1·23	1·23	1·23	1·23
		13	14	—	—	—	—	1·54	1·29	1·23	1·23	1·23	1·23
		12	13	—	—	—	—	1·53	1·29	1·22	1·22	1·22	1·22
		11	12	—	—	—	2·08	1·53	1·28	1·22	1·22	1·22	1·22
		10	11	—	—	—	2·05	1·52	1·27	1·21	1·21	1·21	1·21
		9	10	—	—	—	2·00	1·51	1·26	1·21	1·21	1·21	1·21
		8	9	—	—	—	1·90	1·41	1·22	1·17	1·17	1·17	1·17
		7	8	—	—	—	1·38	1·12	1·04	1·02	1·02	1·02	1·02
		6	7	—	—	1·40	1·05	0·92	0·89	0·89	0·89	0·89	0·89
		5	6	—	1·27	1·00	0·80	0·77	0·76	0·76	0·76	0·76	0·76
		4	5	—	0·82	0·70	0·65	0·63	0·63	0·63	0·63	0·63	0·63
		3	4	0·82	0·55	0·53	0·51	0·50	0·50	0·50	0·50	0·50	0·50
		—	3	0·48	0·39	0·38	0·38	0·38	0·38	0·38	0·38	0·38	0·38

2·2	2·3	16	17	—	—	—	—	1·87	1·50	1·37	1·37	1·37	1·37
		15	16	—	—	—	—	1·87	1·50	1·37	1·37	1·37	1·37
		14	15	—	—	—	—	1·86	1·50	1·37	1·37	1·37	1·37
		13	14	—	—	—	—	1·86	1·49	1·37	1·37	1·37	1·37
		12	13	—	—	—	—	1·85	1·49	1·36	1·36	1·36	1·36
		11	12	—	—	—	—	1·84	1·48	1·36	1·36	1·36	1·36
		10	11	—	—	—	—	1·83	1·47	1·36	1·36	1·36	1·36
		9	10	—	—	—	—	1·79	1·46	1·36	1·36	1·36	1·36
		8	9	—	—	—	—	1·68	1·40	1·31	1·31	1·31	1·31
		7	8	—	—	—	1·67	1·29	1·16	1·13	1·13	1·13	1·13
		6	7	—	—	1·68	1·20	1·00	0·97	0·97	0·97	0·97	0·97
		5	6	—	—	1·17	0·93	0·84	0·82	0·82	0·82	0·82	0·82
		4	5	—	0·95	0·79	0·71	0·68	0·68	0·68	0·68	0·68	0·68
		3	4	0·95	0·60	0·57	0·55	0·55	0·55	0·55	0·55	0·55	0·55
		—	3	0·52	0·42	0·42	0·42	0·42	0·42	0·42	0·42	0·42	0·42
2·1	2·2	16	17	—	—	—	—	2·35	1·78	1·57	1·57	1·57	1·57
		15	16	—	—	—	—	2·34	1·78	1·57	1·57	1·57	1·57
		14	15	—	—	—	—	2·34	1·77	1·57	1·57	1·57	1·57
		13	14	—	—	—	—	2·33	1·77	1·56	1·56	1·56	1·56
		12	13	—	—	—	—	2·32	1·76	1·56	1·56	1·56	1·56
		11	12	—	—	—	—	2·31	1·76	1·56	1·56	1·56	1·56
		10	11	—	—	—	—	2·28	1·75	1·55	1·55	1·55	1·55
		9	10	—	—	—	—	2·22	1·75	1·55	1·55	1·55	1·55
		8	9	—	—	—	—	2·12	1·65	1·49	1·49	1·49	1·49
		7	8	—	—	—	—	1·54	1·36	1·30	1·30	1·30	1·30
		6	7	—	—	—	1·44	1·18	1·13	1·11	1·11	1·11	1·11
		5	6	—	—	1·39	1·09	0·96	0·93	0·93	0·93	0·93	0·93
		4	5	—	1·14	0·92	0·79	0·76	0·76	0·76	0·76	0·76	0·76
		3	4	1·14	0·70	0·64	0·60	0·59	0·59	0·59	0·59	0·59	0·59
		—	3	0·59	0·46	0·46	0·46	0·46	0·46	0·46	0·46	0·46	0·46

†(*a*) Height of foot of glazed portion of opening not exceeding 1·15 metres.
(*b*) The table gives minimum widths for ground floor windows on a level site; the height of window head may be reduced by up to 0·30 metre on floors above the ground floor.

SCHEDULE 9—*continued*

TABLE 15—*continued*

Part II: Kitchens—continued

Height of head of window opening above floor†		Floor area of room		Width of room measured parallel to window, exceeding (metres)									
Exceeding (metres)	Not exceeding (metres)	Exceeding (square metres)	Not exceeding (square metres)	1·2	1·5	1·8	2·1	2·4	2·7	3·0	3·3	3·6	3·9
(1)	(2)	(3)	(4)	Minimum width of window opening (metres) (5)									
2·0	2·1	16	17	—	—	—	—	—	2·22	1·86	1·84	1·83	1·83
		15	16	—	—	—	—	—	2·22	1·86	1·84	1·83	1·83
		14	15	—	—	—	—	—	2·21	1·86	1·84	1·83	1·83
		13	14	—	—	—	—	—	2·21	1·85	1·83	1·82	1·82
		12	13	—	—	—	—	—	2·20	1·85	1·83	1·82	1·82
		11	12	—	—	—	—	—	2·19	1·84	1·82	1·81	1·81
		10	11	—	—	—	—	—	2·17	1·84	1·82	1·81	1·81
		9	10	—	—	—	—	—	2·14	1·83	1·82	1·81	1·81
		8	9	—	—	—	—	—	2·00	1·78	1·73	1·73	1·73
		7	8	—	—	—	—	1·92	1·55	1·49	1·49	1·49	1·49
		6	7	—	—	—	1·85	1·43	1·29	1·27	1·27	1·27	1·27
		5	6	—	—	1·78	1·28	1·11	1·07	1·07	1·07	1·07	1·07
		4	5	—	1·42	1·10	0·93	0·87	0·87	0·87	0·87	0·87	0·87
		3	4	—	0·85	0·75	0·71	0·69	0·69	0·69	0·69	0·69	0·69
		—	3	0·69	0·52	0·52	0·52	0·52	0·52	0·52	0·52	0·52	0·52
—	2·0	16	17	—	—	—	—	—	—	2·35	2·33	2·25	2·20
		15	16	—	—	—	—	—	—	2·35	2·32	2·24	2·19
		14	15	—	—	—	—	—	—	2·34	2·30	2·23	2·18
		13	14	—	—	—	—	—	—	2·34	2·28	2·22	2·17
		12	13	—	—	—	—	—	—	2·33	2·26	2·20	2·16
		11	12	—	—	—	—	—	—	2·32	2·23	2·18	2·15

		10	11	—	—	—	—	—	—	2·31	2·20	2·16	2·13
		9	10	—	—	—	—	—	—	2·30	2·18	2·11	2·11
		8	9	—	—	—	—	—	—	2·18	2·08	2·03	2·03
		7	8	—	—	—	—	—	2·01	1·75	1·75	1·75	1·75
		6	7	—	—	—	—	1·84	1·56	1·50	1·50	1·50	1·50
		5	6	—	—	—	1·62	1·34	1·26	1·26	1·26	1·26	1·26
		4	5	—	—	1·44	1·10	1·04	1·03	1·03	1·03	1·03	1·03
		3	4	—	1·08	0·88	0·84	0·81	0·81	0·81	0·81	0·81	0·81
		—	3	0·85	0·63	0·62	0·62	0·62	0·62	0·62	0·62	0·62	0·62

†(*a*) Height of foot of glazed portion of opening not exceeding 1·15 metres.
(*b*) The table gives minimum widths for ground floor windows on a level site; the height of window head may be reduced by up to 0·30 metre on floors above the ground floor.

SCHEDULE 9—*continued*

TABLE 15—*continued*

Part III: Apartments other than living rooms

Height of head of window opening above floor†		Floor area of room		Width of room measured parallel to window, exceeding (metres)										
Exceeding (metres)	Not exceeding (metres)	Exceeding (square metres)	Not exceeding (square metres)	1·8	2·1	2·4	2·7	3·0	3·3	3·6	3·9	4·2	4·5	4·8
(1)	(2)	(3)	(4)	Minimum width of window opening (metres) (5)										
2·4	2·5	16	17	—	—	1·40	1·02	0·87	0·78	0·70	0·65	0·62	0·62	0·62
		15	16	—	1·65	1·20	0·92	0·72	0·65	0·60	0·57	0·57	0·57	0·57
		14	15	—	1·37	0·97	0·75	0·63	0·57	0·54	0·52	0·52	0·52	0·52
		13	14	—	1·12	0·83	0·65	0·55	0·52	0·49	0·47	0·47	0·47	0·47
		12	13	1·47	0·97	0·70	0·55	0·47	0·44	0·42	0·42	0·42	0·42	0·42
		11	12	1·10	0·82	0·57	0·45	0·42	0·39	0·38	0·38	0·38	0·38	0·38
		10	11	0·90	0·67	0·47	0·40	0·36	0·35	0·35	0·35	0·35	0·35	0·35
		9	10	0·70	0·52	0·40	0·35	0·32	0·32	0·32	0·32	0·32	0·32	0·32
		8	9	0·55	0·40	0·34	0·30	0·28	0·28	0·28	0·28	0·28	0·28	0·28
		7	8	0·42	0·32	0·28	0·25	0·25	0·25	0·25	0·25	0·25	0·25	0·25
		6	7	0·32	0·25	0·22	0·22	0·22	0·22	0·22	0·22	0·22	0·22	0·22
		5	6	0·22	0·20	0·18	0·18	0·18	0·18	0·18	0·18	0·18	0·18	0·18
		—	5	0·17	0·15	0·15	0·15	0·15	0·15	0·15	0·15	0·15	0·15	0·15
2·3	2·4	16	17	—	—	1·75	1·25	1·05	0·95	0·82	0·75	0·70	0·70	0·70
		15	16	—	—	1·45	1·12	0·88	0·82	0·72	0·68	0·65	0·65	0·65
		14	15	—	1·67	1·17	0·90	0·74	0·69	0·65	0·62	0·60	0·60	0·60
		13	14	—	1·37	1·07	0·77	0·66	0·61	0·57	0·55	0·55	0·55	0·55
		12	13	—	1·15	0·82	0·65	0·55	0·52	0·50	0·50	0·50	0·50	0·50
		11	12	1·32	0·92	0·67	0·54	0·50	0·47	0·45	0·45	0·45	0·45	0·45
		10	11	1·07	0·80	0·55	0·45	0·40	0·40	0·40	0·40	0·40	0·40	0·40
		9	10	0·82	0·60	0·47	0·37	0·35	0·35	0·35	0·35	0·35	0·35	0·35
		8	9	0·65	0·47	0·35	0·32	0·30	0·30	0·30	0·30	0·30	0·30	0·30
		7	8	0·50	0·35	0·32	0·28	0·27	0·27	0·27	0·27	0·27	0·27	0·27
		6	7	0·37	0·27	0·24	0·24	0·24	0·24	0·24	0·24	0·24	0·24	0·24
		5	6	0·25	0·22	0·20	0·20	0·20	0·20	0·20	0·20	0·20	0·20	0·20
		—	5	0·20	0·17	0·17	0·17	0·17	0·17	0·17	0·17	0·17	0·17	0·17

2·2	2·3	16	17	—	—	—	1·57	1·27	1·15	1·00	0·87	0·85	0·85	0·85
		15	16	—	—	1·85	1·39	1·10	1·00	0·87	0·82	0·77	0·77	0·77
		14	15	—	—	1·47	1·12	0·90	0·82	0·76	0·72	0·70	0·70	0·70
		13	14	—	1·75	1·35	0·95	0·77	0·71	0·67	0·65	0·64	0·64	0·64
		12	13	—	1·42	1·05	0·80	0·65	0·61	0·58	0·58	0·58	0·58	0·58
		11	12	—	1·15	0·82	0·62	0·56	0·52	0·52	0·52	0·52	0·52	0·52
		10	11	1·32	0·97	0·67	0·55	0·49	0·47	0·47	0·47	0·47	0·47	0·47
		9	10	1·00	0·75	0·57	0·46	0·41	0·41	0·41	0·41	0·41	0·41	0·41
		8	9	0·77	0·55	0·40	0·38	0·36	0·35	0·36	0·36	0·36	0·36	0·36
		7	8	0·60	0·42	0·36	0·33	0·32	0·32	0·32	0·32	0·32	0·32	0·32
		6	7	0·45	0·34	0·30	0·27	0·27	0·27	0·27	0·27	0·27	0·27	0·27
		5	6	0·30	0·25	0·23	0·23	0·23	0·23	0·23	0·23	0·23	0·23	0·23
		—	5	0·20	0·20	0·20	0·20	0·20	0·20	0·20	0·20	0·20	0·20	0·20
2·1	2·2	16	17	—	—	—	2·10	1·67	1·52	1·22	1·10	1·02	0·98	0·95
		15	16	—	—	—	1·92	1·45	1·25	1·07	0·94	0·88	0·88	0·88
		14	15	—	—	1·95	1·50	1·15	1·01	0·92	0·84	0·82	0·82	0·82
		13	14	—	—	1·82	1·20	0·95	0·84	0·79	0·75	0·75	0·75	0·75
		12	13	—	1·87	1·37	1·02	0·80	0·76	0·72	0·69	0·69	0·69	0·69
		11	12	—	1·47	1·05	0·80	0·70	0·67	0·62	0·62	0·62	0·62	0·62
		10	11	—	1·27	0·82	0·67	0·58	0·55	0·55	0·55	0·55	0·55	0·55
		9	10	1·30	0·95	0·70	0·52	0·50	0·48	0·48	0·48	0·48	0·48	0·48
		8	9	0·97	0·70	0·53	0·44	0·42	0·42	0·42	0·42	0·42	0·42	0·42
		7	8	0·72	0·52	0·40	0·37	0·35	0·35	0·35	0·35	0·35	0·35	0·35
		6	7	0·52	0·37	0·32	0·30	0·30	0·30	0·30	0·30	0·30	0·30	0·30
		5	6	0·35	0·30	0·27	0·25	0·25	0·25	0·25	0·25	0·25	0·25	0·25
		—	5	0·25	0·22	0·20	0·20	0·20	0·20	0·20	0·20	0·20	0·20	0·20

†(*a*) Height of foot of glazed portion of opening not exceeding 1·15 metres.

(*b*) The table gives minimum widths for ground floor windows on a level site; the height of window head may be reduced by up to 0·30 metre on floors above the ground floor.

SCHEDULE 9—*continued*

TABLE 15—*continued*

Part III: Apartments other than living rooms—continued

Height of head of window opening above floor†		Floor area of room		Width of room measured parallel to window, exceeding (metres)										
Exceeding (metres)	Not exceeding (metres)	Exceeding (square metres)	Not exceeding (square metres)	1·8	2·1	2·4	2·7	3·0	3·3	3·6	3·9	4·2	4·5	4·8
				Minimum width of window opening (metres)										
(1)	(2)	(3)	(4)	(5)										
2·0	2·1	16	17	—	—	—	—	2·35	2·20	1·70	1·37	1·25	1·22	1·20
		15	16	—	—	—	—	1·90	1·70	1·52	1·22	1·14	1·10	1·10
		14	15	—	—	—	2·12	1·57	1·47	1·17	1·07	1·02	1·00	1·00
		13	14	—	—	—	1·68	1·25	1·12	1·05	0·94	0·91	0·91	0·91
		12	13	—	—	1·95	1·42	1·02	0·94	0·83	0·82	0·82	0·82	0·82
		11	12	—	—	1·42	1·05	0·82	0·77	0·74	0·74	0·74	0·74	0·74
		10	11	—	1·80	1·10	0·85	0·68	0·67	0·67	0·67	0·67	0·67	0·67
		9	10	—	1·30	0·92	0·65	0·60	0·60	0·60	0·60	0·60	0·60	0·60
		8	9	1·30	0·90	0·65	0·54	0·52	0·52	0·52	0·52	0·52	0·52	0·52
		7	8	0·95	0·65	0·49	0·45	0·45	0·45	0·45	0·45	0·45	0·45	0·45
		6	7	0·67	0·45	0·40	0·37	0·37	0·37	0·37	0·37	0·37	0·37	0·37
		5	6	0·42	0·35	0·32	0·30	0·30	0·30	0·30	0·30	0·30	0·30	0·30
		—	5	0·30	0·25	0·22	0·22	0·22	0·22	0·22	0·22	0·22	0·22	0·22
—	2·0	16	17	—	—	—	—	—	—	2·60	1·97	1·70	1·62	1·60
		15	16	—	—	—	—	2·75	2·60	2·10	1·72	1·47	1·40	1·37
		14	15	—	—	—	—	2·45	2·16	1·65	1·45	1·32	1·27	1·25
		13	14	—	—	—	2·45	1·80	1·65	1·42	1·24	1·15	1·13	1·13
		12	13	—	—	—	2·22	1·50	1·45	1·15	1·07	1·02	1·02	1·02
		11	12	—	—	2·17	1·52	1·14	1·07	0·95	0·92	0·92	0·92	0·92
		10	11	—	—	1·55	1·15	0·95	0·88	0·83	0·82	0·82	0·82	0·82
		9	10	—	—	1·22	0·92	0·76	0·72	0·72	0·72	0·72	0·72	0·72
		8	9	—	1·32	0·90	0·67	0·64	0·63	0·63	0·63	0·63	0·63	0·63
		7	8	1·32	0·90	0·65	0·57	0·54	0·54	0·54	0·54	0·54	0·54	0·54
		6	7	0·92	0·60	0·52	0·47	0·45	0·45	0·45	0·45	0·45	0·45	0·45
		5	6	0·57	0·42	0·38	0·36	0·36	0·36	0·36	0·36	0·36	0·36	0·36
		—	5	0·37	0·32	0·27	0·27	0·27	0·27	0·27	0·27	0·27	0·27	0·27

†(*a*) Height of foot of glazed portion of opening not exceeding 1·15 metres.
(*b*) The table gives minimum widths for ground floor windows on a level site; the height of window head may be reduced by up to 0·30 metre on floors above the ground floor.

SCHEDULE 9—*continued*

Schedule 7

TABLE 16—DAYLIGHTING—PERCENTAGE ADDITIONS TO WINDOW OPENING WIDTHS ACCORDING TO TYPE OF WINDOW INSTALLED

Metal windows		Wood casements		Wood sash and case	
Unbarred	Barred	Unbarred	Barred	Unbarred	Barred
+6%	+16%	+12%	+20%	+25%	+30%

Regulations Q5, Q6, Q8 and Q11

TABLE 17—STANDARDS OF HOUSING ACCOMMODATION

Size of house (1)	Number of apartments (other than living room) less than 10 square metres (2)	Minimum area in square metres of— Aggregate area of living room and kitchen‡ (3)	Kitchen (4)	Aggregate area of apartments other than living room (5)	Minimum capacity in cubic metres of— Larder and dry goods store (6)	Linen and general storage (7)
One apartment	—	†23	4·2	†	0·68	4·8
Two apartments	Nil	20	4·6	11	0·85	5·0
	One	16	2·8	8·8	0·68	4·8
Three apartments	Nil	25	7·0	22	1·25	9·3
	One	23	6·5	18	1·25	9·3
	Two	20	4·6	16	0·85	5·0
Four apartments	Nil	28	7·0	33	1·70	9·5
	One	28	7·0	29	1·42	9·5
	Two	25	7·0	25	1·25	9·3
	Three	23	6·5	21	1·25	9·3
Five apartments	Nil	28	7·0	45	1·70	9·6
	One	28	7·0	40	1·70	9·6
	Two	28	7·0	36	1·70	9·5
	Three	28	7·0	32	1·42	9·5
	Four	25	7·0	28	1·25	9·3
Six or more apartments	—	28	7·0	Four of the apartments shall have a minimum area equal to the appropriate area for a five apartment house	1·70	9·6

†In the case of a one apartment house the figure given in column (3) includes sleeping accommodation.

‡The area specified in this column includes any part of a living room or kitchen reserved for dining.

Regulation Q19

SCHEDULE 9—*continued*

TABLE 18—SPACE STANDARDS FOR HOUSES

Part A—Net space and general storage space

House type		Net space (N) General storage space (S)	Minimum area in square metres for a house designed to accommodate the following numbers of persons— (3)						
(1)		(2)	1	2	3	4	5	6	7
Occupancy sub-group A1	Single storey	N	30	44·5	57	67	75·5	84	—
		S	3	4	4	4·5	4·5	4·5	—
	Two storey (detached, semi-detached or end terrace)	N	—	—	—	72	82	92·5	108
		S	—	—	—	4·5	4·5	4·5	6·5
	Two storey (intermediate terrace)	N	—	—	—	74·5	85	92·5	108
		S	—	—	—	4·5	4·5	4·5	6·5
Occupancy sub-group A2	Three storey	N	—	—	—	—	94	98	112
		S	—	—	—	—	4·5	4·5	6·5
	Flat	N	30	44·5	57	70*	79	86·5	—
		S	2·5	3	3	3·5	3·5	3·5	—
	Maisonette	N	—	—	—	72	82	92·5	108
		S	—	—	—	3·5	3·5	3·5	3·5

*(67 square metres if access to the flat is by means of a balcony).

Tolerance: Where any house is designed on a planning grid a negative tolerance not exceeding 1½ per cent is permitted on the net space.

Part B—Kitchen storage space

	Minimum capacity in cubic metres of the ventilated larder	Total minimum capacity in cubic metres of kitchen storage space for a house designed to accommodate the following numbers of persons— (3)						
(1)	(2)	1	2	3	4	5	6	7
Where provision is made for a refrigerator	0·17	1·7	1·7	2·3	2·3	2·3	2·3	2·3
Where no provision is made for a refrigerator	0·34	1·87	1·87	2·47	2·47	2·47	2·47	2·47

Part C—Cupboards for linen storage

	Total minimum capacity in cubic metres for a house designed to accommodate the following numbers of persons— (2)						
(1)	1	2	3	4	5	6	7
Aggregate capacity of cupboard or cupboards for linen storage	0·4	0·4	0·4	0·6	0·6	0·6	0·6

SCHEDULE 10

Regulation A12

Deemed-to-satisfy Specifications

A. Interpretation of Schedule 10

1. Subject to paragraphs (4) and (5) of regulation A3, where any specification in this Schedule requires a material, component, design, method of construction or operation to conform to a British Standard or to be based on the recommendations of a British Standard Code of Practice or other publication the reference in the specification to the British Standard, Code of Practice or other publication shall be taken to be a reference only to so much of the British Standard, Code of Practice or other publication as is relevant to the material, component, design, method of construction or operation in the circumstances in which it is proposed to be used.

2. Any reference in this Schedule to a specification only by a number shall be construed as referring to the specification so numbered which is deemed to satisfy the same provision of the same regulation as that in relation to which the reference appears.

3. Any expression used in or in relation to a specification in this Schedule shall have the same meaning as in the regulation which is deemed to be satisfied by that specification.

4. Any reference in a specification in this Schedule to—

(*a*) a dimension shall, unless the context otherwise requires, be taken to be a reference to any dimension not less than that so stated;

(*b*) a mix of materials by reference to proportionate parts of each material shall, unless the context otherwise requires, be construed as a reference to proportions measured by volume.

5. In this Schedule—

"BS" means British Standard;

"CP" means British Standard Code of Practice.

SCHEDULE 10—*continued*

B. Specifications

Provision of regulation deemed to be satisfied	Element of structure or fitting	Case dealt with or relevant conditions	Specification
		Part B—Materials and durability	
B1	All	The use of a material for a purpose and in conditions dealt with in a British Standard Code of Practice	(*a*) The material conforms to the relevant British Standard†, if any, as to quality; (*b*) it is selected, prepared and used in accordance with the recommendations of the British Standard Code of Practice†, and having regard to the principles and recommendations contained in CP 3: Chapter IX: 1950—"Durability".
		The use of a material for a purpose and in conditions not dealt with in a British Standard Code of Practice	(*a*) The material conforms to a British Standard† as to quality; (*b*) the use of the material is appropriate to the purpose and conditions for and in which it is used.

†Latest edition as at 31st December 1970, including any amendments thereto, published at that date.

Provision of regulation deemed to be satisfied	Element of structure or fitting	Case dealt with or relevant conditions	Specification
		Part C—Structural strength and stability	
C2(1)—as to design and construction	Foundations	Building of not more than two storeys comprising house, houses or school	(1) The design and construction of the foundations are in accordance with CP 101: 1963.
		Building of more than two storeys or if two storeys or less not comprising house, houses or school	(2) The design and construction of the foundations are based on the Institution of Civil Engineers Code of Practice No. 4.
C2(2)—as to design and construction	Loadbearing structure	—of steel	(1) The design and construction of the structure conform to BS 449: Part 2: 1969 as read with Amendments AMD 416, January 1970, AMD 523, May 1970 and AMD 661, December 1970.
		—of reinforced concrete	(2) The design and construction of the structure are in accordance with CP 114: Part 2: 1969.

		—of timber	(3) The design and construction of the structure are in accordance with CP 112: 1967.
		—of natural stone, bricks or blocks or of unreinforced in situ concrete	(4) The design and construction of the structure are in accordance with CP 111: Part 2: 1970.
		—of bricks or blocks in a building of more than two storeys comprising houses	(5) The design of the wall is based on CP 111: Part 2: 1970 and the construction thereof is in accordance with the Scottish Development Department Explanatory Memorandum on the Building Standards (Scotland) Regulations "Structural Strength and Stability".
		—of prestressed concrete	(6) The design and construction of the structure are in accordance with CP 115: Part 2: 1969.
		—of aluminium ..	(7) The design, erection and protection of the structure are in accordance with CP 118: 1969.
		—of pre-cast concrete ..	(8) The design and construction of the structure are in accordance with CP 116: Part 2: 1969 and Addendum No. 1 (1970).
		—of composite construction in structural steel and concrete	(9) The design and construction are in accordance with CP 117: Part 1: 1965 and CP 117: Part 2: 1967.
C3(4)(*b*)—as to localising any structural failure within each storey	Any structural member	Buildings of five or more storeys in height: removal of any portion of any one structural member	The area within which structural failure would occur does not exceed 70 square metres or 15 per cent of the area of the storey, measured in horizontal plane, whichever is the less.

Part D—Structural fire precautions

D20(2)—as to distance of groups of garages from boundary	All	—not exceeding 3 metres in height	No garage shall be nearer the boundary of the site than the distance specified below—

No. of garages to be erected on site	Distance from boundary (metres)
Not more than 4	4·3
Exceeding 4 but not more than 6	4·9
Exceeding 6 but not more than 10	5·5
Exceeding 10 but not more than 24	5·8

SCHEDULE 10—*continued*

Provision of regulation deemed to be satisfied	Element of structure or fitting	Case dealt with or relevant conditions	Specification
D23(6)—as to design and construction	Fuel oil storage tanks	—	The design and construction of the tank conforms to— Sections 6 and 7 of BS 799:Part 1: 1962, or Sections 8 and 9 of BS 799: Part 2: 1964, or BS 2594: 1955 as read with Amendments PD 2242, July 1955, PD 4517, April 1962 and PD 5411, December 1964, or BS 2654: Part 1: 1965 as read with Amendments PD 5942, November 1966, PD 6130, April 1967, PD 6383, April 1968 and AMD 397, January 1970.
D23(6)—as to fitting of safety devices	Safety devices to fuel oil storage tanks	—	Safety devices are fitted conforming to Section 7 of BS 799: Part 1: 1962 or Section 9 of BS 799: Part 2: 1964.
Part F—Chimneys, flues, hearths and the installation of heat producing appliances			
F4(1)(*a*)—as to thickness and strength of cast iron	Flue-pipe	Appliance designed to burn solid fuel or oil	The flue-pipe conforms to BS 41: 1964.
F13(5)—as to linings	Fireplace openings	Opening for inset open fire	The design and construction of the fireback conforms to BS 1251: 1970.
F20	Fireguard fitting	—	The screwed bushes or plugs fitted with screwed eyelets conform to BS 2788: 1956 as read with Amendments PD 2884, August 1957, PD 3615, December 1959 and PD 3801, May 1960.
F21(1)—as to suitability of materials in chimneys and flue-pipes for gas burning appliances	Chimney	Chimney serves any type of gas burning appliance	(1) Constructed of bricks, dense or aerated concrete blocks, or natural stone with one of the following flue linings— (*a*) acid-resistant tiles embedded and pointed in acid-resistant cement mortar; (*b*) glass enamelled or salt-glazed fireclay pipes, jointed and pointed in acid-resistant cement mortar; (*c*) asbestos cement pipes, the inside wall being coated with an acid-resistant compound prepared from— (i) vinyl acetate polymer, or (ii) a rubber derivative base compound; (*d*) parging composed of acid-resistant cement mortar.

		(2) (*a*) Constructed of dense concrete blocks and made either— (i) wholly of acid-resistant cement, or (ii) with the inside wall of acid-resistant cement; (*b*) jointed and pointed with acid-resistant cement mortar.
	Chimney serves boiler, circulator, storage water heater or air heater	(3) (*a*) Any part of chimney more than 3 metres† above appliance—as for Specification (1); (*b*) any other part —constructed of bricks, dense concrete blocks, or natural stone.
		(4) (*a*) Any part of chimney more than 3 metres† above appliance—as for Specification (2); (*b*) any other part—constructed of dense concrete blocks.
	Chimney serves instantaneous water heater or drying cabinet	(5) (*a*) Any part of chimney more than 6 metres† above appliance—as for Specification (1); (*b*) any other part—constructed of bricks, dense concrete blocks, or natural stone.
	Chimney serves— (i) instantaneous water heater or drying cabinet (ii) radiant or convector gas fire	(6) (*a*) Any part of chimney more than 6 metres† above appliance—as for Specification (2); (*b*) any other part—constructed of dense concrete blocks.
	Chimney serves convector gas fire and has flue of aspect ratio not exceeding 3 to 1	(7) (*a*) Any part of chimney more than 9 metres† above appliance—as for Specification (1); (*b*) any other part—constructed of bricks, dense concrete blocks, or natural stone.
		(8) (*a*) Any part of chimney more than 9 metres† above appliance—as for Specification (2); (*b*) any other part—constructed of dense concrete blocks.
	Chimney serves radiant gas fire and has flue of aspect ratio not exceeding 3 to 1	(9) (*a*) Any part of chimney more than 12 metres† above appliance—as for Specification (1); (*b*) any other part—constructed of bricks, dense concrete blocks, or natural stone.

SCHEDULE 10—*continued*

Provision of regulation deemed to be satisfied	Element of structure or fitting	Case dealt with or relevant conditions	Specification
F21(1)—as to suitability of materials in chimneys and flue-pipes for gas burning appliances—*cont.*	Chimney—*cont.*	Chimney serves radiant gas fire and has flue of aspect ratio not exceeding 3 to 1—*cont.*	(10) (*a*) Any part of chimney more than 12 metres† above appliance—as for Specification (2); (*b*) any other part—constructed of dense concrete blocks.
	Flue-pipe	Flue-pipe serves any type of gas burning appliance	(11) Glass enamelled or salt-glazed fireclay pipes, jointed and pointed with acid-resistant cement mortar.
			(12) Asbestos cement pipes with joints of an acid-resistant compound and the inner wall of the pipes coated with an acid-resistant compound prepared from— (*a*) vinyl acetate polymer, or (*b*) a rubber derivative base compound.
			(13) Mild steel or cast iron pipes, in each case the inner wall having a coating of acid-resistant vitreous enamel.
			(14) Double walled pipes with 7 millimetres to 15 millimetres air space between the walls.
		Flue-pipe serves boiler, circulator, storage water heater or air heater	(15) (*a*) Any part of the flue-pipe more than 3 metres‡ above appliance—as for one of the Specifications (11) to (14); (*b*) any other part—asbestos cement pipes, jointed and pointed with acid-resistant cement mortar.
		Flue-pipe serves instantaneous water heater or drying cabinet	(16) (*a*) Any part of the flue-pipe more than 6 metres‡ above appliance—as for one of the Specifications (11) to (14); (*b*) any other part—asbestos cement pipes, jointed and pointed with acid-resistant cement mortar.

		Flue-pipe serves convector gas fire	(17) (*a*) Any part of the flue-pipe more than 9 metres‡ above the appliance—as for one of the Specifications (11) to (14); (*b*) any other part—asbestos cement pipes, jointed and pointed with acid-resistant cement mortar.
		Flue-pipe serves radiant gas fire	(18) (*a*) Any part of the flue-pipe more than 12 metres‡ above the appliance—as for one of the Specifications (11) to (14); (*b*) any other part—asbestos cement pipes, jointed and pointed with acid-resistant cement mortar.
F29—as to construction and design	Heat producing appliance	Appliance burns gas of type in gas groups G3, G4 and G5 as set out in paragraph A2 of Appendix A to BS 1250: Part 1: 1966.	(1) Appliance conforms to— BS 1250: Part 1: 1966, Part 2: 1963 as read with Amendment PD 5391, November 1964, Part 3: 1963 as read with Amendment PD 5852, June 1966, Part 4: 1965, Part 5: 1963 as read with Amendments PD 5449, January 1965 and PD 5587, July 1965 and Part 6: 1965 as read with Amendment PD 5805, March 1966 or BS 2512: 1963 as read with Amendment PD 5676, November 1965.
		Appliance burns butane or propane	(2) Appliance conforms to— BS 2491: 1963 as read with Amendments PD 5016, August 1963, PD 5082, November 1963 and PD 5667, October 1965, BS 2773: 1965 as read with Amendment PD 5779, February 1966 or BS 2883: 1964 as read with Amendment PD 5659, October 1965.

†If the chimney does not form part of an external wall these figures to be doubled.

‡If the flue-pipe is neither attached to the outside of an external wall nor forms part of an external wall these figures to be doubled.

Part G—Preparation of sites and resistance to the passage of moisture—particular specifications†

G2—as to draining of site and ground in vicinity of building	Sub-soil drain	Not passing through or under a building	(*a*) Pipes conform to BS 1194: 1969, BS 1196: 1944 as read with Amendment PD 2069, December 1954 or BS 2760: Part 1: 1966 as read with Amendment AMD 516, May 1970; (*b*) they are laid in accordance with CP 303: 1952.
G6—as to treatment of solum	Solum	Solum for solid floor of concrete laid directly thereon and incorporating a damp-proof course	(1) (*a*) The solum is brought to a level surface; (*b*) a layer of bottoming 100 millimetres thick, free from fine material, as chemically inert as is practicable, is laid thereon; (*c*) the layer is blinded with suitable fine material and consolidated to form a level crack-free surface.

†A number of general specifications relating to this Part of this Schedule and referred to in this Part are set forth in Schedule 11.

SCHEDULE 1C—*continued*

Provision of regulation deemed to be satisfied	Element of structure or fitting	Case dealt with or relevant conditions	Specification
G6—as to treatment of solum—*cont.*	Solum—*cont.*	Solum separated from lowest floor of timber by an air space	(2) (*a*) The level of the solum is upfilled to the level of the adjoining ground with hard dry material; (*b*) and (*c*) as for Specification (1)(*b*) and (*c*); (*d*) the surface is covered by a continuous layer of damp-resisting coating conforming to BS 2832: 1957 applied hot.
		Solum separated from lowest floor of concrete by an air space	(3) The solum is brought to a level surface.
G7—as to resistance to moisture from the ground	Floor	Solid floor of concrete laid directly on the solum and incorporating a damp-proof course	(1) (*a*) The solum is treated in accordance with Specification (1) for regulation G6; (*b*) there is laid thereon a layer of concrete— (i) having a mix of 1:3:6 (cement: fine aggregate: coarse aggregate) using not more than 31 litres suitable mixing water to 50 kilogrammes of cement, and (ii) of a thickness of 90 millimetres, or where a damp-proof course is placed within its thickness, 75 millimetres below the damp-proof course and 50 millimetres above; (*c*) there is provided immediately below, or within the thickness of the concrete layer a damp-proof course which— (i) is of a material conforming to BS 743: 1970, and (ii) is continuous throughout the whole floor area, and (iii) is continuous with or joined and sealed to the damp-proof course or damp-proof structure in every adjoining wall, pier, buttress, column or chimney.
		Lowest floor of timber separated from the solum by an air space	(2) (*a*) The solum is treated in accordance with Specification (2) for regulation G6; (*b*) the separating air space— (i) is of a depth of 150 millimetres measured vertically below the underside of the lowest part of the floor structure, and (ii) is ventilated by openings in the walls surrounding and intersecting it, such openings being so placed as to ensure ventilation of every part of the underside of the floor structure;

		(*c*) there are, in the external walls, openings which allow 3000 square millimetres of open area per metre run of external wall for the purpose of ventilating the said space and are sealed from any cavity in any wall through which they pass, such openings being provided with gratings conforming to BS 493: Part 2: 1970; (*d*) ducts are formed through any solid floor or hearth which interferes with the adequate ventilation of the said space; (*e*) the floor is so positioned in relation to a wall, pier, buttress, column or chimney as to be protected from moisture rising from the ground through any such wall, pier, buttress, column or chimney.
	Lowest floor of concrete separated from the solum by an air space	(3) (*a*) The solum is brought to a level surface; (*b*) the floor is of— (i) in situ concrete, or (ii) precast concrete units having interlocking or mortar filled butt joints.
Wall, pier, buttress, column, chimney or other element of structure in contact with the ground	The element has no damp-proof course	(4) To a height of not less than 150 millimetres above the finished level of the adjoining ground— (*a*) the element is of dense vibrated concrete; (*b*) the concrete is of a mix suitable for the mode of vibration adopted and incorporates— (i) cement conforming to BS 12: 1958 as read with Amendments PD 3729, April 1960, PD 4676, November 1962 and AMD 198, January 1969, or BS 146: 1958 as read with Amendments PD 3733, April 1960, PD 4699, November 1962 and PD 6092, March 1967 (unless the ground conditions require a more chemically resistant cement), and (ii) aggregate conforming to BS 882: 1965, and (iii) is thoroughly compacted by vibrating; (*c*) any joint is so formed as to prevent the passage of moisture to the inner surface of the building.
		(5) To a height of not less than 150 millimetres above the finished level of the adjoining ground— (*a*) the element is built of— (i) clay engineering bricks, or (ii) granite blocks, conforming in either case to the appropriate specification listed in column (1) of Part I of Schedule 11; (*b*) the mortar conforms to the appropriate specification listed in column (1) of Part II of Schedule 11; (*c*) as for Specification (4)(*c*).

SCHEDULE 10—*continued*

Provision of regulation deemed to be satisfied	Element of structure or fitting	Case dealt with or relevant conditions	Specification
G7—as to resistance to moisture from the ground—*cont.*	Wall, etc.—*cont.*	The element has a damp-proof course	(6) (*a*) To a height of not less than 150 millimetres above the finished level of the adjoining ground the element is of dense concrete of a mix of 1:2:4 (cement: fine aggregate: coarse aggregate) incorporating— (i) not more than 29 litres of suitable mixing water per 50 kilogrammes of cement, and (ii) and (iii) cement and aggregate as for Specification (4)(*b*) (i) and (ii); (*b*) the element has a damp-proof course of a material conforming to BS 743: 1970; (*c*) the damp-proof course— (i) is so arranged as to seal any path by which moisture may otherwise pass from the ground to the inner surface of the building, (ii) extends at every point to, or is placed at a height of, not less than 150 millimetres above the finished level of the adjoining ground, (iii) is joined with and sealed to any damp-proof course in any adjoining structure, and (iv) extends through the thickness of each leaf of a cavity structure but not across the cavity; (*d*) any cavity in the element extends to a depth of not less than 150 millimetres below the damp-proof course.
			(7) (*a*) To a height of not less than 150 millimetres above the finished level of the adjoining ground— (i) the element is built of bricks or blocks conforming to the appropriate specification listed in column (1) of Part I of Schedule 11, and (ii) the mortar conforms to the appropriate specification listed in column (1) of Part II of Schedule 11; (*b*), (*c*) and (*d*) as for Specification (6)(*b*), (*c*) and (*d*).
G8—as to resistance to moisture from rain or snow	External wall	Solid wall of bricks, blocks, slabs or natural stone of building in occupancy group A or occupancy sub-group B1, which under nor-	(1) Between the level of the main damp-proof construction and the junction of the wall with the roof— (*a*) the wall is of material conforming to the appropriate specification listed in column (2) of Part I of Schedule 11 and of a thickness of— (i) 250 millimetres when the material is autoclaved aerated concrete blocks or slabs, or

	mal conditions is liable to severe conditions of exposure as specified in the Building Research Station Digest No. 23 (Second Series) "An index of exposure to driving rain".	(ii) 340 millimetres for any other material; (*b*) the mortar conforms to the appropriate specification listed in column (2) of Part II of Schedule 11; (*c*) any external rendering conforms to the appropriate specification listed in columns (1) to (5) of Part III of Schedule 11; (*d*) the wall has a damp-proof course or flashing of material conforming to BS 743: 1970 so arranged at openings and at intrusions of other elements in the wall as to seal any path by which moisture may otherwise pass from the exterior of the building to its inner surface; (*e*) the wall, when a material other than autoclaved aerated concrete blocks or slabs is used, is strapped and lined internally with— (i) timber straps having a thickness of 19 millimetres and treated with an inodorous non-staining preservative, and (ii) lined with plaster on lath or plasterboard or other suitable material.
	Solid wall of bricks, blocks, slabs or natural stone of building in occupancy group A or occupancy sub-group B1, when the wall is not liable under normal conditions to severe conditions of exposure as specified in the Building Research Station Digest No. 23 (Second Series) "An index of exposure to driving rain".	(2) Between the level of the main damp-proof construction and the junction of the wall with the roof— (*a*) the wall is of material conforming to the appropriate specification listed in column (2) of Part I of Schedule 11 and of a thickness of— (i) 200 millimetres when the material is autoclaved aerated concrete blocks or slabs, or (ii) 225 millimetres for any other material; (*b*), (*c*), (*d*) and (*e*) as for Specification (1)(*b*), (*c*), (*d*) and (*e*).
	Cavity wall of bricks, blocks or natural stone	(3) Between the level of the top of the main damp-proof construction and the junction of the wall with the roof— (*a*) any leaf of the wall is 75 millimetres in thickness and the cavity is 50 millimetres in width; (*b*) the wall is built of material conforming to the appropriate specification listed in column (2) of Part I of Schedule 11; (*c*) the mortar conforms to the appropriate specification listed in column (2) of Part II of Schedule 11; (*d*) any external rendering conforms to the appropriate specification listed in columns (1) to (5) of Part III of Schedule 11;

SCHEDULE 10—*continued*

Provision of regulation deemed to be satisfied	Element of structure or fitting	Case dealt with or relevant conditions	Specification
G8—as to resistance to moisture from rain or snow—*cont.*	External wall—*cont.*	Cavity wall of bricks, blocks or natural stone —*cont.*	(*e*) the wall ties are so laid and every duct and pipe that bridges the cavity is so positioned as to resist the passage of moisture from the exterior of the building to its inner surface; (*f*) the wall has a damp-proof course and flashing of material conforming to BS 743: 1970 so arranged as to seal any path by which moisture may otherwise pass from the exterior of the building to its inner surface where— (i) the cavity is bridged other than by a wall-tie, duct or pipe, (ii) any part of the inner leaf or any beam, lintel, plate or other part of the structure bearing on or inserted in the inner leaf of the wall intrudes into the cavity, or (iii) any sill or other part of the structure intrudes into the cavity from the outer leaf of the wall in such a way as would otherwise permit moisture to pass to the inner surface of the wall; (*g*) the wall-ties and any other part of the structure which bridges the cavity are kept clear of all mortar droppings; (*h*) the cavity is cleared of all mortar droppings and building debris.
		No-fines concrete wall . .	(4) Between the level of the top of the main damp-proof construction and the junction of the wall with the roof— (*a*) the wall is built of no-fines concrete to the appropriate specification (*a*) or (*b*) listed in column (2) of Part I of Schedule 11 and its thickness is— (i) if specification (*a*), 250 millimetres, or (ii) if specification (*b*), 300 millimetres; (*b*) the wall is externally rendered and the rendering conforms to the appropriate specification listed in columns (1) to (5) of Part III of Schedule 11; (*c*) the wall has a damp-proof course and flashing as for Specification (1)(*d*); (*d*) the wall is finished internally with— (i) a directly applied plaster finish of a thickness of 12·5 millimetres, or (ii) straps and lining in accordance with Specification (1)(*e*).
		Timber wall which under normal conditions is not liable to severe	(5) Between the level of the top of the main damp-proof construction and the junction of the wall with the roof— (*a*) it has a frame of timber standards and dwangs;

	conditions of exposure as specified in the Building Research Station Digest No. 23 (Second Series) "An index of exposure to driving rain".	(*b*) the exterior of the wall is clad with— (i) boarding not less than 21 millimetres in thickness with rebated or tongued and grooved joints, fixed vertically with boards not more than 100 millimetres wide or fixed horizontally with boards not more than 150 millimetres wide, or (ii) tapered boarding not less than 21 millimetres in thickness at the thicker edge and not more than 150 millimetres wide, fixed horizontally either lapped or with rebated joints and in either case the boarding conforms to the appropriate specification listed in column (2) of Part I of Schedule 11; (*c*) a membrane of bituminous felt conforming to BS 747: Part 2: 1970 type (1C) is fixed between the standards and the boarding mentioned in paragraphs (*a*) and (*b*) of this Specification and sealed where necessary to any damp-proof course mentioned in the next succeeding paragraph of this Specification; (*d*) a damp-proof course of material conforming to BS 743: 1970 is arranged at floor levels and at openings in the wall so as to seal any path by which moisture may otherwise pass from the exterior of the building to its inner surface.
	Solid or cavity wall of bricks, blocks or natural stone which extends to 225 millimetres or more above the junction of the wall with the roof	(6) (*a*) Between the junction of the wall with the roof and the top of the wall— (i) the wall is built of materials conforming to the appropriate specification listed in column (1) of Part I of Schedule 11, (ii) the mortar conforms to the appropriate specification listed in column (1) of Part II of Schedule 11, (iii) any external rendering conforms to the appropriate specification listed in columns (1) to (5) of Part III of Schedule 11, and in the case of a solid parapet wall rendering is applied to one face only; (*b*) the wall is protected at its top by— (i) a damp-resisting cope constructed of stone or of pre-cast dense concrete thoroughly compacted by vibrating or pressing, projecting on both sides of the wall, throated on the underside of the projections and weathered on top to conduct rainwater to the roof side, (ii) copper sheeting conforming to BS 2870: 1968 as read with Amendment AMD 428, February 1970 and of 0·7 millimetre thickness properly laid, dressed and lapped (all laps being clinked) and shaped to form drips clear of the faces of the wall, or (iii) in the case of a solid parapet wall a layer of asphalt conforming to BS 1162, 1410, 1418: 1966; or BS 988, 1097, 1076, 1451: 1966 as read with Amendments PD 6154, May 1967 and AMD 419, January 1970 properly laid and dressed over the wall;

SCHEDULE 10—*continued*

Provision of regulation deemed to be satisfied	Element of structure or fitting	Case dealt with or relevant conditions	Specification
G8—as to resistance to moisture from rain or snow—*cont.*	External wall—*cont.*	Solid or cavity wall of bricks, blocks or natural stone which extends to 225 millimetres or more above the junction of the wall with the roof—*cont.*	(*c*) where the wall is protected at its top by a cope as specified in paragraph (*b*)(i) of this Specification it has a continuous damp-proof course of a material conforming to BS 743: 1970 placed between the cope and the top of the wall and extending throughout the thickness of the wall including any surface finish or cavity; (*d*) where it abuts a roof the wall is provided with a continuous damp-proof course and flashing— (i) of a material conforming to BS 743: 1970, and (ii) at a height of not less than 150 millimetres nor more than 300 millimetres from the highest point at which the wall abuts on the roof and the damp-proof course; (*e*) the damp-proof course extends throughout the thickness of the wall, and if the wall is a cavity wall, is sloped upwards across the cavity from the roof side leaf of the wall to a higher level in the other leaf; (*f*) the flashing is so arranged that— (i) where the roof covering or gutter adjoining the wall is in the form of a continuous sheet it is continuous with the sheet or is so jointed thereto as to prevent the passage of moisture into or through the junction, or (ii) where the roof covering or gutter adjoining the wall is not in the form of a continuous sheet it prevents the passage of moisture to the inner surface of the building in conjunction with the roof covering or gutter.
		Solid or cavity wall of bricks, blocks or natural stone which extends to less than 225 millimetres above the junction of the wall with the roof	(7) (*a*), (*b*) and (*c*) as for Specification (6)(*a*), (*b*) and (*c*); (*d*) the damp-proof course beneath the cope, copper sheeting or asphalt protecting the top of the wall is brought down and so arranged as described for flashings in Specification (6)(*f*).
	Wall partly external	Wall of coursed brick, block or natural stone	(8) (*a*) A damp-proof course and flashing of material conforming to BS 743: 1970 are inserted in the wall so as to extend along the wall the full length of

	with roofs abutting at different levels—flat roof abutting at a lower level than the roof on the other side of the wall	the abutment of the lower roof at a height of not less than 150 millimetres above the abutment; (*b*) where the wall is a cavity wall the damp-proof course is stepped upwards from the lower roof within the thickness of the wall; (*c*) the flashing is so arranged in relation to the lower roof that it conforms to Specification (6)(*f*).
	Wall of coursed brick, block or natural stone with roofs abutting at different levels—pitched roof abutting at a lower level than the roof on the other side of the wall	(9) (*a*) A damp-proof course and flashing of a material conforming to BS 743: 1970 are inserted in the wall; (*b*) the damp-proof course is— (i) laid in several horizontal lengths at different heights within the depth between the levels of the two abutments, each length overlapping the length beneath it in such a manner as to prevent the passage of moisture from the exposed surface of the wall to its inner surface, or (ii) stepped down each course to follow the slope of the lower roof abutment and at any part at a height of not less than 150 millimetres above that abutment, and where the wall is of cavity construction, stepped upwards from the lower roof within the thickness of the wall; (*c*) the flashing is so arranged in relation to the lower roof as to comply with Specification (6)(*f*).
Chimney stack	Chimney stack in contact with roof—of bricks, blocks or natural stone rendered externally where the height from the underside of the upper ceiling joists to the lowest point of intersection of the stack and roof covering is more than 760 millimetres	(10) (*a*) The materials conform to the appropriate specification listed in column (1) of Part I of Schedule 11; (*b*) the mortar conforms to the appropriate specification listed in column (1) of Part II of Schedule 11; (*c*) the rendering conforms to the appropriate specification listed in columns (1) to (5) of Part III of Schedule 11 and is applied at the external surfaces of the stack between the cope and where it contacts the roof; (*d*) the stack is protected at its top by a damp-resisting cope constructed of stone or pre-cast dense concrete thoroughly compacted by vibrating or pressing which projects beyond the face of the stack on all sides, is weathered on top, throated on the underside of the projections and all chimney cans are bedded thereon and haunched in mortar; (*e*) where such a cope is not in one piece, a continuous damp-proof course of material conforming to BS 743: 1970 is placed between the cope and the top of the chimney stack and extends throughout the thickness of the stack including the flues and their linings; (*f*) at the junction of the stack and the roof a flashing of material conforming to BS 743: 1970 is so arranged in conjunction with the roof covering or gutter as to conform to Specification (6)(*f*).

SCHEDULE 10—*continued*

Provision of regulation deemed to be satisfied	Element of structure or fitting	Case dealt with or relevant conditions	Specification
G8—as to resistance to moisture from rain or snow—*cont.*	Chimney stack —*cont.*	Chimney stack in contact with roof— (A) of bricks, blocks or natural stone rendered externally where the height from the underside of the upper ceiling joists to the lowest point of intersection of the stack and roof covering is 760 millimetres or less, or (B) of facing bricks or blocks or natural stone	(11) (*a*) to (*e*) as for Specification (10)(*a*) to (*e*); (*f*) a damp-proof course and flashing of material conforming to BS 743: 1970 is inserted in the stack above its junction with the roof; (*g*) the damp-proof course mentioned in the last foregoing paragraph— (i) is at a height of not less than 150 millimetres nor more than 300 millimetres above the highest point at which the chimney is in contact with the roof, and (ii) extends throughout the chimney stack excluding the flues and their linings; (*h*) the flashing mentioned in paragraph (*f*) of this specification is so arranged that in conjunction with the roof covering or gutter it conforms to Specification (6)(*f*).
	Roof	Slated or tiled roof ..	(12) The slates or tiles are laid and fixed in accordance with CP 142: 1968 as read with Amendments AMD 491, April 1970 and AMD 601, September 1970.
		Lead roof	(13) The lead is laid and fixed in accordance with CP 143: Part 11: 1970.
		Copper roof	(14) The copper is laid and fixed in accordance with CP 143: Part 12: 1970.
		Zinc roof	(15) The zinc shall be laid and fixed in accordance with CP 143: Part 5 : 1964.
		Aluminium roof ..	(16) The aluminium is laid and fixed in accordance with— (*a*) CP 143: Part 1: 1958 as read with Amendment PD 4346, October 1961, and (*b*) CP 143: Part 7: 1965.

	Galvanised corrugated steel roof	(17) The steel is laid and fixed in accordance with CP 143: Part 2: 1961.
	Corrugated asbestos cement roof	(18) The asbestos cement is laid and fixed in accordance with CP 143: Part 6: 1962.
	Flat glass roof in patent glazing	(19) The flat glass is laid and fixed in accordance with CP 145: Part 1: 1969.
	Mastic asphalted roof ..	(20) The mastic asphalt is laid and fixed in accordance with CP 144: Part 4: 1970.
	Bitumen felted roof ..	(21) The bitumen felt is laid and fixed in accordance with CP 144: Part 3: 1970.
	Cedar shingled roof with a slope of not less than 14°	(22) (*a*) The shingles are of timber of Canadian Western Red Cedar of no lower grading commercially than Grade No. 1, and (*b*) they are treated by a vacuum/pressure impregnation process with a wood preservative of water-borne copper/chrome/arsenic composition conforming to BS 4072: 1966, and (*c*) they are laid to a gauge of 95 millimetres with one lap of 216 millimetres, a second lap of 120 millimetres and a third lap of 25 millimetres, and (*d*) they are fixed direct through underslating felt conforming to BS 747: Part 2: 1970 to a background of sarking of not less than 19 millimetres thick, and (*e*) the fixing nails are of copper 30 millimetres × 2·3 millimetres diameter with 4·8 millimetres diameter heads or of silicon bronze 30 millimetres × 1·8 millimetres diameter with 4·8 millimetres diameter heads, and (*f*) each shingle is held by two nails driven in at not more than 19 millimetres from the sides of the shingle and not less than 25 millimetres and not more than 50 millimetres above the gauge line.
	Cedar shingled roof with a slope of not less than 22½°	(23) (*a*) as for Specification (22)(*a*), and (*b*) as for Specification (22)(*b*), and (*c*) as for Specification (22)(*c*), or they are laid to a gauge of 125 millimetres with one lap of 150 millimetres and a second lap of 25 millimetres, and (*d*) as for Specification (22)(*d*), and (*e*) as for Specification (22)(*e*), and (*f*) as for Specification (22)(*f*).

SCHEDULE 10—*continued*

Provision of regulation deemed to be satisfied	Element of structure or fitting	Case dealt with or relevant conditions	Specification
		Part H—Resistance to the transmission of sound	
H2(1)—as to sound insulation of walls	Separating wall†	Walls of houses including flats—solid construction	(1) 225 millimetres brick with 12·5 millimetres plaster on both sides and having a weight of 490 kilogrammes per square metre.
		Condition— Each end of the separating wall either— (*a*) extends for a distance of 460 millimetres beyond an external flanking wall, or (*b*) ties into an external flanking wall— (i) in which any windows and door openings within 690 millimetres on either side of the junction are not less than 690 millimetres apart measured horizontally, and (ii) which is of a construction of a weight and mass not less than one-half the weight and mass of any of the Specifications (1) to (5)	(2) 360 millimetres sandstone with 12·5 millimetres plaster on both sides.
			(3) 175 millimetres dense concrete with 12·5 millimetres plaster on both sides and having a weight of 460 kilogrammes per square metre.
			(4) 200 millimetres dense concrete block with 12·5 millimetres plaster on both sides and having a weight of 460 kilogrammes per square metre.
			(5) 250 millimetres no-fines concrete with 12·5 millimetres plaster on both sides including behind ends of abutting partitions and having a weight of 440 kilogrammes per square metre.

		Walls of houses including flats—cavity construction	(6) Two leaves, 100 millimetres brick 50 millimetres wide cavity, butterfly wire ties, with 12·5 millimetres plaster on both sides and having a weight of 490 kilogrammes per square metre.
		Condition—as for condition to Specifications (1) to (5)	(7) Two leaves, 100 millimetres dense concrete block 50 millimetres wide cavity, butterfly wire ties, with 12·5 millimetres plaster on both sides and having a weight of 460 kilogrammes per square metre.
			(8) Two leaves, 75 millimetres clinker block (1520 kilogrammes per cubic metre) 75 millimetres wide cavity, butterfly wire ties, with 12·5 millimetres plaster on both sides and having a weight of 250 kilogrammes per square metre.
		Walls of flats only—solid construction	(9) 150 millimetres dense in situ concrete with 12·5 millimetres plaster on both sides and having a weight of 415 kilogrammes per square metre.
		Condition—as for condition to Specifications (1) to (5)	(10) 360 millimetres sandstone strapped and plasterboard-lined on each side.
		Walls of flats only—cavity construction	(11) Two leaves, 75 millimetres clinker block (1520 kilogrammes per cubic metre) 50 millimetres wide cavity, butterfly wire ties, with 12·5 millimetres plaster on both sides and having a weight of 250 kilogrammes per square metre.
		Condition—as for condition to Specifications (1) to (5)	(12) Two leaves, 100 millimetres autoclaved aerated concrete (960 kilogrammes per cubic metre and having an absorption coefficient of 4) 75 millimetres wide cavity, butterfly wire ties, with 12·5 millimetres plaster on both sides and having a weight of 250 kilogrammes per square metre.

†In the case of a wall dividing houses within the roof space of a building—

(*a*) where the wall is a solid wall, one-half of the thickness of that specified with no plaster on either side;

(*b*) except in the case of Specification (12), where the wall is a cavity wall, one leaf of the type specified.

SCHEDULE 10—*continued*

Provision of regulation deemed to be satisfied	Element of structure or fitting	Case dealt with or relevant conditions	Specification
H2(1) and H2(2)—as to sound insulation of floors	Separating floors	Floor of a flat separated from another flat by a separating wall—concrete floors	(1) Resilient finish of rubber on sponge rubber underlay 4·5 millimetres thick or of cork tiles, laid on solid concrete slab 150 millimetres thick inclusive of any levelling screed and having a weight of 365 kilogrammes per square metre.
		Condition— The separating floor ties in at opposite ends to an external flanking wall which— (*a*) at each junction extends for not less than 600 millimetres vertically measured from the underside of the floor without any window or door opening therein, other than a window or door opening above a balcony forming an extension to the floor, and (*b*) is of a construction of a weight and mass not less than one-half the weight and mass of any of the Specifications (1) to (5) for regulation H2(1)	(2) Wood raft laid to float upon a resilient layer which conforms to CP 3: Chapter III: 1960 (Appendix B, paragraph 7(*d*)), which will retain its resilience under imposed loading, laid on— (*a*) solid concrete slab 100 millimetres thick and having a weight of 220 kilogrammes per square metre; (*b*) slab of concrete beams and hollow clay or concrete infilling blocks and having a weight of 220 kilogrammes per square metre; (*c*) slab of hollow concrete beams of box section and having a weight of 220 kilogrammes per square metre; or (*d*) slab of concrete beams of inverted trough section and having a weight of 220 kilogrammes per square metre.
			(3) Concrete screed (whether or not incorporating heating elements) and any directly applied covering laid to float upon a resilient layer which conforms to CP 3: Chapter III: 1960 (Appendix B, paragraph 7(*d*)) which will retain its resilience under imposed loading, laid on— (*a*) solid concrete slab 100 millimetres thick and having a weight of 220 kilogrammes per square metre; (*b*) slab of concrete beams and hollow clay or concrete infilling blocks and having a weight of 220 kilogrammes per square metre; (*c*) slab of hollow concrete beams of box section and having a weight of 220 kilogrammes per square metre; or (*d*) slab of concrete beams of inverted trough section and having a weight of 220 kilogrammes per square metre.
		Floor of a flat separated from another flat by a separating wall—timber floors	(4) (*a*) Wood joisted floor bounded by walls of 225 millimetres solid brickwork or other materials equivalent to 225 millimetres brickwork on at least three sides;

		Condition—as for condition to Specifications (1) to (3)	(*b*) with a wood raft laid to float upon a resilient layer which conforms to CP 3: Chapter III: 1960 (Appendix B, paragraph 7(*d*)) retaining its resilience under imposed loading; (*c*) 80 kilogrammes per square metre granular deafening on 12·5 millimetres plasterboard nailed to underside of joists and dwangs; and (*d*) a brandered ceiling of plaster 19 millimetres thick on metal lath.

Part J—Resistance to the transmission of heat

J3(1)—as to thermal insulation	Roof	Pitched roof of slates or tiles on roofing felt on (*a*) boarding (other than sarking) not less than 12·5 millimetres thick, or (*b*) sarking not less than 16 millimetres thick, or (*c*) water-repellent plasterboard foil-faced on one side not less than 9·5 millimetres thick	(1) Any of the following layers laid on and in contact with the ceiling with an air space between the layer and the roof boarding— (*a*) nodulated mineral wool or glass fibre, 25 millimetres thick; (*b*) gypsum granules, 25 millimetres thick; (*c*) exfoliated vermiculite, 25 millimetres thick; (*d*) combined corrugated and flat aluminium foil, corrugations in contact with the ceiling; (*e*) foamed or expanded sheeting of plastic or rubber 19 millimetres thick having a density not exceeding 80 kilogrammes per cubic metre.
			(2) Any of the following layers laid over the ceiling joists but not in contact with the ceiling, with an air space between the layer and the roof boarding— (*a*) mat or quilt of glass fibre or mineral wool, 25 millimetres thick; (*b*) reinforced paper faced with aluminium foil on both sides; (*c*) foamed or expanded sheeting of plastic or rubber 12·5 millimetres thick having a density not exceeding 80 kilogrammes per cubic metre.
			(3) A ceiling of aluminium foil-backed plasterboard and a layer of polythene film or building paper lapped at joints, laid over and securely fixed to the ceiling joists but not in contact with the ceiling and with an air space between the layer and the roof boarding.
			(4) Any of the following layers with an air space between the layer and the roof boarding— (*a*) wood wool slabs, 38 millimetres thick; (*b*) compressed straw slabs, 50 millimetres thick; (*c*) mat of glass fibre or mineral wool, 25 millimetres thick; (*d*) fibre insulation board, 19 millimetres thick; (*e*) foamed or expanded sheeting of plastic or rubber 19 millimetres thick and having a density not exceeding 80 kilogrammes per cubic metre.

SCHEDULE 10—*continued*

Provision of regulation deemed to be satisfied	Element of structure or fitting	Case dealt with or relevant conditions	Specification
J3(1)—as to thermal insulation—*cont.*	Roof—*cont.*	Pitched or flat roof of any waterproof material bonded to a layer of insulation on top of a vapour barrier fixed to (*a*) boarding (other than sarking) not less than 12·5 millimetres thick, or (*b*) sarking not less than 16 millimetres thick	(5) Any of the following layers, the entire surface of which should be bonded to a vapour barrier of bitumen felt which complies with BS 747: Part 2: 1970 (Section 1.5 Type 1C) having a weight of not less than 13 kilogrammes per 10 square metres and nailed or bonded to the boarding or sarking in accordance with CP 144: Part 3: 1970; the roof thus formed to be left exposed on the underside or to be in conjunction with a ceiling comprising 9·5 millimetres thick plasterboard or other sheet or boarding having a minimal thermal resistance and having no insulation laid thereon e.g., (*a*) fibre insulation board not less than 19 millimetres thick; (*b*) foamed or expanded plastic sheeting 19 millimetres thick and having a density not exceeding 80 kilogrammes per cubic metre; (*c*) resin bonded glass or mineral wool 19 millimetres thick; (*d*) cork sheeting 19 millimetres thick; (*e*) compressed straw slabs 50 millimetres thick.
		Pitched or flat roof of in situ concrete with any waterproof covering and with a ceiling comprising any kind of board lining backed by a suitable vapour barrier and fixed to branders not less than 19 millimetres thick secured to the underside of the concrete	(6) Any of the following layers laid over the concrete between it and the waterproof covering— (*a*) wood wool slabs, 38 millimetres thick; (*b*) a screed of concrete made with vermiculite, 63 millimetres thick, having a mix of 1:5 to 1:8 cement and vermiculite; (*c*) a screed of aerated concrete, 63 millimetres thick and having a density not exceeding 640 kilogrammes per cubic metre; (*d*) a screed of concrete made with foamed slag, expanded clay or sintered pulverised fuel ash, 100 millimetres thick, having a mix of 1:8 to 1:10 cement and aggregate.
		Pitched or flat roof of concrete with any waterproof covering	(7) The concrete is reinforced autoclaved aerated concrete not less than 125 millimetres thick and having a density not exceeding 720 kilogrammes per cubic metre.

		Pitched or flat roof of concrete cast in situ or precast with a bitumen felt covering laid in accordance with CP 144: Part 3: 1970 as a system comprising fibre insulation board and layers of bitumen felt and with a ceiling comprising any kind of board lining backed by a vapour barrier, and fixed to branders not less than 19 millimetres thick secured to the underside of the concrete	(8) (*a*) A layer of fibre insulation board 19 millimetres thick either bonded directly to the concrete with hot applied bitumen coating or bonded to a layer of bitumen felt that is lapped and sealed at all joints and is itself bonded to the concrete so that in either case a vapour barrier is formed between the concrete and the fibre insulation board, and (*b*) a covering of three layers of bitumen felt, bonded overall to the fibre insulation board in such a way that at all times the fibre insulation board is protected against the penetration of moisture.
J4(1)—as to thermal insulation	External wall excluding window and other glazed openings	Unventilated cavity wall having a cavity not greater than 75 millimetres nor less than 50 millimetres	(1) (*a*) Outer leaf of clay, concrete, sand-lime brick or block having a density not exceeding 2400 kilogrammes per cubic metre, 100 millimetres thick, rendered or unrendered; (*b*) inner leaf of— (i) clay, concrete, sand-lime brick or block having a density not exceeding 2400 kilogrammes per cubic metre, 100 millimetres thick, or (ii) lightweight concrete block having a density not exceeding 1440 kilogrammes per cubic metre, 75 millimetres thick; (*c*) internal finish of plaster, 12·5 millimetres thick.
			(2) (*a*) Outer leaf of— (i) freestone, 125 millimetres thick, or (ii) whinstone or granite, 250 millimetres thick; (*b*) inner leaf of— (i) clay, concrete, sand-lime brick or block having a density not exceeding 2400 kilogrammes per cubic metre, 100 millimetres thick, or (ii) lightweight concrete block having a density not exceeding 1440 kilogrammes per cubic metre, 75 millimetres thick; (*c*) internal finish of plaster 12·5 millimetres thick.

SCHEDULE 10—*continued*

Provision of regulation deemed to be satisfied	Element of structure or fitting	Case dealt with or relevant conditions	Specification
J4(1)—as to thermal insulation—*cont.*	External wall excluding window and other glazed openings—*cont.*	Unventilated cavity wall having a cavity not greater than 75 millimetres nor less than 50 millimetres—*cont.*	(3) (*a*) As for Specification (1)(*a*) or (2)(*a*); (*b*) inner leaf of— (i) lightweight concrete block having a density not exceeding 1440 kilogrammes per cubic metre, 100 millimetres thick, or (ii) lightweight concrete block having a density not exceeding 1120 kilogrammes per cubic metre, 75 millimetres thick; (*c*) internal finish of plaster, 12·5 millimetres thick.
			(4) (*a*) As for Specification (1)(*a*) or (2)(*a*); (*b*) inner leaf of— clay, concrete, sand-lime brick or block having a density not exceeding 2400 kilogrammes per cubic metre, 100 millimetres thick; (*c*) internal finish of plasterboard 10 millimetres thick, on strapping 19 millimetres thick.
			(5) (*a*) As for Specification (1)(*a*) or (2)(*a*); (*b*) inner leaf of— (i) lightweight concrete block having a density not exceeding 1120 kilogrammes per cubic metre, 100 millimetres thick, or (ii) lightweight concrete block having a density not exceeding 800 kilogrammes per cubic metre, 75 millimetres thick; (*c*) internal finish of plaster, 12·5 millimetres thick.
			(6) (*a*) As for Specification (1)(*a*) or (2)(*a*); (*b*) as for Specification (2)(*b*); and (*c*) (i) internal finish of aluminium foil-backed plasterboard, 10 millimetres thick, on strapping 19 millimetres thick, or (ii) an internal finish of 12·5 millimetres insulation board having a density not exceeding 400 kilogrammes per cubic metre, with a finishing coat of plaster, on strapping 19 millimetres thick.
			(7) (*a*) As for Specification (1)(*a*) or (2)(*a*); (*b*) as for Specification (2)(*b*); and

(*c*) (i) internal finish of 25 millimetres insulation board having a density not exceeding 400 kilogrammes per cubic metre, with a finishing coat of plaster, on strapping 19 millimetres thick, or

(ii) internal finish of 12·5 millimetres aluminium foil-backed insulation board having a density not exceeding 400 kilogrammes per cubic metre with a finishing coat of plaster on strapping 19 millimetres thick.

(8) (*a*) As for Specification (1)(*a*) or (2)(*a*);

(*b*) inner leaf of lightweight concrete block having a density not exceeding 800 kilogrammes per cubic metre, 125 millimetres thick;

(*c*) internal finish of plaster, 12·5 millimetres thick.

(9) (*a*) As for Specification (1)(*a*) or (2)(*a*);

(*b*) inner leaf of—

(i) lightweight concrete block having a density not exceeding 800 kilogrammes per cubic metre, 100 millimetres thick, or

(ii) lightweight concrete block having a density not exceeding 1120 kilogrammes per cubic metre, 125 millimetres thick; and

(*c*) (i) internal finish of plasterboard, 10 millimetres thick on strapping 19 millimetres thick, or

(ii) internal finish of 12·5 millimetres insulation board having a density not exceeding 400 kilogrammes per cubic metre with a finishing coat of plaster on strapping 19 millimetres thick.

(10) (*a*) As for Specification (1)(*a*) or (2)(*a*);

(*b*) inner leaf of lightweight concrete block having a density not exceeding 800 kilogrammes per cubic metre, 100 millimetres thick; and

(*c*) (i) internal finish of plasterboard, 10 millimetres thick, on strapping 19 millimetres thick with the interspace between the blockwork and the plasterboard filled with glass fibre or mineral wool, or

(ii) internal finish of 25 millimetres aluminium foil-backed insulation board having a density not exceeding 400 kilogrammes per cubic metre with a finishing coat of plaster on strapping 19 millimetres thick.

(11) (*a*) As for Specification (1)(*a*) or (2)(*a*);

(*b*) inner leaf of lightweight concrete block having a density not exceeding 640 kilogrammes per cubic metre, 200 millimetres thick;

(*c*) internal finish of plaster, 12·5 millimetres thick.

(12) (*a*) Outer leaf of rendered lightweight aggregate concrete blocks having a density not exceeding 1440 kilogrammes per cubic metre, 75 millimetres thick;

(*b*) inner leaf of lightweight concrete blocks having a density not exceeding 1440 kilogrammes per cubic metre, 75 millimetres thick;

(*c*) internal finish of plaster 12·5 millimetres thick.

SCHEDULE 10—*continued*

Provision of regulation deemed to be satisfied	Element of structure or fitting	Case dealt with or relevant conditions	Specification
J4(1)—as to thermal insulation—*cont.*	External wall excluding window and other glazed openings—*cont.*	Unventilated cavity wall having a cavity not greater than 75 millimetres nor less than 50 millimetres—*cont.*	(13) (*a*) As for Specification (12)(*a*); (*b*) inner leaf of lightweight concrete blocks having a density not exceeding 1120 kilogrammes per cubic metre, 75 millimetres thick; (*c*) internal finish of plaster 12·5 millimetres thick.
			(14) (*a*) As for Specification (12)(*a*); (*b*) as for Specification (13)(*b*); (*c*) internal finish of aluminium foil-backed plasterboard 10 millimetres thick on strapping 19 millimetres thick.
			(15) (*a*) and (*b*) As for Specification (12)(*a*) and (*b*); (*c*) internal finish of plasterboard 10 millimetres thick on strapping 19 millimetres thick with the interspace between the blockwork and the plasterboard filled with glass fibre or mineral wool.
			(16) (*a*) Outer leaf of rendered autoclaved aerated concrete blocks or slabs having a density not exceeding 800 kilogrammes per cubic metre, 100 millimetres thick; (*b*) inner leaf of autoclaved aerated concrete blocks or slabs having a density not exceeding 800 kilogrammes per cubic metre, 100 millimetres thick; (*c*) internal finish of plaster 12·5 millimetres thick.
			(17) (*a*) and (*b*) As for Specification (16)(*a*) and (*b*); (*c*) internal finish of aluminium foil-backed plasterboard 10 millimetres thick on strapping 19 millimetres thick.
		Framed wall having a cavity not greater than 100 millimetres nor less than 50 millimetres	(18) (*a*) Timber standards and dwangs lined with bitumen felt externally and clad with boarding 21 millimetres thick; (*b*) internal lining of— (i) two layers of plasterboard, each 10 millimetres thick, laid to break bond at joints between boards, or (ii) one layer of aluminium foil-backed plasterboard 12·5 millimetres thick and plaster finish 5 millimetres thick.

		Framed wall having two cavities each not less than 38 millimetres	(19) (*a*) Timber standards and dwangs lined with bitumen felt externally and clad with boarding 21 millimetres thick; (*b*) inter-leaf of plasterboard, 10 millimetres thick, fixed to dwangs between the standards; (*c*) internal lining of plasterboard, 10 millimetres thick, fixed to the standards.
			(20) (*a*) and (*b*) As for Specification (19)(*a*) and (*b*); (*c*) internal lining of aluminium foil-backed plasterboard, 10 millimetres thick, with joints between boards sealed, fixed to the standards.
		Solid wall	(21) (*a*) No-fines concrete— (i) 250 millimetres thick, made with whinstone or gravel aggregate and cement, having a density not exceeding 1760 kilogrammes per cubic metre, or (ii) 300 millimetres thick, made with whinstone or gravel aggregate and cement, having a density greater than 1760 kilogrammes per cubic metre; (*b*) external finish of roughcast, 19 millimetres thick; (*c*) internal finish of plaster, 12·5 millimetres thick.
			(22) (*a*) (i) Clay, concrete, sand-lime brick or block having a density not exceeding 2400 kilogrammes per cubic metre, 330 millimetres thick, rendered or unrendered, (ii) freestone, 250 millimetres thick, or (iii) whinstone or granite 460 millimetres thick; (*b*) internal finish of plasterboard, 10 millimetres thick, on strapping 19 millimetres thick.
			(23) (*a*) As for Specification (21)(*a*) or (22)(*a*); and (*b*) (i) internal finish of aluminium foil-backed plasterboard, 10 millimetres thick, on strapping not less than 19 millimetres thick, or (ii) internal finish of 12·5 millimetres insulation board having a density not exceeding 400 kilogrammes per cubic metre with a finishing coat of plaster on strapping 19 millimetres thick.
			(24) (*a*) Autoclaved aerated concrete blocks or slabs 200 millimetres thick having a density not exceeding 800 kilogrammes per cubic metre; (*b*) external finish of rendering or paint harled and internal finish of plaster.
			(25) (*a*) Autoclaved aerated concrete blocks or slabs 250 millimetres thick having a density not exceeding 800 kilogrammes per cubic metre; (*b*) as for Specification (24)(*b*).
			(26) (*a*) Autoclaved aerated concrete 200 millimetres thick having a density not exceeding 640 kilogrammes per cubic metre; (*b*) as for Specification (24)(*b*).

SCHEDULE 10—*continued*

Provision of regulation deemed to be satisfied	Element of structure or fitting	Case dealt with or relevant conditions	Specification
J4(2)—as to thermal insulation	External wall including any window or other glazed openings therein	The wall (excluding any window or other glazed opening) complies with one of the Specifications for regulation J4(1)	(*a*) The wall (excluding any window or other glazed opening) complies with the Specification for regulation J4(1) set out in column (1) of the following table; (*b*) the percentage of total glazing shown in column (2) of the said table is double glazing; and (*c*) the aggregate area of windows and other glazed openings does not exceed the percentage of the total area of the external walls of the house or other building set out in columns (3) to (5) of the said table—

TABLE

(1) Specification for wall for regulation J4(1)		(2)	(3)	(4) For mean U-value	(5)
			2·4	2·7	3·3
No.	Type	Percentage of glazing which is double glazing	Maximum percentage of glazed openings	Maximum percentage of glazed openings	Maximum percentage of glazed openings
		Per cent	Per cent	Per cent	Per cent
1 and 2 18 21 and 22	Unventilated cavity Composite Solid	Nil	17	26	40
		20	21	30	47
		40	24	36	56
		60	30	45	70
		80	40	60	93
		100	60	90	100

3, 4 and 12		Unventilated cavity..........	Nil	23	30	44
19		Composite..................	20	27	35	51
23		Solid	40	32	42	60
			60	38	51	73
			80	50	66	94
			100	68	92	100
5, 6 and 13		Unventilated cavity..........	Nil	28	35	48
20		Composite..................	20	32	40	54
			40	37	47	63
			60	45	56	76
			80	56	70	95
			100	73	93	100
7, 8, 9, 14 and 16		Unventilated cavity..........	Nil	28	35	48
24		Solid	20	32	40	54
			40	37	47	63
			50	40	51	69
			60	50	60	78
			80	61	73	96
			100	77	94	100
10, 11, 15 and 17		Unventilated cavity..........	Nil	28	35	48
25 and 26		Solid	20	32	40	54
			40	37	47	63
			50	40	51	69
			60	54	63	80
			80	64	76	96
			100	80	95	100

SCHEDULE 10—*continued*

Provision of regulation deemed to be satisfied	Element of structure or fitting	Case dealt with or relevant conditions	Specification
J5(2)—as to thermal insulation	Floor	Tongued and grooved boarding on timber joists where the underside is exposed to the open air	(1) Wood wool slab, 50 millimetres thick, fixed under joists.
			(2) Compressed straw slab, 50 millimetres thick, fixed under joists, used in conjunction with a ceiling.
			(3) Fibre insulation board, 19 millimetres thick, used in conjunction with a ceiling.
			(4) Foamed or expanded plastic sheeting 12·5 millimetres thick and having a density not exceeding 80 kilogrammes per cubic metre used in conjunction with a ceiling.
			(5) Mat or quilt of glass fibre or mineral wool, 25 millimetres thick, used in conjunction with a ceiling.
			(6) Combined corrugated and flat aluminium foil, with a cavity on the flat side, used in conjunction with a ceiling.
			(7) Reinforced paper faced with aluminium foil, fixed with a cavity on each side, used in conjunction with a ceiling.
		Concrete—slab or beam construction where the underside is exposed to the open air	(8) Wood wool slab, 38 millimetres thick, fixed under concrete.
			(9) Compressed straw slab, 50 millimetres thick, fixed under concrete, used in conjunction with a ceiling.
			(10) The slab or beam is of reinforced autoclaved aerated concrete not less than 100 millimetres thick and having a density not exceeding 560 kilogrammes per cubic metre.
			(11) The slab or beam is of reinforced autoclaved aerated concrete not less than 125 millimetres thick and having a density not exceeding 720 kilogrammes per cubic metre.

		Part K—Ventilation	
K3 to K7, K9 to K11 and K13—so far as requiring the provision of mechanical ventilation systems	Ventilation system	Mechanical means of ventilation	A system of mechanical ventilation designed and installed in accordance with CP 352: 1958.
		Part M—Drainage and sanitary appliances	
M3(2) proviso (ii)—as to design, location and construction of sewage treatment works	Sewage treatment works		The design, location and construction are in accordance with CP 302.100: 1956.
M4(2)—as to suitability and strength of materials	Pipes and fittings of a drain	Drain laid in firm ground and passing through or under a building	(1) The pipes and fittings conform to BS 78: Part 1: 1961 and Part 2: 1965 as read with Amendment PD 5731, January 1966, BS 437: Part 1: 1970, BS 1130: 1943 as read with Amendment AMD 648, December 1970 or Class B of BS 1211: 1958.
		Drain laid in firm ground and not passing through or under a building	(2) The pipes and fittings conform to BS 65 & 540: 1966 as read with Amendment PD 6410, May 1968, Class B of BS 486: 1966 as read with Amendments PD 6128, April 1967 and PD 6301, January 1968, BS 539: 1968, BS 556: 1966 as read with Amendment AMD 550, August 1970, BS 2760: Part 1: 1966 as read with Amendment AMD 516, May 1970 and Part 2: 1967 as read with Amendment AMD 517, May 1970, BS 3506: 1969 or BS 3656: 1963 as read with Amendments PD 6055, March 1967 and AMD 322, September 1969.
M4(3)—as to jointing	Drain	Joint in asbestos cement, glazed ware, fire-clay and cement concrete drain, or joint between such pipes, or between any one of these pipes and a cast iron pipe—drain laid in firm ground	(1) The joint incorporates a rubber joint ring conforming to BS 2494: Part 2: 1967 as read with Amendment AMD 40, July 1968.
			(2) The joint is made with a gaskin steeped in cement grout or tar caulked tightly home so as not to fill more than one-quarter of the total depth of the socket, and the remainder of the socket is filled with 1:2 (cement: sand) mortar and otherwise in accordance with clause 505(*c*)(i) of CP 301: 1950 as read with Amendment PD 1829, March 1954.
		Joints in cast iron drains—drain laid in firm ground	(3) The joint incorporates a rubber joint ring conforming to BS 2494: Part 2: 1967 as read with Amendment AMD 40, July 1968.
			(4) The joint is made in accordance with clause 505(*c*)(v)(1) or (2) of CP 301: 1950 as read with Amendment PD 1829, March 1954.

SCHEDULE 10—*continued*

Provision of regulation deemed to be satisfied	Element of structure or fitting	Case dealt with or relevant conditions	Specification
M4(3)—as to construction, support and laying	Drain—*cont.*	Drain laid in firm ground	(5) The drain is laid, constructed and supported in accordance with clause 505 (*b*) and clause 508(*a*) of CP 301: 1950 as read with Amendment PD 1829, March 1954.
M4(3)—as to gradient and size			(6) The gradient and size (other than the minimum internal diameter) are in accordance with clauses 303, 304 and 305 of CP 301: 1950 as read with Amendment PD 1829, March 1954.
M4(7)–as to provision of flexible joints		Spigot and socket pipes	The joint incorporates a rubber joint ring conforming to BS 2494: Part 2: 1967 as read with Amendment AMD 40, July 1968.
M5(3)—as to provision for settlement		Drain passes through or under a wall of a building	The wall is supported by a lintel or arch so positioned that no load bears on the drain.
M6(1) — as to strength of concrete infill	Drain tracks	Drain tracks passing near or under walls	The concrete infill is of a mix of 1:15 (cement: all-in graded aggregate).
M6(2)—as to the provision of contraction joints			The contraction joint— (*a*) forms a plane surface in the concrete infill normal to the centre line of the drain; (*b*) separates the lengths of concrete infill with waterproof building paper conforming to Class A of BS 1521: 1965.
M8(1)(*a*)—as to size and form	Manhole		The size and form are in accordance with clause 315 of CP 301: 1950 as read with Amendment PD 1829, March 1954.
M8(1)(*b*)—as to construction		Manhole with brick walls of any size	(1) The design is in accordance with clause 316(*b*) of CP 301: 1950 as read with Amendment PD 1829, March 1954.
		Manhole with brick walls not exceeding 900 millimetres in depth	(2) (*a*) The walls are constructed of common bricks and are 112·5 millimetres in thickness; (*b*) the roof slab is of concrete and is 100 millimetres in thickness.

		Manhole formed of pre-cast concrete	(3) The design is in accordance with clause 316(*d*) of CP 301: 1950 as read with Amendment PD 1829, March 1954.
M8(1)(*c*) — as to access			Access is provided in accordance with clause 318 of CP 301: 1950 as read with Amendment PD 1829, March 1954.
M8(1)(*d*)—as to provision of cover	Manhole cover	Manhole outside a building	(1) The cover and its frame— (*a*) conform to BS 497: 1967 as read with Amendments PD 6398, May 1968 and AMD 554, August 1970, and (*b*) are of a grade appropriate to the superimposed loads they are to support.
		Manhole within a building	(2) (*a*) The cover is fitted in the frame with an airtight rubber seal; (*b*) the cover is secured to the frame by removable gun-metal bolts; and (*c*) the frame is firmly bedded on and anchored to the manhole walls.
M8(2)—as to construction of drain within a manhole	Drain	Drain constructed with access fittings provided with covers	(1) (*a*) The access fittings conform to Part 2 of BS 539: 1968; (*b*) the concrete benching is floated to a smooth hard surface in 1:2 (cement: sand) mortar, and graded towards the access at a slope of 1 in 6.
		Drain constructed with open channels	(2) The channels and benchings are constructed in accordance with clause 317 of CP 301: 1950 as read with Amendment PD 1829, March 1954, save that if the diameter of the drain is greater than 300 millimetres the channels are formed in concrete and finished in 1: 2 (cement: sand) mortar.
M11—as to construction of suitable trap or tank	Oil and grease interceptor	Discharge does not include silt	The interceptor is constructed in accordance with clauses 313 and 314 of CP 301: 1950 as read with Amendment PD 1829, March 1954.
M13—as to adequacy of means of ventilation	Trap in a drain	Trap is not within a building	A shaft of the same material as the drain and of the same diameter as the trap is carried up from the trap to finished ground or paving level, whichever is the higher, and is fitted with a grating conforming to BS 1130: 1943 as read with Amendment AMD 648, December 1970.
M14(1)(*a*) — as to suitability and strength of materials	Soil, soil-waste, waste and ventilating pipes		(1) Cast iron pipes and fittings conforming to BS 416: 1967.
			(2) Cast (spun) iron pipes (Class 'B') conforming to BS 1211: 1958.
			(3) Copper tubes conforming to BS 659: 1967 and fittings conforming to BS 864: 1953 as read with Amendments PD 2915, December 1957, PD 3925, September 1960, PD 5754, February 1966 and PD 6411, May 1968.

SCHEDULE 10—*continued*

Provision of regulation deemed to be satisfied	Element of structure or fitting	Case dealt with or relevant conditions	Specification
M14(1)(*a*) — as to suitability and strength of materials—*cont.*	Soil, soil-waste, waste and ventilating pipes—*cont.*		(4) Copper tubes, in straight lengths, conforming to BS 3931: 1965 as read with Amendment AMD 311, August 1969.
			(5) Lead pipes conforming to BS 602, 1085: 1956 as read with Amendment PD 5862, June 1966 and in accordance with the weights given in Table 5 of BS 602.
			(6) Pitch-impregnated fibre pipes and fittings conforming respectively to BS 2760: Part 1: 1966 as read with Amendment AMD 516, May 1970 and Part 2: 1967 as read with Amendment AMD 517, May 1970.
			(7) Unplasticised polyvinylchloride pipes and fittings conforming to BS 3506: 1969 or BS 4514: 1969.
M14(1)(*b*)—as to manner of jointing			The joints are made in accordance with subsection 4.1 of CP 304: 1968 as read with Amendment AMD 187, January 1969.
M14(2)(*a*) — as to height and position of ventilating pipes	Ventilating pipe	Ventilating pipe to a waste pipe	(1) An offset fitting of the same material and diameter as the pipe is inserted therein immediately below the rainwater inlet, and the ventilating pipe is carried up therefrom to a point which is at least 600 millimetres higher than— (*a*) the eaves of the building to which it is attached or the barge course in any gable of that building, or (*b*) the top of any opening in a roof or any window within a radius of 1·8 metres of the pipe, whichever is higher.
		Ventilating pipe to a soil, or a soil-waste pipe or a drain	(2) The pipe is carried up to a point as required in Specification (1), such point being no less than 900 millimetres above or below the level of the top of any chimney within a radius of 1·8 metres from the pipe.
M14(2)(*b*)—as to the fitting of a wire cage			The pipe is fitted with a wire balloon conforming to BS 416: 1967.

M15(1)—as to size	Soil, soil-waste and ventilating pipes	Internal diameters	The internal diameters are in accordance with section 3 of CP 304: 1968 as read with Amendment AMD 187, January 1969.
M15(3)(*a*) — as to support			The support is in accordance with subsection 4.2 of CP 304: 1968 as read with Amendment AMD 187, January 1969.
M15(3)(*c*) — as to access			The access is in accordance with subsections 3.6 and 3.8 of CP 304: 1968 as read with Amendment AMD 187, January 1969.
M16(1)—as to size	Waste pipe	Internal diameter	As for Specification for regulation M15(1).
M16(1)—as to support			As for Specification for regulation M15(3)(*a*).
M16(2)—as to access			As for Specification for regulation M15(3)(*c*).
M16(2)—as to provision of traps	Trap for waste pipe		(*a*) The trap is fitted on the waste pipe and close to the appliance served by the pipe; (*b*) the trap is a lead trap conforming to BS 504: 1961 as read with Amendment PD 4448, January 1962, or is a non-ferrous trap conforming to BS 1184: 1961 as read with Amendment AMD 201, February 1969, or, in the case of a waste pipe serving a bath, sink or tub, is a ferrous trap conforming to BS 1291: 1946; (*c*) the trap is a plastics trap conforming to BS 3943: 1965 as read with Amendment AMD 32, August 1968.
M17(1)(*a*) to (*d*)—as to materials, design and construction	Sanitary appliances	Watercloset pan	(1) The watercloset pan conforms to BS 1213: 1945 as read with Amendments PD 769, April 1948, PD 1750, November 1953, PD 4462, February 1962, PD 5509, April 1965, AMD 134, November 1968 and AMD 443, February 1970.
		Wash-hand basin	(2) The basin conforms to BS 1188: 1965 or BS 1329: 1956 as read with Amendment PD 5367, October 1964.
		Sink	(3) The sink conforms to BS 1229: 1945 as read with Amendment PD 1361, April 1952, BS 1206: 1945 as read with Amendments PD 1330, January 1952 and PD 4644, September 1962 or BS 1244: 1956 as read with Amendment PD 6361, March 1968.
		Tub	(4) The tub conforms to BS 1229: 1945 as read with Amendment PD 1361, April 1952.
		Bath	(5) The bath conforms to BS 1390: 1947 as read with Amendments PD 772, April 1948 and PD 1872, May 1954 or BS 1189: 1961 as read with Amendment PD 4534, April 1962.

SCHEDULE 10—*continued*

Provision of regulation deemed to be satisfied	Element of structure or fitting	Case dealt with or relevant conditions	Specification
M18—as to provision for maintenance of water seals	Traps		The ventilation of the trap is in accordance with subsections 3.1, 3.2 and 3.5, including Tables 1 and 7, of CP 304: 1968 as read with Amendment AMD 187, January 1969.
M21(1)(*a*)—as to the suitability and strength of materials	Gutter	Cast iron gutter	(1) The gutter, fittings and accessories conform to BS 460: 1964.
		Asbestos cement gutter	(2) The gutter, fittings and accessories conform to BS 569: 1967.
		Aluminium and aluminium alloy gutter	(3) The gutter, fittings and accessories conform to BS 2997: 1958 as read with Amendment PD 6403, May 1968.
		Pressed steel gutter	(4) The gutter, fittings and accessories conform to BS 1091: 1963.
		Wrought copper and wrought zinc gutter	(5) The gutter, fittings and accessories conform to BS 1431: 1960.
M21(1)(*b*) — as to size		Half-round eaves gutter	(*a*) The gutter is one of the sizes specified in column (1) of the following Table; (*b*) the flow capacity specified in the appropriate columns (2) to (4) of the said Table is not less than the flow load from the roof; (*c*) the flow load from the roof for the purposes of this Specification shall be taken to be the number of litres per second obtained by multiplying the area of the roof draining to the gutter (in square metres) by— (i) where the pitch of the roof does not exceed 50 degrees, a factor of 0·021, (ii) where the pitch of the roof exceeds 50 degrees, a factor of the aggregate of 0·021 plus 0·012 x tangent A (where A is the angle of the pitch of the roof)--

TABLE

Flow capacities† *(in litres per second) for half-round gutters with outlet at one end*

Gutter size (millimetres) (1)	Slope of less than 1 in 600 (2)		Slope 1 in 600 and over, and longer than 6 metres (3)		Slope 1 in 600 and over, and length 6 metres or less (4)	
	True‡	Nominal§	True‡	Nominal§	True‡	Nominal§
75	0·4	0·3	0·6	0·5	0·5	0·4
100	0·8	0·7	1·1	0·9	1·1	0·8
115	1·1	0·8	1·6	1·2	1·4	1·1
125	1·5	1·1	2·1	1·5	1·9	1·4
150	2·3	1·8	3·3	2·5	3·0	2·3
†*Note:* Where there is a bend these flow capacities shall be reduced by the percentage shown—						
(*a*) if bend within 1·8 metres of outlet						
(i) sharp bend	20%		25%		25%	
(ii) round bend	10%		25%		25%	
(*b*) bend between 1·8 metres and 3·6 metres of outlet						
(i) sharp bend	10%		12½%		12½%	
(ii) round bend	5%		12½%		12½%	

‡"True" means a true half-round gutter (i.e. pressed steel to BS 1091: 1963 or asbestos cement to BS 569: 1967).

§"Nominal" means a nominally half-round gutter (i.e. aluminium to BS 2997: 1958 as read with Amendment PD 6403, May 1968 or cast iron to BS 460: 1964).

SCHEDULE 10—*continued*

Provision of regulation deemed to be satisfied	Element of structure or fitting	Case dealt with or relevant conditions	Specification
M21(1)(*e*)—as to adequacy of outlet	Gutter—*cont.*	Half-round eaves gutter—*cont.*	(*a*) The gutter is of one of the sizes specified in column (1) of the following Table; (*b*) the outlet is of the appropriate size specified in column (3) or (4) of the said Table—

TABLE

Half-round gutter outlet sizes (diameter in millimetres)

Half-round gutter size (millimetres) (1)	Sharp (S.C.) or round-cornered (R.C.) outlet (2)	Outlet at one end of gutter (3)	Outlet not at one end of gutter (4)
75	S.C. R.C.	50 50	50 50
100	S.C. R.C.	63 50	63 50
115	S.C. R.C.	63 50	75 63
125	S.C. R.C.	75 63	90 75

Provision of regulation deemed to be satisfied	Element of structure or fitting	Case dealt with or relevant conditions	Specification
M22(1)(*a*) — as to suitability and strength of materials	Rainwater pipe	Rainwater pipe within a building	(1) Cast iron pipes and fittings (Medium grade) conforming to BS 416: 1967.
			(2) Cast (spun) iron pipes (Class B) which conform to BS 1211: 1958.
			(3) Copper tubes and fittings which conform to BS 659: 1967 and BS 864: 1953 as read with Amendments PD 2915, December 1957, PD 3925, September 1960, PD 5754, February 1966 and PD 6411, May 1968 respectively.

			(4) Pitch-impregnated fibre pipes and fittings conforming respectively to BS 2760: Part 1: 1966 as read with Amendment AMD 516, May 1970 and Part 2: 1967 as read with Amendment AMD 517, May 1970.
			(5) Unplasticised polyvinylchloride pipes and fittings conforming to BS 3506: 1969 or BS 4514: 1969.
		Rainwater pipe not being within a building	(6) Cast iron pipes and fittings conforming to BS 460: 1964.
			(7) Asbestos cement pipes and fittings conforming to BS 569: 1967.
			(8) Aluminium pipes and fittings conforming to BS 2997: 1958 as read with Amendment PD 6403, May 1968.
			(9) Pressed steel pipes and fittings conforming to BS 1091: 1963.
			(10) As for Specifications (4) and (5).
M22(1)(*b*)—as to size of rainwater pipe		Rainwater pipe from a half-round eaves gutter	(*a*) The size of the gutter is one of those specified in column (1) of the Table annexed to Specification for regulation M21(1)(*e*); (*b*) the internal diameter of the pipe is not less than the appropriate outlet size specified in column (3) or (4) of the said Table.
M22(1)(*d*)—as to the manner of jointing		Rainwater pipe within a building	The joints are made in accordance with subsection 4.1 of CP 304: 1968 as read with Amendment AMD 187, January 1969.
M24(2)—as to type and number of sanitary conveniences in a building	Sanitary conveniences	(1) Art gallery, library or museum (2) Cinema, concert hall or theatre (3) Hospital (4) Hotel (5) Restaurant	(1) to (5) The sanitary conveniences provided contain appliances of a type and to a scale in accordance with CP 3: Chapter VII: 1950 as read with Amendments PD 1468, August 1952, PD 5362, October 1964 and AMD 636, November 1970.
		(6) Office premises	(6) The sanitary conveniences provided contain appliances of a type and to a scale in accordance with the Washing Facilities Regulations 1964**(a)** and the Sanitary Conveniences Regulations 1964**(b)**.
		(7) School	(7) The sanitary conveniences provided contain appliances of a type and to a scale in accordance with the School Premises (General Requirements and Standards) (Scotland) Regulations 1967**(c)**.
		(8) Shop premises	(8) As for Specification (6).

(a) S.I. 1964/965 (1964 II, p. 2178). **(b)** S.I. 1964/966 (1964 II, p. 2183). **(c)** S.I. 1967/1199 (1967 II, p. 3514).

SCHEDULE 10—*continued*

Provision of regulation deemed to be satisfied	Element of structure or fitting	Case dealt with or relevant conditions	Specification
		Part N—Electrical installations	
N3–N11	Electrical installation		It conforms to the provisions of the "Regulations for the Electrical Equipment of Buildings Fourteenth Edition, reprinted in metric units incorporating amendments 1970" issued by the Institution of Electrical Engineers.
		Part Q—Housing standards	
Q2(2)—as to load-bearing capability	Access roadway	(1) Bituminous asphalt finish	(1) (*a*) The site is cleared of vegetable and other harmful matter; (*b*) the roadway is constructed of— (i) a base course of 63 millimetres of granular material, (ii) followed by a layer of 150 millimetres of hard-core bottoming, consolidated, (iii) followed by a fully compacted layer of 50 millimetres of either bituminous macadam conforming to BS 1621: 1961 as read with Amendment PD 6415, May 1968 or tar macadam conforming to BS 802: 1967 as read with Amendment PD 6125, April 1967.
		(2) Concrete roadway	(2) (*a*) The site is cleared of vegetable and other harmful matter; (*b*) the roadway is constructed of 125 millimetres of concrete with not less than 1·9 kilogrammes per square metre of reinforcement; (*c*) the concrete is fully compacted and has a compressive strength of 28 newtons per square millimetre 28 days after construction.
Q2(4)—as to safety and adequacy of surface	Access footpath	(1) Footpath serving only one house	(1) (*a*) The site is cleared of vegetable and other harmful matter; (*b*) the footpath is constructed of 50 millimetres concrete slabs bedded on granular material.
		(2) Footpath serving more than one house	(2) (*a*) The site is cleared of vegetable and other harmful matter; (*b*) the footpath is constructed of— (i) a layer of 100 millimetres of hard-core bottoming, consolidated, (ii) followed by a fully compacted layer of 32 millimetres of tar macadam conforming to BS 1242: 1960 as read with Amendment PD 6241, August 1967.

Q7(1)(*a*) — as to adequacy of size of bath	Bath		The bath conforms to BS 1390: 1947 as read with Amendments PD 772, April 1948 and PD 1872, May 1954 or BS 1189: 1961 as read with Amendment PD 4534, April 1962.
Q7(1)(*b*) — as to adequacy of size of wash-hand basin	Wash-hand basin		The wash-hand basin conforms to BS 1188: 1965.
Q7(2) — as to the enclosure of compartment by materials impervious to moisture	Shower bath compartment		The compartment enclosure consists of— (*a*) waterproof curtains, and (*b*) a wall rendered on the inside with cement plaster 12·5 millimetres in thickness, composed of 1:3 cement: sand, trowelled smooth and finished with one coat of alkali resisting primer and two coats of oil paint.
Q7(2) — as to the operation of spray by anti-scald valve	Anti-scald valve of shower bath		The mixing valve conforms to and is installed in accordance with BS 1415: 1955 as read with Amendment PD 5235, May 1964.
Q8(2)(*a*) — as to adequacy of size of sink	Sink		The sink conforms to BS 1229: 1945 as read with Amendment PD 1361, April 1952, BS 1206: 1945 as read with Amendments PD 1330, January 1952 and PD 4644, September 1962 or BS 1244: 1956 as read with Amendment PD 6361, March 1968.
Q8(2)(*b*) — as to provision of draining board in kitchen	Draining board in kitchen		The draining board conforms to BS 1226: 1945 as read with Amendments PD 404, October 1945 and PD 1305, December 1951.
Q12(1)(*a*) — as to adequacy of size of sink	Sink		The sink conforms to BS 1229: 1945 as read with Amendment PD 1361, April 1952, BS 1206: 1945 as read with Amendments PD 1330, January 1952 and PD 4644, September 1962 or BS 1244: 1956 as read with Amendment PD 6361, March 1968.
Q12(1)(*b*) — as to adequacy of size of tub	Tub		The tub conforms to BS 1229: 1945 as read with Amendment PD 1361, April 1952.
Q13(2)(*a*)—as to provision of clothes posts	Clothes line posts		The posts conform to BS 1373: 1967.

SCHEDULE 10—*continued*

Provision of regulation deemed to be satisfied	Element of structure or fitting	Case dealt with or relevant conditions	Specification
Q17(1)—as to efficiency of power points	Power points	Gas installation	(*a*) Materials are in accordance with CP 331: Part 3: 1965; (*b*) sockets conform to CP 335: Part 1: 1960 as read with Amendments PD 4161, May 1961 and PD 5616, August 1965.
Q17(4)—as to suitability of socket	Electricity outlet socket		The socket conforms to BS 1363: 1967 as read with Amendment AMD 249, May 1969.
Q18	Refuse disposal arrangements	Gravity system by chute and container	The system is in accordance with CP 306: 1960.
Q19(1)(*a*) — as to the adequacy of the accommodation and suitability of its location and planning	Space standards	Houses of occupancy sub-groups A1 and A2	The design of the houses is based on the standards and commentary set out in paragraphs 7 and 8 of the New Scottish Housing Handbook: Bulletin 1: Metric Space Standards, 1968.

SCHEDULE 11

Regulation A12(3)

General Specifications for Preparation of Sites and Resistance to the Passage of Moisture

Part I

Materials of walls and chimney stacks

To a height of not less than 150 millimetres above the finished level of the adjoining ground (1)	Between the level of the top of the main damp-proof construction and the junction of the wall with the roof (2)
1. *Clay facing and common bricks and blocks*— of hard fired durable materials, including 'blaes' and 'bing' material, suitable for the intended use—	
for conditions of extreme exposure where the structure may become saturated and frozen, to BS 3921: Part 2: 1969, Chapter 1, Section Two, Sub-section B.	to BS 3921: Part 2: 1969, Chapter 1, Section Two, Sub-section A.
2. *Clay engineering bricks*—	
to BS 3921: Part 2 :1969 and having an average absorption boiling or vacuum per cent weight not greater than 4·5 when used as a damp-proof course.	to BS 3921: Part 2: 1969.
3. *Sandlime and concrete bricks*—	
(*a*) sandlime bricks to BS 187: Part 2: 1970, Class 3A, 3B, 4, 5 or 7; (*b*) special purpose concrete bricks to BS 1180: 1944 as read with Amendments PD 774, May 1948 and PD 4692, November 1962.	(*a*) sandlime bricks to BS 187: Part 2: 1970, Class 2A or 2B; (*b*) concrete bricks to BS 1180: 1944 as read with Amendments PD 774, May 1948 and PD 4692, November 1962, Class A(i) or A(ii).
4. *Concrete blocks laid in accordance with CP 122: 1952 as read with Amendments PD 1769, December 1953, PD 2531, July 1956 and PD 6102, March 1967*—	
to type A of BS 2028, 1364: 1968 as read with Amendment AMD 411, January 1970 or type B restricted as stated in clause 1.1 of BS 2028, 1364: 1968 as read with Amendment AMD 411, January 1970.	to type A or B of BS 2028, 1364: 1968 as read with Amendment AMD 411, January 1970, save that no type B blocks are used in the outer part of a solid wall or in the outer leaf of a cavity wall in a building of more than three storeys in height in occupancy group A or occupancy sub-group B1.
5. *Cast stone*—	
to BS 1217: 1945 and having an adequate frost resistance.	to BS 1217: 1945.
6. *Natural stone*—	
free from defects that would adversely affect its durability and weather resistance and having an adequate frost resistance and laid on natural bed.	free from defects that would adversely affect its durability and weather resistance and laid on natural bed so far as reasonably practicable.

SCHEDULE 11—*continued*

To a height of not less than 150 millimetres above the finished level of the adjoining ground (1)	Between the level of the top of the main damp-proof construction and the junction of the wall with the roof (2)
7. *No-fines concrete*—	
	(*a*) made from whinstone or gravel aggregate conforming where appropriate to BS 882: 1965 and having a bulk density of not more than 1760 kilogrammes per cubic metre, or (*b*) made from whinstone or gravel aggregate conforming where appropriate to BS 882: 1965 and having a bulk density of more than 1760 kilogrammes per cubic metre in either case the grading of the aggregate is such that it all passes a 19 millimetres sieve but 95 per cent of it by weight is retained on a 10 millimetres sieve.
8. *Timber weather boarding*—	
	(A) *Air-cured Softwoods* of one of the following species and in the case of species (1) to (4), impregnated under pressure with preservative to BS 1282: 1959 as read with Amendment PD 4252, August 1961— *Species* (1) Redwood or whitewood from Northern European source and of no lower commercial grade than "unsorted". (2) Western hemlock, Californian redwood, East Canadian spruce and western white spruce from North American source and of no lower commercial grade than "selected merchantable". (3) British Columbia Douglas fir from North American source and of no lower commercial grade than "No. 2 clear". (4) Scots pine, sitka spruce, and Douglas fir which is home grown and no lower commercial grade than "No. 2". (5) Western red cedar from North American source and of no lower commercial grade than "selected merchantable". (B) *Air-cured Hardwoods* of one of the following species and— (*a*) containing no sapwood; (*b*) any checks, splits or shakes— (i) on either face do not exceed 0·3 millimetre and are not continuous for more than 300 millimetres in length,

SCHEDULE 11—*continued*

To a height of not less than 150 millimetres above the finished level of the adjoining ground (1)	Between the level of the top of the main damp-proof construction and the junction of the wall with the roof (2)
	(ii) are not more than one-quarter of the width of the piece, (iii) do not exceed one in 100 millimetres of width or one in 900 millimetres of length of piece; (*c*) all exposed surfaces are free from knots other than isolated sound and tight knots not exceeding 19 millimetres in diameter and in any case having no splay, arris knots, or decayed or dead knots; (*d*) having no pitch pockets or plugs or inserts; (*e*) free from all signs of decay and active insect attack— *Species* (1) Afrormosia. (2) Opepe. (3) Iroko. (4) African mahogany. (5) Utile. (6) Idigbo. (7) Teak. (8) Agba. (9) Makore. (10) European oak. (11) Sapele.

SCHEDULE 11—*continued*

PART II

Specifications for mortar

To a height of not less than 150 millimetres above the finished level of the adjoining ground (1)	Between the level of the top of the main damp-proof construction and the junction of the wall with the roof (2)
1. *For all conditions of exposure* § *and for construction at all seasons* Mix† A, B or G.	1. *For sheltered and moderate conditions of exposure and for construction in spring and summer* Mix† C, D or E.
2. *For all conditions of exposure* § *and for construction at all seasons* Mix† G when the element is designed specifically to withstand heavy loading.	2. *For sheltered and moderate conditions of exposure and for construction in autumn and winter* Mix† A, B or F save that mix A is not to be used with Class A (ii) sand-lime and concrete bricks.
	3. *For severe exposure conditions and for construction at all seasons* Mix† A, B or F save that mix A is not to be used with Class A (ii) sand-lime and concrete bricks.
	4. *For all conditions of exposure and for construction at all seasons* Mix† G when the element is designed to withstand heavy loading.

†*See details of mixes—Part III.*

§*References to exposure conditions shall be those defined in Building Research Station Digest No.* 23 (*Second Series*) "*An index of exposure to driving rain*".

SCHEDULE 11—*continued*

PART III

Specifications for rendering

Background and type of finish (1)	Undercoat(s)		Final coat	
	Mix† for severe exposure§ (2)	Mix† for moderate or sheltered exposure§ (3)	Mix† for severe exposure§ (4)	Mix† for moderate or sheltered exposure§ (5)
Dense, strong and smooth moderately strong, porous backgrounds				
Wood float	H‡ or A	H‡ A or C	H‡ or A	H‡ A or C
Scraped or textured	A	A or C	A	A or C
Roughcast, wet dash, harling ...	H‡ or A	H‡ or A	H‡ or A	H‡ or A
Dry dash, pebble dash	H	H	H	H
Moderately weak, porous backgrounds				
Wood float	A	A or C	A	A or C
Scraped or textured	A	A or C	A	A or C
Roughcast, wet dash, harling ...	A	A	A	A
Dry dash, pebble dash	H‡ or A	H‡ or A	H‡ or A	H‡ or A
No-fines concrete background				
Wood float	H‡ or A	H‡ A or C	H‡ or A	A or C
Scraped or textured	H‡ or A	H‡ A or C	A	A or C
Roughcast, wet dash, harling ...	H‡ or A	H‡ or A	H‡ or A	H‡ or A
Dry dash, pebble dash	H	H	H	H

†*Details of mixes*

The references in the foregoing specifications to mixes are, subject to the General notes which follow, to be construed as follows—

Mix	*Composition*	
A	1:1:5–6 of cement: lime: sand or 1:5 of masonry cement and sand	All measured by volume
B	1:5–6 of cement: sand with the addition of mortar plasticizer	
C	1:2:8–9 of cement: lime: sand or 1:6 of masonry cement and sand	
D	1:8 of cement: sand with the addition of mortar plasticizer	
E	1:3 of hydraulic lime: sand	
F	1:2 of hydraulic lime: sand	
G	1:3 of cement: sand or 1:3 of masonry cement and sand	
H	1:½:4–4½ of cement: lime: sand or 1:4 of masonry cement and sand	

‡*Mix H to be used for winter construction.*

§*References to exposure conditions shall be those defined in Building Research Station Digest No.* 23 (*Second Series*) "*An index of exposure to driving rain*".

SCHEDULE 11—*continued*

GENERAL NOTES ON MIXES SPECIFIED FOR MORTAR AND RENDERING IN THIS SCHEDULE

Materials

1. *Cement*—to BS 12: 1958 as read with Amendments PD 3729, April 1960, PD 4676, November 1962 and AMD 198, January 1969, BS 146: 1958 as read with Amendments PD 3733, April 1960, PD 4699, November 1962 and PD 6092, March 1967 or BS 1370: 1958 as read with Amendments PD 3734, April 1960, PD 4678, November 1962 and AMD 199, January 1969, or having similar properties.

2. *Sand*

(*a*) Sand to BS 1199: 1955 and BS 1200: 1955 both as read with Amendment PD 4835, March 1963;

(*b*) when a range of sand content is given (e.g. 5–6 and 8–9) the highest to be used for well-graded sand and the lowest for coarse or uniformly fine sand;

(*c*) very fine sand not to be used with hydraulic limes or for construction specifically designed to withstand heavy loading; and

(*d*) in proportioning, allowance to be made for the bulking of damp sand, particularly if fine sand is used.

3. *Lime*

(*a*) Non-hydraulic lime, or semi-hydraulic lime to BS 890: 1966;

(*b*) proportions given are for lime putty;

(*c*) if lime hydrate, to be soaked at least overnight before use if weather conditions permit; and

(*d*) magnesium lime mortar used below main damp-proof course level to be fully hydrated.

4. *Mortar plasticizers*

If used, to be added in accordance with the manufacturer's instructions.

5. *Water-retentive properties*

For units and backgrounds having high suction, mortars and rendering mixes should have high water-retentive properties.

Operations

6. *Pointing*

Pointing is to be done on the bedding mortar as work proceeds, but if this is not possible the mix for pointing as a separate operation is not to be appreciably stronger than the bedding mortar.

7. *Rendering mixes*

(*a*) The mix for a following coat not to be richer in cement than the one to which it is applied;

(*b*) if metal lathing or wire netting fixed to dense, strong and smooth backgrounds to form a key, the first undercoat not to be of a Type C mix;

(*c*) spatterdash used to provide a key on dense, strong and smooth backgrounds to be of a mix 1:1½-2 cement: coarse sand; and

(*d*) spatterdash used to overcome uneven suction on moderately strong and porous backgrounds to be of a mix 1:2-3 cement: coarse sand.

8. *Rendering coats*

(*a*) Not less than two coat work to be applied;

(*b*) the thickness of an undercoat to be not more than 15 millimetres nor less than 10 millimetres; and

(*c*) the thickness of the finishing coat to be not less than 7 millimetres.

EXPLANATORY NOTE

(This Note is not part of the Regulations.)

These Regulations are made for the purpose only of consolidating the regulations thereby revoked and accordingly by virtue of section 1 of the Building (Scotland) Act 1970 the regulations have not been referred to the Building Standards Advisory Committee nor to interested bodies.

These regulations prescribe standards for buildings for the purposes of Part II of the Building (Scotland) Act 1959 as amended by the Building (Scotland) Act 1970. The matters in relation to which standards have been prescribed are described in the Table of Arrangement given at the beginning of this Instrument.

NOTE: Copies of technical and other publications referred to in these regulations may be purchased from the following:—

(*a*) British Standards and British Standard Codes of Practice: British Standards Institution, British Standards House, 2 Park Street, London W1Y 4AA.

(*b*) Institution of Electrical Engineers—Regulations for the Electrical Equipment of Buildings: Institution of Electrical Engineers, Savoy Place, London, WC2.

(*c*) Institution of Civil Engineers—Code of Practice No. 4: Institution of Civil Engineers, 1 Great George Street, London SW1.

(*d*) Scottish Development Department—Explanatory Memorandum on the Building Standards (Scotland) Regulations, "Structural Strength and Stability": Her Majesty's Stationery Office.

(*e*) Electricity Commissioners—Electricity Supply Regulations 1937: Her Majesty's Stationery Office.

(*f*) Building Research Station Digest No. 23 (Second Series): Her Majesty's Stationery Office.

(*g*) Standard Industrial Classification: Her Majesty's Stationery Office.

(*h*) New Scottish Housing Handbook: Bulletin 1: Metric Space Standards, 1968: Her Majesty's Stationery Office.

1971 No. 2053

POULTRY

The Newcastle Disease (England and Wales) Order 1971

Made - - - 16*th December* 1971

Coming into Operation 1*st January* 1972

The Minister of Agriculture, Fisheries and Food and the Secretary of State, acting jointly in exercise of the powers vested in them under sections 1(1), 20(v), 45, 47(1) and 85(1) of the Diseases of Animals Act 1950(**a**), as read with the Transfer of Functions (Animal Health) Order 1955(**b**) and all other powers enabling them in that behalf, hereby order as follows :—

Citation, extent and commencement

1. This order, which may be cited as the Newcastle Disease (England and Wales) Order 1971, applies to England and Wales and shall come into operation on 1st January 1972.

Interpretation

2.—(1) In this order, unless the context otherwise requires—

"carcase" means the carcase of any poultry or any part thereof ;

"licensed vaccine" means either—

(*a*) a vaccine which is the subject of, and which is being used in accordance with the provisions of, a current product licence issued under the Medicines Act 1968(**c**), or an animal test certificate so issued, or

(*b*) a vaccine of which the manufacture for sale or the importation into Great Britain is licensed, as respects England and Wales by the Minister, or as respects Scotland by the Secretary of State, under any order for the time being in force made under Part II of the Diseases of Animals Act 1950 ;

"Minister" means the Minister of Agriculture, Fisheries and Food ;

"poultry" means any live bird or birds of the following species, that is to say, domestic fowls, turkeys, geese, ducks and guinea fowls, and partridges, pheasants, pigeons and quails (**d**) kept in contact with domestic fowls, turkeys, geese, ducks or guinea fowls ;

"Veterinary Inspector" means a veterinary inspector appointed by the Minister.

(2) The Interpretation Act 1889(**e**) applies to the interpretation of this order as it applies to the interpretation of an Act of Parliament.

(**a**) 1950 c. 36. For change of title of the Minister see S.I. 1955/554 (1955 I, p. 1200).

(**b**) S.I. 1955/958 (1955 I, p. 1184). (**c**) 1968 c. 67.

(**d**) For the extension of the definition of poultry in section 84(2) of the Diseases of Animals Act 1950 to include quails see S.I. 1971/311 (1971 I, p. 1046).

(**e**) 1889 c. 63.

Notification of Newcastle disease

3.—(1) Every person having in his possession or under his charge any poultry or carcase which is affected or suspected of being affected with Newcastle disease shall, with all practicable speed, give notice of the fact to a constable of the police force for the area wherein the poultry or carcase is, or to the Veterinary Inspector appointed for the time being by the Minister to receive such information within the area wherein the poultry or carcase is.

(2) A veterinary surgeon who examines any poultry or carcase and suspects that the poultry or carcase is affected with Newcastle disease shall, with all practicable speed, give notice of the fact to a constable of the police force for the area wherein the poultry or carcase is, or to the Veterinary Inspector appointed as aforesaid to receive such information within the area wherein the poultry or carcase is.

(3) A constable receiving any such notice shall immediately transmit the information by the most expeditious means to the Veterinary Inspector appointed as aforesaid to receive such information within the area wherein the poultry or carcase is.

Restrictions on premises

4. The occupier of premises on which there is any poultry or carcase affected with or suspected of being affected with Newcastle disease, shall forthwith and until a Veterinary Inspector attends those premises for the purpose of the diagnosis of the disease—

(*a*) prevent the access of any person (other than a person exercising any right of entry or way granted by law or a person attending the poultry) to the part of the premises on which the poultry or carcase is or has been kept ; and

(*b*) detain on the premises all poultry and carcases, except dressed carcases not affected with or suspected of the disease.

Provision of assistance

5. For the purpose of establishing whether information in any manner received concerning the existence or suspected existence of Newcastle disease on any premises is correct, the occupier of such premises and any person in his employment shall render to a Veterinary Inspector such reasonable assistance as he may require for such purpose as aforesaid and shall permit him to examine any poultry or carcase found on such premises.

Prohibition of vaccination with unlicensed vaccine

6. No person shall vaccinate, or cause or permit to be vaccinated, any poultry against Newcastle disease except with a licensed vaccine.

Local authority to enforce order

7. The provisions of this order shall, except where it is otherwise provided, be executed and enforced by the local authority.

Amendment of the Fowl Pest Order of 1936

8. Article 12(1) of the Fowl Pest Order of 1936(**a**) as amended (**b**) shall, in the application of that order to England and Wales, have effect as if in the definition of "Fowl pest" the words "any of the forms of that disease, including Newcastle disease and" were omitted.

In Witness whereof the Official Seal of the Minister of Agriculture, Fisheries and Food is hereunto affixed on 13th December 1971.

(L.S.)

J. M. L. Prior,
Minister of Agriculture, Fisheries and Food.

Gordon Campbell,
16th December 1971. Secretary of State for Scotland.

EXPLANATORY NOTE

(*This Note is not part of the Order.*)

This order provides that the Fowl Pest Order of 1936, as amended, shall no longer apply in relation to Newcastle disease in poultry in England and Wales. Under the provisions of the new order, which applies to England and Wales, Newcastle disease remains a disease notification of the existence of which is required to be made as soon as practicable to a police constable or to a veterinary inspector of the Ministry of Agriculture, Fisheries and Food. The owner or person in charge making the notification is required to retain on the premises all poultry and carcases, and to prevent, so far as he legally may, the admission of persons until a diagnostic visit has been made. The vaccination of poultry against Newcastle disease with an unlicensed vaccine is prohibited.

(**a**) S. R. & O. 1936/1297 (Rev. XVIII, p. 442; 1936 II, p. 2086).

(**b**) The amending orders are not relevant to the subject matter of this Order.

STATUTORY INSTRUMENTS

1971 No. 2054

INDUSTRIAL ORGANISATION AND DEVELOPMENT

The Textile Council (Dissolution) Order 1971

Laid before Parliament in draft

Made - - - -	16*th December* 1971
Coming into Operation	1*st January* 1972

Whereas the Secretary of State has consulted the development council known as the Textile Council (for the Man-Made Fibre, Cotton and Silk industries of Great Britain) (hereinafter called "the Council") and the organisations appearing to him to be representative of substantial numbers of persons carrying on business in those industries and the organisations representative of persons employed in those industries appearing to him to be appropriate:

And whereas a draft of this Order has been approved by a resolution of each House of Parliament:

Now, therefore, the Secretary of State, in exercise of his powers under section 8 of the Industrial Organisation and Development Act 1947**(a)** and all other powers in that behalf enabling him, hereby orders as follows:—

Citation, Commencement and Interpretation

1.—(1) This Order may be cited as the Textile Council (Dissolution) Order 1971 and shall come into operation on 1st January 1972.

(2) The Interpretation Act 1889**(b)** shall apply to the interpretation of this Order as it applies to the interpretation of an Act of Parliament.

Winding up of the Textile Council

2. On 31st March 1972 or on such later date as the Secretary of State may direct (hereinafter referred to as "the dissolution date"), the property, rights and liabilities which immediately before that date were property, rights and liabilities of the Council shall, by virtue of this Article, vest in the Secretary of State for Trade and Industry and the Council shall be dissolved.

Council's final accounts

3.—(1) The general accounts of the Council shall be prepared for the period commencing on 1st April 1971 and terminating on 29th February 1972 which shall be the Council's last financial year and the Council shall comply with section 7(1) of the Industrial Organisation and Development Act 1947 and deliver the said accounts to the Council's auditors not later than the dissolution date.

(a) 1947 c. 40. **(b)** 1889 c. 63.

(2) Special liquidation accounts, in such form as the Secretary of State may direct, relating to the financial transactions of the Council occurring on and after 1st March 1972 until the dissolution date shall be separately prepared by the Council and delivered to the Secretary of State before the dissolution date.

Powers of the Council pending dissolution

4. After 29th February 1972 the Council shall not exercise any of the functions assigned to them by the Cotton Industry Development Council Order 1948**(a)** (as amended **(b)**) (hereinafter referred to as "the Order") except so far as may be necessary for the beneficial winding up of the Council.

Power to impose and recover charges

5.—(1) If the assets of the Council are insufficient to meet their liabilities and the expenses of the winding up, the Council shall have power with the approval of the Secretary of State to impose a charge or charges on persons carrying on business in the industry consisting of the activities specified in Schedule 1 to the Order.

(2) The provisions of Articles 6, 8 and 9 of the Order shall apply in relation to any such charge, subject to the following modifications:—

(*a*) the omission of paragraphs (1) to (3) of Article 6 and the substitution, for references in that Article to those paragraphs, of references to paragraph (1) of this Article;

(*b*) the omission of paragraphs (8) and (10) of Article 6; and

(*c*) the omission of heads (*a*) and (*b*) of Article 6(11) and the substitution therefor of the words "pay to the Council".

(3) Charges imposed under paragraph (1) of this Article shall be computed to yield, as near as possible, a total amount equal to the amount by which the liabilities of the Council and the expenses of the winding up exceed the assets of the Council.

Surplus Moneys

6. The Council may, from time to time out of any moneys which they are satisfied are not, and will not be, required for the purposes of meeting their liabilities or the expenses of the winding up, make payments for purposes connected with the industry for which the Council was established, being purposes specified in the First Schedule to this Order.

Powers of the Secretary of State

7.—(1) The Secretary of State shall have power to do anything which, in his opinion, is necessary or desirable to facilitate the winding up of the Council and after the Council's dissolution in accordance with Article 2 of this Order may dispose as he thinks fit of all the property vested in the Council on the dissolution date.

(2) The Secretary of State shall have power after the Council's dissolution to pay any moneys which he is satisfied are not, and will not be, required for the purposes of meeting the liabilities of the Council and the expenses of the winding up for the purposes referred to in Article 6.

(a) S.I. 1948/629 (Rev. V, p. 87: 1948 I, p. 1623).
(b) The relevant amending instruments are: S.I. 1951/2173; 1953/421; 1957/508; 1961/899; 1964/662; 1966/1578; (1951 I, p. 1125; 1953 I, p. 862; 1957 I, p. 1174; 1961 II, p. 1713; 1964 II, p. 1236; 1966 III, p. 4862).

Settlement of Council's debts and liabilities

8.—(1) Every creditor of the Council shall notify the Council and, after the dissolution date, the Secretary of State for Trade and Industry of each of his debts or claims against the Council—

(*a*) if the right of action accrued prior to the date on which this Order comes into operation, within three months of that date; or

(*b*) if the right of action accrued on or after the date on which this Order comes into operation, within three months of the date on which they so accrued,

and shall give the Council or the Secretary of State for Trade and Industry, as the case may be, such further information relating thereto as they or he may reasonably require:

Provided that this paragraph shall not apply to any debt or claim which is the subject of any legal proceedings which have been commenced against the Council prior to the date on which this Order comes into operation.

(2) Every creditor in the notification given to the Council or the Secretary of State for Trade and Industry in accordance with paragraph (1) of this Article shall state therein the amount of the debt or claim or, where the debt or claim is subject to a contingency or sounds in damages or bears no specific value, shall include therein as far as possible a just estimate of the debt or claim.

(3) The Council or the Secretary of State for Trade and Industry, as the case may be, may admit or reject each debt or claim notified to them or him in accordance with paragraph (1) of this Article and shall notify the creditor in writing whether they or he admit or reject it in whole or in part, and if they or he reject it shall state in the notification the grounds of the rejection.

Limitation of actions

9. No action or other legal proceedings shall be commenced in respect of any debt or claim or any part thereof against the Council on or after the date on which this Order comes into operation unless—

(*a*) that debt or claim has been notified to the Council or the Secretary of State in accordance with the provisions of Article 8;

(*b*) that debt or claim or that part has been rejected by the Council or the Secretary of State; and

(*c*) not more than two months have elapsed since the Council or the Secretary of State notified the creditor of the grounds of the rejection.

Council's duty to give information

10. It shall be the duty of the Council to give the Secretary of State for Trade and Industry all such information, to prepare all such documents and to do all such other things as appear to him to be necessary or expedient for facilitating the carrying into effect of the provisions of Article 2 of this Order and for assisting him in managing or otherwise dealing with any property, rights or liabilities thereby transferred to him.

Revocations

11. The Orders listed in the Second Schedule to this Order are hereby revoked without prejudice to anything lawfully done thereunder.

Dated 16th December 1971.

John Eden,
Minister for Industry,
Department of Trade and Industry.

Articles 6 and 7

SCHEDULE 1

Specified Purposes

(1) Maintaining productivity services.

(2) Maintaining statistical services.

(3) Developing industrial and commercial policies to improve the efficiency and prosperity of the industry and promoting the representation of its interests.

(4) Scientific research.

(5) The purposes for which the funds of the Cotton War Memorial Trust may be applied.

Article 11

SCHEDULE 2

Regulations Revoked	Reference
The Cotton Industry Development Council Order 1948	SI 1948/629 (Rev. V, p. 87: 1948 I, p. 1623)
The Cotton Industry Development Council (Amendment) Order 1951	SI 1951/2173 (1951 I, p. 1125)
The Cotton Industry Development Council (Amendment No. 2) Order 1953	SI 1953/421 (1953 I, p. 862)
The Cotton Industry Development Council (Amendment No. 3) Order 1957	SI 1957/508 (1957 I, p. 1174)
The Cotton Industry Development Council (Amendment No. 4) Order 1961	SI 1961/899 (1961 II, p. 1713)
The Cotton Industry Development Council (Amendment No. 5) Order 1964	SI 1964/662 (1964 II, p. 1236)
The Cotton Industry Development Council (Amendment No. 6) Order 1966	SI 1966/1578 (1966 III, p. 4862).

EXPLANATORY NOTE

(*This Note is not part of the Order.*)

This Order provides for the winding up and dissolution of the Textile Council, the imposition and recovery of charges to meet their liabilities and the expenses of the winding up, the application of surplus moneys of the Council for specified purposes, and the revocation of the Cotton Industry Development Council Order 1948, as amended.

1971 No. 2056

COTTON INDUSTRY

The Textile Council Committee (Discharge) Order 1971

Laid before Parliament in draft

Made - - - 16*th December* 1971

Coming into Operation 1*st January* 1972

Whereas it appears to the Secretary of State that the Committee of the Textile Council (for the Man-Made Fibre, Cotton and Silk industries of Great Britain) provided for by section 3 of the Cotton Industry Act 1959(**a**) has no remaining functions to discharge:

And whereas a draft of this Order has been approved by a resolution of each House of Parliament:

Now, therefore, the Secretary of State, in exercise of his powers under sub-section (7) of the said section 3 and all other powers in that behalf enabling him, hereby orders as follows:—

1. This Order may be cited as the Textile Council Committee (Discharge) Order 1971 and shall come into operation on 1st January 1972.

2. The Interpretation Act 1889(**b**) shall apply to the interpretation of this Order as it applies to the interpretation of an Act of Parliament.

3. Section 3(1) of the Cotton Industry Act 1959 shall cease to apply.

Dated 16th December 1971.

John Eden,
Minister for Industry,
Department of Trade and Industry.

EXPLANATORY NOTE

(*This Note is not part of the Order.*)

This Order provides for the discharge of the Committee of the Textile Council.

(**a**) 1959 c. 48. (**b**) 1889 c. 63.

STATUTORY INSTRUMENTS

1971 No. 2057

INDUSTRIAL TRAINING

The Industrial Training (Financial Provisions) Order 1971

Made - - -	17*th December* 1971
Laid before Parliament	30*th December* 1971
Coming into Operation	1*st April* 1972

The Secretary of State for Social Services, in exercise of his powers under section 3(6) of the Employment and Training Act 1948(**a**), as amended by section 17 of the Industrial Training Act 1964(**b**), and of all other powers enabling him in that behalf, hereby makes the following Order :—

Citation, commencement and interpretation

1.—(1) This Order may be cited as the Industrial Training (Financial Provisions) Order 1971 and shall come into operation on 1st April 1972.

(2) The rules for the construction of Acts of Parliament contained in the Interpretation Act 1889(**c**) shall apply in relation to this Order as if this Order were an Act of Parliament.

Payment out of the National Insurance Fund

2. The maximum amount which may be paid out of the National Insurance Fund in any year by way of contribution towards expenses incurred by the Secretary of State under section 3 of the Employment and Training Act 1948 in providing training courses shall be £4 million.

Keith Joseph,
Secretary of State for Social Services.

17th December 1971.

(**a**) 1948 c. 46.
(**b**) 1964 c. 16.
(**c**) 1889 c. 63.

EXPLANATORY NOTE

(This Note is not part of the Order.)

This Order increases to £4 million a year the maximum contribution which may be paid out of the National Insurance Fund towards the expenses of the Secretary of State in providing training courses for persons entitled to unemployment benefit or who would be so entitled but for regulations.

The maximum contribution was previously £2 million a year by virtue of the Industrial Training (Financial Provisions) Order 1967 (S.I. 1967/1535).

STATUTORY INSTRUMENTS

1971 No. 2070

ANIMALS

DESTRUCTIVE ANIMALS

The Coypus (Keeping) (Amendment) Regulations 1971

Made - - -	17*th December* 1971
Coming into Operation	1*st January* 1972

The Minister of Agriculture, Fisheries and Food, the Secretary of State for Scotland and the Secretary of State for Wales, acting jointly, in exercise of the powers conferred on them by section 2 of the Destructive Imported Animals Act 1932(**a**), as read with article 3 of, and paragraph 5 of Schedule 2 to, the Transfer of Functions (Wales) Order 1969(**b**), and of all other powers enabling them in that behalf, with the approval of the Treasury hereby make the following regulations :—

Citation, commencement and interpretation

1.—(1) These regulations may be cited as the Coypus (Keeping) (Amendment) Regulations 1971, and shall come into operation on 1st January 1972.

(2) The Interpretation Act 1889(**c**) shall apply to the interpretation of these regulations as it applies to the interpretation of an Act of Parliament.

Amendment of the principal regulations

2. The Coypus (Keeping) Regulations 1967(**d**), as amended (**e**), shall be further amended by substituting in regulation 4(2) thereof for the figure "£4" the figure "£6·50".

In Witness whereof the Official Seal of the Minister of Agriculture, Fisheries and Food is hereunto affixed on 14th December 1971.

(L.S.)

J. M. L. Prior,
Minister of Agriculture, Fisheries and Food.

Gordon Campbell,
Secretary of State for Scotland.

14th December 1971.

Given under my hand on 16th December 1971.

Peter Thomas,
Secretary of State for Wales.

(**a**) 1932 c. 12.
(**b**) S.I. 1969/388 (1969 I, p. 1070).
(**c**) 1889 c. 63.
(**d**) S.I. 1967/1873 (1967 III, p. 5088).
(**e**) S.I. 1968/2006 (1968 III, p. 5442).

Approved on 17th December 1971.

Walter Clegg,
Tim Fortescue,
Two of the Lords Commissioners
of Her Majesty's Treasury.

EXPLANATORY NOTE

(*This Note is not part of the regulations.*)

These amending regulations increase the fee for a licence to keep coypus from £4 to £6·50 with effect from 1st January 1972.

STATUTORY INSTRUMENTS

1971 No. 2071

ANIMALS

DESTRUCTIVE ANIMALS

The Mink (Keeping) (Amendment) Regulations 1971

Made - - - *17th December* 1971

Coming into Operation *1st January* 1972

The Minister of Agriculture, Fisheries and Food, the Secretary of State for Scotland and the Secretary of State for Wales, acting jointly, in exercise of the powers conferred on them by section 2 of the Destructive Imported Animals Act 1932(**a**), as read with article 3 of, and paragraph 5 of Schedule 2 to, the Transfer of Functions (Wales) Order 1969(**b**), and of all other powers enabling them in that behalf, with the approval of the Treasury hereby make the following regulations :—

Citation, commencement and interpretation

1.—(1) These regulations may be cited as the Mink (Keeping) (Amendment) Regulations 1971, and shall come into operation on 1st January 1972.

(2) The Interpretation Act 1889(**c**) shall apply to the interpretation of these regulations as it applies to the interpretation of an Act of Parliament.

Amendment of the principal regulations

2. The Mink (Keeping) Regulations 1967(**d**), as amended (**e**), shall be further amended by substituting in regulation 4(2) thereof for the figure "£6" the figure "£10".

In Witness whereof the Official Seal of the Minister of Agriculture, Fisheries and Food is hereunto affixed on 14th December 1971.

(L.S.)

J. M. L. Prior,
Minister of Agriculture, Fisheries and Food.

Gordon Campbell,
Secretary of State for Scotland.

14th December 1971.

(**a**) 1932 c. 12.
(**b**) S.I. 1969/388 (1969 I, p. 1070).
(**c**) 1889 c. 63.
(**d**) S.I. 1967/1872 (1967 III, p. 5082).
(**e**) S.I. 1968/2007 (1968 III, p. 5444).

Given under my hand on 16th December 1971.

Peter Thomas,
Secretary of State for Wales.

Approved on 17th December 1971.

Walter Clegg,
Tim Fortescue,
Two of the Lords Commissioners
of Her Majesty's Treasury.

EXPLANATORY NOTE

(*This Note is not part of the regulations.*)

These amending regulations increase the fee for a licence to keep mink from £6 to £10 with effect from 1st January 1972.

1971 No. 2072 (S.219)

SEA FISHERIES

The Sea Fisheries (Scotland) Byelaw (No. 85) 1971

Made - - - *1st November* 1971

Coming into Operation *17th December* 1971

The Secretary of State in exercise of the powers conferred on him by section 4 of the Sea Fisheries (Scotland) Amendment Act 1885(**a**), and of all other powers enabling him in that behalf, hereby makes the following Byelaw :—

Citation, commencement and interpretation

1.—(1) This Byelaw may be cited as the Sea Fisheries (Scotland) Byelaw (No. 85) 1971.

(2) This Byelaw shall come into operation on the date of its confirmation by the Secretary of State.

(3) The Interpretation Act 1889(**b**) shall apply for the interpretation of this Byelaw as it applies for the interpretation of an Act of Parliament.

Prohibition of Methods of fishing for herring in Firth of Clyde

2. Except as hereinafter provided it shall not be lawful for any person to use for the purpose of catching herring any of the following methods of fishing, namely—

beam trawling ; otter trawling ; pair trawling ; drift netting ; ring netting ; trammel netting ; purse seining ; seining ;

within that area of the sea lying inside a line drawn from Corsewall Point in the County of Wigtown to the Mull of Kintyre in the County of Argyll during the whole or any part of the period from 1st January to 31st March in any year occurring within the space of five years from the date of coming into operation of this Byelaw ; and where any of the said methods of fishing is used for the purpose of catching sea fish other than herring within the said area during the whole or any part of the said period, any herring taken in such fishing shall be returned to the sea immediately after each haul of the net is completed :

(**a**) 1885 c. 70. (**b**) 1889 c. 63.

Provided that nothing in this Byelaw shall apply in relation to the use within the said area for the purpose of catching herring of (1) any of the said methods of fishing, by a person in the service of the Secretary of State, or (2) any method of fishing specified in a written authority granted by the Secretary of State, by the person thereby authorised.

Made by the Secretary of State on 1st November 1971.

Eric Gillett,
Fisheries Secretary.

Confirmed by the Secretary of State on 17th December 1971.

Eric Gillett,
Fisheries Secretary.

Department of Agriculture and
Fisheries for Scotland,
St. Andrew's House,
Edinburgh.

EXPLANATORY NOTE

(This Note is not part of the Byelaw.)

This Byelaw prohibits specified methods of fishing for herring in the Firth of Clyde during the period 1st January to 31st March for a period of five years commencing on the date on which the Byelaw comes into operation. Operations authorised by the Secretary of State are excepted.

STATUTORY INSTRUMENTS

1971 No. 2073 (L.50)

COMPANIES

The Companies (Winding-up) (Amendment) Rules 1971

Made - - -	*17th December* 1971
Laid before Parliament	*30th December* 1971
Coming into Operation	*1st January* 1972

The Lord Chancellor, in exercise of the powers conferred on him by section 365(1) of the Companies Act 1948(**a**), and with the concurrence of the Secretary of State for Trade and Industry, hereby makes the following Rules :—

1.—(1) These Rules may be cited as the Companies (Winding-up) (Amendment) Rules 1971 and shall come into operation on 1st January 1972.

(2) In these Rules a rule referred to by number means the rule so numbered in the Companies (Winding-up) Rules 1949(**b**), as amended (**c**).

(3) The Interpretation Act 1889(**d**) shall apply to the interpretation of these Rules as it applies to the interpretation of an Act of Parliament.

2. In Rule 1, in the definition of "Registrar", for the words "Liverpool or Manchester" there shall be substituted the words "Leeds, Liverpool, Manchester, Newcastle upon Tyne or Preston".

3. In Rule 46, the words "or a Palatine Court" shall be omitted in the two places where they occur.

4. In Rule 217(1), for the words "Liverpool and Manchester" there shall be substituted the words "Leeds, Liverpool, Manchester, Newcastle upon Tyne and Preston".

5. In Rule 227, the words "Palatine Court and" shall be omitted.

6. Rule 228 shall be omitted.

Dated 17th December 1971.

Hailsham of St. Marylebone, C.

I concur,
Dated 17th December 1971.

John Davies,
Secretary of State for Trade and Industry.

(**a**) 1948 c. 38.
(**b**) S.I. 1949/330 (1949 I, p. 789).
(**c**) There are no relevant amendments.
(**d**) 1889 c. 63.

EXPLANATORY NOTE

(This Note is not part of the Rules.)

These Rules amend the Companies (Winding-up) Rules 1949 by removing references to the Palatine Courts of Lancaster and Durham, which are abolished on merger with the High Court under section 41 of the Courts Act 1971 (c.23), and make provision for the exercise of companies winding-up jurisdiction in the District Registries of Leeds, Newcastle upon Tyne and Preston.

1971 No. 2074

ROAD TRAFFIC

The Goods Vehicles (Plating and Testing) (Amendment) Regulations 1971

Made - - - - -	20*th December* 1971
Laid before Parliament	29*th December* 1971
Coming into Operation	24*th January* 1972

The Secretary of State for the Environment, in exercise of his powers under section 9(1) and (6) of the Road Safety Act 1967**(a)** as amended by section 148 of the Transport Act 1968**(b)** and of all other enabling powers, and after consultation with representative organisations in accordance with the provisions of section 260(2) of the Road Traffic Act 1960**(c)**, as applied by section 29(6) of the said Act of 1967, hereby makes the following Regulations:—

1.—(1) These Regulations shall come into operation on 24th January 1972 and may be cited as the Goods Vehicles (Plating and Testing) (Amendment) Regulations 1971.

(2) The Interpretation Act 1889**(d)** shall apply for the interpretation of these Regulations as it applies for the interpretation of an Act of Parliament.

2. The Goods Vehicles (Plating and Testing) Regulations 1971**(e)** shall be amended in accordance with the following provisions of these Regulations.

3. Regulation 9 (Conditions subject to which motor vehicles accepted for examinations) shall have effect as though in paragraph (3)(*a*) for the words "within thirty minutes after the time" there were substituted the words "at the time".

4. Regulation 10 (Conditions subject to which trailers accepted for examinations) shall have effect as though—

(*a*) in paragraph (2)(*a*) for the words "within thirty minutes after the time" there were substituted the words "at the time";

(*b*) in paragraph (2)(*h*) for the words "section 7 of the Vehicles (Excise) Act 1962**(f)**" there were substituted the words "section 8 of the Vehicles (Excise) Act 1971**(g)**".

(a) 1967 c. 30.
(b) 1968 c. 73.
(c) 1960 c. 16.
(d) 1889 c. 63.
(e) S.I. 1971/352 (1971 I, p. 1098).
(f) 1962 c. 13.
(g) 1971 c. 10.

5. Regulation 21 (Fees for Part II re-tests) shall have effect as though for paragraph (1) there were substituted the following paragraph:—

"*Fees for Part II re-tests*

21.—(1) The fee payable for a Part II re-test of a vehicle carried out in accordance with arrangements made under Regulation 20(2) or (4) shall be of the amount specified in paragraph 1 of Part II of Schedule 4:

Provided that no fee shall be payable for such a re-test of a vehicle submitted within the relevant time, if it is the first re-test of the vehicle carried out following the first examination of the vehicle or following an earlier Part II re-test of the vehicle in respect of which a fee has been paid under this Regulation and if it is a re-test due only to any minor defect.

In this paragraph "relevant time" means the same day as that on which the said first examination or the said Part II re-test was completed or the next following day on which the vehicle testing station is open and "minor defect" means a defect in a vehicle by virtue of which any of the following items of the prescribed construction and use requirements were not complied with in relation to the vehicle, namely, those contained in Schedule 3, in Part I, in paragraphs 2 (insofar as the regulation therein mentioned relates to the emission of any oily substance), 3, 4(*a*) and (*f*), 9, 10, 11, 13, 16(*a*), 16(*c*) (insofar as it relates to any cab door), 22, 23, 24, 25, 26, 27, 28 and 29 and in Part II in paragraphs 1, 2(*a*), 6(*a*), 9, 10, 11, 12, 13 and 14.".

6. Regulation 30 (Relating to expedited certificates) shall have effect as though in paragraph (2)—

(*a*) the words "being a trailer" were omitted;

(*b*) for the words "Regulation 28(2)" there were substituted the words "Regulation 28".

7. Regulation 36 (Fees for Part III re-tests) shall have effect as though for paragraph (1) there were substituted the following paragraph:—

"*Fees for Part III re-tests*

36.—(1) The fee payable for a Part III re-test of a vehicle carried out in accordance with arrangements made under Regulation 35(2) or (4) shall be of the amount specified in paragraph 1 of Part IV of Schedule 4:

Provided that no fee shall be payable for such a re-test of a vehicle submitted within the relevant time, if it is the first re-test of the vehicle carried out following the last periodical test of the vehicle or following an earlier Part III re-test of the vehicle in respect of which a fee has been paid under this Regulation and if it is a re-test due only to any minor defect.

In this paragraph "relevant time" means the same day as that on which the said periodical test or the said Part III re-test was completed or the next following day on which the vehicle testing station is open and "minor defect" has the same meaning as in Regulation 21(1).".

8. For Regulation 50 (General provision as to fees) there shall be substituted the following Regulation:—

"*General provision as to fees*

50.—(1) Where any fee under these Regulations in respect of a first examination of a vehicle, a re-test of a vehicle to be carried out by virtue of Regulation 20(3) or Regulation 35(3), a periodical test of a vehicle or a Part IV test of a vehicle has been paid to the Secretary of State at the Goods Vehicle Centre, Swansea, or at a vehicle testing station, the said fee shall, subject as hereinafter provided in this Regulation, be payable notwithstanding that the vehicle is not submitted for any such examination on the day and at the time fixed under these Regulations for that examination.

(2) If in the following cases—

(*a*) the applicant for the examination in question has not less than 7 days before the day fixed under these Regulations for the carrying out of that examination given the Secretary of State notice (whether in writing or otherwise) at the said Goods Vehicle Centre that the applicant does not propose to submit the vehicle for examination on the said day; or

(*b*) the said applicant satisfies the Secretary of State that the vehicle cannot or, as the case may be, could not be submitted for the examination in question on the day or at the time fixed for the carrying out of that examination because of the effect on his ability so to submit the vehicle of exceptional circumstances occurring not more than 7 days before the said time and of which notice is given to the Secretary of State whether in writing or otherwise within 3 days of the occurrence thereof,

then either—

(i) the said applicant may give notice (whether in writing or otherwise) to the Secretary of State at the time of the notice given under paragraph 2(*a*) or (*b*) of this Regulation, or within 28 days of the date thereof, requesting another examination of the same kind for that vehicle or another vehicle, and in that event the said fee shall be treated as payable in respect of that other examination; or

(ii) the said applicant may give notice to the Secretary of State at the said Goods Vehicle Centre at the time of the notice given under paragraph 2(*a*) or (*b*) of this Regulation or within 28 days of the date thereof, that no other examination of the same kind is required for that vehicle or another vehicle, and in that event the said fee, less a sum of 75 new pence, shall be repaid by the Secretary of State to the said applicant.

(3) In this Regulation "exceptional circumstances" means an accident, a fire, an epidemic, severe weather, a failure in the supply of essential services or other unexpected happening (excluding a breakdown or mechanical defect in a vehicle or non-delivery of spare parts therefor).".

9. Regulation 55 (Provision as to Crown vehicles) shall have effect as though for the reference to the Vehicles (Excise) Act 1962 there were substituted a reference to the Vehicles (Excise) Act 1971.

10. Regulation 56 (Exemption from s.14(1) of the 1967 Act of the use of vehicles for certain purposes) shall have effect as though in paragraph (3) for the words "section 12 of the Vehicles (Excise) Act 1962" there were substituted the words "section 16 of the Vehicles (Excise) Act 1971".

11. Regulation 60 (Certificates of temporary exemption) shall have effect as though—

(*a*) in paragraph (2)(*a*) for the words from "caused by" to "in a vehicle)" there were substituted the words "(as defined in Regulation 50(3)) affecting either a station or a vehicle";

(*b*) in paragraph (3)(*d*) for the words "one month" there were substituted the words "three months".

12. In Schedule 2 (Classes of Vehicle to which regulations do not apply)—

(*a*) in paragraphs 2 and 6 for the words "1962 Act" there shall be substituted the words "1971 Act";

(*b*) in paragraph 7 for the words "section 6(8) of the 1962 Act" there shall be substituted the words "section 4(2) of the 1971 Act";

(*c*) in paragraph 17 for the words "1962 Act by virtue of section 6(6)" there shall be substituted "1971 Act by virtue of section 7(1)";

(*d*) for paragraph 20, there shall be substituted the following paragraph:—

"20. Vehicles to which paragraph 4 or 6 of Schedule 1 to the Goods Vehicles (Operators' Licences) Regulations 1969**(a)** applies.";

(*e*) for paragraph 24, there shall be substituted the following paragraph:—

"24. Motor vehicles brought into Great Britain and displaying a registration mark mentioned in Regulation 5 of the Motor Vehicles (International Circulation) Regulations 1971**(b)**, a period of twelve months not having elapsed since the vehicle in question was last brought into Great Britain.";

(*f*) for paragraph 27, there shall be substituted the following paragraph:—

"27. Trailers brought into Great Britain and having a base or centre in a country outside Great Britain from which the use of the vehicle on a journey is normally commenced, a period of twelve months not having elapsed since the vehicle in question was last brought into Great Britain.";

(*g*) in paragraph 32 after the words "or controlling" there shall be inserted the words "or loading or unloading";

(*h*) for the definition of "the 1962 Act" under the heading "Interpretation" there shall be substituted the following definition:—

"the 1971 Act" means "the Vehicles (Excise) Act 1971;".

13. In Schedule 3 (The Prescribed Construction and Use Requirements)—

(*a*) in Part I, in Section I, at the end of that Section there shall be added:—

"4A. Regulation 25 (relating to an excess fuel device).";

(*b*) in Part I, in Section III in paragraph 12, there shall be added at the end the words "and Regulation 20 (relating to windscreen washers).";

(*c*) in Part I, for Section V there shall be substituted the following Section:—

"*Section V*

The requirements contained in the following provisions of the Road Transport Lighting Act 1957**(c)**:—

(a) S.I. 1969/1636 (1969 III, p. 5141). **(b)** S.I. 1971/937 (1971 II, p 2688).
(c) 1957 c. 51.

22. Section 1(1) and (2) (relating to lights and reflectors).

The requirements contained in the following provisions of the Road Vehicles Lighting Regulations 1971**(a)**:—

23. Regulations 4, 5, 8 and 9 (relating to front lamps).

24. Regulations 15 to 22 other than Regulations 16(3) and 18(2) (relating to headlamps).

25. Regulation 23 (relating to rear lamps).

26. Regulation 30 (relating to reflectors).

27. Regulations 52, 53 and 56 (relating to side facing reflectors).

28. Regulations 72 to 75 (relating to stop lamps).

29. Regulation 76 (relating to maintenance of direction indicators and stop lamps).

The requirements contained in the following provisions of the Motor Vehicles (Rear Markings) Regulations 1970**(b)**:—

30. Regulation 4(1)(*a*), (3)(*a*) and (5)";

(*d*) In Part II, in Section 1, at the end of paragraph 2 there shall be added the words—

"(*e*) landing legs.";

(*e*) in Part II, for Section V there shall be substituted the following Section:—

"*Section V*

The requirements contained in the following provisions of the Road Transport Lighting Act 1957:—

9. Section 1(1)(*b*) and (2) (relating to lights and reflectors).

The requirements contained in the following provisions of the Road Vehicles Lighting Regulations 1971:—

10. Regulation 23 (relating to rear lamps).

11. Regulation 30 (relating to reflectors).

12. Regulations 54, 55 and 56 (relating to side facing reflectors).

13. Regulations 72 to 75 (relating to stop lamps).

14. Regulation 76 (relating to maintenance of direction indicators and stop lamps).

The requirements contained in the following provisions of the Motor Vehicles (Rear Marking) Regulations 1970:—

15. Regulation 4(1)(*b*), (2), (3)(*b*) and (5).".

Signed by authority of the Secretary of State.

John Peyton,

20th December 1971.

Minister for Transport Industries,
Department of the Environment.

(a) S.I. 1971/694 (1971 I, p. 1833). (b) S.I. 1970/1700 (1970 III, p. 5577).

EXPLANATORY NOTE

(*This Note is not part of the Regulations.*)

These Regulations amend the Goods Vehicles (Plating and Testing) Regulations 1971.

The principal changes are:—

1. Regulations 3 and 4 withdraw the concession which allowed a vehicle to be presented for an examination up to half an hour after the appointed time.

2. Regulations 5 and 7 limit free re-tests for vehicles to those cases where the vehicle failed an earlier examination only due to certain prescribed minor defects.

3. Regulation 6 allows greater flexibility for the dates by which periodical tests of motor vehicles have to be undertaken.

4. Regulation 8 prescribes "exceptional circumstances" in which fees will not be forfeited although a vehicle is not presented for an examination at the appointed time.

5. Regulation 11 extends the maximum period of validity of a temporary certificate exempting a vehicle from the need to have a plating certificate or goods vehicle test certificate from one to three months.

6. Regulation 12 brings up to date references to other legislation in Schedule 2, and in particular Regulation 12(*f*) provides that the exemption for trailers temporarily in Great Britain applies only to vehicles which are based outside Great Britain.

7. Regulation 13 provides for amendments to Schedule 3 which contains the requirements in relation to which vehicles are examined and, in particular, includes among the testable items excess fuel devices, windscreen washers, side facing reflectors, rear markings and certain landing gear on trailers.

STATUTORY INSTRUMENTS

1971 No. 2079 (C.54)

TOWN AND COUNTRY PLANNING, ENGLAND AND WALES

The Town and Country Planning Act 1968 (Commencement No. 7) (South Hampshire) Order 1971

Made - - - - 17*th December* 1971

The Secretary of State for the Environment in exercise of the power conferred on him by section 105 of the Town and Country Planning Act 1968(**a**) hereby makes the following Order:—

1.—(1) This Order may be cited as the Town and Country Planning Act 1968 (Commencement No. 7) (South Hampshire) Order 1971.

(2) In this Order:—

"the Act" means the Town and Country Planning Act 1968;

"the principal Act" means the Town and Country Planning Act 1962(**b**); and

"the Order area" means the area described in Schedule 1 to this Order.

2. The provisions of the Act specified in the first column of Schedule 2 hereto (which relate to the matters specified in the second column of the said Schedule) shall come into operation in the Order area on 31st December 1971.

3. The bringing into operation of paragraph 5 of Schedule 9 to the Act shall not prejudice the continued operation of any reference in the principal Act to the carrying out of a survey or the preparation, approval, making or amendment of a development plan under Part II of that Act, or to a plan or amendment approved or made under the said Part II, until the repeal of the said Part II as respects the Order area.

(**a**) 1968 c. 72. (**b**) 1962 c. 38.

SCHEDULE 1

THE ORDER AREA

The county boroughs of Portsmouth and Southampton.

In the administrative county of Hampshire:—

The boroughs of Eastleigh, Gosport and Romsey.

The urban districts of Fareham and Havant and Waterloo.

In the rural district of Droxford, the whole of the following parishes:—

Bishops Waltham
Boarhunt
Curdridge
Denmead
Droxford
Durley
Hambledon
Shedfield
Soberton
Southwick and Widley
Swanmore
Upham
Wickham

In the rural district of New Forest, the whole of the following parishes:—

Copythorne
Dibden
Eling
Fawley
Marchwood
Netley Marsh

In the rural district of Petersfield, the whole of the following parishes:—

Clanfield
Horndean
Rowlands Castle

In the rural district of Romsey and Stockbridge, the whole of the following parishes:—

Ampfield
Chilworth
North Baddesley
Nursling and Rownhams
Romsey Extra

In the rural district of Winchester, the whole of the following parishes:—

Botley
Bursledon
Coldon Common
Compton
Fair Oak
Hamble
Hedge End
Hound
Hursley
Twyford
Olivers Battery
Otterbourne
Owslebury
West End

SCHEDULE 2

PROVISIONS COMING INTO OPERATION IN THE ORDER AREA ON 31ST DECEMBER 1971

Provisions of the Act	Subject matter of provisions
Part I, except sections 13 and 14 and except so far as it enables any matter or thing to be prescribed.	New provisions as to development plans.
In Schedule 9, paragraph 5.	Adaptation of provisions in the principal Act as to surveys and development plans.
In Schedule 9, paragraph 54.	Adaptation of provisions of paragraph 5 of Schedule 2 to the principal Act as to joint advisory committees for development plans, to structure plans and local plans.
In Schedule 11, the entry relating to the principal Act section 210.	Repeal consequential on the bringing into operation of the above-mentioned provisions.

Peter Walker,
Secretary of State for the Environment.

17th December 1971.

EXPLANATORY NOTE

(*This Note is not part of the Order.*)

This Order brings into force for the county boroughs of Portsmouth and Southampton and certain adjacent areas of the administrative county of Hampshire as described in Schedule 1 to the Order the provisions of the Town and Country Planning Act 1968 which are set out in Schedule 2, subject to the transitional provision contained in Article 3. The provisions which are brought into force are the new substantive provisions as to development plans in Part I of the Act and certain provisions in Schedules 9 and 11 to the Act which are consequential on the operation of those provisions.

1971 No. 2080 (C.55)

TOWN AND COUNTRY PLANNING, ENGLAND AND WALES

The Town and Country Planning Act 1968 (Commencement No. 8) (Leicester-Leicestershire) Order 1971

Made - - - *17th December* 1971

The Secretary of State for the Environment in exercise of the power conferred on him by section 105 of the Town and Country Planning Act 1968(**a**) hereby makes the following Order :—

1.—(1) This Order may be cited as the Town and Country Planning Act 1968 (Commencement No. 8) (Leicester-Leicestershire) Order 1971.

(2) In this Order :—

"the Act" means the Town and Country Planning Act 1968 ;

"the principal Act" means the Town and Country Planning Act 1962(**b**) ; and

"the Order area" means the area described in Schedule 1 to this Order.

2. The provisions of the Act specified in the first column of Schedule 2 hereto (which relate to the matters specified in the second column of the said Schedule) shall come into operation in the Order area on 31st December 1971.

3. The bringing into operation of paragraph 5 of Schedule 9 to the Act shall not prejudice the continued operation of any reference in the principal Act to the carrying out of a survey or the preparation, approval, making or amendment of a development plan under Part II of that Act, or to a plan or amendment approved or made under the said Part II, until the repeal of the said Part II as respects the Order area.

SCHEDULE 1

THE ORDER AREA

The county borough of Leicester.

The administrative county of Leicestershire.

(**a**) 1968 c. 72. (**b**) 1962 c. 38.

SCHEDULE 2

PROVISIONS COMING INTO OPERATION IN THE ORDER AREA ON 31ST DECEMBER 1971

Provisions of the Act	Subject matter of provisions
Part I, except sections 13 and 14, and except so far as it enables any matter or thing to be prescribed.	New provisions as to development plans.
In Schedule 9, paragraph 5.	Adaptation of provisions in the principal Act as to surveys and development plans.
In Schedule 9, paragraph 54.	Adaptation of provisions of paragraph 5 of Schedule 2 to the principal Act as to joint advisory committees for development plans, to structure plans and local plans.
In Schedule 11, the entry relating to the principal Act section 210.	Repeal consequential on the bringing into operation of the above-mentioned provisions.

Peter Walker,
Secretary of State for the Environment.

17th December 1971.

EXPLANATORY NOTE

(*This Note is not part of the Order.*)

This Order brings into force for the county borough of Leicester and the administrative county of Leicestershire the provisions of the Town and Country Planning Act 1968 which are set out in Schedule 2 to the Order, subject to the transitional provision contained in Article 3. The provisions which are brought into force are the new substantive provisions as to development plans in Part I of the Act and certain provisions in Schedules 9 and 11 to the Act which are consequential on the operation of those provisions.

1971 No. 2082

SUGAR

The Sugar (Rates of Surcharge and Surcharge Repayments) (No. 10) Order 1971

Made - - - -	21*st December* 1971
Laid before Parliament -	21*st December* 1971
Coming into Operation -	22*nd December* 1971

The Minister of Agriculture, Fisheries and Food, in exercise of the powers conferred on him by sections 7(4), 8(6) and 33(4) of the Sugar Act 1956(**a**) having effect subject to the provisions of section 3 of, and Part II of Schedule 5 to, the Finance Act 1962(**b**), and section 58 of the Finance Act 1968(**c**) and of all other powers enabling him in that behalf, with the concurrence of the Treasury, on the advice of the Sugar Board, hereby makes the following order:—

1.—(1) This order may be cited as the Sugar (Rates of Surcharge and Surcharge Repayments) (No. 10) Order 1971; and shall come into operation on 22nd December 1971.

(2) The Interpretation Act 1889(**d**) shall apply for the interpretation of this order as it applies for the interpretation of an Act of Parliament.

2. Notwithstanding the provisions of Article 2 of the Sugar (Rates of Surcharge and Surcharge Repayments) (No. 9) Order 1971(**e**), the rates of surcharge payable under and in accordance with the provisions of section 7 of the Sugar Act 1956, having effect as aforesaid, in respect of sugar and invert sugar imported or home produced or used in the manufacture of imported composite sugar products shall on and after 22nd December 1971 be the appropriate rates specified in Schedule 1 to this order.

3. For the purpose of section 8(3)(*b*) of the Sugar Act 1956, having effect as aforesaid, the rates of surcharge repayments in respect of invert sugar produced in the United Kingdom from materials on which on or after 22nd December 1971 sugar duty has been paid or, by virtue of paragraph 1 of Part II of Schedule 5 to the Finance Act 1962, is treated as having been paid shall, notwithstanding the provisions of Article 3 of the Sugar (Rates of Surcharge and Surcharge Repayments) (No. 9) Order 1971 be the appropriate rates specified in Schedule 2 to this order.

(**a**) 1956 c. 48.
(**b**) 1962 c. 44.
(**c**) 1968 c. 44.
(**d**) 1889 c. 63.
(**e**) S.I. 1971/1964 (1971 III, p. 5304).

In Witness whereof the Official Seal of the Minister of Agriculture, Fisheries and Food is hereunto affixed on 20th December 1971.

(L.S.)

E. J. G. Smith,
Authorised by the Minister.

We concur.
21st December 1971.

Walter Clegg,
Tim Fortescue,
Two of the Lords Commissioners of Her Majesty's Treasury.

SCHEDULE 1

Part I

Surcharge Rates for Sugar

Polarisation	Rate of Surcharge per ton
	£
Exceeding—	
99°	8·000
98° but not exceeding 99°	7·544
97° ,, ,, ,, 98°	7·360
96° ,, ,, ,, 97°	7·168
95° ,, ,, ,, 96°	6·976
94° ,, ,, ,, 95°	6·784
93° ,, ,, ,, 94°	6·592
92° ,, ,, ,, 93°	6·400
91° ,, ,, ,, 92°	6·208
90° ,, ,, ,, 91°	6·016
89° ,, ,, ,, 90°	5·824
88° ,, ,, ,, 89°	5·632
87° ,, ,, ,, 88°	5·472
86° ,, ,, ,, 87°	5·312
85° ,, ,, ,, 86°	5·168
84° ,, ,, ,, 85°	5·024
83° ,, ,, ,, 84°	4·880
82° ,, ,, ,, 83°	4·736
81° ,, ,, ,, 82°	4·608
80° ,, ,, ,, 81°	4·480
79° ,, ,, ,, 80°	4·352
78° ,, ,, ,, 79°	4·224
77° ,, ,, ,, 78°	4·096
76° ,, ,, ,, 77°	3·968
Not exceeding 76°	3·840

Part II

Surcharge Rates for Invert Sugar

Sweetening matter content by weight	Rate of Surcharge per cwt.
	£
70 per cent. or more	0·25
Less than 70 per cent. and more than 50 per cent.	0·18
Not more than 50 per cent.	0·08

SCHEDULE 2

Surcharge Repayment Rates for Invert Sugar

Sweetening matter content by weight	Rate of Surcharge Repayment per cwt.
	£
More than 80 per cent.	0·30
More than 70 per cent. but not more than 80 per cent.	0·25
More than 60 per cent. but not more than 70 per cent.	0·18
More than 50 per cent. but not more than 60 per cent.	0·14
Not more than 50 per cent. and the invert sugar not being less in weight than 14 lb. per gallon	0·08

EXPLANATORY NOTE

(*This Note is not part of the Order.*)

This order prescribes—

(*a*) reductions equivalent to 20p per cwt. of refined sugar in the rates of surcharge payable on sugar and invert sugar which become chargeable with surcharge on or after 22nd December 1971;

(*b*) correspondingly reduced rates of surcharge repayment in respect of invert sugar produced in the United Kingdom from materials on which surcharge has been paid.

1971 No. 2083

SUGAR

The Composite Sugar Products (Surcharge and Surcharge Repayments—Average Rates) (No. 10) Order 1971

Made - - - -	21*st December* 1971
Laid before Parliament -	21*st December* 1971
Coming into Operation -	22*nd December* 1971

Whereas the Minister of Agriculture, Fisheries and Food (hereinafter called " the Minister ") has on the recommendation of the Commissioners of Customs and Excise (hereinafter called " the Commissioners ") made an order(**a**) pursuant to the powers conferred upon him by sections 9(1) and 9(4) of the Sugar Act 1956(**b**), having effect subject to the provisions of section 3 of, and Part II of Schedule 5 to, the Finance Act 1962(**c**), to the provisions of section 52(2) of the Finance Act 1966(**d**), and to the provisions of section 58 of the Finance Act 1968(**e**), providing that in the case of certain descriptions of composite sugar products surcharge shall be calculated on the basis of an average quantity of sugar or invert sugar taken to have been used in the manufacture of the products, and that certain other descriptions of composite sugar products shall be treated as not containing any sugar or invert sugar, and that in the case of certain descriptions of goods in the manufacture of which sugar or invert sugar is used, surcharge repayments shall be calculated on the basis of an average quantity of sugar or invert sugar taken to have been so used:

Now, therefore, the Minister, on the recommendation of the Commissioners and in exercise of the powers conferred upon him by sections 9(1), 9(4) and 33(4) of the Sugar Act 1956, having effect as aforesaid, and of all other powers enabling him in that behalf, hereby makes the following order:—

1.—(1) This order may be cited as the Composite Sugar Products (Surcharge and Surcharge Repayments—Average Rates) (No. 10) Order 1971, and shall come into operation on 22nd December 1971.

(2) The Interpretation Act 1889(**f**) shall apply for the interpretation of this order as it applies for the interpretation of an Act of Parliament.

2. Surcharge payable on or after 22nd December 1971 under and in accordance with the Sugar Act 1956, having effect as aforesaid, in respect of sugar and invert sugar used in the manufacture of the descriptions of imported composite sugar products specified in the second column of Schedule 1 to this order shall, notwithstanding the provisions of the Sugar (Rates of Surcharge and Surcharge Repayments) (No 10) Order 1971(**g**) and the Composite Sugar Products (Surcharge and Surcharge Repayments—Average Rates) (No. 9) Order 1971(**a**), be calculated by reference to the weight of the products at the appropriate rates specified in relation thereto in the third column of the said Schedule.

(**a**) S.I. 1971/1965 (1971 III, p. 5307). (**b**) 1956 c. 48. (**c**) 1962 c. 44.
(**d**) 1966 c. 18. (**e**) 1968 c. 44. (**f**) 1889 c. 63.
(**g**) S.I. 1971/2082(1971 III, p. 6160).

3. Imported composite sugar products other than those of a description specified in Schedules 1 and 2 to this order shall be treated as not containing any sugar or invert sugar for the purposes of surcharge payable on or after 22nd December 1971.

4. Surcharge repayments payable on and after 22nd December 1971 under and in accordance with the provisions of section 8 of the Sugar Act 1956, having effect as aforesaid, in respect of sugar and invert sugar used in the manufacture of the descriptions of goods specified in the first column of Schedule 3 to this order shall, notwithstanding the provisions of the Sugar (Rates of Surcharge and Surcharge Repayments) (No. 10) Order 1971(**a**) and the Composite Sugar Products (Surcharge and Surcharge Repayments—Average Rates) (No. 9) Order 1971(**b**), be calculated by reference to the quantity of the goods at the appropriate rates specified in relation thereto in the second column of the said Schedule.

In Witness whereof the Official Seal of the Minister of Agriculture, Fisheries and Food is hereunto affixed on 21st December 1971.

(L.S.)

E. J. G. Smith,
Authorised by the Minister.

SCHEDULE 1

In this Schedule:—

" Tariff heading " means a heading or, where the context so requires, a subheading of the Customs Tariff 1959 (see paragraph (1) of Article 2 of the Import Duties (General) (No. 7) Order 1970(**c**)).

Tariff heading	Description of Imported Composite Sugar Products	Rate of Surcharge
		Per cwt. £
04.02 ..	Milk and cream, preserved, concentrated or sweetened, containing more than 10 per cent. by weight of added sugar	0·17

(a) S.I. 1971/2082(1971 III, p. 6160). (b) S.I. 1971/1965 (1971 III, p. 5307).
(c) S.I. 1970/1522 (1970 III, p. 4935).

Tariff heading	Description of Imported Composite Sugar Products	Rate of Surcharge
		Per cwt. £
17.02 (B) (2) and 17.05 (B)	Syrups containing sucrose sugar, whether or not flavoured or coloured, but not including fruit juices containing added sugar in any proportion:—	
	containing 70 per cent. or more by weight of sweetening matter	0·25
	containing less than 70 per cent., and more than 50 per cent., by weight of sweetening matter	0·18
	containing not more than 50 per cent. by weight of sweetening matter	0·08
17.02 (F) ..	Caramel:—	
	Solid	0·40
	Liquid	0·27
17.04 ..	Sugar confectionery, not containing cocoa ..	0·32
18.06 ..	Chocolate and other food preparations containing cocoa and added sugar:—	
	Chocolate couverture not prepared for retail sale; chocolate milk crumb, liquid ..	0·17
	Chocolate milk crumb, solid	0·21
	Solid chocolate bars or blocks, milk or plain, with or without fruit or nuts; other chocolate confectionery consisting wholly of chocolate or of chocolate and other ingredients not containing added sugar, but not including such goods when packed together in retail packages with goods liable to surcharge at a higher rate	0·17
	Other	0·23
19.08 ..	Pastry, biscuits, cakes and other fine bakers' wares containing added sugar:—	
	Biscuits, wafers and rusks containing more than 12½ per cent. by weight of added sugar, and other biscuits, wafers and rusks included in retail packages with such goods	0·10
	Cakes with covering or filling containing added sugar; meringues	0·13
	Other	0·05
20.01 ..	Vegetables and fruit, prepared or preserved by vinegar or acetic acid, containing added sugar:—	
	Containing 10 per cent. or more by weight of added sugar	0·14
	Other	0·02
20.03 ..	Fruit preserved by freezing, containing added sugar	0·05
20.04 ..	Fruit, fruit-peel and parts of plants, preserved by sugar (drained, glacé or crystallised)	0·26
20.05 ..	Jams, fruit jellies, marmalades, fruit purée and fruit pastes, being cooked preparations, containing added sugar	0·25
20.06 ..	Fruit otherwise prepared or preserved, containing added sugar:—	
	Ginger	0·20
	Other	0·05

SCHEDULE 2

Tariff heading	Description of Imported Composite Sugar Products
17.05 (A) and (B)	Sugar and invert sugar, flavoured or coloured.

SCHEDULE 3

Description of goods	Rate of surcharge repayment per bulk barrel of 36 gallons
Lager	£0·029
All beer other than lager	£0·018

EXPLANATORY NOTE

(*This Note is not part of the Order.*)

This order provides for reductions on and after 22nd December 1971 in the average rates of surcharge payable on imported composite sugar products of the descriptions specified in Schedule 1 and in the average rates of surcharge repayment in respect of exported goods of the descriptions specified in Schedule 3. These correspond to the reductions in surcharge rates effected by the Sugar (Rates of Surcharge and Surcharge Repayments) (No. 10) Order 1971 (S.I. 1971/2082). Provision is also made for certain imported composite sugar products to be treated as not containing any sugar or invert sugar.

STATUTORY INSTRUMENTS

1971 No. 2084 (L.51)

CRIMINAL PROCEDURE, ENGLAND AND WALES

The Indictments (Procedure) Rules 1971

Made - - - *20th December* 1971

Coming into Operation *1st January* 1972

The Lord Chancellor, in exercise of the powers conferred upon him by section 2 of the Administration of Justice (Miscellaneous Provisions) Act 1933(**a**), hereby makes the following Rules :—

1. These Rules may be cited as the Indictments (Procedure) Rules 1971 and shall come into operation on 1st January 1972.

2. In these Rules—

"the appropriate officer" means such officer as may be designated for the purpose in question by arrangements made by or on behalf of the Lord Chancellor ;

"the Act" means the Administration of Justice (Miscellaneous Provisions) Act 1933 ;

"committal proceedings" means proceedings before a magistrates' court acting as examining justices ;

"depositions" means depositions taken before justices under the Magistrates' Courts Act 1952(**b**) or under the Children and Young Persons Act 1933(**c**) and includes written statements tendered in evidence under section 2 of the Criminal Justice Act 1967(**d**), any document exhibited to such depositions or statements and the statement of the accused :

Provided that any requirement of these Rules that an application should be accompanied by a copy of any depositions, shall as respects documents exhibited to those depositions, be satisfied if a copy of such parts only of the exhibits as are, in the opinion of the applicant, material, accompanies the application, and the application contains an express statement to that effect.

3. The Interpretation Act 1889(**e**) shall apply to the interpretation of these Rules as it applies to the interpretation of an Act of Parliament.

4. Subject as hereinafter provided, a bill of indictment shall be preferred before the Crown Court by delivering the bill to the appropriate officer of the Crown Court :

Provided that where with the assent of the prosecutor the bill is prepared by, or under the supervision of, the appropriate officer it shall not be nec-

(**a**) 1933 c. 36.
(**b**) 1952 c. 55.
(**c**) 1933 c. 12.
(**d**) 1967 c. 80.
(**e**) 1889 c. 63.

essary for the bill to be delivered to the appropriate officer but as soon as it has been settled to his satisfaction it shall be deemed to have been duly preferred.

5. Where a defendant has been committed for trial, the bill of indictment must be preferred within 28 days of such committal or within such longer period as a judge of the Crown Court may allow.

6. An application under section 2(2)(*b*) of the Act for consent to the preferment of a bill of indictment may be made to a judge of the High Court.

7. Every such application shall be in writing and shall be signed by the applicant or his solicitor.

8. Every such application—

(*a*) shall be accompanied by the bill of indictment which it is proposed to prefer and, unless the application is made by or on behalf of the Director of Public Prosecutions, shall also be accompanied by an affidavit by the applicant, or, if the applicant is a corporation, by an affidavit by some director or officer of the corporation, that the statements contained in the application are, to the best of the deponent's knowledge, information and belief, true ; and

(*b*) shall state whether or not any application has previously been made under these Rules or any Rules revoked by these Rules and whether there have been any committal proceedings, and the result of any such application or proceedings.

9.—(1) Where there have been no committal proceedings, the application shall state the reason why it is desired to prefer a bill without such proceedings and—

(*a*) there shall accompany the application proofs of the evidence of the witnesses whom it is proposed to call in support of the charges ; and

(*b*) the application shall embody a statement that the evidence shown by the proofs will be available at the trial and that the case disclosed by the proofs is, to the best of the knowledge, information and belief of the applicant, substantially a true case.

(2) Where there have been committal proceedings, and the justice or justices have refused to commit the accused for trial, the application shall be accompanied by—

(*a*) a copy of the depositions ; and

(*b*) proofs of any evidence which it is proposed to call in support of the charges so far as that evidence is not contained in the depositions ;

and the application shall embody a statement that the evidence shown by the proofs and (except so far as may be expressly stated to the contrary in the application) the evidence shown by the depositions, will be available at the trial and that the case disclosed by the depositions and proofs is, to the best of the knowledge, information and belief of the applicant, substantially a true case.

(3) Where the accused has been committed for trial the application shall state why the application is made and shall be accompanied by proofs of any evidence which it is proposed to call in support of the charges, so far as that evidence is not contained in the depositions, and, unless the depositions have already been transmitted to the judge to whom the application is made, shall also be accompanied by a copy of the depositions ; and the application shall embody a statement that the evidence shown by the proofs will be available at the trial, and that the case disclosed by the depositions and proofs is, to the best of the knowledge, information and belief of the applicant, substantially a true case.

10. Unless the judge otherwise directs in any particular case, his decision on the application shall be signified in writing on the application without requiring the attendance before him of the applicant or of any of the witnesses, and if the judge thinks fit to require the attendance of the applicant or of any of the witnesses, their attendance shall not be in open court.

Unless the judge gives a direction to the contrary, where an applicant is required to attend as aforesaid, he may attend by a solicitor or by counsel.

11. It shall be the duty of any person in charge of any depositions to give to any person desiring to make an application for leave to prefer a bill of indictment against the person who was accused when the depositions were taken, a reasonable opportunity to inspect the depositions and, if so required by him, to supply him with copies of the depositions or any part thereof.

12. The Indictments (Procedure) Rules 1933(**a**), the Indictments (Procedure) (Amendment) Rules 1964(**b**) and the Indictments (Procedure) (Amendment) Rules 1967(**c**) are hereby revoked.

Dated 20th December 1971.

Hailsham of St. Marylebone, C.

(**a**) S.R. & O. 1933/745 (Rev. V, p. 347: 1933, p. 556).
(**b**) S.I. 1964/2002 (1964 III, p. 5065). (**c**) S.I. 1967/1734 (1967 III, p. 4656).

EXPLANATORY NOTE

(This Note is not part of the Rules.)

These Rules revoke and replace the existing Indictments (Procedure) Rules to take account of the replacement of Assizes and Quarter Sessions by the Crown Court created by section 4 of the Courts Act 1971 (c.23). They set out the procedure for the preferment of bills of indictment and prescribe the period within which such bills may be preferred.

STATUTORY INSTRUMENTS

1971 No. 2085

INDUSTRIAL RELATIONS

The Industrial Relations (Nominations) Regulations 1971

Made - - -	20*th December* 1971
Laid before Parliament	31*st December* 1971
Coming into Operation	28*th February* 1972

The Secretary of State in exercise of the powers conferred on him by section 155 of the Industrial Relations Act 1971(**a**) and of all other powers enabling him in that behalf, hereby makes the following Regulations:—

PART I

PRELIMINARY

Citation, interpretation and commencement

1.—(1) This Order may be cited as the Industrial Relations (Nominations) Regulations 1971.

(2) In these Regulations "trade union" means an organisation of workers which is for the time being registered as a trade union or entered in the provisional register under the Industrial Relations Act 1971.

(3) (*a*) The Interpretation Act 1889(**b**) applies to the interpretation of these Regulations as it applies to the interpretation of an Act of Parliament.

(*b*) The reference in Regulation 10 of these Regulations to the Trade Union Act Amendment Act 1876(**c**) shall be construed as including a reference to that Act as amended or extended by the Provident Nominations and Small Intestacies Act 1883(**d**), the Friendly Societies Act 1955(**e**) and the Administration of Estates (Small Payments) Act 1965(**f**).

(4) These Regulations shall come into operation on 28th February 1972.

PART II

NOMINATIONS

Power to make nominations

2.—(1) Subject to the provisions of these Regulations a member of a trade union being a person who has attained the age of 16 years may nominate any person to receive the whole or part of any moneys not exceeding £500 payable on his death out of any funds of the trade union of which he is a member.

(**a**) 1971 c. 72.
(**b**) 1889 c. 63.
(**c**) 1876 c. 22.
(**d**) 1883 c. 47.
(**e**) 4 & 5 Eliz. 2. c. 19.
(**f**) 1965 c. 32.

(2) Every nomination shall be made in writing in a form approved by the trade union, and shall be signed by the nominator.

(3) A nomination shall be of no effect unless it is delivered at or sent to the principal office of the trade union during the lifetime of the nominator.

(4) The trade union shall register every nomination and notify the registration to the nominator.

(5) The trade union may require the nominator to pay a fee not exceeding 3p in respect of each nomination.

(6) A nomination may be in favour of one person or of several persons (who shall be clearly designated in the nomination) and, where there is more than one nominee, may direct that specific sums shall be paid to one or more of the nominees or that the nominees shall take the money nominated in specified shares, or may give directions to both effects.

(7) A nomination shall not be valid in respect of any nominee who at the date of the nomination is an officer or employee of the trade union unless that person is the husband, wife, father, mother, child, brother, sister, nephew or niece of the nominator.

Revocation of nominations

3.—(1) A nomination shall be revoked :—

(*a*) by the death of the nominee, or, where there is more than one nominee, by the death of all the nominees, in the lifetime of the nominator ;

(*b*) so far as relates to the interest thereunder of any nominee (being one of two or more nominees), by the death of that nominee in the lifetime of the nominator, unless the interest of that nominee is disposed of by the nomination ;

(*c*) by the subsequent marriage of the nominator ;

(*d*) by written notice of revocation signed by the nominator and delivered at or sent to the principal office of the trade union during the lifetime of the nominator ;

(*e*) by a subsequent nomination duly made in accordance with these regulations by the same nominator disposing of either the whole or any part of the moneys disposed of by the earlier nomination, but so far only as respects those moneys or that part of those moneys, as the case may be ;

but a nomination shall not be revoked by any will or by any other act, or means whatsoever.

(2) Notwithstanding that a nomination has been revoked by the marriage of the nominator, where the trade union has paid the money to the nominee in ignorance of that marriage, the payment shall be as valid as if the nomination had not been so revoked.

Nomination covers all funds unless otherwise stated

4. A nomination shall, subject to the provisions of these Regulations, be deemed to extend to all sums to which a nominator is entitled at the time of his death unless a contrary intention appears from the nomination.

Payment under nomination

5. On the death of a nominator, the trade union shall pay to the nominee the amount due to him according to the directions of the nomination:

Provided that, if any nominee is under the age of 16 years, the trade union shall not make any payment to that nominee until he attains that age, but may pay the sum due or any part thereof, to any person who satisfies the trade union that he will apply it for the maintenance or benefit of the said nominee.

PART III

PAYMENTS ON DEATH

6.—(1) Where any money is payable out of the funds of a trade union on the death of a member, the trade union may, without letters of administration or probate of any will or confirmation, pay out or distribute (otherwise than in accordance with a nomination) an amount not exceeding £500 to the person or persons the trade union considers to be entitled by law to receive it.

(2) Where any person to whom a payment may be made under this paragraph is under the age of 16 years the trade union may make the payment to any person who satisfies it that he will apply the moneys for the maintenance or benefit of the first mentioned person.

PART IV

GENERAL

Persons unable to write

7. Where any document is required by the trade union or by these Regulations to be signed by any person and that person is unable to write, it shall be sufficient for the purposes of these Regulations if the document is marked by that person in the presence of a witness.

Receipts to be a good discharge

8. The receipt of any person aged 16 years or over for any money paid to him in accordance with a nomination or payment or distribution made in accordance with these Regulations shall be a good discharge to the trade union for any money so paid.

Proof of death

9. The trade union may accept as conclusive proof of the death of a member any evidence which it considers satisfactory.

Application of Regulations

10.—(1) Any nomination made on or after 28th February 1972 and any payment made (whether or not by virtue of a nomination) on a death occurring on or after that date shall be governed by these Regulations.

(2) Any nomination made prior to 28th February 1972 under section 10 of the Trade Union Act Amendment Act 1876(**a**) shall continue in force as if it had been validly made under these Regulations, and may be varied or revoked accordingly.

(**a**) 1876 c. 22.

(3) Any payment made (otherwise than by virtue of a nomination) on or after 28th February 1972 in respect of a death occurring before that date shall be governed by these Regulations.

(4) Any nomination made or having effect as if made under these Regulations by a member of an organisation shall continue to have effect notwithstanding that the organisation ceases to be a trade union, and may be varied or revoked accordingly.

Signed by order of the Secretary of State.

20th December 1971.

Paul Bryan,
Minister of State,
Department of Employment.

EXPLANATORY NOTE

(*This Note is not part of the Regulations.*)

These Regulations supersede the nomination powers contained in section 10 of the Trade Union Act Amendment Act 1876 as amended and the provision for payments on death contained in section 7 of the Provident Nominations and Small Intestacies Act 1883 as amended. They set out the procedure in greater detail.

These Regulations enable nominators to dispose of sums on death to nominated persons otherwise than under a will or on intestacy. They also allow trade unions (as defined) to distribute up to £500 on the death of a member to persons appearing to be entitled.

STATUTORY INSTRUMENTS

1971 No. 2089 (S.220)

RATING AND VALUATION

Act of Sederunt (Valuation Appeal Rules Amendment No. 2) 1971

Made - - - - 16*th December* 1971

Coming into Operation 13*th January* 1972

The Lords of Council and Session, under and by virtue of the powers conferred upon them by section 6 of the Rating and Valuation (Scotland) Act 1952**(a)** and of all other powers competent to them in that behalf, do hereby enact and declare as follows:

1. A party appealing by way of stated case against the determination of a Valuation Appeal Committee in terms of section 7 of the Valuation of Lands (Scotland) Amendment Act 1879**(b)** shall lodge his grounds of appeal with the Clerk to the Valuation Appeal Committee within ten days after the issue of the determination of the Committee, or, where application has been made under regulation 9 of the Valuation Appeal Committee Procedure (Scotland) Regulations 1965**(c)** for a statement of the reasons for the decision, within seven days after the date on which such statement shall have been supplied to him, and shall at the same time deliver to the respondent a copy thereof; and the respondent may, if so advised, lodge answers to the grounds of appeal with the Clerk to the Committee within ten days thereafter: provided that the Valuation Appeal Committee may, on cause shown, allow to a party such longer time within which to lodge grounds of appeal, or answers thereto, as the case may be, as may seem necessary and reasonable in the circumstances.

2. Within twenty-one days after the date on which a party has lodged his grounds of appeal, the Clerk to the Valuation Appeal Committee shall send a copy of the draft stated case to the appellant or his agent and to the respondent or his agent.

3. Either party to an appeal by way of stated case may, within fourteen days after the date on which a copy of the draft stated case shall have been sent to him as aforesaid, lodge with the Clerk to the Valuation Appeal Committee representations in writing that any finding in fact contained in the draft stated case should be deleted as altered or that additional findings in fact should be included in the stated case: provided that any party lodging such representations shall at the same time send a copy of the same to the other party to the appeal who may, within seven days thereafter, lodge with the Clerk of the Valuation Appeal Committee and send to the opposing party observations in writing as to why effect should not be given to such representations.

(a) 1952 c. 47. **(b)** 1879 c. 42.
(c) S.I. 1965/403 (1965 I, p. 1104).

4. It shall be competent to the Valuation Appeal Committee to revise the findings in fact set forth in the draft stated case in the light of any representations received in terms of paragraph 3 hereof, or otherwise as they may think proper.

5. Appeals by way of stated case in respect of lands and heritages entered in the ordinary valuation roll shall be lodged in the General Department of the Court of Session:

(*a*) In the case of determinations issued on or before the 15th day of October in any year, not later than the 15th day of January following the issue of the determination appealed against;

(*b*) In the case of determinations issued after the 15th day of October, within a period of three months after the issue of the determination appealed against.

6. Appeals by way of stated case in respect of lands and heritages entered in the supplementary valuation roll shall be lodged in the General Department of the Court of Session within a period of three months after the issue of the determination appealed against.

7. Within twenty one days after an appeal by way of stated case shall have been lodged in terms of paragraph 5 or 6 hereof the appellant shall lodge fifteen copies of the stated case and deliver at least ten copies thereof to the solicitor for the respondent; and if the appellant shall fail within the said period of twenty one days to lodge and deliver the said copies, he shall be held to have abandoned his appeal and shall not be entitled to insist therein except upon being reponed as hereinafter provided: provided however that, within seven days after the date of lodging of the stated case, the appellant may enrol a motion for a sist of process, and if, on cause shown, the Lands Valuation Appeal Court or the Vacation Judge grants such sist, the running of the said twenty one days shall be postponed for the duration of the period of sist or until the sist is recalled. An unopposed motion for the recall of such sist may, in vacation or recess, be disposed of by the Vacation Judge.

8. An appellant may, within seven days after an appeal has been held to be abandoned in terms of paragraph 7 hereof, enrol a motion to be reponed. Such motion shall be put out before the Lands Valuation Appeal Court or, in vacation or recess, before the Vacation Judge, and shall only be granted upon cause shown, and upon such conditions as to payment of expenses or otherwise as shall seem just.

9. The respondent may, within fourteen days after an appeal has been held to be abandoned in terms of paragraph 7 hereof, lodge fifteen copies of the stated case and deliver at least ten copies thereof to the solicitor for the appellant, and may thereafter insist in the appeal as if he had been the appellant; in which case the appellant shall also be entitled to insist in the appeal; and the provisions regulating appeals by an appellant shall apply equally to appeals insisted in under this paragraph by the respondent.

10. The instruments referred to in the Schedule hereto are revoked to the extent therein mentioned.

11. This Act of Sederunt may be cited as the Act of Sederunt (Valuation Appeal Rules Amendment No. 2) 1971, and shall come into operation on 13th January 1972.

And the Lords appoint this Act of Sederunt to be inserted in the Books of Sederunt.

Edinburgh,
16th December 1971.

J. L. CLYDE,
I.P.D.

Paragraph 10

SCHEDULE

REVOCATIONS

Citation	Instrument Revoked	Extent of Revocation
1. S.I. 1961/2205 (1961 III, p. 3901)	Act of Sederunt (Valuation Appeal Rules Amendment) 1961	Paragraphs 1 and 2
2. S.I. 1962/1220 (1962 II, p. 1327)	Act of Sederunt (Valuation Appeal Rules Amendment) 1962	The whole Act of Sederunt
3. S.I. 1965/450 (1965 I, p. 1200)	Act of Sederunt (Valuation Appeal Rules Amendment) 1965	Paragraphs 2, 3 and 4

EXPLANATORY NOTE

(*This Note is not part of the Act of Sederunt.*)

This Act of Sederunt consolidates the provisions contained in the Acts of Sederunt (Valuation Appeal Rules Amendment) of 1961, 1962 and 1965, and makes new provision for the lodging of copies of the stated case in appeals to the Lands Valuation Appeal Court.

1971 No. 2094 (C.56)

SOCIAL SECURITY

The National Insurance Act 1966 (Commencement No. 4) Order 1971

Made - - -	21*st December* 1971
Laid before Parliament	30*th December* 1971
Coming into Operation	31*st December* 1971

The Secretary of State for Social Services, in conjunction with the Treasury and in exercise of his powers under section 14(4) of the National Insurance Act 1966(**a**) and of all other powers enabling him in that behalf, hereby makes the following order :—

1. The National Insurance Act 1966 (Commencement No. 3) Order 1971(**b**) (which appointed 1st January 1972 for the coming into force of section 3(1) of the National Insurance Act 1966 for certain purposes) is hereby revoked.

2. This order may be cited as the National Insurance Act 1966 (Commencement No. 4) Order 1971 and shall come into operation on 31st December 1971.

Keith Joseph,
Secretary of State for Social Services.

20th December 1971.

Walter Clegg,
Tim Fortescue,
Two of the Lords Commissioners of Her Majesty's Treasury.

21st December 1971.

(**a**) 1966 c. 6.
(**b**) S.I. 1971/905 (1971 II, p. 2624).

EXPLANATORY NOTE

(This Note is not part of the Order.)

This Order revokes the National Insurance Act 1966 (Commencement No. 3) Order 1971. That Order would have brought into force on 1st January 1972 for the purpose of flat-rate unemployment benefit the provisions of section 3(1) of the National Insurance Act 1966 which deal with days not to be treated as days of unemployment where employment is suspended. The subsection is already in force for the purpose of earnings-related supplement.

STATUTORY INSTRUMENTS

1971 No. 2095

ROAD TRAFFIC

The Traffic Signs (Amendment) Regulations 1971

Made - - - -	21*st December* 1971
Laid before Parliament	31*st December* 1971
Coming into Operation	1*st January* 1972

The Secretary of State for the Environment, the Secretary of State for Scotland and the Secretary of State for Wales, acting jointly in exercise of their powers under section 54(1), (2) and (5) of the Road Traffic Regulation Act 1967**(a)** and of all other enabling powers, and after consultation with representative organisations in accordance with the provisions of section 107(2) of the said Act of 1967, hereby make the following Regulations:—

1.—(1) These Regulations may be cited as the Traffic Signs (Amendment) Regulations 1971 and shall come into operation on 1st January 1972.

(2) The Interpretation Act 1889**(b)** shall apply for the interpretation of these Regulations as it applies for the interpretation of an Act of Parliament.

2. The Traffic Signs Regulations 1964**(c)**, as amended **(d)**, shall have effect as though—

(1) in Regulation 11A(2), for the proviso there were substituted the following proviso—

"Provided that conditions (*b*) and (*c*) above shall not apply if—

(i) on the use by the driver of the telephone placed at the crossing he receives an indication for not less than two minutes that the telephone at the other end of the telephone line is being called but no duly authorised person answers it; and

(ii) the driver then drives the unit on to the crossing with the reasonable expectation of crossing it within times specified in a railway notice at that telephone as being times between which trains do not normally travel over that crossing.";

(2) in Regulation 25(1), in proviso (*b*), for the reference to the year 1971 there were substituted a reference to the year 1973;

(3) in Regulation 31 (3A), in sub-paragraph (*f*), for the words "9 feet 3 inches" there were substituted the words "8 feet 9 inches".

(a) 1967 c. 76. **(b)** 1889 c. 63.
(c) S.I. 1964/1857 (1964 III, p. 4053).
(d) The relevant amending instruments are S.I. 1966/490, 1969/1269, 1970/468, 1970/1972 (1966 I, p. 1001; 1969 III, p. 3786; 1970 I, p. 1567; 1970 III, p. 6420).

Peter Walker,
Secretary of State for the Environment.

20th December 1971.

Gordon Campbell,
Secretary of State for Scotland.

21st December 1971.

Peter Thomas,
Secretary of State for Wales.

21st December 1971.

EXPLANATORY NOTE

(This Note is not part of the Regulations.)

These Regulations further amend the Traffic Signs Regulations 1964. The principal changes are:—

1. Amendment is made to the significance of the sign shown in diagram 649 (already prescribed by the Regulations for use at railway level crossings equipped with automatic barriers) as regards the conditions under which certain of the requirements conveyed by that sign are not to apply. In particular, it will be necessary in future for the driver of a vehicle who is required to use the telephone before driving his vehicle over the railway level crossing to hear an indication that the telephone at the other end of the line is ringing for at least two minutes before he may proceed without permission at specified times. (Regulation 2(1)).

2. The minimum height of the red lenses of traffic signals conforming to Regulation 31 (3A) is lowered. (Regulation 2(3)).

STATUTORY INSTRUMENTS

1971 No. 2096

LOCAL GOVERNMENT, ENGLAND AND WALES

The Local Government (Financial Loss Allowance) Regulations 1971

Made - - -	16*th December* 1971
Laid before Parliament	3*rd January* 1972
Coming into Operation	24*th January* 1972

The Secretary of State for the Environment, in exercise of his powers under sections 112 and 117 of the Local Government Act 1948(**a**) as having effect by virtue of section 16 of the Local Government (Miscellaneous Provisions) Act 1953(**b**), and of all other powers enabling him in that behalf, hereby makes the following regulations:—

Citation and commencement

1. These regulations may be cited as the Local Government (Financial Loss Allowance) Regulations 1971 and shall come into operation on 24th January 1972.

Interpretation

2. The Interpretation Act 1889(**c**) applies for the interpretation of these regulations as it applies for the interpretation of an Act of Parliament.

Financial loss allowance

3. The amount which a member of a body to which Part VI of the Local Government Act 1948 applies shall be entitled to be paid by way of financial loss allowance within the meaning of section 112 of the said Act in respect of any one period of 24 hours shall not exceed—

(a) where the period of time over which earnings are lost or additional expense (other than expense on account of travelling or subsistence) is incurred is not more than 4 hours, the sum of £2·37½

(b) where the said period of time is more than 4 hours, the sum of £4·75.

Revocation

4. The Local Government (Financial Loss Allowance) Regulations 1970(**d**) are hereby revoked.

Peter Walker,
Secretary of State for the Environment.

16th December 1971.

(**a**) 1948 c. 26. (**b**) 1953 c. 26. (**c**) 1889 c. 63.
(**d**) S.I. 1970/89 (1970 I, p. 402).

EXPLANATORY NOTE

(This Note is not part of the Regulations.)

The Regulations supersede the Local Government (Financial Loss Allowance) Regulations 1970 and prescribe new maximum amounts for the financial loss allowance to which members of local authorities, etc., are entitled in respect of the performance of their duties.

1971 No. 2097

LONDON GOVERNMENT

The Greater London Council (Allowances to Members) Regulations 1971

Made - - - -	20*th December* 1971
Laid before Parliament	3*rd January* 1972
Coming into Operation	24*th January* 1972

The Secretary of State for the Environment, in exercise of his powers under section 117 of the Local Government Act 1948**(a)**, as extended by section 23 of the Greater London Council (General Powers) Act 1966**(b)**, and of all other powers enabling him in that behalf, hereby makes the following regulations:—

Title and commencement

1. These regulations may be cited as the Greater London Council (Allowances to Members) Regulations 1971 and shall come into operation on 24th January 1972.

Interpretation

2.—(1) In these regulations—

"the Act of 1966" means the Greater London Council (General Powers) Act 1966;

"the Council" means the Greater London Council; and

"day" means a period of 24 hours commencing at midnight;

and any reference to a period shall be read as referring to a period during which a member of the Council performs any approved duty as a member of the Council.

(2) For the purposes of these regulations a member of a committee or sub-committee of the Council shall be deemed to be a member of the Council.

(3) The Interpretation Act 1889**(c)** shall apply for the interpretation of these regulations as it applies for the interpretation of an Act of Parliament.

Maximum rates of allowance

3. For the purposes of section 23(3) of the Act of 1966, the rate at which a member of the Council shall be entitled to receive an allowance in respect of any period shall not exceed the rate prescribed in column (2) of the following table against the period in column (1) which is appropriate to the case.

(a) 1948 c. 26. **(b)** 1966 c. xxviii.
(c) 1889 c. 63.

TABLE

(1) Period	(2) Rate
1. A morning (up to 1 p.m. in any day)	£3·32½
2. An afternoon (from 1 p.m. onwards in any day)	£3·32½
3. A period which starts before 1 p.m. and continues after 2 p.m. in any day	£6·65
4. A period of absence overnight from the usual place of residence—	
(*a*) which does not exceed 24 hours	£10·25
(*b*) which does exceed 24 hours	£10·25 for each complete 24 hours plus the rate appropriate to the remainder of the period.

Claims for allowances

4. A member of the Council who wishes to claim an allowance under these regulations shall make a declaration that he has not and will not make any claim for financial loss allowance or subsistence allowance from any other authority or body in respect of the approved duty to which the claim relates.

Record of allowances paid

5. The Council shall keep records of all payments to members made by the Council under the Act of 1966, and such records shall be open to inspection at all reasonable hours by any local government elector for the area of the Council.

Revocation

6. The Greater London Council (Allowances to Members) Regulations 1970(**a**) are hereby revoked.

Peter Walker,
Secretary of State for
the Environment.

20th December 1971.

EXPLANATORY NOTE

(*This Note is not part of the Regulations.*)

These Regulations supersede the Greater London Council (Allowances to Members) Regulations 1970. They prescribe new maximum rates of the payments which members of the Greater London Council and its committees and sub-committees are entitled to receive instead of subsistence and financial loss allowances under Part VI of the Local Government Act 1948.

(**a**) S.I. 1970/88 (1970 I, p. 399).

1971 No. 2099

MINISTERS OF THE CROWN

The Minister for the Civil Service Order 1971

Made - - - -	22*nd December* 1971
Laid before Parliament	31*st December* 1971
Coming into Operation	7*th February* 1972

At the Court at Buckingham Palace, the 22nd day of December 1971

Present,

The Queen's Most Excellent Majesty in Council

Her Majesty, in pursuance of section 1 of the Ministers of the Crown (Transfer of Functions) Act 1946(**a**), is pleased, by and with the advice of Her Privy Council, to order, and it is hereby ordered, as follows:—

Citation, interpretation and commencement

1.—(1) This Order may be cited as the Minister for the Civil Service Order 1971.

(2) The Interpretation Act 1889(**b**) applies for the interpretation of this Order as it applies for the interpretation of an Act of Parliament.

(3) Any reference in this Order to an enactment is a reference thereto as amended, and includes a reference thereto as applied, by or under any other enactment.

(4) This Order shall come into operation on 7th February 1972.

Further transfer of functions from Treasury

2.—(1) There are hereby transferred to the Minister for the Civil Service all functions which at the coming into operation of this Order are exercisable by the Treasury—

(*a*) with respect to the appointment or employment of judges and judicial staff (including determination of numbers) or to their continuation in or removal from office or employment; or

(*b*) with respect to the determination of remuneration and, except where it is payable out of the Consolidated Fund, the times of payment of remuneration, of judges and judicial staff, or with respect to the determination of their conditions of service, personal expenses or allowances; or

(*c*) with respect to allowances payable for expenses or otherwise to jurors, witnesses or others by reason of their attendance at or before any court or tribunal or other judicial body or any inquiry.

(2) In this Article—

(*a*) references to judges shall apply—

(i) to all members of any court or tribunal or other judicial body;

(ii) to all other holders of any judicial office;

(**a**) 1946 c. 31. (**b**) 1889 c. 63.

(iii) to all persons appointed to assist any court or tribunal or other judicial body or inquiry as assessors or otherwise;

(iv) to any person other than a person mentioned in paragraphs (i) to (iii) above who is appointed to perform any judicial function or to hold any inquiry;

(*b*) references to judicial staff shall apply to all officers, servants or staff of any judge, or of any court or tribunal or other judicial body.

3. There are hereby also transferred to the Minister for the Civil Service any functions of the Treasury relating to the exercise by any person or body other than the Treasury of any power requiring for its exercise the sanction of the Treasury (whether by approval, consent, agreement or otherwise) being a power to determine the numbers, remuneration, conditions of service, expenses or allowances of persons employed (under whatever title) as agents of any person or any body, whether judicial or not.

Transfer or retransfer of functions under Tax Acts

4.—(1) In section 191 of the Income and Corporation Taxes Act 1970(**a**) (which relates to the deduction of expenses necessarily incurred, and defrayed from official emoluments) for the words " the Minister for the Civil Service " in each place where they occur there shall be substituted the words " the Treasury "; and accordingly—

(*a*) for the word " is " there shall be substituted the word " are ", and

(*b*) for the words " his opinion " there shall be substituted the words " the opinion of the Treasury ".

(2) In the Taxes Management Act 1970(**b**) in section 2(5) (allowances of General Commissioners) for the words " the Treasury " there shall be substituted the words " the Minister for the Civil Service ".

(3) In Schedule 14 to the Income and Corporation Taxes Act 1970 there shall be omitted paragraph 28 (which provides for the continued exercise by the Treasury of functions expressed by that Act or the Taxes Management Act 1970 to be conferred on the Minister for the Civil Service, but not transferred to him by the Minister for the Civil Service Order 1968(**c**)).

Other provisions related to previous transfer of functions from Treasury

5.—(1) There are hereby transferred to the Treasury any functions which at the coming into operation of this Order are exercisable by the Minister for the Civil Service under or by virtue of section 1 of the Polish Resettlement Act 1947(**d**).

(2) There are hereby also transferred to the Treasury any functions exercisable by the Minister for the Civil Service under or by virtue of the following enactments (which relate to Royal Household retired allowances), namely, section 7 of the Civil List Act 1910(**e**), section 8 of the Civil List Act 1936(**f**), section 11 of the Civil List Act 1937(**g**), and section 7(2) of the Civil List Act 1952(**h**).

(3) In Schedule 4 to the Sea Fish Industry Act 1970(**i**), in paragraph 12 (which requires the concurrence of the Treasury to orders varying certain provisions of the Schedule relating to the remuneration, etc., of members of the Herring Industry Board or to the staff of the Board) for the words " the Treasury " there shall be substituted the words " the Minister for the Civil Service ".

(**a**) 1970 c. 10. (**b**) 1970 c. 9. (**c**) S.I. 1968/1656 (1968 III, p. 4485).
(**d**) 1947 c. 19. (**e**) 1910 c. 28. (**f**) 1936 c. 15.
(**g**) 1937 c. 32. (**h**) 1952 c. 37. (**i**) 1970 c. 11.

(4) There are hereby transferred to the Minister for the Civil Service, in consequence of the transfer to him of functions of the Treasury effected by Article 2(1)(*c*) of the Minister for the Civil Service Order 1968 (superannuation functions) all policies of assurance and rights and liabilities under policies of assurance to which at the coming into operation of this Order the Treasury (or any person on their behalf) or the Treasury Solicitor may be entitled or subject in connection with the functions of the Treasury so transferred.

Supplemental

6.—(1) This Order shall not affect the validity of anything done by or in relation to the Treasury or the Minister for the Civil Service before the coming into operation of this Order; and anything which, at the coming into operation of this Order, is in process of being done by or in relation to either may, if it relates to any functions transferred by this Order to the other, be continued by or in relation to the other.

(2) Any approval, consent, direction or appointment given or made or other thing whatsoever done by the Treasury or the Minister for the Civil Service, for the purposes of any functions transferred by this Order to the other shall, if in force at the coming into operation of this Order, continue in force and have effect as if similarly given, made or done by the other.

(3) Article 3(2) of the Minister for the Civil Service Order 1968 (adaptation of references to Treasury) shall cease to apply to the enactments mentioned in Article 5(1) and (2) of this Order.

(4) The provisions so far unrepealed of the Statutory Salaries Act 1937(**a**) are hereby repealed; but in place of the words inserted by that Act after the word " members " in section 3(9) of the Small Landholders (Scotland) Act 1911(**b**) there shall be inserted the words " such salary as may be determined by the Minister for the Civil Service ".

(5) Subject to any express repeal or amendment made by this Order, any enactment or instrument passed or made before the coming into operation of this Order shall have effect, so far as may be necessary for the purpose or in consequence of the transfers effected by Articles 2 and 3 above as if for any references to the Treasury or any officer of the Treasury there were substituted a reference to the Minister for the Civil Service or an officer of his.

W. G. Agnew.

(**a**) 1937 c. 35. (**b**) 1911 c. 49.

EXPLANATORY NOTE

(This Note is not part of the Order.)

This Order in Council transfers to the Minister for the Civil Service the following functions of the Treasury:—

(*a*) functions in relation to the appointment, employment, determination of remuneration, conditions of service, personal expenses or allowances of judges and judicial staff and functions in relation to allowances payable for expenses to jurors, witnesses or others who attend any court, tribunal or other judicial body or any inquiry (Article 2(1));

(*b*) functions relating to the exercise by other persons or bodies of powers enabling them subject to the sanction of the Treasury to determine the remuneration, conditions of service, expenses or allowances of persons employed as agents of any person or body (Article 3);

(*c*) functions relating to allowances of Commissioners for the general purposes of the income tax (Article 4(2));

(*d*) the power of concurrence to orders varying certain provisions relating to remuneration etc. of members of the Herring Industry Board or to the staff of the Board (Article 5(3)).

Article 4(1) transfers back to the Treasury functions relating to the deduction of expenses necessarily incurred and defrayed from official emoluments under the Income and Corporation Taxes Act 1970.

Article 5(1) and (2) makes a similar re-transfer of functions under the Polish Resettlement Act 1947 and the Civil List Acts.

The remaining provisions of the Order are consequential or supplementary.

1971 No. 2100

CARIBBEAN AND NORTH ATLANTIC TERRITORIES

The Cayman Islands (Legislative Assembly—Extension of Duration) Order 1971

Made - - - -	22*nd December* 1971
Laid before Parliament	31*st December* 1971
Coming into operation	22*nd January* 1972

At the Court at Buckingham Palace, the 22nd day of December 1971

Present,

The Queen's Most Excellent Majesty in Council

Her Majesty, by virtue and in exercise of the powers vested in Her by sections 5 and 7 of the West Indies Act 1962(**a**), is pleased, by and with the advice of Her Privy Council, to order, and it is hereby ordered, as follows:—

1.—(1) This Order may be cited as the Cayman Islands (Legislative Assembly—Extension of Duration) Order 1971.

(2) This Order shall be construed as one with the Cayman Islands Constitution Orders 1965 to 1971(**b**).

(3) This Order shall come into operation on 22nd January 1972.

2. Sub-section (2) of section 47 of the Constitution of the Cayman Islands shall have effect as if for the words " three years " there were substituted the words " four years ".

W. G. Agnew.

EXPLANATORY NOTE

(*This Note is not part of the Order.*)

This Order extends the maximum life of the Cayman Islands Legislative Assembly for a further year beyond the period of three years after its first meeting.

(**a**) 1962 c. 19. (**b**) S.I. 1965/1860, 1967/970, 1971/1737 (1965 III, p. 5588; 1967 III, p. 2933; 1971 III p. 4733).

STATUTORY INSTRUMENTS

1971 No. 2101

DIPLOMATIC AND INTERNATIONAL IMMUNITIES AND PRIVILEGES

The Diplomatic Immunities Restriction (Amendment) Order 1971

Made - - - -	*22nd December* 1971
Laid before Parliament	*31st December* 1971
Coming into Operation	*21st January* 1972

At the Court at Buckingham Palace, the 22nd day of December 1971

Present,

The Queen's Most Excellent Majesty in Council

Her Majesty, in pursuance of the powers conferred on Her by sections 3, 6 and 8 of the Diplomatic Privileges Act 1964(**a**), or otherwise in Her Majesty vested, is pleased, by and with the advice of Her Privy Council, to order, and it is hereby ordered, as follows:—

1. This Order may be cited as the Diplomatic Immunities Restriction (Amendment) Order 1971 and shall come into operation on 21st January 1972.

2. The Interpretation Act 1889(**b**) shall apply for the interpretation of this Order as it applies for the interpretation of an Act of Parliament.

3. Article 1, paragraph (*c*) of Article 2, Article 3 and Schedules 1 and 2 of the Diplomatic Immunities Restriction Order 1956(**c**), as amended(**d**), are hereby revoked.

W. G. Agnew.

EXPLANATORY NOTE

(This Note is not part of the Order.)

This Order, by revoking Article 1 and paragraph (*c*) of Article 2 of the Diplomatic Immunities Restriction Order 1956, removes restrictions on personal immunity from suit and legal process which were imposed on certain persons connected with the diplomatic missions of France and the Lebanon by the 1956 Order. After the coming into operation of the present Order the enjoyment of immunity from suit and legal process by these persons will

(**a**) 1964 c. 81. (**b**) 1889 c. 63. (**c**) S.I. 1956/84 (1956 I, p. 683).
(**d**) S.I. 1956/1579, 1966/191, 1016, 1970/1113 (1956 I, p. 685; 1966 I, p. 385; II, p. 2438; 1970 II, p. 3529).

be subject to the provisions of the Diplomatic Privileges Act 1964. The other countries specified in Schedule 1 to the 1956 Order were deleted by previous amending Orders.

This Order also revokes Article 3 of the 1956 Order which restricted the personal immunity from suit and legal process of servants of envoys of certain countries. The conferment of immunity in respect of these persons is now governed by the Diplomatic Privileges Act 1964.

STATUTORY INSTRUMENTS

1971 No. 2102

FUGITIVE CRIMINAL

The Extradition (Hijacking) Order 1971

Made - - - -	*22nd December* 1971
Laid before Parliament	*31st December* 1971
Coming into Operation	*21st January* 1972

At the Court at Buckingham Palace, the 22nd day of December 1971

Present,

The Queen's Most Excellent Majesty in Council

Whereas the Convention for the Suppression of Unlawful Seizure of Aircraft (hereinafter referred to as " the Convention ") signed at The Hague on 16th December 1970, the terms of which are set out in Schedule 1 to this Order, will enter into force for the United Kingdom on 21st January 1972:

And Whereas the States mentioned in Schedule 2 to this Order are foreign States in respect of which the Convention is for the time being in force and with which extradition arrangements are in force:

And Whereas the States mentioned in Part I of Schedule 3 to this Order are foreign States in respect of which the Convention is for the time being in force but with which no extradition arrangements are in force:

And Whereas section 3(2) of the Hijacking Act 1971(**a**) provides that where no such arrangement as is mentioned in section 2 of the Extradition Act 1870(**b**) has been made with a State which is a party to the Convention, an Order in Council applying that Act may be made under that section as if the Convention were such an arrangement with that State:

Now, therefore, Her Majesty, in exercise of the powers conferred upon Her by sections 2 and 17 of the Extradition Act 1870 and sections 3(2) and 6(1) of the Hijacking Act 1971, or otherwise in Her Majesty vested, is pleased, by and with the advice of Her Privy Council, to order, and it is hereby ordered, as follows:—

1. This Order may be cited as the Extradition (Hijacking) Order 1971 and shall come into operation on 21st January 1972.

2.—(1) In this Order any references to the Extradition Acts and to the Act of 1870 are, respectively, references to the Extradition Acts 1870 to 1935 and to the Extradition Act 1870, as amended or extended by any subsequent enactment.

(2) The Interpretation Act 1889(**c**) shall apply for the interpretation of this Order as it applies for the interpretation of an Act of Parliament.

(**a**) 1971 c. 70. (**b**) 1870 c. 52. (**c**) 1889 c. 63.

3. The Extradition Acts shall apply in the case of a State mentioned in Schedule 2 to this Order under and in accordance with the extradition treaties described in the second column of that Schedule as supplemented by paragraphs 1 and 4 of Article 8 of the Convention (set out in Schedule 1 to this Order), which entered into force for those States on the dates specified in the third column of the said Schedule 2.

4. The Extradition Acts shall apply in the case of the States mentioned in Part I of Schedule 3 to this Order (being States in respect of which the Convention entered into force on the dates specified in the second column of that Schedule) subject to the conditions contained in, and in accordance with, Part II of that Schedule.

5. The operation of this Order is limited to the United Kingdom, the Channel Islands, the Isle of Man and the territories specified in Schedule 4 to this Order, being territories to which the application of the Convention is extended.

W. G. Agnew.

Article 3

SCHEDULE 1

The Convention

CONVENTION FOR THE SUPPRESSION OF UNLAWFUL SEIZURE OF AIRCRAFT

Preamble

The States Parties to this Convention

Considering that unlawful acts of seizure or exercise of control of aircraft in flight jeopardize the safety of persons and property, seriously affect the operation of air services, and undermine the confidence of the peoples of the world in the safety of civil aviation ;

Considering that the occurrence of such acts is a matter of grave concern ;

Considering that, for the purpose of deterring such acts, there is an urgent need to provide appropriate measures for punishment of offenders ;

Have agreed as follows:

Article 1

Any person who on board an aircraft in flight:

(*a*) unlawfully, by force or threat thereof, or by any other form of intimidation, seizes, or exercises control of, that aircraft, or attempts to perform any such act, or

(*b*) is an accomplice of a person who performs or attempts to perform any such act

commits an offence (hereinafter referred to as " the offence ").

Article 2

Each Contracting State undertakes to make the offence punishable by severe penalties.

ARTICLE 3

1. For the purposes of this Convention, an aircraft is considered to be in flight at any time from the moment when all its external doors are closed following embarkation until the moment when any such door is opened for disembarkation. In the case of a forced landing, the flight shall be deemed to continue until the competent authorities take over the responsibility for the aircraft and for persons and property on board.

2. This Convention shall not apply to aircraft used in military, customs or police services.

3. This Convention shall apply only if the place of take-off or the place of actual landing of the aircraft on board which the offence is committed is situated outside the territory of the State of registration of that aircraft ; it shall be immaterial whether the aircraft is engaged in an international or domestic flight.

4. In the cases mentioned in Article 5, this Convention shall not apply if the place of take-off and the place of actual landing of the aircraft on board which the offence is committed are situated within the territory of the same State where that State is one of those referred to in that Article.

5. Notwithstanding paragraphs 3 and 4 of this Article, Articles 6, 7, 8 and 10 shall apply whatever the place of take-off or the place of actual landing of the aircraft, if the offender or the alleged offender is found in the territory of a State other than the State of registration of that aircraft.

ARTICLE 4

1. Each Contracting State shall take such measures as may be necessary to establish its jurisdiction over the offence and any other act of violence against passengers or crew committed by the alleged offender in connection with the offence, in the following cases:

(*a*) when the offence is committed on board an aircraft registered in that State ;

(*b*) when the aircraft on board which the offence is committed lands in its territory with the alleged offender still on board ;

(*c*) when the offence is committed on board an aircraft leased without crew to a lessee who has his principal place of business or, if the lessee has no such place of business, his permanent residence, in that State.

2. Each Contracting State shall likewise take such measures as may be necessary to establish its jurisdiction over the offence in the case where the alleged offender is present in its territory and it does not extradite him pursuant to Article 8 to any of the States mentioned in paragraph 1 of this Article.

3. This Convention does not exclude any criminal jurisdiction exercised in accordance with national law.

ARTICLE 5

The Contracting States which establish joint air transport operating organizations or international operating agencies, which operate aircraft which are subject to joint or international registration shall, by appropriate means, designate for each aircraft the State, among them which shall exercise the jurisdiction and have the attributes of the State of registration for the purpose of this Convention and shall give notice thereof to the International Civil Aviation Organization which shall communicate the notice to all States Parties to this Convention.

ARTICLE 6

1. Upon being satisfied that the circumstances so warrant, any Contracting State in the territory of which the offender or the alleged offender is present, shall take him into custody or take other measures to ensure his presence. The custody and other measures shall be as provided in the law of that State but may only be continued for such time as is necessary to enable any criminal or extradition proceedings to be instituted.

2. Such State shall immediately make a preliminary enquiry into the facts.

3. Any person in custody pursuant to paragraph 1 of this Article shall be assisted in communicating immediately with the nearest appropriate representative of the State of which he is a national.

4. When a State, pursuant to this Article, has taken a person into custody, it shall immediately notify the State of registration of the aircraft, the State mentioned in Article 4, paragraph 1(*c*), the State of nationality of the detained person and, if it considers it advisable, any other interested States of the fact that such person is in custody and of the circumstances which warrant his detention. The State which makes the preliminary enquiry contemplated in paragraph 2 of this Article shall promptly report its findings to the said States and shall indicate whether it intends to exercise jurisdiction.

ARTICLE 7

The Contracting State in the territory of which the alleged offender is found shall, if it does not extradite him, be obliged, without exception whatsoever and whether or not the offence was committed in its territory, to submit the case to its competent authorities for the purpose of prosecution. Those authorities shall take their decision in the same manner as in the case of any ordinary offence of a serious nature under the law of that State.

ARTICLE 8

1. The offence shall be deemed to be included as an extraditable offence in any extradition treaty existing between Contracting States. Contracting States undertake to include the offence as an extraditable offence in every extradition treaty to be concluded between them.

2. If a Contracting State which makes extradition conditional on the existence of a treaty receives a request for extradition from another Contracting State with which it has no extradition treaty, it may at its option consider this Convention as the legal basis for extradition in respect of the offence. Extradition shall be subject to the other conditions provided by the law of the requested State.

3. Contracting States which do not make extradition conditional on the existence of a treaty shall recognize the offence as an extraditable offence between themselves subject to the conditions provided by the law of the requested State.

4. The offence shall be treated, for the purpose of extradition between Contracting States, as if it had been committed not only in the place in which it occurred but also in the territories of the States required to establish their jurisdiction in accordance with Article 4, paragraph 1.

ARTICLE 9

1. When any of the acts mentioned in Article 1(*a*) has occurred or is about to occur, Contracting States shall take all appropriate measures to restore control of the aircraft to its lawful commander or to preserve his control of the aircraft.

2. In the cases contemplated by the preceding paragraph, any Contracting State in which the aircraft or its passengers or crew are present shall facilitate the continuation of the journey of the passengers and crew as soon as practicable, and shall without delay return the aircraft and its cargo to the persons lawfully entitled to possession.

ARTICLE 10

1. Contracting States shall afford one another the greatest measure of assistance in connection with criminal proceedings brought in respect of the offence and other acts mentioned in Article 4. The law of the State requested shall apply in all cases.

2. The provisions of paragraph 1 of this Article shall not affect obligations under any other treaty, bilateral or multilateral, which governs or will govern, in whole or in part, mutual assistance in criminal matters.

ARTICLE 11

Each contracting State shall in accordance with its national law report to the Council of the International Civil Aviation Organisation as promptly as possible any relevant information in its possession concerning:

(*a*) the circumstances of the offence;

(*b*) the action taken pursuant to Article 9;

(*c*) the measures taken in relation to the offender or the alleged offender, and, in particular, the results of any extradition proceedings or other legal proceedings.

ARTICLE 12

1. Any dispute between two or more Contracting States concerning the interpretation or application of this Convention which cannot be settled through negotiation, shall, at the request of one of them, be submitted to arbitration. If within six months from the date of the request for arbitration the Parties are unable to agree on the organisation of the arbitration, any one of those Parties may refer the dispute to the International Court of Justice by request in conformity with the Statute of the Court.

2. Each State may at the time of signature or ratification of this Convention or accession thereto, declare that it does not consider itself bound by the preceding paragraph. The other Contracting States shall not be bound by the preceding paragraph with respect to any Contracting State having made such a reservation.

3. Any Contracting State having made a reservation in accordance with the preceding paragraph may at any time withdraw this reservation by notification to the Depositary Governments.

ARTICLE 13

1. This Convention shall be open for signature at The Hague on 16 December 1970, by States participating in the International Conference on Air Law held at The Hague from 1 to 16 December 1970 (hereinafter referred to as The Hague Conference). After 31 December 1970, the Convention shall be open to all States for signature in Moscow, London and Washington. Any State which does not sign this Convention before its entry into force in accordance with paragraph 3 of this Article may accede to it at any time.

2. This Convention shall be subject to ratification by the signatory States. Instruments of ratification and instruments of accession shall be deposited with the Governments of the Union of Soviet Socialist Republics, the United Kingdom of Great Britain and Northern Ireland, and the United States of America, which are hereby designated the Depositary Governments.

3. This Convention shall enter into force thirty days following the date of the deposit of instruments of ratification by ten States signatory to this Convention which participated in The Hague Conference.

4. For other States, this Convention shall enter into force on the date of entry into force of this Convention in accordance with paragraph 3 of this Article, or thirty days following the date of deposit of their instruments of ratification or accession, whichever is later.

5. The Depositary Governments shall promptly inform all signatory and acceding States of the date of each signature, the date of deposit of each instrument of ratification or accession, the date of entry into force of this Convention, and other notices.

6. As soon as this Convention comes into force, it shall be registered by the Depositary Governments pursuant to Article 102 of the Charter of the United Nations and pursuant to Article 83 of the Convention on International Civil Aviation (Chicago, 1944).

ARTICLE 14

1. Any Contracting State may denouce this Convention by written notification to the Depositary Governments.

2. Denunciation shall take effect six months following the date on which notification is received by the Depositary Governments.

IN WITNESS WHEREOF the undersigned Plenipotentiaries, being duly authorised thereto by their Governments, have signed this Convention.

DONE at The Hague, this sixteenth day of December, one thousand nine hundred and seventy, in three originals, each being drawn up in four authentic texts in the English, French, Russian and Spanish languages.

Article 3

SCHEDULE 2

FOREIGN STATES WHICH ARE PARTIES TO THE CONVENTION AND WITH WHICH EXTRADITION TREATIES ARE IN FORCE

State	Date of Extradition Treaty	Date of Entry into force of Convention for the State concerned
Ecuador	20th September 1880	14th October 1971
Hungary	3rd December 1873	14th October 1971
Israel	4th April 1960	14th October 1971
Norway	26th June 1873	14th October 1971
Sweden	26th April 1963	14th October 1971
Switzerland	26th November 1880 19th December 1934	14th October 1971
United States of America ...	22nd December 1931	14th October 1971

SCHEDULE 3

Article 4

PART I

FOREIGN STATES WHICH ARE PARTIES TO THE CONVENTION AND WITH WHICH NO EXTRADITION TREATIES ARE IN FORCE

State	Date of Entry into force of Convention for the State concerned
Bulgaria	14th October 1971
Costa Rica	14th October 1971
Gabonese Republic	14th October 1971
Japan	14th October 1971
Jordan	16th December 1971
Mali	14th October 1971
Mongolia	7th November 1971
Niger	14th November 1971
Union of Soviet Socialist Republics	24th October 1971

PART II

APPLICATION OF THE EXTRADITION ACTS IN THE CASE OF THE STATES MENTIONED IN PART I

1. The Extradition Acts shall have effect as if the only extradition crimes within the meaning of the Act of 1870 were offences under the Hijacking Act 1971 and attempts to commit such offences.

2. The Extradition Acts shall only apply where the case is such that paragraphs 2 and 4 of Article 8 of the Convention apply.

3. No proceedings shall be taken on an application by information or complaint, for a provisional warrant of arrest (that is to say, a warrant issued under section 8 of the Act of 1870 otherwise than in pursuance of sub-paragraph 1 of the first paragraph thereof), and no such warrant shall be issued, unless the application is made with the consent of the Secretary of State signified by an order in the form set out in Part III of this Schedule or in a form to the like effect; but, subject as aforesaid, the signification of consent shall not affect the provisions of the said section 8.

4. Without prejudice to sections 3, 9 and 11 of the Act of 1870, the fugitive criminal shall not be surrendered if—

(*a*) it appears to the Secretary of State, to the magistrate hearing the case in pursuance of section 9 of that Act or to the High Court on an application for a writ of habeas corpus—

(i) that the request for his surrender (though purporting to be made on account of such an offence as is mentioned in paragraph 1 above) is in fact made for the purpose of prosecuting or punishing him on account of his race, religion, nationality or political opinions, or

(ii) that he might, if surrendered, be prejudiced at his trial or punished, detained or restricted in his personal liberty by reason of his race, religion, nationality or political opinions, or

(iii) that if charged in England or Wales with the offence of which he is accused he would be entitled to be discharged under any rule of law relating to previous acquittal or conviction ; or

(*b*) it appears to the Secretary of State or to the High Court on an application for a writ of habeas corpus that—

(i) by reason of the passage of time since the fugitive criminal is alleged to have committed the offence of which he is accused or to have become unlawfully at large, or

(ii) because the accusation against him is not made in good faith in the interests of justice,

it would, having regard to all the circumstances, be unjust or oppressive to surrender him.

5.—(1) Without prejudice to his so deciding on other grounds, the Secretary of State may, in the circumstances mentioned in the following sub-paragraph, decide not to make an order or issue a warrant—

(*a*) for the purposes of paragraph 3 above signifying his consent to an application for a provisional warrant of arrest, or

(*b*) under section 7 of the Act of 1870 requiring the issue of a warrant of arrest, or

(*c*) under section 11 of the Act of 1870 ordering the fugitive criminal to be surrendered.

(2) The circumstances referred to in the preceding sub-paragraph are—

(*a*) that the Secretary of State is not satisfied that provision is made by the law of the State requesting surrender under which a person accused or convicted in the United Kingdom of the like offence as that with which the fugitive criminal is accused or convicted might be surrendered to the United Kingdom if found in that State, or

(*b*) that under the law of the State requesting surrender the fugitive criminal is liable to the death penalty for the offence of which he is accused, or

(*c*) that the fugitive criminal is a citizen of the United Kingdom and Colonies.

PART III

FORM OF CONSENT OF SECRETARY OF STATE TO APPLICATION FOR A PROVISIONAL WARRANT OF ARREST

Whereas AB, a person recognised by the Secretary of State as a diplomatic representative of ...., has requested consent to application being made for the issue of a provisional warrant for the arrest of CD, late of ...., who is [accused] [convicted] of the commission of an offence, or attempt to commit an offence, within the jurisdiction of the said State, being an offence which, if committed in England, would be an offence under the Hijacking Act 1971:

Now I hereby, by this my Order under my hand and seal, signify to you my consent to the said application being made.

Given under the hand and seal of the undersigned, one of Her Majesty's Principal Secretaries of State this day of 19 .

SCHEDULE 4

Article 5

TERRITORIES TO WHICH THE APPLICATION OF THE CONVENTION IS EXTENDED

Bahamas.
Bermuda.
British Antarctic Territory.
British Honduras.
British Indian Ocean Territory.
British Solomon Islands Protectorate.
British Virgin Islands.
Cayman Islands.
Central and Southern Line Islands.
Falkland Islands (and Dependencies).
Gibraltar.
Gilbert and Ellice Islands Colony.
Hong Kong.
Montserrat.
Pitcairn, Henderson, Ducie and Oeno Islands.
St. Helena (and Dependencies).
Seychelles.
Sovereign Base Areas of Akrotiri and Dhekelia.
Turks and Caicos Islands.

EXPLANATORY NOTE

(*This Note is not part of the Order.*)

This Order applies the Extradition Acts 1870 to 1935, as amended, so as to make the offence of hijacking extraditable in the case of States party to the Convention for the Suppression of Unlawful Seizure of Aircraft signed at the Hague on 16th December 1970.

1971 No. 2103

FUGITIVE CRIMINAL

The Extradition (Tokyo Convention) Order 1971

Made - - - -	22*nd December* 1971
Laid before Parliament	31*st December* 1971
Coming into Operation	21*st January* 1972

At the Court at Buckingham Palace, the 22nd day of December 1971

Present,

The Queen's Most Excellent Majesty in Council

Whereas Article 16.1 of the Convention on Offences and certain other Acts Committed on board Aircraft (hereinafter referred to as the "Tokyo Convention") signed at Tokyo on 14th September 1963 and which entered into force for the United Kingdom on 4th December 1969 provides as follows:

"Offences committed on aircraft registered in a Contracting State shall be treated, for the purpose of extradition, as if they had been committed not only in the place in which they have occurred but also in the territory of the State of registration of the aircraft":

And whereas by section 2(1) of the Tokyo Convention Act 1967(**a**) it is provided that, for the purposes of the application of the Extradition Act 1870(**b**) to crimes committed on board an aircraft in flight, any aircraft registered in a country in which the Tokyo Convention is for the time being in force shall at any time while that aircraft is in flight be deemed to be within the jurisdiction of that country, whether or not it is for the time being also within the jurisdiction of any other country:

And whereas the States mentioned in Schedule 1 to this Order are States with which extradition arrangements are in force and in respect of which the Tokyo Convention is for the time being in force:

Now, therefore, Her Majesty, in exercise of the powers conferred upon Her by sections 2 and 17 of the Extradition Act 1870 and section 2(2) of the Tokyo Convention Act 1967, or otherwise in Her Majesty vested, is pleased, by and with the advice of Her Privy Council, to order, and it is hereby ordered, as follows:—

1. This Order may be cited as the Extradition (Tokyo Convention) Order 1971 and shall come into operation on 21st January 1972.

2. The Interpretation Act 1889(**c**) shall apply for the interpretation of this Order as it applies for the interpretation of an Act of Parliament.

(**a**) 1967 c. 52. (**b**) 1870 c. 52. (**c**) 1889 c. 63.

3. The Extradition Acts 1870 to 1935 as amended by section 2 of the Tokyo Convention Act 1967 shall apply in the case of the States mentioned in Schedule 1 to this Order under and in accordance with the extradition treaties described in the second column of that Schedule as supplemented by Article 16.1 of the Tokyo Convention, which entered into force as between those States and the United Kingdom on the dates specified in the third column of that Schedule.

4. The operation of this Order is limited to the United Kingdom, the Channel Islands, the Isle of Man and the territories mentioned in Schedule 2 to this Order, being territories to which the application of the Tokyo Convention is extended.

W. G. Agnew

Article 3 SCHEDULE 1

States with which the United Kingdom has extradition treaties and in respect of which the Tokyo Convention is in force.

State	Date of Extradition Treaty	Date on which Tokyo Convention entered into force as between the United Kingdom and the State concerned
Belgium	29th October 1901/ 5th March 1907/ 3rd March 1911	4th November 1970
Denmark	31st March 1873/ 15th October 1935	4th December 1969
Ecuador	20th September 1880	3rd March 1970
Finland	30th May 1924	1st July 1971
France	14th August 1876/ 13th February 1896 17th October 1908	10th December 1970
The Federal Republic of Germany.	14th May 1872/ 23rd February 1960	16th March 1970
Greece	24th September 1910	29th August 1971
Guatemala	4th July 1885/ 30th May 1914/ 3rd December 1873	15th February 1971
Hungary	26th June 1901/ 18th September 1936	3rd March 1971
Iceland	31st March 1873/ 25th October 1938	14th June 1970
Israel	4th April 1960	18th December 1969
Italy	5th February 1873	4th December 1969

State	Date of Extradition Treaty	Date on which Tokyo Convention entered into force as between the United Kingdom and the State concerned
Mexico	7th September 1886	4th December 1969
Netherlands	26th September 1898	12th February 1970
Norway	26th June 1873/ 18th February 1907	4th December 1969
Panama	25th August 1906	14th February 1971
Poland	11th January 1932	17th June 1971
Portugal	17th October 1892	4th December 1969
Spain	4th June 1878/ 19th February 1889	30th December 1969
Sweden	26th April 1963	4th December 1969
Switzerland	26th November 1880/ 29th June 1904/ 19th December 1934	21st March 1971
United States of America	22nd December 1931	4th December 1969
Yugoslavia	23rd November 1900 & 6th December 1900	13th May 1971

SCHEDULE 2

Article 4

TERRITORIES TO WHICH THE APPLICATION OF THE TOKYO CONVENTION IS EXTENDED

Bahamas.
Bermuda.
British Antarctic Territory.
British Honduras.
British Indian Ocean Territory.
British Virgin Islands.
Cayman Islands.
Central and Southern Line Islands.
Falkland Islands (and Dependencies).
Gibraltar.
Gilbert and Ellice Islands Colony.
Hong Kong.
Montserrat.
Pitcairn, Henderson, Ducie and Oeno Islands.
St. Helena (and Dependencies).
Seychelles.
Sovereign Base Areas of Akrotiri and Dhekelia.
Turks and Caicos Islands.

EXPLANATORY NOTE

(This Note is not part of the Order.)

This Order applies the Extradition Acts 1870 to 1935, as amended by the Tokyo Convention Act 1967, to offences committed on board aircraft in flight registered in States parties to the Tokyo Convention and with whom the United Kingdom has extradition treaties.

1971 No. 2104

FOREIGN COMPENSATION

The Foreign Compensation (Egypt) Order 1971

Made - - - -	22*nd December* 1971
Laid before Parliament	31*st December* 1971
Coming into Operation	1*st February* 1972

At the Court at Buckingham Palace, the 22nd day of December 1971

Present,

The Queen's Most Excellent Majesty in Council

Whereas Her Majesty is authorised to make provision by Order in Council under section 3 of the Foreign Compensation Act 1950(**a**) (hereinafter referred to as " the Act of 1950 ") as amended by section 2(1) of the Foreign Compensation Act 1969(**b**) (hereinafter referred to as " the Act of 1969 ") for the determination by the Foreign Compensation Commission (hereinafter referred to as " the Commission ") of claims to participate in compensation received under an agreement with the Government of any other country, and for the distribution by the Commission of such compensation:

And Whereas an Agreement (hereinafter referred to as " the Agreement ") entered into between Her Majesty's Government and the Government of the Arab Republic of Egypt on 13th September 1971 provides that the Government of the Arab Republic of Egypt shall pay the Government of the United Kingdom the sum of £2,100,000 in settlement of claims for compensation in respect of British nationalised property (subject to a deduction of £200,000 in settlement of all liabilities of entitled British claimants to the Government of the Arab Republic of Egypt, and to other authorities and banks in the Arab Republic of Egypt):

Now, therefore, Her Majesty, by virtue and in exercise of the powers in that behalf by the Acts of 1950 and 1969 or otherwise in Her Majesty vested, is pleased, by and with the advice of Her Privy Council, to order, and it is hereby ordered, as follows:—

PART I

Citation, Commencement and Interpretation

1. This Order may be cited as the Foreign Compensation (Egypt) Order 1971 and shall come into operation on 1st February 1972.

2.—(1) The Interpretation Act 1889(**c**) shall apply for the interpretation of this Order as it applies for the interpretation of an Act of Parliament.

(2) In this Order:—

" Egyptian measure " means any of the laws promulgated by the Government of the Arab Republic of Egypt in respect of expropriation or nationalisation during the years 1960 to 1964, including Agrarian Reform

(**a**) 1950 c. 12. (**b**) 1969 c. 20. (**c**) 1889 c. 63.

Laws No. 127 of 1961 and No. 15 of 1963 but not including Law No. 150 of 1964.

" Material time " means any time or date at which it is material for the purposes of this Order to determine whether or not a person is a United Kingdom national.

" Predecessor in title " means any person from whom, whether directly or indirectly, a person making application under this Order (including a trustee) has succeeded, whether by assignment or otherwise, to the property or claim to which the application relates. For the purpose of considering any question of succession, every claim shall be deemed (i) to have arisen at the relevant date but no claim shall be barred by any lapse of time thereafter, and (ii) to have been capable of transfer and transmission in the same manner as the property to which it relates.

" Property " includes all rights and interests of any kind in property and any claim in respect of property.

" Relevant date " means the date of publication of the Egyptian measure by or under which the property to which the claim relates was affected, or, if such measure was first applied to the property on a date other than the date of publication of the measure, the date on which the applicant, or his predecessor in title, was deprived of title to or enjoyment of the property.

" Rules of the Commission " means rules made by the Commission with the approval of the Lord Chancellor under section 4(2) of the Act of 1950 regulating the procedure of the Commission in determining applications made under this Order.

" Trustee " includes a personal representative of a deceased person or a nominee ; and " beneficiary " shall have a corresponding meaning.

" United Kingdom national " means—

(*a*) any individual who was at the material time a citizen of the United Kingdom and Colonies, a British subject by virtue of section 2, 13 or 16 of the British Nationality Act 1948(**a**) or the British Nationality Act 1965(**b**), or a British protected person within the meaning of the said Act of 1948 ;

(*b*) any individual who was at the material time a citizen of Southern Rhodesia or a citizen of Rhodesia and Nyasaland ;

(*c*) any individual who as regards any material time prior to 17th September 1963 was a citizen of Singapore ;

(*d*) any corporation, firm or association incorporated or constituted under the laws in force in the United Kingdom or in any territory for whose international relations Her Majesty's Government in the United Kingdom were, at the material time, responsible.

Part II

The fund

3. The Commission shall pay into a fund to be called the Egyptian Nationalised Property Compensation Fund (hereinafter referred to as " the Fund ") all such sums as may be paid to them by Her Majesty's Government, being sums received under the Agreement.

4.—(1) Any sums standing to the credit of the Fund may be temporarily invested by the Commission in such manner as the Treasury may authorise.

(**a**) 1948 c. 56. (**b**) 1965 c. 34.

(2) All interest, dividends and other sums received by the Commission as a result of any investment made by them of any sum standing to the credit of the Fund shall be paid into the Fund.

5. When it appears to the Secretary of State that all payments to be made into the Fund have been made and that all payments which it is practicable to make out of the Fund have been made, he may direct that the Fund shall be wound up and that any sum remaining therein shall be paid into the Consolidated Fund.

PART III

Provisions concerning the establishment of claims

6.—(1) An application shall not be entertained by the Commission for the purposes of this Order unless it has reached the Commission on or before 31st August 1972.

(2) An application shall not be entertained by the Commission for the purposes of this Order unless it is made in accordance with the Rules of the Commission.

(3) An application shall not be entertained by the Commission for the purposes of this Order if

(i) the application relates to property owned by a United Kingdom national on 28th February 1959 and referred to in Annex E to the Agreement concerning Financial and Commercial Relations and British Property in Egypt of 28th February 1959 (hereinafter referred to as " the Financial Agreement ") as amended by the Exchange of Notes of 7th August 1962 supplementary to that Agreement ; or

(ii) the application relates to property which was sequestrated by the Government of the Arab Republic of Egypt in accordance with the provisions of Proclamation No. 5 of 1956 and which was neither the subject of an application for release, nor established as British property, in accordance with the Financial Agreement and the Exchange of Notes of 7th August 1962 supplementary to that Agreement.

7. Each application made under this Order shall be determined by not less than two members of the Commission, provided that one member of the Commission may provisionally determine any application which is not the subject of an oral hearing unless it is determined that such application be dismissed wholly or in part or the aggregate amount of the assessed loss thereon exceeds £10,000.

8.—(1) The following persons shall be qualified to make application to the Commission for the purpose of establishing claims under this Order:—

(*a*) any person who was a United Kingdom national on 13th September 1971 ;

(*b*) any person who after 13th September 1971 has succeeded, whether by assignment or otherwise, to the claim of any person qualified under sub-paragraph (*a*) of this paragraph ;

(*c*) a trustee for any person qualified under sub-paragraph (*a*) or (*b*) of this paragraph.

(2) An application under this Order may be made by a trustee qualified under paragraph (1) of this Article or by a beneficiary so qualified. An application by a trustee (other than a nominee) shall, however, be entertained by the Commission only in so far as the beneficial interest in the property or in the claim to which the application relates was, on the relevant date and on 13th September 1971, owned by a United Kingdom national.

(3) If applications under this Order are made by a trustee and by a beneficiary in relation to the same claim, and both the trustee and the beneficiary are qualified under paragraph (1) of this Article, the Commission may entertain the application made by the trustee in preference to that made by the beneficiary, or entertain the application made by the beneficiary in preference to that made by the trustee. The Commission shall dismiss the application by the trustee or by the beneficiary, as the case may be, which it has decided not to entertain.

9.—(1) To establish a claim under this Order, any person making application to the Commission shall be required to establish to the satisfaction of the Commission:—

(*a*) that he is a person qualified under Article 8 of this Order to make such application;

(*b*) that the property to which his application relates was British at the relevant date;

(*c*) that where any succession in respect of his claim (whether legal or beneficial and whether by assignment, inheritance on death or otherwise) has occurred between the relevant date and 14th September 1971, the property was British immediately before and immediately after the date of such succession; and

(*d*) that by or under any Egyptian measure he or his predecessor in title (or, if he is a trustee, the person for whom he is a trustee or the predecessor in title of such person) has before 13th September 1971 been deprived of title to or enjoyment of the property, and has suffered loss thereby.

(2) Property shall be deemed to be British property to the extent that it was owned or held, whether beneficially or as nominee, by a United Kingdom national.

(3) A person holding shares in The Anglo-Egyptian Oilfields Limited or The Egyptian Delta Land and Investment Company Limited shall be deemed to have been deprived of the enjoyment of those shares to the extent that he can establish that the value of his shares depreciated as a direct result of the application of any Egyptian measure to that company.

10.—(1) Subject to the provisions of this Order the Commission shall assess the amount of loss with respect to each claim which is established under this Order as may seem just and equitable to them having regard to all the circumstances and shall dismiss each claim which is not so established.

(2) In assessing the amount of loss in respect of each claim established under this Order the Commission shall have regard to:—

(*a*) any valuation of property concerned which was published in accordance with the relevant Egyptian measure, unless the person making the application establishes to the satisfaction of the Commission that this would lead to an unjust or inequitable result having regard to all the circumstances;

(*b*) any compensation recoupment or payment in respect of that loss from any source other than the Fund that the person making the application or his predecessor in title or any trustee for such person or predecessor in title, or, if the person making the application is a trustee, any beneficiary or any predecessor in title of any beneficiary (i) has received or (ii) may, if he exercises diligence, be reasonably expected to receive or (iii) might, if he had exercised diligence, reasonably have been expected to receive.

(3) Where any amount which is material to the assessment of the amount of loss with respect to any claim established under this Order is expressed in Egyptian currency, the value in sterling of that amount shall be calculated in accordance with the rate of exchange used for official transactions on 13th September 1971 by Her Majesty's Embassy in Cairo, namely 1·040 Egyptian pounds = 1 pound sterling.

PART IV

Payments out of the Fund

11.—(1) The Commission shall make payments out of the Fund to every person who has established a claim under this Order and who applies to the Commission for payment.

(2) If any person who has established a claim under this Order shall have died before the amounts payable to him under Articles 12 and 13 of the Order have been paid to him, such payments or the balance thereof shall be made to his personal representatives if they apply to the Commission for payment, provided that, if the Commission are satisfied that no grant of administration of his estate has been made in the United Kingdom and that the assets of his estate (including the amount payable under this Order) do not exceed £500 in value, the Commission may at their discretion and subject to such conditions as the Commission think proper, make such payment either to any person who has taken out administration in any other part of the Commonwealth, or to the person who shall appear to the Commission to be the person who, being a widower, widow, child, father, mother, brother or sister of the deceased person, would, under the law of England, have the prior right to a grant of administration of the estate of the deceased person if such deceased person had died intestate domiciled in England.

(3) If any person whose claim has been established under this Order is an infant at the date when the amounts payable to him under Articles 12 and 13 of this Order are due to be paid, the Commission may make payment thereof into the Supreme Court, or, if the amount thereof does not exceed £5,000, into the County Court for the district in which the infant resides, under the provisions of the Trustee Act 1925(**a**), or, if the amount does not exceed £50, may place the same on deposit in the name of the Commission in any bank for such time as the person remains an infant.

12.—(1) The payment in respect of each claim established under this Order shall be a fraction of the distributable amount of the Fund equal to the proportion which the assessed amount of the claim bears to the total of the amount assessed with respect to all claims established under the Order, less such sum (if any) as the Secretary of State for Foreign and Commonwealth Affairs shall notify in writing to the Commission as an appropriate deduction in respect of any ex gratia loan made to the applicant or his predecessor in title by Her Majesty's Government.

(2) If it shall appear to the Secretary of State for Foreign and Commonwealth Affairs that any sum notified by him in writing to the Commission as a deduction pursuant to paragraph (1) of this Article was in excess of the sum which in all the circumstances it was appropriate to deduct, he may at any time thereafter notify in writing some lesser sum as an appropriate deduction in lieu of the sum previously notified, and the Commission shall thereupon adjust the amount of the payment and (if the case requires) make an additional payment accordingly.

(**a**) 1925 c. 19.

(3) Where the Foreign Compensation Commission has made a deduction in accordance with paragraphs (1) and (2) of this Article in respect of a loan to the applicant or his predecessor in title made by Her Majesty's Government, the Commission shall pay to the Secretary of State for Foreign and Commonwealth Affairs from the Fund a sum equal to the amount of that deduction.

(4) The distributable amount shall be the total of all sums paid into the Fund, after the deduction of any payments made therefrom into the Consolidated Fund in accordance with any Order in Council made under section 7(2) of the Act of 1950 as originally enacted and as applied by section 3(3) of the Foreign Compensation Act 1962(**a**).

13.—(1) Whether or not all claims under this Order have been finally determined, the Commission may, at such time or times as they may decide, make from the Fund interim payments to any of the persons who have established claims under the Order.

(2) Interim payment made under the provisions of this Article shall be made—

(*a*) on account of payments to be made in accordance with Article 12 of this Order, and

(*b*) at a uniform rate upon the assessed amount of the claim, except that any deduction in accordance with paragraph (1) of Article 12 of this Order shall be made as soon as possible, and the amount deducted shall be paid by the Commission to the Secretary of State for Foreign and Commonwealth Affairs. The uniform rate of payment shall be determined by the Commission ; for this purpose the Commission shall estimate the total liability likely to fall upon the Fund.

(3) For the purposes of this Article—

(*a*) a claim shall be deemed to be established under this Order even though the determination thereof may be provisional and subject to review under the Rules of the Commission.

(*b*) the assessed amount of the claim shall be deemed to be the amount so provisionally determined subject to review unless before the date of payment the Commission shall have made a final determination on review.

14.—(1) Subject to the provisions of paragraph (2) of this Article, the Commission shall, as a condition of the making of any payment to any person under this Order, require him to surrender to the Commission all available documents of title, if any, relating exclusively to the claim to which the payment relates, and shall require him to sign and deliver to the Commission a document in such form as the Commission may determine declaring that he renounces all those claims which he has established under the Order.

(2) If the person for whose benefit a payment is to be made is an infant, the Commission shall, as a condition of the making of any payment into Court or placing the same on deposit under Article 11(3) of this Order, require the person who, in accordance with the Rules of the Commission, has made an application for payment on the infant's behalf to surrender to the Commission the documents of title, if any, under his control relating exclusively to the claim, and to sign and deliver to the Commission a

(**a**) 11 & 12 Eliz. 2. c. 4.

document in such form as the Commission may determine declaring that the infant renounces all claims to which the payment relates; and that the document so signed shall operate as a valid surrender by the infant of all such claims.

(3) The Commission shall retain all documents which are delivered to them under paragraphs (1) and (2) of this Article, and shall dispose of them in accordance with instructions to be given by the Secretary of State for Foreign and Commonwealth Affairs.

W. G. Agnew.

EXPLANATORY NOTE

(*This Note is not part of the Order.*)

This Order provides—

(i) for the determination by the Foreign Compensation Commission of claims to participate in the compensation received by Her Majesty's Government from the Government of the Arab Republic of Egypt under the Agreement between the two Governments of 13th September 1971 regarding Compensation for British Property Rights and Interests affected by Arab Republic of Egypt Measures of Nationalization (Cmnd. 4853); and

(ii) for the distribution of the aforesaid compensation by the Commission to applicants who have established claims under the Order.

The Agreement has not yet been ratified.

1971 No. 2105

ALDERNEY

The Alderney (Transfer of Property, &c.) Order 1971

Made - - - - *22nd December* 1971

At the Court at Buckingham Palace, the 22nd day of December 1971

Present,

The Queen's Most Excellent Majesty in Council

Her Majesty, in exercise of the powers conferred upon Her by section 1 of the Alderney (Transfer of Property, &c.) Act 1923**(a)**, is pleased, by and with the advice of Her Privy Council, to order, and it is hereby ordered, as follows:—

1. This Order may be cited as the Alderney (Transfer of Property, &c.) Order 1971 and shall take effect on 31st January 1972.

2. The Interpretation Act 1889**(b)** shall apply for the purpose of the interpretation of this Order as it applies for the purpose of the interpretation of an Act of Parliament.

3. The property specified in the Schedule to this Order, being the property now representing the personal estate of the late Ernest Perrine Marie Audren (hereinafter referred to as "the deceased") who died intestate on 3rd May 1964 domiciled in the Island of Alderney, is hereby, subject to the terms and conditions next following, transferred to and vested in the Treasury.

4. The said terms and conditions are that the said property in so far as it consists of money shall be invested in the name of Her Majesty's Receiver General for the Bailiwick of Guernsey in such manner as the Treasury may from time to time direct and in so far as it consists of War Stock shall be registered in his name and that the income arising therefrom shall be paid by Her Majesty's Receiver General aforesaid to the Treasurer of the States of Alderney for the account of the States of Alderney; so however that the Treasury may from time to time direct that any part of such income shall be paid by Her Majesty's Receiver General aforesaid to any dependant, whether kindred or not, of the deceased and other persons for whom the deceased might reasonably be expected to have made provision.

W. G. Agnew.

(a) 1923 c. 15. **(b)** 1889 c. 63.

SCHEDULE

Property Transferred to the Treasury

Any amount of 3½% War Stock registered at the Bank of England in the name of the deceased.

Any sum of money now representing the remainder of the personal estate of the deceased credited (*a*) to the deposit account in the names of the Law Officers of the Crown for Guernsey at Lloyds Bank Limited, Smith Street, Saint Peter Port, Guernsey; (*b*) to the names of the said Law Officers in the special investment department and the ordinary department of the Guernsey Savings Bank.

EXPLANATORY NOTE

(*This Note is not part of the Order.*)

This Order vests in the Treasury the property now representing the personal estate which devolved to the Crown as bona vacantia upon the intestacy of a person who died domiciled in Alderney.

STATUTORY INSTRUMENTS

1971 No. 2106

REPRESENTATION OF THE PEOPLE

REDISTRIBUTION OF SEATS

The Parliamentary Constituencies (Abingdon and Newbury) Order 1971

Laid before Parliament in draft

Made - - -	*22nd December* 1971
Coming into Operation	*5th January* 1972

At the Court at Buckingham Palace, the 22nd day of December 1971

Present,

The Queen's Most Excellent Majesty in Council

Whereas in pursuance of section 2(3) of the House of Commons (Redistribution of Seats) Act 1949(**a**) the Boundary Commission for England have submitted to the Secretary of State a report dated 1st October 1971 with respect to the areas comprised in certain constituencies in England and showing the constituencies into which they recommend, in accordance with the provisions of the House of Commons (Redistribution of Seats) Acts 1949 and 1958(**b**), that the areas should be divided :

And whereas the Secretary of State has laid the said report before Parliament together with the draft of this Order in Council to give effect to recommendations contained in the report and each House of Parliament has by resolution approved the said draft :

Now, therefore, Her Majesty, in pursuance of section 3 of the House of Commons (Redistribution of Seats) Act 1949, is pleased, by and with the advice of Her Privy Council, to order, and it is hereby ordered, as follows :—

1.—(1) This Order may be cited as the Parliamentary Constituencies (Abingdon and Newbury) Order 1971.

(2) The Interpretation Act 1889(**c**) shall apply to the interpretation of this Order as it applies to the interpretation of an Act of Parliament.

(3) This Order shall come into operation on the fourteenth day after the day on which it is made:

Provided that the coming into operation of this Order shall not affect any parliamentary election until a proclamation is issued by Her Majesty summoning a new Parliament or affect the constitution of the House of Commons until the dissolution of the Parliament in being on the day on which this Order comes into operation.

(**a**) 1949 c. 66. (**b**) 1958 c. 26.
(**c**) 1889 c. 63.

2. In lieu of the county constituency of Abingdon described in Schedule 1 to the Representation of the People Act 1948(**a**) and the county constituency of Newbury described in Part II of the Schedule to the Parliamentary Constituencies (England) Order 1970(**b**) and specified in Part I of the Schedule to this Order there shall be substituted the county constituencies described in Part II of the Schedule to this Order.

3. The electoral registration officer for the Berkshire registration area shall make such re-arrangement or adaptation of the registers of parliamentary electors as may be necessary to give effect to this Order.

W. G. Agnew.

SCHEDULE

BERKSHIRE

PART I

Existing constituencies described in the case of Abingdon by reference to circumstances as they existed immediately before the end of the year 1947 *and in the case of Newbury by reference to circumstances as they existed on* 1*st January* 1969

Name	County or Borough Constituency	Contents
Abingdon	County ..	(i) The boroughs of Abingdon and Wallingford; (ii) the urban district of Wantage; (iii) the rural districts of Abingdon, Faringdon, Wallingford and Wantage.
Newbury	County ..	(i) The borough of Newbury; (ii) the rural districts of Bradfield, Hungerford and Newbury.

PART II

New constituencies described by reference to circumstances as they existed on 1*st October* 1971 (*being a date subsequent to the County of Berkshire* (*Bradfield, Newbury and Wantage Rural Districts*) *Confirmation Order* 1969)

Name	County or Borough Constituency	Contents
Abingdon	County ..	(i) The boroughs of Abingdon and Wallingford; (ii) the urban district of Wantage; (iii) the rural districts of Abingdon, Faringdon, Wallingford and Wantage.
Newbury	County ..	(i) The borough of Newbury; (ii) the rural districts of Bradfield, Hungerford and Newbury.

(**a**) 1948 c. 65.

(**b**) S.I. 1970/1674 (1970 III, p. 5444).

1971 No. 2107

REPRESENTATION OF THE PEOPLE

REDISTRIBUTION OF SEATS

The Parliamentary Constituencies (Blyth and Hexham) Order 1971

Laid before Parliament in draft

Made - - - *22nd December* 1971

Coming into Operation *5th January* 1972

At the Court at Buckingham Palace, the 22nd day of December 1971

Present,

The Queen's Most Excellent Majesty in Council

Whereas in pursuance of section 2(3) of the House of Commons (Redistribution of Seats) Act 1949(**a**) the Boundary Commission for England have submitted to the Secretary of State a report dated 1st October 1971 with respect to the areas comprised in certain constituencies in England and showing the constituencies into which they recommend, in accordance with the provisions of the House of Commons (Redistribution of Seats) Acts 1949 and 1958(**b**), that the areas should be divided :

And whereas the Secretary of State has laid the said report before Parliament together with the draft of this Order in Council to give effect to recommendations contained in the report and each House of Parliament has by resolution approved the said draft :

Now, therefore, Her Majesty, in pursuance of section 3 of the House of Commons (Redistribution of Seats) Act 1949, is pleased, by and with the advice of Her Privy Council, to order, and it is hereby ordered, as follows :—

1.—(1) This Order may be cited as the Parliamentary Constituencies (Blyth and Hexham) Order 1971.

(2) The Interpretation Act 1889(**c**) shall apply to the interpretation of this Order as it applies to the interpretation of an Act of Parliament.

(3) This Order shall come into operation on the fourteenth day after the day on which it is made:

Provided that the coming into operation of this Order shall not affect any parliamentary election until a proclamation is issued by Her Majesty summoning a new Parliament or affect the constitution of the House of Commons until the dissolution of the Parliament in being on the day on which this Order comes into operation.

(**a**) 1949 c. 66. (**b**) 1958 c. 26.
(**c**) 1889 c. 63.

2. In lieu of the county constituency of Hexham and the borough constituency of Blyth described in Schedule 1 to the Representation of the People Act 1948(**a**) and specified in Part I of the Schedule to this Order there shall be substituted the county and borough constituencies described in Part II of the Schedule to this Order.

3. The electoral registration officers for the aforesaid constituencies shall make such re-arrangement or adaptation of the registers of parliamentary electors as may be necessary to give effect to this Order.

W. G. Agnew.

SCHEDULE

NORTHUMBERLAND

PART I

Existing constituencies described by reference to circumstances as they existed immediately before the end of the year 1947 *except for any subsequent accretion from the sea*

Name	County or Borough Constituency	Contents
Hexham	County ..	(i) The urban districts of Hexham and Prudhoe; (ii) the rural districts of Bellingham, Castle Ward, Haltwhistle and Hexham.
Blyth	Borough ..	(i) The borough of Blyth; (ii) the urban districts of Bedlingtonshire and Seaton Valley.

PART II

New constituencies described by reference to circumstances as they existed on 1*st October* 1971 (*being a date subsequent to the County of Northumberland* (*Seaton Valley Urban District*) *Confirmation Order* 1969) *except for any subsequent accretion from the sea whether occurring before or after the making of this Order*

Name	County or Borough Constituency	Contents
Hexham	County ..	(i) The urban districts of Hexham and Prudhoe; (ii) the rural districts of Bellingham, Castle Ward, Haltwhistle and Hexham.
Blyth	Borough ..	(i) The borough of Blyth; (ii) the urban districts of Bedlingtonshire and Seaton Valley.

(**a**) 1948 c. 65.

1971 No. 2108

REPRESENTATION OF THE PEOPLE

REDISTRIBUTION OF SEATS

The Parliamentary Constituencies (Bosworth and Loughborough) Order 1971

Laid before Parliament in draft

Made - - - *22nd December* 1971

Coming into Operation *5th January* 1972

At the Court at Buckingham Palace, the 22nd day of December 1971

Present,

The Queen's Most Excellent Majesty in Council

Whereas in pursuance of section 2(3) of the House of Commons (Redistribution of Seats) Act 1949(**a**) the Boundary Commission for England have submitted to the Secretary of State a report dated 1st October 1971 with respect to the areas comprised in certain constituencies in England and showing the constituencies into which they recommend, in accordance with the provisions of the House of Commons (Redistribution of Seats) Acts 1949 and 1958(**b**), that the areas should be divided :

And whereas the Secretary of State has laid the said report before Parliament together with the draft of this Order in Council to give effect to recommendations contained in the report and each House of Parliament has by resolution approved the said draft :

Now, therefore, Her Majesty, in pursuance of section 3 of the House of Commons (Redistribution of Seats) Act 1949, is pleased, by and with the advice of Her Privy Council, to order, and it is hereby ordered, as follows :—

1.—(1) This Order may be cited as the Parliamentary Constituencies (Bosworth and Loughborough) Order 1971.

(2) The Interpretation Act 1889(**c**) shall apply to the interpretation of this Order as it applies to the interpretation of an Act of Parliament.

(3) This Order shall come into operation on the fourteenth day after the day on which it is made:

Provided that the coming into operation of this Order shall not affect any parliamentary election until a proclamation is issued by Her Majesty summoning a new Parliament or affect the constitution of the House of Commons until the dissolution of the Parliament in being on the day on which this Order comes into operation.

(**a**) 1949 c. 66. (**b**) 1958 c. 26.
(**c**) 1889 c. 63.

2. In lieu of the county constituencies of Bosworth and Loughborough described in Part II of the Schedule to the Parliamentary Constituencies (England) Order 1970(**a**) and specified in Part I of the Schedule to this Order there shall be substituted the county constituencies described in Part II of the Schedule to this Order.

3. The electoral registration officer for the Leicestershire registration area shall make such re-arrangement or adaptation of the registers of parliamentary electors as may be necessary to give effect to this Order.

W. G. Agnew.

SCHEDULE

LEICESTER

PART I

Existing constituencies described by reference to circumstances as they existed on 1st January 1969

Name	County or Borough Constituency	Contents
Bosworth	County ..	(i) The urban districts of Coalville and Hinckley; (ii) the rural district of Market Bosworth.
Loughborough	County ..	(i) The borough of Loughborough; (ii) the urban districts of Ashby de la Zouch, Ashby Woulds and Shepshed; (iii) the rural districts of Ashby de la Zouch and Castle Donington.

PART II

New constituencies described by reference to circumstances as they existed on 1st October 1971 (*being a date subsequent to the County of Leicester* (*Coalville Urban District*) *Confirmation Order* 1969)

Name	County or Borough Constituency	Contents
Bosworth	County ..	(i) The urban districts of Coalville and Hinckley; (ii) the rural district of Market Bosworth.
Loughborough	County ..	(i) The borough of Loughborough; (ii) the urban districts of Ashby de la Zouch, Ashby Woulds and Shepshed; (iii) the rural districts of Ashby de la Zouch and Castle Donington.

(**a**) S.I. 1970/1674 (1970 III, p. 5444).

STATUTORY INSTRUMENTS

1971 No. 2109

REPRESENTATION OF THE PEOPLE

REDISTRIBUTION OF SEATS

The Parliamentary Constituencies (Bromsgrove and Redditch and Stratford-on-Avon) Order 1971

Laid before Parliament in draft

Made - - - *22nd December* 1971

Coming into Operation *5th January* 1972

At the Court at Buckingham Palace, the 22nd day of December 1971

Present,

The Queen's Most Excellent Majesty in Council

Whereas in pursuance of section 2(3) of the House of Commons (Redistribution of Seats) Act 1949(**a**) the Boundary Commission for England have submitted to the Secretary of State a report dated 1st October 1971 with respect to the areas comprised in certain constituencies in England and showing the constituencies into which they recommend, in accordance with the provisions of the House of Commons (Redistribution of Seats) Acts 1949 and 1958(**b**), that the areas should be divided:

And whereas the Secretary of State has laid the said report before Parliament together with the draft of this Order in Council to give effect to recommendations contained in the report and each House of Parliament has by resolution approved the said draft:

Now, therefore, Her Majesty, in pursuance of section 3 of the House of Commons (Redistribution of Seats) Act 1949, is pleased, by and with the advice of Her Privy Council, to order, and it is hereby ordered, as follows:—

1.—(1) This Order may be cited as the Parliamentary Constituencies (Bromsgrove and Redditch and Stratford-on-Avon) Order 1971.

(2) The Interpretation Act 1889(**c**) shall apply to the interpretation of this Order as it applies to the interpretation of an Act of Parliament.

(3) This Order shall come into operation on the fourteenth day after the day on which it is made:

Provided that the coming into operation of this Order shall not affect any parliamentary election until a proclamation is issued by Her Majesty summoning a new Parliament or affect the constitution of the House of Commons until the dissolution of the Parliament in being on the day on which this Order comes into operation.

(**a**) 1949 c. 66.
(**b**) 1958 c. 26.
(**c**) 1889 c. 63.

2. In lieu of the county constituencies of Bromsgrove and Redditch and Stratford-on-Avon described in Part II of the Schedule to the Parliamentary Constituencies (England) Order 1970(**a**) and specified in Part I of the Schedule to this Order there shall be substituted the county constituencies described in Part II of the Schedule to this Order.

3. The electoral registration officers for the aforesaid constituencies shall make such re-arrangement or adaptation of the registers of parliamentary electors as may be necessary to give effect to this Order.

W. G. Agnew.

SCHEDULE

WARWICKSHIRE AND WORCESTERSHIRE

PART I

Existing constituencies described by reference to circumstances as they existed on 1st January 1969

Name	County or Borough Constituency	Contents
Bromsgrove and Redditch	County ..	(i) The urban districts of Bromsgrove and Redditch; (ii) the rural district of Bromsgrove.
Stratford-on-Avon	County ..	(i) The borough of Stratford-upon-Avon; (ii) the rural districts of Alcester, Shipston on Stour, Southam and Stratford-on-Avon.

PART II

New constituencies described by reference to circumstances as they existed on 1st October 1971 (*being a date subsequent to the Warwickshire and Worcestershire* (*Boundaries*) *Order* 1969(**b**))

Name	County or Borough Constituency	Contents
Bromsgrove and Redditch	County ..	(i) The urban districts of Bromsgrove and Redditch; (ii) the rural district of Bromsgrove.
Stratford-on-Avon	County ..	(i) The borough of Stratford-upon-Avon; (ii) the rural districts of Alcester, Shipston on Stour, Southam and Stratford-on-Avon.

(**a**) S.I. 1970/1674 (1970 III, p. 5444). (**b**) S.I. 1969/361.

STATUTORY INSTRUMENTS

1971 No. 2110

REPRESENTATION OF THE PEOPLE

REDISTRIBUTION OF SEATS

The Parliamentary Constituencies (Hertford and Stevenage and Hitchin) Order 1971

Laid before Parliament in draft

Made - - -	*22nd December* 1971
Coming into Operation	*5th January* 1972

At the Court at Buckingham Palace, the 22nd day of December 1971

Present,

The Queen's Most Excellent Majesty in Council

Whereas in pursuance of section 2(3) of the House of Commons (Redistribution of Seats) Act 1949(**a**) the Boundary Commission for England have submitted to the Secretary of State a report dated 1st October 1971 with respect to the areas comprised in certain constituencies in England and showing the constituencies into which they recommend, in accordance with the provisions of the House of Commons (Redistribution of Seats) Acts 1949 and 1958(**b**), that the areas should be divided:

And whereas the Secretary of State has laid the said report before Parliament together with the draft of this Order in Council to give effect to recommendations contained in the report and each House of Parliament has by resolution approved the said draft:

Now, therefore, Her Majesty, in pursuance of section 3 of the House of Commons (Redistribution of Seats) Act 1949, is pleased, by and with the advice of Her Privy Council, to order, and it is hereby ordered, as follows:—

1.—(1) This Order may be cited as the Parliamentary Constituencies (Hertford and Stevenage and Hitchin) Order 1971.

(2) The Interpretation Act 1889(**c**) shall apply to the interpretation of this Order as it applies to the interpretation of an Act of Parliament.

(3) This Order shall come into operation on the fourteenth day after the day on which it is made:

(**a**) 1949 c. 66. (**b**) 1958 c. 26.
(**c**) 1889 c. 63.

Provided that the coming into operation of this Order shall not affect any parliamentary election until a proclamation is issued by Her Majesty summoning a new Parliament or affect the constitution of the House of Commons until the dissolution of the Parliament in being on the day on which this Order comes into operation.

2. In lieu of the county constituencies of Hertford and Stevenage and Hitchin described in Part II of the Schedule to the Parliamentary Constituencies (England) Order 1970(**a**) and specified in Part I of the Schedule to this Order there shall be substituted the county constituencies described in Part II of the Schedule to this Order.

3. The electoral registration officer for the Hertfordshire registration area shall make such re-arrangement or adaptation of the registers of parliamentary electors as may be necessary to give effect to this Order.

W. G. Agnew.

SCHEDULE

Hertfordshire

Part I

Existing constituencies described by reference to circumstances as they existed on 1st January 1969

Name	County or Borough Constituency	Contents
Hertford and Stevenage	County ..	(i) The borough of Hertford; (ii) the urban districts of Stevenage and Ware; (iii) the rural district of Hertford.
Hitchin	County ..	(i) The urban districts of Baldock, Hitchin, Letchworth and Royston; (ii) the rural district of Hitchin.

(**a**) S.I. 1970/1674 (1970 III, p. 5444).

PART II

New constituencies described by reference to circumstances as they existed on 1*st October* 1971 (*being a date subsequent to the County of Hertford* (*Stevenage Urban District*) *Confirmation Order* 1969)

Name	County or Borough Constituency	Contents
Hertford and Stevenage	County ..	(i) The borough of Hertford; (ii) the urban districts of Stevenage and Ware; (iii) the rural district of Hertford.
Hitchin	County ..	(i) The urban districts of Baldock, Hitchin, Letchworth and Royston; (ii) the rural district of Hitchin.

1971 No. 2111

REPRESENTATION OF THE PEOPLE

REDISTRIBUTION OF SEATS

The Parliamentary Constituencies (Leicester South and Harborough) Order 1971

Laid before Parliament in draft

Made - - - *22nd December* 1971

Coming into Operation *5th January* 1972

At the Court at Buckingham Palace, the 22nd day of December 1971

Present,

The Queen's Most Excellent Majesty in Council

Whereas in pursuance of section 2(3) of the House of Commons (Redistribution of Seats) Act 1949(**a**) the Boundary Commission for England have submitted to the Secretary of State a report dated 1st October 1971 with respect to the areas comprised in certain constituencies in England and showing the constituencies into which they recommend, in accordance with the provisions of the House of Commons (Redistribution of Seats) Acts 1949 and 1958(**b**), that the areas should be divided :

And whereas the Secretary of State has laid the said report before Parliament together with the draft of this Order in Council to give effect to recommendations contained in the report and each House of Parliament has by resolution approved the said draft :

Now, therefore, Her Majesty, in pursuance of section 3 of the House of Commons (Redistribution of Seats) Act 1949, is pleased, by and with the advice of Her Privy Council, to order, and it is hereby ordered, as follows :—

1.—(1) This Order may be cited as the Parliamentary Constituencies (Leicester South and Harborough) Order 1971.

(2) The Interpretation Act 1889(**c**) shall apply to the interpretation of this Order as it applies to the interpretation of an Act of Parliament.

(3) This Order shall come into operation on the fourteenth day after the day on which it is made:

Provided that the coming into operation of this Order shall not affect any parliamentary election until a proclamation is issued by Her Majesty summoning a new Parliament or affect the constitution of the House of Commons until the dissolution of the Parliament in being on the day on which this Order comes into operation.

(**a**) 1949 c. 66. (**b**) 1958 c. 26.
(**c**) 1889 c. 63.

2. In lieu of the county constituency of Harborough and the borough constituency of Leicester South described in Part II of the Schedule to the Parliamentary Constituencies (England) Order 1970(**a**) and specified in Part I of the Schedule to this Order there shall be substituted the county and borough constituencies described in Part II of the Schedule to this Order.

3. The electoral registration officers for the aforesaid constituencies shall make such re-arrangement or adaptation of the registers of parliamentary electors as may be necessary to give effect to this Order.

W. G. Agnew.

SCHEDULE

LEICESTER

PART I

Existing constituencies described by reference to circumstances as they existed on 1st January 1969

Name	County or Borough Constituency	Contents
Harborough	County ..	(i) The urban districts of Market Harborough, Oadby and Wigston; (ii) the rural districts of Billesdon and Market Harborough.
Leicester South	Borough ..	The following wards of the county borough of Leicester, namely, Aylestone, De Montfort, Knighton, Spinney Hill, The Castle and Wycliffe.

PART II

New constituencies described by reference to circumstances as they existed on 1st *October* 1971 (*being a date subsequent to the Leicester* (*Boundaries*) *Order* 1969(**b**))

Name	County or Borough Constituency	Contents
Harborough	County ..	(i) The urban districts of Market Harborough, Oadby and Wigston; (ii) the rural districts of Billesdon and Market Harborough.
Leicester South	Borough ..	The following wards of the county borough of Leicester, namely, Aylestone, De Montfort, Knighton, Spinney Hill, The Castle and Wycliffe.

(**a**) S.I. 1970/1674 (1970 III, p. 5444). (**b**) S.I. 1969/340.

1971 No. 2112

REPRESENTATION OF THE PEOPLE

REDISTRIBUTION OF SEATS

The Parliamentary Constituencies (London Borough of Bromley) Order 1971

Laid before Parliament in draft

Made - - - *22nd December* 1971

Coming into Operation *5th January* 1972

At the Court at Buckingham Palace, the 22nd day of December 1971

Present,

The Queen's Most Excellent Majesty in Council

Whereas in pursuance of section 2(3) of the House of Commons (Redistribution of Seats) Act 1949(**a**) the Boundary Commission for England have submitted to the Secretary of State a report dated 1st October 1971 with respect to the areas comprised in certain constituencies in England and showing the constituencies into which they recommend, in accordance with the provisions of the House of Commons (Redistribution of Seats) Acts 1949 and 1958(**b**), that the areas should be divided:

And whereas the Secretary of State has laid the said report before Parliament together with the draft of this Order in Council to give effect to recommendations contained in the report and each House of Parliament has by resolution approved the said draft:

Now, therefore, Her Majesty, in pursuance of section 3 of the House of Commons (Redistribution of Seats) Act 1949, is pleased, by and with the advice of Her Privy Council, to order, and it is hereby ordered, as follows:—

1.—(1) This Order may be cited as the Parliamentary Constituencies (London Borough of Bromley) Order 1971.

(**a**) 1949 c. 66. (**b**) 1958 c. 26.

(2) The Interpretation Act 1889(**a**) shall apply to the interpretation of this Order as it applies to the interpretation of an Act of Parliament.

(3) This Order shall come into operation on the fourteenth day after the day on which it is made:

Provided that the coming into operation of this Order shall not affect any parliamentary election until a proclamation is issued by Her Majesty summoning a new Parliament or affect the constitution of the House of Commons until the dissolution of the Parliament in being on the day on which this Order comes into operation.

2. In lieu of the borough constituencies of Bromley Beckenham, Bromley Chislehurst, Bromley Orpington and Bromley Ravensbourne described in Part II of the Schedule to the Parliamentary Constituencies (England) Order 1970(**b**) and specified in Part I of the Schedule to this Order there shall be substituted the borough constituencies described in Part II of the Schedule to this Order.

3. The electoral registration officer for the Bromley registration area shall make such re-arrangement or adaptation of the registers of parliamentary electors as may be necessary to give effect to this Order.

W. G. Agnew.

(**a**) 1889 c. 63. (**b**) S.I. 1970/1674 (1970 III, p. 5444).

SCHEDULE

GREATER LONDON (LONDON BOROUGH OF BROMLEY)

PART I

Existing constituencies described by reference to circumstances as they existed on 1st January 1969

Name	County or Borough Constituency	Contents
Bromley, Beckenham	Borough ..	The following wards of the London borough of Bromley, namely, Anerley, Clock House, Copers Cope, Eden Park, Lawrie Park and Kent House, Manor House, Penge and Shortlands.
Bromley, Chislehurst	Borough ..	The following wards of the London borough of Bromley, namely, Bickley, Chislehurst, Mottingham, Plaistow and Sundridge and St. Paul's Cray.
Bromley, Orpington	Borough ..	The following wards, as altered by the Greater London, Kent and Surrey Order 1968(**a**), of the London borough of Bromley, namely, Biggin Hill, Chelsfield, Darwin, Farnborough, Goddington, Petts Wood and St. Mary Cray.
Bromley, Ravensbourne	Borough ..	The following wards of the London borough of Bromley, namely, Bromley Common, Keston and Hayes, Martin's Hill and Town, West Wickham North and West Wickham South.

PART II

New constituencies described by reference to circumstances as they existed on 1*st October* 1971 (*being a date subsequent to the London Borough of Bromley* (*Wards*) *Order* 1970(**b**))

Name	County or Borough Constituency	Contents
Bromley, Beckenham	Borough ..	The following wards of the London borough of Bromley, namely, Anerley, Clock House, Copers Cope, Eden Park, Lawrie Park and Kent House, Manor House, Penge and Shortlands.
Bromley, Chislehurst	Borough ..	The following wards of the London borough of Bromley, namely, Bickley, Chislehurst, Mottingham, Plaistow and Sundridge and St. Paul's Cray.
Bromley, Orpington	Borough ..	The following wards of the London borough of Bromley, namely, Biggin Hill, Chelsfield, Darwin, Farnborough, Goddington, Petts Wood and St. Mary Cray.
Bromley, Ravensbourne	Borough ..	The following wards of the London borough of Bromley, namely, Bromley Common, Keston and Hayes, Martin's Hill and Town, West Wickham North and West Wickham South.

(**a**) S.I. 1968/2020. (**b**) S.I. 1970/1888.

1971 No. 2113

REPRESENTATION OF THE PEOPLE

REDISTRIBUTION OF SEATS

The Parliamentary Constituencies (London Borough of Southwark) Order 1971

Laid before Parliament in draft

Made - - - *22nd December* 1971

Coming into Operation *5th January* 1972

At the Court at Buckingham Palace, the 22nd day of December 1971

Present,

The Queen's Most Excellent Majesty in Council

Whereas in pursuance of section 2(3) of the House of Commons (Redistribution of Seats) Act 1949(**a**) the Boundary Commission for England have submitted to the Secretary of State a report dated 1st October 1971 with respect to the areas comprised in certain constituencies in England and showing the constituencies into which they recommend, in accordance with the provisions of the House of Commons (Redistribution of Seats) Acts 1949 and 1958(**b**), that the areas should be divided :

And whereas the Secretary of State has laid the said report before Parliament together with the draft of this Order in Council to give effect to recommendations contained in the report and each House of Parliament has by resolution approved the said draft :

Now, therefore, Her Majesty, in pursuance of section 3 of the House of Commons (Redistribution of Seats) Act 1949, is pleased, by and with the advice of Her Privy Council, to order, and it is hereby ordered, as follows :—

1.—(1) This Order may be cited as the Parliamentary Constituencies (London Borough of Southwark) Order 1971.

(2) The Interpretation Act 1889(**c**) shall apply to the interpretation of this Order as it applies to the interpretation of an Act of Parliament.

(3) This Order shall come into operation on the fourteenth day after the day on which it is made:

Provided that the coming into operation of this Order shall not affect any parliamentary election until a proclamation is issued by Her Majesty

(**a**) 1949 c. 66. (**b**) 1958 c. 26.
(**c**) 1889 c. 63.

summoning a new Parliament or affect the constitution of the House of Commons until the dissolution of the Parliament in being on the day on which this Order comes into operation.

2. In lieu of the borough constituencies of Southwark Bermondsey, Southwark Dulwich and Southwark Peckham described in Part II of the Schedule to the Parliamentary Constituencies (England) Order 1970(**a**) and specified in Part I of the Schedule to this Order there shall be substituted the borough constituencies described in Part II of the Schedule to this Order.

3. The electoral registration officer for the Southwark registration area shall make such re-arrangement or adaptation of the registers of parliamentary electors as may be necessary to give effect to this Order.

W. G. Agnew.

SCHEDULE

Greater London (London Borough of Southwark)

Part I

Existing constituencies described by reference to circumstances as they existed on 1*st January* 1969

Name	County or Borough Constituency	Contents
Southwark, Bermondsey	Borough ..	The following wards of the London borough of Southwark, namely, Abbey, Bricklayers, Browning, Cathedral, Chaucer, Dockyard, Riverside and Rotherhithe.
Southwark, Dulwich	Borough ..	The following wards of the London borough of Southwark, namely, Alleyn, Bellenden, College, Lyndhurst, Ruskin, Rye, The Lane and Waverley.
Southwark, Peckham	Borough ..	The following wards of the London borough of Southwark, namely, Brunswick, Burgess, Consort, Faraday, Friary, Newington and St. Giles.

(**a**) S.I. 1970/1674 (1970 III, p. 5444).

PART II

New constituencies described by reference to circumstances as they existed on 1st October 1971 (being a date subsequent to the London Borough of Southwark (Wards) Order 1970(a))

Name	County or Borough Constituency	Contents
Southwark, Bermondsey	Borough ..	The following wards of the London borough of Southwark, namely, Abbey, Bricklayers, Browning, Cathedral, Chaucer, Dockyard, Riverside and Rotherhithe.
Southwark, Dulwich	Borough ..	The following wards of the London borough of Southwark, namely, Alleyn, Bellenden, College, Lyndhurst, Ruskin, Rye, The Lane and Waverley.
Southwark, Peckham	Borough ..	The following wards of the London borough of Southwark, namely, Brunswick, Burgess, Consort, Faraday, Friary, Newington and St. Giles.

(a) S.I. 1970/1717.

1971 No. 2114

REPRESENTATION OF THE PEOPLE

REDISTRIBUTION OF SEATS

The Parliamentary Constituencies (Richmond upon Thames, Twickenham and Esher) Order 1971

Laid before Parliament in draft

Made - - - *22nd December* 1971

Coming into Operation *5th January* 1972

At the Court at Buckingham Palace, the 22nd day of December 1971

Present,

The Queen's Most Excellent Majesty in Council

Whereas in pursuance of section 2(3) of the House of Commons (Redistribution of Seats) Act 1949(**a**) the Boundary Commission for England have submitted to the Secretary of State a report dated 1st October 1971 with respect to the areas comprised in certain constituencies in England and showing the constituencies into which they recommend, in accordance with the provisions of the House of Commons (Redistribution of Seats) Acts 1949 and 1958(**b**), that the areas should be divided:

And whereas the Secretary of State has laid the said report before Parliament together with the draft of this Order in Council to give effect to recommendations contained in the report and each House of Parliament has by resolution approved the said draft:

Now, therefore, Her Majesty, in pursuance of section 3 of the House of Commons (Redistribution of Seats) Act 1949, is pleased, by and with the advice of Her Privy Council, to order, and it is hereby ordered, as follows:—

1.—(1) This Order may be cited as the Parliamentary Constituencies (Richmond upon Thames, Twickenham and Esher) Order 1971.

(2) The Interpretation Act 1889(**c**) shall apply to the interpretation of this Order as it applies to the interpretation of an Act of Parliament.

(3) This Order shall come into operation on the fourteenth day after the day on which it is made:

Provided that the coming into operation of this Order shall not affect any parliamentary election until a proclamation is issued by Her Majesty summoning a new Parliament or affect the constitution of the House of Commons until the dissolution of the Parliament in being on the day on which this Order comes into operation.

(**a**) 1949 c. 66. (**b**) 1958 c. 26.
(**c**) 1889 c. 63.

2. In lieu of the borough constituencies of Esher and Richmond upon Thames, Twickenham described in Part II of the Schedule to the Parliamentary Constituencies (England) Order 1970(**a**) and specified in Part I of the Schedule to this Order there shall be substituted the borough constituencies described in Part II of the Schedule to this Order.

3. The electoral registration officers for the aforesaid constituencies shall make such re-arrangement or adaptation of the registers of parliamentary electors as may be necessary to give effect to this Order.

W. G. Agnew.

SCHEDULE

GREATER LONDON (LONDON BOROUGH OF RICHMOND UPON THAMES) AND SURREY

PART I

Existing constituencies described by reference to circumstances as they existed on 1st January 1969

Name	County or Borough Constituency	Contents
Esher	Borough ..	The urban district of Esher.
Richmond upon Thames, Twickenham	Borough ..	The following wards of the London borough of Richmond upon Thames, namely, Central Twickenham, East Twickenham, Hampton, Hampton Hill, Hampton Wick, Heathfield, South Twickenham, Teddington, West Twickenham and Whitton.

PART II

New constituencies described by reference to circumstances as they existed on 1st October 1971 (*being a date subsequent to the Greater London and Surrey Order* 1970(**b**))

Name	County or Borough Constituency	Contents
Esher	Borough ..	The urban district of Esher.
Richmond upon Thames, Twickenham	Borough ..	The following wards of the London borough of Richmond upon Thames, namely, Central Twickenham, East Twickenham, Hampton, Hampton Hill, Hampton Wick, Heathfield, South Twickenham, Teddington, West Twickenham and Whitton.

(**a**) S.I. 1970/1674 (1970 III, p. 5444). (**b**) S.I. 1970/397.

1971 No. 2115

REPRESENTATION OF THE PEOPLE

REDISTRIBUTION OF SEATS

The Parliamentary Constituencies (Stockport) Order 1971

Laid before Parliament in draft

Made - - - *22nd December* 1971

Coming into Operation *5th January* 1972

At the Court at Buckingham Palace, the 22nd day of December 1971

Present,

The Queen's Most Excellent Majesty in Council

Whereas in pursuance of section 2(3) of the House of Commons (Redistribution of Seats) Act 1949(**a**) the Boundary Commission for England have submitted to the Secretary of State a report dated 1st October 1971 with respect to the areas comprised in certain constituencies in England and showing the constituencies into which they recommend, in accordance with the provisions of the House of Commons (Redistribution of Seats) Acts 1949 and 1958(**b**), that the areas should be divided:

And whereas the Secretary of State has laid the said report before Parliament together with the draft of this Order in Council to give effect to recommendations contained in the report and each House of Parliament has by resolution approved the said draft:

Now, therefore, Her Majesty, in pursuance of section 3 of the House of Commons (Redistribution of Seats) Act 1949, is pleased, by and with the advice of Her Privy Council, to order, and it is hereby ordered, as follows:—

1.—(1) This Order may be cited as the Parliamentary Constituencies (Stockport) Order 1971.

(2) The Interpretation Act 1889(**c**) shall apply to the interpretation of this Order as it applies to the interpretation of an Act of Parliament.

(3) This Order shall come into operation on the fourteenth day after the day on which it is made:

(**a**) 1949 c. 66.
(**b**) 1958 c. 26.
(**c**) 1889 c. 63.

Provided that the coming into operation of this Order shall not affect any parliamentary election until a proclamation is issued by Her Majesty summoning a new Parliament or affect the constitution of the House of Commons until the dissolution of the Parliament in being on the day on which this Order comes into operation.

2. In lieu of the borough constituency of Stockport North described in Schedule 1 to the Representation of the People Act 1948(**a**) and the borough constituency of Stockport South described in Part II of Schedule 1 to the House of Commons (Redistribution of Seats) (Stockport South and Cheadle) Order 1953(**b**) and specified in Part I of the Schedule to this Order there shall be substituted the borough constituencies described in Part II of the Schedule to this Order.

3. The electoral registration officer for the Stockport registration area shall make such re-arrangement or adaptation of the registers of parliamentary electors as may be necessary to give effect to this Order.

W. G. Agnew.

SCHEDULE

CHESTER

PART I

Existing constituencies described by reference to circumstances as they existed immediately before the end of the year 1947 *except where otherwise stated*

Name	County or Borough Constituency	Contents
Stockport North	Borough ..	The following wards of the county borough of Stockport, namely, Edgeley, Heaton Lane, Heaton Norris North, Heaton Norris South, Hollywood, Lancashire Hill, Old Road, Reddish North and Reddish South.
Stockport South	Borough ..	The following wards of the county borough of Stockport (as constituted by the Stockport (Extension) Order 1952(**c**)), namely, Cale Green, Davenport, Heaviley, Hempshaw Lane, Portwood, St Mary's, St Thomas's, Shaw Heath and Vernon.

(**a**) 1948 c. 65. (**b**) S.I. 1953/742 (1953 II, p. 1776).
(**c**) S.I. 1952/588.

PART II

New constituencies described by reference to circumstances as they existed on 1st October 1971

Name	County or Borough Constituency	Contents
Stockport North	Borough ..	The following wards of the county borough of Stockport, namely, Cheadle Heath, Edgeley, Heaton Chapel, Heaton Mersey, Heaton Moor, Heaton Norris, Lancashire Hill, Longford and Reddish Green.
Stockport South	Borough ..	The following wards of the county borough of Stockport, namely, Adswood, Brinnington, Cale Green, Davenport, Heaviley, Little Moor, Manor, Offerton and Vernon.

STATUTORY INSTRUMENTS

1971 No. 2116

REPRESENTATION OF THE PEOPLE

REDISTRIBUTION OF SEATS

The Parliamentary Constituencies (Swindon and Devizes) Order 1971

Laid before Parliament in draft

Made - - - *22nd December* 1971

Coming into Operation *5th January* 1972

At the Court at Buckingham Palace, the 22nd day of December 1971

Present,

The Queen's Most Excellent Majesty in Council

Whereas in pursuance of section 2(3) of the House of Commons (Redistribution of Seats) Act 1949(**a**) the Boundary Commission for England have submitted to the Secretary of State a report dated 1st October 1971 with respect to the areas comprised in certain constituencies in England and showing the constituencies into which they recommend, in accordance with the provisions of the House of Commons (Redistribution of Seats) Acts 1949 and 1958(**b**), that the areas should be divided :

And whereas the Secretary of State has laid the said report before Parliament together with the draft of this Order in Council to give effect to recommendations contained in the report and each House of Parliament has by resolution approved the said draft :

Now, therefore, Her Majesty, in pursuance of section 3 of the House of Commons (Redistribution of Seats) Act 1949, is pleased, by and with the advice of Her Privy Council, to order, and it is hereby ordered, as follows :—

1.—(1) This Order may be cited as the Parliamentary Constituencies (Swindon and Devizes) Order 1971.

(2) The Interpretation Act 1889(**c**) shall apply to the interpretation of this Order as it applies to the interpretation of an Act of Parliament.

(3) This Order shall come into operation on the fourteenth day after the day on which it is made:

Provided that the coming into operation of this Order shall not affect any parliamentary election until a proclamation is issued by Her Majesty summoning a new Parliament or affect the constitution of the House of

(**a**) 1949 c. 66. (**b**) 1958 c. 26.
(**c**) 1889 c. 63.

Commons until the dissolution of the Parliament in being on the day on which this Order comes into operation.

2. In lieu of the county constituency of Devizes described in Part II of Schedule 2 to the House of Commons (Redistribution of Seats) (Swindon and Devizes) Order 1952(**a**) and the borough constituency of Swindon described in Part II of Schedule 1 to the said Order and specified in Part I of the Schedule to this Order there shall be substituted the county and borough constituencies described in Part II of the Schedule to this Order.

3. The electoral registration officers for the aforesaid constituencies shall make such re-arrangement or adaptation of the registers of parliamentary electors as may be necessary to give effect to this Order.

W. G. Agnew.

SCHEDULE

WILTSHIRE

PART I

Existing constituencies described in the House of Commons (Redistribution of Seats) (Swindon and Devizes) Order 1952

Name	County or Borough Constituency	Contents
Devizes	County ..	(i) The boroughs of Devizes and Marlborough; (ii) the rural districts of Devizes, Marlborough and Ramsbury and Pewsey; (iii) the rural district of Highworth except the part of the parish of Stratton Saint Margaret added to the borough of Swindon by the Swindon Corporation Act 1951(**b**).
Swindon	Borough ..	The borough of Swindon, as extended by the Swindon Corporation Act 1951.

PART II

New constituencies described by reference to circumstances as they existed on 1*st October* 1971 (*being a date subsequent to the County of Wiltshire* (*Borough of Swindon*) *Confirmation Order* 1969)

Name	County or Borough Constituency	Contents
Devizes	County ..	(i) The boroughs of Devizes and Marlborough; (ii) the rural districts of Devizes, Highworth, Marlborough and Ramsbury and Pewsey.
Swindon	Borough ..	The borough of Swindon.

(**a**) S.I. 1952/1349 (1952 III, p. 2831). (**b**) 1951 c. xl.

STATUTORY INSTRUMENTS

1971 No. 2117

INCOME TAX

The Double Taxation Relief (Taxes on Income) (Trinidad and Tobago) Order 1971

Laid before the House of Commons in draft

Made - - - - *22nd December* 1971

At the Court at Buckingham Palace, the 22nd day of December 1971

Present,

The Queen's Most Excellent Majesty in Council

Whereas a draft of this Order was laid before the Commons House of Parliament in accordance with the provisions of section 497(8) of the Income and Corporation Taxes Act 1970(**a**), and an Address has been presented to Her Majesty by that House praying that an Order may be made in the terms of this Order:

Now, therefore, Her Majesty, in exercise of the powers conferred upon Her by section 497 of the said Income and Corporation Taxes Act 1970, and of all other powers enabling Her in that behalf, is pleased, by and with the advice of Her Privy Council, to order, and it is hereby ordered, as follows:—

1. This Order may be cited as the Double Taxation Relief (Taxes on Income) (Trinidad and Tobago) Order 1971.

2. It is hereby declared—

(*a*) that the arrangements specified in the Supplementary Protocol set out in the Schedule to this Order, which vary the arrangements set out in the Schedule to the Double Taxation Relief (Taxes on Income) (Trinidad and Tobago) Order 1967(**b**) as amended by the arrangements set out in the Schedule to the Double Taxation Relief (Taxes on Income) (Trinidad and Tobago) Order 1970(**c**), have been made with the Government of Trinidad and Tobago with a view to affording relief from double taxation in relation to income tax, or corporation tax and taxes of a similar character imposed by the laws of Trinidad and Tobago; and

(*b*) that it is expedient that these arrangements should have effect.

W. G. Agnew.

(**a**) 1970 c. 10. (**b**) S.I. 1967/484 (1967 I, p. 1529). (**c**) S.I. 1970/483 (1970 I, p. 1630).

SCHEDULE

SUPPLEMENTARY PROTOCOL BETWEEN THE GOVERNMENT OF THE UNITED KINGDOM OF GREAT BRITAIN AND NORTHERN IRELAND AND THE GOVERNMENT OF TRINIDAD AND TOBAGO, AMENDING THE AGREEMENT FOR THE AVOIDANCE OF DOUBLE TAXATION AND THE PREVENTION OF FISCAL EVASION WITH RESPECT TO TAXES ON INCOME, SIGNED AT PORT OF SPAIN ON 29 DECEMBER 1966, AS MODIFIED BY THE PROTOCOL SIGNED AT PORT OF SPAIN ON 10 DECEMBER 1969.

The Government of the United Kingdom of Great Britain and Northern Ireland and the Government of Trinidad and Tobago;

Desiring to conclude a Supplementary Protocol to amend the Agreement between the Contracting Governments for the Avoidance of Double Taxation and the Prevention of Fiscal Evasion with respect to Taxes on Income signed at Port of Spain on 29 December 1966, as modified by the Protocol signed at Port of Spain on 10 December 1969 (hereinafter referred to as " the Agreement ");

Have agreed as follows:

ARTICLE 1

Paragraph (1) of Article 10 of the Agreement shall be deleted and replaced by the following:

" (1) The tax imposed in one of the territories on royalties which arise there and which are derived and beneficially owned by a resident of the other territory shall not exceed 10 per cent of the gross amount of the royalties."

ARTICLE 2

This Supplementary Protocol, which shall form an integral part of the Agreement, shall come into force when the last of all such things shall have been done in the United Kingdom and Trinidad and Tobago as are necessary to give the Supplementary Protocol the force of law in the United Kingdom and Trinidad and Tobago respectively and shall thereupon have effect in relation to royalties payable on or after:

(*a*) 1 January 1972; or

(*b*) the date on which it so comes into force;

whichever date is the later.

In witness whereof the undersigned, duly authorised thereto by their respective Governments, have signed this Supplementary Protocol.

Done in duplicate at Port of Spain this Fifteenth day of November, One Thousand Nine Hundred and Seventy One.

For the Government of the United Kingdom of Great Britain and Northern Ireland:

BERNARD A. PENNOCK.

For the Government of Trinidad and Tobago:

GEO. M. CHAMBERS.

EXPLANATORY NOTE

(*This Note is not part of the Order.*)

The Double Taxation Agreement with Trinidad and Tobago signed on the 29th December 1966 was amended by a Protocol signed on the 10th December 1969. The Supplementary Protocol scheduled to this Order makes a further alteration to the Agreement by providing that in general the rate of tax in the source country on royalties flowing to the other country shall not exceed 10 per cent.

The Supplementary Protocol is to apply to royalties payable on or after 1st January 1972 or the date on which it comes into force, whichever date is the later.

1971 No. 2118

CIVIL AVIATION

The Tokyo Convention (Certification of Countries) Order 1971

Made - - - - *22nd December* 1971

At the Court at Buckingham Palace, the 22nd day of December 1971

Present,

The Queen's Most Excellent Majesty in Council

Her Majesty, in exercise of the powers conferred upon Her by section 7(1) of the Tokyo Convention Act 1967**(a)** (which provides that Her Majesty may by Order in Council certify which countries are Convention countries, that is to say countries in which the Convention on Offences and certain other Acts Committed on board Aircraft signed in Tokyo on 14th September 1963 is for the time being in force) and of all other powers enabling Her in that behalf is pleased, by and with the advice of Her Privy Council, to order, and it is hereby ordered, as follows:

1. This Order may be cited as the Tokyo Convention (Certification of Countries) Order 1971.

2. The Tokyo Convention (Certification of Countries) Order 1970**(b)** is hereby revoked. Section 38(2) of the Interpretation Act 1889**(c)** (which relates to the effect of repeals) shall apply to this Order as if this Order were an Act of Parliament and as if the Order revoked by this Article were an Act of Parliament thereby repealed.

3. It is hereby certified that the countries listed in the Schedule hereto are Convention countries.

W. G. Agnew.

SCHEDULE

The United Kingdom of Great Britain and Northern Ireland
- The Channel Islands
- The Isle of Man
- Bahamas
- Bermuda
- British Antarctic Territory
- British Honduras
- British Indian Ocean Territory
- British Solomon Islands Protectorate
- British Virgin Islands

(a) 1967 c. 52.
(b) S.I. 1970/825 (1970 II, p. 2678).
(c) 1889 c. 63.

SCHEDULE (*continued*)

Cayman Islands
Central and Southern Line Islands
The Sovereign Base Areas of Akrotiri and Dhekelia in the island of Cyprus
Falkland Islands and Dependencies
Gibraltar
Gilbert and Ellice Islands Colony
Hong Kong
Montserrat
Pitcairn
St. Helena and Dependencies
St. Vincent
Seychelles
Turks and Caicos Islands

Australia and all territories subject to the sovereignty or authority of Australia

Belgium

Brazil

Canada

Chad

Denmark and the Faroe Islands

Dominican Republic

Ecuador

Fiji

Finland

France and all territories subject to the sovereignty or authority of France

Gabon

The Federal Republic of Germany

Greece

Guatemala

Hungary

Iceland

Israel

Italy

Ivory Coast

Japan

Kenya

The Republic of Korea

Malagasy Republic

Mali

Mexico

The Netherlands except Surinam and the Netherlands Antilles

Niger

Nigeria

Norway and all territories subject to the sovereignty or authority of Norway

Panama

The Philippines

Poland

Portugal and all territories subject to the sovereignty or authority of Portugal

Rwanda

SCHEDULE (*continued*)

Saudi Arabia
Sierra Leone
Singapore
Spain and all territories subject to the sovereignty or authority of Spain
Sweden
Switzerland
The United States of America and all territories subject to the sovereignty or authority of the United States of America
Upper Volta
Yugoslavia

EXPLANATORY NOTE

(*This Note is not part of the Order.*)

This Order revokes and replaces the Tokyo Convention (Certification of Countries) Order 1970. It certifies in which countries the Convention on Offences and certain other Acts Committed on board Aircraft, signed in Tokyo on 14th September 1963, is for the time being in force. Under section 7(1) of the Tokyo Convention Act 1967 this Order is conclusive evidence of the matters certified.

STATUTORY INSTRUMENTS

1971 No. 2119

MINISTERS OF THE CROWN

The Transfer of Functions (Export Guarantees) Order 1971

Made - - - -	*22nd December* 1971
Laid before Parliament	*31st December* 1971
Coming into Operation	*7th February* 1972

At the Court at Buckingham Palace, the 22nd day of December 1971

Present,

The Queen's Most Excellent Majesty in Council

Her Majesty, in pursuance of sections 1 and 3 of the Ministers of the Crown (Transfer of Functions) Act 1946(**a**) and of section 4 of the Ministers of the Crown Act 1964(**b**), is pleased, by and with the advice of Her Privy Council, to order, and it is hereby ordered, as follows:—

Citation, interpretation and commencement

1.—(1) This Order may be cited as the Transfer of Functions (Export Guarantees) Order 1971.

(2) The Interpretation Act 1889(**c**) applies for the interpretation of this Order as it applies for the interpretation of an Act of Parliament.

(3) This Order shall come into operation on 7th February 1972.

Functions under Export Guarantees Acts 1968 *and* 1970

2.—(1) All functions of the Secretary of State under the Export Guarantees Acts 1968(**d**) and 1970(**e**) (which were conferred on him by the Secretary of State for Trade and Industry Order 1970(**f**) to be exercisable concurrently with the Board of Trade) shall be exercised and performed through the Export Credits Guarantee Department, and no functions under those Acts shall be exercised by the Board of Trade.

(2) For section 7 of the Export Guarantees Act 1968 there shall be substituted the following section:—

" 7. All powers and duties of the Secretary of State under this Act shall be exercised and performed through the Export Credits Guarantee Department, which shall be a Department of the Secretary of State."

(3) In the Export Guarantees Acts 1968 and 1970, as so amended, for any reference to the Board of Trade there shall be substituted a reference to the Secretary of State.

(4) Nothing in this Order shall affect the validity of anything done by the Board of Trade before the coming into operation of this Order.

W. G. Agnew.

(**a**) 1946 c. 31. (**b**) 1964 c. 98. (**c**) 1889 c. 63. (**d**) 1968 c. 26.
(**e**) 1970 c. 15. (**f**) S.I. 1970/1537 (1970 III p. 5293).

EXPLANATORY NOTE

(*This Note is not part of the Order.*)

By this Order the functions of the Secretary of State under the Export Guarantees Acts 1968 and 1970 will be exercised through the Export Credits Guarantee Department. And those functions will be exercisable solely by the Secretary of State, and not concurrently with the Board of Trade.

The Export Credits Guarantee Department will continue as a separate Government department, but it will be under the Secretary of State.

STATUTORY INSTRUMENTS

1971 No. 2120 (C.57)

DANGEROUS DRUGS

The Misuse of Drugs Act 1971 (Commencement No. 1) Order 1971

Made - - - - 20*th December* 1971

In pursuance of section 40(3) of the Misuse of Drugs Act 1971(**a**), I hereby make the following Order:—

1. This Order may be cited as the Misuse of Drugs Act 1971 (Commencement No. 1) Order 1971.

2. Sections 1, 32, 35, 37, 38 and 40 of and Schedule 1 to the Misuse of Drugs Act 1971 shall come into operation on 1st February 1972.

R. Maudling,
One of Her Majesty's Principal
Secretaries of State.

Home Office,
Whitehall.
20th December 1971.

EXPLANATORY NOTE

(*This Note is not part of the Order.*)

This Order brings into force, with effect from 1st February 1972, those provisions of the Misuse of Drugs Act 1971 which relate to the Advisory Council on the Misuse of Drugs and to research concerning the misuse of drugs, together with interpretation and other supplementary provisions.

(**a**) 1971 c. 38.

1971 No. 2124 (S.223)

PENSIONS

The Pensions Appeal Tribunals (Scotland) Rules 1971

Made - - - -	17*th December* 1971
Laid before Parliament	31*st December* 1971
Coming into Operation	17*th January* 1972

ARRANGEMENT OF RULES

The Lord President of the Court of Session, in exercise of the powers conferred on him by paragraph 5 of the Schedule to, and read along with section 13 of, the Pensions Appeal Tribunals Act 1943**(a)** and after consultation with the Council on Tribunals in accordance with section 10 of the Tribunals and Inquiries Act 1971**(b)**, hereby makes the following Rules:—

Citation and commencement

1. These Rules may be cited as the Pensions Appeal Tribunals (Scotland) Rules 1971 and shall come into operation on 17th January 1972.

Interpretation

2.—(1) In these Rules, unless the context otherwise requires,

(*a*) "the Act" means the Pensions Appeal Tribunals Act 1943**(a)** as amended by the Pensions Appeal Tribunals Act 1949**(c)** and by section 23 of the Chronically Sick and Disabled Persons Act 1970**(d)**;

(*b*) "appeal" means an appeal which lies under section 1, 2, 3, 4 or 5 of the Act;

(*c*) "appellant" means the person by whom or on whose behalf the appeal is brought;

(*d*) "assessment appeal" means an appeal brought under section 5 of the Act;

(*e*) "entitlement appeal" means an appeal brought under section 1, 2, 3 or 4 of the Act;

(*f*) "incapax" means a person who by reason of mental disorder within the meaning of the Mental Health (Scotland) Act 1960**(e)**, is incapable of managing his own affairs;

(*g*) "notice of appeal" means notice of an appeal given to the Secretary of State in manner prescribed by these Rules;

(*h*) "Pensions Appeal Office" means the office of the Pensions Appeal Tribunals for Scotland, 20 Walker Street, Edinburgh, EH3 7HS;

(*i*) "the President" means the person appointed by the Lord President of the Court of Session to be President of the Pensions Appeal Tribunals;

(*j*) "the Secretary of State" means the Secretary of State for Social Services;

(*k*) "tribunal" means a Pensions Appeal Tribunal.

(2) The Interpretation Act 1889**(f)** applies to the interpretation of these

(a) 1943 c. 39.
(b) 1971 c. 62.
(c) 1949 c. 12.
(d) 1970 c. 44.
(e) 1960 c. 61.
(f) 1889 c. 63.

Rules as it applies to the interpretation of an Act of Parliament.

(3) Unless the context otherwise requires, reference in these Rules to a numbered rule or schedule is a reference to the rule or schedule so numbered in these Rules.

(4) In these Rules a form referred to by number means the form so numbered in Schedule 1 or a form as near thereto as the circumstances permit.

Persons by whom appeals may be brought

3.—(1) Subject to the provision of this rule—

(*a*) an entitlement appeal shall be brought by the person in respect of whose claim the Secretary of State has given the decision against which the appeal lies; and

(*b*) an assessment appeal shall be brought by the person in respect of whose claim the Secretary of State has made the interim assessment, final decision, or final assessment against which the appeal lies.

(2) Where the person by whom an appeal may be brought is under the age of 16, or is prevented by mental or physical infirmity from acting on his own behalf, the appeal shall be brought by some other person acting for him.

(3) Where an appeal is brought by a person acting on behalf of another, that person may take all such steps and do all such things for the purposes of the appeal as an appellant is by these Rules required or authorised to take or do.

(4) An appeal on behalf of, or in respect of the estate of a minor or pupil or of an incapax may be brought, and an appeal in respect of the estate of a deceased person may be carried on by virtue of directions given by the President under rule 24(2), notwithstanding that no curator or tutor has been appointed or is acting or, as the case may be, that confirmation has not been issued in respect of the deceased's estate.

Method of appealing

4.—(1) An appeal to a tribunal shall be commenced by a notice of appeal given to the Secretary of State on whichever form of notice of appeal set out in Schedule 1 is appropriate:

Provided that where a person who is desirous of commencing an assessment appeal has signified to the Secretary of State his intention to appeal by a prepaid letter sent to the Secretary of State before the time for commencing the appeal has expired, and the appropriate form of notice of appeal is sent to the Secretary of State within six weeks after the form was sent by the Secretary of State to the appellant for completion, the appeal shall be deemed to have been commenced on the date on which the letter was so sent.

(2) The appropriate form of notice of appeal shall be supplied by the Secretary of State on request.

(3) A notice of appeal in Form 1, 3 or 5 shall be signed by the appellant, and a notice of appeal in Form 2, 4 or 6 shall be signed by the person acting on behalf of the appellant, and in each case shall bear the date on which it was signed, and shall be sent by post addressed to "The Secretary of State for Social Services".

Statement of Case and answer

5.—(1) Subject to the provisions of rules 6, 9 and 22, the Secretary of State shall, on receipt by him of a notice of appeal, prepare a document (to be called a Statement of Case) containing the following information—

(*a*) the relevant facts relating to the appellant's case as known to the Secretary of State, including the relevant medical history of the appellant; and

(*b*) in the case of an entitlement appeal, the Secretary of State's reasons for making the decision against which the appeal is brought.

(2) When the Statement of Case has been prepared, the Secretary of State shall send two copies to the appellant and shall inform him that he may, if he so desires, submit (on a form to be supplied by the Secretary of State) an answer to the statement indicating—

(*a*) whether, and in what respects, the facts in the Statement of Case are disputed;

(*b*) any further facts which, in his opinion, are relevant to the appeal; and

(*c*) his reasons for thinking that the decision of the Secretary of State, or the interim assessment, final decision or final assessment, as the case may be, made by the Secretary of State, was wrong.

(3) Where the appellant submits an answer disputing any of the facts in the Statement of Case or putting forward further facts, he shall attach to his answer such documentary evidence in support of his case as is in his possession or as he can reasonably obtain.

(4) The appellant shall send his answer, and any documents submitted therewith, to the Secretary of State within 28 days from the date on which the Statement of Case was sent to him.

(5) The Secretary of State may, if he so desires, comment in writing on the appellant's answer and, if he does so, the Secretary of State shall send a copy of his comments to the appellant.

(6) As soon as may be after the receipt of the answer or, if the appellant does not send an answer, on the expiration of the said 28 days, the Secretary of State shall, subject to the provisions of rule 9, send to the Pensions Appeal Office—

(*a*) three copies of the Statement of Case;

(*b*) three copies of the appellant's answer (if any);

(*c*) any documents submitted by the appellant; and

(*d*) three copies of any comments made by the Secretary of State on the Appellant's answer.

Disclosure of official documents and information

6.—(1) Where for the purposes of his appeal an appellant desires to have disclosed any document, or part of any document, which he has reason to believe is in the possession of a government department, he may, at any time not later than six weeks after the Statement of Case was sent to him, apply to the President for the disclosures of the document or part, and, if the President considers that the document or part is likely to be relevant to any issue to be determined on the appeal, he may give a direction to the department concerned requiring its disclosure (if in the possession of the department) in such manner and upon such terms and conditions as the President may think fit:

Provided that directions given under this rule shall not require the disclosure of—

(i) documents in the nature of departmental minutes or reports; or

(ii) the name of any person in the service of Her Majesty who has given a report or medical certificate relating to the appellant or to the person in respect of whose death the appeal is brought.

For the purposes of this paragraph a certificate given by an officer of the government department concerned (being an officer authorised in that behalf by the Secretary of State or Minister in charge of the department) that a document or name is such a document or name as is described in sub-paragraph (i) or sub-paragraph (ii) shall be final and conclusive.

(2) On receipt of a direction given by the President under this rule, the Secretary of State or Minister in charge of the government department concerned, or any person authorised by him in that behalf, may certify to the President—

(*a*) that it would be contrary to the public interest for the whole or part of the document to which the direction relates to be disclosed publicly; or

(*b*) that the whole or part of the document ought not, for reasons of security, to be disclosed in any manner whatsoever:

and where a certificate is given under sub-paragraph (*a*), the President shall give such directions to the tribunal as may be requisite for prohibiting or restricting the disclosure in public of the document, or part thereof, as the case may be, and where a certificate is given under sub-paragraph (*b*) the President shall direct the tribunal to consider whether the appellant's case will be prejudiced if the appeal proceeds without such disclosure, and, where the tribunal are of opinion that the appellant would be prejudiced if the appeal were to proceed without such disclosure, they shall adjourn the hearing of the appeal until such time as the necessity for non-disclosure on the ground of security no longer exists.

(3) At the hearing the appellant may apply to the tribunal for the disclosure of such a document as is mentioned in this rule, and, where it appears to the tribunal that the document is likely to be relevant to any issue to be determined on the appeal and that the appellant has reasonable excuse for having failed to make the application for disclosure to the President under paragraph (1) before the hearing, the tribunal may, unless the document is produced by the Secretary of State's representative, adjourn the case for an application to the President to be made by the appellant.

(4) It shall be a sufficient compliance with a direction given for the disclosure of a document, or part of a document, under this rule, if there is produced a copy of the document or the part thereof, certified as a true copy by an officer of the department concerned authorised in that behalf by the Secretary of State or Minister in charge of the department.

List of cases for hearing

7. A list of cases for hearing shall be prepared in the Pensions Appeal Office, and on receipt in that office of the documents mentioned in rule 5(6) the case shall be entered in that list.

Date of hearing

8.—(1) Not less than 10 clear days before the date fixed for the hearing, a notice of hearing in Form 7 shall be sent from the Pensions Appeal Office to the appellant, and the Secretary of State shall be informed of the date so fixed.

(2) If, at any time before the date fixed for the hearing, the appellant becomes aware of any circumstances which will prevent him from attending the tribunal

on the date so fixed, he shall (unless the appeal is to be heard in his absence under rule 20) immediately notify the Pensions Appeal Office of his inability to appear, stating the reasons:

Provided that, where the appellant is prevented from attending by reason of circumstances arising within 24 hours of the time of the hearing, the appellant shall, in addition to notifying the Pensions Appeal Office, use his best endeavours to inform the clerk to the tribunal at the place where the appeal is to be heard of his inability to appear.

Withdrawal of appeal

9.—(1) An appellant may at any time before the hearing give notice to the Pensions Appeal Office that he desires to withdraw his appeal, and thereupon the appeal shall be struck out.

(2) Where, after a notice of appeal has been given, the Secretary of State decides the issue arising on the appeal in favour of the appellant, the Secretary of State shall give notice of his decision to the Pensions Appeal Office and to the appellant, and the appeal shall be struck out.

Appeal not prosecuted

10. Subject to the provisions of rule 20, if the appellant fails to prosecute the appeal and does not satisfy the President that he had sufficient reason for his failure to do so, the President may direct the case to be placed in the deferred list.

Representation of the appellant and the Secretary of State

11.—(1) An appellant may conduct his case himself or may be represented by any person (whether holding any legal or other qualification or being a member of any war pensions committee, association of ex-servicemen, trade union or other body or not) whom he may appoint to assist him for the purpose.

(2) The Secretary of State may be represented by any person whom he may appoint for the purpose.

(3) It shall be the duty of the tribunal to assist any appellant who appears to them to be unable to make the best of his case.

Evidence

12.—(1) The appellant may give evidence in support of his appeal and the appellant and the Secretary of State may, subject to the provision of the next following paragraph, call a doctor or any other witness, and may produce at the hearing any further documentary evidence not already in the possession of the tribunal.

(2) Where the appellant or the Secretary of State intends to call a doctor as a witness at the hearing, he shall, unless he has already notified the Pensions Appeal Office of his intention to call the witness, send notice of his intention to the Pensions Appeal Office not less than seven days before the date fixed for the hearing and the Pensions Appeal Office shall notify the Secretary of State or, as the case may be, the appellant who shall then be entitled to call a doctor at the hearing without giving notice.

(3) The tribunal may require the appellant to furnish such evidence of his identity as they may think fit, and, where the appeal is brought by a person acting on behalf of the appellant, the tribunal may require him to satisfy them as to his qualifications for so acting.

(4) The tribunal may summon before it expert or other witnesses.

(5) The tribunal shall not refuse evidence tendered to them on the ground only that such evidence would be inadmissible in a court of law.

(6) Subject to rule 22 and to any direction given by the President under rule 6 or by the chairman under rule 15, every document tendered in evidence or considered by the tribunal for the purposes of the appeal shall be made available to the appellant or his representative (if any) and to the Secretary of State or his representative in such manner as the tribunal may direct.

Procedure at hearing

13.—(1) At the hearing the tribunal shall give an opportunity to the appellant or his representative to address the tribunal and call witnesses and, if the appellant is not represented, the examination of the appellant's witnesses may, if the appellant so desires, be conducted by the chairman of the tribunal on behalf of the appellant. The representative of the Secretary of State may put questions to any witness called by or on behalf of the appellant.

(2) The tribunal shall give the representative of the Secretary of State an opportunity to address the tribunal and call witnesses. The appellant or his representative may put questions to any witness called by or on behalf of the Secretary of State.

Adjournment for further information or evidence

14.—(1) Where during the hearing of an appeal it appears to the tribunal that it is necessary to obtain further information on any point, or that the appellant or the Secretary of State should be allowed or required to procure or produce further evidence, the appeal shall be adjourned for such further information to be obtained in such manner as the tribunal may direct or for the appellant or the Secretary of State to procure or produce such further evidence.

(2) Where the tribunal adjourns the hearing for further information to be obtained, the information, if and when obtained, shall, subject to any direction given by the President under rule 6, be communicated to the appellant and the Secretary of State, together with a statement that the appellant and the Secretary of State may comment thereon in writing if they so desire, or may address the tribunal thereon at a further hearing of the case.

(3) Where the hearing is adjourned for the appellant or the Secretary of State to procure or produce further written evidence, the evidence shall, subject to any directions given by the President under rule 6, be communicated to the Pensions Appeal Office, together with a statement indicating whether or not the appellant or the Secretary of State wishes to address the tribunal on the evidence at a further hearing of the case, and a copy of the evidence shall be sent from the Pensions Appeal Office to the Secretary of State, or, as the case may be, to the appellant, together with a statement that the Secretary of State or, as the case may be, the appellant, may comment thereon in writing if he so desires, or may address the tribunal thereon at a further hearing of the case.

(4) Where the appellant or the Secretary of State informs the Pensions Appeal Office of his desire to address the tribunal on the further information, or on further written evidence, a notice of hearing shall be sent to the appellant and to the Secretary of State not less than 10 days before the date fixed for the case to be further heard.

(5) Where neither the appellant nor the Secretary of State wishes to address the tribunal on the further information or further written evidence, the tribunal may give their decision without a further hearing of the case after taking into

consideration any comments in writing made by the appellant or by the Secretary of State on the further information or evidence.

(6) Where the hearing is adjounred for the appellant or the Secretary of State to procure or produce further oral evidence, a notice of hearing shall be sent to the appellant and to the Secretary of State not less than 10 days before the date fixed for the case to be further heard if a date for the further hearing was not fixed at the adjournment or the date then fixed has to be altered.

(7) Where the appellant fails to procure or produce further evidence which he has been required by the tribunal to procure or produce, and the tribunal is satisfied that the failure was due to the wilful default of the appellant, the case shall be placed on the deferred list.

Power of tribunal to take expert advice.

15.—(1) Where in the case of any appeal the tribunal are of opinion that a difficult medical or other technical question arises, the tribunal may, before giving their decision, take the opinion of a medical specialist or other technical expert in such manner as may appear to them to be convenient.

(2) Where the question is a medical question, the tribunal may arrange for the appellant to be examined by a medical specialist for a report on his condition.

(3) The tribunal shall direct the specialist or other technical expert to send his opinion or report to the Pensions Appeal Office, and copies thereof and of the terms of reference to the specialist or technical expert shall be sent from the Pensions Appeal Office to the appellant and to the Secretary of State together with a statement that the appellant or the Secretary of State may comment on the opinion or report in writing, if he so desires, or may address the tribunal thereon at a further hearing of the case:

Provided that where it appears to the chairman that it would not be in the best interests of the appellant for the opinion or report of a medical specialist to be communicated to him, the chairman may direct that, instead of being sent to the appellant, the opinion or report shall be sent to the appellant's medical adviser (if known to the tribunal) and, if the appellant was represented at the hearing, to his representative.

(4) Where the Pensions Appeal Office is notified by, or on behalf of, the appellant or the Secretary of State that a further hearing is desired on the opinion or report, a notice of hearing shall be sent to the appellant and to the Secretary of State not less than 10 days before the date fixed for the case to be further heard.

(5) Where neither the appellant nor the Secretary of State desires to address the tribunal further, the tribunal may give their decision without a further hearing of the case, after taking into consideration any comments in writing made by the appellant or by the Secretary of State on the opinion or report.

Adjourned hearings

16. Where an appeal has been adjourned by a tribunal or has been remitted back to the tribunal by the Court of Session and the President is of the opinion that it is not practicable, or that it is not possible, without undue delay, for the hearing of the appeal or consideration of the remit to be continued by the same tribunal, he may direct that the appeal be re-heard or the remit considered by another tribunal.

Medical examination of appellant

17. In a case where the appellant is present in person at the hearing and is the person in respect of whose incapacity for work or disablement the appeal is brought, the medical member or members of the tribunal may, with the assent of the appellant, make a medical examination of the appellant.

Decision of the tribunal

18. The decision of the tribunal may, at the discretion of the tribunal, be announced by the chairman immediately after the hearing of the case, or may be communicated in writing to the appellant and the Secretary of State within seven days after the tribunal have reached their decision, and in either case the chairman shall indicate shortly the tribunal's reasons for their decision.

Recording and proof of decisions

19.—(1) The clerk to the tribunal shall enter, in a book to be kept by him for the purpose, a minute of every decision of the tribunal.

(2) The chairman of the tribunal shall sign a document (to be called a "Form of Decision") recording the decision on the appeal and it shall be the duty of the clerk to the tribunal to transmit the Form of Decision to the Pensions Appeal Office.

(3) Copies of the Form of Decision shall be prepared in the Pensions Appeal Office, and shall be certified under the hand of an officer authorised in that behalf by the President, and a copy so certified shall be sent to the appellant and to the Secretary of State.

(4) A copy of a Form of Decision purporting to have been certified as aforesaid shall be conclusive evidence of the decision of the tribunal on the appeal to which that form of decision relates.

Appeal in absence of appellant

20. Subject to any arrangement made by the President under rule 21, an appeal shall not be heard in the absence of the appellant unless he has sent to to the Pensions Appeal Office, or to the tribunal a request that his appeal should be heard in his absence, or the tribunal are satisfied on representation made on behalf of the appellant that he desires that his appeal should be heard in his absence;

Provided that, notwithstanding that such a request or representation has been made, the tribunal may, if they think that the presence of the appellant is necessary for the due determination of the appeal, give directions that the appeal shall not be heard in his absence.

Appellant unable to attend tribunal through infirmity

21. Where the President is satisfied that any appellant is unable, through physical or mental infirmity, to attend the tribunal and that his incapacity is likely to continue for a prolonged period, the President may make such arrangements as may appear to him best suited, in all the circumstances of the case, for disposing fairly of the appeal, and in particular may arrange—

(*a*) for the appellant to be visited at some convenient place by one or more members of the tribunal, or by other person or persons appointed in that behalf by the President, for the purpose of recording the appellant's evidence and any statement which he may wish to make, and for the appellant to be medically examined, so however that in an assessment appeal the visit shall be made by one or both of the medical members of the tribunal or by another duly qualified medical practitioner, as may be appointed by the President;

(*b*) for taking, whether before the tribunal or otherwise, the evidence of medical or other witnesses on behalf of the appellant and the Secretary of State, and in particular the evidence of the near relatives, guardian or other representative of the appellant;

(*c*) for enabling the appellant's representative and the Secretary of State to comment, whether at a hearing of the tribunal or in writing, on the evidence so taken and to make a statement in writing or to address the tribunal;

(*d*) for the determination of the appeal in the absence of the appellant:

Provided that any arrangement made under paragraph (*a*) or (*b*) shall make provision for enabling the representative of the Secretary of State if he so desires, to be present while the evidence of the appellant and other witnesses, is taken and to ask questions of the appellant and other witnesses.

Medical evidence injurious to the appellant

22.—(1) This rule shall apply to any case where the medical history of the appellant or of the person in respect of whose death an appeal is brought comprises material which, in the opinion of the Secretary of State, it would be undesirable in the interests of the appellant to disclose to him.

(2) Where in any case to which this rule applies it comes to the knowledge of the Secretary of State, before the Statement of Case is sent to the appellant under rule 5 that the appellant is to be represented at the hearing of the appeal, the representative shall for the purposes of the provision of that rule relating to the transmission of the statement of the case, the submission of an answer and the transmission of any comments thereon, be treated as the appellant.

(3) If in any case to which this rule applies it appears to the Secretary of State that the appellant does not intend to be represented at the hearing of the appeal, the Secretary of State shall omit from the copies of the Statement of Case sent by him to the appellant under rule 5 those portions which in the opinion of the Secretary of State it would be undesirable in the interest of the appellant to disclose to him, so, however, that the copies of the Statement of Case sent by the Secretary of State to the Pensions Appeal Office under rule 5(6) shall contain the omitted portions and shall be accompanied by a notice stating the fact of the omission and the reasons therefor.

(4) On the receipt of copies of a Statement of Case and a notice under paragraph (3), the President shall use his best endeavours to assist the appellant to obtain a suitable person or organisation to represent him at the hearing of the appeal, and where such a representative is obtained the Secretary of State shall, on being notified to that effect, send to the representative two copies of the omitted portions of the Statement of Case, together with a statement that the omissions were made pursuant to this rule.

(5) In any case to which this rule applies the President shall indicate to the tribunal before the hearing of the appeal which portions of the Statement of Case have not been disclosed to the appellant, and the tribunal shall decide whether, in the interests of the appellant, those portions should or should not be disclosed to him, and accordingly the tribunal may order that all or any of those portions shall be communicated to the appellant forthwith, or may hear the appeal without all or any of those protions being so communicated, so, however, that the tribunal shall take the omitted portions into consideration before deciding the appeal.

Death of appellant before hearing

23.—(1) Where the pensions appeal office is notified that an appellant has died before the appeal is decided—

(*a*) in the case of an entitlement appeal, the case shall be placed in the deferred list;

(*b*) in the case of an assessment appeal, the appeal shall be struck out.

(2) Where the appellant in an entitlement appeal has died before the appeal is decided, the President may, on application made to him under rule 25 by the widow or other dependant of the deceased appellant or by his personal representative, give directions that the appeal shall proceed, so far as may be, as if the widow, dependant or personal representative, as the case may be, had brought the appeal on behalf of the appellant in the first instance and the appellant had not died, and that it shall be heard with any appeal brought by the widow or other dependant in respect of the appellant's death.

Appeal to Court of Session on point of law

24.—(1) Where the appellant or the Secretary of State is dissatisfied with the decision of the tribunal on an entitlement appeal as being erroneous in point of law, he may apply to the tribunal, in manner prescribed by this rule, for leave to appeal to the Court of Session.

(2) An application for leave to appeal may be made—

(*a*) at the hearing of the appeal, immediately after the decision of the tribunal is announced; or

(*b*) by notice in writing sent to the Pensions Appeal Office within six weeks of the communication to the appellant of the decision of the tribunal;

and in making his application the applicant shall state in writing the point of law in respect of which he claims that the decision of the tribunal is erroneous and on which he wishes to appeal.

(3) On receipt of an application in writing for leave to appeal, a copy thereof shall be sent from the Pensions Appeal Office to the Secretary of State or, as the case may be, to the appellant, and a notice shall be sent to the appellant and to the Secretary of State stating that the application will, unless the Secretary of State or the appellant desires to address the tribunal thereon, be determined by the tribunal without a hearing, and, unless within fifteen days of the sending to him of the notice the Secretary of State or the appellant notifies the Pensions Appeal Office that he desires to address the tribunal, the application may be so determined.

(4) Where the appellant or the Secretary of State notifies the Pensions Appeal Office that he desires to address the tribunal a notice of hearing shall be sent to the appellant and to the Secretary of State not less than 10 days before the date fixed for the hearing of the application.

(5) Where the tribunal decide to give leave to appeal to the Court of Session, the chairman shall, within such time and in such manner as may be determined by rules of court, state a case for the opinion of the Court.

(6) At the hearing of an appeal, or of an application for leave to appeal to the Court of Session, the chairman shall, at the request of the appellant or the Secretary of State, take a note—

(*a*) of any question of law raised at the hearing;

(*b*) of the facts in evidence in relation thereto; and

(c) of the decision of the tribunal thereon;

and, where such a note has been taken, the chairman shall (whether an application for leave to appeal is made or not) on the application of the appellant or the Secretary of State, furnish him with a copy of the note, and shall sign the copy.

Deferred list cases

25.—(1) Where a case is placed in the deferred list, notice of the fact shall be sent from the Pensions Appeal Office to the Secretary of State and to the appellant or, where an entitlement appeal has been placed in the deferred list because the appellant has died before the appeal was decided, to his widow or other dependant or personal representative.

(2) An appellant whose case has been placed in the deferred list or, where an entitlement appeal has been placed in the deferred list because the appellant has died before the appeal was decided, the widow or other dependant or personal representative of the appellant, may at any time within 12 months after notice of the fact has been given apply to the President for an order that the case be restored to the list of cases for hearing.

(3) An order under the last foregoing paragraph of this rule may be made unconditionally or subject to such terms and conditions as the President thinks just:

Provided that, where the case has been placed in the deferred list pursuant to a direction given by the President under rule 10, the case shall, on the application of the appellant, be restored unconditionally to the list of cases for hearing unless the President is satisfied that the appellant's failure to prosecute the appeal was due to his wilful default.

(4) Where no application to restore the case to the list of cases for hearing has been made within the time prescribed by paragraph (2), or where any such application has been made and has been refused by the President, the appeal shall be struck out.

Expenses of appellant

26.—(1) There may be allowed—

(a) to an appellant who attends the hearing;

(b) to a relative, guardian or other representative attending the hearing on behalf of an appellant by virtue of arrangements made by the President under rule 21;

(c) to a person who accompanies an appellant at the hearing where the President or the chairman of the tribunal certified that it is necessary for the appellant, by reason of his health, to be accompanied by an attendant;

(d) to an appellant who is examined by a medical specialist pursuant to arrangements made by the tribunal under rule 15(2); and

(e) to a witness other than a medical witness who attends the hearing, where before the hearing an application is made to the President or chairman of the tribunal and he certifies that in the exceptional circumstances of the case the attendance of the witness is necessary;

the travelling expenses actually and reasonably incurred by him for the purpose of attending the tribunal or of undergoing the medical examination, as the case may be, and an allowance in respect of subsistence, not exceeding in amount whichever of the allowances specified in Part I of Schedule 2 is appropriate to his case.

(2) Where it is necessary for the appellant or other person to travel by railway train to and from the tribunal, or, as the case may be, the place where the medical examination is held, a railway warrant shall be sent to him from the Pensions Appeal Office.

(3) Where the appeal is successful, and where the appeal was not successful but the chairman certifies that there were reasonable grounds for the appeal, there may be allowed to the appellant or to any such person as is referred to in paragraph (1)(*b*), (*c*) or (*e*) in addition to the allowances mentioned in that paragraph, such sum as compensation for loss of time as the chairman thinks reasonable, not exceeding the sum of £2.37½ per half day or £4.75 per day.

(4) Where an appellant brings a medical witness to the hearing or, for the purposes of the appeal, has obtained from a medical adviser, or from a hospital, nursing home or other institution in which he has received treatment, a report, certificate or other document and the chairman of the tribunal or the President certifies that the attendance of the medical witness, or the production of the report, certificate or other document, was reasonably necessary for the purposes of the appeal, the appellant may be allowed such sum in respect of the expenses incurred by him in securing such attendance or in obtaining such report, certificate or document as the President thinks reasonable, not exceeding the sum specified in Part II of Schedule 2.

Expenses of appeals to the Court of Session.

27.—(1) Where leave to appeal to the Court of Session on a point of law is given, whether to the appellant or to the Secretary of State, the appellant shall be entitled to be paid the expenses of prosecuting or defending the appeal in the Court of Session and in addition—

(*a*) if the leave is given by the tribunal, the expenses (if any) certified by the President to have been reasonably incurred by the appellant for the purpose of making or opposing an application for the leave of the tribunal;

(*b*) if the leave is given by the Court of Session, the expense of making or opposing an application for the leave of the Court and, where an application has been made to the tribunal and has been refused, the expenses (if any) certified by the President to have been reasonably incurred by the appellant for the purpose of making or opposing the application to the tribunal.

(2) Where leave to appeal to the Court of Session on a point of law is applied for by the Secretary of State and refused, the appellant shall be entitled to be paid—

(*a*) where the leave is refused by the tribunal, the expenses (if any) certified by the President to have been reasonably incurred by the appellant for the purpose of opposing the application; or

(*b*) where the leave is refused by the Court of Session, the expenses of opposing the application to the Court and, where an application for leave has been made to the tribunal and has been refused, the expenses (if any) certified by the President to have been reasonably incurred by the appellant for the purpose of opposing the application to the tribunal.

(3) Where an application for leave to appeal to the Court of Session has been delivered to the Pensions Appeal Office, and the Secretary of State, before such application is heard by a tribunal, decides the issue arising on the application in

favour of the appellant, the Secretary of State shall give notice of his decision to the Pensions Appeal Office and to the appellant and the application shall be struck out and the appellant may be allowed the expenses certified by the President to have been reasonably incurred in making the application up to the date of notification of his decision by the Secretary of State.

(4) An application for expenses payable to an appellant under this rule shall be made in writing to the Pensions Appeal Office within one month after the termination of the proceedings in the Court of Session, or, as the case may be, the refusal of leave to appeal, and for the purpose of ascertaining the sum due to the appellant he shall furnish to the Pensions Appeal Office such certificates or other documents as he may be directed to furnish.

(5) For the purposes of exercising his jurisdiction as to expenses under paragraphs (1), (2) or (3), the President may apply or adapt the regulations and tables of fees and charges applicable to similar proceedings in the Court of Session.

Expenses of applications under section 6(2A) *of the Act*

28.—(1) When an application has been made under section 6(2A) of the Act (which provides for a joint application by an appellant and the Secretary of State to set aside a decision of a tribunal and rehear the appeal) the appellant shall be entitled to be paid the expenses (if any) certified by the President to have been reasonably incurred by the appellant in connection with such application.

(2) An application for expenses payable to an appellant under this rule shall be made in writing to the Pensions Appeal Office, and for the purpose of ascertaining the sum due to the appellant and he shall furnish to the Pensions Appeal Office such certificates or other documents as he may be directed to furnish.

(3) For the purposes of exercising his jurisdiction as to expenses under paragraph (1), the President may apply or adapt the regulations and tables of fees and charges applicable to similar proceedings in the Court of Session.

Other expenses of the tribunal

29.—(1) Where under rule 15 the tribunal take the opinion of a medical specialist or other technical expert, or send the appellant to be examined by a medical specialist, the tribunal may direct the payment to the specialist or expert of a fee of £5.25 or such greater fee not exceeding £17.25 as the President may in special cases direct.

(2) Where the tribunal summon an expert or other witness or obtain from a medical practitioner, hospital or other institution documentary information relating to an appeal, the tribunal may direct the payment to such witness of a fee of £5.25 or such greater fee not exceeding £15.75 as the President may direct or to the medical practitioner, hospital or institution such sums, not exceeding £0.75 in respect of each document or set of documents, as the tribunal may think reasonable.

Claims for expenses

30. An application for any expenses payable to an appellant or other person under rules 26, 27, 28 or 29 shall be made in writing to the clerk to the tribunal or the Pensions Appeal Office.

Applications to the President for directions

31.—(1) The appellant or the Secretary of State may at any time apply to the president for directions on any matter arising in connection with the appeal, or with an application to the tribunal for leave to appeal to the Court of Session.

(2) An application for directions shall state the matter on which the directions are required.

(3) The President shall communicate the nature of the application to the Secretary of State or, as the case may be, to the appellant, together with a statement that the Secretary of State or the appellant may comment thereon in writing if he so desires, and before giving his directions the President shall consider any comments furnished to him.

(4) Any directions given by the President under this rule shall be communicated to the appellant and the Secretary of State.

(5) If an appellant fails to comply with a direction given to him by the President under this rule, the President may direct the case to be placed in the deferred list.

Extension of time

32. The time appointed by these rules for doing any act or taking any step in connection with an appeal may be extended by the tribunal or by the President upon such terms (if any) as the justice of the case may require, and such extension may be ordered although the application therefore is not made until after the expiration of the time appointed.

Notices, etc.

33.—(1) Any notice, document or other communication required or authorised by these rules to be given or sent to the Pensions Appeal Office shall be delivered to, or sent by post addressed to, the Pensions Appeal Office at 20 Walker Street, Edinburgh, EH3 7HS.

(2) Any notice, request, direction, document or other communication required or authorised by these rules to be given or sent to an appellant may be given or sent by sending it by post to the address given by the appellant in his notice of appeal or, where notice of appeal is given on behalf of an appellant, to the address of the person acting on his behalf, or to such other address as may be subsequently notified in writing to the Pensions Appeal Office by the appellant or by the person acting on his behalf.

(3) Any application to be made to the President under these rules may be made by post addressed to the President at the Pensions Appeal Office.

(4) Where under these rules any notice, certificate, request, direction, application or communication is to be given or made, it shall be given or made in writing.

Sittings of the tribunal

34.—(1) Subject to the provisions of this rule, the sittings of the tribunal shall be held in public.

(2) A sitting of the tribunal shall be held in private to such extent as may be necessary to enable the tribunal to comply with a direction given by the President under rule 6.

(3) Where a request is made to a tribunal by or on behalf of the appellant that the appeal, or some part of it, should be heard in private, the tribunal may, if they think that the presentation of the appellant's case will be prejudiced by a public sitting, sit in private to such extent as they think just.

(4) Nothing in this rule shall prevent a member of the Council on Tribunals or a member of the Scottish Committee of the Council on Tribunals from attending the hearing in his capacity as such.

Evidence on oath

35. The tribunal may, if they think fit, take the evidence of the appellant or any other witness on oath and for that purpose the chairman may administer an oath.

Irregularities

36. Non-compliance with any of these Rules shall not render the proceedings on the appeal void unless the tribunal or the President shall so direct, but the tribunal or the President may give such directions for the purpose of mitigating the consequences of the irregularity as the justice of the case may require.

Acting President

37. The functions of the President under these Rules may, if he is for any reason unable to act or during a vacancy in his office, be discharged by a person nominated for that purpose by the Lord President of the Court of Session.

Revocations

38. The rules specified in Schedule 3 to these Rules are hereby revoked.

Dated 17th December 1971.

J. L. Clyde.

SCHEDULE 1

Form 1 Rule 4(3)

NOTICE OF ENTITLEMENT APPEAL

PENSIONS APPEAL TRIBUNALS ACTS 1943 AND 1949

Department Ref:

I, (1)..

(1) Full name(s) of appellant

of (2)..

(2) Address of appellant

hereby give notice that I appeal under the Pensions Appeal Tribunal Acts 1943 and 1949 against the decision of the Secretary of State for Social Services notified to me by letter dated..

Dated..Signed.........................., Appellant

Note:—This form when completed must be sent to the Department of Health and Social Security.

Rule 4(3) Form 2

NOTICE OF ENTITLEMENT APPEAL ON BEHALF OF APPELLANT
PENSIONS APPEAL TRIBUNALS ACTS 1943 AND 1949

Department Ref:

I, (1)..
(1) Full name(s) of person acting on behalf of appellant

of (2)..
(2) Address of person acting on behalf of appellant

acting on behalf of (3)...
(3) Full name(s) of appellant

of (4)..
(4) Address of appellant

as (5)..
(5) State your qualification for acting on behalf of appellant

hereby give notice of appeal under the Pensions Appeal Tribunals Acts 1943 and 1949 against the decision of the Secretary of State notified to (specify person to whom decision was notified) by letter dated................................

Dated.............................. Signed.................................

Note:—
(1) This form is only to be used where the appellant is under the age of 16 years or is prevented by physical or mental infirmity from acting on his own behalf.
(2) This form when completed must be sent to the Department of Health and Social Security.

Rule 4(3) Form 3

NOTICE OF APPEAL AGAINST INTERIM ASSESSMENT
PENSIONS APPEAL TRIBUNALS ACTS 1943 AND 1949

Department Ref:

I, (1)..
(1) Full name(s) of appellant

of (2)..
(2) Address of appellant

hereby give notice that I appeal under the Pensions Appeal Tribunals Acts 1943 and 1949 against the Assessment made by the Secretary of State for Social Services and notified to me by letter dated..

Dated............................ Signed..Appellant

Note:—This form when completed must be sent to the Department of Health and Social Security.

Form 4 Rule 4(3)

NOTICE OF APPEAL AGAINST INTERIM ASSESSMENT ON BEHALF OF APPELLANT
PENSIONS APPEAL TRIBUNALS ACTS 1943 AND 1949

Department Ref:

I, (1)..
(1) Full name(s) of person acting on behalf of appellant

of (2)..
(2) Address of person acting on behalf of appellant

acting on behalf of (3)..
(3) Full name(s) of appellant

of (4)..
(4) Address of appellant

as (5)..
(5) State your qualification for acting on behalf of appellant

hereby give notice of appeal under the Pensions Appeal Tribunals Acts 1943 and 1949 against the Assessment(s) made by the Secretary of State for Social Services and notified to (6)..
(6) Specify person to whom the assessment was notified

by letter dated..

Dated.. Signed..

Note:—

(1) This form is only to be used where the appellant is under the age of 16 years or is prevented by physical or mental infirmity from acting on his own behalf.

(2) This form when completed must be sent to the Department of Health and Social Security.

Form 5

Rule 4(3)

NOTICE OF APPEAL AGAINST FINAL DECISION OR FINAL ASSESSMENT
PENSIONS APPEAL TRIBUNALS ACTS 1943 AND 1949

Department Ref:

I, (1)..
(1) Full name(s) of appellant

of (2)..
(2) Address of appellant

hereby give notice that I appeal under the Pensions Appeal Tribunals Acts 1943 and 1949 against—

(*a*) the decision of the Secretary of State that the circumstances of my case permit a final settlement of the question to what extent, if any, I am disabled;

(*b*) *the final assessment made by the Secretary of State of the degree or nature of my disablement,
*the final decision made by the Secretary of State that on account of

†Delete whichever c these is not applicable

....

....

(1) there is no disablement;
or (2) the disablement has come to an end;
or (3) the disablement is not serious and prolonged;
or (4) the disablement is no longer serious and prolonged.
and notified to me by letter dated..
Dated.. Signed..........................Appellant

Note:—This form, when completed, must be sent to the Department of Health and Social Security.

Rule 4(3)

Form 6

NOTICE OF APPEAL AGAINST FINAL DECISION OR FINAL ASSESSMENT ON BEHALF OF APPELLANT

PENSIONS APPEAL TRIBUNALS ACTS 1943 AND 1949

Department Ref:

I, (1)..

(1) Full name(s) of person acting on behalf of appellant

of (2)..

(2) Address of person acting on behalf of appellant

acting on behalf of (3)...

(3) Full name(s) of appellant

of (4)..

(4) Address of appellant

as (5)..

(5) State your qualification for acting on behalf of appellant

hereby give notice of appeal under the Pensions Appeal Tribunals Acts 1943 and 1949 against—

(*a*) the decision of the Secretary of State that the circumstances of the appellant's case permit a final settlement of the question to what extent, if any, he is disabled;

(*b*) *the final assessment made by the Secretary of State of the degree or nature of his disablement.

*The final decision made by the Secretary of State that on account

....

....

*Delete whichever of these is not applicable

(1) there is no disablement;

or (2) the disablement has come to an end;

or (3) the disablement is not serious and prolonged;

or (4) the disablement is no longer serious and prolonged.

and notified to (6)..

by letter dated..

Dated.. Signed..

(6) specify person etc. to whom final decision or final assessment was notified.

Note:—

(1) This form is only to be used where the appellant is under the age of 16 years or is prevented by physical or mental infirmity from acting on his own behalf.

(2) This form when completed must be sent to the Department of Health and Social Security.

Form 7

Rule 8

NOTICE OF HEARING

(This Notice to be produced at the hearing)

PENSIONS APPEAL TRIBUNALS FOR SCOTLAND

Case No.

To...
....
....

Pensions Appeal Office
20 Walker Street
EDINBURGH EH3 7HS

....19.....

NOTICE OF HEARING

Sir/Madam

1. Your appeal will be considered by the Tribunal appointed by the Lord President of the Court of Session at...
on..the ....of.............
at...o'oclock.

2. A return warrant (No.................) for your railway journey is enclosed.

If it is more convenient to travel by bus, please do so and hand the Railway Warrant to the Clerk of the Tribunal from whom you should claim the actual and necessary expense you have incurred.

3. If for any reason you are unable to attend or are not ready to proceed with your appeal on the date stated, you must immediately inform me in writing, stating the reasons for your inability to appear.

Should you wish your appeal to be disposed of in your absence you must so notify me not later than seven days before the date fixed for the hearing.

In the above circumstances the Rail Warrant issued for your attendance at the hearing must be returned to me without delay.

4. If you intend to call a doctor as a witness you must so notify me not later than seven days before the date fixed for the hearing.

5. You should bring with you the Statement of Case, and, if you are represented by any organisation, **it is suggested that you attend 30 minutes before the appointed time,** in order to discuss the appeal with the representative.

6. If you change your address please inform me immediately.

Yours faithfully

Secretary.

SCHEDULE 2

Rule 26.

SUBSISTENCE ALLOWANCES AND EXPENSES

PART I

SUBSISTENCE ALLOWANCES TO APPELLANTS, ETC

1. The maximum allowance payable under paragraph (1) of Rule 27 to an appellant or other person absent from home for the purpose of attending the tribunal or undergoing a medical examination shall be—

(*a*) for a period of two and a half hours or more but not less than five hours consecutively, £0.15, or for a period of five hours or more but less than ten hours consecutively, £0.27½, or for a period of ten hours or more consecutively, £0.57½;

(*b*) for a night, £1.80 in addition to any sum payable under paragraph (*a*).

2. When the appellant or other person is absent from home for more than twenty-four hours he shall be entitled to a further allowance calculated in accordance with the foregoing provisions for periods of absence during each successive period of twenty-four hours.

PART II

EXPENSES OF MEDICAL EVIDENCE

1. The expenses allowed to the appellant for securing the attendance of a medical witness before the tribunal shall not exceed the aggregate sum of

(*a*) £7.35 or with the leave of the President in special cases £17.25; and

(*b*) the amount of the expenses actually and reasonably incurred by the witness in travelling to and from the tribunal.

2. The expenses allowed to the appellant for obtaining a report, certificate or other document shall not exceed £15.75 in respect of each document or set of documents.

SCHEDULE 3

RULES REVOKED

Title	*Reference*
The Pensions Appeal Tribunals (Scotland) Rules 1946	S.R. & O. 1946/1709 (Rev. XVII, p. 752).
The Pensions Appeal Tribunals (Scotland) (Amendment) Rules 1949	S.I. 1949/2239 (1949 I, p. 3010).
The Pensions Appeal Tribunals (Scotland) (Amendment) Rules 1957	S.I. 1957/1972 (1957 II, p. 1834).
The Pensions Appeal Tribunals (Scotland) (Amendment) Rules 1959	S.I. 1959/2067 (1959 II, p. 2069).
The Pensions Appeal Tribunals (Scotland) (Amendment) Rules 1962	S.I. 1962/2522 (1962 III, p. 3400).
The Pensions Appeal Tribunals (Scotland) (Amendment) Rules 1965	S.I. 1965/2017 (1965 III, p. 5946).
The Pensions Appeal Tribunals (Scotland) (Amendment) Rules 1967	S.I. 1967/27 (1967 I, p. 78).
The Pensions Appeal Tribunals (Scotland) (Amendment) Rules 1969	S.I. 1969/1585 (1969 III, p. 5058).
The Pensions Appeal Tribunals (Scotland) (Amendment) Rules 1970	S.I. 1970/448 (1970 I, p. 1521).

EXPLANATORY NOTE

(*This Note is not part of the Rules.*)

These Rules supersede the Pensions Appeal Tribunals (Scotland) Rules 1946, as amended.

They consolidate the existing rules with amendments of a minor nature, and the addition of Rule 28 which deals with the expenses of a joint application by the appellant and Secretary of State for a rehearing.

1971 No. 2125

TRANSPORT

The London Transport (Lost Property) Regulations 1971

Made - - - -	*22nd December* 1971
Coming into Operation	*31st December* 1971

The Secretary of State for the Environment, in exercise of his powers under section 106 of the London Passenger Transport Act 1933**(a)**, as amended by section 68(1) of the Transport Act 1962**(b)** and section 17 of and paragraph 6(1) of Schedule 3 to the Transport (London) Act 1969**(c)**, and of all other powers enabling him in that behalf, hereby makes the following Regulations:—

Citation and commencement

1. These Regulations may be cited as the London Transport (Lost Property) Regulations 1971 and shall come into operation on 31st December 1971.

Interpretation

2.—(1) In these Regulations, unless the context otherwise requires, the following expressions have the meanings hereby respectively assigned to them, that is to say—

"the Executive" means the London Transport Executive;

"Lost Property Office" means any place designated by the Executive for the safe keeping of lost property, and any reference to the delivery of property to a lost Property Office means delivery to an official at such an office in accordance with any relevant directions of the Executive;

"the 1960 Regulations" means the London Transport (Lost Property) Regulations 1960**(d)**:

(2) Any reference in these Regulations to the conductor of a vehicle shall, as respects a vehicle which has no conductor, be construed as a reference to the driver.

(3) The Interpretation Act 1889**(e)** shall apply for the interpretation of these Regulations as it applies for the interpretation of an Act of Parliament, and as if for the purpose of section 38 of that Act these Regulations were an Act of Parliament and the Regulations revoked by Regulation 13 hereof were an Act of Parliament thereby repealed.

(a) 1933 c. 14.
(b) 1962 c. 46.
(c) 1969 c. 35.
(d) S.I. 1960/2396 (1960 I, p. 432).
(e) 1889 c. 63.

Application of regulations

3.—(1) These Regulations apply in relation to the safe custody, redelivery and disposal of property found on or in any premises or vehicle belonging to the Executive and references in these Regulations to "premises" or "vehicle" shall be construed as references to any such premises or vehicle.

(2) Without prejudice to the generality of paragraph (1) of this Regulation, these Regulations shall apply in relation to the safe custody, redelivery and disposal of any property found on or in any premises or vehicle of the Executive and handed or delivered to the Executive before the coming into operation of these Regulations.

Lost property to be handed to conductor, guard or other official

4. Any person who finds property accidentally left on or in premises or a vehicle shall hand it immediately in the state in which he finds it (i) to the conductor or guard of the vehicle on or in which it is found or (ii) where this is not practicable or where the property is not found on or in a vehicle, to some other appropriate official of the Executive.

Search of vehicles and premises for lost property

5.—(1) In the case of a road vehicle the conductor shall, immediately before or on the termination of any journey, so far as practicable search the vehicle for any property accidentally left on or in the vehicle.

(2) The Executive shall make suitable arrangements for premises and rail vehicles to be searched at reasonable intervals for any property accidentally left thereon or therein.

Delivery of lost property to Lost Property Office

6. Any official of the Executive to whom property has been handed under the 1960 Regulations or under Regulation 4 of these Regulations or who himself finds any property on or in any premises or vehicle shall, as soon as possible and in any case within 24 hours (unless the property has been claimed), deliver the property for safe keeping in the state in which it comes into his possession to a Lost Property Office or to such official of the Executive as the Executive may direct for delivery to a Lost Property Office.

Safe keeping and recording of property

7.—(1) Any property delivered to a Lost Property Office under the 1960 Regulations or under Regulation 6 of these Regulations shall be held for safe keeping by the Executive until claimed by the owner thereof or disposed of in accordance with these Regulations:

Provided that—

(*a*) official documents, including licences, passports and alien's identity books, shall wherever practicable be returned forthwith to the appropriate Government Department, local authority or other body or person responsible for issuing them or for controlling or dealing with them;

(*b*) where the name and address of the owner of any property, other than the documents referred to in the preceding proviso, are readily ascertainable the Executive shall forthwith notify him that the property is in the possession of the Executive and may be claimed in accordance with these Regulations.

(2) The Executive shall keep for a period of not less than twelve months a record showing particulars of all property delivered to a Lost Property Office or claimed before delivery, the circumstances in which it was found, and the ultimate disposal of the property, and such record shall at all reasonable times during the said period be available for inspection by a constable or any person authorised in that behalf by the chairman of the traffic commissioners for the Metropolitan Traffic Area.

Return of claimed property on payment of charges

8.—(1) If any property accidentally left on or in premises or a vehicle is claimed, before it has been delivered to a Lost Property Office, by a claimant who gives his name and address and satisfies the Executive that he is the owner thereof, it shall thereupon be returned to him on payment to the Executive of the charge specified in the second column of the Schedule hereto for property of that kind.

(2) If any such property, while it is held by the Executive for safe keeping at a Lost Property Office, is claimed there by a claimant who gives his name and address and satisfies the Executive that he is the owner thereof, it shall thereupon be returned to him on payment to the Executive of the charge specified in the third column of the Schedule hereto for property of that kind.

Disposal of property by the Executive

9. If any property held by the Executive for safe keeping in accordance with these Regulations is not claimed within one month of the date when it was delivered to a Lost Property Office pursuant to the 1960 Regulations or to Regulation 6 of these Regulations, and proved to the satisfaction of the Executive to belong to the claimant, or if the claimant shall refuse or neglect to pay to the Executive the appropriate sum or sums due under Regulation 8 hereof and to take delivery of the property within the said period, the Property shall thereupon vest in the Executive who shall without undue delay sell the property;

Provided that—

(*a*) property the value of which in the opinion of the Executive exceeds 50p and any other property which for any reason in the opinion of the Executive should be retained for a longer period than one month, shall not vest in the Executive and shall not be so disposed of until the expiration of such longer period, not being less than three months, as the Executive may think fit;

(*b*) any official documents which it has not been practicable to return to the appropriate body or person in accordance with the provisions of proviso (*a*) to Regulation 7 hereof, and any other documents which have not been claimed by a person entitled to their return within the period of one month as provided by this Regulation, shall be dealt with or disposed of in such manner as the Executive may deem appropriate.

Perishable property

10. Notwithstanding the foregoing provisions of these Regulations, if any property held by the Executive under these Regulations appears to the Executive to be of a perishable nature, and if, within 48 hours from the time when it was found, it has not been claimed and proved to the satisfaction of the Executive to belong to a claimant who has paid the amounts payable under Regulation 8 hereof and taken delivery of the property, the property shall thereupon vest in the Executive who may destroy or otherwise dispose of it as they think fit:

Provided that any property which is or which becomes objectionable may be destroyed or disposed of at any time in the discretion of the Executive.

Cost of packing and carriage

11. Where any property is forwarded to a claimant the reasonable costs of packing and carriage shall be paid to the Executive in advance by the claimant.

Examination of property

12. Where any property is contained in a package, bag or other receptacle the Executive may cause such receptacle to be opened and the contents examined, or require the claimant to open it and submit it and its contents for examination, if the Executive deem it necessary to do so for the purpose either—

(*a*) of identifying and tracing the owner of the property, or

(*b*) of ascertaining the nature of the contents or valuing the property.

Revocation

13. The 1960 Regulations are hereby revoked.

Signed by authority of the Secretary of State.
22nd December 1971.

J. Garlick,
An Under Secretary in the
Department of the Environment.

SCHEDULE

Article	Amounts chargeable for article when collected	
	Before delivery to a Lost Property Office	At a Lost Property Office
1. Handbag or purse (not containing money) Book Glove or Pair of Gloves Hat Key or bunch of keys Mackintosh (Plastic) Scarf Smokers' Requisites Spectacles or sunglasses Umbrella Walking Stick Article of small value	15p	30p
2. Money Purse, handbag or other receptacle containing money — Up to £1	15p	30p
— Over £1	30p	60p
3. Livestock	30p	60p
4. Bicycle Perambulator	45p	90p
5. Any article not otherwise provided for	40p	80p
6. Additional daily charge for keeping a dog or other small animal	50p	50p

EXPLANATORY NOTE

(This Note is not part of the Regulations.)

These Regulations make provision as respects property accidentally left in or on vehicles or premises of the London Transport Executive. For the most part they re-enact (with amendments) in relation to the Executive the London Transport (Lost Property) Regulations 1960 which are revoked.

The principal change is that the fee payable on the return of claimed property will depend on the nature of the property instead of its value (Reg. 8 and the Schedule).

1971 No. 2127 (L.52)

COUNTY COURTS

PROCEDURE

The County Court (Amendment No. 3) Rules 1971

Made - - -	21*st December* 1971
Coming into Operation	
All provisions except Rule 11(4)	24*th January* 1972
Rule 11(4)	1*st March* 1972

1.—(1) These Rules may be cited as the County Court (Amendment No. 3) Rules 1971.

(2) In these Rules an Order and Rule referred to by number means the Order and Rule so numbered in the County Court Rules 1936(**a**), as amended (**b**), and a form referred to by number means the form so numbered in Appendix A to those Rules.

(3) The Interpretation Act 1889(**c**) shall apply for the interpretation of these Rules as it applies for the interpretation of an Act of Parliament.

2. Paragraph (9) of Order 5, Rule 19, shall be omitted.

3. The following Rule shall be added at the end of Order 13 :—

Juries

"14.—(1) An application for an order for trial with a jury may be made by any party on notice stating the grounds of the application.

(2) Notice of the application shall, if time allows, regard being had to the date of service of the summons, be given not less than 10 clear days before the return day.

(3) Where notice of the application is given less than 10 clear days before the return day or where for that or any other reason the application is not heard in time for a jury to be summoned, the judge or registrar may, on such terms as he thinks fit, postpone the trial so as to allow time for a jury to be summoned.

(4) The judge may from time to time give the registrar directions as to whether the application is to be heard by the judge or the registrar in every case or in any particular case or class of case.

(**a**) S.R. & O. 1936/626 (1936 I, p. 282).
(**b**) The relevant amending instruments are S.R. & O. 1938/731, S.I. 1950/1231, 1993, 1952/2198, 1954/1394, 1955/1799, 1959/1251, 1960/1275, 1964/353, 1974, 1965/2147, 1969/585, 1970/204, 1971/836 (1938 I, p. 986; 1950 I, pp. 400, 440; 1952 I, p. 635; 1954 I, p. 526; 1955 I, p. 530; 1959 I, p. 795; 1960 I, p. 809; 1964 I, p. 543, III, p. 4477; 1965 III, p. 6292; 1969 I, p. 1551; 1970 I, p. 911; 1971 II, p. 2393).
(**c**) 1889 c. 63.

(5) Notice of an order for trial with a jury shall be communicated by the registrar to any party who was not present or represented at the hearing of the application.

(6) Where an order for trial with a jury has been made, but the proceedings are withdrawn or settled before the return day, it shall be the duty of the party at whose instance the order was made to inform the registrar."

4. Order 16 shall be amended as follows :—

(1) Rule 12 shall be revoked except in relation to any proceedings transferred to a county court before 1st January 1972.

(2) Rule 13 shall be amended as follows :—

(*a*) In paragraph (1) the words "or a widow" shall be omitted and for the words "guardian *ad litem* or widow" there shall be substituted the words "or guardian *ad litem*".

(*b*) In paragraph (4) for the words "person of unsound mind or widow" there shall be substituted the words "or person of unsound mind", and the proviso shall be omitted.

(3) In Rule 15 for the words "guardian *ad litem* or widow" there shall be substituted the words "or guardian *ad litem*".

5. Order 21 shall be revoked.

6. In Order 25, Rule 92(2), the words "or 95" shall be omitted.

7. The following Rule shall be added at the end of Order 27:-

Exercise of powers by registrar

"20. The powers conferred on the judge by Rules 7(4), (5) and (6), 9(1) and 16 and (where the judgment debtor does not appear) by Rule 8 of this Order may be exercised by the registrar."

8. Order 34 shall be amended as follows :—

(1) Rule 4 shall be revoked.

(2) In Rule 6 the words "Section 95 or" shall be omitted.

9. Order 36 shall be amended as follows :—

(1) Rule 1 shall be revoked.

(2) For Rule 2 there shall be substituted the following Rule :—

Parties to action for revocation

"2. Every person who is entitled or claims to be entitled to administer the estate of a deceased person under or by virtue of an unrevoked grant of probate of his will or letters of administration shall be made a party to any action brought in a county court for revocation of the grant."

(3) In Rule 4 for the words "intervene and appear" there shall be substituted the words "apply to be added as a defendant".

(4) In Rule 6 for the words "the plaintiff and the defendant and any party intervening" there shall be substituted the words "each party".

(5) In Rule 9 for the words "of the Probate Division of the High Court" there shall be substituted the words "of the High Court relating to probate causes and matters".

10. In Order 45A, Rule 8(2), for the words "Principal Probate Registry" there shall be substituted the words "Principal Registry of the Family Division".

11. The following amendments shall be made in Order 46:—

(1) Rule 1 shall be amended as follows:—

(*a*) For the heading there shall be substituted the following:—

"GUARDIANSHIP OF MINORS ACT 1971".

(*b*) In paragraph (1) for the words "Guardianship of Infants Act 1886 and 1925" there shall be substituted the words "Guardianship of Minors Act 1971" and in the margin there shall be inserted the note "1971 c.3".

(*c*) In paragraph (2) for the words from "paragraph (2A)" to "an infant" there shall be substituted the words "section 5 of the said Act for the appointment of the applicant to be the guardian of a minor", and the marginal note "15 & 16 Geo. 5, c.45" shall be omitted.

(2) Rule 8 shall be amended as follows:—

(*a*) In paragraph (1) after the words "section 2" there shall be inserted the words "or, as the case may be, section 3A".

(*b*) In paragraph (2) after the words "section 1" there shall be inserted the words "or section 3(2) or (3)".

(*c*) In paragraph (4) after the words "section 2(1)" there shall be inserted the words "or section 3A(1)", and after the words "section 1" there shall be inserted the words "or section 3(2)".

(3) The following Rule shall be added after Rule 21 :—

"THE INDUSTRIAL RELATIONS ACT 1971

22. In deciding whether to stay proceedings in tort under section 131 of the Industrial Relations Act 1971, the court shall take into account all relevant circumstances, including the question whether, notwithstanding that the proceedings are framed in tort, the complaint is in substance one of an unfair industrial practice within the meaning of that Act, or whether the matters in issue in the proceedings are for any other reason more suitable to be determined by the National Industrial Relations Court or an industrial tribunal than by the appropriate mode of trial in the county court (including, where applicable, trial with a jury)."

1971 c. 72.

(4) The following Rule shall be added at the end of Order 46 :—

"PART III OF THE FAMILY LAW REFORM ACT 1969

23.—(1) In this Rule—

"the Act" means Part III of the Family Law Reform Act 1969 ;

1969 c. 46.

"blood samples" and "blood tests" have the meanings assigned to them by section 25 of the Act ;

"direction" means a direction for the use of blood tests under section 20(1) of the Act.

(2) Except with the leave of the court, an application in any proceedings for a direction shall be made on notice to every party to the proceedings (other than the applicant) and to any other person from whom the direction involves the taking of blood samples.

(3) Where an application is made for a direction involving the taking of blood samples from a person who is not a party to the proceedings in which the application is made, the notice of application shall be served on him personally and the court may at any time direct him to be made a party to the proceedings.

(4) Where an application is made for a direction in respect of a person (in this paragraph referred to as a person under disability) who is either—

(*a*) under 16, or

(*b*) suffering from mental disorder within the meaning of the Mental Health Act 1959 and incapable of understanding the nature and purpose of blood tests,

1959 c. 72

the notice of application shall state the name and address of the person having the care and control of the person under disability and shall be served on him instead of on the person under disability.

(5) Where the court gives a direction in any proceedings, the registrar shall send a copy to every party to the proceedings and to every other person from whom the direction involves the taking of blood samples and, unless otherwise ordered, the proceedings shall stand adjourned until the court receives a report pursuant to the direction.

(6) On receipt by the court of a report made pursuant to a direction, the registrar shall send a copy to every party to the proceedings and to every other person from whom the direction involved the taking of blood samples."

12. The following paragraph shall be added at the end of Order 47, Rule 30 :—

"(6) Rule 21(4) of this Order shall apply to an application for a certificate under paragraph (5) of this Rule as it applies to an application for a certificate under that Rule."

13. Forms 123, 124, 125, 126, 127, 263 and 276 shall be omitted.

14. In Form 278 for the words "Section 95 [*or* 84]" and "juror [*or* witness]" there shall be substituted the words "section 84" and "witness" respectively.

15. In Form 309 the words "the Probate, Divorce and Admiralty Division of" and "the said division of" shall be omitted.

16. In Forms 329 and 370 for the words "Probate, Divorce and Admiralty" there shall in each case be substituted the word "Family".

We, the undersigned members of the Rule Committee appointed by the Lord Chancellor under section 102 of the County Courts Act 1959(**a**) having by virtue of the powers vested in us in this behalf made the foregoing Rules, do hereby certify the same under our hand and submit them to the Lord Chancellor accordingly.

D. O. McKee.
Conolly H. Gage.
H. S. Ruttle.
David Pennant.
W. Granville Wingate,
W. Ralph Davies.
E. A. Everett.
K. W. Mellor.
M. J. P. Macnair.
D. A. Marshall.
E. W. Sankey.

I allow these Rules, which shall come into operation on 24th January 1972, with the exception of Rule 11(4) which shall come into operation on 1st March 1972.

Dated 21st December 1971.

Hailsham of St. Marylebone, C.

EXPLANATORY NOTE

(*This Note is not part of the Rules.*)

The amendments made by these Rules are mainly consequential on a number of recent statutes. The provisions of the Law Reform (Miscellaneous Provisions) Act 1971 (c.43) relating to the limitation of actions and the control of widows' damages are dealt with in Rules 2, 4(2) and (3) and 11(2). The matters to be taken into account in deciding whether to stay proceedings in tort under section 131 of the Industrial Relations Act 1971 are defined by Rule 11(3) and blood tests under the Family Law Reform Act 1969 are provided for by Rule 11(4). Changes in the law relating to the summoning of juries and the abolition of the Salford Hundred Court effected by the Courts Act 1971 (c.23) necessitate the amendments made by Rules 3, 4(1), 8, 13 and 14. Other provisions result from the reorganisation of the High Court under the Administration of Justice Act 1970 (c.31) (Rules 9, 10, 15 and 16), the consolidation of enactments by the Guardianship of Minors Act 1971 (c.3) (Rule 11(1)) and the abolition of distress damage feasant under the Animals Act 1971 (c.22) (Rule 13).

Rule 7 enables uncontested garnishee proceedings to be heard by the registrar and Rule 12 provides for the allowance of an increased fee for an expert witness after the day of trial or where an action does not go to trial.

(**a**) 1959 c. 22.

1971 No. 2128

OPTICIANS

The General Optical Council (Registration and Enrolment Rules) Order of Council 1971

Made - - - - *22nd December* 1971

At the Council Chamber, Whitehall, the 22nd day of December 1971

By the Lords of Her Majesty's Most Honourable Privy Council

Whereas in pursuance of section 7 of the Opticians Act 1958(a) the General Optical Council have made rules entitled "The Registration and Enrolment Rules 1971":

And whereas by subsection (5) of the said section such rules shall not come into force until approved by Order of the Privy Council:

Now, therefore, Their Lordships, having taken the said rules into consideration, are hereby pleased to approve the same as set out in the Schedule to this Order.

This Order may be cited as the General Optical Council (Registration and Enrolment Rules) Order of Council 1971.

W. G. Agnew.

SCHEDULE

THE REGISTRATION AND ENROLMENT RULES 1971

The General Optical Council, in exercise of their powers under section 7 of the Opticians Act 1958, hereby make the following rules:—

INTERPRETATION

1. These rules may be cited as the Registration and Enrolment Rules 1971.

2. In these rules, unless the context otherwise requires, the following expressions have the respective meanings hereby assigned to them—

"the Act" means the Opticians Act 1958;

"appropriate form" means an application form issued by the Council for the type

(a) 1958 c. 32.

of application in question and a requirement that an application shall be made on the appropriate form shall imply that the Council are entitled to require the completion of the form;

"the Council" means the General Optical Council established under the Act;

"enrolment period" means the period commencing on the date of the first enrolment of an enrolled body corporate and ending on a date prescribed by the Council in relation to the enrolment of that body corporate;

"practice address" means an address at which the applicant provides ophthalmic services including testing sight as defined by section 30(2) of the Act, or the fitting and supply of optical appliances, or both, except an address at which he provides such services only in the following circumstances:—

(*a*) when working as an employee of a registered medical practitioner or registered optician, or of an authority or person carrying on a hospital, clinic, nursing home or other institution providing medical or surgical treatment, or of a Minister of the Crown or Government department (including a department of the Government of Northern Ireland), or

(*b*) when working as director, secretary or employee of an enrolled body corporate, or

(*c*) in an emergency or in the place of a registered optician who is ill or on holiday;

"the Registrar" means the Registrar of the Council;

"registration period" means the period commencing on the date of the first registration of a registered optician and ending on a date prescribed by the Council in relation to the registration of that optician;

"restoration period" means the period commencing on the date of the restoration of the name of an optician to the register or the date of restoration of the name of a body corporate to the list and ending on a date prescribed by the Council in relation to the restoration of that name to the register or list;

"retention period" means the period of retention in the register or list of one year commencing on the day following the last day of a registration period, enrolment period, restoration period or retention period, or, in the case of a retention which takes effect on 1st April 1972, such lesser period as may be prescribed by the Council.

3. Section 30 of the Act shall apply for the interpretation of these rules as it applies for the interpretation of the Act.

4. The Interpretation Act 1889**(a)** shall apply for the interpretation of these rules as it applies for the interpretation of an Act of Parliament.

The Registers and Lists

5. Each register shall contain the following particulars of each optician registered therein:—

(*a*) full name;

(*b*) permanent address with an indication whether or not he works there as an ophthalmic or dispensing optician;

(*c*) practice addresses, if any, other than the permanent address;

(*d*) qualifications held by the optician and recognised by the Council under section 3(2) or section 3(4), or approved by the Council under section 5, of the Act;

(*e*) other optical, academic or professional qualifications approved by the Council for inclusion in the register.

(a) 1889 c. 63.

6. Each list shall contain the following particulars of each body corporate enrolled therein:—

(*a*) name;

(*b*) principal place of business;

(*c*) the addresses of all places at which the body corporate carries on business as ophthalmic or dispensing opticians and the name under which such business is carried on at each such place.

7. The Registrar shall have authority to refuse to enter a name in a register or list, and to refuse to transfer or restore a name to a register or list, until the fees prescribed by these rules for the registration, enrolment, transfer or restoration, as the case may be, have been paid.

Applications for Registration or Enrolment

8.—(1) An application to the Council for the inclusion of a name in the register or the name of a body corporate in the list shall be made on the appropriate form.

(2) The Council may require in a particular case such evidence in verification of the information given on the appropriate form as in their view is necessary to establish whether the applicant is entitled to be registered or the body corporate to be enrolled.

Transfer from one Register or List to another

9.—(1) An application for the transfer of the name of a registered optician from one register to another or for the transfer of the name of an enrolled body corporate from one list to the other shall be accompanied by such information as the Council may reasonably require for establishing whether the registered optician is entitled to be registered in the other register or the body corporate to be enrolled in the other list.

(2) Where the Council are satisfied that the registered optician or body corporate is so entitled, they shall delete the name of the registered optician from one register and insert it in the other, or, as the case may be, shall delete the name of the body corporate from one list and insert it in the other.

Retention of a name in the Register or List and removal for non-payment of fee

10.—(1) Not later than the seventeenth day before the end of a registration period, restoration period or retention period, the Registrar shall send to every registered optician whose period as aforesaid is about to expire the appropriate form of application for retention of a name in the register.

(2) Not later than the seventeenth day before the end of an enrolment period, restoration period or retention period, the Registrar shall send to every enrolled body corporate the aforesaid period of which is about to expire the appropriate form of application for retention of a name in the list.

(3) When the appropriate form is sent to a registered optician or to an enrolled body corporate in pursuance of this rule it shall be accompanied by a notice of the fees payable to the Council on application for retention of a name in the register or list and a warning that failure to pay the appropriate fees will entail removal from the register or list.

(4) Failure to receive a form or notice shall not constitute a ground for retention in the register or list.

(5) The appropriate form sent to a registered optician or enrolled body corporate in accordance with this rule shall be addressed to the registered optician or enrolled body corporate at his permanent address or, as the case may be, its principal place of business.

(6) For the purpose of this rule a registration period, enrolment period, restoration period or retention period shall be deemed to be about to expire when less than one month of the period remains unexpired.

11. Where the Registrar shall not have received from a registered optician or enrolled body corporate by the last day of a registration period, enrolment period, retention period or restoration period, as the case may be, a retention fee due on that date he shall send a warning to that registered optician or enrolled body corporate that failure to pay the fee will result in the removal from the register or the list of the name in relation to which the fee was due, and if the fee is not received within fourteen days of the issue of the warning he shall remove the name from the register or list.

Changes in particulars notified to the Council

12. A registered optician shall notify the Council within one month of any of the following changes bearing on the particulars entered in the register:—

(*a*) change of name;

(*b*) change or abandonment of any address entered in the register or addition of any further practice address to those entered in the register;

(*c*) loss of any qualification entered in the register.

13. An enrolled body corporate shall notify the Council within one month of any of the following changes bearing on the particulars entered in the list:—

(*a*) change of name;

(*b*) change or abandonment of any address entered in the list;

(*c*) inception by the body corporate of business as ophthalmic or dispensing opticians at an address additional to those entered in the list, the notification to include the name under which business is carried on at the additional address.

14. An enrolled body corporate shall notify the Council forthwith if at any time any particulars supplied by it or in support of its application for enrolment no longer apply in any respect which may materially affect the application to the body corporate of any of the conditions of enrolment set out in section 4(2) of the Act.

Alteration or removal of an entry in the Register or List

15.—(1) When the Registrar receives information that an entry in the register or the list has become incorrect, or application is made by or on behalf of a registered optician or an enrolled body corporate for an entry in the register or list to be altered, if he has satisfied himself by means of a statutory declaration or otherwise that the information is true or the ground of the application is sufficient, he shall make the required correction or alteration.

(2) No charge shall be made for a correction or alteration under this rule unless it involves the inclusion in the register or list of addresses in respect of which additional fees are chargeable under Rule 23 or Rule 29 of these rules, in which case the appropriate fees prescribed in the Appendix to these rules shall be payable.

16. The Registrar may remove from the register or the list the name of any registered optician or enrolled body corporate upon receipt of a written application by or on behalf of the registered optician or enrolled body corporate stating the grounds on which the application is made and accompanied by a statutory declaration that the applicant is not aware of any reason for the institution of proceedings which might lead to the erasure of the name under section 11 or section 13 of the Act.

17. The Registrar shall erase from the register or the list the name of any registered optician or enrolled body corporate in respect of which he shall receive a direction to

that effect from the Disciplinary Committee under section 11 or section 13 of the Act, on the date upon which such direction takes effect in accordance with section 14 of the Act.

Restoration of a name to the Register or List

18. Subject to the provisions of sections 12 and 13 of the Act, the Council may restore a name to the register on receipt of an application accompanied by:—

(*a*) the appropriate fees mentioned in Rules 21, 22 and 23 and prescribed in the Appendix to these rules; and

(*b*) where the name of the applicant has not been included in the register at any time during the five years immediately preceding the date on which the application is made, evidence establishing to the satisfaction of the Council his identity and good character.

19. Subject to the provisions of sections 12 and 13 of the Act, the Council may restore a name to the list on receipt of an application accompanied by:—

(*a*) the appropriate fees mentioned in Rules 27, 28 and 29 and prescribed in the Appendix to these rules; and

(*b*) evidence establishing to the satisfaction of the Council the continuance of entitlement to enrolment.

Fees payable by Ophthalmic and Dispensing Opticians

20.—(1) The fee for the entry of a name of an optician in the register shall be called the registration fee and shall be paid at the time of the application for registration.

(2) Payment of the registration fee shall, subject to sections 11, 13 and 14 of the Act, entitle an optician to the retention of his name in the register until the end of the registration period.

(3) Payment of the registration fee shall not constitute an entitlement for the retention of a name in the register for any period beyond the registration period.

21. The fee for the retention of a name in the register for any retention period or restoration period shall be called the retention fee and, in relation to a retention period, shall be paid before the beginning of the retention period to which it relates.

22. The fee for restoration of a name to the register shall be called the restoration fee and shall be in addition to the retention fee in relation to the restoration period following that restoration.

23.—(1) A fee shall be paid in addition to the registration fee, retention fee and restoration fee in respect of each practice address, other than a permanent address, included in the particulars of an optician entered in the register.

(2) Each such fee shall be called an additional fee and shall be paid at the time of the application for registration, retention or restoration, as the case may be.

24.—(1) The fee for the transfer of a name from one register to another shall be called the transfer fee and shall be paid at the time of the application for transfer.

(2) Additional fees shall not be payable in relation to practice addresses other than a permanent address, included in an entry to be transferred from one register to another.

25. The fees set out in Table A of the Appendix to these rules shall be the fees which shall be charged under Rules 20 to 24.

Fees payable by Bodies Corporate

26.—(1) The fee for the entry of a name of a body corporate in the list shall be called the enrolment fee and shall be paid at the time of the application for enrolment.

(2) Payment of the enrolment fee shall, subject to sections 11, 13 and 14 of the Act, entitle a body corporate to the retention of its name in the list until the end of the enrolment period.

(3) Payment of the enrolment fee shall not constitute an entitlement for the retention of a name in the list for any period beyond the enrolment period.

27. The fee for the retention of a name in the list for any retention period or restoration period shall be called the retention fee and, in relation to a retention period, shall be paid before the beginning of the retention period to which it relates.

28. The fee for restoration of a name to the list shall be called the restoration fee and shall be in addition to the retention fee in relation to the restoration period following that restoration.

29.—(1) A fee shall be paid in addition to the enrolment fee, retention fee and restoration fee in respect of each address, other than the address of the principal place of business of a body corporate, included in the particulars of the body corporate entered in the list.

(2) Each such fee shall be called an additional fee and shall be paid at the time of the application for enrolment, retention or restoration, as the case may be.

30.—(1) The fee for the transfer of a name from one list to the other shall be called the transfer fee and shall be paid at the time of the application for transfer.

(2) Additional fees shall not be payable in relation to business addresses other than the address of a principal place of business included in an entry to be transferrred from one list to the other.

31. The fees set out in Table B of the Appendix to these rules shall be the fees which shall be charged under Rules 26 to 30.

Transitional provisions

32.—(1) A registered optician:—

(*a*) whose registration period, retention period or restoration period, as the case may be, expires on 31st March 1972 and

(*b*) whose retention period immediately following that date will be a period of less than one year,

shall be given the opportunity by the Council of electing to apply for retention in the register either for the retention period or for a period comprising the retention period and an additional year (in this rule and Rule 33 referred to as an extended retention period).

(2) A registered optician to whom this rule applies and who, in applying for retention of his name in the register, does not unequivocably elect to apply for retention for an extended retention period shall be taken as electing to apply for retention for the retention period.

33. The fee for the retention on the register of the name of a registered optician to whom Rule 32 applies, notwithstanding Rule 21 and the Appendix to these rules, shall be as follows:—

(*a*) in relation to a retention period, a sum equal to 40p for each month in the retention period relating to that registered optician, and (*b*) in relation to an extended retention period, a sum equal to £5 increased by 40p for each month in the retention period.

34. The additional fees in respect of the practice addresses, other than the permanent address, of a registered optician to whom Rule 32 applies and who applies for a name to be retained in the register, shall not be payable; but an applicant for retention in the register shall pay a fee for each such address:—

(*a*) in relation to a retention period, a sum equal to 8p for each month in the retention period; or

(*b*) in relation to an extended retention period, a sum equal to £1 increased by 8p for each month in the retention period.

35.—(1) An enrolled body corporate:—

(*a*) the enrolment period, retention period or restoration period of which, as the case may be, expires on 31st March 1972; and

(*b*) the retention period of which immediately following that date will be a period of less than one year,

shall be given the opportunity by the Council of electing to apply for retention in the list either for the retention period or for a period comprising the retention period and an additional year (in this rule and Rule 36 referred to as an extended retention period).

(2) An enrolled body corporate to which this rule applies which, in applying for retention of its name in the list, does not unequivocably elect to apply for retention for an extended retention period, shall be taken as electing to apply for retention for the retention period.

36. The fee for the retention on the list of the name of an enrolled body corporate to which Rule 35 applies, notwithstanding Rule 27 and the Appendix to these rules shall be as follows:—

(*a*) in relation to a retention period, a sum equal to 40p for each month in the retention period relating to that enrolled body corporate; and

(*b*) in relation to an extended retention period, a sum equal to £5 increased by 40p for each month in the retention period.

37. The additional fees in respect of the addresses, other than the address of the principal place of business, of an enrolled body corporate to which Rule 35 applies and which applies for a name to be retained in the list, shall not be payable; but an applicant for retention in the list shall pay a fee for each such address:—

(*a*) in relation to a retention period, a sum equal to 8p for each month in the retention period; or

(*b*) in relation to an extended retention period, a sum equal to £1 increased by 8p for each month in the retention period.

Operation of these Rules

38. These rules shall come into operation on the 1st day of April 1972 and shall apply to applications for registration, enrolment, retention, restoration or transfer to take effect on or after the 1st day of April 1972, whether made before, on or after that date.

39. The Registration and Enrolment Rules 1968**(a)** as amended by the Registration and Enrolment (Amendment) Rules 1970**(b)** shall cease to have effect on 1st day of April 1972.

(a) S.I. 1968/1965 (1968 III, p. 5366). **(b)** S.I. 1970/226 (1970 I, p. 953).

Sealed on the 10th
day of November 1971.

Attested by:

G. R. Rougier,
Member of Council.

Ronald Russell,
Member of Council.

J. Daniel Devlin,
Registrar.

APPENDIX

Fees

Table A

Fees payable by Ophthalmic and Dispensing Opticians
(*Rules* 20 *to* 24)

Registration fee	£5
Retention fee	£5
Additional fee:	
in respect of each practice address other than a permanent address ...	£1
Restoration fee	£2
Transfer fee	£2

Table B

Fees payable by bodies corporate
(*Rules* 26 *to* 30)

Enrolment fee	£5
Retention fee	£5
Additional fee:	
in respect of each address other than the address of the principal place of business	£1
Restoration fee	£2
Transfer fee	£2

EXPLANATORY NOTE

(*This Note is not part of the Order.*)

The rules approved by this Order consolidate, with amendments, the rules relating to the registration of opticians and the enrolment of bodies corporate.

The principal change effected by the rules is in the system of annual renewals of registration and enrolment. Hitherto all of these have expired simultaneously; as from the 1st April 1972, a proportion of them will expire at the end of each month.

1971 No. 2129

WAGES COUNCILS

The Wages Regulation (General Waste Materials Reclamation) Order 1971

Made - - - -	*22nd December* 1971
Coming into Operation	*24th January* 1972

Whereas the Secretary of State has received from the General Waste Materials Reclamation Wages Council (Great Britain) the wages regulation proposals set out in the Schedule hereto;

Now, therefore, the Secretary of State in exercise of his powers under section 11 of the Wages Councils Act 1959**(a)**, and of all other powers enabling him in that behalf, hereby makes the following Order:—

1. This Order may be cited as the Wages Regulation (General Waste Materials Reclamation) Order 1971.

2.—(1) In this Order the expression "the specified date" means the 24th January 1972, provided that where, as respects any worker who is paid wages at intervals not exceeding seven days, that date does not correspond with the beginning of the period for which the wages are paid, the expression "the specified date" means, as respects that worker, the beginning of the next such period following that date.

(2) The Interpretation Act 1889**(b)** shall apply to the interpretation of this Order as it applies to the interpretation of an Act of Parliament and as if this Order and the Order hereby revoked were Acts of Parliament.

3. The wages regulation proposals set out in the Schedule hereto shall have effect as from the specified date and as from that date the Wages Regulation (General Waste Materials Reclamation) Order 1970**(c)** shall cease to have effect.

Signed by order of the Secretary of State.

22nd December 1971.

J. R. Lloyd Davies,
Assistant Secretary,
Department of Employment.

(a) 1959 c. 69. **(b)** 1889 c. 63.
(c) S.I. 1970/1314 (1970 III, p. 4396).

ARRANGEMENT OF SCHEDULE

Article 3

SCHEDULE

The following minimum remuneration shall be substituted for the statutory minimum remuneration fixed by the Wages Regulation (General Waste Materials Reclamation) Order 1970 (Order D.B. (73)).

STATUTORY MINIMUM REMUNERATION

PART I—GENERAL

1. The minimum remuneration payable to a worker to whom this Schedule applies for all work except work to which a minimum overtime rate applies under Part IV is:—

(1) in the case of a time worker, the general minimum time rate payable to the worker under Part II or Part III of this Schedule;

(2) in the case of a male worker employed on piece work, piece rates each of which would yield, in the circumstances of the case, to an ordinary worker at least the same amount of money as the general minimum time rate which would be payable to the worker under Part II of this Schedule if he were a time worker;

(3) in the case of a female worker employed on piece work, piece rates each of which would yield, in the circumstances of the case, to an ordinary worker at least the same amount of money as the piece work basis time rate applicable to the worker under Part III of this Schedule:

Provided that where a guaranteed time rate is applicable to a female worker under paragraph 8 and the remuneration calculated on a time work basis at that rate exceeds the remuneration calculated under sub-paragraph (3) of this paragraph on the basis of the said piece rates, the worker shall be paid not less than that guaranteed time rate.

PART II

MALE WORKERS

GENERAL MINIMUM TIME RATES

2. The general minimum time rates payable to male workers employed in any section of the trade are:—

	Per hour p
Aged under 16 years	*18*
„ 16 and under 16½ years	*21*
„ 16½ „ „ 17 „	*23*
„ 17 „ „ 17½ „	*27*
„ 17½ „ „ 18 „	*32*
„ 18 years or over	*35*

PART III

FEMALE WORKERS

GENERAL MINIMUM TIME RATES

3. Subject to the provisions of paragraphs 4 and 9, the general minimum time rates payable to female workers employed—

(1) wholly or mainly on one or more of the operations of the sorting or grading of either woollen rags or woollen and worsted waste materials, or of both such rags and materials, to shade or quality or to both shade and quality, or

(2) in receiving, stripping, packing, compressing, teagling, craning, despatching or warehousing, when carried on in, or in association with, or in conjunction with, any establishment or department in which the sorting or grading of either woollen rags or woollen and worsted waste materials, or of both such rags and materials, to shade or quality or to both shade and quality, constitutes the sole or main work of the establishment or department,

are as follows:—

	Per hour p
Aged under 16 years	*15*
„ 16 and under 16½ years	*19*
„ 16½ „ „ 17 „	*21*
„ 17 „ „ 17½ „	*25*
„ 17½ „ „ 18 „	*27*
„ 18 years or over	*31*

4. Notwithstanding the provisions of paragraph 3, where a worker is employed for the first time after reaching the age of 18 years on any work therein mentioned and her employer causes her to be well and sufficiently instructed in the sorting and grading of woollen rags or woollen and worsted waste materials or of both such rags and materials, to shade or quality or to both shade and quality, the general minimum time rate payable during the periods following shall be:—

	Per hour p
during the first *six* months of such employment	*30*

5. Subject to the provisions of paragraphs 6 and 9, the general minimum time rates payable to female workers other than the workers specified in paragraph 3 or 4 are as follows:—

	Per hour p
Aged under 16 years	*15*
„ 16 and under 16½ years	*18*
„ 16½ „ „ 17 „	*21*
„ 17 „ „ 17½ „	*24*
„ 17½ „ „ 18 „	*27*
„ 18 years or over	*30*

6. Notwithstanding the provisions of paragraph 5, where a worker is employed for the first time after reaching the age of 18 years and her employer causes her to be well and sufficiently instructed in the sorting and grading of waste paper, rags, and paper-making materials, or of paper-making materials, the general minimum time rate payable shall be:—

	Per hour p
during the first six months of such employment	*29*

PIECE WORK BASIS TIME RATES

7. The following piece work basis time rates are applicable to female workers employed on piece work:—

	Per hour p
(1) the workers specified in paragraph 3 or 4	*31*
(2) all other workers	*30*

GUARANTEED TIME RATE

8. The guaranteed time rate applicable to a female worker specified in paragraph 4 or 6 when employed on piece work during the period of six months therein mentioned is a rate equal to the general minimum time rate which would be payable to her if she were employed on time work.

DETERMINATION OF AGE RATES

9. The general minimum time rate payable under paragraph 3 or 5 to a female worker aged under 18 years shall be determined (1) during the period 1st January to 30th June in any year by reference to her age or prospective age on 31st March in that year; and (2) during the period 1st July to 31st December in any year by reference to her age or prospective age on 30th September in that year:

Provided that the rate for a female worker aged 17½ and under 18 years having become payable under the provisions of this paragraph shall continue to be payable only until her 18th birthday.

PART IV

OVERTIME AND WAITING TIME

MINIMUM OVERTIME RATES

10. Minimum overtime rates are payable to a worker to whom this Schedule applies as follows:—

(1) On any day other than a Saturday, Sunday or customary holiday—

for all time worked in excess of 7¼ hours ... ... time-and-a-half

Provided that where it is, or may become, the established practice of the employer to require the worker's attendance only on Monday, Tuesday, Wednesday, Thursday and Friday in the week, the overtime rate of *time-and-a-half* shall be payable—

after 8 hours' work on any of these days.

(2) On a Saturday, not being a customary holiday—
for all time worked in excess of 3¾ hours ... ... time-and-a-half

(3) On a Sunday or a customary holiday, for all time worked... double time

(4) In any week, for all time worked in excess of 40 hours, exclusive of any time for which a minimum overtime rate is payable under the foregoing provisions of this paragraph ... *time-and-a-half*

11. In this Part of this Schedule—

(1) The expression "customary holiday" means—

(*a*) (i) in England and Wales—

Christmas Day (or, if Christmas Day falls on a Sunday, such other week day as may be appointed by national proclamation, or, if none is so appointed, the next following Tuesday), Boxing Day, Good Friday, Easter Monday, Whit Monday (or where another day is substituted therefor by national proclamation, that day), August Bank Holiday and any day proclaimed to be a national holiday;

(ii) in Scotland—

New Year's Day (or, if New Year's Day falls on a Sunday, the following Monday);
the local Spring holiday;
the local Autumn holiday;
three other days (being days on which the worker normally works) in the course of a calendar year, to be fixed by the employer and notified to the worker not less than three weeks before the holiday, and any day proclaimed to be a national holiday; or

(*b*) in the case of each of the said days (other than a day fixed by the employer in Scotland and notified to the worker as aforesaid) a day substituted by the employer therefor, being either a day recognised by local custom as a day of holiday in substitution for the said day, or a day agreed between the employer and the worker or his representative.

(2) The expressions "time-and-a-half" and "double time" mean respectively:—

(*a*) in the case of a time worker:—

one and a half times and twice the general minimum time rate otherwise applicable to the worker;

(*b*) in the case of a female worker employed on piece work:—

(i) a time rate equal respectively to one half and the whole of the piece work basis time rate otherwise applicable to the worker, and, in addition thereto,

(ii) the minimum remuneration otherwise applicable to the worker under paragraph 1(3);

(*c*) in the case of a male worker employed on piece work:—

(i) a time rate equal respectively to one half and the whole of the general minimum time rate which would be applicable to the worker if he were a time worker and a minimum overtime rate did not apply, and, in addition thereto,

(ii) the minimum remuneration otherwise applicable to the worker under paragraph 1(2).

WAITING TIME

12.—(1) A worker is entitled to payment of the minimum remuneration specified in this Schedule for all time during which he is present on the premises of his employer, unless he is present thereon in any of the following circumstances:—

(*a*) without the employer's consent, express or implied;

(*b*) for some purpose unconnected with his work and other than that of waiting for work to be given to him to perform;

(*c*) by reason only of the fact that he is resident thereon;

(*d*) during normal meal times in a room or place in which no work is being done, and he is not waiting for work to be given to him to perform.

(2) The minimum remuneration payable under sub-paragraph (1) of this paragraph to a piece worker when not engaged on piece work is that which would be payable if he were a time worker.

PART V

APPLICABILITY OF STATUTORY MINIMUM REMUNERATION

13. This Schedule does not apply to male workers engaged in the loading or discharging of water-borne craft in any section of the trade, but, save as aforesaid, this Schedule applies to workers in relation to whom the General Waste Materials Reclamation Wages Council (Great Britain) operates, that is to say, workers employed in Great Britain in the Waste Materials Reclamation Trade (General Waste Branch) specified in the Schedule to the General Waste Materials Reclamation Wages Council (Great Britain) (Variation) Order 1970(a), which Schedule reads as follows:—

"1. For the purposes of this Schedule:—

The expression 'reclamation' means all operations (including the operations of willowing and garnetting) performed on any waste material or waste article.

The expression 'general waste materials establishment' means an establishment in which the operations specified in paragraph 2(*a*) hereof and operations connected therewith constitute the principal business carried on.

The expression 'establishment' means any establishment or any branch or department of an establishment.

2. Subject to the provisions of this Schedule the General Waste Branch of the Waste Materials Reclamation trade consists of the following operations:—

(*a*) reclamation wherever performed of any of the following waste materials or waste articles, that is to say:—rags, waste paper and paper salvage (including paper damaged by fire, newspaper reel-ends, damaged paper reels, outer wrappers of reels and news off-cuts), paper stock, woollen, worsted, flax, or other textile waste (not being jute or cotton waste), textile clippings or cuttings, used bags, used sacks, used sackings, or used tares, scrap rubber, scrap iron or other scrap metals (other than unbroken heavy machinery or plant), fur cuttings, rabbit skins, bones and fat, used tins, used bottles or jars, old ropes or string and broken glass or earthenware;

(*b*) reclamation of any other waste material or article where performed in or in connection with a general waste materials establishment;

(*c*) making (whether from new or waste material) or repairing sacks or bags in a general waste materials establishment except where the bags are made or repaired:—

(i) otherwise than for use in the establishment, and

(ii) in an establishment wholly or mainly engaged in the making or repairing of sacks or bags;

and operations connected therewith.

3. Notwithstanding anything in this Schedule the following operations are not operations in the General Waste branch of the Waste Materials Reclamation trade:—

(*a*) reclamation of any waste material or waste article in an establishment (other than a general waste materials establishment) in which that material or article is produced or is used as material for manufacture or as a container or wrapper for other articles manufactured in the establishment; and operations connected therewith;

(*b*) reclamation of any waste material or waste article produced in the business of breaking up ships or breaking up or dismantling buildings or machinery or tramway or railway installations or heavy plant when performed in the course of such business; and operations connected therewith;

(*c*) reclamation of scrap rubber in an establishment in which the scrap rubber is broken down or devulcanised; and operations connected therewith;

(a) S.I. 1970/1175 (1970 II, p. 3956).

(*d*) reclamation of rabbit skins where performed in an establishment in which such reclamation constitutes the principal business carried on or in connection with an establishment in which the principal business carried on is the manufacture of hatters' fur; and operations connected therewith;

(*e*) reclamation of bottles or jars preliminary to their use in the same establishment as containers, or when such bottles or jars are the property of a trader and are used by him for the purpose of delivering the contents to a customer and are recovered when empty from the customer by or on behalf of the trader; and operations connected therewith;

(*f*) reclamation of jute textile cuttings and clippings where carried on in an establishment mainly engaged in operations included in the Trade Boards (Jute) Order, 1919(**a**), or any amendment thereof;

(*g*) production of shoddy or mungo or woollen flock (including sorting, willowing or garnetting) or any operations performed in an establishment in which the production of shoddy or mungo or woollen flock is the principal business carried on;

(*h*) de-tinning of metal or refining of old gold or silver;

(*i*) repairing or overhauling machinery or plant;

(*j*) collecting, transporting, packing, warehousing or despatching, when performed by workers in the direct employment of an employer who is not otherwise engaged in the Waste Materials Reclamation trade;

(*k*) cleaning or washing when performed in an establishment where the cleaning or washing is mainly of articles other than those specified in paragraph 2 hereof;

(*l*) cleaning of premises by charwomen;

(*m*) caretaking;

(*n*) clerical work;

(*o*) operations performed in or in connection with a cotton waste establishment as defined in the Schedule to the Trade Boards (Waste Materials Reclamation Trade, Great Britain) (Cotton Waste Branch) (Constitution and Proceedings) Regulations, 1929(**b**);

(*p*) all operations performed in an establishment in which the manual sorting to shade and quality of the wastes and by-products of the woollen and worsted textile processes is the sole or main activity."

EXPLANATORY NOTE

(*This Note is not part of the Order.*)

This Order, which has effect from 24th January 1972, sets out the statutory minimum remuneration payable in substitution for that fixed by the Wages Regulation (General Waste Materials Reclamation) Order 1970 (Order D.B. (73)), which Order is revoked.

New provisions are printed in italics.

(**a**) S.R. & O. 1919/859 (1919 II, p. 517).
(**b**) S.R. & O. 1929/3 (1929 p. 1378).

1971 No. 2130 (S.224)

LOCAL GOVERNMENT, SCOTLAND

The Local Government (Financial Loss Allowance) (Scotland) Amendment Regulations 1971

Made - - - -	*22nd December* 1971
Laid before Parliament	*3rd January* 1972
Coming into Operation	*24th January* 1972

In exercise of the powers conferred on me by sections 112 and 117 as read with section 118 of the Local Government Act 1948**(a)** and as amended by section 16 of the Local Government (Miscellaneous Provisions) Act 1953**(b)**, and of all other powers enabling me in that behalf, I hereby make the following regulations:—

1. These regulations may be cited as the Local Government (Financial Loss Allowance) (Scotland) Amendment Regulations 1971 and shall come into operation on 24th January 1972.

2. The Interpretation Act 1889**(c)** shall apply for the interpretation of these regulations as it applies for the interpretation of an Act of Parliament.

3. For "£2" in paragraph (i) and "£4" in paragraph (ii) of Schedule 1 to the Local Government (Financial Loss Allowance) (Scotland) Regulations 1970**(d)**, there shall be substituted "£2·37½" and "£4·75" respectively.

Gordon Campbell,
One of Her Majesty's Principal
Secretaries of State.

St. Andrew's House,
Edinburgh.
22nd December 1971.

(a) 1948 c. 26.
(b) 1953 c. 26.
(c) 1889 c. 63.
(d) S.I. 1970/106 (1970 I, p. 454).

EXPLANATORY NOTE

(This Note is not part of the Regulations.)

These Regulations prescribe in pursuance of section 16 of the Local Government (Miscellaneous Provisions) Act 1953, revised maximum amounts which may be paid to members of any body to which Part VI of the Local Government Act 1948 applies by way of financial loss allowance for loss of earnings or additional expenses (other than travelling or subsistence) incurred in the performance of their duties as such members.

1971 No. 2131 (S.225)

LOCAL GOVERNMENT, SCOTLAND

The Local Government (Travelling Allowances, etc.) (Scotland) Amendment Regulations 1971

Made - - - -	*22nd December* 1971
Laid before Parliament	*3rd January* 1972
Coming into Operation	*24th January* 1972

In exercise of the powers conferred on me by sections 113 and 117 as read with section 118 of the Local Government Act 1948**(a)**, and of all other powers enabling me in that behalf, I hereby make the following regulations:—

1. These regulations may be cited as the Local Government (Travelling Allowances, etc.) (Scotland) Amendment Regulations 1971 and shall come into operation on 24th January 1972.

2. The Interpretation Act 1889**(b)** shall apply for the interpretation of these regulations as it applies for the interpretation of an Act of Parliament.

3. In paragraph 3 of Schedule 1 to the Local Government (Travelling Allowances, etc.) (Scotland) Regulations 1970**(c)**, for the sums of ½d, 1d, 2¾d, 3½d, 4d, 5¾d, 11¼d, 1s. 0¾d, 1s. 2¼d, 1s. 6d and 2s. 6d there shall be substituted the sums of 0·2p, 0·4p, 1·1p, 1·5p, 1·7p, 2·4p, 4·7p, 5·3p, 5·9p, 7·5p and 12·5p respectively.

4. In Schedule 2 to the said Regulations for the sums of 10s, 19s, 35s, 50s, 59s and 110s there shall be substituted the sums of £0·50, £0·95, £1·75, £2·50, £2·95 and £5·50 respectively.

5. After paragraph 2 of Schedule 2 to the said Regulations there shall be added—

"3. An amount payable by any body by way of subsistence allowance shall be reduced by an appropriate sum in respect of any meal provided for the claimant by that body, free of charge, during the period to which the allowance relates."

Gordon Campbell,
One of Her Majesty's Principal
Secretaries of State.

St Andrew's House,
Edinburgh.
22nd December 1971.

(a) 1948 c. 26. **(b)** 1889 c. 63.
(c) S.I. 1970/107 (1970 I, p. 458).

EXPLANATORY NOTE

(This Note is not part of the Regulations.)

These Regulations decimalise the maximum rates of travelling and subsistence allowances provided for by the Local Government (Travelling Allowances, etc.) (Scotland) Regulations 1970. They also add to Schedule 2 of the 1970 Regulations a third paragraph in terms of which subsistence allowance is to be reduced in certain circumstances.

1971 No. 2133

DISTRESS

The Distress for Rent (Amendment No. 2) Rules 1971

Made - - - *23rd December* 1971

Coming into Operation *24th January* 1972

The Lord Chancellor, in exercise of the powers conferred on him by section 8 of the Law of Distress Amendment Act 1888(**a**), hereby makes the following Rules :—

1.—(1) These Rules may be cited as the Distress for Rent (Amendment No. 2) Rules 1971 and shall come into operation on 24th January 1972.

(2) The Interpretation Act 1889(**b**) shall apply to the interpretation of these Rules as it applies to the interpretation of an Act of Parliament.

2. In Rule 7 of the Distress for Rent Rules 1953(**c**), as amended (**d**), after the words "hold it, and" there shall be inserted the words ", in particular, does not carry on the business of buying debts, and who".

Dated 23rd December 1971.

Hailsham of St. Marylebone, C.

EXPLANATORY NOTE

(*This Note is not part of the Rules.*)

These Rules require an applicant for a certificate authorizing him to levy distress for rent to satisfy the court that he is not carrying on the business of buying debts.

(**a**) 1888 c. 21.
(**b**) 1889 c. 63.
(**c**) S.I. 1953/1702 (1953 I, p. 574).
(**d**) S.I. 1971/1333 (1971 II, p. 3822).

STATUTORY INSTRUMENTS

1971 No. 2135

CLEAN AIR

The Smoke Control Areas (Authorised Fuels) (No. 4) Regulations 1971

Made - - -	21*st December* 1971
Laid before Parliament	7*th January* 1972
Coming into Operation	28*th January* 1972

The Secretary of State for the Environment, in exercise of the powers conferred on him by section 34(1) of the Clean Air Act 1956(**a**), and of all other powers enabling him in that behalf, hereby makes the following regulations :—

Title and commencement

1. These regulations may be cited as the Smoke Control Areas (Authorised Fuels) (No. 4) Regulations 1971 and shall come into operation on 28th January 1972.

Interpretation

2. The Interpretation Act 1889(**b**) shall apply for the interpretation of these regulations as it applies for the interpretation of an Act of Parliament.

Authorised fuels for purposes of the Clean Air Act 1956

3. The following fuel is hereby declared to be an authorised fuel for the purposes of the Clean Air Act 1956 :—

"Fireglo" briquettes which have been manufactured by Société Charentaise de Défumage, Tonnay-Charente and which—

(i) comprise anthracite duff (as to approximately 93 per cent. of total weight) and pitch (as to the remaining weight) and

(ii) have been subjected to a mild heat treatment process.

Peter Walker,
Secretary of State
for the Environment.

21st December 1971.

(**a**) 1956 c. 52. (**b**) 1889 c. 63.

EXPLANATORY NOTE

(This Note is not part of the Regulations.)

Section 11 of the Clean Air Act 1956 makes it an offence to emit smoke from a chimney of a building within a smoke control area unless it can be shown that the emission of smoke arose solely from use of an authorised fuel. These Regulations declare "Fireglo" briquettes manufactured by Société Charentaise de Défumage, Tonnay-Charente, to be an authorised fuel.

1971 No. 2147

PENSIONS

The Superannuation (Teaching and Public Boards) Interchange (Amendment) Rules 1971

Made - - - -	30*th December* 1971
Laid before Parliament	10*th January* 1972
Coming into Operation	1*st February* 1972

The Secretary of State for Education and Science, with the consent of the Minister for the Civil Service, in exercise of the powers conferred on her by sections 2 and 15 of the Superannuation (Miscellaneous Provisions) Act 1948**(a)**, as amended by section 11 of the Superannuation (Miscellaneous Provisions) Act 1967**(b)** and as read with the Minister for the Civil Service Order 1968**(c)**, hereby makes the following Rules:—

1. These Rules may be cited as the Superannuation (Teaching and Public Boards) Interchange (Amendment) Rules 1971 and shall come into operation on 1st February 1972.

2. The Interpretation Act 1889**(d)** shall apply for the interpretation of these Rules as it applies for the interpretation of an Act of Parliament.

3. Schedule 3 to the Superannuation (Teaching and Public Boards) Interchange Rules 1968**(e)**, as amended**(f)**, is hereby further amended by the addition thereto of the following bodies and dates:—

The Arts Council of Great Britain	1st January 1967
The British Airports Authority	1st April 1966
The British Productivity Council	1st April 1968
The British Steel Corporation	1st July 1969
The Church Commissioners	1st April 1948
The Meat and Livestock Commission	1st October 1968

4. In relation to a person becoming, or ceasing to be, employed by a body named in rule 3 the operative date for the purposes of the Superannuation (Teaching and Public Boards) Interchange Rules 1968 shall be the date of the coming into operation of these Rules.

(a) 1948 c. 33.
(b) 1967 c. 28.
(c) S.I. 1968/1656 (1968 III, p. 4485).
(d) 1889 c. 63.
(e) S.I. 1968/1120 (1968 II, p. 3078).
(f) S.I. 1970/138 (1970 I, p. 592).

Given under the Official Seal of the Secretary of State for Education and Science on 23rd December 1971.

(L.S.)

Margaret H. Thatcher,
Secretary of State for Education
and Science.

Consent of the Minister for the Civil Service given under his Official Seal on 30th December 1971.

(L.S.)

K. H. McNeill,
Authorised by the Minister for
the Civil Service.

EXPLANATORY NOTE

(*This Note is not part of the Rules.*)

These Rules extend to the Arts Council of Great Britain, the British Airports Authority, the British Productivity Council, the British Steel Corporation, the Church Commissioners and the Meat and Livestock Commission the existing arrangements for the preservation of superannuation rights on changes of employment between teaching and other public boards.

The Rules may have retrospective effect in certain cases under the express powers of, and subject to the safeguards required by, section 2(5) of the Superannuation (Miscellaneous Provisions) Act 1948.

STATUTORY INSTRUMENTS

1971 No. 2152 (L.53)

COUNTY COURTS

PROCEDURE

The County Court (New Procedure) Rules 1971

Made - - - -	31*st December* 1971
Coming into Operation	1*st March* 1972

1.—(1) These Rules may be cited as the County Court (New Procedure) Rules 1971.

(2) In these Rules an Order and Rule referred to by number means the Order and Rule so numbered in the County Court Rules 1936**(a)**, as amended **(b)**; Appendices A and D mean respectively Appendices A and D to those Rules, and a form referred to by number means the form so numbered in Appendix A.

(3) The Interpretation Act 1889**(c)** shall apply for the interpretation of these Rules as it applies for the interpretation of an Act of Parliament.

2. In Order 2, Rule 1(3), the words "then, unless" to "exceeds £100" shall be omitted.

3. In Order 5, Rule 14(*a*), for the words "at the trial" there shall be substituted the words "on the return day" and for the words "in court" there shall be substituted the word "present".

4. Order 6 shall be amended as follows:—

(1) The following Rule shall be substituted for Rule 2:—

"2.—(1) Any action to recover a debt or liquidated demand shall be a default action except where it is brought—

(*a*) against a person under disability;

(*b*) to recover money lent by a moneylender within the meaning of the Moneylenders Acts 1900 to 1927**(d)**, or interest on money so lent, or to enforce any agreement made or security taken in respect of money so lent;

(*c*) to recover money secured by a mortgage or charge;

(*d*) on a claim arising out of a hire-purchase agreement unless the claim is for no more than the amount of any instalment or instalments of the hire-purchase price which is or are due and unpaid; or

(*e*) to recover interest accruing after the commencement of the action.

(a) S.R. & O. 1936/626 (1936 I, p. 282).

(b) The relevant amending instruments are S. R. & O. 1938/1475, 1939/815, 1943/1120, 1944/63, S.I. 1950/1231, 1993, 1952/2198, 1953/1728, 1955/1799, 1956/1243, 1851, 1957/1136, 1959/1251, 1960/1275, 1961/1526, 1962/1293, 1963/403, 1964/353, 1974, 1965/2147, 1969/585, 1970/204, 673, 1201, 1971/836, 2127 (1938 I, p. 990; 1939 I, p. 469; 1943 I, p. 121; 1944 I, p. 50; 1950 I, pp. 400, 440; 1952 I, p. 635; 1953 I, p. 404; 1955 I, p. 530; 1956 I pp. 541, 545; 1957 I, p. 517; 1959 I, p. 795; 1960 I, p. 809; 1961 II, p. 3177; 1962 II, p. 1383; 1963 I, p. 475; 1964 I, p. 543; III, p. 4477; 1965 III, p. 6292; 1969 I, p. 1551; 1970 I, p. 911; II, pp. 2180, 3984; 1971 II, p 2393).

(c) 1889 c. 63.

(d) 1900 c. 51; 1927 c. 21.

(2) Any other action shall be an ordinary action.

(3) Nothing in this Rule applies to an Admiralty action or a rent action."

(2) Rule 3 shall be amended as follows:—

(*a*) In paragraph (2)(*a*) for the words "a day for the hearing" there shall be substituted the words "the return day".

(*b*) In paragraph (2)(*c*) for the words "Form 18A or Form 20A" there shall be substituted the words "Form 18A, 20A or 20B" and in the marginal note after "20A" there shall be added ", 20B".

(*c*) After paragraph (2) there shall be added the following paragraph:—

"(3) In the case of an ordinary action other than an action for recovery of land, the return day shall, unless the court otherwise directs, be a day fixed for the preliminary consideration of the action under Order 21."

(3) The following paragraph shall be added to Rule 7:—

"(3) Where proceedings which ought to have been brought by ordinary action are brought by default action or proceedings which ought to have been brought by default action are brought by ordinary action, the court may either strike out the proceedings or order them to continue in accordance with the procedure prescribed for an ordinary action, and may direct that any necessary or desirable amendments shall be made."

5. Order 8 shall be amended as follows:—

(1) In the definition of "An originating process" in Rule 40 the words from "means" to "and" shall be omitted.

(2) For Rule 45 there shall be substituted the following Rule:—

"45. When giving leave to serve a process out of England and Wales the judge shall—

(*a*) in the case of a default summons, fix the time for delivering an admission or defence or paying the total amount of the claim and costs into court, and

(*b*) in any other case, fix the return day,

and in so doing shall have regard to the distance of the country of service."

6. Order 9 shall be amended as follows:—

(1) In Rule 1(5) for the words "at the hearing of the action" and "at the hearing" there shall in each case be substituted the words "on the return day".

(2) In Rule 2(1) for the words from "the title" to "the immediate possession thereof" there shall be substituted the words "the plaintiff's right to recover possession of the land".

(3) In Rule 4(10) for the words "in court" there shall be substituted the words "at court".

(4) Rule 5 shall be revoked.

7. Order 10 shall be amended as follows:—

(1) In Rules 3 and 4(3)(*b*) after the words "a day for the hearing of the action" there shall in each case be inserted the words "or, if he thinks fit, a day for the preliminary consideration of the action under Order 21".

(2) In Rule 4(4) for the words "at the disposal or hearing" there shall be substituted the words "on the day fixed pursuant to Rule 3 or 4(3) of this Order" and for the words "at the hearing" in sub-paragraph (*c*) there shall be substituted the words "on the day aforesaid".

(3) Rule 8 shall be revoked.

8. In Order 12, Rule 1(3), for the words "and as to the date of trial" there shall be substituted the words "and as to the further conduct of the proceedings".

9. Order 13 shall be amended as follows:—

(1) In Rule 3 paragraph (3), (4), (6), (7) and (8) shall be omitted and paragraph (5) shall stand as paragraph (3).

(2) Paragraph (5) of Rule 4 shall be omitted.

(3) For Rule 6 there shall be substituted the following Rule:—

Striking out pleadings

"6.—(1) The court may at any stage of the proceedings order the whole or any part of any particulars of claim or defence to be amended or struck out on the ground that—

(*a*) it discloses no reasonable cause of action or defence, as the case may be; or

(*b*) it is scandalous, frivolous or vexatious; or

(*c*) it may prejudice, embarrass or delay the fair trial of the action; or

(*d*) it is otherwise an abuse of the process of the court,

and may order the action to be stayed or dismissed or judgment to be entered accordingly, as the case may be.

(2) Any application for an order under paragraph (1) of this Rule shall be made on notice to the party affected thereby.

(3) This Rule shall apply with the necessary modifications to a matter as it applies to an action."

10. Order 15 shall be amended as follows:—

(1) In Rule 4 for the words "the day fixed for the hearing" there shall be substituted the words "the return day" and for the words "at the hearing" there shall be substituted the words "on the return day".

(2) In Rule 11 for the words "at the trial" there shall be substituted the words "on the return day".

11. In Order 16, Rule 7, for the words "and send notice of hearing" there shall be substituted the words "or, if he thinks fit, a day for the preliminary consideration of the action under Order 21 and send notice thereof".

12. Order 20, Rule 8, shall be amended as follows:—

(1) In paragraph (1) the words "at the hearing in court", wherever they appear, shall be omitted.

(2) In paragraph (4) for the words "the day fixed for the hearing" there shall be substituted the words "the return day".

13. The following Order shall be inserted after Order 20:—

"ORDER 21

PRELIMINARY CONSIDERATION OF ACTION OR MATTER

Matters to be considered on pre-trial review

1. On any day fixed under Order 6, Rule 3(3), or Order 10, Rule 3 or 4(3)(*b*), for the preliminary consideration of an action (in this Order referred to as a pre-trial review), the registrar shall, subject to the following provisions of this Order, consider the course of the proceedings and give all such directions as appear to him necessary or desirable for securing the just, expeditious and economical disposal of the action.

Securing admissions and agreements

2. The registrar shall endeavour on the pre-trial review to secure that the parties make all such admissions and agreements as ought reasonably to be made by them in relation to the proceedings and may record in the order made on the review any admission or agreement so made or any refusal to make any admission or agreement.

Application for particular direction

3. Every party shall, so far as practicable, apply on the pre-trial review for any particular direction he may desire and shall give to the registrar and every other party notice of his intention to do so, and if an application which might have been made on the review is made subsequently, the applicant shall pay the costs of and occasioned by the application, unless the court is of opinion that there was sufficient reason for the application not having been made on the review.

Rules as to interlocutory applications to apply

4. The provisions of these Rules relating to interlocutory applications shall have effect as if the pre-trial review were the hearing of an interlocutory application and accordingly the registrar may, on the review, exercise any of the powers exercisable by him on an interlocutory application and may do so of his own motion if no application is made for the exercise of the power.

Evidence by affidavit

5. Evidence on the pre-trial review may be given by affidavit unless the court otherwise directs.

Admission by defendant of plaintiff's claim

6. If, on or before the pre-trial review, the defendant admits the plaintiff's claim or such part thereof as the plaintiff accepts in satisfaction of his claim, the registrar may proceed as if the review were the day fixed for the disposal of a default summons.

Non-appearance by defendant who has not delivered defence

7. If the defendant does not appear on the pre-trial review and has not delivered an admission or defence, the registrar may, if he thinks fit, enter judgment for the plaintiff.

Non-appearance by defendant who has delivered defence

8. If the defendant has delivered a defence but does not appear on the pre-trial review, the registrar may, if the plaintiff so requests, exercise on the appointment such powers as are exercisable by him under Order 23, Rule 4, on the hearing of an action.

Fixing date of trial

9. On or as soon as practicable after completing his consideration of the matters referred to in Rule 1 of this Order the registrar shall, if the action remains to be tried, fix a day for the trial and give notice thereof to every party.

Pre-trial review in other proceedings

Form 367

10. If in any proceedings in which no pre-trial review has been fixed the registrar is nevertheless of opinion that the question of giving directions ought to be considered, he may, with a view to obtaining assistance in such consideration, give to the parties notice in Form 367 requiring them to appear before him on a day named in the notice and thereupon the preceding provisions of this Order shall have effect, with the necessary modifications, as if that day were the day fixed for a pre-trial review."

14. Order 22 shall be amended as follows:—

(1) In Rule 4(2) after the word "court" there shall be inserted the words "or an ordinary action is so fixed under Order 21, Rule 9".

(2) Rule 5 shall be amended as follows:—

(*a*) In paragraph (1) for the words from "receipt by him" to the end there shall be substituted the words "receipt by him—

(*a*) in a case to which Rule 4(1) of this Order applies, of the plaint note, and

(*b*) in any other case, of notice of the day fixed for the hearing."

(*b*) In paragraph (2) for the words "in an ordinary action" to the end there shall be substituted the following words:—

"(*a*) in a case to which Rule 4(1) of this Order applies, in his defence, and

(*b*) in any other case, within 3 days of the receipt by him of notice of the day fixed for the hearing."

15. Order 23 shall be amended as follows:—

(1) In Rule 2(1) for the words from the beginning to "action or matter" there shall be substituted the words "If in any action or matter the plaintiff does not appear on the return day".

(2) In Rule 2(3) for the words "at the hearing", in both places where they appear, there shall be substituted the words "on the return day".

(3) In Rules 3(1) and 4(1) after the word "appears" there shall in each case be inserted the words "at the hearing".

16. Order 24 shall be amended as follows:—

(1) Rule 7 shall stand as paragraph (1) of that Rule and Rule 10 shall be added to Rule 7 as paragraph (2) of that Rule.

(2) The following Rule shall be inserted after Rule 9:—

Final and interlocutory judgment where defendant debarred

"10.—(1) Where a defendant is debarred from defending altogether or the whole of his defence is struck out, the plaintiff may have judgment entered for the amount of his claim and costs.

Form 127(1)

(2) If the plaintiff's claim is for unliquidated damages, any judgment entered under paragraph (1) of this Rule shall be an interlocutory judgment for damages to be assessed and costs.

Form 127(2)

(3) An application for the assessment of damages pursuant to an interlocutory judgment shall be made on notice under Order 13, Rule 1, and for the purposes of any provision of these Rules authorising the registrar to hear and determine any proceedings the assessment shall be treated as the hearing of an action for the damages claimed.

(4) Paragraphs (2) and (3) of this Rule shall apply to a judgment entered on the preliminary consideration of an action under Order 21 as they apply to a judgment entered under paragraph (1) of this Rule, unless at the time of the entry of judgment the plaintiff adduces evidence as to the amount of his damages."

17. Order 26 shall be amended as follows:—

(1) For the title there shall be substituted the following title:—

"SUMMARY PROCEEDINGS FOR THE RECOVERY OF LAND OR RENT

PART I—LAND"

(2) The following Part shall be added after Rule 7:—

"PART II—RENT

Claim for arrears of rent by rent action

8. Where a landlord claims arrears of rent from a tenant or former tenant of his who is still in occupation of the land to which the claim relates, the claim may be brought by action (in these Rules referred to as a "rent action") in accordance with the provisions of this Part of this Order and, subject to those provisions, these Rules shall apply with the necessary modifications to a rent action as they apply to an ordinary action.

Venue

9. A rent action shall be brought in the court for the district in which the land is situated and the praecipe shall contain a statement that the plaintiff requires a summons in Form 410.

Form of summons and service Form 410

10. The summons, which shall be in Form 410 with a copy of the particulars of claim attached, shall be served on the defendant in accordance with Order 8, Rule 39, not less than 7 clear days before the return day.

Certain Rules not to apply

11.—(1) Order 6, Rule 3(2)(*c*) and (3), Order 9 and Order 11 (except Rules 1, 2, 5, 6 and 10 thereof) shall not apply to a rent action.

(2) Nothing in paragraph (1) of this Rule shall prejudice the exercise by the court of its power to give directions under Order 13, Rule 3, and the court may at any time direct that the proceedings shall continue as an ordinary action."

18. Order 46, Rule 10(3), shall be amended as follows:—

(*a*) In sub-paragraph (*b*)(ii) for the words "the date fixed for the hearing of the action" there shall be substituted the words "the return day".

(*b*) In sub-paragraph (*c*) for the words "the hearing" there shall be substituted the words "on the return day".

19. The following paragraph shall be substituted for Order 47, Rule 5(4):—

"(4) Where the sum of money does not exceed £20, no solicitors' charges shall be allowed unless—

(*a*) a certificate is granted under Rule 13 of this Order;

(*b*) the sum exceeds £5, in which case there may be allowed—

(i) in respect of the charges of the plaintiff's solicitor, the costs stated on the summons;

(ii) the costs of enforcing any judgment or order otherwise than by warrant of execution."

20. Order 49 shall be amended as follows:—

(1) The following definition shall be added at the end of Rule 2:—

" "Praecipe" means a request for the issue of process or the doing of some other act by the registrar."

(2) The following Rule shall be added at the end:—

"5. A claim in an action for the cost of repairs executed to a vehicle in consequence of damage which it is alleged to have sustained in an accident on land due to the defendant's negligence shall, unless the court otherwise orders, be treated as a liquidated demand for the purposes of these Rules."

21. In Forms 6 and 172 for the word "praecipe" there shall in each case be substituted the words "request for the summons".

22. In Forms 7, 7A, 8, 9, 9A, 10, 11, 30, 44, 115, 158, 158A, 158B, 170, 183, 281, 286, 296, 300, 302, 306, 307 and 315 for the word "praecipe", wherever it appears, there shall be substituted the word "request".

23. In Form 8 the words "and does not exceed £100", in both places where they appear, shall be omitted.

24. In Form 14 for the words "and will be heard" there shall be substituted the words "and you must attend", and after the word "o'clock" there shall be inserted the words "when the proceedings will be heard [*or* when the Registrar will consider giving directions for securing the just, expeditious and economical disposal of the proceedings. If you intend to ask the Registrar to give any particular direction, you must give notice of your intention to him and to the Defendant.]"

25. Form 18 shall stand as Form 18(1) and the Instructions on the form shall be amended as follows:—

(*a*) The words from "Unless you pay" to "stated above" shall stand as paragraph (5) and the following paragraphs shall be re-numbered accordingly.

(*b*) After paragraph (10) as so re-numbered there shall be added the following paragraph:—

"(11) If the Court issuing this summons is not the Court for the district in which you reside or carry on business, you may write to the Registrar of the issuing Court asking for the action to be transferred to the Court for your district. In deciding whether to order the transfer, the Court will take into account the question whether the claim is disputed. Transfer of the action may add to the costs which you may have to pay if you lose."

26. The following form shall be inserted in Appendix A after Form 18(1):—

"18(2)

ORDINARY SUMMONS (PRE-TRIAL REVIEW)

County Court

Order 6,
Rule 3(2)(*b*)

Mention Plaint No.
Plaintiff
Defendant

TO THE DEFENDANT

Seal

The Plaintiff claims

Debt or Damages.................................. £
(*Particulars are attached*)

Costs:

Court Fee..

Solicitor's Charge.............................

Total

YOU ARE HEREBY SUMMONED to appear at the Court Office at on , the day of , 19 , at o'clock when the Registrar will consider giving directions for securing the just, expeditious and economical disposal of this action.

Issued this day of 19 .

Registrar

IMPORTANT—FOR INSTRUCTIONS TURN OVER

[*Back*]

INSTRUCTIONS

[*As on Form* 18(1) *but adding to paragraph* (5) *the following words:* and be prepared to give the Registrar information about the nature of your case. The Registrar will then give directions as to how the action is to be dealt with. If you intend to ask the Registrar to give any particular direction, you should give notice of your intention to him and the Plaintiff. **If you do not attend as stated above, judgment may be entered against you.**]"

27. The following Form shall be substituted for Form 18A:—

"18A

Order 6, Rule 3(2)(*c*)

FORM OF ADMISSION, DEFENCE AND COUNTERCLAIM TO ACCOMPANY FORMS 18(1) AND (2), 19 AND 22

No. of Plaint ....

.... v. ....

ADMISSION

1. Do you admit the plaintiff's claim in full? Yes/No

2. Do you admit *part* of the plaintiff's claim? Yes/No

If so—

How much do you admit? £......................

What are your reasons for disputing the balance?

....

....

....

3. Do you want time to pay the amount admitted? Yes/No

4. If you want time to pay, answer these questions:—

Pay and means:—

(*a*) What is your basic pay before deductions? £...................... per week/month

(*b*) What overtime, bonuses, fees, allowances or commission do you receive?

(*c*) What deductions are normally made from your pay? £...................... per week/month

(*d*) What is your usual take-home pay? £...................... per week/month

(*e*) Do you receive a pension or any other income? Please give details. No/Yes: Details:—

(*f*) What contributions, if any, are made by any member of your household?

Liabilities:—

(*a*) What persons, if any, are financially dependent on you? Please give details, including the ages of any dependent children.

(*b*) What rent or mortgage instalments do you have to pay? £...................... per week/month

(*c*) What rates, if any, do you have to pay?	£...................... per week/month
(*d*) Do you have to pay under any Court orders? Please give details.	
(*e*) What other regular payments have you to make?	
(*f*) Have you any other liabilities which you would like the court to take into account? Please give details.	
What offer of payment do you make? *or*	Payment on by instalments of £.........per month.

[*In an action to which section* 35 *of the Hire-Purchase Act* 1965 *applies add:—*

5. Are the goods in your possession? Yes/No

I understand that if the plaintiff accepts my offer of payment by instalments, the Court will make an order for the return of the goods but the plaintiff will not be able to enforce this order so long as I pay the instalments punctually].

DEFENCE

1. Do you dispute the plaintiff's claim? Yes/No

2. If so, what are your reasons for disputing the plaintiff's claim?

....

....

....

COUNTERCLAIM

1. Do you wish to make a claim against the plaintiff? Yes/No

2. If so, for how much? £...................

3. What is the nature of the claim?

....

....

....

Note: If your claim against the plaintiff is bigger than his claim against you, you may have to pay a fee before it can be dealt with. You can find out whether a fee is payable by inquiring at any county court office.

SIGN HERE...

DATE.............day of....................................19..............

Where should notices about this case be sent to you? ....

....

If you have any difficulty in filling in this form, ask for help at your local Citizens' Advice Bureau or at any county court office. Immediately after you have filled in this form, send it by post or take it to the Court Office as stated on the summons."

28. The following paragraph shall be inserted as paragraph (10) in the Instructions on Form 19 and as paragraph (9) in the Instructions on Form 22:—

"If the Court issuing this summons is not the Court for the district in which you reside or carry on business, you may write to the Registrar of the issuing Court asking for the action to be transferred to the Court for your district. In deciding whether to order the transfer, the Court will take into account the question whether the claim is disputed. Transfer of the action may add to the costs which you may have to pay if you lose."

29. In the title of Form 20A for the words "FORMS 20, 21(1) AND (2)" there shall be substituted the words "FORM 20".

30. The following form shall be inserted after Form 20A:—

"20B

FORM OF ADMISSION AND DEFENCE TO ACCOMPANY FORMS 21(1) AND (2)

Order 6, Rule 3(2)(*c*)

County Court

No. of Plaint

.... v. ....

1. Do you admit that the plaintiff is entitled to recover possession of the premises? Yes/No

If yes, what facts do you wish the Court to take into account in deciding upon its order?

....

....

....

If no, what are your reasons for disputing the plaintiff's claim?

....

....

....

2. Do you admit the plaintiff's money claim *in full*? Yes/No

3. Do you admit *part* of the plaintiff's money claim? Yes/No

If so, how much? £

4. If you dispute the whole or part of the plaintiff's money claim, what are your reasons for doing so?

....

....

....

SIGN HERE:.......................................

DATE.................day of.............19.....

Where should notices about this case be sent to you? ....

...."

31. In Form 21(1) for paragraph (1) of the Instructions there shall be substituted the following paragraph:—

"(1) Complete the form of admission and defence attached and attend at the Court on the day and at the time stated above."

32. In Form 21(2) for paragraph 2 of the Instructions there shall be substituted the following paragraph:—

"2. Unless you pay the rent in arrear and costs in accordance with paragraph 1, complete the form of admission and defence attached and attend the Court on the day and at the time stated above."

33. In Form 27(1) for the words "this action will be heard at a Court to be held" there shall be substituted the words "you must attend", and for the words "and that if" there shall be substituted the words "when this action will be heard [*or* when the Registrar will consider giving directions for securing the just, expeditious and economical disposal of this action. If you intend to ask the Registrar to give any particular direction, you must give notice of your intention to him and to every other party to the action.] If".

34. In the title of Form 27(2) the words "in default action" shall be omitted.

35. In Form 49 for the word "trial" at the end of the first paragraph there shall be substituted the words "hearing of the action".

36. In Form 60 for the words "on the day of hearing" and "the hearing" there shall in each case be substituted the words "on the return day".

37. In Form 61 for the words "on the day of hearing" and "on the day fixed for the hearing", wherever they appear, there shall in each case be substituted the words "on the return day".

38. Form 62 shall be amended as follows:—

(*a*) For paragraph 1 there shall be substituted the following paragraph:—

"1. The defendant has delivered an admission of your claim and a copy is attached."

(*b*) In paragraph 2 for the words "and stated above" there shall be substituted the words "in the document attached".

39. Form 63 shall be omitted.

40. In Form 88 for the words "at the hearing [*or* disposal] of this action" there shall be substituted the words "on the day of 19 ."

41. Form 91 shall be amended as follows:—

(*a*) In the title the words "of day of hearing" shall be omitted.

(*b*) For the words "and will be heard" there shall be substituted the words "and you must attend".

(*c*) After the word "o'clock" there shall be added the words "when the proceedings will be heard [*or* when the Registrar will consider giving directions for securing the just, expeditious and economical disposal of the proceedings. If you intend to ask the Registrar to give any particular direction, you must give notice of your intention to him and to every other party to the proceedings.]".

42. In Form 109 for the words "at the hearing of this Action" there shall be substituted the words "at Court".

43. In Forms 113 and 114 for the words "until the above action or matter is tried" there shall in each case be substituted the words "until the proceedings are heard".

44. The following forms shall be inserted in Appendix A before Form 128:—

"127(1)

INTERLOCUTORY JUDGMENT FOR PLAINTIFF
(DAMAGES TO BE ASSESSED)

Seal

Order 24, Rule 10(2)

[*General Title— Form* 1]

IT IS ADJUDGED that the plaintiff do recover against the defendant damages to be assessed and costs.

127(2)

FINAL JUDGMENT FOR PLAINTIFF
AFTER ASSESSMENT OF DAMAGES

Order 24, Rule 10(3)

[*General Title—Form* 1]

The plaintiff in this action having on the day of 19 obtained interlocutory judgment against the defendant for damages to be assessed, and the Registrar having assessed the damages at £

IT IS ADJUDGED that the plaintiff do recover against the defendant the said sum of £ and his costs of this action to be taxed on scale

IT IS ORDERED [*proceed as in Form* 133 *or as appropriate*]."

45. In Form 128 for the words "not having appeared at the hearing of this action [*or* matter]" there shall be substituted the words "in this action [*or* matter] not having appeared on the return day".

46. In the marginal note to Form 367 for the words "Order 13, Rule 3(5)" there shall be substituted the words "Order 21, Rule 10".

47. In Form 368 for the words "Rule 3(5)" there shall be substituted the words "Rule 3(3)".

48. Form 369 shall be omitted.

49. The following Form shall be inserted in Appendix A after Form 409:—

"410

Order 26, Rule 10

SUMMONS FOR RENT

County Court

Mention plaint No.

Plaintiff

Defendant

Seal

TO THE DEFENDANT

The Plaintiff claims

Arrears of rent..................................£

(*Particulars are attached*)

Costs:

Court Fee..

Solicitor's Charge ....

TOTAL

YOU ARE HEREBY SUMMONED TO APPEAR AT COUNTY COURT [*here insert address of Court House*] on the day of 19 , at o'clock to answer the claim.

Dated this day of 19 .

Registrar

IMPORTANT—FOR INSTRUCTIONS TURN OVER

[*Back*]

INSTRUCTIONS

(1) If you admit the claim or any part of it, pay the amount admitted and costs into Court as soon as possible. Delay may add to the costs.

(2) If you dispute the claim or any part of it or if you require time for payment, you must attend the Court at the time above stated, otherwise judgment may be given in your absence.

(3) Remittances to the Court [*proceed as in Instruction* (10) *in Form* 18(1)]."

50.—(1) Paragraph 1 of Part I of Appendix D shall be amended as follows:—

(*a*) In sub-paragraph (*a*) after the word "money" there shall be inserted the words "(other than a rent action)", and after the words "Rule 7" there shall be inserted the words "Order 47, Rule 5(4)".

(*b*) At the end of sub-paragraph (*c*) there shall be inserted the word "or" and after that sub-paragraph there shall be inserted the following sub-paragraph:—

"(*d*) in a rent action, for the purpose of Part II of this Appendix and of fixing the amount which the plaintiff may receive in respect of solicitors' charges without taxation in the event of the defendant paying the amount claimed in sufficient time to prevent the plaintiff's attendance at the hearing."

(2) In the first paragraph of the Directions in Part II of the said Appendix after the word "shall" there shall be inserted the words "subject to Order 47, Rule 5(4)".

51. Notwithstanding anything in Rules 21 and 22 of these Rules, the forms mentioned in those Rules may continue to be used in the form hitherto prescribed until the Lord Chancellor otherwise directs.

We, the undersigned members of the Rule Committee appointed by the Lord Chancellor under section 102 of the County Courts Act 1959**(a)** having by virtue of the powers vested in us in this behalf made the foregoing Rules, do hereby certify the same under our hand and submit them to the Lord Chancellor accordingly.

D. O. McKee.
Conolly H. Gage.
H. S. Ruttle.
David Pennant.
W. Granville Wingate.
W. Ralph Davies.
E. A. Everett.
K. W. Mellor.
M. J. P. Macnair.
D. A. Marshall.
E. W. Sankey.

I allow these Rules, which shall come into operation on 1st March 1972 so however that nothing in these Rules shall apply to any action or matter begun before that date.

Dated 31st December 1971.

Hailsham of St. Marylebone, C.

(a) 1959 c. 22.

EXPLANATORY NOTE

(This Note is not part of the Rules.)

These Rules make a number of important changes in county court procedure:—

(1) With minor exceptions, every claim for a liquidated demand (including a claim for negligent damage to a vehicle on land) will be required to be brought by default action (Rules 4(1) and (3) and 20(2)).

(2) The return day of an ordinary summons will, in nearly every case, be a day fixed for the preliminary consideration of the action by the registrar (Rules 4(2), 24 and 26). On this "pre-trial review" the registrar will be required to give directions for securing the just, expeditious and economical disposal of the action and he will be empowered to give judgment if the claim is admitted or the defendant does not appear (Rule 13). A pre-trial review may also be fixed in a defended default action, a transferred action or a matter (Rules 7(1) and (2), 11, 13, 33 and 41).

(3) The court is given extended powers to strike out pleadings where, for example, they disclose no reasonable cause of action or defence (Rule 9(3)).

(4) In appropriate cases where the claim is for unliquidated damages an interlocutory judgment may be entered for damages to be assessed (Rules 16 and 44).

(5) A revised form of admission, defence and counterclaim is prescribed for use in ordinary and default actions (Rule 27) and a new form of admission is introduced for use in actions for the recovery of land (Rules 6(2) and (4), 30, 31 and 32).

(6) A new summary procedure is provided for the recovery of rent on the lines recommended by the Committee on the Enforcement of Judgment Debts (Cmnd. 3909) (Rules 17 and 49).

(7) An action for money due under a hire-purchase agreement or instalment contract is required to be brought in the defendant's court notwithstanding that the claim exceeds £100 (Rules 2 and 23).

(8) A defendant who does not reside or carry on business in the district of the court in which he has been sued will be informed of his right to ask for the action to be transferred to his local court (Rules 25 and 28).

(9) In all county court forms the term "praecipe" is replaced by "request" (Rules 20(1), 21 and 22).

(10) In the absence of a special order no costs will be allowable on a claim not exceeding £20 (instead of £5 as at present) except the costs on the summons (Rule 19).

A number of minor and consequential amendments are also made.

1971 No. 2154

AGRICULTURE

The Price Stability of Imported Products (Rates of Levy) (Cereals) (No. 14) Order 1971

Made - - - -	*31st December* 1971
Coming into Operation	*1st January* 1972

The Minister of Agriculture, Fisheries and Food, in exercise of the powers conferred upon him by section 1(2), (4), (5), (6) and (7) of the Agriculture and Horticulture Act 1964(**a**) and of all other powers enabling him in that behalf, hereby makes the following order:—

1. This order may be cited as the Price Stability of Imported Products (Rates of Levy) (Cereals) (No. 14) Order 1971, and shall come into operation on 1st January 1972.

2.—(1) In this order—

"the Principal Order" means the Price Stability of Imported Products (Levy Arrangements) (Cereals) Order 1971(**b**), as amended by any subsequent order and if any such order is replaced by any subsequent order the expression shall be construed as a reference to such subsequent order;

AND other expressions have the same meaning as in the Principal Order.

(2) The Interpretation Act 1889(**c**) shall apply to the interpretation of this order as it applies to the interpretation of an Act of Parliament and as if this order and the order hereby revoked were Acts of Parliament.

3. In accordance with and subject to the provisions of Part II of the Principal Order (which provides for the charging of levies on imports of certain specified commodities) the rate of levy for such imports into the United Kingdom of any specified commodity as are described in column 2 of the Schedule to this order in relation to a tariff heading indicated in column 1 of that Schedule shall be the rate set forth in relation thereto in column 3 of that Schedule.

4. The Price Stability of Imported Products (Rates of Levy) (Cereals) (No. 13) Order 1971(**d**) is hereby revoked.

In Witness whereof the Official Seal of the Minister of Agriculture, Fisheries and Food is hereunto affixed on 31st December 1971.

(L.S.)

A. Jeffrey Smith,
Assistant Secretary.

(**a**) 1964 c. 28. (**b**) S.I. 1971/631 (1971 I, p. 1660). (**c**) 1889 c. 63.
(**d**) S.I. 1971/1986(1971 III, p. 5668).

SCHEDULE

1. Tariff Heading	2. Description of Imports	3. Rate of Levy
		per ton £
	Imports of:—	
10.01	Denatured wheat	2·00
	Wheat (other than denatured wheat)..	6·50
10.03	Barley other than barley having a potential diastatic activity of not less than 170 degrees	5·25
10.04	Oats	4·00
10.05	Maize (other than sweet corn on the cob)	3·75
10.07	Grain sorghum	2·00
11.02	Cereal groats, meals (including denatured wheat meal), kibbled or cut cereals, rolled, flaked, crushed or bruised cereals and other processed cereals—	
	of wheat	5·00
	of barley	6·00
	of maize	4·75

EXPLANATORY NOTE

(This Note is not part of the Order.)

This order, which comes into operation on 1st January 1972, supersedes the Price Stability of Imported Products (Rates of Levy) (Cereals) (No. 13) Order 1971. It:—

(*a*) increases the rates of levy to be charged on imports of wheat (other than denatured wheat) and grain sorghum;

(*b*) reduces the rate of levy to be charged on imports of processed wheat within tariff heading 11.02;

(*c*) removes the levy on imports of processed oats and processed cereals other than processed wheat, barley and maize within tariff heading 11.02; and

(*d*) reimposes unchanged the remaining rates of levy in force immediately before the commencement of the order.

STATUTORY INSTRUMENTS

1971 No. 2161

LOCAL GOVERNMENT, ENGLAND AND WALES

The Isles of Scilly (Scrap Metal Dealers) Order 1971

Made - - -	30*th December* 1971
Coming into Operation	20*th January* 1972

The Secretary of State for the Environment, upon the application of the Council of the Isles of Scilly and in exercise of his powers under section 292 of the Local Government Act 1933(**a**) and of all other powers enabling him in that behalf, hereby makes the following order:—

1. This order may be cited as the Isles of Scilly (Scrap Metal Dealers) Order 1971 and shall come into operation on 20th January 1972.

2. This order shall be read and construed as one with the Isles of Scilly Orders 1943 and 1957(**b**).

3. The Council shall exercise and perform the functions conferred or imposed on local authorities by the Scrap Metal Dealers Act 1964(**c**).

J. E. Beddoe,
An Under Secretary in the Department of the Environment.

Signed by authority of the Secretary of State.
30th December 1971.

(**a**) 1933 c. 51.
(**b**) S.R. & O. 1943/107 (Rev. XII, p. 558; 1943 I, p. 602), S.I. 1957/1315 (1957 I, p. 1332).
(**c**) 1964 c. 69.

1971 No. 2162

CIVIL AVIATION

The Air Navigation (Fees) (Fourth Amendment) Regulations 1971

Made - - - 31*st December* 1971

Coming into Operation 1*st February* 1972

The Secretary of State with the consent of the Treasury and in exercise of his powers under Article 78 of the Air Navigation Order 1970(**a**), as amended (**b**), and of all other powers enabling him in that behalf, hereby makes the following Regulations:

1. These Regulations may be cited as the Air Navigation (Fees) (Fourth Amendment) Regulations 1971 and shall come into operation on 1st February 1972.

2. The Interpretation Act 1889(**c**) shall apply for the purpose of the interpretation of these Regulations as it applies for the purpose of the interpretation of an Act of Parliament.

3. The Schedule to the Air Navigation (Fees) Regulations 1970(**d**), as amended (**b**), shall be further amended by substituting for paragraph 14 of that Schedule the following paragraph:

"14.—(1) The fees to be paid in respect of the grant or renewal of an air traffic controller's licence or a student air traffic controller's licence, the inclusion or renewal of a rating in such a licence and the naming of an aerodrome or place, or an additional aerodrome or place, in pursuance of Article 60(1) of the Order and Rule 58 of the Rules of the Air and Air Traffic Control shall be as follows:

	£
(*a*) on application for the air traffic controller's licence technical examination	6·00
(*b*) on application for the grant of an air traffic controller's or a student air traffic controller's licence ...	4·00
(*c*) on application for the renewal of an air traffic controller's or a student air traffic controller's licence ...	4·00
(*d*) on application for the inclusion or renewal of:	
(i) an aerodrome control rating	4·00
(ii) an approach control rating	8·00
(iii) an approach radar control rating	12·00

(**a**) S.I. 1970/954 (1970 II, p. 2964).
(**b**) There is no relevant amending instrument.
(**c**) 1889 c. 63.
(**d**) S.I. 1970/1085 (1970 II, p. 3426).

	£
(iv) a precision approach radar control rating ...	10·00
(v) an area control rating	12·00
(vi) an area radar control rating	12·00
(*e*) on application for the naming of an aerodrome or place, or of any additional aerodrome or place, in respect of each rating to which the application relates	8·00

(2) The fees to be paid on application for the resitting of an examination or part of an examination in respect of the licence and ratings specified in the following sub-paragraphs, and in respect of the naming of an aerodrome or place or an additional aerodrome or place shall be as follows:

	£
(*a*) air traffic controller's licence:	
technical examination, for each part	2·00
(*b*) aerodrome control rating:	
written examination	2·00
oral examination	2·00
(*c*) approach control rating:	
written examination	2·00
oral examination	2·00
practical examination	4·00
(*d*) approach radar control rating:	
written examination, for each part	2·00
oral examination	2·00
practical examination	6·00
(*e*) precision approach radar control rating:	
written examination	2·00
oral examination	2·00
practical examination	6·00
(*f*) area control rating:	
written examination, for each part	2·00
oral examination	2·00
practical examination	6·00
(*g*) area radar control rating:	
written examination, for each part	2·00
oral examination	2·00
practical examination	6·00
(*h*) naming of an aerodrome or place, or additional aerodrome or place:	
oral examination	2·00
practical examination	6·00"

D. F. Hubback,
A Deputy Secretary,
Department of Trade and Industry.

31st December 1971.

We consent to the making of these Regulations.

Tim Fortescue,
P. L. Hawkins,
Lords Commissioners of
Her Majesty's Treasury.

31st December 1971.

EXPLANATORY NOTE

(*This Note is not part of the Regulations.*)

These Regulations amend the Schedule to the Air Navigation (Fees) Regulations 1970, as amended. They increase the fees payable for the grant or renewal of an air traffic controller's and student air traffic controller's licence, and for the ratings contained in the air traffic controller's licence, and prescribe separate fees (*a*) for the technical examination for the air traffic controller's licence and the naming of an aerodrome or place and (*b*) for the re-sitting of any examination or part of an examination for such ratings, technical examination or naming of an aerodrome (Paragraph 14).

STATUTORY INSTRUMENTS

1971 No. 2167

BETTING AND GAMING

The Pool Competitions (Licence Fees) Order 1971

Made - - - -	31*st December* 1971
Laid before Parliament	11*th January* 1972
Coming into Operation	1*st February* 1972

In pursuance of section 5(1)(*a*) and (*c*) and (2) of the Pool Competitions Act 1971(**a**), I hereby make the following Order:—

1. This Order may be cited as the Pool Competitions (Licence Fees) Order 1971 and shall come into operation on 1st February 1972.

2. There shall be payable to the Gaming Board for Great Britain—

(*a*) in respect of the grant of a licence under the Pool Competitions Act 1971 (otherwise than by way of renewal of such a licence), a fee of such amount, being not less than £100 nor more than £3,000, as the Board may determine;

(*b*) in respect of an application for the variation or withdrawal of terms or conditions attached to a licence under that Act, a fee of such amount, not exceeding £10, as the Board may determine;

(*c*) in respect of the variation or withdrawal of any term or condition attached to a licence under that Act being a variation or withdrawal in pursuance of an application in that behalf, a fee of such amount, not exceeding £100, as the Board may determine.

R. Maudling,
One of Her Majesty's Principal
Secretaries of State.

Home Office,
Whitehall.
31st December 1971.

EXPLANATORY NOTE

(*This Note is not part of the Order.*)

This Order makes provision for the fees to be payable in respect of licences under the Pool Competitions Act 1971, otherwise than on the renewal of a licence.

(**a**) 1971 c. 57.

APPENDIX
OF CERTAIN INSTRUMENTS NOT REGISTERED AS S.I.

Orders in Council, Letters Patent and Royal Instructions

relating to the Constitutions etc. of Overseas Territories or to appeals to the Judicial Committee,

Royal Proclamations, etc.

PACIFIC ISLANDS

The Gilbert and Ellice Islands (Amendment) Order 1971

At the Court at Buckingham Palace the 27th day of October 1971

Present,

The Queen's Most Excellent Majesty in Council

Her Majesty, by virtue and in exercise of the powers in Her Majesty vested, is pleased, by and with the advice of Her Privy Council, to order, and it is hereby ordered, as follows:—

Citation, construction and commencement.

1.—(1) This Order may be cited as the Gilbert and Ellice Islands (Amendment) Order 1971 and shall be construed as one with the Gilbert and Ellice Islands Order in Council 1915(**a**) and the Gilbert and Ellice Islands Order 1970(**b**), and those Orders and this Order may be cited together as the Gilbert and Ellice Islands Orders 1915 to 1971.

(2) This Order shall be published by exhibition at the Public Office of the Resident Commissioner and printed in the Gazette as soon as may be after the date of such publication and shall come into operation on such date as the Resident Commissioner, acting in his discretion, by notice published and printed in like manner respectively, shall appoint.

Interpretation.

2.—(1) In this Order, unless the context otherwise requires—

"the appointed day" means the date appointed in accordance with the provisions of section 1(2) of this Order;

"the Order of 1970" means the Gilbert and Ellice Islands Order 1970;

"law" means any Act of Parliament, Order of Her Majesty in Council, Ordinance, proclamation, regulation, order, rule or other like instrument having the force of law.

(2) Subject to the provisions of the preceding subsection, the provisions of section 2 of the Order of 1970 shall apply for the purpose of interpreting this Order, and otherwise in relation thereto, as they apply for the purpose of interpreting and in relation to the Order of 1970.

Revocation of Chapter III of the Gilbert & Ellice Islands Order 1970.

3. Chapter III of the Order of 1970 is hereby revoked.

Amendment of part of Chapter IV of the same Order.

4. Sections 22, 23, 24 and 25 of the Order of 1970 are hereby revoked and replaced by the following provisions:

"The Governor, his functions.

22.—(1) There shall be a Governor for the Colony who shall be appointed by Her Majesty by commission under Her Sign Manual and Signet and shall hold office during Her Majesty's pleasure.

(**a**) Rev. IX, p. 655 (1915 III, p. 315). (**b**) S.I. 1970 III, p. 6765.

(2) The Governor shall have such functions as may be conferred upon him by or under this Order or any other law for the time being in force in the Colony and such other functions as Her Majesty may assign to him and, subject to the provisions of this Order (and, in the case of functions conferred upon him by or under any other law, subject to the provisions of that law or any law amending that law) shall perform all the functions of his office according to such instructions as may be given to him by Her Majesty:

Provided that the question whether or not the Governor has in any matter complied with any such instructions shall not be inquired into in any court.

Publication of commission and making of oaths.

23. Every person appointed to the office of Governor shall, before assuming the functions of his office—

(*a*) cause the commission appointing him to be Governor to be read and published in the presence of the Chief Justice, or such person as the Chief Justice may designate for the purpose, and of such members of the Executive Council as can conveniently attend; and

(*b*) make before the above-mentioned persons the oaths of allegiance and for the due execution of his office in the forms set out in Schedule 2 to this Order, which oaths the Chief Justice, or person designated by him, shall administer.

Succession to Government.

24.—(1) Whenever the office of Governor is vacant or the person holding the office of Governor is absent from the Colony or is for any other reason unable to perform the functions of his office those functions shall be performed and the Government of the Colony administered by—

(*a*) such person as Her Majesty may have designated by instructions given through a Secretary of State (hereinafter referred to as " the person designated "); or

(*b*) if no person has been so designated, by the Chief Secretary.

(2) For the purposes of the preceding subsection the person holding the office of Governor shall not be regarded as absent from the Colony or unable to perform the functions of his office—

(*a*) by reason only of the fact that he is in passage from one part of the Colony to another; or

(*b*) at any time when there is a subsisting appointment of a deputy under the next following section.

(3) Before assuming the administration of the Government of the Colony the person designated or the Chief Secretary, as the case may be, shall take and subscribe oaths of allegiance and for the due execution of the office of Governor in the forms set out in Schedule 2 to this Order.

(4) The person designated or the Chief Secretary, as the case may be, shall not continue to administer the Government of the Colony after the person holding the office of Governor has informed him that he is about to assume or resume the administration of the Government.

Governor's deputy.

25.—(1) Whenever the Governor—

(*a*) has occasion to be absent from Tarawa but not from the Colony; or

(*b*) has occasion to be absent from the Colony for a period which he has reason to believe will be of short duration; or

(*c*) is suffering from an illness which he has reason to believe will be of short duration,

he may, acting in his discretion, by instrument under the public seal, appoint any public officer in the Colony to be his deputy during his absence or illness and in that capacity to perform on his behalf such of the functions of his office as may be specified in the instrument.

(2) The powers and authority of the Governor shall not be abridged, altered or in any way affected by the appointment of a deputy under this section otherwise than as Her Majesty may at any time think proper to direct by instructions to the Governor through a Secretary of State and the deputy shall conform to and observe all instructions that may from time to time be given to him by the Governor, acting in his discretion:

Provided that the question whether or not the deputy has in any matter complied with any such instructions shall not be enquired into in any court.

(3) A person appointed as deputy under this section shall hold that office for such period as may be specified in the instrument by which he is appointed but his appointment may be revoked at any time by Her Majesty by instructions given to the Governor through a Secretary of State or by the Governor, acting in his discretion.

(4) In this section "Governor" does not include a deputy appointed under this section."

Adaptation of existing laws.

5.—(1) Subject to the following provisions of this section, the existing laws shall, as from the appointed day, be construed with such adaptations and modifications as may be necessary to bring them into conformity with the provisions of this Order.

(2) (*a*) The Governor, acting in his discretion, may, by order published by exhibition at the Public Office of the Governor, at any time within twelve months after the appointed day, provide that any existing law shall be read and construed with such adaptations and modifications as may appear to him to be necessary or expedient for bringing that

law into conformity with the provisions of this Order or otherwise for giving effect or enabling effect to be given to those provisions; and any existing law shall have effect accordingly from such date as may be specified in the order.

(*b*) An order made under this subsection may be amended or revoked in relation to any law affected thereby by the authority competent to amend or revoke that law.

(3) In the existing laws any reference to the High Commissioner or to the Resident Commissioner shall in their application to the Colony be construed as a reference to the Governor, and any reference to the Assistant Resident Commissioner shall be construed as a reference to the Chief Secretary:

Provided that the provisions of this subsection shall not apply to references to the High Commissioner in—

(*a*) the British Solomon Islands and Gilbert and Ellice Islands (Probate and Administration) Order in Council 1914(**a**); and

(*b*) the Western Pacific (Courts) Order in Council 1961(**b**), as amended(**c**).

(4) Without prejudice to the generality of the preceding subsection, the Emergency Powers Order in Council 1939(**d**), as amended(**e**), shall be amended by deleting the words "and the Gilbert and Ellice Islands Colony," in section 2(1)(*b*).

(5) In this section "existing law" means any law that has effect as part of the law of the Colony immediately before the appointed day and is not revoked by this Order.

Governor may revoke certain provisions.

6. If he is satisfied that proper and adequate provision has been made in the law of the Colony with respect to any matter provided for in the British Solomon Islands and Gilbert and Ellice Islands (Probate and Administration) Order in Council 1914, the Governor, acting in his discretion, may by order direct that on such day, to be specified in such order, such provisions of the said Order as he considers are no longer required shall cease to apply to the Colony on such conditions and subject to such exceptions and qualifications as may be prescribed in such order.

Revocations.

7. The Orders in Council described in the first column of the Schedule to this Order are hereby revoked as respects the Colony to the extent specified in the second column of that Schedule.

W. G. Agnew.

(**a**) S.R. & O. 1914/150 (Rev. VIII, p. 691; 1914 I, p. 634). (**b**) S.I. 1961/1506 (1961 II, p. 3066). (**c**) S.I. 1966/1183, 1967/586, 1970/1435, 1971/715 (1966 III, p. 3071; 1967 I, p. 1791; 1970 III, p. 4684; 1971 II, p. 1933).
(**d**) 1952 I, p. 621. (**e**) S.I. 1956/731, 1963/88, 1963/1633, 1963/2084, 1964/267, 1964/1199, 1965/131, 1968/724 (1956 I, p. 512; 1963 I, p. 105; 1963 III, p. 3084; 1963 III, p. 4403; 1964 I, p. 467; 1964 II, p. 2781; 1965 I, p. 270; 1968 II, p. 2077).

Section 7

THE SCHEDULE

ORDERS REVOKED

Title	*Extent of Revocation*
The Pacific Order in Council 1893(**a**).	Articles 50, 84(1), 86, 134, 137 and 139.
The British Solomon Islands Protectorate and Gilbert and Ellice Islands Colony (Currency) Order in Council 1937(**b**).	The whole Order.

EXPLANATORY NOTE

(*This Note is not part of the Order.*)

This Order separates the government of the Gilbert and Ellice Islands Colony from the High Commissioner for the Western Pacific, with the exception of certain judicial matters. It provides for the office of Governor and makes various consequential amendments to the law of the Colony.

(**a**) Rev. VIII, p. 597; 1893, p. 312.
(**b**) S.R. & O. 1937/627 (Rev. VIII, p. 696; 1937, p. 622).

PACIFIC ISLANDS

The Gilbert and Ellice Islands (Boundaries) Order 1971

At the Court at Buckingham Palace the 27th day of October 1971

Present,

The Queen's Most Excellent Majesty in Council

Whereas the Colonial Boundaries Act 1895(**a**) provides that where the boundaries of a Colony have, either before or after the passing of that Act, been altered by an Order in Council or by Letters Patent, the boundaries as so altered shall be, and be deemed to have been from the date of the alteration, the boundaries of the Colony:

And whereas it is expedient that the boundaries of the Gilbert and Ellice Islands Colony should be altered so as to include the Central and Southern Line Islands in the Pacific Ocean:

Now, therefore, Her Majesty, by virtue and in exercise of the powers in Her Majesty vested, is pleased, by and with the advice of Her Privy Council, to order, and it is hereby ordered, as follows:

1.—(1) This Order may be cited as the Gilbert and Ellice Islands (Boundaries) Order 1971 and shall be published by exhibition at the Public Office of the Resident Commissioner and in the official Gazette of the Colony.

2. As from 1st January 1972 the boundaries of the Gilbert and Ellice Islands Colony shall be extended so as to include:

Caroline Island (Lat. 10°00′S ; Long. 150°14′W.)

Flint Island (Lat. 11°26′S ; Long. 151°48′W.)

Malden Island (Lat. 4°04′S ; Long. 154°58′W.)

Starbuck Island (Lat. 5°37′S ; Long. 155°53′W.)

Vostock Island (Lat. 10°06′S ; Long. 152°23′W.)

3. As from 1st January 1972 the provisions of Article 108 of the Pacific Order in Council 1893(**b**) shall cease to apply to the islands described in the preceding section.

W. G. Agnew.

EXPLANATORY NOTE

(*This Note is not part of the Order.*)

This Order includes, with effect from 1st January 1972, the Central and Southern Line Islands within the boundaries of the Gilbert and Ellice Islands Colony.

(**a**) 1895 c. 34.

(**b**) Rev. VIII, p. 597; S.R. & O. 1893, p. 312.

PACIFIC ISLANDS

The Gilbert and Ellice Islands Royal Instructions 1971

Dated the 30th November 1971.

ELIZABETH R.

INSTRUCTIONS to Our Governor in and over Our Colony of the Gilbert and Ellice Islands or other Officer Administering the Government of the Colony.

We do hereby direct and enjoin and declare Our will and pleasure as follows: —

Citation, publication, commencement and revocation.

1.—(1) These Instructions may be cited as the Gilbert and Ellice Islands Royal Instructions 1971.

(2) These Instructions shall be published by exhibition at the Public Office of the Resident Commissioner and thereafter as soon as may be in the Gazette and shall take effect on the day on which the Gilbert and Ellice Islands (Amendment) Order 1971(**a**) (in these Instructions referred to as " the Order of 1971 ") comes into operation.

(3) Without prejudice to anything lawfully done thereunder, the Gilbert and Ellice Islands Royal Instructions 1970(**b**) shall cease to have effect on the taking effect of these Instructions.

Interpretation.

2. The provisions of section 2 of the Order of 1971 shall apply for the purpose of interpreting these Instructions as they apply for the purpose of interpreting that Order.

Instructions to be observed by deputy.

3.—(1) These Instructions, so far as they apply to any functions to be performed by a person appointed under section 25 of the Gilbert and Ellice Islands Order 1970(**c**), as amended by the Order of 1971, (in these Instructions referred to as " the Order of 1970 ") shall be deemed to be addressed to, and shall be observed by, that person.

(2) Such person may, if he thinks fit, apply to Us through a Secretary of State for instructions in any matter; but he shall forthwith transmit to the Governor a copy of every despatch or other communication so addressed to Us.

Rules for the making of laws.

4. In the making of laws under the powers conferred by section 51 of the Order of 1970 the following rules shall be observed as far as practicable:—

(*a*) All laws shall be styled " Ordinances " and the words of enactment shall be—

" Enacted by the Governor with the advice and consent of the Legislative Council ":

Provided that in the case of any law made by the Governor under section 57 of the Order of 1970 the words of enactment shall be " Enacted by the Governor in accordance with the

(**a**) S.I. 1971, III, p. 6330. (**b**) S.I. 1970, III, p. 6802. (**c**) S.I. 1970, III, p. 6765.

provisions of section 57 of the Gilbert and Ellice Islands Order 1970 ".

(*b*) All Ordinances shall be distinguished by titles, and shall be divided into successive sections consecutively numbered, and to every section there shall be annexed in the margin or at its head a short indication of its contents.

(*c*) All Ordinances shall be numbered consecutively in a separate series for each year, commencing with the number one, so that—

(i) an Ordinance passed by the Legislative Council (or deemed to have been so passed under section 57 of the Order of 1970) and assented to by the Governor is included in the series for the year in which it is so passed, and its position in the series is determined with reference to the day on which the Governor has assented to it ;

(ii) an Ordinance assented to by Us through a Secretary of State is included in the series for the year in which the Governor has signified Our assent by proclamation, and its position in the series is determined with reference to the day on which Our assent has been so signified.

(*d*) Matters having no proper relation to each other shall not be provided for by the same Ordinance ; no Ordinance shall contain anything foreign to what the title of the Ordinance imports ; and no provision having indefinite duration shall be included in any Ordinance expressed to have limited duration.

Certain Bills not to be assented to without instructions.

5. Without having previously obtained Our instructions through a Secretary of State the Governor shall not assent to any Bill within any of the following classes, unless the Bill contains a provision suspending its operation until the signification of Our pleasure, that is to say, any Bill—

(*a*) for the divorce of married persons ;

(*b*) whereby any grant of land or money or other donation be made to himself ;

(*c*) affecting the currency of the Colony or relating to the issue of bank notes ;

(*d*) establishing any banking association, or altering the constitution, powers or privileges of any banking association ;

(*e*) imposing differential duties ;

(*f*) affecting the discipline or control of Our naval, military or air forces ;

(*g*) the provisions of which appear to him to be inconsistent with obligations imposed on Us by treaty, convention, agreement or arrangement relating to any country or international or similar organisation outside the Colony ;

(*h*) of an extraordinary nature and importance whereby Our prerogative, or the rights or property of Our subjects not residing in the Colony, or the trade, transport or communications of any part of Our dominions or any territory under Our protection or in which We have for the time being jurisdiction, may be prejudiced ;

(*i*) the provisions of which appear to him as likely to cause a financial liability which the Government of the Colony might find difficulty in meeting out of its own resources ; or

(*j*) containing provisions to which Our assent has been refused or which have been disallowed by Us:

Provided that if the Governor is satisfied that it is urgently necessary in the public interest that a Bill falling within any of the said classes (other than a Bill falling within paragraph (*g*) of this clause) be brought into immediate operation, he may assent to that Bill without such instructions as aforesaid and although the Bill contains no provision as aforesaid ; but he shall forthwith transmit to Us the Bill together with his reasons for so assenting to it.

Ordinances and Bills to be sent through a Secretary of State.

6. When any Ordinance has been enacted or any Bill has been reserved for the signification of Our pleasure, the Governor shall forthwith transmit to Us through a Secretary of State for the signification of Our pleasure, a transcript in duplicate of the Ordinance or Bill, duly authenticated by his own signature, together with an explanation of the reasons and occasion for the enactment of the Ordinance or the passing of the Bill.

Collection of Ordinances to be published annually.

7. As soon as practicable after the commencement of each year the Governor shall cause a complete collection of all Ordinances enacted during the preceding year to be published for general information.

Purchase of property by Governor.

8. The Governor shall not, directly or indirectly, purchase for himself any land or building in the Colony to Us belonging without Our special permission given through a Secretary of State.

Oath of allegiance by public officers, etc.

9. The Governor may, whenever he thinks fit, require any person in the public service of the Colony or holding any office constituted by or under the Order of 1970 to make an oath or affirmation of allegiance in the form set out in Schedule 2 to the Order of 1970 together with any other oath or affirmation that may be prescribed in relation to his office by any law for the time being in force in the Colony.

Given at Our Court at St. James's this thirtieth day of November 1971 in the twentieth year of Our Reign.

CLASSIFIED LIST

OF THE

LOCAL STATUTORY INSTRUMENTS

REGISTERED DURING

1971

TABLE OF CONTENTS

NOTES

1. In the following list the number in round brackets is the S.I. number of that instrument in the 1971 series.

2. Instruments indicated with an asterisk were not printed and sold by H.M.S.O. Copies will usually be obtainable from the local authority or Government Department concerned.

3. The list does not show ministerial orders (including special procedure orders) which are not statutory instruments. Information as to any such orders may be obtained from the local authority or Government Department concerned.

(1) Bridges and tunnels

(*a*) *England and Wales*

Severn Bridge Tolls (Temporary Reduction) O., *made by Secretary of State under Severn Bridge Tolls Act 1965* (*c. 24*), *ss. 6*(*1*) *and* (*2*)...(1444).

Secretary of State—Confirmation Instruments under Highways (*Miscellaneous Provisions*) *Act 1961* (*c. 63*), *s. 3*†.

Bedford Inner Relief Road (Southern Section) Bridges Scheme 1966 (2150).
Warley County Borough Council (Roebuck Lane Improvement) Scheme 1968 (2170).

(*b*) *Scotland*

Erskine Bridge Tolls O., *made by Secretary of State under Erskine Bridge Tolls Act 1968* (*c. 4*), *ss. 1 and 2* ... (975).

Roads (S.) Act 1970 (Local Enactments) O., *made by Secretary of State under Roads* (*S.*) *Act 1970* (*c. 20*), *s. 47*(*2*) ... (1150).

(2) Establishment as highways

(*a*) TRUNK ROADS

Restriction of traffic on trunk roads—*see* (4) below.
Trunk roads in built-up areas—*see* (4) below.

(*i*) *England and Wales*

Secretary of State—Orders under Highways Act 1959 (*c. 25*), *s. 7*†, *sch. 24 para. 29; Local Government Act 1966* (*c. 42*), *s. 27.*

Chester–Bangor Trunk Road (East of Abergele to County Boundary) (465).
Penrith–Middlesbrough Trunk Road (Greta Bridge By-Pass) (2176).

Secretary of State—Orders under Highways Act 1959 (*c. 25*), *s. 7*†, *and, where indicated in square brackets, one or more of the following:—Highways Act 1959, ss. 20, 44 or 286, or Local Government Act 1966* (*c. 42*), *s. 27.*

A.1 London–Edinburgh–Thurso Trunk Road (Lemsford to Welwyn Detrunking) [1966 s. 27] (59).
A.23 London–Brighton Trunk Road (Hooley Interchange) (662).
Bath–Lincoln Trunk Road (Oxenton Diversion) [1966 s. 27] (361).
Bilston Link Trunk Road and Slip Roads [1959 ss. 20 and 44] (1685).
Birmingham–Great Yarmouth Trunk Road (King's Lynn Southern By-Pass) [1959 ss. 20, 44 and 286; 1966 s. 27] (294).
Bootle–Southport–South of Preston Trunk Road (Crosby Road South Diversion) (1112).
Bootle–North of Aintree Trunk Road (Litherland Lift Bridge Diversion) (Detrunking) [1966 s. 27] (1016).
Carlisle–Sunderland Trunk Road (Whooff House–Plains Road) (1349).
Dolgellau–South of Birkenhead Trunk Road (Llanarman Road Junction near Llanferres) (395).

†Orders made under this section are liable to special Parliamentary procedure.

Class 1.—Roads, Bridges, Road Traffic and Rights of Way—*cont.*

(2) Establishment as highways—*cont.*

(*a*) TRUNK ROADS—*cont.*

(*i*) *England and Wales—cont.*

East of Birmingham–Birkenhead Trunk Road (Rock Ferry By-Pass) [1959 s. 44; 1966 s. 27] (826).
East of Snaith–Sunderland Trunk Road (Teeside Diversion Stage 1)—
  [1959 ss. 20 and 44] (1363).
  (Slip Roads)—
    [1959 s. 44] (1364).
    (No. 2) [1959 s. 44] (1365).
Exeter–Leeds Trunk Road (Silver Street and other Roads, Taunton) [1966 s. 27] (508).
Exeter–Leeds and Nottingham–Stoke-on-Trent Trunk Roads (Mickleover By-Pass and Link Road) (Manor Hospital and Kingsway Junctions) (1657).
Folkeston–Honiton Trunk Road—
  (Amdt. of Route, Winchelsea) [1966 s. 27] (2092).
  (Arundel Relief Road) [1959 ss. 20 and 44; 1966 s. 27] (507).
  (Shoreham By-Pass De-trunking) [1966 s. 27] (332).
  (Stony Head, Near Bridport, Diversion) [1959 s. 44] (1620).
  (Yarty Bridge Diversion) (509).
Ipswich–Weedon Trunk Road—
  (Bury St. Edmunds By-Pass and Slip Roads) [1959 s. 44; 1966 s. 27] (506).
  (Stowmarket to Claydon By-Pass) [1959 ss. 44 and 286] (1532).
Leeds–Scarborough Trunk Road (Staxton Diversion) (1804).
Levens Bridge–Carlisle Trunk Road (Thwaites Mill and Slapestones Diversions) [1959 s. 44] (1350).
London–Birmingham Trunk Road—
  (Bourne End Diversion) [s. 44] (1184).
  (Detrunking of Birmingham Road Service Road) (1829).
London–Brighton Trunk Road (Balcombe Road Gyratory System) [1959 s. 44] (535).
London–Cambridge–King's Lynn and Royston–Huntingdon–Alconbury Trunk Roads (Queens Road, Mill Road and High Street, Royston Trunking and Detrunking) (325).
London–Cambridge–King's Lynn Trunk Road (Littleport Bridge Diversion) [1959 ss. 20 and 44] (886).
London–Cambridge Trunk Road—
  (Hoddesdon By-Pass) [1959 s. 44; 1966 s. 27] (130).
  (Ware By-Pass [1959 ss. 20 and 44; 1966 s. 27] (140).
London–Carlisle–Glasgow–Inverness Trunk Road—
  (Diversion North of Sharnbrook Crossroads) [1959 s. 44] (2151).
  (Gretna Diversion, Cumberland) (Connecting Roads) (53).
London–Carlisle–Glasgow Trunk Road (Kempley Bank Roundabout to Stoneybeck Roundabout Detrunking) [1966 s. 27] (1266).
London 'D' (Ring Road—
  A.1–A.111 Section) [1959 s. 44; 1966 s. 27] (1382).
  A.111–A.10 Section) [1959 s. 44] (1367).
London–Great Yarmouth Trunk Road—
  (Colchester Northern By-Pass)—
    [1959 s. 44] (1516).
    (Crown Interchange, Park Lane and Birchwood Slip Roads) [1959 s. 44; 1966 s. 27] (1517).
  (Marine Parade and other roads, Lowestoft Trunking) (706).
London–Holyhead Trunk Road—
  (Allesly By-Pass Slip Roads) (1567).
  (Dinas Hill, near Betwys-y-Coed) (523).
London to Holyhead and Newport–Shrewsbury Trunk Roads (Meole Brace Diversion) (1764).

Class 1.—Roads, Bridges, Road Traffic and Rights of Way—*cont.*

(2) Establishment as highways—*cont.*

(*a*) TRUNK ROADS—*cont.*

(*i*) *England and Wales—cont.*

London–Inverness Trunk Road and Liverpool–Leeds–Hull Trunk Road (Irlams o' th' Height Underpass) [1959 s. 44] (418).

London North Circular Trunk Road (Waterworks Corner Improvement Stage 2) [1959 s. 44; 1966 s. 27] (1763).

London–North Orbital Trunk Road (Hunton Bridge–Maple Cross Section) [1959 s. 44] (428).

London–Norwich Trunk Road (Woodford New Road/High Road, Woodford Green Improvement) [1959 s. 44; 1966 s. 27] (630).

London–Penzance Trunk Road—
(Ashburton–Buckfastleigh Diversion) [1959 s. 44; 1966 s. 27] (302).
(Camborne and Scorrier By-Pass) [1959 s. 44; 1966 s. 27] (1678).
(Drumbridge–Caton Cross Diversion) [1959 s. 44; 1966 s. 27] (921).
(Drybridge–Syon Abbey) [1959 s. 44; 1966 s. 27] (1226).
(Ivybridge By-Pass) [1959 s. 44; 1966 s. 27] (27).
(Liskeard By-Pass) [1959 s. 44; 1966 s. 27] (1594).
(Second Crossing of the Exeter Canal) [1959 s. 20] (796).
(South Brent By-Pass) [1959 s. 44; 1966 s. 27] (1225).

London–Portsmouth Trunk Road—
(Cannonball Corner and Gravel Hill Diversion) (1710).
(Hogs Back Junction) [1959 s. 44] (443).
(Scilly Isles Gyratory System) [1959 s. 44] (1138).

London–Thurso Trunk Road (Allerton Park Flyover Link Roads) (419).

Maentwrog–East of Conway Trunk Road (Teiliau Isaf Ffestiniag) (529).

Newport–Shrewsbury Trunk Road—
(Diversion South of Cherry Tree Cottage) (1568).
(Diversion near The Green, Wellington) [1959 s. 44; 1966 s. 27] (1523).
(Diversion at Hunger Hill) [1959 s. 44; 1966 s. 27] (1837)
(Leominster Inner Relief Road) [1959 s. 44; 1966 s. 27] (1007).

Newtown–Aberystwyth Trunk Road (Llanidloes Road, Newtown) (1174).

Norman Cross–Grimsby Trunk Road (Partney Hill Diversion) (427).

North of Oxford–South of Coventry Trunk Road (Shipton-on-Cherwell Diversion) [1959 s. 44; 1966 s. 27] (536).

North West of Doncaster–Kendal Trunk Road (Clapham Outer By-Pass) [1959 ss. 44, 286] (2126).

Oxford–Market Deeping Trunk Road—
(Stamford) [1966 s. 27] (1910).
(Thorpeville, Northampton) [1966 s. 27] (2049).

Raglan–Llandovery Trunk Road (Abergavenny Inner Relief Road) [1959 s. 44; 1966 s. 27] (2177).

Royston–Alconbury Trunk Road (Huntingdon and Godmanchester By-Pass) [1959 ss. 20, 40 and 286] (1601).

Seaforth–North of Aintree Trunk Road (Litherland Lift Bridge Diversion) [1959 ss. 20, 44] (1015).

Winchester–Preston Trunk Road—
(Abingdon By-Pass) [1959 s. 44; 1966 s. 27] (75).
(Abingdon By-Pass Slip Roads) [1959 s. 44] (74).
(Chilton–Drayton) [1959 s. 44; 1966 s. 27] (73).

Worcester–Wolverhampton–South of Stafford Trunk Road (Ombersley By-Pass) (Slip Roads and Variation) [1959 s. 286; 1966 s. 27] (1282).

Workington–Barons Cross Trunk Road (Chapel Brow–Fitz Cottage) [1959 s. 44; 1966 s. 27] (1909).

York–Hull Trunk Road (Barmby Newton Diversion) [1959 s. 44] (1957).

Class 1.—Roads, Bridges, Road Traffic and Rights of Way—*cont.*

(2) Establishment as highways—*cont.*

(*a*) Trunk Roads—*cont.*

(ii) Scotland

Secretary of State—Orders under Trunk Roads Act 1946 (c. 30), s. 1(2),† and, where indicated in square brackets, s. 2(3) of Trunk Roads Act 1946 or s.1 of Roads (S.) Act 1970 (c. 20).

Abingdon–Lanark–Airdrie–Cumbernauld Trunk Road—
(Castlehill Diversion) (774).
(Duneatonfoot Bridge Diversion) (861).
Edinburgh–Carlisle Trunk Road (Bridgeheugh and Lindean Diversions) [1970 s. 1] (402).
Edinburgh–Newcastle upon Tyne Trunk Road—
(Broomhill, Drygrange Bridge and Drygrange Diversions) [1970 s. 1] (373).
(Drygrange Mains and Packman's Bridge Diversions) [1970 s. 1] (399).
Edinburgh–Stirling–Perth Trunk Road (Keir Roundabout Trunking) (1816).
Fort William–Mallaig Trunk Road—
(Drochaid Sgainnir and Drochaid na Saille Diversions) (799).
(Fassfern Diversion) (1768).
Glasgow–Stirling Trunk Road (Pirnhall to Bannockburn Diversion) and the Edinburgh–Stirling–Perth Trunk Road (Detrunking) [1946 s. 2(3)] (615).
Gretna–Stranraer–Glasgow Trunk Road—
(Cairneyhill Diversion) [1970 s. 1] (433).
(Old Hermitage and Other Diversions) (2178).
London–Edinburgh–Thurso Trunk Road—
(Alness to Kildary Trunking and Detrunking) (1063).
(Danachton Lodge Diversions) (2091).
(Lamberton and Greystonelees Diversions) (372).
North of Abingdon–Edinburgh Trunk Road (Clydes Bridge Diversion) (867).
Perth–Aberdeen–Inverness Trunk Road (Mormond House Diversion) [1970 s. 1] (1943).
Stirling–Callander–Crianlarich Trunk Road (Craigforth Diversion Trunking) (1817).

Secretary of State—Orders under Trunk Roads Acts 1936 (c. 5), s. 13(2); 1946 (c. 30), ss. 1(2)†, 6(1), 11(4).

Invergarry–Kyle of Lochalsh Trunk Road (West of Invergarry and Other Diversions) (Amdt.) (800).
London–Carlisle–Glasgow–Inverness Trunk Road—
(Alexandria By-Pass Stage II Slip Roads) (Variation) (1911).
(Ballachulish Bridge Diversion) (2090).
London–Edinburgh–Thurso Trunk Road (Evelnix Bridge and Other Diversions) (Variation) (1470).

(*b*) Special Roads

(i) England and Wales

Secretary of State—Motorways Traffic (Speed Limit) Regs., under Road Traffic Act 1967 (c. 76), s. 13(2).

A.57(M) (Mancunian Way) (1006).
Leeds Inner Ring Road (1842).
M.4 (1502).

†Orders made under this section are liable to special Parliamentary procedure.

Class 1.—Roads, Bridges, Road Traffic and Rights of Way—*cont.*

(2) Establishment as highways—*cont.*

(*b*) SPECIAL ROADS—*cont.*

(*i*) *England and Wales—cont.*

Secretary of State—Schemes under Highways Act 1959 (c. 25), s. 11†, *and, where indicated in square brackets, ss. 12, 14, 20 or 286.*

A.1(M) Motorway (Hatfield–The Clock Roundabout, Welwyn) Scheme [ss. 12 and 14] (58).
Beaconsfield and Gerrards Cross By-Pass Special Road (Extension at Denham) Scheme [ss. 12 and 14] (379).
Cheshire County Council (Ellesmere Port) Motorway Scheme 1967 Confirmation (524).
City and County of Bristol (Bristol Parkway) (Lower Ashley Road to Muller Road) Special Roads Scheme 1970 Confirmation (331).
Greater London Council (Blackwall Tunnel Southern Approach) Motorway Scheme 1970 Confirmation (1932).
Lancashire County Council—
(Kirkby to Tarbock) Special Road Scheme 1968 Confirmation (1940).
Outer Ring Road (Kirkby to Tarbock) Special Connecting Roads Scheme 1970 Confirmation (1941).
Manchester City Council (Mancunian Way) Special Road Scheme 1968 Confirmation (1005).
M.3/M.25 Motorways (Thorpe Interchange) Connecting Roads Scheme [ss. 12 and 14] (1417).
M.5 Motorway (Huntsworth–Willand) Scheme [ss. 12, 14 and 20] (641).
M.23 Motorway (Woodmansterne–Merstham Section) Connecting Roads Scheme [ss. 12 and 14] (663).
M.25 Motorway (Wrotham Spur) Scheme [ss. 12 and 14] (1418).
M.25 South Orbital Motorway—
(Egham–Chertsey Section) [ss. 12 and 14] (1416).
(Godstone to Sevenoaks Section) [ss. 12 and 14] (1425).
(Reigate–Godstone Section) Connecting Roads Scheme [ss. 12 and 14] (607).
M.27 South Coast Motorway (Chilworth–Windhover Section) Scheme [ss. 12 and 14] (1029).
M.56 North Cheshire Motorway (Preston Brook to Bowden Section) and Connecting Roads Scheme [ss. 12 and 14] (1397).
M.62 Motorway (Lofthouse–South of Ferrybridge Section)—
(Alteration and Extension of Route) (Variation) [s. 286] (1304).
Connecting Roads—
[ss. 12 and 14] (1305).
(No. 2) [ss. 12 and 14] (1306).
M.62 Motorway (Rawcliffe to Balkholme Section)—
[ss. 12, 14 and 20] (1958).
(No. 2) [ss. 12 and 14] (1960).
Connecting Roads [ss. 12 and 14] (1959).
M.66 Motorway (Bury Easterly By-Pass Southern Section) and Connecting Roads [ss. 12 and 14] (1307).
Reading County Borough Council A.329 Relief Road Special Road Scheme 1969 Confirmation (109).
Royal County of Berkshire A.329 Relief Road Special Road Scheme 1969—
No. 1 Confirmation (110).
No. 2 Confirmation (268).

---

†Orders made under this section are liable to special Parliamentary procedure.

Class 1.—Roads, Bridges, Road Traffic and Rights of Way—*cont.*

(2) Establishment as highways—*cont.*

(*b*) Special Roads—*cont.*

(*ii*) *Scotland*

Secretary of State—Schemes under Special Roads Act 1949 (*c. 32*), *ss. 1*†, *2, 9, and, where indicated in square brackets, s. 17.*

Bishopton By-Pass (Stage II)—
(Connecting Roads) Special Roads Scheme (1252).
Special Road Scheme (1251).
Ingliston to Pirnhall Special Road Scheme (614).
Newbridge to Lathallan—
(Connecting Roads) Special Roads (Variation)—
[s. 17] (401).
(No. 2) [s. 17] (1071).
Special Road (Variation) [s. 17] (400).
Stirling By-Pass—
(Connecting Roads) Special Roads Scheme (616).
Extension Special Roads Scheme (613).

Secretary of State—Schemes under Special Roads Act 1949 (*c. 32*), *ss. 1*†, *8.*

A.814 Glasgow–Helensburgh–Dumbarton Road Diversion (Bridge over the River Leven) Scheme 1971 Confirmation (925).
Glasgow–Monkland Motorway (Stage I)—
Special Road Scheme 1970 Confirmation—
(1790).
(Connecting Roads) (1791).

(*c*) Metropolitan Roads*

Secretary of State—Orders under London Government 1963 (*c. 33*), *s. 17.*

London Government (Metropolitan Roads) (628).

(*d*) County Roads*

Bedfordshire County Roads (Polhill Avenue, Bedford) O., *made by Secretary of State under Highways Act 1959* (*c. 25*), *s. 21*(*7*)...(1892).‡

County Roads Cesser Orders made by Secretary of State under Highways Act 1959 (*c. 25*) *s. 22.*

Essex (1391).
Leicester (No. 1) (1086).

(3) Rights of Way (extinguishment, stopping up, etc.)*

Stopping Up of Highways Orders made by Secretary of State under Town and Country Planning (*S.*) *Act 1947* (*c. 53*) *s. 46*†

Aberdeen—
Union Lane (1104).
Upper Denburn (1055).
Tanfield Place (920).
Clydebank—
MacArthur Street (1693).
North Bank Street (1692).
Rander Street (1694).
Cowdenbeath, Valleyfield Place (989).
Dumbarton—
Bowie Street (1293).
Graham Road (1622).
Edinburgh (Brister Street and General's Entry) (1347).
Glasgow—
Royston (732).
Townhead (1177).
Kilmarnock, Mill Lane (1355).
Kilsyth, Westport Street and Newtown Street (1825).
Kilwinning, Cranberry Moss Road (34).
Stirling, Ladysneuk Road (862).

Stopping Up of Highways Orders made by Secretary of State under Town and Country Planning (*S.*) *Act 1969* (*c. 30*), *s. 90.*

Allanton, Mill Road and Church Road, Bonkle (County of Lanark) (1580).
Mill Street etc. (Burgh of Rutherglen) (1581).

†Orders made under this section are liable to special Parliamentary procedure.
*Not printed for sale in the S.I. series.
‡This instrument (1892) was printed and put on sale.

Class 1.—Roads, Bridges, Road Traffic and Rights of Way—*cont.*

(4) Traffic regulation

(a) England and Wales (b) Scotland

(*a*) ENGLAND AND WALES*

(i) General regulation

†Crown Roads (Admiralty Arch, Whitehall, London) (Application of Road Traffic Enactments) O., *made by Secretary of State under Transport Act 1968* (*c. 73*), *s. 149*...(1073).

Secretary of State—Orders under Road Traffic Regulation Act 1967 (*c. 76*), *ss. 1*(*1*), (*2*), (*3*), (*6*) *and 84D*(*1*).

BOX JUNCTIONS—
Bedford, St. John's Street and the Broadway (1888).
Colchester, London Road (839).
Derby, Osmaston Park Road (208).
High Wycombe (1486).
Ipswich, Chevallier Street and Yarmouth Road (2069).
Penwortham, Liverpool Road (23).
Peterborough, London Road (1461).
Stockton Heath, Victoria Square (1068).
Stratford-upon-Avon, Evesham Road and Evesham Place (2137).
Warminster, Market Place (820).

BOXED AREA—
Sunningdale Level Crossing (833).

CLOSURE OF GAP—
Cambridge, Chesterton Bridge (890).
Felling By-Pass (22).

NO RIGHT-HAND TURN—
Raglan, Usk Road (Revn.) (1230).

ONE-WAY TRAFFIC—
Cardigan, Pendre and Morgan Street (1640).
Cowbridge By-Pass (Access Road) (1096).
Jordanston, Pembrokeshire (Slip Road) (1399).
Llanwrda (1344).
Streethay, Lichfield Eastern By-Pass (1700).

ONE-WAY TRAFFIC AND PROHIBITION OF WAITING—
Huntley (1969).

ONE-WAY TRAFFIC AND PROHIBITION AND RESTRICTION OF WAITING—
Rochester, Various Streets (Amdt.) (455).

ONE-WAY WORKING—
Alnwick By-Pass Slip Road (71).

PRESCRIBED ROUTES—
Bagshot, Surrey, Cricketers Bridge (995).

PRESCRIBED ROUTES AND PROHIBITION AND RESTRICTION OF WAITING—
Haverfordwest (1346).

PROHIBITION OF CYCLING—
Thetford Inner Relief Road Subway (1487).

PROHIBITION OF DRIVING—
Adwick-le-Street, Skellow Cross Roads (1125).
Alfreton (9).
Allerton Park (49).
Allesley, Junction with Oak Lane (1800).
Bridgewater, Monmouth Street (1485).
Broughton Astley (137).
Bucklow, Chester Road—
(1458).
(No. 2) (2138).
Chester-le-Street, Cowan Gardens (2139).
Derby, Burton Road (1625).
Egham (1699).
Fareham, West Street, Porchester (1724).
Felton, Mouldshaugh Lane (1831).
Gosforth, Great North Road (1099).

PROHIBITION OF DRIVING—*cont.*
Haltwhistle, West End (1782).
Haydock, East Lancashire Road (784).
Hexham, Haydon Bridge (5).
Liverpool, East Lancashire Road (4).
Oadby, Harborough Road (791).
Peterborough, Lincoln Road (1928).
Prees Heath, Heath Lane (484).
Preston, Longton By-Pass (1193).
St. Albans, St. Peter's Street (1926).
Sale, Cross Street (205).
Slough, High Street (606).
Spenborough (597).
Staplegrove, Somerset (1723).
Turnford, North of New River Arms Roundabout (1433).
Wall Lane, Watling Street (1801).
Warrington, Sankey Canal Lift Bridge Diversion (582).
Whiston, Warrington Road (1464).

PROHIBITION OF DRIVING, ONE-WAY TRAFFIC AND PROHIBITION AND RESTRICTION OF WAITING—
Royston, Various Roads (56).

PROHIBITION OF ENTRY—
Bampton—
(658).
(Revn.) (1351).
Lancaster, Back George Street (48).
Maidenhead, Castle Hill (758).

PROHIBITION OF EXIT—
Darton (1246).

PROHIBITION OF GOODS VEHICLES—
Brampton, Warren Bank (46).

PROHIBITION OF LEFT-HAND TURN—
Peterborough, Albert Place (1341).

PROHIBITION OF RIGHT-HAND TURN—
Altrincham, Shaftesbury Avenue (1375).
Beaconsfield, Bucks. (1866).
Bodicote, Oxfordshire (1513).
Colchester, Cymbeline Way (892).
Copdock, London Road (1890).
Coventry, Kenpas Highway—
(893).
(Revn.) (1362).
Crosby, Seaforth Road (1925).
Faxton, Level Crossing (1617).
Guildford, Ladymead (956).
Hebden Bridge (267).
High Wycombe, High Street (Revn.) (1595).
Loughborough, Leicester Road (1126).
Newcastle-under-Lyme, Talke Road (1452).
Peterborough, London Road (1249).
Potters Bar, Barnet By-Pass (1868).
St. Albans, North Orbital Road (1474).
Sale, Cross Street (54).
Stretford, Chester Road (1802).
Tyldesley, East Lancashire Road (891).
West Moors, Ringwood Road (1360).

---

*Not printed for sale in the S.I. series.

†This instrument was printed and put on sale.

Class 1.—Roads, Bridges, Road Traffic and Rights of Way—*cont.*

(4) Traffic Regulation—*cont.*

(*a*) England and Wales* —*cont.*

(*i*) *General Regulation—cont.*

PROHIBITION OF RIGHT-HAND TURNS AND U-TURNS—
Gosforth, Great North Road (1229).

PROHIBITION OF RIGHT-HAND TURNS AND U-TURNS AND PRESCRIBED ROUTES—
Oxford, Northern By-Pass (1832).

PROHIBITION OF U-TURNS—
Cambridge, Elizabeth Way (2014).
Hampreston, Ringwood Road (1374).
Northwich By-Pass (1453).
Nut Hill, West Riding of Yorkshire (120).
Rayleigh, Southend Arterial Road (55).
Slough (10).
Watford, North-Western Avenue (1085).
Worsley, East Lancashire Road—
(3).
(No. 2) (1948).

PROHIBITION OF WAITING—
Barham, Kent (1074).
Boston, Spilsby Road (967).
Box, Wiltshire (1597).
Broadoak (789).
Broxbourne, High Road and High Street, Hoddesdon (504).
Cannock, Walsall Road (1462).
Cheltenham (Promenade and Montpelier Walk) (1512).
Chudleigh (485).
Claydon, Greyhound Corner (1396).
Colchester, Ipswich Road (2016).
Coventry (889).
Cricklade, High Street and Calcutt Street (1865).
Cross Hands, Carmarthen Road (2173).
Derby, Burton Road (1671).
Dunstable, High Street North (762).
Earn, Bridge of (1608).
Eastburn and Steeton, Various Roads (1595).
East Dereham, Norfolk (2015).
Ewloe, Holywell Road—
(411).
(Variation) (1097).
Folkestone—
(850).
Sandgate Esplanade, Hill Road (1673).
Frodsham, High Street (840).
Froncysyllte, Llangollen Road (431).
Gravesend, Watling Street (1051).
Haydon Bridge, Ratcliffe Road (1598).
Hilton, Main Street and Derby Road (1893).
Hoddesdon (504).
Kenilworth, New Street (559).
Knutsford, Toft Road (581).
Llanymynech (24).
Longbenton, Great North Road (1313).
Lower Fishguard (1456).
Marlborough (877).
Micklefield (1451).
Northchurch, High Street (672).
Norton, Yorkshire (1167).
Nuneaton, Camp Hill Road and Coleshill Road, Harthill (1815).
Peterborough, Lincoln Road (1192).
Petersfield, Dragon Street (2140).
Rawtenstall (763).
Red Lodge, West Suffolk (1889).
Ripley, Various Roads (1596).
St. Clears, Tenby Road (410).
Stanstead Mountfitchet, Silver Street (841).
Swaffham, Lynn Road, Lynn Street, Market Place and Margate Street (2136).
Talgarth, Various Streets (1428).
Thirsk, Topcliffe Road and Westgate (35).
Wilnecote (1383).
Wormley, High Road (578).

PROHIBITION OF WAITING (CLEARWAYS)—
A.2 and A.282 (Variation) (1390).
Birmingham—Great Yarmouth (795).
Chester—Bangor (933).
Exeter—Leeds (1283).
Folkestone—Honiton (1314).
Hungerford—Gloucester—Ross—Hereford (1064).
Kings Lynn—Sleaford—Newark (2033).
Liverpool—Preston—Leeds (965).
London—Cambridge—King's Lynn (2086).
London—Edinburgh—Thurso—
(894).
(No. 2) (2005).
(No. 3) (2006).
London, Fishguard—
(1484).
Golden Valley By-Pass (442).
London—Folkestone—Dover—
(761).
(Dartford) (1676).
London—Great Yarmouth (1927).
Newport—Monmouth—Ross-on-Wye—Worcester (Wales) (No. 1) (204).
North West of Doncaster—Wakefield—Bradford—Skipton—Kendal (1858).
Winchester—Preston (1950).

PROHIBITION OF WAITING AND LOADING—
Keith (2145).
Stevenston (1583).
Vale of Leven (1643).

PROHIBITION OF WAITING AND LOADING AND NO ENTRY—
Millerston and Stepps (1765).

PROHIBITION OF WAITING, LOADINGANDUNLOADING—
Boston, Various Roads (2141).
Gosforth, High Street and Great North Road (1803).
Swallownest (865).
Trentham, Stone Road (1248).

PROHIBITION OF WAITING AND RESTRICTION OF LOADING AND UNLOADING—
Altrincham, Manchester Road (1155).
Sale, Washway Road (123).

PROHIBITION OF WAITING AND RIGHT-HAND TURN—
Nottingham, Western Boulevard and Valley Road (2028).

PROHIBITION AND RESTRICTION OF WAITING—
Arundel, Sussex, Various Roads (1659).
Batheaston, Somerset (1997).
Cannock, Walsall Road and Market Place (579).
Folkestone (1562).
Harwarden, Highway and Glynne Way (1345).
Hebden Bridge, Mytholmroyd and Luddenden Foot (269).
Hove and Portslade-by-Sea (1589).
Hythe (1838).
Ilchester (12).
Lancaster, Various Roads (1431).
Longrock (955).
Market Deeping and Deeping St. James (1873).
Mytholmroyd and Luddenden Foot (269).
Newmarket, High Street and Bury Road (1310).
Nuneaton, Midland Road (1460).
Ormskirk, Various Roads—
(876).
(Variation) (1785).
Rainhill, Warrington Road (1886).
Rhayader, Various Roads (466).
Ross-on-Wye, Gloucester Road (576).
St. Columb Major—
(757).
(Variation) (1563).
Scarborough, Various Roads (1277).
Selby, Various Roads (1324).
Wretham, High Street (664).

*Not printed for sale in the S.I. series.

Class 1.—Roads, Bridges, Road Traffic and Rights of Way—*cont.*

(4) Traffic Regulation—*cont.*

(*a*) ENGLAND AND WALES*—*cont.*

(*i*) *General Regulation—cont.*

PROHIBITION AND RESTRICTION OF WAITING, LOADING AND UNLOADING—
- Bedford, Various Roads (292).
- Bridgwater, Various Roads (1952).
- Cambridge, Various Roads (1575).
- Denton, Manchester Road and Hyde Road (1139).
- Dover, Various Roads—
  - (604).
  - (Variation) (1372).
- Gillingham and Chatham, Various Roads (2148).
- Gloucester (1672).
- St. Albans (1312).
- Shrewsbury, Various Streets (1496).
- Stroud, Various Roads (1722).
- Swindon and Pendlebury, Chorley Road (1854).
- Taunton, Various Roads (977).
- Warminster, Various Roads (788).
- West Bridgford, Various Roads (786).
- Whaley Bridge (2172).

RESTRICTION OF WAITING—
- Abergavenny, Hereford Road (1359).
- Appleby, The Sands (1610).
- Ashbourne, Station Street and Derby Road (1182).
- Batley (787).
- Belper (1783).
- Bushey, North Western Avenue (6).
- Cheltenham, College Road (520).
- Chorley, Preston Road (1924).
- Horncastle (521).
- Kettering, St. Mary's Road (1181).
- King's Lynn, Wisbech Road and Hardwick Road (1637).
- Llangollen, Berwyn Street, Regent Street and Queen Street (1204).
- Nantgarw, Cardiff Road (Revn.) (38).
- Newburn, Herxham Road (11).
- New Romney, Lydd Road and High Street (978).
- Newbridge, Newbridge Road (2168).
- Newton Hill, Leeds Road (1408).
- Norwich, Dereham Road (1721).
- Radlett, Watling Street (1867).
- Sawbridgeworth, London Road and Cambridge Road (72).
- Sittingbourne, West Street (1627).
- Standish, Preston Road, High Street and Wigan Road (1459).
- Stowmarket, Various Streets (1639).

RESTRICTION OF WAITING, LOADING AND UNLOADING—
- Cheadle, Various Roads (1342).
- Cheltenham, Shurdington Road (1373).
- Ely, St Mary's Street (1463).
- Fulwood, Garstang Road (1361).
- Ipswich, Various Roads (849).
- Slough (106).

TRAFFIC REGULATION—
- Abingdon (1154).
- Aylesbury, Various Roads (1250).
- Brigg (1949).
- Chippenham, Various Roads (785).
- Oswestry, Various Streets (1674).
- Totton, Various Roads (322).

WEIGHT RESTRICTION—
- Beverley, North Bar (Variation) (790).
- Cambridge, Various Roads (1998).

Secretary of State—Orders under Road Traffic Regulation Act 1967 (c. 76), s. 6.

PRESCRIBED ROUTES—
- Ealing, Hanger Lane and North Circular Road (728).
- Enfield, Great Cambridge Road—
  - (1702).
  - (No. 2) (1936).
- Havering, Southend Arterial Road (1536).
- Redbridge, Eastern Avenue (1170).

PROHIBITION OF CYCLING—
- Redbridge, Eastern Avenue and Woodford Avenue (1701).

RESTRICTION OF TRAFFIC—
- Ealing and Brent, North Circular Road (1183).
- Haringey, Great Cambridge Road (1107).
- Newham, East Ham and Barking By-Pass (1407).

(*ii*) *Miscellaneous restrictions*

Trunk Roads (Restricted Roads) Orders made by Secretary of State under Road Traffic Regulation Act 1967 (c. 76) ss. 72(3), 73(1), 84D.

No. 1 A.259 Dymchurch (330).
No. 2 A.69 Heddon-on-the-Wall (640).
No. 3 A.50 Sudbury (1014).

Trunk Roads (40 m.p.h. Speed Limit) Orders made by Secretary of State under Road Traffic Regulation Act 1967 (c. 76), ss. 72(3), 73(1), 74(1), 84D, 108.

No. 1	A.18	Edenthorpe (97).
No. 2	A.453	Nottingham (119).
No. 3	A.1079	Bishop Burton (158).
No. 4	A.18	Great Limber (278).
No. 5	A.40	Stokenchurch (277).
No. 6	A.64	Tadcaster (323).
No. 7	A.259	Dymchurch (345).
No. 8	A.15	Peterborough (336).
No. 9	A.41	Kings Langley (338).
No. 10	A.2	Bexley (417).
No. 11	A.4	Quemerford (441).
No. 12	A.69	West Denton (505).
No. 13	A.19	York (540).
No. 14	A.57	Denton (794).
No. 15	A.16	Stickney (864).
No. 16	A.6	Disley (961).
No. 17	A.650	Morley (1127).
No. 18	A.439	Salford Priors (1140).
No. 19	A.30	Summercourt (1256).
No. 20	A.54	Kelsall (1262).
No. 21	A.30	Cheriton Cross (1320).
No. 22	A.51	Nantwich (1321).
No. 23	A.34	Grea tBarr (1409).
No. 24	A.259	Bexhill (1476).
No. 25	A.630	Hooton Roberts (1490).
No. 26	A.57	Rainhill (1495).
No. 27	A.18	Melton Ross (1535).
No. 28	A.46	Cheltenham (1561).
No. 29	A.38	Bittaford (1611).
No. 30	A.30	Sunningdale (1618).
No. 31	A.35	Wilmington (1762).
No. 32	A.38	Streethay (1860).
No. 33	A.523	Macclesfield (1887).
No. 34	A.596	Workington (1934).
No. 35	A.30	Crockernwell (1929).
No. 36	A.638	Bentley (2087).

*Not printed for sale in the S.I. series.

Class 1.—Roads, Bridges, Road Traffic and Rights of Way—*cont.*

(4) Traffic Regulation—*cont.*

(*a*) ENGLAND AND WALES*—*cont.*

(*ii*) *Miscellaneous restrictions—cont.*

Trunk Road (40 m.p.h. Speed Limit) Orders made by Secretary of State under Road Traffic Regulation Act 1967 (c. 76), ss. 74(1), 108.

No. 1 A.470 Glamorgan (186).
No. 2 A.487 Aberystwyth.
No. 3 A.477 Sageston (432).
No. 4 A.494 Loggerheads (1205).
No. 5 A.4056 and A.48 Cardiff (1611).

Trunk Roads (50 m.p.h. Speed Limit) Orders made by Secretary of State under Road Traffic Regulation Act 1967 (c. 76), s. 74(1).

No. 1 A.46 Warwick (359).
No. 2 A.38 Dursley (693).
No. 3 A.27 Falmer (878).
No. 4 A.12 East Suffolk (938).
No. 5 A.23 Newtimber (1008).
No. 6 A.56—A.556 Bowdon (1261).
No. 7 A.5 Warwick (1996).

Trunk Roads (50 m.p.h. Speed Limit) (England) (Variation) Orders made by Secretary of State under Road Traffic Regulation Act 1967 (c. 76), ss. 74(1) and 84D(1).

No. 1 A.61 Tankersley (1286).
No. 2 A.1 Huntingdon, Peterborough and Bedford (1711).
No. 3 A.38 Tewkesbury (1906).
No. 4 A.10 Cambridgeshire (1907).

(*iii*) *Temporary restrictions*

Secretary of State—Orders under Road Traffic Regulation Act 1967 (c. 76), ss. 12, 108.

CLOSURE—
Settle Footbridge (1322).

NO RIGHT-TURN—
Greenock, Spango Valley (2134).

ONE-WAY—
Cambridge, Magdalene Street (481).
Cardigan, North Road (94).
Hythe, East Street (722).
Market Harborough (1315).
Sonning Cutting (1472).
Stowmarket, Combs Ford (929).
Streatley, Barbon Cutting (1276).
Wetherby (1999).

PRESCRIBED ROUTES—
Barnet, West Hendon Broadway (1830).

PROHIBITION OF DRIVING—
Bedale, Yorkshire (316).
Fareham, West Street, Porchester (337).
Swanley By-Pass (931).

PROHIBITION OF FOOT PASSENGERS—
Pontlliw Railway Bridge, Glamorgan (1931).

PROHIBITION OF LEFT-HAND TURN—
Plympton By-Pass (954).
Shrewsbury, High Street (358).

PROHIBITION OF RIGHT-HAND TURN—
Crosby, Crosby Road South and Seaforth Road (821).

PROHIBITION OF TRAFFIC—
Altrincham Level Crossing—
(121).
(No. 2) (764).
Ashburton By-Pass—
(47).
(No. 2) (1612).
Barnet, North Circular Road (580).
Bawtry, West Riding of Yorkshire (542).
Beverly, Toll Gavel (1624).
Brent, North Circular Road—
(734).
(No. 2) (1872).
Bridestowe, East Bridge (314).
Bromsgrove, Hanover Street (1047).

PROHIBITION OF TRAFFIC—*cont.*
Buttington Bridge, Montgomeryshire (1828).
Cannock, Watling Street (1989).
Dolgellau—Bala—Ruthin—Queensferry—South of Birkenhead (A.494)—
(528).
(No. 2)(590).
Ealing, Western Avenue—
(949).
(No. 2) (1100).
(No. 3) (1278).
Findern, Burton Road (122).
Gloucestershire, Berkely Road (635).
Greenock—Monkton (1824).
Harcombe, New Exeter Road (682).
Haydock, East Lancashire Road (1851).
Hexham, Dilston Level Crossing (639).
Hogarth Flyover (651).
Kington Level Crossing (994).
Kirkby, East Lancashire Road—
(1044).
(No. 2) (1457).
(No. 3) (1590).
Litherland, Church Road (838).
London—Basingstoke Motorway (M.3) (1511).
London—Oxford Motorway (M.40)—
(705).
(No. 2) (1558).
London–South Wales Motorway (M.4) (704).
London–South Wales Motorway (M.4) and Birmingham–Bristol Motorway (M.5) (1560).
London–Yorkshire Motorway (M.1) Northamptonshire and Leicestershire (930).
M.1 Motorway—
(652).
(No. 2) (1043).
(No. 2) (Amdt.) (1168)
(No. 3) (1559)
M.4 Motorway—
(1228).
(No. 2) (1343).
Market Weighton (105).
Merstham, Rockshaw Road Bailey Bridge (1669)
Oswestry, Ifton Colliery Railway Bridge (483).
Penrith, Scotland Road and Strickland Gate (159).
Plympton St. Mary (1658).

*Not printed for sale in the S.I. series.

Class 1.—Roads, Bridges, Road Traffic and Rights of Way—*cont.*

(4) Traffic Regulation—*cont.*

(*a*) ENGLAND AND WALES*—*cont.*

(*iii*) *Temporary Restrictions—cont.*

PROHIBITION OF TRAFFIC—*cont.*
- Raglan–Abergavenny–Brecon–Llandovery (A.40) (1827).
- Ross By-Pass (950).
- Ross Spur Motorway—
  - (1046).
  - (No. 2) (1432).
- Rowsley, Derbyshire (98).
- St. Columb Major, Various Roads (1884).
- St. Thomas, Haldon Hill (312).
- South of Haysgate–East of Christchurch Special Road (M.4) (522).
- Theale—
  - (1247).
  - (Variation) (1389).
- Turvey, Bedford Road (605).
- Walton-le-Dale, Bamber Bridge Station Level Crossing (1340).
- Weldon (1564)
- Yeovil, South Petherton Bridge—
  - (313).
  - (Variation)—
    - (365).
    - (No. 2) (671).

PROHIBITION OF TRAFFIC AND ONE-WAY TRAFFIC—
- Whitfield, Gloucestershire—
  - (541).
  - (No. 2) (1514).

PROHIBITION OF TRAFFIC AND PROHIBITION OF OVERTAKING—
- M.5 Motorway—
  - (1588).
  - Halesowen (1638).
  - Near Quinton (315).
  - New Tewkesbury (321).
- M.50 Motorway Near Tewkesbury (440).

PROHIBITION OF WAITING, LOADING AND UNLOADING AND ONE-WAY TRAFFIC—
- Shrewsbury, Wyle Cop (700).

PROHIBITION AND RESTRICTION OF TRAFFIC—
- Hereford, Ross Road (148).

RESTRICTION OF TRAFFIC—
- Barnet, North Circular Road—
  - (138).
  - (No. 2) (653).
- Barnet and Brent, West Hendon Broadway (1784).
- Bexley, Rochester Way—
  - (96).
  - (No. 2) (147).
- Brent, North Circular Road (1626).
- Cardiff, Western Avenue (1869).
- Havering, Southend Arterial Road—
  - (335).
  - (No. 2) (1045).
- Hounslow—
  - Bath Road (334).
  - Great West Road—
    - (336).
    - (No. 2) (429).
    - (No. 3) (1185).
  - Various Roads (1371).
- Kingston-upon-Thames, Malden Way (1534).
- London–South Wales Motorway (M.4) (456).
- M.6 Motorway, Croft Interchange (1935).
- Newham—
  - Beckton Road (1670).
  - Beckton Road and East Ham and Barking By-Pass (2027).
- Oxfordshire, Old Woodstock Bridge (360).
- St. Albans—
  - Chequer Street (1169).
  - Holywell Hill (996).
  - St. Peter's Street (1473).
- Yorkshire, West Riding—
  - (634).
  - (Variation) (1798).

SPEED LIMIT—
- Ffynnon, Pembrokeshire (326).
- Trunk Road (A.38) (No. 1) (293).

TRAFFIC REGULATION—
- Camborne, Various Streets (1885).
- Lichfield (1080).
- St. Thomas, Haldon Hill (1098).

WEIGHT RESTRICTION—
- Buckland Bridge, Bucks. (1988).
- Dover, Limekiln Road (279).
- Teesside, Mandale Road (482).
- Thurrock, Hairpin Bridge (1973).

(*iv*) *Experimental traffic schemes*

Secretary of State—Orders under Road Traffic Regulation Act 1967 (*c. 76*), *ss. 9, 84D*(*1*), *108.*

BOX JUNCTION—
- Thirsk, Westgate and Market Place (36).

BOX JUNCTIONS AND PROHIBITION OF RIGHT-HAND TURN—
- Malton, Yorkersgate and Castlegate (598).

ONE-WAY TRAFFIC
- Camarthen, Coracle Way and Carmarthen Bridge (650).
- Peterborough, Bridge Street (577).
- Wimborne Minster (966).

PRESCRIBED ROUTES—
- Barnet, Edgware Way (1471).

PRESCRIBED ROUTES—*cont.*
- Ealing—
  - Hanger Lane and North Circular Road (Revn.) (727).
  - Western Circus (1945).
- Enfield, Great Cambridge Road (1066).
- Kingston-upon-Thames, Tolworth Rise (1576).
- Redbridge, Eastern Avenue (1905).

PROHIBITION OF DRIVING—
- Hythe, High Street (2149).

PROHIBITION OF TRAFFIC—
- Kingston-upon-Thames, Malden Way (692).

TRAFFIC REGULATION—
- Stockton and Thornaby—
  - (1255).
  - (Variation) (2171).

---

*Not printed for sale in the S.I. series.

Class 1.—Roads, Bridges, Road Traffic and Rights of Way—*cont.*

(4) Traffic Regulation—*cont.*

(*b*) SCOTLAND*

(i) General regulation

Secretary of State—Orders under Road Traffic Regulation Act 1967 (c. 76), ss. 1(1), (3), (12), 84D.

CLEARWAYS—
Glasgow–Carlisle Trunk Road (160).

PROHIBITION OF OVERTAKING—
Dunkeld Bridge (A.9) (695).

PROHIBITION OF WAITING—
A.75 at Minnigaff (1386).
Auchtermuchty (355).
Kirkoswald (742).
Selkirk (733).
Thirsk, Topcliffe Road and Westgate (35).

PROHIBITION OF WAITING AND LOADING—
Linlithgow (959).
Musselburgh (572).
Vale of Leven (637).

RESTRICTION OF WAITING—
Bucksburn (125).
Fort William (612).

TRAFFIC REGULATION—
Lanark (1881).

(ii) Miscellaneous restrictions

Glasgow Inner Ring Road (West and North Flanks) (Speed Limit) Regs., *made by Secretary of State under Road Traffic Regulation Act 1967 (c. 76), s. 13*...(951)†

Trunk Roads (Restricted Roads) S.O., *made by Secretary of State under Road Traffic Regulation Act 1967 (c. 76), ss. 72, 73*...(696).

Secretary of State—Trunk Roads (40 m.p.h. Speed Limit) Orders made under Road Traffic Regulation Act 1967 (c. 76), s. 74.

No. 1 A.76 Closeburn (678).
No. 2 A.82 Onich (1294).
No. 3 A.75 Castle Douglas (1665).
No. 4 A.96 Lhanbryde (1792).
No. 5 A.9 Pitlochry (2098).
No. 6 A.9 Aberuthven (2132).

(iii) Temporary restrictions

Secretary of State—Orders under Road Traffic Regulation Act 1967 (c. 76), s. 12.

PROHIBITION OF TRAFFIC—
Blackford Level Crossing (1586).
Kinross, Kincardine Bridge (777).
Penrith, Scotland Road and Stricklandgave (159).
Renfrew By-Pass (M.8) New Arkleston Road (89).

REGULATION OF ACCESS—
A.9 Turnhouse (573).

WEIGHT RESTRICTION—
A.75 Various Bridges (31).
A.76 Newbridge, Dumfriesshire (32).

WEIGHT RESTRICTION—*cont.*
A.77 Ayrshire, Bridge Hill—
(33).
(173).
A.78 (1002).
A.83 (1030).
A.702 (1001).
Edinburgh–Carlisle Trunk Road (Various Bridges) (236).
Inverness–Wick Trunk Road (Various Bridges) (1000).

---

*Not printed for sale in the S.I. series.

†This instrument (951) was printed and put on sale.

CLASS 2.—RAILWAYS, TRAMWAYS AND TROLLEY VEHICLES

Light Railway Orders made by Secretary of State under Light Railways Act 1896 (c. 48) (enabling sections in square brackets) as amended by Light Railways Act 1912 (c. 19) and Railways Act 1921 (c. 55).

British Railways Board—
(Totton Hythe and Fawley) [7, 9, 10, 24] (1619).
(Whitby and Pickering) [7, 9, 10, 18] (1129).
Corringham Light Railway (Winding-up) [7] (1494).

Secretary of State—Orders under Transport Act 1968 (c. 73), s. 20.

Merseyside Passenger Transport Area (Railway Passenger Services) (1114).
South East Lancashire and North East Cheshire Passenger Transport Area (Railway Passenger Services) (1111).
Tyneside Passenger Transport Area (Railway Passenger Services) (1113).
West Midlands Passenger Transport Area (Railway Passenger Services) (1115).

CLASS 3.—RIVERS AND INLAND WATERWAYS

(1) *Land drainage schemes and orders*
(2) *Rivers (prevention of pollution)*
(3) *Salmon and freshwater fisheries*

(1) Land drainage schemes and orders

General Drainage Charge (Ascertainment) O., *made by Minister of Agriculture, Fisheries and Food under Agriculture (Miscellaneous Provisions) Act 1968 (c. 34), ss. 22(2)(4), 51(4)*...(501).

Lower Avon Navigation Trust (Conferment of Powers to make Byelaws) O., *made by the Secretary of State under Transport Act 1968 (c. 73), s. 113* ... (765).

Trent and Lincolnshire River Authies. (Alteration of Areas) O., *made by Secretary of State and Minister of Agriculture, Fisheries and Food under Water Resources Act 1963 (c. 38), s. 10* ... (1641).

Minister of Agriculture, Fisheries and Food—Orders under Land Drainage Act 1930 (c. 44), s. 4, and, where indicated in square brackets, s. 14.*

Cumberland River Authority—
(Abolition of the River Marron Internal Drainage District) [s. 14] (901).
(Abolition of the Upper Derwent Internal Drainage District) [s. 14] (1059).
Great Ouse River Authority (Littleport and Downham Internal Drainage District) [s. 14] (404).
Lancashire River Authority—
(Reconstitution of the Croston Internal Drainage Bd.) [s. 14] (1052).
(River Kent Estuary Internal Drainage District) [s. 14] (948).
(Windermoor Internal Drainage District) [s. 14] (434).
Lincolnshire River Authority—
(Alford Drainage District) [s. 14] (1667).
(Witham Fourth District Internal Drainage District) [s. 14] (1011).
Welland and Nene River Authority (Alteration of Boundaries of the Hundred of Wisbech and the Wingland Internal Drainage Districts) [s. 14] (935).

Secretary of State—Orders made under Water Resources Act 1963 (c. 38), s. 133.

Furness Water Bd. (1289).
Southampton Corporation Water—
(No. 2) (738).
(No. 3) (1767).
West Glamorgan Water Bd. (Cray Reservoir) (768).
Winchester Corporation Water (939).

---

*Not printed for sale in the S.I. series.

Class 3.—Rivers and inland waterways—*cont.*

(2) Rivers (prevention of pollution)

Secretary of State—Orders under Rivers (Prevention of Pollution) Act 1951 (c. 64), (enabling sections in square brackets).

Rivers Pollution (Rivers Rheidol, Ystwyth and Tributaries)—
(No. 1) [s. 2(4)] (828).
(No. 2) [s. 1(2)] (829).

(3) Salmon and freshwater fisheries

Diseases of Fish (Infected Area) No. 1 O., *made by Minister of Agriculture, Fisheries and Food under Diseases of Fish Act 1937 (c. 33), s. 2* ... (406).

Minister of Agriculture, Fisheries and Food—Orders under Salmon and Freshwater Fisheries Act 1923 (c. 16), ss. 37† and 38†.
East Suffolk and Norfolk River Authy. (Fisheries) Revn. (407).
Usk River Authy. (Fisheries) (1681).

CLASS 4.—SHIPPING, HARBOURS, DOCKS, PORTS, &c.

(1) *Dockyard ports*
(2) *Harbour development and improvement*
(3) *Pilotage*
(4) *Revision of charges*

(1) Dockyard ports

Clyde Dockyard Port of Gareloch and Loch Long (Amdt.) O., *made under Dockyard Ports Regulation Act 1865 (c. 125), s. 7; as amended by Defence (Transfer of Functions) Act 1964 (c. 15), s. 3* ... (210).

(2) Harbour development and improvement

Secretary of State—Harbour Revision Orders made under Harbours Act 1964 (c. 40), s. 14†.

Cowes Harbour (806).
Manchester Ship Canal (191).
Port of London Authority (Borrowing Powers) (1227).
Tees and Hartlepool Port Authority (2004).

(3) Pilotage

Clyde Pilotage (Amdt.) O., *made by Secretary of State under Pilotage Act 1913 (c. 31), s. 7* ... (887).

(4) Revision of charges*

Mersey Tunnels O., *made by Secretary of State under Mersey Tunnel Act 1925 (c. 110), s. 66* ... (1042).

Secretary of State—Revision of Charges Orders under Transport Charges, etc. (Miscellaneous Provisions) Act 1954 (c. 64), s. 6.

Blyth Ferries (1951).
Dartmouth–Kingswear Higher Ferry (235).
Merseyside Passenger Executive (Seacombe and New Brighton Ferries) (112).
Pembrokeshire County Council (Neyland–Hobbs Point Ferry) (1852).
Port of Tyne Authority (Market Place Ferry) (1143).
Tamar Bridge and Torpoint Ferry Tolls (895).

---

*Not printed for sale in the S.I. series.

†Orders made under this section are liable to special Parliamentary procedure.

(1) *Accounts and audit*
(2) *Adaption of enactments*
(3) *Clean air*
(4) *Fire services*
(5) *Housing*
(6) *Licensing*
(7) *Local government areas*
(8) *Pensions*
(9) *Police*
(10) *Powers and duties of local authorities*
(11) *Miscellaneous*

(1) Accounts and audit*

Secretary of State—Amalgamation of Fund Orders made under Local Govt. (Miscellaneous Provisions) Act 1953 (c. 26), s. 1(4).

Coventry (587).
Denton Urban District (863).
Eton Rural District (642).

(2) Adaption of enactments

Lowestoft (Amdt. of Local Enactments) O., *made by Secretary of State under Public Health Act 1961 (c. 64), s. 82* ... (1915).

(3) Clean air*

Secretary of State—Suspension of Smoke Control Orders made under Clean Air Acts 1956 (c. 52), s. 11; 1968 (c. 62), s. 9.

Ashton-under-Lyne (95).
Castle Ward Rural District (1118).
Church Urban District (14).
Gravesend (69).
Harlow (70).
Middleton (68).
Northfleet Urban District (42).
Rothwell Urban District (1191).
Southport (88).
Stockport (85).

(4) Fire services

Suffolk and Ipswich Fire Services (Combination) (Amdt.) O., *made by Secretary of State under Fire Services Act 1947 (c. 41), ss. 5, 9* ... (1050).

(5) Housing*

County Borough of Plymouth (Town Development) (No. 2) O., *made by Secretary of State under Housing Act 1961 (c. 65), s. 34* ... (2018).

(6) Licensing

Stansted Airport Licensing (Liquor) O., *made by Secretary of State under Licensing Act 1964 (c. 26), s. 87* ... (691).

**Secretary of State—Orders made under Licensing Act 1964 (c. 26), s. 120(4): as amended by Expiring Laws Continuance Act 1970 (c. 58), s. 1(2).*

Coventry Licensing Planning Area (Revn.) (396).
Licensing Planning Area (Revn.) (284).
Southampton Licensing Planning Area (2153).

(7) Local government areas

(*a*) ENGLAND AND WALES

(*i*) *County electorial divisions*

County of Chester (Electoral Divisions) O., *made under Local Govt. Act 1933 (c. 51), s. 11; as amended by Local Govt. Act 1958 (c. 55), sch. 8 para. 3*...(135).

*Not printed for sale in the S.I. series.

Class 5.—Local Government—*cont.*

(7) Local government areas—*cont.*

(*a*) ENGLAND AND WALES*—*cont.*

(*ii*) *Alteration of areas*

Northamptonshire and Northampton (Boundaries) O., *under Local Govt. Act 1933* (*c. 51*), *s. 143; as amended by Local Govt. Act 1958* (*c. 55*), *sch. 8 para. 9.*

(*iii*) *City, Borough and Metropolitan borough wards*

Secretary of State—Orders under London Government Act 1963 (*c. 33*), (*enabling sections in square brackets*).

Camden [Sch. 1 Pt. III paras. 5 and 6] ... (600).
Hounslow (Wards) [Sch. 1 Pt. III para. 1] ... (141).

(*b*) SCOTLAND*

Secretary of State—Local Govt. (*S.*) *Orders made under Local Govt.* (*S.*) *Act 1947* (*c. 43*) (*enabling sections in square brackets*).

(*i*) *County councils and electoral divisions*

West Lothian (Representation of the Burgh of Whitburn) [13 and 372] (1010).

(*ii*) *Burgh councils and wards*

East Kilbride [16(4) and 21(1)] (286).

(8) Pensions*

Mr. Speaker Morrison's Retirement Act 1959 (Pensions Increase) O., *made by Minister for the Civil Service under Pensions* (*Increase*) *Act 1969* (*c. 7*), *s. 1*(*4*), *sch. 2 paras. 12, 14* ... (1414).

(9) Police

Police (Amalgamation) (Amdt. of Specified Schemes) O., *made by Secretary of State under Cts. Act 1971* (*c. 23*), *s. 53*(*7*) ... (2055).

Police (*Amalgamation*) (*Amdt.*) *Orders made by Secretary of State under Police Act 1964* (*c. 48*), *ss. 21, 22.*

Bedfordshire and Luton (2163).
Cheshire, Birkenhead Chester Stockport and Wallasey (2157).
Cumbria (2143).
Dorset and Bournemouth (2061).
Durham (2122).
Dyfed-Powys (2165).
Essex and Southend-on-Sea (2142).
Gwynedd (2146).
Hampshire (2062).
Kent (1916).
Lancashire (2063).
Leicester and Rutland (2064).
Lincolnshire (2164).
Mid-Anglia (2065).
Monmouthshire and Newport (2158).
Norfolk (2123).
Northampton and County (2160).
Northumberland (2066).
Somerset and Bath (2166).
South Wales (2155).
Staffordshire County and Stoke-on-Trent (2077).
Suffolk (2067).
Sussex (2159).
Thames Valley (2076).
Warwickshire and Coventry (2075).
West Mercia (2156).
West Yorkshire (2068).

*Not printed for sale in the S.I. series.

Class 5.—Local Government—*cont.*

(10) Powers and duties of local authorities*

(*a*) General Powers

(*i*) *Borough and district councils*

Wolverhampton (Highways Act 1959) O., *made by Secretary of State under Highways Act 1959* (*c. 25*), *s. 290*(*3*) ... (347).

Secretary of State—Orders under Public Health Act 1875 (*c. 55*), *s. 276, and, where indicated in square brackets, Public Health Acts 1925* (*c. 71*), *s. 4*(*2*), *or Local Government Act 1933* (*c. 51*), *s. 190.*

Amesbury (552).
Brecknock (2060).
Caistor [1925 s. 4] (735).
Caistor [1933 s. 190] (84).
Chepstow (1480).
Cowbridge [1925 s. 4] (897).
Loddon [1933 s. 190] (1565).
Louth (285).
Pershore [1925 s. 4(2)] (206).
Pewsey [1933 s. 190] (1435).
Ripon and Pateley [1925 s. 4(2)] (397).
Ruthin (1395).
St. Faith's and Aylsham [1933 s. 190] (142).
Warminster and Westbury [1933 s. 190] (1540).
West Penwith (1424).

Secretary of State—Declarations under Public Health Acts Amdt. Act 1890 (*c. 59*), *s. 5.*

Axbridge (19).
Dulverton (488).
East Elloe (489).
Frome (1753).
Gipping (458).
Glanford Brigg (699).
Langport (2121).
Lothingland (970).
Samford (812).
South Westmorland (971).
Uttoxeter (599).
Wainford (1274).
Wellingborough (1273).
Wells (771).
Wincanton (1499).
Yeovil (57).

Secretary of State—Orders under Public Health Acts Amdt. Act 1907 (*c. 53*), *s. 3.*

Pleasure Boats (Lymington) (1110).
Seashore Byelaws—
(Gwyrfai) (1550).
(Queenborough-in-Sheppey) (1902).

Secretary of State—Orders under Public Health Act 1936 (*c. 49*), *s. 3.*

Axbridge (611).
Boston (586).
Downham (250).
Gwyfai (898).
Spalding (1587).

Secretary of State—(*Advance Payments for Street Works*) *Orders made under Highways Act 1959* (*c. 25*), *sch. 14 para. 6.*

Cornwall (8).
Glamorgan (703).

(*ii*) *Special expenses*

Secretary of State—Orders under Local Govt. Act 1933 (*c. 51*), *s. 190.*

Battle (1709).
Chepstow (1481).
Easingwold (2059).
Gipping (26).
Ripon and Pateley Bridge (1776).
Spilsby (51).
Thirsk (1599).
Witney (2058).

(*b*) Extension of Powers

Secretary of State—Orders under Local Government Act 1933 (*c. 51*), *s. 271.*

Chichester (1318).
Stourport-on-Severn (776).

(11) Miscellaneous

Bowhouse Incineration Joint Ctee. (S.) O., *made by Secretary of State under Local Govt.* (*S.*) *Act 1947* (*c. 43*), *s. 119*(*4*) ... (2088).

Glasgow Corporation (Burgh Rate Partial Exemptions) (Amdt.) O., *made by Secretary of State under Local Govt.* (*S.*) *Act 1947* (*c. 43*), *s. 224*(*1*) ... (168).

*Not printed for sale in the S.I. series.

Class 5.—Local Government—*cont.*

(11) Miscellaneous—*cont.*

Leicester Corporation Act 1956 (Amdt.) O., *made by Secretary of State under Local Authority Social Services Act 1970* (*c. 47*), *s. 14*(*3*) ... (983).

Lever Park (Rivington Pike Tower Agreement) Approval Instrt., *made by Secretary of State under Lever Park Act 1969* (*c. 36*), *s. 5* ... (811).

Secretary of State—Suspension of Loan Repayment Orders made under Local Govt. (*Financial Provisions etc.*) (*S.*) *Act 1962* (*c. 9*), *s. 6.*

Perth (638).

Secretary of State—Water Undertaking (*Valuation*) *Orders made under General Rate Act 1967* (*c. 9*), *sch. 4 para. 10.*

Craven (1224).
Pembrokeshire (852).
South Wilts. (452).

CLASS 6.—PUBLIC HEALTH

(1) *Authorities*
(2) *National Health Service*

(1) Authorities

Heckmondwike Sewerage O., *made by Secretary of State under Public Health* (*Drainage of Trade Premises*) *Act 1937* (*c. 40*), *s. 12*(*1*) ... (2038).

South Hampshire Main Drainage O., *made by Secretary of State under Public Health Act 1936* (*c. 49*), *s. 6* ... (1606).

Medical Officer of Health—Orders made by Secretary of State under Local Govt. Act 1933 (*c. 51*), *s. 112.*†

Cotswold United Districts (Amdt.) (908).
North Gloucestershire United Districts Revn. (910).
West Gloucestershire United Districts (Amdt.) (909).

(2) National Health Service

(*a*) ENGLAND AND WALES

National Health Service (East Sussex, Eastbourne and Hastings) Executive Council O., *made by Secretary of State under National Health Service Act 1946* (*c. 81*), *s. 31* ... (1548).

Secretary of State—National Health Service Orders made under National Health Service Act 1946 (*c. 81*), *s. 11.*

Bradford Hospital Management Ctee. (177).
Cornwall Hospital Management Ctee. (298).
East Liverpool University Hospital Management Ctee. (697).
Farnham and Brookwood Hospital Management Ctee. (2078).
Maidstone and District Hospital Management Ctee. (1962).
Newcastle University Hospital Management Ctee. (153).
North Sheffield University Hospital Management Ctee. (299).
Plymouth and District Hospital Management Ctee. (276).
Portsmouth Hospital Management Ctee. (1653).
Royal Buckinghamshire and St. John's Hospital Management Ctee. (266).
South West London Hospital Management Ctee. (1488).
Southampton University Management Ctee. (247).
Swindon and District Hospital Management Ctee. (328).
Tunbridge Wells and Leybourne Hospital Management Ctee. (255).
Warrington Hospital Management Ctee. (1438).

---

*Not printed for sale in the S.I. series.

†Orders made under this section are liable to special Parliamentary procedure.

Class 6.—Public Health—*cont.*

(*b*) SCOTLAND

Secretary of State—Endowments Scheme Confirmation Orders made under National Health Service (S.) Act 1947 (c. 27), s. 8(6).

Angus Hospitals (1021).
Edinburgh—
Northern Hospitals Amdt. (708).
Royal Victoria and Associated Hospitals Amdt. (710).
Foresterhill and Associated Hospitals (883).
Royal Infirmary of Edinburgh and Associated Hospitals Amdt. (709).

CLASS 7.—TOWN AND COUNTRY PLANNING, OPEN SPACES, ACCESS TO THE COUNTRYSIDE

(1) *Byelaws under Military Lands Act 1892*
(2) *New Forest*
(3) *Open spaces*

(1) Byelaws under Military Lands Act 1892*

Byelaws made by the Secretary of State under Military Lands Act 1892 (c. 43), Pt. II.

Dockyard Port of Rosyth (917).
Faslane, Coulport and Rhu Narrows (918).
Otterburn Training Area (919).

(2) New Forest

Cadnam–Lymington Road (Power to Enclose) (Appointed Day) O., *made by Secretary of State under New Forest Act 1970 (c. 21), s. 2* ... (280).

(3) Open spaces

Strensall Common (Use for Military Purposes) Regs., *made by Secretary of State under Strensall Common Act 1884, s. 6 and Defence (Transfer of Functions) Act 1964, s. 2* ... (1376).

Secretary of State—Regulations under Parks Regulation (Amdt.) Act 1926 (c. 36), s. 2.

Holyrood Park (593).
Linlithgow Peel and Loch (592).

CLASS 8.—WATER SUPPLY

*Birmingham (Water Charges) O., *made by Secretary of State under Birmingham (Water and Gas) O. 1914, article 1(1)* ... (104).

Secretary of State—Orders made under one or more of the following sections of Water Act 1945 (c. 42), Water Act 1948 (c. 22) and Compulsory Purchase Act 1965 (c. 56).

1945: ss. 9†, 10†, 19, 23†, 32†, 33†, 40, 50.
1948: ss. 2†, 3, 14.
1965: s. 33.

Brighton Corporation (Water Charges) (282).
Bristol Waterworks (1053).
Bucks. Water—
(Hawridge Pumping Station) (1412).
(Mill End Additional Boreholes) (1338).
Cambridge Water (Duxford and Thriplow) (1547).
Central Flintshire Water Bd. (Charges) (1691).
Central Nottinghamshire Water Bd. (421).
Claro Water Bd. (Borehole at Baldersby St. James) (1180).
Colchester and District Water Bd. (Water Charges) (566).
Colne Valley Water (Financial Provisions)—
(986).
(No. 2) (1908).
Coventry, Birmingham and Rugby (1509).
Coventry (Water Charges) (180).

---

†Orders made under this section are liable to special Parliamentary procedure.

*Not printed for sale in the S.I. series.

Class 8.—Water Supply—*cont.*

Craven Water Bd.—
(Charges) (1645).
(Extension of Operation of Byelaws) (654).
(Ponden and Lower Laithe Reservoirs) (497).
(Vale Mills Mains) (310).
Dorset (681).
Durham County Water Bd. (1041).
East Anglian Water (Financial Provisions) (846).
East Devon Water—
(657).
(No. 2) (1317).
(No. 3) (1864).
(Pynes Intake) (1978).
East Shropshire Water Bd.—
(Diddlebury Borehole) (237).
(Tern Hill Boreholes) (2039).
East Yorkshire (Wolds Area) Water Bd. (Etton Borehole No. 2) (1571).
East Yorkshire (Wolds Area) and Kingston upon Hull (Variation of Limits of Supply) (182).
Eastbourne—
(Water Charges) (1268).
Water (Financial Provisions) (1279).
Eden Water Bd. (Cliburn Borehole) (238).
Eryri Water Bd. (Bwrdd Dwr Eryri) (Marchlyn Bach Dam) (1574).
Essex Water (307).
Furness Water Bd. (No. 2) (1311).
Fylde Water Bd.—
(900).
(Extension of Operation of Byelaws) (1546).
Great Ouse (2169).
Herefordshire Water Bd. (1855).
Ipswich Water—
(1439).
(Winston Borehole (1131).
Lee Valley Water (Charges) (565).
Leicester Water (Consolidation, etc.) (1148).
Lune Valley Water Bd. (Charges) (83).
Makerfield Water Bd.—
(Eller Brook) (1231).
(Pocket Nook No. 2 and Lanside Boreholes) (1826).
Metropolitan Water Bd. (251).
Mid Cheshire Water Bd. (1302).
Mid Southern Water (968).
Mid Sussex Water—
(498).
(No. 2) (928).
Newcastle and Gateshead Water (R.A.F. Acklington) (409).
North Derbyshire Water Bd. (River Derwent) (369).
North Devon Water (Stratton) (281).
North East Warwickshire Water Bd. (Charges) (430).
North Lindsey Water—
(1760).
(Winterton Carrs and Hibaldstow) (723).
North West Leicestershire Water Bd. (Charges) (539).
North West Norfolk Water Bd.—
(Amdt.) (1436).
(Sedgeford Borehole) (305).
North West Sussex Water (1572).
North Wilts. Water Bd.—
(Bishops Cannings Borehole) (712).
(Holt Borehole No. 2) (713).
Northallerton and the Dales Water—
(564).
(Charges) (1336).
(Stubbing Nook Borehole) (1385).
Norwich (Royston Bridge and Witton Park) Water (2037).
Oxfordshire and District Water Bd. (Charges) (530).
Portsmouth Water (Financial Provisions) (363).
Rickmansworth and Uxbridge Valley Water (Charges) (567).
Royal Tunbridge Wells Water (Extension of Operation of Byelaws) (1208).
St. Helens (Eccleston Park) (1207).
Scarborough (Westerdale Waterworks) (283).
South Derbyshire Water Bd. (Water Rates) (2030).
South East Breconshire Water Bd.—
(320).
(No. 2) (1400).
South Lincolnshire Water—
(Aslackby and Rippingale) (1337).
(Wilsthorpe and Greatford) (760).
South West Devon Water Bd. (371).
South West Suburban (1718).
Southampton Corporation (568).
Staffordshire Potteries Water Bd.—
(1106).
(Tottenhall Boreholes) (257).
Sunderland and South Shields (514).
Sutton District (270).
Tendring Hundred (Extension of Operation of Byelaws) (982).
Thames Valley Water (Fognam Down Pumping Station) (368).
Thanet (Water Charges) (143).
Watford (Water Charges) (537).
West Cornwall Water Bd. (Charges) (179).
West Pennine Water (Green Vale Pipeline, Littleborough) (1384).
West Shropshire Water Bd. Condover Borehole (1644).
West Shropshire and East Shropshire (Variation of Limits of Supply) (2017).
West Somerset Water Bd. (Charges) (258).
West Suffolk Water Bd. (Honington Airfield) (1646).
Woking (Water Charges) (1258).
Wrexham and East Denbighshire—
(Financial Provisions) (349).
(Water Charges) (350).

**Secretary of State—Drought Orders made under Water Act 1958 (c. 67), s. 1(1), (3), 2(1).*

Kesteven Water Bd. (River Witham) (39).

Mid Calder Water Bd. (1301).

North Devon Water Bd.—
(896).
(No. 2) (999).
(No. 3) (1339).
West Pennine Water Bd. (1853).

Secretary of State—Orders made under one or more of the following sections of Water (S.) Act 1946 (c. 42), (as amended by Water (S.) Act 1949 (c. 31)) and Water (S.) Act 1967 (c. 78).

1946: ss. 21†, 44†.
1967: s. 12.

Argyll Water Bd. (Financial Provisions) (685).

Ayrshire and Bute Water Bd. (Financial Provisions) (646).

East of Scotland Water Bd.—
(Allt Coire, Ardrain, Crianlarich) (515).
(Burn of Ample, Lochearnhead) (1442).
(Financial Provisions) (645).
(Milton Glen Burn, Brig O'Turk) (41).

---

*Not printed for sale in the S.I. series.

†Orders made under this section are liable to special Parliamentary procedure.

Class 8.—Water Supply—*cont.*

Inverness-shire Water Bd.—
(Allt Currachan and Loch na Beinne Moire) (2174).
(Financial Provisions) (766).
(Loch nam Bat and Loch Gorm) (1323).
(Loch Eilean Iain and Loch Fada, Benbecula) (223).
(Loch Strathaid) (1966).
Mid-Scotland Water Bd. (Financial Provisions) (647).
North of Scotland Water Bd.—
(Financial Provisions) (686).
(Loch na Caorach) (2175).
North-East of Scotland Water Bd. (Lower Deveron) (526).
Ross and Cromarty Water Bd. (Financial Provisions) (759).

**Secretary of State—Orders made under Water Act 1958* (c. 67), *s. 1.*

Fife and Kinross Water Bd.—
(River Farg) (Emergency) (1794).
(River Leven) (Emergency) (1793).
North-East of Scotland Water Bd.—
(River Dee) Kincardine O'Neil (Emergency) (1656).
(River Deveron) (Emergency)—
(924).
(Extension) (1944).
(River Don) Kintore (Emergency) (1863).
(River Urie) Inverurie (1862).

CLASS 9.—EDUCATION

Secretary of State—Endowment Schemes made under Education (*S.*) *Act 1962* (*c. 47*), *ss. 118, 125, and, where indicated in square brackets, s. 129.*

Banff Bursary Fund (1232).
Clackmannanshire Educational Trust (Amdt.) [s. 129] (737).
Heriot-Watt College, Edinburgh (1308).

CLASS 10.—LIGHTING, POWER AND HEATING

Mines and Quarries*

Manton Mine Tip O., *made by Secretary of State under Mines and Quarries* (*Tips*) *Act 1969* (*c. 10*), *s. 2*(*3*) ... (879).

(*a*) Special Regulations

Secretary of State—regulations under Mines and Quarries Act 1954 (*c. 70*), *ss. 141, 143 revoking special mines regs.*

Brewers No. 9 (Explosives) (1756).
Close Quarry—
No. 1 (Explosives) (1758).
No. 2 (Explosives) (1759).
Goonamarris (Explosives) (1755).
Hendra (China Stone) No. 2 (Explosives) (1757).
Meldon (Explosives) (976).
Rostowrack (Explosives) (1754).
Slip Quarry (Explosives) (1669).
Wearmouth (Precautions Against Inrushes) (1799).
Wheal Prosper Quarry (Explosives) (1663).

Secretary of State—Special Regulations made under Mines and Quarries Act 1954 (*c. 70*).

regs. relating to automatic shaft signalling (*made under s. 141*):

Coventry (815).

regs. relating to cable reel shuttle cars (*made under ss. 40, 68, 141, 143*):

Ellington (Amdt.) (139).
Horden (18).
Lynemouth (Amdt.) (111).

regs. relating to cinematograph lighting (*made under ss. 68, 141, 143*):

Pye Hill (677).
Sharleston (16).

regs. relating to diesel vehicles (*made under ss. 40, 83, 141, 143*):

Sallet Hole (44).
West Cannock No. 5 (28).

regs. relating to diesel vehicles and storage battery vehicles (*made under ss. 39, 68, 83, 141, 143*):

Winsford Rock Salt (50).

*Not printed for sale in the S.I. series.

Class 10.—Lighting, Power and Heating—*cont.*

Mines and Quarries*—*cont.*

(*a*) Special Regulations—*cont.*

regs. relating to dowcast shafts (made under ss. 141 and 143):

Coventry (815).
Kimblesworth (1840).

regs. relating to electric lighting (made under ss. 68, 141, 143):

Ashington (80).
Castlehill (1834).
Desford (816).
Frances (1841).
Gomersal (772).
Murton (17).
Solsgirth (1787).

regs. relating to friction winding (made under ss. 47, 141, 143):

Dawdon (81).
Wyndham/Western (866).

regs. relating to methane gas-fired steam boilers (made under ss. 84, 141, 143):

Silverwood (1325).

regs. relating to precautions against inrushes (made under ss. 141, 143):

Bagworth (1334).
Blackburn Fell Drift (Amdt.) (1379).

regs. relating to refuge holes (made under ss. 40, 141, 143):

Littleton (1703).

regs. relating to rope hauled sledge (made under ss. 47, 141, 143):

Riddings (1704).

regs. relating to rope haulage (made under ss. 47, 141, 143):

Ashington (1578).
Shillbottle (1579).

regs. relating to shafts (made under ss. 141, 143):

Coventry (No. 1) (319).
Frickley/South Elmsall (No. 3) (1789).
Wheal Jane (No. 2) (2081).

regs. relating to storage battery locomotives (made under ss. 68, 83, 141):

Mount Wellington (1270.)

regs. relating to upcast shafts (made under ss. 141, 143):

Whittle (318).

regs. relating to winding and haulage apparatus (made under ss. 141, 143):

Methley Junction (2093).

CLASS 11.—ADMINISTRATION OF JUSTICE

Petty sessional divisions

(*a*) Petty Sessions Generally

Secretary of State—Petty Sessional Divisions Orders made under Justices of the Peace Act 1949 (c. 101), s. 18.

Cheshire (1084).
Herefordshire (464).
South-West London (495).

*Not printed for sale in the S.I. series.

Class 11.—Administration of Justice—*cont.*

(*b*) Juvenile Court Panels*

Secretary of State—Juvenile Court Panel Orders made under Children and Young Persons Act 1933 (*c. 12*), *sch. 2 para. 4.*

Bath (301).
Furness (660).
Norfolk (1808).
Stratford and Henley (425).

CLASS 12.—AGRICULTURE, FISHERIES AND FORESTRY

(1) *Diseases of animals*
(2) *Forestry*
(3) *Protection of birds*

(1) Diseases of animals*

Importation of Pedigree Animals (No. 1) O., *made by Minister of Agriculture, Fisheries and Food and Secretary of State under Diseases of Animals Act 1950* (*c. 36*), *ss. 24 and 26* ... (1310).

Minister of Agriculture, Fisheries and Food or Secretary of State—Orders made under Diseases of Animals Act 1950 (*c. 36*), *s. 5.*

Brucellosis (Eradication Areas)—
(E. and W.)—
(533).
(Amdt.) (1716).
(S.)—
(571).
(No. 2) (2144).

(2) Forestry

Forestry Commission Byelaws *made by Forestry Commissioners under Forestry Act 1967* (*c. 10*), *s. 46* ... (997).

(3) Protection of birds

Wild Birds (Gibraltar Point Sanctuary) O., *made by Secretary of State under Protection of Birds Acts 1954* (*c. 30*), *s. 3*(*1*); *1967* (*c. 46*), *s. 4*(*2*) ... (557).

CLASS 13.—MISCELLANEOUS

(1) Atomic Energy and Radioactive Substances

Urenco Limited (Designation) O., *made by Secretary of State under Atomic Energy Authority Act 1971* (*c. 11*), *s. 19*(*2*) ... (1434).

(2) Banks and banking

Co-Operative Bank Act 1971 (Appointed Day) O., *made by Secretary of State under Co-operative Bank Act 1971* (*c. xxii*), *s. 3*(*1*) ... (962).

National Westminster Bank (North Central Finance and Lombard Banking) Act 1971 (Appointed Day) O., *made by Secretary of State under National Westminster Bank* (*North Central Finance and Lombard Banking*) *Act 1971* (*c. xxiii*), *s. 3* ... (1173).

(3) Charities

Charities (Highland Society of London) O., *made by Secretary of State under Charities Act 1960* (*c. 58*), *s. 19*(*1*) ... (1982).

Charities (Richmond Parish Charity Lands) O., *made by Secretary of State under Charities Act 1960* (*c. 58*), *s. 19*(*2*) ... (805).

*Not printed for sale in the S.I. series.

Class 13.—Miscellaneous—*cont.*

(4) Civil aviation

Airport Traffic (Edinburgh) O., *made by Secretary of State under Airports Authy. Act 1965* (*c. 16*), *s. 12; Civil Aviation Act 1968* (*c. 61*), *s. 10*) ... (551).

Civil Aviation (Designation of Aerodromes) O., *made by Secretary of State under Civil Aviation Act 1971* (*c. 75*), *s. 29*(*11*) *and Interpretation Act 1889* (*c. 63*), *s. 37* ... (1687).

Air Navigation (*Restriction of Flying*)*—Regulations made by Secretary of State under Air Navigation O. 1970, art. 61.*

Chequers—
(1552).
(No. 2) (1719).

Long Kesh Aerodrome (1609).

(5) Cotton industry*

Cotton Industry War Memorial Trust Act (Amdt.) O., *made by Secretary of State under Cotton Industry War Memorial Trust Act 1947* (*c. v*), *s. 2* ... (380).

(6) Decimal currency

Secretary of State—Orders made under Decimal Currency Act 1969 (*c. 19*), *s. 11.*

Amdt. of Local Enactments etc. (25).
Bridge and Ferry Undertakings (183).
Local Enactments (Water Undertakings, etc.) (538).
Water Rates and Charges (Wales) (494).

(7) Landlord and tenant

Leasehold Reform Act 1967 (Wimbledon and Putney Commons Conservators) O., *made by Secretary of State under Leasehold Reform Act 1967* (*c. 88*), *s. 28*(*7*) ... (1009).

(8) Local employment

Intermediate Areas O., *made by Secretary of State under Local Employment Act 1970* (*c. 7*), *s. 1*(*1*) ... (329).

(9) National Gallery and Tate Gallery

Secretary of State—Orders under National Gallery and Tate Gallery Act 1954 (*c. 65*), *s. 4*(*2*).

National Gallery (Lending Outside the United Kingdom –
No. 1) (424).
No. 2) (436).

*Not printed for sale in the S.I. series.

TABLES OF EFFECT
of the Statutory Instruments of 1971

(With certain additional information)

Table A

A CHRONOLOGICAL TABLE OF ACTS OF PARLIAMENT
WHOSE OPERATION WAS AFFECTED BY
STATUTORY INSTRUMENTS OF 1971

Table B

A CHRONOLOGICAL TABLE OF SUBORDINATE LEGISLATION
(S.R. & O. AND S.I.) AND CERTAIN PREROGATIVE INSTRUMENTS
WHOSE OPERATION WAS AFFECTED BY
LEGISLATION OF 1971 (ACTS AND INSTRUMENTS)

TABLE A

NOTES

1. For List of Abbreviations used in this Table, see p. ix.

2. A comprehensive table showing the effect of Acts, Measures and S.I. of 1971 on Acts and Measures is printed in the *Annual Volume of Public General Acts*.

PART I

EFFECT ON PUBLIC GENERAL ACTS

Short Title	How affected and Instrument by which affected
1838 Judgments Act 1838 (c.110)	s. 17 **am.**, 1971/491.
1857 Probates and Letters of Administration Act (Ireland) 1857 (c. 79)	s. 63 **am.**, 1971/875.
1859 Ct. of Probate Act (Ireland) 1859 (22 & 23 Vict. c. 31)	s. 8 **r.**, 1971/875.
1870 Common Law Procedure Amendment Act (Ireland) 1870 (c. 109)	**r.**, 1971/875.
1872 Pawnbrokers Act 1872 (c. 93)	s. 52 **am.**, 1971/1292.
1874 Civil Bill Cts. (Ireland) Act 1874 (c. 66) ...	**r.**, 1971/875.
1876 Sheriff Cts. (S.) Act 1876 (c. 70)	s. 44 **replaced** ,1971/1655.
1877 County Officers and Cts. (Ireland) Act 1877 (c. 56)	ss. 35, 36, 51, 52, 57, 58 **r.**, 1971/875.
Supreme Court of Judicature Act (Ireland) 1877 (c. 57)	s. 60 **r.**, 1971/875.
1890 Public Health Acts Adt. Act 1890 (c. 59)...	s. 7 **am.**, 1971/1292.
1898 Canals Protection (London) Act 1898 (c. 16)	s. 5 **am.**, 1971/1292.
1907 Limited Partnerships Act 1907 (c. 24) ...	s. 4(2) **mod.**, 1971/782.
Sheriff Cts. (S.) Act 1907 (c. 51)	sch. 1 rule 5 **am.**, 15B **inserted**, 1971/1214.
Public Health Acts Adt. Act 1907 (c. 53)...	s. 7 **am.**, 1971/1292.
1910 Civil List Act 1910 (c. 28)	s. 7 functions transfd. to the Treasury, 1971/2099.
1911 Small Landholders (S.) Act 1911 (c. 49) ...	s. 3(9) **am.**, 1971/2099.
1915 Indictments Act 1915 (c. 90)	sch. **am.**, 1971/1253.

	Short Title	How affected and Instrument by which affected
1925	Performing Animals (Regulation) Act 1925 (c. 38)	s. 2(2) **am.**, 1971/1292.
	Theatrical Employers Registration Act 1925 (c. 50)	s. 6(1) **am.**, 1971/1292.
1927	Moneylenders Act 1927 (c. 21)	s. 2(7) **am.**, 1971/1292.
1933	Pharmacy and Poisons Act 1933 (c. 25) ...	s. 21(2) **am.**, 1971/1292.
1936	Civil List Act 1936 (c. 15)	s. 8 functions transfd. to the Treasury, 1971/2099.
1937	Statutory Salaries Act 1937 (c. 35)... ...	residue **r.**, 1971/2099.
1939	Marriage (S.) Act 1939 (c. 34) ... ... H. of C. Members' Funds Act 1939 (c. 49)...	sch. 1 **replaced**, 1971/1159. sch. 1 **am.**, 1971/770.
1942	Supreme Court (N.I.) Act 1942 (6 & 7 Geo. 6 c. 2)	s. 1(1)(2) **r.**, 1971/875.
1946	National Health Service Act 1946 (c. 81) ...	sch. 3 Pt. II **mod.**, 1971/676.
1947	Exchange Control Act 1947 (c. 14) ...	sch. 1 **am.**, 1971/1406, 1556 para. 18 **r.**, 1971/2002.
	Polish Resettlement Act 1947 (c. 19) ...	s. 1 functions transfd. to the Treasury, 1971/2099.
	Civil List Act 1947 (c. 32)	s. 11 functions transfd. to the Treasury, 1971/2099.
	Statistics of Trade Act 1947 (c. 39) ...	s. 17(3) **replaced**, 1971/719.
	Industrial Organisation and Development Act 1947 (c. 40)	s. 1(2) **am.**, 1971/719.
	Crown Proceedings Act 1947 (c. 44) ...	s. 20(2) **am.**, 1971/875.
1948	Companies Act 1948 (c. 38)	sch. 8 para. 13(A)(5) **am.**, 1971/2044.
	Representation of the People Act 1948 (c. 65)	sch. 1 **am.**, 1971/2106, 2107, 2115.
1949	Special Roads Act 1949 (c. 32)	sch. 2 **am.**, 1971/1211.
	Patents Act 1949 (c. 87)	s. 18 **am.**, 1971/719.
1950	Diseases of Animals Act 1950 (c. 36) ...	s. 84(2) **am.**, 1971/311. 84(1) **am.**, 1971/2045.
1951	National Health Service Act 1951 (c. 31)...	sch. 1 **am.**, (E.) 1971/340, (S.) 1971/420.
1952	National Health Service Act 1952 (c. 25)...	s. 2 **am.**, (E.) 1971/340, (S.) 1971/420.
	Civil List Act 1952 (c. 37)	s. 7(2) functions transfd. to the Treasury, 1971/2099.

	Short Title	How affected and Instrument by which affected
1952	Customs and Excise Act 1952 (c. 44) ...	s. 88(4) **am.**, 1971/1033.
	Magistrates' Courts Act 1952 (c. 55) ...	sch. 4 Pt. 1 **am.**, 1971/188.
1955	Air Force Act 1955 (c. 19)	ss. 17, 20 **am.**, 1971/510.
1957	H. of C. Disqualification Act 1957 (c. 20)...	sch. 2 **am.**, 1971/719. sch. Pt. II **am.**, 1971/1175.
	Housing Act 1957 (c. 56)	s. 14(5) **am.**, 1971/1292.
1958	Land Powers (Defence) Act 1958 (c. 30) ...	ss. 7, 8(1), 10(1) **am.**, 1971/719. s. 10(8) **r.**, 1971/719. s. 11(1), sch. 3 para. 1 **am.**, 1971/719.
	Defence Contracts Act 1958 (c. 38) ...	s. 6(1) **am.**, 1971/719.
	Housing (Financial Provisions) Act 1958 (c. 42)	sch. 5 paras. 1, 2 **mod.**, 1971/231.
	Adoption Act 1958 (7 & 8 Eliz. 2 c. 5) ...	sch. 2 **replaced**, 1971/1160. sch. 1 **mod.**, 1971/1880.
1959	Highways Act 1959 (c. 25)	s. 276 **r.**, 1971/1292. sch. 4 **am.**, 1971/1156.
	Cotton Industry Act 1959 (c. 48)	sch. 3(1) **r.**, 1971/2056.
1960	Road Traffic Act 1960 (c. 16)	s. 253(5) **am.**, 1971/451. s. 117(3) **am.**, 1971/1142. s. 97(1) **am.**, 1971/1978.
1961	Army and Air Force Act 1961 (c. 52) ...	ss. 8–12 **r.**, s. 13 **am.**, 14, 15 **r.**, sch. 2 **am.**, 1971/510.
1962	Health Visiting and Social Work (Training) Act 1962 (c. 33)	sch. 1 **am.**, 1971/1241.
1963	Betting, Gaming and Lotteries Act 1963 (c. 2)	sch. 1 para. 21(1) **am.**, 22 **r.**, 1971/1292. 28(2) **am.**, 1971/1292. 2 para. 6 **am.**, 1971/1292. 3 para. 13(2) **am.**, 1971/1292. 7 para. 5 **am.**, 1971/1292.
	Purchase Tax Act 1963 (c. 9)	sch. 1 Pt. I groups 9, 26 **am.**, 1971/155. sch. 1 Pt. I group 28 **am.**, 1971/731. sch. 1 Pt. I group 11, 12 **am.**, 1971/1078. sch. 1 Pt. I **am.**, 1971/1145. sch. 1 Pt. I **am.**, 1971/1166. sch. 1 Pt. I group 5 **am.**, 1971/1781.
	British Museum Act 1963 (c. 24)	sch. 3 Pt. I **am.**, 1971/82.
	London Govt. Act 1963 (c. 33)	ss. 22(4), 24(3)(4A)(5)(8), 25–27, 28(1), 29(1), 45, 46(1), 47, 49 **am.**, 1971/1732. sch. 14 para. 1, 10 **am.**, 1971/1732. 17 para. 2 **am.**, 1971/1732.
1964	Television Act 1964 (c. 21)	s. 13 **am.**, 1971/309.
	Licensing Act 1964 (c. 26)	s. 22(1)(3) **am.**, 1971/1292.
	Emrgency Laws (Re-enactments and Repeals) Act 1964 (c. 60)	s. 4(2) **am.**, 1971/422.

	Short Title	How affected and Instrument by which affected
1964	Shipping Contracts and Commercial Documents Act 1964 (c. 87)	s. 2(1) **am.,** 1971/719. s. 2(2) **r.,** 1971/719.
	Ministers of the Crown Act 1964 (c. 98) ...	sch. 1 para. 5–7 **mod.,** sch. 2 **am.,** 1971/719.
1965	Science and Technology Act 1965 (c. 4) ...	s. 5(1) **am.,** 1971/719.
	Ministerial Salaries and Members' Pensions Act 1965 (c. 11)	Pt. II **am.,** 1971/623.
	Ministerial Salaries Consolidation Act 1965 (c. 58)	sch. 1 **am.,** 1971/719.
	Superannuation Act 1965 (c. 74)	sch. 8 **am.,** 1971/1648.
	Southern Rhodesia 1965 (c. 76)	s. 2 cont. 1971/1847.
1966	National Health Service Act 1966 (c. 8) ...	s. 6 **am.,** 1971/382.
	Ministry of Social Security Act 1966 (c. 20)	sch. 2 para. 23 **am.,** 1971/457. sch. 2 Pt. II para. 9–11 **replaced,** 12A **inserted,** 13, 14, 17 **am.,** 1971/1054.
1967	General Rate Act 1967 (c. 9)	s. 7 (1) **am.,** 1971/1292. sch. 8 **am.,** (*retrosp.*), 1971/2007.
	Parliamentary Commissioner Act 1967 (c. 13)	sch. 2 **am.,** 1971/719.
	Decimal Currency Act 1967 (c. 47) ...	s. 4(2) **r.,** 1971/1175.
	Road Traffic Regulation Act 1967 (c. 76)...	sch. 5 para. 2 **am.,** 1971/602.
	Water (S.) Act 1967 (c. 78)	s. 12 **am.,** 1971/527.
	Companies Act 1967 (c. 81)	s. 6(6) **am.,** 1971/2044.
1968	National Loans Act 1968 (c. 13)	s. 4(2) **am.,** 1971/1930.
	Export Guarantees Act 1968 (c. 26) ...	gen **am.,** 1971/2119. s. 7 **replaced** 1971/2119.
	Firearms Act 1968 (c. 27)	sch. 5 para. 4 **am.,** 1971/1292. 6, 8 **r.,** 1971/1292.
	Housing (Financial Provns.) (S.) Act 1968 (c. 31)	s. 29(1)(*bb*) **am.,** 1971/1411.
	Social Work (S.) Act 1968 (c. 49)	sch. 7 para. 4 **am.,** 1971/184.
	Gaming Act 1968 (c. 65)	sch. 2 para. 29(1) **am.,** 30(1) **r.,** 30(2) **am.,** 1971/1292. sch. 3 para. 12, 15 **am.,** 1971/1292. sch. 7 para. 11, 20 **am.,** 1971/1292. sch. 9 para. 14(1) **r.,** 14(2) **am.,** 1971/1292.
	Medicines Act 1968 (c. 67)	s. 10 **am.,** 1971/1445.
	Transport Act 1968 (c. 73)	ss. 96(2)–(4), (6), (7) 103 **am.,** 1971/818. s. 32(4) **am.,** 1971/1878.

	Short Title	How affected and Instrument by which affected
1969	Housing Act 1969 (c. 33)	s. 50(2) **am.**, 1971/570.
	Housing (S.) Act 1969 (c. 34)	s. 51(2) **am.**, 1971/624.
	Childrens and Young Persons Act 1969 (c. 54)	s. 3(8) **am.**, 1971/1292. sch. 4 Pt. II **am.**, 1971/589.
1970	Taxes Management Act 1970 (c. 9) ...	s. 2(5) **am.**, 1971/2099.
	Income and Corporation Taxes Act 1970 (c. 10)	s. 191 **am.**, sch. 14 **am.**, 1971/2099.
	Sea Fish Act 1970 (c. 11)	sch. 4 para. 12 **am.**, 1971/2099.
	Export Guarantees Act 1970 (c. 15) ...	gen **am.**, 1971/2119.
	Family Income Supplements Act 1970 (c. 55)	ss. 2, 3 **am.**, 1971/702.
1971	Hijacking Act 1971 (c. 70)	s. 1–5 **mod.**, 1971/1739.

PART II

EFFECT ON LOCAL AND PERSONAL ACTS

Short Title	How affected and Instrument by which affected
Manchester Corporation Act 1920 (c. xcvii)	s. 59 **am.**, 1971/25.
Nottingham Corporation Act 1923 (c. c) ...	s. 112 **am.**, 1971/25.
City of London (Various Powers) Act 1931 (c. xiv)	s. 8 **am.**, 1971/25.
Brighton Corporation Act 1931 (c. cix) ...	s. 191 **am.**, 1971/25.
Gloucester Corporation Act 1935 (c. lxxxvii)	s. 129 **am.**, 1971/25.
Nottingham Corporation Act 1935 (c. cxix)	s. 41 **am.**, 1971/25.
Grimsby Corporation (Grimsby, Cleethorpes and District Water &c.) Act 1937 (c. xli)	s. 181 **am.**, 1971/25.
Lancashire County Council (Rivers Bd. and General Powers) Act 1938 (c. xciv)	ss. 106, 107 **am.**, 1971/25.
Nottingham Corporation Act 1938 (c. xcv)	s. 78 **am.**, 1971/25.
Northampton Corporation Act 1943 (c. xv)	ss. 112, 128 **am.**, 1971/25.
Nottingham Corporation Act 1947 (c. xxxvi)	s. 44 **am.**, 1971/25.
Beverley Corporation Act 1948 (c. li) ...	s. 83 **am.**, 1971/25.

Short Title	How affected and Instrument by which affected
West Riding County Council (General Powers) Act 1948 (c. lii)	ss. 48, 49 **am.**, 1971/25.
Slough Corporation Act 1949 (c. xxxviii)...	ss. 131, 141 **am.**, 1971/25.
Lancashire County Council (General Powers) Act 1951 (c. xxxv)	ss. 21, 23 **am.**, 1971/25.
West Riding County Council (General Powers) Act 1951 (c. xliii)	ss. 104, 107, 114 **am.**, 1971/25.
Leamington Corporation Act 1952 (c. xvi)	ss. 127, 131 **am.**, 1971/25.
Birkenhead Corporation Act 1954 (c. xlvii)	ss. 149, 174, 176 **am.**, 1971/25.
Leicester Corporation Act 1956 (c. xlix) ...	ss. 221, 235 **am.**, 1971/25.
Kent County Council Act 1958 (c. vi) ...	ss. 66, 68 **am.**, 1971/25.
Gloucester Corporation Act 1958 (c. xxxv)	s. 94 **am.**, 1971/25.
Durham County Council Act 1963 (c. xxxvii)	ss. 55, 58, 105 **am.**, 1971/25.
West Riding County Council (General Powers) Act 1964 (c. xxxix)	s. 19 **am.**, 1971/25.
Lee Valley Regional Park Act 1966 (c. xli)	s. 48 **am.**, 1971/25.
Lancashire County Council (General Powers) Act 1968 (c. xxix)	s. 32 **am.**, 1971/25.
Port of London Act 1968 (c. xxxii) ...	sch. 3, rule 5, 6, 17 **am.**, 1971/189.
Dudley Corporation Act 1969 (c. liii) ...	s. 103 **am.**, 1971/25.

TABLE B

A CHRONOLOGICAL TABLE OF SUBORDINATE LEGISLATION (S.R. & O. AND S.I. AND CERTAIN PREROGATIVE INSTRUMENTS) WHOSE OPERATION WAS AFFECTED BY LEGISLATION OF 1971 (ACTS AND INSTRUMENTS)

NOTES

1. For List of Abbreviations used in this Table, see p. ix.
2. In Col. 2, Volume references given in brackets after the titles of instruments have the following significance:—

   " Rev., 1903 " indicates *Statutory Rules and Orders Revised* (2nd Edition, to 31 Dec. 1903).

   " Rev." indicates *Statutory Rules and Orders and Statutory Instruments Revised* (3rd Edition, to 31 Dec. 1948).

   Where neither of these appears, the reference is to the Annual Volume of S.R. & O. (1890 to 1947) or S.I. (1948 onwards) for the year shown (in heavy type) in col. 1.

   The Roman numeral indicates the Volume or Part number of the Edition or year concerned.

Year and Number (or date)	Title or Description	How affected and Act or Instrument by which affected
1893		
15 Mar.	Pacific O. in C. 1893 (Rev. VIII, p. 597)	arts. 38–46 **r.** (*prosp.*), 1971/1741. arts. 50 **r.**, 84 **am.**, 86, 134, 137, 139 **r.**, O. 27.10.71 (p. 6330). art. 108 **r.**, (Gilbert and Ellice Is. and Dependencies), O. 27.10.71 (p. 6335).
1897		
6	Friendly Society Regs. 1897 (Rev. VIII, p. 815)	regs. 19, 20, 25 **r.**, 53, 60, 65, 70 **am.**, 1971/461. regs. 18, 21–24, 33–43 **r.**, 44 **am.**, 46, 49, 54, 59, 68, 70 **r.**, 75 **am.**, sch. Forms J, K, L, T, U, V, W, X, Y, Z, AA, AX, AY, CI, UI, XI **r.**, 1971/1956.
1900		
Instrt. not S.I. 29 Oct.	Constitution of Office of Governor of the State of Tasmania and its Dependencies—L.P. 1900 (Rev. II, p. 1081)	Cl. XIII **am.**, L.P. 25.5.71.
1909		
10 Aug.	Hong Kong (Appeal to Privy Council) O. in C. 1909 (Rev. XI, p. 374)	rules 2, 4 **am.**, 1971/1239.
1911		
433	Land Values (Referee) (S.) Rules 1911 (Rev. XII, p. 187)	**r.** (*prosp.*), 1971/218
1912		
69	Irish Land (Finance) Rules 1912 (1912, p. 405)	rule 16 **am.**, 1971/1883.

Year and Number (or date)	Title or Description	How affected and Act or Instrument by which affected
1912		
348	Public Trustee Rules 1912 (Rev. XXIII, p. 311)	rule 30 **replaced,** 1971/1894.
861	Land Values (Referee) (S.)— Addnl. Rules 1912 (Rev. XII, p. 187)	**r.** (*prosp.*), 1971/218.
1913		
1275	Land Values (Referee) (S.)—Addnl. Rules 1913 (Rev. XII, p. 187)	**r.** (*prosp.*), 1971/218.
1914		
152	Pacific (Fugitive Criminals Surrender) O. 1914 (Rev. VIII, p. 699)	sch. 1 **am.,** 1971/1739.
1916		
282	Indictment Rules 1916 (Rev. V, p. 331)	**r.,** 1971/1253.
323	Indictment (Criminal Informations and Inquisitions) Rules 1916 (Rev. V, p. 335)	**r.,** 1971/1253.
1920		
1250	Writs of Fieri Facias, sheriffs' or sheriffs' officers' fees—O. 1920 (Rev. XX, p. 734)	sch. fees 1–4, 8 **am.,** 10 **replaced,** residue **am.,** 1971/808.
1921		
352	Anthrax, control of imports—O. in C. 1921 (1921, p. 38)	**r.,** 1971/1234.
622	Fees for certificates of Savings Bank Rules, Awards, etc.—Warrant 1921 (Rev. XX, p. 606)	art. 1 **am.,** 1971/981.
827	Sheriffs' and sheriffs' officers' fees—O. 1921 (Rev. XX, p. 736)	sch. fees 1 **am.,** 7A, 7B, 7C **inserted,** 8 **replaced,** 1971/808.
1922		
846	Ct. of Session, fees and books of Account—A.S. 1922 (Rev. XXII, p. 306)	**r.,** 1971/67.
1923		
713	Industrial Assurance (Fees) Regs. 1923 (Rev. VIII, p. 905)	**r.,** 1971/448.
919	Friendly Society (Amdt. of Fees) Reg. 1923 (Rev. VIII, p. 815)	**r.,** 1971/461.
1364	Indictment Rules 1923 (Rev. V, p. 336)	**r.,** 1971/1253.
1925		
1093	Land Registration Rules 1925 (Rev. XII, p. 81)	rule 82 **replaced,** 1971/1197.
1926		
671	Industrial Assurance (Amdt. of Fees) Reg. 1926 (Rev. VIII, p. 906)	**r.,** 1971/448.
1423	Public Trustee (Custodian Trustee) Rules 1926 (Rev. XXIII, p. 311)	**r.,** 1971/1894.

Year and Number (or date)	Title or Description	How affected and Act or Instrument by which affected
1927		
1184	Supreme Ct. Funds Rules 1927 (1927, p. 1638)	rules 3, 70, 77, 78 **am.**, 1971/259.
1928		
922	Importation of Dogs and Cats O. 1928 (Rev. II, p. 399)	art. 12 **am.**, 1971/2045.
1931		
157	Acquisition of Land (Assessment of Compensation) (Fees) Rules 1931 (Rev. XI, p. 797)	**r.** (*prosp.*), 1971/218.
1933		
48	Sheriffs' ordinary and small debt cts., forms of procedure—A.S. 1933 (Rev. XX, p. 829)	s. 5 **am.**, sch. D **replaced**, 1971/1164.
745	Indictments (Procedure) Rules 1933 (Rev. V, p. 347)	**r.**, 1971/2084.
1149	Savings Certificates Regs. 1933 (Rev. XV, p. 309)	reg. 4 **am.**, 1971/549.
1934		
581	Acquisition of Land (Assessment of Compensation) (S.) Act 1934—Rules (Rev. XI, p. 792)	**r.**, 1971/218.
1346	London Cab O. 1934 (Rev. XIV, p. 795)	paras. 40, 41 **replaced**, para. 50 **am.**, sch. E **replaced**, 1971/333.
26 Nov.	Rules of the Salford Hundred Ct. of Record 1935	O. LXV **am.**, Appx. N **replaced**' 1971/798.
1935		
488	Sheriff Ct., solicitors' etc. fees—A.S. 1935 (Rev. XX, p. 880)	c. II **replaced**, 1971/194. c. II **am.**, 1971/904.
1936		
626	County Ct. Rules 1936 (1936 I, p. 282)	O. 5 **am.**, 8 heading Pt. II **replaced**, 8–13, 16, 28, 35, 37, 46 **am.**, Appx. A (forms) **am.**, B (forms) **am.**, 1971/781. O. 8, 25, 46 **am.**, Appx. A (forms) **am.**, 1971/836. O. 5, 13, 16 **am.**, 21 **r.**, 25, 27, 34, 36, 45A, 46, 47 **am.**, Appx. A (forms) **am.**, 1971/2127. O. 2, 5, 6, 8–10, 12, 13, 15, 16, 20 **am.**, new 21 **inserted**, 22–24, 26, 46, 47, 49 **am.**, Appx. A (forms) **am.**, D **am.**, 1971/2152.
1297	Fowl Pest O. 1936 (Rev. XVIII, p. 442)	art. 12 **am.** (E. and W.), 1971/2053.
1317	Admin. Order Rules 1936 (Rev. V. p. 164)	**r.**, 1971/1095.
1937		
627	British Solomon Is. Protectorate and Gilbert and Ellice Is. Colony (Currency) O. in C. 1937 (Rev. VIII, p. 696)	**r.**, O, 27.10.71.

Year and Number (or date)	Title or Description	How affected and Act or Instrument by which affected
1937		
993	Methylated Spirits (Sale by Retail) (S.) O. 1937 (Rev. XXI, p. 474)	art. 2 **am.**, 1971/813.
1217	Indian Civil Service Family Pension Fund Rules 1937 (Rev. X, p. 715)	rules 7, 11, 26, 27 **am.**, schs. 1, 7 **replaced**, 8 **am.**, 1971/823.
1225	Superior Services (India) Family Pension Fund Rules 1937 (Rev. X, p. 597)	rules 7, 12, 14, 15, 22, 32 **am.**, schs. 4 **replaced**, 6 **am.**, 1971/825.
1226	Indian Military Service Family Pension Fund Rules 1937 (Rev. X, p. 632)	rules 2, 8, 18, 35A, 36, 37 **am.**, schs. 2, 3, 7 **replaced**, 8 **am.**, 1971/822.
		rule 34 **am.**, sch. 7 **replaced**, 1971/1771.
1227	Indian Military Widows' and Orphans' Fund Rules 1937 (Rev. X, p. 662)	rules 2, 8, 13A, 19, 35A, 36, 37 **am.**, schs. 4, 5, 9 **replaced**, 10 **am.**, 1971/824.
1938		
202	Rabies O. 1938 (Rev. II, p. 578)	arts. 2, 5, 12, 14 **am.**, 1971/2045.
661	Trade Marks Rules 1938 (Rev. XXIII, p. 3)	sch. 1 **replaced** 1971/261.
1940		
784	Friendly Society (Amdt. of Fees) Reg. 1940 (Rev. VIII, p. 815)	**r.**, 1971/461.
1492	Trade Bds. (Laundry Trade, G.B.) (Constitution and Proceedings) Regs. 1940 (1940 I, p. 1038)	sch. **r.**, 1971/998.
1941		
1534	Public Trustee (Custodian Trustee) Rules 1941 (Rev. XXIII, p. 311)	**r.**, 1971/1894.
1946		
1708	Pensions Appeal Tribunals (E. and W.) Rules 1946 (Rev. XVII, p. 733)	**r.**, 1971/769.
1709	Pensions Appeal Tribunals (S.) Rules 1946 (Rev. XVII, p. 752)	**r.**, 1971/2124.
2157	Private Legislation Procedure (S.) General O. 1946 (Rev. XVIII, p. 719)	O. 22, 28–30, 32, 35, 39, 43, 69, 70, 70A, 78A, 93, 97, 99 **am.**, 100, 103 **r.**, 106, 107, 123 **am.**, 124 **replaced**, 1971/1413.
1947		
2050	Exchange Control (Traders in Coin) O. 1947 (Rev. VI, p. 1031)	**r.**, 1971/516.
2243	New Towns Compulsory Purchase (Contemporaneous Procedure) (S.) Regs. 1947 (Rev. XXII, p. 978)	**r.**, 1971/128.
1948		
35	Atomic Energy (Assessment of Compensation for Work done in Searching for Minerals) (S.) Rules 1948 (Rev. II p. 1020)	**r.** (*prosp.*), 1971/218.

Year and Number (or date)	Title or Description	How affected and Act or Instrument by which affected
1948		
55	National Insurance (Pensions, Existing Beneficiaries and Other Persons) (Transitional) Regs. 1948 (Rev. XVI, p. 36)	regs. 9, 10 **am.**, schs. 1–3 **am.**, 1971/1220.
226	Electricity (Pension Schemes) Regs. 1948 (Rev. VI, p. 917)	reg. 1 **am.**, 1971/936.
604	Firemen's Pension Scheme O. 1948 (Rev. VII, p. 776)	arts. 4, 7, 10, 24, 37B **am.**, schs. 3, 7 **am.**, 16 **r.**, 1971/1329. art. 6 **am.**, 1971/1468.
612	National Insurance (Pensions, Existing Contributors) (Transitional) Regs. 1948 (Rev. XVI, p. 18)	regs. 6, 11 **am.**, sch. 2, 5 **am.**, 1971/1720.
629	Cotton Industry Development Council O. 1948 (Rev. V, p. 87)	**r.**, 1971/2054.
712	Local Govt. Audit (S.) Regs. 1948 (Rev. XII, p. 621)	reg. 4 **r.**, 1971/2023.
714	Local Govt. (Payment of Accounts) (S.) Regs. 1948 (Rev. XII, p. 624)	sch. **am.**, 1971/767.
1041	National Insurance (Claims and Payments) Regs. 1948 (Rev. XVI, p. 313)	**r.**, 1971/707.
1261	National Insurance (Widow's Benefit and Retirement Pensions) Regs. 1948 (Rev. XVI p. 207)	reg. 12 **am.**, sch. **am.**, 1971/1220. reg. 11 **am.**, 1971/1419.
1274	National Insurance and Industrial Injuries (Collection of Contributions) Regs. 1948 (Rev. XVI, p. 148)	reg. 6A **inserted**, 1971/993. regs. 10A, 11 **am.**, 1971/1421.
1275	National Insurance (Residence and Persons Abroad) Regs. 1948 (Rev. XVI, p. 88)	regs. 7 **am.**, 7A, 7B **inserted**, 1971/1419.
1276	National Insurance (Sickness Benefit, Maternity Benefit and Miscellaneous Provns.) (Transitional) Regs. 1948 (Rev. XVI, p. 49)	regs. 3 **am.**, 6 **replaced**, 1971/1419.
1425	National Insurance (Classification) Regs. 1948 (Rev. XVI, p. 95)	sch. 1 paras. 8, 11, 17, 32, 34–44A, 46–53 **am.**, 1971/1421. sch. 1 paras. 5C **am.**, 7 **inserted**, sch. 3 para. 8 **replaced**, 1971/1728.
1456	National Insurance (Industrial Injuries) (Insurable and Excepted Employments) Regs. 1948 (Rev. XVI, p. 423)	sch. 2 Pt. I **am.**, sch. 3 **am.**, 1971/1729.
1462	Superannuation (Policy and Local Govt. Schemes) (S.) Rules 1948 (Rev. XVII, p. 582)	rules. 4 **replaced**, 5 **am.**, 6 **replaced**, 7 **inserted**, 1971/1879.
1466	National Insurance (Airmen) Regs. 1948 (Rev. XVI, p. 108)	regs. 4, 7 **am.**, 1971/1419.

Year and Number (or date)	Title or Description	How affected and Act or Instrument by which affected
1948		
1470	National Insurance (Married Women) Regs. 1948 (Rev. XVI, p. 123)	reg. 8C **replaced,** 1971/906. reg. 8A **am.,** 1971/1419.
1506	National Health Service (Medical Practices Compensation) Regs. 1948 (Rev. XV, p. 758)	reg. 13 **am.,** 1971/1684.
1768	National Health Service (Medical Practices Compensation) (S.) Regs. 1948 (Rev. XV, p. 1021)	reg. 15 **am.,** 1971/1833.
2172	Electricity (Pension Rights) Regs. 1948 (Rev. VI, p. 918)	reg. 9 **am.,** 1971/936.
2188	Public Trustee (Custodian Trustee) Rules 1948 (Rev. XXIII, p. 311)	**r.,** 1971/1894.
2361	Airways Corporations (General Staff Pensions) Regs. 1948 (Rev. I p. 1275)	sch. **am.,** 1971/176. reg. 7 **r.,** 1971/927.
2711	National Insurance (Overlapping Benefits) Regs. 1948 (Rev. XVI, p. 196)	Pt. II reg. 9 **inserted,** 1971/621. regs. 2, 8, 12 **am.,** sch. **am.,** 1971/1419. sch. **am.,** 1971/1633.
1949		
330	Companies (Winding-up) Rules 1949 (1949 I, p. 789)	rules 1, 46, 217, 227 **am.,** 228 **r.,** 1971/2073.
352	National Insurance (New Entrants Transitional) Regs. 1949 (1949 I, p. 2737)	reg. 5, sch. 2 **am.,** 1971/1220.
744	Gas (Pension Scheme) Regs. 1949 (1949 I, p. 1997)	reg. 1 **am.,** 1971/915.
790	Gas (Meter) Regs. 1949 (1949 I, p. 1985)	sch. 1 **replaced,** 1971/170.
1204	National Insurance (Death Grant) Regs. 1949 (1949 I, p. 2708)	reg. 12, sch. 2 **r.,** 1971/707.
1461	National Insurance (Hospital In-Patients) Regs. 1949 (1949 I, p. 2718)	regs. 3–6, 6A **am.,** 1971/1220. regs. 3, 5 **am.,** 5A **inserted,** 6C, 8 **am.,** 13A **inserted,** 1971/1419. reg. 8 am., 1971/1440.
1836	Northern Ireland (Crown Proceedings) O. 1949 (1949 I, p. 1261)	arts. 3 **am.,** 8A **inserted,** 14 **replaced,** 15 **replaced** by 15, 15A, 17 **replaced,** 1971/212.
2042	Exchange Control (Traders in Coin) (Amdt.) O. 1949 (1949 I, p. 1631)	**r.,** 1971/516.
2105	Pensions Appeal Tribunal (E. and W.) (Amdt.) Rules 1949 (1949 I, p. 3008)	**r.,** 1971/769.
2239	Pensions Appeal Tribunals (S.) (Amdt.) Rules 1949 (1949 I, p. 3010)	**r.,** 1971/2124.
2275	Administration Order (Amdt.) Rules 1949 (1949 I, p. 1200)	**r.,** 1971/1095.
2368	Designs Rules 1949 (1949 I, p. 1417)	sch. 1 **replaced** 1971/262.

Year and Number (or date)	Title or Description	How affected and Act or Instrument by which affected
1950		
376	Coal Industry Nationalisation (Superannuation) Regs. 1950 (1950 I, p. 356)	reg. 1 **am.,** 1971/914.
392	Patents Appeal Tribunal Rules 1950 (1950 II, p. 201)	rule 7A **inserted,** 1971/394.
1195	Double Taxation Relief (Taxes on Income) (Denmark) O. 1950 (1950 I, p. 1019)	art. 12 **r.,** 1971/717.
1206	Gas (Pension Rights) Regs. 1950 (1950 I, p. 814)	reg. 9 **am.,** 1971/915.
1539	Superannuation (Transfers between the Civil Service and Public Bds.) Rules 1950 (1950 II, p. 291)	sch. **am.,** 1971/752.
1951		
1232	National Insurance (Increase of Benefit, Re-entry into Regular Employment and Miscellaneous Provns.) Regs. 1951 (1951 I, p. 1457)	reg. 17 **r.,** 1971/707. reg. 11 **am.,** 1971/1419.
2173	Cotton Industry Development Council (Amdt.) O. 1951 (1951 I, p. 1125)	**r.,** 1971/2054.
1952		
60	Injury Warrant 1952 (1952 II, p. 2400)	para. 16 **replaced,** 1971/1209.
944	Firemen's Pension Scheme O. 1952 (1952 I, p. 1003)	arts. 4, 5, 7, 8, 10, 23A, 23B, 23C, 24, 37B **am.,** sch. 3 **am.,** sch. 5 Pt I **am.,** Pt. 2 **r.,** schs. 7, 8 **am.,** sch. 8A **inserted,** sch. 16 **r.,** 1971/1329. art. 6 **am.,** 1971/1468.
1207	National Insurance (Claims and Payments) Amdt. Regs. 1952 (1952 II, p. 2122)	**r.,** 1971/707.
1349	H. of C. (Redistribution of Seats) (Swindon and Devizes) O. 1952 (1952 III, p. 2831)	**superseded,** 1971/2116.
1869	Marriage (Authorised Persons) Regs. 1952 (1952 II, p. 1691)	reg. 17 **am.,** 1971/1216.
1906	A.S. (Valuation Appeal Rules) 1952 (1952 III, p. 2967)	para. 3 **replaced,** 1971/375.
2115	Industrial Assurance (Amdt. of Fees) Regs. 1952 (1952 I, p. 1231)	**r.,** 1971/448
2158	Friendly Societies (Amdt. of Fees) Regs. 1952 (1952 I, p. 1098)	**r.,** 1971/461
2228	Aircraft (Customs) Regs. 1952 (1952 I, p. 669)	**r.,** 1971/848
1953		
65	Meals Service (S.) Regs. 1953 (1953 I, p. 642)	**r.,** 1971/1537
130	Pensions Appeal Tribunals (E. and W.) (Amdt.) Rules 1953 (1953 II, p. 1544)	**r.,** 1971/769

Year and Number (or date)	Title or Description	How affected and Act or Instrument by which affected
1953		
168	Assessor of Public Undertakings Valuation Roll (Procedure Dates) (S.) O. 1953 (1953 II, p. 1737)	sch. **am.**, 1971/591
421	Cotton Industry Development Council (Amdt. No. 2) O. 1953 (1953 I, p. 862)	**r.**, 1971/2054
650	Drawback (Isle of Man) Regs. 1953 (1953 I, p. 529)	**r.**, 1971/1503
742	H. of C. (Redistribution of Seats) (Stockport South and Cheadle) O. 1953 (1953 II, p. 1776)	sch. 1 **superseded** 1971/2115
1174	Therapeutic Substances (Supply of Antibiotics for Agricultural Purposes) Regs. 1953 (1953 II, p. 2292)	**r.**, 1971/459
1702	Distress for Rent Rules 1953 (1953 I, p. 574)	Appx. 1 **replaced**, Appx. 2 form 5 (back) **replaced**, 1971/1333 rule 7 **am.**, 1971/2133.
1709	Ecclesiastical Officers Remuneration O. No. 2, 1953 (1953 I, p. 598)	sch. **am.**, 1971/1130.
1776	A.S. (Fees of Town Clerks and Clerks of the Peace) 1953 (1953 II, p. 2299)	**r.**, 1971/91.
1954		
189	National Insurance (Maternity Benefit and Miscellaneous Provns.) Regs. 1954 (1954 I, p. 1387)	reg. 13 **am.**, 1971/1220. reg. 19, sch. I pts III to V, **r.**, 1971/707
268	Virus Hepatitis O. 1954 (1954 II, p. 1826)	**r.**, 1971/405
370	Pedestrian Crossings Regs. 1954 (1954 II, p. 1948)	**r.** (30 .11.73), 1971/1524.
448	Removal of Bodies Regs. 1954 (1954 II, p. 1915)	reg. 5 **am.**, sch. 1 **replaced** 1971/1354.
796	Non-Contentious Probate Rules 1954 (1954 II, p. 2202)	rules 2, 4–6, 21, 34 **am.**, 38 **replaced**, 39, 40, **r.**, 41 **am.**, 41A **inserted**, 44, 47, 49, 56 **am.**, sch. 1 forms 1, 2 **replaced**, 3–7 **am.**, 1971/1977
815	Local Education Authies. Recoupment (Further Education) Regs. 1954 (1954 I, p. 721)	reg. 4 **am.**, 1971/701 reg. 14 **am.**, 1971/1821
898	British Transport Commission (Male Wages Grades Pensions) Regs. 1954 (1954 I, p. 175)	Tables I–V **am.**, 1971/189
1647	Therapeutic Substances (Supply of Oxytetracycline for Agricultural Purposes) Regs. 1954 (1954 II, p. 2392)	**r.**, 1971/459
1743	Telegraph (Inland Written Press Telegram) Regs. 1954 (1954 II, p. 2279)	**r.**, P.O. Scheme 11.1.71.*

* Not S.I. *See* London Gazette 27.1.71. p. 37s.

Year and Number (or date)	Title or Description	How affected and Act or Instrument by which affected
1955		
147	Poultry Carcases (Landing) O. 1955 (1955 II, p. 2652)	**r.,** 1971/1593
222	Local Education Authies. Recoupment (Further Education) Amdt. Regs. 1955 (1955 I, p. 713)	**superseded,** 1971/1821
346	Town and Country Planning (Minerals) (S.) Regs. 1955 (1955 II, p. 2665)	**r.,** 1971/778
690	Potato Marketing Scheme 1955 (1955 I, p. 148)	annex paras. 40, 56, 84 **am.,** 1971/711.
842	Trustee Savings Banks (Pensions) O. 1955 (1955 II, p. 2388)	art. 5 **r.,** 1971/1316.
1125	Cinematograph (Safety) (S.) Regs. 1955 (1955 I, p. 326)	regs. 8 **am.,** 8A **inserted,** 10 **am.,** 31B **inserted** 1971/471.
1803	Merchant Shipping (Safety Convention (Countries) (Various) (No. 2) O. 1955 (1955 I, p. 1139)	**superseded** (Monaco), 1971/217.
1892	Telegraph (Inland Written Press Telegram) Amdt. (No. 1) Regs. 1955 (1955 II, p. 2568)	**r.,** P.O. Scheme 11.1.71.*
1893	Commonwealth Telegraphs (Cable and Wireless Ltd. Pension) Regs. 1955 (1955 I, p. 500)	regs. 2, 5–8, 10, 11, 13–16, 18–20, 26 **am.,** (*retrosp)* 1971/61.
1956		
84	Diplomatic Immunities Restriction O. 1956 (1956 I, p. 683)	arts. 1 **r.,** 2 **am.,** 3 **r.,** schs. 1, 2 **r.,** 1971/2101.
630	Bd. of Inquiry (Army) Rules 1956 (1956 I, p. 207)	rule 7 **am.,** 1971/1257.
732	National Insurance (Mod. of the London Transport and Railway Pension Schemes) Regs. 1956 (1956 I, p. 1645)	schs. 1–3 **am.,** 1971/189.
894	Schools (S.) Code 1956 (1956 I, p. 735)	reg. 4 **am.,** 1971/1079.
1002	Merchant Shipping (Colonies etc.) Tonnage Measurement O. 1956 (1956 I, p. 1208)	**r.,** 1971/383.
1022	Firemen's Pension Scheme O. 1956 (1956 I, p. 953)	arts. 10, 11, 17, 46, 53, 55–57 **am.** sch. 2 Pt. I, III, **am.,** sch. 3 Pt. I, III **am.,** sch. 4 **r.,** sch. 8 **am.,** 1971/1329. art 4 **am.,** 1971/1468.
1078	National Health Service (Supplementary Ophthalmic Services) Regs. 1956 (1956 I, p. 1524)	sch. 3 **am.,** 1971/340.
1239	Increase of Pensions (Mod.) (No. 3) Regs. 1956 (1956 II, p. 1736)	reg. 3 **am.,** 1971/146.

* Not S.I. *see* London Gazette 27.1.71. p. 37s.

Year and Number (or date)	Title or Description	How affected and Act or Instrument by which affected
1956		
1456	Trustee Savings Banks (Increase of Pensions) O. 1956 (1956 II, p. 2197)	**r.,** 1971/1316.
1657	Premium Savings Bonds Regs. 1956 (1956 I, p. 1489)	reg. 2A **am.,** 1971/550. reg. 2B **inserted,** 1971/1870.
1901	Metropolitan Police Staffs (Increase of Superannuation Allowances) O. 1956 (1956 I, p. 1210)	**r.,** 1971/1316.
1957		
87	Airways Corporations (General Staff, Pilots and Officers Pensions) (Amdt.) Regs. 1957 (1957 I, p. 395)	reg. 1 **am.,** 1971/927.
488	National Health Service (Designation of London Teaching Hospitals) O. 1957 (1957 I, p. 1452)	sch. 1 **am.,** 1971/300, 362.
508	Cotton Industry Development Council (Amdt. No. 3) O. 1957 (1957 I, p. 1174)	**r.,** 1971/2054.
578	National Insurance (Claims and Payments) Amdt. Regs. 1957 (1957 I, p. 1516)	**r.,** 1971/707.
669	Indictment Rules 1957 (1957 I, p. 533)	**r.,** 1971/1253.
787	Live Poultry (Restrictions) O. 1957 (1957 II, p. 1919)	**r.,** 1971/311.
1074	Motor Vehicles (International Circulation) O. 1957 (1957 II, p. 2154)	sch. 2 **am.,** 1971/100. arts. 1 **am.,** 5 **replaced,** schs. 1 **am.,** 2 **replaced,** 1971/869.
1357	National Insurance (Claims and Payments) Amdt. (No. 2) Regs. 1957 (1957 I, p. 1518)	**r.,** 1971/707.
1372	Merchant Shipping (Safety Convention Countries) (Various) (No. 1) O. 1957 (1957 I, p. 1373)	**superseded** (Hungary), 1971/217.
1421	Town and Country Planning (Minerals) (Amdt.) (S.) Regs. 1957 (1957 II, p. 2574)	**r.,** 1971/778.
1800	Local Govt. (Allowances for Attendance at Road Safety Conferences) Regs. 1957 (1957 I, p. 1328)	**r.,** 1971/753.
1827	Pensions Appeal Tribunals (E. and W.) (Amdt.) Rules 1957 (1957 II, p. 1833)	**r.,** 1971/769.
1835	National Insurance (Child's Special Allowance) Regs. 1957 (1957 I, p. 1523)	sch. **am.,** 1971/707.
1972	Pensions Appeal Tribunals (S.) (Amdt.) Rules 1957 (1957 II, p. 1834)	**r.,** 1971/2124.

Year and Number (or date)	Title or Description	How affected and Act or Instrument by which affected
1957		
2179	National Insurance (Death Grant) (Consequential Provns.) Regs. 1957 (1957 I, p. 1527)	reg. 2, sch. Pt. I **r.,** 1971/707.
2201	Public Trustee (Custodian Trustee) Rules 1957 (1957 II, p. 2577)	**r.,** 1971/1894.
2224	Judicial Ctee. Rules 1957 (1957 I, p. 1205)	sch. B Pt. II **r.,** 1971/213.
1958		
101	Royal Irish Constabulary (Widows' Pensions) Regs. 1958 (1958 I, p. 354)	**r.,** 1971/1469.
305	Pedestrian Crossings (E. and W.) (Amdt.) Regs. 1958 (1958 II, p. 2107)	**r.** (30.11.73), 1971/1524.
310	Pedestrian Crossings (Amdt.) (S.) Regs. 1958 (1958 II, p. 2108)	**r.** (30.11.73), 1971/1524.
341	Superannuation and other Trust Funds (Fees) Regs. 1958 (1958 II, p. 2246)	**r.,** 1971/462.
765	Judicial Ctee. (Medical Rules) O. 1958 (1958 I, p. 1330)	**r.,** 1971/214.
787	Savings Bank (Fees) (Amdt.) Warrant 1958 (1958 II, p. 2123)	**r.,** 1971/981.
956	Cereals (Protection of Guarantees) O. (1958 I, p. 78)	**r.,** 1971/290.
1872	A.S. (Legal Aid Rules) 1958 (1958 I, p. 389)	rules. 1, 2, 4, 5 **am.,** 1971/174. rule 2 **am.,** 1971/1796.
1959		
3	Magistrates Cts. (Maintenance Orders Act 1958) Rules 1959 (1959 I, p. 1646)	rules 10–20 **r.,** 23 **am.,** sch. forms 13, 14, 20 **r.,** 1971/809.
278	Patents Appeal Tribunal Rules 1959 (1959 II, p. 2002)	**r.,** 1971/394.
337	Removal of Defence Works Grant Regs. 1959 (1959 I, p. 1050)	reg. 4 **am.,** 1971/534.
364	School Regs. 1959 (1959 I, p. 1584)	reg. 16, sch. **am.,** 1971/342.
365	Handicapped Pupils and Special School Regs. 1959 (1959 I, p. 1024)	regs. 15 **am.,** 16A **inserted,** 1971/342.
466	Live Poultry (Restrictions) Amdt. O. 1959 (1959 II, p. 2209)	**r.,** 1971/311.
476	Abolition of the Education (S.) Fund (Consequential Provns.) Regs. 1959 (1959 I, p. 1095)	reg. 11 **r.,** 1971/1537.
479	Adoption (High Ct.) Rules 1959 (1959 I, p. 631)	**r.,** 1971/1520.

Year and Number (or date)	Title or Description	How affected and Act or Instrument by which affected
1959		
748	National Health Service (Designation of Teaching Hospitals) O. 1959 (1959 I, p. 1813)	sch. 1 **am.**, 1971/152, 1437.
763	A.S. (Adoption of Children) 1959 (1959 I, p. 649)	para. 15 **am.**, 1971/1163.
833	Grant-Aided Secondary Schools (S.) Grant Regs. 1959 (1959 I, p. 1104)	reg. 4, sch. **replaced,** 1971/558.
890	Standards for School Premises Regs. 1959 (1959 I, p. 1006)	regs. 4, 16 **am.**, 1971/1553.
955	General Optical Council (Companies Ctee. Rules) O. of C. 1959 (1959 II, p. 1981)	rule 6 **replaced,** 1971/1525.
956	General Optical Council (Education Ctee. Rules) O. of C. 1959 (1959 II, p. 1983)	rule 7 **replaced,** 1971/1527.
1147	Motorways Traffic Regs. 1959 (1959 II, p. 2507)	reg. 11A **inserted** (E)., 1971/1087.
1262	County Ct. Fees O. 1959 (1959 I, p. 803)	**r.** (saving), 1971/1649.
1334	Postal Order Warrant 1959 (1959 II, p. 2201)	**r.**, P.O. Scheme 15.1.71.*
1340	Pensions Appeal Tribunals (E. and W.) (Amdt.) Rules 1959 (1959 II, p. 2068)	**r.**, 1971/769.
1362	Town and Country Planning (Limit of Annual Value) (S.) O. 1959 (1959 II, p. 2660)	**r.**, 1971/1634.
1534	Trustee Savings Banks (Increase of Pensions) O. 1959 (1959 II, p. 2468)	**r.**, 1971/1316.
1787	Poultry Carcases (Landing) Amdt. O. 1959 (1959 II, p. 2208)	**r.**, 1971/1593.
1831	Increase of Pensions (Mod.) (No. 2) Regs. 1959 (1959 II, p. 2064)	reg. 2 **am.**, 1971/146.
1832	Direct Grant Schools Regs. 1959 (1959 I, p. 1034)	reg. 4 **am.**, 1971/1788.
2067	Pensions Appeal Tribunals (S.) (Amdt.) Rules 1959 (1959 II, p. 2069)	**r.**, 1971/2124.
2099	Telegraph (British Commonwealth and Foreign Written Telegram) Regs. 1959 (1959 II, p. 2580)	**r.**, P.O. Scheme 7.1.71.†
2100	Telegraph (British Commonwealth and Foreign Written Press Telegram) Regs. 1959 (1959 II, p. 2576)	**r.**, P.O. Scheme 7.1.71.†

* Not S.I. *see* London Gazette 3.2.71. p. 19s.
† Not S.I. *see* London Gazette 27.1.71. pp. 40s, 50s.

Year and Number (or date)	Title or Description	How affected and Act or Instrument by which affected
1959		
2296 *Instrt. not S.I.*	Pedestrian Crossings (E. and W.) (Amdt.) Regs. 1959 (1959 II, p. 2379)	**r.** (30.11.73), 1971/1524.
22 Dec.	Montserrat L.P. 1959 (1959 II, p. 3386)	arts. 12, 13 **am.,** 1971/873. art. 3 **am.,** 1971/1740.
1960		
13	Pedestrian Crossings (Amdt.) (S.) Regs. 1960 (1960 III, p. 2929)	**r.** (30.11.73), 1971/1524.
250	Cycle Racing on Highways Regs. 1960 (1960 III, p. 3047)	reg. 5 **am.** (*temp.*), 1971/346.
1099	Metropolitan Police Staffs (Increase of Superannuation Allowances) O. 1960 (1960 II, p. 2022)	**r.,** 1971/1316.
1139	Mental Health Review Tribunal Rules 1960 (1960 II, p. 1962)	sch. 1 **mod.** (W.), 1971/1772.
1241	Mental Health (Hospital and Guardianship) Regs. 1960 (1960 II, p. 1903)	reg. 4, sch. **mod.,** 1971/178.
1270	National Insurance (Modification of the Superannuation Acts) Regs. 1960 (1960 II, p. 2297)	reg. 4 **am.,** 1971/1441.
1395	Legal Aid (S.) (Assessment of Resources) Regs. 1960 (1960 II, p. 1807)	reg. 11, sch. 1 rule 5 **am.,** 1971/275.
1471	Legal Aid (Assessment of Resources) Regs. 1960 (1960 II, p. 1749)	reg. 9 **am.,** 1971/63. sch. 1 rule 5 **am.,** 1971/103
1505	Goods Vehicles (Licences and Prohibitions) Regs. 1960 (1960 III, p. 3020)	**r.,** 1971/2020.
1934	General Optical Council (Disciplinary Ctee. Rules) O. of C. 1960 (1960 II, p. 2643)	rules 10 **replaced,** 17, 19 **am.,** 1971/1526.
1935	General Optical Council (Investigating Ctee. Rules) O. of C. 1960 (1960 II, p. 2646)	rule 6 **replaced,** 1971/1528.
2195	Legal Aid (S.) (General) Regs. 1960 (1960 II, p. 1817)	regs. 3, 8, 10, 11 **am.,** 1971/194. arrangement of regs. **am.,** regs. 3 **am.,** 4A **inserted,** 8, 10 **am.,** 1971/1914.
2396	London Transport (Lost Property) Regs. 1960 (1960 I, p. 432)	**r.,** 1971/2125.
1961		
153	Tribunals and Inquiries (Air Operators' Certificates) O. 1961	**r.,** 1971/831.
243	Food (Meat Inspection) (S.) Regs. 1961	reg. 22 **am.,** 1971/1196.
251	Financial Statements (Parishes) Regs. 1961	**r.,** 1971/819.

Year and Number (or date)	Title or Description	How affected and Act or Instrument by which affected
1961		
355	County Ct. Fees (Amdt.) O. 1961	**r.** (saving), 1971/1649.
402	Royal Irish Constabulary (Widows' Pensions) Regs. 1961	**r.**, 1971/1469.
557	National Insurance (Graduated Retirement Benefit and Consequential Provisions) Regs. 1961	schs. 2 Pt I, 3 Pt, I **r.**, 1971/707.
559	National Insurance (Mod. of Transport Undertaking Superannuation Funds) Regs. 1961	reg. 4 **am.**, 1971/189.
899	Cotton Industry Development Council (Amdt. No. 4) O. 1961	**r.**, 1971/2054.
1071	Cereals (Protection of Guarantees) (Amdt.) O. 1961	**r.**, 1971/290.
1210	Special Roads (Classes of Traffic) O. 1961	**r.**, 1971/1156.
1246	Injuries in War (Shore Employments) Compensation (Amdt.) Scheme 1961	para. 1 **am.**, *see* 1971/1987.
1389	Rag Flock and Other Filling Materials Regs. 1961	**r.**, 1971/1652.
1398	National Health Service (Superannuation) (S.) Regs. 1961	regs. 2, 19, 30, 51, 58, 75 **am.**, sch. 2 **am.**, 1971/1430.
1405	Live Poultry (Restrictions) Amdt. O. 1961	**r.**, 1971/311.
1506	Western Pacific (Cts.) O. in C. 1961	s. 19 **am.**, 1971/715.
1894	County Ct. Fees (Amdt. No. 2) O. 1961	**r.** (saving), 1971/1649.
2040	Anthrax Prevention (Goat, Hair and Shaving Brushes) O. 1961	**r.**, 1971/1234.
2102	Civil Aviation (Aerial Advertising) Regs. 1961	**r.**, 1971/1968.
2205	A.S. (Valuation Appeal Rules Amdt.) 1961	paras. 1, 2 **r.**, 1971/2089.
1962		
148	Legal Aid (General) Regs. 1962	**r.**, 1971/62.
927	Goods Vehicles (Licences and Prohibitions) (Amdt.) Regs. 1962	**r.**, 1971/2020.
1000	Superannuation (Teaching and Local Government) Interchange (S.) Rules 1962	**r.**, 1971/2025.
1001	Public Trustee (Custodian Trustee) Rules 1962	**r.**, 1971/1894.

Year and Number (or date)	Title or Description	How affected and Act or Instrument by which affected
1962		
1220	A.S. (Valuation Appeal Rules Amdt.) 1962	**r.,** 1971/2089.
1271	Functions of Traffic Wardens (S.) O. 1962	**r.,** 1971/374.
1319	Special Roads and Trunk Roads (Procedure) Regs. 1962	regs. 1, 4 **am.,** 1971/1706.
1532	Preservatives in Food Regs. 1962	reg. 3, sch. 1 **am.,** 1971/882.
1614	Pensions Appeal Tribunals (E. and W.) (Amdt.) Rules 1962	**r.,** 1971/769.
1714	Legal Aid (General) (Amdt.) Regs. 1962	**r.,** 1971/62.
1926	Preservatives in Food (S.) Regs. 1962	reg. 4, sch. 1 **am.,** 1971/988.
2045	Building Societies (Forms and Fees) Regs. 1962	sch. 2 **replaced,** 1971/449.
2086	Students' Allowances (S.) Regs. 1962	**r.,** 1971/124.
2334	A.S. (Fees of Town Clerks and Clerks of the Peace)1962	**r.,** 1971/91.
2522	Pensions Appeal Tribunals (S.) (Amdt.) Rules 1962	**r.,** 1971/2124.
2758	British Transport Reorganisation (Pensions of Employees) (No. 3) Order 1962	art. 17 **r.,** 1971/1128.
1963		
372	Judicial Ctee. (Fees) Rules 1963	sch. B Pt. I, **r.,** 1971/213.
558	Telegraph (Inland Written Telegram) Regs. 1963	**r.,** P.O. Scheme 11.1.71.*
559	Telegraph (Inland Written Press Telegram) Amdt. (No. 2) Regs. 1963	**r.,** P.O. Scheme 11.1.71.*
616	Double Taxation Relief (Taxes on Income) (Israel) O. 1963	arts. I, II **am.,** VI **replaced,** VII, VIII **am.,** VIIIA **inserted,** XVIII, XXI, XXIV **am.,** 1971/391.
766	Friendly Societies (London and Edinburgh Gazette Fees) Regs. 1963	**r.,** 1971/461.
897	County Ct. Fees (Amdt.) O. 1963	**r.** (saving), 1971/1649.
901	Trustee Savings Banks (Increase of Pensions) O. 1963	**r.,** 1971/1316.
920	Royal Irish Constabulary (Widows' Pensions) Regs. 1963	**r.,** 1971/1469.
1064	Superannuation (Teaching and N.I. Local Govt.) Interchange Rules 1963	**r.** (saving), 1971/907.

* Not S.I. *see* London Gazette 27.1.71 pp. 31s, 37s.

Year and Number (or date)	Title or Description	How affected and Act or Instrument by which affected
1963		
1221	Town and Country Planning (Minerals) Regs. 1963	**r.,** 1971/756.
1229	Meat Inspection Regs. 1963	reg. 12 **am.,** 1971/1179.
1311	Increase of Pensions (Mod.) (No. 4) Regs. 1963	reg. 3 **am.,** 1971/146.
1450	Therapeutic Substances (Manufacture and Importation) General Regs. 1963	reg. 11 **am.,** 1971/666.
1459	Therapeutic Substances (Manufacture of Vaccines, Toxins and Antigens) Regs. 1963	reg. 5 **am.,** Pt. XX **r.,** new Pt. XX (regs. 96–101),Pt. XXA (regs. 102–108), Pt. XXB (regs. 109–109F), Pt. XXX (regs. 173–178), Pt. XXXA (regs. 179–184), Pt. XXXB (regs. 185–190) **inserted** 1971/118.
1557	Town and Country Planning (Limit of Annual Value) (S.) O. 1963	**r.,** 1971/1634.
1979	Metropolitan Police Staffs (Increase of Superannuation Allowances) O. 1963.	**r.,** 1971/1316.
2006	Live Poultry (Restrictions) Amdt. O. 1963	**r.,** 1971/311.
2149	Poultry Carcasses (Landing) Amdt. O. 1963	**r.,** 1971/1593.
1964		
73	National Insurance (Industrial Injuries) (Claims and Payments) Regs. 1964	reg. 24A **inserted,** 1971/1201.
205	Road Vehicles Lighting Regs. 1964	**r.,** 1971/694.
388	Prison Rules 1964	rule 6, 8, 10, 19, 25, 26, 34, 41, 43, 46, 51, 52, 56, 74, 75, 88 **am.,** 89–91 **r.,** 93–97, 99 **am.,** 1971/2019.
404	Road Vehicles (Index Marks) Regs. 1964	**r.,** 1971/450.
409	Importation of Potatoes (Health) (G.B.) O. 1964	**r.,** 1971/438.
463	Fatstock (Guarantee Payments) O. 1964	art. 2, 4, 8 **am.,** 9, **replaced,** sch. Pt. II **replaced,** 1971/801.
504	National Insurance (Industrial Injuries) (Benefit) Regs. 1964	regs.11, 16, 31 **am.,** 1971/1019. regs. 9, 11, 18 **am.,** 26 **replaced by** 26, 26A, regs. 39, 42, 44 **am.,** 1971/1201.
662	Cotton Industry Development Council (Amdt. No. 5) O. 1964	**r.,** 1971/2054.
690	Copyright (International Conventions) O. 1964	sch. 1 Pts. 1, 2 **am.,** schs. 3, 5, 6 **am.,** 1971/1850.
711	Building (Forms) (S.) Regs. 1964	**r.,** 1971/747.

Year and Number (or date)	Title or Description	How affected and Act or Instrument by which affected
1964		
712	Building (S.) Act 1959 (Procedure) Regs. 1964	**r.**, 1971/746.
814	Price Stabilisation Levies (Supplementary Provns.) Regs. 1964	reg. 5 **replaced**, 1971/1033.
840	Cereals (Guarantee Payments) O. 1964	**r.**, 1971/289.
853	Justices' Allowances Regs. 1964	**r.**, 1971/413.
872	Justices' Allowances (S.) Regs. 1964	**r.**, 1971/490.
879	Trade Union Regs. 1964	**r.**, 1971/1542.
904	Probation (Allowances) Rules 1964	**r.**, 1971/414.
1033	Legal Officers Fees O. 1964	sch. Tables I, IV **am.**, 1971/1130.
1071	Civil Aviation (Navigation Services Charges) Regs. 1964	**r.**, 1971/1135.
1084	Special Roads (Classes of Traffic) (S.) O. 1964	**r.**, 1971/1211.
1086	Industrial Training (Engineering Bd.) O. 1964	sch. 1 **replaced**, 1971/1530.
1110	National Insurance (Claims and Payments) Amdt. Regs. 1964	**r.**, 1971/707.
1116	Civil Aviation (Licensing) Regs. 1964	sch. 2 paras. 1 **replaced**, para. 3 **am.**, 1971/1981.
1148	Firemen's Pension Scheme O. 1964	**am.**, (so far as still in force), 1971/145. arts. 10, 11, 17, 51, 58, 61–63, 80 **am.**, sch. 2 Pt. I, III **am.**, sch. 3 Pt. I, III **am.**,sch. 4 **r.**, sch. 9 **am.**, 1971/1329. art. 4 **a.m.**, 1971/1468.
1177	Local Government (Executive Councils) (Compensation) Regs. 1964	**mod.**, 1971/52.
1178	Road Vehicles (Registration and Licensing) Regs. 1964	**r.**, 1971/450.
1329	British Transport Reorganisation (Pensions of Employees) (No. 1) O. 1964	**mod.**, 1971/116, 117.
1386	Control of Harbour Development O. 1964	art. 3 **am.**, 1971/1874.
1410	Act of Adj. (Criminal Legal Aid Fees) 1964	ss. 3–10 **replaced**, 1971/926.
1556	Police Authorities (Appointment of Magistrates) Rules 1964	**r.**, 1971/2048.
1575	Merchant Shipping (Safety Convention Countries) (Various) (No. 9) O. 1964	**superseded** (Senegal), 1971/217.
1592	Protection of Depositors (Registration of Documents) (Fees) Regs. 1964	**r.**, 1971/574.

Year and Number (or date)	Title or Description	How affected and Act or Instrument by which affected
1964		
1857	Traffic Signs Regs. 1964	regs. 11A, 25, 31 **am.**, 1971/2095.
1892	Land Drainage (Compensation) Regs. 1964	regs. 2, 7, 17–19, 27 **am.**, 30A **inserted**, 31 **replaced**, 32 **am.**, 42 **inserted**, 1971/1303.
1893	Legal Aid (General) (Amdt.) Regs. 1964	**r.**, 1971/62
1966	European Free Trade Association (Origin of Goods) Regs. 1964	sch. 1, cc. 28, 29, 31, 32, 34, 35, 44, 68–70, 73–76, 82–85, 87, 89, 90 **am.**, sch. 2 cc. 57, 59, **am.**, sch. 3 cc. 25, 28, 38, 57 **am.**, 1971/2046.
1967	Registration of Births and Deaths (High Commissioners) Regs. 1964	regs. 1, 12, **am.**, 16 **r.**, 1971/608.
2002	Indictments (Procedure) (Amdt.) Rules 1964	**r.**, 1971/2084.
2077	Personal Injuries (Civilians) Scheme 1964	arts. 17 **am.**, 17A **inserted**, 21, 23, 29, 49, 66 **am.**, schs. 3, 4 **am.**, 1971/1178.
1965		
237	Road Vehicles (Index Marks) (Amdt.) Regs. 1965	**r.**, 1971/450.
260	Precepts Rules 1965	sch. Pt. I **am.**, 1971/1843.
261	Rate-demands Rules 1965	sch. 1 Pts. I–V **am.**, 1971/1844.
273	Pensions Appeal Tribunals (E. and W.) (Amdt.) Rules 1965	**r.**, 1971/769.
283	Justices of the Peace Act 1949 (Compensation) Regs. 1965	regs. 2, 8, 18 **am.**, 33A **inserted**, 34, 35 **am.**, 1971/1119.
321	A.S. (Rules of Ct., Consolidation and Amdt.) 1965	rule 168 **am.**, 1971/202. rule 289A **inserted**, 1971/203. rule 291 **am.**, 1971/265. rule 347 c. IV **replaced**, 1971/1161. rule 230 **am.**, 1971/1162. rules 72, 75 **am.**, 75A **inserted**, 1971/1215. rules 2, 3 **am.**, 1971/1714. rule 75A **am.**, 1971/1797. c. IV, s. 8 heading **am.**, rule 249A **inserted**, 1971/1809.
329	Motor Vehicles (International Circulation) Regs. 1965	**r.**, 1971/937.
395	County Ct. Fees (Amdt.) O. 1965	**r.** (saving), 1971/1649.
450	A.S. (Valuation Appeal Rules Amdt.) 1965	paras. 2–4 **r.**, 1971/2089.
500	Royal Irish Constabulary (Widows' Pensions) Regs. 1965	**r.**, 1971/1469.

Year and Number (or date)	Title or Description	How affected and Act or Instrument by which affected
1965		
516	Income Tax (Employments) Regs. 1965	reg. 17 **am.,** 1971/21. regs 2, 16, 17 **am.,** 21 **r.,** 24 **am.,** 1971/1896. regs. 43 **am.,** 44–47 **r.** (*prosp.*), 48 **mod.,** 1971/1947.
517	Clerks of the Peace and Justices' Clerks (Compensation) Regs. 1965	regs. 2, 8, 18 **am.,** 33A **inserted,** 34 35 **am.,** 1971/1122.
543	Police (Discipline) Regs. 1965	reg. 17 **am.,** 1971/133.
544	Police (Discipline) (Deputy Chief Constables, Assistant Chief Constables and Chief Constables) Regs. 1965	reg. 16 **am.,** 1971/134.
563	Fire Services (Compensation) Regs. 1965	regs. 6 **am.,** 26A **inserted,** 27, 37 **am.,** 1971/1121.
620	Probation (Compensation) Regs. 1965	regs. 2, 8, **am.,** 33A **inserted,** 34, 35 **am.,** 1971/1120.
654	London Govt. O. 1965	art. 4 **am.,** 1971/753.
718	Resolution of the H. of C. dated 9th March 1965 passed in pursuance of the H. of C. Members' Fund Act 1948 s. 3 (11 & 12 Geo. 6 c. 36) (1965 I, p. 2567)	**superseded,** 1971/770 (1971 II, p. 4028).
722	Probation (Conditions of Service) Rules 1965	rule 3 **am.,** schs. 1, 2 **replaced,** 1971/1615.
723	Probation Rules 1965	rules 43, 48 **am.,** 1971/480.
865	Legal Aid (General) (Amdt.) Regs. 1965	**r.,** 1971/62.
870	Road Vehicles Lighting (Amdt.) Regs. 1965	**r.,** 1971/694.
901	Administration Orders (Amdt.) Rules 1965	**r.,** 1971/1095.
1046	Merchant Shipping (Pilot Ladders) Rules 1965	rule 4 **am.,** 1971/724.
1101	Industrial Tribunals (E.W.) Regs. 1965	reg. 5 **am.,** 1971/1660.
1157	Industrial Tribunals (S.) Regs. 1965	reg. 5 **am.,** 1971/1661.
1192	Telex Regulations 1965	**r.,** P.O. Scheme, 11.1.71.*
1343	Wages Regulation (Stamped or Pressed Metal-Wares) (Holidays) O. 1965	**r.,** 1971/1089.
1373	Building Regs. 1965	regs. A2, A4 **am.,** A13 **replaced,** B3 **am.,** D1, D2 **replaced,** D3, D8, D14, D15, D19 **am.,** D21 **inserted,** E7 **am.,** E14 **replaced,** E14A, E16, G1 **am.,** G2 **replaced,** G3 **am.,** G4 **replaced,** L1, L2 **am.,** L22 **inserted,** M1 **replaced,** M3, M4 **am.,** M6A **inserted,** M7, M8 **am.,** M11 **inserted,** sch. 1 Pt. A **replaced,** sch. 3A **am.,** sch. 5 **r.,** sch. 6 rule 2 **am.,** sch. 7 rule 11 **am.,** sch. 8 Pt. V B **am.,** sch. 10 Pt. I–III, IV (B) **am.,** sch. 12 **inserted,** 1971/1600.

* Not S.I. *see* London Gazette 27.1.71. p. 26s.

Year and Number (or date)	Title or Description	How affected and Act or Instrument by which affected
1965		
1412	Milk (N.I.) O. 1965	**r.,** 1971/1037.
1421	Superannuation (Teaching and Belfast Corporation) Interchange Rules 1965	**r.** (saving), 1971/907.
1426	Importation of Plants and Plant Produce (Health) (G.B.) O. 1965	**r.,** 1971/438.
1437	Rag Flock and Other Filling Materials Regs. 1695	**r.,** 1971/1652.
1500	County Ct. Funds Rules 1965	rules 2, 20, 23, 24 **am.,** 1971/260.
1506	Performing Right Tribunal Rules 1965	rules 2–5, 7, 9, 14, 17, 18 **am.,** sch. 1 forms 3A, 4A **inserted,** sch. 2 **am.,** 1971/636.
1521	Probation (Allowances) Rules 1965	**r.,** 1971/414.
1522	Justices' Allowances Regs 1965	**r.,** 1971/413.
1599	Anti-Dumping Duty O. 1965	**r.,** 1971/2001.
1611	A.S. (Alteration of Sheriff Ct. Fees) 1965	**r.** (as to proceedings commenced after 15.2.71), 1971/90.
1707	Mayor's and City of London Ct. Funds Rules 1965	rules 2, 17, 20, 21 **am.,** 1971/453.
1734	British Commonwealth and Foreign Parcel Post Regs. 1965	**r.,** by P.O. Scheme 15.6.71*.
1735	British Commonwealth and Foreign Post Regs. 1965	**r.,** by P.O. Scheme 15.6.71.*
1776	Rules of Supreme Ct. (Revision) 1965	O. 62, 72, 97 Appx. A forms 1, 2, 8, 9, 17, 20, B. 12, 9 **am.,** 1971/354. O. 104 **am.,** Appx. A form 104, 105 **am.,** 106 **r.,** 1971/835. O. 80, 110 **am.,** 1971/1132. Arrangement of Orders, O. 1, 4, 11, 12, 15, 17, 24, 28, 29, 30, 32, 34, 35, 37, 41, 43, 46, 50, 51, 54, 56–59, 61–64, 67, 68, 72, 74, 75 **am.,** 76 **replaced,** 77, 80, 81, 89 **am.,** 90 renumbered as 91, new 90 **inserted,** 91 **r.,** 99, 104, 106, 107, 109 **am.,** 112 **r.,** Appx. A forms 4, 6, 14, 37, 87-90, 104 Appx B. forms 1, 2 **am.,** 1971/1269. Order 1. 4, 6–9, 11, 12, 15, 22, 28, 29, 32–35, 38, 39, 42, 53, 56, 62–64, 67, 68, 72, 79, 86, 90, 92, 102, 106 **am.,** 112 **inserted,** Appx. A forms 2, 7, 15, 28, 37, 46 **am.,** 60, 61 **r.,** 97, 98, 98A, 101 **am.,** 102 **r.,** 103 **am.,** 1971/1955.
1788	Act of Adj. (Criminal Legal Aid Fees Amdt.) 1965	**superseded,** 1971/926.

* Not S.I. *see* London Gazette 30.6.71. pp. 14s, 26s.

Year and Number (or date)	Title or Description	How affected and Act or Instrument by which affected
1965		
1825	Nuclear Installations Regs. 1965	**r.,** 1971/381.
1839	Registration of Births, Still Births, Deaths and Marriages (Prescription of Forms) (S.) Regs. 1965	schs. 1, 2, 5, 10, 16–18, 27 **replaced,** 1971/1158.
1841	Registration of Births, Deaths and Marriages (Adopted Children Register) (S.) Regs. 1965	**r.,** 1971/1160.
1843	Registration of Births, Deaths and Marriages (Civil Marriage Schedule) (S.) Regs. 1965	**r.,** 1971/1159.
1860	Cayman Is. (Constitution) O. 1965	s. 3 **am.,** 1971/1737. s. 47 **am.,** 1971/2100.
1993	Ship's Report, Importation and Exportation by Sea Regs. 1965	regs. 8A **inserted,** 9 **am.,** 1971/1300.
1995	Industrial and Provident Societies Regs. 1965	sch. 2 **replaced,** 1971/463.
2017	Pension Appeal Tribunals (S.) Amdt. Rules 1965	**r.,** 1971/2124.
2071	Adoption (High Ct.) (Amdt.) Rules 1965	**r.,** 1971/1520.
1966		
10	Witnesses' Allowances Regs. 1966	**r.,** 1971/107.
11	Coroners (Fees and Allowances) Rules 1966	**r.,** 1971/108.
30	Road Vehicles Lighting (Amdt.) Regs. 1966	**r.,** 1971/694.
164	Pneumoconiosis, Byssinosis and Miscellaneous Diseases Benefit Scheme 1966	arts. 4, 5 **am.,** 6 **replaced,** 7 **am.,** schs. 2, 3 **am.,** 1971/1222.
165	Workmen's Compensation (Supplementation) Scheme 1966	arts. 7, 10 **am.,** sch. 1 **replaced** 1971/1223.
222	Functions of Traffic Wardens (S.) O. 1966	**r.,** 1971/374.
224	Road Vehicles (Excise) (Prescribed Particulars) Regs. 1966	**r.,** 1971/1628.
243	County Ct. Fees (Amdt.) O. 1966	**r.** (saving), 1971/1649.
250	Road Vehicles (Index Marks) (Amdt.) Regs. 1966	**r.,** 1971/450.
346	Public Health Aircraft (S.) Regs. 1966	**r.,** 1971/131.
438	Exchange Control (Gold Coins Exemption) O. 1966	**r.,** 1971/516.

Year and Number (or date)	Title or Description	How affected and Act or Instrument by which affected
1966 465	Civil Aviation (Navigation Services Charges) (Amdt.) Regs. 1966	**r.**, 1971/1135.
476	Pedestrian Crossings (W.) (Amdt.) Regs. 1966	**r.** (30.11.73), 1971/1524.
484	Cereals (Guarantee Payments) (Amdt.) O. 1966	**r.**, 1971/289.
485	Cereals (Protection of Guarantees) (Amdt.) O. 1966	**r.**, 1971/290.
492	Pedestrian Crossings (E.) (Amdt.) Regs. 1966	**r.** (30.11.73), 1971/1524.
505	Therapeutic Substances (Manufacture of Antibiotics) Regs. 1966	Pt. XVIII (reg. 94–97) **inserted,** 1971/888.
519	Pedestrian Crossings (S.) (Amdt.) Regs. 1966	**r.** (30.11.73), 1971/1524.
530	Motorways Traffic (E.) (Amdt.) Regs. 1966	**r.**, 1971/1087.
810	Metropolitan Police Staffs (Increase of Superannuation Allowances) O. 1966	**r.**, 1971/1316.
822	Increase of Pensions (Police and Fire Services) Regs. 1966	reg. 3 **am.**, 1971/146.
898	Petroleum (Production) Regs. 1966	sch. 2 para. 6 **replaced,** sch. 4 cl. 1, 3, 4 **am.,** 5, 6 **replaced,** 7, 11 **am.,** 12 **replaced,** 23 **am.,** 25 **replaced,** sch. 5 cl. 15 **replaced,** 1971/814.
914	Postal Order Amdt. (No. 1) Regs. 1966	**r.**, P.O. Scheme, 15.1.71.*
936	Price Stability of Imported Products (Levy Arrangements) O. 1966	**r.**, 1971/631.
951	Live Poultry (Restrictions) Amdt. O. 1966	**r.**, 1971/311.
959	National Insurance (Earnings-related Benefit) Regs. 1966	reg. 3 **am.**, sch. **replaced,** 1971/1497.
980	Motor Vehicles (Speed Limit on Motorways) Regs. 1966	**r.**, 1971/601.
1010	National Insurance (Miscs. Consequential Amdts. and Transitional Provns.) Regs. 1966	reg. 2 **r.**, 1971/707.
1045	Firemen's Pension Scheme O. 1966	**r.** (saving), 1971/145. (so far as still in force). arts. 10, 11, 11A, 17, 53, 60, 63–65, 82 **am.**, sch. 2 Pts. I, II, IV, VI, **am.**, sch. 3 Pts. I, III **am.**, sch. 4 **r.**, sch. 10 **am.**, 1971/1329. art. 4 **am.**, 1971/1468.

* Not S.I. *see* London Gazette 3.2.71, p. 19s.

Year and Number (or date)	Title or Description	How affected and Act or Instrument by which affected
1966		
1065	Supplementary Benefit (General) Regs. 1966	regs. 5A **inserted**, 6 **am.**, 1971/1549.
1066	Supplementary Benefit (Appeal Tribunals) Rules 1966	**r.**, 1971/680.
1067	Supplementary Benefit (Claims and Payments) Regs. 1966	reg. 12 **replaced**, 1971/1331.
1142	Firemen's Pension Scheme (Amdt.) O. 1966	**r.** (saving), 1971/145.
1143	Alkali, &c. Works O. 1966	schs. 1, 2 **am.**, 1971/1960.
1164	LondonTransport (Male Wages Grades Pensions) O. 1966	Tables I–IV **am.**, 1971/189.
1189	District Registries O. in C. 1966	**r.**, 1971/392.
1233	National Health Service (General Medical and Pharmaceutical Services) (S.) Regs. 1966	regs. 2 **am.**, 29 **replaced**, 32 **am.**, sch. 1 Pt. I **am.**, sch. 3 **replaced**, sch. 4 Pts. I, II **am.**, 1971/472.
1305	London Govt. O. 1966	art. 3 **am.**, 1971/753.
1308	Importation of Plants and Plant Produce (Health) (G.B.) (Amdt.) O. 1966	**r.**, 1971/438.
1381	Electricity (Borrowing Powers) O. 1966	**superseded**, 1971/339.
1421	Pension Appeal Tribunals (E. and W.) (Amdt.) Rules 1966	**r.**, 1971/769.
1493	Wages Regulations (Ready-made and Wholesale Bespoke Tailoring) (Holidays) O. 1966	sch. para. 2 **am.**, 1971/1651.
1547	County Cts. (Admiralty Jurisdiction) O. 1966	**r.**, 1971/1152.
1548	County Cts. (Bankruptcy and Companies Winding-up Jurisdiction) O. 1966	**r.**, 1971/656.
1570	Public Health (Ships) (S.) Regs. 1966	**r.**, 1971/132.
1578	Cotton Industry Development Council (Amdt. No. 6) O. 1966	**r.**, 1971/2054.
1579	Apple and Pear Development Council O. 1966	arts. 2 **am.**, 8 **r.**, 10, 13 **am.**, 1971/511.
1582	Police Pensions Regs. 1966	**r.**, 1971/232.
1590	Special Constables (Pensions) Regs. 1966	**r.**, 1971/233.
1625	Special Constables (Pensions) (S.) Regs. 1966	**r.**, 1971/234.

Year and Number (or date)	Title or Description	How affected and Act or Instrument by which affected
1967		
25	Double Taxation Relief (Taxes on Income) (Federal Republic of Germany) O. 1967	arts. I **replaced,** II, VI, VII **am.,** VIII **replaced,** XII **am.,** XVII, XVIII **replaced,** XVIIIA **inserted,** XIX, XXIV **replaced,** 1971/874.
27	Pensions Appeal Tribunals (S.) (Amdt.) Rules 1967	**r.,** 1971/2124.
38	Coroners (Fees and Allowances) Rules 1967	**r.,** 1971/108.
39	Witnesses' Allowances Regs. 1967	**r.,** 1971/107.
72	Jurors' Allowances Regs. 1967	**r.,** 1971/136.
144	Jurors' Allowances (S.) Regs. 1967	**r.,** 1971/220.
226	Dominica Constitution O. 1967	Annex—s. 26 **am.,** 1971/714.
315	Road Vehicles (Index Marks) (Amdt.) Regs. 1967	**r.,** 1971/450.
330	National Insurance (Unemployment and Sickness Benefit) Regs. 1967	reg. 7 **am.,** 1971/807. sch. 2 **am.,** 1971/1220. regs. 4, 5, 7 **am.,** 7A **inserted,** 10-12, 14 **am.,** 1971/1949. reg. 14 **replaced,** 1971/1633.
363	Rate Support Grant Regs. 1967	reg. 4 sch. **am.,** 1971/1898.
372	Fishing Vessels (Acquisition and Improvement) (Grants) Scheme 1967	paras. 2, 10, 11 **am.,** 1971/797.
386	National Insurance (Mariners) Regs. 1967	regs. 10, 13, 14, 18, 20, 21 **am.,** schs. 5, 6 **replaced,** sch. 7 **r.,** 1971/1420
422	Supplementary Benefit (Claims and Payments) (Amdt.) Regs. 1967	**r.,** 1971/1331.
453	Police Pensions (Amdt.) Regs. 1967	**r.,** 1971/232.
455	Milk (G.B.) O. 1967	**r.,** 1971/1038.
467	Rate Support Grants (Pooling Arrangements) Regs. 1967	reg. 2 **am.,** 1971/1654.
471	Virgin Islands (Constitution) O. 1967	s. 3 **am.,** 1971/1240.
484	Double Taxation Relief (Taxes on Income) (Trinidad and Tobago) O. 1967	sch. art. 10 **am.,** 1971/2117.
489	Teachers' Superannuation Regs. 1967	regs. 6, 13, 16, 29, 50, 70 sch. 1 Pt. I **am.,** sch. 4 **replaced,** sch. 5 **am.,** 1971/403.
520	National Insurance (Medical Certification) Regs. 1967	reg. 2 **am.,** 1971/1419.

Year and Number (or date)	Title or Description	How affected and Act or Instrument by which affected
1967		
553	Anti-Dumping Duty O. 1967	**r.,** 1971/2.
577	Premium Savings Bonds (Amdt.) Regs. 1967	**r.,** 1971/550.
599	Veterinary Surgeons (Examination of Commonwealth and Foreign Candidates) Regs. 1967	regs. 2 **am.,** 10 **inserted,** 1971/749.
601	Valuation (Water Undertakings) (S.) (No. 1) O. 1967	para. 3 **am.,** 1971/1212.
628	Wages Regulation (Rubber Proofed Garment) (Holidays) O. 1967	sch. para. 2 **am.,** 1971/1836.
633	Royal Air Force (Determination of Service) (No. 2) Regs. 1967	**r.,** 1971/510.
646	Wages Regulation (Retail Bespoke Tailoring) (S.) O. 1967	**r.,** 1971/934.
668	Road Vehicles (Registration and Licensing) (Amdt.) Regs. 1967	**r.,** 1971/450.
709	Oil in Navigable Waters (Prohibited Sea Areas) O. 1967	sch. 1 **am.,** 1971/1822.
760	National Insurance (Computation of Earnings) Regs. 1967	regs. 4, 6–8 **am.,** 9 **replaced,** 1971/1419.
801	Money Order Regs. 1967	regs. 1, 3, 4, 16 **am.,** schs. 1, 2 **replaced as am.,** by P.O. Scheme 15.1.71.*
815	Commonwealth Countries and Republic of Ireland (Immunities) (No. 2) O. 1967	**r.,** 1971/1237.
844	National Insurance (Assessment of Graduated Contributions) Regs. 1967	regs. 2, 3, 9 **am.,** schs. 4, 5 **replaced,** 1971/1202.
876	Injury Warrant 1967	para. 1 **am.,** 1971/1209.
924	Industrial Training (Construction Bd.) O. 1967	**r.,** 1971/1766.
937	National Health Service (General Dental Services) Regs. 1967	regs. 2, 23 **am.,** sch. 1 Pt. I paras. 7, 8 **am.,** sch. 4 Pt. II, III **am.,** sch. 6 paras. 1, 3 **replaced,** 1971/1984.
981	Iron Casting Industry (Scientific Research Levy) O. 1967	**r.,** 1971/253.
1018	Army Terms of Service Regs. 1967	regs. 4A, 6A, 8A **inserted,** 1971/502. sch. 2 **am.,** 1971/1585.
1021	Police (Discipline) (S.) Regs. 1967	regs. 14, 38 **am.,** 1971/843.
1022	Hydrocarbon Oil Duties (Drawback) (No. 1) O. 1967	**r.,** 1971/1233.

* Not S.I. *see* London Gazette 3.2.71 p. 18s.

Year and Number (or date)	Title or Description	How affected and Act or Instrument by which affected
1967		
1082	Iron and Steel (Pension Schemes) Regs. 1967	regs. 2, 3, 9 **am.**, 1971/916.
1125	National Insurance (Claims and Payments) Amdt. Regs. 1967	**r.**, 1971/707.
1162	Teachers (Education Training and Registration) (S.) Regs. 1967	sch. I paras. 1–3 **am.**, 1971/903.
1164	Valuation (Scottish Gas Bd.) (S.) O. 1967	**r.**, 1971/1213.
1189	Exchange Control (Payments) O. 1967	art. 1 **r.**, 1971/1632
1230	Firemen's Pension Scheme (Amdt.) O. 1967	**r.** (saving), 1971/145.
1265	National Insurance (Increase of Benefit and Miscellaneous Provns.) Regs. 1967	reg. 7 **am.**, 1971/1220.
1286	Teachers' (Part Time) Superannuation Regs. 1967	reg. 8 **am.**, 1971/403.
1294	A.S. (Alteration of Sheriff Ct. Fees) 1967	**r.** (as to proceedings commenced after 15.2.71),1971/90.
1361	Wages Regulation (Shirtmaking) (Holidays) O. 1967	sch. paras. 2, 6 **am.**, 1971/1919.
1362	Wages Regulation (Corset) (Holidays) O. 1967	sch. paras. 2, 6 **am.**, 1971/1918.
1500	Police Pensions (Amdt.) (No. 2) Regs. 1967	**r.**, 1971/232.
1501	Royal Irish Constabulary (Widows' Pensions) Regs. 1967	**r.**, 1971/1469.
1535	Industrial Training (Financial Provisions) O. 1967	**superseded** 1971/2057.
1546	Special Constables (Pensions) (Amdt.) Regs. 1967	**r.**, 1971/233.
1553	Special Constables (Pensions) (S.) Amdt. Regs. 1967	**r.**, 1971/234.
1555	Beef Cow (E. and W.) Scheme 1967 ...	paras. 4, 6, 7 **am.**, 1971/1025.
1570	National Insurance (Determination of Claims and Questions) (No. 2) Regs. 1967	reg. 15 **am.**, 1971/621, 1419.
1611	Merchant Shipping (Fees) Regs. 1967	**r.**, 1971/643.
1626	Wages Regulations (Retail Newsagency, Tobacco and Confectionery) (S.) O. 1967	**r.**, 1971/1666.
1640	Road Vehicles Lighting (Amdt.) Regs. 1967.	**r.**, 1971/694.

Year and Number (or date)	Title or Description	How affected and Act or Instrument by which affected
1967		
1659	Magistrates' Cts. (Attachment of Earnings) Rules 1967	**r.**, 1971/809.
1734	Indictments (Procedure) (Amdt.) Rules 1967	**r.**, 1971/2084.
1776	Witnesses' Allowances (Amdt.) Regs. 1967	**r.**, 1971/107.
1821	Royal Navy Terms of Service Regs. 1967	regs. 3A–3E **inserted** 1971/517.
1844	Road Vehicles (Registration and Licensing) (Amdt.) (No. 2) Regs. 1967	**r.**, 1971/450.
1861	Building Societies (Special Advances) O. 1967	**r.** (saving), 1971/1067.
1862	Hill and Upland Sheep (S.) Scheme 1967	sch. **am.**, 1971/1818.
1863	Hill and Upland Sheep Subsidy Payment (S.) O. 1967	art. 3 **am.**, 1971/1819.
1870	Hill Sheep Subsidy Payment (E. and W.) O. 1967	art. 3 **am.**, 1971/945.
1872	Mink (Keeping) Regs. 1967	reg. 4 **am.**, 1971/2071.
1873	Coypus (Keeping) Regs. 1967 ...	reg. 4 **am.**, 1971/2070.
1934	Road Vehicles Lighting (Amdt.) (No. 2) Regs. 1967	**r.**, 1971/694.
1976	Beef Cow (N.I.) Scheme 1967	paras. 4, 6, 7 **am.**, 1971/942.
1968		
25	Police Cadets Regs. 1968	regs. 12, 14 **am.**, 1971/151. schs. 1, 2 **am.**, 1971/804.
26	Police Regulations 1968	**r.** (saving), 1971/156. regs. 36, 48, sch. 6 **am.** (so far as still in force), 1971/156. schs. 3, 4 **am.** (so far as still in force), 1971/659. sch. 3 Pt. II **am.** (so far still in force), 1971/1901.
35	Assistance for House Purchase and Improvement (Housing Assocns.) Regs. 1968	sch. **am.**, 1971/1577.
71	Agricultural Drainage (Standard Costs) (S.) Regs. 1968	reg. 3 **am.**, 1971/195.
114	Consular Fees O. 1968	**r.**, 1971/211.
157	Firemen's Pension Scheme (Amdt.) O. 1968	**r.** (saving), 1971/145.
165	Importation of Potatoes (Health) (G.B.) (Amdt.) O. 1968	**r.**, 1971/438.

Year and Number (or date)	Title or Description	How affected and Act or Instrument by which affected
1968		
208	Police Cadets (S.) Regs. 1968	regs. 13, 15 **am.**, 1971/185. schs. 1, 2 **am.**, 1971/810.
219	Matrimonial Causes Rules 1968	**r.** (saving), 1971/953.
281	Matrimonial Causes (Costs) Rules 1968	**r.**, 1971/987.
282	Agricultural and Horticultural Improvements (Standard Costs) Regs. 1968	reg. 2 **am.**, 1971/193.
314	Divorce County Courts O. 1968	**r.**, 1971/1954.
355	Road Vehicles (Index Marks) (Amdt.) Regs. 1968	**r.**, 1971/450.
373	Police (Common Police Services) (S.) O. 1968	**r.**, 1971/447.
384	Anti-Dumping Duty O. 1968	**r.**, 1971/1812.
388	Matrimonial Causes Fees O. 1968	**r.** (saving), 1971/102.
389	Welfare Foods Order 1968	**r.**, 1971/457.
397	Firemen's Pension Scheme (Amdt.) (No. 2) O. 1968	**r.** (saving), 1971/145.
423	Civil Aviation (Navigation Services Charges) (Second Amdt.) Regs. 1968	**r.**, 1971/1135.
431	Clean Air (Measurement of Grit and Dust) Regs. 1968	**r.**, 1971/161.
464	Commonwealth Countries and Republic of Ireland (Immunities) (Amdt.) O. 1968	**r.**, 1971/1237.
530	Police Pensions (Amdt.) Regs. 1968	**r.**, 1971/232.
552	Police (Amdt.) Regs. 1968	**r.** (saving), 1971/156.
570	Petroleum (Inflammable Liquids) O. 1968	**r.**, 1971/1040.
579	District Registries O. in C. 1968	**r.**, 1971/392.
594	Road Vehicles (Registration and Licensing) (Amdt.) Regs. 1968	**r.**, 1971/450.
601	Goods Vehicles (Plating and Testing) Regs. 1968	**r.** (saving), 1971/352.
619	Plant Breeders' Rights (Fees) Regs. 1968	sch. 2 **am.**, 1971/1102.
710	Domestic Water Rate Product (S.) Rules 1968	rules 3, 4 **am.**, 1971/416.

Year and Number (or date)	Title or Description	How affected and Act or Instrument by which affected
1968		
716	Police (S.) Regs. 1968	regs. 6, 14, 22, 23, 29, 33, 38, 39, 42, 44, 45, 46, schs. 2, 5, 6, 7, 11 **am.**, 1971/196. reg. 50 **am.**, sch. 3 **replaced**, sch. 4 **am.**, sch. 6 **replaced** 1971/683 regs. 29 **replaced**, 32 **am.**, 44A **inserted**, 46, sch. 9 **am.**, 1971/1203.
717	Police (Promotion) (S.) Regs. 1968 ...	regs. 2, 4 **replaced**, sch. **am.**, 1971/344.
759	National Health Service (Charges for Drugs and Appliances) Regs. 1968	regs. 2A, 3, 5-8 **am.**, 1971/1340.
766	Police (Amdt.) (No. 2) Regs. 1968 ...	**r.** (saving), 1971/156.
767	Cereals (Guarantee Payments) (Amdt.) O. 1968	**r.**, 1971/289.
818	National Health Service (Charges for Drugs and Appliances) (S.) Regs. 1968	regs. 2A, 3, 5–8 **am.**, 1971/420.
827	National Insurance (Members of the Forces) Regs. 1968	reg. 8 **am.**, 1971/1419. schs. 3–5, 5A **replaced** 1971/1422.
831	Hill Sheep Subsidy Payment (N.I.) O. 1968	art. 3 **am.**, 1971/946.
892	Continental Shelf (Jurisdiction) O. 1968	art. 1 **am.**, 1971/721.
927	Inflammable Liquids (Conveyance by Road) Regs. 1968	**r.**, 1971/1061.
928	Inflammable Substances (Conveyance by Road) (Labelling) Regs. 1968	**r.**, 1971/1062.
939	County Cts. (Bankruptcy and Companies Winding-up Jurisdiction) (Amdt.) O. 1968	**r.**, 1971/656.
981	Hill Cattle (S.) Scheme 1968	para. 2 **am.**, 1971/1187.
987	Redundant Mineworkers (Payments Scheme) O. 1968.	art. 2, sch. arts. 3, 8 **am.**, 1971/553.
1033	Industrial Training (Food, Drink and Tobacco Bd.) O. 1968	sch. 1 **replaced**, 1971/648.
1074	Police (Promotion) Regs. 1968 ...	regs. 1, 8, 9 **am.**, 1971/157.
1077	Cinematograph Films (Collection of Levy) Regs. 1968	reg. 3 **am.**, 1971/1206.
1117	Merchant Shipping (Load Lines) (Fees) Regs. 1968	regs. 2 **r.**, 3, 5 **am.**, sch. Pt. I **replaced**, Pt. II **am.**, 1971/644. sch. Pt. II **am.**, 1971/1352.
1120	Superannuation (Teaching and Public Bds.) Interchange Rules 1968	sch. 3 **am.**, 1971/2147.

Year and Number (or date)	Title or Description	How affected and Act or Instrument by which affected
1968		
1132	Price Stability of Imported Products (Minimum Import Price Levels) O. 1968	**r.,** 1971/632.
1169	Goods Vehicles (Plating and Testing) (Amdt.) Regs. 1968	**r.** (saving), 1971/352.
1170	Iron and Steel (Compensation to Employees) Regs. 1968	reg. 2 **am.,** 1971/2026.
1196	Pedestrian Crossings (Amdt.) Regs. 1968	**r.** (30.11.73), 1971/1524.
1207	Police (Amdt.) (No. 3) Regs. 1968	**r.** (saving), 1971/156.
1235	White Fish and Herring Subsidies (U.K.) Scheme 1968	**r.,** 1971/1295.
1240	Countervailing Duty O. 1968	**r.,** 1971/2001.
1247	Road Vehicles Lighting (Amdt.) Regs. 1968	**r.,** 1971/694.
1253	Inland Postal Regs. 1968	regs. 1, 4, 5, 11, 12, 14 **am.,** 16 **r.,** 17, 18, 21, 23, 24, 28, 31, 33, 34, 41, 44 **am.,** 52 **replaced,** 55 **am.,** schs. 1–3, sch. 4 Pt. I **replaced,** sch. 5 **r.,** schs. 6, 7 **replaced.** P.O. Scheme 14.1.71.* regs. 1, 21, 55A **am.,** P.O. Scheme 15.6.71.†
1256	Telephone Regs. 1968	**r.,** P.O. Scheme 11.1.71.‡
1257	Telephone (Channel Is.) Regs. 1968	**r.,** P.O. Scheme 11.1.71.‡
1258	Telex Amdt. (No. 1) Regs. 1968	**r.,** P.O. Scheme 11.1.71.‡
1271	Clean Air (Measurement of Grit and Dust) (S.) Regs. 1968	**r.,** 1971/626.
1315	Theatres (Licence Application Fees) O. 1968	arts. 1–3 **am.,** 1971/1.
1333	Industrial Training (Engineering Bd.) O. 1968	**r.,** 1971/1530.
1374	Commonwealth Countries and Republic of Ireland (Immunities) (Amdt.) (No. 2) O. 1968	**r.,** 1971/1237.
1389	Patents Rules 1968	sch. 1 **replaced,** 1971/263. rules 67, 68, 127 **replaced,** sch. 1 para. 25 **am.,** sch. 2 forms 24, 26 **replaced,** 1971/1917.
1406	Health and Welfare Services (Provision of Instruction) Regs. 1968	**r.,** 1971/86.

* Not S.I. *see* London Gazette 3.2.71 p. ls.
† Not S.I. *see* London Gazette 30.6.71 p. 27s.
‡ Not S.I. *see* London Gazette 27.1.71 pp. ls, 52, 26s.

Year and Number (or date)	Title or Description	How affected and Act or Instrument by which affected
1968		
1407	Health and Welfare Services (Provision of Instruction) (S.) Regs. 1968	**r.**, 1971/99.
1452	Theatres (Licence Application Fees) (S.) O. 1968	arts. 1–3 **am.**, 1971/175.
1558	Customs Duty (Personal Reliefs) (No. 1) O. 1968.	para. 2 **am.**, 1971/911.
1561	Customs Duty (Personal Reliefs) (No. 4) O. 1968	paras. 1, 2 **am.**, 1971/1974.
1605	Welfare Foods (Amdt.) O. 1968 ...	**r.**, 1971/457.
1609	Wages Regulation (Dressmaking and Women's Light Clothing) (S.) O. 1968	**r.**, 1971/87.
1714	Motor Vehicles (TestRegs) s. 1968 ...	regs. 19, 23, 25, 27, schs. 2, 5, Pt. I Table of Fees, Pt. II **am.**, 1971/165.
1761	Police (Amdt.) (No. 4) Regs. 1968 ...	**r.** (saving), 1971/156.
1801	Armed Forces (Discharge by Purchase) Regs. 1968	regs. 3, 4 **am.**, 1971/503.
1854	Goods Vehicles (Plating and Testing) (Amdt.) (No. 2) Regs. 1968	**r.** (saving), 1971/352.
1869	Double Taxation Relief (Taxes on Income) (France) O. 1968	art. 9 **am.**, 1971/718.
1881	Import Duty Drawbacks (No. 10) O. 1968	**r.**, 1971/274.
1913	Public Health (Ships) (S.) Amdt. Regs. 1968	**r.**, 1971/132.
1929	London Cab O. 1968	**superseded** 1971/333.
1934	Divorce County Cts. (Amdt.) O. 1968	**r.**, 1971/1954.
1956	Rate Support Grant O. 1968 ...	reg. 3 **am.**, 1971/2031.
1965	Registration and Enrolment Rules 1968	**r.** (1.4.72), 1971/2128.
1966	Special Roads (Classes of Traffic) (E. and W.) O. 1968	**r.**, 1971/1156.
1978	County Cts. (Race Relations Jurisdiction) O. 1968	sch. **am.**, 1971/454, 1985.
1982	Special Roads (Classes of Traffic) (S.) O. 1968	**r.**, 1971/1211.
1989	Special Constables (Pensions) (Amdt.) Regs. 1968	**r.**, 1971/233.
1995	Special Constables (Pensions) (S.) Amdt. Regs. 1968	**r.**, 1971/234.

Year and Number (or date)	Title or Description	How affected and Act or Instrument by which affected
1968		
2006	Coypus (Keeping) (Amdt.) Regs. 1968	**superseded** 1971/2070.
2011	British Transport (Pensions of Employees) (No. 1) O. 1968	art. 12 **r.,** 1971/1128.
2049	Registration of Births, Deaths, and Marriages Regs. 1968	**mod.** (W.), 1971/129. reg. 68 **am.,** 1971/1218
1969		
35	Wages Regulation (Retail Newsagency, Tobacco and Confectionery) (E. and W.) O. 1969	**r.,** 1971/1443.
77	Teachers Superannuation (S.) Regs. 1969	regs. 5, 7, 8, 14, 28, schs. 1, 3 **am.,** sch. 4 **replaced,** sch. 5 **am.,** 1971/1995.
78	Teachers Superannuation (Family Benefits) (S.) Regs. 1969	**r.,** 1971/1775.
85	Motor Cars (Driving Instruction) Regs. 1969	reg. 11 **am.,** 1971/351.
137	Police (Amdt.) Regs. 1969	**r.** (saving), 1971/156.
142	Commonwealth Countries and Republic of Ireland (Immunities) (Amdt.) O. 1969	**r.,** 1971/1237.
148	Trial of the Pyx O. 1969	art. 4 **am.,** 1971/596.
167	Salmon and Migratory Trout (Prohibition of Drift-net Fishing) (Extension) O. 1969	**superseded,** 1971/242.
187	Eggs (Protection of Guarantees) O. 1969	**r.,** 1971/475.
213	Coroners (Fees and Allowances) (Amdt.) Rules 1969	**r.,** 1971/108.
214	Witnesses' Allowances (Amdt.) Regs. 1969	**r.,** 1971/107.
224	Approved Schools (Contributions by Education Authies.) (S.) Regs. 1969	**r.,** 1971/248.
289	National Insurance (Claims and Payments) Amdt. Regs. 1969	**r.,** 1971/707.
297	National Health Service (Functions of Regional Hospital Bds., etc.) Regs. 1969	reg. 4 am., 1971/264.
321	Motor Vehicles (Construction and Use) Regs. 1969	regs. 25A, 85A **inserted,** 1971/444. regs. 31–32C, 81A, 81B, schs. 3, 12 **r.,** 1971/694. regs. 3, 4 **am.,** 12C **inserted,** 53 **r.,** 106 **replaced,** 110, 111 **am.,** sch. 8 **am.,** 1971/979.

Year and Number (or date)	Title or Description	How affected and Act or Instrument by which affected
1969		
322	Goods Vehicles (Plating and Testing) (Amdt.) Regs. 1969	**r.** (saving), 1971/352.
339	National Insurance (Claims and Payments) Amdt. (No. 2) Regs. 1969	**r.,** 1971/707.
344	Motor Vehicles (Authorisation of Special Types) General O. 1969	arts. 8 **am.,** 11 **replaced,** 14, 16, 19–21, 24–27 **am.,** 30 **inserted**, schs. 1, 2 **am.,** 1971/980.
371	Anguilla (Temporary Provns.) O. 1969	**r.,** 1971/1235.
401	Eggs (Guaranteed Prices) O. 1969	**r.,** 1971/474.
419	Motor Vehicles (Tests) (Exemption) Regs. 1969	reg. 4 **am.,** 1971/1814.
420	Goods Vehicles (Licences and Prohibitions) (Amdt.) Regs. 1969	**r.,** 1971/2020.
463	Local Authies'. Traffic Orders (Procedure) (E. and W.) Regs. 1969	regs. 2, 4–6 **am.,** 20 **inserted,** 1971/1493.
471	White Fish and Herring Subsidies (U.K.) (Amdt.) Scheme 1969	**r.,** 1971/1295.
481	Designs (Amdt.) Rules 1969	**r.,** 1971/262.
482	Patents (Amdt.) Rules 1969	**r.,** 1971/263.
483	Provision of Milk and Meals Regs. 1969	sch. 1 **am.,** 1971/169. regs. 4, 10 sch. 1 **am.,** 1971/1368.
487	Local Authies'. Traffic Orders (Procedure) (S.) Regs. 1969	regs. 2, 4, 5 **am.,** 20 **inserted,** 1971/1521.
506	Grant-Aided Secondary Schools (S.) Grant (Amdt.) Regs. 1969	**superseded,** 1971/558.
510	Civil Aviation (Navigation Services Charges) (Third Amdt.) Regs. 1969	**r.,** 1971/1135.
513	Public Trustee (Fees) O. 1969	paras. 12, 15, 22, 24 **am.,** 25A **inserted,** 26 **am.,** 1971/291.
519	Companies (Bd. of Trade) Fees O. 1969	sch. Table A **am.,** 1971/1020.
521	Importation of Potatoes (Health) (G.B.) (Amdt.) O. 1969	**r.,** 1971/438.
522	Trade Marks (Amdt.) Rules 1969	**r.,** 1971/261.
567	Increase of Pensions (Police and Fire Services) Regs. 1969	reg. 6 **am.,** 1971/146.
610	Wages Regulation (Coffin Furniture and Cerement-making) O. 1969	**r.,** 1971/922.
611	Wages Regulation (Coffin Furniture and Cerement-making) (Holidays) O. 1969	**r.,** 1971/923.

Year and Number (or date)	Title or Description	How affected and Act or Instrument by which affected
1969		
618	Remuneration of Teachers (Primary and Secondary Schools) O. 1969	**r.,** 1971/1539.
628	Fishing Nets (Northwest Atlantic) O. 1969	**r.,** 1971/1172.
667	Motor Vehicles (International Circulation (Amdt.) Regs. 1969	**r.,** 1971/937.
668	Motor Vehicles (International Motor Insurance Card) Regs. 1969	**r.,** 1971/792.
672	Cereals (Guarantee Payments) (Amdt.) O. 1969	**r.,** 1971/289.
677	Importation of Plants and Plant Produce (Health) (G.B.) (Amdt.) O. 1969	**r.,** 1971/438.
723	Police Pensions (Amdt.) Regs. 1969	**r.,** 1971/232.
724	Special Constables (Pensions) (Amdt.) Regs. 1969	**r.,** 1971/233.
735	Foreign Compensation (Union of Soviet Socialist Republics) O. 1969	arts. 15, 23, 26 **am.,** 27 **replaced,** 28 **am.,** 1971/1738.
756	Urban District Council Election Rules 1969	sch. 1 rule 10A **inserted,** 1971/545.
757	Rural District Council Election Rules 1969	sch. 1 rule 10A **inserted,** 1971/546.
758	Price Stability of Imported Products (Levy Arrangements) (Amdt.) O. 1969	**r.,** 1971/631.
763	Matrimonial Causes (Amdt.) Rules 1969	**r.** (saving), 1971/953.
842	Foreign Compensation Commission (Union of Soviet Socialist Republics) Rules Approval Instrt. 1969	rule 43 **am.,** 1971/1807.
851	Irish Land (Finances) (Amdt.) Rules 1969	**r.,** 1971/1883.
903	Heavy Goods Vehicles (Drivers' Licences) Regs. 1969	regs. 2–4 **am.,** 5 **replaced,** 9, 10, 12, 14–16, 21, 24, 26–28 **am.,** 1971/736.
911	Police (Amdt.) (No. 2) Regs. 1969	**r.** (saving), 1971/156.
915	Equine Animals (Importation) O. 1969	art. 4 **am.,** 1971/1137.
923	Legal Aid (General) (Amdt.) Regs. 1969	**r.,** 1971/62.
929	Wages Regulation (Hollow-ware) (Holidays) O. 1969	**r.,** 1971/1697.
930	Wages Regulation (Hollow-ware) O. 1969	**r.,** 1971/1696.

Year and Number (or date)	Title or Description	How affected and Act or Instrument by which affected
1969		
931	Pensions Appeal Tribunals (E. and W.) (Amdt.) Rules 1969	**r.**, 1971/769.
972	Milk (G.B.) (Amdt.) O. 1969	**r.**, 1971/1038.
973	Milk (N.I.) (Amdt.) O. 1969	**r.**, 1971/1037.
989	Special Constables (Pensions) (S.) Amdt. Regs. 1969	**r.**, 1971/234.
997	Superannuation (Local Govt. and Approved Employment) Interchange Rules 1969	rule 2 sch. 2 **am.**, 1971/114.
1001	Firemen's Pension Scheme (Amdt.) O. 1969	**r.** (saving), 1971/145.
1021	Plant Breeders' Rights Regs. 1969	regs. 12–14, 16, 20, 22 **am.**, sch. 2 **am.**, sch. 3 Pts. II, V, VI **am.**, Pt. XXIX, XXX, XXXI **inserted**, 1971/1094.
1024	Plant Breeders' Rights (Trees, Shrubs and Woody Climbers) Scheme 1969	sch. **am.**, 1971/1093.
1034	Import Duty Drawbacks (No. 1) O. 1969	**r.**, 1971/274.
1046	Superannuation (Teaching and Public Bds.) Interchange (S.) Rules 1969	sch. 3 **am.**, 1971/2024.
1086	Motor Vehicles (International Circulation) (Amdt.) O. 1969	**superseded**, 1971/869.
1110	Gaming Clubs (Licensing) Regs. 1969	reg. 3 sch. 1 **r.**, 1971/1538.
1115	Gaming Clubs (Licensing) (S.) Regs. 1969	reg. 3 sch. 1, **r.**, 1971/1557
1135	Family Allowances, National Insurance and Industrial Injuries (Post Office Act 1969 Consequential) Regs. 1969	reg. 3 **r.**, 1971/707.
1141	Mines and Quarries (Notification of Tipping Operations) Regs. 1969	**r.**, 1971/1377.
1170	County Cts. (Bankruptcy and Companies Winding-up Jurisdiction) (Amdt.) O. 1969	**r.**, 1971/656.
1173	Wages Regulation (Paper Box) (Holidays) O. 1969	**r.**, 1971/1569.
1232	District Registries O. in C. 1969	**r.**, 1971/392.
1265	National Assistance (Charges for Accommodation) Regs. 1969	**r.**, 1971/1404.
1307	Control of Hiring O. 1969	**r.**, 1971/1146.
1308	Hire Purchase and Credit Sale Agreements (Control) O. 1969	**r.**, 1971/1147.

Year and Number (or date)	Title or Description	How affected and Act or Instrument by which affected
1969		
1324	Goods Vehicles (Plating and Testing) (Amdt.) (No. 2) Regs. 1969	**r.** (saving), 1971/352.
1331	Road Vehicles (Registration and Licensing) (Amdt.) Regs. 1969	**r.**, 1971/450.
1346	Legal Aid (General) (Amdt. No. 2) Regs. 1969	**r.**, 1971/62.
1376	Industrial Training (Engineering Bd.) O. 1968 (Amdt.) O. 1969	**r.**, 1971/1530.
1399	Postal Packets (Customs and Excise) Regs. 1969	**r.**, 1971/1057.
1443	National Assistance (Charges for Accommodation) (S.) Regs. 1969	**r.**, 1971/1500.
1484	Police Pensions (Amdt.) (No. 2) Regs. 1969	**r.**, 1971/232.
1514	Special Constables (Pensions) (Amdt.) (No. 2) Regs. 1969	**r.**, 1971/233.
1517	Royal Irish Constabulary (Widows' Pensions) Regs. 1969	**r.**, 1971/1469.
1529	Special Constables (Pensions) (S.) Amdt. (No. 2) Regs. 1969	**r.**, 1971/234.
1549	National Insurance (Modification of the Superannuation Acts) Regs. 1969	**r.**, 1971/1441.
1564	Price Stability of Imported Products (Levy Arrangements) (Amdt. No. 2) O. 1969	**r.**, 1971/631.
1585	Pensions Appeal Tribunals (S.) (Amdt.) Rules 1969	**r.**, 1971/2124.
1589	Road Vehicles (Registration and Licensing) (Amdt.) (No. 2) Regs. 1969	**r.**, 1971/450.
1633	Fees of Appointed Factory Doctors O. 1969	**r.**, 1971/1060.
1638	Goods Vehicles (Licences and Prohibitions) (Amdt.) (No. 2) Regs. 1969	**r.**, 1971/2020.
1647	Road Vehicles (Headlamps) Regs. 1969	**r.**, 1971/694.
1658	Import Duty Drawbacks (No. 2) O. 1969	**r.**, 1971/274.
1696	National Insurance (Contributions) Regs. 1969	regs. 3, 5, 15, 25 **am.**, 1971/1421.
1706	Patents (Amdt. No. 2) Rules 1969	**r.**, 1971/263.
1737	Exotic Animals (Importation) O. 1969	**r.**, 1971/2045.
1739	Wages Regulation (Sack and Bag) O. 1969	**r.**, 1971/207.

Year and Number (or date)	Title or Description	How affected and Act or Instrument by which affected
1969		
1743	Importation of Dogs and Cats (Amdt.) O. 1969	**r.** (exc. dogs and cats) 1971/2045.
1762	Goods Vehicles (Plating and Testing) (Amdt.) (No. 3) Regs. 1969	**r.** (saving), 1971/352.
1782	Road Vehicles (Excise) (Prescribed Particulars) (Amdt.) Regs. 1969	**r.**, 1971/1628.
1787	Police Federation Regs. 1969	regs. 9, 12, 16, 19 sch. 4 Pt. II **am.**, sch. 5 **am.**, 1971/1498.
1799	Goods Vehicles (Carriers' and Operators' Licences) (Fees) Regs. 1969	**r.**, 1971/149.
1800	Road Vehicles (Registration and Licensing) (Amdt.) (No. 3) Regs. 1969	**r.**, 1971/450.
1816	Divorce County Court (Amdt.) O. 1969	**r.**, 1971/1954.
1823	Fishing Nets (North-East Atlantic) O. 1969	**r.**, 1971/1171.
1824	British Transport (Pensions of Employees) (No. 1) O. 1969	art. 3, 4, **mod.**, 1971/116, 117.
1849	Police Pensions (Amdt.) (No. 3) Regs. 1969	**r.**, 1971/232.
1850	Special Constables (Pensions) (Amdt.) (No. 3) Regs. 1969	**r.**, 1971/233.
1861	Injuries in War (Shore Employments) Compensation (Second Amdt.) Scheme 1969	**superseded**, 1971/1987.
1880	Special Constables (Pensions) (S.) Amdt. (No. 3) Regs. 1969	**r.**, 1971/234.
1970		
16	County Ct. Districts O. 1970	sch. 1 **am.**, 1971/1081.
28	Remuneration of Teachers (Primary and Secondary Schools) (Amdt.) O. 1970	**r.**, 1971/1539.
29	Matrimonial Causes (Amdt.) Rules 1970	**r.** (saving), 1971/953.
48	Road Vehicles Lighting (Amdt.) Regs. 1970	**r.**, 1971/694.
49	Motor Vehicles (Construction and Use) (Amdt.) Regs. 1970	regs. 3 **am.**, 5, 6, 8–10 **r.**, 1971/694.
60	Wages Regulation (Retail Drapery, Outfitting and Footwear) O. 1970	**r.**, 1971/845.
66	Police (Amdt.) Regs. 1970	**r.** (saving), 1971/156.
88	Greater London Council (Allowances to Members) Regs. 1970	**r.**, 1971/2097.

Year and Number (or date)	Title or Description	How affected and Act or Instrument by which affected
1970		
89	Local Govt. (Financial Loss Allowance) Regs. 1970	**r.**, 1971/2096.
92	Greater London Council Election Rules 1970	sch. 1 rule 10A **inserted,** 1971/1602.
95	Import Duty Drawbacks (No. 1) O. 1970	**r.**, 1971/274.
98	Anti-Dumping Duty (Temporary Suspension) O. 1970	**r.**, 1971/2.
106	Local Govt. (Financial Loss Allowance) (S.) Regs. 1970	sch. 1 **am.**, 1971/2130.
107	Local Govt. (Travelling Allowances, etc.) (S.) Regs. 1970	sch. 1 para. 3 **am.**, sch. 2 para. 3 **inserted,** 1971/2131.
123	Drivers' Hours (Goods Vehicles) (Keeping of Records) Regs. 1970	reg. 12 **am.**, 1971/847.
131	London Borough Council Election Rules 1970	sch. 1 rule 10A **inserted,** 1971/1603.
163	Pensions Appeal Tribunals (E. and W.) (Amdt.) Rules 1970	**r.**, 1971/769.
170	Motor Vehicles (Driving Licences) Regs. 1970	**r.**, 1971/451.
174	Coroners (Fees and Allowances) (Amdt.) Rules 1970	**r.**, 1971/108.
175	Jurors' Allowances (Amdt.) Regs. 1970	**r.**, 1971/136.
176	Witnesses' Allowances (Amdt.) Regs. 1970	**r.**, 1971/107.
177	A.S. (Increase of Fees of Shorthand Writers in the Sheriff Cts.) 1970	**superseded,** 1971/197.
197	Rural Borough Council Election Rules 1970	sch. 1 rule 10A **inserted,** 1971/547.
198	Fixed Penalty (Procedure) Regs. 1970	reg. 4 **replaced,** 1971/479. reg. 4 **am.**, 1971/1505.
201	Parish Council Election Rules 1970	sch. 1 rule 10A **inserted,** 1971/548.
202	Goods Vehicles (Operators' Licences) Temporary Use in G.B. Regs. 1970	regs. 4B **inserted,** 12 **am.**, sch. 2 Pt. II **am.**, 1971/353.
226	Registration and Enrolment (Amdt.) Rules 1970	**r.** (1.4.72), 1971/2128.
228	County Ct. Funds (Amdt. Rules) 1970	**superseded,** 1971/260.
229	Mayor's and City of London Ct. Funds (Amdt.) Rules 1970	**superseded,** 1971/453.
231	Justices' Clerks Rules 1970	sch. **am.**, 1971/809.

Year and Number (or date)	Title or Description	How affected and Act or Instrument by which affected
1970		
233	Road Vehicles Lighting (Amdt.) (No. 2) Regs. 1970	**r.**, 1971/694.
239	Is. of Scilly (Civic Amenities) O. 1970	sch. **am.**, 1971/324.
242	Gaming Clubs (Licensing) (Amdt.) Regs. 1970	**r.**, 1971/1538.
250	Firemen's Pension Scheme (Amdt.) O. 1970	**r.** (saving), 1971/145.
251	Remuneration of Teachers (Primary and Secondary Schools) (Amdt. No. 2) O. 1970	**r.**, 1971/1539.
257	Drivers' Hours (Goods Vehicles) (Modifications) O. 1970	arts. 3, 4 **am.**, 1971/818.
262	Jurors' Allowances (S.) Amdt. Regs. 1970	**r.**, 1971/220.
270	Import Duty Drawbacks (No. 2) O. 1970	**r.**, 1971/274.
283	Wages Regulation (Hairdressing) O. 1970	**r.**, 1971/1136.
296	Wages Regulation (Stamped or Pressed Metal-Wares) O. 1970	**r.**, 1971/1088.
311	Wages Regulation (Pin, Hook and Eye, and Snap Fastener) O. 1970	**r.**, 1971/868.
325	Transitional Relief for Interest and Royalties paid to Non-Residents (Extension of Period) O. 1970	**superseded**, 1971/563.
326	Non Residents' Transitional Relief from Income Tax on Dividends (Extension of Period) O. 1970	**superseded**, 1971/562.
348	Wool Textile Industry (Export Promotion Levy) O. 1970	arts. 7, 8 **am.**, 1971/880.
349	Wool Textile Industry (Scientific Research Levy) O. 1970	arts. 7, 8 **am.**, 1971/881.
356	Drivers' Hours (Passenger Vehicles) (Modifications) O. 1970	**r.**, 1971/818.
358	Importation of Dogs and Cats (Amdt.) (No. 1) O. 1970	**r.** (exc. dogs and cats) 1971/2045.
359	Price Stability of Imported Products (Levy Arrangements) (Eggs) O. 1970	sch. Pt. I **am.**, 1971/947, 1642.
360	Price Stability of Imported Products (Minimum Import Price Levels) (Eggs) O. 1970	**r.**, 1971/473.
364	Purchase Tax (No. 1) O. 1970	**r.**, 1971/1166.

Year and Number (or date)	Title or Description	How affected and Act or Instrument by which affected
1970		
365	Rate Support Grant (Increase) (S.) O. 1970	art. 2 **am.**, 1971/470.
376	National Insurance (Industrial Injuries) (Colliery Workers Supplementary Scheme) Amdt. and Consolidation O. 1970	sch. 1 art. 7 **am.**, 1971/1263.
409	Road Vehicles (Registration and Licensing) (Amdt.) Regs. 1970	**r.**, 1971/450.
417	Police (Amdt.) (No. 2) Regs. 1970	**r.** (saving), 1971/156.
428	Wages Regulation (Retail Food) (S.) O. 1970	**r.**, 1971/1023.
441	Importation of Dogs and Cats (Amdt.) (No. 2) O. 1970	art. 3 **r.** (exc. dogs and cats) 1971/2045.
446	Eggs (Guaranteed Prices) (Amdt.) O. 1970	**r.**, 1971/474.
448	Pensions Appeal Tribunals (S.) (Amdt.) Rules 1970	**r.**, 1971/2124.
464	Import Duty Drawbacks (No. 3) O. 1970	**r.**, 1971/274.
466	Public Trustee (Fees) O. 1970	**superseded**, 1971/291.
475	Therapeutic Substances (Supply of Zinc Bacitracin for Agricultural Purposes) Regs. 1970	**r.**, 1971/1398.
480	Foreign Compensation (Financial Provisions) O. 1970	**expired**, 30.3.71.
497	Awards (First Degree etc. Courses) Regs. 1970	**r.**, 1971/1297.
498	Wages Regulation (Toy Manufacturing) O. 1970	**r.**, 1971/1393.
499	Wages Regulation (Toy Manufacturing) (Holidays) O. 1970	**r.**, 1971/1394.
503	Docks and Harbours (Valuation) O. 1970	**r.** (saving), 1971/561.
504	Consular Fees Regs. 1970	**r.**, 1971/398.
548	Wireless Telegraphy (Broadcast Licence Charges and Exemption) Regs. 1970	regs. 3, 4 sch. 2 **am.**, 1971/13. reg. 4 sch. 3 **am.**, 1971/295.
557	Land Registration Fee O. 1970	para. 14 **replaced,** sch. para. VI **am.,** 1971/1082.
562	Wages Regulation (Retail Newsagency, Tobacco and Confectionery) (E. and W.) (Amdt.) O. 1970	**r.**, 1971/1443.

Year and Number (or date)	Title or Description	How affected and Act or Instrument by which affected
1970		
567	Television Act 1964 (Addnl. Payments) O. 1970	**r.**, 1971/309.
573	Wages Regulation (Retail Bread and Flour Confectionery) (E. and W.) O. 1970	**r.**, 1971/1058.
587	Police Pensions (Amdt.) Regs. 1970	**r.**, 1971/232.
601	Police (Amdt.) (No. 3) Regs. 1970	**r.** (saving), 1971/156.
617	Wages Regulation (Retail Food) (E. and W.) O. 1970	**r.**, 1971/990.
624	Wages Regulation (Retail Bookselling and Stationery) O. 1970	sch. paras. 2–4 **replaced,** 1971/1482.
645	Wages Regulation (Retail Bread and Flour Confectionery) (S.) O. 1970	**r.**, 1971/1483.
656	Wages Regulation (Brush and Broom) O. 1970	**r.**, 1971/859.
690	Legal Aid (General) (Amdt.) Regs. 1970	**r.**, 1971/62.
691	Exchange Control (Authorised Dealers and Depositaries) O. 1970	**r.**, 1971/477.
702	Wages Regulation (Keg and Drum) O. 1970	**r.**, 1971/885.
703	Wages Regulation (Keg and Drum) (Holidays) O. 1970	sch. paras. 6 **replaced,** 11 **am.**, 1971/885.
721	Opencast Coal (Rate of Interest on Compensation) (No. 2) O. 1970	**r.**, 1971/674.
722	Wages Regulation (Boot and Shoe Repairing) O. 1970	**r.**, 1971/150.
723	Wages Regulation (Boot and Shoe Repairing) (Holidays) O. 1970	**r.**, 1971/1605.
739	Remuneration of Teachers (Primary and Secondary Schools) (Amdt. No. 3) O. 1970	**r.**, 1971/1539.
743	Wages Regulation (Retail Newsagents, Tobacco and Confectionery) (S.) (Amdt.) O. 1970	**r.**, 1971/1666.
758	Motor Vehicles (Driving Licences) (Amdt.) Regs. 1970	**r.**, 1971/451.
771	Import Duty Drawbacks (No. 4) O. 1970	**r.**, 1971/274.
782	Industrial Training Levy (Air Transport and Travel) O. 1970	arts. 2, 3 **am.**, 1971/496.
783	Wages Regulation (Retail Bespoke Tailoring) (E. and W.) O. 1970	**r.**, 1971/830.

Year and Number (or date)	Title or Description	How affected and Act or Instrument by which affected
1970		
787	Legal Aid (General) (Amdt. No. 2) Regs. 1970	**r.,** 1971/62.
797	Poisons List O. 1970	**superseded,** 1971/725.
798	Poisons Rules 1970	**r.,** 1971/726.
809	Wages Regulation (Fur) O. 1970	**r.,** 1971/1381.
810	Wages Regulation (Fur) (Holidays) O. 1970	sch. para. 11 **am.,** 1971/1381.
825	Tokyo Convention (Certification of Countries) O. 1970	**r.,** 1971/2118.
860	Wages Regulation (Retail Food) (S.) (Amdt.) O. 1970.	**r.,** 1971/1023.
862	Teachers' Superannuation (Family Benefits) Regs. 1970	regs. 27, 33–35, 38 **am.,** 40 **replaced,** 41, 45–47, 49 **am.,** 50 **replaced,** 53, **am.,** 55A, 55B **inserted,** 58, 69, 71, 72, 74, 83 **am.,** 1971/679.
867	Awards (First Degree, etc. Courses) (Amdt.) Regs. 1970	**r.,** 1971/1297.
877	Hill Cattle (Breeding Herds) (E. and W.) (Amdt.) Scheme 1970	para. 2 **am.,** 1971/940.
878	Hill Cattle Subsidy (Breeding Herds) (E. and W.) Payment O. 1970	art. 3 **am.,** 1971/941.
883	Wages Regulation (Hat, Cap and Millinery) O. 1970	**r.,** 1971/1022.
905	County Cts. (Bankruptcy and Companies Winding up Jurisdiction) (Amdt.) O. 1970	**r.,** 1971/656.
954	Air Navigation O. 1970	arts. 6, 8, 10, 17, 19, 25, 26, 30, 32, 40, 47, 53, 63, 85, 87 **am.,** sch. 5 para, 4 **am.,** sch. 6, sch. 9 Pts. A, C **am.,** 1971/1733.
978	Wages Regulation (Rope, Twine and Net) O. 1970	**r.,** 1971/750.
991	Exchange Control (Authorised Dealers and Depositaries) (Amdt.) (No. 3) O. 1970	**r.,** 1971/477.
1005	Wages Regulation (Licensed Non-residential Establishment) O. 1970	**r.,** 1971/991.
1013	Anti-Dumping Duty O. 1970	**r.,** 1971/2001.
1038	Justices' Allowances (Amdt.) Regs. 1970	**r.,** 1971/413.
1039	Probation (Allowances) (Amdt.) Rules 1970	**r.,** 1971/414.
1053	Industrial Training (Distributive Bd.) O. 1970	sch. paras 1, 2, 4 appx. **am.,** 1971/1876.

Year and Number (or date)	Title or Description	How affected and Act or Instrument by which affected
1970		
1070	Wages Regulation (Linen and Cotton Handkerchief, etc.) O. 1970	**r.**, 1971/1454.
1078	Milk (G.B.) (Amdt.) O. 1970	**r.**, 1971/1038.
1079	Milk (N.I.) (Amdt.) O. 1970	**r.**, 1971/1037.
1081	Air Navigation (General) Regs. 1970	regs. 4 **am.**, 15 **inserted**, 1971/271. regs. 4, 12-13, 14 sch. **am.**, 1971/1750.
1082	Rules of the Air and Air Traffic Control Regs. 1970	sch. rules 11, 14, 56 **am.**, 1971/1751. sch. rule 16 **replaced**, 1971/1972.
1085	Air Navigation (Fees) Regs. 1970	sch. paras. 1, 2, 11, 12 **am.**, 13 **replaced**, 16, 17 **am.**, 1971/468. sch. paras. 1, 4–6, 17 **am.**, 1971/1105. sch. paras. 1, 3, 4, 6, 12, 15 **am.**, 1971/1980. sch. para. 14 **replaced**, 1971/2162.
1097	Justices Allowances (S.) Amdt. Regs. 1970	**r.**, 1971/490.
1105	Wages Regulation (Licensed Non-Residential Establishment) O. 1970	**r.**, 1971/991.
1106	Wages Regulation (Licensed Non-Residential Establishment) (Managers and Club Stewards) O. 1970	**r.**, 1971/992.
1136	Wages Regulations (Dressmaking and Women's Light Clothing) (E. and W.) O. 1970	**r.**, 1971/308.
1137	Building Standards (S.) (Consolidation) Regs. 1970	regs. A3, D5, D6, E6, F32, J1, J4, K2, K5, L6, L7 **am.**, L10 **replaced**, Q1, Q5, Q7, Q9, Q10, Q11 **am.**, Q21 **inserted**, schs. 3, 4, 9, 10 **am.**, 1972/748. gen. **am.**, (Metrication) Arrangements of Regs. **am.**, regs. D22, E5, E8, E10, F27, J2, J3 **am.**, J4 **replaced**, J5, K7, K8, K10, K13, Q14, Q15 **am.**, sch. 9 Tables 2, 4, 5, 7, 9, 10, 13, 16, 18 **replaced**, sch. 10 Pts. A, B **am.**, 1971/1032. regs. A3, A6 **am.**, C1–C4 **replaced**, D1, D6, D12 **am.**, D13 **replaced**, D18 **am.**, D21 **replaced**, D21A **inserted**, D22, E4–6 **am.**, E7 **replaced**, E8 **am.**, E11 **r.**, E20, F8, F10 **am.**, F18 **r.**, K2, K5, K10, K11, L4, M15, N3, N4, N12 **am.**, P1, P6 **r.**, Q1, Q2 **am.**, Q3 **r.**, Q4 **am.**, Q5 **r.**, Q6 **am.**, Pt. S (regs. S1–S6) added, schs. 1 **am.**, sch. 2 **replaced**, sch. 3 **am.**, sch. 9 tables sch. 3 **r.**, 4, 5 **am.**, 8 **replaced**, sch. 10 Pts. A, B **am.**, sch. 11 Pt. I **am.**, 1971/1811. **r.** (9.2.72), 1971/2052.

Year and Number (or date)	Title or Description	How affected and Act or Instrument by which affected
1970		
1148	Anti-Dumping Duty (No. 2) O. 1970	**r.**, 1971/2001.
1160	Matrimonial Causes (Costs) (Amdt.) Rules 1970	**r.**, 1971/987.
1161	Matrimonial Causes (Amdt. No. 2) Rules 1970	**r.** (saving), 1971/953.
1202	Wages Regulation (Paper Box) O. 1970	**r.**, 1971/1679.
1209	Fixed Penalty (Procedure) (Amdt.) (No. 4) Regs. 1970	**superseded**, 1971/479.
1210	Wages Regulation (Laundry) O. 1970	**r.**, 1971/1591.
1214	London Cab O. 1970	**r.**, 1971/333.
1220	Road Vehicles (Registration and Licensing) (Amdt.) (No. 2) Regs. 1970	**r.**, 1970/450.
1221	Road Vehicles (Excise) (Prescribed Particulars) (Amdt.) Regs. 1970	**r.**, 1971/1628.
1227	Wages Regulation (Made-up Textiles) O. 1970	**r.**, 1971/1280.
1240	Wages Regulation (Milk Distributive) (E. and W.) O. 1970	**r.**, 1971/1698.
1259	Import Duty Drawbacks (No. 5) O. 1970	**r.**, 1971/274.
1266	Awards (First Degree, etc. Courses) (Amdt. No. 2) Regs. 1970	**r.**, 1971/1297.
1271	Importation of Dogs and Cats (Amdt.) (No. 3) O. 1970	art. 4 **am.** (exc. dogs and cats), 1971/2045.
1277	Milk (Eradication of Brucellosis) Scheme 1970	paras. 2–4, **am.**, 1971/532.
1280	National Insurance (Old Persons' Pensions) Regs. 1970	reg. 7 **am.**, 1971/1220. regs. 1 **am.**, 2A **inserted**, 7, 8, 11, 12 **am.**, 1971/1419.
1281	Wages Regulation (Flax and Hemp) O. 1970	**r.**, 1971/1415.
1288	Export of Goods (Control) O. 1970	art 5 sch. 1 Group 8 **am.**, 1971/113.
1301	Wages Regulation (Retail Bread and Flour Confectionery) (E. and W.) (Amdt.) O. 1970	**r.**, 1971/1058.
1314	Wages Regulation (General Waste Materials Reclamation) O. 1970	**r.**, 1971/2129.
1349	Matrimonial Causes (Amdt. No. 3) Rules 1970	**r.** (saving), 1971/953.

Year and Number (or date)	Title or Description	How affected and Act or Instrument by which affected
1970		
1351	Goods Vehicles (Plating and Testing) (Amdt.) Regs. 1970	**r.** (saving), 1971/352.
1366	Wages Regulation (Milk Distributive) (S.) O. 1970	**r.**, 1971/649.
1370	Weights Regs. 1970	regs. 2, 6, 7, schs. 2, 4 **am.**, 1971/40.
1372	Diseases of Animals (Approved Disinfectants) O. 1970	sch. Pts. I–IV **replaced,** 1971/1287.
1389	Acquisition of Land (Rate of Interest after Entry) (S.) (No. 2) Regs. 1970	**r.**, 1971/65.
1390	Acquisition of Land (Rate of Interest after Entry) (No. 2) Regs. 1970	**r.**, 1971/64.
1401	Savings Certificates (Amdt.) Regs. 1970	**r.**, 1971/549.
1402	Police Cadets (Amdt.) (No. 2) Regs. 1970	**superseded,** 1971/804.
1407	National Health Service (General Dental Services) Amdt. (No. 3) Regs. 1970	**superseded,** 1971/984.
1409	Wages Regulation (Aerated Waters) (S.) O. 1970	**r.**, 1971/1369.
1444	Civil Aviation (Aerial Advertising) (Amdt.) Regs. 1970	**r.**, 1971/1968.
1445	Hill Cattle Subsidy (Breeding Herds) (N.I.) Payment O. 1970	art.3 **am.**, 1971/944.
1446	Beef Cow Subsidy Payment (N.I.) O. 1970	art.3 **am.**, 1971/943.
1459	Brucellosis (Payments for Cows in Accredited Herds) (S.) Scheme 1970	paras. 2–4 **am.**, 1971/1072.
1480	Wages Regulation (Ready-made and Wholesale Bespoke Tailoring) O. 1970	**r.**, 1971/1651.
1519	Motor Vehicles (Driving Licences) (Amdt.) (No. 2) Regs. 1970	**r.**, 1971/451.
1522	Import Duties (General) (No. 7) O. 1970	**r.**, 1971/1971.
1528	Wages Regulation (Shirtmaking) (No. 2) O. 1970	**r.**, 1971/1919.
1529	Wages Regulation (Corset) (No. 2) O. 1970	**r.**, 1971/1918.
1537	Secretary of State for Trade and Industry O. 1970	art 7 **am.**, 1971/716.

Year and Number (or date)	Title or Description	How affected and Act or Instrument by which affected
1970		
1558	Anti-Dumping Duty (No. 3) O. 1970	**r.,** 1971/2001.
1559	Exchange Control (Authorised Dealers and Depositaries) (Amdt.) (No. 4) O. 1970	**r.,** 1971/477.
1570	Police Pensions (Amdt.) (No. 2) Regs. 1970	**r.,** 1971/232.
1571	Special Constables (Pensions) (Amdt.) Regs. 1970	**r.,** 1971/233.
1583	Special Constables (Pensions) (S.) Amdt. Regs. 1970	**r.,** 1971/234.
1587	British Sugar Corporation Limited (Financial Year) O. 1970	art. 2 **am.,** 1971/617.
1640	Wages Regulation (Retail Furnishing and Allied Trades) (No. 2) O. 1970	**r.,** 1971/1518.
1641	Anti-Dumping Duty (No. 4) O. 1970	**r.,** 1971/2001.
1649	Hill Cattle Subsidy Payment (S.) Order 1970	**superseded,** 1971/1188.
1650	Beef Cow (S.) (Amdt.) Scheme 1970	para. 2 **am.,** 1971/1189.
1651	Beef Cow Subsidy Payment (S.) O. 1970	**superseded,** 1971/1190.
1659	Police (Amdt.) (No. 4) Regs. 1970	**r.** (saving), 1971/156.
1674	Parliamentary Constituencies (E.) O. 1970	sch. Pt. II **am.,** 1971/2106, 2108, 2109, 2110, 2111, 2112, 2113, 2114.
1683	Consular Fees (Amdt.) O. 1970	**r.,** 1971/211.
1686	Awards (First Degree, etc. Courses) (Amdt. No. 3) Regs. 1970	**r.,** 1971/1297.
1712	Cubic Measures (Sand, Ballast and Agricultural Materials) Regs. 1970	regs. 6, 11, 14 **am.,** 1971/827.
1724	Wages Regulation (Rubber Proofed Garment) (No. 2) O. 1970	**r.,** 1971/1836.
1746	A.S. (Rules of Court Amendment No. 5) 1970	c. IV **replaced,** 1971/1161.
1759	Farm Capital Grant Scheme 1970	para. 5 sch. 3 **am.,** 1971/1077.
1770	National Insurance (Collection of Graduated Contributions) Regs. 1970	regs. 1, 2, 5 **am.,** sch. re-numbered sch. 1 sch. 1 regs. 19, 26–29, 32 **am.,** Pt. V (regs. 35–42) **r.,** sch. 2 **inserted,** 1971/2050.
1800	Hill Sheep Subsidy Payment (N.I.) (Amdt.) O. 1970	**superseded,** 1971/946.

Year and Number (or date)	Title or Description	How affected and Act or Instrument by which affected
1970		
1801	Hill Sheep Subsidy Payment (E. and W.) (Amdt.) O. 1970	**superseded,** 1971/945.
1805	Farm Capital Grant (S.) Scheme 1970	para. 5 sch. 2 **am.,** 1971/1076.
1818	Import Duty Drawbacks (No. 6) O. 1970	**r.,** 1971/274.
1819	Import Duties (Temporary Exemptions) (No. 11) O. 1970	**r.,** 1971/2010.
1840	Matrimonial Causes Fees (Amdt.) O. 1970	**r.** (saving), 1971/102.
1846	Anti-Dumping Duty (No. 5) O. 1970	**r.,** 1971/2001.
1848	Wages Regulation (Wholesale Mantle and Costume) (No. 2) O. 1970	**r.,** 1971/1922.
1853	Superannuation (Local Govt. and Approved Employment) Interchange (S.) Rules 1970	rule 2 sch. 2 **am.,** 1971/1031.
1863	Irish Land (Finance) (Amdt.) (No. 2) Rules 1970	**r.,** 1971/860.
1865	Matrimonial Causes (Costs) (Amdt. No. 2) Rules 1970	**r.,** 1971/987.
1870	Supreme Ct. Fees O. 1970	art. 5 sch. s. 11 **am.,** 1971/1245. 245.
1875	Rate Support Grant (Increase) O. 1970	**superseded,** 1971/2031.
1887	Merchant Shipping (Fees) (Amdt.) Regs. 1970	**r.,** 1971/643.
1959	Approved Schools and Classifying Centres (Contributions by Local Authies.) Regs. 1970	**r.,** 1971/222.
1981	National Insurance (General Benefit) Regs. 1970	reg. 13 **am.,** 1971/621. regs. 5, 11 **am.,** 1971/1018. regs. 4, 5 **am.,** 5A **inserted,** 7–9, 11, 13 **am.,** 1971/1419. reg. 13 **am.,** 1971/1478. reg. 5, 5A, 7 **am.,** 1971/1633.
1982	Exchange Control (Authorised Dealers and Depositaries) (Amdt.) (No. 5) O. 1970	**r.,** 1971/477.
1993	Price Stability of Imported Products (Rates of Levy) (Eggs) (No. 16) O. 1970	**r.,** 1971/7.
2005	Sugar (Rates of Surcharge) and Surcharge Repayments) (No. 10) O. 1970	**superseded,** 1971/78.

Year and Number (or date)	Title or Description	How affected and Act or Instrument by which affected
1970		
2006	Composite Sugar Products (Surcharge and Surcharge Repayments—Average Rates) (No. 11) O. 1970	**superseded,** 1971/79.
2007	Bankruptcy Fees O. 1970	sch. Table A Pt. II **am.,** 1971/1017.
2024	Beef Cow Subsidy Payment (E. and W.) O. 1970	art 3 **am.,** 1971/1026.
2032	Divorce County Courts (Amdt.) O. 1970	**r.,** 1971/1954.
Instrts. not S.I.		
11 Nov.	Gilbert and Ellice Is. O. 1970 (1970 III, p. 6765)	ss. 20, 21 **r.,** 22–25 **replaced,** O. 27.10.71
27 Nov.	Gilbert and Ellice Is. R. Instructions 1970 (1970 III, p. 6802)	**r.,** R. Instructions 30.11.71.
1971		
7	Price Stability of Imported Products (Rates of Levy) (Eggs) (No. 1) O. 1971	**r.,** 1971/37.
29	Wages Regulation (Licensed Non-residential Establishment) (Amdt.) O. 1971	**r.,** 1971/991.
30	Wages Regulation (Licensed Non-residential Establishment) (Managers and Club Stewards) (Amdt.) O. 1971	**r.,** 1971/992.
37	Price Stability of Imported Products (Rates of Levy) (Eggs) (No. 2) O. 1971	**r.,** 1971/166.
43	Import Duties (Temporary Exemptions) (No. 1) O. 1971	**r.,** 1971/2010.
62	Legal Aid (General) Regs. 1971	arrangement of regs. **am.,** 1971/1877. regs. 5, 6 **am.,** 26(A) **inserted** 1971/1877.
64	Acquisition of Land (Rate of Interest after Entry) Regs. 1971	**r.,** 1971/673.
65	Acquisition of Land (Rate of Interest after Entry) (S.) Regs. 1971	**r.,** 1971/675.
66	A.S. (Rules of Ct. Amdt. No. 1) 1971	commencement date **am.,** 1971/201.
76	National Insurance and Industrial Injuries (Collection of Contributions) Amdt. Provn. Regs. 1971	**r.,** 1971/993.
77	Welfare Foods (Amdt.) O. 1971	**r.,** 1971/457.
78	Sugar (Rates of Surcharge and Surcharge Repayments) O. 1971	**superseded,** 1971/163.

Year and Number (or date)	Title or Description	How affected and Act or Instrument by which affected
1971		
79	Composite Sugar Products (Surcharge and Surcharge Repayments—Average Rates) O. 1971	**superseded,** 1971/164.
100	Motor Vehicles (International Circulation) (Decimal Currency) O. 1971	**superseded,** 1971/869.
101	County Ct. Fees (Decimalisation) O. 1971	**r.** (saving), 1971/1649.
107	Witnesses' Allowances Regs. 1971	regs. 5, 15 **am.,** 1971/1259.
108	Coroners (Fees and Allowances) Rules 1971	rules 4, 5 **am.,** 1971/1260.
115	Import Duties (General) (No. 1) O. 1971	**r.,** 1971/1971.
126	A.S. (Citation of Witnesses) 1971	**expired,** 8.3.71.
127	A.S. (Citation of Jurors) 1971	**expired** 8.3.71.
129	Registration of Marriages (Welsh Language) Regs. 1971	sch. 2 **am.,** 1971/1217.
136	Jurors' Allowances Regs. 1971	**r.** (saving), 1971/2046.
145	Firemen's Pension Scheme O. 1971	arts. 8, 21–23, 29, 65, 72, 75–77, **am.,** sch. 2 Pts. I, II, IV, V, **am.,** sch. 3 Pts. I, III **am.,** sch. 4 **r.,** sch. 10 **am.,** 1971/1329. art. 15 **am.,** 1971/1468.
150	Wages Regulation (Boot and Shoe Repairing) O. 1971	sch. Pts. II–IV **replaced,** 1971/1604.
154	Anti-Dumping Duty O. 1971	**r.,** 1971/2001.
156	Police Regs. 1971	schs. 5, 6 **am.,** 1971/659. regs. 33 **replaced,** 36, 37 **am.,** 49A **inserted,** 51 **am.,** sch. 11 **am.,** 1971/1141. regs. 37 **replaced,** 47, 49 **am.,** sch. 5 Pt. II **am.,** 1971/1901.
163	Sugar (Rates of Surcharge and Surcharge Repayments) (No. 2) O. 1971	**superseded,** 1971/240.
164	Composite Sugar Products (Surcharge and Surcharge Repayments—Average Rates) (No. 2) O. 1971	**superseded,** 1971/241.
166	Price Stability of Imported Products (Rates of Levy) (Eggs) (No. 3) O. 1971	**r.,** 1971/192.
167	A.S. (Citation of Defenders in the Sheriff Ct.) 1971	**expired,** 8.3.71.
192	Price Stability of Imported Products (Rates of Levy) (Eggs) (No. 4) O. 1971	**r.,** 1971/327.

Year and Number (or date)	Title or Description	How affected and Act or Instrument by which affected
1971		
198	A.S. (Rules of Ct. Amdt. No. 5 1970) (Alteration of Fees of Shorthand Writers) 1971	**superseded**, 1971/1161.
209	Lands Tribunal (Temporary Provs.) Rules 1971	**expired** 5.4.71.
214	Judicial Ctee., (Medical Rules) O. 1971	**r.**, 1971/393.
219	A.S. (Legal Aid Fees) 1971	para. 1 **renumbered** 1A, paras. 1, 2A, 4A **inserted**, 1971/1796.
220	Jurors' Allowances (S.) Regs. 1971	reg. 5 **am.**, 1971/2022.
232	Police Pensions Regs. 1971	regs. 3, 30, 33, 35 **am.**, sch. 3 Pt. VI **am.**, 1971/583. regs. 34, 89, 90 **am.**, Pt. XIII (regs. 106–113) **replaced** by new Pt. XIII (regs. 106–108), sch. 2 Pt. I para. 4 **r.**, Pt. II paras. 5 **r.**, Pt. VI para. 3 **r.**, sch. 3 Pt. I para. 3, 4 **replaced**, Pt. II scheme I **am.**, Pt. IV para. 2 **replaced**, sch. 4 Pts. I, III Tables **replaced**, 1971/1327. regs. 22, 30, 33, 35 **am.**, sch. 3 Pt. VI **replaced**, sch. 4 Pt. III **am.**, 1971/1466.
233	Special Constables (Pensions) Regs. 1971	regs. 3, 4 **am.**, 12 **r.**, 1971/1328. reg. 3 **am.**, 1971/1467.
234	Special Constables (Pensions) (S.) Regs. 1971	reg. 3, **am.**, 1971/585. regs. 3, 4 **am.**, 12 **r.**, 1971/1402. reg. 3 **am.**, 1971/1501.
240	Sugar (Rates of Surcharge and Surcharge Repayments) (No. 3) O. 1971	**superseded**, 1971/512.
241	Composite Sugar Products (Surcharge and Surcharge Repayments) (No. 3) O. 1971	**superseded**, 1971/513.
272	Import Duties (General) (No. 2) O. 1971	**r.**, 1971/1971.
273	Import Duties (Temporary Exemptions) (No. 2) O. 1971	**r.**, 1971/2010.
274	Import Duty Drawbacks (No. 1) O. 1971	schs. 1, 2 **am.**, 1971/1186. sch. 1 **am.**, 1971/2009.
287	A.S. (Legal Aid) (Children) 1971	para. 1 **am.**, 1971/1795.
288	Legal Aid (S.) (Children) Regs. 1971	reg. 9 **am.**, 1971/554.
303	Therapeutic Substances (Control of Sale and Supply) Regs. 1971	**r.**, 1971/459.
304	Therapeutic Substances (Supply of Antibiotics and Chemotherapeutic Substances for Agricultural Purposes) Regs. 1971	sch. 1 **am.**, 1971/1405.

Year and Number (or date)	Title or Description	How affected and Act or Instrument by which affected
1971		
311	Live Poultry (Restrictions) O. 1971	arts. 3 **am.**, 11 **r.**, schs. 3, 4 **r.**, 1971/1036.
327	Price Stability of Imported Products (Rates of Levy) (Eggs) (No. 5) O. 1971	**r.**, 1971/603.
352	Goods Vehicles (Plating and Testing) Regs. 1971	regs. 9, 10, 21, 30, 36 **am.**, 50 **replaced,** 55, 56, 60 sch. 2, sch. 3 Pts. I, II **am.**, 1971/2074.
356	A.S. (Extension of Prescribed Time) 1971	**expired** 8.3.71.
357	A.S. (Removal Notices) 1971	**expired** 8.3.71.
364	Anti-Dumping (Provisional Charge to Duty) O. 1971	**r.**, 1971/518.
413	Justices' Allowances Regs. 1971	reg. 5 **am.**, 1971/1975.
414	Probation (Allowances) Rules 1971	rule 5 **am.**, 1971/1976.
437	Remuneration of Teachers (Primary and Secondary Schools) (Amdt.) O. 1971	**r.**, 1971/1539.
445	Import Duties (Temporary Exemptions) (No. 3) O. 1971	**r.**, 1971/2010.
450	Road Vehicles (Registration and Licensing) Regs. 1971	reg. 26 **am.**, 1971/1285.
457	Welfare Food O. 1971	arts. 2 **am.**, 6 **replaced,** sch. 2 **am.**, 1971/1920.
460	Industrial Training Levy (Knitting, Lace and Net) O. 1971	arts. 3, 5 **am.**, 1971/1070.
461	Friendly Societies (Amdt.) Regs. 1971	reg. 3 **am.**, sch. 1 **r.**, 1971/1956.
477	Exchange Control (Authorised Dealers and Depositaries) O. 1971	sch. 2 **am.**, 1971/1028, 1370, 1566, 2034. sch. 3 **am.**, 1971/1566.
490	Justices Allowances (S.) Regs. 1971	sch. 3 **am.**, 1971/1990.
499	Import Duties (Temporary Exemptions) (Amdt.) O. 1971	**r.**, 1971/2010.
512	Sugar (Rates of Surcharge and Surcharge Repayments) (No. 4) O. 1971	**superseded,** 1971/739.
513	Composite Sugar Products (Surcharge and Surcharge Repayments—Average Rates) (No. 4) O. 1971	**superseded,** 1971/740.
519	Anti-Dumping (Provisional Charge to Duty) (No. 2) O. 1971	**r.**, 1971/1048.
584	Special Constables (Pensions) (Amdt.) Regs. 1971	**superseded,** 1971/1328.

Year and Number (or date)	Title or Description	How affected and Act or Instrument by which affected
1971		
603	Price Stability of Imported Products (Rates of Levy) (Eggs) (No. 6) O. 1971	**r.,** 1971/684.
621	National Insurance (Attendance Allowance) Regs. 1971	reg. 12 **r.,** 1971/707. reg. 14 **am.,** 1971/1854.
643	Merchant Shipping (Fees) Regs. 1971	sch. Pt. 1 **am.,** 1971/1003. sch. Pts. 1–6, 8–11, 21 **am.,** 1971/1353.
649	Wages Regulation (Milk Distributive) (S.) O. 1971	**r.,** 1971/1531.
656	County Cts. (Bankruptcy and Companies Winding-up Jurisdiction) O. 1971	sch. 1 **am.,** 1971/1983.
667	Import Duties (Temporary Exemptions) (No. 4) O. 1971	**r.,** 1971/2010.
673	Acquisition of Land (Rate of Interest after Entry) (No. 2) Regs. 1971	**r.,** 1971/1544.
674	Opencast Coal (Rate of Interest on Compensation) O. 1971	**r.,** 1971/1551.
675	Acquisition of Land (Rate of Interest after Entry) (S.) (No. 2) Regs. 1971	**r.,** 1971/1545.
684	Price Stability of Imported Products (Rates of Levy) (Eggs) (No. 7) O. 1971	**r.,** 1971/773.
707	National Insurance (Claims and Payments) Regs. 1971	reg. 10A **inserted,** 1971/1219. regs. 9 **am.,** 15A **inserted,** schs. 1–3 **am.,** 1971/1419. sch. 3 **am.,** 1971/1478.
726	Poisons Rules 1971	rule 18A **inserted,** sch. 3 group II **am.,** 1971/1835.
739	Sugar (Rates of Surcharge and Surcharge Repayments) (No. 5) O. 1971	**superseded,** 1971/957.
740	Composite Sugar Products (Surcharge and Surcharge Repayments—Average Rates) (No. 5) O. 1971	**superseded,** 1971/958.
745	Building Standards (Relaxation by Building Authies.) (S.) Regs. 1971	**r.,** 1971/2051.
748	Building Standards (S.) Amdt. Regs. 1971	**r.** (9.2.72), 1971/2052.
769	Pensions Appeal Tribunals (E. and W.) Rules 1971	rule 27 **am.,** 1971/1856.
773	Price Stability of Imported Products (Rates of Levy) (Eggs) (No. 8) O. 1971	**r.,** 1971/817.

Year and Number (or date)	Title or Description	How affected and Act or Instrument by which affected
1971		
817	Price Stability of Imported Products (Rates of Levy) (Eggs) (No. 9) O. 1971	**r.**, 1971/912.
845	Wages Regulation (Retail Drapery, Outfitting and Footwear) O. 1971	sch. paras. 5, 7 **replaced,** 19 **am.,** 1971/1631.
848	Aircraft (Customs) Regs. 1971	reg. 7 **am.,** 1971/1299.
851	Import Duties (General) (No. 3) O. 1971	**r.,** 1971/1971.
858	Import Duties (General) (No. 4) O. 1971	**r.,** 1971/1971.
860	Irish Land (Finance) (Amdt.) Rules 1971	**r.,** 1971/1883.
884	Awards (First Degree, etc. Courses) (Amdt.) Regs. 1971	**r.,** 1971/1297.
904	A.S. (Alteration of Fees of Shorthand Writers in the Sheriff Ct.) 1971	para. 2 **am.,** 1971/1810.
905	National Insurance Act 1966 (Commencement No. 3) O. 1971	**r.,** 1971/2094.
912	Price Stability of Imported Products (Rates of Levy) (Eggs) (No. 10) O. 1971	**r.,** 1971/952.
952	Price Stability of Imported Products (Rates of Levy) (Eggs) (No. 11) O. 1971	**r.,** 1971/985.
953	Matrimonial Causes Rules 1971	rules 2, 9, 18, 21, 30, 34, 43, 44, 46, 47, 62, 79, 102, 107 **am.,** Appx. 1 **r.,** forms 2, 4, 9, 14, 20, 21 **am.,** 1971/1923.
957	Sugar (Rates of Surcharge and Surcharge Repayments) (No. 6) O. 1971	**superseded,** 1971/1507.
958	Composite Sugar Products (Surcharge and Surcharge Repayments—Average Rates) (No. 6) O. 1971	**superseded,** 1971/1508.
985	Price Stability of Imported Products (Rates of Levy) (Eggs) (No. 12) O. 1971	**r.,** 1971/1027.
1012	Import Duties (TemporaryExemptions) (No. 5) O. 1971	**r.,** 1971/2010.
1022	Hydrocarbon Oil Duties (Drawback) (No. 1) O. 1971	**r.,** 1971/1233.
1027	Price Stability of Imported Products (Rates of Levy) (Eggs) (No. 13) O. 1971	**r.,** 1971/1157.

Year and Number (or date)	Title or Description	How affected and Act or Instrument by which sffected
1971 1032	Building Standards (S.) Amdt. 2 (Metrication) Regs. 1971	**r.** (9.2.72), 1971/2052.
1048	Anti-Dumping Duty (No. 3) O. 1971	**r.**, 1971/2001.
1056	Import Duties (General) (No. 5) O. 1971	**r.**, 1971/1971.
1069	Price Stability of Imported Products (Rates of Levy) (Cereals) (No. 1) O. 1971	**r.**, 1971/1264.
1075	Anti-Dumping (Provisional Charge to Duty) (No. 3) O. 1971	**r.**, 1971/1635.
1083	County Ct. Fees (Amdt.) O. 1971	**r.** (saving), 1971/1649.
1135	Civil Aviation (Navigation Services Charges) Regs. 1971	regs. 4, 5 **am.**, 6A **inserted**, 7 **am.**, 15 **replaced**, 1971/1730.
1152	County Cts. (Admiralty Jurisdiction) O. 1971	sch. **am.**, 1971/1984.
1157	Price Stability of Imported Products (Rates of Levy) (Eggs) (No. 14) O. 1971	**r.**, 1971/1271.
1164	Act of Sederunt (Confirmation of Executors Amdt.) O. 1971	**am.**, 1971/1655.
1264	Price Stability of Imported Products (Rates of Levy) (Cereals) (No. 2) O. 1971	**r.**, 1971/1429.
1271	Price Stability of Imported Products (Rates of Levy) (Eggs) (No. 15) O. 1971	**r.**, 1971/1319.
1284	Road Vehicles (Excise) (Prescribed Particulars) (Amdt.) Regs. 1971	**r.**, 1971/1628.
1287	Diseases of Animals (Approved Disinfectants) (Amdt.) O. 1971	art. 4 **am.**, 1971/1839.
1319	Price Stability of Imported Products (Rates of Levy) (Eggs) (No. 16) O. 1971	**r.**, 1971/1401.
1348	Anti-Dumping (Provisional Charge to Duty) (No. 3) (Amdt.) 1971	**r.**, 1971/1635.
1357	Anti-Dumping (Provisional Charge to Duty) (No. 4) O. 1971	**r.**, 1971/1897.
1387	Import Duties (General) (No. 6) O. 1971	**r.**, 1971/1971.
1388	Import Duties (Temporary Exemptions) (No. 6) O. 1971	**r.**, 1971/2010.

Year and Number (or date)	Title or Description	How affected and Act or Instrument by which affected
1971		
1401	Price Stability of Imported Products (Rates of Levy) (Eggs) (No. 17) O. 1971	**r.**, 1971/1475.
1427	Remuneration of Teachers (Primary and Secondary Schools) (Amdt. No. 2) O. 1971	**r.**, 1971/1539.
1429	Price Stability of Imported Products (Rates of Levy) (Cereals) (No. 3) O. 1971	**r.**, 1971/1465.
1443	Wages Regulation (Retail Newsagency, Tobacco and Confectionery) (E. and W.) O. 1971	**r.**, 1971/1942.
1465	Price Stability of Imported Products (Rates of Levy) (Cereals) (No. 4) O. 1971	**r.**, 1971/1607.
1475	Price Stability of Imported Products (Rates of Levy) (Eggs) (No. 18) O. 1971	**r.**, 1971/1506.
1506	Price Stability of Imported Products (Rates of Levy) (Eggs) (No. 19) O. 1971	**r.**, 1971/1541.
1507	Sugar (Rates of Surcharge and Surcharge Repayments) (No. 7) O. 1971	**superseded,** 1971/1769.
1508	Composite Sugar Products (Surcharge and Surcharge Repayments—Average Rates) (No. 7) O. 1971	**superseded,** 1971/1770.
1538	Gaming Clubs (Permitted Areas) Regs. 1971	reg. 3 **am.**, 1971/2029.
1541	Price Stability of Imported Products (Rates of Levy) (Eggs) (No. 20) O. 1971	**r.**, 1971/1584.
1543	Import Duties (Temporary Exemptions) (No. 7) O. 1971	**r.**, 1971/2010.
1544	Acquisition of Land (Rate of Interest after Entry) (No. 3) Regs. 1971	**r.**, 1971/1993.
1545	Acquisition of Land (Rate of Interest after Entry) (S.) (No. 3) Regs. 1971	**r.**, 1971/1994.
1584	Price Stability of Imported Products (Rates of Levy) (Eggs) (No. 21) O. 1971	**r.**, 1971/1621.
1607	Price Stability of Imported Products (Rates of Levy) (Cereals) (No. 5) O. 1971	**r.**, 1971/1629.

Year and Number (or date)	Title or Description	How affected and Act or Instrument by which affected
1971		
1621	Price Stability of Imported Products (Rates of Levy) (Eggs) (No. 22) O. 1971	**r.**, 1971/1650.
1629	Price Stability of Imported Products (Rates of Levy) (Cereals) (No. 6) O. 1971	**r.**, 1971/1647.
1635	Anti-Dumping Duty (No. 4) O. 1971	**r.**, 1971/2001.
1647	Price Stability of Imported Products (Rates of Levy) (Cereals) (No. 7)O. 1971	**r.**, 1971/1695.
1650	Price Stability of Imported Products (Rates of Levy) (Eggs) (No. 23) O. 1971	**r.**, 1971/1689.
1668	Price Stability of Imported Products (Rates of Levy) (Cereals) (No. 8) O. 1971	**r.**, 1971/1695.
1689	Price Stability of Imported Products (Rates of Levy) (Eggs) (No. 24) O. 1971	**r.**, 1971/1720.
1695	Price Stability of Imported Products (Rates of Levy) (Cereals) (No. 9) O. 1971	**r.**, 1971/1713.
1708	Dutch Elm Disease (Local Authorities) O. 1971	sch. **am.**, 1971/1823, 1963.
1712	Import Duties (Temporary Exemptions) (No. 8) O. 1971	**r.**, 1971/2010.
1713	Price Stability of Imported Products (Rates of Levy) (Cereals) (No. 10) O. 1971	**r.**, 1971/1774.
1720	Price Stability of Imported Products (Rates of Levy) (Eggs) (No. 25) O. 1971	**r.**, 1971/1778.
1769	Sugar (Rates of Surcharge and Surcharge Repayments) (No. 8) O. 1971	**superseded**, 1971/1964.
1770	Composite Sugar Products (Surcharge and Surcharge Repayments—Average Rates) (No. 8) O. 1971	**superseded**, 1971/1965.
1774	Price Stability of Imported Products (Rates of Levy) (Cereals) (No. 11) O. 1971	**r.**, 1971/1937.
1778	Price Stability of Imported Products (Rates of Levy) (Eggs) (No. 26) O. 1971	**r.**, 1971/1895.

Year and Number (or date)	Title or Description	How affected and Act or Instrument by which affected
1971		
1811	Building Standards (S.) Amdt. No. 3 Regs. 1971	**r.** (9.2.72.), 1971/2052.
1813	Import Duties (General) (No. 7) O. 1971	**expired.**
1875	Rate Support Grant (Increases) O. 1970	**superseded,** 1971/2031.
1882	Import Duties (Developing Countries) O. 1971	sch. 2 **am.,** 1971/2021.
1891	Import Duties (General) (No. 8) O. 1971	art. 2 **am.,** 1971/2041.
1895	Price Stability of Imported Products (Rates of Levy) (Eggs) (No. 27) O. 1971	**r.,** 1971/1938.
1897	Anti-Dumping Duty (No. 5) O. 1971	**r.,** 1971/2001.
1937	Price Stability of Imported Products (Rates of Levy) (Cereals) (No. 12) O. 1971	**r.,** 1971/1986.
1964	Sugar (Rates of Surcharge and Surcharge Repayments) (No. 10) O. 1971	**superseded,** 1971/2082.
1965	Composite Sugar Products (Surcharge and Surcharge Repayments—Average Rates) (No. 10) O. 1971	**superseded,** 1971/2083.
1971	Import Duties (General) (No. 7) O. 1971	sch. 1 c. 5, 7, 12, 15, 27–29, 32, 38, 39, 44, 51, 58, 59, 69, 70, 73, 74, 76, 81, 85, 90, 95 **am.,** 1971/2010. c. 32 **am.,** 1971/2011. c. 20 **am.,** 1971/2012. c. 7, 8, 33, 47 **am.,** 1971/2021. c. 20 **am.,** 1971/2041. c. 15, 25, 28–30, 34, 38, 39, 48, 50, 73, 76, 81, 85, 88 **am.,** 1971/2042. c. 39 **am.,** 1971/2043.
1986	Price Stability of Imported Products (Rates of Levy) (Cereals) (No. 13) O. 1971	**r.,** 1971/2154.

NUMERICAL LIST

of those Statutory Instruments of 1971 which were printed and sold under the Statutory Instruments Act 1946

No.	Subject	Part	Page
1	Theatres (Licence Application Fees) [11 Jan.] ...	I,	1
2	Anti-Dumping Duty O. 1967 (Revn.) [11 Jan.] ...	I,	2
7	Price Stability of Imported Products (Rates of Levy) (Eggs) [7 Jan.]	I,	3
8	Cornwall (Advance Payments for Street Works) [14 Jan.]	(n) III,	6357
13	Wireless Telegraphy (Broadcast Licence Charges & Exemption) [18 Jan.]	I,	5
15	Industrial Training Levy (Iron and Steel) [15 Jan.]	I,	7
20	Remuneration of Teachers (S.) [15 Jan.]	I,	12
21	Income Tax (Employments) [15 Jan.]	I,	15
25	Decimal Currency (Amdt. of Local Enactments etc.) [18 Jan.]	(n) III,	6364
27	London–Penzance Trunk Road (Ivybridge By-Pass) [18 Jan.]	(n) III,	6343
29	Wages Regulation (Licensed Non-residential Establishment) [20 Jan.]	I,	23
30	Wages Regulation (Licensed Non-residential Establishment) (Managers and Club Stewards) [20 Jan.]	I,	27
37	Price Stability of Imported Products (Rates of Levy) (Eggs) [14 Jan.]	I,	32
40	Weights [20 Jan.]	I,	34
41	East of Scotland Water Bd. (Milton Glen Burn, Brig O'Turk) Water [19 Jan.]	(n) III,	6360
43	Import Duties (Temp. Exemptions) [14 Jan.] ...	I,	36
52	National Health Service (Compensation) [25 Jan.]	I,	38
53	London–Carlisle–Glasgow–Inverness Trunk Road (Gretna Diversion (Cumberland) Connecting Roads) [25 Jan.]	(n) III,	6342
58	A.1(M) Motorway (Hatfield–The Clock Roundabout, Welwyn) [20 Jan.]	(n) III,	6345
59	A.1 London–Edinburgh–Thurso Trunk Road (Lemsford to Welwyn Detrunking) [20 Jan.] ...	(n) III,	6341

(**n**) Instrument classified as local, noted in the Classified List of Local S.I. at the page shown above, but not set out in full.

No.	Subject	Part	Page
60	Commonwealth Telegraphs (Pension Rights of Former Cable and Wireless Ltd. Staff) [21 Jan.]...	I,	69
61	Commonwealth Telegraphs (Cable and Wireless Ltd. Pension) [21 Jan.]	I,	70
62	Legal Aid (General) [26 Jan.]	I,	75
63	Legal Aid (Assessment of Resources) [26 Jan.] ...	I,	120
64	Acquisition of Land (Rate of Interest after Entry) [22 Jan.]	I,	122
65	Acquisition of Land (Rate of Interest after Entry) (S.) [22 Jan.]	I,	123
66	A.S. (Rules of Ct. Amdt. No. 1) [9 Feb.]	I,	124
67	A.S. (Fees in the Ct. of Teinds) [9 Feb.]	I,	125
73	Winchester–Preston Trunk Road (Chilton–Drayton) [22 Jan.]	(n) III,	6343
74	Winchester–Preston Trunk Road (Abingdon By-Pass Slip Roads) [22 Jan.]	(n) III,	6343
75	Winchester–Preston Trunk Road (Abingdon By-Pass) [22 Jan.]	(n) III,	6343
76	National Insurance and Industrial Injuries (Collection of Contributions) [1 Feb.]	I,	128
77	Welfare Foods [28 Jan.]	I,	130
78	Sugar (Rates of Surcharge and Surcharge Repayments) [20 Jan.]	I,	132
79	Composite Sugar Products (Surcharge and Surcharge Repayments—Average Rates) [20 Jan.]...	I,	135
82	British Museum (Authorised Repositories) [27 Jan.]	I,	139
83	Lune Valley Water Bd. (Charges) [28 Jan.] ...	(n) III,	6360
86	Health and Welfare Services (Provision of Instruction) [26 Jan.]	I,	140
87	Wages Regulation (Dressmaking and Women's Light Clothing) (S.) [29 Jan.]	I,	142
90	A.S. (Alteration of Sheriff Ct. Fees) [27 Jan.] ...	I,	151
91	A.S. (Fees of Town Clerks and Clerks of the Peace) [12 Feb.]	I,	161
92	A.S. (Social Work) (Sheriff Ct. Procedure Rules) [22 Feb.]	I,	167
93	A.S. (Sessions of Ct.) [12 Feb.]	I,	183
99	Health and Welfare Services (Provision of Instruction) (S.) [26 Jan.]	I,	184
100	Motor Vehicles (International Circulation) (Decimal Currency) [28 Jan.]...	I,	186
101	County Ct. Fees (Decimalisation) [27 Jan.] ...	I,	188
102	Matrimonial Causes Fees [27 Jan.]	I,	190
103	Legal Aid (Assessment of Resources) (Decimalisation) [27 Jan.]	I,	193
107	Witnesses' Allowances [29 Jan.]	I,	195
108	Coroners (Fees and Allowances) [29 Jan.] ...	I,	200
109	Reading County Borough Council A.329 Relief Road Special Road Scheme 1969 Confirmation [28 Jan.]	(n) III,	6345

(n) Instrument classified as local, noted in the Classified List of Local S.I. at the page shown above, but not set out in full.

No.	Subject	Part	Page
110	Royal County of Berkshire A.329 Relief Road Special Road Scheme 1969 No. 1 Confirmation [28 Jan.]	(n) III,	6345
113	Export of Goods (Control) [28 Jan.]	I,	205
114	Superannuation (Local Govt. and Approved Employment) Interchange [28 Jan.]	I,	206
115	Import Duties (General) [29 Jan.]	I,	209
116	National Freight Corporation (Alteration of Pension Schemes) [29 Jan.]	I,	210
117	National Freight Corporation (Alteration of Pension Schemes) [29 Jan.]	I,	217
118	Therapeutic Substances (Manufacture of Vaccines, Toxins and Antigens) [2 Feb.]	I,	224
124	Students' Allowances (S.) [29 Jan.]	I,	238
126	A.S. (Citation of Witnesses) [23 Feb.]	I,	241
127	A.S. (Citation of Jurors) [17 Feb.]	I,	242
128	New Towns Compulsory Purchase (Contemporaneous Procedure) (S.) [29 Jan.]	I,	244
129	Registration of Marriages (Welsh Language) [3 Feb.]	I,	246
130	London–Cambridge Trunk Road (Hoddesdon By-Pass) [3 Feb.]	(n) III,	6342
131	Public Health (Aircraft) (S.) [4 Feb.]	I,	263
132	Public Health (Ships) (S.) [4 Feb.]	I,	283
133	Police (Discipline) [3 Feb.]	I,	311
134	Police (Discipline) (Deputy Chief Constables, Assistant Chief Constables and Chief Constables) [3 Feb.]	I,	313
135	County of Chester (Electoral Divisions) [4 Feb.] ...	(n) III,	6355
136	Jurors' Allowances [4 Feb.]	I,	315
140	London–Cambridge Trunk Road (Ware By-Pass) [3 Feb.]	(n) III,	6342
141	London Borough of Hounslow (Wards) [4 Feb.] ...	(n) III,	6356
143	Thanet (Water Charges) [5 Feb.]	(n) III,	6360
144	National Health Service (Newcastle University Designation) [5 Feb.]	I,	318
145	Firemen's Pension Scheme [9 Feb.]	I,	320
146	Increase of Pensions (Fire Services) [9 Feb.] ...	I,	384
149	Goods Vehicles (Operators' Licences) (Fees) [5 Feb.]	I,	387
150	Wages Regulation (Boot and Shoe Repairing) [12 Feb.]	I,	389
151	Police Cadets [5 Feb.]	I,	432
152	National Health Service (Designation of Teaching Hospitals) [5 Feb.]	I,	433
153	National Health Service (Newcastle University Hospital Management Ctee.) [5 Feb.]	(n) III,	6358
154	Anti-Dumping Duty [1 Feb.]	I,	436
155	Purchase Tax [5 Feb.]	I,	438
156	Police [11 Feb.]	I,	439
157	Police (Promotion) [11 Feb.]	I,	495
161	Clean Air (Measurement of Grit and Dust from Furnaces) [8 Feb.]	I,	497

(**n**) Instrument classified as local, noted in the Classified List of Local S.I. at the page shown above, but not set out in full.

No.	Subject	Part	Page
162	Clean Air (Emission of Grit and Dust from Furnaces) [8 Feb.]	I,	500
163	Sugar (Rates of Surcharge and Surcharge Repayments) [3 Feb.]	I,	505
164	Composite Sugar Products (Surcharge and Surcharge Repayments—Average Rates) [3 Feb.] ...	I,	508
165	Motor Vehicles (Tests) [11 Feb.]	I,	512
166	Price Stability of Imported Products (Rates of Levy) (Eggs) [3 Feb.]	I,	516
167	A.S. (Citation of Defenders in the Sheriff Ct.) [25 Feb.]	I,	518
169	Provision of Milk and Meals [9 Feb.]	I,	520
170	Gas (Meter) [11 Feb.]	I,	522
171	Salmon (Northwest Atlantic) [11 Feb.]	I,	524
172	Salmon and Migratory Trout (Restrictions on Landing) [11 Feb.]	I,	526
174	A.S. (Legal Aid Rules Amdt.) [22 Feb.]	I,	530
175	Theatres (Licence Application Fees) (S.) [9 Feb.]...	I,	532
176	Air Corporations (General Staff, Pilots and Officers Pensions) [11 Feb.]	I,	533
177	National Health Service (Bradford Hospital Management Ctee.) [11 Feb.]	(n) III,	6358
178	Mental Health (Hospital and Guardianship) (Welsh Forms) [11 Feb.]	I,	537
179	West Cornwall Water Bd. (Charges) [12 Feb.] ...	(n) III,	6360
180	Coventry (Water Charges) [12 Feb.]	(n) III,	6359
181	Salmon and Migratory Trout (Sea Fishing) Licensing [11 Feb.]	I,	544
182	East Yorkshire (Wolds Area) and Kingston upon Hull (Variation of Limits of Supply) [12 Feb.] ...	(n) III,	6360
183	Bridge and Ferry Undertakings (Decimal Currency) [12 Feb.]	(n) III,	6364
184	Social Work (S.) Act 1968 (Commencement) [15 Feb.]	I,	547
185	Police Cadets (S.) [12 Feb.]	I,	555
187	Education (Handicapped Children) Act 1970 (Appointed Day) [16 Feb.] ...	I,	557
188	Magistrates' Cts. Fees (Decimalisation) [12 Feb.]...	I,	558
189	Transport Pension Schemes (Decimal Currency) [12 Feb.]	I,	560
190	Legal Aid (S.) Act 1967 (Commencement) [16 Feb.]	I,	564
191	Manchester Ship Canal Revision [12 Feb.] ...	(n) III,	6354
192	Price Stability of Imported Products (Rates of Levy) (Eggs) [11 Feb.]	I,	566
193	Agricultural and Horticultural Improvements (Standard Costs) [12 Feb.]	I,	568
194	Legal Aid (S.) (General) [16 Feb.]	I,	570
195	Agricultural Drainage (Standard Costs) (S.) [18 Feb.]	I,	572
196	Police (S.) [18 Feb.]	I,	574
197	A.S. (Alteration of Fees of Shorthand Writers in the Sheriff Cts.) [17 Feb.]	I,	583

(n) Instrument classified as local, noted in the Classified List of Local S.I. at the page shown above, but not set out in full.

No.	Subject	Part	Page
198	A.S. (Rules of Ct. Amdt. No. 5 1970) (Alteration of Fees to Shorthand Writers) [1 Mar.]	I,	585
199	Conveyancing and Feudal Reform (S.) Act 1970 (Commencement) [18 Feb.]	I,	587
200	Allocation of Feuduty etc. (Form of Notice) [18 Feb.]	I,	588
201	A.S. (Rules of Ct. Amdt. No. 1) (Alteration of Operative Date) [1 Mar.]	I,	590
202	A.S. (Rules of Ct. Amdt. No. 2) [1 Mar.]	I,	591
203	A.S. (Rules of Ct. Amdt. No. 3) [1 Mar.]	I,	592
207	Wages Regulation (Sack and Bag) [18 Feb.] ...	I,	594
209	Lands Tribunal (Temporary Provisions) [17 Mar.]	I,	600
210	Clyde Dockyard Port of Gareloch and Loch Long [16 Feb.]	(n) III,	6354
211	Consular Fees [16 Feb.]	I,	601
212	Northern Ireland (Crown Proceedings) [15 Feb.]	I,	609
213	Judicial Committee (Fees) [15 Feb.]	I,	612
214	Judicial Committee (Medical Rules) [16 Feb.] ...	I,	620
215	Lands Tribunal Act 1949 (Appointed Day) (S.) [18 Feb.]	I,	626
216	Merchant Shipping (Load Lines Convention) (Various Countries) [16 Feb.]	I,	627
217	Merchant Shipping (Safety Convention) (Various Countries) [16 Feb.]	I,	628
218	Lands Tribunal for Scotland [19 Feb.]	I,	629
219	A.S. (Legal Aid Fees) [3 Mar.]	I,	648
220	Jurors' Allowances (S.) [19 Feb.]	I,	651
221	Civil Defence (Posts and Telecommunications) [24 Feb.]	I,	655
222	Approved Schools and Classifying Centres (Contributions by Local Authorities) [19 Feb.] ...	I,	657
223	Inverness-shire Water Bd. (Loch Eilean Iain and Loch Fada, Benbecula) Water [18 Feb.] ...	(n) III,	6361
224	Northern Pennines Rural Development Bd. (Dissolution) [18 Feb.]	I,	659
225	Family Income Supplements Act 1970 (Commencement) [22 Feb.]	I,	661
226	Family Income Supplements (General) [22 Feb.] ...	I,	662
227	Family Income Supplements (Claims and Payments) [22 Feb.]	I,	668
228	London Authorities (Parks and Open Spaces) [19 Feb.]	I,	673
229	London Authorities (Parks and Open Spaces) (Staff) [19 Feb.]	I,	681
230	London Authorities (Parks and Open Spaces) (Misc. Property) [19 Feb.]	I,	685
231	London Authorities (Transfer of Housing Estates etc.) [19 Feb.]	I,	688
232	Police Pensions [1 Mar.]	I,	700
233	Special Constables (Pensions) [15 Feb.]	I,	802
234	Special Constables (Pensions) (S.) [22 Feb.] ...	I,	814

(n) Instrument classified as local, noted in the Classified List of Local S.I. at the page shown above, but not set out in full.

No.	Subject	Part	Page
237	East Shropshire Water Bd. (Diddlebury Borehole) [22 Feb.]	(n) III,	6360
238	Eden Water Bd. (Cliburn Borehole) [23 Feb.] ...	(n) III,	6360
239	Police Cadets (Pensions) [19 Feb.]	I,	826
240	Sugar (Rates of Surcharge and Surcharge Repayments) [16 Feb.]	I,	832
241	Composite Sugar Products (Surcharge and Surcharge Repayments—Average Rates) [16 Feb.]	I,	835
242	Salmon and Migratory Trout (Prohibition of Fishing) [22 Feb.]	I,	839
244	Vehicle and Driving Licences Act 1969 (Commencement) [19 Feb.]	I,	842
245	Industrial Training Levy (Agricultural, Horticultural and Forestry) [22 Feb.]	I,	843
246	Police Cadets (Pensions) (S.) [19 Feb.]	I,	849
247	National Health Service (Southampton University Hospital Management Ctee.) [23 Feb.]	(n) III,	6358
248	Approved Schools (Contributions by Education Authorities) (S.) [25 Feb.]	I,	855
249	Residential Establishments (Payments by Local Authorities) (S.) [25 Feb.]	I,	857
251	Metropolitan Water Bd. [23 Feb.]	(n) III,	6360
252	Programme Distribution Systems (General Licence Charges) [24 Feb.]	I,	859
253	Iron Casting Industry (Scientific Research Levy) [25 Feb.]	I,	863
254	National Health Service (Compensation) (S.) [24 Feb.]	I,	867
255	National Health Service (Tunbridge Wells and Leybourne Hospital Management Ctee.) [25 Feb.]	(n) III,	6358
256	Isles of Scilly (Road Traffic Regulation) [26 Feb.]	I,	896
257	Staffordshire Potteries Water Bd. (Tattenhall Boreholes) [26 Feb.]	(n) III,	6360
258	West Somerset Water Bd. (Charges) [26 Feb.] ...	(n) III,	6360
259	Supreme Ct. Funds [23 Feb.]	I,	898
260	County Ct. Funds [23 Feb.]	I,	900
261	Trade Marks [26 Feb.]	I,	902
262	Designs [26 Feb.]	I,	913
263	Patents [26 Feb.]	I,	918
264	National Health Service (Functions of Regional Hospital Bds., etc.) [25 Feb.]	I,	926
265	A.S. (Rules of Ct. Amdt.) [10 Mar.]	I,	928
266	National Health Service (Royal Buckinghamshire and St. John's Hospital Management Ctee.) [26 Feb.]	(n) III,	6358
268	Royal County of Berkshire A.329 Relief Road Special Road Scheme 1969 No. 2 Confirmation [26 Feb.]	(n) III,	6345
270	Sutton District Water [26 Feb.]	(n) III,	6360
271	Air Navigation (General) [26 Feb.]	I,	929

(n) Instrument classified as local, noted in the Classified List of Local S.I. at the page shown above, but not set out in full.

No.	Subject	Part	Page
272	Import Duties (General) [26 Feb.]	I,	934
273	Import Duties (Temp. Exemptions) [26 Feb.] ...	I,	935
274	Import Duty Drawbacks [26 Feb.]	I,	939
275	Legal Aid (S.) (Assessment of Resources) [26 Feb.]	I,	990
276	National Health Service (Plymouth and District Hospital Management Ctee.) [2 Mar.]	(n) III,	6358
280	Cadnam–Lymington Road (Power to Enclose) (Appointed Day) [12 Mar.]	(n) III,	6359
281	North Devon Water (Stratton) [2 Mar.]	(n) III,	6360
282	Brighton Corporation (Water Charges) [2 Mar.] ...	(n) III,	6359
283	Scarborough (Westerdale Waterworks) [2 Mar.] ...	(n) III,	6360
287	A.S. (Legal Aid) (Children) [18 Mar.]	I,	992
288	Legal Aid (S.) (Children) [2 Mar.]	I,	996
289	Cereals (Guarantee Payments) [2 Mar.]	I,	1002
290	Cereals (Protection of Guarantees) [2 Mar.] ...	I,	1007
291	Public Trustee (Fees) [2 Mar.]	I,	1011
294	Birmingham–Great Yarmouth Trunk Road (King's Lynn Southern By-Pass) [5 Mar.]	(n) III,	6341
295	Wireless Telegraphy (Broadcast Licence Charges & Exemption) [1 Mar.]	I,	1013
296	General Teaching Council (Deduction of Fees for Renewal of Registration) (S.) [3 Mar.]	I,	1015
297	National Insurance (Old persons' and widows' pensions and attendance allowance) Act 1970 (Commencement) [3 Mar.]	I,	1017
298	National Health Service (Cornwall Hospital Management Ctee.) [5 Mar.]	(n) III,	6358
299	National Health Service (North Sheffield University Hospital Management Ctee.) [5 Mar.]	(n) III,	6358
300	National Health Service (Designation of London Teaching Hospitals) [5 Mar.]	I,	1018
302	London–Penzance Trunk Road (Ashburton–Buckfastleigh Diversion) [3 Mar.]	(n) III,	6343
303	Therapeutic Substances (Control of Sale and Supply) [3 Mar.]	I,	1021
304	Therapeutic Substances (Supply of Antibiotics and Chemotherapeutic Substances for Agricultural Purposes) [3 Mar.]	I,	1024
305	North-West Norfolk Water Bd. (Sedgeford Borehole) [8 Mar.]	(n) III,	6360
306	Anti-Dumping Duty [2 Mar.]	I,	1031
307	Essex Water [8 Mar.]	(n) III,	6360
308	Wages Regulation (Dressmaking and Women's Light Clothing) (E. and W.) [9 Mar.]	I,	1033
309	Television Act 1964 (Additional Payments) [4 Mar.]	I,	1044
310	Craven Water Bd. (Vale Mills Mains) [8 Mar.] ...	(n) III,	6360
311	Live Poultry (Restrictions) [4 Mar.]	I,	1046
317	Legal Aid (S.) (Extension of Proceedings) [8 Mar.]	I,	1054
320	South-East Breconshire Water Bd. [8 Mar.] ...	(n) III,	6360
324	Isles of Scilly (Civic Amenities) [9 Mar.]	I,	1055

(n) Instrument classified as local, noted in the Classified List of Local S.I. at the page shown above, but not set out in full.

No.	Subject	Part	Page
325	London–Cambridge–King's Lynn and Royston–Huntingdon–Alconbury Trunk Roads (Queens Road, Mill Road and High Street, Royston Trunking and Detrunking) [11 Mar.]	(n) III,	6342
327	Price Stability of Imported Products (Rates of Levy) (Eggs) [3 Mar.]	I,	1057
328	National Health Service (Swindon and District Hospital Management Ctee.) [10 Mar.]	(n) III,	6358
329	Intermediate Areas [9 Mar.]	(n) III,	6364
331	City and County of Bristol (Bristol Parkway) (Lower Ashley Road to Muller Road) Special Roads Scheme 1970 Confirmation [10 Mar.]	(n) III,	6345
332	Folkestone–Honiton Trunk Road (Shoreham By-Pass Detrunking) [18 Mar.]	(n) III,	6342
333	London Cab [10 Mar.]	I,	1059
339	Electricity (Borrowing Powers) [9 Mar.]	I,	1066
340	National Health Service (Charges) [10 Mar.] ...	I,	1067
341	Education of Handicapped Children (Transfer of of Staff and Property) [11 Mar.]	I,	1075
342	Qualified Teachers and Teachers in Special Schools [12 Mar.]	I,	1082
343	Payments in Aid of Agricultural Schemes (Extension) [11 Mar.]	I,	1085
344	Police (Promotion) (S.) [11 Mar.]	I,	1087
346	Cycle Racing on Highways (Special Authorisation) (E. and W.) [12 Mar.]	I,	1090
348	Children and Young Persons (Designation of Guernsey Order) [12 Mar.]	I,	1095
349	Wrexham and East Denbighshire Water (Financial Provisions) [15 Mar.]	(n) III,	6360
350	Wrexham and East Denbighshire (Water Charges) [15 Mar.]	(n) III,	6360
351	Motor Cars (Driving Instruction) [16 Mar.] ...	I,	1096
352	Goods Vehicles (Plating and Testing) [17 Mar.] ...	I,	1098
353	Goods Vehicles (Operators' Licences) (Temporary Use in G.B.) [16 Mar.]	I,	1141
354	Rules of the Supreme Ct. [16 Mar.]	I,	1144
356	A.S. (Extension of Prescribed Time) [26 Mar.] ...	I,	1147
357	A.S. (Removal Notices) [26 Mar.]	I,	1148
361	Bath–Lincoln Trunk Road (Oxenton Diversion) [16 Mar.]	(n) III,	6341
362	National Health Service (Designation of London Teaching Hospitals) [16 Mar.]	I,	1149
363	Portsmouth Water (Financial Provisions) [15 Mar.]	(n) III,	6360
364	Anti-Dumping (Provisional Charge to Duty) [12 Mar.]	I,	1152
367	Sugar Beet (Research and Education) [16 Mar.] ...	I,	1154
368	Thames Valley Water (Fognam Down Pumping Station) [17 Mar.]	(n) III,	6360
369	North Derbyshire Water Bd. (River Derwent) [17 Mar.]	(n) III,	6360

(n) Instrument classified as local, noted in the Classified List of Local S.I. at the page shown above, but not set out in full.

No.	Subject	Part	Page
370	Industrial Training (Financing of Agricultural Training) [16 Mar.]	I,	1158
371	South West Devon Water Bd. [17 Mar.]	(n) III,	6360
372	London–Edinburgh–Thurso Trunk Road (Lamberton and Greystoneless Diversions) [23 Mar.]	(n) III,	6344
373	Edinburgh – Newcastle-upon-Tyne Trunk Road (Broomhill, Drygrange Bridge and Drygrange Diversions) [22 Mar.]	(n) III,	6344
374	Functions of Traffic Wardens (S.) [18 Mar.] ...	I,	1160
375	A.S. (Valuation Appeal Rules Amdt.) [5 Apr.] ...	I,	1163
376	Vehicle and Driving Licences Act 1969 (Commencement) [18 Mar.]	I,	1165
377	Vehicle and Driving Licences (Transfer of Functions) (Appointed Date) [18 Mar.]	I,	1166
378	Vehicle and Driving Licences (Transfer of Functions) (Supplementary Provisions) [18 Mar.]	I,	1167
379	Beaconsfield and Gerrards Cross By-Pass Special Road (Extension at Denham) [16 Mar.] ...	(n) III,	6345
381	Nuclear Installations [17 Mar.]	I,	1169
382	General Practice Finance Corporation (Increase of Borrowing Powers) [18 Mar.]	I,	1173
383	Merchant Shipping (Tonnage) (Overseas Territories) [17 Mar.]	I,	1175
384	Foreign Compensation (Financial Provisions) [17 Mar.]	I,	1180
391	Double Taxation Relief (Taxes on Income) (Israel) [18 Mar.]	I,	1182
392	District Registries [19 Mar.]	I,	1189
393	Judicial Ctee. (Medical Rules) [17 Mar.]	I,	1195
394	Patents Appeal Tribunal [18 Mar.]	I,	1201
395	Dolgellau–South of Birkenhead Trunk Road (Llanarmon Road Junction near Llanferres) [25 Mar.]	(n) III,	6341
398	Consular Fees [22 Mar.]	I,	1203
399	Edinburgh – Newcastle-upon-Tyne Trunk Road (Drygrange Mains and Packman's Bridge Diversions) [22 Mar.]	(n) III,	6344
400	Newbridge to Lathallan Special Road (Variation) [24 Mar.]	(n) III,	6346
401	Newbridge to Lathallan (Connecting Roads) Special Roads (Variation) [24 Mar.]	(n) III,	6346
402	Edinburgh–Carlisle Trunk Road (Bridgeheugh and Lindean Diversions) [25 Mar.]	(n) III,	6344
403	Teachers' Superannuation [19 Mar.]	I,	1206
404	Great Ouse River Authy. (Littleport and Downham Internal Drainage District) [19 Mar.]	(n) III,	6353

(n) Instrument classified as local, noted in the Classified List of Local S.I. at the page shown above, but not set out in full.

No.	Subject	Part	Page
405	Virus Hepatitis [18 Mar.]	I,	1214
406	Diseases of Fish (Infected Area) [19 Mar.] ...	(n) III,	6354
407	East Suffolk and Norfolk River Authy. (Fisheries) [19 Mar.]	(n) III,	6354
408	Police Act 1969 (Commencement) [13 Mar.] ...	I,	1215
409	Newcastle and Gateshead Water (R.A.F. Acklington) [23 Mar.]	(n) III,	6360
412	Justices of the Peace Act 1968 (Commencement) [22 Mar.]	I,	1216
413	Justices' Allowances [22 Mar.]	I,	1217
414	Probation (Allowances) [22 Mar.]	I,	1225
415	Agricultural and Horticultural Co-operation [22 Mar.]	I,	1232
416	Domestic Water Rate Product (S.) [22 Mar.] ...	I,	1239
418	London–Inverness Trunk Road and The Liverpool–Leeds–Hull Trunk Load (Irlams o' th' Height Underpass) [19 Mar.]	(n) III,	6343
419	London–Thurso Trunk Road (Allerton Park Fly-over Link Roads) [19 Mar.]	(n) III,	6343
420	National Health Service (Charges) (S.) [19 Mar.]...	I,	1240
421	Central Nottinghamshire Water Bd. [24 Mar.] ...	(n) III,	6359
422	Welfare Food (Extension of Definition) [22 Mar.]	I,	1248
423	Health Services and Public Health Act 1968 (Commencement) [24 Mar.]	I,	1250
426	British Overseas Airways Corporation [19 Mar.] ...	I,	1252
427	Norman Cross–Grimsby Trunk Road (Partney Mill Diversion) [23 Mar.]	(n) III,	6343
428	London North Orbital Trunk Road (Hunton Bridge—Maple Cross Section) [22 Mar.]	(n) III,	6343
430	North East Warwickshire Water Bd. (Charges) [25 Mar.]	(n) III,	6360
433	Gretna–Stranraer–Glasgow–Stirling Trunk Road (Cairneyhill Diversion) [26 Mar.]	(n) III,	6344
434	Lancashire River Authy. (Windermoor Internal Drainage District) [24 Mar.]	(n) III,	6353
435	Residential Establishments (Prescribed Deductions from Contributions etc.) (S.) [24 Mar.]	I,	1254
436	National Gallery (Lending Outside the U.K.) [26 Mar.]	(n) III,	6364
437	Remuneration of Teachers (Primary and Secondary Schools) [25 Mar.]	I,	1255
438	Importation of Plants, Plant Produce and Potatoes (Health) (G.B.) [29 Mar.]	I,	1261
439	Eggs Authy. (Rates of Levy) [25 Mar.]	I,	1288
443	London–Portsmouth Trunk Road (Hogs Back Junction) [6 Apr.]	(n) III,	6343
444	Motor Vehicles (Construction and Use) [25 Apr.]...	I,	1291
445	Import Duties (Temp. Exemptions) [22 Mar.] ...	I,	1293

(n) Instrument classified as local, noted in the Classified List of Local S.I. at the page shown above, but not set out in full.

No.	Subject	Part	Page
446	Act of Adj. (Summary Proceedings) (Children) [7 Apr.]	I,	1294
447	Police (Common Police Services) (S.) [25 Mar.] ...	I,	1298
448	Industrial Assurance (Fees [25 Mar.]	I,	1300
449	Building Societies (Fees) [25 Mar.]	I,	1303
450	Road Vehicles (Registration and Licensing) [26 Mar.]	I,	1305
451	Motor Vehicles (Driving Licences) [26 Mar.] ...	I,	1338
452	South Wilts Water Undertaking (Valuation) [25 Mar.]	(n) III,	6358
453	Mayors and City of London Ct. Funds [25 Mar.]...	I,	1353
454	County Cts. (Race Relations Jurisdiction) [25 Mar.]	I,	1355
457	Welfare Food [25 Mar.]	I,	1358
459	Therapeutic Substances (Control of Sale and Supply [25 Mar.]	I,	1368
460	Industrial Training Levy (Knitting, Lace and Net) [29 Mar.]	I,	1371
461	Friendly Societies [29 Mar.]	I,	1376
462	Superannuation and other Trust Funds (Fees) [29 Mar.]	I,	1380
463	Industrial and Provident Societies (Amdt. of Fees) [29 Mar.]	I,	1382
464	Petty Sessional Divisions (Herefordshire) [25 Mar.]	(n) III,	6362
465	Chester–Bangor Trunk Road (East of Abergele to County Boundary) [31 May.]	(n) III,	6341
467	Assistance for House Purchase and Improvement (Qualifying Lenders) [30 Mar.]	I,	1385
468	Air Navigation (Fees) [25 Mar.]	I,	1387
469	Rate Support Grant (S.) [30 Mar.]	I,	1392
470	Rate Support Grant (Increase) (S.) [30 Mar.] ...	I,	1400
471	Cinematograph (Safety) (S.) [29 Mar.]	I,	1402
472	National Health Service (General Medical and Pharmaceutical Services) (S.) [30 Mar.] ...	I,	1405
473	Price Stability of Imported Products (Minimum Import Price Levels) (Eggs) [26 Mar.]	I,	1409
474	Eggs (Guaranteed Prices) [26 Mar.]	I,	1412
475	Eggs (Protection of Guarantees) [26 Mar.]... ...	I,	1416
476	Foundries (Protective Footwear and Gaiters) [30 Mar.]	I,	1421
477	Exchange Control (Authorised Dealers and Depositaries) [1 Apr.]	I,	1425
478	Atomic Energy Authy. Act 1971 (Appointed Day) [26 Mar.]	I,	1431
479	Fixed Penalty (Procedure) [29 Mar.]	I,	1432
480	Probation [29 Mar.]	I,	1431
486	Children and Young Persons (Definition of Independent Persons) [30 Mar.]	I,	1436
487	Industrial Training (Financing of Agricultural Training) (N.I.) [30 Mar.]	I,	1438
490	Justices' Allowances (S.) [30 Mar.]	I,	1440
491	Judgement Debts (Rate of Interest) [29 Mar.] ...	I,	1446

(**n**) Instrument classified as local, noted in the Classified List of Local S.I. at the page shown above, but not set out in full.

No.	Subject	Part	Page
492	Children's Hearings (S.) [31 Mar.]	I,	1447
493	Social Work (S.) Act 1968 (Transitional Cases) [31 Mar.]	I,	1482
494	Water Rates and Charges (Decimal Currency) (W.) [30 Mar.]	(n) III,	6364
495	Petty Sessional Divisions (S.W. London) [1 Apr.] ...	(n) III,	6362
496	Industrial Training Levy (Air Transport and Travel) [31 Mar.]	I,	1488
497	Craven Water Bd. (Ponden and Lower Laithe Reservoirs) [1 Apr.]	(n) III,	6360
498	Mid-Sussex Water [1 Apr.]	(n) III,	6360
499	Import Duties (Temp. Exemptions) [30 Mar.] ...	I,	1490
500	Calf Subsidies (U.K.) [31 Mar]	I,	1491
501	General Drainage Charge (Ascertainment) [31 Mar.]	(n) III,	6353
502	Army Terms of Service [30 Mar.]	I,	1496
503	Armed Forces (Discharge by Purchase) [30 Mar.]...	I,	1498
506	Ipswich–Weedon Trunk Road (Bury St. Edmunds By-Pass and Slip Roads) [31 Mar.]	(n) III,	6342
507	Folkestone–Honiton Trunk Road (Arundel Relief Road) [5 Apr.]	(n) III,	6342
508	Exeter–Leeds Trunk Road (Silver Street and other roads, Taunton) [30 Mar.]	(n) III,	6342
509	Folkestone–Honiton Trunk Road (Harty Bridge Diversion) [31 Mar.]	(n) III,	6342
510	Royal Air Force Terms of Service [1 Apr.] ...	I,	1500
511	Apple and Pear Development Council [31 Mar.] ...	I,	1507
512	Sugar (Rates of Surcharge and Surcharge Repayments) [26 Mar.]	I,	1509
513	Composite Sugar Products (Surcharge and Surcharge Repayments—Average Rates) [26 Mar.]...	I,	1512
514	Sunderland and South Shields Water [1 Apr.] ...	(n) III,	6360
515	East of Scotland Water Bd. (Allt Coire Ardrain, Crianlarich) Water [5 Apr.]	(n) III,	6360
516	Exchange Control (Gold Coins Exemption) [31 Mar.]	I,	1516
517	Royal Navy Terms of Service [31 Mar.]	I,	1518
518	Anti-Dumping (Provisional Charge to Duty) [31 Mar.]	I,	1520
519	Anti-Dumping (Provisional Charge to Duty) [31 Mar.]	I,	1521
523	London–Holyhead Trunk Road (Dinas Hill, near Betws-y-Coed) [14 Apr.]	(n) III,	6342
524	Cheshire County Council (Ellesmere Port) Motorway Scheme 1967 Confirmation [7 Apr.] ...	(n) III,	6345
525	Reporter's Duties and Transmission of Information, etc. (S.) [2 Apr.]	I,	1523
526	North-East of Scotland Water Bd. (Lower Deveron) Water [5 Apr.]	(n) III,	6361
527	Regional Water Bds. (Requisitions) (Decimal Currency) [2 Apr.]	I,	1529

(**n**) Instrument classified as local, noted in the Classified List of Local S.I. at the page shown above, but not set out in full.

No.	Subject	Part	Page
529	Maentwrog–East of Conway Trunk Road (Teiliau Isaf, Ffestiniog) [7 Apr.]	(n) III,	6343
530	Oxfordshire and District Water Bd. (Charges) [5 Apr.]	(n) III,	6360
531	Diseases of Animals (Extension of Definitions) [2 Apr.]	I,	1530
532	Milk (Eradication of Brucellosis) (Variation) [1 Apr.]	I,	1532
533	Brucellosis (Eradication Areas) (E. and W.) [2 Apr.]	(n) III,	6363
534	Removal of Defence Works (Grants) [5 Apr.] ...	I,	1535
535	London–Brighton Trunk Road (Balcombe Road Gyratory System) [15 Apr.]	(n) III,	6342
536	North of Oxford–South of Coventry Trunk Road (Shipton-on-Cherwell Diversion) [5 Apr.] ...	(n) III,	6343
537	Watford (Water Charges) [7 Apr.]	(n) III,	6360
538	Local Enactments (Water Undertakings, etc.) (Decimal Currency) [5 Apr.]	(n) III,	6364
539	North West Leicestershire Water Bd. (Charges) [7 Apr.]	(n) III,	6360
543	British Overseas Airways Corporation (Govt. Investment) [6 Apr.]	I,	1537
544	Representation of the People Act 1969 (Commencement) [7 Apr.]	I,	1539
545	Urban District Council Election [7 Apr.]	I,	1540
546	Rural District Council Election [7 Apr.]	I,	1541
547	Rural Borough Council Election [7 Apr.]	I,	1542
548	Parish Council Election [7 Apr.]	I,	1543
549	Savings Certificates [31 Mar.]	I,	1544
550	Premium Savings Bonds [31 Mar.]	I,	1545
551	Airport Traffic (Edinburgh) [14 Apr.]	(n) III,	6364
553	Redundant Mineworkers [6 Apr.]	I,	1546
554	Legal Aid (S.) (Children) [6 Apr.]	I,	1547
555	Health Services and Public Health Act 1968 (Commencement) (S.) [7 Apr.]	I,	1549
556	Social Work (S.) Act 1968 (Commencement) [7 Apr.]	I,	1550
557	Wild Birds (Gibraltar Point Sanctuary) [7 Apr.] ...	(n) III,	6363
558	Grant-Aided Secondary Schools (S.) Grant [7 Apr.]	I,	1551
560	Mines and Quarries (Valuation) [13 Apr.] ...	I,	1555
561	Docks and Harbours (Valuation) [13 Apr.] ...	I,	1560
562	Non-Residents' Transitional Relief from Income Tax on Dividends (Ext. of Period) [5 Apr.] ...	I,	1565
563	Transitional Relief for Interest and Royalties paid to Non-Residents (Ext. of Period) [5 Apr.] ...	I,	1567
564	Northallerton and the Dales Water [13 Apr.] ...	(n) III,	6360
565	Lee Valley Water (Charges) [13 Apr.]	(n) III,	6360
566	Colchester and District Water Bd. (Water Charges) [13 Apr.]	(n) III,	6359
567	Rickmansworth and Uxbridge Valley Water (Charges) [13 Apr.]	(n) III,	6360
568	Southampton Corporation Water [13 Apr.] ...	(n) III,	6360
569	Nuclear Installations (Application of Security Provisions) [7 Apr.]	I,	1569

(n) Instrument classified as local, noted in the Classified List of Local S.I. at the page shown above, but not set out in full.

No.	Subject	Part	Page
570	Regulated Tenancies (Conversion from Control) (E. and W.) [8 Apr.]	I,	1570
571	Brucellosis (Eradication Areas) (S.) [13 Apr.] ...	(n) III,	6363
574	Protection of Depositors (Registration of Documents) (Fees) [7 Apr.]	I,	1572
575	Northamptonshire and Northampton (Boundaries) [14 Apr.]	(n) III,	6356
583	Police Pensions [13 Apr.]	I,	1573
584	Special Constables (Pensions) [5 Apr.]	I,	1576
585	Special Constables (Pensions) (S.) [8 Apr.] ...	I,	1578
588	Children and Young Persons Act 1969 (Commencement) [13 Apr.]	I,	1580
589	Children and Young Persons (Termination of Transitional Provisions) [13 Apr.]	I,	1582
591	Assessor of Public Undertakings Valuation Roll (Procedure Dates) (S.) [14 Apr.]	I,	1584
592	Linlithgow Peel and Loch [15 Apr.]	(n) III,	6359
593	Holyrood Park [15 Apr.]	(n) III,	6359
594	Continental Shelf (Designation of Additional Areas) [13 Apr.]	I,	1586
595	Kuwaiti Tonnage [13 Apr.]	I,	1589
596	Trial of the Pyx [13 Apr.]	I,	1591
600	London Borough of Camden (Wards) [15 Apr.] ...	(n) III,	6356
601	Motor Vehicles (Speed Limits on Motorways) [14 Apr.]	I,	1592
602	Motor Vehicles (Variation of Speed Limits) [14 Apr.]	I,	1594
603	Price Stability of Imported Products (Rates of Levy) (Eggs) [8 Apr.]	I,	1596
607	M.25 South Orbital Motorway (Reigate–Godstone Section) Connecting Roads [15 Apr.]	(n) III,	6345
608	Registration of Births and Deaths (High Commissioners) [19 Apr.]	I,	1598
609	Industrial Training Levy (Carpet) [20 Apr.] ...	I,	1600
610	Industrial Training Levy (Clothing and Allied Products) [20 Apr.]	I,	1605
613	Stirling By-Pass Extension Special Roads [20 Apr.]	(n) III,	6346
614	Ingliston to Pirnhall Special Road [20 Apr.] ...	(n) III,	6346
615	Glasgow–Stirling Trunk Road (Pirnhall to Bannockburn Diversion) and the Edinburgh–Stirling–Perth Trunk Road (Detrunking) [20 Apr.] ...	(n) III,	6344
616	Stirling Bypass (Connecting Roads) Special Roads [20 Apr.]	(n) III,	6346
617	British Sugar Corporation Limited (Financial Year) (Variation) [19 Apr.]	I,	1610
618	Corrosive Substances (Conveyance by Road) [19 Apr.]	I,	1611
619	Baking Wages Council (E. and W.) (Abolition) [20 Apr.]	I,	1620
620	Post Office (Borrowing Powers) [19 Apr.]	I,	1622

(n) Instrument classified as local, noted in the Classified List of Local S.I. at the page shown above, but not set out in full.

No.	Subject	Part	Page
621	National Insurance (Attendance Allowance) [20 Apr.]	I,	1623
622	Family Income Supplements (Appeal Tribunal) [20 Apr.]	I,	1636
623	Members' Contributory Pension Fund (Increase of Benefits) [21 Apr.]	I,	1640
624	Regulated Tenancies (Conversion from Control) (S.) [19 Apr.]	I,	1642
625	Clean Air (Emission of Grit and Dust from Furnaces) (S.) [20 Apr.]	I,	1644
626	Clean Air (Measurement of Grit and Dust from Furnaces) (S.) [20 Apr.]	I,	1650
627	Salmon and Migratory Trout (Enforcement) [19 Apr.]	I,	1653
629	British Waterways Bd. (Alteration of Pension Schemes) [21 Apr.]	I,	1655
630	London–Norwich Trunk Road (Woodford New Road/High Road, Woodford Green Improvement) [26 Apr.]	**(n)** III,	6343
631	Price Stability of Imported Products (Levy Arrangements) (Cereals) [22 Apr.]	I,	1660
632	Price Stability of Imported Products (Minimum Import Price Levels) (Cereals) [22 Apr.]... ...	I,	1670
633	Northern Ireland Loans (Increase of Limit) [21 Apr.]	I,	1681
636	Performing Right Tribunal [22 Apr.]	I,	1682
641	M.5 Motorway (Huntworth–Willand) [23 Apr.] ...	**(n)** III,	6345
643	Merchant Shipping (Fees) [29 Apr.]	I,	1686
644	Merchant Shipping (Load Lines) (Fees) [29 Apr.]	I,	1706
645	East of Scotland Water Bd. (Financial Provisions) [26 Apr.]	**(n)** III,	6360
646	Ayrshire and Bute Water Bd. (Financial Provisions) [26 Apr.]	**(n)** III,	6360
647	Mid-Scotland Water Bd. (Financial Provisions) [26 Apr.]	**(n)** III,	6361
648	Industrial Training (Food, Drink and Tobacco Bd.) [30 Apr.]	I,	1709
649	Wages Regulation (Milk Distributive) (S.) [30 Apr.]	I,	1720
654	Craven Water Bd. (Extension of Operation of Byelaws) [28 Apr.]	**(n)** III,	6360
655	Industrial Training Levy (Food, Drink and Tobacco) [30 Apr.]	I,	1731
656	County Cts. (Bankruptcy and Winding-up Jurisdiction) [28 Apr.]	I,	1737
657	East Devon Water [28 Apr.]...	**(n)** III,	6360
659	Police [28 Apr.]	I,	1744
661	Slaughter of Poultry (Humane Conditions) [28 Apr.]	I,	1756
662	A.23 London—Brighton Trunk Road (Hooley Interchange) [28 Apr.]	**(n)** III,	6341
663	M.23 Motorway (Woodmansterne—Merstham Section) Connecting Roads [28 Apr.]	**(n)** III,	6345

(n) Instrument classified as local, noted in the Classified List of Local S.I. at the page shown above, but not set out in full.

No.	Subject	Part	Page
665	Industrial Reorganisation Corporation Dissolution (Appointed Day) [29 Apr.]	I,	1759
666	Therapeutic Substances (Manufacture and Importation) General [29 Apr.]	I,	1761
667	Import Duties (Temp. Exemptions) [29 Apr.] ...	I,	1763
668	Industrial Training Levy (Electricity Supply) [30 Apr.]	I,	1768
669	Remuneration of Teachers (S.) [30 Apr.]	I,	1772
670	Land Commission (Dissolution) (Appointed Day) [28 Apr.]	I,	1781
673	Acquisition of Land (Rate of Interest after Entry) [29 Apr.]	I,	1782
674	Opencast Coal (Rate of Interest on Compensation) [29 Apr.]	I,	1783
675	Acquisition of Land (Rate of Interest after Entry) (S.) [29 Apr.]	I,	1784
676	National Health Service (East Liverpool University Hospital Designation) [3 May]	I,	1785
679	Teachers' Superannuation (Family Benefits) [30 Apr.]	I,	1787
680	Supplementary Benefit (Appeal Tribunal) [30 Apr.]	I,	1798
681	Dorset Water [30 Apr.]	**(n)** III,	6360
683	Police (S.) [30 Apr.]	I,	1804
684	Price Stability of Imported Products (Rates of Levy) (Eggs) [28 Apr.]	I,	1814
685	Argyll Water Bd. (Financial Provisions) [6 May] ...	**(n)** III,	6360
686	North of Scotland Water Bd. (Financial Provisions) [6 May]	**(n)** III,	6361
687	Herring (North Sea Fishing) Licensing [30 Apr.] ...	I,	1816
688	Herring (North Sea) Restrictions on Landing [30 Apr.]	I,	1819
689	Industrial Training Levy (Footwear, Leather and Fur Skin) [6 May]	I,	1822
690	Industrial Training Levy (Paper and Paper Products) [6 May]	I,	1827
691	Stansted Airport Licensing (Liquor) [30 Apr.] ...	**(n)** III,	6355
694	Road Vehicles Lighting [12 May]	I,	1833
697	National Health Service (East Liverpool University Hospital Management Ctee.) [10 May]	**(n)** III,	6358
698	Chronically Sick and Disabled Persons Act 1970 (Commencement) [6 May]	I,	1904
701	Local Education Authorities Recoupment (Further Education) [6 May]	I,	1905
702	Family Income Supplements (Computation) [5 May]	I,	1907
703	Glamorgan (Advance Payments for Street Works) [6 May]	**(n)** III,	6357
706	London—Great Yarmouth Trunk Road (Marine Parade and other roads, Lowestoft Trunking) [13 May]	**(n)** III,	6342
707	National Insurance (Claims and Payments) [1 May]	I,	1908

(n) Instrument classified as local, noted in the Classified List of Local S.I. at the page shown above, but not set out in full.

No.	Subject	Part	Page
708	Edinburgh Northern Hospitals Endowments [7 May]	(n) III,	6359
709	Royal Infirmary of Edinburgh and Associated Hospitals Endowments [7 May]	(n) III,	6359
710	Edinburgh Royal Victoria and Associated Hospitals Endowments [7 May]	(n) III,	6359
711	Potato Marketing [7 May]	I,	1926
712	North Wilts. Water Bd. (Bishops Cannings Borehole) [11 May]	(n) III,	6360
713	North Wilts. Water Bd. (Holt Borehole) [11 May]	(n) III,	6360
714	Dominica Constitution [6 May]	II,	1931
715	Western Pacific (Cts.) [6 May]	II,	1933
716	Transfer of Functions (Supplementary) [6 May] ...	II,	1935
717	Double Taxation Relief (Taxes on Income) (Faroe Is.) [7 May]	II,	1937
718	Double Taxation Relief (Taxes on Income) (France) [7 May]	II,	1940
719	Ministry of Aviation Supply (Dissolution) [4 May]	II,	1943
720	Hovercraft (Civil Liability) [11 May]	II,	1947
721	Continental Shelf (Jurisdiction) [6 May]	II,	1968
723	North Lindsey Water (Winterton Carrs and Hibaldstow) [11 May]	(n) III,	6360
724	Merchant Shipping (Pilot Ladders) [10 May] ...	II,	1970
725	Poisons List [12 May]	II,	1972
726	Poisons [12 May]	II,	1982
728	Trunk Road (Hanger Lane and North Circular Road, Ealing) (Prescribed Routes) [7 May] ...	(n) III,	6349
729	Farm and Garden Chemicals [10 May]	II,	2036
730	Greater London Council (Sewerage Area) [12 May]	II,	2046
731	Purchase Tax [7 May]	II,	2048
736	Heavy Goods Vehicles (Drivers' Licences) [11 May]	II,	2049
737	Clackmannanshire Educational Trust [17 May] ...	(n) III,	6361
738	Southampton Corporation Water [11 May] ...	(n) III,	6353
739	Sugar (Rates of Surcharge and Surcharge Repayments) [6 May]	II,	2054
740	Composite Sugar Products (Surcharge and Surcharge Repayments—Average Rates) [6 May] ...	II,	2057
741	Trustee Savings Banks (Pensions) (Civil Service Transfers) [17 May]	II,	2061
743	Sheriff of Chancery (Transfer of Jurisdiction) [13 May]	II,	2065
744	Building (S.) Act 1970 (Commencement) [17 May]...	II,	2066
745	Building Standards (Relaxation by Buildings Authorities) (S.) [17 May]	II,	2067
746	Building (Procedure) (S.) [17 May]	II,	2069
747	Building (Forms) (S.) [17 May]	II,	2097
748	Building Standards (S.) [18 May]	II,	2153
749	Veterinary Surgeons (Examination of Commonwealth and Foreign Candidates) [14 May] ...	II,	2163
750	Wages Regulation (Rope, Twine and Net) [19 May]	II,	2165

(n) Instrument classified as local, noted in the Classified List of Local S.I. at the page shown above, but not set out in full.

No.	Subject	Part	Page
751	Industrial Training Levy (Chemical and Allied Products) [17 May]	II,	2182
752	Superannuation (Transfers between the Civil Service and Public Bds.) [18 May]	II,	2187
753	Local Govt. (Allowances for Attendance at Road Safety Conferences) [13 May]	II,	2189
754	Hearing Aid Council Disciplinary Ctee. (Procedure) [14 May]	II,	2192
755	Hearing Aid Council (Disciplinary Proceedings) Legal Assessor [14 May]	II,	2202
756	Town and Country Planning (Minerals) [17 May]...	II,	2204
759	Ross and Cromarty Water Bd. (Financial Provisions) [13 May]	(n) III,	6361
760	South Lincolnshire Water Bd. (Wilsthorpe and Greatford) [20 May]	(n) III,	6360
765	Lower Avon Navigation Trust (Conferment of Powers to make Byelaws) [14 May]	(n) III,	6353
766	Inverness-shire Water Bd. (Financial Provisions) [13 May]	(n) III,	6361
767	Local Govt. (Payment of Accounts) (S.) [14 May]	II,	2208
768	West Glamorgan Water Bd. (Cray Reservoir) [18 May]	(n) III,	6353
769	Pensions Appeal Tribunals (E. and W.) [19 May]...	II,	2210
770	Resolution of the House of Commons [18 May] ...	II,	4028
773	Price Stability of Imported Products (Rates of Levy) (Eggs) [12 May]	II,	2235
774	Abington—Lanark—Airdrie—Cumberland Trunk Road (Castlehill Diversion) [27 May]	(n) III,	6344
775	Gaming Act 1968 (Commencement) [18 May] ...	II,	2237
778	Town and Country Planning (Minerals) (S.) [20 May]	II,	2238
779	Valuation (Mines and Quarries) (S.) [19 May] ...	II,	2244
780	Rating of Industry (S.) [19 May]	II,	2246
781	County Cts. [19 May]	II,	2247
782	Limited Partnerships (Unrestricted Size) [19 May]	II,	2253
783	British Overseas Airways Corporation [18 May] ...	II,	2255
792	Motor Vehicles (International Motor Insurance Card) [20 May]	II,	2256
793	Capital Gains Tax (Exempt Gilt-edged Securities) [21 May]	II,	2271
796	London—Penzance Trunk Road (Second Crossing of the Exeter Canal) [21 May]	(n) III,	6343
797	Fishing Vessels (Acquisition and Improvement) (Grants) [19 May]	II,	2272
798	Salford Hundred Ct. of Record [27 May]	II,	2275
799	Fort William—Mallaig Trunk Road (Drochaid Sgainnir and Drochaid Druim na Saille Diversions) [25 May]	(n) III,	6344
800	Invergarry—Kyle of Lochlash Trunk Road (West of Invergarry and other Diversions) [25 May] ...	(n) III,	6344
801	Fatstock (Guarantee Payments) [19 May]	II,	2294

(n) Instrument classified as local, noted in the Classified List of Local S.I. at the page shown above, but not set out in full.

No.	Subject	Part	Page
802	Price Stability of Imported Products (Specified Commodities) (Beef and Veal) [19 May] ...	II,	2299
803	Price Stability of Imported Products (Specified Commodities) (Milk and Milk Products) [19 May]	II,	2301
804	Police (Cadets) [21 May]	II,	2303
805	Charities (Richmond Parish Charity Lands) [24 May]	(n) III,	6363
806	Cowes Harbour [21 May]	(n) III,	6354
807	National Insurance (Unemployment and Sickness Benefit) [27 May]	II,	2305
808	Sheriff's Fees [24 May]	II,	2307
809	Magistrates' Cts. (Attachment of Earnings) [21 May]	II,	2310
810	Police Cadets (S.) [24 May]	II,	2323
813	Methylated Spirits (Sale by Retail) (Variation of Fees) (S.) [24 May]...	II,	2325
814	Petroleum (Production) [24 May]	II,	2327
817	Price Stability of Imported Products (Rates of Levy) (Eggs) [19 May]	II,	2333
818	Drivers' Hours (Passenger and Goods Vehicles) [25 May]	II,	2335
819	Financial Statements (Parishes) [27 May]	II,	2341
822	Indian Military Service Family Pension Fund [27 May]	II,	2346
823	Indian Civil Service Family Pension Fund [27 May]	II,	2353
824	Indian Military Widows' and Orphans' Fund [27 May]	II,	2358
825	Superior Services (India) Family Pension Fund [27 May]	II,	2365
826	East of Birmingham–Birkenhead Trunk Road (Rock Ferry By-pass) [1 June]	(n) III,	6342
827	Cubic Measures (Sand, Ballast and Agricultural Materials) [25 May]	II,	2368
828 } 829 }	Rivers Pollution (Rivers Rheidol, Ystwyth and Tributaries) [27 May]	(n) III,	6354
830	Wages Regulation (Retail Bespoke Tailoring) (E. and W.) [1 June]	II,	2370
831	Tribunals and Inquiries (Firemens' Pension Scheme Appeal Tribunals and Air Operators' Certificates) [27 May]	II,	2381
832	Livestock Rearing Land Improvement Schemes (Terminal Date) [26 May]	II,	2383
834	Administration of Justice Act 1970 (Commencement) [27 May]	II,	2385
835	Rules of Supreme Ct. [27 May]	II,	2388
836	County Ct. [27 May]	II,	2393
837	Industrial Training Levy (Construction Bd.) [27 May]	II,	2412
842	Town and Country Planning Act 1968 (Commencement) [2 June]	II,	2421
843	Police (Discipline) (S.) [26 May]	II,	2423

(n) Instrument classified as local, noted in the Classified List of Local S.I. at the page shown above, but not set out in full.

No.	Subject	Part	Page
844	Agricultural Wages Ctees. (Wages Structure) [27 May]	II,	2426
845	Wages Regulation (Retail Drapery, Outfitting and Footwear) [4 June]	II,	2431
846	East Anglian Water (Financial Provisions) [2 June]	(n) III,	6360
847	Drivers' Hours (Goods Vehicles) (Keeping of Records) [27 May]	II,	2454
848	Aircraft (Customs) [26 May]	II,	2455
851	Import Duties (General) [25 May]	II,	2458
852	Pembrokeshire Water Undertaking (Valuation) [2 June]	(n) III,	6358
853	Livestock Rearing Land Improvement Schemes (Terminal Date) (S.) [27 May]	II,	2460
854	Price Stability of Imported Products (Levy Arrangements) (Beef and Veal) [26 May]	II,	2462
855	Price Stability of Imported Products (Minimum Import Price Levels) (Beef and Veal) [26 May]...	II,	2466
856	Price Stability of Imported Products (Levy Arrangements) (Milk and Milk Products) [26 May] ...	II,	2470
857	Price Stability of Imported Products (Minimum Import Price Levels) (Milk and Milk Products) [26 May]	II,	2474
858	Import Duties (General) [27 May]	II,	2478
859	Wages Regulation (Brush and Broom) [7 June] ...	II,	2479
860	Irish Land (Finance) [27 May]	II,	2533
861	Abington - Lanark - Airdrie - Cumbernauld Trunk Road (Duneaton Foot Bridge Diversion) [14 June]	(n) III,	6344
867	North of Abington–Edinburgh Trunk Road (Clyde's Bridge Diversion) [14 June]	(n) III,	6344
868	Wages Regulation (Pin, Hook and Eye, and Snap Fastener) [4 June]	II,	2535
869	Motor Vehicles (International Circulation) [1 June]	II,	2541
870	British Solomon Islands Protectorate (Entitled Officers) [2 June]	II,	2545
871	New Hebrides (British Service) (Entitled Officers) [2 June]	II,	2562
872	Merchant Shipping (Registration of South Australian Government Ships) [2 June]...	II,	2579
873	Montserrat [2 June]...	II,	2583
874	Double Taxation Relief (Taxes on Income) (Germany) [4 June]	II,	2585
875	N.I. (Remittal and Removal of Proceedings) [3 June]	II,	2593
880	Wool Textile Industry (Export Promotion Levy) [4 June]	II,	2597
881	Wool Textile Industry (Scientific Research Levy) [4 June]	II,	2599
882	Preservatives in Food [4 June]	II,	2601
883	Foresterhill and Associated Hospitals Endowments [8 June]	(n) III,	6359
884	Awards (First Degree, etc. Courses) [7 June] ...	II,	2604

(**n**) Instrument classified as local, noted in the Classified List of Local S.I. at the page shown above, but not set out in full.

No.	Subject	Part	Page
885	Wages Regulation (Keg and Drum) [7 June] ...	II,	2606
886	London–Cambridge–King's Lynn Trunk Road (Littleport Bridge Diversion) [14 June]	(**n**) III,	6342
887	Clyde Pilotage [14 June]	(**n**) III,	6354
888	Threapeutic Substances (Manufacture of Antibiotics) [8 June]	II,	2613
889	Lands Tribunal for Scotland (Fees) [8 June] ...	II,	2616
900	Fylde Water Bd. [8 June]	(**n**) III,	6360
901	Cumberland River Authority (Abolition of the River Marron Internal Drainage District) [8 June]	(**n**) III,	6353
902	Home-Grown Cereals Authority (Rates of Levy) [8 June]	II,	2617
903	Teachers (Education, Training and Registration) (S.) [8 June]	II,	2620
904	A.S. (Alteration of Fees of Shorthand Writers in the Sheriff Ct.) [8 June]	II,	2623
905	National Insurance Act 1966 (Commencement) [8 June]	II,	2624
906	National Insurance (Married Women) [8 June] ...	II,	2626
907	Superannuation (Teaching and N.I. Local Govt.) Interchange [11 June]	II,	2629
911	Customs Duty (Personal Reliefs) [9 June]	II,	2641
912	Price Stability of Imported Products (Rates of Levy) (Eggs) [3 June]	II,	2642
913	Fertilisers (U.K.) [9 June]	II,	2644
914	Coal Industry (Pension Schemes) [10 June] ...	II,	2650
915	Gas (Pension Schemes) [10 June]	II,	2652
916	Iron and Steel (Pension Schemes) [10 June] ...	II,	2654
921	London–Penzance Trunk Road (Drumbridge–Caton Cross Diversion) [8 June]	(**n**) III,	6343
922	Wages Regulation (Coffin Furniture and Cerement-making) [11 June]	II,	2656
923	Wages Regulation (Coffin Furniture and Cerement-making) (Holidays) [11 June]	II,	2664
925	A.814 Glasgow–Helensburgh–Dumbarton Road Diversion (Bridge over River Leven) [10 June] ...	(**n**) III,	6346
926	Act of Adj. (Criminal Legal Aid Fees) [24 June]	II,	2671
927	Air Corporations (General Staff, Pilots and Officers Pensions) [10 June]...	II,	2674
928	Mid-Sussex Water [11 June]	(**n**) III,	6360
932	Oil in Navigable Waters Act 1971 (Commencement) [11 June]	II,	2676
934	Wages Regulation (Retail Bespoke Tailoring) (S.) [14 June]	II,	2678
935	Welland and Nene River Authority (Alteration of Boundaries of the Hundred of Wisbech and the Wingland Internal Drainage Districts [14 June]	(**n**) III,	6353
936	Electricity (Pension Schemes) [10 June]	II,	2686
937	Motor Vehicles (International Circulation) [11 June]	II,	2688
939	Winchester Corporation [14 June]	(**n**) III,	6353

(**n**) Instrument classified as local, noted in the Classified List of Local S.I. at the page shown above, but not set out in full.

No.	Subject	Part	Page
940	Hill Cattle (Breeding Herds) (E. and W.) [11 June]	II,	2695
941	Hill Cattle Subsidy (Breeding Herds) (E. and W.) Payment [11 June]	II,	2697
942	Beef Cow (N.I.) [14 June]	II,	2699
943	Beef Cow Subsidy Payment (N.I.) [14 June] ...	II,	2701
944	Hill Cattle Subsidy (Breeding Herds) (N.I.) Payment [14 June]	II,	2703
945	Hill Sheep Subsidy Payment (E. and W.) [14 June]	II,	2705
946	Hill Sheep Subsidy Payment (N.I.) [14 June] ...	II,	2707
947	Price Stability of Imported Products (Levy Arrangements) (Eggs) [14 June]	II,	2709
948	Lancashire River Authority (River Kent Estuary Internal Drainage District [15 June]	(n) III,	6353
951	Glasgow Inner Ring Road (West and North Flanks) (Speed Limit) [14 June]	(n) III,	6352
952	Price Stability of Imported Products (Rates of Levy) (Eggs) [9 June]	II,	2711
953	Matrimonial Causes [23 June]	II,	2713
957	Sugar (Rates of Surcharge and Surcharge Repayments) [9 June]	II,	2792
958	Composite Sugar Products (Surcharge and Surcharge Repayments—Average Rates) [9 June] ...	II,	2795
960	Alkali, &c. Works [16 June]	II,	2799
962	Co-operative Bank Act 1971 (Appointed Day) [16 June]	(n) III,	6363
963	Industrial Training Levy (Petroleum) [18 June] ...	II,	2802
964	Motor Vehicles (Passenger Insurance) Act 1971 (Commencement) [17 June]	II,	2807
968	Mid Southern Water [21 June]	(n) III,	6360
969	Isles of Scilly (Explosives) [21 June]	II,	2808
972	Medicines (Standard Provisions for Licences and Certificates) [24 June]	II,	2809
973	Medicines (Applications for Product Licences and Clinical Trial and Animal Test Certificates) [24 June]	II,	2816
974	Medicines (Applications for Manufacturer's and Wholesale Dealer's Licences) [24 June]	II,	2836
975	Erskine Bridge Tolls [18 June]	(n) III,	6341
979	Motor Vehicles (Construction and Use) [24 June]	II,	2841
980	Motor Vehicles (Authorisation of Special Types) [22 June]	II,	2848
981	Savings Banks (Fees) [23 June]	II,	2856
982	Tendring Hundred (Ext. of Operation of Byelaws) [22 June]	(n) III,	6360
983	Leicester Corporation [21 June]	(n) III,	6358
984	National Health Service (General Dental Services) [22 June]	II,	2858
985	Price Stability of Imported Products (Rates of Levy) (Eggs) [16 June]	II,	2867
986	Colne Valley Water (Financial Provisions) [23 June]	(n) III,	6359
987	Matrimonial Causes (Costs) [23 June]	II,	2869

(n) Instrument classified as local, noted in the Classified List of Local S.I. at the page shown above, but not set out in full.

No.	Subject	Part	Page
988	Preservatives in Food (S.) [22 June]	II,	2883
990	Wages Regulation (Retail Food) (E. and W.) [30 June]	II,	2886
991	Wages Regulation (Licensed Non-residential Establishment) [30 June]	II,	2909
992	Wages Regulation (Licensed Non-residential Establishment) (Managers and Club Stewards) [30 June]	II,	2924
993	National Insurance and Industrial Injuries (Collection of Contributions) [25 June]	II,	2940
997	Forestry Commission Byelaws [28 June]	II,	2942
998	Laundry Wages Council (Gt. Britain) [24 June] ...	II,	2945
1003	Merchant Shipping (Fees) [22 June]	II,	2947
1004	Smoke Control Areas (Authorised Fuels) [25 June]	II,	2949
1005	Manchester City Council (Mancunian Way) Special Road [24 June]	(n) III,	6345
1006	Motorways Traffic (A.57(M)) (Mancurian Way) (Speed Limit) [28 June]	(n) III,	6344
1007	Newport–Shrewsbury Trunk Road (Leominster Inner Relief Road) [25 June]	(n) III,	6343
1009	Leasehold Reform Act 1967 (Wimbledon and Putney Commons Conservators) [25 June]	(n) III,	6364
1011	Lincolnshire River Authority (Witham Fourth District Internal Drainage District [25 June] ...	(n) III,	6353
1012	Import Duties (Temp. Exemptions) [25 June] ...	II,	2951
1013	Import Duties (Temp. Reductions) [25 June] ...	II,	2957
1015	Seaforth–North of Aintree Trunk Road (Litherland Lift Bridge Diversion) [30 June]	(n) III,	6343
1016	Bootle–North of Aintree Trunk Road (Litherland Lift Bridge Diversion) [30 June]	(n) III,	6341
1017	Bankruptcy Fees [25 June]	II,	2958
1018	National Insurance (General Benefit) [29 June] ...	II,	2959
1019	National Insurance (Industrial Injuries) (Benefit) [29 June]	II,	2962
1020	Companies (Bd. of Trade) Fees [25 June]	II,	2966
1021	Angus Hospitals Endowments Scheme Confirmation [28 June]	(n) III,	6358
1022	Wages Regulation (Hat, Cap and Millinery) [1 July]	II,	2967
1023	Wages Regulation (Retail Food) (S.) [5 July] ...	II,	2975
1024	Industrial Training Levy (Hotel and Catering) [30 June]	II,	2994
1025	Beef Cow (E. and W.) [28 June]	II,	3003
1026	Beef Cow Subsidy Payment (E. and W.) [28 June]	II,	3005
1027	Price Stability of Imported Products (Rates of Levy) (Eggs) (No. 13) [23 June]	II,	3007
1028	Exchange Control (Authorised Dealers and Depositaries) [30 June]	II,	3009
1029	M.27 South Coast Motorway (Chilworth –Windhover Section) [28 June]	(n) III,	6345
1031	Superannuation (Local Govt. and Approved Employment) Interchange (S.) [29 June]	II,	3010

(n) Instrument classified as local, noted in the Classified List of Local S.I. at the page shown above, but not set out in full.

No.	Subject	Part	Page
1032	Building Standards (S.) Amdt. No. 2 (Metrication) [8 July]	II,	3013
1033	Price Stabilisation Levies (Supplementary Provns.) [30 June]	II,	3095
1034	Industrial Training Levy (Water Supply) [1 July] ...	II,	3097
1035	Mineral Royalties (Tax) [30 June]	II,	3101
1036	Live Poultry (Restrictions) [30 June]	II,	3103
1037	Milk (N.I.) [30 June]	II,	3105
1038	Milk (G.B.) [30 June]	II,	3108
1039	Reciprocal Enforcement of Foreign Judgements (Israel) [30 June]	II,	3114
1040	Petroleum (Inflammable Liquids) [29 June] ...	II,	3125
1041	Durham County Water Bd. [1 July]	(n) III,	
1048	Anti-Dumping Duty [29 June]	II,	3133
1049	Industrial Training Levy (Road Transport) [1 July]	II,	3135
1050	Suffolk and Ipswich Fire Services (Combination) [1 July]	(n) III,	6355
1052	Lancashire River Authority (Reconstitution of the Croston Internal Drainage Bd.) [1 July] ...	(n) III,	6353
1053	Bristol Waterworks [2 July]	(n) III,	6359
1054	Supplementary Benefit (Determination of Requirements) [5 July]	II,	3141
1056	Import Duties (General) [30 June]	II,	3145
1057	Postal Packets (Customs and Excise) [1 July] ...	II,	3146
1058	Wages Regulation (Retail Bread and Flour Confectionery (E. and W.) [9 July]	II,	3154
1059	Cumberland River Authority (Abolition of the Upper Derwent Internal Drainage District) [2 July]	(n) III,	6353
1060	Fees of Appointed Factory Doctors [7 July] ...	II,	3177
1061	Inflammable Liquids (Conveyance by Road) [8 July]	II,	3181
1062	Inflammable Substances (Conveyance by Road) (Labelling) [8 July]	II,	3184
1063	London–Edinburgh–Thurso Trunk Road (Alness to Kildary Trunking and Detrunking) [8 July] ...	(n) III,	6344
1065	Rent Assessment Ctees. (E. and W.) [7 July] ...	II,	3194
1067	Building Societies (Special Advances) [8 July] ...	II,	3198
1069	Price Stability of Imported Products (Rates of Levy) (Cereals) [2 July]	II,	3200
1070	Industrial Training Levy (Knitting, Lace and Net) [9 July]	II,	3202
1071	Newbridge to Lathallan (Connecting Roads) Special Roads [9 July]	(n) III,	6346
1072	Brucellosis (Payments for Cows in Accredited Herds) (S.) [7 July]	II,	3204
1073	Crown Roads (Admiralty Arch, Whitehall, London) (Application of Road Traffic Enactments) [9 July]	(n) III,	6347
1075	Anti-Dumping (Provisional Charge to Duty) [7 July]	II,	3206
1076	Farm Capital Grant (S.) [8 July]	II,	3208
1077	Farm Capital Grant [8 July]...	II,	3210

(n) Instrument classified as local, noted in the Classified List of Local S.I. at the page shown above, but not set out in full.

No.	Subject	Part	Page
1078	Purchase Tax [9 July]	II,	3213
1079	Schools (S.) Code [9 July]	II,	3215
1081	County Ct. Districts [9 July]	II,	3217
1082	Land Registration Fee [12 July]	II,	3220
1083	County Ct. Fees [12 July]	II,	3222
1084	Petty Sessional Divisions (Cheshire) [13 July] ...	**(n)** III,	6362
1087	Motorways Traffic (E. and W.) [13 July]	II,	3225
1088	Wages Regulation (Stamped or Pressed Metal-Wares) [16 July]	II,	3227
1089	Wages Regulation (Stamped or Pressed Metal-Wares) (Holidays) [16 July]	II,	3238
1090	Plant Breeders' Rights (Lettuces) [14 July] ...	II,	3245
1091	Plant Breeders' Rights (Runner Beans) [14 July] ...	II,	3247
1092	Plant Breeders' Rights (Cymbidiums) [14 July] ...	II,	3249
1093	Plant Breeders' Rights (Trees, Shrubs and Woody Climbers) [14 July]	II,	3251
1094	Plant Breeders' Rights [14 July]	II,	3253
1095	Administration Order [16 July]	II,	3257
1101	Rent Assessment Ctees. (S.) [14 July]	II,	3276
1102	Plant Breeders' Rights (Fees) [14 July]	II,	3280
1103	Foreign Sea-Fishery Officers (International Commission for the North-West Atlantic Fisheries Scheme) [15 July]	II,	3282
1105	Air Navigation (Fees) [16 July]	II,	3287
1106	Staffordshire Potteries Water Bd. [22 July] ...	**(n)** III,	6360
1107	Trunk Road (Gt. Cambridge Road, Haringey) (Restriction of Traffic) [16 July]	**(n)** III,	6349
1108	Town and Country Planning Act 1968 (Commencement) [15 July]	II,	3289
1109	Town and Country Planning (Structure and Local Plans) [15 July]	II,	3291
1111	South East Lancashire and North East Cheshire Passenger Transport Area (Railway Passenger Services) [19 July]	**(n)** III,	6353
1112	Bootle-Southport-South of Preston Trunk Road (Crosby Road South Diversion) [22 July]... ...	**(n)** III,	6341
1113	Tyneside Passenger Transport Area (Railway Passenger Services) [19 July]	**(n)** III,	6353
1114	Merseyside Passenger Transport Area (Railway Passenger Services) [19 July]	**(n)** III,	6353
1115	West Midlands Passenger Transport Area (Railway Passenger Services) [19 July]	**(n)** III,	6353
1116	Employers' Liability (Compulsory Insurance) Act 1969 (Commencement) [20 July]	II,	3314
1117	Employers' Liability (Compulsory Insurance) [20 July]	II,	3315
1119	Justices of the Peace Act 1949 (Compensation) [21 July]	II,	3319
1120	Probation (Compensation) [21 July]	II,	3322
1121	Fire Services (Compensation) [21 July]	II,	3325

(n) Instrument classified as local, noted in the Classified List of Local S.I. at the page shown above, but not set out in full.

No.	Subject	Part	Page
1122	Clerks of the Peace and Justices' Clerks (Compensation) [21 July]	II,	3328
1123	Decimal Currency (End of Transitional Period) [15 July]	II,	3331
1124	Price Stability of Imported Products (Specified Commodities) (Poultry Meat) [20 July]	II,	3332
1128	British Transport (Pensions of Employees) [21 July]	II,	3334
1129	British Railways Bd. (Whitby and Pickering) Light Railway [21 July]	(n) III,	6353
1130	Legal Officers Fees [20 July]	II,	3336
1131	Ipswich (Winston Borehole) [22 July]	(n) III,	6360
1132	Rules of the Supreme Ct. [20 July]	II,	3339
1133	Civil Aviation Act 1968 (Commencement) [22 July]	II,	3341
1134	Civil Aviation (Airport Charges) (Sale of Detained Aircraft) [22 July]	II,	3342
1135	Civil Aviation (Navigation Service Charges) [22 July]	II,	3345
1136	Wages Regulation (Hairdressing) [27 July] ...	II,	3353
1137	Equine Animals (Importation) [26 July]	II,	3371
1138	London–Portsmouth Trunk Road (Scilly Isles Gyratory System) [12 Aug.]	(n) III,	6343
1141	Police [23 July]	II,	3373
1142	Public Service Vehicles (Definition of Express Carriage) [26 July]	II,	3376
1144	Iron and Steel (Borrowing Powers) [23 July] ...	II,	3377
1145	Purchase Tax [19 July]	II,	3378
1146	Control of Hiring [19 July]	II,	3379
1147	Hire Purchase and Credit Sale Agreements [19 July]	II,	3380
1148	Leicester Water [28 July]	(n) III,	6360
1149	National Insurance Act 1971 (Commencement) [23 July]	II,	3381
1150	Roads (S.) Act 1970 (Local Enactments) [26 July]	(n) III,	6341
1151	Courts Act 1971 (Commencement) [27 July] ...	II,	3387
1152	County Cts. (Admiralty Jurisdiction) [28 July] ...	II,	3389
1153	Medicines (First Appointed Day) [27 July] ...	II,	3393
1156	Special Roads (Classes of Traffic) [23 July] ...	II,	3395
1157	Price Stability of Imported Products (Rates of Levy) (Eggs) [21 July]	II,	3399
1158	Registration of Births, Still-births, Deaths and Marriages (Prescription of Forms) (S.) [27 July]	II,	3401
1159	Registration of Births, Deaths and Marriages (Civil Marriage Schedule) (S.) [27 July]	II,	3412
1160	Registration of Births, Deaths and Marriages (Adopted Children Register) (S.) [27 July] ...	II,	3415
1161	A.S. (Rules of Ct.) [6 Aug.]	II,	3419
1162	A.S. (Rule of Ct.) [5 Aug.]	II,	3421
1163	A.S. (Adoption of Children) [5 Aug.]	II,	3422
1164	A.S. (Confirmation of Executors) [6 Aug.] ...	II,	3423
1165	A.S. (Edictal Citations, Commissary Petitions and Petitions of Service) [6 Aug.]	II,	3425
1166	Purchase Tax [28 July]	II,	3428

(n) Instrument classified as local, noted in the Classified List of Local S.I. at the page shown above, but not set out in full.

No.	Subject	Part	Page
1170	Trunk Road (Eastern Avenue, Redbridge) (Prescribed Routes) [9 Aug.]	(n) III,	6349
1171	Fishing Nets (North-East Atlantic) [27 July] ...	II,	3446
1172	Fishing Nets (North-West Atlantic) [27 July] ...	II,	3453
1173	National Westminster Bank (North Central Finance and Lombard Banking) Act 1971 (Appointed Day) [28 July]	(n) III,	6363
1174	Newtown–Aberystwyth Trunk Road (Llanidloes Road, Newtown) [4 Aug.]...	(n) III,	6343
1175	Decimal Currency Bd. (Dissolution) [30 July] ...	II,	3461
1176	Industrial Training Levy (Shipbuilding) [28 July]...	II,	3463
1178	Personal Injuries (Civilians) [28 July]	II,	3468
1179	Meat Inspection [28 July]	II,	3478
1180	Claro Water Bd. (Borehole at Baldersby St. James) [30 July]	(n) III,	6359
1183	Trunk Road (North Circular Road, Ealing and Brent) (Restriction of Traffic) [3 Aug.]	(n) III,	6349
1184	London–Birmingham Trunk Road (Bourne End Diversion) [3 Aug.]	(n) III,	6342
1186	Import Duty Drawbacks [29 July]	II,	3480
1187	Hill Cattle (S.) Scheme [29 July]	II,	3483
1188	Hill Cattle Subsidy Payment (S.) [29 July] ...	II,	3485
1189	Beef Cow (S.) Scheme [29 July]	II,	3487
1190	Beef Cow Subsidy Payment [29 July]	II,	3489
1194	Industrial Training Levy (Distributive Bd.) [2 Aug.]	II,	3491
1195	Electricity (Borrowing Powers) (S.) [2 Aug.] ...	II,	3496
1196	Food (Meat Inspection) (S.) [28 July]	II,	3498
1197	Land Registration (Powers of Attorney) [4 Aug.]...	II,	3500
1198	Medicines (Exportation of Specific Products for Human Use) [2 Aug.]	II,	3502
1199	Smoke Control Areas (Authorised Fuels) [30 July]	II,	3504
1200	Medicines (Control of Substances for Manufacture) [3 Aug.]	II,	3506
1201	National Insurance (Industrial Injuries) (Increase of Benefit and Miscellaneous Provisions) [4 Aug.]	II,	3514
1202	National Insurance (Assessment of Graduated Contributions) [2 Aug.]	II,	3522
1203	Police (S.) [30 July]	II,	3527
1206	Cinematograph Films (Collection of Levy) [4 Aug.]	II,	3530
1207	St. Helens (Eccleston Park) Water [4 Aug.] ...	(n) III,	6360
1208	Royal Tunbridge Wells (Ext. of Operation of Byelaws) [4 Aug.]	(n) III,	6360
1209	Injury Warrant [2 Aug.]	II,	3532
1210	Valuation (Post Office and Telecommunication Services) (S.) [3 Aug.]	II,	3534
1211	Special Roads (Classes of Traffic) (S.) [5 Aug.] ...	II,	3536
1212	Valuation (Water Undertakings) (S.) [5 Aug.] ...	II,	3539
1213	Valuation (Scottish Gas Bd.) (S.) [5 Aug.] ...	II,	3541
1214	A.S. (Sheriff Ct. Procedure) [13 Aug.]	II,	3543
1215	A.S. (Rule of Ct.) [13 Aug.]	II,	3545
1216	Marriage (Authorised Persons) [4 Aug.]	II,	3547

(n) Instrument classified as local, noted in the Classified List of Local S.I. at the page shown above, but not set out in full.

No.	Subject	Part	Page
1217	Registration of Marriages (Welsh Language) [4 Aug.]...	II,	3549
1218	Registration of Births, Deaths and Marriages [4 Aug.]...	II,	3551
1219	National Insurance (Age Addition) [5 Aug.] ...	II,	3553
1220	National Insurance (Increase of Benefit and Miscellaneous Provisions) [5 Aug.]	II,	3556
1221	Local Authority Social Services Act 1970 (Commencement) [5 Aug.]	II,	3576
1222	Pneumoconiosis, Byssinosis and Miscellaneous Diseases Benefit) [5 Aug.]	II,	3576
1223	Workmen's Compensation (Supplementation) [5 Aug.]...	II,	3580
1224	Craven Water Undertaking (Valuation) [4 Aug.] ...	(n) III,	6358
1225	London–Penzance Trunk Road (South Brent By-Pass) [4 Aug.]	(n) III,	6343
1226	London–Penzance Trunk Road (Drybridge–Syon Abbey) [4 Aug.]	(n) III,	6343
1227	Port of London Authy. (Borrowing Powers) [5 Aug.]	(n) III,	6354
1231	Makerfield Water Bd. (Eller Brook) [5 Aug.] ...	(n) III,	6360
1232	County of Banff Bursary Fund [6 Aug.]	(n) III,	6361
1233	Hydrocarbon Oil Duties (Drawback) [3 Aug.] ...	II,	3583
1234	Anthrax Prevention [3 Aug.]	II,	3584
1235	Anguilla (Administration) [3 Aug.]	II,	3587
1236	Antarctic Treaty (Specially Protected Area) [3 Aug.]	II,	3595
1237	Commonwealth Countries and Republic of Ireland (Immunities and Privileges) [3 Aug.]	II,	3597
1238	Consular Conventions (Polish People's Republic) [3 Aug.]	II,	3601
1239	Hong Kong (Appeal to Privy Council) [3 Aug.] ...	II,	3602
1240	Virgin Islands Constitution [3 Aug.]	II,	3604
1241	Central Council for Education and Training in Social Work [3 Aug.]	II,	3606
1242	Fugitive Offenders (Designated Commonwealth Countries) [3 Aug.]	II,	3610
1243	Transfer of Functions (Development Fund) [3 Aug.]	II,	3611
1244	Administration of Justice Act 1970 (Commencement) [4 Aug.]	II,	3613
1245	Supreme Ct. Fees [4 Aug.]	II,	3615
1251	Bishopton By-Pass (Stage II) [6 Aug.]	(n) III,	6346
1252	Bishopton By-Pass (Stage II) (Connecting Roads) [6 Aug.]	(n) III,	6346
1253	Indictment Rules [6 Aug.]	II,	3617
1254	Transport Holding Company (Transfer of Assets) [5 Aug.]	II,	3620
1257	Board of Inquiry (Army) [6 Aug.]	II,	3622
1258	Woking (Water Charges) [6 Aug.]	(n) III,	6360
1259	Witnesses Allowances [6 Aug.]	II,	3624
1260	Coroners (Fees and Allowances) [6 Aug.]	II,	3625
1263	National Insurance (Industrial Injuries) (Colliery Workers Supplementary Scheme) [10 Aug.] ...	II,	3626

(n) Instrument classified as local, noted in the Classified List of Local S.I. at the page shown above, but not set out in full.

No.	Subject	Part	Page
1264	Price Stability of Imported Products (Rates of Levy) (Cereals) [3 Aug.]	II,	3628
1265	Smoke Control Areas (Exempted Fireplaces) [10 Aug.]...	II,	3630
1266	London–Carlisle–Glasgow Trunk Road (Kempley Bank Roundabout to Stonybeck Roundabout Detrunking) [12 Aug.]	**(n)** III,	6342
1267	Medicines (Surgical Materials) [10 Aug.]	II,	3632
1268	Eastbourne (Water Charges) [10 Aug.]	**(n)** III,	6360
1269	Rules of the Supreme Ct. [10 Aug.]	II,	3634
1271	Price Stability of Imported Products (Rates of Levy) (Eggs) [4 Aug.]	II,	3661
1272	Housing Subsidies (Representative Rates of Interest) [10 Aug.]	II,	3663
1275	Investment Grants Termination [12 Aug.] ...	II,	3665
1279	Eastbourne Water (Financial Provisions) [12 Aug.]	**(n)** III,	6360
1280	Wages Regulation (Made-up Textiles) [13 Aug.] ...	II,	3667
1281	Smoke Control Areas (Exempted Fireplaces) (S.) [10 Aug.]	II,	3675
1282	Worcester–Wolverhampton–South of Stafford Trunk Road (Ombersley By-Pass) (Slip Roads and Variation) [13 Aug.]	**(n)** III,	6343
1284	Road Vehicles (Excise) (Prescribed Particulars) [12 Aug.]	II,	3677
1285	Road Vehicles (Registration and Licensing) [12 Aug.]...	II,	3679
1287	Diseases of Animals (Approved Disinfectants) [13 Aug.]...	II,	3681
1288	Children and Young Persons (Designation of Isle of Man Order) [13 Aug.]	II,	3692
1289	Furness Water Bd. [13 Aug.]	**(n)** III,	6353
1290	Housing Corporation Advances (Increase of Limit) [16 Aug.]	II,	3693
1291	Social Security Act 1971 (Commencement) [13 Aug.]	II,	3695
1292	Crown Ct. Rules [16 Aug.]	II,	3696
1295	White Fish (Inshore Vessels) and Herring Subsidies (U.K.) [16 Aug.]	II,	3710
1296	Housing Subsidies (Representative Rates of Interest) (S.) [12 Aug.]	II,	3720
1297	Awards (First Degree, etc. Courses) [19 Aug.] ...	II,	3722
1298	Finance Act 1971 Schedule 1 (Customs Procedures, etc.) (Commencement) [11 Aug.]...	II,	3739
1299	Aircraft (Customs) Regs. 1971 [11 Aug.]	II,	3740
1300	Ship's Report, Importation and Exportation by Sea Regs. 1965 [11 Aug.]	II,	3743
1302	Mid Cheshire Water Bd. [16 Aug.]	**(n)** III,	6360
1303	Land Drainage (Compensation) [16 Aug.] ...	II,	3745
1304	M.62 Motorway (Lofthouse–South of Ferrybridge Section) (Alteration and Extension of Route) (Variation) [16 Aug.]	**(n)** III,	6345

(n) Instrument classified as local, noted in the Classified List of Local S.I. at the page shown above, but not set out in full.

No.	Subject	Part	Page
1305	M.62 Motorway (Lofthouse–South of Ferrybridge Section) Connecting Roads Scheme [16 Aug.] ...	(n) III,	6345
1306	M.62 Motorway (Lofthouse–South of Ferrybridge Section) Connecting Roads Scheme [16 Aug.] ...	(n) III,	6345
1307	M.66 Motorway (Bury Easterly By-Pass Southern Section) and Connecting Roads Scheme [16 Aug.]	(n) III,	6345
1308	Heriot-Watt College, Edinburgh Scheme [16 Aug.]	(n) III,	6361
1309	Medicines (Exportation of Specified Veterinary Products) [16 Aug.]	II,	3749
1311	Furness Water Bd. [17 Aug.]	(n) III,	6360
1316	Pensions (Preservation of Increases) [17 Aug.] ...	II,	3752
1317	East Devon Water [18 Aug.]	(n) III,	6360
1319	Price Stability of Imported Products (Rates of Levy) (Eggs) [11 Aug.]	II,	3788
1323	Inverness-shire Water Bd. (Lochnam Bat and Loch Gorm) [19 Aug.]	(n) III,	6361
1326	Medicines (Importation of Medicinal Products for Re-exportation) [18 Aug.]	II,	3790
1327	Police Pensions [19 Aug.]	II,	3794
1328	Special Constables (Pensions) [19 Aug.]	II,	3799
1329	Firemen's Pension Scheme [19 Aug.]	II,	3801
1330	Increase of Pensions (Police and Fire Services) [19 Aug.]...	II,	3813
1331	Supplementary Benefit (Claims and Payments) [20 Aug.]...	II,	3819
1332	National Insurance Act 1971 (Commencement) [19 Aug.]...	II,	3821
1333	Distress for Rent [19 Aug.]	II,	3822
1335	Road Traffic Act 1962 (Commencement) [19 Aug.]	II,	3825
1336	Northallerton and Dales Water (Charges) [20 Aug.]	(n) III,	6360
1337	South Lincolnshire (Aslackby and Rippingale) Water [20 Aug.]	(n) III,	6360
1338	Bucks. Water (Mill End Additional Boreholes) [20 Aug.]...	(n) III,	6359
1348	Anti-Dumping (Provisional Charge to Duty) [19 Aug.]...	II,	3826
1349	Carlisle–Sutherland Trunk Road (Whooff House–Plains Road) [27 Aug.]	(n) III,	6341
1350	Levens Bridge–Carlisle Trunk Road (Thwaites Mill and Slapestones Diversions) [23 Aug.]	(n) III,	6342
1352	Merchant Shipping (Load Lines) (Fees) [17 Aug]...	II,	3828
1353	Merchant Shipping (Fees) [17 Aug.]	II,	3830
1354	Removal of Bodies [23 Aug.]	II,	3832
1356	Temporary Importation (Magnetic Tapes) [23 Aug.]	II,	3835
1357	Anti-Dumping (Provisional Charge to Duty) [23 Aug.]...	II,	3837
1358	Iron and Steel (Pension Schemes) (Transfer) [24 Aug.]...	II,	3839
1363	East of Snaith–Sunderland Trunk Road (Teesside Diversion Stage 1) [23 Aug.]	(n) III,	6342

(n) Instrument classified as local, noted in the Classified List of Local S.I. at the page shown above, but not set out in full.

No.	Subject	Part	Page
1364	East of Snaith–Sunderland Trunk Road (Teesside Diversion Stage 1) (Slip Roads) [23 Aug.] ...	(n) III,	6342
1365	East of Snaith–Sunderland Trunk Road (Teesside Diversion Stage 1) (Slip Roads) [23 Aug.] ...	(n) III,	6342
1366	Capital Gains Tax (Exempt Gilt-edged Securities) [20 Aug.]	II,	3843
1367	London 'D' Ring Road (A.111–A.10 Section) [23 Aug.]...	(n) III,	6342
1368	Provision of Milk and Meals [25 Aug.]	II,	3844
1369	Wages Regulation (Aerated Waters) (S.) [26 Aug.]	II,	3851
1370	Exchange Control (Authorised Dealers and Depositaries) [1 Sept.]	II,	3855
1377	Mines and Quarries (Tips) [26 Aug.]	II,	3857
1378	Mines and Quarries (Tipping Plans) [26 Aug.] ...	II,	3871
1380	Superannuation (Teaching and Police) Interchange [27 Aug.]	II,	3873
1381	Wages Regulation (Fur) [27 Aug.]	II,	3882
1382	London 'D' Ring Road (A.1–A.111 Section) [24 Aug.]...	(n) III,	6342
1384	West Pennine Water (Green Vale Pipeline, Littleborough) [27 Aug.]...	(n) III,	6360
1385	Northallerton and the Dales Water (Stubbing Nook Borehole) [27 Aug.]	(n) III,	6360
1387	Import Duties (General) [26 Aug.]...	II,	3901
1388	Import Duties (Temp. Exemptions) [26 Aug.] ...	II,	3903
1392	Industrial Training Levy (Furniture and Timber) [31 Aug.]	II,	3907
1393	Wages Regulation (Toy Manufacturing) [31 Aug.]	II,	3912
1394	Wages Regulation (Toy Manufacturing) (Holidays) [31 Aug.]	II,	3919
1397	M.56 North Cheshire Motorway (Preston Brook to Bowdon Section) and Connecting Roads Scheme [31 Aug.]	(n) III,	6345
1398	Therapeutic Substances (Supply of Zinc Bacitracin for Agricultural Purposes) [31 Aug.]	II,	3926
1400	South-East Breconshire Water Bd. [31 Aug.] ...	(n) III,	6360
1401	Price Stability of Imported Products (Rates of Levy) (Eggs) [25 Aug.]	II,	3930
1402	Special Constables (Pensions) (S.) [31 Aug.] ...	II,	3932
1403	Scottish Hospital Trust (Administration) [31 Aug.]	II,	3934
1404	National Assistance (Charges for Accommodation) [31 Aug.]	II,	3938
1405	Therapeutic Substances (Supply of Antibiotics and Chemotherapeutic Substances for Agricultural Purposes) [31 Aug.]	II,	3941
1406	Exchange Control (Scheduled Territories) [1 Sept.]	II,	3943
1407	Trunk Road (East Ham and Barking By-Pass Newham) (Restriction of Traffic) [3 Sept.] ...	(n) III,	6349
1410	Medicines (Exemption from Licences) (Foods and Cosmetics) [3 Sept.]	II,	3945

(n) Instrument classified as local, noted in the Classified List of Local S.I. at the page shown above, but not set out in full.

No.	Subject	Part	Page
1411	Housing (Amount of Improving Grant) (S.) [1 Sept.]	II,	3949
1412	Bucks Water (Hawridge Pumping Station) [3 Sept.]	(n) III,	6359
1413	Private Legislation Procedure (S.) [2 Sept.] ...	II,	3951
1415	Wages Regulation (Flax and Hemp) [8 Sept.] ...	II,	3955
1416	M.25 South Orbital Motorway (Egham–Chertsey Section) [6 Sept.]	(n) III,	6345
1417	M.3/M.25 Motorway (Thorpe Interchange) Connecting Roads Scheme [6 Sept.]	(n) III,	6345
1418	M.25 Motorway (Wrotham Spur) Scheme [6 Sept.]	(n) III,	6345
1419	National Insurance [3 Sept.]	II,	3964
1420	National Insurance (Mariners) [3 Sept.]	II,	3983
1421	National Insurance and Industrial Injuries (Classification, Contributions and Collection of Contributions) [3 Sept.]	II,	3992
1422	National Insurance (Members of the Forces) [3 Sept.]	II,	3996
1423	Merchant Shipping (Oil Pollution) Act 1971 (Commencement) [6 Sept.]	II,	4006
1425	M.25 South Orbital Motorway (Godstone to Sevenoaks Section) Scheme [6 Sept.]	(n) III,	6345
1426	Remuneration of Teachers (Further Education) [8 Sept.]	II,	4008
1427	Remuneration of Teachers (Primary and Secondary Schools) [8 Sept.]	II,	4011
1429	Price Stability of Imported Products (Rates of Levy) (Cereals) [1 Sept.]	II,	4014
1430	Superannuation (Teaching and National Health Service) Interchange (S.) [7 Sept.]	II,	4016
1434	Urenco Limited (Designation) [8 Sept.]	(n) III,	6363
1436	North-West Norfolk Water Bd. [8 Sept.]	(n) III,	6360
1437	National Health Service (Designation of Teaching Hospitals) [8 Sept.]	III,	4049
1438	National Health Service (Warrington Hospital Management Ctee.) [8 Sept.]	(n) III,	6358
1439	Ipswich Water [9 Sept.]	(n) III,	6360
1440	National Insurance (Industrial Injuries) (Hospital In-Patients) [17 Sept.]	III,	4052
1441	National Insurance (Modification of the Superannuation Acts) [9 Sept.]	III,	4056
1442	East of Scotland Water Bd. (Burn of Ample, Lochearnhead) Water [8 Sept.]	(n) III,	6360
1443	Wages Regulation (Retail Newsagency, Tobacco and Confectionery) (E. and W.) [13 Sept.] ...	III,	4058
1444	Severn Bridge Tolls (Temp. Reduction) [7 Sept.]	(n) III,	6341
1445	Medicines (Retail Pharmacists—Exemptions from Licensing Requirements) [9 Sept.]	III,	4078
1446	Medicines (Data Sheet) (Transitional) [9 Sept.] ...	III,	4082
1447	Medicines (Applications for Product Licences of Right and Clinical Trial and Animal Test Certificates of Right) [9 Sept.]	III,	4085

(n) Instrument classified as local, noted in the Classified List of Local S.I. at the page shown above, but not set out in full.

No.	Subject	Part	Page
1448	Medicines (Applications for Manufacturer's and Wholesale Dealer's Licences of Right) [9 Sept.]	III,	4096
1449	Medicines (Fees) [9 Sept.]	III,	4102
1450	Medicines (Exemption from Licences) (Special and Transitional Cases) [9 Sept.]	III,	4118
1454	Wages Regulation (Linen and Cotton Handerchief etc.) [10 Sept.]	III,	4123
1455	Industrial Training Levy (Printing and Publishing) [9 Sept.]	III,	4128
1465	Price Stability of Imported Products (Rates of Levy) (Cereals) [7 Sept.]	III,	4134
1466	Police Pensions [14 Sept.]	III,	4136
1467	Special Constables (Pensions) [14 Sept.]	III,	4142
1468	Firemen's Pension Scheme [14 Sept.]	III,	4144
1469	Royal Irish Constabulary (Widows' Pensions) [14 Sept.]	III,	4147
1470	London–Edinburgh–Thurso Trunk Road (Evelix Bridge and Other Diversions) (Variation) [13 Sept.]	(n) III,	6344
1475	Price Stability of Imported Products (Rates of Levy) (Eggs) [8 Sept.]	III,	4152
1477	Vehicle and Driving Licences Act 1969 (Commencement) [15 Sept.]	III,	4154
1478	National Insurance (General Benefit and Claims and Payments) [17 Sept.]	III,	4155
1479	Social Security (Financial Adjustments) [15 Sept]	III,	4157
1482	Wages Regulation (Retail Bookselling and Stationery) [17 Sept.]	III,	4159
1483	Wages Regulation (Retail Bread and Flour Confectionery) (S.) [20 Sept.]	III,	4162
1488	National Health Service (South West London Hospital Management Ctee.) [20 Sept.]	(n) III,	6358
1489	Land Registration and Land Charges Act 1971 (Commencement) [17 Sept.]	III,	4174
1491	Chronically Sick and Disabled Persons Act 1970 (Commencement) [17 Sept.]	III,	4175
1492	Disabled Persons (Badges for Motor Vehicles) [17 Sept.]	III,	4177
1493	Local Authies. Traffic Orders (Exemptions for Disabled Persons) (E. and W.) [17 Sept.]	III,	4185
1494	Corringham Light Railway (Winding-Up) [20 Sept.]	(n) III,	6353
1497	National Insurance (Earnings-related Benefit) [17 Sept.]	III,	4190
1498	Police Federation [20 Sept.]	III,	4194
1500	National Assistance (Charges for Accommodation) (S.) [17 Sept.]	III,	4197
1501	Special Constables (Pensions) (S.) [17 Sept.] ...	III,	4204
1502	Motorways Traffic (M.4) (Speed Limit) [21 Sept.] ...	(n) III,	6344
1503	Drawback (Isle of Man) Regs. 1953 (Revn.) [24 Sept.]	III,	4202

(n) Instrument classified as local, noted in the Classified List of Local S.I. at the page shown above, but not set out in full.

No.	Subject	Part	Page
1504	Industrial Training Levy (Ceramics, Glass and Mineral Products) [23 Sept.]	III,	4203
1505	Fixed Penalty (Procedure) [22 Sept.]	III,	4209
1506	Price Stability of Imported Products (Rates of Levy) (Eggs) [15 Sept.]	III,	4211
1507	Sugar (Rates of Surcharge and Surcharge Repayments) [15 Sept.]	III,	4213
1508	Composite Sugar Products (Surcharge and Surcharge Repayments—Average Rates) [15 Sept.]	III,	4216
1509	Coventry, Birmingham and Rugby Water [22 Sept.]	(n) III,	6359
1516	London–Great Yarmouth Trunk Road (Colchester Northern By-Pass) [21 Sept.]	(n) III,	6342
1517	London–Great Yarmouth Trunk Road (Colchester Northern By-Pass) (Crown Interchange, Park Lane and Birchwood Road Slip Roads) [21 Sept.]	(n) III,	6342
1518	Wages Regulation (Retail Furnishing and Allied Trades) [27 Sept.]	III,	4220
1519	Industrial Training Levy (Wool, Jute and Flax) [23 Sept.]	III,	4241
1520	Adoption (High Ct.) [24 Sept.]	III,	4249
1521	Local Authies. Traffic Orders (Exemptions for Disabled Persons) (S.) [22 Sept.]	III,	4270
1522	Industrial Relations Act 1971 (Commencement) [23 Sept.]	III,	4274
1523	Newport–Shrewsbury Trunk Road (Diversion near ' The Green ', Wellington) [23 Sept.]	(n) III,	6343
1524	' Zebra ' Pedestrian Crossings [28 Sept.]	III,	4281
1525	General Optical Council (Companies Ctee. Rules) [23 Sept.]	III,	4294
1526	General Optical Council (Disciplinary Ctee. Rules) [22 Sept.]	III,	4296
1527	General Optical Council (Education Ctee. Rules) [23 Sept.]	III,	4298
1528	General Optical Council (Investigating Ctee. Rules [22 Sept.]	III,	4300
1529	Industrial Training Levy (Cotton and Allied Textiles) [27 Sept.]	III,	4302
1530	Industrial Training (Engineering Bd.) [27 Sept.] ...	III,	4309
1531	Wages Regulation (Milk Distributive) (S.) [28 Sept.]	III,	4324
1532	Ipswich–Weedon Trunk Road (Stowmarket–Claydon By-Pass) [24 Sept.]	(n) III,	6342
1533	Industrial Training Levy (Gas) [27 Sept.]	III,	4336
1536	Trunk Road (Southend Arterial Road, Havering) (Prescribed Routes) [30 Sept.]	(n) III,	6349
1537	Milk and Meals (Education) (S.) [27 Sept.] ...	III,	4340
1538	Gaming Clubs (Permitted Areas) [24 Sept.] ...	III,	4345
1539	Renumeration of Teachers (Primary and Secondary Schools) [28 Sept.]	III,	4347
1541	Price Stability of Imported Products (Rates of Levy) (Eggs) [22 Sept.]	III,	4350

(n) Instrument classified as local, noted in the Classified List of Local S.I. at the page shown above, but not set out in full.

No.	Subject	Part	Page
1542	Employers' and Workers' Organisations (Amalgamations etc.) [27 Sept.]	III,	4352
1543	Import Duties (Temp. Exemptions) [27 Sept.]	III,	4358
1544	Acquisition of Land (Rate of Interest after Entry) [27 Sept.]	III,	4359
1545	Acquisition of Land (Rate of Interest after Entry) (S.) [27 Sept.]	III,	4360
1546	Fylde Water Bd. (Extension of Operation of Byelaws) [29 Sept.]	**(n)** III,	6360
1547	Cambridge Water (Duxford and Thriplow) [29 Sept.]	**(n)** III,	6359
1548	National Health Service (East Sussex, Eastbourne and Hastings) Executive Council [30 Sept.] ...	**(n)** III,	6358
1549	Supplementary Benefit (General) [30 Sept.] ...	III,	4361
1551	Opencast Coal (Rate of Interest on Compensation) [27 Sept.]	III,	4363
1552	Air Navigation (Restriction of Flying) (Chequers) [27 Sept.]	**(n)** III,	6364
1553	Standards for School Premises [30 Sept.]	III,	4364
1554	Price Stability of Imported Products (Levy Arrangements) (Poultry Meat) [29 Sept.]	III,	4366
1555	Price Stability of Imported Products (Minimum Import Price Levels) (Poultry Meat) [29 Sept.] ...	III,	4369
1556	Exchange Control (Scheduled Territories) [30 Sept.]	III,	4373
1557	Gaming Clubs (Permitted Areas) (S.) [28 Sept.] ...	III,	4375
1566	Exchange Control (Authorised Dealers and Depositaries) [1 Oct.]	III,	4377
1567	London–Holyhead Trunk Road (Allesley By-Pass Slip Roads) [30 Sept.]	**(n)** III,	6342
1568	Newport–Shrewsbury Trunk Road (Diversion South of Cherry Tree Cottage) [30 Sept.]	**(n)** III,	6343
1569	Wages Regulation (Paper Box) (Holidays) [1 Oct.]...	III,	4379
1570	British Sugar Corporation Limited (Incentive Agreement) (Variation) [29 Sept.]	III,	4387
1571	East Yorkshire (Wolds Area) Water Bd. (Etton Borehole) [4 Oct.]	**(n)** III,	6360
1572	North West Sussex Water [1 Oct.]	**(n)** III,	6360
1573	Civil Aviation Act 1971 (Commencement) [30 Sept.]	III,	4390
1574	Eryri Water Bd. (Bwrdd Dwr Eryri) (Marchlyn Bach Dam) [7 Oct.]	**(n)** III,	6360
1577	Assistance for House Purchase and Improvement (Housing Associations) [1 Oct.]	III,	4391
1582	Sheriff Courts (S.) Act 1971 (Commencement) [30 Sept.]	III,	4393
1584	Price Stability of Imported Products (Rates of Levy) (Eggs) [29 Sept.]	III,	4395
1585	Army Terms of Service [4 Oct.]	III,	4397
1591	Wages Regulation (Laundry) [8 Oct.]	III,	4399
1592	Inspection of Registers and Documents [6 Oct.] ...	III,	4407
1593	Poultry Carcases (Landing) [7 Oct.]	III,	4408

(n) Instrument classified as local, noted in the Classified List of Local S.I. at the page shown above, but not set out in full.

No.	Subject		Part	Page
1594	London–Penzance Trunk Road (Liskeard By-Pass) [7 Oct.]	(n)	III,	6343
1600	Building [6 Oct.]		III,	4411
1601	Royston–Alconbury Trunk Road (Huntingdon and Godmanchester By-Pass) [5 Oct.]	(n)	III,	6343
1602	Greater London Council Election [6 Oct.] ...		III,	4435
1603	London Borough Council Election [6 Oct.] ...		III,	4437
1604	Wages Regulation (Boot and Shoe Repairing) [11 Oct.]		III,	4439
1605	Wages Regulation (Boot and Shoe Repairing) (Holidays) [11 Oct.]		III,	4444
1606	South Hampshire Main Drainage (8 Oct.]	(n)	III,	6358
1607	Price Stability of Imported Products (Rates of Levy) (Cereals) [4 Oct.]		III,	4452
1609	Air Navigation (Restriction of Flying) (Long Kesh Aerodrome) [5 Oct.]	(n)	III,	6364
1613	Pool Competition (Fee for Certificate) [8 Oct.] ...		III,	4454
1614	Increase of Pensions (Teachers' Family Benefits) [7 Oct.]		III,	4455
1615	Probation (Conditions of Service) [12 Oct.] ...		III,	4459
1616	Pensions Increase (Injury Warrant Pensions) [6 Oct.]		III,	4464
1619	British Railways Bd. (Totton Hythe and Fawley Light Railway) [13 Oct.]	(n)	III,	6353
1620	Folkestone–Honiton Trunk Road (Stony Head, Near Bridport, Diversion) [14 Oct.]	(n)	III,	6342
1621	Price Stability of Imported Products (Rates of Levy) (Eggs) [6 Oct.]		III,	4466
1623	Herring (Celtic Sea) (Prohibition of Fishing Method) [12 Oct.]		III,	4468
1628	Road Vehicles (Excise) (Prescribed Particulars) [14 Oct.]		III,	4470
1629	Price Stability of Imported Products (Rates of Levy) (Cereals) [7 Oct.]		III,	4489
1631	Wages Regulation (Retail Drapery, Outfitting and Footwear) [15 Oct.]		III,	4491
1632	Exchange Control (Payment) [13 Oct.]		III,	4495
1633	National Insurance [12 Oct.]		III,	4496
1634	Town and Country Planning (Limit of Annual Value) (S.) [14 Oct.]		III,	4499
1635	Anti-Dumping Duty [13 Oct.]		III,	4501
1636	Civil Aviation Act 1971 (Commencement) [13 Oct.]		III,	4504
1641	Trent and Lincolnshire River Authies. (Alteration of Areas) [15 Oct.]...	(n)	III,	6353
1642	Price Stability of Imported Products (Levy) Arrangements) (Eggs) [14 Oct.]		III,	4505
1644	West Shropshire Water Bd. (Condover Borehole) [15 Oct.]	(n)	III,	6360
1645	Craven Water Bd. (Charges) [15 Oct.]	(n)	III,	6360
1646	West Suffolk Water Bd. (Honington Airfield) [15 Oct.]	(n)	III,	6360

(n) Instrument classified as local, noted in the Classified List of Local S.I. at the page shown above, but not set out in full.

No.	Subject	Part	Page
1647	Price Stability of Imported Products (Rates of Levy) (Cereals) [12 Oct.]	III,	4507
1648	Superannuation (Commission on Industrial Relations) [18 Oct.]	III,	4509
1649	County Ct. Fees [20 Oct.]	III,	4511
1650	Price Stability of Imported Products (Rates of Levy) (Eggs) [13 Oct.]	III,	4531
1651	Wages Regulation (Ready Made and Wholesale Bespoke Tailoring) [21 Oct.]	III,	4533
1652	Rag Flock and Other Filling Materials [20 Oct.] ...	III,	4543
1653	National Health Service (Portsmouth Hospital Management Ctee.) [19 Oct.]	(n) III,	6358
1654	Rate Support Grants (Pooling Arrangements) [19 Oct.]	III,	4555
1655	A.S. (Confirmation of Executors) [1 Nov.] ...	III,	4557
1657	Exeter–Leeds and Nottingham–Stoke-on-Trent Trunk Roads (Mickleover By-Pass and Link Road) (Manor Hospital and Kingsway Junctions) [18 Oct.]	(n) III,	6342
1660	Industrial Tribunals (E. and W.) [20 Oct.] ...	III,	4559
1661	Industrial Tribunals (S.) [20 Oct.]	III,	4561
1662	Industrial Training Levy (Engineering) [20 Oct.] ...	III,	4563
1666	Wages Regulation (Retail Newsagency, Tobacco and Confectionery) (S.) [26 Oct.]	III,	4569
1667	Lincolnshire River Authy. (Alford Drainage District) [21 Oct.]	(n) III,	6353
1668	Price Stability of Imported Products (Rates of Levy) (Cereals) [18 Oct.]	III,	4585
1675	Wireless Telegraphy (Control of Interference from Radio-Frequency Heating Apparatus) [21 Oct.]	III,	4587
1678	London–Penzance Trunk Road (Camborne and Scorrier By-Pass) [21 Oct.]	(n) III,	6343
1679	Wages Regulation (Paper Box) [25 Oct.]	III,	4595
1680	Certificates of Appointment of Factory Inspectors [26 Oct.]	III,	4604
1681	Usk River Authy. [22 Oct.]	(n) III,	6354
1682	Industrial Relations Act 1971 (Commencement) [25 Oct.]	III,	4606
1683	Social Security Act 1971 (Commencement) [25 Oct.]	III,	4608
1684	National Health Service (Medical Practices Compensation) [25 Oct.]	III,	4609
1685	Bilston Link Trunk Road and Slip Roads (27 Oct.]	(n) III,	6341
1686	Civil Aviation (Notices) [26 Oct.]	III,	4611
1687	Civil Aviation (Designation of Aerodromes) [26 Oct.]	(n) III,	6364
1688	Income Tax (Certification of Sub-Contractors in the Construction Industry) [26 Oct.]	III,	4612
1689	Price Stability of Imported Products (Rates of Levy) (Eggs) [20 Oct.]	III,	4615
1690	Pensions Increase (Past Prime Ministers) [25 Oct.]	III,	4617

(n) Instrument classified as local, noted in the Classified List of Local S.I. at the page shown above, but not set out in full.

No.	Subject	Part	Page
1691	Central Flintshire Water Bd. (Charges) [27 Oct.] ...	(n) III,	6359
1695	Price Stability of Imported Products (Rates of Levy) (Cereals) [21 Oct.]	III,	4619
1696	Wages Regulation (Hollow-ware) [28 Oct.] ...	III,	4621
1697	Wages Regulation (Hollow-ware) (Holidays) [28 Oct.]	III,	4628
1698	Wages Regulation (Milk Distributive) (E. and W.) [1 Nov.]	III,	4635
1701	Trunk Roads (Eastern Avenue and Woodford Avenue, Redbridge) (Prohibition of Cycling) [1 Nov.]	(n) III,	6349
1702	Trunk Road (Great Cambridge Road, Enfield) (Prescribed Routes) [1 Nov.]	(n) III,	6349
1705	Highways Act 1971 (Commencement) [27 Oct.] ...	III,	4649
1706	Special and Other Roads (Maps etc.) [27 Oct.] ...	III,	4652
1707	Stopping up of Accesses to Premises (Procedure) ...	III,	4654
1708	Dutch Elm Disease (Local Authies.) [27 Oct.] ...	III,	4994
1710	London–Portsmouth Trunk Road (Cannonball Corner and Gravel Hill Diversion) [4 Nov.] ...	(n) III,	6343
1712	Import Duties (Temp. Exemptions) [1 Nov.] ...	III,	4658
1713	Price Stability of Imported Products (Rates of Levy) (Cereals) [26 Oct.]	III,	4662
1714	A.S. Rules of Ct. [11 Nov.]	III,	4664
1715	Civil Aviation (Route Charges for Navigation Services) [1 Nov.]	III,	4666
1716	Brucellosis (Eradication Areas) (E. and W.) [4 Nov.]	(n) III,	6364
1717	Brucellosis (Area Eradication) (E. and W.) [4 Nov.]	III,	4673
1718	South West Suburban Water [1 Nov.]	(n) III,	6360
1719	Air Navigation (Restriction of Flying) (Chequers) [1 Nov.]	(n) III,	6364
1720	Price Stability of Imported Products (Rates of Levy) (Eggs) [27 Oct.]	III,	4682
1725	Census of Production (1972) (Returns and Exempted Persons) [3 Nov.]	III,	4684
1726	Superannuation (Pest Infestation and Civil Service) Transfer [2 Nov.]	III,	4686
1727	Commons Commissioners [4 Nov.]	III,	4688
1728	National Insurance (Classification) [4 Nov.] ...	III,	4709
1729	National Insurance (Industrial Injuries) (Insurable and Excepted Employments) [4 Nov.]	III,	4713
1730	Civil Aviation (Navigation Service Charges) [1 Nov.]	III,	4716
1731	Radioactive Substances Act 1948 Appropriate Minister Designation [2 Nov.]	III,	4718
1732	Temples [2 Nov.]	III,	4720
1733	Air Navigation [2 Nov.]	III,	4725
1734	Hijacking Act 1971 (Commencement) [2 Nov.] ...	III,	4729
1735	Oil in Navigable Waters (Convention Countries) (New Zealand) [2 Nov.]	III,	4730
1736	Oil in Navigable Waters (Shipping Casualties) [2 Nov.]	III,	4731
1737	Cayman Islands Constitution [2 Nov.]	III,	4733

(**n**) Instrument classified as local, noted in the Classified List of Local S.I. at the page shown above, but not set out in full.

No.	Subject	Part	Page
1738	Foreign Compensation (Union of Soviet Socialist Republics) [2 Nov.]	III,	4735
1739	Hijacking Act 1971 (Overseas Territories) [2 Nov.]	III,	4737
1740	Montserrat (Governor) [2 Nov.]	III,	4741
1741	Pacific [2 Nov.]	III,	4743
1742	National Insurance (Republic of Ireland) [3 Nov.]...	III,	4745
1743	Carriage of Goods by Road (Guernsey) [2 Nov.] ...	III,	4752
1744	Hijacking Act 1971 (Guernsey) [2 Nov.]	III,	4754
1745	Hijacking Act 1971 (Isle of Man) [2 Nov.] ...	III,	4756
1746	Hijacking Act 1971 (Jersey) [2 Nov.]	III,	4758
1747	Sea Fisheries (Isle of Man) [2 Nov.]	III,	4760
1748	Sea Fishing (Manx Boats) [2 Nov.]	III,	4763
1749	Health Service (Northern Ireland Agreement) [3 Nov.]	III,	4764
1750	Air Navigation (General) [2 Nov.]	III,	4766
1751	Rules of the Air and Air Traffic Control [2 Nov.] ...	III,	4768
1752	Brucellosis (Area Eradication) (S.) [5 Nov.]... ...	III,	4769
1760	North Lindsey Water [5 Nov.]	**(n)** III,	6360
1761	Industrial Relations Act 1971 (Commencement) [4 Nov.]	III,	4779
1763	London North Circular Trunk Road (Waterworks Corner Improvement Stage 2) [4 Nov.]	**(n)** III,	6343
1764	London–Holyhead and Newport–Shrewsbury Trunk Roads (Meole Brace Diversion) [5 Nov.] ...	**(n)** III,	6342
1766	Industrial Training (Construction Bd.) [8 Nov.] ...	III,	4784
1767	Southampton Corporation Water [4 Nov.] ...	**(n)** III,	6353
1768	Fort William–Malliag Trunk Road (Fassfem Diversion) [9 Nov.]	**(n)** III,	6344
1769	Sugar (Rates of Surcharge and Surcharge Repayments) [1 Nov.]	III,	4793
1770	Composite Sugar Products (Surcharge and Surcharge Repayments—Average Rates) [1 Nov.] ...	III,	4796
1771	Indian Military Service Family Pension Fund [4 Nov.]	III,	4800
1772	Mental Health Review Tribunal (Welsh Forms) [8 Nov.]	III,	4804
1773	International Development Association (Third Replenishment: Interim Payments) [5 Nov.] ...	III,	4809
1774	Price Stability of Imported Products (Rates of Levy) (Cereals) [2 Nov.]	III,	4811
1775	Teachers Superannuation (Family Benefits) (S.) [9 Nov.]	III,	4813
1777	Industrial Ct. [10 Nov.]	III,	4869
1778	Price Stability of Imported Products (Rates of Levy) (Eggs) [3 Nov.]	III,	4901
1779	Income Tax (Payments to Sub-Contractors in the Construction Industry) [9 Nov.]	III,	4903
1780	British Waterways Bd. (Alteration of Pension Schemes) [11 Nov.]	III,	4910
1781	Purchase Tax [8 Nov.]	III,	4916

(n) Instrument classified as local, noted in the Classified List of Local S.I. at the page shown above, but not set out in full.

No.	Subject	Part	Page
1786	Capital Gains Tax (Exempt Gilt-edged Securities) [9 Nov.]	III,	4918
1788	Direct Grant Schools [11 Nov.]	III,	4919
1790	Glasgow–Monkland Motorway (Stage I) Special Roads Scheme 1970 Confirmation [11 Nov.] ...	(n) III,	6346
1791	Glasgow–Monkland Motorway (Stage 1) (Connecting Roads) Special Roads Scheme 1970 Confirmation [11 Nov.]	(n) III,	6346
1795	A.S. (Legal Aid) (Children) [23 Nov.]	III,	4921
1796	A.S. (Legal Aid Rules and Legal Aid Fees) [23 Nov.]	III,	4922
1797	A.S. (Rules of Ct.) [23 Nov.]	III,	4924
1804	Leeds–Scarborough Trunk Road (Staxton Diversion) [15 Nov.]	(n) III,	6342
1805	Road Safety Act 1967 (Commencement) [15 Nov.]	III,	4926
1806	Baking and Sausage Making (Christmas and New Year) [12 Nov.]	III,	4928
1807	Foreign Compensation Commission (Union of Soviet Socialist Republics) [12 Nov.]	III,	4930
1809	A.S. (Rules of Ct.) [25 Nov.]	III,	4932
1810	A.S. (Alteration of Fees of Shorthand Writers in the Sheriff Ct.) (Citation) [22 Nov.]	III,	4935
1811	Building Standards (S.) [17 Nov.]	III,	4936
1812	Anti-Dumping Duty Order 1968 (Revn.) [12 Nov.]	III,	4979
1813	Import Duties (General) [19 Nov.]	Expired	
1814	Motor Vehicles (Tests) (Exemption) [1 Nov.] ...	III,	4980
1816	Edinburgh–Stirling–Perth Trunk Road (Keir Roundabout Trunking) [15 Nov.]	(n) III,	6344
1817	Stirling–Callender–Crianlarich Trunk Road (Craigforth Diversion Trunking) [15 Nov.]	(n) III,	6344
1818	Hill and Upland Sheep (S.) [12 Nov.]	III,	4982
1819	Hill and Upland Sheep Subsidy Payment (S.) [12 Nov.]	III,	4984
1820	Crofting Counties Agricultural Grants (S.) [12 Nov.]	III,	4986
1821	Local Education Authies. Recoupment (Further Education) [16 Nov.]	III,	4990
1822	Oil in Navigable Waters (Prohibited Sea Areas) [15 Nov.]	III,	4992
1823	Dutch Elm Disease (Local Authies.) [15 Nov.] ...	III,	4994
1826	Makerfield Water Bd. (Pocket Nook No. 2 and Lanside Boreholes) [17 Nov.]	(n) III,	6360
1829	London–Birmingham Trunk Road (Detrunking of Birmingham Road Service Road) [17 Nov.] ...	(n) III,	6342
1833	National Health Service (Medical Practices Compensation) (S.) [16 Nov.]	III,	5001
1835	Poisons [17 Nov.]	III,	5003
1836	Wages Regulation (Rubber Proofed Garment) [22 Nov.]	III,	5005
1837	Newport–Shrewsbury Trunk Road (Diversion at Hunger Hill) [18 Nov.]	(n) III,	6343

(n) Instrument classified as local, noted in the Classified List of Local S.I. at the page shown above, but not set out in full.

No.	Subject	Part	Page
1839	Diseases of Animals (Approved Disinfectants) [22 Nov.]	III,	5019
1842	Motorways Traffic (Leeds Inner Ring Road) (Speed Limit) [18 Nov.]	(n) III,	6344
1843	Precepts [22 Nov.]	III,	5021
1844	Rate-demands [22 Nov.]	III,	5023
1845	Consular Conventions (Hungarian People's Republic) [18 Nov.]	III,	5024
1846	Consular Relations (Merchant Shipping and Civil Aviation) (Hungarian People's Republic) [18 Nov.]	III,	5025
1847	Southern Rhodesia Act 1965 (Continuation) [18 Nov.]	III,	5027
1848	Copyright (Isle of Man) [18 Nov.]	III,	5028
1849	University of Edinburgh (Fellowships, Scholarships and Bursaries) Scheme 1971 [24 Nov.]	III,	5029
1850	Copyright (International Conventions) [18 Nov.]...	III,	5087
1854	National Insurance (Attendance Allowance) [22 Nov.]	III,	5089
1855	Herefordshire Water Bd. [24 Nov.]	(n) III,	6360
1856	Pensions Appeal Tribunals (E. and W.) [19 Nov.]...	III,	5091
1857	Family Law Reform Act 1969 (Commencement) [22 Nov.]	III,	5092
1861	Blood Tests (Evidence of Paternity) [24 Nov.] ...	III,	5093
1864	East Devon Water [25 Nov.]	(n) III,	6360
1870	Premium Savings Bonds [22 Nov.]	III,	5103
1871	Act of Adj. (Sittings of the High Ct. of Justiciary on Circuit) [6 Dec.]	III,	5104
1874	Control of Harbour Development [23 Nov.] ...	III,	5106
1875	Smoke Control Areas (Authorised Fuels) [24 Nov.]	III,	5107
1876	Industrial Training (Distributive Bd.) Order 1970 [25 Nov.]	III,	5109
1877	Legal Aid (General) [24 Nov.]	III,	5114
1878	New Bus Grants (Increase of Rate and Extension of Period) [24 Nov.]	III,	5117
1879	Superannuation (Policy and Local Government Schemes) (Interchange (S.) [24 Nov.]	III,	5119
1880	Adoption Orders (Welsh Cts.) [25 Nov.]	III,	5122
1882	Import Duties (Developing Countries) [26 Nov.] ...	III,	5125
1883	Irish Land (Finance) (Amdt.) (No. 2) Rules [30 Nov.]	III,	5138
1891	Import Duties (General) [26 Nov.]	III,	5140
1892	Bedfordshire County Roads (Polhill Avenue, Bedford) [29 Nov.]	(n) III,	6346
1894	Public Trustee (Custodian Trustee) [29 Nov.] ...	III,	5142
1895	Price Stability of Imported Products (Rates of Levy) (Eggs) [24 Nov.]	III,	5145
1896	Income Tax (Employments) [30 Nov.]	III,	5147
1897	Anti-Dumping Duty [26 Nov.]	III,	5149
1898	Rate Support Grant [30 Nov.]	III,	5151

(n) Instrument classified as local, noted in the Classified List of Local S.I. at the page shown above, but not set out in full.

No.	Subject	Part	Page
1899	Friendly Societies Act 1971 (Commencement) [30 Nov.]	III,	5154
1900	Friendly Societies (Fees) [30 Nov.]	III,	5155
1901	Police [1 Dec.]...	III,	5156
1903	Industrial Ct. [30 Nov.]	III,	5160
1904	Legal Aid (Extension of Proceedings) [30 Nov.] ...	III,	5162
1908	Colne Valley Water (Financial Provisions) [1 Dec.]	(n) III,	6359
1909	Workington–Barons Cross Trunk Road (Chapel Brow-Fitz Cottage) [1 Dec.]	(n) III,	6343
1910	Oxford–Market Deeping Trunk Road (Stamford) [1 Dec.]	(n) III,	6343
1911	London–Carlisle–Glasgow–Inverness Trunk Road (Alexandria By-pass Stage II Slip Roads) (Variation) [2 Dec.]	(n) III,	6344
1912	Legal Aid (S.) (Extension of Proceedings) [30 Nov.]	III,	5163
1913	Industrial Ct. (Appeals) (S.) [30 Nov.]	III,	5164
1914	Legal Aid (S.) (General) [30 Nov.]	III,	5166
1915	Lowestoft (Local Enactments) [1 Dec.]	(n) III,	6355
1916	Kent Police (Amalgamation) [2 Dec.]	(n) III,	6356
1917	Patents [2 Dec.]	III,	5170
1918	Wages Regulation (Corset) [3 Dec.]	III,	5174
1919	Wages Regulation (Shirtmaking) [3 Dec.]	III,	5182
1920	Welfare Food [3 Dec.]	III,	5190
1921	Developing Countries (Origin of Goods) [3 Dec.]...	III,	5192
1922	Wages Regulation (Wholesale Mantle and Costume) [6 Dec.]	III,	5232
1923	Matrimonial Causes [3 Dec.]	III,	5234
1930	Local Loans (Increase of Limit) [3 Dec.]	III,	5247
1932	Greater London Council (Blackwall Tunnel Southern Approach) Motorway Scheme 1970 Confirmation [6 Dec.]	(n) III,	6345
1933	Employers' Liability (Compulsory Insurance) Exemption [7 Dec.]	III,	5248
1936	Trunk Road (Great Cambridge Road, Enfield) (Prescribed Routes) [10 Dec.]	(n) III,	6349
1937	Price Stability of Imported Products (Rates of Levy) (Cereals) [1 Dec.]	III,	5251
1938	Price Stability of Imported Products (Rates of Levy) (Eggs) [1 Dec.]	III,	5253
1939	Shipbuilding Industry (Dissolution Provisions) [7 Dec.]		
1940	Lancashire County Council (Kirby to Tarbock) Special Road Scheme 1968 Confirmation [8 Dec.]	(n) III,	6345
1941	Lancashire County Council Liverpool Outer Ring Road (Kirkby to Tarbock) Special Connecting Roads Scheme 1970 Confirmation [8 Dec.] ...	(n) III,	6345
1942	Wages Regulation (Retail Newsagency, Tobacco and Confectionery) (E. and W.) [8 Dec.]... ...	III,	5257
1943	Perth–Aberdeen–Inverness Trunk Road (Mormond House Diversion) [8 Dec.]	(n) III,	6344
1946	Friendly Societies (Proxy Voting) [9 Dec.] ...	III,	5260

(n) Instrument classified as local, noted in the Classified List of Local S.I. at the page shown above, but not set out in full.

No.	Subject	Part	Page
1947	Income Tax (Employments) [8 Dec.]	III,	5262
1953	White Fish Subsidy (Deep Sea Vessels) (U.K.) [8 Dec.]	III,	5264
1954	Divorce County Cts. [10 Dec.]	III,	5271
1955	Rule of the Supreme Ct. [10 Dec.]	III,	5274
1956	Friendly Societies (Forms and Fees) [15 Dec.] ...	III,	5284
1957	York–Hull Trunk Road (Barmby New Inn Diversion) [9 Dec.]	(**n**) III,	6343
1958	M62 Motorway (Rawcliffe to Balkholme Section) [9 Dec.]	(**n**) III,	6345
1959	M62 Motorway (Rawcliffe to Balkholme Section) Connecting Roads [9 Dec.]	(**n**) III,	6345
1960	M62 Motorway (Rawcliffe to Balkholme Section) [9 Dec.]	(**n**) III,	6345
1961	Electric Blankets (Safety) [10 Dec.]...	III,	5298
1962	National Health Service (Maidstone and District Hospital Management Ctee.) [10 Dec.]	(**n**) III,	6358
1963	Dutch Elm Disease (Local Authies.) [9 Dec.] ...	III,	5302
1964	Sugar (Rates of Surcharge and Surcharge Repayments) [6 Dec.]	III,	5304
1965	Composite Sugar Products (Surcharge and Surcharge Repayments—Average Rates) [6 Dec.] ...	III,	5307
1966	Inverness-shire Water Bd. (Loch Shnathaid) Water [10 Dec.]	(**n**) III,	6361
1967	Brucellosis Payments [10 Dec.]	III,	5311
1968	Civil Aviation (Aerial Avertising) [10 Dec.] ...	III,	5318
1970	Superannuation (Teaching and Public Transport Services) Interchange (S.) [10 Dec.]	III,	5320
1971	Import Duties (General) [6 Dec.]	III,	5330
1972	Rules of the Air and Air Traffic Control [13 Dec.]...	III,	5644
1974	Customs Duty (Personal Reliefs) (No. 4) O. 1968 [10 Dec.]	III,	5646
1975	Justices' Allowances [13 Dec.]	III,	5648
1976	Probation (Allowances) [13 Dec.]	III,	5649
1977	Non-Contentious Probate [13 Dec.]	III,	5650
1978	East Devon Water (Pynes Intake) [14 Dec.] ...	(**n**) III,	6360
1979	Motor Vehicles (Minimum Age for Driving) (Motor Cycles) [15 Dec.]	III,	5658
1980	Air Navigation (Fees) [14 Dec.]	III,	5660
1981	Civil Aviation (Licensing) [14 Dec.]	III,	5662
1982	Charities (Highland Society of London) [14 Dec.]...	(**n**) III,	6363
1983	County Cts. (Bankruptcy and Companies Winding-up Jurisdiction) [15 Dec.]	III,	5664
1984	County Cts. (Admiralty Jurisdiction) [15 Dec.] ...	III,	5665
1985	County Cts. (Race Relations Jurisdiction) [15 Dec.]	III,	5667
1986	Price Stability of Imported Products (Rates of Levy) (Cereals) [9 Dec.]	III,	5668
1987	Injuries in War (Shore Employments) Compensation [15 Dec.]	III,	5670
1990	Justices' Allowances (S.) [14 Dec.]	III,	5672
1991	Magistrates' Cts. (Blood Tests) [16 Dec.]	III,	5673

(**n**) Instrument classified as local, noted in the Classified List of Local S.I. at the page shown above, but not set out in full.

No.	Subject		Part	Page
1992	Civil Aviation Act 1971 (Commencement) [16 Dec.]		III,	5679
1993	Acquisition of Land (Rate of Interest after Entry) [16 Dec.]		III,	5681
1994	Acquisition of Land (Rate of Interest after Entry) (S.) [16 Dec.]		III,	5682
1995	Teachers' Superannuation (S.) [15 Dec.]		III,	5683
2000	Import Duty Reliefs [15 Dec.]		III,	5690
2001	Anti-Dumping and Countervailing Duties (Metric Rates [14 Dec.]		III,	5691
2002	Exchange Contro! (Scheduled Territories) [14 Dec.]		III,	5693
2003	Highways Act 1971 (Commencement) [17 Dec.] ...		III,	5695
2004	Tees and Hartlepool Port Authy. Revision [17 Dec.]	(n)	III,	6354
2007	Rating (Charitable Institutions) [17 Dec.]		III,	5698
2008	Cts. (Compensation to Officers) [17 Dec.]		III,	5700
2009	Import Duty Drawbacks [17 Dec.]		III,	5738
2010	Import Duties (Temp. Exemptions) [17 Dec.] ...		III,	5740
2011	Import Duties (Temp. Reductions) [17 Dec.] ...		III,	5779
2012	Import Duties (Temp. Reductions) [17 Dec.] ...		III,	5780
2013	Superannuation (Civil Service and Northern Ireland Teaching Service) Transfer [16 Dec.]		III,	5782
2017	West Shropshire and East Shropshire (Variation of Limits of Supply) [20 Dec.]	(n)	III,	6360
2019	Prison [20 Dec.]		III,	5788
2020	Goods Vehicles (Prohibitions) (Exemptions and Appeals) [21 Dec.]		III,	5790
2021	Import Duties (General) [17 Dec.]		III,	5793
2022	Jurors' Allowances (S.) [20 Dec.]		III,	5795
2023	Local Govt. Audit (S.) [20 Dec.]		III,	5797
2024	Superannuation (Teaching and Public Bds.) Interchange (S.) [20 Dec.]		III,	5798
2025	Superannuation (Teaching and Local Government) Interchange (S.) [22 Dec.]		III,	5800
2026	Iron and Steel (Compensation to Employees) [22 Dec.]		III,	5818
2029	Gaming Clubs (Permitted Areas) [22 Dec.]... ...		III,	5820
2030	South Derbyshire Water Bd. (Water Rates) [21 Dec.]	(n)	III,	6360
2031	Rate Support Grant (Increase) [22 Dec.]		III,	5821
2032	Rate Support Grant (Increase) [22 Dec.]		III,	5825
2034	Exchange Control (Authorised Dealers and Depositaries) [30 Dec.]		III,	5829
2035	Increase of Pensions (Governers) [21 Dec.] ...		III,	5831
2036	Increase of Pensions (Teachers Family Benefits) (S.) [20 Dec.]		III,	5833
2037	Norwich (Royston Bridge and Witton Park) Water [23 Dec.]	(n)	III,	6360
2038	Heckmondwike Sewerage [29 Dec.]	(n)	III,	6358
2039	East Shropshire Water Bd. (Tern Hill Boreholes) [23 Dec.]	(n)	III,	6360
2040	European Free Trade Association (Origin of Goods) [22 Dec.]		III,	5837

(n) Instrument classified as local, noted in the Classified List of Local S.I. at the page shown above, but not set out in full.

No.	Subject	Part	Page
2041	Import Duties (General) [20 Dec.]	III,	5843
2042	Import Duties (Temporary Exemptions) [23 Dec.]	III,	5844
2043	Import Duties (General) [20 Dec.]	III,	5851
2044	Companies (Accounts) [23 Dec.]	III,	5852
2045	Rabies (Importation of Mammals) [29 Dec.] ...	III,	5853
2046	Jurors' Allowances [22 Dec.]...	III,	5866
2047	Circuit Judges' Superannuation (Transitional) [22 Dec.]	III,	5869
2048	Police Authies. (Appointment of Magistrates) [29 Dec.]	III,	5871
2049	Oxford–Market Deeping Trunk Road (Thorpeville, Northampton) [3 Jan.]	(n) III,	6343
2050	National Insurance (Collection of Graduated Contributions) [6 Jan]	III,	5874
2051	Building Standards (Relaxation by Building Authies.) (S.) [31 Dec.]	III,	5880
2052	Building Standards (S.) (Consolidation) [19 Jan.]...	III,	5883
2053	Newcastle Disease (E. and W.) [29 Dec.]	III,	6130
2054	Textile Council (Dissolution) [29 Dec]	III,	6133
2055	Police (Amalgamation) [30 Dec.]	(n) III,	6356
2056	Textile Council Ctee. (Discharge) [29 Dec.] ...	III,	6138
2057	Industrial Training (Financial Provisions) [30 Dec.]	III,	6139
2061	Dorset and Bournemouth Police (Amalgamation) [30 Dec.]	(n) III,	6356
2062	Hampshire Police (Amalgamation) [30 Dec.] ...	(n) III,	6356
2063	Lancashire Police (Amalgamation) [30 Dec.] ...	(n) III,	6356
2064	Leicester and Rutland Police (Amalgamation) [30 Dec.]	(n) III,	6356
2065	Mid-Anglia Police (Amalgamation) [30 Dec.] ...	(n) III,	6356
2066	Northumberland Police (Amalgamation) [30 Dec.]	(n) III,	6356
2067	Suffolk Police (Amalgamation) [30 Dec.]	(n) III,	6356
2068	West Yorkshire Police (Amalgamation) [30 Dec.] ...	(n) III,	6356
2070	Coypus (Keeping) [30 Dec.]	III,	6141
2071	Mink (Keeping) [30 Dec.]	III,	6143
2072	Sea Fisheries (S.) [31 Dec.]	III,	6145
2073	Companies (Winding-up) [30 Dec.]	III,	6147
2074	Goods Vehicles (Plating and Testing) [29 Dec.] ...	III,	6149
2075	Warwickshire and Coventry Police (Amalgamation) [30 Dec.]	(n) III,	6356
2076	Thames Valley Police (Amalgamation) [30 Dec.]	(n) III,	6356
2077	Staffordshire County and Stoke-on-Trent Police (Amalgamation) [30 Dec.]	(n) III,	6356
2078	National Health Service (Farnham and Brookwood Hospital Management Ctee.) [31 Dec.]	(n) III,	6358
2079	Town and Country Planning Act 1968 (Commencement) (South Hampshire) [31 Dec.]	(n) III,	6155
2080	Town and Country Planning Act 1968 (Commencement) (Leicester–Leicestershire) [31 Dec.] ...	III,	6158
2082	Sugar (Rates of Surcharge and Surcharge Repayments) [22 Dec.]	III,	6160

(**n**) Instrument classified as local, noted in the Classified List of Local S.I. at the page shown above, but not set out in full.

No.	Subject		Part	Page
2083	Composite Sugar Products (Surcharge and Surcharge Repayments—Average Rates) [22 Dec.]...		III,	6163
2084	Indictments (Procedure) [31 Dec.]		III,	6167
2085	Industrial Relations (Nominations) [31 Dec.] ...		III,	6171
2089	A.S. (Valuation Appeal Rules) [14 Jan.]		III,	6175
2090	London–Carlisle–Inverness Trunk Road (Ballachulish Bridge Diversion) [6 Jan.]	(n)	III,	6344
2091	London–Edinburgh–Thurso Trunk Road (Dunachton Lodge Diversion) [6 Jan.]	(n)	III,	6344
2092	Folkestone–Honiton Trunk Road (Amendment of Route, Winchelsea) [14 Jan.]	(n)	III,	6342
2094	National Insurance Act 1966 (Commencement) [30 Dec.]		III,	6178
2095	Traffic Signs [31 Dec.]		III,	6180
2096	Local Govt. (Financial Loss Allowance) [3 Jan.]...		III,	6182
2097	Greater London Council (Allowances to Members) [3 Jan.]		III,	6184
2099	Minister for the Civil Service [3 Jan.]		III,	6186
2100	Cayman Islands (Legislative Assembly—Extension of Duration) [3 Jan.]		III,	6190
2101	Diplomatic Immunities Restriction [3 Jan.] ...		III,	6191
2102	Extradition (Hijacking) [3 Jan.]		III,	6193
2103	Extradition (Tokyo Convention) [3 Jan.] ...		III,	6202
2104	Foreign Compensation (Egypt) O. [25 Jan.] ...		III,	6206
2105	Alderney (Transfer of Property, &c.) [31 Dec.] ...		III,	6213
2106	Parliamentary Constituencies (Abingdon and Newbury) [4 Jan.]		III,	6215
2107	Parliamentary Constituencies (Blyth and Hexham) [4 Jan.]		III,	6217
2108	Parliamentary Constituencies (Bosworth and Loughborough) [4 Jan.]		III,	6219
2109	Parliamentary Constituencies (Bromsgrove and Redditch and Stratford-on-Avon) [4 Jan.] ...		III,	6221
2110	Parliamentary Constituencies (Hertford and Stevenage and Hitchin) [4 Jan.]		III,	6223
2111	Parliamentary Constituencies (Leicester South and Harborough) [4 Jan.]		III,	6226
2112	Parliamentary Constituencies (London Borough of Bromley) [4 Jan.]		III,	6228
2113	Parliamentary Constituencies (London Borough of Southwark) [4 Jan.]		III,	6231
2114	Parliamentary Constituencies (Richmond upon Thames, Twickenham and Esher) [4 Jan.] ...		III,	6234
2115	Parliamentary Constituencies (Stockport) [4 Jan.]		III,	6236
2116	Parliamentary Constituencies (Swindon and Devizes) [4 Jan.]		III,	6239
2117	Double Taxation Relief (Taxes and Income) (Trinidad and Tobago) [4 Jan.]		III,	6241
2118	Tokyo Convention (Certification of Countries) [31 Dec.]		III,	6244
2119	Transfer of Functions (Export Guarantees) [3 Jan.]		III,	6247

(n) Instrument classified as local, noted in the Classified List of Local S.I. at the page shown above, but not set out in full.

No.	Subject	Part	Page
2120	Misuse of Drugs Act 1971 (Commencement) [3 Jan.]	III,	6249
2122	Durham Police (Amalgamation) [3 Jan.]	(n) III,	6356
2123	Norfolk Joint Police (Amalgamation) [3 Jan.] ...	(n) III,	6356
2124	Pensions Appeal Tribunals (S.) [31 Dec.]	III,	6250
2125	London Transport (Lost Property) [4 Jan.] ...	III,	6271
2126	North West of Doncaster–Kendal Trunk Road (Clapham Outer By-Pass) [11 Jan.]	(n) III,	6343
2127	County Ct. [4 Jan.]	III,	6276
2128	General Optical Council (Registration and Enrolment Rules) [4 Jan.]	III,	6281
2129	Wages Regulation (General Waste Materials Reclamation) [6 Jan.]	III,	6289
2130	Local Govt. (Financial Loss Allowance) (S.) [3 Jan.]	III,	6296
2131	Local Govt. (Travelling Allowances, etc.) (S.) [3 Jan.]	III,	6298
2133	Distress for Rent [5 Jan.]	III,	6300
2135	Smoke Control Areas (Authorised Fuels) [7 Jan.]	III,	6301
2142	Essex and Southend-on-Sea Police (Amalgamation) [7 Jan.]	(n) III,	6356
2143	Cumbria Police (Amalgamation) [7 Jan.]	(n) III,	6156
2144	Brucellosis (Eradication Areas) (S.) [6 Jan.] ...	(n) III,	6363
2146	Gwynedd Police (Amalgamation) [7 Jan.] ...	(n) III,	6356
2147	Superannuation (Teaching and Public Boards) Interchange [7 Jan.]	III,	6303
2150	Bedford Inner Relief Road (Southern Section) Bridges Scheme A.66 Confirmation [14 Jan.] ...	(n) III,	6341
2151	London–Carlisle–Glasgow–Inverness Trunk Road (Diversion North of Sharnbrook Crossroads) [11 Jan.]	(n) III,	6342
2152	County Ct. (New Procedure) [10 Jan.]	III,	6305
2154	Price Stability of Imported Products (Rates of Levy) (Cereals) [4 Jan.]	III,	6321
2155	South Wales Police (Amalgamation) [7 Jan.] ...	(n) III,	6356
2156	West Mercia Police (Amalgamation) [7 Jan.] ...	(n) III,	6356
2157	Cheshire, Birkenhead, Chester, Stockport and Wallasey Police (Amalgamation) [7 Jan.] ...	(n) III,	6356
2158	Monmouthshire and Newport Police (Amalgamation) [7 Jan.]	(n) III,	6356
2159	Sussex Police (Amalgamation) [7 Jan.]	(n) III,	6356
2160	Northampton and County Police (Amalgamation) [7 Jan.]	(n) III,	6356
2161	Isles of Scilly (Scrap Metal Dealers) [11 Jan.] ...	III,	6323
2162	Air Navigation (Fees) [10 Jan.]	III,	6324
2163	Bedfordshire and Luton Police (Amalgamation) [10 Jan.]	(n) III,	6356
2164	Lincolnshire Police (Amalgamation) [10 Jan.] ...	(n) III,	6356
2165	Dyfed-Powys Police (Amalgamation) [10 Jan.] ...	(n) III,	6356
2166	Somerset and Bath Police (Amalgamation) [10 Jan.]	(n) III,	6356
2167	Pool Competitions (Licence Fees) [11 Jan.] ...	III,	6327
2169	Great Ouse Water [19 Jan.]	(n) III,	6360

(n) Instrument classified as local, noted in the Classified List of Local S.I. at the page shown above, but not set out in full.

No.	Subject	Part	Page
2170	Warley County Borough Council (Roebuck Lane Improvement) Scheme 1968 Confirmation [19 Jan.]	(n) III,	6341
2174	Inverness-shire Water Bd. (Allt Currachan and Loch na Beinne More) Water [12 Jan.]	(n) III,	6361
2175	North of Scotland Water Bd. (Loch na Carrach) Water [12 Jan.]	(n) III,	6361
2176	Penrith–Middlesbrough Trunk Road (Greta Bridge By-Pass) [24 Jan.]	(n) III,	6341
2177	Raglan–Llandovery Trunk Road (Abergavenny Inner Relief Road) [18 Jan.]	(n) III,	6343
2178	Gretna–Stranraer–Glasgow–Stirling Trunk Road (Old Hermitage and Other Diversions) [25 Jan.]	(n) III,	6344

(n) Instrument classified as local, noted in the Classified List of Local S.I. at the page shown above, but not set out in full.

Index to Parts I, II and III

Volume Reference

SBN 11 840093 2*